PAGE 62 | ON THE ROAD

YOUR COMPLETE DESTINATION GUIDE
In-depth reviews, detailed listings
and insider tips

Santiago de Compostela & Galicia p507

Cantabria & Asturias p463

Basque Country, Navarra & La Rioja p406

Castilla y León p135

Aragón p369

Catalonia p306

⦿ Barcelona p235

★ Madrid p61

Castilla-La Mancha p203

Extremadura p779

Valencia & Murcia p550

Mallorca, Menorca & Ibiza p608

Seville & Andalucía p657

PAGE 849 | SURVIVAL GUIDE

VITAL PRACTICAL INFORMATION TO
HELP YOU HAVE A SMOOTH TRIP

THIS EDITION WRITTEN AND RESEARCHED BY

Anthony Ham
Stuart Butler, Anna Kaminski, John Noble, Miles Roddis
Brendan Sainsbury, Regis St Louis, Andy Symington

welcome to Spain

An Epic Land

Spain's diverse landscapes stir the soul. The Pyrenees and the Picos de Europa are as beautiful as any mountain range on the continent, while the snowcapped Sierra Nevada rises up improbably from the sun-baked plains of Andalucía; these are hiking destinations of the highest order. The wildly beautiful cliffs of Spain's Atlantic northwest are the scene for some of Europe's most spectacular drives, even as the charming coves of the Mediterranean are still the continent's summer destination of choice; despite decades of overdevelopment, numerous unspoiled corners remain. And everywhere you go, villages of timeless beauty perch on hilltops, huddle in valleys and cling to coastal outcrops as tiny but resilient outposts of Old Spain. Spend as long as you can in places like these.

A Culinary Feast

Food and wine are national obsessions in Spain, and with good reason. Yes, there's paella, tapas, *jamón* and olive oil in abundance, but these are merely the best-known ingredients of a national cuisine that continues to take the world by storm. The touchstones of Spanish cooking are deceptively simple: incalculable variety, strong traditions of recipes handed down through the generations, and an innate willingness to experiment and see what

Passionate, sophisticated and devoted to living the good life, Spain is at once a stereotype come to life and a country more diverse than you ever imagined.

(left) Menorca's prehistoric Cova d'en Xoroi
(below) The colourful Feria de Abril in Seville

comes out of the kitchen-laboratory. You may experience the best meal ever over tapas in an earthy bar where everyone's shouting, or over a meal prepared by a celebrity chef in the refined surrounds of a Michelin-starred restaurant. Either way, the breadth of gastronomic experience that awaits you is breathtaking.

Art Imitates Life

Spain's story is told with endless creativity through its arts and architecture. Poignantly windswept Roman ruins, cathedrals of rare power and incomparable jewels of Islamic architecture speak of a country where the great civilisations of history have always risen, fallen and left behind their indelible mark. More recently, what other country could produce such rebellious and relentlessly creative spirits as Salvador Dalí, Pablo Picasso and Antoni Gaudí and place them front and centre in public life? Here, grand monuments to the past coexist alongside architectural creations of such daring that it becomes clear that Spain's future will be every bit as original as its past. For all such talk, this is a country that lives very much in the present. Perhaps you'll sense it along a crowded postmidnight street when all the world has come out to play. Or maybe that moment will come when a flamenco performer touches something deep in your soul. Whenever it happens, you'll find yourself nodding in recognition: *this* is Spain.

Picos de Europa
Enjoy Spain's most dramatic peaks (p495)

ATLANTIC OCEAN

Bay of Biscay

Costa da Morte

Ferrol · Gijón · Santander

Parque Natural · Avilés · Torrelavega
Fragas do Eume · Oviedo

A Coruña · Parque Nacional de los · Bilbao
Picos de Europa · (Bilbo)
Cordillera Cantábrica

Lugo · Miranda
Parque · de Ebro
Natural
Santiago de · de Somiedo
Compostela · León · Burgos

Pontevedra

Ourense · Río Sil

Santiago de Compostela
Walk softly through
this sacred city (p509)

Palencia · Aranda
de Duero

Benavente · Valladolid
Río Du

Zamora · Segovia

Salamanca
The high point of Renaissance
architecture (p143)

Salamanca · Guadalaj
Ávila · Cordillera Central · MADRI

Madrid
Linger in three of the world's
finest art galleries (p64)

Sierra de · Aranjue
Gredos

PORTUGAL · Plasencia · Toledo

Río Tajo

Toledo
Search for the signs of
its multifaith past (p205)

Río Guadiana · Ciudad
Real

LISBON · Badajoz · Mérida

Córdoba
Explore the perfection of
Islamic architecture (p733)

Zafra · Los Pedroches · Parque
Natural Sierra
de Andújar

Sierra Morena

Seville
Immerse yourself in
Easter celebrations (p659)

Parque Natural · Córdoba
Sierra Norte

Cordillera Bética · Parque
Seville · Natural
Sierra

Huelva · Granada · Nevada
Sierra
Nevada

Granada
Marvel at the exquisite
Alhambra's perfection (p741)

Parque
Natural Los · Málaga
Alcornocales

Cádiz

Costa de la · Costa del
Luz · Sol

Algeciras · Gibraltar

Strait of Gibraltar · Ceuta
(Spain)

MOROCCO · Tangier

43°N · 41°N · 40°N · 39°N · 38°N · 37°N

9°W · 8°W · 7°W · 4°W

3

San Sebastián
Eat in Spain's culinary capital (p425)

FRANCE

Nîmes

Montpellier

Aragonese Pyrenees
Hike the Pyrenean high country (p379)

Biarritz

Costa Brava
Seek out Dalí along a picturesque coast (p308)

San Sebastián

Pamplona (Iruña)

Perpignan

Pyrenees

ANDORRA

ANDORRA LA VELLA

Figueras

Golfe du Lion

Logroño

Río Segre

Girona

Riu Ter

Costa Brava

Zaragoza

Lleida

Barcelona

La Rioja
Meander through Spain's premier wine region (p454)

Río Ebro

Costa Daurada

Golfo de Valencia

Teruel

Costa del Azahar

Barcelona
Admire the extraordinary Sagrada Família (p235)

Menorca

Cuenca

Río Turia

Valencia
Experience the finest modern architecture (p552)

Palma de Mallorca

Valencia

Río Cabriel

Mallorca

Balearic Islands (Islas Baleares)

Albacete

Ibiza

Parque Natural Sierras de Cazorla, Segura y las Villas

Río Segura

Alicante (Alacant)

Costa Blanca

Formentera

Menorca
Laze on the Mediterranean's best beaches (p625)

Elche (Elx)

MEDITERRANEAN SEA

Murcia

Cartagena

Costa Cálida

0°

1°E

2°E

ELEVATION

	2000m
	1500m
	1000m
	700m
	500m
	300m
	200m
	100m
	0

Almería

Parque Natural de Cabo de Gata-Níjar

ALGERIA

N

0 — 100km
0 — 50 miles

Cabo de Gata
Discover the Mediterranean as it once was (p775)

25
TOP
EXPERIENCES

Alhambra

1 The palace complex of Granada's Alhambra (p742) is close to architectural perfection. It is perhaps the most refined example of Islamic art anywhere in the world, not to mention the most enduring symbol of 800 years of Moorish rule in what was known as Al-Andalus. From afar, the Alhambra's red fortress towers dominate the Granada skyline, set against a backdrop of the Sierra Nevada's snowcapped peaks. Up close, the Alhambra's perfectly proportioned Generalife gardens complement the exquisite detail of the Palacios Nazaríes. Put simply, this is Spain's most beautiful monument.

La Sagrada Família

2 One of Spain's top sights, the Modernista brainchild of Antoni Gaudí remains a work in progress more than 80 years after its creator's death. Fanciful and profound, inspired by nature and barely restrained by a Gothic style, Barcelona's quirky temple (p257) soars skyward with an almost playful majesty. The improbable angles and departures from architectural convention will have you shaking your head in disbelief, but the detail of the decorative flourishes on the Passion Facade, Nativity Facade and elsewhere are worth studying for hours.

KUTLAYEV DMITRY / SHUTTERSTOCK ©

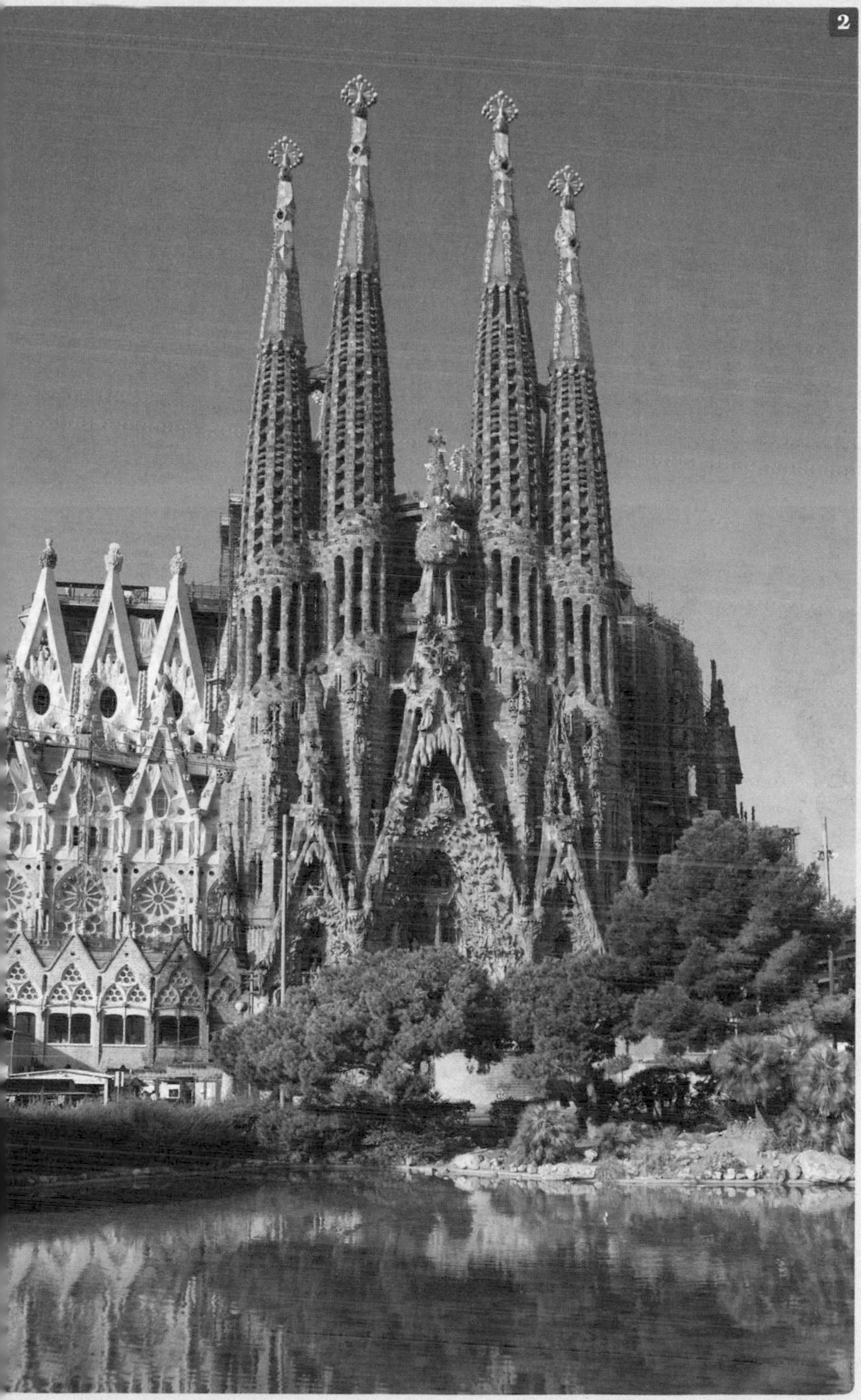

2

JEAN-PIERRE LESCOURRET / GETTY IMAGES ©

Mezquita

3 A church that became a mosque before reverting to a church, Córdoba's Mezquita (p733) charts the evolution of western and Islamic architecture over a 1000-year trajectory. Its most innovative features include some early horseshoe arches, an intricate mihrab, and a veritable 'forest' of 856 columns, many of them recycled from Roman ruins. The sheer scale of the Mezquita reflects Córdoba's erstwhile power as the most cultured city in 10th-century Europe. It was also inspiration for even greater buildings to come, most notably in Seville and Granada.

Easter in Seville

4 Return to Spain's medieval Christian roots and join Seville's masses for the dramatic Easter celebration of Semana Santa (p672). Religious fraternities parade elaborate *pasos* (figures) of Christ and the Virgin Mary around the city to the emotive acclaim of the populace; the most prestigious procession is the *madrugada* (early hours) of Good Friday. Seen for the first time, it's an unforgettable experience, an exotic and utterly compelling fusion o pageantry, solemnity and deep religious faith. There are processions in towns across Spain, but none on the scale of Seville's.

Madrid Nightlife

5 Madrid is not the only European city with nightlife (see p113 and p117), but few others can match its intensity and street clamour. As Ernest Hemingway said, 'Nobody goes to bed in Madrid until they have killed the night'. There are wall-to-wall bars, small clubs, live venues, cocktail bars and mega-clubs beloved by A-list celebrities all across the city, with unimaginable variety to suit all tastes. But it's in Huertas, Malasaña, Chueca and La Latina that you'll really understand what we're talking about. Why Not? bar, Chueca

Ciudad de las Artes y las Ciencias

6 Created by Santiago Calatrava, one of the nation's star architects, the City of Arts and Sciences in Valencia (p552) has helped transform Spain's third-largest city into one of the country's most vibrant. A daring and visually stunning piece of contemporary architecture, the complex includes a state-of-the-art theatre (Palau de les Arts Reina Sofía), grand aquarium (Oceanogràfic), planetarium (Hemisfèric) and science museum (Museo de las Ciencias Príncipe Felipe).

La Rioja Wine Country

7 La Rioja (p454) is the sort of place where you could spend weeks meandering along quiet roads in search of the finest drop. Bodegas offering wine tastings and picturesque villages that shelter excellent wine museums are the mainstay in this region. The Frank Gehry–designed Hotel Marqués de Riscal (p460), close to Elciego, has been likened to Bilbao's Guggenheim in architectural scale and ambition, and it has become the elite centre for wine tourism in the region.

Pintxos in San Sebastián

8 Chefs here have turned bar snacks into an art form. Sometimes called 'high cuisine in miniature', *pintxos* (Basque tapas) are piles of flavour often mounted on a slice of baguette. On stepping into any bar in central San Sebastián (p432), the choice lined up along the counter will leave first-time visitors gasping. In short, this is Spain's most memorable eating experience. Although the atmosphere is always casual, the serious business of experimenting with taste combinations (a Basque trademark) ensures that it just keeps getting better.

Renaissance Salamanca

9 Luminous when floodlit, the elegant central square of Salamanca (p143), the Plaza Mayor, is possibly the most attractive in all of Spain. It is just one of many highlights in a city which has few peers in the country when it comes to architectural splendour. Salamanca is home to one of Europe's oldest and most prestigious universities, so student revelry also lights up the nights. It's this combination of grandeur and energy that makes so many people call Salamanca their favourite city in Spain.

Sierra Nevada & Las Alpujarras

10 Dominated by the Mulhacén (3479m), mainland Spain's highest peak, the Sierra Nevada (p755) is a stunning backdrop to the warm city of Granada. Skiing and hiking can be mixed with exploration of the fascinating Las Alpujarras (p759), arguably Andalucía's most engaging collection of *pueblos blancos* (white villages). Among the last outposts of Moorish settlement on Spanish soil, these hamlets resemble North Africa, oasis-like and set amid woodlands and the deep ravines for which the region is renowned. Sierra Nevada National Park

Asturian Coast

11 According to one count, the emerald-green northern Spanish region of Asturias (p477) boasts more than 600 beaches. While the coolness of the Atlantic may be a drawback for those planning on catching some sun, the beauty of many of these frequently wild and unspoiled stretches is utterly breathtaking. Even better, the villages of the coast and hinterland are among the prettiest anywhere along the Spanish shoreline, and the food served in this part of the country is famous throughout Spain.

Madrid's Golden Art Triangle

12 Madrid may lack architectural landmarks, but it more than compensates with extraordinary art galleries. Housing works by Goya, Velázquez, El Greco and masters from across Europe, the showpiece is the Museo del Prado (p82), but within a short stroll are the Centro de Arte Reina Sofía (p79), showcasing Picasso's *Guernica,* plus works by Dalí and Miró, and the Museo Thyssen-Bornemisza (p87), with all the big names spanning centuries. Roy Lichtenstein's *Brochazo* at Centro de Arte Reina Sofía (designed by Jean Nouvel)

13

DAVID C TOMLINSON / GETTY IMAGES ©

14

ANDREA PISTOLESI / GETTY IMAGES ©

15

ALEX SCHLEIF / J. LAMY ©

Staying in a Beautiful Parador

13 Sleeping like a king has never been easier than in Spain's state-run chain of *paradores* (p852) – often palatial, always supremely comfortable former castles, palaces, monasteries and convents. There are (at last count) 94 of them scattered across the country. Ranking among Europe's most atmospheric sleeping experiences, many are sited on prime real estate (eg inside the grounds of Granada's Alhambra), and prices are more reasonable than you might imagine, especially if you book online and far in advance.

Flamenco in Andalucía

14 Who needs rock 'n' roll? Like all great anguished music, flamenco (p844) has the power to lift you out of the doldrums and stir your soul. It's as if by sharing in the pain of innumerable generations of dispossessed misfits you open a door to a secret world of musical ghosts and ancient Andalucian spirits. On the other side of the coin, flamenco culture can also be surprisingly jolly, jokey and tongue-in-cheek. There's only one real proviso: you have to hear it live, preferably in its Seville-Jerez-Cádiz heartland.

Hiking the Aragonese Pyrenees

15 Spain is a walker's destination of exceptional variety, but we reckon Aragón's Pyrenees offer the most special hiking country. The Parque Nacional de Ordesa y Monte Perdido (p386) is one of the high points (pun intended) of the Pyrenees. Centred on Monte Perdido (3348m), it offers plenty of opportunities for tough excursions along great rock walls and glacial cirques, accompanied by the occasional chamois. Even better, there are limits on the number of people in the park at any one time.

Sample the Best Jamón

16 *Jamón* (cured ham; p841) is Spain's culinary constant and one of the few things that unite the country. If there is a national dish, this is it, more so even than paella. Nearly every bar and restaurant in Spain has at least one *jamón* on the go at any one time, strapped into a cradle-like frame called a *jamonera*. Wafer-thin slices of the best *jamón* (known as *jamón ibérico de bellota,* although there are many different kinds) is simplicity itself and our idea of Spanish culinary heaven.

Galicia's Costa da Morte & Cabo Ortegal

17 The wild Atlantic bluffs of the Galician coast remind us of how small we are. Close to Cabo Ortegal (p529), powerful winds whip around you and great Atlantic rollers seem little more than sea spray as they crash against the walls of the cape far below. And along the Costa da Morte (Coast of Death; p520), where the stories of shipwrecks are legion, long and empty sweeps of sand are separated by dramatic rocky headlands. If only all stretches of Spain's coastline were this unspoiled. Costa da Morte

CRAIG PERSHOUSE / GETTY IMAGES ©

MAN / IMAGEBROKER ©

MATTHEW M. SCHOENFELDER / GETTY IMAGES ©

Santiago de Compostela

18 As the reputed final resting place of St James, one of the 12 Apostles, Santiago de Compostela (p509) in Galicia in Spain's far northwest resonates with the sacred like no other place in the country. Its splendid cathedral contains a majestic Romanesque portico behind its elaborate baroque facade; the cathedral is the suitably extravagant objective of pilgrims traversing the Camino de Santiago across northern Spain. But look beyond the cathedral and you'll find a smattering of other gilt-edged monuments and an eating culture that is Galicia in a nutshell.

Cabo de Gata

19 For a cherished memory of what the Spanish coastline used to look like before megaresorts gate-crashed the Costa del Sol, come to Cabo de Gata (p775), a wild, rugged, golf-course-free zone where fishing boats still reel in the day's catch and bold cliffs clash with the azure Mediterranean. Considering it's one of the driest areas of Europe, the Cabo is abundant with feathered fauna and scrubby vegetation. It's also a protected area, so you can wave goodbye to your car; cycling and hiking are the best means of transport.

Picos de Europa

20 Jutting out in compact form just back from the rugged and ever-changing coastline of Cantabria and Asturias, the Picos (p495) comprise three dramatic limestone massifs, unique in Spain but geologically similar to the Alps and jammed with inspiring trails. These ridgelines, an integral part of Spain's second-largest national park, boast some of the most spectacular mountain scenery in the country – no small claim considering the presence of the Pyrenees and Sierra Nevada. The Picos de Europa deservedly belong in such elite company.

BORGESE MAURIZIO / HEMIS / CORBIS ©

Segovia

21 One of the most beautiful medium-sized towns in Spain, Segovia (p155) has the usual glittering array of Castilian churches and a fine location, strung out along a ridge against a backdrop of often snowcapped mountains. But two buildings of legend set Segovia apart. Its multi-turreted Alcázar provided the inspiration for Walt Disney's castle confection, while a gigantic but elegant Roman aqueduct of granite blocks (held together by not a drop of mortar) has stood the test of time in the heart of town for almost 2000 years.

Beaches of Menorca

22 At a time when the Spanish Mediterranean has become a byword for mass tourism, Menorca (p625) is just a little bit different. Saved from the worst effects of overdevelopment, most of the island is a Unesco Biosphere Reserve with 216km of coastline and beaches that defy description. Some assert that reaching them by sea is the height of pleasure, but happening upon them from the interior brings equal joy. Among the best are Cala Macarelleta and Cala en Turqueta.

Camino de Santiago

23 Every year, tens of thousands of pilgrims and walkers with all manner of motivations set out to walk across northern Spain. Their destination, Santiago de Compostela, is a place of untold significance for Christians, but the appeal of this epic walk (p45) goes far beyond the religious. With numerous routes across the north, there is no finer way to get under Spain's skin and experience the pleasures and caprices of its natural world. And even completing one small stage will leave you with a lifetime of impressions.

Three Cultures in Toledo

24 Symbolic home to Spain's Catholic Church and the army, the medieval core of Toledo (p205) is an extraordinary piece of world heritage. Known as 'the city of the three cultures' (where Muslims, Jews and Christians once rubbed shoulders), it remains a fascinating labyrinth today with former mosques, synagogues and churches; the latter are still very much in use and the cathedral is one of Spain's most imposing. Given Toledo's proximity to Madrid, the city can get overrun with day-trippers. Stay overnight – that's when Toledo really comes into its own.

Costa Brava

25 Easily accessible by air and land from the rest of Europe, and filled with villages and beaches of the kind that spawned northern Europe's summer obsession with the Spanish coast, the Costa Brava (p308) in Catalonia is one of our favourite corners of the Mediterranean. Beyond this, however, the spirit of Salvador Dalí lends so much personality and studied eccentricity to the Costa Brava experience, from his one-time home in Port-lligat near Cadaqués (p323) to Dalí-centric sites in Figueres (p326) and Castell de Púbol (p314).

24

CHRISTOPHER GROENHOUT / GETTY IMAGES ©

25

PETER ADAMS PHOTOGRAPHY LTD / ALAMY ©

need to know

Currency
» The euro (€)

Language
» Spanish (castellano).
Also Catalan, Basque
and Galician.

When to Go

Santiago de Compostela
GO May–Sep

Barcelona
GO year-round

Madrid
GO Mar–May, Sep & Oct

Valencia
GO year-round

Seville
GO Oct–Apr

- Dry climate
- Warm to hot summers, cold winters
- Mild to hot summers, cold winters
- Cold climate

High Season
(Jun–Aug, public
holidays)
» Accommodation
books out and prices
increase by up to
50%.
» Low season in
parts of inland Spain.
» Expect warm, dry
and sunny weather;
more humid in
coastal areas.

Shoulder
(Mar–May,
Sep & Oct)
» A good time to
travel with mild, clear
weather and fewer
crowds.
» Local festivals can
send prices soaring.

Low Season
(Nov–Feb)
» Cold in central
Spain; rain in the
north and northwest.
» Mild temperatures
in Andalucía and the
Mediterranean coast.
» This is high season
in ski resorts.

Your Daily Budget

Budget less than
€75
» Dorm beds: €17
to €22
» Doubles in *hostales*:
€55 to €65 (more in
Madrid & Barcelona)
» Supermarkets and
lunch *menú del día*
» Use museum and
gallery 'free admission'
afternoons

Midrange
€75–175
» Room in midrange
hotel: €65 to €140
» Lunch and/or dinner
in local restaurant
» Car hire: from €25
per day

Top end over
€175
» Room in top-end
hotel: €140 and up
(€200 in Madrid and
Barcelona)
» Fine dining for lunch
and dinner
» Regularly stay in
paradores

Money
» ATMs widely available. Credit cards accepted in most hotels, restaurants and shops.

Visas
» Generally not required for stays up to 90 days (not at all for members of EU or Schengen countries). Some nationalities need a Schengen visa.

Mobile Phones
» Local SIM cards widely available and can be used in European and Australian mobile phones.

Driving
» Drive on the right; steering wheel is on the left side of the car.

Websites
» **Fiestas.net** (www. fiestas.net) Festivals around the country.

» **Lonely Planet** (www.lonelyplanet. com/spain) Destination information, hotel bookings, traveller forums and more.

» **Renfe** (Red Nacional de los Ferrocarriles Españoles; www.renfe. com) Spain's rail network.

» **Tour Spain** (www. tourspain.org) Culture, food and links to hotels and transport.

» **Turespaña** (www. spain.info) Spanish tourist office's site.

Exchange Rates

Australia	A$1	€0.79
Canada	C$1	€0.78
Japan	¥100	€0.98
New Zealand	NZ$1	€0.63
UK	UK£1	€1.24
US	US$1	€0.77

For current exchange rates see www.xe.com.

Important Numbers
There are no area codes in Spain.

International access code	☏00
Country code	☏34
International directory inquiries	☏11825
Domestic operator	☏1009
National directory Inquiries	☏11818
Emergencies	☏112

Arriving in Spain
» **Barajas airport (p128), Madrid**
Metro & Buses – €4.50; every five to 10 minutes from 6.05am to 2am; 30 to 40 minutes to the centre
Taxis – €25 to €35; 20 minutes to the centre

» **Aeroport del Prat (p302), Barcelona**
Buses – €5.65; every six to 15 minutes from 6.10am to 1.05am; 30 to 40 minutes to the centre
Trains – €3.60; from 5.42am to 11.38pm; 35 minutes to the centre
Taxis – €25 to €30; 30 minutes to the centre

Staying in Touch
Internet access in Spain is reasonably easy with some cafes, most hotels and even some budget accommodation having (usually) free wireless internet access for guests. Be wary, however, of hotels promising in-room wi-fi as connection speeds can vary considerably from room to room; always make it clear that you require a room with a fast connection when making a reservation. Good internet cafes are increasingly difficult to find; most corner *locutorios* (private call centres) have a few computer terminals out the back. Internet-connected telephone calls (eg Skype) are easily the cheapest way to call home. Otherwise, phonecards are your next best bet (*locutorios* have the widest selection). Buying a local prepaid SIM card for your mobile phone will work out much cheaper than racking up (often exorbitant) roaming charges.

first time

Everyone needs a helping hand when they visit a country for the first time. There are phrases to learn, customs to get used to and etiquette to understand. The following section will help demystify Spain so your first trip goes as smoothly as your fifth.

Language

English is quite widely spoken throughout Spain. This is especially true in larger cities and popular tourist areas, less so in rural villages and among older Spaniards. Even Spaniards with only a few English words are generally happy to try them out. Learning a little Spanish before you come will, however, greatly increase your appreciation of the country, not least in your ability to converse with locals. Many restaurants (but by no means all) now have English-language menus, but some museums have labels only in Spanish.

Booking Ahead

Reserving a room is always recommended in high season (especially along the coast in summer or anywhere at Easter), and is usually a good idea at other times too. Most hotels and even some *hostales* (budget hotels) allow you to book online via their websites, while email enquiries in English will most often be understood. The following phrases should see you through a call if English isn't spoken.

Hello.	Hola.
I'd like to book a room.	Quisiera reservar una habitación.
a single/double room	una habitación individual/doble
My surname is ...	Mi apellido es ...
from ... to ... (date)	desde ... hasta ...
How much is it?	¿Cuánto cuesta?
per night/person	por noche/persona
Thank you (very much).	(Muchas) Gracias.

What to Wear

Spain has come a long way since the 1950s when visiting tourists were fined and escorted from Spanish beaches by police for wearing bikinis. Just about anything goes now, and you'll rarely feel uncomfortable because of what you're wearing. Northern Spain and much of the interior can be bitterly cold in winter – bring plenty of warm clothing. Also carry some form of wet-weather gear if you're in the northwest. Spaniards are generally quite fashion-conscious and well-dressed – in the cities they rarely dip below smart casual, perhaps a little more if they're going somewhere special in the evening.

What to Pack

- » Passport and/or national ID card (EU citizens)
- » Credit card
- » Drivers licence
- » Phrasebook
- » Money belt
- » Travel plug
- » Mobile (cell) phone charger
- » Earplugs for noisy Spanish nights
- » Sunscreen
- » Hat
- » Swimming towel
- » Waterproof clothing
- » Padlock for your suitcase/backpack
- » English-language reading matter

Checklist

» With huge airfare differences, check *all* airlines before booking your flight

» Check if you can use your phone in Spain (p859) and ask about roaming charges

» At the very least, book your first night's accommodation to ensure an easy start to your trip

» Check the calendar (p26) to work out which festivals to visit or avoid

» Organise travel insurance (p856)

Etiquette

Spain is fairly relaxed when it comes to etiquette. There are a few things to remember:

» **Greetings**
Spaniards almost always greet friends and strangers alike with a kiss on each cheek, although two males only do this if they're close friends, and foreigners may be excused. Say 'Hola, buenos días' – or 'Hola, buenas tardes' (in the afternoon or evening) – when meeting someone.

» **Eating & Drinking**
Spanish waiters won't expect you to thank them every time they bring you something, but they will expect you to keep your cutlery between courses in more casual bars and restaurants.

» **Civilities**
Don't necessarily expect thanks when letting someone pass.

» **Visiting Churches**
It is considered disrespectful to visit churches as a tourist during Mass and other worship services. Taking photos at such times is a definite no-no.

» **Escalators**
Always stand on the right to let people pass, especially in the metro systems of Madrid and Barcelona.

Tipping

» **When to Tip**
Tipping is customary (but by no means universal) in restaurants but optional elsewhere.

» **Restaurants**
Many Spaniards leave small change, others up to 5%, which is considered generous.

» **Taxis**
Optional, but most locals round up to the nearest euro.

» **Bars**
It's rare to leave a tip in bars (even though they may give you your change on a small dish).

Money

Paying with a credit card is almost universal in Spain, although there may be a minimum amount of €5 or €10. Visa and MasterCard are almost always accepted, American Express is widely accepted (although it's far from universal) and Diners Club is less frequently accepted. When paying with a credit card, a photo ID (such as a passport or driving licence) is usually required, even for chip cards where you're required to enter your PIN. ATMs are seemingly on every street corner and the overwhelming majority of them allow you to use international credit or debit cards to withdraw money in euros – always check the display on the ATM showing which cards you can use. Remember also that there is usually a charge (around 1.5% to 2%) on ATM cash withdrawals abroad – check with your bank to see if some Spanish banks charge less than others.

what's new

For this new edition of Spain, our authors have hunted down the fresh, the transformed, the hot and the happening. These are some of our favourites. For up-to-the-minute recommendations, see lonelyplanet.com/spain.

Barcelona Reinvented

1 Bullfighting's gone; master chef Ferran Adrià has opened a new restaurant; Gaudí's Palau Güell has reopened after two decades; new museums; new cultural hubs from La Ribera to El Raval... What can we say, it's Barcelona. (p235)

Museo del Prado, Madrid

2 Not only does the Prado now open seven days a week, but it has also unveiled a near-perfect copy of the *Mona Lisa* that came from the studio of Leonardo da Vinci. (p82)

Santiago's Guggenheim

3 Cidade da Cultura de Galicia is Galicia's grand answer to Bilbao's Guggenheim. Inaugurated in 2011, it will eventually include major performance and exhibition spaces and the Library and Archive of Galicia. (p513)

Archaeology's New Home

4 After an eight-year revamp, Oviedo's Museo Arqueológico de Asturias does full justice to a heritage spanning millennia from prehistoric cave art to the medieval kingdom that launched the Reconquista. (p480)

Metropol Parasol, Seville

5 Seville's giant 'flying waffle' has injected a dose of modernism into the city's traditional urban core. It's sparking predictable controversy, and the jury's still out on its architectural merits. (p670)

Museo Carmen Thyssen, Málaga

6 Look out for Málaga! Andalucía's emerging art capital has just added a new string to its bow in this showcase of 19th-century Spanish and Andalucian art. (p718)

France by Boat

7 A new ferry service now operates between Gijón and Saint-Nazaire (close to Nantes in northwestern France). If you're driving from the UK, the 14- to 15-hour crossing cuts days off the long drive. (p487)

A Bull Museum

8 Pamplona's Running of the Bulls now has a museum worthy of the fiesta's fame. The new Museo del Encierro has a 3D re-creation of the run and child-friendly exhibits. (p444)

Unesco's Spain

9 Mallorca's Serra de Tramuntana was elevated to Unesco's World Heritage List in 2011, while flamenco and the Mediterranean diet were added to its lists of Intangible Cultural Heritage a year before. (p617)

Toledo's Alcázar

10 We've been waiting for years for them to reopen Toledo's Alcázar, one of inland Spain's most iconic buildings, and it was worth the wait. It's home to Spain's best military museum, and the architecture is something special. (p207)

if you like...

Art Galleries

Spain's artistic tradition is one of Europe's richest and most original. Royal patronage of the arts ensured that works by the great painters from all over Europe also found a home in Spain. The result? Art galleries of astonishing depth.

Museo del Prado, Madrid Quite simply one of the world's best galleries (p82)

Centro de Arte Reina Sofía, Madrid Picasso's *Guernica*, Dalí and Miró (p79)

Museo Thyssen-Bornemisza, Madrid Works by seemingly every European master (p87)

Museo Picasso, Málaga More than 200 works by Picasso, Málaga's favourite son (p716)

Museu Picasso, Barcelona Unrivalled collection from Picasso's early years (p249)

Teatre-Museu Dalí, Figueres As weird and wonderful as Salvador Dalí himself (p326)

Museo Guggenheim, Bilbao Showpiece architecture and world-class modern art (p409)

Museo de Bellas Artes, Valencia City Another stunning gallery with many big names (p556)

Cidade da Cultura de Galicia, Santiago de Compostela Galicia's stunning new riposte to the Guggenheim (p513)

Islamic Architecture

Spain's almost seven centuries of Muslim empires left behind Europe's finest accumulation of Islamic architecture. Outstanding extant remains are found in the former Moorish heartland of al-Andalus (Andalucía), especially in Unesco World Heritage–listed Granada, Córdoba and Seville.

Alhambra, Granada An extraordinary monument to the extravagance of al-Andalus (p742)

Mezquita, Córdoba Perfection wrought in stone in Córdoba's one-time great mosque (p733)

Albayzín, Granada Like a white-washed North African medina climbing up the hillside (p745)

Alcázar, Seville Exquisite detail amid a perfectly proportioned whole (p663)

Giralda, Seville The former minaret represents a high point in Seville's Islamic skyline (p662)

Aljafería, Zaragoza A rare Moorish jewel in the north (p373)

Alcazaba, Málaga An 11th-century palace-fortress (p717)

Teruel A splendid collection of Mudéjar design, proof that Islam's influence outlasted Islamic rule (p399)

Roman Ruins

Spain, or Hispania as it was then called, was an important part of the ancient Roman Empire for almost five centuries and it left behind a legacy of extraordinary sites scattered around the country. The ruins abandoned to their fate in the countryside speak eloquently of this epic past.

Mérida The most extensive Roman remains in the country (p798)

Tarragona Major public buildings peek out from beneath the new (p361)

Segovia Astonishing Roman aqueduct bisects the city (p155)

Lugo Spain's finest preserved Roman walls encircle this Galician city (p548)

Itálica Iberia's oldest Roman town with a fine amphitheatre close to Seville (p681)

Baelo Claudia, Bolonia Intact Roman town with views of Africa on Andalucía's far southern coast (p708)

Zaragoza A fine theatre, beautifully restored forum and a former river port (p371)

Villa Romana La Olmeda Spain's best-preserved Roman villa laid with exquisite mosaic floors (p180)

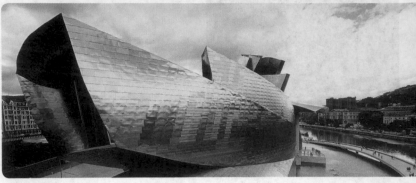

» Bilbao's Museo Guggenheim (p409), designed by Frank Gehry

Cathedrals

Catholicism stands at the heart of Spanish identity, and cathedrals form the monumental and spiritual centrepiece of many Spanish towns. This legacy of profound faith and the rich accumulation of architectural styles tell the story of the country's past writ large.

La Sagrada Família, Barcelona Gaudí's unfinished masterpiece rises like an apparition of some fevered imagination (p257)

Catedral de Santiago de Compostela One of Spain's most sacred and beautiful sites, with an extravagant facade (p511)

Catedral de León Perfectly proportioned and truly astonishing stained-glass windows (p178)

Catedral de Burgos A Gothic highpoint with legends of El Cid lording it over the old town (p186)

Catedral Nueva and Catedral Vieja, Salamanca Sandstone Gothic and Romanesque splendour side by side (p146)

Catedral de Toledo Extravagant monument to the power of Catholic Spain in its most devout heartland (p205)

Capilla Real, Granada An Isabelline-Gothic fantasy adjoining the main cathedral in a Christian response to the Alhambra (p745)

Beaches

Spain's beaches draw foreign and Spanish tourists in their millions every summer. But such is the country's surfeit of coastal riches that the unspoiled beach experience which made the Spanish coastline world-famous remains a possibility. You just need to know where to look.

Cabo de Gata, Almería A wildly beautiful reminder of the Andalucian coast as it once was (p775)

Costa de la Luz, Andalucía Unbroken stretches of sand along a beautiful coast from Tarifa to Cádiz (p705)

Playa de la Concha, San Sebastián One of the most beautiful city beaches anywhere in the world (p425)

Menorca The Balearics before mass tourism arrived and an insight into why it did (p625)

Rías Altas, Galicia Spain's most breathtaking coast with cliffs and isolated, sweeping beaches (p527)

Costa Brava Rugged coast with windswept cliffs, pristine hidden coves and wide sandy beaches (p308)

Nightlife

Nights that never end rank among the most accessible symbols of the Spanish good life. From sophisticated cocktail bars to beachside *chiringuitos* (bars), from dance-until-dawn nightclubs to outdoor *terrazas* (pavement cafes), the Spanish night is diverse, relentless and utterly intoxicating.

Ibiza Europe's after-dark club and chill-out capital and the enduring icon of Mediterranean cool (p646)

Madrid Bars, clubs, live-music venues and nights that roll effortlessly into another (p118)

Valencia Barrio del Carmen nights are famous in Spain, with a roaring soundtrack in the city's oldest quarter (p566)

Barcelona Glamorous and gritty nightspots for an international crowd (p292)

Salamanca Feel-good nights with the university crowd beneath floodlit Renaissance buildings (p149)

Zaragoza The heartbeat of Aragón with fabulous tapas bars and drinking bars that crank up well after midnight (p376)

Cádiz The essence of the Andalucian summer, where informal fun and good-natured outdoor drinking dominate the night (p692)

If you like...unspoiled coastlines
Galicia's Atlantic shoreline is wildly beautiful, especially the Costa da Morte (p520)

If you like...flamenco
Seville in Andalucía is the best place to catch flamenco live (p677)

Spanish Food

Spain obsesses about food and keeps a watchful eye over its chefs, with an eating public as eager to try something new as they are wary lest these same chefs stray too far from one of Europe's richest culinary traditions.

Pintxos in San Sebastián Spain's culinary capital, with more Michelin stars than Paris and the country's best *pintxos* (Basque tapas; p432)

Paella in Valencia The birthplace of paella and still the place for the most authentic version – think chicken, beans and rabbit (p565)

Catalonian cooking in Barcelona Home city for Catalonia's legendary cooking fuelled by Spain's finest food markets (p287)

Tapas in La Latina, Madrid Rising above Madrid's modest home-grown cuisine, this inner-city *barrio* (district) showcases the best tapas from around Spain (p111)

Seafood in Galicia The dark arts of boiling an octopus and the Atlantic's sea creatures (goose barnacles, anyone?) are pure culinary pleasure (p515)

Spanish Wine

In many parts of the country you won't find anything *but* wines from Spain: many Spaniards simply don't see the need for anything else. La Rioja is the king of Spanish wine regions, but there's so much more to Spanish wines.

La Rioja wine region Bodegas, wine museums and vineyards to the horizon – this is Spanish wine's heartland (p459)

Ribera del Duero Spain's favourite wine region in waiting with bodegas lining the riverbank (p197)

Cava bodegas, Penedès wine country The sparkling wines that are Spain's favourite Christmas drink (p359)

Sherry bodegas, El Puerto de Santa María The sherry capital of the world with numerous bodegas open for visits and tastings (p694)

Cider-drinking, Asturias A local passion poured straight from a great height (p482)

Somontano, Aragón One of Spain's most underrated wine regions with dozens of vineyards open to the public (p396)

Zalacaín, Madrid Around 35,000 bottles and 800 different wine varieties at this upscale restaurant (p113)

Hiking

Spanish landscapes are continental in their variety and are one of Europe's premier hiking destinations, from the Pyrenees in the north to the quiet valleys of Andalucía in the south. A superb network of protected areas is the starting point.

Parque Nacional de Ordesa y Monte Perdido Pyrenean high country at its most spectacular (p386)

Parc Nacional d'Aigüestortes i Estany de Sant Maurici More Pyrenean splendour in Catalonia (p343)

Camino de Santiago One of the world's most famous walks, which can last a day or weeks (p45)

Picos de Europa Jagged peaks and steep trails inland from the Bay of Biscay (p495)

Serra de Tramuntana The finest hiking in the Balearics, along Mallorca's west coast (p617)

Sierra Nevada Wildlife and stunning views in the shadow of mainland Spain's highest mountain (p755)

Sierra de Grazalema White villages and precipitous mountains in Andalucía (p703)

month by month

Top Events

1 Semana Santa (Holy Week), usually March or April

2 Las Fallas, March

3 Bienal de Flamenco, September

4 Carnaval, February or March

5 Feria de Abril, April

January

In January the ski resorts in the Pyrenees in the northeast and the Sierra Nevada, close to Granada in the south, are in full swing. School holidays run until around 8 January so book ahead.

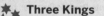 **Three Kings**
The Día de los Reyes Magos (Three Kings' Day), or simply Reyes, on 6 January, is the most important day on a Spanish kid's calendar. The evening before, three local politicians dress up as the three wise men and lead a sweet-distributing frenzy of Cabalgata de Reyes through the centre of most towns.

February

This is often the coldest month in Spain, with temperatures close to freezing, especially in the north and inland regions such as Madrid. If you're heading to Carnaval, you'll find accommodation at a premium in Cádiz, Sitges and Ciudad Rodrigo.

 Life's a Carnaval
Riotously fun Carnaval, ending on the Tuesday 47 days before Easter Sunday, involves fancy-dress parades and festivities. It's wildest in Cádiz (p689), Sitges (p357) and Ciudad Rodrigo (p151). Other curious celebrations are held at Vilanova i La Geltrú and Solsona.

Return to the Middle Ages
In one of Spain's coldest corners, Teruel's inhabitants don their medieval finery and step back to the Middle Ages with markets, food stalls and a re-enactment of a local lovers' legend during the Fiesta Medieval (p401).

Contemporary-Art Fair
One of Europe's biggest celebrations of contemporary art, Madrid's Feria Internacional de Arte Contemporánea (Arco; p102) draws gallery reps and exhibitors from all over the world. It's a thrilling counterpoint to the old masters on display year-round in galleries across the capital.

March

With the arrival of spring, Spain begins to shake off its winter blues (such as they are), the weather starts to warm up ever so slightly and Spaniards start dreaming of a summer by the beach.

 Las Fallas
The extraordinary festival of Las Fallas consists of several days of all-night dancing and drinking, first-class fireworks and processions from 15 to 19 March. Its principal stage is Valencia City (see the boxed text, p567) and the festivities culminate in the ritual burning of effigies in the streets.

April

Spain has a real spring in its step with wildflowers in full bloom, Easter celebrations and school holidays. It requires some advance planning (ie book ahead), but it's a great time to be here.

Semana Santa (Holy Week)

Easter (the dates change each year) entails parades of *pasos* (holy figures), hooded penitents and huge crowds. It's extravagantly celebrated in Seville (p672), as well as Málaga (p720), Córdoba, Toledo (p205), Ávila (p140), Cuenca (p226), Lorca (p606) and Zamora (p172).

Dance of Death

The Dansa de la Mort (Dance of Death) on Holy Thursday in the Catalan village of Verges (see the boxed text, p318) is a chilling experience. This nocturnal dance of skeleton figures is the centrepiece of Holy Week celebrations.

Los Empalaos

On Holy Thursday, Villanueva de la Vera, in northeast Extremadura, plays out an extraordinary act of Easter self-abnegation; the devotion and self-inflicted suffering of the barefoot penitents leaves most onlookers breathless. See the boxed text, p794, for details.

Moros y Cristianos (Moors & Christians)

Late-April colourful parades and mock battles between Christian and Muslim 'armies' in Alcoy (see the boxed text, p591), near Alicante, make this one of the most spectacular of many such festivities staged in Valencia and Alicante provinces.

Feria de Abril (April Fair)

This weeklong party (p673), held in Seville in the second half of April, is the biggest of Andalucía's fairs. *Sevillanos* (Seville residents) ride around on horseback and in elaborate horse-drawn carriages by day and, dressed up in their best traditional finery, dance late into the night.

Feria del Queso (Cheese Fair)

On the last weekend in April, medieval Trujillo (p785), in Extremadura, hosts this pungent cheese fair with the overwhelming aroma of cheeses from all over Spain. It's sometimes held at the beginning of May.

Romería de la Virgen

On the last Sunday in April, hundreds of thousands of people make a mass pilgrimage to the Santuario de la Virgen de la Cabeza near Andújar, in Jaén province. A small statue of the Virgin is paraded about, exciting great passions.

May

A glorious time to be in Spain, May sees the countryside carpeted with spring wildflowers and the weather can feel like summer's just around the corner. In Jerez de la Frontera, the Feria de Caballo is one of Spain's most iconic festivals and you'll need to book accommodation weeks, if not months, in advance.

Feria del Caballo (Horse Fair)

A colourful equestrian fair (p699) in Andalucía's horse capital, Jerez de la Frontera, the Feria del Caballo (p699) is one of Andalucía's most festive and extravagant fiestas. It features parades, horse shows, bullfights and plenty of music and dance.

World Music in Cáceres

For three days Cáceres is taken by musical storm for the World of Music, Arts and Dance festival (Womad; p782). Performers from all over the planet take to stages in the medieval squares of the city.

Córdoba's Courtyards Open Up

Scores of beautiful private courtyards in Córdoba are opened to the public for two weeks for the Concurso de Patios Cordobeses (p738). It's a rare chance to see an otherwise-hidden side of Córdoba strewn with flowers and freshly painted.

Muslim Pirates

Sóller, in northern Mallorca, is invaded by Muslim pirates in early May. The resulting 'battle' between townsfolk and invaders (see the boxed text, p621), known as Es Firó, re-creates an infamous (and unsuccessful) 16th-century assault on the town.

Fiesta de San Isidro

Madrid's major fiesta (p102) celebrates the city's patron saint with bullfights, parades, concerts and more. Locals dress up in traditional costumes, and some of the events, such as the bullfighting season, last for a month.

June

By June, the north is shaking off its winter chill and the Camino de Santiago's trails are becoming crowded. In the south, it's warming up as the coastal resorts ready themselves for the summer onslaught.

Romería del Rocío

Focused on Pentecost weekend (the seventh after Easter), this festive pilgrimage is made by up to one million people to the shrine of the Virgin in El Rocío (see the boxed text, p685). This is Andalucía's Catholic tradition at its most curious and compelling.

Feast of Corpus Christi

On the Thursday in the ninth week after Easter (sometimes May, sometimes June), religious processions and celebrations take place in Toledo (p209) and other cities. The strangest celebration is the baby-jumping tradition of Castrillo de Murcia (see the boxed text, p193).

Bonfires & Fireworks

Midsummer bonfires, fireworks and roaming giants and other figures feature on the eve of the Fiesta de San Juan (24 June; Dia de Sant Joan), notably along the Mediterranean coast, particularly in Barcelona (p283) and in Ciutadella, Menorca, where you can see splendid horsemanship in parades.

Electronica Festival

Performers and spectators come from all over the world for Sónar (p283), Barcelona's two-day celebration of electronic music which is said to be Europe's biggest festival of its kind. Dates vary each year.

Wine Battle

On 29 June Haro, one of the premier wine towns of La Rioja, enjoys the Batalla del Vino (p461), squirting wine all over the place in one of Spain's messiest playfights, pausing only to drink the good stuff.

July

Temperatures in Andalucía and much of the interior can be fiercely hot, but it's a great time to be at the beach and is one of the best months for hiking in the Pyrenees.

Festival Internacional de la Guitarra

Córdoba's contribution to Spain's impressive calendar of musical events, this fine international guitar festival (p738) ranges from flamenco and classical to rock, blues and beyond. Headline performances take place in the Alcázar gardens at night.

Running of the Bulls

The Fiesta de San Fermín (Sanfermines) is the weeklong nonstop festival and party in Pamplona (see the boxed text, p444) with the daily *encierro* (running of the bulls) as its centrepiece. Anything can happen, but it rarely ends well for the bull. The anti-bullfighting event,

the Running of the Nudes, takes place two days earlier.

Celtic Pride

Groups from as far off as Nova Scotia come to celebrate their Celtic roots with the *gallegos* (Galicians) in this bagpipe- and fiddler-filled music fest in the Festival Ortigueira (see the boxed text, p530) in Galicia.

Día de la Virgen del Carmen

Around 16 July in most coastal towns, particularly in some parts of Andalucía, the image of the patron of fisherfolk is carried into the sea or paraded on a flotilla of small boats.

Feast of St James

The Día de Santiago marks the day of Spain's national saint and is spectacularly celebrated in Galicia at Santiago de Compostela (p514). With so many pilgrims in town, it's the city's most festive two weeks of the year.

Festival Internacional de Jazz e Blues de Pontevedra

Top jazz and blues musicians converge on the pretty Galician town of Pontevedra (p534) for four days of good listening near the end of July. The international get-together is preceded by several days of local acts.

Festival Internacional de Benicàssim

Spain is awash with outdoor concert festivals attracting big-name acts from around the country and abroad, especially in summer. This one, in the Valencian town of Benicàssim (p572), remains one of the original and best.

August

Spaniards from all over the country join Europeans in converging on the coastal resorts of the Mediterranean. Although the weather can be unpredictable, Spain's northwestern Atlantic coast offers a more nuanced summer experience.

☆ Festival del Teatro Clásico

The peerless Roman theatre and amphitheatre in Mérida, Extremadura (p801), become the stage for the classics of ancient Greece and Rome, and the occasional newbie such as Will Shakespeare. Performances are held most nights during July and August.

 More Muslim Pirates

In northwest Mallorca, Pollença (p622) is the scene of fierce mock combat between invading Muslim pirates and townsfolk during the Festes de la Patrona. The afternoon of processions and combat in the streets of the town is preceded by much all-night merriment.

⚔ La Tomatina

Buñol's massive tomato-throwing festival (see the boxed text, p570), held in late August, must be one of the messiest get-togethers in the country. Thousands of people launch about 100 tonnes of tomatoes at one another in just an hour or so!

All About Cheese

In Arenas de Cabrales (p502) at the foot of the Picos de Europa, cheese lovers are treated to cheese tasting, making, judging and more. They live for their cheese and cider in this part of the world, and there are both in abundance.

Natural Cider Festival

Gijón's Fiesta de la Sidra Natural (p484) gives expression to the Asturian obsession with cider and even includes an annual world-record attempt for the number of people simultaneously pouring cider in one place. It also involves musical concerts.

September

This is the month when Spain returns to work after a seemingly endless summer. Numerous festivals take advantage of the fact that weather generally remains warm until late September at least.

☆ Bienal de Flamenco

There are flamenco festivals all over Spain throughout the year, but this is the most prestigious of them all. Held in Seville (p673) in even-numbered years (and Málaga every other year), it draws the biggest names in the genre.

Fiesta de la Virgen de Guadalupe

The pretty town of Guadalupe in Extremadura celebrates its very own Virgin Mary (p789). A statue is paraded about on the evening of the 6th and again on the 8th, which also happens to be Extremadura's regional feast day.

Feria de Pedro Romero

The honouring of Pedro Romero, one of the legends of bullfighting, is a good excuse for the people of Ronda to host weeks of partying (p727). Highlights include a flamenco festival, an unusual program of bullfighting and much all-night partying.

🍷 La Rioja's Grape Harvest

Logroño celebrates the feast day of St Matthew (Fiesta de San Mateo) and the year's grape harvest (p455). There are grape-crushing ceremonies and endless opportunities to sample the fruit of the vine in liquid form.

Barcelona's Big Party

Barcelona's Festes de la Mercè (p283) marks the end of summer with four days of parades, concerts, theatre, fire running and more. Barcelona's always fun, but this is a whole new level.

☆ San Sebastián Film Festival

It may not be Cannes, but San Sebastián's annual two-week celebration of film (p429) is one of the most prestigious dates on Europe's film-festival circuit. It's held in the second half of the month and has been gathering plaudits since 1957.

Romans & Carthaginians

In the second half of the month, locals dress up to

re-enact ancient battles during the festival of Carthagineses y Romanos (p602) in Cartagena. It's among the more original mock battles staged around Spain to honour the distant past.

October

Autumn can be a lovely time to be in Spain, with generally mild temperatures throughout the country, although the winter chill can start to bite in central and northern parts of the country.

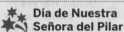 **Día de Nuestra Señora del Pilar**

In Zaragoza on 12 October, the faithful mix with hedonists to celebrate this festival dedicated to Our Lady of the Pillar (p374); the pillar in question is in the cathedral, but much of the fun happens in the bars nearby.

Fiesta de Santa Teresa

The patron saint of Ávila is honoured with 10 days of processions, concerts and fireworks around her feast day (p140). Huddled behind medieval walls, the festival brings to life the powerful cult of personality surrounding Ávila's most famous daughter.

November

A quiet time on the festival calendar, November is cool throughout the country. Depending on the year, the ski season usually begins in this month in the Pyrenees and Sierra Nevada.

Festival Jazz Madrid

One of two annual jazz festivals in the capital (the other one is in the spring), this increasingly prestigious jazz festival (p102) plays out in the famous jazz clubs and larger theatres across the city.

La Matanza

One of Andalucía's more macabre spectacles is November's pig massacre, known as *la matanza*, which traditionally starts on 11 November – St Martin's Day. It's an upbeat affair replicated in many mountain villages with plenty of eating and drinking.

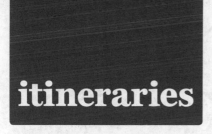

itineraries

Whether you've got six days or 60, these itineraries provide a starting point for the trip of a lifetime. Want more inspiration? Head online to lonelyplanet. com/thorntree to chat with other travellers.

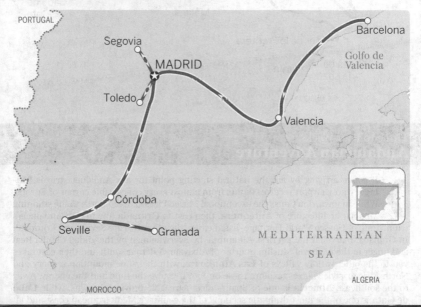

Two Weeks
The Grand Tour

So many Spanish trails begin in **Barcelona**, Spain's second-biggest city and one of the coolest places on earth. Explore the architecture and sample the food, before catching the train down the coast to **Valencia** for another dose of nightlife and the 21st-century wonders of the Ciudad de las Artes y las Ciencias. A fast train whisks you inland to the capital, mighty **Madrid**, for the irresistible street energy and one of the richest concentrations of art museums on the planet. Allow time for a day trip to **Toledo**, a medieval jewel, and/or **Segovia** with its fairytale castle, Roman aqueduct and gorgeous setting. Yet another fast train takes you deep into Andalucía, with **Córdoba**, especially its 7th-century Mezquita, the essence of the country's formerly Islamic south. The charms of **Seville**, too, span the centuries with fabulous tapas, fine flamenco and a smattering of Islamic-era monuments. But we've saved the best until last: **Granada**, the one-time capital of Muslim Al-Andalus, boasts the extraordinary Alhambra, its soulful alter ego, the Albayzín, and an eating and drinking scene that embraces Spanish culinary culture in all its variety.

Three to Four Weeks
Andalucian Adventure

If you're arriving by air, the natural starting point for any Andalucía trip is **Málaga**, whose airport receives flights from almost every conceivable corner of Europe. While in town, don't miss the exceptional Museo Picasso. Head north to the stunning Mudéjar architecture of **Antequera**, then east to **Granada**, the first in Andalucía's triumvirate of Unesco World Heritage–listed cities (the other two are Seville and Córdoba). In Granada, marvel at the peerless Alhambra, be overwhelmed by the gilded Capilla Real and linger in the medieval Muslim quarter of Albayzín. A detour south and then east takes you to the otherworldly valleys of **Las Alpujarras** with their fine mountain scenery and North African–style villages; explore these on foot if you've the time and the energy. Away to the southeast, **Almería** is one of Spain's most agreeable provincial towns, while **Cabo de Gata** is one of the most dramatic sections of the country's Mediterranean coast and an antidote to its otherwise overdeveloped shoreline.

Returning into the Andalucian heartland, via Granada, make for **Córdoba**, home to the magnificent Mezquita and an enchanted *judería* (Jewish quarter). Next stop, **Seville**, the heartbeat of Andalucía with its glorious architecture (especially the Alcázar and cathedral), fine food and soul-stirring live flamenco. There's more flamenco, as well as fine Andalucian horsemanship, at **Jerez de la Frontera**, while **Cádiz** is at once fun-loving and Europe's oldest settlement; if you're in Cádiz during Carnaval in particular you'll understand what we mean. The region's hill villages don't come any more beautiful than cliff-top **Arcos de la Frontera**, which conforms wonderfully to the stereotype of Andalucía's *pueblos blancos* (white villages). After breaking up your journey here, meander along quiet country roads east through the pretty whitewashed villages and mountain trails of **Parque Natural Sierra de Grazalema** and on to spectacularly sited **Ronda**, where a night in its palatial and precipitous *parador* is one of Spain's great sleeping experiences. **Vejer de la Frontera** is another hill town par excellence, while the sandy Atlantic beaches of the **Costa de la Luz** are some of Spain's best. End your journey in hip **Tarifa**, the southernmost tip of mainland Spain, and a centre for summer whale-watching, windsurfing and, of course, much lazing on the fine beach.

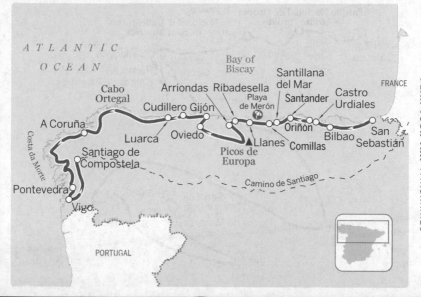

Three Weeks
Spain's Northwest

> Spain's well-drenched northern coast, at times rugged and wildly beautiful, forms
a green band from the Basque Country to Galicia, backed by the Cordillera Cantábrica. This route takes you through what is arguably Spain's most spectacular (and
certainly least developed) stretch of coastline, with gorgeous villages and fine food
thrown in for good measure.

There is no finer introduction to the country than **San Sebastián**, its two dramatic headlands giving way to a perfect crescent bay. Its old town is arguably Spain's spiritual home of
tapas (or *pintxos* as they call them here) and spending an evening wandering from bar to
bar with their counters groaning under the weight of bite-sized morsels is close to gastronomic paradise. West of San Sebastián, **Bilbao** is best known as the home of the showpiece
Guggenheim Museum. Heading west, hug the coast of Cantabria and Asturias and drop by
the old centre of **Castro Urdiales**, to surf at **Oriñón** and to promenade along the waterfront at **Santander**. Following Cantabria's eastern coast, explore the cobblestone medieval
marvel that is **Santillana del Mar** and admire the Modernista architecture in **Comillas**.
The eastern Asturias coast is best travelled by train, stopping off at **Llanes** and **Ribadesella**,
two of many achingly picturesque villages along Asturias' coast. **Arriondas**, the next stop,
is one gateway to the majestic **Picos de Europa** with their vertiginous rock walls, outstanding scenery and fine hiking opportunities. Next make your way to **Oviedo**, Asturias' capital,
for its pre-Romanesque architecture, and **Gijón**, a substantial port where cider, one of the
great Asturian passions, flows freely. West of Gijón, secluded beaches await between the
picturesque fishing harbours of **Cudillero** and **Luarca**. Galicia's coastline is one of Spain's
great natural wonders, punctuated with secluded fishing villages and stunning cliffs. As
you make your way around the coast, don't miss **Cabo Ortegal**, dynamic **A Coruña** and
the **Costa da Morte**. On the cusp of Portugal, **Pontevedra** and **Vigo** are worth continuing
down the coastline for, before doubling back to **Santiago de Compostela**, a thoroughly
Galician city, a place of pilgrim footfalls, fine regional cuisine and a cathedral of rare power.

Those with more time could make the final approach on foot along the Camino Portugues
route of the **Camino de Santiago** pilgrim route. Alternatively, discover the area with the
Transcantábrico scenic train.

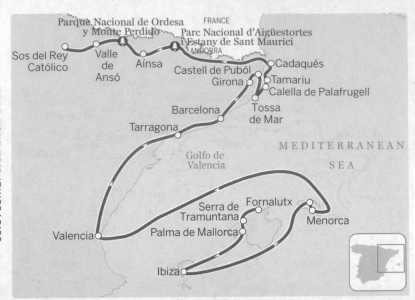

Three to Four Weeks
Balearics to the Pyrenees

> You could spend weeks exploring the Balearic Islands, depending, of course, on how long you need passing long, lazy days on its wonderful beaches. Begin, like so many holidaymakers, in pretty **Palma de Mallorca**, lingering in particular over its astonishing cathedral. Before leaving the island, set aside time to leave the crowds behind by trekking into the **Serra de Tramuntana** and exploring the villages of Mallorca's northwestern coast, such as **Fornalutx**, and the fine coastal scenery at Cap de Formentor. Take a ferry to **Ibiza** and dive into its world-famous nightlife, before island-hopping again, this time to **Menorca** and its wonderful south-coast beaches.

Catch one last ferry from Menorca to **Valencia** and dine on paella by the sea, admire the breathtaking Ciudad de las Artes y las Ciencias and stay out late in the Barrio del Carmen. Follow the Mediterranean northeast to **Tarragona**, one of the most significant Roman sites in the country. Follow the Costa Brava, acquaint yourself with **Barcelona**, then head inland to **Girona** and Salvador Dalí's fantasy castle **Castell de Puból**. Returning to the coast, dip into pretty villages such as **Tossa de Mar**, **Calella de Palafrugell** and **Tamariu** en route to **Cadaqués**, Dalí's beautiful one-time home.

Leave the Mediterranean behind and climb up into the Pyrenees, passing through the increasingly spectacular northwestern valleys to the **Parc Nacional d'Aigüestortes i Estany de Sant Maurici**, before crossing the provincial frontier into Aragón. Medieval, stone-built **Aínsa** is the prettiest among many Aragonese villages in the Pyrenean foothills; linger here for a couple of days before drawing near to the **Parque Nacional de Ordesa y Monte Perdido**, perhaps the most shapely mountains of all on the Spanish side of the frontier. Apart from being staggeringly beautiful, this is one of Europe's premier hiking destinations and its restrictions on the number of visitors make this a top-notch wilderness destination. As you head west in the shadow of the snow-capped peaks, detour up the **Valle de Ansó** and then end your journey in the idyllic hill village of **Sos del Rey Católico**.

Legend:
- Castile & Aragón
- Extreme West

(Map showing: FRANCE, ANDORRA, León, Puebla de Sanabria, Burgos, Covarrubias, Zaragoza, Sierra de Francia/La Alberca, Zamora, Salamanca, Medinaceli, Daroca, Ciudad Rodrigo, Ávila, Albarracín, Plasencia, Parque Nacional de Monfragüe, MADRID, Teruel, COSTA DEL AZAHAR, Cáceres, Guadalupe, Trujillo, PORTUGAL, Mérida, Jerez de los Caballeros, Zafra, Seville, MEDITERRANEAN SEA)

Three to Four Weeks
Castilla & Aragón

From **Madrid**, head west to some of the loveliest towns of the Spanish heartland: walled **Ávila**, sleepy **Ciudad Rodrigo** and vibrant **Salamanca**. In the latter, wander with wonder at night through the pulsating streets, amid its splendid plateresque public buildings, luminous and floodlit. Salamanca is also a gateway to some of Spain's least-visited backcountry villages, especially in the timeworn **Sierra de Francia**. The pick of a very fine bunch is probably **La Alberca**. Meander north to provincial **Zamora**, a little-visited Romanesque gem, and on to the medieval village of **Puebla de Sanabria**. The cathedral towns of **León** and **Burgos** take you into the Castilian heartland, while eastern Castilian villages such as **Covarrubias** and **Medinaceli** are beautiful places to rest. Cross the border into Aragón and make for **Zaragoza**, one of Spain's most vibrant cities with a wealth of monuments and great tapas. Heading south, **Daroca** is a picturesque place to break up the journey, while **Teruel** has a compact old quarter studded with Mudéjar gems. Finish your journey in nearby **Albarracín**, one of Spain's most spectacular villages.

Two Weeks
Extreme West

Extremadura is one of Spain's least-known corners, which is all the more reason to visit. Begin in Extremadura's north, in **Plasencia**, which is jammed with notable buildings, churches and convents; for centuries it was the region's principal city, and makes a good base for excursions up the northeast valleys. From Plasencia, a circuit takes you first to the birders' paradise that is the **Parque Nacional de Monfragüe** and then on to the charming hill town and pilgrims' destination of **Guadalupe**, lorded over by the monastery complex dedicated to Our Lady of Guadalupe. Country roads then lead westwards to the medieval town of **Trujillo**, a warren of cobbled lanes, churches and the newer Renaissance-era additions that were the fruit of conquistador gold. A short drive further west lies the medieval splendour of **Cáceres**. To the south stand some of Spain's most impressive Roman ruins in **Mérida**. Further south again across the dry plains lies the white town of **Zafra**, a precursor to Andalucía in both spirit and geography. Rather than continue straight into Andalucía, make a westwards detour to the hilly town of **Jerez de los Caballeros** before finally heading south for magical **Seville**.

Eat & Drink Like a Local

Food Calendar

Andalucía is unusual in Europe in that, due to the balmy climate and exceptionally fertile soil, fruit and vegetables can be grown year-round.

Winter: Stews & Meats

Across inland Spain, winter is the time for fortifying stews (such as *cocido*) and roasted meats, especially *cochinillo* (suckling pig) and *cordero* (spring lamb).

Winter–Spring: Catalonia's Calçots

From November through to March or April, Catalans salivate over these large spring onions that are eaten with your hands, *romesco* (a rich sauce made from red peppers, ground almonds, olive oil and vinegar) and a bib.

Summer: Soups

Few dishes are quite so seasonal as the cold soups gazpacho and *salmorejo* – specialties of Andalucía, they only appear in summer when they're perfect.

Autumn: Grape Harvest, La Rioja

The Fiesta de San Mateo in Logroño (21 September) brings Spain's premier wine region to life.

For Spaniards, eating is so much more than a functional pastime to be squeezed between other more important tasks. Instead, it's one of life's great pleasures, a social event to be enjoyed with friends. Savoured like all good things in life, eating is always taken seriously enough to have adequate hours allocated for the purpose.

At one level, joining locals in enjoying Spanish food requires nothing more than turning up and placing your order – it's that easy. And yet, even a little advance knowledge and planning will greatly enhance your eating experience and could mean the difference between ordering a mediocre meal and one that lives long in the memory. Understanding the regional differences of Spanish food could make all the difference as you map out your itinerary.

And one other thing... Having joined Spaniards around the table for years, we've come to understand what eating Spanish-style is all about. If we could distil the essence of how to make food a highlight of your trip into a few simple rules, it would be this: *always* ask for the local speciality; *never* be shy about looking around to see what others have ordered before choosing; *always* ask the waiter for their recommendations; and, wherever possible, make your meal a centrepiece of your day.

For a more detailed look at some of the essential elements in Spanish cuisine – paella, *jamón* (cured ham), tapas, olive oil – turn to our essay The Spanish Table (p840).

ORDERING TAPAS

Too many travellers miss out on the joys of tapas because, unless you speak Spanish, the art of ordering can seem one of the dark arts of Spanish etiquette. Fear not – it's not as difficult as it first appears.

In the Basque Country, Zaragoza and many bars in Madrid, Barcelona and elsewhere, it couldn't be easier. With tapas varieties lined up along the bar, you either take a small plate and help yourself or point to the morsel you want. If you do this, it's customary to keep track of what you eat (by holding on to the toothpicks for example) and then tell the bar staff how many you've had when it's time to pay. Otherwise, many places have a list of tapas, either on a menu or posted up behind the bar. If you can't choose, ask for *'la especialidad de la casa'* (the house speciality) and it's hard to go wrong. Another way of eating tapas is to order *raciones* (literally 'rations'; large tapas servings) or *media raciones* (half-rations; smaller tapas servings). These plates and half-plates of a particular dish are a good way to go if you particularly like something and want more than a mere tapa. Remember, however, that after a couple of *raciones* you'll almost certainly be full; the *media ración* is a good choice if you want to experience a broader range of tastes. In some bars you'll also get a small (free) tapa when you buy a drink.

Spanish Food Experiences

Food & Wine Festivals

» **Feria del Queso, Trujillo** (p785) An orgy of cheese tasting and serious competition in late April or early May.

» **Feria del Vino del Ribeiro, Ribadavia** (p544) Galicia's south hosts the region's biggest wine festival in early July.

» **Batalla del Vino, Haro** (p461) Every 29 June in Haro, La Rioja, they have a really messy wine fight.

» **Fiesta del Albariño, Cambados** (p533) Galicia's most decorated white is worshipped at the end of July or early August.

» **Fiesta de la Sidra Natural, Gijón** (p484) Includes an annual world-record attempt on the number of people simultaneously pouring cider.

» **Certamen de Queso, Arenas de Cabrales** (p502) A pungent cheese festival in late August in Asturias.

» **Fiesta de San Mateo, Logroño** (p455) La Rioja's September grape harvest is celebrated with grape-crushing ceremonies and tastings.

» **Festa do Marisco, O Grove** (p534) Galicia's love affair with seafood overflows in mid-October.

Meals of a Lifetime

» **Arzak** (p434), San Sebastián

» **Martín Berasategui Restaurant** (p434), San Sebastián

» **El Celler de Can Roca** (p319), Girona

» **Sergi Arola Gastro** (p112), Madrid

» **Tickets** (p291), Barcelona

» **Can Fabes** (p319), south of Barcelona

» **La Cuchara de San Telmo** (p432), San Sebastián

» **Santceloni** (p113), Madrid

Street Foods & Snacks

Spain gave birth to possibly the world's most ingenious form of snacking – tapas (see p840 for more information).

One of the finest comfort foods in the world, *chocolate con churros* (deep-fried doughnut strips dipped in thick hot chocolate) is a particular Spanish favourite for breakfast or at dawn on your way home from a night out. Madrid's Chocolatería de San Ginés (p113) is the most famous place to try them.

Spain's fresh food markets make for an interesting alternative to bars and restaurants. Many have been transformed to meet all of your food needs at once. The trend began years ago in Barcelona's Mercat de la Boqueria (p290), but it really gathered pace in Madrid in recent years in the Mercado de San Miguel (p107) and **Mercado de San Antón** (www.mercadosananton.com; Calle de Augusto Figueroa 24; meals €10-30; ⊗10am-midnight Mon-Thu, to 1.30am Fri-Sun; ⓂChueca).

FAMOUS CHEFS

» **Ferran Adrià** The Catalan poster boy for Spain's food revolution, his El Bulli was regularly voted the world's best restaurant: El Bulli may have closed, but Tickets (p291) in Barcelona heralds a whole new direction.

» **Juan Mari Arzak** One of the leading lights in the world of *nuevo cocina vasca* (Basque nouvelle cuisine), San Sebastián's Arzak (p434) has three Michelin stars and Juan Mari Arzak could just be Spain's finest chef.

» **Sergi Arola** One of a number of young Catalan chefs to emerge from the kitchens (and shadow) of Ferran Adrià to rival the great man himself. He runs the Sergi Arola Gastro (p112) in Madrid.

» **Martín Berasategui** Another Basque master chef with a penchant for experimentation, Berasategui earned his first Michelin star at age 26 and now has a total of four. Try the Martín Berasategui Restaurant (p434) in San Sebastián.

Cooking Courses

Alambique (p97) Cooking classes in Madrid covering Spanish and international themes.

Apunto – Centro Cultural del Gusto (p101) Fun and varied classes in Madrid.

Catacurian (☑97 782 53 41; www.catacurian. com) English-language wine and cooking classes in the Priorat region with Catalan chef Alicia Juanpere and her American partner.

Cook and Taste (p281) One of Barcelona's best cooking schools.

Cooking Club (☑91 323 29 58; www.club -cooking.com; Calle de Veza 33; Ⓜ Valdeacederas) Respected program of classes (in Madrid) across a range of cooking styles.

Dom's Gastronom Cookery School (☑93 674 51 60; www.domsgastronom.com; Passeig del Roser 43; 8 hours of classes over 4 days €100) Cordon-bleu chef Dominique Heathcoate runs the full gamut of Catalan, Spanish and French cuisine. In Barcelona.

L'Atelier (☑958 857 501; http://www.ivu. org/atelier/index-eng; Calle Alberca 21; cooking classes per person per day €50) Award-winning vegetarian chef Jean-Claude Juston runs vegetarian cooking courses in Andalucía's Las Alpujarras.

Regional Specialities

Spaniards love to travel in their own country and, given the riches on offer, they especially love to do so in pursuit of the perfect meal. Tell a Spaniard that you're on your way to a particular place and they're sure to start salivating at the mere thought of the local speciality and they'll surely have a favourite restaurant at which to enjoy it. Here's our pick of what to order wherever you find yourself in Spain. Note that many of our destination chapters also contain boxed texts on the relevant region's cuisine.

Basque Country & Catalonia

If Spaniards elsewhere in the country love their food, the Basques and Catalans are obsessed with it. They talk about it endlessly. They plan their day around it. And then they spend the rest of their time dreaming about it.

The confluence of sea and mountains has bequeathed to the Basque Country an extraordinary culinary richness, a cuisine as much defined by the fruits of the Bay of Biscay as by the fruits of the land. You're as likely to find great *anchoas* (anchovies), *gambas* (prawns) and *bacalao* (salted cod) as you are heaving steaks and *jamón,* and often in surprising *mar y montaña* (sea-and-mountain) combinations. It's in San Sebastián that you understand how deeply ingrained food is in Basque culture; the city is home to everything from secret gastronomic societies and exclusive sit-down restaurants with the full complement of Michelin stars to the more accessible *pintxos* (Basque tapas) bars of the Parte Vieja. It was from the kitchens of San Sebastián that *nueva cocina vasca* (Basque nouvelle cuisine) emerged, announcing Spain's arrival as a culinary superpower.

Considered by many to be the Basque Country's equal when it comes to food excellence, Catalonia blends traditional Catalan flavours and extraordinary geographical diversity with an openness to influences from the rest of Europe. All manner of seafood, paella, rice and pasta dishes are regulars

» (above) A staple of Spanish cuisine,
paella (p842) has its roots in Valencia
» (left) In San Sebastián Basque chefs
have refined *pintxos* (tapas; p430)
to an art form

TOP FIVE BASQUE EATING EXPERIENCES

» **Pintxos (Basque tapas)** In the bars of San Sebastián's Parte Vieja, washed down with *txacoli* (a sharp, local white wine).

» **Bacalao al pil-pil** Salted cod and garlic in an olive-oil emulsion.

» **Chipirones en su tinta** Baby squid served in its own ink.

» **Chuleton de buey** Enormous steaks at various *sidrerías* (cider bars) in the mountains around San Sebastián.

» **Nueva cocina vasca (Basque nouvelle cuisine)** At Arzak (p434), one of Spain's best restaurants.

on Catalonian menus, usually with a creative local twist. Sauces are more prevalent here than elsewhere in Spain, and the further you head inland, the more likely you are to see the mainstays of Pyrenean cooking with *jabalí* (wild boar), *conejo* (rabbit), *caracoles* (snails, especially in Lleida) and delicious hotpots such as *suquet* (fish and potato stew). Watch out also for *botifarra* (the local version of cured pork sausage) and *garrotxa,* a formidable Catalan cheese that almost lives up to its name. Desserts are also a feature, notably *crema catalana* (the Catalan version of crème brûlée).

Inland Spain

Central Spain's high *meseta* (plateau) has a food culture all of its own. The best *jamón ibérico* comes from Extremadura and Salamanca, while *cordero asado lechal* (roast spring lamb) and *cochinillo asado* (roast suckling pig) are winter mainstays, drawing locals from all over the country on winter weekends, especially in Castilla y León. Other mainstays include *legumbres* (legumes) such as *garbanzos* (chickpeas), *judías* (beans) and *lentejas* (lentils). Of the hearty stews, the king is *cocido*, a hotpot or stew with a noodle broth, carrots, cabbage, chickpeas, chicken, *morcilla* (blood sausage), beef and lard – it's a special favourite in Madrid and León.

In Aragón it's all about meat, where a love for *ternasco* (suckling lamb, usually served as a steak or ribs with potatoes) is elevated almost to the status of a local religion. Another signature dish, especially in Teruel, is *jarretes* (stewed Mozarabic hock of lamb). Teruel's *jamón* is also considered to be among Spain's finest.

In Extremadura you should always order *solomillo ibérico con Torta del Casar* (pork sirloin with creamy Torta del Casar cheese made from sheep's milk) if it's on the menu,

while *frito de cordero* (lamb stew), *migas* (breadcrumbs, often cooked with cured meats and served with grapes) and even frog legs are other delicacies to watch for.

Castilla-La Mancha is famous for its *queso manchego* (a hard cheese made from sheep's milk), as well as snails and quirky dishes such as bread embedded with sardines that you'll find in Alcalá de Júcar.

In Madrid the local *cocido a la madrileña* (meat and chickpea stew) inspires considerable passion among its devotees; it's echoed throughout the region, including in Astorga in northern Castilla y León, where the elements (soup, meats etc) are eaten in reverse order and known as *cocido maragato.*

Galicia & the Northwest

Perhaps more than any other Spaniards, *gallegos* (Galicians) are defined by their relationship with the sea. A large proportion of them still make their livelihoods from fishing, and their cuisine, their fiestas and, some would say, their whole reason for living revolves around fish and seafood. Yes, they're proud of their empanadas (savoury pies) and *pimientos de padron* (grilled and often spicy green capsicum). But these are merely diversions from the main event, which is *pulpo gallego* (spicy boiled octopus, spelled *pulpo á galega* in the local Galician tongue), a dish whose constituent elements (octopus, oil, paprika and garlic) are so simple yet whose execution is devilishly difficult. The trick is in the boiling: dipping the octopus into the water, then drawing it out and dipping again cooks it at just the right rate. September to April is the best season for *pulpo*, not to mention *centollo* (spider crab). Other Galician mainstays include a bewildering litany of sea creatures such as *navajas* (razor clams), *coquinas* (large clams), *percebes* (goose barnacles), *mejillones* (mussels), *berberechos* (cockles), *almejas* (baby clams) and *vieiras* (a form of scallop).

Not to be outdone, neighbouring Asturias and Cantabria also give to Spain a handful of seafood delicacies, the best known of which are *anchoas*. If you're anywhere in Spain and you spy *anchoas de santoña* on the menu, don't hesitate for a second. Better still, go straight to the source and visit Santoña.

In the high mountains in the coastal hinterland, the cuisine is as driven by mountain pasture as it is by the daily comings and goings of fishing fleets. Cheeses are particularly sought-after, with special fame reserved for the untreated cow's-milk cheese, *queso de Cabrales*. River fish (trout, eels and salmon in particular) are also popular. But if *asturianos* (Asturians) get excited about one food above all others, then it would have to be *fabada asturiana* (a stew made with pork, blood sausage and white beans). This is winter food, the sort of meal that will have you rising from the table on suddenly heavy legs and longing for a siesta. The saving grace is that the fresh taste of *sidra* (cider) straight from the barrel will not, unless you overindulge, cast such a long shadow over the rest of your afternoon.

Valencia, Murcia & the Balearic Islands

There's so much more to the cuisine of this region than oranges and paella, but these signature products capture the essence of the Mediterranean table. There's no dish better suited to a summer's afternoon spent with friends overlooking the sea than paella, a dish filled with flavour. You can get a paella just about anywhere in Spain, but to get one cooked as it should be cooked, look no further than the restaurants in Va-

lencia's waterfront Las Arenas district or La Albufera. For more on paella, see p842.

Murcia's culinary fame brings us back to the oranges. The littoral is known simply as 'La Huerta' ('the garden'). Since Moorish times, this has been one of Spain's most prolific areas for growing fruit and vegetables. Great plates of grilled vegetables are, not surprisingly, a common order, but *arroz caldoso* (rice cooked in fish stock) and *arroz con conejo* (rice with rabbit) are also popular.

The cooking style of the Balearic Islands owes much to its watery locale and to its cultural similarities with Catalonia and Valencia. As such, paella, rice dishes and lashings of seafood are recurring themes, with a few local variations. One particularly tasty local dish in Ibiza is *arròs caldós* (saffron rice cooked in the broth of local fish, with herbs and potatoes).

Andalucía

Seafood is an obvious and consistent presence the length and breadth of the Andalucian coast, the far reach of local fishing fleets into deep Atlantic waters adding depth to your eating experience. The result is all the usual suspects, alongside *pez espada* (swordfish), *cazón* (dogfish or shark that feeds on shellfish to produce a strong, almost sweet flavour), *salmonetes* (red mullet) and *tortilla de camarones* (shrimp fritters).

Andalucians eat fish in a variety of ways, but they're famous above all for their *pescaito frito* (fried fish). A particular speciality of Cádiz, El Puerto de Santa María and the Costa de la Luz, fried fish Andalucian-style is an art form with more subtlety than first appears. Just about anything that emerges from the sea is rolled in chickpea and wheat flour, shaken to remove the surplus, then deep-fried

---

ATLANTIC CHEESES

» **San Simón** A slightly smoked Galician mountain cheese that's dense, yellow and has a creamy texture.

» **Cabrales** A creamy, powerful blue cheese from Asturias cured in the cool, deep caves of the Picos de Europa.

» **Afuega'l Pitu** An Asturian valley cheese that's drier and nuttier than most Atlantic cheeses. Sometimes made with paprika.

» **Tetilla** Literally translated as 'nipple', this Galician cheese is so named for its remarkable resemblance to a perfectly shaped breast. It's mild, sweet and creamy.

» **Ahumado de Aliva** A Cantabrian cheese smoked over juniper wood and with a mild, smoky taste.

ever so briefly in olive oil, just long enough to form a light, golden crust that seals the essential goodness of the fish or seafood within.

In a region where summers can be fierce, a primary local preoccupation is keeping cool, and there's no better way to do so than with a *gazpacho andaluz* (Andalucian gazpacho), a cold soup with many manifestations. The base is almost always tomato, cucumber, vinegar and olive oil, but also often incorporates green peppers and soaked bread, and you'll find cooks who won't use anything but sherry vinegar. Other similar cold soups typical of the region include *ajo blanco* (white gazpacho, cooked using almonds and no tomato), and *salmorejo cordobés* (a cold tomato-based soup from Córdoba where soaked bread is essential).

Andalucía is also Spain's spiritual home of bullfighting. In season (roughly May to September), bars and restaurants will proudly announce '*hay rabo de toro*', which roughly translates as, 'yes, we have bull's tail for those of you who not only like to see a bull chased around the ring but also like to pursue it to its ultimate conclusion'. If you don't think about where it came from, it's really rather tasty.

Spanish Wines

Spaniards invariably accompany their meal with a Spanish wine. Extremely loyal to the local drop, they're often heard to wonder out loud what need they have for foreign wines when their own vineyards produce prodigiously, at such a reasonable price and to such high quality. Spanish wines have a complicated classification system; see p843 for more details.

Wine Regions

Probably the most common premium red table wine you'll encounter will be from La Rioja, in the north (see the boxed text, p459). The principal grape of Rioja is the tempranillo, widely believed to be a mutant form of the pinot noir. Its wine is smooth and fruity, seldom as dry as its supposed French counterpart. Look for the 'DOC Rioja' classification on the label and you'll find a good wine.

Not far behind are the wine-producing regions of Ribera del Duero (p197) in Castilla y León, Navarra, the Somontano wines (p396) of Aragón, and the Valdepeñas region of southern Castilla-La Mancha, which is famous for its quantities rather than quality, but is generally well priced and remains popular.

For white wines, the Ribeiro wines of Galicia (see the boxed text, p533) are well regarded. Also from the area is one of Spain's most charming whites – Albariño. This crisp, dry and refreshing drop is a rare wine as it's designated by grape rather than region.

The Penedès region in Catalonia (see the boxed text, p360) produces whites and sparkling wine such as *cava*, the traditional champagnelike toasting drink of choice for Spaniards at Christmas.

Sherry

Sherry, the unique wine of Andalucía, is Spain's national dram and is found in almost every bar, *tasca* (tapas bar) and restaurant in the land. Dry sherry, called fino, begins as a fairly ordinary white wine of the palomino grape, but it's 'fortified' with grape brandy. This stops fermentation and gives the wine taste and smell constituents that enable it to age into something sublime. It's taken as an *aperitivo* (aperitif) or as a table wine with seafood. Amontillado and oloroso are sweeter sherries, good for after dinner. Manzanilla is grown only in Sanlúcar de Barrameda near the coast in southwestern Andalucía and develops a slightly salty taste that's very appetising. When ordering it be sure to say '*vino de Manzanilla*', since manzanilla alone means chamomile tea. It's possible to visit a number of bodegas (wineries) in Sanlúcar, as well as in Jerez de la Frontera and El Puerto de Santa María.

WHAT'S FOR BREAKFAST?

Desayuno (breakfast) Spanish-style is generally a no-nonsense affair taken at a bar on the way to work. A *café con leche* (half coffee and half milk) with a *bollo* (pastry) is the typical breakfast. Croissants or a cream-filled pastry are also common. Some people prefer a savoury start – try a *sandwich mixto*, a toasted ham-and-cheese sandwich, or a Spanish *tostada*, which is simply buttered toast. Others, especially those heading home at dawn after a night out, go for a *chocolate con churros* (deep-fried doughnut strips dipped in thick hot chocolate).

THE TRAVELLERS' FRIEND – MENÚ DEL DÍA

One great way to cap prices at lunchtime Monday to Friday is to order the *menú del día*, a full three-course set menu (usually with several options), water, bread and wine. These meals are priced from around €10, although €12 and up is increasingly the norm. You'll be given a menu with a choice of five or six starters, the same number of mains and a handful of desserts – you choose one from each category; it's possible to order two starters, but not two mains. Filling as it may be, it's worth remembering that the *menú del día* usually doesn't include the most exciting dishes on the menu; for those you'll need to order à la carte.

The philosophy behind the *menú del día* is that lunch is the main meal of the day, but during the working week few Spaniards have time to go home for lunch. Taking a packed lunch is just not the done thing, so most people end up eating in restaurants, and all-inclusive three-course meals are as close as they can come to eating homestyle food without breaking the bank.

Reading the Menu

Starters

The typical *carta* (menu) begins with starters such as *ensaladas* (salads), *sopas* (soups) and *entremeses* (hors d'oeuvres). The latter can range from a mound of potato salad with olives, asparagus, anchovies and a selection of cold meats – a meal in itself – to simpler cured meat platters, slices of cheese and olives.

Mains

The main courses on many Spanish menus are divided into *carne* (meat) and *pescado* (fish); the latter includes *marisco* (seafood). Meat may be subdivided into *cerdo* (pork), *ternera* (beef) and *cordero* (lamb). *Arroz* (rice) is often listed under its own heading but usually requires a minimum of two people to make up an order. If you want a *guarnición* (side order), eg *verduras* (vegetables), you may have to order separately.

When it comes to fish, the Spanish mainstays are *bonito* (tuna), *sardinas* (sardines), *anchoas* (anchovies), *merluza* (hake), *dorada* (bream), *lubina* (sea bass), *rodaballo* (turbot) and *lenguado* (sole). Shellfish is another favourite.

But the fish with which Spaniards have the closest relationship historically is *bacalao*. For centuries roving Spanish fishermen have harvested codfish from Newfoundland and Norway, salting it and bringing it home looking more like a rock than food. After soaking it several times in water it's rehydrated and relieved of its salt content, which enriches the flavour and improves the texture. Originally it was considered food for the poor and some called it 'vigil day beef' for its use during fasts. The best place to enjoy it is in the Basque Country, where it's revered.

Desserts

For *postre* (dessert), Spanish menus are just as likely to include *fruta* (fruit) and *tarta de queso* (cheesecake) as they are more traditional Spanish desserts like *crema catalana* or *tarta de santiago* (cinnamon and almond tart). Spaniards always ask if a dessert is *casero* (homemade) – if it's not, they're unlikely to order it.

Outdoor Activities

Best Hiking

Pyrenees
Parque Nacional de Ordesa y Monte Perdido (June to August; p386): the best of the Pyrenees and Spain's finest hiking.

Cantabria & Asturias
Picos de Europa (June to August; p495): a close second to the Pyrenees for Spain's best hiking.

Andalucía
Las Alpujarras (July and August; p759): classic white villages in the Sierra Nevada foothills.

Pilgrimage
Camino de Santiago (June to September) one of the world's favourite pilgrimages, across northern Spain from Roncesvalles to Santiago de Compostela.

Coast to Coast
GR11 (Senda Pirenáica; July and August): traverses the Pyrenees from the Atlantic to the Med.

Coastal Walks
Serra de Tramuntana (year-round; p617): Mallorca's jagged western coast with fine villages en route.

Spain's landscapes are almost continental in their scale and variety, something which few countries in Europe can match. Its never-ending coastline takes in everything from the snakelike *rías* (inlets or estuaries) of rugged Galicia to the olive-backed shores of the Mediterranean, while jagged mountain ranges, such as Andalucía's mighty Sierra Nevada and the Pyrenean peaks in the north, reach for the skies. This landscape makes for a wonderful adventure playground; there's something for everyone no matter what age or fitness level.

Spain is famous for superb walking trails that criss-cross mountains and hills from the snowy Pyrenees and Picos to the sultry Cabo de Gata coastal trail in Andalucía, but none come more famous than the Camino de Santiago – the pilgrimage route to the cathedral in Galicia's Santiago de Compostela.

Away from the trails, Spain's beaches offer fantastic opportunities for water sports, whether hanging in the tube at Mundaka or reef diving in Catalonia.

Other heart-pumping activities include superb skiing, cycling and river rafting, as well as a string of national parks offering the best wildlife-viewing in western Europe.

Hiking

Spain is one of the premier walking destinations in Europe, and a snapshot of the possibilities shows why: conquering Spain's highest mainland peak, Mulhacén (3479m) above Granada; following in the footsteps of Carlos V in Extremadura; walking along Galicia's Costa da Morte (Death Coast); or sauntering through alpine meadows anywhere in the Pyrenees.

When to Go

Spain encompasses a number of different climate zones, ensuring that it's possible to hike year-round. In Andalucía conditions are at their best from March to June and in September and October: they're unbearable in midsummer, but in winter most trails remain open, except in the high mountains.

If you prefer to walk in summer, do what Spaniards have traditionally done and escape to the north. The Basque Country, Asturias, Cantabria and Galicia are best from June to September. The Pyrenees are accessible from mid-June until (usually) September, while July and August are the ideal months for the high Sierra Nevada. August is the busiest month on the trails, so if you plan to head to popular national parks and stay in *refugios* (mountain refuges), book ahead.

Hiking Destinations

For good reason, the Pyrenees, separating Spain from France, are Spain's premier walking destinations. The range is utterly beautiful: prim and chocolate-box pretty on the lower slopes, wild and bleak at higher elevations, and relatively unspoilt compared to some European mountain ranges. The Pyrenees contain two outstanding national parks: Aigüestortes i Estany de Sant Maurici and Ordesa y Monte Perdido. The spectacular GR11 (Senda Pirenáica) traverses the range, connecting the Atlantic (at Hondarribia in the Basque Country) with the Mediterranean (at Cap de Creus in Catalonia). Walking the whole 45-day route is an unforgettable challenge, but there are also magnificent day hikes in the national parks and elsewhere.

Breathtaking and accessible limestone ranges with distinctive craggy peaks (usually hot rock-climbing destinations too) are the hallmark of Spain's first national park, the Picos de Europa, which straddles the Cantabria, Asturias and León provinces and is fast gaining a reputation as *the* place to walk in Spain. Less well-known, but just as rewarding, are Valencia's Els Ports area, and the Sierra de Cazorla and Sierra de Grazalema in Andalucía.

To walk in mountain villages, the classic spot is Las Alpujarras, near the Parque Nacional Sierra Nevada in Andalucía.

Great coastal walking abounds, even in heavily visited areas such as the south coast (eg Andalucía's Cabo de Gata) and Mallorca.

Information

For the full low-down on these walks, including the Camino de Santiago, check out Lonely Planet's *Hiking in Spain*. Region-specific walking (and climbing) guides are published by **Cicerone Press** (www.cicerone.co.uk). Madrid's **La Tienda Verde** (☑91 535 38 10; www.tiendaverde.es; Calle Maudes 23) and **Librería Desnivel** (☑902 248848; www.libreriadesnivel.com; Plaza de Matute 6) both sell maps (the best Spanish ones are *Prames* and *Adrados*) and guides. The website www.andarines.com gives route descriptions for many Spanish regions.

Camino de Santiago

'The door is open to all, to sick and healthy, not only to Catholics but also to pagans, Jews, heretics and vagabonds.'

So go the words of a 13th-century poem describing the Camino. Eight hundred years later these words still ring true. The Camino de Santiago (Way of St James) originated as a medieval pilgrimage and, for more than 1000 years, people have taken up the Camino's age-old symbols – the scallop shell and staff – and set off on the adventure of a lifetime to the tomb of St James the Apostle,

---

PILGRIM HOSTELS

There are around 300 *refugios* (mountain refuges) along the Camino, owned by parishes, 'friends of the Camino' associations, private individuals, town halls and regional governments. While in the early days these places were run on donations and provided little more than hot water and a bed, today's pilgrims are charged €5 to €10 and can expect showers, kitchens and washing machines. Some things haven't changed though – the *refugios* still operate on a first-come, first-served basis and are intended for those doing the Camino solely under their own steam.

Camino de Santiago

in Santiago de Compostela, in the Iberian Peninsula's far northwest.

Today this magnificent long-distance walk, spanning 783km of Spain's north from Roncesvalles, on the border with France, to Santiago de Compostela in Galicia, attracts walkers of all backgrounds and ages, from countries across the world. And no wonder: its list of assets (culture, history, nature) is impressive, as are its accolades. Not only is it the Council of Europe's first Cultural Route and a Unesco World Heritage site but, for pilgrims, it's a pilgrimage equal to visiting Jerusalem, and by finishing it you're guaranteed a healthy chunk of time off purgatory.

To feel, absorb, smell and taste northern Spain's diversity; for a great physical challenge; for a unique perspective on rural and urban communities; and to meet intriguing travel companions, this is an incomparable walk. *'The door is open to all'* ...so step on in.

History

Sometime in the 9th century a remarkable event occurred in the poor Iberian hinterlands: following a shining star, Pelayo, a religious hermit, unearthed the tomb of the apostle James the Great (Spanish: Santiago). The news was confirmed by the local bishop, the Asturian king and later the pope. Its impact is hard to imagine today, but it was instant and indelible: first a trickle, then a flood of Christian Europeans began to journey towards the setting sun in search of salvation.

Compostela became the most important destination for Christians after Rome and Jerusalem. Its popularity increased with an 11th-century papal decree granting it Holy Year status: pilgrims could receive a plenary indulgence – a full remission of one's lifetime's sins – during a Holy Year. These occur when Santiago's feast day (25 July) falls on a Sunday: the next one isn't until 2021.

The 11th and 12th centuries marked the pilgrimage's heyday. The Reformation was devastating for Catholic pilgrimages and, by the 19th century, the Camino nearly died out. In its startling late-20th-century re-animation, which continues today, it's most popular as a personal and spiritual journey of discovery, rather than one primarily motivated by religion.

Routes

Although in Spain there are many *caminos* (paths) to Santiago, by far the most popular is, and was, the Camino Francés, which originated in France, crossed the Pyrenees at Roncesvalles and then headed west for 783km across the regions of Navarra, La Rioja, Castilla y León and Galicia. Waymarked with cheerful yellow arrows and scallop shells, the 'trail' is a mishmash of rural lanes, paved secondary roads and footpaths all strung together. Starting at Roncesvalles, the Camino takes roughly two weeks cycling or five weeks walking.

A very popular alternative is to walk only the last 100km (the minimum distance allowed) from Sarria in Galicia in order to earn a 'Compostela' certificate of completion given out by the Catedral de Santiago de Compostela.

Information

For more information about the *Credencial* (like a passport for the Camino, in which pilgrims accumulate stamps at various points along the route) and the 'Compostela' certificate, visit the cathedral's **Oficina de Acogida de Peregrinos** (Pilgrim's Office; www.peregrinos santiago.es; Rúa do Vilar 1, Santiago de Compostela).

There are a number of excellent Camino websites packed with useful practical information for the would-be pilgrim:

» **Caminolinks** (www.caminolinks.co.uk) Annotated guide to many Camino websites.

» **Mundicamino** (www.mundicamino.com) Excellent, thorough descriptions and maps.

» **Camino de Santiago** (www.caminode santiago.me) A huge selection of news groups, where you can get all of your questions answered.

When to Walk

People walk and cycle the Camino year-round. In May and June the wildflowers are glorious and the endless fields of cereals turn from green to toasty gold, making the landscapes a huge drawcard. July and August bring crowds of summer holidaymakers and scorching heat, especially in Castilla y León. September is less crowded and the weather is generally pleasant. From November to May there are fewer people on the road as the season can bring snow, rain and bitter winds. Santiago's feast day, 25 July, is a popular time to converge on the city.

National & Natural Parks

Much of Spain's most spectacular and ecologically important terrain – about 40,000 sq km or 8% of the country, if you include national hunting reserves – is under some kind of official protection. Nearly all of these areas are at least partly open to walkers, naturalists and other outdoor enthusiasts, but degrees of conservation and access vary.

The *parques nacionales* (national parks) are areas of exceptional importance and are the country's most strictly controlled protected areas. Spain has 14 national parks – nine on the mainland, four on the Canary Islands and one in the Balearic Islands. The hundreds of other protected areas fall into at least 16 classifications and range in size from 100-sq-metre rocks off the Balearics to Andalucía's 2140-sq-km Parque Natural de Cazorla.

Other Activities

Peddle up a mountain and then blast back down on a pair of skis, clamber up a chasm and then sail above it on a hang-glider, go below the waves on a scuba-diving course or get above them on a surfboard or kayak. If walking isn't your thing, then Spain has plenty of other opportunities to work off that rather delicious lunch.

Canyoning

For exhilarating descents into steep-walled canyons by any means possible (but in the care of professional guides), look no further than Alquézar in Aragón, one of Europe's prime locations for this popular sport. Alquézar's numerous activities operators

---

CAMINO BOOKS

Camino books abound. The best of each category are as follows:

» **Background history** William Melczer's essential history and translation of the 12th-century *Pilgrim's Guide to Santiago de Compostela*.

» **Culture** David Gitlitz and Linda Davidson's *The Pilgrimage Road to Santiago: The Complete Cultural Handbook* is well worth its weight.

» **Analysis** Anthropologist Nancy Frey explores the pilgrimage's modern resurgence in *Pilgrim Stories: On and Off the Road to Santiago*.

» **Guidebook** Millán Bravo Lozano's *A Practical Guide for Pilgrims* has great maps and route descriptions.

» **Religious/spiritual account** Joyce Rupp gives a compelling account of the inner journey in *Walk in a Relaxed Manner*.

» **Esoteric** Paulo Coelho's mystical journey described in *The Pilgrimage* is an international best seller.

» **Travel** Cees Nooteboom meanders through Spain en route to Santiago in *Roads to Santiago*.

SPAIN'S BEST PARKS

PARK	FEATURES	ACTIVITIES	BEST TIME TO VISIT
Parc Nacional d'Aigüestortes i Estany de Sant Maurici (p343)	beautiful Pyrenees lake region	walking, wildlife-watching	Jun-Sep
Parque Nacional de Doñana (p683)	bird and mammal haven in Guadalquivir delta	4WD tours, walking, wildlife-watching, horse riding	year-round
Parque Nacional de Ordesa y Monte Perdido (p386)	spectacular section of the Pyrenees, with chamois, raptors and varied vegetation	walking, rock climbing	mid-Jun–Jul & mid-Aug–Sep
Parque Nacional de los Picos de Europa (p495)	beautiful mountain refuge for chamois, and a few wolves and bears	walking, rock climbing, caving	May-Jul & Sep
Parques Nacional and Natural Sierra Nevada (p755)	mainland Spain's highest mountain range, with ibexes, 60 endemic plants and the beautiful Alpujarras valleys on its southern slopes	walking, rock climbing, mountain biking, skiing, horse riding	year-round, depending on activity
Parque Natural de Cazorla (p770)	abundant wildlife, 2300 plant species and beautiful mountain scenery	walking, driving, mountain biking, wildlife-watching, 4WD tours	Apr-Oct
Áreas Naturales Serra de Tramuntana (p617)	spectacular mountain range on Mallorca	walking, birdwatching	late Feb-early Oct
Parque Nacional de Monfragüe (p797)	spectacular birds of prey	birdwatching	Mar-Oct
Parque Natural Sierra de Grazalema (p703)	lovely, green, mountainous area with rich bird life	walking, caving, canyoning, birdwatching, paragliding, rock climbing	Sep-Jun
Parc Natural del Cadí-Moixeró	steep pre-Pyrenees range	rock climbing, walking	Jun-Sep
Parc Natural de la Zona Volcànica de la Garrotxa (p334)	beautiful wooded region with 30 volcanic cones	walking	Apr-Oct
Parque Natural Sierra de Gredos (p142)	beautiful mountain region, home to Spain's biggest ibex population	walking, rock climbing, mountain biking	Mar-May & Sep-Nov
Parque Natural de Somiedo	dramatic section of Cordillera Cantábrica	walking	Jul-Sep
Parque Natural de Cabo de Gata-Níjar (p775)	sandy beaches, volcanic cliffs, flamingo colony and semidesert vegetation	swimming, birdwatching, walking, horse riding, diving, snorkelling	year-round

can also arrange rock climbing and rafting in the surrounding Sierra de Guara.

Canyoning is also possible in Cangas de Onís in the Picos de Europa.

Cycling

Spain has a splendid variety of cycling possibilities, from gentle family rides to challenging two-week expeditions. If you avoid the cities (where cycling can be somewhat nerve-racking), Spain is also a cycle-friendly country, with drivers accustomed to sharing the roads with platoons of Lycra-clad cyclists. The excellent network of secondary roads, usually with comfortable shoulders to ride on, is ideal for road touring.

Cycling Destinations

Every Spanish region has both off-road (called BTT in Spanish, from *bici todo terreno,* meaning 'mountain bike') and touring trails and routes. Mountain bikers can head to just about any sierra (mountain range) and use the extensive *pistas forestales* (forestry tracks).

One highly recommended and challenging off-road excursion takes you across the snowy Sierra Nevada. Classic long-haul touring routes include the Camino de Santiago, the Ruta de la Plata and the 600km Camino del Cid, which follows in the footsteps of Spain's epic hero, El Cid, from Burgos to Valencia. Guides in Spanish exist for all of these, available at bookshops and online.

Information

An indispensable cycling website is www.amigosdelciclismo.com, which gives useful information on restrictions, updates on laws, circulation norms, contact details for cycling clubs and lists of guidebooks, as well as a lifetime's worth of route descriptions organised region by region.

Bike Spain (p101) in Madrid is one of the better cycling tour operators.

Most of the cycling guidebooks in publication are in Spanish. The following are recommended:

» *España en bici,* by Paco Tortosa and María del Mar Fornés – a good overview guide, but quite hard to find.

» *Cycle Touring in Spain: Eight Detailed Routes,* by Harry Dowdell – a helpful planning tool; also practical once you're in Spain.

» *The Trailrider Guide – Spain: Single Track Mountain Biking in Spain,* by Nathan James and Linsey Stroud – another good resource.

Skiing & Snowboarding

For winter powder, Spain's skiers (including the royal family) head to the Pyrenees of Aragón and Catalonia. Outside of the peak periods (the beginning of December, 20 December to 6 January, Carnaval and Semana Santa), Spain's top resorts are relatively quiet, cheap and warm in comparison with their counterparts in the Alps.

The season runs from December to April, though January and February are generally the best, most reliable times for snow. However, in recent years snow fall has been a bit unpredictable.

ROCK CLIMBING

Spain offers plenty of opportunities to see the mountains and gorges from a more vertical perspective. For an overview of Spanish rock climbing, check out the websites of **Rockfax** (www.rockfax.com) and **Climb Europe** (www.climb-europe.com). Both include details on the best climbs in Spain. Rockfax also publishes various climbing guidebooks covering Spain.

Skiing & Snowboarding Destinations

In Aragón, two popular resorts are Formigal and Candanchú. Just above the town of Jaca, Candanchú has some 42km of runs with 51 pistes (as well as 35km of cross-country track). For more information on skiing in Aragón, see the boxed text, p378. In Catalonia, Spain's first resort, La Molina, is still going strong and is ideal for families and beginners. Considered by many to have the Pyrenees' best snow, the 72-piste resort of Baqueira-Beret boasts 30 modern lifts and 104km of downhill runs for all levels.

Spain's other major resort is Europe's southernmost: the Sierra Nevada, outside Granada. The 80km of runs here are at their prime in March, and the slopes are particularly suited for families as well as novice-to-intermediate skiers.

Information

If you don't want to bring your own gear, Spanish ski resorts have equipment hire, as well as ski schools. Lift tickets cost between €35 and €45 per day for adults, and €25 and €35 for children; equipment hire costs from around €20 per day. If you're planning ahead, Spanish travel agencies frequently advertise affordable single- or multi-day packages with lodging included.

An excellent source of information on snowboarding and skiing in Spain is www.skisnowboardeurope.com.

Water Sports

Scuba Diving & Snorkelling

There's more to Spain than what you see on the surface – literally! Delve under the ocean

DESIGN PICS / BEN WELSH / GETTY IMAGES ©

» (above) The rugged coast of Cabo
Gata around Las Negras (p777) off
exhilarating walks and terrific views
» (left) Tarifa's legendary winds mak
it one of Europe's top windsurfing
destinations (p707)

waves anywhere along the country's almost 5000km of shoreline and a whole new Spain opens up, crowded with marine life and including features such as wrecks, sheer walls and long cavern swim-throughs. The numerous Mediterranean dive centres cater to an English-speaking market and offer single- and multi-day trips, equipment rental and certification courses. Their Atlantic counterparts (in San Sebastián, Santander and A Coruña) deal mostly in Spanish but, if that's not an obstacle for you, the colder waters of the Atlantic will offer a completely different, and very rewarding, underwater experience.

A good starting point is the reefs along the Costa Brava, especially around the Illes Medes marine reserve, off L'Estartit (near Girona). On the Costa del Sol, operators launch to such places as La Herradura Wall, the *Motril* wreck and the Cavern of Cerro Gordo. Balearic Islands are also popular dive destinations with excellent services.

Paco Nadal's book *Buceo en España* provides information province by province, with descriptions of ocean floors, dive centres and equipment rental.

Surfing

The opportunity to get into the waves is a major attraction for beginners and experts alike along many of Spain's coastal regions. The north coast of Spain has, debatably, the best surf in mainland Europe.

The main surfing region is the north coast, where numerous high-class spots can be found, but Atlantic Andalucía gets decent winter swells. Despite the flow of vans loaded down with surfboards along the north coast in the summer, it's actually autumn through to spring that's the prime time for decent swell, with October probably the best

month overall. The variety of waves along the north coast is impressive: there are numerous open, swell-exposed beach breaks for the summer months, and some seriously heavy reefs and points that only really come to life during the colder, stormier months.

Surfing Destinations

The most famous wave in Spain is the legendary river-mouth left at Mundaka. On a good day, there's no doubt that it's one of the best waves in the world. However, it's not very consistent and, when it's on, it's always very busy and ugly.

Heading east, good waves can be found throughout the Basque Country. Going west, into neighbouring regions of Cantabria and Asturias, you'll also find a superb range of well-charted surf beaches, such as Rodiles in Asturias and Liencres in Cantabria. If you're looking for solitude, some isolated beaches along Galicia's beautiful Costa da Morte remain empty even in summer. In southwest Andalucía there are a number of powerful, winter beach breaks, and weekdays off Conil de la Frontera (located just northwest of Cabo de Trafalgar) can be sublimely lonely.

Information

In summer a shortie wetsuit (or, in the Basque Country, just board shorts) is sufficient along all coasts except Galicia, which picks up the icy Canaries current – you'll need a light full suit here.

Surf shops abound in the popular surfing areas and usually offer board and wetsuit hire. If you're a beginner joining a surf school, ask the instructor to explain the rules and to keep you away from the more experienced surfers.

There are a number of excellent surf guidebooks to Spain. The following are recommended:

» Stuart Butler's English-language *Big Blue Surf Guide: Spain*.

» José Pellón's Spanish-language *Guía del surf en España*.

» Low Pressure's superb *Stormrider Guide: Europe – the Continent*.

Windsurfing & Kitesurfing

Spain is blessed with excellent windsurfing and kitesurfing (kiteboarding) conditions along much of its Mediterranean coast.

SPAIN'S TOP BEACHES

Spain has 4964km of coastline (including offshore islands) and a never-ending variety of pebbly coves, sandy strips and hidden bays, so any discussion about its best beaches is sure to lead to some of life's more pleasurable arguments.

» **Playa de la Concha** (p425) A scallop-shaped stretch of sand in the heart of San Sebastián, and possibly Europe's finest city beach.

» **Playa del Silencio** (p491) A long sandy cove backed by a natural rock amphitheatre make this Asturian jewel hard to beat.

» **Praia de Lourido** (p521) Unbeatable for lonely walks along a mist-shrouded beach, although Galicia's bleak Costa da Morte is no place for a swim.

» **Illas Cíes** (p540) A pocket-sized, highly protected archipelago off the end of Spain, with beaches so stunning they'll have you rubbing your eyes in disbelief.

» **Aiguablava** and **Fornells** (p313) Two neighbouring Costa Brava coves so divine we couldn't choose between them.

» **Benidorm** (p582) The king of package-holiday beach resorts might not be to everyone's taste, but there's a reason it draws over two million visitors a year.

» **Menorca's north coast** (p635) Rugged, rocky and dotted with scenic coves; it's the Balearic Islands before the tourists arrived.

» **Cabo de Gata** (p775) Andalucía's most dramatic, remote Mediterranean corner.

» **Zahara de los Atunes** A 12km stretch of pristine sand, the jewel of Andalucía's unspoiled Costa de la Luz.

Windsurfing & Kitesurfing Destinations

The best sailing conditions are around Tarifa, which has such strong and consistent winds that it's said that the town's once-high suicide rate was due to the wind turning people mad. Whether or not this is true, one thing is without doubt: Tarifa's 10km of white, sandy beaches and perfect year-round conditions have made this small town the windsurfing capital of Europe. The town is crammed with windsurf and kite shops, windsurfing schools and a huge contingent of passing surfers. However, the same wind that attracts so many devotees also makes it a less-than-ideal place to learn the art.

If you can't make it as far south as Tarifa, then the less-well-known Empuriabrava in Catalonia also has great conditions, especially from March to July, while the family resort of Oliva near Valencia is also worth considering. If you're looking for waves, try Spain's northwest coast, where Galicia can have fantastic conditions.

Information

An excellent guidebook to windsurfing and kitesurfing spots across Spain and the rest of Europe is Stoked Publications' *The Kite and Windsurfing Guide: Europe*.

The Spanish-language website www.windsurfesp.com has thorough descriptions of spots, conditions and schools all over Spain.

Kayaking, Canoeing & Rafting

With 1800 rivers and streams, Spain has lots of opportunities to take off downstream in search of white-water fun. As most rivers are dammed for electric power at some point along their flow, there are many reservoirs with excellent low-level kayaking and canoeing, where you can also hire equipment.

In general, May and June are best for kayaking, rafting, canoeing and hydrospeeding (water tobogganing). Top white-water rivers are Catalonia's Noguera Pallaresa, Aragón's Gállego, Cantabria's Carasa and Galicia's Miño. Kayaking in the Parque Natural Fragas do Eume is great for families to get paddling together on a beautiful reservoir in the middle of a dense Atlantic forest.

For fun and competition, the crazy 22km, en-masse Descenso Internacional del Sella canoe race is a blast, running from Arriondas in Asturias to coastal Ribadesella. It's held on the first weekend in August.

Patrick Santal's *White Water Pyrenees* thoroughly covers 85 rivers in France and Spain for kayakers, canoeists and rafters.

Travel with Children

Best Regions for Kids

Mediterranean Spain
Spain's coastline may be a summer-holiday cliché, but it's a fabulous place for a family holiday. From Catalonia in the north to Andalucía in the south, most beaches have gentle waters and a host of child-friendly attractions and activities (from water parks to water sports for older kids).

Barcelona
Theme parks, a wax museum, a chocolate museum, all manner of other museums with interactive exhibits, beaches, gardens... Barcelona is one of Spain's most child-friendly cities – even its architecture seems to have sprung from a child's imagination.

Inland Spain
Spain's interior may not be the first place you think of for a family holiday, but its concentrations of castles, tiny villages and fascinating and easily negotiated cities make it worth considering.

Spain is a child- and family-friendly destination with excellent and varied transport and accommodation infrastructure, a cuisine guaranteed to offer something to even the fussiest of eaters, and an extraordinary range of attractions that appeal to adults and children alike. Visiting as a family does require careful planning, but no more so than for visiting any other European country.

Spain for Kids
Spain's tourism industry – from its reception clerks to waiters – are accustomed to Spaniards travelling in family groups, and most will go out of their way to make sure children are looked after.

Eating Out
Food and children are two of the great loves for Spaniards, which means that children are usually welcome, whether in a sit-down restaurant or in a chaotically busy bar. Indeed, it's rare that you'll be made to feel uncomfortable as your children run amok, although a good rule of thumb is that the more formal the place, the more uncomfortable you're likely to feel. In summer, the abundance of outdoor terraces with tables is ideal for families although it can be easy to lose sight of wandering young ones amid the scrum of people.

You cannot rely on restaurants having *tronas* (high chairs), although many do these days. Those that do, however, rarely have more than one (a handful at most), so

ACTIVITIES

There aren't that many organised activities around Spain that really young kids can get involved in, but once they're nearing double figures the possibilities for hiking, rafting, snorkelling and even snow-related fun grow with each passing year.

make the request when making your reservation. If high chairs or risers aren't available, staff will sometimes improvise with double-decker chairs and cushions.

Very few restaurants (or other public facilities) have nappy-changing facilities – this is changing, albeit at a glacial pace.

As for the food, a small but growing number of restaurants offer a *menú infantil* (children's menu), which usually includes a main course (hamburger, chicken nuggets, pasta and the like), drink and an ice cream or milkshake for dessert.

Spanish fare is rarely spicy and kids tend to like it; Spanish toddlers are often fed straight from their parents' plate.

One challenge can be adapting to Spanish eating hours – when kids get hungry between meals it's usually easy to zip into the nearest *tasca* (tapas bar) and get them a snack, and there are also sweet shops every few blocks. That said, we also recommend carrying some emergency supplies from a supermarket for those times when there's simply nothing open.

Transport

Spain's transport infrastructure is world-class, and the long distances between some major cities can be rendered irrelevant if you're travelling on a high-speed AVE train. Apart from anything else, most kids love the idea that they're travelling at nearly 300km/h.

Discounts are available for children (usually under 12) on public transport. Children under four generally go free.

You can hire car seats (usually for an additional cost) for infants and children from most car-hire firms, but you should always book them in advance. This is especially true during busy travel periods, such as Spanish school holidays, Navidad (Christmas) and Semana Santa (Holy Week).

It's extremely rare that taxis have child seats – unless you're carrying a portable version from home, you're expected to sit the child on your lap, with the seatbelt around you both.

Children's Highlights

Spain has a surfeit of castles, horse shows, fiestas and ferias, interactive museums, flamenco shows and even the Semana Santa processions, to name just a few highlights for kids.

For a number of cities throughout this guidebook, we've included boxed texts that highlight child-friendly attractions.

Beaches

Spain's beaches, especially those along the Mediterranean coast, can seem custom-made for children – many (particularly along the Costa Brava and in the Balearic Islands) are sheltered from the open ocean by protective coves, while most others are characterised by waveless waters that quietly lap the shore. Yes, some can get a little overcrowded in the height of summer, but there are still plenty of tranquil stretches of sand if you choose carefully.

» **Playa de la Concha, San Sebastián** Spain's most easily accessible city beach.

» **Aiguablava and Fornells** Sheltered, beautiful Costa Brava coves.

» **Cala Sant Vincenç** Four of Mallorca's loveliest cove beaches.

» **Benidorm** So much to do if the terrific beach gets too crowded.

» **Menorca** Quiet north-coast beaches, even in summer.

» **Zahara de los Atunes** Few beachside developments and pristine sand.

Architecture of the Imagination

There has been something of a sea change in attitudes in Spain when it comes to high culture and children: many museums have started to incorporate an interactive element into what were once staid and static exhibits. Numerous major sights (such as the Alhambra and most art galleries) also have guidebooks aimed specifically at children. And then there's live flamenco, something that every child should see once in their lives.

» **Alcázar, Segovia** The inspiration for Sleeping Beauty's castle.

» **Park Güell and Casa Batlló** Gaudí's weird-and-wonderful Barcelona creations.

» **Castillo do Loarre** The stereotypically turreted castle in Aragón.

» **Cuenca** Houses that hang out over the cliff.

» **Estadio Santiago Bernabéu (Madrid) and Camp Nou (Barcelona)** Football, football, football…

» **Museo Guggenheim, Bilbao** Watch them gaze in wonder.

Gardens, Theme Parks & Horse Shows

For better or worse, Spain has seen an explosion of Disneyfied theme parks in recent years. While nonparents may turn up their nose at the mere thought of them, most parents will see the value of such places when trying to make sure their kids get as much out of their Spanish visit as they do. Parks range from places that re-create the era of the dinosaurs or Wild West to more traditional parks with rides and animals.

» **Dinopolis, Teruel** A cross between Jurassic Park and a funfair.

» **Port Aventura** Fine amusement park close to Tarragona.

» **Terra Mítica, Benidorm** Where the spirit of Disneyland meets the Med.

» **Mini Hollywood** Wild West movie sets in the deserts of Almería.

» **Zoo-Aquarium de Madrid** Probably Spain's best zoo.

» **Parc d'Atraccions, Barcelona** Great rides and a puppet museum.

» **La Ciudad de los Niños, Córdoba** Award-winning, expansive children's play area.

» **Parque del Buen Retiro, Madrid** One of Europe's finest city parks.

» **Real Escuela Andaluza del Arte Ecuestre** Andalucian horse shows in all their finery.

Planning

For general advice on travelling with young ones, see Lonely Planet's *Travel with Children*. Also check out the websites www.travelwithyourkids.com and www.familytravelnetwork.com.

What to Bring

Although you might want to bring a small supply of items that you're used to having back home (this is particularly true for baby products), in case of emergency (or a Sunday when most pharmacies and supermarkets are closed), Spain is likely to have everything you need.

You can buy baby formula in powder or liquid form, as well as sterilising solutions such as Milton, at *farmacias* (pharmacies). Disposable *panales* (nappies, or diapers) are widely available at supermarkets and *farmacias*. Fresh cow's milk is sold in cartons and plastic bottles in supermarkets in big cities, but can be hard to find in small towns, where UHT is often the only option.

When to Go

If you're heading for the beach, summer (especially July and August) is the obvious choice – but it's also when Spaniards undertake a mass pilgrimage to the coast, so book well ahead. It's also a good time to travel to the mountains (the Pyrenees, Sierra

---

TIPS FOR TRAVELLING WITH CHILDREN

Some of our authors have travelled throughout Spain with their children. Here are a few of their tips:

» Expect your children to be kissed, offered sweets, have their cheeks pinched and their hair ruffled (especially if it's anything lighter than black) at least once a day.

» Always ask for extra tapas in bars, such as olives or cut raw carrots.

» Adjust your children to Spanish time (ie late nights) as quickly as you can – otherwise they'll miss half of what's worth seeing.

» Pray for the day when all bars and restaurants are made nonsmoking – it's on its way and may even have begun by the time you read this.

» Unlike in the US, crayons and paper are rarely given out in restaurants – bring your own.

» If you're willing to let your child share your bed you won't incur a supplement. Extra beds usually (though not always) incur a €20 to €30 charge.

» Always ask the local tourist office for the nearest children's playgrounds.

Nevada). During the summer months, however, the interior can be unbearably hot – Seville and Córdoba regularly experience daytime temperatures of almost 50°C.

Our favourite time for visiting Spain is in spring and autumn, particularly May, June, September and October. In all but the latter month, you might be lucky and get weather warm enough for the beach, but temperatures in these months are generally mild and the weather often fine.

Winter can be bitterly cold in much of Spain – fine if you come prepared and even better if you're heading for the snow.

Accommodation

Most hotels (but rarely *hostales* – budget hotels – and other budget places) have cots for small children, although most only have a handful, so reserve one when booking your room. If you're asking for a cot, it can be a good idea to ask for a larger room as many Spanish hotel or *hostal* rooms can be on the small side, making for very cramped conditions. Cots sometimes cost extra, while other hotels offer them for free.

In top-end hotels you can sometimes arrange for childcare, and in some places child-minding agencies cater to temporary visitors. Some top-end hotels – particularly resorts, but also some *paradores* (luxurious state-owned hotels) – have play areas and/or children's playgrounds, and many also have swimming pools.

regions at a glance

⭐

Madrid
Galleries ✓✓✓
Nightlife ✓✓✓
Food ✓✓

Art's Golden Mile
Madrid is one of the world's premier cities for public art. World-class galleries scattered across the city exist in the long shadow cast by the Museo del Prado, the Centro de Arte Reina Sofía and the Museo Thyssen-Bornemisza. Together these three museums, all within easy walking distance of each other, are like a roll-call of fine art's grand elite and a fascinating journey through the Spanish soul.

Killing the Night
Nightclubs that don't really get busy until 3am. Sophisticated cocktail bars where you mingle with A-list celebrities while sipping

p64

your mojito. A live-music scene that begins with flamenco before moving on to jazz and every other genre imaginable. In this city with more bars than any other city in the world, nights are the stuff of legend, reflecting as they do the *madrileño* passion for having a good time.

Spain's Table
You could travel all around Spain to try the best in regional cuisine, or you could simply come to Madrid. Traditional Madrid food is nothing to get excited about, but the best cooking from every corner of Spain and further afield finds a home here. And the neighbourhood of La Latina has one of the country's finest concentrations of tapas bars.

Castilla y León
Medieval Towns ✓✓✓
Villages ✓✓✓
Food ✓✓

City as Art
Rich in history, cathedrals and other grand public monuments, the heart of old Castilla is home to some of Spain's prettiest medium-sized towns. Salamanca, Ávila, Segovia, León and Burgos are only the start.

Quiet Pueblos
The villages of Castilla y León feel like Spain before mass tourism and the modern world arrived on Iberian shores, from the Sierra de Francia in the far southwest to quiet, medieval hamlets like Covarrubias, Puebla de Sanabria and Calatañazor.

Hearty Inland Fare
Roasted and grilled meats are a speciality in the Spanish interior, so much so that Spaniards travel here from all over the country for a special meal. *Jamón* and other cured meats are also a regional passion, and some of the best of their kind come from here.

p135

Castilla-La Mancha

History ✓✓
Literature ✓✓
Villages & Castles ✓✓✓

City of Three Faiths
In the Middle Ages, Toledo was one of the most cosmopolitan cities in Spain, as shown by some fine landmarks of the era – a poignant mosque, fine Jewish sites and a cathedral of real power adorned with works by El Greco, Zurbarán and Velázquez.

Tilting at Windmills
The Don Quijote trail through Castilla-La Mancha offers the rare opportunity to follow the terrain trod by one of literature's most eccentric figures. Windmills and sweeping plains evoke Cervantes' novel to such an extent that you can almost hear Sancho Panza's patter.

Beautiful Villages
Amid the often-empty horizons of La Mancha, pretty villages can seem like oases. Atienza, Almagro, Sigüenza and Alcalá del Júcar are our favourites, while the region's castles – this was a longtime frontier between Moorish and Christian Spain – are simply magnificent.

p203

Barcelona

Architecture ✓✓✓
Food ✓✓✓
Art & History ✓✓✓

Modernista Masterpieces
From Gaudí's unfinished masterpiece – La Sagrada Família – to Domènech i Montaner's celestial Palau de la Música Catalana, Catalan visionaries have transformed Barcelona into one of Europe's great Modernista centres, a showcase for the imaginative, surreal and utterly captivating.

Culinary Gems
Barcelona's artistry doesn't end at the drawing board. Feasting on seafood by the Mediterranean, munching on tapas at the magnificent Boqueria market, indulging in Michelin-starred restaurants: it's all part of the Barcelona experience.

Artistry of the Past
Once a vibrant settlement of ancient Rome, Barcelona hides over 2000 years of history in its old lanes. The old Gothic centre has 14th-century churches and medieval mansions with more recent treasures, from a sprawling Picasso collection to pre-Columbian masterpieces.

p235

Catalonia

Food ✓✓✓
Beaches ✓✓
Hiking ✓✓✓

The Catalan Kitchen
Vying with the Basque Country for Spain's highest per-capita ratio of celebrity chefs, Catalonia is something of a pilgrimage for gastronomes. Here, even in the smallest family establishments, they fuse ingredients from land and sea, always keeping faith with rich culinary traditions even as they head off in innovative new directions.

The Catalan Coast
The picturesque coastlines known as the Costa Brava and Costa Daurada are studded with pretty-as-a-postcard villages and beaches that are generally less crowded than those further south. And not far away, signposts to Salvador Dalí sights and Roman ruins make for fine day trips.

Spain's Table
Northern Catalonia means the Pyrenees, where shapely peaks and quiet valleys offer some of the best hiking anywhere in the country.

p306

Aragón

Mountains ✓✓✓
Villages ✓✓
History ✓

Head for the Hills
Perhaps the prettiest corner of the Pyrenees, northern Aragón combines the drama of impossibly high summits with the quiet pleasures of deep valleys and endless hiking trails. The Parque Nacional de Ordesa y Monte Perdido is arguably Spain's most picturesque national park.

Stone Villages
Aragón has numerous finalists in the competition for Spain's most beautiful village, among them Aínsa, Sos del Rey Católico and Albarracín. Many sit in the Pyrenean foothills against a backdrop of snowcapped mountains.

Romans, Moors & Christians
Centred on one of Spain's most important historical kingdoms, Aragón is strewn with landmarks from the great civilisations of ancient and medieval times. Zaragoza in particular spans the millennia with grace and fervour, but Mudéjar Teruel is an often-missed jewel.

p369

Basque Country, Navarra & La Rioja

Food ✓✓✓
Wine ✓✓✓
Villages ✓✓

Spain's Culinary Capital
To understand the buzz surrounding Spanish food, head for San Sebastián, at once *pintxos* (Basque tapas) heaven and home to outrageously talented chefs. You eat well everywhere in the Basque Country, with seafood and perfectly prepared meats the mainstay.

The Finest Drop
La Rioja is to wine what the Basque Country is to food. Wine museums, wine tastings and vineyards stretching to the horizon make this Spain's most accessible wine region. And, of course, it accompanies every meal here, from picnics to bars and restaurants.

Villages
There are stunning villages to be found throughout the Basque Country and La Rioja, but those in the Pyrenean foothills and high valleys of Navarra are a match for anything France or the rest of Spain have to offer.

p406

Cantabria & Asturias

Coastal Scenery ✓✓✓
Mountains ✓✓✓
Food ✓✓

The Scenic Coast
While beach-lovers head for the Mediterranean, those looking for something more head to Cantabria and Asturias. It's all about dramatic landforms, gorgeous villages and marvellous sights in the hinterland (including the astonishing Cueva de Altamira).

Picos de Europa
The vertiginous Picos de Europa might not be Spain's most extensive mountain range, but it's easily one of the most beautiful. Jagged summits and ridgelines are the perfect drawcard for hikers and day-trippers alike.

Cheese & Cider
Mention to any Spaniard that you're on your way to Asturias and chances are they'll start waxing lyrical about the pleasures of Asturian food. The tangy Cabrales cheese is one of Spain's best, while cider poured straight from the barrel is a much-lauded Asturian institution.

p463

Santiago de Compostela & Galicia

Coastal Scenery ✓✓✓
Food ✓✓✓
History ✓✓

The Wildest Coast

Galicia's wild and wind-swept coast is one of Europe's most dramatic. Cliffs plunge from a great height into the roiling waters of the Atlantic, and elsewhere shelter isolated fishing villages and deserted beaches of rare beauty.

Fruits of the Sea

Food dominates life in Galicia, even more than elsewhere in Spain. The culture here owes much to the fishing fleets that have sustained the region through the centuries, while most of the region's festivals have food as their centrepiece.

A Sacred Past

There's no more sacred site in Spain than Santiago de Compostela, the reputed final resting place of St James and endpoint of that great pilgrimage, the Camino de Santiago. And don't forget Lugo, encircled as it is by fine Roman-era walls.

p507

Valencia & Murcia

Fiestas ✓✓✓
Cuisine ✓✓
Beaches ✓✓

Bulls, Fire & Knights in Armour

The biggest and noisiest party is Valencia City's Las Fallas in March. But almost every *pueblo* has its fiesta, usually with fireworks and often with bulls. Lorca's Semana Santa (Holy Week) festivities rival those of Andalucía, while Romans battle Carthaginians in Cartagena in September.

Simmering Rice

Paella first simmered over an open fire in Valencia. Rice dishes are everywhere, with fish and seafood from the Mediterranean and the freshest of vegetables grown along the fertile coast down into Murcia. Murcia City is one of Spain's most underrated tapas experiences.

Strands & Rocky Coves

From small bays to vast beaches stretching over kilometres, from tiny rocky coves to the sandy sweeps of Denia, Benidorm and Murcia's Costa Cálida (Hot Coast), there's always room to stretch out your towel.

p550

Mallorca, Menorca & Ibiza

Beaches ✓✓
Walking & Cycling ✓✓
Nightlife ✓✓

Beaches

White sand, black sand, pebbles or rocky inlets: each of the islands offers variety with, in general, fine sand on their southern shores, rougher stuff to the north.

Outdoor Adventure

Indulge in watery fun, sailing, windsurfing, diving or simply splashing about in all the major coastal resorts. Choose between magnificent trekking in the Tramontana, Mallorca's wild, craggy north, and more gentle striding in the hills of Menorca. Or go cycling along the well-signed routes of all four islands.

Through the Night

It's not only the megavenues of Ibiza that pound until dawn. In season, Ciutadella, on Menorca, draws in clubbers from all over the island, Palma de Mallorca is the big draw for locals there, while the smaller music bars of diminutive Formentera hold their own.

p608

Seville & Andalucía

Music ✓✓✓
White Towns ✓✓
Moorish Heritage ✓✓✓

Stylistic Flamenco

Music in Andalucía is the tale of flamenco which, in turn, is a tale of three cities. Look no further than the *bulerías* of Jerez, the *alegrías* of Cádiz and the *soleares* of Seville, all of them still performed in local *tablaos* and *peñas*.

Hilltop Citadels

They're all here, the famous white towns, with their ruined hilltop castles, geranium-filled flowerboxes and small somnolent churches. Arcos, Jimena, Vejer...the ancient sentinels on a once-volatile frontier that divided two cultures.

Architectural Evolution

A hybrid church-mosque, an Alcázar conceived to re-create heaven on earth, and a palace-fortress that argu-ably marked the high point of Moorish majesty in Europe; Córdoba, Seville and Granada are where Spain's Moorish heritage burns the strongest.

p657

Extremadura

Medieval Towns ✓✓✓
Roman Ruins ✓✓
Monasteries ✓✓

Medieval Film Sets

Spain may be replete with wonderfully preserved old towns that date back to the Middle Ages, but Cáceres and Trujillo are up there with the best. Meandering along their cobblestoned lanes is a journey back into an epic past. Check out Granadilla for the village version.

Roman Mérida

Spain's most beautiful Roman theatre, its longest Roman-era bridge, a breath-taking museum and other ruined glories – welcome to Emerita Augusta, now known as Mérida and Spain's finest Roman site. The fabulous bridge at Alcántara also merits a visit.

Holy Orders

Monkish contemplation required remote corners, and Extremadura fit the bill perfectly. The magnificent sanctuary of Guadalupe, the working convent at Zafra, and an emperor's retire-ment home at Yuste are among Spain's most intrigu-ing religious complexes.

p779

❯ **Every listing is recommended by our authors, and their favourite places are listed first**

❯ **Look out for these icons:**

 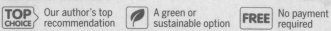

| **TOP CHOICE** | Our author's top recommendation | 🌿 | A green or sustainable option | **FREE** | No payment required |

On the Road

Madrid

Best Places to Eat

» Mercado de San Miguel (p107)

» Restaurante Sobrino de Botín (p107)

» Enotaberna del León de Oro (p107)

» Casa Alberto (p109)

» Sula Madrid (p110)

Best Places to Stay

» Hotel Meninas (p103)

» Praktik Metropol (p103)

» Posada del Dragón (p104)

» Hotel Óscar (p106)

» Hotel Puerta América (p106)

Why Go?

No city on earth is more alive than Madrid, a beguiling place whose sheer energy carries a simple message: this city knows how to live.

It's true Madrid doesn't have the immediate cachet of Paris, the monumental history of Rome or the reputation for cool of that other city up the road. But it's a city in which contradictory impulses are legion, the perfect expression of Europe's most passionate country writ large.

This city has transformed itself into Spain's premier style centre and its calling cards are many: astonishing art galleries; relentless nightlife; an exceptional live-music scene; a feast of fine restaurants and tapas bars; and a population that's mastered the art of the good life. It's not that other cities don't have these things: it's just that Madrid has all of them in bucketloads.

When to Go
Madrid

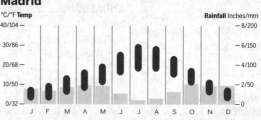

Feb Five days of Spain's best flamenco during the Festival Flamenco Caja Madrid.

May Two of Madrid's biggest fiestas: Fiesta de la Comunidad de Madrid and Fiesta de San Isidro.

Sep Madrid shakes off its summer torpor with (usually) lovely autumn weather.

Madrid Baroque

The Spanish capital's contribution to world architectural textbooks is known as *barroco madrileño* (Madrid baroque). Its creation is largely attributed to Juan de Herrera (1530–97), perhaps the greatest figure of the Spanish Renaissance, who fused the sternness of the Renaissance style with a muted approach to its successor, the more voluptuous, ornamental baroque. Prime examples in Madrid include the Plaza Mayor, the former *ayuntamiento* (town hall) on Plaza de la Villa and the Convento de la Encarnación.

DON'T MISS

La Latina, southwest of Plaza Mayor, is one of Spain's best tapas neighbourhoods. Start along Calle de la Cava Baja, and finish with a mojito on Plaza de la Paja.

MADRID'S BARRIOS IN A NUTSHELL

Los Austrias, Sol and **Centro** form Madrid's oldest quarter, home to some of the city's grandest monuments, as well as bars, restaurants and hotels. Next door, the **La Latina** and **Lavapiés** neighbourhoods are the preserve of narrow medieval streets, great bars for tapas and drinking, and restaurants. Away to the east, the **Huertas** and **Atocha** area is one of Madrid's nightlife capitals and home to the Centro de Arte Reina Sofía.

Down the hill and a world away, the **Paseo del Prado** and **El Retiro** area is downtown Madrid's greenest corner, with world-class art galleries along the Paseo's shores and the Parque del Buen Retiro up the hill to the east. **Salamanca** is upmarket and Madrid's home of old money, not to mention the city's home of designer shopping; while **Malasaña** and **Chueca** are two inner-city *barrios* with eclectic nightlife, shopping and outstanding eating options: the latter is the heartbeat of Madrid's gay community.

To the north, **Chamberí** and **Argüelles** are residential *barrios* with a glimpse of Madrid away from the tourist crowds, while **Northern Madrid** has high-class restaurants and is the home of Real Madrid football club.

Fast Facts

» Population: 3.26 million (city), 6.2 million (Comunidad)

» Area: 505 sq km (city), 7995 sq km (Comunidad)

» Number of visitors (2010): 8 million

» Average annual income: €25,860

Planning Your Trip

» Book your accommodation: www.hotels.lonely planet.com.

» Avoid the queues and book your Museo del Prado tickets online: www.museo delprado.es.

» Beat the rush – book your tickets in advance to see Real Madrid play.

Madrid's Best Art Galleries

» **Museo del Prado** (p82) One of the great art galleries of the world, with Goya and Velázquez the highlights.
» **Centro de Arte Reina Sofía** (p79) Stunning art gallery that's home to Picasso's Guernica.
» **Museo Thyssen-Bornemisza** (p87) Private art gallery with masters from every era.
» **Real Academia de Bellas Artes de San Fernando** (p76) Goya, Picasso, Velázquez, Rubens...
» **Ermita de San Antonio de la Florida** (p91) Exquisite Goya frescoes in their original setting.

Resources

» Tourism in Madrid city: www.esmadrid.com.
» Tourism in Madrid region: www.turismomadrid.es.
» English-language guide to what's happening: www.in-madrid.com.

Madrid Highlights

1 Watch the masterpieces of Velázquez and Goya leap off the canvas at the world-famous **Museo del Prado** (p82)

2 Search for treasure in the Sunday **El Rastro** (p77) flea market, then join the crowds in the **Parque del Buen Retiro** (p88)

3 Soak up the buzz with a *caña* (small beer) or glass of Spanish wine on **Plaza de Santa Ana** (p79)

4 Go on a **tapas crawl** (p111) in the medieval *barrio* (district) of La Latina

5 Order *chocolate con churros* (deep-fried doughnut strips dipped in hot chocolate) close to dawn at the **Chocolatería de San Ginés** (p113)

6 Make a sporting pilgrimage to see the stars of Real Madrid play at **Estadio Santiago Bernabéu** (p124)

7 Dance the night away in one of the city's world-famous **nightclubs** (p118)

8 Feast on roast suckling pig at **Café de la Iberia** (p132) in Chinchón

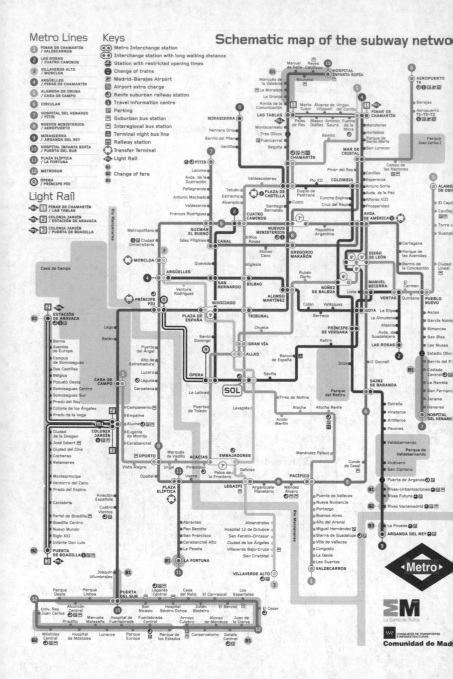

History

When Iberia's Christians began the Reconquista (c 722) – the centuries-long campaign by Christian forces to reclaim the peninsula – the Muslims of Al-Andalus constructed a chain of fortified positions through the heart of Iberia. One of these was built by Muhammad I, emir of Córdoba, in 854, on the site of what would become Madrid. The name they gave to the new settlement was Mayrit (or Magerit), which comes from the Arabic word *majira*, meaning water channel.

A WORTHY CAPITAL?

Madrid's strategic location in the centre of the peninsula saw the city change hands repeatedly, but it was not until 1309 that the travelling Cortes (royal court and parliament) sat in Madrid for the first time. Despite the growing royal attention, medieval Madrid remained dirt poor and small-scale: 'In Madrid there is nothing except what you bring with you', observed one 15th-century writer. It simply bore no comparison with other major Spanish, let alone European, cities.

By the time Felipe II ascended the Spanish throne in 1556, Madrid was surrounded by walls that boasted 130 towers and six stone gates, but these fortifications were largely built of mud and designed more to impress than provide any meaningful defence of the city. Madrid was nonetheless chosen by Felipe II as the capital of Spain in 1561.

Madrid took centuries to grow into its new role and despite a handful of elegant churches, the imposing Alcázar and a smattering of noble residences, the city consisted of, for the most part, precarious whitewashed houses. The monumental Paseo del Prado, which now provides Madrid with so much of its grandeur, was a small creek.

During the 17th century, Spain's golden age, Madrid began to take on the aspect of a capital and was home to 175,000 people, making it the fifth-largest city in Europe (after London, Paris, Constantinople and Naples).

Carlos III (r 1759–88) gave Madrid and Spain a period of comparatively commonsense government. After he cleaned up the city, completed the Palacio Real, inaugurated the Real Jardín Botánico and carried out numerous other public works, he became known as the best 'mayor' Madrid had ever had.

Madrileños (residents of Madrid) didn't take kindly to Napoleon's invasion and subsequent occupation of Spain in 1805 and, on 2 May 1808, they attacked French troops around the Palacio Real and what is now Plaza del Dos de Mayo. The ill-fated rebellion was quickly put down by Murat, Napoleon's brother-in-law and the most powerful of his military leaders.

WARS, FRANCO & TERRORISM

Turmoil continued to stalk the Spanish capital. The upheaval of the 19th-century Carlist Wars was followed by a two-and-a-half-year siege of Madrid by Franco's Nationalist forces from 1936 to 1939, during which the city was shelled regularly from Casa de Campo and Gran Vía became known as 'Howitzer Alley'.

After Franco's death in 1975 and the country's subsequent transition to democracy, Madrid became an icon for the new Spain as the city's young people unleashed a flood of pent-up energy. This took its most colourful form in the years of *la movida*, the endless party that swept up the city in a frenzy of creativity and open-minded freedom that has in some ways yet to abate.

On 11 March 2004, just three days before the country was due to vote in national elections, Madrid was rocked by 10 bombs on four rush-hour commuter trains heading into the capital's Atocha station. The bombs had been planted by terrorists with links to al-Qaeda, reportedly because of Spain's then support for the American-led war in Iraq. When the dust cleared, 191 people had died and 1755 were wounded, many seriously. Madrid was in shock and, for 24 hours at least, this most clamorous of cities fell silent. Then, 36 hours after the attacks, more than three million *madrileños* streamed onto the streets to protest against the bombings, making it the largest demonstration in the city's history. Although deeply traumatised, Madrid's mass act of defiance and pride began the process of healing. Visit Madrid today and you'll find a city that has resolutely returned to normal.

In the years since, Madrid has come agonisingly close in the race to host the Summer Olympics, coming third behind London and Paris in the race for 2012 and second behind Rio for 2016. The town hall has yet to decide whether to mount another bid, but many *madrileños* are hoping it will be third time lucky. And, of course, Madrid was the scene of one of the biggest celebrations in modern Spanish history when the Spanish World Cup–winning football team returned home in July 2010. These celebrations were almost matched two years later when Spain won the 2012 European Football Championships, again bringing much-needed cheer to

MADRID IN...

One Day

Begin in the **Plaza Mayor** with its architectural beauty, fine *terrazas* and endlessly fascinating passing Madrid parade. Wander down Calle Mayor, passing the delightful **Plaza de la Villa** en route, and head for the **Palacio Real**. By then you'll be ready for a coffee (or something stronger) and there's no finer place to rest than in the **Plaza de Oriente**. Double back up towards the **Plaza de la Puerta del Sol** then lose yourself in the Huertas area around **Plaza de Santa Ana**, the ideal place for a long, liquid lunch. Stroll down the hill to the incomparable **Museo del Prado**, one of Europe's best art galleries. In anticipation of a long night ahead, catch your breath in the **Parque del Buen Retiro** before heading up along **Gran Vía** and into Chueca for Madrid's famously noisy and eclectic nightlife.

Three Days

Three days is a minimum for getting a real taste of Madrid. Spend a morning each on days two and three at **Centro de Arte Reina Sofía** and **Museo Thyssen-Bornemisza**. Otherwise, pause in **Plaza de la Cibeles** to admire some of the best architecture in Madrid as you work your way north to the **Gran Café de Gijón**, one of Madrid's grand old cafes. A quick metro ride across town takes you to the astonishing Goya frescoes in the **Ermita de San Antonio de la Florida**. While you're in the area, consider a chicken-and-cider meal at **Casa Mingo**. On another day, head for La Latina and the great restaurants and tapas bars along Calle de la Cava Baja, or some cod tapas at **Casa Revuelta**. If it's a Sunday, precede these outings with a wander through **El Rastro**, one of the best flea markets in Europe. In Malasaña, Calle de Manuela Malasaña offers rich pickings for a meal and the august and old-world **Café Comercial** is a fine old pit stop at any time of the day.

One Week

If you're in town for a week, begin day four with some shopping. Calle de Serrano has just about everything for the designer-conscious, while Calle de Fuencarral (casual streetwear) or Calle de Augusto Figueroa (shoes) could also occupy an hour or two. Check out the bullring at **Plaza de Toros**, and **Estadio Santiago Bernabéu**, home to Real Madrid. Other possibilities that will deepen your Madrid experience include wandering through medieval and multicultural **Lavapiés** or seeing a live **flamenco performance**. Day trips could include **Toledo** and **Segovia**. Of the numerous royal residences in the Madrid vicinity, the most impressive is **San Lorenzo de El Escorial**, but **Chinchón** is an enchanted alternative with ramshackle village charm written all over its colonnaded Plaza Mayor.

a city affected deeply by Spain's severe economic downturn.

⊙ Sights

Madrid has three of the finest art galleries in the world: if ever there existed a golden mile of fine art, it would have to be the combined charms of the Museo del Prado, the Centro de Arte Reina Sofía and the Museo Thyssen-Bornemisza. Beyond the museums' walls, the combination of stately architecture and feel-good living has never been easier to access than in the beautiful plazas, where *terrazas* (cafes with outdoor tables) provide a front-row seat for Madrid's fine cityscape and endlessly energetic street life. Throw in some outstanding city parks (the Parque del Buen Retiro, in particular) and areas like Chueca, Malasaña and Salamanca, which each have their own identity, and you'll quickly end up wondering why you decided to spend so little time here.

LOS AUSTRIAS, SOL & CENTRO

These *barrios* are where the story of Madrid began. As the seat of royal power, this is where the splendour of imperial Spain was at its most ostentatious and where Spain's overarching Catholicism was at its most devout – think expansive palaces, elaborate private mansions, ancient churches and imposing convents amid the clamour of modern Madrid.

TOP CHOICE Plaza Mayor SQUARE

(Map p72; Plaza Mayor; MSol) Ah, the history the plaza has seen! Designed in 1619 by Juan Gómez de Mora and built in typical Herrerian style, of which the slate spires are the most obvious expression, its first public ceremony was suitably auspicious – the beatification of San Isidro Labrador (St Isidro the Farm Labourer), Madrid's patron saint. Thereafter it was as if all that was controversial about Spain took place in this square. Bullfights, often in celebration of royal weddings or births, with royalty watching on from the balconies and up to 50,000 people crammed into the plaza, were a recurring theme until 1878. Far more notorious were the *autos-da-fé* (the ritual condemnations of heretics during the Spanish Inquisition) followed by executions – burnings at the stake and deaths by garrotte on the north side of the square, hangings to the south. These continued until 1790 when a fire largely destroyed the square, which was subsequently reproduced under the supervision of Juan de Villanueva, who lent his name to the building that now houses the Museo del Prado (p82).These days, the plaza is an epicentre of Madrid life, from the outdoor tables to the life coursing across its cobblestones.

The grandeur of the plaza is due in large part to the warm colours of the uniformly ochre apartments, with 237 wrought-iron balconies offset by the exquisite frescoes of the 17th-century Real Casa de la Panadería (Royal Bakery). The present frescoes date to just 1992 and are the work of artist Carlos Franco, who chose images from the signs of the zodiac and gods (eg Cybele) to provide a stunning backdrop for the plaza. The frescoes were inaugurated to coincide with Madrid's 1992 spell as European Capital of Culture.

TOP CHOICE Palacio Real PALACE

(Map p72; www.patrimonionacional.es; Calle de Bailén; adult/concession €10/5, guide/audioguide/pamphlet €7/4/1, EU citizens free 5-8pm Wed & Thu; ⊙10am-8pm; MÓpera) Spain's lavish Palacio Real is a jewel box of a palace, although it's used only occasionally for royal ceremonies; the royal family moved to the modest Palacio de la Zarzuela years ago.

When the Alcázar burned down on Christmas Day 1734, Felipe V, the first of the Bourbon kings, decided to build a palace that would dwarf all its European counterparts. Felipe died before the palace was finished, which is perhaps why the Italianate baroque colossus has a mere 2800 rooms, just one-quarter of the original plan.

The official tour leads through 50 of the palace rooms, which hold a good selection of Goyas, 215 absurdly ornate clocks, and five Stradivarius violins still used for concerts and balls. The main stairway is a grand statement of imperial power, leading first to the Halberdiers' rooms and eventually to the sumptuous Salón del Trono (Throne Room), with its crimson-velvet wall coverings and Tiepolo ceiling. Shortly after, you reach the Salón de Gasparini, with its exquisite stucco ceiling and walls resplendent with embroidered silks.

Outside the main palace, visit the Farmacia Real (Royal Pharmacy) at the southern end of the patio known as the Plaza de la Armería (or Plaza de Armas). Westwards across the plaza is the Armería Real (Royal Armoury), a shiny collection of weapons and armour, mostly dating from the 16th and 17th centuries.

Plaza de Oriente SQUARE

(Map p72; Plaza de Oriente; MÓpera) A royal palace that once had aspirations to be the Spanish Versailles. Sophisticated cafes watched over by apartments that cost the equivalent of a royal salary. The Teatro Real, Madrid's opera house and one of Spain's temples to high culture. Some of the finest sunset views in Madrid... Welcome to Plaza de Oriente, a living, breathing monument to imperial Madrid.

At the centre of the plaza, which the palace overlooks, is an equestrian statue of Felipe IV (Map p72; MÓpera). Designed by Velázquez, it's the perfect place to take it all in, with marvellous views wherever you look. If you're wondering how a heavy bronze statue of a rider and his horse rearing up can actually maintain that stance, the answer is simple: the hind legs are solid, while the front ones are hollow. That idea was Galileo Galilei's. Nearby are some 20 marble statues, mostly of ancient monarchs. Local legend has it that these ageing royals get down off their pedestals at night to stretch their legs.

The adjacent Jardines Cabo Naval, a great place to watch the sunset, adds to the sense of a sophisticated oasis of green in the heart of Madrid.

Campo del Moro & Jardines de Sabatini GARDENS

In proper palace style, lush gardens surround the Palacio Real. To the north are the formal French-style Jardines de Sabatini

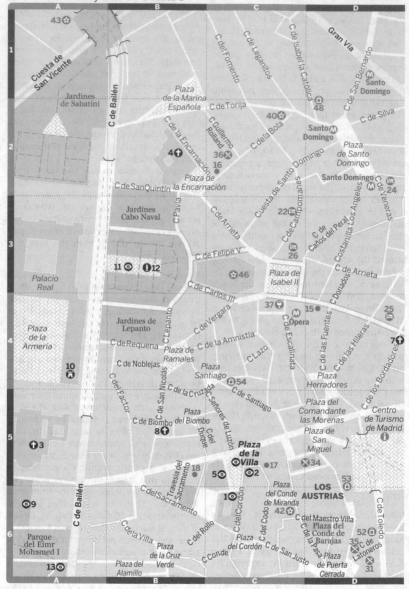

(⊙9am-9pm May-Sep; Ⓜ Ópera). Directly behind the palace are the fountains of the **Campo del Moro** (☑91 454 88 00; www.patrimonionacional.es; Paseo de la Virgen del Puerto; ⊙10am-8pm Mon-Sat, 9am-8pm Sun & holidays Apr-Sep, 10am-6pm Mon-Sat, 9am-6pm Sun & holidays Oct-Mar; Ⓜ Príncipe Pío), so named because this is where the Muslim army camped before a 12th-century attack on the Alcázar. Now, shady paths, a thatch-roofed pagoda and palace views are the main attractions.

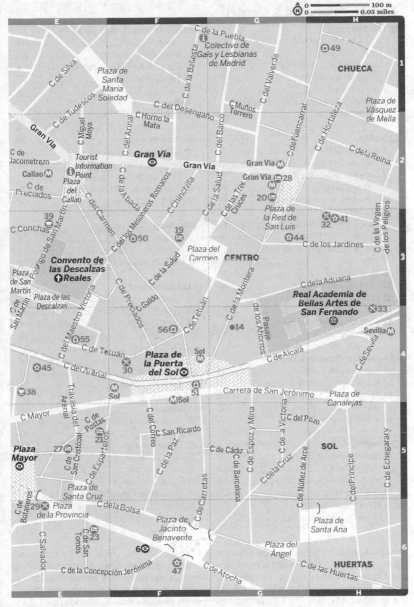

Catedral de Nuestra Señora de la Almudena
CATHEDRAL

(Map p72; ☎91 542 22 00; www.museocatedral.archimadrid.es; Calle de Bailén; cathedral & crypt by donation, museum adult/child €6/4; ⊙9am-8.30pm Mon-Sat, for Mass Sun, museum 10am-2.30pm Mon-Sat; Ⓜ Ópera) Paris has Notre Dame and Rome has St Peter's Basilica. In fact, almost every European city of stature has its signature cathedral, a standout monument to a glorious Christian past. Not Madrid. Although the exterior of the Catedral de Nuestra Señora de la

Los Austrias, Sol & Centro

Almudena sits in harmony with the adjacent Palacio Real, Madrid's cathedral is cavernous and largely charmless within; its colourful, modern ceilings do little to make up for the lack of old-world gravitas that so distinguishes great cathedrals.

Carlos I first proposed building a cathedral here back in 1518, but building didn't actually begin until 1879. It was finally finished in 1992 and its pristine, bright-white neo-Gothic interior holds no pride of place in the affections of *madrileños*.

It's possible to climb to the cathedral's summit, with fine views. En route you climb through the cathedral's museum; follow the signs to the **Museo de la Catedral y Cúpola** on the northern facade, opposite the Palacio Real.

Muralla Árabe WALLS
(Map p72; Cuesta de la Vega; ⓜÓpera) Behind the cathedral apse, down Cuesta de la Vega, is a short stretch of the so-called Muralla Árabe, the fortifications built by Madrid's

early medieval Islamic rulers. Some of it dates as far back as the 9th century, when the initial Islamic fort was raised. Other sections date from the 12th and 13th centuries, by which time the city was in Christian hands.

Plaza de la Villa · SQUARE

(Map p72; Plaza de la Villa; mÓpera) The intimate Plaza de la Villa is one of Madrid's prettiest. Enclosed on three sides by wonderfully preserved examples of 17th-century *barroco madrileño* (Madrid-style baroque architecture – a pleasing amalgam of brick, exposed stone and wrought iron), it was the permanent seat of Madrid's city government from the Middle Ages until recent years when Madrid's city council relocated to the grand Palacio de Comunicaciones on Plaza de la Cibeles (p89).

On the western side of the square is the 17th-century **former ayuntamiento** (Map p72; mÓpera) (town hall), in Habsburg-style baroque with Herrerian slate-tile spires. On the opposite side of the square is the Gothic **Casa de los Lujanes** (Map p72; mÓpera), whose brickwork tower is said to have been 'home' to the imprisoned French monarch François I after his capture in the Battle of Pavia (1525). The plateresque (15th- and 16th-century Spanish baroque) **Casa de Cisneros** (Map p72; mÓpera), built in 1537 with later Renaissance alterations, also catches the eye.

Convento de las Descalzas Reales · CONVENT

(Convent of the Barefoot Royals; Map p72; www.patrimonionacional.es; Plaza de las Descalzas 3; adult/child €7/4, incl Convento de la Encarnación €10/5, EU citizens free Wed & Thu afternoon; ☺10.30am-2pm & 4-6.30pm Tue-Sat, 10am-3pm Sun; mÓpera, Sol) The grim plateresque walls of the Convento de las Descalzas Reales offer no hint that behind the facade lies a sumptuous stronghold of the faith. Founded in 1559 by Juana of Austria, the widowed daughter of the Spanish king Carlos I, the convent quickly became one of Spain's richest religious houses thanks to gifts from Juana's noble friends. On the obligatory guided tour you'll see a gaudily frescoed Renaissance stairway, a number of extraordinary tapestries based on works by Rubens, and a wonderful painting entitled *The Voyage of the 11,000 Virgins*. Some 33 nuns still live here and there are 33 chapels dotted around the convent.

Convento de la Encarnación · CONVENT

(Map p72; ☎91 454 88 00; www.patrimonionacional.es; Plaza de la Encarnación 1; adult/concession €7/4, incl Convento de las Descalzas Reales €10/5, EU citizens free Wed & Thu afternoon; ☺10am-2pm & 4-6.30pm Tue-Sat, 10am-3pm Sun; mÓpera) Founded by Empress Margarita de Austria, this 17th-century mansion built in the Madrid baroque style is still inhabited by nuns of the Augustine order. The large art collection dates mostly from the 17th century, and among the many gold and silver reliquaries is one that contains the blood of San Pantaleón, which purportedly liquefies each year on 27 July.

Iglesia de San Nicolás de los Servitas · CHURCH

(Map p72; ☎91 548 83 14; Plaza de San Nicolás 6; ☺8am-1.30pm & 5.30-8.30pm Mon, 8-9.30am & 6.30-8.30pm Tue-Sat, 9.30am-2pm & 6.30-9pm Sun & holidays; mÓpera) Considered Madrid's oldest surviving church, Iglesia de San Nicolás de los Servitas may have been built on the site of Muslim Magerit's second mosque. It offers a rare glimpse of medieval Madrid, although apart from the restored 12th-century Mudéjar bell tower, most of the present church dates back to the 15th century.

MADRID CARD

If you intend to do some intensive sightseeing and travelling on public transport, it might be worth looking at the **Madrid Card** (☎91 360 47 72; www.madridcard.com; 1/2/3 days adult €39/49/59, child age 6-12 €20/28/34). It includes free entry to more than 50 museums in and around Madrid (some of these are already free, but it does include the Museo del Prado, Museo Thyssen-Bornemisza, Centro de Arte Reina Sofía, Estadio Santiago Bernabéu and Palacio Real); free walking tours; and discounts in a number of restaurants, shops, bars and car rental. The Madrid Card can be bought online, or in person at the tourist offices on Plaza Mayor or Terminal 4 in Barajas airport, the Metro de Madrid ticket office in Terminal 2 of the airport, the Museo Thyssen-Bornemisza, and in some tobacconists and hotels. A list of sales outlets appears on the website.

MADRID SIGHTS

DON'T MISS

MADRID'S BEAUTIFUL PLAZAS

» Plaza Mayor (p71)

» Plaza de Oriente (p71)

» Plaza de Santa Ana (p79)

» Plaza de la Villa (p75)

» Plaza de la Paja (p100)

» Plaza de la Puerta del Sol (p76)

» Plaza de la Cibeles (p89)

Iglesia de San Ginés
CHURCH

(Map p72; Calle del Arenal 13; ⊙8.45am-1pm & 6-9pm Mon-Sat, 9.45am-2pm & 6-9pm Sun; Ⓜ Sol, Ópera) Due north of Plaza Mayor, San Ginés is one of Madrid's oldest churches: it has been here in one form or another since at least the 14th century. It is speculated that, prior to the arrival of the Christians in 1085, a Mozarabic community (Christians in Muslim territory) lived around the stream that later became Calle del Arenal and that its parish church stood on this site. What you see today was built in 1645 but largely reconstructed after a fire in 1824. The church houses some fine paintings, including El Greco's *Expulsion of the Moneychangers from the Temple* (1614), which is beautifully displayed; the glass is just 6mm from the canvas to avoid reflections.

Plaza de la Puerta del Sol
SQUARE

(Map p72; Plaza de la Puerta del Sol; Ⓜ Sol) The official centre point of Spain is a gracious hemisphere of elegant facades that's often very crowded. It is, above all, a crossroads. People here are forever heading somewhere else, on foot, by metro (three lines cross here) or by bus (many lines terminate and start nearby). In Madrid's earliest days, the Puerta del Sol (Gate of the Sun) was the eastern gate of the city.

Plaza de la Puerta del Sol comes into its own on New Year's Eve, when *madrileños* pack into the square in their tens of thousands, waiting for the clock that gives Spain its official time to strike midnight, as the rest of the country watches on TV. Look out for the statue of a bear nuzzling a *madroño* (strawberry tree) off the plaza's northeastern corner; this is the official symbol of the city.

The plaza has always been a place to gauge the political winds of the day and has been the scene for so many of Spain's most important political protests. In 2011, the *indignados* – a mass sit-in that lasted months and served as a forerunner for similar protests around the world – took over the square, while massive protests against government austerity cuts in 2012 also began here.

Real Academia de Bellas Artes de San Fernando
MUSEUM

(Map p72; ☑91 524 08 64; http://rabasf.insde.es; Calle de Alcalá 13; adult/child €5/free, free Wed; ⊙9am-3pm Tue-Sat, 9am-2.30pm Sun Sep-Jun, hours vary Jul & Aug; Ⓜ Sol, Sevilla) In any other city, the Royal Fine Arts Academy would be a standout attraction, but in Madrid it too often gets forgotten in the rush to the Prado, Thyssen or Reina Sofía. An academic centre for up-and-coming artists since Fernando VI founded it in the 18th century (both Picasso and Dalí studied here), it houses works by some of the best-loved old masters. Highlights include works by Zurbarán, El Greco, Rubens, Tintoretto, Goya, Sorolla and Juan Gris, not to mention a couple of minor portraits by Velázquez and a few drawings by Picasso.

Gran Vía
STREET

(Map p72; Gran Vía; Ⓜ Gran Vía, Callao) It's difficult to imagine Madrid without Gran Vía, the grand boulevard that climbs through the city centre from Plaza de España down to Calle de Alcalá, but it has only existed since 1910, when it was bulldozed through what was then a lively labyrinth of old streets.

On a rise about one-third of the way along stands the 1920s-era **Telefónica building** (Map p94) (Edificio Telefónica), which was for years the tallest building in the city. During the civil war, the boulevard became known as 'Howitzer Alley' as shells rained down from Franco's forces in the Casa de Campo. At the southern end of Gran Vía, the stunning French-designed **Metrópolis building** (Edificio Metrópolis; 1905) has a winged statue of victory sitting atop its dome.

LA LATINA & LAVAPIÉS

La Latina combines some of the best things about Madrid: the Spanish capital's best selection of tapas bars and a medieval streetscape studded with elegant churches. The *barrio's* heartland is centred on the area between (and very much including) Calle de la Cava Baja and the beautiful Plaza de la Paja.

Lavapiés, on the other hand, is a world away from the sophistication of modern Madrid. This is at once one of the city's oldest and most traditional *barrios* and home to more immigrants than any other central-Madrid *barrio*. It's quirky, alternative and a melting pot all in one. It's not without its problems, and the *barrio* has a reputation both for anti-glamour cool and as a no-go zone, depending on your perspective.

Basílica de San Francisco El Grande
CHURCH

(Map p78; Plaza de San Francisco 1; adult/concession €3/2; ⊘Mass 8-10.30am Mon-Sat, museum 10.30am-12.30pm & 4-6pm Tue-Sun; MLa Latina, Puerta de Toledo) One of the largest churches in the city, the Basílica de San Francisco el Grande dominates the skyline at the southern reaches of La Latina. Its extravagantly frescoed dome is, by some estimates, the largest in Spain and the fourth-largest in the world, with a height of 56m and diameter of 33m. The baroque basilica has some outstanding features, including frescoed cupolas and chapel ceilings by Francisco Bayeu. Goya's *The Prediction of San Bernardino of Siena for the King of Aragón* is here, too, in the Capilla de San Bernardino. According to legend, the basilica sits atop the site where St Francis of Assisi built a chapel in 1217.

Although entry is free during morning Mass times, there is no access to the museum and the lights in the Capilla de San Bernardino won't be on (to illuminate the Goya).

Iglesia de San Andrés & Around
CHURCH, MUSEUM

(Map p78; Plaza de San Andrés 1; ⊘8am-1pm & 6-8pm Mon-Sat, 8am-1pm Sun; MLa Latina) The stately Iglesia de San Andrés crowns the plaza of the same name, providing a lovely backdrop for the impromptu parties that fill this square on Sunday afternoons as the El Rastro crowd drifts in. Gutted during Spain's civil war, it was restored to its former glory and is at its best when illuminated at night.

Around the back, overlooking the delightful Plaza de la Paja, is the Capilla del Obispo, where San Isidro Labrador, patron saint of Madrid, was first buried. When the saint's body was discovered here in the late 13th century, two centuries after his death, decomposition had not yet set in. San Isidro made his last move to the Basílica de Nuestra Señora del Buen Consejo (Map p80; Calle de Toledo 37; ⊘8am-1pm & 6-9pm; MTirso de Molina, La Latina) in the 18th century.

From Tuesday to Friday at 12.30pm, stop by for the sung service 'Oficio del Mediodía'.

The nearby Museo de los Orígenes (Casa de San Isidro; Map p78; ☎91 366 74 15; www.madrid.es; Plaza de San Andrés 2; ⊘9.30am-8pm Tue-Fri, 10am-2pm Sat & Sun Sep-Jul, 9.30am-2.30pm Tue-Sat Aug; MLa Latina) occupies the spot where San Isidro Labrador is said to have ended his days in 1172. Displays range from archaeological finds from the Roman period to maps, scale models, paintings and photos of Madrid down through the ages.

Viaducto & Jardines de las Vistillas
VIEWPOINT, GARDENS

(Map p72; MLa Latina) For a great view out to the west, take a stroll down Calle de Segovia, where a *viaducto* (viaduct) provides a good vantage point. The outdoor tables in the adjacent Jardines de las Vistillas are another good spot, with views out towards Sierra de Guadarrama. During the civil war, Las Vistillas was heavily bombarded by Nationalist troops from the Casa de Campo, and they in turn were shelled from a Republican bunker here.

La Morería
NEIGHBOURHOOD

(Map p78; MLa Latina) The area stretching southeast from the *viaducto* to the Iglesia de San Andrés was the heart of the *morería*. This is where the Muslim population of Magerit was concentrated in the wake of the 11th-century Christian takeover of the town. Strain the imagination a little and the maze of winding and hilly lanes even now retains a whiff of the North African medina.

Iglesia de San Pedro El Viejo
CHURCH

(Map p78; ☎91 365 12 84; Costanilla de San Pedro; MLa Latina) With its clearly Mudéjar bell tower, Iglesia de San Pedro El Viejo is one of the few remaining windows onto the world of medieval Madrid. The church was built atop the site of the old Mezquita de la Morería (Mosque of the Muslim Quarter).

El Rastro
MARKET

(Ribera de Curtidores; ⊘8am-3pm Sun; MLa Latina) The crowded Sunday flea market was, back in the 17th and 18th centuries, largely a meat market (*rastro* means 'stain', in reference to the trail of blood left behind by animals dragged down the hill). The road leading through the market, Ribera de Curtidores, translates as Tanners' Alley and further evokes this sense of a slaughterhouse past. On Sunday mornings this is *the* place

La Latina

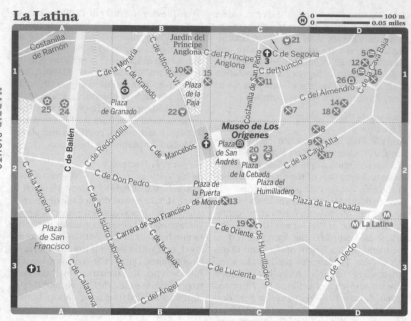

La Latina

to be, with all of Madrid (in all its diversity) here in search of a bargain.

HUERTAS & ATOCHA

If Huertas is known for anything, it's for nightlife that never seems to abate once the sun goes down. Such fame is well deserved, but there's so much more to Huertas than immediately meets the eye. Enjoy the height of sophisticated European cafe culture in the superb Plaza de Santa Ana, then go down the hill through Barrio de las Letras to the Centro de Arte Reina Sofía, one of the finest contemporary art galleries in Europe. Across the Plaza del Emperador Carlos V from the gallery, the Antigua Estación de Atocha marks the beginning of the Atocha district.

TOP CHOICE **Centro de Arte Reina Sofía** MUSEUM
(Map p82; www.museoreinasofia.es; Calle de Santa Isabel 52; adult/concession €6/free, free Sun, 7-9pm Mon-Fri & 2.30-9pm Sat; ⊙10am-9pm Mon, Wed, Thu & Sat, 10am-11pm Fri, 10am-7pm Sun, closed Tue; ⓂAtocha) Home to Picasso's *Guernica,* arguably Spain's single most famous artwork, the Centro de Arte Reina Sofía is Madrid's premier collection of contemporary art. In addition to plenty of paintings by Picasso, other major drawcards are works by Salvador Dalí (1904–1989) and Joan Miró (1893–1983). The collection principally spans the 20th century up to the 1980s (for more recent works, check to see if the Museo Municipal de Arte Contemporáneo (Map p94; ☑91 588 59 28; www.munimadrid.es/museoartecontemporaneo; Calle del Conde Duque 9-11; ⓂPlaza de España, Ventura Rodríguez, San Bernardo), which was closed for renovations at the time of writing, has reopened). The occasional non-Spaniard artist makes an appearance (including Francis Bacon's *Lying Figure;* 1966), but most of the collection is strictly peninsular.

The permanent collection is displayed on the 2nd and 4th floors of the main wing of the museum, the **Edificio Sabatini**. *Guernica's* location never changes – you'll find it in room 206 on the 2nd floor. Beyond that, the location of specific paintings can be a little confusing. After a period of grouping together works by the same artist, the museum has moved towards a more theme-based approach, which ensures that you may find works by Picasso or Miró, for example, spread across the two floors. The only solution if you're looking for something specific is to pick up the latest copy of the *Planos de museo* (Museum Floorplans) from the information desk just inside the main entrance; it lists the rooms in which each artist appears.

In addition to Picasso's *Guernica,* which is worth the admission fee on its own, don't neglect the artist's preparatory sketches in the rooms surrounding room 206; they offer an intriguing insight into the development of this seminal work. If Picasso's cubist style has captured your imagination, the work of the Madrid-born Juan Gris (1887–1927) or Georges Braque (1882–1963) may appeal.

The work of Joan Miró is defined by often delightfully bright primary colours, but watch out also for a handful of his equally odd sculptures. Since his paintings became a symbol of the Barcelona Olympics in 1992, his work has begun to receive the international acclaim it so richly deserves – the museum is a fine place to get a representative sample of his innovative work.

The Reina Sofía is also home to 20 or so canvases by Salvador Dalí, of which the most famous is perhaps the surrealist extravaganza that is *El gran masturbador* (1929). Among his other works is a strange bust of a certain *Joelle,* which Dalí created with his friend Man Ray (1890–1976). Another well-known surrealist painter, Max Ernst (1891–1976), is also worth tracking down.

If you can tear yourself away from the big names, the Reina Sofía offers a terrific opportunity to learn more about sometimes lesser-known 20th-century Spanish artists. Among these are Miquel Barceló (b 1957); *madrileño* artist José Gutiérrez Solana (1886–1945); the renowned Basque painter Ignazio Zuloaga (1870–1945); Benjamin Palencia (1894–1980), whose paintings capture the turbulence of Spain in the 1930s; Barcelona painter Antoni Tàpies (1923–2012); pop artist Eduardo Arroyo (b 1937); and abstract painters such as Eusebio Sempere (1923–85) and members of the Equipo 57 group (founded in 1957 by a group of Spanish artists in exile in Paris), such as Pablo Palazuelo (1916–2007). Better known as a poet and playwright, Federico García Lorca (1898–1936) is represented by a number of his sketches.

Of the sculptors, watch in particular for Pablo Gargallo (1881–1934), whose work in bronze includes a bust of Picasso, and the renowned Basque sculptors Jorge Oteiza (1908–2003) and Eduardo Chillida (1924–2002).

Plaza de Santa Ana SQUARE
(Map p80; Plaza de Santa Ana; ⓂSevilla, Sol, Antón Martín) The Plaza de Santa Ana is a delightful confluence of elegant architecture and irresistible energy. Situated in the heart of Huertas, it was laid out in 1810 during the controversial reign of Joseph Bonaparte, giving breathing space to what had hitherto

Huertas

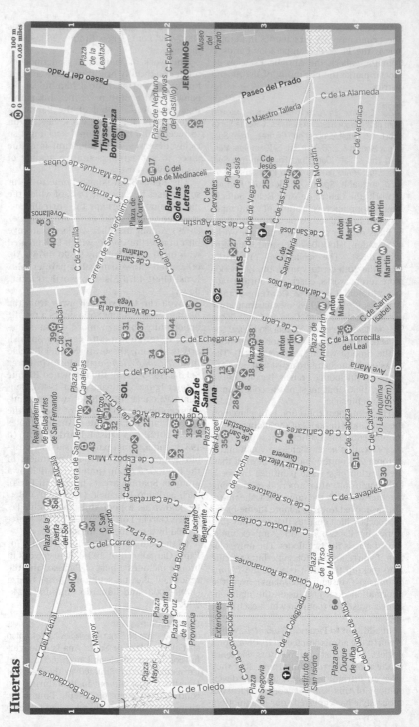

Huertas

been one of Madrid's most claustrophobic *barrios*. The plaza quickly became a focal point for intellectual life, and the cafes surrounding the plaza thronged with writers, poets and artists engaging in endless *tertulias* (literary and philosophical discussions). Echoes of this literary history survive in the statues of the 17th-century writer Calderón de la Barca and Federíco García Lorca, and in the Teatro Español (formerly the Teatro del Príncipe) at the plaza's eastern end, and continue down into the Barrio de las Letras. Apart from anything else, the plaza is the starting point for many a long Huertas night.

Barrio de las Letras   NEIGHBOURHOOD
(Map p80; ⓂAntón Martín) The area that unfurls down the hill east of Plaza de Santa Ana is referred to as the Barrio de las Letras (District of Letters), because of the writers who lived here during Spain's golden age of the 16th and 17th centuries. Miguel de Cervantes Saavedra (1547–1616), the author of *Don Quijote,* spent much of his adult life in Madrid and lived and died at Calle de Cervantes 2 (Map p80; Calle de Cervantes 2; ⓂAntón Martín); a plaque (dating from 1834) sits above the door. Sadly, the original building was torn down in the early 19th century. When Cervantes died his body was interred around the corner at the Convento de las Trinitarias (Map p80; Calle de Lope de Vega 16; ⓂAntón Martín), which is marked by another plaque. Still home to cloistered nuns, the convent is closed to the public, which saves the authorities embarrassment: no one really knows where in the convent the bones

Atocha

of Cervantes lie. A commemorative Mass is held for him here every year on the anniversary of his death, 23 April. Another literary landmark is the **Casa de Lope de Vega** (Map p80; ✆91 429 92 16; Calle de Cervantes 11; ⊙guided tours every 30min 10am-2pm Tue-Sat; Ⓜ Antón Martín), the former home of Lope de Vega (1562–1635), Spain's premier playwright. It's now a museum containing memorabilia from Lope de Vega's life and work.

Antigua Estación de Atocha NOTABLE BUILDING
(Map p82; Plaza del Emperador Carlos V; Ⓜ Atocha Renfe) In 1992 the northwestern wing of the Antigua Estación de Atocha (Old Atocha train station) was given a stunning overhaul. The structure of this grand iron-and-glass relic from the 19th century was preserved, while its interior was artfully converted into a light-filled tropical garden with more than 500 plant species (and a resident turtle population), in addition to shops, cafes and the Renfe train information offices. The project was the work of architect Rafael Moneo, the man behind the Museo del Prado extension and the Thyssen-Bornemisza museum, and his landmark achievement was to create a thoroughly modern space that resonates with the stately European train stations of another age.

PASEO DEL PRADO & EL RETIRO

If you've just come down the hill from Huertas, you'll feel like you've left behind a madhouse for an oasis of greenery, fresh air and high culture. The Museo del Prado and the Museo Thyssen-Bornemisza are among the richest galleries of fine art in the world, and

other museums lurk in the quietly elegant streets just behind the Prado. Rising up the hill to the east are the stately gardens of the glorious Parque del Buen Retiro.

TOP CHOICE Museo del Prado   MUSEUM

(Map p86; www.museodelprado.es; Paseo del Prado; adult/child €12/free, free 6-8pm Mon-Sat & 5-7pm Sun, audio guides €3.50; ⊙10am-8pm Mon-Sat, 10am-7pm Sun; Ⓜ Banco de España) Welcome to one of the world's premier art galleries. The more than 7000 paintings held in the Museo del Prado's collection (although only around 1500 are currently on display) are like a window onto the historical vagaries of the Spanish soul, at once grand and imperious in the royal paintings of Velázquez, darkly tumultuous in *Las pinturas negras* (The Black Paintings) of Goya, and outward-looking with sophisticated works of art from all across Europe. Spend as long as you can at the Prado or, better still, plan to make a couple of visits because it can be a little overwhelming if you try to absorb it all at once.

Entrance to the Prado is via the western Puerta de Velázquez or northern Puerta de Goya. Either way, tickets must first be purchased from the ticket office at the northern end of the building, opposite the Hotel Ritz and beneath the Puerta de Goya. Once inside, pick up the free *Plan* from the ticket office or information desk just inside the entrance – it lists the location of 50 of the Prado's most famous works and gives room numbers for all major artists.

Francisco José de Goya y Lucientes (Goya) is found on all three floors of the Prado, but we recommend starting at the southern end of the ground or lower level. In room 89, Goya's *El dos de mayo* and *El tres de mayo* rank among Madrid's most emblematic paintings; they bring to life the 1808 anti-French revolt and subsequent execution of insurgents in Madrid. Alongside, in rooms 87 and 88, are some of his darkest and most disturbing works, *Las pinturas negras*; they are so called in part because of the dark browns and black that dominate, but more for the distorted animalesque appearance of their characters.

There are more Goyas on the 1st floor in rooms 69 to 73. Among them are two more of Goya's best-known and most intriguing oils: *La maja vestida* and *La maja desnuda*. These portraits, in room 73, of an unknown woman, commonly believed to be the Duquesa de Alba (who may have been

Goya's lover), are identical save for the lack of clothing in the latter. There are further Goyas on the top floor.

Diego Rodriguez de Silva y Velázquez (Velázquez) is another of the grand masters of Spanish art who brings so much distinction to the Prado. Of all his works, *Las meninas* (room 50) is what most people come to see. Completed in 1656, it is more properly known as *La família de Felipe IV* (The Family of Felipe IV). The rooms surrounding *Las meninas* (rooms 51 and 52) contain more fine works by Velázquez: watch in particular for his paintings of various members of royalty who seem to spring off the canvas – Felipe II, Felipe IV, Margarita de Austria (a younger version of whom features in *Las meninas*), El Príncipe Baltasar Carlos and Isabel de Francia – on horseback.

Having experienced the essence of the Prado, you're now free to select from the astonishingly diverse works that remain. If Spanish painters have piqued your curiosity, Bartolomé Esteban Murillo, José de Ribera and the stark figures of Francisco de Zurbarán should be on your itinerary. The vivid, almost surreal works by the 16th-century master and adopted Spaniard El Greco, whose figures are characteristically slender and tortured, are also perfectly executed.

Another alternative is the Prado's outstanding collection of Flemish art. The fulsome figures and bulbous cherubs of Peter Paul Rubens (1577–1640) provide a playful antidote to the darkness of many of the other Flemish artists. His signature works are *Las tres Gracias* (The Three Graces) and *Adoración de los Reyes Magos*. Other fine works in the vicinity include *The Triumph of Death* by Pieter Bruegel, Rembrandt's *Artemisa,* and those by Anton Van Dyck. And on no account miss the weird-and-wonderful *The Garden of Earthly Delights* (room 3) by Hieronymus Bosch (c 1450–1516). No one has yet been able to provide a definitive explanation for this hallucinatory work, although many have tried.

And then there are the paintings by Dürer, Rafael, Tiziano (Titian), Tintoretto, Sorolla, Gainsborough, Fra Angelico, Tiepolo...

The western wing (Edificio Villanueva) was completed in 1785, as the neoclassical Palacio de Villanueva. Originally conceived as a house of science, it later served, somewhat ignominiously, as a cavalry barracks for Napoleon's troops during their occupation of Madrid between 1808 and 1813. In 1814 King Fernando VII decided to use the palace as a museum, although his purpose was more about finding a way of storing the hundreds of royal paintings gathering dust than any high-minded civic ideals – his was an era where art was a royal preserve. Five years later the Museo del Prado opened with 311 Spanish paintings on display.

In contrast, the eastern wing (Edificio Jerónimos) is part of the Prado's stunning modern extension, which opened in 2007.

DON'T MISS

TOP ARTWORKS IN THE CENTRO DE ARTE REINA SOFÍA

» *Guernica* (Pablo Picasso; room 206)

» *Naturaleza muerta* (Pablo Picasso; 1912)

» *El gran masturbador* (Salvador Dalí; 1929)

» *Muchacha en la ventana* (Salvador Dalí; 1925)

» *Monumento imperial a la mujer niña* (Salvador Dalí; 1929)

» *Pastorale* (Joan Miró; 1923–24)

» *Danseuse Espagnole* (Joan Miró; 1928)

» *L'atelier aux Sculptures* (Miquel Barceló; 1993)

» *Los cuatro dictadores* (Eduardo Arroyo; 1963)

» *Retrato de Josette* (Juan Gris; 1916)

» *Cartes et Dés* (Georges Braque; 1914)

» *El peine del viento I* (Eduardo Chillida; 1962)

» *Homenaje a Mallarmé* (Jorge Oteiza; 1958)

» *Pintura* (Antoni Tàpies; 1955)

» *Otoños* (Pablo Palazuelo; 1952)

Museo del Prado

PLAN OF ATTACK

Begin on the 1st floor with **Las Meninas 1** by Velázquez. Although alone worth the entry price, it's a fine introduction to the 17th-century golden age of Spanish art; nearby are more of Velázquez' royal paintings and works by Zurbarán and Murillo. While on the 1st floor, seek out Goya's **La Maja Vestida and La Maja Desnuda 2** with more of Goya's early works in neighbouring rooms. Downstairs at the southern end of the Prado, Goya's anger is evident in the searing **El Dos de Mayo** and **El Tres de Mayo 3** , and the torment of Goya's later years finds expression in the adjacent rooms with his **Pinturas Negras 4** , or Black Paintings. Also on the lower floor, Hieronymus Bosch's weird-and-wonderful **Garden of Earthly Delights 5** is one of the Prado's signature masterpieces. Returning to the 1st floor, El Greco's **Adoration of the Shepherds 6** is an extraordinary work, as is Peter Paul Rubens' **Las Tres Gracias 7** which forms the centrepiece of the Prado's gathering of Flemish masters. (This painting may have been moved to the 2nd floor.) A detour to the 2nd floor takes in some lesser-known Goyas, but finish in the **Edificio Jerónimos 8** with a visit to the cloisters and the outstanding bookshop.

ALSO VISIT:

Nearby are Museo Thyssen-Bornemisza and Centro de Arte Reina Sofía. They form an extraordinary trio of galleries.

Las Tres Gracias (Rubens)
A late Rubens masterpiece, *The Three Graces* is a classical and masterly expression of Rubens' preoccupation with sensuality, here portraying Aglaia, Euphrosyne and Thalia, the daughters of Zeus.

PETER BARRITT/ALAMY ©

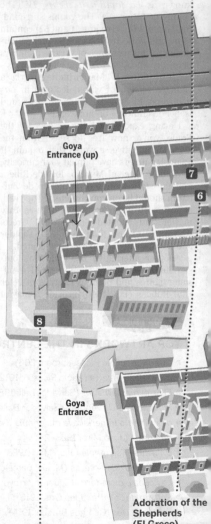

Goya Entrance (up)

Goya Entrance

Edificio Jerónimos
Opened in 2007, this state-of-the-art extension has rotating exhibitions of Prado masterpieces held in storage for decades for lack of wall space, and stunning 2nd-floor granite cloisters that date back to 1672.

Adoration of the Shepherds (El Greco)
There's an ecstatic quality to this intense painting. El Greco's distorted rendering of bodily forms came to characterise much of his later work.

Las Meninas (Velázquez)

This masterpiece depicts Velázquez and the Infanta Margarita, with the king and queen whose images appear, according to some experts, in mirrors behind Velázquez.

La Maja Vestida & La Maja Desnuda (Goya)

These enigmatic works scandalised early-19th-century Madrid society, fuelling the rumour mill as to the woman's identity and drawing the ire of the Spanish Inquisition. (La Maja Vestida pictured above.)

Edificio Villanueva

El Dos de Mayo & El Tres de Mayo (Goya)

Few paintings evoke a city's sense of self quite like Goya's portrayal of Madrid's valiant but ultimately unsuccessful uprising against French rule in 1808. (El Dos de Mayo pictured here.)

Jerónimos Entrance

Murillo Entrance

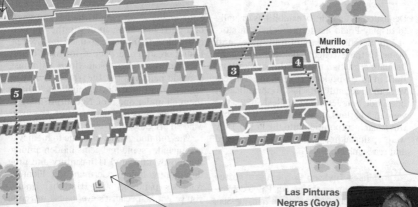

Velázquez Entrance

The Garden of Earthly Delights (Bosch)

A fantastical painting in triptych form, this overwhelming work depicts the Garden of Eden and what the Prado describes as 'the lugubrious precincts of Hell' in exquisitely bizarre detail.

Las Pinturas Negras (Goya)

Las Pinturas Negras are Goya's darkest works. *Saturno Devorando a Su Hijo* evokes a writhing mass of tortured humanity, while *La Romería de San Isidro* and *El Akelarre* are profoundly unsettling.

Paseo del Prado & El Retiro

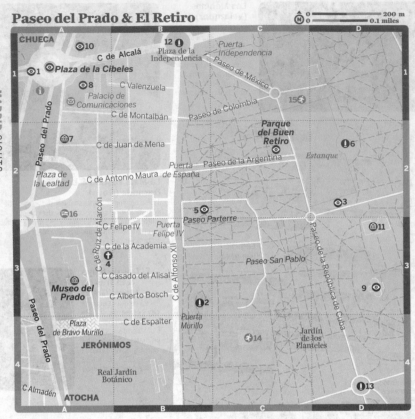

Dedicated to temporary exhibitions (usually to display Prado masterpieces held in storage for decades for lack of wall space), and home to the excellent bookshop and cafe, its main attraction is the 2nd-floor cloisters. Built in 1672 with local granite, the cloisters were until recently attached to the adjacent Iglesia de San Jerónimo El Real (p89), but were in a parlous state. As part of their controversial incorporation into the Prado, they were painstakingly dismantled, restored and reassembled.

TOP
CHOICE **Museo Thyssen-Bornemisza** MUSEUM
(Map p80; www.museothyssen.org; Paseo del Prado 8; adult/child €9/free; ⊙10am-7pm Tue-Sun; Ⓜ Banco de España) One of the most extraordinary private collections of predominantly European art in the world, the Museo Thyssen-Bornemisza is a worthy member of Madrid's 'Golden Triangle' of art. Where the Museo del Prado or Centro de Arte Reina Sofía enable you to study the body of work of a particular artist in depth, the Thyssen is the place to immerse yourself in a breathtaking breadth of artistic styles. Most of the big names are here, sometimes with just a single painting, but the Thyssen's gift to Madrid and the art-loving public is to have them all under one roof. Not surprisingly, it often ends up being many visitors' favourite Madrid art gallery.

The 2nd floor, which is home to medieval art, includes some real gems hidden among the mostly 13th- and 14th-century and predominantly Italian, German and Flemish religious paintings and triptychs. Unless you've got a specialist's eye, pause in room 5 where you'll find one work by Italy's Piero della Francesca (1410–92) and the instantly recognisable *Portrait of King Henry VIII* by Holbein the Younger (1497–1543), before continuing on to room 10 for the evocative 1586 *Massacre of the Innocents* by Lucas

Paseo del Prado & El Retiro

Van Valckenberch. Room 11 is dedicated to El Greco (with three pieces) and his Venetian contemporaries Tintoretto and Titian, while Caravaggio and the Spaniard José de Ribera dominate room 12. A single painting each by Murillo and Zurbarán add further Spanish flavour in the two rooms that follow, while the exceptionally rendered views of Venice by Canaletto (1697–1768) should on no account be missed.

Best of all on this floor is the extension (rooms A to H) built to house the collection of Carmen Thyssen-Bornemisza. Room C houses paintings by Canaletto, Constable and Van Gogh, while the stunning room H includes works by Monet, Sisley, Renoir, Pissarro and Degas.

Before heading downstairs, a detour to rooms 19 through 21 will satisfy those devoted to 17th-century Dutch and Flemish masters, such as Anton van Dyck, Jan Brueghel the Elder, Rubens and Rembrandt (one painting).

If all that sounds impressive, the 1st floor is where the Thyssen really shines. There's a Gainsborough in room 28 and a Goya in room 31 but, if you've been skimming the surface of this overwhelming collection, room 32 is the place to linger over each and every painting. The astonishing texture of Van Gogh's *Les Vessenots* is a masterpiece, but the same could be said for *Woman in Riding Habit* by Manet, *The Thaw at Véthueil* by Monet, Renoir's *Woman with a Parasol in a Garden* and Pissarro's quintessentially Parisian *Rue Saint-Honoré in the Afternoon*. Room 33 is also something special, with Cézanne, Gauguin, Toulouse-Lautrec and Degas, while the big names continue in room 34 (Picasso, Matisse and Modigliani) and 35 (Edvard Munch and Egon Schiele).

In the 1st floor's extension (rooms I to P), the names speak for themselves. Room K has works by Monet, Pissaro, Sorolla and Sisley, while room L is the domain of Gauguin (including his iconic *Mata Mua*), Degas and Toulouse-Lautrec. Rooms M (Munch), N (Kandinsky), O (Matisse and Georges Braque) and P (Picasso, Matisse, Edward Hopper and Juan Gris) round out an outrageously rich journey through the masters. On your way to the stairs there's Edward Hopper's *Hotel Room*.

On the ground floor, the foray into the 20th century that you began in the 1st-floor extension takes over with a fine spread of paintings from cubism through to pop art.

In room 41 you'll see a nice mix of the big three of cubism, Picasso, Georges Braque and Madrid's own Juan Gris, along with several other contemporaries. Kandinsky is the main drawcard in room 43, while there's an early Salvador Dalí alongside Max Ernst and Paul Klee in room 44. Picasso appears again in room 45, another one of the gallery's standout rooms; its treasures include works by Marc Chagall and Dalí's hallucinatory *Dream Caused by the Flight of a Bee Around a Pomegranate, One Second Before Waking Up*.

Room 46 is similarly rich, with Joan Miró's *Catalan Peasant with a Guitar*, the splattered craziness of Jackson Pollock's *Brown and Silver I*, and the deceptively simple but strangely pleasing *Green on Maroon* by Mark Rothko taking centre stage. In rooms 47 and 48 the Thyssen builds to a stirring climax, with Francis Bacon, Roy Lichtenstein, Henry Moore and Lucian Freud, Sigmund's Berlin-born grandson, all represented.

TOP CHOICE **Parque del Buen Retiro** GARDENS (Map p86; ⊙6am-midnight May-Sep, to 11pm Oct-Apr; MRetiro, Príncipe de Vergara, Ibiza, Atocha) The glorious gardens of El Retiro are as beautiful as any you'll find in a European city. Littered with marble monuments, landscaped lawns, the occasional elegant building and abundant greenery, it's quiet and contemplative during the week but comes to life on weekends. Put simply, this is one of our favourite places in Madrid.

Laid out in the 17th century by Felipe IV as the preserve of kings, queens and their intimates, the park was opened to the public in 1868 and ever since, whenever the weather's fine and on weekends in particular, *madrileños* from all across the city gather here to stroll, read the Sunday papers in the shade, take a boat ride or nurse a cool drink at the numerous outdoor *terrazas*.

The focal point for so much of El Retiro's life is the artificial lake *(estanque)*, which is watched over by the massive ornamental structure of the Monument to Alfonso XII (Map p86) on the east side, complete with marble lions; as sunset approaches on a Sunday afternoon in summer, the crowd grows, bongos sound out across the park and people start to dance. Row boats (Map p86; per boat per 45min €4.65; ⊙10am-8.30pm Apr-Sep, 10am-5.45pm Oct-Mar) can be rented from the lake's northern shore – an iconic Madrid experience. On the southern end of the lake, the odd structure decorated with sphinxes is the Fuente Egipcia (Egyptian Fountain; Map p86): legend has it that an enormous fortune buried in the park by Felipe IV in the mid-18th century rests here. Hidden among the trees south of the lake is the Palacio de Cristal (Map p86; ☎91 574 66 14; ⊙11am-8pm Mon-Sat, 11am-6pm Sun May-Sep, 10am-6pm Mon-Sat, 10am-4pm Sun Oct-Apr), a magnificent metal-and-glass structure that is arguably El Retiro's most beautiful architectural monument. It was built in 1887 as a winter garden for exotic flowers and is now used for temporary exhibitions organised by the Centro de Arte Reina Sofía. Just north of here, the 1883 Palacio de Velázquez (Map p86) is also used for temporary exhibitions.

At the southern end of the park, near La Rosaleda (Rose Garden), with its more than 4000 roses, is a statue of El Ángel Caído (the Fallen Angel, aka Lucifer; Map p86). Strangely, it sits 666m above sea level... In the same vein, the Puerta de Dante, in the extreme southeastern corner of the park, is watched over by a carved mural of Dante's Inferno. Occupying much of the southwestern corner of the park is the Jardín de los Planteles, one of the least-visited sections of El Retiro, where quiet pathways lead beneath an overarching canopy of trees. West of here is the moving Bosque del Recuerdo (Memorial Forest; Map p86), an understated memorial to the 191 victims of the 11 March 2004 train bombings. For each victim stands an olive or cypress tree. To the north, just inside the Puerta de Felipe IV, stands what is thought to be Madrid's oldest tree (Map p86), a Mexican conifer *(ahuehuete)* planted in 1633.

In the northeastern corner of the park is the Ermita de San Isidro (Map p92), a small country chapel noteworthy as one of the few, albeit modest, examples of Romanesque architecture in Madrid. When it was built, Madrid was a small village more than 2km away.

Real Jardín Botánico GARDENS (Royal Botanical Garden; ☎91 420 04 38; www.rjb.csic.es; Plaza de Bravo Murillo 2; adult/child €3/free; ⊙10am-9pm May-Aug, reduced hours Sep-Apr; MAtocha) With its manicured flower beds and neat paths, the Real Jardín Botánico is more intimate than El Retiro. First created in 1755 on the banks of Río Manzanares, the garden was moved here in 1781 by Carlos III. Today there are thousands of plant species.

FREE CaixaForum MUSEUM, ARCHITECTURE (www.fundacio.lacaixa.es; Paseo del Prado 36; ⊙10am-8pm; MAtocha) This extraordinary

---

BEST MUSEUMS FOR SPANISH ARTISTS

» **Museo del Prado** (p82) Goya, Velázquez, Zurbarán

» **Centro de Arte Reina Sofía** (p79) Picasso, Dalí, Miró

» **Real Academia de Bellas Artes de San Fernando** (p76) Goya, Velázquez, Picasso, Juan Gris

» **Ermita de San Antonio de la Florida** (p91) Goya

» **Museo Sorolla** (p93) Joaquín Sorolla

structure down towards the southern end of the Paseo del Prado is one of Madrid's most eye-catching architectural innovations. Seeming to hover above the ground, this brick edifice is topped by an intriguing summit of what looks like rusted iron. On an adjacent wall is the *jardín colgante* (hanging garden), a lush vertical wall of greenery almost four storeys high. Inside there are four floors of exhibition and performance space awash in stainless steel and with soaring ceilings. The exhibitions here are always worth checking out and include photography, contemporary painting and multimedia shows.

Plaza de la Cibeles SQUARE
(Map p86; Plaza de la Cibeles; Ⓜ Banco de España) Of all the grand roundabouts that punctuate the Paseo del Prado, Plaza de la Cibeles most evokes the splendour of imperial Madrid.

The jewel in the crown is the astonishing **Palacio de Comunicaciones** (Map p86). Built between 1904 and 1917 by Antonio Palacios, Madrid's most prolific architect of the belle époque, it combines elements of the North American monumental style of the period with Gothic and Renaissance touches. It serves as Madrid's **town hall** *(ayuntamiento)*, with the **main post office** occupying the southwestern corner. Other landmark buildings around the plaza's perimeter include the **Palacio de Linares and Casa de América** (Map p86; ☎ 91 595 48 00; www.casamerica.es; Plaza de la Cibeles 2; adult/child/student & senior €7/free/4; ⊙ guided tours 11am, noon & 1pm Sat & Sun, ticket office 9am-8pm Mon-Fri, 11am-1pm Sat & Sun; Ⓜ Banco de España), the **Palacio Buenavista** (Map p94; Plaza de la Cibeles) (1769) and the national **Banco de España** (Map p86) (1891). There are fine views east towards the Puerta de Alcalá or, even better, west towards the Edificio Metrópolis.

The spectacular **fountain of the goddess Cybele** at the centre of the plaza is one of Madrid's most beautiful. Ever since it was erected in 1780 by Ventura Rodríguez, it has been a Madrid favourite. Carlos III liked it so much that he tried to have it moved to the royal gardens of the Granja de San Ildefonso, on the road to Segovia, but *madrileños* kicked up such a fuss that he let it be. The Cibeles fountain has been the venue for joyous and often-destructive celebrations by players and supporters of Real Madrid whenever the side has won anything of note.

DON'T MISS

PAINTINGS IN THE MUSEO DEL PRADO

» *Las meninas* (Velázquez)

» *La rendición de Breda* (Velázquez)

» *La maja desnuda & La maja vestida* (Goya)

» *El tres de mayo* (Goya)

» *Las pinturas negras* (The Black Paintings; Goya)

» *El jardín de las delicias* (The Garden of Earthly Delights; Hieronymus Bosch)

» *Adam & Eve* (Adán y Eva; Dürer)

» *El lavatorio* (Tintoretto)

» *La Trinidad* (El Greco)

» *David vencedor de Goliat* (Caravaggio)

» *El sueño de Jacob* (Ribera)

» *Las tres Gracias* (The Three Graces; Rubens)

» *Artemisa* (Rembrandt)

FREE **Museo Naval** MUSEUM
(Map p86; ☎ 91 523 87 89; www.armada.mde.es/museonaval; Paseo del Prado 5; ⊙ 10am-7pm Tue-Sun; Ⓜ Banco de España) A block south of Plaza de la Cibeles, this museum will appeal to those who love their ships or who have always wondered what the Spanish Armada really looked like. On display are quite extraordinary models of ships, from the earliest days of Spain's maritime history to the 20th century. Lovers of antique maps will also find plenty of interest, especially Juan de la Cosa's parchment map of the known world, put together in 1500. The accuracy of Europe and Africa is astounding, and it's supposedly the first map to show the Americas (albeit with considerably greater fantasy than fact).

Iglesia de San Jerónimo El Real CHURCH
(Map p86; ☎ 91 420 35 78; Calle de Ruiz de Alarcón; ⊙ 10am-1pm & 5-8.30pm Mon-Sat Oct-Jun, hours vary Jul-Sep; Ⓜ Atocha, Banco de España) Tucked away behind the Museo del Prado, this chapel was traditionally favoured by the Spanish royal family, and King Juan Carlos I was crowned here in 1975 upon the death of Franco. The sometimes-sober, sometimes-splendid mock-Isabelline interior is actually a 19th-century reconstruction that took its

MADRID SIGHTS

cues from the Iglesia de San Juan de los Reyes in Toledo; the original was largely destroyed in the Peninsular War. What remained of the former cloisters has been incorporated into the Museo del Prado (p82).

Puerta de Alcalá   MONUMENT
(Map p86; Plaza de la Independencia; MRetiro) The first gate to bear this name was built in 1599, but Carlos III was singularly unimpressed and had it demolished in 1764 to be replaced by another – the one you see today. Twice a year, in autumn and spring, cars abandon the roundabout and are replaced by flocks of sheep being transferred in an age-old ritual from their summer to winter pastures (and vice versa).

SALAMANCA

The *barrio* of Salamanca is Madrid's most exclusive quarter, defined by grand and restrained elegance. This is a place to put on your finest clothes and be seen (especially along Calle de Serrano or Calle de José Ortega y Gasset); to stroll into shops with an affected air and resist asking the prices; or to promenade between the fine museums and parks that make you wonder whether you've arrived at the height of civilisation.

FREE Museo
Arqueológico Nacional   MUSEUM
(Map p92; http://man.mcu.es; Calle de Serrano 13; ☻9.30am-8pm Tue-Sat, 9.30am-3pm Sun; MSerrano) The showpiece National Archaeology Museum contains a sweeping accumulation of artefacts behind its towering facade. The large collection includes stunning mosaics taken from Roman villas across Spain, intricate Muslim-era and Mudéjar handiwork, sculpted figures such as the *Dama de Ibiza* and *Dama de Elche*, examples of Romanesque and Gothic architectural styles and a partial copy of the prehistoric cave paintings of Altamira (Cantabria). Until late 2012 (and more likely 2013), the museum was closed for a major and much-needed overhaul of the building.

Museo Lázaro Galdiano   MUSEUM
(www.flg.es; Calle de Serrano 122; adult/concession €6/3, last hr free; ☻10am-4.30pm Wed-Sat & Mon, 10am-3pm Sun; MGregorio Marañón) In an imposing early-20th-century Italianate stone mansion, the Museo Lázaro Galdiano has some 13,000 works of art and objets d'art. Apart from works by Bosch, Zurbarán, Goya, Claudio Coello, El Greco and Con-

stable, this is a rather oddball assembly of all sorts of collectables. In room 14 some of Goya's more famous works are hung together to make a collage, including *La maja* and the frescoes of the *Ermita de San Antonio de la Florida*.

Plaza de Toros & Museo Taurino   STADIUM
(Calle de Alcalá 237; MLas Ventas) The Plaza de Toros Monumental de Las Ventas (often known simply as Las Ventas) is not the most beautiful bullring in the world – that honour probably goes to Ronda in Andalucía – but it is the most important.

A classic example of the neo-Mudéjar style, it opened in 1931 and hosted its first *corrida* (bullfight) three years later. Like all bullrings, the circle of sand enclosed by four storeys, which can seat up to 25,000 spectators, evokes more a sense of a theatre than a sports stadium – it also hosts concerts. To be carried high on the shoulders of aficionados out through the grand and decidedly Moorish Puerta de Madrid is the ultimate dream of any *torero* (bullfighter) – if you've made it at Las Ventas, you've reached the pinnacle of the bullfighting world. The gate is known more colloquially as the 'Gate of Glory'. Guided visits (conducted in English and Spanish) take you out onto the sand and into the royal box, last 40 minutes and start on the hour. For reservations, contact Las Ventas Tour (☑687 739 032; www.lasventastour.com; adult/child €7/5; ☻10am-6pm, days of bullfight 10am-2pm).

If your curiosity is piqued, wander into the Museo Taurino (☑91 725 18 57; www.las-ventas.com; Calle de Alcalá 237; admission free; ☻9.30am-2.30pm Mon-Fri), and check out the collection of paraphernalia, costumes, photos and other bullfighting memorabilia up on the top floor above one of the two courtyards by the ring.

The area where the Plaza de Toros is located is known as Las Ventas because, in times gone by, several wayside taverns *(ventas)*, along with houses of ill repute, were to be found here.

FREE Museo al Aire Libre   SCULPTURE
(Map p92; www.munimadrid.es/museoairelibre; cnr Paseo de la Castellana & Paseo de Eduardo Dato; ☻24hr; MRubén Darío) This fascinating open-air collection of 17 abstract sculptures includes works by the renowned Basque artist Eduardo Chillida, the Catalan master Joan Miró as well as Eusebio Sempere and Alberto Sánchez, one of Spain's foremost sculptors of the 20th century. The sculptures are beneath

the overpass where Paseo de Eduardo Dato crosses Paseo de la Castellana, but somehow the hint of traffic grime and pigeon shit only adds to the appeal. All but one are on the eastern side of Paseo de la Castellana.

MALASAÑA & CHUECA

The inner-city *barrios* of Malasaña and Chueca are where Madrid gets up close and personal. Yes, there are rewarding museums and examples of landmark architecture sprinkled throughout. But these *barrios* are more about doing than seeing; more about experiencing life as it's lived by *madrileños* than ticking off a list of wonderful, if more static, attractions. These attractions may have made the city famous, but they only tell half the story. Malasaña and Chueca are neighbourhoods with attitude and personality, where Madrid's famed nightlife, shopping and eating thrive. Malasaña is streetwise and down to earth, while Chueca, as Madrid's centre of gay culture, is more stylish and flamboyant.

FREE **Museo de Historia**　　　MUSEUM
(Map p94; www.munimadrid.es/museodehistoria; Calle de Fuencarral 78; ⊙9.30am-8pm Tue-Fri, 10am-2pm Sat & Sun; MTribunal) The fine Museo de Historia (formerly the Museo Municipal) has an elaborate and restored baroque entrance, raised in 1721 by Pedro de Ribera. The interior is dominated by paintings and other memorabilia charting the historical evolution of Madrid, of which the highlight is Goya's *Allegory of the City of Madrid*. Also worth lingering over is the expansive model of 1830s Madrid.

Sociedad General de Autores y Editores　　　ARCHITECTURE
(General Society of Authors & Editors; Map p94; Calle de Fernando VI 4; MAlonso Martínez) This swirling, melting, wedding cake of a building is as close as Madrid comes to the work of Antoni Gaudí, which so illuminates Barcelona. It's a joyously self-indulgent ode to *modernismo* and is virtually one of a kind in Madrid. Casual visitors are actively discouraged, although what you see from the street is impressive enough. The only exceptions are on the first Monday of October, International Architecture Day, and during the Noche en Blanco (p102) festivities.

Antiguo Cuartel del Conde Duque　　　NOTABLE BUILDING
(Map p94; Calle del Conde Duque 9; MPlaza de España, Ventura Rodríguez, San Bernardo) This

grand former barracks dominates Conde Duque on the western fringe of Malasaña, with its imposing, recently restored facade stretching 228m down the hill. Its highlight is the extravagant 18th-century doorway, a masterpiece of the baroque churrigueresque style. These days it's home by day to a cultural centre, which hosts government archives, libraries, the Hemeroteca Municipal (the biggest collection of newspapers and magazines in Spain), temporary exhibitions and the Museo Municipal de Arte Contemporáneo (p79). The latter was closed for renovations at the time this book went to print.

CHAMBERÍ & ARGÜELLES

You don't come to Chamberí or Argüelles for the sights, although there are some fine museums, as well as outstanding places to eat, drink and watch live music. Chamberí and, to a lesser extent, Argüelles may be fairly well off today, but they lack the snootiness of Salamanca. As such, it's here perhaps more than anywhere else in Madrid that you get a sense of the city as the *madrileños* experience it, away from the tourist crowds.

TOP
CHOICE **Ermita de San Antonio de la Florida**　　　CHURCH
(Glorieta de San Antonio de la Florida 5; admission free; ⊙9.30am-8pm Tue-Fri, 10am-2pm Sat & Sun, hours vary Jul & Aug; MPríncipe Pío) The frescoed ceilings of the Ermita de San Antonio de la Florida are one of Madrid's most surprising secrets. Recently restored and also known as the **Panteón de Goya**, the southern of the two small chapels is one of the few places to see Goya's work in its original setting, as painted by the master in 1798 on the request of Carlos IV. The frescoes on the dome depict the miracle of St Anthony, who is calling on a young man to rise from the grave and absolve his father, unjustly accused of his murder. Around them swarms a typical Madrid crowd.

The painter is buried in front of the altar. His remains (minus the mysteriously missing head) were transferred in 1919 from Bordeaux (France), where he died in self-imposed exile in 1828.

FREE **Templo de Debod**　　　RUIN
(www.munimadrid.es/templodebod; Paseo del Pintor Rosales; ⊙10am-2pm & 6-8pm Tue-Fri, 10am-2pm Sat & Sun; MVentura Rodríguez) Remarkably,

Salamanca

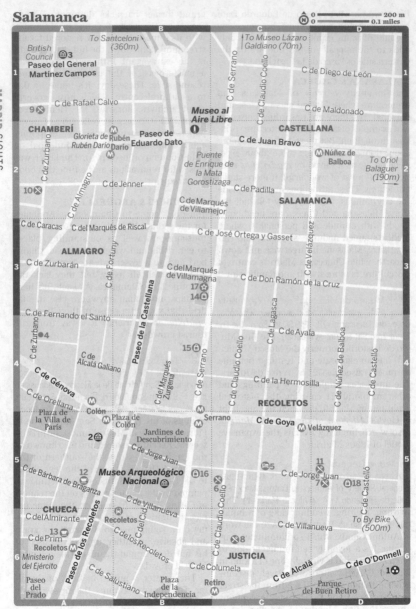

this authentic 4th-century-BC Egyptian temple sits in the heart of Madrid, in the Parque de la Montaña. The Templo de Debod was saved from the rising waters of Lake Nasser, formed by the Aswan High Dam in Egypt, and sent block by block to Spain in 1968. The views from the surrounding gardens towards the Palacio Real are quite special.

Museo de América MUSEUM
(museodeamerica.mcu.es; Avenida de los Reyes Católicos 6; adult/concession €3/1.50, free Sun;

Salamanca

⊙9.30am-8.30pm Tue-Sat, 10am-3pm Sun; Ⓜ Moncloa) Travel to, and trade with, the newly discovered Americas was a central part of Spain's culture and economy from 1492 until the early 20th century. The Museo de América has a representative display of ceramics, statuary, jewellery and instruments of hunting, fishing and war, along with some of the paraphernalia brought back by the colonisers. The Colombian gold collection, dating back to the 2nd century AD, is particularly eye-catching.

Museo Sorolla GALLERY
(Map p92; http://museosorolla.mcu.es; Paseo del General Martínez Campos 37; adult/child €3/free, free Sun; ⊙9.30am-8pm Tue-Sat, 10am-3pm Sun; Ⓜ Iglesia, Gregorio Marañón) The Valencian artist Joaquín Sorolla immortalised the clear Mediterranean light of the Valencian coast. His Madrid house, a quiet mansion surrounded by lush gardens that he designed himself, was inspired by what he had seen in Andalucía and now contains the most complete collection of the artist's works.

On the ground floor there's a cool *patio cordobés,* an Andalucian courtyard off which is a room containing collections of Sorolla's drawings. The 1st floor, with the main salon and dining areas, was mostly decorated by the artist himself. On the same floor are three separate rooms that Sorolla used as studios. In the second one is a collection of his Valencian beach scenes. The third was where he usually worked. Upstairs, works spanning Sorolla's career are organised across four adjoining rooms.

BEYOND THE CENTRE
Casa de Campo PARK
(Ⓜ Batán) This 1700-hectare, somewhat unkempt semi-wilderness, stretches west of Río Manzanares. There are prettier and more central parks in Madrid, but such is the scope here that nearly half a million *madrileños* visit every weekend, when cyclists, walkers and picnickers overwhelm the byways and trails that criss-cross the park.

Inside the Casa de Campo is the Zoo Aquarium de Madrid (☑902 345014; www.zoomadrid.com; Casa de Campo; adult/child €21.35/17.60; ⊙10.30am-8.30pm Jul & Aug, reduced hours Sep-Jun; ☑37 from Intercambiador de Príncipe Pío, Ⓜ Casa de Campo), home to around 3000 animals, as well as the Parque de Atracciones (☑91 463 29 00; www.parquedeatracciones.es; Casa de Campo; >120cm/90-120cm/<90cm €29.90/23.90/free; ⊙noon-midnight Sun-Fri, noon-1am Sat Jul & Aug, reduced hours Sep-Jun; ☑37 from Intercambiador de Príncipe Pío, Ⓜ Batán), a decent amusement park sure to keep the kids entertained.

A fun way to get to the Casa de Campo is the Teleférico (☑91 541 11 18; www.teleferico.com; one way/return €3.75/5.50; ⊙noon-9pm Mon-Fri, noon-9.30pm Sat & Sun Jun-Aug, reduced hours Sep-May; Ⓜ Argüelles) cable car. It starts at Paseo del Pintor Rosales, on the corner of Calle del Marqués de Urquijo, and ends at a high point in the middle of the park.

Malasaña & Chueca

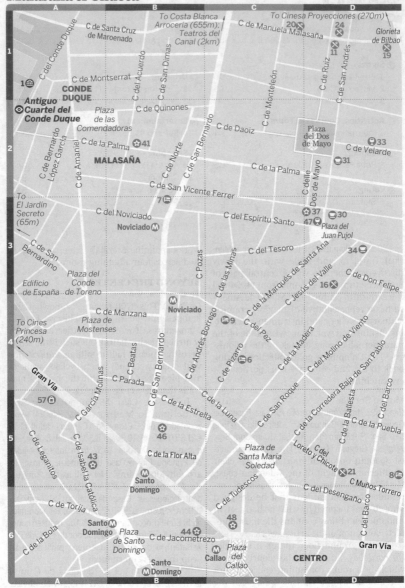

🏃 Activities

Madrid is not Europe's most bicycle-friendly city, but a ride in the Casa de Campo or El Retiro is a fantastic way to spend an afternoon.

There are public gyms scattered throughout Madrid. They generally charge a modest €3.50 to €7 for one-day admission. Privately owned health centres are more expensive (€10 to €15), but usually have less-crowded workout rooms.

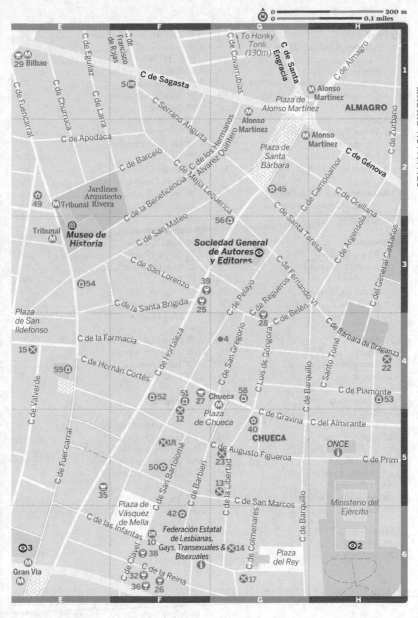

Madrid Xanadú   SKIING
(☎902 36 13 09; www.madridsnowzone.com; Calle
Puerto de Navacerrada; per hr adult/child €22/19,
day pass €36/33, equipment rental €18; ☺10am–
midnight; 🚍528, 534) This is the largest covered ski centre in Europe. Open year-round,

it's kept at a decidedly cool -2°C. Within the
same complex you will find a mammoth
mall, cinemas, a kart track and an amusement park. Madrid Xanadú is approximately 23km west of Madrid, just off the A5. To

Malasaña & Chueca

get here, take bus 528 or 534 from the Inter-cambiador de Príncipe Pío.

Hammam al-Andalus　　　　　　DAY SPA
(Map p72; http://madrid.hammamalandalus.com;
Calle de Atocha 14; treatments €24-76.50; ⊙10am-midnight; ⓂSol) A beautiful imitation traditional Arab bathhouse; bookings required.

By Bike　　　　　　BICYCLE RENTAL
(www.bybike.info; Avenida de Menédez Pelayo 35;
per hr/day from €4/30; ⊙10am-9pm Mon-Fri &
9.30am-9.30pm Sat & Sun Jun-Sep, reduced hours
Oct-May; Ⓜlbiza) Ideally placed for the Parque del Buen Retiro and with child seats/trailers, roller blades and electric bikes for hire. Prices vary depending on the length of hire and number of people.

Centro Deportivo La Chopera   GYM
(Map p86; ☑91 420 11 54; Parque del Buen Retiro; 1/10 sessions €4.45/38.25, court hire per adult €5.75; ☺8.30am-9.30pm, closed Aug; ⓂAtocha) With a fine workout centre and several football fields, this *centro deportivo* (sports centre and gym) in the southwestern corner of the Parque del Buen Retiro is one of Madrid's most attractive and central. It also has tennis courts, but you'll need your own racquet.

Canal de Isabel II   SWIMMING
(Avenida de Filipinas 54; from €4.20; ☺11am-8pm late May-early Sep; ⓂRíos Rosas, Canal) Open only in summer, this large outdoor pool is easily accessible by metro from the city centre. The complex also has a football field, a basketball court and a weights room, and across the road there's a running track and a golf driving range. It's around 3km north of the centre, close to where Calle de Bravo Murillo intersects with Avenida de Filipinas.

Courses

Language
Spanish-language schools abound in Madrid. Non-EU citizens who are wanting to study at a university or language school in Spain should, in theory, have a study visa.

Academia Inhispania   LANGUAGE COURSE
(Map p72; ☑91 521 22 31; www.inhispania.com; Calle de la Montera 10-12; ⓂSol) Intensive four-week courses start at €520.

Academia Madrid Plus   LANGUAGE COURSE
(Map p72; ☑91 548 11 16; www.madridplus.es; 6th fl, Calle del Arenal 21; ⓂÓpera) Four-week courses start from €335; intensive courses cost up to €735.

International House   LANGUAGE COURSE
(Map p92; ☑902 14 15 17; www.ihmadrid.es; Calle de Zurbano 8; ⓂAlonso Martínez) Four-week intensive courses cost from €746 (20 hours per week) to €1066 (30 hours per week). Staff can organise accommodation with local families.

Universidad Complutense   LANGUAGE COURSE
(☑91 394 53 25; www.ucm.es/info/cextran/Index.htm; Secretaría de los Cursos para Extranjeros, Facultadole Filologia (Edificio A) Universidad Complutense; ⓂCuidad Universitaria) A range of language and cultural courses throughout the year. An intensive semester course of 120 contact hours costs €1155, while month-long courses (48 hours) start at €462.

Cooking

Alambique   COOKING COURSE
(Map p72; ☑91 547 42 20; www.alambique.com; Plaza de la Encarnación 2; per person from €50; ⓂÓpera, Santo Domingo) Most classes here last from 2½ to 3½ hours and cover a range of cuisines. Most are conducted in Spanish, but some are in English.

MADRID FOR CHILDREN

Madrid has plenty to keep the little ones entertained. A good place to start is Casa de Campo (p93), with swimming pools, the Zoo Aquarium de Madrid and the Parque de Atracciones amusement park, which has a 'Zona Infantil' with sedate rides for the really young. To get to Casa de Campo, take the Teleférico (p93), one of the world's most horizontal cable cars, which putters for 2.5km out from the slopes of La Rosaleda.

Another possibility is Faunia (☑91 301 62 10; www.faunia.es; Avenida de las Comunidades 28; adult/child €25.50/19.50; ☺10am-8pm Mon-Fri & 10am-9pm Sat & Sun Jun-Aug, reduced hours Sep-May; ⓂValdebernardo), a modern animal theme park with an 'Amazon Jungle' and a 'Polar Ecosystem'. Faunia is located east of the M-40, about 7km from the city centre.

The Museo del Ferrocarril (☑902 228822; www.museodelferrocarril.org; Paseo de las Delicias 61; adult/child €4.50/3; ☺10am-3pm Tue-Sun Sep-Jul; ⓂDelicias) is home to old railway cars, train engines and more. The free Museo Naval (p89) will appeal to those fascinated by ships.

The Museo de Cera (Map p92; ☑91 319 26 49; www.museoceramadrid.com; Paseo de Recoletos 41; adult/child €16/12; ☺10am-2.30pm & 4.30-8.30pm Mon-Fri, 10am-8.30pm Sat & Sun; ⓂColón) is Madrid's modest answer to Madame Tussaud's, with more than 450 wax characters.

Other possibilities include seeing Real Madrid play at the Estadio Santiago Bernabéu (p124), wandering through the soothing greenery of the Parque del Buen Retiro (p88), where in summer there are puppet shows and boat rides, or skiing at Madrid Xanadú (p95).

Madrid – Killing the Night

BRUCE BI / GETTY IMAGES ©

An All-Night Itinerary

Nights in the capital are long and loud, and what Hemingway wrote in the '30s remains true to this day: 'Nobody goes to bed in Madrid until they have killed the night.'

» Start late afternoon with a quiet drink at **Café Comercial** (p116), one of Madrid's grandest old cafes.

» Move on to something a little stronger, namely a mojito at **Café Belén** (p116), the epitome of Chueca cool.

» Head next for one of Europe's most famous bars, **Museo Chicote** (p116), with its creative cocktails, fine lounge music and celebrity crowd.

» Not far away, **Costello Café & Niteclub** (p123) is New York style wedded to an irresistible Madrid buzz.

» It's time for some live jazz at the art-deco **Café Central** (p122), one of Europe's most prestigious live-music venues.

» You have just enough time for an atmospheric tipple at the timeless **La Venencia** (p115) before it closes.

» Resist the urge to linger in the nearby Plaza de Santa Ana, and climb up to look down upon it all from on high at the sophisticated **Penthouse** (p115).

» It's time for a dance, and **Kapital** (p119) is one of the biggest and the best of Madrid's mega nightclubs.

» One of the stalwarts of the Madrid night, **Teatro Joy Eslava** (p118) inhabits a converted theatre and will keep you going until dawn.

» And no Madrid night is complete without a *chocolate con churros* (deep-fried doughnut strips dipped in hot chocolate) close to sunrise at **Chocolatería de San Ginés** (p113).

Clockwise from top left
1. Mercado de San Miguel (p107) 2. Teatro Joy Eslava (p118) 3. Café Central (p122) 4. Malasaña street (p115)

START PLAZA DE LA PUERTA DEL SOL
FINISH PLAZA DE LA CIBELES
DISTANCE 5KM
DURATION 3 TO 4 HOURS

Walking Tour
Historic Madrid

❭ Start in the pulsating, geographic centre of Spain, **❶ Plaza de la Puerta del Sol**, then head northwest along Calle del Arenal to the **❷ Iglesia de San Ginés**, the site of one of Madrid's oldest places of Christian worship. Behind it is the wonderful **❸ Chocolatería de San Ginés**, a place of worship for lovers of *chocolate con churros* (deep-fried doughnut strips dipped in hot chocolate).

Continue up to and across Calle Mayor until you reach **❹ Plaza Mayor**, then turn west and head down the hill to the historic **❺ Plaza de la Villa**, home to some of the city's oldest surviving buildings.

Take the street down the left side of the Casa de Cisneros, cross Calle del Sacramento at the end, go down the stairs and follow the cobbled Calle del Cordón out onto Calle de Segovia. Almost directly in front of you is the Mudéjar tower of the 15th-century **❻ Iglesia de San Pedro El Viejo**; proceed up Costanilla de San Pedro, lingering en route in the charming **❼ Plaza de la Paja**.

From here, twist down through lanes of La Morería to Calle de Bailén and the wonderful (if expensive) *terrazas* (cafes with outdoor tables) on the edge of the **❽ Jardines de las Vistillas**. After a soothing *cerveza* (beer), follow Calle de Bailén past the cathedral and royal palace to the supremely elegant **❾ Plaza de Oriente**.

Head to the western side of the square and follow the walkway extension of Calle de Bailén, which leads into **❿ Plaza de España**, surrounded by monumental towers. The eastern flank of Plaza de España marks the start of **⓫ Gran Vía**, a Haussmann-esque boulevard that was slammed through tumbledown slums in the 1910s and 1920s. Head up and then down the hill past the elegant facades to the superb dome of the **⓬ Metrópolis building**, where Gran Vía meets Calle de Alcalá. Down the hill you go to **⓭ Plaza de la Cibeles**, Madrid's favourite roundabout.

Apunto – Centro Cultural del Gusto
COOKING COURSE

(Map p94, ☑91 702 10 41; www.apuntolibreria.com; Calle de Pelayo 60; per person €40-60; ⓂChueca) This engaging little bookstore, whose subtitle translates as 'Cultural Centre of Taste', runs cooking classes across a range of cuisines.

Flamenco

Fundación Conservatorio Casa Patas
FLAMENCO

(Map p80; www.conservatorioflamenco.org; Calle de Cañizares 10; per month €30-75, plus €33 joining fee; ⓂAntón Martín, Tirso de Molina) Every conceivable type of flamenco instruction, including dance, guitar, singing and much more. It's upstairs from the Casa Patas flamenco *tablao* (flamenco venue). Single classes are also possible.

☞ Tours

It you're pushed for time and want to fit a lot of sightseeing into a short visit, guided tours can be the ideal way to see the city.

Visitas Guiadas Oficiales
GUIDED TOUR

(Official Guided Tours; Map p72; ☑902 221424; www.esmadrid.com; Plaza Mayor 27; adult/child €3.90/free; ⓂSol) Over 20 highly recommended walking and cycling tours conducted in Spanish and English. Organised by the Centro de Turismo de Madrid (p127).

Wellington Society
WALKING TOUR

(☑609 143203; www.wellsoc.org; tours €50-85) A handful of quirky historical tours laced with anecdotes and led by the inimitable Stephen Drake-Jones. Membership costs €50 and includes a day or evening walking tour.

Letango Tours
WALKING TOUR

(Map p80; ☑91 369 47 52; www.letangospaintours.com; Plaza Tirso de Molina 12, 1ºD; Mon-Fri/Sat & Sun €95/135; ⓂTirso de Molina) Eight different walking tours through Madrid with additional excursions to San Lorenzo El Escorial, Segovia and Toledo.

Insider's Madrid
WALKING TOUR

(☑91 447 38 66; www.insidersmadrid.com; tours from €60) An impressive range of tailor-made tours, including walking, tapas, flamenco and bullfighting tours.

Madrid Bike Tours
CYCLING

(☑680 581782; www.madridbiketours.com; 4hr tours €55) Londoner Mike Chandler offers a

---

WANT MORE?

For in-depth information, reviews and recommendations at your fingertips, head to the Apple App Store to purchase Lonely Planet's *Madrid City Guide* iPhone app.

Alternatively, head to Lonely Planet (p128) for planning advice, author recommendations, traveller reviews and insider tips.

---

guided two-wheel tour of Madrid as well as tours further afield.

Bike Spain
CYCLING

(Map p72; ☑91 559 06 53; www.bikespain.info; Plaza de la Villa 1, Calle del Codo ; tours €35; ☺10am-2pm & 4-7pm Mon-Fri, 10am-2pm Sat & Sun; ⓂÓpera) English-language guided city tours by bicycle, by day or (Friday) night, plus longer expeditions to San Lorenzo de El Escorial (€105).

Madrid Segway Tours
GUIDED TOUR

(☑659 824499; www.madsegs.com; 3hr tour per person €65, plus €15 refundable deposit) Most of these Segway tours start in Plaza de España.

Madrid City Tour
BUS TOUR

(☑902 02 47 58; http://www.esmadrid.com/en/tourist-bus; 1-day ticket adult €20, child free-€9; ☺9am-10pm Mar-Oct, 10am-6pm Nov-Feb) Hop-on, hop-off open-topped buses that run every 10 minutes or so along two routes. Information, including maps, is available at tourist offices, most travel agencies and some hotels, or you can get tickets on the bus. One of the major stops is outside the Museo del Prado on Calle Felipe IV. It also runs night tours in summer. Two-day tickets also available.

Adventurous Appetites
WALKING TOUR

(☑639 331073; www.adventurousappetites.com; 4hr tours €50; ☺8pm-midnight Mon-Sat) English-language tapas tours through central Madrid. Prices include the first drink but they exclude food.

✪ Festivals & Events

Madrid loves to party, and seemingly any excuse is good for a fiesta. For details about national festivals and events in the city, check online at www.esmadrid.com.

February

Festival de Flamenco
FLAMENCO

Five days of fine flamenco music in one of the city's theatres. Dates are movable. Big names in recent years have included Enrique Morente, Carmen Linares and Diego El Cigala.

Arco
ART

(Feria Internacional de Arte Contemporánea; www.ifema.es) One of Europe's biggest celebrations of contemporary art, Arco draws galleries and exhibitors from all over the world to the Parque Ferial Juan Carlos I exhibition centre near Barajas airport in mid-February.

March

La Noche de los Teatros
THEATRE

(www.lanochedelosteatros.com) On 'The Night of the Theatres', Madrid's streets become the stage for all manner of performances, with a focus on comedy and children's plays. It usually takes place on the last Saturday of March.

May & June

Fiesta de la Comunidad de Madrid
CITY FESTIVAL

On 2 May 1808 Napoleon's troops quelled an uprising in Madrid, and commemoration of the day has become an opportunity for much festivity. The day is celebrated with particular energy in the bars of Malasaña.

Fiesta de San Isidro
CITY FESTIVAL

Around 15 May Madrid's patron saint is honoured with a week of nonstop processions, parties and bullfights. Free concerts are held throughout the city, and this week marks the start of the city's bullfighting season.

HAVE YOUR SAY

Found a fantastic restaurant that you're longing to share with the world? Disagree with our recommendations? Or just want to talk about your most recent trip?

Whatever your reason, head to lonelyplanet.com, where you can post a review, ask or answer a question on the Thorntree forum, comment on a blog, or share your photos and tips on Groups. Or you can simply spend time chatting with like-minded travellers. So go on, have your say.

Festimad
MUSIC

(www.festimad.es) Bands from all over the country and beyond converge on Móstoles or Leganés (on the MetroSur train network) for two days of indie music indulgence. Although usually held in May, Festimad sometimes spills over into April or June.

Fiesta de Otoño en Primavera
MUSIC, THEATRE

(www.esmadrid.com) The 'Autumn Festival in Spring' involves a busy calendar of musical and theatrical activity.

Suma Flamenca
FLAMENCO

(www.madrid.org/sumaflamenca) A soul-filled flamenco festival that draws some of the biggest names in the genre to the Teatros del Canal in June.

Día del Orgullo de Gays, Lesbianas y Transexuales
GAY PRIDE

(www.orgullogay.org) The colourful Gay Pride Parade, on the last Saturday in June, sets out from the Puerta de Alcalá in the early evening, and winds its way around the city in an explosion of music and energy, ending up at the Puerta del Sol.

July & August

Veranos de la Villa
SUMMER FESTIVAL

(http://veranosdelavilla.esmadrid.com) Madrid's town hall stages a series of cultural events, shows and exhibitions throughout July and August, known as 'Summers in the City'.

Summer Festivals
SUMMER FESTIVAL

Small-time but fun, the neighbourhood summer festivals (held during the period from mid-August to September), such as San Cayetano in Lavapiés, and San Lorenzo and La Paloma in La Latina, are great for cheap entertainment.

September–November

La Noche en Blanco
NIGHT FESTIVAL

(http://lanocheenblanco.esmadrid.com) On September's 'White Night', Madrid stays open all night with a citywide extravaganza of concerts and general revelry in more than 100 venues.

Festival Jazz Madrid
MUSIC

(www.esmadrid.com/festivaljazz) This fine jazz festival in November (and sometimes into December) sees groups from far and wide converge on the capital for a series of concerts in venues across town.

🛏 Sleeping

Madrid has high-quality accommodation across all price ranges and caters to every taste. Where you decide to stay will play an important role in your experience of Madrid. Los Austrias, Sol and Centro put you in the heart of the busy downtown area, while La Latina (the best *barrio* for tapas), Lavapiés and Huertas (good for nightlife) are ideal for those who love Madrid nights and don't want to stagger too far to get back to their hotel in the wee small hours. Staying along the Paseo del Prado is ideal for those here to spend most of their time in galleries, while Salamanca is quiet, up-market and perfect for serial shoppers. You don't have to be gay to stay in Chueca, but you'll love it if you are, while Malasaña is another inner-city *barrio* with great restaurants and bars.

LOS AUSTRIAS, SOL & CENTRO

TOP CHOICE **Hotel Meninas** BOUTIQUE HOTEL €€
(Map p72; ☎91 541 28 05; www.hotelmeninas.com; Calle de Campomanes 7; s/d from €69/87; ❋🛜; ⓂÓpera) This is a classy, cool choice. Opened in 2005, it's the sort of place where an interior designer licked his or her lips and created a master work of understated, minimalist luxury. The colour scheme is blacks, whites and greys, with dark-wood floors and splashes of fuchsia and lime green. Flat-screen TVs in every room, modern bathroom fittings, internet access points, and even a laptop in some rooms, round out the clean lines and latest innovations. Past guests include Viggo Mortensen and Natalie Portman.

Praktik Metropol BOUTIQUE HOTEL €€
(Map p72; ☎91 521 29 35; www.hotelpraktikmetropol.com; Calle de la Montera 47; s/d €59/75; ❋🛜; ⓂGran Vía) You'd be hard-pressed to find better value anywhere in Europe than here in this recently overhauled hotel. The rooms have a fresh, contemporary look with white wood furnishings, and some (especially the corner rooms) have brilliant views down to Gran Vía and out over the city. It's spread over six floors and there's a roof terrace if you don't have a room with a view.

Hostal Madrid HOSTAL, APARTMENT €
(Map p72; ☎91 522 00 60; www.hostal-madrid.info; 2nd fl, Calle de Esparteros 6; s €35-62, d €45-78, apt per night €60-150, per month €1200-2100; ❋🛜; ⓂSol) The 19 excellent apartments here range in size from 33 sq metres to 200 sq metres and each has a fully equipped kitchen, its own sitting area, bathroom and, in the case of the larger ones (room 51 on the 5th floor is one of the best), an expansive terrace with good views over central Madrid. The *hostal* rooms are comfortable and well-sized and the service is friendly.

Hotel Plaza Mayor HOTEL €€
(Map p72; ☎91 360 06 06; www.h-plazamayor.com; Calle de Atocha 2; s/d from €50/75; ❋🛜; ⓂSol, Tirso de Molina) We love this place. Sitting just across from the Plaza Mayor, here you'll find stylish decor, helpful staff and charming original elements of this 150-year-old building. The rooms are attractive, some with a light colour scheme and wrought-iron furniture. The attic rooms (doubles from €130) boast dark wood and designer lamps, and have lovely little terraces with wonderful rooftop views of central Madrid.

Los Amigos Sol Backpackers' Hostel HOSTEL €
(Map p72; ☎91 559 24 72; www.losamigoshostel.com; 4th fl, Calle de Arenal 26; dm incl breakfast €17-19; @🛜; ⓂÓpera, Sol) If you arrive in Madrid keen for company, this could be the place for you – lots of students stay here, the staff are savvy (and speak English) and there are bright dorm style rooms (with free lockers) that sleep from two to four people. There's also a kitchen for guests.

Mario Room Mate BOUTIQUE HOTEL €€
(Map p72; ☎91 548 85 48; www.room-matehoteles.com; Calle de Campomanes 4; s €80-125, d €100-150; ❋🛜; ⓂÓpera) Entering this swanky boutique hotel is like crossing the threshold of Madrid's latest nightclub: staff dressed all in black, black walls and swirls of red lighting in the lobby. Rooms can be small, but have high ceilings, simple furniture and light tones contrasting smoothly with muted colours and dark surfaces. Some rooms are pristine white; others have splashes of colour with zany murals.

Hostal Luis XV HOSTAL €
(Map p72; ☎91 522 10 21; www.hrluisxv.net; 8th fl, Calle de la Montera 47; s/d from €45/59; ❋🛜; ⓂGran Vía) Everything here – especially the spacious rooms and the attention to detail – makes this family-run place feel pricier than it is. You'll find it hard to tear yourself away from the balconies outside every exterior room, from where the views are superb (especially from the triple in room 820),

and you're so high up that noise is rarely a problem.

Hostal Acapulco
HOSTAL €

(Map p72; ☑91 531 19 45; www.hostalacapulco. com; 4th fl, Calle de la Salud 13; s/d €55/65; ✱☎; ⓂGran Vía) A cut above many other *hostales* in Madrid, this immaculate little place has marble floors, recently renovated bathrooms (with bathtubs), double-glazed windows and comfortable beds. Street-facing rooms have balconies overlooking a sunny plaza and are flooded with natural light.

Petit Palace Posada del Peine
BOUTIQUE HOTEL €€

(Map p72; ☑91 523 81 51; www.hthoteles.com; Calle de Postas 17; d from €125; ✱☎; ⓂSol) This hotel combines a splendid historic building (dating from 1610), a brilliant location (just 50m from the Plaza Mayor) and modern hi-tech rooms. The bathrooms sparkle with stunning fittings and hydromassage showers, and the rooms are beautifully appointed. Many historical architectural features remain in situ in the public areas. It's just a pity some of the rooms aren't larger.

Hotel Preciados
BUSINESS HOTEL €€

(Map p72; ☑91 454 44 00; www.preciadoshotel. com; Calle de Preciados 37; d from €125; ✱☎; ⓂSanto Domingo, Callao) With a classier feel than many of the other business options around town, the Preciados gets rave reviews for its service. Soft lighting, light shades and plentiful glass personalise the rooms and provide an intimate feel.

LA LATINA & LAVAPIÉS

TOP CHOICE Posada del Dragón
BOUTIQUE HOTEL €€

(Map p78; ☑91 119 14 24; www.posadadeldragon. com; Calle de la Cava Baja 14 ; s €62-90, d €80-144; ✱☎; ⓂLa Latina) At last, a boutique hotel in the heart of La Latina. This restored 19th-century inn sits on one of our favourite Madrid streets (and one of the best streets for tapas in the country), and rooms either look out over the street or over the pretty internal patio. The rooms? Some are on the small side, but bold, brassy colour schemes and designer everything distract (for the most part). There's a terrific bar-restaurant downstairs.

Posada del León de Oro
BOUTIQUE HOTEL €€

(Map p78; ☑91 119 14 94; www.posadadelleonde oro.com; Calle de la Cava Baja 12; r €89-219; ✱☎; ⓂLa Latina) This rehabilitated inn has muted colour schemes and well-sized rooms. It also

has a patio at its core and thoroughly modern rooms along one of Madrid's best-loved streets. The downstairs bar is terrific.

Mad Hostel
HOSTEL €

(Map p80; ☑91 506 48 40; www.madhostel.com; Calle de la Cabeza 24; dm €18-24; ✱@☎; ⓂAntón Martín) Mad Hostel is filled with life. The 1st-floor courtyard – with retractable roof – re-creates an old Madrid *corrala* (a traditional Madrid tenement block with long communal balconies built around a central courtyard), and is a wonderful place to chill. The four- to eight-bed rooms are smallish but clean. There's a small, rooftop gym with state-of-the-art equipment.

HUERTAS & ATOCHA

Hotel Alicia
BOUTIQUE HOTEL €€

(Map p80; ☑91 389 60 95; www.room-matehoteles. com; Calle del Prado 2; d €100-175, ste from €200; ✱☎; ⓂSol, Sevilla, Antón Martín) One of the landmark properties of the designer Room Mate chain of hotels, Hotel Alicia overlooks Plaza de Santa Ana with beautiful, spacious rooms. The style (the work of designer Pascua Ortega) is a touch more muted than in other Room Mate hotels, but the supermodern look remains intact, the downstairs bar is oh-so-cool, and the service is young and switched on.

Hotel Urban
LUXURY HOTEL €€

(Map p80; ☑91 787 77 70; www.derbyhotels.com; Carrera de San Jerónimo 34; d/ste from €150/250; ✱☎☀; ⓂSevilla) This towering glass edifice is the epitome of art-inspired designer cool. With its clean lines and original artworks from Africa and Asia (there's a small museum dedicated to Egyptian art in the basement), it's a wonderful antidote to the more classic charm of Madrid's five-star hotels of longer standing. Dark-wood floors and dark walls are offset by plenty of light, while the dazzling bathrooms have wonderful designer fittings – the washbasins are sublime. The rooftop swimming pool is one of Madrid's best and the gorgeous terrace is heaven on a candlelit summer's evening.

Chic & Basic Colors
HOSTEL €

(Map p80; ☑91 429 69 35; www.chicandbasic.com; 2nd fl, Calle de las Huertas 14; r €50-75; ✱☎☀; ⓂAntón Martín) At this fine little hostel they claim to have Madrid's most colourful rooms: they're minimalist, with free internet, flat-screen TVs and dark hardwood floors, with bright colour schemes superimposed over white (every room is a different shade). It's all very comfortable, contemporary and casual. The owners also run the slightly more upmarket hotel **Chic & Basic Atocha** (☎91 369 28 95; Calle de Atocha 113; s/d from €80/100; ❀❀; Ⓜ Antón Martín).

Cat's Hostel
HOSTEL €
(Map p80; ☎91 369 28 07; www.catshostel.com; Calle de Cañizares 6; dm €17-22; ❀@❀; Ⓜ Antón Martín) Forming part of a 17th-century palace, the internal courtyard here is one of Madrid's finest – lavish Andalucian tilework, a fountain, a spectacular glass ceiling and stunning Islamic decoration, surrounded on four sides by an open balcony. There's also a super-cool basement bar with free internet and fiestas, often with live music.

Hostal Adriano
HOSTAL €
(Map p80; ☎91 521 13 39; www.hostaladriano.com; 4th fl, Calle de la Cruz 26; s/d €49/60; ❀❀; Ⓜ Sol) They don't come any better than this bright and friendly *hostal* wedged in the streets that mark the boundary between Sol and Huertas. Most rooms are well sized and each has its own well-considered colour scheme. On the same floor, the owners run the **Hostal Adria Santa Ana** (Map p80; www.hostal adriasantaana.com; s/d €59/68; ❀❀), which is a step up in price, style and comfort.

Hostal Sardinero
HOSTAL €
(Map p80; ☎91 429 57 56; www.hostalsardin ero.com; Calle del Prado 16; d €54-62; ❀@; Ⓜ Sol, Antón Martín) A change of owners a few years ago brought a fresh lick of paint, new mattresses and new TVs, and we're pleased to see that this commitment to a comfortable stay continues. The cheerful rooms, which have high ceilings, air-conditioning, safes, hairdryers and renovated bathrooms, are complemented nicely by the owners who are attentive without being in your face.

Me by Meliá
LUXURY HOTEL €€€
(Map p80; ☎91 701 60 00; www.memadrid.com; Plaza de Santa Ana 14; d with/without plaza view €254/199; ❀❀; Ⓜ Sol, Antón Martín) Once the landmark Gran Victoria Hotel, the Madrid home of many a famous bullfighter, this audacious new hotel is fast becoming a landmark of a different kind. Overlooking the western end of Plaza de Santa Ana, this luxury hotel is decked out in minimalist white with curves and comfort in all the right places; this is one place where it's definitely worth paying extra for the view.

Hotel Miau
BOUTIQUE HOTEL €€
(Map p80; ☎91 369 71 20; www.hotelmiau.com, Calle del Príncipe 26; s/d incl breakfast €85/95; ❀❀; Ⓜ Sol, Antón Martín) If you want to be close to the Huertas nightlife or can't tear yourself away from the lovely Plaza de Santa Ana, Hotel Miau is your place. Light tones, splashes of colour and modern art adorn the walls of the large and well-equipped rooms. It can be noisy, but you did choose Huertas…

Hotel El Pasaje
HOTEL €€
(Map p80; ☎91 521 29 95; www.elpasajehs.com; Calle del Pozo 4; d incl breakfast €87-105; ❀❀; Ⓜ Sol) If you were to choose your ideal location in Huertas, Hotel El Pasaje would be hard to beat. Set on a quiet lane largely devoid of bars, yet just around the corner from the Plaza de la Puerta del Sol, it combines a central location with a quiet night's sleep (at least by the standards of Huertas). The feel is intimate and modern, with good bathrooms, minibars and enough space to leave your suitcase without tripping over it.

PASEO DEL PRADO & EL RETIRO

TOP CHOICE Hotel Ritz
LUXURY HOTEL €€€
(Map p86; ☎91 701 67 67; www.ritzmadrid.com; Plaza de la Lealtad 5; d from €280, ste €850-5000; ❀❀; Ⓜ Banco de España) The grand old lady of Madrid, the Hotel Ritz is the height of exclusivity. One of the most lavish buildings in the city, it has classic style and impeccable service that is second to none. Unsurprisingly it's the favoured hotel of presidents, kings and celebrities. The public areas are palatial and awash with antiques, while the rooms are extravagantly large, opulent and supremely comfortable.

Westin Palace
LUXURY HOTEL €€€
(Map p80; ☎91 360 80 00; www.westinpalace madrid.com; Plaza de las Cortes 7; d/ste from €275/575; ❀❀; Ⓜ Banco de España, Antón Martín) An old Madrid classic, this former palace of the Duque de Lerma opened as a hotel in 1911, and was Spain's second luxury hotel. Ever since, it has looked out across Plaza de Neptuno at its rival, the Ritz, like a lover unjustly scorned. Its name may not have the world-famous cachet of the Ritz, but it's not called the Palace for nothing and is extravagant in all the right places.

SALAMANCA

Petit Palace Art Gallery
HOTEL €€
(Map p92; ☎91 435 54 11; www.hthoteles.com; Calle de Jorge Juan 17; d €80-200; ❀❀; Ⓜ Serrano)

Occupying a stately 19th-century Salamanca building, this landmark property of the Petit Palace chain is a lovely designer hotel that combines hi-tech facilities with an artistic aesthetic, with loads of original works dotted around the public spaces and even in some of the rooms. Hydro-massage showers, laptop computers and exercise bikes in many rooms are just some of the extras, and the address is ideal for the best of Salamanca.

MALASAÑA & CHUECA

TOP CHOICE Hotel Óscar BOUTIQUE HOTEL €€
(Map p94; ✆91 701 11 73; www.room-matehoteles.com; Plaza de Vázquez de Mella 12; d €90-200, ste €150-280; ❄️🅂🏊; MGran Vía) Outstanding. Hotel Óscar belongs to the highly original Room Mate chain of hotels, and the designer rooms ooze style and sophistication. Some have floor-to-ceiling murals, the lighting is always funky, and the colour scheme is asplash with pinks, lime greens, oranges or more-minimalist black and white. There's a fine street-level tapas bar and a rooftop terrace.

Hotel Abalú BOUTIQUE HOTEL €€
(Map p94; ✆91 531 47 44; www.hotelabalu.com; Calle del Pez 19; s/d/ste from €68/89/128; ❄️🅂; MNoviciado) Malasaña's very own boutique hotel is an oasis of style amid the *barrio's* time-worn feel. Suitably located on cool Calle del Pez, each room here has its own design drawn from the imagination of Luis Delgado, from retro chintz to Zen, baroque and pure white (and most aesthetics in between). You're close to Gran Vía, but away from the tourist scrum.

Antigua Posada del Pez HOTEL €€
(Map p94; ✆91 531 42 96; www.antiguaposadadelpez.com; Calle de Pizarro 16; s €50-110, d €60-140; ❄️🅂; MNoviciado) This place inhabits the shell of a historic Malasaña building, but the rooms are slick and contemporary with designer bathrooms. You're also just a few steps up the hill from Calle del Pez, one of Malasaña's most happening streets. It's an exceptionally good deal, even when prices head upwards.

Flat 5 Madrid HOSTAL €
(Map p94; ✆91 127 24 00; www.flat5madrid.com; 5th fl, Calle de San Bernardo 55; d with/without bathroom from €60/40; ❄️🅂; MNoviciado) Unlike so many other *hostales* in Madrid, where the charm depends on a time-worn air, Flat 5 Madrid has a fresh, clean-lined look with bright colours, flat-screen TVs and flower boxes on the window sills. Even the rooms that face onto a patio have partial views over the rooftops. If the rooms and bathrooms were a little bigger, we'd consider moving in.

Hostal La Zona HOSTAL €
(Map p94; ✆91 521 99 04; www.hostallazona.com; 1st fl, Calle de Valverde 7; s/d incl breakfast €50/60; ❄️🅂; MGran Vía) Catering primarily to a gay clientele, the stylish Hostal La Zona has exposed brickwork, subtle colour shades and wooden pillars. We like a place where a sleep-in is encouraged – breakfast is served from 9am to noon, which is exactly the understanding Madrid's nightlife merits. Arnaldo and Vincent are friendly hosts.

Albergue Juvenil HOSTAL €
(Map p94; ✆91 593 96 88; www.ajmadrid.es; Calle de Mejía Lequerica 21; dm incl breakfast €20-27; ❄️@🅂; MBilbao, Alonso Martínez) The Albergue has spotless rooms, no dorm houses more than six beds (each has its own bathroom), and facilities include a pool table, gymnasium, wheelchair access, free internet, laundry and a TV/DVD room with a choice of movies. Yes, there are places with more character or a more central location, but we'd still rate this as one of Madrid's best hostels for backpackers.

BEYOND THE CENTRE

TOP CHOICE Hotel Puerta América LUXURY HOTEL €€
(✆91 744 54 00; www.hotelpuertamerica.com; Avenida de América 41; d/ste from €125/250; ❄️🅂; MCartagena) When the owners of this hotel saw their location – halfway between the city and the airport – they knew they had to do something special, to build a self-contained world so innovative and luxurious that you'd never want to leave. Their idea? Give 22 of world architecture's most creative names (eg Zaha Hadid, Sir Norman Foster, Ron Arad, David Chipperfield, Jean Nouvel) a floor each to design. The result? An extravagant pastiche of styles, from zany montages of 1980s chic to bright-red bathrooms that feel like a movie star's dressing room. To get here, take Avenida de América in the direction of the airport; it's about 4km northwest of the city centre.

✕ Eating

After holding fast to its rather unexciting local cuisine for centuries (aided by loyal locals who never saw the need for anything else), Madrid has finally become a worthy culinary capital.

There's everything to be found here, not least the rich variety of regional Spanish specialities from across the country. And there's not a *barrio* where you can't find a great meal. Restaurants in Malasaña, Chueca and Huertas range from glorious old *tabernas* (taverns) to boutique eateries across all price ranges. For more classically classy surrounds, Salamanca and Northern Madrid are generally pricey but of the highest standard, and ideal for a special occasion. In the central *barrios* of Los Austrias, Sol and Centro there's a little bit of everything. Splendid tapas bars abound everywhere, but La Latina is the undoubted queen.

LOS AUSTRIAS, SOL & CENTRO

Mercado de San Miguel   TAPAS €

(Map p72; www.mercadodesanmiguel.es; Plaza de San Miguel; tapas from €1; ⊗10am-midnight Sun-Wed, 10am-2am Thu-Sat; ⋈Sol) One of Madrid's oldest and most beautiful markets, the Mercado de San Miguel has undergone a stunning major renovation and bills itself as a 'culinary cultural centre'. Within the early-20th-century glass walls, the market has become an inviting space strewn with tables. You can order tapas and sometimes more substantial plates at most of the counter bars, and everything here (from caviar to chocolate) is as tempting as the market is alive.

Restaurante Sobrino de Botín   CASTILIAN €€

(Map p72; ☎91 366 42 17; www.botin.es; Calle de los Cuchilleros 17; mains €18.50-28; ⋈La Latina, Sol) It's not every day that you can eat in the oldest restaurant in the world (the *Guinness Book of Records* has recognised it as the oldest – established in 1725). And it has also appeared in many novels about Madrid, from Ernest Hemingway to Frederick Forsyth. The secret of its staying power is fine *cochinillo* (roast suckling pig; €24) and *cordero asado* (roast lamb; €24) cooked in wood-fired ovens. Eating in the vaulted cellar is a treat.

La Terraza del Casino   MODERN SPANISH €€€

(Map p72; ☎91 521 87 00; www.casinodemadrid.es; Calle de Alcalá 15; set menus from €100; ⊗lunch & dinner Mon-Fri, dinner Sat; ⋈Sevilla) Perched atop the landmark Casino de Madrid building, this temple of haute cuisine is overseen, albeit from afar, by Ferran Adrià (Spain's premier celebrity chef), but is mostly in the hands of his acolyte Paco Roncero. It's all about culinary experimentation, with a menu that changes as each new idea emerges from the laboratory and moves into the kitchen.

Taberna La Bola   MADRILEÑO €€

(Map p72; ☎91 547 69 30; www.labola.es; Calle de la Bola 5; mains €16-24; ⊗lunch & dinner Mon-Sat, lunch Sun, closed Aug; ⋈Santo Domingo) In any poll of food-loving locals seeking the best and most traditional Madrid cuisine, Taberna La Bola (going strong since 1870 and run by the sixth generation of the Verdasco family) always features near the top. We're inclined to agree and, if you're going to try *cocido a la madrileña* (meat-and-chickpea stew; €19.50) while in Madrid, this is a good place to do so. It's busy and noisy and very Madrid.

Casa Revuelta   TAPAS €

(Map p72; ☎91 366 33 32; Calle de Latoneros 3; tapas from €2.60; ⊗10.30am-4pm & 7-11pm Tue-Sat, 10.30am-4pm Sun, closed Aug; ⋈Sol, La Latina) Casa Revuelta puts out some of Madrid's finest tapas of *bacalao* (dried and salted cod; €2.60), bar none. While aficionados of Casa Labra (p111) may disagree, the fact that the octogenarian owner, Señor Revuelta, painstakingly extracts every fish bone in the morning and serves as a waiter in the afternoon wins the argument for us. Early on a Sunday afternoon, as the Rastro crowd gathers here, it's filled to the rafters. It's also famous for its *callos* (tripe), *torreznos* (bacon bits) and *albóndigas* (meatballs).

La Gloria de Montera   SPANISH €

(Map p72; www.lagloriademontera.com; Calle del Caballero de Gracia 10; mains €7-10; ⋈Gran Vía) From the same stable as La Finca de Susana (p110), La Gloria de Montera combines classy decor with eminently reasonable prices. It's not that the food is especially creative, but rather the tastes are fresh and the surroundings sophisticated. You'll get a good initiation into Spanish cooking without paying too much for the experience.

LA LATINA & LAVAPIÉS

Enotaberna del León de Oro   SPANISH €€

(Map p78; ☎91 119 14 94; www.posadadlleondeoro. com; Calle de la Cava Baja 12; mains €13-15; ⋈La Latina) The stunning restoration work that brought to life the Posada del León de Oro (p104) also bequeathed to La Latina a fine

BEST FOR...

Cocido a la Madrileña (meat-and-chickpea stew)
» Taberna La Bola (p107)
» Lhardy

Roast lamb or suckling pig
» Restaurante Sobrino de Botín (p107)
» Posada de la Villa

Tortilla de patatas (potato-and-onion omelette)
» Juana La Loca (p111)
» Bodega de la Ardosa (p111)
» Estado Puro (p110)
» Las Tortillas de Gabino (p113)

Croquetas
» Casa Julio (p111)
» Casa Labra (p111)
» Casa Alberto (p109)
» Baco y Beto (p111)
» Las Tortillas de Gabino (p113)

Patatas bravas (roast potatoes in a spicy tomato sauce)
» Las Bravas (p111)
» Vi Cool (p109)
» Bodega de la Ardosa (p111)

Huevos rotos (fried eggs with potato & jamón)
» Almendro 13 (p111)
» Casa Lucio (p109)

Rice & paella
» Costa Blanca Arrocería (p113)

Chocolate con churros
» Chocolatería de San Ginés (p113)
» Chocolatería Valor (p114)

new bar-restaurant. The emphasis is on matching carefully chosen wines with creative dishes (such as baby squid with potato emulsion and ruccola pesto) in a casual atmosphere. It's a winning combination.

Posada de la Villa　　MADRILEÑO €€€
(Map p78; ☑91 366 18 80; www.posadadelavilla.com; Calle de la Cava Baja 9; mains €20-28; ☺lunch & dinner Mon-Sat, lunch Sun, closed Aug; Ⓜ La Latina) This wonderfully restored 17th-century *posada* (inn) is something of a local landmark. The atmosphere is formal, the decoration sombre and traditional (heavy timber and brickwork), and the cuisine is decidedly local – roast meats, *cocido* (meat-and-chickpea stew), *callos* (tripe) and *sopa de ajo* (garlic soup).

Naïa Restaurante　　FUSION €€
(Map p78; ☑91 366 27 83; www.naiarestaurante.com; Plaza de la Paja 3; mains €12-19; ☺lunch & dinner Tue-Sun; Ⓜ La Latina) On the lovely Plaza de la Paja, Naïa has a real buzz about it, with a cooking laboratory overseen by Carlos López Reyes, modern Spanish cuisine and a chill-out lounge downstairs. The empha-

sis throughout is on natural ingredients, healthy food and exciting tastes.

Ene Restaurante
MODERN SPANISH €€
(Map p78; ☎91 366 25 91; www.enerestaurante. com; Calle del Nuncio 19; mains €11-22, brunch €22; ☺lunch & dinner daily, brunch 12.30-4.30pm Sat & Sun; Ⓜ La Latina) Just across from Iglesia de San Pedro El Viejo, one of Madrid's oldest churches, Ene is anything but old world. The design is cutting edge and awash with reds and purples, while the young and friendly waiters circulate to the tune of lounge music. The food is Spanish-Asian fusion and there are also plenty of *pintxos* (Basque tapas) to choose from.

El Estragón
VEGETARIAN €€
(Map p78; ☎91 365 89 82; www.elestragonveg etariano.com; Plaza de la Paja 10; mains €8-14; ✍; Ⓜ La Latina) A delightful spot for crêpes, vegie burgers and other vegetarian specialities, El Estragón is undoubtedly one of Madrid's best vegetarian restaurants, although attentive vegans won't appreciate the use of butter. Apart from that, we're yet to hear a bad word about it, and the *menu del día* (from €8) is one of Madrid's best bargains.

Casa Lucio
SPANISH €€
(Map p78; ☎91 365 32 52; www.casalucio.es; Calle de la Cava Baja 35; mains €12-25; ☺lunch & dinner Sun-Fri, dinner Sat, closed Aug; Ⓜ La Latina) Lucio has been wowing *madrileños* with his light touch, quality ingredients and home-style local cooking for ages – think roasted meats and, a Lucio speciality, eggs in abundance. There's also *rabo de toro* (bull's tail) during the Fiestas de San Isidro Labrador, and plenty of *rioja* (red wine) to wash away the mere thought of it. The lunchtime *guisos del día* (stews of the day, including *cocido* on Wednesdays) are also popular. Casa Lucio draws an august, always-well-dressed crowd.

HUERTAS & ATOCHA

Casa Alberto
SPANISH €€
(Map p80; ☎91 429 93 56; www.casaalberto.es; Calle de las Huertas 18; mains €16-20; ☺lunch & dinner Tue-Sat, lunch Sun; Ⓜ Antón Martín) One of the most atmospheric old *tabernas* of Madrid, Casa Alberto has been around since 1827. The secret to its staying power is vermouth on tap, excellent tapas at the bar and fine sit-down meals; Casa Alberto's *rabo de toro* is famous among aficionados. As the antique wood-panelled decoration will suggest straight away, the *raciones* have none

of the frilly innovations that have come to characterise Spanish tapas. *Jamón*, Manchego cheese and *croquetas* are recurring themes.

Vi Cool
MODERN SPANISH €€
(Map p80; ☎91 429 49 13; www.vi-cool.com; Calle de las Huertas 12; mains €8-18; Ⓜ Antón Martín) Catalan master chef Sergi Arola is one of the most restless and relentlessly creative culinary talents in the country. Aside from his showpiece Sergi Arola Gastro (p112), he has dabbled in numerous new restaurants around the capital and in Barcelona, but this is one of his most interesting yet – a modern bar-style space with prices that enable the average mortal to sample his formidable gastronomic skills. Dishes are either tapas or larger *raciones,* ranging from his trademark Las Bravas de Arola (a different take on the well-loved Spanish dish of roast potatoes in a spicy tomato sauce), to fried prawns with curry and mint.

Maceiras
GALICIAN €€
(Map p80; ☎91 429 15 84; Calle de las Huertas 66; mains €7-14; Ⓜ Antón Martín) Galician tapas (think octopus, green peppers etc) never tasted so good as in this agreeably rustic bar down the bottom of the Huertas hill, especially when washed down with a crisp white Ribeiro. The simple wooden tables, loyal customers and handy location make this a fine place to rest after (or en route to) the museums along the Paseo del Prado.

Sidrería Vasca Zeraín
BASQUE €€
(Map p80; ☎91 429 79 09; www.restaurante-vasco -zerain-sidreria.es; Calle Quevedo 3; mains €14-32; ☺lunch & dinner Mon-Sat, lunch Sun, closed Aug; Ⓜ Antón Martín) In the heart of the Barrio de las Letras, this sophisticated Basque restaurant is one of the best places in town to sample Basque cuisine. The essential staples include cider, *bacalao* and wonderful steaks, while there are also a few splashes of creativity thrown in (the secret's in the sauce). We highly recommend the *menú sidrería* (cider-house menu; €38).

Lhardy
MADRILEÑO €€€
(Map p80; ☎91 521 33 85; www.lhardy.com; Carrera de San Jerónimo 8; mains €18.50-39; ☺lunch & dinner Mon-Sat, lunch Sun, closed Aug; Ⓜ Sol, Sevilla) Downstairs at this Madrid landmark (since 1839) is an elegant treasure trove of takeaway gourmet tapas, while the six upstairs dining areas are the upmarket preserve of traditional Madrid dishes with an

A TAPAS TOUR OF MADRID

La Latina

Madrid's home of tapas is La Latina, especially along Calle de la Cava Baja and the surrounding streets. **Almendro 13** (Map p78; ✆91 365 42 52; Calle del Almendro 13; mains €7-15; ⓂLa Latina) is famous for quality rather than frilly elaborations, with cured meats, cheeses, tortillas and *huevos rotos* (literally, 'broken eggs') the house specialities. Down on Calle de la Cava Baja, **Txacolina** (Map p78; ✆91 366 48 77; Calle de la Cava Baja 26; tapas from €3; ⓢdinner Mon & Wed-Fri, lunch & dinner Sat, lunch Sun; ⓂLa Latina) does Basque 'high cuisine in miniature', although these are some of the biggest *pintxos* (Basque tapas) you'll find; wash it all down with a *txacoli,* a sharp Basque white. On the same street, **Casa Lucas** (Map p78; ✆91 365 08 04; www.casalucas.es; Calle de la Cava Baja 30; tapas/raciones from €5/12; ⓢlunch & dinner Thu-Tue, dinner Wed; ⓂLa Latina) and **La Chata** (Map p78; ✆91 366 14 58; Calle de la Cava Baja 24; mains €8-20; ⓢlunch & dinner Thu-Mon, dinner Wed; ⓂLa Latina) are also hugely popular. Not far away, **Juana La Loca** (Map p78; ✆91 364 05 25; Plaza de la Puerta de Moros 4; tapas from €4, mains €8-19; ⓢlunch & dinner Tue-Sun, dinner Mon; ⓂLa Latina) does a magnificent *tortilla de patatas* (potato and onion omelette), as does **Txirimiri** (Map p78; ✆91 364 11 96; www.txirimiri.es; Calle del Humilladero 6; tapas from €4; ⓢlunch & dinner Mon-Sat, closed Aug; ⓂLa Latina). **Taberna Matritum** (Map p78; ✆91 365 82 37; Calle de la Cava Alta 17; mains €13-18; ⓢlunch & dinner Wed-Sun, dinner Mon & Tue; ⓂLa Latina) serves great tapas and desserts by the master chocolatier Oriol Balaguer.

Los Austrias, Sol & Centro

La Latina's tapas experience spills over into neighbouring Los Austrias, Sol and Centro, with **Amaya** (Map p72; ✆91 366 82 07; Plaza de la Provincia 3; meals €25-30; ⓢnoon-5pm & 8pm-late Tue-Sat, noon-5pm Sun; ⓂSol) combining traditional Spanish flavours with some surprising twists. For *bacalao* (cod), **Casa Labra** (Map p72; ✆91 532 14 05; www.casalabra.es; Calle de Tetuán 11; tapas from €1; ⓢ9.30am-3.30pm & 5.30-11pm; ⓂSol) has been around since 1860 and was a favourite of the poet Federico García Lorca. However, many *madrileños* wouldn't eat *bacalao* anywhere except Casa Revuelta (p107), clinched by the fact that the owner painstakingly extracts every fish bone in the morning.

Huertas

In Huertas, **La Casa del Abuelo** (Map p80; ✆91 000 01 33; www.lacasadelabuelo.es; Calle de la Victoria 12; raciones from €9.50; ⓢ8.30am-midnight Sun-Thu, 8am-1am Fri & Sat; ⓂSol)

occasional hint of French influence. House specialities include *cocido a la madrileña* (€35.50), pheasant and wild duck in an orange perfume. The quality and service are unimpeachable.

La Finca de Susana SPANISH €€
(Map p80; www.lafinca-restaurant.com; Calle de Arlabán 4; mains €7-12; ⓂSevilla) It's difficult to find a better combination of price, quality cooking and classy atmosphere anywhere in Huertas. The softly lit dining area is bathed in greenery and the sometimes innovative, sometimes traditional food draws a hip young crowd. The duck confit with plums, turnips and couscous is a fine choice. No reservations.

PASEO DEL PRADO & EL RETIRO

Estado Puro TAPAS €
(Map p80; ✆91 330 24 00; www.tapasenestadopuro.com; Plaza de Cánovas del Castillo 4; tapas €5-12.50; ⓢ11am-1am Tue-Sat, 11am-4pm Sun; ⓂBanco de España, Atocha) A slick but casual tapas bar, Estado Puro serves up fantastic tapas, many of which have their origins in Catalonia's world-famous elBulli restaurant, such as the *tortilla española siglo XXI* (21st-century Spanish omelette, served in a glass). The kitchen here is overseen by Paco Roncero, the head chef at La Terraza del Casino (p107), who learned his trade with master chef Ferran Adrià.

SALAMANCA

[TOP CHOICE] **Sula Madrid** MODERN SPANISH €€€
(Map p92; ✆91 781 61 97; www.sula.es; Calle de Jorge Juan 33; mains €23.50-27.50, set menus

is famous for *gambas a la plancha* (grilled prawns) or *gambas al ajillo* (prawns sizzling in garlic on little ceramic plates) and a *chato* (small glass) of the heavy, sweet El Abuelo red wine; they cook over 200kg of prawns here on a good day. For *patatas bravas* (fried potatoes lathered in a spicy tomato sauce), **Las Bravas** (Map p80; ☑91 522 85 81; Callejón de Álvarez Gato 3; raciones €3.50-10; Ⓜ Sol, Sevilla) is the place, while **La Trucha** (Map p80; ☑91 532 08 90; Calle de Núñez de Arce 6; mains €8.50-13.50; Ⓜ Sol) has a counter overloaded with enticing Andalucian tapas and 95 items on the menu. Another good choice down the bottom of the Huertas hill is **Los Gatos** (Map p80; ☑91 429 30 67; Calle de Jesús 2; tapas from €3.50; ⊙noon-1am Sun-Thu, noon-2am Fri & Sat; Ⓜ Antón Martín) with eclectic decor and terrific canapés.

Paseo del Prado & Salamanca

Along the Paseo del Prado, there's only one choice for tapas and it's one of Madrid's best: Estado Puro. In Salamanca, **Biotza** (Map p92; www.biotzarestaurante.com; Calle de Claudio Coello 27; tapas €2.50-3.50; ⊙9am-midnight Mon-Thu, 9am-1am Fri & Sat; Ⓜ Serrano) offers creative Basque *pintxos* in stylish surrounds, while La Colonial de Goya serves up a staggering choice of *pintxos*, including 63 varieties of canapés.

Chueca

Chueca is another stellar tapas *barrio*. Don't miss **Bocaito** (Map p94; ☑91 532 12 19; www.bocaito.com; Calle de la Libertad 4-6; tapas from €3.50, mains €12-20; ⊙lunch & dinner Mon-Fri, dinner Sat; Ⓜ Chueca, Banco de España), another purveyor of Andalucian *jamón* (ham) and seafood and a favourite haunt of film-maker Pedro Almodóvar. **Bodega de La Ardosa** (Map p94; ☑91 521 49 79; Calle de Colón 13; tapas & raciones €3.50-11; ⊙8.30am-1am; Ⓜ Tribunal) is extremely popular for its *salmorejo* (cold, tomato-based soup), *croquetas*, *patatas bravas* and *tortilla de patatas*, while **Casa Julio** (Map p94; ☑91 522 72 74; www.barcasajulio. com; Calle de la Madera 37; 6/12 croquetas €5/10; ⊙lunch & dinner Mon-Sat; Ⓜ Tribunal) is widely touted as the home of Madrid's best *croquetas*. Other brilliant choices include **Le Cabrera** (Map p94; ☑91 319 94 57; www.lecabrera.com; Calle de Bárbara de Braganza 2; tapas €3-22, caviar €85; ⊙lunch & dinner Tue-Sat; Ⓜ Colón, Alonso Martínez), **Baco y Beto** (Map p94; ☑91 522 84 81; www.bacoybeto.com; Calle de Pelayo 24; tapas from €4; ⊙dinner Mon-Fri, lunch & dinner Sat; Ⓜ Chueca) and **Gastromaquia** (Map p94; ☑91 522 64 13; Calle de Pelayo 8; tapas from €4; ⊙lunch Mon-Thu & Sat, dinner Tue-Sat; Ⓜ Chueca).

€30 60; ⊙lunch & dinner Mon-Sat; Ⓜ Velázquez) A gastronomic temple that combines stellar cooking with clean-styled sophistication, Sula Madrid – a superstylish tapas bar, topnotch restaurant and ham-and-champagne tasting centre all rolled into one – is one of our favourite top-end restaurants in Madrid. And we're not the only ones: when master chef Ferran Adrià was asked to nominate his favourite restaurant, he chose Sula.

La Galette   SPANISH €€
(Map p92; ☑91 576 06 41; Calle del Conde de Aranda 11; mains €9.50-19.50; ⊙lunch & dinner Mon-Sat, lunch Sun; ☑; Ⓜ Retiro) This lovely little restaurant combines an intimate dining area with checked tablecloths and cuisine that the owner describes as 'baroque vegetarian'. The

food (both veg and non-veg) is a revelation, blending creative flavours with a strong base in traditional home cooking. The *croquetas de manzana* (apple croquettes) are a house speciality.

La Colonial de Goya   TAPAS €
(Map p92; www.restauranterincondegoya.es; Calle de Jorge Juan 34; tapas €3-4.50; ⊙8am-midnight Mon-Fri, noon-1am Sat & Sun; Ⓜ Velázquez) A mere 63 varieties of canapé should be sufficient for most, but they also serve a range of carpaccios, croquettes and main dishes at this engaging little tapas bar. The atmosphere is casual, the all-white decor of wood and exposed brick walls is classy, and some of the dishes (such as the sirloin, brie and quail's eggs) are Spanish nouvelle cuisine at its best.

MADRID EATING

MALASAÑA & CHUECA

TOP CHOICE La Musa
SPANISH, FUSION €€

(Map p94; [phone]91 448 75 58; www.lamusa.com.es; Calle de Manuela Malasaña 18; mains €7-15; [clock]9am-1am Mon-Thu, 9am-2am Fri, 1pm-2am Sat, 1pm-1am Sun; [M]San Bernardo) Snug yet loud, a favourite of Madrid's hip young crowd yet utterly unpretentious, La Musa is all about designer decor, lounge music on the sound system and fun food (breakfast, lunch and dinner) that will live long in the memory. The menu is divided into three types of tapas – hot, cold and BBQ; among the hot varieties is the fantastic *jabalí con ali-oli de miel y sobrasada* (wild boar with honey mayonnaise and *sobrasada* – a soft, mildly spicy sausage from Mallorca). If you don't fancy waiting, try the sister restaurant/lounge bar nearby, Ojalá Awareness Club (p117).

Bazaar
MODERN SPANISH €

(Map p94; www.restaurantbazaar.com; Calle de la Libertad 21; mains €6.50-10; [M]Chueca) Bazaar's popularity among the well heeled and famous shows no sign of abating. Its pristine white interior design, with theatre-style lighting and wall-length windows, may draw a crowd that looks like it stepped out of the pages of *Hola!* magazine, but the food is extremely well priced and innovative and the atmosphere is casual. It doesn't take reservations, so get there early or be prepared to wait, regardless of whether you're famous or not.

Nina
MODERN SPANISH €€

(Map p94; [phone]91 591 00 46; Calle de Manuela Malasaña 10; mains €11.50-16; [M]Bilbao) Sophisticated, intimate and enduringly popular, Nina has an extensive menu (available in English) of Mediterranean nouvelle cuisine that doesn't miss a trick: boned pig's trotters filled with boletus mushrooms, foie gras and truffles with fried Dublin Bay prawns is as weird and wonderful as it sounds. The weekend brunch (two courses, plus juice and coffee for €22; noon to 5.30pm Saturday and Sunday) is excellent.

Albur
TAPAS, SPANISH €€

(Map p94; [phone]91 594 27 33; www.restaurantealbur.com; Calle de Manuela Malasaña 15; mains €13-18; [clock]noon-1am Sun-Thu, noon-2am Fri & Sat; [M]Bilbao) One of Malasaña's best deals, this place has a wildly popular tapas bar and a classy-but-casual restaurant out the back. Albur is known for terrific rice dishes and tapas, and has a well-chosen wine list. The restau-

rant waiters never seem to lose their cool, and its extremely well-priced rice dishes are the stars of the show, although in truth you could order anything here and leave well satisfied.

La Tasquita de Enfrente
MODERN SPANISH €€€

(Map p94; [phone]91 532 54 49; www.latasquitadeenfrente.com; Calle de la Ballesta 6; mains €20-32; [clock]lunch & dinner Tue-Sat; [M]Gran Vía) To succeed on the international stage, Spain's celebrity chefs have to take experimentation to new levels, but to succeed at home they usually have to maintain a greater fidelity to traditional bases before heading off in new directions. And therein lies the success of chef Juanjo López. His seasonal menu never ceases to surprise but also combines simple Spanish staples to stunning effect. His *menú degustación* (€48) and *menú de Juanjo* (€65) would be our choice if this is your first time. Reservations essential.

La Isla del Tesoro
VEGETARIAN €€

(Map p94; [phone]91 593 14 40; www.isladeltesoro.net; Calle de Manuela Malasaña 3; mains €12.50-14.50; [phone]; [M]Bilbao) Unlike some vegetarian restaurants that seem to work on the philosophy that basic decor signifies healthy food, the dining area here is like someone's fantasy of a secret garden come to life. The cooking is assured and wide-ranging in its influences; the jungle burger is typical in a menu that's full of surprises.

El Original
SPANISH €€

(Map p94; [phone]91 522 90 69; www.eloriginal.es; Calle de las Infantas 44; mains €8-12, set menus €25-38; [clock]lunch & dinner Mon-Sat; [M]Chueca, Banco de España) With the best products and signature dishes from most Spanish regions, El Original turns out well-priced cooking, and instead of messing with some of Spain's favourite dishes, it's gone for creativity with the pleasingly contemporary decor.

CHAMBERÍ & ARGÜELLES

TOP CHOICE Sergi Arola Gastro
MODERN SPANISH €€€

(Map p92; [phone]91 310 21 69; www.sergiarola.es; Calle de Zurbano 31; mains €43-52, set menus €105-135; [clock]lunch & dinner Mon-Fri, dinner Sat; [M]Alonso Martínez) Sergi Arola, a stellar Catalan acolyte of the world-renowned chef Ferran Adrià, runs this highly personalised temple to all that's innovative in Spanish gastronomy. The menus change with the seasons – a recent sample included smoked beetroot ravioli with celery consommé, or Jerusalem artichoke soft cream, truffled poultry mousse, mascarpone cheese and fine herbs. You pay for the privilege of eating here. But this is culinary indulgence at its finest, the sort of place where creativity, presentation and taste are everything. And oh, what tastes... With just 26 seats, booking well in advance is necessary.

Las Tortillas de Gabino SPANISH €€
(Map p92; ☑91 319 75 05; www.lastortillasdegabino.com; Calle de Rafael Calvo 20; tortillas €9-15.50, mains €12-18; ☺lunch & dinner Mon-Fri, dinner Sat; ⓂIglesia) It's a brave Spanish chef who messes with the iconic *tortilla de patatas* (potato-and-onion omelette), but the results here are delicious – such as tortilla with octopus, and with all manner of surprising combinations. This place also gets rave reviews for its *croquetas*. The service is excellent and the bright yet classy dining area adds to the sense of a most agreeable eating experience. Reservations are highly recommended.

Costa Blanca Arrocería SPANISH €€
(☑91 448 58 32; Calle de Bravo Murillo 3; mains €9-18; ⓂQuevedo) Even if you don't have plans to be in Chamberí, it's worth a trip across town to this casual bar-restaurant that offers outstanding rice dishes, including paella. The quality is high and prices are among the cheapest in town. Start with *almejas a la marinera* (baby clams) and follow it up with *paella de marisco* (seafood paella) for the full experience. As always in such places, you'll need two people to make up an order.

NORTHERN MADRID

TOP CHOICE Santceloni CATALAN €€€
(☑91 210 88 40; www.restaurantesantceloni.com; Paseo de la Castellana 57; mains €43-69, set menus €150-180; ☺lunch & dinner Mon-Fri, dinner Sat; ⓂGregorio Marañón) The Michelin-starred Santceloni is one of Madrid's best restaurants, with luxury decor that's the work of star interior designer Pascual Ortega, and nouvelle cuisine from the kitchen of chef Óscar Velasco, protege of master chef, the late Santi Santamaría. Each dish is an exquisite work of art and the menu changes with the seasons, but we'd recommend one of the *menús gastronómicos* to really sample the breadth of surprising tastes on offer. Make no mistake: this is one of Madrid's best restaurants.

Zalacaín BASQUE, NAVARRAN €€€
(☑91 561 48 40; www.restaurantezalacain.com; Calle de Álvarez de Baena 4; mains €35-50, menú degustación €104; ☺lunch & dinner Mon-Fri, dinner Sat, closed Aug; ⓂGregorio Marañón) Where most other fine-dining experiences centre on innovation, Zalacaín is a bastion of tradition, with a refined air and a loyal following among Spain's great and good. Everyone who's anyone in Madrid, from the king down, has eaten here since the doors opened in 1973; it was the first restaurant in Spain to receive three Michelin stars. The pig's trotters filled with mushrooms and lamb is a house speciality, as is the lobster salad. The wine list is purported to be one of the best in the city (it stocks an estimated 35,000 bottles with 800 different varieties). You should certainly dress to impress (men will need a tie and a jacket). To get here from Gregorio Marañón metro station, turn onto Calle de María de Molina from Paseo de la Castellana and take the first left.

🍷 Drinking

To get an idea of how much *madrileños* like to go out and have a good time, consider one simple statistic: Madrid has more bars than any city in the world – six, in fact, for every 100 inhabitants.

LOS AUSTRIAS, SOL & CENTRO
Old taverns and the odd hidden gem rub shoulders in Madrid's centre. As a general rule, the further you stray from Plaza Mayor, the more prices drop and the fewer tourists you'll see.

Chocolatería de San Ginés CAFE
(Map p72; Pasadizo de San Ginés 5; ☺9.30am-7am; ⓂSol) One of the grand icons of the Madrid night, this *chocolate con churros* cafe sees a sprinkling of tourists throughout the day, but locals usually pack it out in their search for sustenance on their way home from a nightclub sometime close to dawn. It closes for only a couple of hours a day, and only then to give it a quick scrub. Only in Madrid...

Café del Real COCKTAIL BAR, CAFE
(Map p72; Plaza de Isabel II 2; ☺9am-1am Mon-Thu, 9am-3am Fri & Sat; ⓂÓpera) A cafe and cocktail bar in equal parts, this intimate little place serves up creative coffees and a few cocktails to the soundtrack of chill-out music. The best seats are upstairs, where the low ceilings, wooden beams and leather chairs

are a great place to pass an afternoon with friends.

Chocolatería Valor
CAFE

(Map p72; www.chocolateriasvalor.es; Postigo de San Martín; ☺9am-10.30pm Sun, 8am-10.30pm Mon-Thu, 8am-1am Fri, 9am-1am Sat; MCallao) It may be Madrid tradition to indulge in *chocolate con churros* around sunrise on your way home from a nightclub, but for everyone else who prefers a more reasonable hour, this is possibly the best *chocolatería* in town. It serves traditional *churros,* but they're only the side event to the astonishing array of chocolates in which to dip them. Our favourite has to be *cuatro sentidos de chocolate* (four senses of chocolate; €8), but we'd happily try everything on the menu to make sure.

LA LATINA & LAVAPIÉS

Most nights (and Sunday afternoons), crowds of happy *madrileños* hop from bar to bar across La Latina. This is a *barrio* beloved by discerning 20- and 30-something urban sophisticates who ensure there's little room to move in the good places and the bad ones don't survive long. The crowd is a little more diverse on Sundays as hordes fan out from El Rastro. Most of the action takes place along Calle de la Cava Baja (where the dividing line between drinking and tapas bars is decidedly blurred), the western end of Calle del Almendro and Plaza de la Paja. Working-class, multicultural Lavapiés is a completely different kettle of fish – quirky bars brimful of personality that draw an alternative, often bohemian crowd. Not everyone loves Lavapiés, but we do.

TOP CHOICE Gaudeamus Café
CAFE

(www.gaudeamuscafe.com; 4th fl, Calle de Tribulete 14; ☺3pm-midnight Mon-Sat; MLavapiés) What a place! Decoration that's light and airy, with pop-art posters of Audrey Hepburn and James Bond. A large terrace with views over the Lavapiés rooftops. A stunning backdrop of a ruined church atop which the cafe sits. With so much else going for it, it almost seems incidental that it also serves great teas, coffees and snacks (and meals). The only criticism we can think of is that it doesn't stay open later. The terrace is filled to bursting on summer evenings. The cafe is around 300m southwest of Plaza de Lavapiés along Calle de Tribulete; look for the glass doors.

Delic
BAR, CAFE

(Map p78; www.delic.es; Costanilla de San Andrés 14; ☺11am-2am Fri-Sun & Tue-Thu, 7pm-2am Mon; MLa Latina) We could go on for hours about this long-standing cafe-bar, but we'll reduce it to its most basic elements: nursing an exceptionally good mojito (€8) or three on a warm summer's evening at Delic's outdoor tables on one of Madrid's prettiest plazas is one of life's great pleasures. Bliss. Due to local licensing restrictions, the outdoor tables close two hours before closing time, whereafter the intimate interior is almost as good.

La Escalera de Jacob
COCKTAIL BAR, LIVE MUSIC

(Map p80; www.laescaleradejacob.es; Calle de Lavapiés 11; concerts from €6; ☺8pm-2am Wed & Thu, 8pm-2.30am Fri, 11am-2.30am Sat, 5pm-1am Sun; MAntón Martín, Tirso de Molina) As much a cocktail bar as a live-music venue or theatre, 'Jacob's Ladder' is one of Madrid's most original stages. Magicians, storytellers, children's theatre, live jazz and other genres are all part of the mix. This alternative slant on life makes for some terrific live performances, and regardless of what's on, it's worth stopping by here for its creative cocktails that you won't find anywhere else – the *fray aguacate* (Frangelico, vodka, honey, avocado and vanilla) should give you an idea of how far they go.

Bonanno
WINE BAR

(Map p78; ☎91 366 68 86; Plaza del Humilladero 4; ☺noon-2am; MLa Latina) If much of Madrid's nightlife starts too late for your liking, Bonanno could be for you. It made its name as a cocktail bar, but many people come here for the great wines and it's usually full of young professionals from early evening onwards. Be prepared to snuggle up close to those around you if you want a spot at the bar.

Café del Nuncio
BAR, CAFE

(Map p78; Calle de Segovia 9; ☺noon-2am Sun-Thu, noon-3am Fri & Sat; MLa Latina) Café del Nuncio straggles down a laneway to Calle de Segovia. You can drink on one of several cosy levels inside or, better still, in summer enjoy the outdoor seating that one local reviewer likened to a slice of Rome. By day it's an old-world cafe, but by night it's one of the best bars in the *barrio*.

La Inquilina
BAR

(www.lainquilina.es; Calle del Ave María 39; ☺7pm-3am Tue-Sat, 1pm-1am Sun; MLavapiés) One of our favourite bars in Lavapiés, La Inquilina has a cool-and-casual vibe and deep roots in the Lavapiés soil. Contemporary artworks by budding local artists adorn the walls and you can either gather around the bar or take a table out the back. It serves tapas for €1 until 10pm if your night is starting early.

Taberna Tempranillo   WINE BAR
(Map p78; Calle de la Cava Baja 38; ☺1-3.30pm & 8pm-midnight Tue-Sun, 8pm-midnight Mon; Ⓜ La Latina) You could come here for the tapas, but we recommend Taberna Tempranillo primarily for its wines, of which it has a selection that puts many Spanish bars to shame, and many are sold by the glass. It's not a late-night place, but it's always packed in the early evening and on Sundays after El Rastro.

HUERTAS & ATOCHA
Huertas comes into its own after dark and stays that way until close to sunrise. Bars are everywhere, from Sol down to the Paseo del Prado hinterland, but it's in Plaza de Santa Ana and along Calle de las Huertas that most of the action is concentrated.

[TOP CHOICE] **La Venencia**   BAR
(Map p80; Calle de Echegaray 7; ☺1-3.30pm & 7.30pm-1.30am; Ⓜ Sol) This is how sherry bars should be – old-world vibe, drinks poured straight from the dusty wooden barrels, and none of the frenetic activity for which Huertas is so famous. La Venencia is a *barrio* classic, with fine sherry from Sanlúcar and manzanilla from Jeréz, accompanied by a small selection of tapas with an Andalucian bent. Otherwise, there's no music, no flashy decorations; it's all about you, your *fino* (sherry) and your friends. As one reviewer put it, it's 'a classic among classics'.

El Imperfecto   BAR, LIVE MUSIC
(Map p80; Plaza de Matute 2; ☺3pm-2am Mon-Thu, 3pm-2.30am Fri & Sat; Ⓜ Antón Martín) Its name notwithstanding, the 'Imperfect One' is our ideal Huertas bar, with live jazz most Tuesdays at 9pm and a drinks menu as long as a saxophone, ranging from cocktails (€7) and spirits to milkshakes, teas and creative coffees. Its pina colada is one of the best we've tasted and the atmosphere is agreeably buzzy yet chilled.

The Penthouse   COCKTAIL BAR
(Map p80; ☎91 701 60 20; www.thepenthouse.es; Plaza de Santa Ana 14; admission €25; ☺9pm-3am Wed & Thu, 9pm-3.30am Fri & Sat; Ⓜ Antón Martín, Sol) High above the Plaza de Santa Ana, this sybaritic, open-air (7th floor) cocktail bar

has terrific views over Madrid's rooftops. The high admission price announces straight away that riff-raff are not welcome – this is a place for sophisticates, with chill-out areas strewn with cushions, funky DJs and a dress policy designed to sort out the classy from the wannabes. If you suffer from vertigo, consider the equally classy **Midnight Rose** on the ground floor.

Taberna Alhambra   BAR
(Map p80; www.tabernaalhambra.es; Calle de la Victoria 9; ☺11am-1.30am Sun-Wed, 11am-2am Thu, 11am-2.30am Fri & Sat; ✐; Ⓜ Sol) There can be a certain sameness about the bars between Sol and Huertas, which is why this fine old *taberna* (tavern) stands out. The striking facade and exquisite tile work of the interior are quite beautiful; however, this place is anything but stuffy and the feel is cool, casual and busy. It serves tapas and, later at night, there are some fine flamenco tunes.

Cervecería Alemana   BAR
(Map p80; Plaza de Santa Ana 6; ☺11am-12.30am Sun-Thu, 11am-2am Fri & Sat, closed Aug; Ⓜ Antón Martín, Sol) If you've only got time to stop at one bar on Plaza Santa Ana, let it be this classic *cervecería* (beer bar), renowned for its cold, frothy beers and a wider selection of Spanish beers than is the norm. It's fine inside, but snaffle a table outside in the plaza on a summer's evening and you won't be giving it up without a fight. This was one of Hemingway's haunts, and neither the wood-lined bar nor the bow-tied waiters have changed much since his day.

Viva Madrid   BAR
(Map p80; www.barvivamadrid.es; Calle de Manuel Fernández y González 7; ☺1pm-2am; Ⓜ Antón Martín, Sol) The tiled facade of Viva Madrid is one of Madrid's most recognisable and it's an essential landmark on the Huertas nightlife scene. It's packed to the rafters on weekends, and you come here in part for fine mojitos and also for the casual, friendly atmosphere. The recently improved tapas offerings are another reason to stop by.

MALASAÑA & CHUECA
Drinking in Malasaña and Chueca is like a journey through Madrid's multifaceted past. Around the Glorieta de Bilbao and along the Paseo de los Recoletos you encounter stately old literary cafes that revel in their grandeur and late-19th-century ambience. Throughout Malasaña, rockers nostalgic for the

hedonistic Madrid of the 1970s and 1980s will find ample bars to indulge their memories. At the same time, across both *barrios*, but especially in gay-focussed Chueca and away to the west in Conde Duque, modern Madrid is very much on show, with chill-out spaces and swanky, sophisticated cocktail bars.

TOP CHOICE Museo Chicote
COCKTAIL BAR

(Map p94; www.museo-chicote.com; Gran Vía 12; ⊘6pm-3am Mon-Thu, 6pm-4am Fri & Sat; MGran Vía) The founder of this Madrid landmark is said to have invented more than 100 cocktails, which the likes of Hemingway, Ava Gardner, Grace Kelly, Sophia Loren and Frank Sinatra have all enjoyed at one time or another. It's still frequented by film stars and top socialites, and it's at its best after midnight, when a lounge atmosphere takes over, couples cuddle on the curved benches and some of the city's best DJs do their stuff. The 1930s-era interior only adds to the cachet of this place. We don't say this often, but if you haven't been here, you haven't really been to Madrid – it's that much of an icon.

TOP CHOICE Café Comercial
CAFE

(Map p94; Glorieta de Bilbao 7; ⊘7.30am-midnight Mon-Thu, 7.30am-2am Fri, 8.30am-2am Sat, 9am-midnight Sun; MBilbao) This glorious old Madrid cafe proudly fights a rearguard action against progress with heavy leather seats, abundant marble and old-style waiters. Café Comercial, which dates back to 1887, is the largest of the *barrio's* old cafes and has changed little since those days, although the clientele has broadened to include just about anyone, from writers and their laptops to old men playing chess.

Splash Óscar
LOUNGE

(Map p94; Plaza de Vázquez de Mella 12; ⊘5pm-2am Mon-Thu, 4pm-3am Fri-Sun; MGran Vía) Occupying one of the stunning rooftop terraces (this one with a small swimming pool) atop Hotel Óscar (p106), this chilled space with gorgeous skyline views has become a cause célèbre among A-list celebrities.

El Jardín Secreto
BAR, CAFE

(Calle de Conde Duque 2; ⊘5.30pm-12.30am Sun-Thu, 6.30pm-2.30am Fri & Sat; MPlaza de España) 'The Secret Garden' is intimate and romantic in a *barrio* that's one of Madrid's best-kept secrets. Lit by Spanish designer candles, draped in organza from India and serving up chocolates from the Caribbean, El Jardín Secreto ranks among our favourite drinking corners in Conde Duque. They serve milkshakes, cocktails and everything in between. It's at its best on a summer's evening, but the atmosphere never misses a beat, with a loyal, young professional crowd.

Café Belén
BAR

(Map p94; Calle de Belén 5; ⊘3.30pm-3am; MChueca) Café Belén is cool in all the right places – lounge and chill-out music, dim lighting, a great range of drinks (the mojitos are especially good) and a low-key crowd that's the height of casual sophistication. In short, it's one of our favourite Chueca watering holes.

Lolina Vintage Café
CAFE

(Map p94; Calle del Espíritu Santo 9; ⊘9am-2.30am Mon-Fri, 10am-2.30am Sat, 11am-2.30am Sun; MTribunal) Lolina Vintage Café seems to have captured the essence of the *barrio* in one small space. With a studied retro look (comfy old-style chairs and sofas, gilded mirrors and 1970s-era wallpaper), it confirms that the new Malasaña is not unlike the old, but is a whole lot more sophisticated. It's low-key and full from breakfast to closing time, catering to every taste from salads to cocktails.

La Vía Láctea
BAR, CLUB

(Map p94; Calle de Velarde 18; ⊘9pm-3am; MTribunal) A living, breathing and delightfully grungy relic of *la movida,* La Vía Láctea remains a Malasaña favourite for a mixed, informal crowd that seems to live for the 1980s. The music ranges across rock, pop, garage, rockabilly and indie. There are plenty of drinks to choose from, and by late Saturday night anything goes. Expect long queues to get in on weekends.

Café-Restaurante El Espejo
CAFE

(Map p92; Paseo de los Recoletos 31; ⊘8am-midnight Sun-Thu, 10am-3am Fri & Sat; MColón) Once a haunt of writers and intellectuals, this architectural gem blends Modernista and art-deco styles, and its interior could well overwhelm you with all the mirrors, chandeliers and bow-tied service of another era. The atmosphere is suitably quiet and refined, although our favourite corner is the elegant glass pavilion out on the Paseo de los Recoletos, where the outdoor tables are hugely popular in summer.

Café Pepe Botella
CAFE, BAR

(Map p94; Calle de San Andrés 12; ☺10am-2am Mon-Thu, 10am-2.30am Fri & Sat, 11am-2am Sun; Ⓜ️Bilbao, Tribunal) Pepe Botella has hit on a fine formula for success. As good around midnight as it is in the afternoon when its wi-fi access draws the laptop-toting crowd, it's a classy bar with green velvet benches, marble-topped tables and old photos and mirrors covering the walls. The faded elegance gives the place the charm that has made it one of the most enduringly popular drinking holes in the *barrio*.

Areia
LOUNGE

(Map p94; www.areiachillout.com; Calle de Hortaleza 92; ☺1pm-3am; Ⓜ️Chueca, Alonso Martínez) The ultimate lounge bar by day (cushions, chill-out music and dark secluded corners, where you can hear yourself talk or even canoodle quietly), this place is equally enjoyable by night. That's when groovy DJs take over (from 11pm Sunday to Wednesday, and from 9pm the rest of the week) with deep and chill house, nu jazz, bossa and electronica. It's cool, funky and low-key all at once.

Gran Café de Gijón
CAFE

(Map p92; www.cafegijon.com; Paseo de los Recoletos 21; ☺7am-1.30am; Ⓜ️Chueca, Banco de España) This graceful old cafe has been serving coffee and meals since 1888 and has long been a favourite with Madrid's literati for a drink or a meal – *all* of Spain's great 20th-century literary figures came here for coffee and *tertulias* (literary discussions). You'll find yourself among intellectuals, conservative Franco diehards and young *madrileños* looking for a quiet drink.

Ojalá Awareness Club
LOUNGE

(Map p94; Calle de San Andrés 1; ☺8.30am-1am Sun-Wed, 8.30am-2am Thu-Sat; Ⓜ️Tribunal) From the people who brought you La Musa (p112), Ojalá is every bit as funky and has a lot more space to enjoy. Yes, you eat well here, but we love it first and foremost for a drink (especially a daiquiri) at any time of day. Its lime-green colour scheme, zany lighting and hip, cafe-style ambience make it an extremely cool place to hang out, but the sandy floor and cushions downstairs take chilled to a whole new level.

Café Manuela
CAFE

(Map p94; Calle de San Vicente Ferrer 29; ☺9am-2am Mon-Fri, 10am-3am Sat, 10am-2am Sun; Ⓜ️Tribunal) Stumbling into this graciously

---

CHUECA COCKTAIL BARS

Chueca has Madrid's richest concentration of sophisticated cocktail bars beloved by the city's A-list celebrities. In addition to Museo Chicote, there's **Del Diego** (Map p94; ☑91 523 31 06; Calle de la Reina 12; ☺7pm-3am Mon-Thu, 7pm-3.30am Fri & Sat; Ⓜ️Gran Vía), where the decor blends old-world-cafe with New York style and there are 75 cocktails to choose from. Other places we highly recommend include old-world **Bar Cock** (Map p94; ☑91 532 28 26; www.barcock.com; Calle de la Reina 16; ☺8pm-3am; Ⓜ️Gran Vía), achingly chic **Le Cabrera** (Map p94; ☑91 319 94 57; www.lecabrera.com; Calle de Bárbara de Braganza 2; ☺4pm-2.30am Mon-Fri, 1pm-2.30am Sat; Ⓜ️Colón, Alonso Martínez) and **Stromboli** (Map p94; ☑91 319 46 28; Calle de Hortaleza 96; ☺9pm-3am Wed & Thu, 9pm-3.30am Fri & Sat; Ⓜ️Chueca, Tribunal).

---

restored throwback to the 1950s along one of Malasaña's grittier streets is akin to discovering hidden treasure. There's a luminous quality to it when you come in out of the night and, like so many Madrid cafes, it's a surprisingly multifaceted space, serving cocktails, delicious milkshakes and offering board games atop the marble tables in the unlikely event that you get bored.

☆ Entertainment

All of the publications and websites in the following list provide comprehensive and updated listings of what's showing at Madrid's various theatres, cinemas and concert halls:

EsMadrid Magazine (www.esmadrid.com) Monthly tourist-office listings for concerts and other performances; available at tourist offices, some hotels and online.

Guía del Ocio (www.guiadelocio.com) Spanish-only weekly magazine available for €1 at news kiosks.

In Madrid (www.in-madrid.com) Monthly English-language expat publication given out free (check the website for locations) with lots of information about what to see and do in town.

La Netro (http://madrid.lanetro.com) Comprehensive online guide to Madrid events.

LA MOVIDA MADRILEÑA

Anyone who went wild when they first moved out of their parents' house can identify with *la movida madrileña* (literally, 'the Madrid scene'). After the long, dark years of dictatorship and conservative Catholicism, Spaniards, especially *madrileños*, emerged onto the streets in the late 1970s with all the zeal of ex-convent schoolgirls. Nothing was taboo as *madrileños* discovered the '60s, '70s and early '80s all at once. Drinking, drugs and sex suddenly were OK. All-night partying was the norm, cannabis was virtually legalised and the city howled.

La movida was presided over by Enrique Tierno Galván, an ageing former university professor who had been a leading opposition figure under Franco and was affectionately known throughout Spain as 'the old teacher'. A socialist, he became mayor of Madrid in 1979 and, for many, launched *la movida* by telling a public gathering 'a colocarse y ponerse al loro', which loosely translates as 'get stoned and do what's cool'. Not surprisingly, he was Madrid's most popular mayor ever. When he died in 1986, a million *madrileños* turned out for his funeral.

But *la movida* was not just about rediscovering the Spanish art of *salir de copas* (going out to drink). It was also accompanied by an explosion of creativity among the country's musicians, designers and film-makers.

The most famous of these was film director Pedro Almodóvar. Still one of Europe's most creative directors, his riotously colourful films captured the spirit of *la movida*, featuring larger-than-life characters who pushed the limits of sex and drugs. When he wasn't making films, Almodóvar immersed himself in the spirit of *la movida*, doing drag acts in smoky bars. Among the other names from *la movida* that still resonate, the designer Agatha Ruiz de la Prada stands out. And start playing anything by Alaska, Los Rebeldes, Radio Futura or Nacha Pop and watch *madrileños'* eyes glaze over with nostalgia.

Metropoli (www.elmundo.es/metropoli) *El Mundo's* Friday supplement magazine has information on the week's offerings.

On Madrid (www.elpais.com) *El País* also has a Friday supplement with weekly listings.

What's on When (www.whatsonwhen.com) The Madrid page covers the highlights of sport and cultural activities, with information on getting tickets.

Nightclubs

No *barrio* in Madrid is without a decent club or disco, but the most popular dance spots are in the centre. Don't expect the dance clubs or *discotecas* to really get going until after 1am, and some won't even bat an eyelid until 3am, when the bars elsewhere have closed.

Club prices vary widely, depending on the time of night you enter, the way you're dressed and the number of people inside. The standard admission fee is €12, which usually includes the first drink, although megaclubs and swankier places charge a few euros more. Even those that let you in free will play catch-up with hefty prices

for drinks, so don't plan your night around looking for the cheapest ticket.

LOS AUSTRIAS, SOL & CENTRO

Teatro Joy Eslava CLUB
(Joy Madrid; Map p72; ☎91 366 37 33; www.joy-eslava.com; Calle del Arenal 11; admission €12-15; ☉11.30pm-6am; MSol) The only things guaranteed at this grand old Madrid dance club (housed in a 19th-century theatre) are a crowd and the fact that it'll be open (it claims to have operated every single day for the past 29 years). 'Loco Monday' kicks off the week in spectacular fashion, Thursday is student night, Friday's 'Fabulush' is all about glamour and there's even the no-alcohol, no-smoking 'Joy Light' on Saturday evenings (5.30pm to 10pm) for those aged between 14 and 17. Throw in occasional live acts and cabaret-style performances on stage and it's a point of reference for Madrid's professional party crowd.

Cool CLUB
(Map p94; ☎91 733 35 05; www.fsmgroup.es; Calle de Isabel la Católica 6; admission from €10; ☉midnight-6am Thu-Sat; MSanto Domingo) Cool by name, cool by nature. One of the hottest clubs in the city, the Phillipe Starck–designed

curvy white lines, discreet lounge chairs in dark corners and pulsating dance floor here are accompanied by gorgeous people, gorgeous clothes and a strict entry policy. Saturdays draw a predominantly gay clientele, but whatever the night, the sexy, well-heeled crowd includes a lot of sleek-looking gay men and model-like women.

Charada
CLUB

(Map p72; www.charadaclubdebaile.com; Calle de la Bola 13; admission €12; ⊘midnight-6am Thu-Sun; MSanto Domingo) Charada took the Madrid nightlife scene by storm in 2009 and has since settled back into a reliable regular on the Madrid clubbing scene. Its two rooms (one red, one black) are New York chic (with no hint of the building's former existence as a brothel). The cocktails are original, the clientele is well heeled and often famous, and it's the home turntable for some of the best DJs in town. We especially like it when they turn their attention to indie dance and electronica.

HUERTAS & ATOCHA

Kapital
CLUB

(☑91 420 29 06; www.grupo-kapital.com; Calle de Atocha 125; admission from €10; ⊘5.30-10.30pm & midnight-6am Fri & Sat, midnight-6am Thu & Sun; MAtocha) One of the most famous megaclubs in Madrid, this massive, seven-storey nightclub has something for everyone: from cocktail bars and dance music to karaoke, salsa, hip hop and more chilled spaces for R&B and soul, as well as an area devoted to 'Made in Spain' music. It's such a big place that a cross section of Madrid society (VIPs and the Real Madrid set love this place) hangs out here without ever getting in each other's way.

Stella
CLUB

(Map p80; ☑91 531 63 78; www.web-mondo.com; Calle de Arlabán 7; admission €12; ⊘12.30-6am Thu-Sat; MSevilla) One of the enduring success stories of the Madrid night, Stella is one of the city's best nightclubs. If you arrive here after 3am, there simply won't be room and those inside have no intention of leaving until dawn. The DJs here are some of Madrid's best and the great visuals will leave you cross-eyed if you weren't already from the music in this heady place. Thursday and Saturday nights ('Mondo', for electronica) rely on resident and invited DJs, while Friday nights are more house-oriented.

SALAMANCA

Serrano 41
CLUB

(Map p92; ☑91 578 18 65; www.serrano41.com; Calle de Serrano 41; admission €10; ⊘11pm-5.30am Wed-Sun; MSerrano) If bullfighters, Real Madrid stars and other A-listers can't drag themselves away from Salamanca, chances are that you'll find them here. Danceable pop and house dominate the most popular Friday and Saturday nights, funk gets a turn on Sunday, and it's indie night on Thursday. As you'd imagine, the door policy is stricter than most. Its outdoor terrace opens in late May and is *very* cool thereafter.

MALASAÑA & CHUECA

Morocco
CLUB

(Map p94; ☑91 531 51 67; www.morocco-madrid.com; Calle del Marqués de Leganés 7; admission €10; ⊘midnight-6am Fri & Sat; MSanto Domingo or Noviciado) Owned by the zany Alaska, the standout musical personality of *la movida*, Morocco has decor that's so kitsch it's cool, and a mix of musical styles that never strays too far from 1980s Spanish and international tunes, with electronica another recurring theme. The bouncers have been known to show a bit of attitude, but then that kind of comes with the profession. We've heard it said that they need to turn the volume up, but we doubt that the neighbours agree.

Nasti Club
CLUB, LIVE MUSIC

(Map p94; ☑91 521 76 05; www.nasti.es; Calle de San Vicente Ferrer 33; admission free-€10; ⊘10pm-6am Thu-Sat; MTribunal) It's hard to think of a more off-putting entrance than Nasti Club's graffiti and abandoned-building look. You also won't find the name outside – if you want to come here, you're supposed to know where to find it. Indie rock and post-punk are the mainstays. But it's not as nasty as it sounds and the crowd can span the full range of 1970s throwbacks from a who's who of Madrid's underground to some surprisingly respectable types. Above all it's a place with attitude and, as their own publicity says, they're *not* from Barcelona, they *don't* play electronica, people who come here *are* cool and no one's ever heard of the live acts who appear here until they become famous two years later. Says it all really. Very Malasaña.

Tupperware
BAR, CLUB

(Map p94; ☑91 446 42 04; Calle de la Corredera Alta de San Pablo 26; ⊘8pm-3.30am Tue-Sat; MTribunal) A Malasaña stalwart and prime candidate for the bar that best catches the enduring *rockero* spirit of Malasaña, Tupperware draws a 30-something crowd, spins indie rock with a bit of soul and classics from the '60s and '70s, and generally revels in kitsch (eyeballs stuck to the ceiling, and plastic TVs with action-figure dioramas lined up behind the bar). It can get pretty packed on a weekend after 1am. By the way, locals pronounce it 'Tupper-warry'.

Cinemas

Cine Doré
CINEMA

(Map p80; ☎91 369 11 25; www.mcu.es/cine/MC/FE/CineDore/Programacion; Calle de Santa Isabel 3; tickets €2.50; ☉Tue-Sun; MAntón Martín) The National Film Library offers fantastic classic and vanguard films.

Cinesa Proyecciones
CINEMA

(☎902 333231; www.cinesa.es; Calle de Fuencarral 136; tickets €8; MBilbao, Quevedo) Wonderful art-deco exterior; modern cinema within.

Cines Princesa
CINEMA

(☎902 229122, 91 541 41 00; www.cinesrenoir.com; Calle de Princesa 3; from €7.50; MPlaza de España) Screens all kinds of original-version films, from Hollywood blockbusters to arty flicks.

Yelmo Cineplex Ideal
CINEMA

(Map p72; ☎902 220922; www.yelmocines.es; Calle del Doctor Cortezo 6; tickets €8; MSol, Tirso de Molina) Close to Plaza Mayor; offers a wide selection of films.

Theatre & Dance

Madrid's theatre scene is a year-round affair. Most shows are in Spanish, but those who don't speak the language may still enjoy musicals or *zarzuela,* Spain's own singing and dancing version of musical theatre. Tickets for all shows start at around €10 and run up to around €50.

Compañía Nacional de Danza
DANCE

(☎91 354 50 53; www.cndanza.net) Under director José Carlos Martínez, this dynamic company performs worldwide and has won accolades for its innovation, marvellous technicality and style. The company, made up mostly of international dancers, performs original, contemporary pieces and is considered a leading player on the international dance scene.

Ballet Nacional de España
DANCE

(☎91 517 99 99; http://balletnacional.mcu.es) A classical company that's known for its unique mix of ballet and traditional Spanish styles, such as flamenco and *zarzuela.*

When in Madrid, it's usually on stage at the Teatro Real or the Teatro de la Zarzuela.

Teatro de la Zarzuela
THEATRE

(Map p80; ☎91 524 54 00; http://teatrodelazarzuela.mcu.es; Calle de Jovellanos 4; tickets €5-42; ☉box office noon-6pm Mon-Fri, 3-6pm Sat & Sun; MBanco de España) This theatre, built in 1856, is the premier place to see *zarzuela*. It also hosts a smattering of classical music and opera performances, as well as the cutting-edge Compañía Nacional de Danza.

Teatro Español
THEATRE

(Map p80; ☎91 360 14 84; www.teatroespanol.es; Calle del Príncipe 25; MSevilla, Sol, Antón Martín) This theatre, which fronts onto the Plaza de Santa Ana, has been here in one form or another since the 16th century and is still one of the best places to catch mainstream Spanish drama, from the works of Lope de Vega to more recent playwrights.

Teatros del Canal
THEATRE

(☎91 308 99 99; www.teatrosdelcanal.org; Calle de Cea Bermúdez 1; MCanal) A state-of-the-art theatre complex opened in 2009, Teatros del Canal hosts major theatre performances, as well as musical and dance concerts. It also runs numerous concerts during the Suma Flamenca (p102) festival in June.

Live Music
FLAMENCO

Madrid may not be the spiritual home of flamenco, and its big names may feel more at home in the atmospheric flamenco taverns of Andalucía, but Madrid remains one of Spain's premier flamenco stages.

Seeing flamenco in Madrid is, with some worthy exceptions, expensive – at the *tablaos* (restaurants where flamenco is performed) expect to pay €25 to €35 just to see the show. The admission price usually includes your first drink, but you pay extra for meals that, put simply, are rarely worth the money (up to €50 per person). For that reason, we suggest you eat elsewhere and simply pay for the show (after having bought tickets in advance), albeit on the understanding that you won't have a front-row seat. The other important thing to remember is that most of these shows are geared towards tourists. That's not to say that the quality isn't often top-notch. On the contrary, often it's magnificent, spine-tingling stuff. It's just that they sometimes lack the genuine, raw emotion of real flamenco.

GAY & LESBIAN MADRID

Madrid is one of Europe's most gay-friendly cities. The heartbeat of gay Madrid is the inner-city *barrio* of Chueca, where Madrid didn't just come out of the closet, but ripped the doors off in the process. But even here the crowd is almost always mixed gay/straight. The best time of all to be in town if you're gay or lesbian is around the last Saturday in June, for Madrid's gay and lesbian pride march, Día del Orgullo de Gays, Lesbianas y Transexuales (p102).

Chueca has an abundance of gay-friendly bars, restaurants and shops. **Librería Berkana** (Map p94; ☎91 522 55 99; www.libreriaberkana.com; Calle de Hortaleza 64; ☉10.30am-9pm Mon-Fri, 11.30am-9pm Sat, noon-2pm & 5-9pm Sun; ⓂChueca) operates like an unofficial information centre for gay Madrid; here you'll find the biweekly *Shanguide*, jammed with listings and contact ads, as well as books, magazines and videos. **A Different Life** (Map p94; ☎91 532 96 52; www.adifferentlife.es; Calle de Pelayo 30; ☉11am-10pm Mon-Fri, 11am-midnight Sat, 11am-3pm & 5-10pm Sun; ⓂChueca) is another bookshop geared towards gays and lesbians.

Another good place to get the low-down on gay Madrid is the laid-back **Mamá Inés** (Map p94; www.mamaines.com; Calle de Hortaleza 22; ☉10am-2am Sun-Thu, 10am-3am Fri & Sat, ⓂChueca), a cafe where you'll hear the word on where that night's hotspot will be. **Café Acuarela** (Map p94; www.cafeacuarela.es; ⓂChueca) is a dimly lit centrepiece of gay Madrid – a huge statue of a nude male angel guards the doorway. Also good for a low-key night out is the sophisticated **Café La Troje** (Map p94; Calle de Pelayo 26; ☉2pm-2am; ⓂChueca).

Two of the most popular Chueca nightspots are **Club 54 Studio** (Map p94; www.studio54madrid.com; Calle de Barbieri 7; ☉11.30am-3.30am Wed-Sat; ⓂChueca), which is modelled on the famous New York club Studio 54, and **Liquid Madrid** (Map p94; www.liquid.es; ☉9pm-3am Mon-Thu, 9pm-3.30am Fri & Sat; ⓂChueca). For something that stays open later, **Why Not?** (Map p94; www.whynotmadrid.com; Calle de San Bartolomé 7; admission €10; ☉10.30pm-6am; ⓂChueca) is the sort of place where nothing's left to the imagination (the gay and straight crowd who come here are pretty amorous) and it's full nearly every night of the week. Pop and top-40s music are the standards here.

Other clubs popular with a predominantly gay crowd include **Sala Bash/Ohm** (Map p94; www.ohmclub.es; Plaza del Callao 4; admission €12; ☉midnight-6am Thu-Sun; ⓂCallao), **Black & White** (Map p94; www.discoblack-white.net; Calle de la Libertad 34; ☉10pm-5.30am Sun-Thu, 10pm-6am Fri & Sat; ⓂChueca) and Saturday nights at Cool (p118).

For a place to rest your head, look no further than the excellent Hostal La Zona (p106), which has a mainly gay clientele.

Corral de la Morería FLAMENCO
(Map p78; ☎91 365 84 46; www.corraldelamoreria.com; Calle de la Morería 17; admission incl drink €42-45; ☉8.30pm-2.30am, shows 9.30pm & 11.30pm Sun-Fri, 7pm, 10pm & midnight Sat; ⓂÓpera) This is one of the most prestigious flamenco stages in Madrid, with 50 years' experience as a leading flamenco venue and top performers most nights. The stage area has a rustic feel, and tables are pushed up close. We'd steer clear of the restaurant, which is overpriced (from €43), but the performances have a far better price:quality ratio. This is where international celebrities (Marlene Dietrich, Marlon Brando, Muhammad Ali, Omar Sharif) have all gone for their flamenco fix when in town.

Las Carboneras FLAMENCO
(Map p72; ☎91 542 86 77; www.tablaolascarboneras.com; Plaza del Conde de Miranda 1; admission €30; ☉shows 8.30pm & 10.30pm Mon-Thu, 8.30pm & 11pm Fri & Sat; ⓂÓpera, Sol, La Latina) Like most of the *tablaos* around town, this place sees far more tourists than locals, but the quality is nonetheless unimpeachable. It's not the place for gritty, soul-moving spontaneity, but it's still an excellent introduction and one of the few places that flamenco aficionados seem to have no complaints about.

Las Tablas FLAMENCO
(Map p72; ☎91 542 05 20; www.lastablasmadrid.com; Plaza de España 9; admission €26; ☉shows 10.30pm Sun-Thu, 8pm & 10pm Fri & Sat; ⓂPlaza de

España) Las Tablas has a reputation for quality flamenco and reasonable prices; it could just be the best choice in town. Most nights you'll see a classic flamenco show, with plenty of throaty singing and soul-baring dancing. Antonia Moya and Marisol Navarro, leading lights in the flamenco world, are regular performers here.

Casa Patas
FLAMENCO

(Map p80; ☎91 369 04 96; www.casapatas.com; Calle de Cañizares 10; admission €32; ◎shows 10.30pm Mon-Thu, 9pm & midnight Fri & Sat; ⓂAntón Martín, Tirso de Molina) One of the top flamenco stages in Madrid, this *tablao* offers flawless quality and serves as a good introduction to the art. It's not the friendliest place in town, especially if you're only here for the show, and you're likely to be crammed in a little, but no one complains about the standard of the performances.

Villa Rosa
FLAMENCO

(Map p80; ☎91 521 36 89; Plaza de Santa Ana 15; admission €17; ◎shows 8.30pm & 10.45pm Sun-Thu, 8.30pm, 10.45pm & 12.15am Fri & Sat; ⓂSol) The extraordinary tiled facade (the 1928 work of Alfonso Romero, who was responsible for the tile work in Madrid's Plaza de Toros) of this long-standing nightclub is a tourist attraction in itself; the club even appeared in the Pedro Almodóvar film *Tacones lejanos* (High Heels; 1991). It's been going strong since 1914 and has seen many manifestations – it made its name as a flamenco venue and it has recently returned to its roots with well-priced shows and meals that won't break the bank.

CLASSICAL MUSIC & OPERA

Auditorio Nacional de Música
CLASSICAL MUSIC

(☎91 337 01 40; www.auditorionacional.mcu.es; Calle del Príncipe de Vergara 146; ⓂCruz del Rayo) When it's not playing the Teatro Real, Madrid's venerable Orquesta Sinfonía plays at this modern venue, which also attracts famous conductors from across the world to its two concert halls. It's usually fairly easy to get your hands on tickets at the box office. It's north of the Salamanca neighbourhood, 1km beyond Calle del Príncipe de Vergara's intersection with Avenida de América.

Teatro Real
OPERA, CLASSICAL MUSIC

(Map p72; ☎902 24 48 48; www.teatro-real.com; Plaza de Oriente; ⓂÓpera) After spending €100 million-plus on a long rebuilding project, the Teatro Real is as technologically advanced as any venue in Europe, and is the city's grandest stage for elaborate operas, ballets and classical music. You'll pay as little as €6 for a spot so far away you'll need a telescope, although the sound quality is consistent throughout. For the best seats, don't expect change from €127.

JAZZ

⊤OP CHOICE Café Central
JAZZ

(Map p80; ☎91 369 41 43; www.cafecentralmadrid.com; Plaza del Ángel 10; admission €10-15; ◎1.30pm-2.30am Sun-Thu, 1.30pm-3.30am Fri & Sat; ⓂAntón Martín, Sol) In 2011, the respected jazz magazine *Down Beat* included this art-deco bar on the list of the world's best jazz clubs, the only place in Spain to earn the prestigious accolade (said by some to be the jazz equivalent of earning a Michelin star) and with well over 9000 gigs under its belt, it rarely misses a beat. Big international names like Chano Domínguez, Tal Farlow and Wynton Marsalis have all played here, and you'll hear everything from Latin jazz and fusion to tango and classical jazz. Performers usually play here for a week and then move on, so getting tickets shouldn't be a problem (except on weekends). Shows start at 10pm and tickets go on sale an hour before the set starts.

Populart
JAZZ

(Map p80; ☎91 429 84 07; www.populart.es; Calle de las Huertas 22; admission free; ◎6pm-2.30am Sun-Thu, 6pm-3.30am Fri & Sat; ⓂAntón Martín, Sol) One of Madrid's classic jazz clubs, this place offers a low-key atmosphere and top-quality music, which is mostly jazz with occasional blues, swing and even flamenco thrown into the mix. Compay Segundo, Sonny Fortune and the Canal Street Jazz Band have all played here. Shows start at 10.45pm but, if you want a seat, get here early.

El Berlín Jazz Café
JAZZ

(Map p94; ☎91 521 57 52; www.berlincafe.es; Calle de Jacometrezo 4; admission €8; ◎7pm-2.30am Tue-Sun Sep-Jul; ⚧; ⓂCallao, Santo Domingo) El Berlín has been something of a Madrid jazz stalwart since the 1950s and it's the kind of place that serious jazz fans rave about as the most authentic in town – it's all about classic jazz here, with none of the fusion performances that you find elsewhere. The art-deco interior ads to the charm and the headline acts are a who's who of world jazz; in the past Al Foster (Miles Davis' drummer), Santiago de Muela and the Calento

Jazz Orchestra have all taken to the stage. Headline acts play at 11.30pm on Fridays and Saturdays, with other performances sprinkled throughout the week, including a Tuesday jam session.

El Junco Jazz Club

JAZZ, CLUB

(Map p94; ☑91 319 20 81; www.eljunco.com; Plaza de Santa Bárbara 10; concerts €6-10; ⊙8pm-3.30pm Mon, 8pm-6am Tue-Fri, 11pm-6am Sat & Sun, concerts 11pm Tue-Sun; MAlonso Martínez) El Junco has established itself on the Madrid nightlife scene by appealing as much to jazz aficionados as to clubbers. Its secret is high-quality live jazz gigs from Spain and around the world, followed by DJs spinning funk, soul, nu jazz, blues and innovative groove beats. There are also jam sessions at 11pm in jazz (Tuesday) and blues (Sunday). The emphasis is on music from the American South and the crowd is classy and casual.

OTHER LIVE MUSIC

Costello Café & Niteclub

LIVE MUSIC

(Map p72; www.costelloclub.com; Calle del Caballero de Gracia 10; admission €5-10; ⊙6pm-1am Sun-Wed, 6pm-2.30am Thu-Sat; MGran Vía) Very cool. Costello Café & Niteclub is smooth-as-silk ambience wedded with an innovative mix of pop, rock and fusion in Warholesque surrounds. There's live music at 9.30pm every night except Sundays, with resident and visiting DJs keeping you on your feet until closing time from Thursday to Saturday. Our only complaint is that it closes earlier than we'd like.

Sala El Sol

LIVE MUSIC

(Map p72; ☑91 532 64 90; www.elsolmad.com; Calle de los Jardines 3; admission €8-25; ⊙11pm-5.30am Tue-Sat Jul-Sep; MGran Vía) Madrid institutions don't come any more beloved than Sala El Sol. It opened in 1979, just in time for *la movida,* and quickly established itself as a leading stage for all the icons of the era. *La movida* may have faded into history, but it lives on at El Sol, where the music rocks and rolls and usually resurrects the '70s and '80s, while soul and funk also get a run. It's a terrific venue and although most concerts start at 11pm and despite the official opening hours, some acts take to the stage as early as 10pm. After the show, DJs spin rock, fusion and electronica from the awesome sound system. Check the website (which also allows you to book online) for upcoming acts.

ContraClub

LIVE MUSIC

(Map p78; ☑91 365 55 45; www.contraclub.es; Calle de Bailén 16; admission €6-12; ⊙10pm-6am Wed-Sat; MLa Latina) ContraClub is a crossover live-music venue and nightclub, with live flamenco on Wednesday and an eclectic mix of other live music (jazz, blues, world music and rock) from Thursday to Saturday. After the live acts (which start at 10.30pm), the resident DJs serve up equally eclectic beats (indie, pop, funk and soul) to make sure you don't move elsewhere.

Café La Palma

LIVE MUSIC

(Map p94; ☑91 522 50 31; www.cafelapalma. com; Calle de la Palma 62; admission free-€12; ⊙4.30pm-3am; MNoviciado) It's amazing how much variety Café La Palma has packed into its labyrinth of rooms. Live shows featuring hot local bands are held at the back, while DJs mix it up at the front. Some rooms have a cafe style, while others evoke an Arab tea room, pillows on the floor and all. There are always two shows – at 10pm and midnight – from Thursday to Saturday, but you might find live music other nights as well.

Clamores

LIVE MUSIC

(☑91 445 79 38; www.clamores.es; Calle de Alburquerque 14; admission €5-15; ⊙6pm-3am; MBilbao) Clamores is a one-time classic jazz cafe that has morphed into one of the most diverse music stages in Madrid – it's been going for three decades and hasn't changed the decor once, we're pleased to say. Jazz is still a staple, but world music, flamenco, soul fusion, singer-songwriter, pop and rock all make regular appearances. Live shows can begin as early as 7pm on weekends, but sometimes really only get going after 1am. It's in the neighbourhood of Chamberí, just off Calle de Trafalgar.

Honky Tonk

LIVE MUSIC

(☑91 445 61 91; www.clubhonky.com; Calle de Covarrubias 24; admission free; ⊙9pm-5am; MAlonso Martínez) Despite the name, this is a great place to see blues or local rock 'n' roll, though many acts have a little country, jazz or R&B thrown into the mix. It's a fun vibe in a smallish club that's been around since the heady 1980s and opens 365 days a year. It's a reliable late-night option, and the range of malt whiskies is impressive.

La Boca del Lobo

LIVE MUSIC

(Map p80; ☑91 429 70 13; www.labocadellobo.com; Calle de Echegaray 11; admission free-€10; ⊙9pm-3.30am; MSol, Sevilla) Known for offering

BULLFIGHTING

From the Fiesta de San Isidro (p102) in mid-May until the end of October, Spain's top bullfighters come to swing their capes at Plaza de Toros Monumental de Las Ventas (p90), one of the largest rings in the bullfighting world. During the six weeks of the fiesta's main bullfighting season that begins with the Fiesta de San Isidro, there are *corridas* (bullfights) almost every day.

Although bullfighting's popularity is waning in Madrid and the average age of paying spectators is increasing with each passing year, the bullfights during Fiesta de San Isidro remain hugely popular, particularly with celebrities wanting to be seen. And don't mistake the sport's falling popularity with any likelihood of Madrid following the lead of Barcelona and banning bullfights – Madrid remains one of Spain's most important bastions of this enduring and controversial Spanish tradition. For a more in-depth discussion of bullfighting, turn to p847.

mostly rock and alternative concerts, La Boca del Lobo (The Wolf's Mouth) is as dark as its name suggests and has broadened its horizons to include just about anything – roots, reggae, jazz, soul, ska, flamenco, funk and fusion. Amid all the variety are some mainstays – Wednesdays at 11pm are set aside for a roots-and-groove jam session, for example. Concerts start between 9.30pm and 11pm (check the website) Wednesday to Saturday, then DJs take over until closing time.

Sport
FOOTBALL

Estadio Santiago Bernabéu   FOOTBALL
(☎902 291709, 91 398 43 00; www.realmadrid.com; Avenida de Concha Espina 1; tour adult/child €16/11; ☺10am-7pm Mon-Sat, 10.30am-6.30pm Sun, except match days; ⓂSantiago Bernabéu) The home of **Real Madrid**, Estadio Santiago Bernabéu is a temple to football and is one of the world's great sporting arenas; watching a game here is akin to a pilgrimage for sports fans. When the players strut their stuff with 80,000 passionate *madrileños* in attendance, you'll get chills down your spine. If you're fortunate enough to be in town when Real Madrid wins a major trophy, head to Plaza de la Cibeles and wait for the all-night party to begin.

For a self-guided *tour* of the stadium, buy your ticket at ticket window 10 (next to gate 7). The tour takes you through the extraordinary Exposición de Trofeos (Trophy Exhibit), the presidential box, the press room, dressing rooms and the players' tunnel, and even onto the pitch itself. On match days, tours cease five hours before the game is scheduled to start, although the Exposición de Trofeos is open until two hours before game time.

Tickets for matches start at around €40 and run up to the rafters for major matches. Unless you book through a ticket agency, turn up at the ticket office at gate 42 on Avenida de Concha Espina early in the week before a scheduled game. Tickets can also be bought online at www.realmadrid.com, while the all-important telephone number for booking tickets (which you later pick up at gate 42) is 902 324324, which only works if you're calling from within Spain.

The stadium is north of the city, along the Paseo de la Castellana, around 3.5km north of the Plaza de la Cibeles.

🔒 Shopping

Eager to change your look to blend in with the casual-but-sophisticated Spanish crowd? Tired of bull postcards and tacky flamenco posters? Convinced that your discerning friends back home have taste that extends beyond polka-dot flamenco dresses? In Madrid, you'll find it all. This is a fantastic city in which to shop and *madrileños* are some of the finest exponents of the art.

The peak shopping season is during *las rebajas,* the annual winter and summer sales period when prices are slashed on just about everything. The winter sales begin around 7 January, just after Three Kings' Day, and last well into February. Summer sales begin in early July and last into August.

All shops may (and many usually do) open on the first Sunday of every month and throughout December.

LOS AUSTRIAS, SOL & CENTRO
Antigua Casa Talavera   CERAMICS
(Map p72; Calle de Isabel la Católica 2; ☺10am-1.30pm & 5-8pm Mon-Fri, 10am-1.30pm Sat; ✳; ⓂSanto Do-

mingo) The extraordinary tiled façade of this wonderful old shop conceals an Aladdin's cave of ceramics from all over Spain. This is not the mass-produced stuff aimed at a tourist market, but comes from the small family potters of Andalucía and Toledo, ranging from the decorative (tiles) to the useful (plates, jugs and other kitchen items). The old couple who run the place are delightful.

El Arco Artesanía
HANDICRAFTS
(Map p72; www.artesaniaelarco.com; Plaza Mayor 9; ⊙11am-9pm; Ⓜ Sol, La Latina) This original shop in the southwestern corner of Plaza Mayor sells an outstanding array of home-made designer souvenirs, from stone and glass work to jewellery and home fittings. The papier mâché figures are gorgeous, but there's so much else here to turn your head.

El Flamenco Vive
FLAMENCO
(Map p72; www.elflamencovive.es; Calle Conde de Lemos 7; ⊙10.30am-2pm & 5-9pm Mon-Sat; Ⓜ Ópera) This temple to flamenco has it all, from guitars and songbooks to well-priced CDs, polka-dotted dancing costumes, shoes, colourful plastic jewellery and literature about flamenco. It's the sort of place that will appeal as much to curious first timers as to serious students of the art. It also organises classes in flamenco guitar.

Casa de Diego
ACCESSORIES
(Map p72; www.casadediego.com; Plaza de la Puerta del Sol 12; ⊙9.30am-8pm Mon-Sat; Ⓜ Sol) This classic shop has been around since 1858, making, selling and repairing Spanish fans, shawls, umbrellas and canes. Service is old style and occasionally grumpy, but the fans are works of antique art. There's another branch (Map p72; ☎91 531 02 23; www.casadediego.com; Calle del los Mesoneros Romanos 4; ⊙9.30am-1.30pm & 4.45-8pm Mon-Sat; Ⓜ Callao, Sol) nearby.

Salvador Bachiller
ACCESSORIES
(Map p94; www.salvadorbachiller.com; Gran Vía 65; ⊙10am-9.30pm Mon-Sat, 11am-9pm Sun; Ⓜ Plaza de España, Santo Domingo) The stylish and high-quality leather bags, wallets, suitcases and other accessories of Salvador Bachiller are a staple of Spanish shopping aficionados. This is leather with a typically Spanish twist – the colours are dazzling in bright pinks, yellows and greens. Sound garish? You'll change your mind once you step inside. It also has an outlet (Map p94; ☎91 523 30 37; Calle de Gravina 11; ⊙10.30am-9.30pm Mon-Thu, 10.30am-11pm Fri & Sat, noon-9pm Sun; Ⓜ Chueca) in Chueca for superseded stock.

Casa Hernanz
SHOES
(Map p72; Calle de Toledo 18; ⊙9am-1.30pm & 4.30-8pm Mon-Fri, 10am-2pm Sat; Ⓜ La Latina, Sol) Comfy, rope-soled *alpargatas* (espadrilles), Spain's traditional summer footwear, are worn by everyone from the King of Spain down, and you can buy your own pair at this humble workshop, which has been hand-making the shoes for five generations; you can even get them made to order. Prices range from €5 to €40 and queues form whenever the weather starts to warm up.

Maty
FLAMENCO
(Map p72; ☎91 531 32 91; Calle del Maestro Victoria 2; ⊙10am-1.45pm & 4.30-8pm Mon-Fri, 10am-2pm & 4.30-8pm Sat; Ⓜ Sol) Wandering around central Madrid, it's easy to imagine that flamenco outfits have been reduced to imitation dresses sold as souvenirs to tourists. That's why places like Maty matter. Here you'll find dresses, shoes and all the accessories that go with the genre, with sizes for children and adults. It also does quality disguises for Carnaval. These are the real deal, with prices to match, but they make brilliant gifts.

LA LATINA & LAVAPIÉS

TOP CHOICE El Rastro
MARKET
(Calle de la Ribera de Curtidores; ⊙8am-3pm Sun; Ⓜ La Latina, Puerta de Toledo, Tirso de Molina) A Sunday morning at El Rastro is a Madrid institution. You could easily spend an entire morning inching your way down the Calle de la Ribera de Curtidores and through the maze of streets that hosts El Rastro flea market every Sunday morning. Cheap clothes, luggage, old flamenco records, even older photos of Madrid, faux designer purses, grungy T-shirts, household goods and electronics are the main fare. For every 10 pieces of junk, there's a real gem (a lost masterpiece, an Underwood typewriter) waiting to be found.

A word of warning: pickpockets love El Rastro as much as everyone else, so keep a tight hold on your belongings and don't keep valuables in easy-to-reach pockets.

Helena Rohner
JEWELLERY
(Map p78; www.helenarohner.com.es; Calle del Almendro 4; ⊙9am-8.30pm Mon-Fri, noon-2.30pm & 3.30-8pm Sat, noon-3pm Sun; Ⓜ La Latina, Tirso de Molina) One of Europe's most creative jewellery designers, Helena Rohner has a spacious boutique in La Latina. Working with silver, stone, porcelain, wood and Murano glass, she makes inventive pieces and her

work is a regular feature of Paris fashion shows. In her own words, she seeks to recreate 'the magic of Florence, the vitality of London and the luminosity of Madrid'.

HUERTAS & ATOCHA

Gil
ACCESSORIES

(Map p80; Carrera de San Jerónimo 2; ⊙9.30am-1.30pm & 4.30-8pm Mon-Sat; MSol) You don't see them much these days, but the exquisite fringed and embroidered *mantones* and *mantoncillos* (traditional Spanish shawls worn by women on grand occasions) and delicate *mantillas* (Spanish veils) are stunning and uniquely Spanish gifts. Gil also sells *abanicos* (Spanish fans). Inside this dark shop, dating back to 1880, the sales clerks still wait behind a long counter to attend to you; the service hasn't changed in years and that's no bad thing.

María Cabello
WINE

(Map p80; Calle de Echegaray 19; ⊙9.30am-2.30pm & 5.30-9pm Mon-Fri, 10am-2.30pm & 6.30-9.30pm Sat; MSevilla, Antón Martín) All wine shops should be like this. This family-run corner shop really knows its wines and the interior has scarcely changed since 1913, with wooden shelves and even a faded ceiling fresco. There are fine wines in abundance (mostly Spanish, and a few foreign bottles), with some 500 labels on show or tucked away out the back.

SALAMANCA

TOP CHOICE Agatha Ruiz de la Prada
FASHION

(Map p92; www.agatharuizdelaprada.com; Calle de Serrano 27; ⊙10am-8.30pm Mon-Sat; MSerrano) This boutique has to be seen to be believed, with pinks, yellows and oranges everywhere you turn. It's fun and exuberant, but not just for kids. It also has serious and highly original fashion. Agatha Ruiz de la Prada is one of the enduring icons of *la movida,* Madrid's 1980s outpouring of creativity.

Gallery
CLOTHING, ACCESSORIES

(Map p92; www.gallerymadrid.com; Calle de Jorge Juan 38; ⊙10.30am-8.30pm Mon-Sat; MPríncipe de Vergara, Velázquez) This stunning showpiece of men's fashions and accessories (shoes, bags, belts and the like) is the new Madrid in a nutshell – stylish, brand-conscious and all about having the right look. There are creams and fragrances to indulge the metrosexual in you, as well as quirkier items such as designer crash helmets. With an interior designed by Tomas Alia, and a growing line

in women's fashions, it's one of the city's coolest shops.

Oriol Balaguer
FOOD

(www.oriolbalaguer.com; Calle de José Ortega y Gasset 44; ⊙9am-9pm Mon-Sat, 9am-2.30pm Sun; MNuñez de Balboa) Catalan pastry chef Oriol Balaguer has a formidable CV – he worked in the kitchens of Ferran Adrià in Catalonia and won the prize for the World's Best Dessert (his 'Seven Textures of Chocolate') in 2001. His chocolate boutique is presented like a small art gallery, except that it's dedicated to exquisite, finely crafted chocolate collections and cakes. You'll never be able to buy ordinary chocolate again.

Camper
SHOES

(Map p92; www.camper.es; Calle de Serrano 24; ⊙10am-9pm Mon-Sat, 11am-8pm Sun; MSerrano) Spanish fashion is not all haute couture, and this world-famous cool and quirky shoe brand from Mallorca offers bowling-shoe chic with colourful, fun designs that are all about quality coupled with comfort. There are other outlets throughout the city, including a branch (Map p72; ☑91 531 23 47; www.camper.com; Calle de Fuencarral 42; MGran Vía, Tribunal) in Malasaña – check out the website for locations.

MALASAÑA & CHUECA

TOP CHOICE Mercado de Fuencarral
CLOTHING

(Map p94; www.mdf.es; Calle de Fuencarral 45; ⊙11am-9pm Mon-Sat; MTribunal) Madrid's home of alternative club cool is still going strong, revelling in its reverse snobbery. With shops like Fuck, Ugly Shop and Black Kiss, it's funky, grungy and filled to the rafters with torn T-shirts and more black leather and silver studs than you'll ever need. This is a Madrid icon and when it was threatened with closure in 2008, there was nearly an uprising.

Lurdes Bergada
FASHION

(Map p94; ☑91 531 99 58; www.lurdesbergada.es; Calle del Conde de Xiquena 8; ⊙10am-8.30pm Mon-Sat; MChueca, Colón) Lurdes Bergada and Syngman Cucala, a mother-and-son designer team from Barcelona, offer classy and original men's and women's fashions using neutral colours and all-natural fibres. They've developed something of a cult following for their clothes that are stylish yet casual in a very Chueca kind of way. It's difficult to leave without finding something that you just *have* to have. They have another

branch (Map p94; www.lurdesbergada.es; Calle de Fuencarral 70; ☺10.30am-8.30pm Mon-Sat; ⓂTribunal) in Malasaña.

Patrimonio Comunal Olivarero FOOD
(Map p94; www.pco.es; Calle de Mejía Lequerica 1; ☺10am-2pm & 5-8pm Mon-Fri, 10am-2pm Sat; ⓂAlonso Martínez) To catch the essence of the country's olive oil varieties (Spain is the world's largest producer), Patrimonio Comunal Olivarero is perfect. With examples of the extra-virgin variety (and nothing else) from all over Spain, you could spend ages agonising over the choices. The staff know their oil and are happy to help out if you speak a little Spanish.

NORTHERN MADRID

Tienda Real Madrid SPORTS
(Gate 57, Estadio Santiago Bernabéu, Avenida de Concha Espina 1; ☺10am-8.30pm; ⓂSantiago Bernabéu) The Real Madrid club shop sells replica shirts, posters, caps and just about everything under the sun to which it could attach a club logo. From the shop window, you can see down onto the stadium itself. There's another **branch** (Map p72; ☎521 79 50; Calle del Carmen 3; ☺10am-8.45pm Mon-Sat, 10am-6.45pm Sun; ⓂSol) in the centre of town.

ℹ Information

Dangers & Annoyances

Madrid is a generally safe city although you should, as in most European cities, be wary of pickpockets in the city centre, on the metro and around major tourist sights. You need to be especially careful in the most heavily touristed parts of town, notably the Plaza Mayor and surrounding streets, the Puerta del Sol, El Rastro and the Museo del Prado. Tricks abound and they usually involve a team of two or more (sometimes one of them is an attractive woman to distract male victims). While one diverts your attention, the other empties out your pockets. But don't be paranoid: remember that the overwhelming majority of travellers to Madrid rarely encounter any problems.

More unsettling than dangerous, the central Calle de la Montera has long been the haunt of prostitutes, pimps and a fair share of shady characters, although the street has recently been pedestrianised, and furnished with CCTV cameras and a police station.

The *barrio* of Lavapiés is a gritty, multicultural melting pot. We love it, but it's not without its problems, with drug-related crime an occasional but persistent problem. It's probably best avoided if you're on your own at night.

Emergency

Emergency (☎112)

Policía Nacional (☎091)

Servicio de Atención al Turista Extranjero (Foreign Tourist Assistance Service; ☎902 102112, 91 548 85 37, 91 548 80 08; www. esmadrid.com/satemadrid; Calle de Leganitos 19; ☺9am-10pm; ⓂPlaza de España, Santo Domingo) To report thefts or other crime-related matters, cancel your credit cards, contact your embassy and other related matters, this is your best bet.

Teléfono de la Víctima (☎902 180995) Hotline for victims of racial or sexual violence.

Internet Access

In this era of wi-fi and laptop-bearing travellers, most of Madrid's better internet cafes have fallen by the wayside. You'll find plenty of small *locutorios* (small shops selling phonecards and cheap phone calls) all over the city and many have a few computers out the back, but we haven't listed these as they come and go with monotonous regularity. In the downtown area, your best options include the Centro de Turismo de Madrid, which has a couple of computers with time-limited access.

Café Comercial (Glorieta de Bilbao 7; per 50min €1; ☺7.30am-midnight Mon, 7.30am-1am Tue-Thu, 7.30am-2am Fri, 8.30am-2am Sat, 9am-midnight Sun; ⓂBilbao) One of Madrid's grandest old cafes, with internet upstairs.

Medical Services

Unidad Medica (Anglo American; ☎91 435 18 23; www.unidadmedica.com; Calle del Conde de Aranda 1; ☺9am-8pm Mon-Fri, 10am-1pm Sat; ⓂRetiro) A private clinic with a wide range of specialisations and where all doctors speak Spanish and English, with some also speaking French and German. Each consultation costs around €125.

Farmacia Mayor (☎91 366 46 16; Calle Mayor 13; ☺24hr; ⓂSol)

Farmacia Velázquez 70 (☎91 575 60 28; Calle de Velázquez 70; ☺24hr; ⓂVelázquez)

Hospital General Gregorio Marañón (☎91 586 80 00; www.hggm.es; Calle del Doctor Esquerdo 46; ⓂSáinz de Baranda, O'Donnell, Ibiza) One of the city's main (and more central) hospitals.

Post

Main post office (www.correos.es; Paseo del Prado 1; ☺8.30am-9.30pm Mon-Fri, 8.30am-2pm Sat; ⓂBanco de España) The main post office is in the gigantic Palacio de Comunicaciones on Plaza de la Cibeles.

Tourist Information

Centro de Turismo de Madrid (☎91 588 16 36; www.esmadrid.com; Plaza Mayor 27; ☺9.30am-8.30pm; @; ⓂSol) Excellent city tourist office with a smaller office underneath Plaza de Colón and information points at **Plaza de la Cibeles** (Plaza de la Cibeles; ☺9.30am-8.30pm; MBanco de España), **Plaza del Callao** (Plaza del Callao; ☺9am-midnight; MCallao), outside the **Centro de Arte Reina Sofía** (cnr Calle de Santa Isabel & Plaza del Emperador Carlos V; ☺9.30am-8.30pm; MAtocha) and at the T4 terminal at Barajas airport.

Websites

EsMadrid.com (www.esmadrid.com) The *ayuntamiento's* (town hall) supersexy website with info on upcoming events.

Le Cool (www.madrid.lecool.com) Weekly updates on upcoming events in Madrid with an emphasis on the alternative, offbeat and avant-garde.

Lonely Planet (www.lonelyplanet.com) An overview of Madrid with hundreds of useful links, including to the Thorn Tree, Lonely Planet's online bulletin board.

Turismo Madrid (www.turismomadrid.es) Portal of the regional Comunidad de Madrid tourist office that's especially good for areas outside the city but still within the Comunidad de Madrid.

ⓘ Getting There & Away

Air

Madrid's **Barajas airport** (☑902 404704; www.aena.es; MAeropuerto T1, T2 & T3, Aeropuerto T4) lies 15km northeast of the city. It's Europe's fourth-busiest hub (more than 52 million passengers pass through here annually), trailing only London Heathrow, Paris Charles de Gaulle and Frankfurt.

Although all airlines conduct check-in *(facturación)* in the airport's departure areas, some also allow check-in at the Nuevos Ministerios metro stop and transport interchange in Madrid itself – ask your airline.

A full list of airlines flying to Madrid (and which of Madrid's four terminals they use) is available on the Madrid-Barajas section of www.aena.es; click on 'Airlines'. For more on international and domestic flights to Madrid, see p863 and p866.

Bus

Estación Sur de Autobuses (☑91 468 42 00; www.estaciondeautobuses.com; Calle de Méndez Álvaro 83; MMéndez Álvaro), just south of the M30 ring road, is the city's principal bus station. To get here, take Calle de Méndez Alvaro around 2km southeast of Atocha train station. It serves most destinations to the south and many in other parts of the country. Most bus companies have a ticket office here, even if their buses depart from elsewhere.

Major bus companies include the following:

ALSA (☑902 422242; www.alsa.es) One of the largest Spanish companies with many services throughout Spain. Most depart from Estación Sur but some buses headed north (including to Bilbao and Zaragoza, and some services to Barcelona) leave from the Intercambiador de Avenida de América with occasional services from T4 of Madrid's Barajas airport.

Avanzabus (☑902 020052; www.avanzabus. com) Services to Extremadura (eg Cáceres), Castilla y León (eg Salamanca and Zamora) and Valencia via Cuenca, as well as Lisbon in Portugal. All leave from the Estación Sur.

Car & Motorcycle

Madrid is surrounded by two main ring roads, the outermost M40 and the inner M30; there are also two partial ring roads, the M45 and the more-distant M50. The R5 and R3 are part of a series of toll roads built to ease traffic jams.

The big-name car-rental agencies have offices all over Madrid and offices at the airport, and some have branches at Atocha and Chamartín train stations.

Avis (☑902 180854; www.avis.es; Gran Vía 60; MSanto Domingo, Plaza de España)

Europcar (☑902 105030; www.europcar.es; Calle de San Leonardo de Dios 8; MPlaza de España)

Hertz (☑902 402405; www.hertz.es; Edificio de España, Calle de Princesa 14; MPlaza de España)

National/Atesa (☑902 100101; www.atesa. es; Plaza de España, underground parking area; MPlaza de España)

Pepecar (☑807 414243; www.pepecar.com; Plaza de España, underground parking area; MPlaza de España)

Train

Madrid is served by two main train stations. The bigger of the two is **Puerta de Atocha** (MAtocha Renfe), at the southern end of the city centre, while **Chamartín** (MChamartín) lies in the north of the city. The bulk of trains for Spanish destinations depart from Atocha, especially those going south. International services arrive at and leave from Chamartín. For bookings, contact **Renfe** (☑902 240202; www.renfe.es) at either train station.

High-speed **Tren de Alta Velocidad Española (AVE)** services connect Madrid with Seville (via Córdoba), Valladolid (via Segovia), Toledo, Valencia (via Cuenca), Málaga and Barcelona (via Zaragoza and Huesca or Tarragona). Most high-speed services operate from Madrid's Puerta de Atocha station. The Madrid–Segovia/Valladolid service leaves from the Chamartín station.

❶ Getting Around

Madrid is well served by an excellent and ever-expanding **metro** system and an extensive **bus** service. In addition, you can get from the north to the south of the city quickly by using **local trains** (cercanías) between Chamartín and Atocha train stations. **Taxis** are also a reasonably priced option.

To/From the Airport

A **taxi** to the city centre will cost you around €25 (up to €35 from T4), depending on traffic and where you're going; in addition to what the meter says, you pay a €5.50 airport supplement.

Exprés Aeropuerto (Airport Express; www.emtmadrid.es; €5; ⊘24hr) The recently inaugurated Exprés Aeropuerto runs between Puerta de Atocha train station and the airport. Buses run every 13 to 23 minutes from 6am to 11.30pm, and every 35 minutes throughout the rest of the night. The trip takes 40 minutes. From 11.55pm to 5.35am, departures are from the Plaza de la Cibeles, not the train station.

Metro (www.metromadrid.es; entrances in T2 & T4) Line 8 of the metro runs from the airport to the Nuevos Ministerios transport interchange on Paseo de la Castella, where it connects with lines 10 and 6. It operates from 6.05am to 2am. A one-way ticket to/from the airport costs €4.50 (10-trip Metrobús ticket €12). Even if you have a 10-trip ticket, you'll need to buy the airport supplement from machines in any metro station. The journey to Nuevos Ministerios takes around 15 minutes; around 25 minutes from T4.

AeroCITY (☏91 747 75 70; www.aerocity.com; per person €5-19) Private minibus service.

Bus

Buses operated by **Empresa Municipal de Transportes de Madrid** (EMT; ☏902 507850; www.emtmadrid.es) travel along most city routes regularly between about 6.30am and 11.30pm. There are 26 night-bus búhos (owls) routes operating from midnight to 6am, with all routes originating in Plaza de la Cibeles.

Cercanías

The short-range cercanías regional trains operated by **Renfe** (www.renfe.es/cercanias) go as far afield as El Escorial, Alcalá de Henares, Aranjuez and other points in the Comunidad de Madrid. Tickets range between €1.50 and €5.05 depending on how far you're travelling. In Madrid itself they're handy for making a quick, north–south hop between Chamartín and Atocha train stations (with stops at Nuevos Ministerios and Sol).

Metro

Madrid's modern metro, Europe's second-largest, is a fast, efficient and safe way to navigate Madrid, and generally easier than getting to grips with bus routes. There are 11 colour-coded lines in central Madrid, in addition to the modern southern suburban MetroSur system, as well as lines heading east to the major population centres of Pozuelo and Boadilla del Monte. Colour maps showing the metro system are available from any metro station (see also p68). The metro operates from 6.05am to 2am, although there is talk of ceasing the service at midnight. A single ticket costs €1.50; a 10-ride Metrobús ticket is €12.

Taxi

You can pick up a taxi at ranks throughout town or simply flag one down. Flag fall is €2.15 from 6am to 10pm daily, €2.20 from 10pm to 6am Sunday to Friday, and €3.10 from 10pm Saturday to 6am Sunday. You pay between €1 and €1.20 per kilometre depending on the hour. Several supplementary charges, usually posted inside the taxi, apply; these include €5.50 to/from the airport, €3 from taxi ranks at train and bus stations, and €3 to/from the Parque Ferial Juan Carlos I. There's no charge for luggage.

Radio-Teléfono Taxi (☏91 547 82 00; www.radiotelefono-taxi.com)

Tele-Taxi (☏91 371 21 31; www.tele-taxi.es)

AROUND MADRID

The Comunidad de Madrid may be small but there are plenty of rewarding excursions that allow you to escape the clamour of city life without straying too far. Imposing San Lorenzo de El Escorial and graceful Aranjuez guard the western and southern gateways to Madrid. Also to the south, the beguiling village of Chinchón is a must-see, while Alcalá de Henares is a stunning university town east of the capital. To the north, picturesque villages (and skiing opportunities) abound in Sierra de Guadarrama and Sierra del Pobre.

San Lorenzo de El Escorial

POP 18,447 / ELEV 1032M

The imposing palace and monastery complex of San Lorenzo de El Escorial is an impressive place, rising up from the foothills of the mountains that shelter Madrid from the north and west. The one-time royal getaway is now a prim little town overflowing with quaint shops, restaurants and hotels catering primarily to throngs of weekending *madrileños*. The fresh, cool air here has been drawing city dwellers since the complex was first ordered

MADRID SAN LORENZO DE EL ESCORIAL

to be built by Felipe II in the 16th century. Most visitors come on a day trip from Madrid.

History

After Felipe II's decisive victory in the Battle of St Quentin against the French on St Lawrence's Day, 10 August 1557, he ordered the construction of the complex in the saint's name above the hamlet of El Escorial. Several villages were razed to make way for the huge monastery, royal palace and mausoleum for Felipe's parents, Carlos I and Isabel. It all flourished under the watchful eye of the architect Juan de Herrera, a towering figure of the Spanish Renaissance.

The palace-monastery became an important intellectual centre, with a burgeoning library and art collection, and even a laboratory where scientists could dabble in alchemy. Felipe II died here on 13 September 1598.

In 1854 the monks belonging to the Hieronymite order, who had occupied the monastery from the beginning, were obliged to leave during one of the 19th-century waves of confiscation of religious property by the Spanish state, only to be replaced 30 years later by Augustinians.

⊙ Sights

The main entrance to the **Real Monasterio de San Lorenzo** (📞91 890 78 18; www.patri monionacional.es; adult/concession €10/5, guide/audio guide €7/4, EU citizens free 5-8pm Wed & Thu; ⊙10am-8pm Apr-Sep, 10am-6pm Oct-Mar, closed Mon) is on its western facade. Above the gateway a statue of St Lawrence stands guard, holding a symbolic gridiron, the instrument of his martyrdom (he was roasted alive on one). From here you'll first enter the **Patio de los Reyes**, which houses the statues of the six kings of Judah.

Directly ahead lies the sombre **basilica**. As you enter, look up at the unusual flat vaulting by the choir stalls. Once inside the church proper, turn left to view Benvenuto Cellini's white Carrara marble statue of Christ crucified (1576).

The remainder of the ground floor contains various treasures, including some tapestries and an El Greco painting – impressive as it is, it's a far cry from El Greco's dream of decorating the whole complex. Continue downstairs to the northeastern corner of the complex. You pass through the **Museo de Arquitectura** and the **Museo de Pintura**. The former tells (in Spanish) the story of how the complex was built; the latter

contains a range of 16th- and 17th-century Italian, Spanish and Flemish art.

Head upstairs into a gallery around the eastern part of the complex known as the **Palacio de Felipe II** or **Palacio de los Austrias**. You'll then descend to the 17th-century **Panteón de los Reyes** (Crypt of the Kings), where almost all Spain's monarchs since Carlos I are interred. Backtracking a little, you'll find yourself in the **Panteón de los Infantes** (Crypt of the Princesses).

Stairs lead up from the **Patio de los Evangelistas** (Patio of the Gospels) to the **Salas Capitulares** (chapter houses) in the southeastern corner of the monastery. These bright, airy rooms, with their richly frescoed ceilings, contain works by El Greco, Titian, Tintoretto, José de Ribera and Hieronymus Bosch (known as 'El Bosco' to Spaniards).

Just south of the monastery is the **Huerta de los Frailes** (Friars Garden; ⊙10am-7pm Apr-Sep, 10am-6pm Oct-Mar, closed Mon), which merits a stroll, while the **Jardín del Príncipe** (⊙10am-9pm Apr-Sep, 10am-6pm Oct-Mar, closed Mon), which leads down to the town of El Escorial (and the train station), contains the **Casita del Príncipe** (guided visits adult/student €3.60/2; ⊙10am-8pm Apr-Sep, 10am-6pm Oct-Mar, closed Mon), a little neoclassical gem built in 1772 by Juan de Villanueva under Carlos III for his heir, Carlos IV.

ℹ Information

Tourist office (📞91 890 53 13; www.sanloren zoturismo.org; Calle de Grimaldi 4; ⊙10am-2pm & 3-6pm Tue-Sat, 10am-2pm Sun)

ℹ Getting There & Away

Every 15 minutes (every 30 minutes on weekends) buses 661 and 664 run to El Escorial (€3.55, one hour) from platform 30 at the Intercambiador de Autobuses de Moncloa in Madrid.

San Lorenzo de El Escorial is 59km northwest of Madrid and it takes 40 minutes to drive there. Take the A6 highway to the M600, then follow the signs to El Escorial.

A few dozen **Renfe** (📞902 240202; www.renfe.es) C8 *cercanías* make the trip daily from Madrid's Atocha or Chamartín train station to El Escorial (€1.65, one hour).

South of Madrid

ARANJUEZ
POP 55,755

Aranjuez was founded as a royal pleasure retreat, away from the riff-raff of Madrid, and it remains an easy day trip to escape the rigours of city life. The palace is opulent, but the fresh air and ample gardens are what really stand out.

Sights

Palacio Real PALACE

(✆91 891 07 40; www.patrimonionacional.es; palace adult/concession €9/4, guide/audio guide €6/4, EU citizens free 5-8pm Wed & Thu, gardens free; ☉palace 10am-8pm Tue-Sun Apr-Sep, 10am-6pm Tue-Sun Oct-Mar, gardens 8am-9.30pm mid-Jun–mid-Aug, reduced hours mid-Aug–mid-Jun) The Royal Palace started as one of Felipe II's modest summer palaces but took on a life of its own as a succession of royals, inspired by the palace at Versailles in France, lavished money upon it. By the 18th century its 300-plus rooms had turned the palace into a sprawling, gracefully symmetrical complex filled with a cornucopia of ornamentation. Of all the rulers who spent time here, Carlos III and Isabel II left the greatest mark.

The obligatory guided tour (in Spanish) provides insight into the palace's art and history. And a stroll in the lush gardens takes you through a mix of local and exotic species, the product of seeds brought back by Spanish botanists and explorers from Spain's colonies all over the world. Within their shady perimeter, which stretches a few kilometres from the palace, you'll find the Casa de Marinos, which contains the Museo de Falúas, a museum of royal pleasure boats from days gone by. The 18th-century neoclassical Casa de Labrador is also worth a visit. Further away, towards Chinchón, is the Jardín del Príncipe, an extension of the massive gardens.

Eating

Casa José SPANISH €€€

(✆91 891 14 88; www.casajose.es; Calle de Abastos 32; mains €20-30, set menus €63-74; ☉lunch & dinner Tue-Sat, lunch Sun) The quietly elegant Casa José is the proud owner of a Michelin star and is packed on weekends with *madrileños,* drawn by the beautifully prepared meats and local dishes with some surprising innovations. It's pricey but worth every euro.

Pabelete TAPAS €

(Calle de Stuart 108; tapas from €3.50, raciones €7-12; ☉lunch & dinner Wed-Mon, closed Aug) Going strong since 1946, this casual tapas bar has a loyal following far beyond Aranjuez. Its *croquetas* are a major drawcard, as is the stuffed squid, and it's all about traditional cooking at its best without too many elaborations.

Information

Tourist office (✆91 891 04 27; www.aranjuez. es; Antigua Carretera de Andalucía; ☉10am-8.30pm May-Oct) The tourist office is in the heart of town, a few hundred metres southwest of the Palacio Real.

Getting There & Away

Coming by car from Madrid, take the N-IV south to the M305, which leads to the city centre.

AISA Bus Company (✆902 198788; www. aisa-grupo.com) bus 423 runs to Aranjuez from Madrid's Estación Sur every 15 minutes or so (€4.20, 45 minutes).

From Madrid's Atocha station, C3 *cercanías* trains leave every 15 or 20 minutes for Aranjuez (€3.20, 45 minutes) .

CHINCHÓN
POP 5389

Chinchón is just 45km from Madrid but worlds apart. Although it has grown beyond its village confines, visiting its antique heart is like stepping back into a charming, ramshackle past. It's worth an overnight stay to really soak it up, and lunch in one of the *mesón* (tavern)-style restaurants around the plaza is another must.

Sights

The heart of town is its unique, almost circular Plaza Mayor, which is lined with sagging, tiered balconies – it wins our vote as one of the most evocative *plazas mayores* in Spain. In summer the plaza is converted into a bullring, and it's also the stage for a popular Passion play shown at Easter.

Chinchón's historical monuments won't detain you long, but you should take a quick look at the 16th-century Iglesia de la Asunción, which rises above Plaza Mayor, and the late-16th-century Renaissance Castillo de los Condes, out of town to the south. The castle was abandoned in the 1700s and was last used as a liquor factory. Ask at the tourist office to see if they're open.

Festivals & Events

Fiesta Mayor VILLAGE FESTIVAL

Chinchón's main annual festival, with religious processions, bullfights and other merriment centred on the Plaza Mayor. It starts in the second week of August and usually lasts for a week.

Sleeping

Hostal Chinchón HOSTAL €

(✆91 893 53 98; www.hostalchinchon.com; Calle Grande 16; s/d/tr €40/50/65; ❋❀⊛) The public areas here are nicer than the smallish

THE STRAWBERRY TRAIN

You could take a normal train from Madrid to Aranjuez, but for romance it's hard to beat the **Tren de la Fresa** (Strawberry Train; ☎902 240202; www.museodelferrocarril.org; return adult/child €28/20; ☺10am Sat & Sun early May-late Oct). Begun in 1985 to commemorate the Madrid–Aranjuez route (Madrid's first and Spain's third rail line, which was inaugurated in the 1850s) the Strawberry Train is a throwback to the time when Spanish royalty would escape the summer heat and head for the royal palace at Aranjuez.

The journey begins when an antique Mikado 141F-2413 steam engine pulls out from Madrid's Museo del Ferrocarril, pulling behind it four passenger carriages that date from the early 20th century and have old-style front and back balconies. During the 50-minute journey, rail staff in period dress provide samples of local strawberries: one of the original train's purposes was to allow royalty to sample the summer strawberry crop from the Aranjuez orchards. Upon arrival in Aranjuez, your ticket fare includes a guided tour of the Palacio Real, Museo de Falúas and other Aranjuez sights, not to mention more strawberry samplings. The train leaves Aranjuez for Madrid at 6.25pm for the return journey.

rooms, which are clean but worn around the edges. The highlight is the surprise rooftop pool overlooking Plaza Mayor.

Parador Nacional   LUXURY HOTEL €€€
(☎91 894 08 36; www.parador.es; Avenida Generalísimo 1; d €173; ❇☎) The former Convento de Agustinos (Augustine Convent), Parador Nacional is one of the town's most important historical buildings and can't be beaten for luxury. It's worth stopping by for a meal or coffee (and a peek around) even if you don't stay here.

✖ Eating

Chinchón is loaded with traditional-style restaurants dishing up *cordero asado* (roast lamb). But if you're after something a little lighter, there is nothing better than savouring a few tapas and drinks on sunny Plaza Mayor.

Mesón Cuevas del Vino   SPANISH €€
(☎91 894 02 06; www.cuevasdelvino.com; Calle Benito Hortelano 13; mains €14-27; ☺noon-5pm & 8-11pm Mon-Fri, noon-11pm Sat, noon-8pm Sun) From the huge goatskins filled with wine and the barrels covered in famous signatures, to the atmospheric caves underground, this is sure to be a memorable eating experience with delicious home-style cooking.

Café de la Iberia   SPANISH €€
(☎91 894 08 47; www.cafedelaiberia.com; Plaza Mayor 17; mains €13-22) This is definitely our favourite of the *mesones* (home-style restaurants) on the Plaza Mayor perimeter. It offers wonderful food, including succulent roast lamb, served by attentive staff in an atmospheric dining area set around a light-filled internal courtyard (where Goya is said to have visited). Or, if you can get a table, you can eat out on the balcony.

❶ Information

Tourist office (☎91 893 53 23; www.ciudad-chinchon.com; Plaza Mayor 6; ☺10am-7pm) A small office with helpful staff.

❶ Getting There & Away

La Veloz (☎91 409 76 02; Avenida del Mediterráneo 49; Ⓜ Conde de Casal) runs bus 337 half-hourly from Madrid to Chinchón (€3.55, 50 minutes). Buses leave from Avenida del Mediterráneo, 100m east of Plaza del Conde de Casal.

Sitting 45km southeast of Madrid, Chinchón is easy to reach by car. Take the N-IV motorway and exit onto the M404, which makes its way to Chinchón.

Alcalá de Henares

POP 203,686

East of Madrid, Alcalá de Henares is full of surprises with historical sandstone buildings seemingly at every turn. Throw in some sunny squares and a legendary university, and it's a terrific place to escape the capital for a few hours.

⊙ Sights

FREE **Universidad de Alcalá**   UNIVERSITY
(☎91 883 43 84; guided tours €4; ☺9am-9pm) Founded in 1486 by Cardinal Cisneros, this is one of the country's principal seats of learning. A guided tour gives a peek into the Mudéjar chapel and the magnificent Paraninfo auditorium, where the King and Queen

of Spain give out the prestigious Premio Cervantes literary award every year.

Museo Casa Natal de Miguel de Cervantes   MUSEUM
(📞91 889 96 54; www.museo-casa-natal-cervantes.org; Calle Mayor 48; ⊙10am-6pm Tue-Sun) The town is dear to Spaniards because it's the birthplace of literary figurehead Miguel de Cervantes Saavedra. The site believed to be Cervantes' birthplace is re-created in this illuminating museum, which lies along the beautiful, colonnaded Calle Mayor.

✖ Eating

Baratería   TAPAS €€
(📞91 888 59 25; Calle de los Cerrajeros 18; tapas from €3.50, mains €8-13; ⊙lunch & dinner Mon-Sat, lunch Sun) A wine bar, tapas bar and restaurant all rolled into one, Baratería is a fine place to eat whatever your mood. Grilled meats are the star of the show: the ribs with honey, in particular, are a local favourite.

Hostería del Estudiante   CASTILIAN €€
(📞91 888 03 30; Calle de los Colegios 3; mains €13-21) Based in the *parador,* this charming restaurant has wonderful Castilian cooking and a classy ambience in a dining room decorated with artefacts from the city's illustrious history.

ⓘ Information

Tourist office (📞91 881 06 34; www.turismoalcala.com; Plaza de los Santos Niños; ⊙10am-8pm) Free guided tours of 'Alcalá Monumental' (Alcalá's monuments/architecture) at noon and 4.30pm Saturday and Sunday.

ⓘ Getting There & Away

Alcalá de Henares is just 35km east of Madrid, heading towards Zaragoza along the A2.

Buses depart every five to 15 minutes from Madrid's Intercambiador de Avenida de América (€3.60, one hour).

The C2 and C7 *cercanías* trains make the trip to Alcalá de Henares daily (€2.40, 50 minutes).

Sierra de Guadarrama

North of Madrid lies the Sierra de Guadarrama, a popular skiing destination and home of several charming towns. In Manzanares El Real you can explore the small 15th-century Castillo de los Mendoza (📞91 853 00 08; admission incl guided tour €3; ⊙10am-5pm Tue-Fri, 10am-7.30pm Sat & Sun), a storybook

castle with round towers at its corners and a Gothic interior patio.

Cercedilla is a popular base for hikers and mountain bikers. There are several marked trails, the main one known as the Cuerda Larga or Cuerda Castellana. This is a forest track that takes in 55 peaks between the Puerto de Somosierra in the north and Puerto de la Cruz Verde in the southwest. Small ski resorts, such as Valdesqui (📞902 886446; www.valdesqui.es; Puerto de Cotos; lift tickets day/afternoon €37/21; ⊙9am-4pm) and Navacerrada (📞902 882328; www.puertonavacerrada.com; lift tickets €25-30; ⊙9.30am-5pm) welcome weekend skiers from the city.

ⓘ Information

Centro de Información Valle de la Fuenfría (📞91 852 22 13; Carretera de las Dehesas; ⊙10am-6pm) Information centre located 2km outside Cercedilla on the M614.

Navacerrada tourist office (📞91 856 03 08; www.navacerrada.es; ⊙9am-5pm)

ⓘ Getting There & Away

By car from Madrid, take the A-6 motorway to Cercedilla.

Bus 724 runs to Manzanares El Real from Plaza de Castilla in Madrid (€3.50, 45 minutes). From Madrid's Intercambiador de Autobuses de Moncloa, bus 691 heads to Navacerrada (€3.70, one hour) and bus 684 runs to Cercedilla (€3.70, one hour).

From Chamartín train station you can get to Puerto de Navacerrada on the C8B *cercanías* line (€6, two hours with train change in Cercedilla, four daily), and Cercedilla on the C2 *cercanías* line (€3.20, 1½ hours, 15 daily).

El Pardo

Just beyond Madrid's city limits, El Pardo is an easy escape from the clamour of the city with a fine palace and lovely gardens. If possible, avoid weekends when the whole area can be overrun with visitors.

⊙ Sights

Palacio Real de el Pardo   PALACE
(www.patrimonionacional.es; Calle de Manuel Alonso; adult/concession incl guided tour €9/4, EU citizens free 5-8pm Wed & Thu; ⊙10am-8pm Apr-Sep, 10am-6pm Oct-Mar; ✿) Built in the 15th century and remodelled in the 17th, this opulent palace was Franco's favourite residence. It's surrounded by lush gardens (which close

one hour later than the palace) and on Sunday fills with *madrileño* families looking for a bit of fresh air and a hearty lunch. Of the art on display inside, the tapestries stand out, particularly those based on cartoons by Goya.

❶ Getting There & Away

If you're driving from Madrid take the M40 to the C601, which leads to El Pardo. The 13km trip takes just 15 minutes. You can also take bus 601 (€1.60, 25 minutes), which leaves every five to 10 minutes from the Intercambiador de Autobuses de Moncloa in Madrid.

Buitrago & Sierra Pobre

The 'Poor Sierra' is a toned-down version of its more refined western neighbour, the Sierra de Guadarrama. Popular with hikers and others looking for nature without quite so many creature comforts or crowds, the sleepy Sierra Pobre has yet to develop the tourism industry of its neighbours. And that's just why we like it.

Head first to Buitrago, the largest town in the area, where you can stroll along part of the old city walls. You can also take a peek into the 15th-century Mudéjar and Romanesque Iglesia de Santa María del Castillo and into the small and unlikely Picasso Museum (☑91 868 00 56; www.madrid.org/museo_picasso/principal; Plaza Picasso 1; ☺11am-

1.45pm & 4-6pm Tue, Thu & Fri, 11am-1.45pm Wed, 10am-2pm & 4-7pm Sat, 10am-2pm Sun), which contains a few works that the artist gave to his barber, Eugenio Arias.

Hamlets are scattered throughout the rest of the sierra; some, like Puebla de la Sierra and El Atazar, make for pretty walks and are the starting point for winding hill trails.

Eating

El Arco SPANISH €€
(☑91 868 09 11; Calle Arco 6; mains €14-24; ☺lunch Tue-Sun, dinner Tue-Sat mid-Jun–mid-Sep, lunch Fri-Sun mid-Sep–mid-Jun) The best restaurant in the region, El Arco is located in Villavieja del Lozoya, close to Buitrago, and is known for its fresh, creative cuisine based on local ingredients and traditional northern Spanish dishes. The desserts and wine list also stand out.

❶ Information

Buitrago tourist office (☑91 868 16 15; Calle Tahona 19; ☺9am-3pm Jul-Sep) For more information on Picasso Museum, visit the tourist office.

❶ Getting There & Away

By car from Madrid, take the N-I highway to Buitrago.

Bus 191 leaves hourly from Madrid's Plaza de la Castilla to Buitrago (€5.60, 1½ hours).

Castilla y León

Includes »

Best Places to Eat

» Restaurante El Fogón Sefardí (p162)

» La Cocina de Toño (p148)

» Los Zagales de Abadía (p167)

» Casa Duque (p162)

» Cervecería Morito (p190)

Best Places to Stay

» Posada Real La Cartería (p174)

» Microtel Placentinos (p147)

» Hotel Alcázar (p159)

» Casa de Tepa (p185)

» Hospedería La Gran Casa Mudéjar (p159)

Why Go?

If you're looking for a window on the Spanish soul, head to Castilla y León. This is Spain without the stereotypes, with vast plains, spectacular mountain peaks and evocative medieval towns. Experience fabled cities like Salamanca, with its lively student population, and Segovia, famed for a fairytale fortress that inspired Disneyland's Sleeping Beauty castle. The multiturreted walls of Avila have similar magical appeal, while the lofty cathedrals of León and Burgos are among Europe's most impressive. And like most of Spain, food here is an agreeable obsession, promising the country's best *jamón* (cured ham), roast lamb and suckling pig.

The region's story is equally told through its quiet back roads, half-timbered hamlets and imposing isolated castles. From the scenic Sierra de Francia in the southwest to Covarrubias, Calatañazor and Medinaceli in the east or the Montaña Palentina in the north, this is the hidden Spain most travellers never imagined still existed.

When to Go

Leon

Mar-Apr Enjoy wild flowers in the countryside and soul-stirring Semana Santa processions.	**Jun** Get into holiday mode during annual fiesta time in Burgos, Soria and Segovia.	**Sep** Capture the youthful buzz of Salamanca as universities return to class.

Castilla y León Highlights

1 Spend as long as you can amid the architectural elegance and irresistible energy of **Salamanca** (p143)

2 Savour the sepulchral light in **León's** (p177) cathedral, a kaleidoscope of glass and stone

3 Leave well-travelled paths behind and explore the **Montaña Palentina** (p176)

4 Dine on roast lamb like a Castilian in the pretty hilltop towns of **Lerma** (p194) or **Sepúlveda** (p195)

5 Escape city life in the historic villages of **Covarrubias** (p192) or **Medinaceli** (p201)

6 Imagine yourself somewhere between ancient Rome and Disneyland in **Segovia** (p155)

7 Go in search of wolves in the **Sierra de la Culebra** (p175), close to medieval **Puebla de Sanabria** (p173)

8 Shop for honey and other gourmet goodies at the Saturday morning market in picturesque **La Alberca** (p153)

THE SOUTHWEST

Ávila

POP 59,010 / ELEV 1130M

Ávila's old city, surrounded by imposing city walls comprising eight monumental gates, 88 watchtowers and more than 2500 turrets, is one of the best-preserved medieval bastions in all Spain. In winter, when an icy wind whistles in off the plains, the old city huddles behind the high stone walls as if seeking protection from the harsh Castilian climate. At night, when the walls are illuminated to magical effect, you'll wonder if you've stumbled into a fairy tale. Within the walls, Ávila can appear caught in a time warp. It's a deeply religious city that, for centuries, has drawn pilgrims to the cult of Santa Teresa de Ávila, with many churches, convents and high-walled palaces. As such, Ávila is the essence of Castilla, the epitome of old Spain.

◎ Sights

Murallas WALLS
(adult/child €4/2.50; ⊙10am-8pm Tue-Sun) Ávila's splendid 12th-century walls rank among the world's best-preserved medieval defensive perimeters. Raised to a height of 12m between the 11th and 12th centuries, the walls stretch for 2.5km atop the remains of earlier Roman and Muslim battlements. They have been much restored and modified, with various Gothic and Renaissance touches, and even some Roman stones reused in the construction. At dusk the walls attract swirls of swooping and diving swallows.

Two sections of the walls can be climbed – a 300m stretch that can be accessed from just inside the **Puerta del Alcázar**, and a longer 1300m stretch that runs the length of the old city's northern perimeter, in the process connecting the two access points at **Puerta de los Leales** (⊙10am-8pm Tue-Sun for both) and **Puerta del Puente Adaja**; it's possible to climb down (but not up) from the latter stretch at Puerta del Carmen. The same ticket allows you to climb both sections; the last ones are sold at 7.15pm. The regional tourist office runs free guided tours.

FREE **Convento de Santa Teresa** MUSEUM
(⊙8.45am-1.30pm & 3.30-9pm Tue-Sun) Built in 1636 over the saint's birthplace, this is the epicentre of the cult surrounding Teresa. There are three attractions in one

here: the church (built around the room where the saint was born), a relics room and museum. Inside the main church, to the left of the main altar as you enter, the room where Teresa was born in 1515 is now a chapel smothered in gold and lorded over by a baroque altar by Gregorio Fernández; it features a statue of the saint. An adjoining relics room is crammed with Teresa relics, some of which, such as her ring finger (complete with ring), border on the macabre; that didn't stop Franco from keeping it by his bedside throughout his rule. There's also a basement museum dedicated to the saint, accessible from Calle Aizpuru.

Catedral CATHEDRAL
(Plaza de la Catedral; admission €4; ⊙10am-7.30pm Mon-Fri, 10am-8pm Sat, noon-6.30pm Sun) Ávila's 12th-century cathedral is at once a house of worship and an ingenious fortress: its stout granite apse forms the central bulwark in the heavily fortified eastern wall of the old city. Although the main facade hints at the cathedral's 12th-century, Romanesque origins, the church was finished 400 years later in a predominantly Gothic style, making it the first Gothic church in Spain. The sombre grey facade betrays some unhappy 18th-century meddling in the main portal.

The interior is a different story, with an exquisite altar painting showing the life of Jesus in 24 scenes; it was begun by Pedro de Berruguete and completed by Juan de Borgoña in 1515, the year of Santa Teresa's birth. Above, the stunning ochre-stained limestone columns and cantilevered ceilings in the side aisles produce an effect unlike any other cathedral in the country. Renaissance-era carved walnut choir stalls are another highlight of the inner sanctum. Push the buttons to illuminate both the altar and choir stalls. Off the fine cloisters, a small museum contains a painting by El Greco and a splendid silver monstrance by Juan de Arfe.

Monasterio de la Encarnación MONASTERY
(Calle de la Encarnación; admission €2; ⊙9.30am-1.30pm & 3.30-6pm Mon-Fri, 10am-1pm & 4-6pm Sat & Sun) North of the city walls, this unadorned Renaissance monastery is where Santa Teresa fully took on the monastic life and lived for 27 years. By a strange twist of divine fate, it was inaugurated the same month that the infant Teresa was baptised. There are three main rooms open to the public. The most interesting is the third (up

Ávila

Ávila

the stairs where the saint is said to have had a vision of the baby Jesus), where you'll find relics such as the piece of wood used by Teresa as a pillow and the chair upon which St John of the Cross made his confessions. To reach here, head north from Plaza de Fuente el Sol, via Calle de la Encarnación, for approximately 500m.

Los Cuatro Postes   VIEWPOINT

Northwest of the city, on the road to Salamanca, this viewpoint provides the best views of Ávila's walls. It also marks the place where Santa Teresa and her brother were caught by their uncle as they tried to run away from home (they were hoping to achieve martyrdom at the hands of the Muslims). The best views are at night.

Iglesia de San Andrés   CHURCH

(Plaza de San Andrés; ⊙10am-2pm & 4-6pm Mon-Sat Easter-Oct) North of the old city and dating from the 12th century, this is Ávila's oldest church and a fine example of Romanesque architecture, although the exterior is a little scarred by later restorations. Opening hours can be unreliable; check at the tourist office.

Basílica de San Vicente   CHURCH

(www.basilicasanvicente.com; Plaza de San Vicente; admission €2; ⊙10am-6.30pm Mon-Sat, 4-6pm Sun) Unlike much of Ávila's often sombre and brooding religious architecture, this graceful church is a masterpiece of Romanesque simplicity: a series of largely Gothic modifications in sober granite contrasted with the warm sandstone of the Romanesque original. Work started in the 11th century, supposedly on the site where three martyrs – San Vicente and his sisters – were slaughtered by the Romans in the early 4th century. Their canopied cenotaph is an outstanding piece of Romanesque style with nods to the Gothic, and stands in stark contrast to the weathered headstones on the floor of the main nave, some dating back to the 17th century; don't forget to take a peek at the crypt. The Jardín de San Vicente across the road was once a Roman cemetery.

Murallito   TOURIST TRAIN

(www.murallitoavila.com; adult/child & senior €4/3) This nifty tourist train makes a complete 30-minute circuit of the city walls with a few other sights thrown in.

Museo Provincial   MUSEUM

(Plaza de los Nalvillos; incl Iglesia de Santo Tomé El Viejo €1.20, Sat & Sun free; ⊙10am-2pm & 5-8pm Tue-Sat, 10am-2pm Sun) This regional museum includes local ethnographic exhibits (the 1932 photos by Albert Klemm are particularly interesting) as well Roman artefacts and some fine medieval paintings.

Iglesia de Santo Tomé El Viejo   CHURCH, MUSEUM

(Plaza de Italia; incl Museo Provincial €1.20, Sat & Sun free; ⊙10am-2pm & 5-8pm Tue-Sat, 10am-2pm Sun) This church dates from the 13th century, and it was from this pulpit that Santa Teresa was castigated most vehemently for her reforms. It has been restored to house mostly Roman foundation stones and a splendid floor mosaic.

Monasterio de Santo Tomás   MONASTERY

(www.monasteriosantotomas.com; Plaza de Granada 1; admission €4; ⊙10.30am-2pm & 3.30-7.30pm) Although it is a good 10 minutes' walk southeast from the city walls, this monastery is well worth the side step. Commissioned by the Reyes Católicos (Catholic Monarchs), Fernando and Isabel, and completed in 1492, it is an exquisite example of Isabelline architecture, rich in historical resonance. Three interconnected cloisters lead up to the church that contains the alabaster tomb of Don Juan, the monarchs' only son. It's backed by an altarpiece by Pedro de Berruguete depicting scenes from the life of St Thomas Aquinas. The magnificent choir stalls, in Flemish Gothic style, are accessible from the upper level of the second cloister, the Claustro del Silencio. It's thought that the Grand Inquisitor Torquemada is buried in the sacristy. Off the Claustro de los Reyes, named thus because Fernando and Isabel often attended Mass here, there's the impressive Museo Oriental (Oriental Museum) with 11 rooms of art from the Far East, as well as a more modest Museo de Historia Natural (Natural History Museum); both are included in the admission price.

To get here, head southeast from Jardín de San Vicente along Calle de Ferrol Hernandez and Avenida del Alférez Provisional.

Iglesia de San Pedro   CHURCH

(Plaza de Santa Teresa; ⊙10.30am-noon & 7-8pm) One of the city's later churches, its light, sandstone exterior is a pleasant complement to the granite austerity that reigns inside the city walls.

FREE Iglesia de San Juan Bautista CHURCH
(Plaza de la Victoria; ☺before & after Mass (10am
& 7.30pm Mon-Sat, noon Sun)) This quiet parish church dates from the 16th century and
contains the font in which Santa Teresa was
baptised on 4 April 1515.

Festivals & Events

Semana Santa HOLY WEEK
Ávila is one of the best places in Castilla y
León to watch the solemn processions of
Easter. It all begins on Holy Thursday and
the most evocative event is the early morning (around 5am) Good Friday procession
which circles the city wall.

Fiesta de Santa Teresa PATRON SAINT FESTIVAL
Annual festival during the second week of
October honouring the city's patron saint
with processions, concerts and fireworks.

Sleeping

TOP CHOICE Hotel El Rastro HISTORIC HOTEL €
(☎920 35 22 25; www.elrastroavila.com; Calle Ce-
pedas; s/d €35/55; ❄⬤) This superb choice
occupies a former 16th-century palace with
original natural stone, exposed brickwork
and a warm earth-toned colour scheme ex-
uding a calm understated elegance. Each
room has a different form, but most have
high ceilings and plenty of space. Rooms
205 to 209 are more modern – avoid these
to really soak up the atmosphere.

Hotel Las Leyendas HISTORIC HOTEL €€
(☎920 35 20 42; www.lasleyendas.es; Calle de Francisco Gallego 3; s/d €56/79; ❄⬤) Occupying the
house of 16th-century Ávila nobility, this intimate hotel overflows with period touches
wedded to modern amenities. Some rooms
have views out across the plains, others look
onto an internal garden. Some rooms have
original wooden beams, exposed brick and
stonework, others are more modern with
muted tones.

Hostal Arco San Vicente HOSTAL €€
(☎920 22 24 98; www.arcosanvicente.com; Calle de
López Núñez 6; s/d €40/65; ❄⬤) This gleaming *hostal* (budget hotel) has small, blue-
carpeted rooms with pale paintwork and
wrought-iron bedheads. Rooms on the 2nd
floor have attic windows and air-con, some
on the 1st floor look out at the Puerta de San
Vicente; room 109 is particularly spacious
and attractive.

Hostal San Juan HOSTAL €
(☎920 25 14 75; www.hostalsanjuan.es; Calle de
los Comuneros de Castilla 3; s/d Sun-Thu €24/30,
Fri & Sat €30/38.50; ⬤) With warm tones
throughout, well-kept rooms and a location
close to everything in Ávila, Hostal San Juan
is pleasant, friendly and outrageously good
value. The recent addition of a small fitness
room, complete with exercise machines, is a
real one-off in this budget category.

Hospedería La Sinagoga HISTORIC HOTEL €
(☎920 35 23 21; Calle de los Reyes Católicos 22;
s/d €50/60; ❄) This delightful small hotel
incorporates details from Ávila's main 15th-
century synagogue. Choose carefully as
some rooms can be a little dark, while others
are large and adorned in period brickwork.

WHO WAS SANTA TERESA?

Teresa de Cepeda y Ahumada, probably the most important woman in the history of
the Spanish Catholic Church, was born in Ávila on 28 March 1515, one of 10 children of a
merchant family. Raised by Augustinian nuns after her mother's death, she joined the Carmelite order at age 20. After her early, undistinguished years as a nun, she was shaken by a
vision of hell in 1560, which crystallised her true vocation: she would reform the Carmelites.

In stark contrast to the opulence of the church in 16th-century Spain, her reforms called
for the church to return to its roots, taking on the suffering and simple lifestyle of Jesus
Christ. The Carmelites demanded the strictest of piety, went *descalzadas* (barefoot), lived
in extremely basic conditions and even employed flagellation to atone for their sins. Not
surprisingly, all this proved extremely unpopular with the mainstream Catholic Church.

With the help of many supporters, Teresa founded convents of the Carmelitas Descalzas (Shoeless Carmelites) all over Spain. She also co-opted San Juan de la Cruz (St John
of the Cross) to undertake a similar reform in the masculine order, a task that earned him
several stints of incarceration. Santa Teresa's writings were first published in 1588 and
proved enormously popular, perhaps partly for their earthy style. She died in 1582 in Alba
de Tormes, where she is buried. She was canonised by Pope Gregory XV in 1622.

✖ Eating

Ávila is famous for its *chuleton de Ávila* (T-bone steak) and *judías del barco de Ávila* (white beans, often with chorizo, in a thick sauce).

TOP CHOICE Hostería Las Cancelas CASTILIAN €€
(📞920 21 22 49; www.lascancelas.com; Calle de la Cruz Vieja 6; mains €16-25; ⏰Feb-Dec) This courtyard restaurant occupies a delightful interior patio dating back to the 15th century; across the road, the summer-only terrace occupies part of a former cathedral courtyard. Renowned for being a mainstay of Ávila cuisine, traditional meals are prepared with a salutary attention to detail; the *solomillo con salsa al ron y nueces* (sirloin in a rum and walnut sauce) is a rare deviation from tradition. Reservations recommended.

La Bruja CONTEMPORARY CASTILIAN €€
(📞920 35 24 96; www.la-bruja.es; Paseo del Rastro 1; menú del día €14.50, mains €15-23) In the shadow of the old city walls, 'The Witch' combines a beautifully adapted 16th-century space with creative tapas that have won a host of gastronomic awards and meat and fish mainstays. With advance notice (in the morning for an evening meal), you can order the 'Menú Maridaje', a tasting menu of seven dishes with seven wines for €75.

Mesón del Rastro CASTILIAN €€
(www.elrastroavila.com; Plaza del Rastro 1; menú del día €13, mains €9-22; ⏰Thu-Sat, lunch only Sun-Wed) The dark-wood beamed interior announces immediately that this is a bastion of robust Castilian cooking and has been since 1881. Expect delicious mainstays such as *judías del barco de Ávila* and *cordero asado*, mercifully light salads and, regrettably, the occasional coach tour. We especially like its *menú castellano* (Castilian set menu; €24), but only if you're *really* hungry.

Restaurante Reyes Católicos CASTILIAN €€
(www.restaurante-reyescatolicos.com; Calle de los Reyes Católicos 6; menú del día €16, mains €16-24) Fronted by a popular tapas bar, this place has bright decor and an accomplished kitchen that churns out traditional dishes that benefit from a creative tweak. Its range of set menus includes the stellar *menú degustacion cocina tradicional de Ávila* (tasting menu of traditional Ávila cooking; €12).

Posada de la Fruta CASTILIAN €
(www.posadadelafruta.com; Plaza de Pedro Dávila 8; bar mains €7.90-12.90, restaurant €10.90-19.80; ⏰bar lunch & dinner daily, restaurant lunch & dinner Wed-Mon) Simple tasty meals can be had in a light-filled, covered courtyard, while the traditional *comedor* (dining room) is typically all about hearty meat dishes offset by simple fresh salads. The unusual international meat dishes, which include gazelle, kangaroo and eland, are the standout here.

🍺 Drinking

Ávila is long on saints but short on discos, so nights aren't particularly lively.

TOP CHOICE La Bodeguita de San Segundo WINE BAR
(www.vinoavila.com; Calle de San Segundo 19; ⏰11am-midnight Thu-Tue) Situated in the 16th-century Casa de la Misericordia, this superb wine bar is standing-room only most nights and more tranquil in the quieter afternoon hours. Its wine list is renowned throughout Spain with over 1000 wines to choose from, with tapas-sized servings of cheeses and cured meats the perfect accompaniment.

La Taberna After Work BAR
(Calle del Tostado; ⏰4pm-2am Sun-Wed, 4pm-3am Thu-Sat; 📶) A strange mix of underground medieval arches and the ambience of a wood-pannelled British pub, this agreeable bar has an especially good range of gins.

ℹ Information

Centro de Recepción de Visitantes (📞920 35 40 00, ext 790; www.avilaturismo.com;

WHAT'S COOKING IN CASTILLA Y LEÓN?

Castilla y León's cuisine owes everything to climate. There's no better way to fortify yourself against the bitterly cold winters of the high plateau than with *cordero asado* (roast lamb), a signature dish from Sepúlveda to Burgos and every town in between. *Cochinillo asado* (roast suckling pig) is a speciality of Segovia. Other regional specialities include *morcilla de Burgos* (blood sausage mixed with rice, from Burgos) and *chuleton de Ávila* (T-bone steak, from Ávila). An estimated 60% of Spain's *jamón* (cured ham) comes from the Salamanca region and *jamón* from Guijelo, south of Salamanca, ranks among Spain's most prestigious.

Avenida de Madrid 39; ◎9am-8pm) Municipal tourist office.

Regional tourist office (☑920 21 13 87; www.turismocastillayleon.com; Casa de las Carnicerías, Calle de San Segundo 17; ◎9am-8pm)

❶ Getting There & Away

BUS Frequent services to Segovia (€5, one hour), Salamanca (€6.08, 1½ hours) and Madrid (€8.06, 1½ hours); a couple of daily buses also head for the main towns in the Sierra de Gredos.

CAR & MOTORCYCLE From Madrid the driving time is around one hour; the toll costs €8.

TRAIN There are services to Madrid (from €6.80, 1¼ to two hours), Salamanca (from €8.55, 1¼ hours, eight daily) and León (from €24.80, three hours, three daily).

❶ Getting Around

Local bus 1 runs past the train station to Plaza de la Catedral.

Sierra de Gredos

West of Madrid and south of Ávila, the plains of Castilla yield to the precipitous Sierra de Gredos, a secret world of lakes and granite mountains rising up to the Pico de Almanzor (2592m). While the occasional castle or sanctuary may catch the eye, the overriding appeal is the scenery. The sierra is also popular with walkers, mountain bikers and rock climbers, the best seasons being spring (March to May) and autumn (September to November). Summer (June to August) can be stifling, while in winter (December to February) the trails are covered in snow.

◎ Sights & Activities

A convenient gateway to the southern Sierra de Gredos, Arenas de San Pedro is the sort of place you would use as a base rather than visit for its own sake. In the town centre, check out the stout 15th-century Castillo de la Triste Condesa, the sober 14th-century Gothic parish church and the Roman bridge. A 10-minute walk north of here is the neoclassical Palacio del Infante Don Luis de Borbón, a gilded cage for Carlos III's imprisoned brother. Not far from Arenas de San Pedro, Guisando, El Hornillo and El Arenal, a trio of villages at a distance of 5km, 6km and 9km from Arenas, respectively, have access to walking trails.

To escape the weekend and summer crowds, head for the Sierra de Gredos' less-frequented northern flank of mountains, which are normally snowcapped until Easter. Running west off the N502, near Puerta de Pico, the scenic C500 leads past Navarredonda de Gredos and on to Hoyos del Espino, from where the small AV931 leads into the sierra, ending after 12km at La Plataforma. This is the jumping-off point for one of the most picturesque walks, leading to the Laguna Grande, a glassy mountain lake in the shadow of the Pico de Almanzor. The easy-to-moderate walk along a well-marked 8km trail takes about 2½ hours each way. Next to the lake is a *refugio* (mountain shelter), which is often full, and good camping. From here it's possible to climb to the top of the Pico de Almanzor (difficult) in about two hours or continue for two hours west to the Circo de Cinco Lagunas (easy to moderate). From there you could either backtrack or descend via the Garganta del Pinar towards the town of Navalperral de Tormes, a rigorous undertaking that can take five hours. For organised activities, including horse riding, trekking and abseiling, check out Alternativas en el Medio Natural (☑920 34 83 85; www.amngredos.com; Hoyos del Espino).

⎆ Sleeping & Eating

TOP CHOICE El Milano Real   BOUTIQUE HOTEL €€
(☑920 34 91 08; www.elmilanoreal.com; Calle de Toledo, Hoyos del Espino; r €107, mains €15-19.50;

(P❄🛜🏊) This is a gorgeous place to stay, with wonderful views, a peaceful setting and a fine restaurant. The accommodation is super stylish hiding behind the old-world facade. Each room's decor reflects the name it has been given; there is a Zen-feel Japanese room, the minimalist-look Manhattan suite and an English suite decorated in country-garden-style floral fabrics. All have luxuries like hydro-massage baths and DVD players, and breakfast is a gourmet affair. There is also a spa.

La Casa de Arriba   RURAL HOTEL €€
(✏920 34 80 24; www.casadearriba.com; Calle de la Cruz 19, Navarredonda de Gredos; s/d €67/79; 🛜) Located at the top of the village and well signposted, this lovely hotel brims with rustic charm: wooden beams, wood floors, antique furnishings and thick stone walls. The restaurant is highly regarded.

El Fogon de Gredos   RURAL HOTEL €
(✏920 37 40 18; www.fogondegredos.com; Carretera Linarejos, Guisando; s/d incl breakfast €26/52) This is the most attractive option in Guisando, offering attractive, spacious rooms with sweeping pine-clad mountain views. The *hostal* is even better known as a restaurant (meals €20) for satisfying, meat-dominated local cuisine. It's located (and well signposted) around 1.5km beyond the town centre, by the Rio Pelayo.

Camping Los Galayos   CAMPGROUND €
(✏920 37 40 21, www.campinglosgalayos.com; Carretera Linarejos; adult/sites/car €3.90/3.80/3.60, 4-person bungalow €93; 🚐) One of the best camping grounds in the region, Los Galayos has a stunning position on the Rio Pelayo with mountain views. Ideal for families, there is easy access to a small waterfall and pools of shallow turquoise water for paddling tots. The restaurant offers a reduced-price menu for campers (€9.90).

🛈 Information

Tourist office (✏920 37 23 68; Plaza de San Pedro; ⏱10am-1.30pm & 4-8pm) Has walking suggestions.

🛈 Getting There & Away

Public transport to and throughout the sierra is intermittent at best – renting a car is essential. Daily buses connect Arenas de San Pedro with Madrid (€11.75, 2½ hours, two daily) and Ávila (€6.20, 1¼ hours), except on Sunday.

Salamanca
POP 153,470

Whether floodlit by night or bathed in the light of sunset, there's something magical about Salamanca. This is a city of rare beauty, awash with golden sandstone overlaid with ochre-tinted Latin inscriptions, an extraordinary virtuosity of plateresque and Renaissance styles. The monumental highlights are many, with the exceptional Plaza Mayor (illuminated to stunning effect at night) an unforgettable highlight. But this is also Castilla's liveliest city; home to a massive Spanish and international student population that throngs the streets at night and provides the city with so much youth and vitality.

History

In 220 BC Celtiberian Salamanca was besieged by Hannibal. Later, under Roman rule, it was an important staging post on the Vía Lata (Ruta de la Plata, or Silver Route) from the mines in Asturias to Andalucía. After the Muslim invasion of Spain, it changed hands repeatedly. The greatest turning point in the city's history was the founding of the university in 1218. It became the equal of Oxford and Bologna and, by the end of the 15th century, was the focal point of some of the richest artistic activity in the country. The city followed the rest of Castilla into decline in the 17th century, although by the time Spanish literary hero Miguel de Unamuno became rector at the university in 1900, Salamanca had essentially recovered. Throughout the 20th century, especially during the civil war and the almost four decades of Franco's rule that followed, Salamanca's university became both the centre for liberal resistance to fascism and the object of Franco's efforts to impose a compliant

CASTILLA Y LEÓN SALAMANCA

SALAMANCA CARD

If you plan on visiting most of Salamanca's attractions, consider the Salamanca Card (www.salamancacard.com), which entitles you to free entry to most museums, an MP3 audio guide to the city, and discounts at some restaurants, hotels and shops. It can be purchased online or from both tourist offices, and costs €16/22 for 24/48 hours.

Salamanca

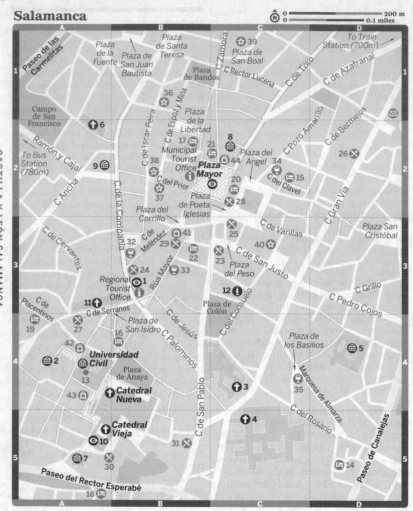

academic philosophy in Spain's most prestigious university. To a small degree, that liberal–conservative tension still survives and defines the character of the town.

◉ Sights & Activities

Plaza Mayor SQUARE

Built between 1729 and 1755, Salamanca's exceptional grand square is widely considered to be Spain's most beautiful central plaza. The square is particularly memorable at night when illuminated (until midnight) to magical effect. Designed by Alberto Churriguera, it's a remarkably harmonious and control-led baroque display. The medallions placed around the square bear the busts of famous figures. Look for the controversial inclusion of Franco in the northeast corner – it looks different from the others, being moulded in a special easy-to-clean plastic to counter its regular subjection to vandalism. Bullfights were held here well into the 19th century; the last ceremonial *corrida* (bullfight) took place here in 1992.

Universidad Civil HISTORIC BUILDING

(Calle de los Libreros; adult/child €4/2, Mon morning free; ⊙9.30am-1.30pm & 4-6.30pm Mon-Fri,

Salamanca

10am-1.30pm Sun) The visual feast of the entrance facade to Salamanca's university is a tapestry in sandstone, bursting with images of mythical heroes, religious scenes and coats of arms. It's dominated in the centre by busts of Fernando and Isabel.

Founded initially as the Estudio Generál in 1218, the university came into being in 1254 and reached the peak of its renown in the 15th and 16th centuries. Behind the facade, the highlight of an otherwise modest collection of rooms lies upstairs: the extraordinary university library, the oldest university library in Europe. With some 2800 manuscripts gathering dust, it's a real cemetery of forgotten books. Note the fine late-Gothic features and beautiful *techumbre* (carved wooden ceiling).

Among the small lecture rooms arranged around the courtyard downstairs, the Aula de Fray Luis de León was named after the celebrated 16th-century theologian and writer whose statue adorns the Patio de las Escuelas Menores outside. It conserves the original benches and lectern from Fray Luis' day. Arrested by the Inquisition for having translated the Song of Solomon into Spanish, the sardonic theologian returned to his class after five years in jail and resumed lecturing with the words, 'As I was saying yesterday...' It was here, too, that the famous Spanish philosopher and essayist, Miguel de Unamuno, claimed the Nationalist rising was 'necessary to save Western Civilization', and was saved from the fury of the crowd by Franco's wife.

The Escalera de la Universidad (University Staircase) that connects the two floors has symbols carved into the balustrade, seemingly of giant insects having a frolic with several bishops – to decode them was seen as symbolic of the quest for knowledge.

FREE **Catedral Nueva**   CATHEDRAL
(Plaza de Anaya; ⊘9am-8pm) The tower of the late-Gothic Catedral Nueva lords over the centre of Salamanca, its compelling *churrigueresco* (ornate style of baroque) dome visible from almost every angle. The interior is similarly impressive, with elaborate choir stalls, main chapel and retrochoir all courtesy of the prolific José Churriguera. The ceilings are also exceptional. It is, however, the magnificent Renaissance doorways, particularly the Puerta del Nacimiento on the western face, that stand out as one of several miracles worked in the city's native sandstone. The Puerta de Ramos, facing Plaza de Anaya, contains an encore to the 'frog spotting' challenge on the university facade. Look for the little astronaut and ice-cream cone chiselled into the portal by stonemasons during restorations.

Catedral Vieja   CATHEDRAL
(Plaza de Anaya; admission €4.75; ⊘10am-7.30pm) The Catedral Nueva's largely Romanesque predecessor, the Catedral Vieja is adorned with an exquisite 15th-century altarpiece, with 53 panels depicting scenes from the lives of Christ and Mary, topped by a representation of the Final Judgment – it's one of the most beautiful Renaissance altarpieces outside Italy. The cathedral was begun in 1120 and remains something of a hybrid: there are Gothic elements, while the unusual ribbed cupola, the Torre del Gallo, reflects a Byzantine influence. The cloister was largely ruined in the 1755 earthquake, but the Capilla de Anaya houses an extravagant alabaster sepulchre and one of Europe's oldest organs, a Mudéjar work of art dating from the 16th century. The entrance is inside the Catedral Nueva.

Puerta de la Torre   VIEWPOINT
(Jeronimus; Plaza de Juan XXIII; admission €3.75; ⊘10am-7.15pm; 🚹) For fine views over Salamanca, head to the tower at the southwestern corner of the Catedral Nueva's facade. From here, stairs lead up through the tower, past labyrinthine but well-presented exhibitions of cathedral memorabilia, then along the interior balconies of the sanctuaries of the Catedral Nueva and Catedral Vieja and out onto the exterior balconies. There's another entrance inside the Catedral Vieja.

Convento de San Esteban   CONVENT
(Plaza del Concilio de Trento; adult/concession €3/2; ⊘10am-1.30pm & 4-7.30pm) Just down the hill from the cathedral, the lordly Convento de San Esteban's church has an extraordinary altar-like facade, with the stoning of San Esteban (St Stephen) as its central motif. Inside is a well-presented museum dedicated to the Dominicans, a splendid Gothic-Renaissance cloister and an elaborate church built in the form of a Latin cross and adorned by an overwhelming 17th-century altar by José Churriguera.

Convento y Museo de las Úrsulas CONVENT
(Calle de las Úrsulas 2; admission €2; ⊘11am-1pm & 4.30-6pm Tue-Sun) A late-Gothic nunnery founded by Archbishop Alonso de Fonseca in 1512, the religious museum is fairly modest with some interesting paintings by Juan de Borgoña, who completed the stunning altar in Ávila Cathedral (p137), but do take a look at the magnificent marble tomb within the church, sculpted by Diego de Siloé.

Palacio de Monterrey   HISTORIC BUILDING
(Calle del Prior) Off the southwestern corner of Plaza Mayor, take Calle del Prior, which leads to the Palacio de Monterrey, a 16th-century holiday home of the Duques de Alba and a seminal piece of Spanish Renaissance architecture; it's not open to the public but the facade is superb.

FREE **Casa de las Conchas**   HISTORIC BUILDING
(Calle de la Compañía 2; ⊘9am-9pm Mon-Fri, 10am-2pm & 4-7pm Sat & Sun) One of the city's most endearing buildings, the House of the Shells is named after the scallop shells clinging to its facade. Its original owner, Dr Rodrigo Maldonado de Talavera, was a doctor at the court of Isabel and a member of the Order of Santiago, whose symbol is the shell. It now houses the public library, entered via a charming bi-level courtyard.

FREE **Cielo de Salamanca**   HISTORIC BUILDING
(Patio de las Escuelas Menores; ⊘9.30am-1.30pm Tue-Fri, 10am-2pm Sat & Sun) The main (and only) attraction here is the beautiful pale-blue ceiling fresco of the zodiac; give yourself a few moments to adjust to the light before gazing aloft.

Convento de Santa Clara   MUSEUM
(Calle Santa Clara 2; adult/child €3/0.50; ⊘9.30am-12.45pm & 4.20-6.10pm Mon-Fri, 9.30am-2.10pm Sat & Sun) This much-modified convent started life as a Romanesque structure and now houses a small museum. You can admire the beautiful frescoes and climb up some stairs

> **DON'T MISS**
>
> ## FROG-SPOTTING
>
> Arguably a lot more interesting than trainspotting (and you don't have to drink tea from a thermos flask), a compulsory task facing all visitors to Salamanca is to search out the frog sculpted into the facade of the Universidad Civil. Once pointed out, it's easily enough seen, but the uninitiated can spend considerable time searching. Why bother? Well, they say that those who detect it without help can be assured of good luck and even marriage within a year. Some hopeful students see a guaranteed examination's victory in it. If you believe all this, stop reading now: if you need help, look at the busts of Fernando and Isabel. From there, turn your gaze to the largest column on the extreme right of the front. Slightly above the level of the busts is a series of skulls, atop the left-most of which sits our little amphibious friend (or what's left of his eroded self).

to inspect at close quarters the 14th- and 15th-century *artesonado* (wooden Mudéjar ceiling). You can only visit as part of a (Spanish-language) guided tour that takes 50 minutes.

Convento de las Dueñas CONVENT
(Calle Gran Vía; admission €2; ⊘11am-12.45pm & 4.30-6.45pm Mon-Sat) This Dominican convent is home to the city's most beautiful cloister, with some decidedly ghoulish carvings on the capitals.

Museo de Art Nouveau y Art Decó MUSEUM
(Casa Lis; Calle de Gibraltar; adult/concession €4/2, Thu morning free; ⊘11am-2pm & 5-9pm Tue-Fri, 11am-9pm Sat & Sun) Utterly unlike any other Salamanca museum, this playful collection of scultpure, paintings and art deco and art nouveau pieces inhabits a stunning, light-filled *Modernista* (Catalan art nouveau) house. There's abundant stained glass, Beatrix Potter bronzes, 19th-century children's dolls and so much more. There's a cafe and a fabulous shop; later head for Paseo del Rector Esperabé for excellent views of the house.

Real Clerícia de San Marcos CHURCH
(Universidad Pontificia; Calle de la Compañia; admission €3; ⊘10.30am-12.30pm & 5-6.30pm Wed-Fri, 10am-1pm & 5-7.15pm Sat, 10am-1pm Sun) Visits to this colossal baroque church and the attached Catholic university are via obligatory guided tours (in Spanish), which run every 45 minutes. There are also plans to run tours up the church spire; ask at the municipal tourist office.

Torre del Clavero TOWER
(Calle del Consuelo) This 15th-century octagonal fortress has an unusual square base and smaller cylindrical towers.

Museo Taurino MUSEUM
(Calle de Doctor Piñuela 5-7; adult/senior/child €3/2/free; ⊘11.30am-1.30pm & 6-8pm Tue-Sat, 11.30am-1.30pm Sun; ⊛) Salamanca lies in one of Spain's bullfighting heartlands and this small museum is packed with bullfighting memorabilia.

🎓 Courses

In addition to the following, the municipal tourist office has a list of accredited private colleges.

University of Salamanca LANGUAGE COURSE
(Cursos Internacionales, Universidad Civil; ☏923 29 44 18; www.usal.es; Patio de las Escuelas Menores) Salamanca is one of the most popular places in Spain to study Spanish and the University of Salamanca is the most respected language school. Courses range from a three-hour daily course spread over two weeks (€415) to a 10-week course of five hours daily (€1870). Accommodation can also be arranged.

☞ Tours

Both the Municipal tourist office (p150) and the Regional tourist office (p150) organise guided tours of the city. These depart at noon daily and cost €6 (daytime) to €7 (night tours). The duration is roughly 1½ hours but you must reserve in advance. They're conducted in Spanish, but you may also be able to arrange tours in English and French.

🛏 Sleeping

TOP CHOICE **Microtel Placentinos** BOUTIQUE HOTEL €€
(☏923 28 15 31; www.microtelplacentinos.com; Calle de Placentinos 9; s/d incl breakfast Sun-Thu €56/72, Fri & Sat €86/99; ⊛⊜) One of Salamanca's most charming boutique hotels, Microtel Placentinos is tucked away on a quiet

street and has rooms with exposed stone walls and wooden beams. The service is faultless, and the overall atmosphere is one of intimacy and discretion. All rooms have a hydromassage shower or tub and there's a summer-only outside whirpool spa.

Aparthotel El Toboso
APARTMENT €

(☑923 27 14 62; www.hoteltoboso.com; Calle del Clavel 7; s/d €30/45, 3-/4-/5-person apt €75/85/95; ❋🐾🛜) These rooms have a homey spare-room feel and are super value, especially the enormous apartments, which come with kitchens (including washing machines) and renovated bathrooms. It's ideal for families or if you're planning to stay in Salamanca for more than a night. Don't miss the fabulous 100-year-old tiled mural of Don Quijote in the bar.

Hostal Concejo
HOSTAL €

(☑923 21 47 37; www.hconcejo.com; Plaza de la Libertad 1; s/d €45/60; P❋🛜) A cut above the average *hostal,* the stylish Concejo has polished-wood floors, tasteful furnishings, light-filled rooms and a superb central location. Try and snag one of the corner rooms (like number 104) with its traditional glassed-in balcony, complete with a table, chairs and people-watching views.

Pensión Los Ángeles
PENSIÓN €

(☑923 21 81 66; www.pensionlosangeles.com; Plaza Mayor 10; s/d €25/45, without bathroom €20/30; 🛜) In a prime location on Plaza Mayor and with bargain prices to boot, this place is a winner. The rooms have original colourful floor tiles, and the best rooms are large and have balconies overlooking the square. On the downside, it's a steep climb if you're lugging heavy luggage.

Hostal Catedral
HOSTAL €

(☑923 27 06 14; http://hostalcatedralsalamanca.com; Rúa Mayor 46; s/d €30/48; ❋🛜) Just across from the cathedrals, this pleasing *hostal* has just six extremely pretty, impeccable, bright bedrooms with showers. All look out onto the street or cathedral, which is a real bonus, as is the motherly owner, who treats her visitors as honoured guests.

Hotel Rector
HOTEL €€€

(☑923 21 84 82; www.hotelrector.com; Paseo del Rector Esperabé 10; r incl breakfast from €150; ❋🛜) This luxurious hotel is an oasis of calm and luxury, and the antithesis of the cookie-cut homogeneity of the five-star chains. Expect vases of orchids, stained-glass win-

dows, intricately carved antiques and excellent service, as well as sumptuous, carpeted rooms.

Albergue Juvenil
HOSTEL €

(☑923 26 91 41; www.alberguesalamanca.com; Calle de Escoto 13-15; dm/s/d €14/28/38; 🛜) Salamanca's youth hostel is a popular, well-run place, with large, clean dorms. It's a 10-minute walk down the hill from the old city.

Rúa Hotel
HOTEL €€

(☑923 27 22 72; www.hotelrua.com; Calle de Sánchez Barbero 11; r incl breakfast €80-120; ❋@🛜) The former apartments here have been converted to seriously spacious rooms. Light-wood floors, pastel painted walls and arty prints set the tone. You couldn't be more central than this.

Petit Palace Las Torres
HOTEL €€

(☑923 21 21 00; www.hthotels.com; Calle de Concejo 4-6; d from €85; ❋@🛜) Part of the quality High-Tech chain, this slick hotel has designer lamps, computers and a sophisticated feel. On the downside, the rooms overlooking Plaza Mayor demand a considerable hike in price and some interior rooms are a little small. Guests have free use of bikes.

🍴 Eating

🔝 La Cocina de Toño
TAPAS €€

(www.lacocinadetoño.es; Calle Gran Vía 20; menú del día €17, tapas €1.30-3.80, mains €6.90-23; ⏰lunch & dinner Tue-Sat, lunch Sun) We're yet to hear a bad word about this place and its loyal following owes everything to its creative *pinchos* (snacks) and half-servings of dishes such as escalope of foie gras with roast apple and passionfruit gelatin. The restaurant serves more traditional fare as befits the decor, but the bar is one of Salamanca's gastronomic stars. Slightly removed from the old city, it draws a predominantly Spanish crowd.

El Pecado
MODERN SPANISH €€

(☑923 26 65 58; www.elpecadorestaurante.es; Plaza de Poeta Iglesias 12; menú del día €15, mains €15-33) A trendy place that regularly attracts Spanish celebrities (eg Pedro Almodóvar and Ferran Adrià), El Pecado (The Sin) has an intimate dining room and a quirky, creative menu; it's a reasonably priced place to sample high-quality, innovative Spanish cooking. The hallmarks are fresh tastes, intriguing combinations and dishes that regularly change according to what's fresh at the market that day. Reservations recommended.

Mesón Las Conchas
CASTILIAN €€
(Rúa Mayor 16; menú del día €12, mains €10-21; ☻noon-midnight) Enjoy a choice of outdoor tables (in summer), an atmospheric bar or the upstairs, wood-beamed dining area. The bar caters mainly to locals who know their *embutidos* (cured meats). For sit-down meals, there's a good mix of roasts, *platos combinados* and *raciones* (full-plate-size tapas serving). It serves a couple of cured meat platters (€17 to €20) that can be good to share. If you're craving fish, the oven-baked turbot is delicious.

Mesón Cervantes
CASTILIAN €€
(www.mesoncervantes.com; Plaza Mayor 15; menú del día €13.50, mains €10-22; ☻10am-midnight) Although there are outdoor tables on the square, the dark wooden beams and atmospheric buzz of the Spanish crowd on the 1st floor should be experienced at least once; if you snaffle a window table in the evening, you've hit the jackpot. The food's a mix of *platos combinados*, salads and *raciones*.

Víctor Gutiérrez
MODERN SPANISH €€€
(☎923 26 29 73; www.restaurantevictorgutierrez.com; Calle de San Pablo 66-80; set menus €36-130; ☻lunch & dinner Tue-Sat, lunch Sun) Justifiably exclusive vibe with emphasis on innovative dishes with plenty of colourful drizzle. The choice of what to order is largely made for you with some excellent set menus. Reservations essential.

Restaurante Lis
CONTEMPORARY MEDITERRANEAN €€
(☎923 21 62 60; www.restaurantelis.es; Patio Chico 18; mains €14.50, set menus €32; ☻lunch & dinner Tue-Sat, lunch Sun) This classy restaurant has a revolutionary idea – all three-course meals add up to €28, unless you choose one of the tasting menus for a little more. The atmosphere is intimate and the cooking assured with riffs on well-known dishes such as duck hamburger or mango ravioli.

Mandala Café
MEDITERRANEAN €
(Calle de Serranos 9-11; set menus €10-12; ☻) Cool and casual Mandala specialises in a superb daily menu (unusually available for lunch *and* dinner) with choices like black rice with prawns and *calamares* (squid), and vegetarian moussaka. There are also more salads than you can shake a carrot stick at, cakes,

45 types of milkshakes, 56 juice combinations and more teas than we could count.

Casa Paca
CASTILIAN €€
(☎923 21 89 93; www.casapaca.com; Plaza del Peso 10; mains €15-33) Established in 1928 and still going strong, Casa Paca is rumoured to be where the king dines when in town. There's nothing too innovative here – it's all about high-quality, traditional Castilian cooking with hearty dishes like *cochinillo asado* (roast suckling pig) alongside dozens of grilled fish and red meat choices. Reservations essential.

El Bardo
TAPAS €€
(Calle de la Compañía 8; tapas from €2.50, mains €6-19) High-calibre tapas, toasts (topped with combinations like cod carpaccio with sun-dried tomatoes) and a reliable daily menu aimed at the locals make this an excellent choice. It's also a good place to try the local *farinato* (filled pastries).

🍷 Drinking

Salamanca, with its myriad bars and large student population, is the perfect after-dark playground. Nightlife here starts very late, with many bars not filling until after midnight. The so-called 'litre bars' on Plaza de San Juan Bautista are fun night-time hang-outs mainly for students.

TOP CHOICE Tío Vivo
MUSIC BAR
(www.tiovivosalamanca.com; Calle del Clavel 3-5; ☻4pm-late) Sip drinks by flickering candlelight to a background of '80s music, enjoying the whimsical decor of carousel horses and oddball antiquities. There is live music Tuesday to Thursday from midnight, sometimes with a €5 admission.

Taberna La Rayuela
BAR
(Rúa Mayor 19; ☻6pm-1am Sun-Thu, to 2am Fri & Sat) This low-lit upstairs bar buzzes with a 20-something crowd and is an intimate place. It's probably our favourite spot in town for first drinks.

Vinodiario
WINE BAR
(Plaza de los Basilios 1; ☻9.30am-1am Sun-Thu, to 1.30am Fri & Sat) Away from the crowds of the old city, this quiet but classy neighbourhood wine bar is staffed by knowledgeable bar staff and loved by locals who, in summer, fill the outdoor tables for early evening drinks. There are a couple of imported beers, but the wines are resolutely Spanish. The tapas are innovative and delicious.

Café El Corrillo
MUSIC BAR

(www.cafecorrillo.com; Calle de Meléndez; ⊘8.30am-3am) Great for a beer and tapas at any time, with live music on Wednesday and Thursday nights from 10pm. The *terraza* (terrace) at the back is perfect on a warm summer's evening.

 Entertainment

Many of Salamanca's cafe-bars morph into dance clubs after midnight; there's usually no cover charge.

Posada de las Almas
CLUB

(Posada de las Animas; www.posadadelasanimas.com; Plaza de San Boal; ⊘6pm-late) Decked out in a curious design mix of looming papier-mâché figures and velvet curtains, this place attracts a mixed crowd – gay and straight, Spanish and foreign.

Cum Laude
CLUB

(Calle del Prior 7; ⊘10pm-late Tue-Sun) One of Salamanca's most enduring bars, Cum Laude has a sprawling mock-palace interior. Tuesday is Cabaret, Thursday is Ladies Night (both from 11pm) and the rest of the week is just plain good fun.

Garamond
CLUB

(Calle del Prior 24; ⊘9pm-late) An enduring stalwart of the Salamanca night with medieval-style decor, Garamond has music that's good to dance to without straying too far from the mainstream.

Potemkin
LIVE MUSIC

(Calle del Consuelo; ⊘11pm-late) Salamanca's grungy alternative to the sophisticates elsewhere can be found at Potemkin, where you'll catch live rock music most nights. The neighbouring bars are similar, so dress down.

Cubic Club
CLUB

(Calle de Iscar Peira 30; ⊘midnight-6am Fri & Sat) The only thing that seems guaranteed about this space is that there will be a nightclub here – every time we return, it has a different name. Expect house, electro and techno with two dance floors, but don't be surprised if it's got a new name by the time you get here.

🔒 Shopping

Salamanca overflows with souvenir shops, running the whole gamut from the tasteful to the tacky; the following fall into the former category. In addition, the **Municipal tourist office shops** (Plaza Mayor 27; ⊘10am-2pm & 5-8pm Mon-Sat, 10am-2pm Sun) have excellent souvenirs. All over the centre of town, you'll come across places serving the finest Salamanca *jamón serrano* (type of cured ham), usually vacuum sealed and ready to carry home.

Mercatus
SOUVENIRS

(http://mercatus.usal.es; Calle de Cardenal Pla y Deniel; ⊘10am-8.15pm Mon-Sat, 10.15am-2pm Sun) The official shop of the University of Salamanca has a stunning range of stationery items, leather-bound books and other carefully selected reminders of your visit.

El Fotografo
SOUVENIRS

(Calle de Meléndez 5; ⊘10.30am-1.30pm & 5-8pm Mon-Fri, 11am-2pm & 6-8.30pm Sat) This small photography shop sells beautiful B&W photos of Salamanca, coffee-table books and photographic equipment.

La Galatea
BOOKS

(Calle de los Libreros 28; ⊘4.30-8.30pm Mon, 10.30am-2.30pm & 4.30-8.30pm Tue-Sat, 10.30am-2.30pm Sun) The first bookshop in decades to open along Salamanca's 'Street of the Booksellers' (there were once more than 50), this fine space combines a bargain table (with some books in English), some gorgeous Spanish-language rare antique books and a carefully chosen collection of LPs.

❶ Information

Municipal tourist office (☎923 21 83 42; www.turismodesalamanca.com; Plaza Mayor 14; ⊘9am-2pm & 4.30-8pm Mon-Fri, 10am-8pm Sat, 10am-2pm Sun)
Regional tourist office (☎923 26 85 71; www.turismocastillayleon.com; Casa de las Conchas; Rúa Mayor; ⊘9am-8pm)

❶ Getting There & Away

The bus and train stations are a 10- and 15-minute walk northwest and northeast, respectively, of the Plaza Mayor.

BUS There are buses to the following destinations: Madrid (regular/express €12.88/20.30, 2½ to three hours, hourly), Ávila (€6.08, 1½ hours, one to four daily), Ciudad Rodrigo (€6.10, one hour, five to 13 daily), León (€13.70, three hours, two daily), Segovia (€11.08, 2½ hours, two daily), Valladolid (€8, 1½ hours, two daily) and Zamora (from €4.70, one hour, five to 13 daily). There is a limited service to smaller towns with just one daily bus, except on Sunday, to La Alberca (€5.25, around 1½ hours), with stops in the villages of the Sierra de Francia such as Mogarraz and San Martín del Castañar.

TRAIN Regular departures to Madrid's Chamartín station (€19.85, 2½ hours), Ávila (€10.05, 1¼ hour) and Valladolid (from €8.55, 1½ hours).

ℹ Getting Around

Bus 4 runs past the bus station and around the old-city perimeter to Calle Gran Vía. From the train station, the best bet is bus 1, which heads into the centre along Calle de Azafranal. Going the other way, it can be picked up at the Mercado Central.

Around Salamanca

The town of Alba de Tormes makes for an interesting and easily accomplished half-day excursion from Salamanca. People come here from far and wide to pay homage to Santa Teresa, who is buried in the Convento de las Carmelitas she founded in 1570. There's also the stout and highly visible Torreón, the only surviving section of the former castle of the Dukes of Alba. There are regular buses (every two hours on weekends) from Salamanca's bus station to Alba de Tormes.

Ciudad Rodrigo

POP 13,710

Close to the Portuguese border and away from well-travelled tourist routes, somnambulant Ciudad Rodrigo is one of the prettier towns in western Castilla y León. It's an easy day trip from Salamanca, 80km away, but sleeping within the sanctuary of its walls enables you to better appreciate its medieval charm – and you'll have the sloping Plaza Mayor all to yourself after the tourist crowds return home.

◉ Sights

Ciudad Rodrigo's walled Old Town is compact and home to some of the best-preserved plateresque architecture outside Salamanca.

Catedral   CATHEDRAL

(Plaza de San Salvador; adult/concession/under 12yr €3/2.50/free, Sun afternoon free, tower €2; ⊙11.45am-2pm Mon, 11.45am-2pm & 4-7pm Tue-Sat, 12.45-2pm & 4-6pm Sun) The elegant, weathered sandstone cathedral, begun in 1165, towers over the Old Town. Of particular interest are the Puerta de las Cadenas, with splendid Gothic reliefs of Old Testament figures; the elegant Pórtico del Perdón; and, inside, the exquisite carved-oak choir stalls. It's also possible to climb the tower at 1.15pm on Saturday and Sunday; the views are Ciudad Rodrigo's best.

Plaza Mayor   SQUARE

The long, sloping Plaza Mayor is a fine centrepiece for this beautiful town. At the top of the hill, the double-storey arches of the Casa Consistorial (Town Hall; ⊙1st floor gallery 9am-2pm Mon-Fri) are stunning, but the plaza's prettiest building is the Casa del Marqués de Cerralbo, an early 16th-century town house with a wonderful facade.

Muralla   WALLS

There are numerous stairs leading up onto the crumbling ramparts of the city walls that encircle the Old Town. You can follow their length of about 2.2km around the town for good views over the surrounding plains.

Casa de los Vázquez   ARCHITECTURE

(Correos; Calle de San Juan 12; ⊙8.30am-2.30pm Mon-Fri, 9.30am-1pm Sat) Even if you've nothing to post, the *correos* (post office) is worth passing by to admire the *artesonado*.

Iglesia de San Pedro & San Isidro   CHURCH

(Plaza Cristobal de Castillo; ⊙before & after Mass) The fusion of 12th-century Romanesque-Mudéjar elements with later Gothic modifications makes the Iglesia de San Isidoro worth seeking out. Don't miss the porticoes in the cloister. Discovered in 1994, the 12th-century reliefs of a Roman queen, Arab king and Catholic bishop reflect the various cultures of the region over the years.

Palacio de los Ávila y Tiedra   ARCHITECTURE

(Plaza del Conde 3; ⊙9am-7pm Mon-Sat) The 16th-century Palacio de los Ávila y Tiedra boasts one of the town's most engaging plateresque facades, and it's the pick of a handful of fine examples that surround the Plaza del Conde.

✦ Festivals & Events

Carnaval   CARNIVAL

Celebrated with great enthusiasm in Ciudad Rodrigo in February. In addition to the outlandish fancy dress, you can witness (or join in) a colourful *encierro* (running of the bulls) and *capeas* (amateur bullfights).

🛏 Sleeping

TOP CHOICE Hospedería **Audiencia Real**   HISTORIC HOTEL €€

(☏923 49 84 98; www.audienciareal.com; Plaza Mayor 17; d €60-80; ❄🎧) Right on Plaza

---

DON'T MISS

GOING POTTY

Chamber pots, commodes, bed pans... Ciudad Rodrigo's **Museo del Orinal** (Chamber Pot Museum; admission €2; ⊙11am-2pm Tue, Wed, Fri & Sun, 11am-2pm & 4-7pm Sat & Mon; 🖪) is home to Spain's (possibly the world's) only museum dedicated to the not-so-humble chamber pot (or potty, as it is known in the UK). The private collection of former local resident José Maria del Arco, the collection comprises a staggering 1300 exhibits. Originating from 27 countries, there are some truly historic pieces here, including a 12th-century Islamic version from Cordoba and some wonderful one-offs, like a 19th-century French chamber pot shaped like a bra and a Chinese example with a narrow opening, apparently used on rice boats. Among the considerable number of UK potties here there are beautifully painted Victorian ceramic pieces and the more rustic wooden-seated style. Incidentally, if you need a tinkle yourself, you will have to go elsewhere; there are no public toilets at the Museo del Orinal.

Mayor, this fine 16th-century *hospedería* (inn) has been beautifully reformed and retains a tangible historic feel with lovely exposed stone walls. Rooms have wrought-iron furniture and several have balconies overlooking the square; rooms at the back cost €20 less.

Hotel Conde Rodrigo 1 HOTEL €€
(☑923 46 14 08; www.hotelesciudadrodrigo.com; Plaza de San Salvador 9; s/d €78/85; ✸🛜) Housed in a 16th-century former palace, the refurbished rooms are washed in pale yellow with dark-wood furnishings, shiny parquet floors and burgundy-and-white fabrics. The large flat-screen TV, minibar and well-equipped bathroom are similarly agreeable, given the price. The wi-fi signal only reaches the rooms on the 1st floor.

Parador Enrique II HISTORIC HOTEL €€
(☑923 46 01 50; www.parador.es; Plaza del Castillo 1; r €125-145; 🅿✸@🛜) Ciudad Rodrigo's premier address is a plushly renovated 14th-century castle built into the town's western wall. Converted in 1931, it's the third-oldest *parador* (luxurious state-owned hotel) in Spain. The views are good, the rooms brimming with character and the restaurant easily the best in town. The delightful terraced gardens at the back overlook Río Agueda.

Hostal Puerta del Sol HOSTAL €€
(☑923 46 06 71; www.puertadelsolhostal.com; Rúa del Sol 33; d €40-60; @) This attractive *hostal* has comfortable bright rooms featuring modern pine furniture, sunny yellow paintwork and elegant cream fabrics. The bathrooms are expensively marbled in natural colours.

🍴 Eating & Drinking

TOP CHOICE Parador Enrique II SPANISH €€
(☑923 46 01 50; Plaza del Castillo 1; set menu €32, mains €17.50-20) As you'd expect from this high-quality chain, this is Ciudad Rodrigo's finest restaurant, with classy surrounds, attentive service and a menu that changes regularly but always includes the pick of local dishes – the finest *jamón* from the Salamanca region, *cochinillo asado* and *cordero* (spring lamb). Reservations are essential if you're not staying here.

El Sanatorio TAPAS, RACIONES €
(Plaza Mayor 12; raciones €5.50-10, mains €4.50-11; ⊙11am-late) Dating from 1937, the interior here doubles as a fascinating social history of the town. The walls are papered floor to ceiling with B&W photos (the oldest dated 1928), mainly of the annual Carnaval when the square used to be used as a bullring. Order a beer and peruse the pics. The tapas and *raciones* are good, as well.

La Artesa TAPAS €
(Rúa del Sol 1; pinchos €1, raciones €3.50-13; ⊙Tue-Sun; 🖪) The €1 *pinchos* here are excellent value. There are 21 to choose from, ranging from *pulpo a la vinagreta* (octupus in vinaigrette) to *patatas al roquefort* (roast potatoes in a Roquefort sauce). The portions are generous; the house wine (€1 a glass) surprisingly palatable.

❶ Information

Tourist office (☑923 49 84 00; www.aytociu dadrodrigo.es; Plaza Mayor 27; ⊙10am-1.30pm & 4-7pm Tue-Sun)

Regional tourist office (www.turismocastilla yleon.com; Plaza de Amayuelas 5; ⊙9am-2pm

& 5-7pm Mon-Fri, 10am-2pm & 5-8pm Sat & Sun) Can arrange guided tours of the Old Town (€5).

❶ Getting There & Away

BUS From the **bus station** (Campo de Toledo) there are up to 13 daily services (fewer on weekends) to Salamanca (€6.10, one hour). For the Sierra de Francia, you'll need to go via Salamanca.

Sierra de Francia

Hidden away in a remote corner of southwestern Castilla y León and, until recently, secluded for centuries, this mountainous region with wooded hillsides and pretty stone and timber villages is among Castilla y León's best-kept secrets. Quiet mountain roads connect villages that you could easily spend days exploring and where the pace of life remains relatively untouched by the modern world. This was once one of Spain's most godforsaken regions. Malaria-ridden until the early 20th century, the region hadn't improved much in 1932 when Luis Buñuel came to film *Las Hurdes – Terre Sans Pain* (Land Without Bread). When King Alfonso XIII visited in June 1922, the only milk available for his coffee was human! Touched by this abject misery, or perhaps hoping for something a little more palatable on his next visit, he was supposedly responsible for the introduction of the area's first cows.

Having your own car enables you to immerse yourself in quiet villages such as Mogarraz, east of La Alberca, which has some of the most evocative old houses in the region and is famous for its *embutidos*. Miranda del Castañar, further east again, is similarly intriguing, strung out along a narrow ridge, but San Martín del Castañar is the most enchanting, with half-timbered stone houses, flowers cascading from balconies, a bubbling stream and a small village bullring at the top of the town, next to the ruined castle (now a cemetery).

Hotels are rare in these parts, but *casas rurales* (village or farmstead accommodation) abound, with a handful in each village. Alternatively, Abadía de San Martín (☑923 43 73 50; www.abadiadesanmartin.com; Calle Paipérez 24, San Martín del Castañar; d/ste €75/85) and Hotel Spa Villa de Mogarraz (http://hotelspamogarraz.com; Calle Miguel Ángel Maillo 54, Mogarraz; s/d €70/100; ☎) are wonderful choices.

For further information and maps of this area, visit the tourist offices in Salamanca or Ciudad Rodrigo.

La Alberca

POP 1210 / ELEV 1048M

La Alberca is one of the largest and most beautifully preserved of the Sierra de Francia's villages, a historic and harmonious huddle of narrow alleys flanked by gloriously ramshackle houses built of stone, wood beams and plaster. Look for the date they were built (typically late 18th century) carved into the door lintels. Numerous stores sell local products such as *jamón* and

CASTILLA Y LEÓN SIERRA DE FRANCIA

CASTILLA Y LEÓN'S PICTURE-PERFECT VILLAGES

San Martín del Castañar Sierra de Francia's prettiest village.

Candelario (p155) Stone-and-wood village huddling beneath the Sierra de Béjar.

Pedraza de la Sierra (p163) Lovely walled hamlet watched over by a castle.

Puebla de Sanabria (p173) A return to the past with medieval streetscapes.

Castrillo de los Polvazares Rustic stone buildings emblematic of northwestern Castilla y León.

Covarrubias (p192) Arguably Castilla y León's most postcard-perfect village.

Santo Domingo de Silos (p193) Quiet streets, a stunning cloister and Gregorian chants in the Burgos hinterland.

Peñaranda de Duero (p195) A palace, churches and a ruined castle on the banks of the Río Duero.

Calatañazor (p200) Movie-set, cobbled charm just off the highway but a world away.

Medinaceli (p201) Splendid old-world feel high above eastern Castilla y León.

WORTH A TRIP

ROAD TRIP: NORTH OF CIUDAD RODRIGO

Hidden from the outside and one of the most dramatic landforms in Castilla y León, the Parque Natural Arribes del Duero is one of the region's least-known gems, and this road trip takes you through some picturesque country and attractive villages en route to the heart of the park. Although the park can be visited from both Zamora and Salamanca, the road north from Ciudad Rodrigo is the prettiest approach.

The quiet SA324 north from Ciudad Rodrigo gives no hint of what lies ahead. At Castillo de Martín Viejo, 17km northwest of Ciudad Rodrigo, take the turn-off for **Siega Verde** (guided visit adult/concession €5/4; ⊙11am-2pm & 4-7pm Thu-Sun), the Unesco World Heritage–listed archaeological site with 645 prehistoric rock carvings of animals and ancient symbols – it's one of the richest such collections in Europe. **San Felices de los Gallegos**, 40km north of Ciudad Rodrigo, has a pretty Plaza Mayor and a well-preserved castle. After **Lumbrales**, a further 10km to the north, the road (now the SA330) narrows and passes among stone walls and begins to buck and weave with the increasingly steep contours of the land. The **Mirador del Cachón de Caneces** (lookout) offers the first precipitous views. The road then drops down to the **Puerto de la Molinero**, before climbing again to **Saucelle** (24km from Lumbrales) and then on to **Vilvestre** (31km), from where there are reasonable views out towards the Río Duero and Portugal.

But it's at **Aldeadávila**, around 35km to the north, that you find the views that make this trip worthwhile. Before entering the village, turn left at the large purple sign. After 5.1km a 2.5km walking track leads down to the **Mirador El Picón de Felipe**, with fabulous views down into the canyon. Returning to the road, it's a further 1km down to the **Mirador del Fraile** – the views of the impossibly deep canyon with plunging cliffs on both sides are utterly extraordinary. This is prime birdwatching territory with numerous raptors nesting on the cliffs and griffon vultures wheeling high overhead on the thermals.

For an entirely different perspective, return to Aldeadávila, and at the eastern exit to the town follow the signs down to the lovely **Playa del Rostro**, from where 1½-hour **boat journeys** (☑627 637349; www.corazondelasarribes.com; adult/3-9yr €16/8; ⊙noon & 6pm Aug, 6pm Mon-Fri, noon & 6pm Sat & Sun Jun & Jul, shorter hours rest of year) follow the canyon to the base of the cliffs.

turrón (nougat), as well as baskets and the inevitable tackier souvenirs. The centre is pretty-as-a-postcard Plaza Mayor; there's a market here on Saturday mornings.

🛏 Sleeping & Eating

Weekends are the busiest time, when Spanish tourists threaten to overwhelm the town. Come during the week and make an overnight stop to see La Alberca at its best. Restaurants and hotels are concentrated in and around Plaza Mayor.

Hotel Doña Teresa   HOTEL €€
(☑923 41 53 08; www.hoteldeteresa.com; Carretera Mogarraz; s/d €60/90; P ❄ 🛜) Doña Teresa is a perfect modern fit for the village's old-world charm and just a short stroll from Plaza Mayor. The large rooms combine character (wooden beams and exposed stonework) with all the necessary mod cons; some rooms open onto a garden. There's also a small fitness centre with sauna and Turkish bath, and a good restaurant. It is, less happily, popular with Spanish tour groups.

Hostal La Alberca   HOSTAL €
(☑923 41 51 16; www.hostallaalberca.com; Plaza Padre Arsenio; s/d/tr €29/35/49) Housed in one of La Alberca's most evocative half-timbered buildings, this charming place has comfortable, renovated rooms and small balconies overlooking the square. There's a handy restaurant and bar downstairs.

El Soportal   CASTILIAN €€
(Plaza Mayor 10; mains €11-15) Rumbling tummies may want to consider the gut-busting *parrillada* (grill) of various meats, plus potatoes and peppers (€24 for two) at this central spot.

ℹ Getting There & Away

Buses travel between La Alberca and Salamanca (€5.25, around 30 minutes) twice daily on weekdays and once a day on weekends.

Valle de las Batuecas

The drive south into Extremadura through this dreamy valley is spectacular. Just beyond La Alberca, a sweeping panorama of cascading lower mountain ranges opens up before you. The road corkscrews down into the valley before passing through beautiful terrain that has been praised by poets and the writer/academic Miguel de Unamuno. Time your visit for spring when purple heather and brilliant yellow rapeseed blanket the hillsides.

Peña de Francia

Head north from La Alberca along the C512 and you'll soon strike the turn-off to the highest peak in the area, Peña de Francia (1732m), topped by a monastery and reached by a road that turns perilous after rain. Views extend east to the Sierra de Gredos, south into Extremadura and west towards Portugal.

Sierra de Béjar

Between the Sierra de Francia and the Sierra de Gredos, the Sierra de Béjar is home to more delightful villages and rolling mountain scenery, normally snowcapped until well after Easter. It is an excellent region for outdoor activities. The centre of the region is Béjar, whose partly walled old quarters straddle the western end of a high ridge. Among the worthwhile sights is the eye-catching 16th-century Palacio Ducal, just west of Plaza Mayor. A charming place to stay in town is the Hospedaría Real de Béjar (☎923 40 84 94; www.hospederiarealdebejar. com; Plaza de la Piedad 34; s/d €75/100; P❋🛋) with elegant rooms and a good restaurant.

Just east of the mountains, the C500 leads to El Barco de Ávila, which has an appealing setting on Río Tormes and is lorded over by a proud, if ruined, castle.

The most scenic village in the region is tiny Candelario (population 1033), a 5km detour from Béjar. Nudging against a steep rock face, this charming village is dominated by mountain architecture of stone-and-wood houses clustered closely together to protect against the harsh winter climate. It is a popular summer resort and a great base for hiking. Contact Tormes (☎923 40 80 89; www.aventur.es; Calle Tormes 7) for organised hikes and other activities.

Béjar and Candelario are served by sporadic bus services from Salamanca and various other destinations, including Madrid and Plasencia.

THE CENTRAL PLATEAU

There's something soul-stirring about the high *meseta* (plateau) with its seemingly endless horizon. But from the plains spring the delightful towns of the Castilian heartland – magical Segovia, energetic Valladolid, the Romanesque glories of Zamora and the exceptional cathedral of Palencia.

Segovia

POP 55,220 / ELEV 1002M

Unesco World Heritage–listed Segovia has always had a whiff of legend about it, not least in the myths that the city was founded by Hercules or by the son of Noah. It may also have something to do with the fact that nowhere else in Spain has such a stunning monument to Roman grandeur (the soaring aqueduct) survived in the heart of a vibrant modern city. Or maybe it's because art really has imitated life Segovia-style – Walt Disney is said to have modelled Sleeping Beauty's castle in California's Disneyland on Segovia's Alcázar. Whatever it is, the effect is stunning: a city of warm terracotta and sandstone hues set amid the rolling hills of Castilla and against the backdrop of the Sierra de Guadarrama.

History

Founded by Celtiberian tribes, Segovia was occupied by the Romans in 80 BC and rose to become an important town of Roman Hispania. As Christian Spain recovered from the initial shock of the Muslim attack, Segovia became something of a frontline city until the invaders were definitively evicted in 1085. Later a favourite residence of Castilla's roaming royalty, the city backed Isabel and saw her proclaimed queen in the Iglesia de San Miguel in 1474. After backing the wrong side in the Guerra de las Comunidades (War of the Communities) in 1520, Segovia slid into obscurity until the 1960s, when tourism helped regenerate the town. This rebirth gained added momentum in 1985 when the Old Town and aqueduct were added to Unesco's World Heritage list, bringing Segovia to the attention of the world and sparking a tourist boom that has not yet abated.

Segovia

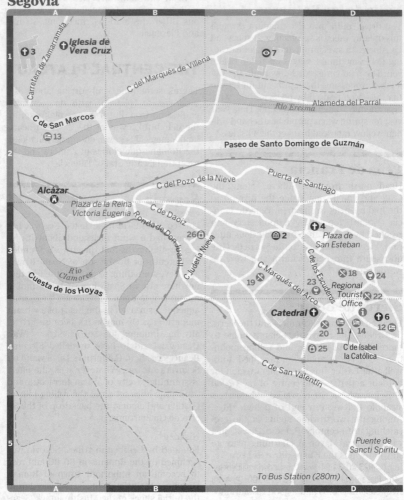

◉ Sights

TOP CHOICE Acueducto ROMAN AQUEDUCT

Segovia's most recognisable symbol is El Acueducto (Roman Aqueduct), an 894m-long engineering wonder that looks like an enormous comb plunged into Segovia. First raised here by the Romans in the 1st century AD, the aqueduct was built with not a drop of mortar to hold the more than 20,000 uneven granite blocks together. It's made up of 163 arches and, at its highest point in Plaza del Azoguejo, rises 28m high. It was most probably built around AD 50 as part of a complex system of aqueducts and un-derground canals that brought water from the mountains more than 15km away. By some accounts, it once reached as far as the Alcázar. The aqueduct's pristine condition is attributable to a major restoration project in the 1990s. For a different perspective, climb the stairs next to the aqueduct that begin be-hind the tourist office.

Alcázar CASTLE

(www.alcazardesegovia.com; Plaza de la Reina Vic-toria Eugenia; adult/child €4/3, tower €2, EU citi-zens free 3rd Tue of month; ☉10am-7pm Apr-Sep) Rapunzel towers, turrets topped with slate

Segovia

witches' hats and a *deep* moat at its base make the Alcázar a prototype fairy-tale castle, so much so that its design inspired Walt Disney's vision of Sleeping Beauty's castle.

Fortified since Roman days, the site takes its name from the Arabic *al-qasr* (fortress). It was rebuilt and expanded in the 13th and 14th centuries, but the whole lot burned down in 1862. What you see today is an evocative, over-the-top reconstruction of the original. Highlights include the **Sala de las Piñas**, with its ceiling of 392 pineapple-shaped 'stalactites', and the **Sala de Reyes**, featuring a three-dimensional frieze of 52 sculptures of kings who fought during the Reconquista. The views from the summit of the Torre de Juan II are truly exceptional and put the Old Town's hilltop location into full context.

Iglesia de Vera Cruz CHURCH
(Carretera de Zamarramala; admission €1.75; ⊙10.30am-1.30pm & 4-7pm Tue-Sun, closed Nov) This 12-sided church is the most interesting of Segovia's churches, and one of the best-preserved of its kind in Europe. Built in the

THE DEVIL'S WORK

Although no one really doubts that the Romans built the aqueduct, a local legend asserts that two millennia ago a young girl, tired of carrying water from the well, voiced a willingness to sell her soul to the devil if an easier solution could be found. No sooner said than done. The devil worked through the night, while the girl recanted and prayed to God for forgiveness. Hearing her prayers, God sent the sun into the sky earlier than usual, catching the devil unawares with only a single stone lacking to complete the structure. The girl's soul was saved, but it seems like she got her wish anyway. Perhaps God didn't have the heart to tear down the aqueduct.

early 13th century by the Knights Templar and based on Jerusalem's Church of the Holy Sepulchre, it once housed a piece of the Vera Cruz (True Cross), now in the nearby village church of Zamarramala (on view only at Easter).

The curious two-storey chamber in the circular nave (the inner temple) is where the knights' secret rites took place and where they stood vigil over the holy relic. For fantastic views of the town and the Sierra de Guadarrama, walk uphill behind the church for approximately 1km.

Catedral CATHEDRAL

(Plaza Mayor; adult/concession €3/2; ◉9.30am-6.30pm) Started in 1525 after its Romanesque predecessor had burned to the ground in the War of the Communities, Segovia's cathedral is a final, powerful expression of Gothic architecture in Spain that took almost 200 years to complete. The austere three-nave interior is anchored by an imposing choir stall and enlivened by 20-odd chapels. One of these, the **Capilla del Cristo del Consuelo**, which leads into the cloister, houses a magnificent Romanesque doorway preserved from the original church. The **Capilla de la Piedad** contains an important altarpiece by Juan de Juni, while the **Capilla del Cristo Yacente** (with its fine ceiling) and **Capilla del Santísimo Sacramento** are also especially beautiful. The Gothic cloister is lovely, while the attached **Museo Catedralicio** will appeal to devotees of religious art.

Plaza de San Martín SQUARE

This is one of the most captivating small plazas in Segovia. The square is presided over by a statue of Juan Bravo, the 14th-century **Torreón de Lozoya** (admission free; ◉5-9pm Tue-Fri, noon-2pm & 5-9pm Sat & Sun), a tower that now houses exhibitions, and the **Iglesia de San Martín** (Plaza de San Martín; ◉before & after Mass), a pièce de Romanesque résistance with its Mudéjar tower and arched gallery. The interior boasts a Flemish Gothic chapel.

Museo de Arte Contemporáneo Esteban Vicente GALLERY

(www.museoestebanvicente.es; Plazuela de las Bellas Artes; adult/concession €3/1.50, Thu free; ◉11am-2pm & 4-7pm Tue & Wed, 11am-2pm & 4-8pm Thu & Fri, 11am-8pm Sat, 11am-3pm Sun) This adventurous art space occupies a 15th-century palace, complete with Renaissance chapel and Mudéjar ceiling. Some 153 abstract paintings, lithographs and sculptures by Segovia-born artist Esteban Vicente (1903–2000), a fine painter of the abstract expressionist school, form the core of the exhibit.

Casa-Museo de Antonio Machado MUSEUM

(Calle de los Desamparados 5; admission €2, Wed free; ◉11am-2pm & 4.30-7.30pm Wed-Sun) This museum commemorates Antonio Machado, a *segoviano* and one of Spain's pre-eminent 20th-century poets. He lived here from 1919 to 1932 and his former home contains his furnishings and personal effects. Obligatory guided tours leave hourly.

Convento de los Carmelitas Descalzos CONVENT

(Carretera de Zamarramala; admission by donation; ◉10am-1.30pm & 4-8pm Tue-Sun, 4-8pm Mon) This is where San Juan de la Cruz is buried. The area immediately south of the convent affords fine views up to the Alcázar, and it's worth coming down here just for the views.

Monasterio del Parral MONASTERY

(Calle Del Marqués de Villena; admission by donation; ◉10am-12.30pm & 4.15-6.30pm Mon-Sat, 10-11.30am & 4.15-6.30pm Sun) Ring the bell to see part of the cloister and church; the latter is a proud, flamboyant Gothic structure. The monks chant a Gregorian Mass at noon on Sundays, and at 1pm daily in summer.

Convento de San Antonio El Real CONVENT

(Calle de San Antonio El Real 6; adult/child €2/free; ◉10am-2pm Wed-Sun) About 1.3km southeast of the aqueduct, this was once the summer residence of Enrique IV. The Gothic-Mudéjar church has a splendid ceiling.

Iglesia de San Miguel
CHURCH

(Plaza Mayor; ☺before & after Mass) On Plaza Mayor, this church – where Isabel was proclaimed Queen of Castile – recedes humbly into the background before the splendour of the cathedral across the square.

Iglesia de San Esteban
CHURCH

(Plaza de San Esteban; ☺before & after Mass) Has a lovely six-level sandstone tower and baroque interior.

✦ Festivals & Events

Fiestas de San Juan y San Pedro
PILGRIMAGE

(☺24-29 Jun) On San Juan's day (29 June), a pilgrimage takes place to a hermitage outside town, where, says a tourist office handout, 'according to tradition and owing to the profound state of merriment caused by the abundant consumption of spirits, the sun is supposed to rise going around in circles'. Throughout the six days of festivities, there are parades, concerts and bullfights.

Fiesta San Frutos
PATRON SAINT FESTIVAL

(☺25 Oct) Segovia celebrates the town's patron saint, who is said to be the healer of hernias and bodily fractures. The event is marked in the cathedral with choral singing.

🛏 Sleeping

⭐TOP CHOICE Hospedería La Gran Casa Mudéjar
HISTORIC HOTEL €€

(☎921 46 62 50; www.lacasamudejar.com; Calle de Isabel la Católica 8; r €90; ❄@🐾) Spread over two buildings, this place has been magnificently renovated, blending genuine, 15th-century Mudéjar carved wooden ceilings in some rooms with modern amenities. In the newer wing, the rooms on the top floors have fine mountain views out over the rooftops of Segovia's old Jewish quarter. Adding to the appeal, there's a small spa and the hotel's El Fogón Sefardi restaurant comes highly recommended.

Hotel Alcázar
BOUTIQUE HOTEL €€€

(☎921 43 85 68; www.alcazar-hotel.com; Calle de San Marcos 5; s/d incl breakfast €135/163; ❄🐾) Sitting by the riverbank in the valley beneath the Alcázar, this charming, tranquil little hotel has lavish rooms beautifully styled to suit those who love old-world luxury. Breakfast on the back terrace is a lovely way to pass the morning, and there's an intimacy and graciousness about the whole experience.

Hostal Fornos
HOSTAL €

(☎921 46 01 98; www.hostalfornos.com; Calle de la Infanta Isabel 13; s/d €41/55; ❄) This tidy little *hostal* is a cut above most other places in this price category. It has a lovely cheerful atmosphere and rooms with a fresh white-linen-and-wicker-chair look. Some rooms are larger than others, but the value is unbeatable.

Natura – La Hostería
HOTEL €

(☎921 46 67 10; www.naturadesegovia.com; Calle de Colón 5-7; r €60; ❄🐾) An eclectic choice a few streets back from Plaza Mayor. The owner obviously has a penchant for Dalí prints and the rooms have plenty of character, with chunky wooden furnishings and bright paintwork.

Hotel Infanta Isabel
HOTEL €€

(☎921 46 13 00; www.hotelinfantaisabel.com; Plaza Mayor 12; r €60-116; ❄🐾) The colonnaded building fits well with the hotel's interior of period furnishings in most of the spacious rooms. The style may be classic in orientation, but there's a lovely sense of light and space here. Some rooms overlook Plaza Mayor.

Hotel Los Linajes
HOTEL €€

(☎921 46 04 75; www.hotelloslinajes.com; Calle del Doctor Valesco 9; s/d €87/118; ❄🐾) The rooms are large and filled with character, and all look out onto the hills; many also have cathedral and/or Alcázar views.

✕ Eating

Segovianos love their pigs to the point of obsession. Just about every restaurant boasts its *horno de asar* (roasts). The main speciality is *cochinillo asado*, but *judiones de la granja* (butter beans with pork chunks) also looms large.

🛈 BEST VIEWS OF TOWN

For *the* shot of Segovia to impress the folks back home, head out of town due north (towards Cuéllar) for around 2km. The view of the city unfolds in all its movie-style magic, with the aqueduct taking a star role – as well it should. Other fine views are to be had from the Convento de los Carmelitas Descalzos and from the car park next to the Alcázar.

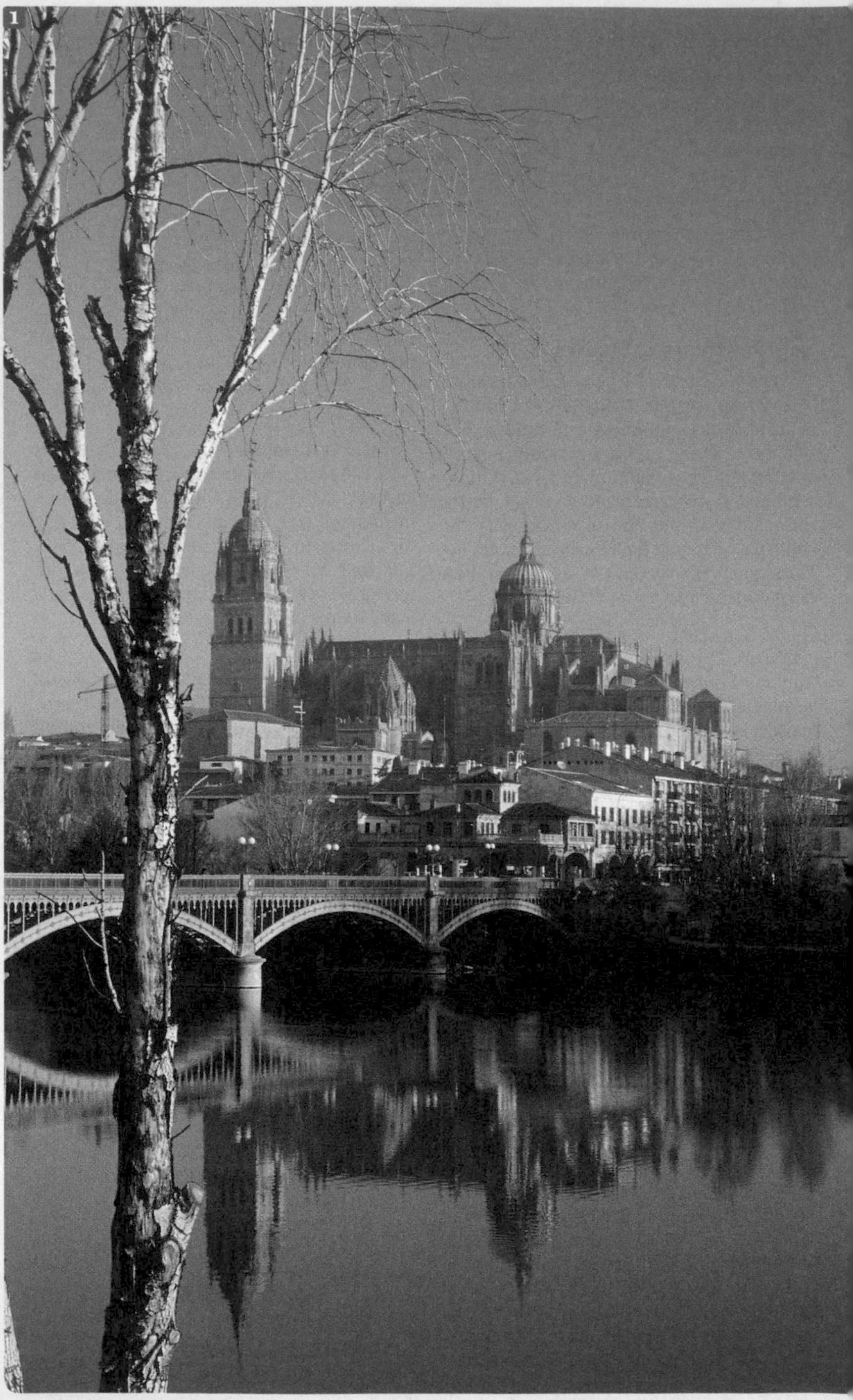
1

2

4

LAR CITYSCAPES / ALAMY ©

1. Salamanca (p143)
A city of rare architectural splendour, with a virtuosity of plateresque and Renaissance styles.

2. León Cathedral (p178)
A 13th-century cathedral with soaring towers, flying buttresses and a truly breathtaking interior.

3. Lerma (p194)
A pretty hilltop town with cobblestoned streets, delightful plazas and a 17th-century convent.

4. Peñaranda de Duero (p195)
Originally a Celtic fortress village, offering superb views from its 15th-century castle ruins.

3

TOP CHOICE Restaurante El Fogón Sefardí
SEPHARDIC €€

(☑921 46 62 50; www.lacasamudejar.com; Calle de Isabel la Católica 8; meals €30-40; 🍴) Located within the Hospedería La Gran Casa Mudéjar, this is one of the most original places in town. Sephardic cuisine is served on the intimate patio or in the splendid dining hall with original, 15th-century Mudéjar flourishes. The theme in the bar is equally diverse, with dishes from all continents and some fabulous set menus. Downstairs, the tapas are similarly creative. Reservations recommended.

TOP CHOICE Casa Duque
GRILL €€

(☑921 46 24 87; www.restauranteduque.es; Calle de Cervantes 12; menús del día €21-40, meals €25-35) *Cochinillo asado* has been served here since the 1890s. For the uninitiated, try the *menú segoviano* (€30), which includes *cochinillo*, or the *menú gastronómico* (€43.50). Downstairs is the informal *cueva* (cave), where you can get tapas and full-bodied *cazuelas* (stews). Reservations recommended.

Mesón de Cándido
GRILL €€

(☑921 42 81 03; www.mesondecandido.es; Plaza del Azoguejo 5; meals €30-40; 🍴) Set in a delightful 18th-century building in the shadow of the aqueduct, Mesón de Cándido is famous for its *cochinillo asado* and the roast boar with apple. Reservations recommended.

Di Vino
MODERN SPANISH €€

(☑921 46 16 50; www.restaurantedivino.com; Calle de Valdeláguila 7; mains €15-25; ⊗lunch & dinner Wed-Mon; 🍴) Dine in snazzy modern surroundings on dishes that combine the traditional, like *pierna de cabrito al horno* (roasted leg of lamb), with the innovative, like the starter of *bacalau bloody mary* (cod-infused bloody mary) or risotto with artichokes and prawns. The restaurant prides itself on its extensive wine list. Reservations recommended.

La Almuzara
ITALIAN €

(Calle Marqués del Arco 3; mains €7.50-11; ⊗Tue-Sat, dinner only Sun; 🍴) If you're a vegetarian, you don't need to feel like an outcast in this resolutely carnivorous city. La Almuzara features lots of vegetarian dishes, pizzas, pastas and salads, and the ambience is warm and artsy.

Mesón José María
CASTILIAN €€

(www.rtejosemaria.com; Calle del Cronista Lecea 11; mains €14-26) Offers great tapas in the bar and five dining rooms serving exquisite *cochinillo asado* and other local specialities.

Drinking & Entertainment

In fine weather Plaza Mayor is the obvious place for hanging out and people-watching. Calle de la Infanta Isabel is one of those Spanish streets that you'll definitely hear before you see; locals call it 'Calle de los Bares' (Street of the Bars). Another good street for bars and nightclubs is nearby Calle de los Escuderos.

La Tasquina
WINE BAR

(Calle de Valdeláguila 3; ⊗9pm-late) This wine bar draws crowds large enough to spill out onto the pavement, nursing their good wines, *cavas* (sparkling wines) and cheeses.

Buddha Bar
CLUB

(Calle de los Escuderos 3; ⊗9pm-late) This place has lounge music that turns more towards house as the night wears on.

🛍 Shopping

Artesanía La Gárgola
CRAFT

(www.gargolart.com; Calle Judería Vieja 4; ⊗11.30am-2.30pm & 5-8pm Tue-Sat) There are many shops worth browsing in Segovia but make sure you check out these unusual, high-quality handmade crafts and souvenirs in ceramic, wood and textile.

Montón de Trigo Montón de Paja
SOUVENIRS

(www.montondetrigomontondepaja.com; Plaza de la Merced 1; ⊗11am-2.30pm & 3.30-7.30pm Mon-Fri, 11.30am-3pm & 4-7.30pm Sat & Sun) With handcrafted handbags, block prints of Sego-

---

DON'T MISS

SWEET TREATS

If you are one of those people who scoffs all the marzipan off the Christmas cake, you will love Segovia's speciality: *ponche segoviano* (literally 'Segovian punch'), but far removed from that insipid low-alcohol drink you used to consume as a spotty teenager. This is a rich lemon-infused sponge cake coated with marzipan and topped with icing sugar in a distinctive criss-cross pattern. A good place to indulge in your *ponche* passion is the patisserie **Limón y Menta** (Calle de Isabel La Católica 2; ⊗8am-11pm), just off Plaza Mayor.

via and a host of other artsy, locally made items, this shop is ideal for creative gifts.

❶ Information

Centro de Recepción de Visitantes (tourist office; www.turismodesegovia.com; Plaza del Azoguejo 1; ◉10am-7pm Sun-Fri, 10am-8pm Sat) Segovia's main tourist office has plenty of information and also runs guided tours, departing daily at 11.15am for a minimum of four people.

Regional tourist office (www.segoviaturismo. es; Plaza Mayor 10; ◉9am-8pm Sun-Thu, 9am-9pm Fri & Sat)

❶ Getting There & Away

BUS The bus station is just off Paseo de Ezequiel González, near Avenida de Fernández Ladreda. Buses run half-hourly to Segovia from Madrid's Paseo de la Florida bus stop (€6.70, 1½ hours). Buses depart to Ávila (€5, one hour, five daily), Salamanca (€11.08, 2½ hours, two daily) and almost hourly to Valladolid (€8.20, 2¾ hours).

CAR & MOTORCYCLE Of the two main roads down to the AP6, which links Madrid and Galicia, the N603 is the prettier. The alternative N110 cuts southwest across to Ávila and northeast to the main Madrid–Burgos highway.The nearest underground car park to the historic centre is in Plaza de la Artillería near the aqueduct.

TRAIN There are two options by train: up to nine normal trains run daily from Madrid to Segovia (€6.75, two hours), leaving you at the main train station 2.5km from the aqueduct. The faster option is the high-speed Avant (€10.60, 28 minutes), which deposits you at the newer Segovia-Guiomar station, 5km from the aqueduct.

❶ Getting Around

Bus 9 does a circuit through the Old Town, bus 8 goes to Segovia train station and bus 11 goes to Segovia-Guiomar station. All services cost €0.90 and leave from just outside the aqueduct.

Around Segovia

LA GRANJA DE SAN ILDEFONSO

It's not hard to see why the Bourbon King Felipe V chose this site to recreate in miniature his version of Versailles, the palace of his French grandfather Louis XIV. In 1720 French architects and gardeners, together with some Italian help, began laying out the elaborate and decidedly baroque **gardens** (admission free; ◉10am-8pm; ⏹) in the western foothills of the Sierra de Guadarrama, 12km southeast of Segovia. La Granja's most famous for its 28 extravagant fountains, situated throughout the gardens, that depict ancient myths, such as those featuring Apollo and Diana. There is also a maze. If you time your visit for Wednesday, Saturday or Sunday at 5.30pm you can see the fountains in action (adult/child €4/2).

The 300-room **Palacio Real** (☎921 47 18 95; www.patrimonionacional.es; adult/concession €9/4; ◉10am-8pm), once a favoured summer residence for Spanish royalty and restored after a fire in 1918, is impressive but perhaps the lesser of La Granja's jewels. The palace includes the colourful **Museo de Tapices** (Tapestry Museum).

Up to a dozen daily buses to La Granja depart regularly from Segovia's bus station (€1.50, 20 minutes).

PEDRAZA DE LA SIERRA
POP 200

The captivating walled village of Pedraza de la Sierra, about 37km northeast of Segovia, is eerily quiet during the week; its considerable number of restaurants, bars and eclectic shops spring to life with the swarms of weekend visitors. Bus services to Pedraza are sporadic at best.

◉ Sights

At the far end of town stands the lonely **Castillo de Pedraza** (admission €5; ◉11am-2pm & 5-8pm Wed-Sun), unusual for its intact outer wall. The 14th-century **Plaza Mayor** is similarly evocative with its ancient columned arcades.

✷ Festivals & Events

Concierto de las Velas   MUSIC
On the first and second Sunday in July, Pedraza hosts the atmospheric Conciertos de las Velas, when the electricity is shut down and live music is performed in a village lit only by candles.

🛏 Sleeping

Hospedería de Santo Domingo   HOTEL €€
(☎921 50 99 71; www.hospederiadesantodomingo. com; Calle Matadero 3; d from €89) The excellent Hospedería de Santo Domingo has terrific rooms decked out in warm ochre and earth colours. Most have large terraces overlooking the low hills nearby, criss-crossed with dry stone walls.

🔒 Shopping

De Natura   ANTIQUES
(☎921 50 98 52; Calle Calzada 8) For a wonderful rural shopping experience, visit this three-storey barn-house filled with quality

---

DON'T MISS

CASTILLA Y LEÓN'S BEST CASTLES

While Segovia's Disneyesque Alcázar may get all the attention, lonely hilltop castles are something of a regional specialty. Our favourites include the following:

Pedraza de la Sierra (p163) An unusually intact outer wall northeast of Segovia.

Turégano A unique 15th-century castle-church complex 30km north of Segovia.

Coca (guided tours €2.50; ☉tours 10am-1.30pm & 4.30-7pm Mon-Fri, 11am-1pm & 4-7pm Sat & Sun) An all-brick, virtuouso piece of Gothic-Mudéjar architecture 50km northwest of Segovia.

Ponferrada (adult/concession €4/2; ☉10am-2pm & 4.30-8.30pm Tue-Sun) A fortress-monastery built by the Knights Templar in the 13th century west of León.

Peñafiel (p195) One of the longest in Spain and now a wine museum.

Gormaz A 10th-century, Muslim-era fortress with 21 towers 14km south of El Burgo de Osma.

Castilian bric-a-brac, including furnishings and traditional clay and porcelain crockery.

Valladolid

POP 313,440

Connected by air to London, Brussels and Milan, and by fast train to Madrid, Valladolid is a city on the upswing and a convenient gateway to northern Spain. An attractive place with a very Spanish character, the city's appeal is in its sprinkling of monuments, the fine Plaza Mayor and its excellent museums. By night, Valladolid comes alive as its large student population overflows from the city's boisterous bars.

☉ Sights

The old heart of Valladolid is compact and easy to cover on foot, with most sights in the narrow streets north and east of the Plaza Mayor.

Museo Nacional de Escultura   MUSEUM
(http://museoescultura.mcu.es; Calle de San Gregorio 2; adult/concession €3/1.50, Sat afternoon & Sun free; ☉10am-2pm & 4-7.30pm Tue-Sat, 10am-2pm Sun) Spain's premier showcase of polychrome wood sculpture is housed in the former Colegio de San Gregorio (1496), a flamboyant example of the Isabelline Gothic style where exhibition rooms line a splendid two-storey galleried courtyard. Works by Alonso de Berruguete, Juan de Juní and Gregorio Fernández are the star attractions, especially some enormously expressive fragments from Berruguete's high altar for Valladolid's Iglesia de San Benito. Downstairs is a small wing dedicated to Fernández, whose melodramatic intensity is especially well reflected in his painfully lifelike sculpture of a dead Christ.

Plaza de San Pablo   SQUARE
Virtually next to the Museo Nacional de Escultura, this open square is dominated by the exquisite Iglesia de San Pablo. The church's main facade is an extravagant masterpiece of Isabelline Gothic, with every square centimetre finely worked, carved and twisted to produce a unique fabric in stone. Also fronting the square is the Palacio de Pimentel, where, on 12 July 1527, Felipe II was born. A tiled mural in the palace's entrance hall depicts scenes from the life of the king. The palace hosts occasional exhibitions.

Museo Patio Herreriano   GALLERY
(www.museopatioherreriano.org; Calle de Jorge Guillén 6; adult/concession €3/2, Wed & Sun €1; ☉11am-2pm & 5-8pm Tue-Fri, 11am-8pm Sat, 10am-3pm Sun) Dedicated to post-WWI Spanish art, this museum contains works by Salvador Dalí, Joan Miró, Basque sculptor Eduardo Chillida, Jorge Oteiza, Antoni Tàpies and Esteban Vicente, arrayed around the cloisters of a former monastery.

Casa-Museo de Colón   MUSEUM
(Calle de Colón; adult/child €2/free, Wed €1; ☉10am-2pm & 5-8.30pm Tue-Sun; ⊞) The Casa-Museo de Colón is a superb museum spread over four floors. It has interactive exhibits, and wonderful old maps take you on a journey through Christopher Columbus' (Cristóbal Colón in Spanish) journeys to the Americas. The top floor describes Valladolid in the days of the great explorer (who died here in 1506).

Catedral   CATHEDRAL

(Calle de Arribas 1; museum adult/concession €3/1.50; ☺10am-1.30pm & 4.30-7pm Tue-Sat, 10am-2pm Sun) Valladolid's 16th-century cathedral is not Castilla's finest, but it does have an extravagant altarpiece by Juní and a processional monstrance by Juan de Arfe in the attached **Museo Diocesano y Catedralicio**. Outside, check out the 13th-century **ruins of the Collegiate Church** (atop which the cathedral was built) on the cathedral's northeastern perimeter.

Casa de Cervantes   MUSEUM

(http://museocasacervantes.mcu.es; Calle del Rastro; adult/child €3/free, Sun free; ☺9.30am-3pm Tue-Sat, 10am-3pm Sun) Cervantes was briefly imprisoned in Valladolid; his house is happily preserved behind a quiet little garden.

FREE Colegio de Santa Cruz   HISTORIC BUILDING

(Calle Cardenal Mendoza; ☺hours vary) Check out the colonnaded patio and chapel with super-realistic *Cristo de la Luz* sculpture. The Colegio, which often hosts temporary exhibitions, is located just east of Plaza de Santa Cruz.

Iglesia de Santa María la Antigua   CHURCH

(Calle Antigua 1; ☺before & after Mass) Stunning 14th-century Gothic church with elegant Romanesque tower.

Iglesia de San Benito El Real   CHURCH

(Calle de San Benito; ☺before & after Mass) One of the loveliest church facades in Valladolid with unusual 16th-century octagonal columns.

🛏 Sleeping

Valladolid's hotels see more businesspeople than tourists during the week, so prices at many hotels drop considerably from Friday to Sunday.

Hostal París   HOSTAL €

(☎983 37 06 25; www.hostalparis.com; Calle de la Especería 2; s/d €40/50; ❄🐾) One of the closest places to Plaza Mayor, Hostal París has had the interior designers in. Washed in pale pastel colours with striking abstract art panels, good-size desks and flat-screen TVs, the rooms successfully combine comfort with a classy feel.

Hotel Meliá Recoletos   HOTEL €€

(☎983 21 62 00; www.solmelia.com; Acera de Recoletos 13; s/d €75/100; 🅿❄@🐾) This excellent four-star hotel has a touch of class that elevates it above other hotels in this category. Part of a chain but with a boutique-hotel intimacy, it offers large luxurious rooms with a classic look and impeccable service. With a predominantly business clientele, the hotel lowers its rates considerably from Friday to Sunday.

Hostal Los Arces   HOTEL €

(☎983 35 38 53; www.hostallosarces.com; Calle de San Antonio de Padua 2; d/tr €40/50, s with washbasin €18) This place is outstanding value, with pleasant, renovated rooms with TV, most of which overlook a reasonably quiet street. The owner is friendly in an understated, Castilian kind of way.

Hotel El Nogal   HOTEL €

(☎983 34 03 33; www.hotelelnogal.com; Calle del Conde Ansúrez 10-12; s/d €50/60; 🅿❄) Hotel El Nogal's rooms sport polished floorboards, colourful crimson drapes and bedspreads, and modern bathrooms, most equipped

---

IT COULD HAVE BEEN SO DIFFERENT

Wondering why some of the great names of Spanish history – El Cid, Cervantes, Christopher Columbus and the merciless Inquisitor General Fray Tomás de Torquemada – were all connected with Valladolid? It's because the city was considered Spain's capital-in-waiting. In short, Valladolid could have been Madrid.

Fernando of Aragón and Isabel of Castilla (the Reyes Católicos, or Catholic Monarchs) discreetly married here in 1469. As Spain's greatest-ever ruling duo, they carried Valladolid to the height of its splendour. Its university was one of the most dynamic on the peninsula and Carlos I made Valladolid the seat of imperial government. Felipe II was born here in 1527 but, 34 years later, chose to make Madrid the capital, even though Madrid was considerably smaller. Valladolid, which had become too powerful for its own good, was aghast. In 1601 Felipe III moved the royal court back to Valladolid, but the move was so unpopular that the court returned to Madrid, there to remain in perpetuity.

With Spain's return to democracy after 1975, the *vallisoletanos* (people from Valladolid) had to be content with their city becoming the administrative capital of Castilla y León.

Valladolid

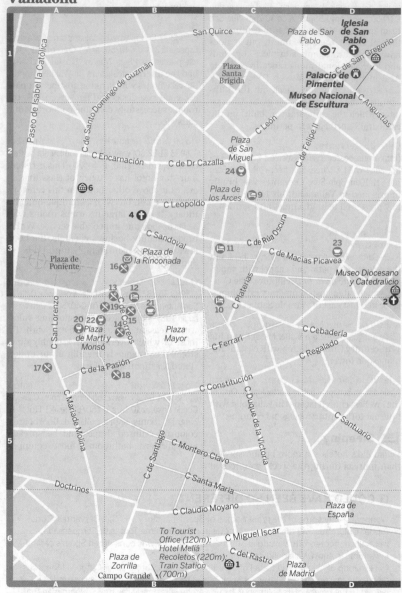

with hydro-massage showers. All rooms face either a square or a quiet street.

Hotel Imperial HOTEL **€€**
(☎983 33 03 00; www.himperial.com; Calle Peso 4; s/d €60/65; ❄️🀫) This solid, comfortable hotel around the corner from Plaza Mayor has a warm old-fashioned feel in its public spaces, while the carpeted rooms are more modern, with sunny cream-and-yellow paintwork. The bathrooms are large and glossy.

Valladolid

⊙ Top Sights
Iglesia de San Pablo...........................D1
Museo Nacional de Escultura............D1
Palacio de Pimentel...........................D1

⊙ Sights
1 Casa de Cervantes..........................C6
2 Catedral...D4
3 Colegio de Santa Cruz.....................F4
4 Iglesia de San Benito El Real...........B3
5 Iglesia de Santa María la
 Antigua...E3
6 Museo Patio Herreriano...................A2
7 Plaza de San Pablo..........................D1
8 Ruins of the Collegiate Church.........E3

⊜ Sleeping
9 Hostal Los Arces..............................C2
10 Hostal París......................................C4
11 Hotel El Nogal..................................C3
12 Hotel Imperial..................................B4

⊗ Eating
13 Bar Zamora.......................................B3
14 El Caballo de Troya..........................B4
15 Herbe..B4
16 Jero...B3
17 La Parrilla de San Lorenzo...............A4
18 Los Zagales de Abadía.....................B4
19 Vinotinto...B4

⊙ Drinking
20 Be Bop...A4
21 Café Continental..............................B4
22 Café de la Comedia..........................A4
23 El Minuto..D3
24 Harlem Music Club...........................C2

hanging local produce, all represented in the prize-winning tapas displayed along the bar – this place has done well not just at local competitions but nationwide and it could be our favourite tapas bar in town. Even so, Los Zagales is best known for its restaurant, where the servings are generous and the food excellent. Reservations recommended.

El Caballo de Troya SPANISH €€
(☎983 33 93 55; www.restaurantesanti.es; Calle de Correos 1; mains €9.20-32; ☺Mon-Sat) The 'Trojan Horse' is a Valladolid treat, ranged around a stunning Renaissance-style courtyard with a *taberna* downstairs for brilliant *raciones* – choose the *bandeja surtidas* (tasting platters) for a rich and varied combination of tastes. The restaurant is as sophisticated in

✗ Eating
Los Zagales de Abadía CONTEMPORARY CASTILIAN €€
(☎983 38 08 92; www.loszagales.com; Calle de la Pasión 13; set menus €19-26, mains €18-21; ☺Mon-Sat, lunch Sun) The bar here is awash with

flavours as the dining room is classy in design. Reservations recommended.

Herbe
CASTILLAN €€

(Calle de Correos 6; menus €12, mains €8-18; ⊗Mon-Sat) A tad more down-to-earth than some of its grander neighbours, Herbe's set menu is, unusually, available both lunchtime and evening. You could go down the tapas road but its *lechazo asado* (roast lamb) is outstanding. The friendly service also stands out.

Vinotinto
CASTILLAN €€

(Calle de Campanas 4; mains €12-20) This is where wine bar meets steakhouse, sizzling nightly with local gossip, spare ribs and other grilled meats in a cavernous tavern atmosphere. The local *jamón ibérico* is particularly good, sliced so finely as to melt in the mouth. The modern Vinotinto Joven, opposite, has a more intimate, younger feel and does some fabulous tapas such as *brocheta de calabacin y cigala* (zucchini and prawn brochette).

La Parrilla de San Lorenzo
CASTILLAN €€

(⊘983 33 50 88; www.hotel-convento.com; Calle de Pedro Niño; mains €14-22; ⊗bar 10.30am-late, restaurant Mon-Sat, lunch Sun) Both a rustic stand-up bar and a much-lauded restaurant in the evocative setting of a former monastery, La Parilla de San Lorenzo specialises in upmarket Castilian cuisine (hearty stews, legumes and steaks). Reservations recommended.

Bar Zamora
TAPAS €€

(Calle de Correos 5; ⊗closed Wed) This prize-winning tapas bar courts flavours from western Castilla.

Jero
TAPAS €

(Calle de Correos 11) For an excellent range of Basque-style *pinchos* check out Jero, with innovative choices like *crema de yogur con gambas y melocotón* (creamy yoghurt with prawns and peach).

☕ Drinking & Entertainment

Café de la Comedia
COCKTAIL BAR

(Plaza de Martí y Monsó; ⊗3.30pm-late) Has that winning combo of a convivial atmosphere with killer cocktails.

Harlem Music Club
CLUB

(Calle de San Antonio de Padua; ⊗6pm-1.30am Sun-Wed, 6pm-2am Thu, 6pm-2.30am Fri & Sat) Plaza de San Miguel is a minor epicentre of the Valladolid night, and the sophisticated Harlem Music Club, around the corner and with

music from America's Deep South, is a real cut above the rest.

El Minuto
CAFE, BAR

(Calle de Macias Picavea 15; ⊗8am-1.30am) Near Valladolid's cathedral, this smooth cafe-bar is popular with students and is flanked by several other prospects for late-night drinking. The nearby Calle de Librería is an epicentre of early evening student drinking.

Café Continental
CAFE, CLUB

(Plaza Mayor 23; ⊗8am-late) This hip spot on the square features live music most nights.

Be Bop
CLUB

(Plaza de Martí y Monsó; ⊗4pm-late) All pink stilettos, G&Ts and a super-cool crowd.

ℹ Information

Tourist office (⊘983 21 93 10; www.asomateavalladolid.org; Acera de Recoletos; ⊗9am-8pm)

ℹ Getting There & Away

AIR **Air Ryanair** (www.ryanair.com) has flights to Valladolid from London (Stansted), Brussels (Charleroi), Barcelona and Málaga. **Iberia** (www.iberia.es) operates up to five daily flights to Barcelona, with connections to other cities in Spain.

TRAIN More than a dozen daily high-speed AVE train services connect Valladolid with Madrid (€36.50, one hour), but there are slower services (23/4 hours) for as little as €19.85. Other regular trains run to León (from €14.90, about two hours), Burgos (from €9.35, about 1½ hours) and Salamanca (from €8.55, 1½ hours).

ℹ Getting Around

AIR Valladolid's airport is 15km northwest of the city centre. **Linecar** (www.linecar.es) has up to five daily bus services from Valladolid to the airport (€4). A taxi between the airport and the city centre costs around €20, a little more on Sunday and holidays.

BUS Local buses 2 and 10 pass the train and bus stations on their way to Plaza de España.

Around Valladolid

MEDINA DE RIOSECO
POP 5000

Medina de Rioseco, a once-wealthy trading centre, still has a tangible medieval feel, particularly along the narrow pedestrian main street with its colonnaded arcades held up by ancient wooden columns; market stalls set up under the columns on Wednesday

THE DARK PRINCE OF THE INQUISITION

There were few more notorious personalities of the Spanish Inquisition than the zealot Fray Tomás de Torquemada (1420–98). Immortalised by Dostoevsky as the articulate Grand Inquisitor who puts Jesus himself on trial in *The Brothers Karamazov*, and satirised by Monty Python in the *Flying Circus*, Torquemada was born in Valladolid to well-placed Jewish *conversos* (converts to Christianity).

A Dominican, Fray Tomás was appointed Queen Isabel's personal confessor in 1479. Four years later, Pope Sixtus IV appointed this rising star to head the Castilian Inquisition. Deeply affected by the Spanish cult of *sangre limpia* (pure blood), the racist doctrine that drove the 800-year struggle to rid Spain of non-Christian peoples, Torquemada gleefully rooted out *conversos* and other heretics, including his favourite targets, the *marranos* (Jews who pretended to convert but continued to practise Judaism in private).

The 'lucky' sinners had their property confiscated, which served as a convenient fundraiser for the war of Reconquista against the Muslims. They were paraded through town wearing the *sambenito*, a yellow shirt emblazoned with crosses that was short enough to expose their genitals, then marched to the doors of the local church and flogged. If you were unlucky, you underwent unimaginable tortures before going through an *auto-da-fé*, a public burning at the stake. Those who recanted and kissed the cross were garrotted before the fire was set, while those who recanted only were burnt quickly with dry wood. If you stayed firm and didn't recant, the wood used for the fire was green and slow-burning.

In the 15 years Torquemada was Inquisitor General of the Castilian Inquisition, he ran some 100,000 trials and sent about 2000 people to burn at the stake. Many of the trials were conducted in Valladolid's Plaza Mayor; the executions in Plaza de Zorrilla. On 31 March 1492 Fernando and Isabel, on Torquemada's insistence, issued their Edict of Expulsion, forcing all Jews to leave Spain within two months on pain of death. The following year Torquemada retired to the monastery of Santo Tomás in Ávila, from where he continued to administer the affairs of the Inquisition. In his final years he became obsessed with the fear that he might be poisoned, and refused to eat anything without having (what he believed to be) a unicorn's horn nearby as an antidote. Unlike many of his victims, he died in his sleep in 1498.

mornings. There are also some museums and monuments.

◉ Sights

Iglesia de Santa María de Mediavilla CHURCH
(Calle Santa María; guided visits €2; ⊙11am-noon & 5-7pm Tue-Sun) This grandiose Isabelline Gothic work has three star-vaulted naves and the rightfully famous **Capilla de los Benavente** chapel. Anchored by an extravagant altarpiece by Juan de Juní and carved over eight years from 1543, it's sometimes referred to as the 'Sistine Chapel of Castilla'; it's certainly one of Spain's finest examples of Renaissance-era religious art. If you don't fancy the hour-long guided visit (although we think it's worth it), you can usually be let into the chapel for a look.

Museo de Semana Santa MUSEUM
(Calle de Lázaro Alonso; admission €3.50; ⊙11am-2pm & 4-7pm Tue-Sun) Medina de Rioseco is famous for its Easter processions, but if you can't be here during Holy Week, this museum provides an insight into the ceremonial passion of Easter here. Like its sister museum in Zamora (p172), it's dedicated to *pasos* (figures carried in Semana Santa processions) and an extensive range of other Easter artefacts.

Iglesia de Santiago CHURCH
(Calle Santa María; admission €2; ⊙11am-noon & 4-7pm Tue-Sun) Down the hill from the Iglesia de Santa María, the portals of this church blend Gothic, neoclassical and plateresque architectural styles. Access to the interior outside of summer is only possible as part of the guided tour of the Iglesia de Santa María de Mediavilla.

Museo de San Francisco CHURCH, MONASTERY
(www.museosanfrancisco.es; Paseo de San Francisco 1; admission €3; ⊙hourly guided visits 11am-1pm & 4-6pm Tue-Sun) This 16th-century former convent has an extravagant *retablo* (altarpiece) by Fray Jacinto de Sierra and a wide-ranging collection of sacred art.

COMBINED TICKETS

If you plan on visiting all four of Medina de Rioseco's sights, consider buying the combined 'Un Viaje a la Emoción' ticket for €7. It can be purchased at each of the four participating sights, and will save you €3.50.

Sleeping & Eating

Vittoria Colonna HOTEL €€
(☑983 72 50 87; www.hotelvittoriacolonna.es; Calle de San Juan 2b; s/d €55/75; ❄️🌐) This elegant modern three-star hotel opened in 2009 and offers well-sized and well-appointed rooms. Some are nicer than others, but all have smart grey-and-white bathrooms. It has a good restaurant.

Hostal Duque de Osuna HOSTAL €
(☑983 70 01 79; www.hostalduquedeosuna.com; Avenida de Castilviejo 16; s/d €20/33; @🌐) Handily located for the bus station, this modern, well-run *hostal* has clean, simply decorated rooms.

Restaurante Pasos CASTILIAN €€
(☑983 72 00 21; www.restaurantepasos.es; Calle de Lázaro Alonso 44; mains €13-22) Recognised as the town's top restaurant, you can expect well-prepared typical Castilian fare that courts various flavours but stays firmly in classical mould with reliable dishes such as *chuletillas de lechazo* (lamb chops). Reservations recommended.

ⓘ Information

Tourist office (☑983 72 03 19; www.medina derioseco.com; Paseo de San Francisco 1; ⏰10am-2pm & 4-6pm Tue-Sat, 10am-2pm Sun) Alongside the Museo de San Francisco.

ⓘ Getting There & Away

Up to eight daily buses run to León (€6.40, 1¼ hours) and up to 10 go to Valladolid (€2.95, 30 minutes).

TORDESILLAS

POP 8760

Commanding a rise on the northern flank of Río Duero, this pretty little town has a historical significance that belies its size. Originally a Roman settlement, it later played a major role in world history when, in 1494, Isabel and Fernando, the Catholic Monarchs, sat down with Portugal here to hammer out a treaty determining who got what in Latin America. Portugal got Brazil and much of the rest went to Spain.

Sights

Real Convento de Santa Clara CONVENT
(☑983770071; www.patrimonionacional.es; adult/ concession incl Arab baths €7/4, EU citizens & residents free Wed & Thu afternoon; ⏰10am-2pm & 4-6.30pm Tue-Sat, 10.30am-3pm Sun) The history of Tordesillas has been dominated by this Mudéjar-style convent, which is still home to a few Franciscan nuns living in near-total isolation from the outside world. First begun in 1340 as a palace for Alfonso XI, it was here, in 1494, that the Treaty of Tordesillas was signed. A 50-minute guided tour (included in the entry fee) of the convent takes in some remarkable rooms, including a wonderful Mudéjar patio left over from the palace, and the church – the stunning *techumbre* (roof) is a masterpiece. The Mudéjar door, Gothic arches and Arabic inscriptions are superb, as are the Arab baths, which are included in the tour as long as it's not raining. Note that the ticket office closes an hour earlier than the advertised time.

FREE **Museo del Tratado del Tordesillas** MUSEUM
(Calle de Casas del Tratado; ⏰10am-1.30pm & 5-7.30pm Tue-Sat, 10am-2pm Sun) Dedicated to the 1494 Treaty of Tordesillas, the informative displays in this museum look at the world as it was before and after the treaty with some fabulous old maps taking centre stage. There's a reproduction of the treaty itself and a map that suggests Spain did very well out of the negotiations. There's also a multilingual video presentation.

Exposición Permanente de Maquetas MUSEUM
(Calle de Casas del Tratado; ⏰10am-1.30pm & 5-7.30pm Tue-Sat, 10am-2pm Sun) This small display of scale models is worth a quick look. The six impressive models include Leon's Gaudí-designed Casa de Botines. It's in the building adjacent to the Museo del Tratado del Tordesillas.

Plaza Mayor SQUARE
The heart of town is formed by the pleasantly ramshackle and porticoed Plaza Mayor, its mustard-yellow paintwork offset by dark-brown woodwork and black grilles.

Sleeping & Eating

Parador de Tordesillas LUXURY HOTEL €€€
(☑983 77 00 51; www.parador.es; Carretera de Salamanca 5; r €148; 🅿❄🌐☲) Tordesillas' most

sophisticated hotel is the low-rise ochre-toned *parador*, surrounded by pine trees just outside town. Some rooms have four-poster beds, all are large and many look out onto the tranquil gardens where there's a pool and small children's playground. In the classy restaurant, the set menu costs €32, while there's also a cheaper bar/cafeteria serving snacks and lighter meals.

Hostal San Antolín   HOSTAL €
(☑983 79 67 71; www.hostalsanantolin.com; Calle San Antolín 8; s/d/tr €25/40/50; ❋❅) This place is terrific value in the Old Town, although the overall aesthetic is modern – rooms are painted in bright pastel tones, which suggests a level of care lacking in some Spanish *hostales*. Its main focus is the attached restaurant, with *raciones* downstairs in the bar, a pretty flower-decked inner patio and a fancy restaurant (set menus €11 to €24, mains €10 to €19) upstairs, which serves roasted meats. It's just off Plaza Mayor.

Viky   TAPAS €
(Plaza Mayor 14; tapas from €0.60, mains €5-16; ❅Tue-Sun) The pick of the eateries that encircle the Plaza Mayor, Viky has tapas lined up along the bar, and a varied menu of canapés, *raciones* and other tapas.

ⓘ Information

Tourist office (☑983 77 10 67; www.tordesillas.net; Calle de Casas del Tratado; ❅10am-1.30pm & 5-7.30pm Tue-Sat, 10am-2pm Sun May-Sep) In Casas del Tratado, near the Iglesia de San Antolín.

ⓘ Getting There & Away

The **bus station** (☑983 77 00 72; Avenida de Valladolid) is near Calle de Santa María. Regular buses depart for Madrid (€11.80, 2¼ hours), Salamanca (€6.50, 1¼ hours), Valladolid (€3.50, 30 minutes) and Zamora (€6, one hour).

TORO

POP 9650

With a name that couldn't be more Spanish and a stirring history that overshadows its present, Toro is your archetypal Castilian town in every sense. It was here that Fernando and Isabel cemented their primacy in Christian Spain at the Battle of Toro in 1476. These days, the town, which sits on a rise high above the north bank of Río Duero, has a charming historic centre with half-timbered houses and Romanesque churches seemingly on every street corner.

⦿ Sights

Colegiata Santa María La Mayor   CHURCH
(admission €1; ❅10.30am-2pm & 5-7.30pm Tue-Sun) This 12th-century church rises above the town and boasts the magnificent Romanesque-Gothic **Pórtico de la Majestad**. Treasures inside include the famous 15th-century painting called *Virgen de la mosca* (Virgin of the Fly); see if you can spot the fly on the virgin's robe. Entrance to the splendid main sanctuary is free; the admission fee applies to the sacristy.

Monasterio Sancti Spiritus   MONASTERY
(admission €4; ❅guided tours 10.30am-12.30pm & 4.30-5.30pm Tue-Sun) Southwest of town, this monastery features a fine Renaissance cloister and the striking alabaster tomb of Beatriz de Portugal, wife of Juan I. Guided tours run regularly during the hours indicated.

Alcázar   CASTLE
(Paseo del Espolón) Not far from the Colegiata Santa María La Mayor, this former fortress dates to the 10th century and still boasts seven towers. On the walk back to the Colegiata, admire the superb views south across the fields to the Puente Mayor de Toro, a 12th-century bridge with Roman origins over the Río Duero.

⊨ Sleeping & Eating

Plaza Mayor and nearby streets bustle with plenty of places to eat and sample local wines.

Hotel Juan II   HOTEL €€
(☑980 69 03 00; www.hotelesentoro.es; Paseo del Espolón 1; s/d €54/72; ❒❋❅❅) Request room 201 if you can for its fabulous double-whammy vista of the Río Duero to one side and the Colegiata Santa María La Mayor to the other. If it's full, ask for a south-facing room with balcony. The rooms have warm terracotta-tiled floors, dark-wood furniture and large terraces. The restaurant is one of Toro's best (mains €15.80 to €24.90) with all the usual hearty meat dishes with a few fish options.

Zaravencia   HOTEL €
(☑980 69 49 98; www.hotelzaravencia.com; Plaza Mayor 17; s/d incl breakfast €38/54; ❋@) Overlooking the lovely Plaza Mayor, this friendly place has a bar-restaurant downstairs and good-sized rooms, albeit with an anaemic decor of light pine furniture and cream walls. In-room internet access is via cable only.

ℹ️ Information

Tourist office (☎980 69 47 47; www.turismo castillayleon.com; Plaza Mayor 6; ◎10am-2pm & 4-8pm)

ℹ️ Getting There & Away

Regular buses operate to Valladolid (€4.80, one hour) and Zamora (€2.20, 30 minutes), and there are two direct services to Salamanca (€5.75, 1½ hours) on weekdays.

Zamora

POP 65,530

First appearances can be deceiving: as in so many Spanish towns, your introduction to provincial Zamora is likely to be non-descript apartment blocks. But persevere you should: Zamora's *casco historico* (old town) is hauntingly beautiful with sumptuous medieval monuments that have earned Zamora the popular sobriquet 'Romanesque Museum'. It's a subdued encore to the monumental splendour of Salamanca and one of the best places to be during Semana Santa.

◉ Sights

Catedral CATHEDRAL
(adult/concession €4/2; ◎10am-2pm & 5-8pm) Crowning medieval Zamora's southwestern extremity, the largely Romanesque cathedral features a square tower, an unusual Byzantine-style dome surrounded by turrets, and the ornate Puerta del Obispo. To enter the cathedral, you pass through the **Museo Catedralicio**, where the star attraction (on the 2nd floor) is the collection of Flemish tapestries. The oldest tapestry depicts the Trojan War and dates from the 15th century. Inside the 12th-century cathedral itself, the early-Renaissance choir stalls are a masterpiece: carvings depict clerics, animals and a naughty encounter between a monk and a nun. The other major highlights are the **Capilla de San Ildefonso**, with its lovely Gothic frescoes, and some fine Flemish tapestries in the adjoining antechamber.

Museo de Semana Santa MUSEUM
(Plaza de Santa María La Nueva; adult/concession €3/1.50; ◎10am-2pm & 5-8pm Tue-Sat, 10am-2pm Sun) This museum will initiate you into the weird-and-wonderful rites of Easter, Spanish-style. It showcases the carved and painted *pasos* that are paraded around town during the colourful processions. The hooded models are eerily lifelike.

Churches CHURCHES
(◎10am-1pm & 5-8pm Tue-Sun) Among those churches retaining some of their Romanesque charm are the **Iglesia de San Pedro y San Ildefonso** (Rúa de Francos 39), with Gothic touches, **Iglesia de la Magdalena** (Rúa de los Francos) – the southern doorway is considered the city's finest, with its preponderance of floral motifs – and **Iglesia de San Juan de Puerta Nueva** (Plaza Mayor). **Iglesia de Santa María La Nueva** (Calle de San Martín Carniceros) is actually a medieval replica of a 7th-century church destroyed by fire in 1158.

FREE **Castillo** CASTLE
(◎10am-2pm & 7-10pm Tue-Sun; 🅿️) This fine, recently restored castle of 11th-century origin is filled with local sculptures and you can climb the tower and walk the ramparts. The surrounding park is a lovely place for a picnic.

✸ Festivals & Events

Semana Santa HOLY WEEK
If you're in Spain during Holy Week, make your way to Zamora, a town made famous for its elaborate celebrations; it's one of the most evocative places in the country to view the hooded processions. Watching the penitents weave their way through the historic streets, sometimes in near-total silence, is an experience you'll never forget. During the rest of the year, the Museo de Semana Santa will provide the appropriate initiation.

🛏️ Sleeping

Prices can almost double here during Semana Santa.

Parador Condes de Alba y Aliste HISTORIC HOTEL €€€
(☎980 51 44 97; www.parador.es; Plaza Viriato 5; r €100-168; ❄️@🛜🏊) Set in a sumptuous 15th-century palace (previous 'guests' included Isabel and Fernando), this is modern luxury with myriad period touches (mostly in the public areas). There's a swimming pool out the back and, unlike many *paradores*, it's right in the heart of town. On the downside, there is very limited parking available (just eight places).

NH Palacio del Duero HOTEL €€
(☎980 50 82 62; www.nh-hotels.com; Plaza de la Horta 1; r €70; 🅿️❄️@🛜) As usual, NH has snagged a superb position for one of its latest hotels. Next to a lovely Romanesque

church, the seemingly modern building has cleverly encompassed part of the former convent, as well as (somewhat bizarrely) a 1940s power station; the lofty brick chimney still remains. Rooms are large and plushly furnished.

Hostal La Reina HOSTAL €
(☑980 53 39 39; Plaza Mayor 1 & 3; s/d €22/30, with shared bathroom €15/20) Watched over by delightful older owners, Hostal La Reina offers large rooms, the best of which have balconies overlooking Plaza Mayor.

✗ Eating & Drinking

The richest pickings for restaurants are close to Plaza Mayor (which is also good for cafes and bars). One local dish worth seeking out is *arroz a la zamorana* (rice with pork and ham). A good area for tapas bars is around Plaza del Maestro.

El Rincón de Antonio CONTEMPORARY CASTILIAN €€€
(☑980 53 53 70; www.elrincondeantonio.com; Rúa de los Francos 6; mains €19.50-26, set menus €11-65; ☺Mon-Sat, lunch Sun) A fine place boasting Zamora's only Michelin star, 'Antonio's Corner' offers tapas in the bar as well as sit-down meals in a classy, softly lit dining area. Amid the range of tasting menus, there's one consisting of four tapas for €11, including a glass of wine. In the restaurant, we recommend starting with the award-winning chickpea and wild mushroom, followed by the Galician scallops in onion leaves. Reservations recommended.

Agape TAPAS €
(Plazuela de San Miguel 3; tapas from €1.70) Of the many bars, cafes and restaurants fanning out from Plaza Mayor, this is probably the best. Ignore the pizza and pasta menu and order one of its artful and well-sized tapas – we particularly enjoyed the *salmorejo* (cold tomato soup, served in a Martini glass) and *tosta de solomillo de tres mostazas* (sirloin toast with three mustards). The service could be more attentive.

❶ Information

Municipal tourist office (☑980 54 82 00; ww.zamora.es; Plaza de Arias Gonzalo; ☺10am-2pm & 4-7pm Oct-Mar, 10am-2pm & 5-8pm Apr-Sep)
Regional tourist office (☑980 53 18 45; www.turismocastillayleon.com; Avenida Príncipe de Asturias 1; ☺9am-8pm) Organises guided tours

(free to €7), including nocturnal explorations of the city.

❶ Getting There & Away

BUS Almost hourly bus services operate to/from Salamanca (from €4.70, one hour, five to 13 daily), with less-frequent departures on weekends. Other regular services include to León (€8.15, 1½ hours), Valladolid (€7.75, 1½ hours) and Burgos (€15.45, 4½ hours).

TRAIN Trains head to Valladolid (€10.15, 1½ hours, one daily) and Madrid (€30.10, two to four hours, two daily).

Around Zamora

The lonely 7th-century **San Pedro de la Nave** (admission free; ☺10am-1pm & 5-8pm Tue-Sun), about 24km northwest of Zamora, is a rare and outstanding example of Visigoth church architecture, with blended Celtic, Germanic and Byzantine elements. Of special note are the intricately sculpted capitals. The church was moved to its present site in Campillo during the construction of the Esla reservoir in 1930. To get there from Zamora, take the N122, then follow the signs to Campillo.

PUEBLA DE SANABRIA
POP 1570
Close to the Portuguese border, this captivating little village is a tangle of medieval alleyways that unfold around a 15th-century castle and trickle down the hill. This is one of Spain's loveliest hamlets and it's well worth stopping overnight: the quiet cobblestone lanes make it feel like you've stepped back centuries.

◉ Sights

Castillo CASTLE
(adult/concession €3/2; ☺11am-2pm & 4-8pm Mon-Sat, 4-7pm Sun) Crowning the village's high point and dominating its skyline for kilometres around, Puebla de Sanabria's castle hosts some interesting displays on local history, flora and fauna; kids will love the chance to try on the pieces of armour. The views from the ramparts are splendid in all directions.

Plaza Mayor SQUARE
At the top of the village, this pretty town square is surrounded by some fine historical buildings. The 17th-century *ayuntamiento* (town hall) has a lovely arched facade and faces across the square to **Iglesia de Nuestra Señora del Azogue** (admission free; ☺11am-

2pm & 4-8pm Sat & Sun), a pretty village church which was first built in the 12th century.

🛏 Sleeping

TOP CHOICE Posada Real La Cartería
HISTORIC HOTEL €€

(☎980 62 03 12; www.lacarteria.com; Calle de Rúa 16; r €136; 🖜) This stunning old inn is one of the best hotels in this part of the country. It blends modern comforts with all the old-world atmosphere of the village itself, featuring delightful, large rooms with exposed stone walls and wooden beams, not to mention a small gym and professional service. Some rooms have fine views over the valley.

La Hoja de Roble
HISTORIC HOTEL €€

(☎980 62 01 90; www.lahojaderoble.com; Calle Constanilla 13; r €55-85; 🅿🖜) At the bottom of the hill where you begin the climb up into the Old Town, this hotel is an outstanding choice. The building dates to the 17th century and the rooms have a real sense of history (exposed stone walls, original wooden beams) without ever being oppressive.

Posada de las Misas
HOTEL €€

(☎980 62 03 58; www.posadadelasmisas.com; Plaza Mayor 13; r €136; 🅿🖜) Run by the same people who brought you Posada Real La Cartería, this place at the top of the village has modern but charming rooms.

✕ Eating

TOP CHOICE Posada Real La Cartería
CASTILIAN €€

(Calle de Rúa 16; mains €7.50-18) The local obsession with wild mushrooms (*setas, boletus*) and *trucha* (trout) caught in the river down below the village is alive and well here.

La Posada de Puebla de Sanabria
CASTILIAN €€

(www.laposadadelavilla.com; Plaza Mayor 3; mains €8-18) This excellent restaurant right on Plaza Mayor serves up local steaks and the wild mushrooms for which this region is famed.

❶ Information

Tourist office (☎980 62 07 34; www.turismos anabria.es; ⊗11am-2pm & 5-8pm) Inside the castle.

❶ Getting There & Away

There are sporadic bus services to Puebla de Sanabria from Zamora (from €7, 1¼ hours).

PARQUE NATURAL LAGO DE SANABRIA

Around 15km north of Puebla de Sanabria, this protected area centres on Spain's largest glacier lake – Lago de Sanabria covers 368 hectares and is an astonishing 55m deep. At least 10 hiking trails fan out across the park and surrounding areas, while the main Lago de Sanabria and the lovely high-altitude Lago de los Peces, deep in the park, can be reached by car. For maps and further information, stop at the Casa del Parque (⊗10am-2pm & 5-8pm Jul & Aug, Sat & Sun only Sep-Jun), 5km before reaching the park entrance, close to the village of Rabanillo on the road from Puebla de Sanabria; in addition to an information office, there's also an informative interpretation centre with information on the park's wildlife and geology (admission €1).

Palencia

POP 81,550

Subdued Palencia boasts an immense Gothic cathedral, the sober exterior of which belies the extraordinary riches that await within; it's widely known as 'La Bella Desconocida' (Unknown Beauty). Otherwise, you'll find some pretty squares, a colonnaded main street (Calle Mayor) and a slew of other churches. King Alfonso VIII founded Spain's first university here in 1208.

◉ Sights

Catedral
CATHEDRAL

(Calle Mayor Antigua 29; admission cathedral & crypt €2, museum, cathedral & crypt €3; ⊗10am-1.30pm & 4.30-7.30pm Mon-Fri, 10am-2pm & 4-5.30pm Sat, 4.30-8pm Sun) The Puerta del Obispo (Bishop's Door) is the highlight of the facade of the imposing cathedral which, at 130m long, 56m wide and 30m high, is one of the largest of the Castilian cathedrals. The interior contains a treasure trove of art.

One of the most stunning chapels is the Capilla El Sagrario: its ceiling-high altarpiece tells the story of Christ in dozens of exquisitely carved and painted panels. The stone screen behind the choir stalls (*trascoro*) is a masterpiece of bas-relief attributed to Gil de Siloé and is considered by many to be the most beautiful retrochoir in Spain. From here, a plateresque stairwell leads down to the crypt, a remnant of the original, 7th-century Visigoth church and a later Romanesque replacement. Near the stairwell is the oak pulpit, with delicate carvings of the Evangelists by Juan de Ortiz. In the attached Museo Catedralicio you'll see some fine Flemish tapestries and a painting of San Se-

WORTH A TRIP

LOOKING FOR WOLVES

Spain is home to Western Europe's largest contingent of wolves – an estimated 2000 to 2500 survive, which represents 30% of Europe's wolves outside of Eastern Europe. Spain's wolves are largely restricted to the country's northwest, with the largest population present in the Sierra de la Culebra, southeast of Puebla de Sanabria. If you're keen to catch a glimpse of this charismatic predator, contact Zamora Natural (☑655 821899; www.zamoranatural.com; per person €35; ⊙10am-2pm Tue-Fri), which runs year-round excursions in search of wolves, including a handful every month devoted to tracking wolves; sightings are certainly not guaranteed with the chances ranging between 20% and 40%. An interpretation centre devoted to the region and its wolves is also under construction in the small village of Robledo, around 8km southwest of Puebla de Sanabria.

bastián by El Greco. A whimsical highlight is a trick painting by 16th-century German artist Lucas Cranach the Elder. Looking straight on, it seems to be a surreal dreamscape that predates Dalí by some 400 years. Only when viewed from the side is the true image revealed – a portrait of Emperor Carlos V.

Iglesia de San Miguel
CHURCH
(Calle de Mayor Antigua; ⊙9.30am-1.30pm & 6.30-7.30pm Mon-Sat, 9.30am-1.30pm & 6.30-8pm Sun) This church stands out for its tall Gothic tower with a castle-like turret. San Miguel's interior is unadorned and austerely beautiful, a welcome antidote to the extravagant interiors of other Castilian churches. According to legend, El Cid was betrothed to his Doña Jimena here.

Museo Diocesano
MUSEUM
(Calle de Mayor Antigua; guided tours €4; ⊙tours 10.30am & 11.30am Mon-Sat) Located within the 18th-century Palacio Episcopal, this museum showcases art from the Middle Ages through to the Renaissance. Pride of place goes to works by Pedro de Berruguete and an altarpiece starring the Virgin (attributed to Diego de Siloé).

Modernista Architecture
ARCHITECTURE
Palencia is embellished with some real architectural gems, including the 19th-century Modernista Mercado de Abastos (Fresh Food Market) on Calle Colón, the eye-catching Collegio Vallandrando on Calle Mayor and the extraordinarily ornate neoplateresque Palacio Provincial on Calle Burgos. Step into the lobby of the latter to admire the ceiling frieze of the city under attack by the Roman legions, dating from 1904 and painted by local artist Eugenio Oliva. The tourist office has more information.

Iglesia de San Pablo
CHURCH
(Plaza de San Pablo) The main facade of this church is an extravagant masterpiece of Isabelline Gothic, with every square centimetre finely worked, carved and twisted to produce a unique fabric in stone.

🛏 Sleeping

TOP CHOICE Hotel Colón 27
HOTEL €
(☑979 74 07 00; www.hotelcolon27.com; Calle de Colón 27, s/d/tr €36/46/58; ❉ 🐾) This place is excellent value, with comfortable carpeted rooms sporting light pine furniture, good firm mattresses, shiny green-tiled bathrooms and small flat-screen TVs. It closes over Christmas and New Year to give the place a fresh coat of paint.

Diana Palace
HOTEL €€
(☑979 01 80 50; www.eurostarsdianapalace.com; Avenida Santander 12; s/d incl breakfast €60/80; 🅿 ❉ 🐾) A comfortable, albeit modern, block of a hotel within walking distance of the town centre.

🍴 Eating & Drinking

Restaurante Casa Lucio
CASTILIAN €€
(☑979 74 81 90; www.restaurantecasalucio.com; Calle de Don Sancho 2; mains €14.50-33; ⊙closed Sun) That great Spanish tradition of an over-crowded bar laden with tapas yielding to a quieter, more elegant restaurant is alive and well. Sidle up to the bar for creative tapas or consider the Castilian speciality of *cordero asado* (€43 for two) at Palencia's most famous restaurant. Reservations recommended.

Taberna Plaza Mayor
SPANISH €
(Plaza Mayor 8; mains €10.50-18) Grab an outdoor table here and choose from a selection of *raciones*, or go for more substantial

meals like the epic *chuletón de ternera* (T-bone steak); the tapas and house wine are also good.

ℹ Information

Municipal tourist office (☏979 74 99 74; www.palencia-turismo.com; Plaza de San Pablo; ⊙10.30am-2pm & 5-8.30pm)

Patronato de Turismo (☏979 70 65 23; www.palencia-turismo.com; Calle Mayor 31; ⊙9am-2pm & 5-8pm Mon-Fri, 10.30am-2.30pm Sat) Information about Palencia province.

Regional tourist office (www.turismocastillayleon.com; Calle Mayor 105; ⊙9am-8pm) Information about the entire Castilla y León region as well as some city info.

ℹ Getting There & Away

BUS From the **bus station** (Carerra del Cementerio) there are regular services to Valladolid (€3.95, 45 minutes), Madrid (€16.79, 3½ hours), Aguilar de Campóo (€5.55, 1½ hours), Frómista (€3.30, 30 minutes) and Paredes de Nava (€1.60, 25 minutes).

TRAIN Regular trains run to Madrid (from €24.80, 3¼ hours), Burgos (from €5.05, 45 minutes), León (from €9.35, 1¼ hours) and Valladolid (from €4.25, 45 minutes).

Around Palencia

BAÑOS DE CERRATO

Close to the singularly unattractive rail junction of Venta de Baños lies Spain's oldest church, the 7th-century Basílica de San Juan (admission €2, Wed free; ⊙10am-1.30pm & 4.50-8pm Tue-Sun Apr-Sep, 10.30am-1.30pm & 4-6pm Tue-Sun Oct-Mar) in Baños de Cerrato. Built by the Visigoths in 661 and modified many times since, its stone-and-terracotta facade exudes a pleasing, austere simplicity and features a 14th-century alabaster statue of St John the Baptist. To get there, take a train from Palencia to Venta de Baños, then walk the final 2km.

FRÓMISTA
POP 830

The main (some would say only) reason for stopping here is the village's exceptional Romanesque church.

☉ Sights

Iglesia de San Martín   CHURCH
(admission €1; ⊙9.30am-2pm & 4.30-8pm) Dating from 1066 and restored in the early 20th century, this harmoniously proportioned church is one of the premier Roman-esque churches in rural Spain, adorned as it is with a veritable menagerie of human and zoomorphic figures just below the eaves. The capitals within are also richly decorated.

🛏 Sleeping

Hotel San Martín   HOTEL €
(☏979 81 00 00; http://hotelsanmartin.es; Plaza San Martín 7; s/d €38/50; 🖭) Some of the rooms at this one-star hotel punch above their weight, with deep-red walls and contemporary art, while others are simple with tired wood furnishings. The location is ideal, right next to the Iglesia de San Martín. There's a decent bar-restaurant downstairs.

ℹ Getting There & Away

There are two buses daily from Palencia (€3.30, 30 minutes).

Montaña Palentina

These hills in the far north of Castilla y León offer a beautiful preview of the Cordillera Cantábrica, which divides Castilla from Spain's northern Atlantic regions. And the driving around here is some of the prettiest in the region.

AGUILAR DE CAMPÓO
POP 7230

Aguilar de Campóo is a bustling town with a sprinkling of interesting monuments. It's also the primary base for exploring the stunning scenery and Romanesque churches of the Montaña Palentina.

☉ Sights

Overlooking the town and providing its picturesque backdrop is a 12th-century castillo and the graceful Romanesque Ermita de Santa Cecilia (admission €1; ⊙11am-2pm & 5-8pm Tue-Sun).

Down in the town itself, the elongated Plaza de España is capped at its eastern end by the Colegiata de San Miguel, a 14th-century Gothic church with a fine Romanesque entrance.

Just outside town, on the highway to Cervera de Pisuerga, is the restored Romanesque Monasterio de Santa María la Real (☏979 12 30 53; Carretera de Cervera; admission with/without guided visit €5/3; ⊙4-7pm Mon-Fri, 10.30am-2pm & 4.30-7.30pm Sat & Sun Oct-Jun, 10.30am-2pm & 4.30-7.30pm Jul-Sep). Its 13th-century Gothic cloister with delicate capitals is glorious.

📛 Sleeping & Eating

There's plenty of accommodation around town and the square is swarming with cafes, bars and a couple of restaurants.

**Posada Santa
María La Real** HISTORIC HOTEL €€
(📞979 12 20 00; www.alojamientosconhistoria.
com; Carretera de Cervera; s/d €80/90; 🛜) Inhabiting part of the Romanesque monastery of the same name, this charming *posada* (rural home) is the most atmospheric place to stay in the region. Some rooms have stone walls, others are split-level and all are decked out in wood. The restaurant serves a well-priced evening set menu (€15).

Hotel Restaurante Valentín HOTEL €€
(📞979 12 21 25; www.hotelvalentin.com; Avenida Ronda 23; s/d €50/68; 🛜) This sprawling, central hotel has little character but does boast large comfortable rooms, and there's a bustling on-site restaurant.

❶ Information

Tourist office (www.turismocastillayleon.
com; Plaza de España 30; ⊙10am-1.45pm & 4-5.45pm Tue-Sat, 10am-1.45pm Sun)

❶ Getting There & Away

Regular trains link Aguilar de Campóo with Palencia (from €6.45, 1¼ hours), but the station is 4km from town. Buses bound for Burgos, Palencia and Santander depart at least once daily.

ROMANESQUE CIRCUIT

There are no fewer than 55 Romanesque churches in the cool, hilly countryside surrounding Aguilar de Campóo and you could easily spend a day tracking them as you meander along quiet country trails.

At Olleros de Pisuerga there's a little church carved into rock; it's signposted as 'Ermita Rupestre'. Ask at Bar Feli on the main road through town for someone to open it up for you.

Further south, on a quiet back road, the Benedictine Monasterio de Santa María de Mave (admission free) has an interesting 13th-century Romanesque church, the only part of the complex open to visitors; ask at the cafe next door for the key. It's off the main highway around 8km south of Aguilar de Campóo. Nearby, the Monasterio de San Andrés de Arroyo (guided tours €2; ⊙10am-12.30pm & 3-6pm) is an outstanding Romanesque gem, especially its cloister, which dates from the 13th century. Guided tours run hourly.

CERVERA DE PISUERGA & AROUND

Around 25km northwest of Aguilar de Campóo along the CL626, Cervera de Pisuerga is an important regional crossroads. If you decide to stay, the parador (r with/without views €184/144; 🛜), 3km west of town along the P210, is classy and the west-facing rooms have fabulous mountain views.

From Cervera you've a choice of routes. The N621 north from Cervera is a lovely road into Cantabria and to the southern face of the Picos de Europa.

If you have time, the sinuous P210 that follows the mountainous foothills for 61km from Cervera to Guardo is one of the loveliest drives in Castilla y León. The road climbs to the mountain pass Alto de La Varga (1413m), while the prettiest views are further on, along the shores of the Embalse de Camporredondo, particularly around Alba de Cardaños. From comparatively ugly Guardo, it's possible to loop back to Aguilar de Campóo along the CL626, or head south to the Roman villa of La Olmeda (p180) near Saldaña.

THE NORTHWEST

León

POP 132,740 / ELEV 527M

León is a wonderful city, combining stunning historical architecture with an irresistible energy. Its standout attraction is the cathedral, one of the most beautiful in all of Spain. By day you'll encounter a city with its roots firmly planted in the soil of northern Castilla, with its grand monuments, loyal Catholic heritage and role as an important staging post along the Camino de Santiago. By night León is taken over by its large student population, who provide it with a deep-into-the-night soundtrack of revelry that floods the narrow streets and plazas of the picturesque old quarter, the Barrio Húmedo. It's a fabulous mix.

History

A Roman legion set up camp here in AD 70 as a base for controlling the gold mines of Las Médulas. In the 10th century the Asturian king Ordoño II moved his capital here from Oviedo and, although it was later sacked by the Muslim armies of Al-Mansour, León was maintained by Alfonso V as the capital of his growing kingdom. As the centre of power shifted south, León went into

León

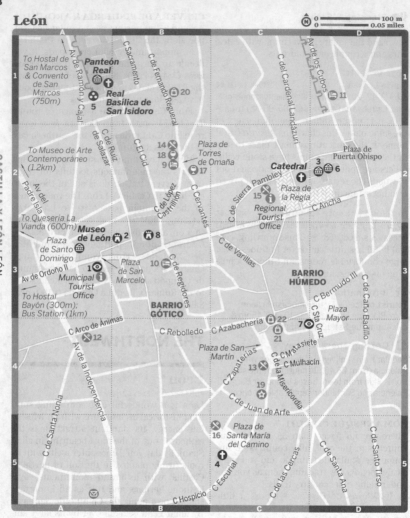

decline. Mining brought the city back to life in the 1800s. Throughout the 20th century, León's fame revolved around its role as a major staging post along the Camino de Santiago. The city came within the newly autonomous region of Castilla y León in 1983, which some locals saw as an indignity after its proudly independent history.

◉ Sights

TOP CHOICE **Catedral**   CATHEDRAL

(www.catedraldeleon.org; adult/concession/child €5/4/free; ☉8.30am-1.30pm & 4-8pm Mon-Sat,

8.30am-2.30pm & 5-8pm Sun) León's 13th-century cathedral, with its soaring towers, flying buttresses and truly breathtaking interior, is the city's spiritual heart. Whether spotlit by night or bathed in the glorious northern sunshine, the cathedral, arguably Spain's premier Gothic masterpiece, exudes a glorious, almost luminous quality.

The extraordinary facade has a radiant rose window, three richly sculpted doorways and two muscular towers. After going through the main entrance, lorded over by the scene of the Last Supper, an extraordinary gallery of *vidrieras* (stained-glass

León

windows) awaits. French in inspiration and mostly executed from the 13th to the 16th centuries, the windows evoke an atmosphere unlike that of any other cathedral in Spain; the kaleidoscope of coloured light is offset by the otherwise gloomy interior. There seems to be more glass than brick – 128 windows with a surface of 1800 sq metres in all – but mere numbers cannot convey the ethereal quality of light permeating this cathedral.

Other treasures include a silver urn on the altar, by Enrique de Arfe, containing the remains of San Froilán, León's patron saint. Also note the magnificent choir stalls and the recently restored frescoes in the Capilla de Santa Teresa. The peaceful, light-filled claustro (cloister; admission €1), with its 15th-century frescoes, is a perfect complement to the main sanctuary and an essential part of the cathedral experience. The Museo Catedralicio-Diocesano, off the cloisters, has an impressive collection encompassing works by Juní and Gaspar Becerra alongside a precious assemblage of early-Romanesque carved statues of the Virgin Mary.

Part of the cathedral is under restoration, but this has been turned cleverly to its advantage, by allowing you to climb up to one of the platforms high in the main sanctuary. Even if you don't understand a word of the Spanish-language explanations, it's worth it for the extraordinary views and

the chance to get up close to the stained glass. Guided visits leave on the hour and are accessed from outside the cathedral next to its northern wall. In addition to the official opening hours, ask about its summer-only night visits, which begin at 11.30pm and coincide with the turning off of the external floodlights and turning on of the church's interior lighting. The change is extraordinary.

Real Basílica de San Isidoro   CHURCH

Even older than León's cathedral, the Real Basílica de San Isidoro provides a stunning Romanesque counterpoint to the former's Gothic strains, with extraordinary frescoes the main highlight among many.

Fernando I and Doña Sancha founded the church in 1063 to house the remains of the saint, as well as the remains of themselves and 21 other early Leónese and Castilian monarchs. Sadly, Napoleon's troops sacked San Isidoro in the early 19th century, although there's still plenty to catch the eye.

The main basilica is a hotchpotch of styles, but the two main portals on the southern facade are pure Romanesque. Of particular note is the Puerta del Perdón (on the right, and under restoration when we visited), which has been attributed to Maestro Mateo, the genius of the cathedral at Santiago de Compostela. The church remains open night and day by historical royal edict. The attached Panteón Real houses

WORTH A TRIP

VILLA ROMANA LA OLMEDA

On the fertile plains south of the Montaña Palentina, Villa Romana La Olmeda (www.villaromanalaolmeda.com; off CL615; adult/concession/child under 12yr €5/3/free, free to all 3-6.30pm Tue; ⊙10.30am-6.30pm Tue-Sun) contains some of the most beautiful remnants of a Roman villa anywhere in the Iberian Peninsula. The villa was built around the 1st or 2nd centuries AD, but was completely overhauled in the middle of the 4th century. It was then that the simply extraordinary mosaics were added; the hunting scenes in El Oecus (reception room) are especially impressive. The whole museum is wonderfully presented – elevated boardwalks guide you around the floor plan of the 4400-sq-metre villa, with multimedia presentations in Spanish, English and French showing how the villa might once have appeared.

The turn-off to the site is 3km south of Saldaña along the CL615, and you'll need your own vehicle to visit the site.

the remaining sarcophagi, which rest with quiet dignity beneath a canopy of some of the finest Romanesque frescoes in Spain. Motif after colourful motif drenches the vaults and arches of this extraordinary hall, held aloft by marble columns with intricately carved capitals. Biblical scenes dominate and include the Annunciation, King Herod's slaughter of the innocents, the Last Supper and a striking representation of Christ Pantocrator. The agricultural calendar on one of the arches is equally superb. The pantheon, which once formed the portico of the original church, also houses a small museum where you can admire the shrine of San Isidoro, a mummified finger of the saint (!) and other treasures. A library houses a collection of manuscripts, including a priceless 10th-century Visigoth-Mozarabe Bible.

Abutting the southwestern corner of the basilica is a fragment of the former muralla (old city wall), a polyglot of Roman origins and medieval adjustments.

Barrio Gótico   HISTORIC QUARTER

On the fringes of León's Old Town, Plaza de San Marcelo is home to the ayuntamiento (town hall), which occupies a charmingly compact Renaissance-era palace. The Renaissance theme continues in the form of the splendid Palacio de los Guzmanes (1560), where the facade and patio stand out; the latter is accessible only on a free guided tour that leaves most hours. Next door is Antoni Gaudí's contribution to León's skyline, the castle-like, neo-Gothic Casa de Botines (1893). The zany architect of Barcelona fame seems to have been subdued by sober León and a statue of the great man adorns a park bench at the front.

Down the hill, the delightful Plaza de Santa María del Camino (also known as Plaza del Grano) feels like a cobblestone Castilian village square and is overlooked by the careworn Romanesque Iglesia de Santa María del Mercado.

At the northeastern end of the Old Town is the beautiful and time-worn 17th-century Plaza Mayor. Sealed off on three sides by porticoes, this sleepy plaza is home to a bustling fruit-and-vegetable market on Wednesday and Saturday. On the west side of the square is the superb late-17th-century baroque old town hall.

Museo de Arte Contemporáneo   MUSEUM

(Musac; www.musac.org.es; Avenida de los Reyes Leóneses 24; admission €5, free 5-9pm Sun; ⊙10am-3pm & 5-8pm Tue-Fri, 11am-3pm & 5-9pm Sat & Sun) León's showpiece Museo de Arte Contemporáneo won the Spanish architecture prize a few years back and has been acclaimed for the 37 shades of coloured glass that adorn the facade; they were gleaned from the pixelisation of a fragment of one of the stained-glass windows in León's cathedral. Even if the revolving exhibitions don't appeal, come here to admire the architecture. Although the museum has a growing permanent collection, it mostly houses temporary displays of cutting-edge Spanish and international photography, video installations and other similar forms. Musac also hosts musical performances and is fast becoming one of northern Spain's most dynamic cultural spaces.

To get here, head northwest of the city centre along Avenida del Padre Isla and follow the signs.

Museo de León
MUSEUM

(Plaza de Santo Domingo 8; admission €1.20, Sat & Sun free; ⏱10am-2pm & 4-7pm Tue-Sat, 10am-2pm Sun) Spread over four floors, the exhibits in this well-presented city museum begin with stone artefacts in the basement, and thereafter journey through the Middle Ages up to the 19th century. There are rooftop views towards the cathedral from the 3rd floor. The informative descriptions are in Spanish and English.

Convento de San Marcos
CONVENT

More than 100m long and blessed with a glorious facade, the Convento de San Marcos (lying within the Hostal de San Marcos) looks more like a palace than the pilgrim's hospital it was from 1173. The plateresque exterior, sectioned off by slender columns and decorated with delicate medallions and friezes, dates to 1513, by which time the edifice had become a monastery of the Knights of Santiago. Much of the former convent is now a supremely elegant *parador,* which is off limits to nonguests. To visit the former chapter house and magnificent cloister, head to the eastern end of the facade, signposted as the Museo de León.

★ Festivals & Events

Semana Santa
RELIGIOUS

León is an excellent place to see solemn Holy Week processions of hooded penitents.

Fiestas de San Juan
y San Pedro
LOCAL FIESTA

The city lets its hair down on the cusp of summer (from 21 to 30 June) with concerts, street stalls and general merriment.

🛏 Sleeping

TOP CHOICE La Posada Regia
HISTORIC HOTEL €€

(☑987 21 31 73; www.regialeon.com; Calle de Regidores 9-11; s/d €65/120; ✷🛜) You won't find many places better than this in northern Spain. The secret is a 14th-century building, magnificently restored (wooden beams, exposed brick and understated antique furniture), with individually styled rooms, character that overflows into the public areas, and supremely comfortable beds and bathrooms. Even the artwork is well thought out, including abstract and classical styles. Prices drop considerably when things are slow. As with anywhere in the Barri Gótic, weekend nights can be noisy.

Hostal San Martín
HOTEL €

(☑987 87 51 87; www.sanmartinhostales.com; 2nd fl, Plaza de Torres de Omaña 1; s/d/tr €31/43/55, s without bathroom €20) In a splendid central location, this recently overhauled 18th-century building has light, airy rooms painted in candy colours with small terraces. The spotless bathrooms have excellent water pressure and tubs, plus showers. There's a comfortable sitting area and the friendly owner can provide advice and a map.

Hostal de San Marcos
HISTORIC HOTEL €€€

(☑987 23 73 00; www.parador.es; Plaza de San Marcos 7; d from €198; ✷@🛜) León's sumptuous *parador* is one of the finest hotels in Spain. With palatial rooms fit for royalty and filled with old-world luxury and decor, this is one of the Parador chain's flagship properties, and as you'd expect, the service and attention to detail are faultless. It also houses the Convento de San Marcos.

Hostal Bayón
HOSTAL €

(☑987 23 14 46; 2nd fl, Calle del Alcázar de Toledo 6; s/d with washbasin €20/30, with shower €25/37; 🛜) At this long-standing León favourite, the laid-back owner presides over simple but inviting rooms with high ceilings and pine floors. It's a five-minute walk from the Old Town and the recent addition of a lift is great news. To reach the *hostal* head west from Plaza de Santo Domingo along Avenida de Ordoño II and right on Calle del Alcázar de Toledo.

Q!H
HOTEL €

(☑987 87 55 80; www.qhhoteles.com; Avenida de los Cubos 6; s/d €45/60; ✷🛜✷) Located within confessional distance of the cathedral, this boutique spa hotel opened in March 2010. The historic 19th-century building provided a suitable aesthetic canvas for the sharp modern design of the interior. Rooms have cathedral views, a bold accented colour scheme and steely grey bathrooms. Prices increase with use of the spa and treatments.

✕ Eating

TOP CHOICE El Llar
TAPAS €€

(Plaza de San Martín 9; meals €25-30; 🍴) This old León *taberna* is a great place to *tapear* (eat tapas) with its innovative selection of *raciones* that includes baked potatoes filled with wild mushrooms and prawns au gratin. The upstairs restaurant has a fine classic look and the menu has vegetarian options like a grilled vegetable platter and other fine dishes such as León trout in a crab sauce. There's an excellent wine list too.

El Picoteo de la Jouja
TAPAS €

(Plaza de Torres de Omaña) This intimate little bar has earned a loyal following for its concentration on traditional local tapas (try the six tapas for €13.50) and local wines, including some from the nearby Bierzo region. The tapas include cured meats, snails and all manner of León specialities.

La Trébede
TAPAS €

(Plaza de Torres de Omaña; tapas from €2.50) As good for tapas (try the *picadillo con patatas* – minced meat with potatoes) as for first drinks (wines by the glass start at €1.50), La Trébede is always full. The decor is eclectic – deer's antlers, a saddle and the scales of justice – and the sign outside promising 350km to Santiago may just prompt you to abandon the Camino and stay a little longer.

Alfonso Valderas
SEAFOOD €€

(☎987 20 05 05; Calle Arco de Ánimas 1; mains €13.65-18.90; ⊗lunch & dinner Mon-Sat, lunch Sun) The city's most famous restaurant for *bacalao* (salt cod), prepared around 20 different ways. If this is your first encounter with this versatile fish, order it *al pil-pil* (with a mild chilli sauce). Otherwise, you might want to try the pig's trotters filled with cod. The dining room is grandly elegant, with a magnificent grandfather clock and a baffling display cabinet of antique shoes. Reservations recommended.

Taberna La Piconera
SPANISH €€

(Plaza de Santa María del Camino; menú del día €14.80, mains €12.70-18.50) When the sun's out, there's no more agreeable corner of León than at La Piconera's outdoor tables. There are all the usual staples with a wide selection of red meats in particular, but there are also lighter tapas dishes to share. The *croquetas de cecina* (cured beef croquettes) and *cecina de chivo* (cured wild goat) are good local specialities to start with.

Restaurante Zuloaga
MODERN SPANISH €€

(☎987 23 78 14; www.restaurantezuloaga.com; Calle de Sierra Pambley 3; menú del día €16, mains €16-20; ⊗Tue-Sat) Located in the vaults of an early-20th-century palace, this sophisticated place has a well-stocked cellar and a classy adventurous menu – the Icelandic cod confit on a bed of deboned pig's trotters is typical of what was on offer when we visited.

Drinking & Entertainment

TOP CHOICE Camarote Madrid
WINE BAR

(www.camarotemadrid.com; Calle Cervantes 8) We could equally recommend this fantastic and enduringly popular bar for its tapas (the little ceramic cup of *salmorejo* is rightly famous). But the extensive wine list wins the day amid the buzz of a happy crowd swirling around the central bar. Bullfighting photos on the walls notwithstanding, the recent renovations have thrust this sophisticated place into the 21st century.

Rebote
BAR

(Plaza de San Martín 9; ⊗8pm-1am Mon-Sat) A reliably popular bar at the lower end of Plaza de San Martín, Rebote is a good place for first drinks; the *croquetas* here are rightly famous.

Delicatessen
MUSIC BAR

(Calle de Juan de Arfe 10; ⊗11pm-3am) Just down the hill from Plaza de San Martín, Delicatessen serves up indie rock in a busy downstairs space, with a smarter feel upstairs where every night is different. Monday begins with jazz, and the DJ-spun beats get faster as the week gathers momentum.

Shopping

El Escribano
HANDICRAFTS

(Calle de Fernando González Regueral 6; ⊗11.30am-1.30pm & 6-8.30pm Mon-Fri) Some lovely etchings and reproductions of medieval art are among the many attractions of this classy shop.

Quesería La Vianda
FOOD, DRINK

(Gran Vía de San Marcos 45; ⊗10am-3pm & 6-9pm Mon-Fri, 10am-3pm Sat) This small shop overflows with *productos artesanales* (homemade products) – ranging from chestnuts in cinnamon to trout cake to *nicanores* (a local sweet pastry) – most of which come from León province.

La Casa de los Quesos
FOOD

(Calle de Plegarias 14; ⊗10am-2pm & 5.30-8.30pm Mon-Fri, 9.30am-3pm & 6-8.30pm Sat, 11.30am-2.30pm Sun) Cheese lovers will want to make a stop here; you'll find every imaginable variety with plenty of regional choices.

Iguazú
BOOKS

(Calle de Plegarias 7; ⊗10am-2pm & 5-8.30pm Mon-Fri, 10.30am-2.30pm Sat) A fine little travel bookshop, with hiking maps of the region.

ℹ Information

Municipal tourist office (☏987 87 83 27; Plaza de San Marcelo; ☺9.30am-2pm & 5-7.30pm) The regional tourist office may have better town maps, but here you can rent bicycles (per half-/full day €3/5).

Regional tourist office (☏987 23 70 82; www.turismocastillayleon.com; Calle el Cid 2; ☺9am-8pm)

ℹ Getting There & Away

The train and bus stations lie on the western bank of Río Bernesga, off the western end of Avenida de Ordoño II.

BUS From the **bus station** (Paseo del Ingeniero Sáez de Miera) there are buses to Madrid (€22.60, 3½ hours, seven daily), Astorga (€3.40, one hour, 12 daily), Burgos (€14.50, two hours, three daily), Ponferrada (€8.20, two hours, 14 daily) and Valladolid (€9.23, two hours, six daily).

CAR & MOTORCYCLE Parking bays (€9 to €13 for 12 hours) are found in the streets surrounding Plaza de Santo Domingo.

TRAIN Regular daily trains travel to Valladolid (from €12.65, two hours), Burgos (from €20.80, two hours), Oviedo (from €8.20, two hours), Madrid (from €34.75, 4¼ hours) and Barcelona (from €70.70, nine hours).

East of León

Rising from Castilla's northern plains, Monasterio de San Miguelde Escalada (admission by donation; ☺10.15am-2pm & 4.30-8pm Tue-Sun) is one of the region's little-known treasures, a typically remote Castilian church rich in history. It was built in the 9th century by refugee monks from Córdoba on the remains of a Visigoth church dedicated to the Archangel Michael, and various orders of monks and nuns lived here from the 9th century until the 19th century. It's best known for its beautifully simple horseshoe arches of the kind that are rarely seen this far north in Spain. The graceful exterior porch with its portico is balanced by the impressive marble columns within; all of the interior columns (and three of those outside) are of Roman origin. Inside, two stone slabs and an arch are all that remains of the original Visigoth church, while other features are clearly Mozarabic (post Islamic). Note also the windows with alabaster instead of glass. To get here, take the N601 southeast of León. After about 14km, take the small LE213 to the east; the church is 16km after the turn-off.

SAHAGÚN

POP 2820 / ELEV 807M

An unremarkable place today, Sahagún was once home to one of Spain's more powerful abbeys and these days it's an important way-station for pilgrims en route to Santiago.

◉ Sights

Iglesia de San Tirso   CHURCH
(Plaza de San Tirso; admission free; ☺10.15am-2pm & 4.30-8pm Wed-Sat, 10.15am-2pm Sun) The early 12th-century Iglesia de San Tirso, at the western entrance to town, is an important stop on the Camino de Santiago, known for its pure Romanesque design and Mudéjar bell tower laced with rounded arches. The Iglesia San Lorenzo, just north of Plaza Mayor, has a similar bell tower.

Santuario de La Peregrina   CONVENT
(off Avenida Fernando de Castro; admission €2; ☺noon-2pm & 6-8pm Tue-Sun) This 13th-century former convent has been stunningly restored with glimpses of elaborate 13th-century frescoes and exceptional Islamic-style 17th-century Mudéjar plasterwork; the latter is in the chapel to the right of the main nave. A modern addition to the convent houses some excellent scale models of Sahagún's major monuments, and there are plans for an interpretation centre dedicated to the Camino de Santiago. It's on the southwestern corner of town.

Museo Benedictinas   MUSEUM
(Avenida de Doctores Bermejo y Calderón; admission by donation; ☺guided visits hourly 10am-noon & 4-5pm Tue-Sat, 10am-noon Sun) The more important remnants of Sahagún's abbey are kept in this small museum. Entry is by guided visit only.

🛏 Sleeping & Eating

Hostal La Codorniz   HOSTAL €
(☏987 78 02 76; www.hostallacodorniz.com; Avenida de la Constitución 97-99; s/d €40/50; ☎) Right across the road from the tourist office, this comfortable *hostal* has large, unadorned rooms. The better ones are those facing north with balconies, so ask for one of these. Downstairs, there's a bar (*raciones* €7 to €15) and a traditional restaurant (mains €16 to €26) complete with original Mudéjar ceiling and specialising in roasted meats.

ℹ Information

Tourist office (☏987 78 21 17; www.sahagun. org; Calle del Arco 87; ☺noon-2pm & 6-9pm Mon-Thu, 11am-2pm & 4-9pm Fri-Sun) Located

Camino in Castilla y León

within the Albergue de Peregrinos (Hostel for Pilgrims).

ℹ Getting There & Away

Trains run regularly throughout the day from León (from €5.05, 40 minutes) and Palencia (from €5.05, 35 minutes).

West of León

ASTORGA
POP 11,900 / ELEV 870M

Perched on a hilltop on the frontier between the bleak plains of northern Castilla and the mountains that rise up to the west towards Galicia, Astorga is a fascinating little town with a wealth of attractions out of proportion to its size. In addition to its fine cathedral, the city boasts a Gaudí-designed palace, a smattering of Roman ruins and a personality dominated by the Camino de Santiago.

History

The Romans built the first settlement, Astúrica Augusta, at the head of the Ruta del Oro. In the Middle Ages Astorga was well established as a way station along one of Europe's most important pilgrimage routes. By the 15th century its growing significance inspired the construction of the cathedral and the rebuilding of its 3rd-century walls.

◉ Sights

Catedral   CATHEDRAL
(☑987 61 58 20; Plaza de la Catedral; cathedral free, museum €3, incl Palacio Episcopal €5; ⊙church 9-10.30am Mon-Sat, 11am-1pm Sun, museum 10am-2pm & 4-8pm Tue-Sat, 10am-2pm & 5-6.30pm Sun)

The cathedral's striking plateresque southern facade is made from caramel-coloured sandstone with elaborate sculptural detail. Work began in 1471 and proceeded in stop-start fashion over three centuries, resulting in a mix of styles. The mainly Gothic interior has soaring ceilings and a superb 16th-century altarpiece by Gaspar Becerra. The attached Museo Catedralicio features the usual religious art, documents and artefacts. When the museum is open, visits to the cathedral are possible, but the admission fee is charged.

Palacio Episcopal   MUSEUM, ARCHITECTURE
(Museo de los Caminos; Calle de Los Sitios; admission €3, incl Museo Catedralicio €5; ⊙10am-2pm & 4-8pm Tue-Sat, 10am-2pm Sun) The Catalan architect Antoni Gaudí may have spurned Madrid, but he left his mark on Astorga in the fairy-tale turrets, frilly facade and surprising details of the Palacio Episcopal. Built for the local bishop from the end of the 19th century, it now houses the Museo de los Caminos, an eclectic collection with Roman artefacts and coins in the basement; contemporary paintings on the top floor; and medieval sculpture, Gothic tombs and silver crosses dominating the ground and 1st floors. The highlight is the chapel, with its stunning murals, tilework and stained glass.

Museo del Chocolate   MUSEUM
(Calle de José María Goy 5; admission €2.50, incl Museo Romano €3; ⊙10.30am-2pm & 4-6pm Tue-Sat, 11am-2pm Sun; ⊡) Proof that Astorga does not exist solely for the virtuous souls of the Camino comes in the form of this small and quirky private museum. Chocolate ruled

Astorga's local economy in the 18th and 19th centuries, as evidenced by this eclectic collection of old machinery, colourful advertising and fascinating lithographs. It offers a refreshing, indulgent (some would say sinful) break from Castilla's religious-art circuit. Best of all, you get a free chocolate sample at the end.

Museo Romano   MUSEUM
(Plaza de San Bartolomé 2; admission €2.50, incl Museo del Chocolate €3; ◷10am-2pm & 4-6pm Tue-Sat, 10.30am-2pm Sun) Housed in the Roman *ergástula* (slave prison), the Museo Romano has a modest selection of artefacts and an enjoyable big-screen slide show on Roman Astorga.

✸ Festivals & Events
Festividad de Santa Marta   RELIGIOUS
(◷last week of Aug) Astorga awakes from its customary slumber to celebrate this saint with fireworks and bullfights.

▣ Sleeping
Casa de Tepa   HISTORIC HOTEL €€
(☏987 60 32 99; www.casadetepa.com; Calle de Santiago Postas 2; s/d €80/100; ❄@☏) This handsome 18th-century building has been reinvented several times, serving as a noble mansion, convent and pilgrims' hospital down through the centuries. Tastefully restored with antiques, plush fabrics and

art work, the *posada* offers luxurious large rooms in the heart of town. It has plans for a small restaurant.

Hotel Gaudí   HOTEL €€
(☏987 61 56 54; www.gaudihotel.es; Calle de Eduardo de Castro 6; s €45-60, d €60-80; ❄☏) There aren't many places in the world where you can see a Gaudí flight of fancy from your bed, so ask for a street-facing room here. The rooms themselves, especially the bathrooms, are in need of an overhaul with somewhat tired decor, but they're clean, large and the friendly family service is unmatched in Astorga.

Hotel Astur Plaza   HOTEL €€
(☏987 61 89 00; www.hotelasturplaza.com; Plaza de España 2; s/d/ste from €55/75/110; ❄@☏) A recent change of owner has brought newly professional service to this place, where some of the supremely comfortable rooms face pretty Plaza de España. On weekends, you'll want to forsake the view for a quieter room out the back.

✗ Eating
The local speciality is *cocido maragato,* a stew of chickpeas, various meats, potatoes and cabbage – the *cocido* here differs from elsewhere in that the soup is served last. Portions are huge, so one order usually feeds two. Several pastry shops sell the traditional

---

CAMINO DE SANTIAGO

Burgos to León

Many pilgrims avoid this stretch of the Camino and take the bus, which is a pity as they are missing out on the subtle and ever-changing play of colours on the *meseta* (the high tableland of central Spain). Contrary to popular opinion, it is not flat. Villages here are set low in long valleys, with occasional rivers, which rise up to the high barren plains. There are large limestone rocks everywhere and evocative sights, such as flocks of sheep led by solitary shepherds and isolated adobe villages. The path passes via Castrojeriz, with its castle dominating the town, while, in better-known Frómista, the Iglesia de San Martín (p176) is one of the jewels of early Spanish Romanesque architecture with its 315 well-preserved corbels and fine interior capitals. Between Carrión de los Condes and Calzadilla de la Cueza, the Camino coincides with a stretch of Roman road. Further on, despite appearances, Sahagún was an immensely powerful and wealthy Benedictine centre by the 12th century. The Mudéjar-influenced brick Romanesque churches merit a visit (look for the horseshoe arches and the clever way the bricks are placed in geometric patterns). Before reaching León, the Camino becomes monotonous, running through a long series of villages along paved, busy roads.

Day Walk

The comparatively short stretch between Rabé de las Calzadas and Hontanas (18.8km, five hours) is best in springtime – this rolling *meseta* walk brings solitude amid the wheat, allowing you to appreciate the region's uniquely lonely landscapes and villages.

local *mantecadas,* a cake-like sweet peculiar to Astorga.

Restaurante Serrano
MODERN SPANISH €€

(☑987 61 78 66; www.restauranteserrano.es; Calle de la Portería 2; mains €12-20; ⊙Tue-Sun) The upmarket Restaurante Serrano is a little different from the other more homey restaurants around town. The menu has a subtle gourmet flourish, with fresh summery starters like *ensalada de mango y centollo* (mango and crab salad), innovative meat and fish mains, and plenty of tempting desserts with chocolate. It also serves *cocido* and supplements it with other rarely seen dishes with their roots in the region. Reservations recommended.

Restaurante Las Termas
CASTILIAN €€

(☑987 60 22 12; Calle de Santiago Postas 1; mains €7-17.80; ⊙lunch Tue-Sun; 🖨) This restaurant is run by Santiago (a popular name in these parts) who, apart from being a charming host, oversees a menu renowned for the quality of its *cocido* and *ensalada maragata* (salad of chickpeas and cod).

Cervecería La Esquina
TAPAS €

(Plaza de España 5; raciones €5-11; ⊙closed Wed) Best for local tapas specialities, including the unsurpassed *patatas esquinadas* (lightly seasoned potato slices), plus 18 varieties of beer.

❶ Information
Tourist office (☑987 61 82 22; www.turismo castillayleon.com; ⊙10am-2pm & 4-8pm) In the northwestern corner of the Old Town.

❶ Getting There & Away
Regular bus services connect Astorga with León (€3.40, one hour, 12 daily) and Madrid (from €22.97, 4½ hours, up to 11 daily). The train station is inconveniently a couple of kilometres north of town.

LAS MÉDULAS
The ancient Roman gold mines at Unesco World Heritage–listed Las Médulas, about 20km southwest of Ponferrada, once served as the main source of gold for the entire Roman Empire – the final tally came to a remarkable 3 million kilograms. An army of slaves honeycombed the area with canals and tunnels (some over 40km long!) through which they pumped water to break up the rock and free it from the precious metal. The result is a singularly unnatural natural phenomenon and one of the more bizarre landscapes you'll see in Spain. It's breathtaking at sunset.

To get to the heart of the former quarries, drive beyond Las Médulas village (4km south of Carucedo and the N536 Hwy). Several trails weave among chestnut trees and bizarre formations left behind by the miners. There are also fine views to be had in the vicinity of neighbouring Orellan.

THE EAST

Burgos
POP 179,250 / ELEV 861M

The extraordinary Gothic cathedral of Burgos is one of Spain's glittering jewels of religious architecture and it looms large over the city and skyline. On the surface, conservative Burgos seems to embody all the stereotypes of a north-central Spanish town, with sombre grey-stone architecture, the fortifying cuisine of the high *meseta* (plateau) and a climate of extremes. But this is a city that rewards deeper exploration: below the surface lie good restaurants and, when the sun's shining, pretty streetscapes that extend far beyond the landmark cathedral. There's even a whiff of legend about the place: beneath the majestic spires of the cathedral lies Burgos' favourite and most roguish son, El Cid.

History
Burgos began life in 884 as a strategic fortress on the frontline between the Muslims and the rival kingdom of Navarra. It was surrounded by several *burgos* (villages), which eventually melded together to form the basis of a new city. Centuries later, Burgos thrived as a staging post for pilgrims on the Camino de Santiago and as a trading centre between the interior and the northern ports. During the Spanish Civil War, General Franco used Burgos as the base for his government-in-waiting.

◉ Sights

Catedral
CATHEDRAL

(Plaza del Rey Fernando; adult/child €5/2.50; ⊙9.30am-6.30pm) The World Heritage–listed cathedral is a masterpiece that's probably worth the trip to Burgos on its own. It had humble origins as a modest Romanesque church, but work began on a grander scale in 1221. Remarkably, within 40 years most of the French Gothic structure that you see today had been completed.

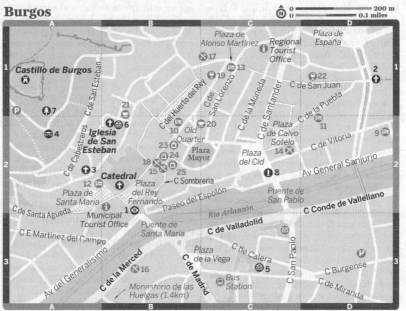

Burgos

◎ Top Sights

Castillo de Burgos	A1
Catedral	B2
Iglesia de San Esteban	B2

◎ Sights

1	Arco de Santa María	B2
2	Iglesia de San Lesmes	D1
3	Iglesia de San Nicolás	A2
4	Mirador	A2
5	Museo de Burgos	C3
6	Museo del Retablo	B2
7	Parque de Castillo	A1
8	Statue of El Cid	C2

🛏 Sleeping

9	Hostal Acacia	D2
10	Hotel Entrearcos	B2
11	Hotel La Puebla	D2
12	Hotel Meson del Cid	A2

13	Hotel Norte y Londres	C1

⊗ Eating

14	Casa Ojeda	C2
15	Cervecería Morito	B2
16	La Fabula	B3
17	La Favorita	C1
18	La Mejillonera	B2

◎ Drinking

19	Café de Las Artes	C1
20	Café España	C2
21	Chocolatería Candilejas	B1
22	El Bosque Encantado	D1

◎ Shopping

23	Casa Quintanilla	B2
24	Jorge Revilla	B2
25	Teodoro	B2

The cathedral's twin towers, which went up later in the 15th century, each represent 84m of richly decorated Gothic fantasy and they're surrounded by a sea of similarly intricate spires. Probably the most impressive of the portals is the **Puerta del Sarmental**, the main entrance for visitors, although

the honour could also go to the **Puerta de la Coronería**, on the northwestern side, which shows Christ surrounded by the Evangelists.

It's possible to enter the cathedral from Plaza de Santa María for free, but doing so leaves the most worthwhile sections off-limits. Nonetheless, you will still have access to the Capilla del Santísimo Cristo, which harbours a much-revered 13th-century crucifix (known as the Cristo de Burgos) made from buffalo hide, and the Capilla de Santa Tecla, with its extraordinary ceiling.

Inside the main sanctuary, a host of other chapels showcase the diversity of the interior, from the light and airy Capilla de la Presentación to the Capilla de la Concepción with its gilded, 15th-century altar. The main altar is a typically overwhelming piece of gold-encrusted extravagance, while directly beneath the star-vaulted central dome lies the tomb of El Cid. Another highlight is the Escalera Dorada (Gilded Stairway; 1520) on the cathedral's northwestern flank, the handiwork of Diego de Siloé. The Capilla del Condestable, on the eastern end of the ambulatory behind the main altar, is a remarkable late-15th-century production. Bridging Gothic and plateresque styles, its highlights include three altars watched over by unusual star-shaped vaulting in the dome. The sculptures facing the entrance to the chapel are astonishing 15th- and 16th-century masterpieces of stone carving, portraying the Passion, death, resurrection and ascension of Christ.

Also worth a look is the peaceful cloister, with its sculpted medieval tombs. Off the cloister is the Capilla de Corpus Cristi, where, high on the northwestern wall, hangs the coffin of El Cid. The adjoining Museo Catedralicio has a wealth of oil paintings, tapestries and ornate chalices, while the lower cloister, downstairs, covers the history of the cathedral's development, with a scale model to help you take it all in.

Old Quarter   NEIGHBOURHOOD

Burgos' old quarter, on the north bank of Río Arlanzón, is austerely elegant in the manner of so many cathedral towns of old Castilla, guarded by monumental gates and with the cathedral as its centrepiece. Coming from the south, old Burgos can be accessed via two main bridges. One of these is the Puente de San Pablo, beyond which looms a romanticised statue of El Cid with his swirling cloak and his sword held aloft. About 300m to the west, the Puente de Santa María leads to the splendid Arco de Santa María (☏947 28 88 68; admission free; ⏰11am-2pm & 5-9pm Tue-Sat, 11am-2pm Sun), once the main gate to the old city and part of the 14th-century walls. It now hosts temporary exhibitions. Running along the riverbank between the two bridges is the Paseo del Espolón, a lovely tree-lined pedestrian area. Just back from the *paseo* (promenade) is the oddly shaped Plaza Mayor, with some lovely facades.

Monasterio de las Huelgas   MONASTERY

(guided tours adult/child €5/2.50, free Wed; ⏰10am-1pm & 3.45-5.30pm Tue-Sat, 10.30am-2pm Sun) A 30-minute walk west of the city centre on the southern bank of Río Arlanzón, this monastery was once among the most prominent monasteries in Spain. Founded in 1187 by Eleanor of Aquitaine, daughter of Henry II of England and wife of Alfonso VIII of Castilla, it's still home to 35 Cistercian nuns.

If you've come this far, join a guided tour (otherwise only a small section of the church is accessible), which takes you through the three main naves of the church. This veritable royal pantheon contains the tombs of numerous kings and queens, as well as a spectacular gilded Renaissance altar topped by a larger-than-life Jesus being taken off the cross. The highlight, though, is the Museo de Ricas Telas, reached via a lovely Romanesque cloister known as Las Claustrillas. It contains bejewelled robes and royal garments.

To get here follow the river via Calle de la Merced and Avenida de Palencia, turning left on Calle Reina Leonor. The monastery is signposted.

Iglesia de San Esteban   CHURCH

(Calle de Pozo Seco; admission incl museum €2; ⏰10am-2pm & 5-8pm Mon-Sat) Located just west of the cathedral, this is a solid 14th-century Gothic structure with an unusual porch and a Museo del Retablo (Altar Museum) with a display of some 15 altars dating from the 15th to 18th centuries.

FREE Cartuja de Miraflores   MONASTERY

(⏰10.15am-3pm & 4-6pm Mon, Tue & Thu-Sat, 11am-3pm & 4-6pm Sun) Located in peaceful woodlands 4km east of the city centre, this monastery contains a trio of 15th-century masterworks by Gil de Siloé. The walk to the monastery along Río Arlanzón takes about one hour. To get here, head north along Paseo de la Quinta (flanking the river) from where the monastery is clearly signposted.

Castillo de Burgos   CASTLE

(admission €2.60, guided visit extra €1.10; ⏰11am-2pm & 4-7pm Sat & Sun; ⊞) Crowning the leafy

EL CID: THE HEROIC MERCENARY

Few names resonate through Spanish history quite like El Cid, the 11th-century soldier of fortune and adventurer whose story tells in microcosm the tumultuous years when Spain was divided into Muslim and Christian zones. That El Cid became a romantic, idealised figure of history, known for his unswerving loyalty and superhuman strength, owes much to the 1961 film starring Charlton Heston and Sophia Loren. Reality, though, presents a different picture.

El Cid (from the Arabic *sidi* for 'chief' or 'lord') was born Rodrígo Diaz in Vivar, a hamlet about 10km north of Burgos, in 1043. After the death of Ferdinand I, he dabbled in the murky world of royal succession, which led to his banishment from Castilla in 1076. With few scruples as to whom he served, El Cid offered his services to a host of rulers, both Christian and Muslim. With each battle, he became ever more powerful and wealthy.

It's not known whether he suddenly developed a loyalty to the Christian kings or smelled the wind and saw that Spain's future would be Christian. Either way, when he heard that the Muslim armies had taken Valencia and expelled all the Christians, El Cid marched on the city, recaptured it and became its ruler in 1094 after a devastating siege. At the height of his powers and reputation, the man also known as El Campeador (Champion) retired to spend the remainder of his days in Valencia, where he died in 1099. His remains were returned to Burgos, where he lies buried along with his wife, Jimena, in the town's cathedral.

hilltop **Parque de Castillo** are the massive fortifications of the rebuilt Castillo de Burgos. Dating from the 9th century, the castle has witnessed a turbulent history, suffering a fire in 1736 before finally being blown up by Napoleon's retreating troops in 1813. There's a small **museum** here covering the history of the town and, thanks to recent excavations, some of the original foundations of the castle are on view. Just south of the car park is a **mirador** (lookout), which offers terrific views over the town.

Museo de Burgos   MUSEUM
(Calle de Calera 25; admission €1.20, Sat & Sun free; ⊙10am-2pm & 5-8pm Tue-Sat, 10am-2pm Sun) This museum, housed in the 16th-century Casa de Miranda, contains some fine Gothic tombs and other archeological artefacts covering a wide period.

Iglesia de San Nicolás   CHURCH
(Calle de San Nicolás; admission €1.50, Mon free; ⊙10am-2pm & 5-7pm Mon-Sat) Close to the cathedral, this place boasts an enormous stone-carved altar by Francisco de Colonia, with scenes from the life of St Nicolas.

Iglesia de San Lesmes   CHURCH
(Plaza de San Juan; ⊙before & after Mass) Dating to the 15th century, San Lesmes is notable for its three naves and rustic charm.

✯ Festivals & Events

Festividad de San Pedro y San Pablo   RELIGIOUS
The Feast of Sts Peter and Paul is celebrated with bullfights, processions and much merry-making, particularly on the first Sunday of July, the **Día de las Peñas**.

Festividad de San Lesmes   PATRON SAINT FESTIVAL
This festival celebrates the city's patron saint on 30 January.

🛏 Sleeping

TOP CHOICE **Hotel Norte y Londres**   HISTORIC HOTEL €€
(☎947 26 41 25; www.hotelnorteylondres.com; Plaza de Alonso Martínez 10; s/d €66/100; P@🕾) Set in a former 16th-century palace and with understated period charm, this fine hotel promises spacious rooms with antique furnishings, polished wooden floors and pretty balconies; those on the 4th floor are more modern. The bathrooms are exceptionally large, the service exceptionally efficient.

Hotel La Puebla   BOUTIQUE HOTEL €€
(☎947 20 00 11; www.hotellapuebla.com; Calle de la Puebla 20; s/d €50/65; ❋@🕾) This boutique hotel adds a touch of style to the Burgos hotel scene. The rooms aren't huge and most don't have views, but they're softly lit, beautifully designed and supremely comfortable.

They come in a range of styles, from colourful to minimalist black and white.

Hotel Meson del Cid
HISTORIC HOTEL €€

(947 20 87 15; www.mesondelcid.es; Plaza de Santa María 8; s/d €70/100; P✻🛜) Facing the cathedral, this hotel occupies a centuries-old building. Rooms have Regency-style burgundy-and-cream fabrics, aptly combined with dark-wood furnishings and terracotta tiles. Most have stunning front-row seats of the cathedral.

Hotel Entrearcos
BOUTIQUE HOTEL €

(947 25 29 11; www.hotelentrearcos.com; Calle de la Paloma 4; s/d €52/59; ✻🛜) A fine addition to the Burgos hotel scene, this stylish little hotel is as central as you'll find. Its rooms are beautifully presented and the terrific bathrooms have hydromassage showers. Some rooms look onto the main pedestrian street, while rooms 502 and 503 have castle and partial cathedral views. Our only complaint? The really large beds don't leave room for much else in some rooms.

Hostal Acacia
HOSTAL €

(947 20 51 34; www.hostalacacia.com; Calle de Bernabé Perez Ortiz 1; s/d €55/59) This *hostal* is especially popular with pilgrims. The simple rooms have plain bedspreads and renovated bathrooms, and some have attractive ochre-painted walls. Bike rental is also available.

✖ Eating

Burgos is famous for its *queso* (cheese), *morcilla* (blood sausage) and *cordero asado*.

TOP CHOICE Cervecería Morito
TAPAS €

(Calle de la Sombrerería 27; tapas €3, raciones €5-7) Cervecería Morito is the undisputed king of Burgos tapas bars and it's always crowded, deservedly so. A typical order is *alpargata* (lashings of cured ham with bread, tomato and olive oil) or the *pincho de morcilla* (small tapa of local blood sausage). The presentation is surprising nouvelle, especially the visual feast of salads.

La Fabula
MODERN CASTILIAN €€

(947 26 30 92; Calle de la Merced; menú del día €15, meals €25-30) With local celebrity chef Isabel Alvarez at the helm, fabulous La Fabula offers innovative slimmed-down dishes in a bright, modern dining room filled with classical music. The menu includes tasty rice dishes and creative flights of fancy such as pyramids of wild mushroom with a pinch of salty nougat. Leave plenty of space for one of the delectable desserts. Reservations essential.

La Favorita
TAPAS €

(www.lafavorita-taberna.com; Calle de Avellanos 8; tapas from €2; ⏰10am-midnight Mon-Fri, noon-1.30am Sat & Sun) Away from the main Burgos tapas hub and close to the cathedral, La Favorita has a barn-like interior of exposed brick and wooden beams, and attracts slicked-back-hair businessmen at midday. The emphasis is on local cured meats and cheeses (try the cheese platter for €11.90), and wine by the glass starts at €1.50. The tapas include beef sirloin with foie gras.

Casa Ojeda
CASTILIAN €€

(947 20 90 52; www.grupojeda.com; Calle de Vitoria 5; mains €15-25, platos combinados from €12.40; ⏰Mon-Sat, lunch Sun) Dating from 1912, this Burgos institution, all sheathed in dark wood with stunning mullioned windows, is one of the best places in town to try *cordero asado* or *morcilla de Burgos*. The upstairs dining room has outstanding food and faultless service. A more limited range of *platos combinados* (meat-and-three-veg dish) is available in the downstairs bar. Reservations recommended.

La Mejillonera
SEAFOOD €

(Calle de la Paloma 33; tapas from €2.50) A popular stand-up place, La Mejillonera serves great mussels, while the *patatas bravas* (potatoes with spicy tomato sauce) and *calamares* (calimari) are other popular orders.

🍷 Drinking

There are two main hubs of nightlife. The first is along Calle de San Juan and Calle de la Puebla. For later nights on weekends, Calle del Huerto del Rey, northeast of the cathedral, has dozens of bars.

Pick up a copy of the Burgos edition of *Go!* (www.laguiago.com) from the tourist office to find out what's on.

Chocolatería Candilejas
CAFE

(Calle de Fernán González 36; desserts from €3; ⏰6.30-11pm Mon-Thu, to 1am Fri & Sat) For killer milkshakes, including unusual flavours like raspberry and walnut, *chocolate con churros* (deep-fried doughnut strips dipped in hot chocolate) and homemade cakes, check out this cross between a Spanish bar and tea room. The lovely owners were due to

WORTH A TRIP

THE OLDEST EUROPEAN

The archeological site of Atapuerca (☎902 02 42 46; www.atapuerca.org; guided tours in Spanish €6; ⏱tours 11am, 1pm & 5.30pm), around 15km west of Burgos, has long excited students of early human history. But archeologists made their greatest discovery here in July 2007 when they uncovered a jawbone and teeth of what is believed to be the oldest-known European: 1.2 million years old, some 500,000 years older than any other remains discovered in Western Europe. A Unesco World Heritage–listed site, there are also remains of occupation in the area by homo sapiens around 40,000 years ago and human settlements from the Neolithic age. Ceramics, cave paintings, carvings and burial sites have been discovered here, as well as evidence of cannibalism. Although Atapuerca is still under excavation, the site is open to visitors. There's a diverse program of courses and study groups for adults, students and children (in Spanish). Advance reservations are essential for all visitors.

retire at the end of 2012 – we hope their successors realise the treasure they've inherited.

Café España   CAFE
(Calle de Lain Calvo 12; ⏱10am-11pm) With its old-world elegance, Café España has been a bastion of the Burgos cafe scene for more than 80 years. A pianist plays jazz here most weekends.

Café de Las Artes   BAR, CAFE
(Calle de Lain Calvo 31; ⏱10am-midnight) An artsy vibe and occasional live music.

El Bosque Encantado   BAR
(Calle de San Juan 31; ⏱4.30pm-1am) 'The Enchanted Garden' revels in its kitsch decor and is good for early evening drinks.

🛍 Shopping

Jorge Revilla   JEWELLERY
(www.jorgerevilla.com; Calle de la Paloma 29; ⏱10am-2pm & 5-8pm Mon-Fri, 10am-2pm Sat) Local Burgos jewellery designer Jorge Revilla is becoming a global name with his exquisite and sophisticated silver pieces.

Casa Quintanilla   FOOD
(Calle de la Paloma 22; ⏱10am-8.30pm Mon-Sat, 10am-2pm Sun) This is the pick of many stores around the town centre offering local produce that's ideal for a picnic or a gift for back home.

Teodoro   ACCESSORIES
(Calle Sombreria 4; ⏱10am-2pm & 5-8pm Mon-Fri, 10am-2pm Sat) Step back in time at this 1860s hat shop with its original interior, including the magnificent American-made (National) cash register. The elderly owner, Teodoro, is a charmer, the hats a delight.

ℹ Information

Municipal tourist office (☎947 28 88 74; www.aytoburgos.es; Plaza de Santa María; ⏱10am-8pm) Pick up its 24-hour, 48-hour and 72-hour guides to Burgos; they can also be downloaded as PDFs online.

Regional tourist office (www.turismocastillayleon.com; Plaza de Alonso Martínez 7; ⏱9am-8pm Sun-Thu, 9am-9pm Fri & Sat)

ℹ Getting There & Away

The **bus station** (Calle de Miranda 4) is south of the river, in the newer part of town. The new train station is a considerable hike northeast of the town centre - bus 2 (€0.95) connects the train station with Plaza de España.

Renfe (☎947 20 91 31; Calle de la Moneda 21; ⏱9.30am-1.30pm & 4.30-7.30pm Mon-Fri), the national rail network, has a convenient sales office in the centre of town.

BUS Regular buses run to Madrid (€17.07, three hours, up to 20 daily), Bilbao (€12.16, two hours, eight daily) and León (€14.50, two hours, three daily).

TRAIN Destinations include Madrid (from €31.45, 2½ to 4½ hours, seven daily), Bilbao (from €19.30, three hours, four daily), León (from €20.80, two hours) and Salamanca (from €19.85, 2½ hours, three daily).

Around Burgos

ERMITA DE SANTA MARÍA DE LARA

If you take the N234 southeast of Burgos, a worthwhile stop some 35km out is the 7th-century Ermita de Santa María de Lara, close to Quintanilla de las Viñas. This modest Visigothic hermitage has some fine bas-reliefs around its external walls, which are among the best surviving regional examples of religious art from the 7th century.

WORTH A TRIP

HIDDEN VILLAGES

The N623 Hwy carves a pretty trail from Burgos, particularly between the mountain passes of **Portillo de Fresno** and **Puerto de Carrales**. About 15km north of the former, a side road takes you through a series of intriguing villages in the **Valle de Sedano**. The town of the same name has a fine 17th-century church, but more interesting is the little Romanesque one above **Moradillo de Sedano**: the sculpted main doorway is outstanding.

Villages flank the highway on the way north, but **Orbaneja del Castillo** is the area's best-kept secret. Take the turn-off for Escalada and follow the signs. A dramatic backdrop of strange rock walls lends this spot an enchanting air. The N623 then continues north into the Valderredible region of Cantabria with its rock-hewn churches.

COVARRUBIAS
POP 630 / ELEV 975M

The picturesque hamlet of Covarrubias is one of Castilla y León's hidden gems. Spread out along the shady banks of Río Arlanza, its distinctive arcaded half-timbered houses overlook intimate cobblestone squares.

A good time to be here is the second weekend of July, when the village hosts its **Medieval Market and Cherry Festival**.

◉ Sights

Although the main attraction of Covarrubias is simply wandering its charming cobbled streets, there are a few sights to provide focus for your visit.

Torreón de Doña Urraca   TOWER
This squat 10th-century tower dominates the remains of the town's medieval walls.

Colegiata de San Cosme y Damián CHURCH
(admission €2.50; ◎10.30am-2pm & 4-7pm Mon & Wed-Sat, 4.30-6pm Sun) This late-Gothic church is home to Castilla's oldest still-functioning church organ and has attractive cloisters. It also contains the stone tomb of Fernán González, the 10th-century founder of Castilla. Check the door for times of guided visits of the church and cloister.

🛏 Sleeping & Eating

Casa Galín   HOSTAL €
(☑947 40 65 52; www.casagalin.com; Plaza de Doña Urraca 4; s/d €25/42; 🕸) A cut above your average provincial Castilian *hostal,* Casa Galín has comfortable, pastel-painted rooms in an old-fashioned timbered building overlooking the main square. It's home to a popular restaurant for tapas, fish and roasted meats, with a well-priced menu (€10).

Hotel Rey Chindasvinto   HOTEL €
(☑947 40 65 60; hotelchindas@wanadoo.es; Plaza del Rey Chindasvinto 5; s/d incl breakfast €35/55; 🕸🖩🕸) The best hotel in town, the Rey Chindasvinto has lovely spacious rooms with wooden beams, exposed brickwork and a good restaurant. The owners are friendly but the service sometimes goes missing.

La Posada del Conde   RURAL HOTEL €
(☑609 406698; www.laposadadelconde.es; Calle Fernán González 8; s/d incl breakfast €50/60; 🕸) The large rooms here are brightly painted, while the bathrooms have a designer touch. The communal sitting room is large and comfortable, although the snarling mounted wolf's head may not appeal to all. Activities, ranging from mountain climbing to fishing, can be organised.

Restaurante de Galo   CASTILIAN €€
(www.degalo.com; Calle Monseñor Vargas 10; mains €8.50-31; ◎lunch Thu-Tue) This fine restaurant in the heart of the village is recommended for its robust traditional dishes cooked in a wood-fired oven. This is a good place to sample the regional speciality of *cordero asado*.

🛍 Shopping

La Alacena   FOOD
(Calle de Monseñor Vargas 8; ◎10am-2pm & 5-7.30pm Tue-Sun) For homemade chocolates, local honey and other gourmet goodies, step inside this friendly shop.

❶ Information

Tourist office (☑947 40 64 61; www.eco varrubias.com; Calle de Monseñor Vargas; ◎10.30am-2pm & 5-8pm Tue-Sat, 11am-2pm Sun) Located under the arches of the village's imposing northern gate, pick up the free *Covarrubias: Castile Birthplace,* a handy pocket-sized guide to the sights around town. The tourist office runs Spanish-language guided tours of the town (€3) at noon and 5pm Tuesday to Saturday and at noon on Sunday.

ⓘ Getting There & Away

Two buses travel between Burgos and Covarrubias on weekdays, and one runs on Saturday (€3.20, one hour).

SANTO DOMINGO DE SILOS
POP 320

Nestled in the rolling hills south of Burgos, this tranquil, pretty village has an unusual claim to fame: monks from its monastery made the British pop charts in the mid-1990s with recordings of Gregorian chants. The monastery is one of the most famous in central Spain, known for its stunning cloister.

◎ Sights

For sweeping views over the town, pass under the **Arco de San Juan** and climb the grassy hill to the south to the **Ermita del Camino y Via Crucis**.

Church   CHURCH
(admission free; ⊙6am-2pm & 4.30-10pm, chant 6am, 7.30am, 9am, 1.45pm, 4pm, 7pm and 9.30pm) Notable for its pleasingly unadorned Romanesque sanctuary dominated by a multi-domed ceiling, this is where you can hear the monks chant; times of the chants are subject to change.

Cloister   MONASTERY
(admission €3.50; ⊙10am-1pm & 4.30-6pm Tue-Sat, 4.30-6pm Sun) The jewel in the village monastery's crown is this two-storey treasure chest of some of the most imaginative Romanesque art anywhere in the country. Although the overall effect is spectacular, the sculpted capitals are especially exquisite, with lions intermingled with floral and geometrical motifs betraying the never-distant influence of Islamic art in Spain. Look for the unusually twisted column on the western side. The pieces executed on the corner pillars represent episodes from the life of Christ, while the galleries are covered by Mudéjar ceilings from the 14th century. In the northeastern corner sits a 13th-century image of the Virgin Mary carved in stone, and nearby is the original burial spot of Santo Domingo.

Although much of the monastery is off limits to visitors, the guided tour will show you inside the 17th-century **botica** (pharmacy) and a small **museum** containing religious artworks, Flemish tapestries and the odd medieval sarcophagus. Guided tours are in Spanish only, and other visitors are usually allowed to wander more freely.

Museo Los Sonidos de la Tierra   MUSEUM
(Calle Las Condesas 10; admission free; ⊙10.30am-2pm & 5-7pm May-Oct, Sat & Sun only Mar, Apr, Nov & Dec, closed Jan & Feb) This engaging museum showcases musical instruments from the region and around the world.

ⓘ Sleeping & Eating

Hotel Tres Coronas   HISTORIC HOTEL €€
(☑947 39 00 47; www.hoteltrescoronasdesilos.com; Plaza Mayor 6; s incl breakfast €57-73, d €71-93; ❋☎) Set in a former 17th-century palace, this hotel is brimming with character (the suit of armour at the top of the grand staircase sets the scene), with rooms of thick stone walls and old-world charm. The rooms at the front have lovely views over the square. The restaurant (mains €7.20 to €25), which specialises in meats roasted in a wood-fire oven, is the village's best and most atmospheric.

ONLY IN SPAIN...

Spain's weird and wonderful fiestas have always left the rest of the world shaking their heads, from the Running of the Bulls in Pamplona to the tomato-throwing extravaganza of La Tomatina in Buñol. But surely there's no festival quite as strange as the baby-jumping festival of **Castrillo de Murcia**, a small village just south of the A231, 25km west of Burgos.

Every year since 1620, this tiny village of around 250 inhabitants has marked the feast of Corpus Cristi by lining up the babies of the village on a mattress, while grown men dressed as 'El Colacho', a figure representing the devil, leap over up to six prostrate and, it must be said, somewhat bewildered babies at a time. Like all Spanish rites, it does have a purpose: the ritual is thought to ward off the devil. But why jumping over babies? We have no idea and the villagers aren't telling. They do, however, assure us that no baby has been injured in the recorded history of the fiesta.

Hotel Santo Domingo de Silos
HOTEL, HOSTAL €

(☎947 39 00 53; www.hotelsantodomingodesilos.
com; Calle Santo Domingo 14; s €30-48, d €40-62,
apt €70-105; ☎☒) This place combines a simple *hostal* with a three-star hotel with large,
comfortable rooms, some with whirlpool
bathtubs, right opposite the monastery. It
also has some new apartments nearby in the
village, and plans for a swimming pool and
underground parking.There is also a reasonable restaurant (mains €5 to €17).

Padre Hospedero
MONASTERY €

(☎947 39 00 68; r incl meals €32) Men can rent
a heated room in the monastery, but you'll
need to book well ahead. Call between 10am
and 1.30pm Monday to Friday. You can stay
for a period of three to 10 days.

ⓘ Information
Tourist office (☎947 39 00 70; www.turismo
castillayleon.com; Calle de Cuatro Cantones 10;
☺10am-1.30pm & 4-6pm Tue-Sun)

ⓘ Getting There & Away
There is one daily bus from Burgos to Santo
Domingo de Silos (€6.25, 1½ hours) from Mon-
day to Saturday.

DESFILADERO DE YECLA
A mere 1.3km down the back road (BU911)
to Caleruega from Santo Domingo, the
spectacular Desfiladero de Yecla, a splendid
gorge of limestone cliffs, opens up. It's easily
visited thanks to a walkway – the stairs lead
down from just past the tunnel exit.

South to Río Duero

LERMA
POP 2830 / ELEV 827M

If you're travelling between Burgos and Madrid and finding the passing scenery none
too eye-catching, Lerma rises up from the
roadside like a welcome apparition. An ancient settlement, Lerma hit the big time in
the early 17th century when Grand Duke Don
Francisco de Rojas y Sandoval, a minister under Felipe II, launched an ambitious project
to create another El Escorial. He failed, but
the cobbled streets and delightful plazas of
the Old Town are his most enduring legacy.

◎ Sights
Pass through the Arco de la Cárcel (Prison
Gate), off the main road to Burgos, climbing up the long Calle del General Mola to the
massive Plaza Mayor, which is fronted by
the oversized Palacio Ducal, now a *parador*

notable for its courtyards and 210 balconies.
To the right of the square is the Dominican
nuns' Convento de San Blas, which can be
visited as part of the tourist- office tour.

A short distance northwest of Plaza
Mayor, a pretty passageway and viewpoint,
Mirador de los Arcos, opens up over Río
Arlanza. Its arches connect with the 17th-
century Convento de Santa Teresa.

The Pasadizo de Duque de Lerma (admission €2) is a restored 17th-century subterranean passage that connects the palace
with the Iglesia Colegial de San Pedro
Apóstol – buy tickets at the tourist office.

🛏 Sleeping & Eating

Parador de Lerma
HISTORIC HOTEL €€€

(☎947 17 71 10; www.parador.es; Plaza Mayor 1; r
€185; ⓟ☀@☎) Undoubtedly the most elegant place to stay is this *parador*, which
occupies the renovated splendour of the old
Palacio Ducal. As in any *parador*, the rooms
have luxury and character, and the service
is impeccable.

Posada La Hacienda de Mi Señor
HISTORIC HOTEL €€

(☎947 17 70 52; www.lahaciendademisenor.com;
Calle El Barco 6; s/d incl breakfast €50/75; ☀@☎)
This is your best midrange bet, with enormous rooms in a renovated, historic building a couple of blocks down the hill from the
square. The candy-floss colour scheme will
start to grate if you stay too long; request
room 205 for a more muted paint palette.

Asador Casa Brigante
CASTILIAN €€

(☎947 17 05 94; www.casabrigante.com; Plaza
Mayor 5; mains €15-22; ☺lunch daily) You're in
the heart of Castilian wood-fired-oven territory and Plaza Mayor is encircled by high-
quality restaurants with *cordero asado* on
the menu (€35 for two is a good price to
pay). A favourite is the cosy and friendly
Asador Casa Brigante – you won't taste better roast lamb anywhere. Ask about its accommodation options nearby.

ⓘ Information
Tourist office (☎947 17 70 02; www.citlerma.
com; Casa Consistorial; ☺10am-2pm & 4-7pm
Tue-Sun) Offers 1¼-hour guided tours (€4)
of the town and most of its monuments up to
three times daily.

ⓘ Getting There & Away
There are eight daily buses from Burgos (€3.40,
30 minutes), with only four on Saturday or Sunday. Some buses coming from Aranda de Duero
or Madrid also pass through.

PEÑARANDA DE DUERO
POP 580 / ELEV 877M

About 20km east of Aranda de Duero on the C111, the village of Peñaranda de Duero exudes considerable charm. Originally a Celtic fortress village, most of its surviving riches are grouped around the stately Plaza Mayor. The **Palacio Condes de Miranda** (947 55 20 13; admission free; 10am-2pm & 4-7.30pm Tue-Sun) is a grand Renaissance palace with a fine plateresque entrance, double-arched patio and beautiful ceilings in various styles. Obligatory guided tours run on the hour.

The 16th-century Iglesia de Santa Ana integrates columns and busts found at the Roman settlement of Clunia into an otherwise baroque design. Enjoy superb views of the village and surrounding country by taking a walk up to the sprawling 15th-century castle ruins.

For more information, visit the tourist office (947 55 20 63; Calle de Trinquete 7; 10am-2pm & 4-8pm Tue-Sun).

There are half a dozen or so *casas rurales* in the area for you to choose from should you wish to stay. Most buses between Valladolid (€6.90, 1½ hours) and Soria (€6.75, 1½ hours) pass through town.

SEPÚLVEDA
POP 1230 / ELEV 1313M

With its houses staggered along a ridge carved out by the gorge of Río Duratón, and famous for its *cordero asado* and *cochinillo*, Sepúlveda is a favourite weekend escape for *madrileños* (Madrid residents). Indeed, the Tuscan-style warm tones of Sepúlveda's buildings, fronting the central Plaza de España, are an enviable setting for a hot Sunday roast. Wednesday is market day.

The *ayuntamiento* backs onto what remains of the old castle, while high above it all rises the 11th-century **Iglesia del Salvador**. It's considered the prototype of Castilian Romanesque, marked by the single arched portico.

Sleeping & Eating

Mirador del Castilla HOSTAL €
(921 54 03 53; www.miradordelcastilla.com; Calle del Conde Sepúlveda 26; s/d €35/45) Most visitors don't stay overnight, but if you'd like to enjoy the town's sleepy post-crowd aspect, Mirador del Castilla, just off Plaza de España, has comfortable rooms, several with views (room 4 is a good choice).

Restaurante Cristóbal CASTILIAN €€
(921 54 01 00; www.restaurantecristobal.com; Calle del Conde de Sepúlveda 9; mains €11-24) This is a long-standing favourite, with good wine lists. Reservations are essential on weekends.

Restaurante Figón Zute el Mayor CASTILIAN €€
(921 54 01 65; www.figondetinin.com; Calle de Lope Tablada 6; mains €11-24) A warmly recommended place, Figón Zute el Mayor is impossibly crowded on winter weekends.

Getting There & Away
At least two buses link Sepúlveda daily with Madrid.

PARQUE NATURAL DEL HOZ DEL DURATÓN

A sizeable chunk of land northwest of Sepúlveda has been constituted as a natural park, the centrepiece of which is the Hoz del Duratón (Duratón Gorge). A dirt track leads 5km west from the hamlet of Villaseca to the Ermita de San Frutos. In ruins now, the hermitage was founded in the 7th century by San Frutos and his siblings, San Valentín and Santa Engracia. They lie buried in a tiny chapel nearby. This is a magical place, overlooking one of the many serpentine bends in the gorge, with squadrons of buzzards and eagles soaring above. The Parque Natural del Hoz del Duratón is a popular weekend excursion and some people take kayaks up to Burgomillodo to launch themselves down the waters of the canyon.

There is an excellent Centro de Interpretación (921 54 05 86; www.miespacionatural.es; Calle del Conde de Sepúlveda 34; 10am-7pm;) in Sepúlveda that also has an informative permanent exhibition about all aspects of the natural park, including the flora and fauna. It is housed in part of the Iglesia de Santiago.

West along Río Duero

PEÑAFIEL
POP 5620

Peñafiel is the gateway to the Ribera del Duero wine region and it makes a wonderful base for getting to know the region's celebrated wines.

Sights
Castillo de Peñafiel CASTLE, MUSEUM
(Museo Provincial del Vino; admission castle €3, incl museum €6, audio guides €2; 11am-2.30pm & 4.30-8.30pm Tue-Sun) Dramatically watching

over Peñafiel from on high, this castle is also home to the state-of-the-art Museo Provincial del Vino. Telling a comprehensive story of the region's wines, this wonderful museum is informative and entertaining with interactive displays, dioramas, backlit panels and computer terminals. The pleasures of the end product are not neglected: wine tasting costs €6 if you do it solo, €9 if you've an expert on hand to explain it all. If you don't speak Spanish, an audio guide (available in English and French) is essential.

The castle itself, one of the longest and narrowest in Spain, is also worth exploring. Its crenulated walls and towers stretch over 200m, but are little more than 20m across, and were raised and modified over 400 years from the 11th century onwards. The sight of it in the distance alone is worth the effort of getting here.

Plaza del Coso   SQUARE
One of Spain's more unusual plazas, this rectangular 15th-century 'square' was one of the first to be laid out for this purpose and is considered one of the most important forerunners to the *plazas mayores* across Spain. It's still used for bullfights on ceremonial occasions, and it's watched over by distinctive half-wooden facades.

🛏 Sleeping & Eating

Hotel Convento Las Claras   HISTORIC HOTEL €€
(☑983 87 81 68; www.hotelconventolasclaras.com; Plaza de los Comuneros 1; s/d €115/130; ❉🌐🏊) This cool, classy hotel is an unexpected find in little Peñafiel. A former convent, the rooms are luxurious and there's a full spa available with thermal baths and treatments, and an excellent restaurant with, as you'd expect, a carefully chosen wine list. There are also lighter meals available in the cafeteria.

Hotel Castillo de Curiel   HISTORIC HOTEL €€€
(☑983 88 04 01; www.castillodecuriel.com; r from €140) Just north of Peñafiel, in the village of Curiel de Duero, this should be the hotel of choice for castle romantics. Occupying the oldest castle, dating from the 9th century, in the region (albeit extensively reformed), the hotel has lovely antique-filled rooms, all with sweeping views. It also has a well-regarded restaurant.

ℹ Information

Tourist office (www.turismopenafiel.com; Plaza del Coso 31-32; ⏲10.30am-2.30pm & 5-8pm Tue-Sun)

ℹ Getting There & Away

Four or five buses a day run to Valladolid (€4.70, 45 minutes), 60km west of Peñafiel.

East along Río Duero

EL BURGO DE OSMA
POP 5270 / ELEV 943M

Some 12km east of San Esteban de Gormaz, El Burgo de Osma is a real surprise. Once important enough to host its own university, it's now a somewhat run-down little old town, dominated by a quite remarkable cathedral and infused with an air of decaying elegance.

👁 Sights

Your initiation into the Old Town is likely to be along the broad Calle Mayor, its portico borne by an uneven phalanx of stone and wooden pillars. Not far along, it leads into Plaza Mayor, fronted by the 18th-century ayuntamiento and the more sumptuous Hospital de San Agustín, which is where you'll find the tourist office.

If you exit El Burgo from near the cathedral on Plaza de San Pedro de Osma, take a left for the village of Osma, high above which stand the ruins of the 10th-century Castillo de Osma.

Catedral   CATHEDRAL
(Plaza de San Pedro de Osma; ⏲10.30am-1pm & 4-7pm Tue-Sun) This cathedral was begun in the 12th century as a Romanesque building, continued in a Gothic vein and finally topped with a weighty baroque tower that rivals many of the great cathedrals of Spain. The sanctuary is filled with art treasures, including the 16th-century main altarpiece and the so-called Beato de Osma, a precious 11th-century codex (manuscript) that can be seen in the Capilla Mayor. Also of note is the light-flooded, circular Capilla de Palafox, a rare example of the neoclassical style in this region.

🛏 Sleeping & Eating

Posada del Canónigo   HISTORIC HOTEL €€
(☑975 36 03 62; www.posadadelcanonigo.es; Plaza San Pedro de Osma 19; s/d incl breakfast €50/65; ❉🌐) This is certainly the most imaginative choice, with some rooms overlooking the cathedral from a handsome 16th-century building. There are two comfortable sitting rooms, one with a fireplace and library, and the rooms, all of them different, are over-

RIBERA DEL DUERO WINE REGION

The Ribero del Duero vintage wines are possibly the oldest in Spain and discerning Spanish wine lovers frequently claim that the wines of this region are the equal of the more famous Rioja wines.

This is the largest wine-growing region in Castilla y León, covering some 9229 hectares. Tempranillo, cabernet sauvignon, malbec and merlot are the most popular grape varieties and Spain's most celebrated (and expensive) wine, Vega Sicilia, comes from here.

Not all the 200-plus wineries here are open for tours and/or tasting (including, unfortunately, Vega Sicilia), but several are. For a full list, pick up the *Guía Enoturística* brochure from the tourist office in Peñafiel. Another good resource is the website www.rutadelvinoriberadelduero.es. All bodegas require you to ring ahead, rather than simply turn up – if that sounds daunting, Peñafiel's tourist office can help make the calls.

Some of the better-known wineries that do run tours and tastings include the following, although it's a far from comprehensive list:

Matarromera (983 10 71 00; www.matarromera.es; Valbuena de Duero)

Legaris (983 87 80 88; www.legaris.es; Curiel de Duero)

Protos (983 87 80 11; www.bodegasprotos.com; Calle Bodegas Protos 24-28; tours €10; 10am-1pm & 4.30-6pm Tue-Fri, 10am-1pm & 4.30-6.30pm Sat & Sun) Unusually, it's right in Peñafiel.

Aside from cellar-door sales at the wineries themselves, Peñafiel has numerous wine sellers dotted around the village. They really know their wines and most have every conceivable Ribera del Duero wine. They include the following:

Ánagora (Calle Derecha al Coso 31; 10.30am-2pm & 4.30-8pm Mon-Sat, 10.30am-2pm Sun)

Enoteca Zaguán (Calle Derecha al Coso 45; 10.15am-2pm & 4.15-8.30pm Tue-Sat, 10.15am-2pm Mon)

Vinos Ojos Negros (Plaza de San Miguel de Reoyo 1; 9am-2pm & 5-8pm Mon-Fri, 9am-2pm & 4-8pm Sat)

Palacio del Vino (Plaza de los Comuneros 2; 10am-2pm & 5-8pm Mon-Sat, 10am-2pm Sun)

flowing with period charm, although it's rarely overdone.

Hotel II Virrey HOTEL €€
(975 34 13 11; www.virreypalafox.com; Calle Mayor 2; s/d/ste €65/95/135; ❄🐾) This place has recently overhauled its decor, and it's now a curious mix of old Spanish charm and contemporary – public areas remain dominated by heavily gilded furniture, porcelain cherubs, dripping chandeliers and a sweeping staircase. Room rates soar on weekends in February and March, when people flock here for the ritual slaughter *(matanza)* of pigs, after which diners indulge in all-you-can-eat feasts. At €46 per head it's not bad for one of the more unusual dining experiences. There's even a pig museum. It also has a good restaurant, or a cafeteria for lighter meals.

Hostal Mayor 71 HOSTAL €
(975 36 80 24; www.mayor71.es; Calle Mayor 71; s/d €42/48; 🐾) This is a good central option,

with modern, simple rooms. The best ones overlook Calle Mayor, and it has some apartments nearby.

Casa Engracia GRILL €
(Calle Ruiz Zorrilla 3; mains €8-14; Tue-Sun, lunch Mon) One of a rare breed of restaurants in this town that opens during the week. Expect sound rather than sensational meals, with an emphasis on grilled meats and fish.

❶ Information
Tourist office (www.burgosma.es; Plaza Mayor 9; 10am-2pm & 4-7pm Wed-Sun)

❶ Getting There & Away
Buses link El Burgo with Soria (€3.50, 50 minutes, two daily, one on Sunday) and Valladolid (€10.15, two hours, three daily).

PARQUE NATURAL DEL CAÑÓN DEL RÍO LOBOS
Some 15km north of El Burgo de Osma, this park promises forbidding rockscapes and a magnificent, deep river canyon, not to

mention abundant vultures and various other birds of prey. About 4km in from the road stands the Romanesque Ermita de San Bartolomé. You can walk deeper into the park, but free camping is forbidden. If you're driving through the park between El Burgo de Osma and San Leonardo de Yagüe, don't miss the wonderful views from the Mirador de La Galiana, which is signposted off the SO920.

Camping Cañón del Río Lobos (☎975 36 35 65; camping.riolobos@hotmail.com; sites per person/tent/car €5/5/6.25; ☺Easter–mid-Sep; 🅿) is near Ucero. If you're heading north along the switchback road that climbs up the canyon, you'll have some fine views back towards Ucero.

BERLANGA DE DUERO
POP 1020 / ELEV 978M

About 15km east of Gormaz, Berlanga de Duero is lorded over by an imposing but ruined castle made larger by its continuous ramparts at the base of its hill. Down below, the squat Colegiata de Santa María del Mercado is a fine late-Gothic church, with star-shaped vaulting inside. The area around the pretty Plaza Mayor, with the occasional Renaissance house, has a certain dusty charm. To find out more, visit the tourist office (☎975 34 34 33; www.berlangadeduero.es; Plaza Mayor 9; ☺10am-2pm & 4-7pm, Sat & Sun only Oct-May).

AROUND BERLANGA DE DUERO
About 8km southeast of Berlanga de Duero stands the Ermita de San Baudelio (admission €1; ☺10am-2pm & 5-9pm Jun-Aug, shorter hours rest of year), whose simple exterior conceals a remarkable 11th-century Mozarabic interior. A great pillar in the centre of the only nave opens up at the top like a palm tree to create delicate horseshoe arches.

Another 17km south, the hilltop stone village of Rello retains much of its medieval defensive wall and feels like the place time forgot. The views from the village's southern ledge are superb. There's at least one *casa rural* if you love peace and quiet.

Soria
POP 39,990 / ELEV 1055M

Small-town Soria is one of Spain's smaller and least-visited provincial capitals, and also one of its better-kept secrets. Set on Río Duero in the heart of backwoods Castilian countryside, it's a great place to escape tourist Spain, with an appealing and compact old centre, and a sprinkling of stunning monuments down by the river.

Sights

Monasterio de San Juan de Duero   RUIN
(Camino Monte de las Ánimas; admission €0.60, Sat & Sun free; ☺10am-2pm & 5-8pm Tue-Sat, 10am-2pm Sun) The most striking of Soria's sights, this wonderfully evocative and partially ruined cloister boasts exposed and gracefully interlaced arches; the arches artfully blend Mudéjar and Romanesque influences and no two capitals are the same. Inside the church, the carvings are worth a closer look for their intense iconography. It's on the riverbank down the hill from the Old Town.

Ermita de San Saturio   HISTORIC BUILDING
(Paseo de San Saturio; admission free; ☺10.30am-2pm & 4.30-7.30pm Tue-Sun) A lovely riverside walk south for 2.3km from the Monasterio de San Juan de Duero will take you past the 13th-century church of the former Knights Templar, the Monasterio de San Polo (not open to the public), and on to the fascinating, baroque Ermita de San Saturio.

The hermitage is one of Castilla y León's most beautifully sited structures, an octagonal structure that perches high on the riverbank and over the cave where Soria's patron saint spent much of his life. Climb through a series of fascinating rooms hewn from the rock, but linger most of all in the Capilla, an extravagantly frescoed chapel near the building's summit.

Concatedral de San Pedro   CHRISTIAN
(Calle de San Agustín; cloister admission €1; ☺cloister 11am-1pm Mon, 10.30am-1.30pm & 4.30-7.30pm Tue-Sun) Climbing back up the hill towards the Old Town, the Concatedral de San Pedro has a plateresque facade. The 12th-century cloister is the most charming feature here. Its delicate arches are divided by slender double pillars topped with capitals adorned with floral, human and animal motifs.

Casco Viejo   OLD TOWN
The narrow streets of Soria's Casco Viejo (Old Town) centre on Plaza Mayor. The plaza's appeal lies in its lack of uniformity, and in the attractive Renaissance-era ayuntamiento and the Iglesia de Santa María la Mayor, with its unadorned Romanesque facade and gloomy, though gilt-edged, interior. A block north is the majes-

tic, sandstone, 16th-century Palacio de los Condes Gomara (Calle de Aguirre). Upstairs from the wonderfully old-world Bar Casino Amistad, Soria's newest museum, Casa de las Poetas (3rd fl, Calle Mayor 23; admission free; ⊙10am-2pm & 4-8pm Tue-Sun), pays homage to Antonio Machado and other Spanish poets with a connection to the town. Further north is Soria's most beautiful church, the Romanesque Iglesia de Santo Domingo (Calle de Santo Tomé Hospicio; ⊙7am-9pm). Its small but exquisitely sculpted portal is something special, particularly at sunset when its reddish stone seems to be aglow. At the Iglesia de San Juan de Rabanera (Calle de San Juan de Rabanera; ⊙before & after Mass), which was first built in the 12th century, hints of Gothic and even Byzantine art gleam through the mainly Romanesque hue.

Museo Numantino   MUSEUM
(Paseo del Espolón 8; adult/concession €1.20/free; ⊙10am-2pm & 5-8pm Tue-Sat, 10am-2pm Sun) Archeology buffs with a passable knowledge of Spanish should enjoy this well-organised museum, dedicated to finds from ancient sites across the province of Soria (especially Numancia). It has everything from mammoth bones to ceramics and jewellery, accompanied by detailed explanations of the historical developments in various major Celtiberian and Roman settlements.

🎊 Festivals & Events

Fiestas de San Juan y de la Madre de Dios   LOCAL FIESTA
Since the 13th century, the 12 *barrios* (districts) of Soria have celebrated this annual festival with considerable fervour. Held during the second half of June, the main festivities take place on Jueves (Thursday) La Saca, when each of the districts presents a bull to be fought the next day. The day following the bullfight some of the animals' meat is auctioned off, after which general carousing continues until the small hours of Sunday – and beyond.

🛏 Sleeping

Hostería Solar de Tejada   BOUTIQUE HOTEL €
(☑975 23 00 54; www.hosteriasolardetejada.es; Calle de Claustrilla 1; s/d €52/56; ❄🔊) This handsome boutique hotel right along the Old Town's pedestrianised zone is one of the best choices in Soria. Individually designed rooms have whimsical decor, bohemian touches and beautifully tiled bathrooms.

Hotel Soria Plaza Mayor   HOTEL €€
(☑975 24 08 64; www.hotelsoriaplazamayor.com; Plaza Mayor 10; s/d/ste €65/72/91; ❄@) This hotel has terrific rooms, each with its own style of decor, overlooking either Plaza Mayor or a quiet side street. There are so many balconies that even some bathrooms have their own. The suites are *very* comfortable.

Hotel Ruiz   HOSTAL €
(☑975 22 67 01; www.hostalruiz.com; Calle Numancia 49; s/d €35/50; ❄@) A cut above those of your average *hostal,* rooms here are polished and comfortable with light-wood floors and dazzling white fabrics. It's just a few minutes from the bustle of the city centre.

Hotel Leonor Centro   HOTEL €€
(☑975 23 93 03; www.hotel-leonor.com; Plaza Ramón y Cajal 5; s/d €64.50/113; ❄🔊) Just off the main pedestrian street through the Old Town and within walking distance of just about everything, this fine four-star hotel has classy, contemporary rooms with strong colours and slate-walled modern bathrooms.

🍴 Eating & Drinking

Soria's restaurants are mainly centred around the main squares, namely Plaza El Salvador, Plaza Ramón Benito Aceñal and Plaza Mayor. Soria's surprisingly raucous drinking scene has its epicentre on Plaza Ramón Benito Aceñal, with Plaza San Clemente, just off Calle Mayor, offering strong competition.

Casa Augusto   CONTEMPORARY CASTILIAN €€
(☑975 21 30 41; www.casaaugusto.com; Plaza Mayor 5; mains €12-20) This is classy, with an intimate dining area, an extensive wine list and professional service. If you can't decide what to eat, ask the waiter for the list of the year's most popular orders. For some reason, *pie sucio rellenos* (stuffed pig's trotters) is always there. The *albondigas caseras con setas* (home-made meatballs with wild mushrooms) is among our favourites. Reservations recommended.

Mesón Castellano   CASTILIAN €€
(☑975 21 30 45; Plaza Mayor 2; mains €13-30) With beamed ceilings, dangling flanks of ham, and the wall papered with proud photos of the local football team, this local institution serves some of the best tapas in town and delicious full meals in its *comedor.* The *cabrito asado* (roast goat kid) is a good order.

Fogon del Salvador CASTILIAN €€
(Plaza El Salvador 1; mains €14.50-22; 🍴) A Soria culinary stalwart, Fogon del Salvador has a wine list as long as your arm (literally) and a fabulous wood-fired oven churning out succulent meat-based dishes. There is also (surprisingly) a healthy list of vegetarian dishes and the *raciones* include some rarely found dishes, such as *anguila ahumada* (smoked baby eels).

Capote SANDWICHES €
(Plaza Ramón Benito Aceñal; montaditos €1.20; 🍴) You'll have to fight through the crowd to reach the counter at this popular (cheap) bar where you can fill up happily on the tasty and varied *montaditos* (open sandwiches).

❶ Information

Municipal tourist office (Plaza de Mariano Granados 1; ◷10am-2pm & 4-8pm Tue-Sun)
Regional tourist office (📞975 21 20 52; www. turismocastillayleon.com; Calle de Medinaceli 2; ◷9.30am-2pm & 5-8pm)

❶ Getting There & Away

BUS From the **bus station** (📞975 22 51 60; Avenida de Valladolid), a 15-minute walk west of the city centre, there are regular services to Burgos (€10.85, 2½ hours), Madrid (€14.99, 2½ hours) and Valladolid (€15.15, three hours), as well as main provincial towns.
TRAIN The **train station** (Carretera de Madrid) is 2.5km southwest of the city centre. Trains connect Soria with Madrid (€18.25, 2¾ hours, three daily), but there are few other direct services.

Around Soria

NUMANCIA

The mainly Roman ruins of Numancia (www.numanciasoria.es; adult/concession/child under 13yr €4/3/free, free Sat & Sun; ◷10am-2pm & 4-8pm Tue-Sat, 10am-2pm Sun), 8km north of Soria, have a lonely, windswept aspect with little to suggest the long history of a settlement inhabited as early as the Bronze Age. Numancia proved one of the most resistant cities to Roman rule. Finally Scipio, who had crushed Carthage, starved the city into submission in 134 BC. Under Roman rule, Numancia was an important stop on the road from Caesaraugustus (Zaragoza) to Astúrica Augusta (Astorga). Now the city exists in outline only and will appeal more to budding archeologists than to casual visitors.

To get here, take the N111 for around 5km north of Soria, then follow the signs to Garray.

SIERRA DE URBIÓN & LAGUNA NEGRA

The Sierra de Urbión, northwest of Soria, is home to the beautiful Laguna Negra (Black Lake), a small glacial lake that resembles a black mirror at the base of brooding rock walls amid partially wooded hills. Located 18km north of the village of Vinuesa, the lake is reached by a winding and scenic road (there's no public transport) that's bumpy in patches. The road ends at a car park, where there's a small information office (◷Jun-Oct). It's a further 2km uphill to the lake, either on foot or via the bus (return €1, departing half-hourly from 10am to 2pm and 4pm to 6.30pm June to October), which leaves you 300m short of the lake. From the lake, a steep trail leads up to the Laguna de Urbión in La Rioja or to the summit of the Pico de Urbión, above the village of Duruelo de la Sierra, and on to a series of other tiny glacial lakes.

CALATAÑAZOR
POP 40 / ELEV 1071M
One of Castilla y León's most romantic tiny hilltop villages, Calatañazor is a charming detour. It's not visible from the highway just 1km away, and has a crumbling medieval air. Pass through the town gate and climb the crooked, cobbled lanes, wandering through narrow streets lined by ochre stone and adobe houses topped with red-tiled roofs and conical chimneys. Scenes from the movie *Doctor Zhivago* were shot here.

Towering above the village is the one-time Muslim fortress that gave Calatañazor its name (which comes from the Arabic Qala'at an-Nassur, literally 'The Vulture's Citadel'). Now in ruins, it has exceptional views from the walls and watchtowers, both down over the rooftops and north over a vast field called Valle de la Sangre (Valley of Blood). This was the setting of an epic 1002 battle that saw the Muslim ruler Almanzor defeated.

There's also a church and a handful of artisan shops selling local products. There are three well-signposted *casas rurales* if you fancy staying the night.

There's no regular public transport to Calatañazor. If you're driving, the village lies around 1km north of the N122 – the well-signposted turn-off is about 29km west of Soria and about 27km northeast of El Burgo de Osma.

South of Soria

MEDINACELI
POP 820 / ELEV 1270M

Modern Medinaceli, along a slip road just north of the A2 motorway, is the contemporary equivalent of a one-horse town, but don't be fooled: old Medinaceli is one of Castilla y León's most beautiful *pueblos* (villages), draped along a high, windswept ridge 3km to the north.

◉ Sights

In addition to the sights listed following, there's the moderately interesting Gothic Colegiata de Santa María (Plaza de la Iglesia; admission by donation; ⊙11am-2pm & 4-7pm Tue-Sun), and the evocative remains of a synagogue: San Román.

But Medinaceli's charm consists of rambling through tranquil cobblestone lanes and being surrounded by delightful stone houses redolent of the noble families that lived here after the town fell to the Reconquista in 1124. The area between Plaza de Santiuste and the lovely, partly colonnaded Plaza Mayor is Medinaceli at its best. The oldest remaining building is the 16th-century Alhóndiga, formerly used for storing and selling grain.

Palacio Ducal   ARCHITECTURE, GALLERY
(Plaza Mayor; admission €2; ⊙10am-8pm) This largely 17th-century palace overlooks the Plaza Mayor, and hosts regular and high-quality exhibitions of contemporary art in rooms arrayed around the stunning two-storey Renaissance courtyard. In one of the rooms is a 2nd-century Roman mosaic.

Roman Sites   RUIN
Once a strategic Roman outpost, Medinaceli boasts a 1st-century-AD Arco Romano (Roman triumphal arch) at the entrance to town, a mosaic (from a Roman villa) in situ under glass on Plaza San Pedro and another mosaic in the Palacio Ducal.

✦ Festivals & Events

Festival Internacional de Música   MUSIC
(⊙weekends Jul) On Saturdays and/or Sundays in July, the Colegiata de Santa María hosts mostly classical concerts by international performers.

⌑ Sleeping & Eating

Both of the sleeping options have good restaurants – La Ceramica is cosier, Bavieca more creative.

La Ceramica   RURAL HOTEL €€
(☎975 32 63 81; www.laceramicacasarural.es; Calle de Santa Isabel 2; s/d €50/55, d incl breakfast & dinner €91; ⊙closed mid-Dec–Jan; ☞) Lovely La Ceramica wins our vote for the friendliest staff, best location in the Old Town and all-round greatest deal. The rooms are intimate and comfortable, with a strong dose of rustic charm; the attic room 22 is lovely, but the CR2 apartment which sleeps four feels just like home. There's sometimes a two-night minimum stay. The restaurant is similarly excellent.

Hostal Rural Bavieca   BOUTIQUE HOTEL €€
(☎975 32 61 06; ww.bavieca.net; Calle Campo de San Nicolás 6; s/d incl breakfast €55/75; ☞) The style of the rooms here may not be to everyone's taste, but this is unmistakably a boutique hotel that offers high-quality rooms and ambience.

Asador de la Villa El Granero   CASTILIAN €€
(☎975 32 61 89; Calle de Yedra 10; mains €13.75-19.75; ⊙lunch & dinner daily Jul & Aug, lunch Wed-Mon Sep-Dec & Feb-Jun, closed Jan) This well-signposted place, with a shop selling local food products at the front, is thought by many to be Medinaceli's best restaurant. The *setas de campo* (wild mushrooms) are something of a local speciality. Book ahead on weekends.

Iglesia Convento Santa Isabel   SWEETS €
(Calle de Campo San Nicolás; cookies from €6; ⊙10am-2pm & 4-7pm) The nuns at this pretty convent bake up tasty cookies and other sweets; ring the bell and then make your selection through the revolving window.

❶ Information

Tourist office (☎975 32 63 47; Calle Campo de San Nicolás; ⊙10am-2pm & 4-7pm Wed-Sun) At the entrance to town, just around the corner from the arch.

❶ Getting There & Away

Two daily buses to Soria (€5.50, 45 minutes) leave from outside the *ayuntamiento* in the new town. There's no transport between the old and new towns; it's a steep hike.

SANTA MARÍA DE LA HUERTA
POP 370

This largely insignificant village, just short of the Aragonese frontier, contains a wonderful Cistercian monastery (admission €3; ⊙10am-1pm & 4-6pm Mon-Sat, 10-11.15am & 4-6.30pm Sun), founded in 1162, where monks lived until the monastery was expropriated in 1835. The order was allowed to return in 1930 and 25 Cistercians are now in residence. Before entering the monastery, note the church's impressive 12th-century facade with its magnificent rose window.

Inside the monastery you pass through two cloisters, the second of which is the more beautiful. Known as the **Claustro de los Caballeros**, it's Spanish-Gothic in style, although the medallions on the 2nd floor,

bearing coats of arms and assorted illustrious busts, such as that of Christopher Columbus, are a successful plateresque touch. Off this cloister is the *refectorio* (dining hall). Built in the 13th century, it's notable for the absence of columns to support the vault.

A couple of buses per day connect the village with Soria.

Castilla-La Mancha

Best Places to Eat

» Calle Mayor (p233)
» Alfileritos 24 (p212)
» El Corregidor (p220)

Best Places to Stay

» Casa de Cisneros (p209)
» Palacio de la Serna (p217)
» La Casa del Rector (p220)
» Posada de San José (p226)
» Hotel Albamanjón (p220)
» Antiguo Palacio de Atienza (p234)
» Parador de Sigüenza (p231)

Why Go?

Castilla-La Mancha's landscape is richly patterned and dramatic: undulating plains of rich henna-coloured earth, neatly striped and spotted with olive groves, and golden wheat fields and grapevines – all stretching to a horizon you never seem to reach. This is Don Quijote country, and you'll find references to the fictional knight throughout the region, including a fistful of picturesque windmills. And in many ways, this really is storybook Spain, a land of hearty meals, cheese and wine, lonely hilltop castles and towns stocked with churches.

The area's best-known city is glorious Toledo, an open-air museum of medieval buildings and cultural sights. Cuenca is another wondrous place, seemingly about to topple off its eagle's-eyrie perch high above a gorge. There are quiet mountainous stretches here as well, including the Sierra de Alcaraz and the Serranía de Cuenca.

When to Go
Toledo

Mar & Apr Enjoy the countryside's colourful dazzle of wild flowers against a lush green landscape.

May Stroll the evocative streets of medieval Toledo and Cuenca before the sizzle of high summer.

Sep & Oct Hike across Castilla-La Mancha's natural parks and picturesque villages.

Castilla-La Mancha Highlights

1 Stroll the tangle of medieval streets and explore the monuments of **Toledo** (p205)

2 Wind down in the picture-perfect medieval town of **Atienza** (p233)

3 Take *the* Don Quijote shot of the windmills overlooking **Consuegra** (p221)

4 Kick back with a beer at a riverside bar in **Alcalá del Júcar** (p223) beneath its castle

5 Visit the Museo de Arte Abstracto Español, in one of **Cuenca's** (p224) extraordinary hanging houses

6 Marvel at the handsome plaza and historic theatre in enticing **Almagro** (p217)

7 Be king or queen of the castle by visiting the region's fascinating **castillos**

8 Enjoy local wines with a crumbly wedge of well-aged, local **Manchego cheese**

9 Check out the chunky cathedral, hilltop castle and great restaurants in pleasing **Sigüenza** (p231)

Toledo

POP 83,110 / ELEV 655M

Though one of the smaller of Spain's provincial capitals, Toledo looms large in the nation's history and consciousness as a religious centre, bulwark of the Spanish church, and once-flourishing symbol of a multicultural medieval society. The Old Town today is a treasure chest of churches, museums, synagogues and mosques set in a labyrinth of narrow streets, plazas and inner patios in a lofty setting high above Río Tajo.

Toledo's charms, and its proximity to Madrid, mean that it can get choked with tour groups during the day. Try to stay till dusk, when the city returns to the locals and the streets take on a moody, other-worldly air.

History

Already an important pre-Roman settlement, Toledo was eventually chosen as capital of the post-Roman Visigothic kingdom. After being taken by the Moors in 711, the city rapidly grew to become the capital of an independent Arab *taifa* (small kingdom) and the centre of learning and arts in Spain.

Alfonso VI marched into Toledo in 1085 and, shortly thereafter, the Vatican recognised Toledo as a seat of the Spanish Church. Initially, Toledo's Christians, Jews and Muslims coexisted tolerably well. However, the eventual convert-or-get-out dictats issued to the Jews and Muslims stripped this multifaith city of the backbone of its social and economic life. Once Felipe II chose Madrid as his capital in the mid-16th century, Toledo went into decline.

◎ Sights

Most of Toledo's sights are within easy strolling distance of each other in the Old Town.

TOP CHOICE Catedral CATHEDRAL
(Plaza del Ayuntamiento; adult/child €7/free; ◎10.30am-6.30pm Mon-Sat, 2-6.30pm Sun) Toledo's cathedral reflects the city's historical significance as the heart of Catholic Spain.

From the earliest days of the Visigothic occupation, the current site of the cathedral has been a centre of worship. During Muslim rule, it contained Toledo's central mosque, destroyed in 1085. Dating from the 13th century and essentially a Gothic structure, the cathedral is nevertheless a melting pot of styles, including Mudéjar and Renaissance. The Visigothic influence continues

TAKE THE ESCALATOR

A remonte peatonal (◎7am-10pm Mon-Fri, 8am-2am Sat, 8am-11pm Sun), which starts near the Puerta de Alfonso VI and ends near the Monasterio de Santo Domingo El Antiguo, is a good way to avoid the steep uphill climb to reach the historic quarter of town.

today in the unique celebration of the Mozarabic Rite, a 6th-century liturgy that was allowed to endure after Cardinal Cisneros put its legitimacy to the test by burning missals in a fire of faith; they survived more or less intact.

The heavy interior, with sturdy columns dividing the space into five naves, is on a monumental scale. Every one of the numerous side chapels has artistic treasures.

The tesoro, however, deals in treasure of the glittery kind. It's dominated by the extraordinary Custodia de Arfe: with 18kg of pure gold and 183kg of silver, this 16th-century processional monstrance bristles with some 260 statuettes. Its big day out is the Feast of Corpus Christi, when it is paraded around Toledo's streets.

In the centre of things, the coro (choir) is a feast of sculpture and carved wooden stalls. The 15th-century lower tier depicts the various stages of the conquest of Granada.

The high altar sits in the extravagant Capilla Mayor, whose masterpiece is the *retablo* (altarpiece), with painted wooden sculptures depicting scenes from the lives of Christ and the Virgin Mary; it's flanked by royal tombs. The oldest of the cathedral's magnificent stained-glass pieces is the rose window above the Puerta del Reloj. Behind the main altar lies a mesmerising piece of 18th-century *churrigueresco* (lavish Baroque ornamentation), the Transparente, which is illuminated by a light well carved into the dome above.

Other noteworthy features include the sober cloister, off which is the 14th-century Capilla de San Blas, with Gothic tombs and stunning frescoes, the gilded Capilla de Reyes Nuevos, and the sala capitular (chapterhouse), with its remarkable 500-year-old *artesonado* (wooden Mudéjar ceiling) and portraits of all the archbishops of Toledo.

The highlight of all, however, is the sacristía (sacristy), which contains a gallery

Toledo

N

0 — 100 m
0 — 0.05 miles

To Bus Station
(330m)

Paseo del Miradero

C de Santa Fe

24

C de Cervantes

5

Alféreces
Provisionales

Alcázar

Arco de
la Sangre

Cuesta de Carlos V

C de las Armas

C de Recoletos

Plaza de
Zocodover

C Juan Labrador

C de la Sillería

Plaza de
San Nicolás

C Nueva

C de Azacanes

Escalator

C de Gerardo Lobo

C Núñez de Arce

21

C de las Cadenas

29

C de Comercio

C Barrio Rey

C de la Plata

C de la
Sinagoga

18

10

C de los Alfileritos

11

To Train
Station
(1.2km)

Puerta
del Sol

C del Cristo de la Luz

4

15

C Real del Arrabal

30

19

C Nuncio Viejo

C de la Plata

Puerta
Nueva de
Bisagra

Puerta de
Alfonso VI

C Airosas

13

Remonte Peatonal
(Escalator)

Subida de la Granja

23

C Alfonso X el Sabio

3

C de San Román

Av de Carlos III

Provincial
Tourist Office

C de la Merced

C de las Tendillas

26

C Real

1

C del Colegio

Paseo de Recaredo

Av de la Cava

C Santa Leocadia

C de Pinto Matías Moreno

C de las Bulas

Monasterio
San Juan de
los Reyes

with paintings by such masters as El Greco, Zurbarán, Caravaggio, Titian, Raphael and Velázquez. It can be difficult to appreciate the packed-together, poorly lit artworks, but it's a stunning assemblage in a small space. In an adjacent chamber, don't miss the spectacular Moorish standard captured in the Battle of Salado in 1340.

An extra €3 gets you entrance to the upper level of the cloister and the belltower, which offers predictably wonderful views over the centre of historic Toledo.

Alcázar
FORTRESS, MUSEUM

(Museo del Ejército; Calle Alféreces Provisionales; adult/child €5/free; ⊙10am-9pm Thu-Tue Jun-Sep, to 7pm Oct-May) At the highest point in the city looms the foreboding Alcázar. Abd ar-Rahman III raised an *al-qasr* here in the 10th century, which was thereafter altered by the Christians. Alonso Covarrubias rebuilt it as a royal residence for Carlos I, but the court moved to Madrid and the fortress eventually became a military academy.

The Alcázar was heavily damaged during the siege of the garrison by loyalist militias at the start of the Civil War in 1936. The soldiers' dogged resistance, and the commander, Moscardó's, famous refusal to give it up in exchange for his son's life, made it a powerful Nationalist symbol.

Rebuilt under Franco, it has recently been reopened as an absolutely enormous military museum, with strict staff barking orders adding to the martial experience. The usual displays of uniforms and medals are here, but the best part is the exhaustive historical section, with an in-depth overview of the nation's history in Spanish and English. By the time you get to the end of the 19th century your feet will be begging for mercy, but relief is at hand: sensibly the Civil War is essentially skipped over in one paragraph to avoid controversy. You can, however, see a re-creation of Moscardó's office; other highlights include the monumental central patio decorated with Habsburg coats of arms, and archaeological remains from Moorish times.

Sinagoga del Tránsito
SYNAGOGUE

(http://museosefardi.mcu.es; Calle Samuel Leví; adult/child €3/1.50, with Museo del Greco €5; ⊙9.30am-8pm Tue-Sat Apr-Sep, to 6.30pm Oct-Mar, 10am-3pm Sun) This magnificent synagogue was built in 1355 by special permission of Pedro I. Toledo's former *judería* (Jewish quarter) was once home to 10

CASTILLA-LA MANCHA TOLEDO

Toledo

synagogues and comprised some 10% of the walled city's area. After the expulsion of the Jews from Spain in 1492, it was variously used as a priory, hermitage and military barracks. The synagogue now houses the **Museo Sefardí**. The vast main prayer hall has been expertly restored and the Mudéjar decoration and intricately carved pine ceiling are striking. Exhibits provide an insight into the history of Jewish culture in Spain, and include archaeological finds, a memorial garden, costumes and ceremonial artefacts. Entry is free from 2pm on Saturday and all day Sunday.

Museo del Greco MUSEUM, GALLERY
(☑925 22 44 05; http://museodelgreco.mcu.es; Paseo del Tránsito; adult/child €3/1.50, with Sinagoga del Tránsito €5; ☺9.30am-8pm Tue-Sat Apr-Sep, to 6.30pm Oct-Mar, 10am-3pm Sun) In the early 20th century, an aristocrat bought what he thought was El Greco's house and did a stunning job of returning it to period style. He was wrong, but this museum is well worth visiting anyway. As well as the house itself, with its lovely patio, there are excavated cellars from a Jewish-quarter palace and a good selection of paintings, including a set of the apostles by El Greco, a Zurbarán, and works by El Greco's son and various followers. There's good information on the painter's life and times and a pleasant garden. Entry is free on Saturday after 2pm and all day Sunday.

Monasterio San Juan de los Reyes MONASTERY
(Calle San Juan de los Reyes 2; admission €2.50; ☺10am-6.45pm) This imposing 15th-century Franciscan monastery and church of San Juan de los Reyes was provocatively founded in the heart of the Jewish quarter by the Catholic Monarchs Isabel and Fernando to demonstrate the supposed supremacy of their faith. The rulers had planned to be buried here but eventually ended up in their prize conquest, Granada.

The highlight is the amazing two-level cloister, a harmonious fusion of late ('flamboyant') Gothic downstairs and Mudéjar architecture upstairs, with superb statuary, arches, vaulting, elaborate pinnacles and gargoyles surrounding a lush garden with orange trees and roses. It takes the breath away at first glimpse. The adjacent church has a series of enormous coats of arms of the Catholic Monarchs, who were never shy about self-publicising.

Sinagoga de Santa María La Blanca SYNAGOGUE

(Calle de los Reyes Católicos 4; admission €2.50; ☉10am-6.45pm) This pretty Mudéjar synagogue has five naves divided by rows of horseshoe and multifoil arches. Originally the upper arches opened onto rooms where women worshipped; the men were down below. Admire the stucco work and ornate capitals; the presence of nuns and a curious exhibition sponsored by a Catholic organisation founded by a converted Jew might offend some visitors.

Mezquita del Cristo de la Luz MOSQUE

(Calle Cristo de la Luz; admission €2.50; ☉10am-2pm & 3.30-6.45pm Mon-Fri, 10am-6.45pm Sat & Sun) On the northern slopes of town you'll find a modest, yet beautiful, mosque where architectural traces of Toledo's medieval Muslim conquerors are still in evidence. Built around 1000AD, it suffered the usual fate of being converted to a church (hence the religious frescoes), but the original vaulting and arches survived.

FREE Museo de Santa Cruz MUSEUM

(Calle Cervantes 3; ☉10am-6.30pm Mon-Sat, to 2pm Sun) The 16th-century Museo de Santa Cruz is a beguiling combination of Gothic and Plateresque styles. The cloisters and carved wooden ceilings are superb, as is the collection of Spanish ceramics. Also upstairs is an atmospheric cruciform gallery that contains an archaeological display, some fine Flemish religious art, a number of El Grecos, a crucifixion attributed to Goya, a flag from the battle of Lepanto, and the wonderful 15th-century *Tapestry of the Astrolabes*.

🎓 Courses

Universidad de Castilla-La Mancha SPANISH

(www.uclm.es/fundacion/esto) The University of Castilla-La Mancha runs an ESTO (Spanish in Toledo) program with various language courses. Visit its website for more details.

🎊 Festivals & Events

Corpus Christi RELIGIOUS

This is one of the finest Corpus Christi celebrations in Spain, taking place on the Thurs-

PULSERA TURÍSTICA

The **Pulsera Turística** is a bracelet (€8) that gets you into six key Toledo sights, all of which cost €2.50 on their own. There's no time limit, but make sure it doesn't fall off! Buy the bracelet at any of the sights covered, which are Monasterio San Juan de los Reyes, Sinagoga de Santa María La Blanca, Iglesia de Santo Tomé, Iglesia del Salvador, Iglesia San Ildefonso and Mezquita del Cristo de la Luz.

day 60 days after Easter Sunday. Several days of festivities reach a crescendo with a procession featuring the massive Custodia de Arfe.

Virgen del Sagrario LOCAL FIESTA

Taking place on 15 August (Assumption Day), this is when you can drink of the cathedral's well water, believed to have miraculous qualities – the queues for a swig from an earthenware *botijo* (jug) can be equally astonishing. It's also the city's main fiesta, with plenty of partying guaranteed.

🛏 Sleeping

Toledo's plentiful accommodation is offset by the visiting tourists, especially from July to September. Book ahead to avoid endless suitcase-trundling over cobbles.

TOP CHOICE Casa de Cisneros BOUTIQUE HOTEL €€

(☎925 22 88 28; www.hostal-casa-de-cisneros.com; Calle Cardenal Cisneros; s/d incl breakfast €55/75; ❄🛜) Right by the cathedral, this lovely 16th-century house was once the home of the cardinal and Grand Inquisitor Cisneros (often known as Ximénes). It's a top choice, with cosy, seductive rooms with original wooden beams and walls and voguish bathrooms. Guests get to visit and sip a wine in the wonderful downstairs space where archaeological works have revealed the remains of Roman baths and part of an 11th-century Moorish palace.

Casa de los Mozárabes APARTMENT €€

(☎925 21 17 01; www.casadelosmozarabes.com; Callejón de Menores 10; apt €96-170; ❄🛜❄) Occupying an historic Toledo house on a quiet central lane, these excellent apartments have modern furnishings that combine well with the exposed brick and historic

TOP VISTAS

For superb city views, head over the Puente de Alcántara to the other side of Río Tajo and head along the road that rises to your right, where the vista becomes more marvellous with every step. You can also climb the towers at the Iglesia San Ildefonso (Iglesia de los Jesuitas; Plaza Juan de Mariana 1; admission €2.50; ⊙10am-6.45pm), surely one of the few churches to boast a Coke machine, for more camera-clicking views of the cathedral and Alcázar. For a meal with superb city panoramas, you can't beat La Ermita (www.laermitarestaurante.com; Carretera de Circunvalación; mains €18-22, degustation menu €48), with a short quality menu of elaborate Spanish cuisine.

features of the building. There's a common lounge area with a pool table and a few weights.

Hostal del Cardenal
HISTORIC HOTEL €€

(☑925 22 49 00; www.hostaldelcardenal.com; Paseo de Recaredo 24; s/d incl breakfast €90/120; ❄️🛜) This wonderful 18th-century mansion has soft ochre-coloured walls, arches and columns. The rooms are grand, yet welcoming, with dark furniture, plush fabrics and parquet floors. Several overlook the glorious terraced gardens.

Hotel Abad
HOTEL €€

(☑925 28 35 00; www.hotelabad.com; Calle Real del Arrabal 1; d midweek/weekend €74/123; P❄️🛜) Compact, pretty and pleasing, this hotel sits on the lower slopes of the Old Town and offers good value, with prices usually lower than those we list here. Rooms blend modern comfort with exposed old brick very successfully; some have small balconies, but those at the back are notably quieter. There are also apartments available next door.

La Posada de Manolo
BOUTIQUE HOTEL €€

(☑925 28 22 50; www.laposadademanolo.com; Calle de Sixto Ramón Parro 8; s/d incl breakfast €46/76; ❄️🛜) This memorable hotel has themed each floor with furnishings and decor reflecting one of the three cultures of Toledo: Christian, Islamic and Jewish. There are stunning views of the Old Town and cathedral from the terrace.

Parador Conde de Orgaz
HOTEL €€€

(☑925 22 18 50; www.parador.es; Cerro del Emperador; s/d €141/177; P❄️🛜🏊) High above the southern bank of Río Tajo, Toledo's low-rise *parador* (luxurious state-owned hotel) boasts a classy interior and breathtaking city views. The parador is well signposted: turn right just after crossing the bridge northeast of the old centre.

Hostal Santo Tomé
HOSTAL €

(☑925 22 17 12; www.hostalsantotome.com; Calle de Santo Tomé 13; s/d €42/55; P❄️🛜) This friendly and good-value *hostal* (budget hotel), run out of the souvenir shop downstairs, has larger-than-most rooms with light wood floors and furniture, plus bathrooms with five-star attitude, offering extras like shoe polish and hairdryers. Try for a room with a streetside balcony if you can handle a bit of weekend noise. Parking costs €10.

Hotel Eurico
HOTEL €€

(☑925 28 41 78; www.hoteleurico.com; Calle de Santa Isabel 3; s/d €79/89; ❄️🛜) With a cracking location just below the cathedral, this has comfortable, unadventurous modern rooms in a handsome old building set around a patio. Service is helpful, and prices lower substantially midweek. Try for an upstairs room: the ones on the ground floor are a little dark. The hotel has a deal with a car park, but it's a long walk away so drop your bags first. A good central option.

Cigarral de Caravantes
HOTEL €€

(☑925 28 36 80; www.cigarraldecaravantes.com; Ctra Circunvalación 2; r midweek/weekend €80/100; P❄️🛜🏊) A pleasant alternative to staying in the centre of Toledo is to be located out here, on the road across the Tajo, where you can enjoy sublime views of the city without the lack of space and parking. This friendly rural hotel is just a few minutes from the Old Town and has three levels of rooms offering great vistas from their balconies. There's also a beautiful bar annexe. To get here, turn left after crossing the bridge to the northwest of the old centre.

Albergue San Servando
HOSTEL €

(☑925 22 45 58; www.reaj.com; Subida del Castillo; dm under/over 30yr €14.05/16.90; ❄️@🛜) Want to be king or queen of the castle? Then head to this well-appointed official hostel with modern installations inside a 14th-century fort. Dorms have either two single beds or two double bunks, and there's a cafeteria

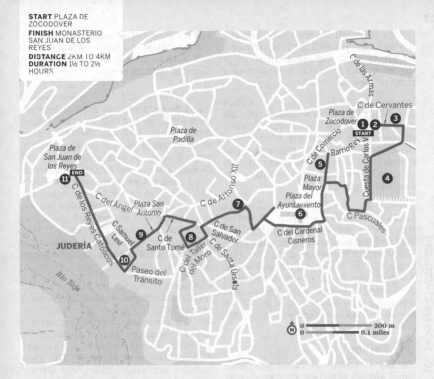

Walking Tour
A Stroll through History

❭ Stock up on Band-Aids and explore Toledo on foot in a walk with plenty of opportunities for detours and diversions.

Start off in central ❶ **Plaza de Zocodover**, for centuries the city's marketplace and scene for bullfights and Inquisition-led burnings at the stake, then pass through the ❷ **Arco de la Sangre** on the eastern side of the square to admire the facade of the ❸ **Museo de Santa Cruz**. Up the hill to the south is Toledo's signature ❹ **Alcázar**, beyond which there are some fine views over the Río Tajo. Follow the spires down the hill to the west, passing the remnants of a mosque, ❺ **Mezquita de las Tornerías**, before reaching the ❻ **Catedral**, the spiritual home of Catholic Spain. Twist your way northwest to the ❼ **Centro Cultural San Marcos**, housed in the 17th-century San Marcos church where the original domed roof, complete with ceiling frescoes, creates an evocative gallery space for temporary art exhibitions. Southwest of here, the 14th-century ❽ **Taller del Moro** is interesting for its classic Mudéjar architecture.

Down the hill you enter the heart of Toledo's old Jewish quarter. Admire the swords in the shops along ❾ **Calle de San Juan de Dios** and head past the ❿ **Sinagoga del Tránsito** to admire further clifftop views over the river. The synagogue takes on a special poignancy if you continue along Calle de los Reyes Católicos to the splendid ⓫ **Monasterio San Juan de los Reyes**. Spain's Catholic rulers hoped this church would represent the ultimate triumph of their religion over others. This is a fine spot to end your walk, but you could drop down from here to the riverside pathway that will take you on a half-circuit of the Old Town back to near your starting point.

serving meals. HI members only: you can buy the card here for €5, or €12 if you're over 30. To get here, cross the bridge northeast of the centre, keep going and the hostel is up a street on the right.

Hostal Alfonso XII
HOSTAL €

(☏925 25 25 09; www.hostal-alfonso12.com; Calle de Alfonso XII; r €65; ❄️🛜) In a great location, this occupies an 18th-century Toledo house, meaning twisty passages and stairs, and compact rooms in curious places. It's got plenty of charm and the non-Saturday room rate (€45) is a bargain.

Cerro de Bú
HOSTEL €

(☏925 25 85 41; www.cerrodebu.es; Travesía del Potro 1; dm €14; ❄️🛜) It's a little tough to find, but this small, cosy hostel set in a quiet residential area at the bottom of the town (but within the city walls) is a tranquil haven. Ten dorm beds upstairs, spotless bathroom downstairs, a lounge, small kitchen and a peaceful patio are the sum of it, but the helpful personal welcome is what makes the place special.

Eating

The city is heaving with restaurants, many aimed squarely at tourists. For a good range of choices, head for Calle Alfonso X el Sabio and the surrounding pedestrian streets, including Calle de los Alfileritos and Calle de la Sillería. Restaurants close very early (for Spain) at night midweek.

TOP CHOICE Alfileritos 24
MODERN SPANISH €€

(www.alfileritos24.com; Calle de los Alfileritos 24; mains €15-21, bar food €6-11; ⊙bar food 9.30am-midnight, to 1am Fri & Sat) The 14th-century surroundings of columns, beams and barrel-vault ceilings are snazzily coupled with modern artwork and bright dining rooms in an atrium space spread over four floors. The menu demonstrates an innovative flourish in the kitchen, with dishes like red-tuna tartare with seaweed and guacamole, and loins of venison with baked-in-the-bag Reineta apple. The ground-floor bar offers good-value tapas and cheaper fare designed for sharing.

La Abadía
TAPAS €

(www.abadiatoledo.com; Plaza de San Nicolás 3; raciones €4-15) In a former 16th-century palace, this atmospheric bar and restaurant is ideal for romancing couples. Arches, niches and subtle lighting are spread over a warren of brick-and-stone-clad rooms. The menu includes lightweight dishes and tapas – perfect for small (distracted) appetites.

LOCAL KNOWLEDGE

ALEJANDRA ABULAFIA, DIRECTOR OF DESTINO SEFARAD

What's the importance of Toledo in Sephardic (Spanish Jewish) history? It's a key place and the major sight is the Sinagoga del Tránsito. It's a real jewel, built by Samuel Levi, who was treasurer to King Pedro I. At that time building synagogues was prohibited, but as Pedro trusted Samuel he was given permission. It's so impressive, both for its decoration and dimensions. There's also Sinagoga Santa María La Blanca and the Puerta del Cambrón, the entrance gate to the Jewish quarter.

What other places would you recommend in Spain? Segovia has a marvellously reconstructed *judería* (Jewish quarter), with lovely facades. There you'll find the Centro Didáctico, a must-visit. Girona in Catalunya also has a spectacular *judería*. Córdoba is another city you should visit: the synagogue there is the only one that was never converted to a church, and nearby Casa Sefarad is lovely.

What's the Jewish population now compared with before the expulsion of 1492? The official figure now is 40,000, though I'm not sure if we're that many. Every historian has a different figure for the past so I wouldn't like to guess. They say that at least 200,000 were expelled and many more converted.

Is there much intolerance or racism against Jews in Spain today? No. Many people are against Israel, and some think Jews and Israelis are one and the same. But attitudes in general have changed: people are very interested in our Sephardic history these days.

Destino Sefarad (www.destinosefarad.es) is a cultural organisation running tours and disseminating knowledge of Spain's Jewish history.

Taberna El Embrujo
TAPAS €€

(Calle Santa Leocadia 6; raciones €8-22) Near the top of the escalator up to the Old Town, this friendly bar has an appealing stone-clad dining area and an outdoor terrace across the street. It does a great line in high-quality deli-style tapas, with tasty tomato salads, delicious foie gras and toothsome seafood options, all served with a smile.

Hostal del Cardenal
SPANISH €€€

(925 22 49 00; www.hostaldelcardenal.com; Paseo de Recaredo 24; mains €16-27) This hotel-restaurant enjoys one of Toledo's most magical locations for eating alfresco; it's tucked into a private garden entered via its own gate in the city walls. The food is classic Spanish, with roast meats – suckling pig and lamb are the best dishes on show here – to the fore. It's a bit touristy, but the location is unforgettable on a warm summer's night.

Madre Tierra
VEGETARIAN €€

(925 21 34 24; www.restaurantemadretierra.com; Bajanda de la Tripería 2; mains €9-13; ⏰lunch & dinner Wed-Sun, lunch Mon; 🖉) A cool cavernous space, with exposed brick arches, a soft ochre colour scheme and muted light, creates a romantic atmosphere for enjoying Indian-, Asian- and Mediterranean-inspired vegetarian meals, including sushi, moussaka, pastas, *pakoras* (vegetables in a spicy batter) and salads. Reservations recommended.

Casa Aurelio
SPANISH €€€

(925 22 77 16; www.casa-aurelio.com; Plaza del Ayuntamiento 4; mains €21-24; ⏰lunch & dinner Tue-Sat, lunch Mon) The three restaurants under this name are among the best of Toledo's traditional eateries (the other locations are Calle de la Sinagoga 1 and 6). Game, fresh produce and time-honoured dishes are prepared with panache.

Taberna El Botero
SPANISH €€

(925 22 90 88; www.tabernaelbotero.com; Calle de la Ciudad 5; mains €18-24) Handy for the cathedral, this atmospheric bar and restaurant offers up elaborately presented dishes based on traditional Spanish ingredients like octopus, hake and game. It also does a nice line in expertly prepared cocktails and mixed drinks.

Asador Palencia de Lara
GRILL €€

(925 25 67 46; www.asadorpalenciadelara.es; Calle Nuncio Viejo 6; mains €17-20) This smart place with a modern dining room set in an historic patio specialises in grilled meats

MIDWEEK DISCOUNTS

Bear in mind that the hotel rates in Toledo, Cuenca and many other tourist-driven towns and villages in the province vary drastically during the week, being popular weekend destinations for city folk from Madrid. Prices can drop by as much as 30% midweek.

and it does them pretty well. Eschew the overpriced starters and start your meal in the bar area, which turns out a delicious series of €2 tapas, then head through for the meaty mains. The wine list looks amazingly cheap, but be aware that €8 is added to each bottle – don't ask us why.

Palacios
SPANISH €

(www.hostalpalaciostolodo.com; Calle Alfonso X el Sabio 3; set menus €8.50-15.90, raciones €5-10; ⏰noon-11pm) An unpretentious place, where stained glass, beams and efficient old-fashioned service combine with traditional no-nonsense cuisine. Hungry? Try a gut-busting bowl of traditional *judías con perdiz* (white beans with partridge) for starters. It's very popular so be prepared to wait a while for a table.

Santa Fe
SPANISH €

(Calle de Santa Fe 6; menus €8) You can eat better here, and for half the price, than in the restaurants on nearby Plaza de Zocodover. It also does good-value *bocadillos* (filled rolls) for lighter meals.

Drinking & Entertainment

Aside from the following listings, the outdoor tables of the bars in the leafy courtyard just off Plaza de Magdalena are a delight in summer, and Calle Cristo de la Luz has several options. For student-oriented nightlife, shimmy down to the streets around Plaza de San Nicolás.

Enebro
BAR

(www.barenebro.com; Plaza San Justo 9; ⏰8am-midnight Mon-Fri, noon-1am Sat & Sun) Ease into your evening out with a drink under the trees in this pretty square, enjoying generous free tapas and Hendrix (or similar) on the sound system.

Círculo de Arte
LIVE MUSIC

(www.circuloartetoledo.org; Plaza de San Vicente 2) There are several venues where you can enjoy foot-tapping live sounds, including this classy place in a converted chapel, with its regular concerts (many free) and theatre productions. Even if there's nothing on, it's still an atmospheric place for a drink and opens late.

Garcilaso   BAR
(www.garcilasocafe.com; Calle Rojas 5; ⊙7pm-late Mon-Thu, 4pm-6am Fri & Sat, 4pm-late Sun) This attractive multilevel place has a bit of everything, from trashy late-night dancing on weekends to comedy nights and quiet afternoons with a coffee or a cocktail. The chill-out zone upstairs gives you respite from the dance floor.

Pícaro   BAR, CAFE
(☑925 22 13 01; www.picarotoledo.com; Calle de las Cadenas 6; ⊙4pm-2.30am Sun-Wed, to 6am Thu-Sat) Pícaro is a popular bar-cafe serving an eclectic range of *copas* (mixed drinks) and there's live music most Friday nights. It really gets going after 2.30am on weekends.

Shopping

For centuries Toledo was renowned for the excellence of its swords and you'll see them for sale everywhere (although be wary of taking them in your hand luggage through customs!). Another big seller is anything decorated with *damasquinado* (damascene), a fine inlay of gold or silver in the Arab artistic tradition. A reliable outlet is Pedro Maldonado (☑925 21 38 16; Calle San Juan de Dios 10), one of several shops on this street.

❶ Information

There are lots of *locutorios* (private call centres) dealing in cheap calls and internet access around the city centre.

ALMOND NUTS

Not a marzipan fan? Think again. You probably won't have tasted it so good anywhere else. Toledo is famed for this wonderful almond-based confectionery, which every shop seems to sell. The Santo Tomé marzipan brand is highly regarded and there are several outlets in town, including one on Plaza de Zocodover. Even the local nuns get in on the marzipan act; most of the convents sell the sweets.

Main tourist office (☑925 25 40 30; www.toledo-turismo.com; Plaza del Ayuntamiento; ⊙10am-6pm)
Provincial tourist office (www.diputoledo.es; Subida de la Granja; ⊙10am-5pm Mon-Sat, to 3pm Sun)

❶ Getting There & Away

For most major destinations, you'll need to backtrack to Madrid.

From Toledo's **bus station** (Avenida de Castilla La Mancha), buses depart for Madrid roughly every half-hour (from €5.25, one hour), some direct, some via villages. There are also services to Albacete (€15, 2¾ hours) and Cuenca (€12.80, 2¼ hours).

From the pretty **train station** (☑902 24 02 02; Paseo de la Rosa) high-speed AVE services run every hour or so to Madrid (€10.60, 30 minutes).

❶ Getting Around

Bus Buses (€1.40) run between Plaza de Zocodover and the bus station (bus 5) and train station (buses 61 and 62). Bus 12 does a circuit within the Old Town.

Car Driving in the Old Town is a nightmare. There are several underground car parks throughout the area. Zones blocked off by bollards can be accessed if you have a hotel reservation. At the base of the Old Town are several large free car parks.

Around Toledo

CASTLES

The area around Toledo is rich with castles in varying states of upkeep. Most are only accessible by car.

Situated some 20km southeast of Toledo along the CM42 is the dramatic ruined Arab castle of Almonacid de Toledo. A few kilometres further down the road is a smaller castle in the village of Mascaraque. Continue on to Mora, where the 12th-century Castillo Peñas Negras, 3km from town, is on the site of a prehistoric necropolis; follow the sandy track to reach the castle for stunning big-sky views of the surrounding plains. Next, head for the pretty, small town of Orgaz, which has a handsome, well-preserved 15th-century castle (admission €3; ⊙10am-1pm Sat & Sun). Visits run on the hour on weekends; you'll need to buy tickets in advance at the tourist office (Calle Prado de Lucas; ⊙9am-2pm & 4-6pm Tue-Fri, 10am-1.30pm Sat & Sun) opposite.

Around 30km southwest of Toledo, the hulking 12th-century Templar ruin of Cas-

EL GRECO IN TOLEDO

Born in Crete in 1541, Domenikos Theotokopoulos, more succinctly known as 'El Greco' (The Greek), laid his wildly individual style over a background as an icon painter and colour training from the likes of Titian and Tintoretto to produce works that hold a lofty position in the pantheon of European art.

After being schooled as a Renaissance artist in Venice and Rome, El Greco came to Spain in 1577 and settled in Toledo, where there were several patrons to support him. The painter did not suffer from a lack of modesty: 'As surely as the rate of payment is inferior to the value of my sublime work, so will my name go down to posterity as one of the greatest geniuses of Spanish painting', he pronounced.

Controversial, arrogant and extravagant, El Greco liked the high life; as Toledo's fortunes declined, however, so did the artist's personal finances. Although his final paintings are among his best, he often found himself unable to pay the rent. At the time of his death in 1614, he wasn't rated highly, and it was only in the late 19th century that people began to appreciate his work again. His striking use of colour and the almost abstract nature of some of his figures make his Spanish paintings instantly recognisable.

Iglesia de Santo Tomé (www.santotome.org; Plaza del Conde; admission €2.50; ⊙10am-6pm, to 7pm summer) contains El Greco's masterpiece *El Entierro del Conde de Orgaz* (The Burial of the Count of Orgaz). When the count was buried in 1322, St Augustine and St Stephen supposedly descended from heaven to attend the funeral. El Greco's work depicts the event, complete with miracle guests including himself, his son and Cervantes. The nearby Museo del Greco has a solid collection of works by El Greco and his followers.

One of the oldest convents in Toledo, the 11th-century **Convento de Santo Domingo El Antiguo** (☎925 22 29 30; Plaza de Santo Domingo el Antiguo; admission €2; ⊙11am-1.30pm & 4-7pm Mon-Sat, 4-7pm Sun) includes some of El Greco's early commissions, other copies and signed contracts of the artist. Visible through a hole in the floor is the crypt and wooden coffin of the painter himself.

Other spots in Toledo where you can contemplate El Greco's works include the Museo de Santa Cruz and the cathedral's *sacristía* (sacristy).

tillo de Montalbán stands majestically over the Río Torcón valley. It's open only sporadically, but there's little to stop you wandering around at any time.

THE WEST

Heavily wooded in parts and with a compelling combination of sweeping plains and dramatic mountains, the west of this region has plenty of surprises up its sleeve.

Talavera de la Reina

POP 88,670

Talavera de la Reina, long famous for its ceramics, has a laid-back appeal. The finest example of its many tiled buildings is the gold-and-blue facade of the **Teatro Victoria**, just off Plaza del Padre Juan de Mariana.

Within the old city walls is **Museo Ruiz de Luna** (Plaza de San Agustín; admission €0.60; ⊙10am-2pm & 4-6.30pm Tue-Sat, 10am-2pm Sun), housing local ceramics dating from the 16th to 20th centuries in a handsome brick monastery. To buy contemporary ceramics, check out the factories and shops along the road leading west to the A5 motorway.

The **tourist office** (☎925 82 63 22; www.turismo.talavera.org; Calle Palenque 2; ⊙9.30am-2pm & 5-7pm Mon-Fri, 10am-2pm Sat & Sun) doubles as a gallery displaying (you guessed it) ceramics.

The bus station is in the town centre. Regular buses between Madrid and Badajoz stop in Talavera de la Reina, and there are services to Toledo (from €5.30, 1½ hours) roughly hourly.

Around Talavera de la Reina

OROPESA

The delightful village of Oropesa, 34km west of Talavera, makes an appealing overnight

EATING & DRINKING IN CASTILLA-LA MANCHA

The region's dry and occasionally arid landscapes belie the fact that Castilla-La Mancha is one of Spain's important food-producing areas; you'll encounter products and dishes in shops and restaurants here that are part of a distinctively local gastronomy.

Things to look out for on menus come from a rural hand-to-mouth tradition of simple dishes made with basic ingredients. They include the renowned *pisto manchego*, a ratatouille-like medley of fried vegetables; *gachas*, a delicious porridge made from grass peas given a kick with peppers, garlic and cured pork belly; *asadillo*, a combination of fried tomatoes and peppers with boiled eggs; *morteruelo*, a tasty paste made from stewed pork liver and other meats; and *migas*, breadcrumbs fried in garlic with chorizo and pork fat. Castilla-La Mancha has always been a zone for small game, so *perdiz* (partridge) and *conejo* (rabbit) dishes are ubiquitous.

More than two dozen local foods and wines have been given DO (Denominación de Origen) status, offering both protection and recognition of high-quality traditional products. *Queso manchego* (Manchego cheese) is the best known of these. Peer into any cheese counter in the country and you'll find great wheels of this cheese in varying sizes and displaying a baffling range of labels and prices. For many visitors, their Manchego initiation will be the neat little tapas triangles often served free with a drink. These are usually *semicurado* (semi-cured) rather than the crumbly stronger (and more expensive) *curado* (cured); the former is aged for approximately three to four months, the latter six to eight months. To receive the Manchego denomination, the milk must come from a local Manchegan breed of sheep that has evolved over hundreds of years.

Many of the DO products are wines, ranging from the huge centre of Valdepeñas, which produces eight times more wine than La Rioja, and the medium-sized Jumilla, to the excellent single-vineyard denomination of Finca Élez in Albacete province. Other distinctive DO foods include olive oils, rice, brown garlic, the famous green aubergines (eggplants) of Almagro, the marzipan of Toledo and the seductive honey from La Alcarria.

stop. Atop the town is the 14th-century **castle** (adult/child €3/1.50; ⏲10am-2pm & 4-6pm Tue-Sat, 11am-2pm Sun; 👪) looking north across the plains to the mighty Sierra de Gredos.

Across from here, sharing a courtyard, is a 14th-century palace that houses Spain's second-oldest **parador** (☎925 43 00 00; www.parador.es; s/d €114/142; P❄📶), which has managed to retain a heady historical feel without 'over-heritaging'. The rooms are large and luxurious, with heavy brocade curtains and antiques. Read Somerset Maugham's rave review of the place in the lobby and ask to see San Pedro de Alcántara's sleeping quarters, hidden in the bowels of this former palace.

There's also **La Hostería** (☎925 43 08 75; www.lahosteriadeoropesa.com; Plaza del Palacio 5; s/d incl breakfast €50/65; P❄), just below the castle, which has pretty, individually decorated rooms with beamed ceilings and a popular restaurant (mains €8 to €14) with tables spilling out into a flower-festooned courtyard.

From Talavera de la Reina, buses travel here three or four times daily.

THE SOUTH

This is the terrain that typifies La Mancha for many people: flat plains stretching to the horizon, punctuated by the occasional farmhouse or emblematic windmill. The southeast, however, is surprisingly verdant and lush with rivers, natural parks and some of the prettiest villages in the province.

Ciudad Real

POP 74,800

Despite being the one-time royal counterpart of Toledo, these days Ciudad Real is an unspectacular Spanish working town. The centre has a certain charm, however, with its pedestrianised shopping streets and distinctive Plaza Mayor, complete with carillon clock (topped by Cupid), flamboyant neo-Gothic town-hall facade and modern tiered fountain.

Sights

FREE **Museo del Quijote** MUSEUM

(Ronda de Alarcos 1; ⏲10am-2pm & 6-9pm Mon-Sat, 10am-2pm Sun) For Don Quijote fans, the

Museo del Quijote has audiovisual displays, plus a Cervantes library stocked with hundreds of Don Quijote books, including some in Esperanto and Braille, and others dating back to 1724. It helps if you speak Spanish. Entry is by guided tour every half-hour. At the time of research it was closed for renovations.

🛏 Sleeping & Eating

TOP CHOICE **Palacio de la Serna**　　HOTEL €€
(📞926 84 22 08; www.hotelpalaciodelaserna.com; Calle Cervantes 18; r €108-173; 🅿🌡🛰🐕) Just 20 minutes' drive south of Ciudad Real (and an equivalent distance from Almagro), this superb hotel feels a world away. Located in the sleepy village of Ballesteros de Calatrava, it's a perfect haven for relaxation and a useful base for exploration of the province. Set around a courtyard, it combines rural comfort with most appealing design; the owner's evocative modern sculptures feature heavily. Rooms are commodious and a little avant-garde, with open showers and numerous thoughtful touches. There's a good on-site restaurant.

Hostal Plaza　　HOSTAL €
(📞926 25 43 35; Plaza de Agustín Salido 2; s/d €50/65; 🌡🛰) Situated on a pretty quiet square, this comfortable place has smart rooms and a bustling breakfast bar and cafeteria. It's much cheaper outside peak season.

La Vinoteca　　SPANISH €€
(Calle Hernán Pérez de Pulgar 3; lunch menus €15, mains €12-17) Willing service and high-quality dishes with a daily changing menu make this one of Ciudad Real's best lunching options. On weekends the set menu rises to €18, but you might get *arroz con bogavante* (rice with lobster) and roast lamb.

ℹ Information

Tourist office (📞926 21 64 86; www.ciudad realturismo.com; Plaza Mayor 1; ⊙10am-2pm & 5-7pm Tue-Sat, 10am-2pm Sun) Can advise on city sights, hotels and restaurants.

ℹ Getting There & Away

The **bus station** (Carretera Calzada) is southwest of the town centre. Services include up to three daily buses to Albacete (€15, 2¾ hours) and Toledo (€9, two hours), and four per day head off to Madrid (€12, 2½ hours).

The **train station** (Avenida Europa) lies east of the town centre. Most trains linking Madrid with Andalucía stop at Ciudad Real. There are regular departures to several cities and towns, including more than hourly services to Madrid (€22.50, one hour) – the 'AVANT' services offer the best price/duration ratio.

ℹ Getting Around

Local bus 5 swings past both the train and bus stations bound for the town centre; catch it from Plaza del Pilar when you're leaving town.

Ciudad Real Province

ALMAGRO
POP 9080

The jewel in Almagro's crown is the extraordinary 16th-century Plaza Mayor, with its wavy tiled roofs, stumpy columns and faded bottle-green porticoes. The town is a delight to wander around.

◉ Sights

Corral de Comedias　　NOTABLE BUILDING
(www.corraldecomedias.com; Plaza Mayor 18; adult/child incl audioguide in English €3/free; ⊙10-11.30am & 4-7pm Mon-Fri, 10am-1pm & 4-6pm Sat & Sun, afternoon opening & closing 1hr later Apr-Oct) Opening onto the plaza is the oldest theatre in Spain: the 17th-century Corral de Comedias, an evocative tribute to the golden age of Spanish theatre, with rows of wooden balconies facing the original stage, complete with dressing rooms. At various intervals visits become 'theatrised' with costumed actors replacing the audioguide: this costs €1 more. It's still used for performances on weekends from spring to autumn; buy tickets via the website.

Museo Nacional de Teatro　　MUSEUM
(http://museoteatro.mcu.es; Calle de Gran Maestre 2; adult/child €3/free, free Sat afternoon & Sun; ⊙10am-2pm & 4-7pm Tue-Fri, 11am-2pm & 4-6pm Sat, 11am-2pm Sun) Just off the main square, this museum has exhibits on Spanish theatre from the golden age of the 17th century displayed in rooms surrounding a magnificent 13th-century courtyard.

★☆ Festivals & Events

Festival Internacional de Teatro Clásico　　THEATRE
(www.festivaldealmagro.com) In July the Corral de Comedias holds a month-long international theatre festival, attracting world-class theatre companies performing, primarily, classical plays.

CASTILLA-LA MANCHA CIUDAD REAL PROVINCE

1. Cuenca (p224)

Casas colgadas (hanging houses) cling like swallows' nests above deep gorges.

2. Consuegra (p221)

Molinos de viento (windmills) flank Consuegra's 12th-century Knights of Malta castle.

3. Corpus Christi, Toledo (p209)

One of the finest Corpus Christi celebrations in Spain, with several days of festivities.

4. Alcalá del Júcar (p223)

A landmark 12th-century castle towers over houses that spill down the steep bank of Júcar gorge.

BRUCE BI / GETTY IMAGES ©

🛏 Sleeping

TOP CHOICE La Casa del Rector HOTEL €€
(☎926 26 12 59; www.lacasadelrector.com; Calle Pedro Oviedo 8; s/d €93/114; ❄@🐕🏊) This extraordinary hotel has a wide variety of rooms ranging from sumptuous antique-filled classics to those reflecting cutting-edge modern design, complete with vast private hot tubs and dramatic artwork. Facilities include a classy spa.

Retiro del Maestre HOTEL €€
(☎926 26 11 85; www.retirodelmaestre.com; Calle San Bartolomé 5; s/d incl breakfast €95/119; 🅿❄🐕) Enjoy five-star treatment and style without the hurly-burly of a big hotel. The rooms are spacious and washed in warm yellow and blue; go for those on the upper floor with private balconies. You can bag cheap deals online here.

Hostal San Bartolomé HOSTAL €
(☎926 26 10 73; www.hostalsanbartolome.com; Calle San Bartolomé 12; s/d €54/64; ❄🐕) Friendly and central, this *hostal* has rather bare rooms surrounding a courtyard. It's a decent summer budget option, but the heating struggles to cope in winter. It's a lot cheaper outside summer.

🍴 Eating

TOP CHOICE El Corregidor SPANISH €€€
(☎658 819367; www.elcorregidor.com; Calle de Jerónimo Ceballos 2; mains €18-26, menus €25-40; ⏰Tue-Sun) The town's best restaurant has several lively bars flanking a leafy courtyard and a hotchpotch decor that somehow works. The upstairs restaurant features high-quality Manchegan cooking; check out the wall of culinary awards. Reservations recommended.

Bar El Gordo TAPAS €
(Plaza Mayor 12; raciones €6-11) The best and liveliest tapas option on the square, this has a good mix of visitors and locals and buzzes with good cheer on weekend evenings. El Gordo means 'The Fat Man', and the cheerful boss Domingo lives up to his name.

ℹ Information

Tourist office (☎926 86 07 17; www.ciudad-almagro.com; Plaza Mayor 1; ⏰10am-2pm & 5-8pm Tue-Fri, to 7pm Sat, 10am-2pm Sun) Afternoon opening and closing is one hour earlier from October to March.

ℹ Getting There & Away

Two trains go daily to Madrid (€16 to €22, 2½ hours); for destinations to the south, change in Ciudad Real (€3.05, 15 minutes). Buses run to Ciudad Real (€2.60, 30 minutes, up to five daily Monday to Saturday).

CASTILLO DE CALATRAVA

This magnificent castle-monastery (Calatrava La Nueva; ⏰11am-2pm & 5.30-8.30pm Tue-Fri, 10am-2pm & 5.30-8.30pm Sat, 10am-2pm & 5-9pm Sun Apr-Sep, 11am-2pm & 4-6pm Tue-Fri, 10am-2pm & 4-6pm Sat, 10am-6pm Sun Oct-Mar) looms high in the sky some 6km south of the town of Calzada de Calatrava and 30km south of Almagro. A steep stony road takes you to the top, where breathtaking views, as well as the imposingly preserved fortress, are your reward. The complex was once a base of the medieval order of knights who controlled this frontier area during the Reconquista.

PARQUE NACIONAL TABLAS DE DAIMIEL

Forty kilometres northeast of Ciudad Real, this small wetland national park is great for birdwatching. From the visitor centre (☎926 69 31 18; www.mma.es/parques; ⏰9am-6pm Oct-Mar, to 9pm Apr-Sep), which has an exhibition on the fragile local ecosystem, three trails lead out along the lakeshore and over boardwalks. From these, and the various observation hides – bring binoculars – you can see an astonishing variety of wildlife, including ducks, geese, kingfishers, flamingos, herons and other waders, tortoises and otters. Early morning and late afternoon are the best times. The park is 10km from the town of Daimiel, which is linked by regular buses to Ciudad Real.

PARQUE NATURAL DE LAS LAGUNAS DE RUIDERA

This ribbon of 14 small lakes is surrounded by lush parkland, camping grounds, picnic areas, and discreetly situated restaurants and hotels. Turn off along the lakeshore in the town of Ruidera; along this road there are several places hiring pedalos, canoes and bikes, or offering horse riding to explore the area.

A great place to stay is Hotel Albamanjón (☎926 69 90 48; www.albamanjon.net; Laguna de San Pedro 16; d incl breakfast €112-186; ❄🐕). Running up the hill behind the main building, these super suites are all separate from each other and have a private terrace with lake views, wood fires for winter, and most have a jacuzzi. The windmill suite has a vista of the turquoise lake that's worth pushing the boat out for. The restaurant has

IN SEARCH OF DON QUIJOTE

Part of the charm of a visit to Castilla-La Mancha is the chance to track down the real-life locations in which Miguel de Cervantes placed his picaresque hero. These days it requires less puzzling over maps as the 250km Route of Don Quijote covers the area, with signposts that direct you along paths, cattle ways and historic routes in the region.

Of all the places and sights you can ponder along the way, the *molinos de viento* (windmills) are the most obvious, for it was these 'monstrous giants' that so haunted El Quijote and with which he tried to battle. Although Consuegra's are the most attractive, those that are specifically mentioned in Cervantes' novel are the windmills of Campo de Criptana and Mota del Cuervo. Other highlights on the trail include the castle of Belmonte and El Toboso, where the knight discovered the lovely Dulcinea.

great views and is decorated exuberantly with tiles and curios. Leafy camping ground Camping Los Batanes (926 69 90 20; www. losbatanes.com; sites incl 2 people, tent and car €23-31; bungalows €75-120; P ≋ ⚑) is on Laguna Redondilla. During summer there's an entertainment program for children.

VILLANUEVA DE LOS INFANTES
POP 5780

Villanueva de los Infantes is an attractive and busy provincial town. A highlight is its Plaza Mayor, with ochre-coloured buildings, wood-and-stone balconies, and lively bars and restaurants. On the square stands the 15th-century Iglesia de San Andrés, where the 16th-century poet Francisco de Quevedo is buried.

Exceptionally welcoming and intelligent hosts combined with a prime location just off the main square make La Morada de Juan de Vargas (926 36 17 09; www.lamora dadevargas.com; Calle Cervantes 3; d €76-85; ✳ 🔊) the best of the town's several appealing rural hotel options.

Buses run to Ciudad Real three times daily Monday to Friday and once on Saturday (€7.45, two hours).

Southeast to Albacete

CONSUEGRA

This is *the* place for the novice windmill spotter, where you can get that classic shot of nine *molinos de viento* (windmills) flanking Consuegra's 12th-century castle (adult/child €4/free; ⊙10.10am-5.45pm Mon-Fri, 10.40am-1.45pm & 3.40-5.45pm Sat & Sun; ⚑). Consuegra once belonged to the Knights of Malta; a few rooms in the castle have been re-created to give a good indication of how the knights would have lived. Information boards include English and French.

There's a tourist office (925 47 57 31; www.consuegra.es; ⊙9am-2pm & 4.30-7pm Mon-Fri, from 10.30am Sat & Sun) in the Bolero mill, which is the first you come to as the road winds up from the town. You can climb the steps here and see the original machinery.

There are a few accommodation options in town, among them charming La Vida de Antes (925 48 06 09; www.lavidadeantes.com; Calle Colón 2; s/d incl breakfast €50/70; P ✳ @ 🔊 ≋ ⚑) whose old tiled floors, antique furnishings and pretty patio really do evoke a bygone era. The duplex rooms are particularly cosy and there's interesting art exhibited throughout the building.

There are regular weekday buses (three on weekends) running between Consuegra and Toledo (€6, one hour) and up to seven buses daily to Madrid (€8.20, two hours).

CAMPO DE CRIPTANA & AROUND

It's all about the top of the town here: 10 spectacular windmills straddle the summit and their proximity to the surrounding houses makes an interesting contrast with Consuegra. One of the windmills has a ticket office (admission €0.60 per mill; ⊙10am-2pm & 5-7pm Tue-Sat, 11am-2pm Sun) selling admission to three other mills that hold a variety of displays, including one on Sara Montiel, femme fatale of the Spanish silver screen in the 1950s and '60s, who was born in this town.

If you want to stay overnight, lovely Hospedería Casa de la Torrecilla (926 58 91 30; www.casadelatorrecilla.com; Calle Cardenal Monescillo 17; s/d €44/76; ✳ @ 🔊) has a vividly patterned and tiled interior patio. Housed in an early-20th-century nobleman's house, the rooms have parquet floors and are atmospheric. It's cheaper midweek. The best place to eat is atmospheric Cueva La Martina (www.cuevalamartina.com; Rocinante 13; mains

€16-20), opposite the windmills. The cave-like dining area is dug into the rock, and there's a breezy upstairs terrace with views over town.

The **tourist office** (☑926 56 22 31; www.campodecriptana.info; ☉10am-2pm & 5-7pm Tue-Sat, 10am-2pm Sun) is located in a low-rise building opposite the Inca Garcilaso windmill. There's an interesting handcrafts exhibition (€0.50) in the basement.

Campo de Criptana and Ciudad Real are linked by two buses Monday to Friday and one on Saturday (€7.73, 1¼ hours).

There are seven more pretty windmills gracing the horizon overlooking **Mota del Cuervo**, 28km northeast of Campo de Criptana, at the junction of the N301.

EL TOBOSO

This is a town that has really cashed in on its Don Quijote heritage; the most entertaining of the numerous Cervantes-influenced locations is the 16th-century **Casa-Museo de Dulcinea** (Calle Don Quijote 1; admission €0.60; ☉10am-2pm & 4.30-7.30pm Tue-Sat, 10am-2pm Sun). This was apparently the home of Doña Ana, the *señorita* who inspired Cervantes' Dulcinea, the platonic love of Quijote.

There's a **tourist office** (☑925 56 82 26; www.turismocastillalamancha.com; Plaza Mayor; ☉10am-2pm & 4-6pm Tue-Sat, 10am-2pm Sun) on the main square. A bus runs Monday to Saturday to/from Toledo (€8.72, 2½ hours); there are also direct buses from Madrid.

BELMONTE

About 17km northeast of Mota del Cuervo, Belmonte has one of the better-preserved 15th-century Castilian **castles** (www.castillodebelmonte.com; adult/child €8/2; ☉10am-2pm & 4.30-8.30pm Tue-Sat Jun-Sep, afternoon hours 3.30-6.30pm Oct–mid-Feb, 4-7pm mid-Feb–May). This is how castles *should* look, with turrets, largely intact walls and a commanding position over the village. It's been recently done up inside, and has a slick display with multilingual audio commentary. Also well worth a visit is **Iglesia Colegial de San Bartolomé** (Colegiata; www.colegiatadebelmonte .blogspot.com; ☉11am-2pm & 4.30-7.30pm Tue-Sat, 11am-2pm Sun), a magnificent golden-sandstone church with an impressive altarpiece.

Palacio Buenavista Hospedería (☑967 18 75 80; www.palaciobuenavista.es; Calle José Antonio González 2; s/d/ste incl breakfast €50/80/120; P☀☎) is a classy boutique hotel set in a 17th-century palace next to the Colegiata. Rooms are stylish and set around a sumptuous central patio with a skylight; several have views of the castle. There's an excellent restaurant (mains €8 to €15).

There are buses to Belmonte from Cuenca (€5.35, 1¼ hours), with more connections changing in nearby Alcázar de San Juan.

Albacete

POP 171,390

Famous in Spain for two things – its knives, and the saying *Albacete – caga y vete* (defecate and leave), this provincial capital is a transport hub and redeems its lack of attractions with a lively free tapas scene.

In the centre of town, the **Pasaje Lodares** is a lovely shopping arcade built in 1925 in Modernista style: it's well worth a look. The other standout attraction is the **Museo Arquéologico** (Parque Abelardo Sánchez; admission €1.20; ☉10am-2pm & 4.30-7pm Mon-Sat, 10am-2pm Sun), with well-documented archaeological exhibits, including a famous collection of Roman ivory and amber articulated dolls. Opposite the cathedral, behind an exuberant green neo-Gothic facade, the **Museo de la Cuchillería** (www.museo-mca.com; Plaza de la Catedral; adult/child €3/1; ☉10am-2pm & 5:30am-8pm Tue-Sat, 10am-3pm Sun) details the city's famous knife industry.

If you want to stay, **Hotel Altozano** (☑967 21 04 62; www.hotelaltozano.es; Plaza del Altozano 7; s/d €30/43; P☀☎) has an ace location on a pretty main square. It's great to see a place run by staff with real enthusiasm for what they do: the compact rooms are remarkably good value – the exterior ones have a little more space – and there's tight parking available for €7.50.

Albacete has good tapas bars and restaurants: head for the streets around Calle Nueva and Calle Tejaras. A couple of blocks from here, it's worth seeking out **Rubia y Tinto** (Calle Muelle 22; raciones €6-13; ☉Tue-Sun) for a choice of free tapas with every drink – try the brochettes – and a good-time atmosphere.

The **tourist office** (☑967 58 05 22; www.turismocastillalamancha.com; Calle del Tinte 2; ☉9.30am-7pm Mon-Thu, 10am-2pm & 4-8pm Fri, 10am-2pm Sat & Sun) is in the town centre.

The adjacent bus and train stations are at the northeastern end of town. There are buses at least daily to Ciudad Real (€15, 2¾ hours), Toledo (€15, 2¾ hours) and Cuenca

(€11.25, two hours), as well as Madrid (€17, three hours), Valencia (€13.20, 2½ hours) and provincial destinations. Trains to Madrid (€25 to €50, 1½ to three hours) leave roughly hourly.

Around Albacete
ALCALÁ DEL JÚCAR

Northeast of Albacete, the deep, tree-filled gorge of Río Júcar makes for a stunning detour. About halfway along the CM3201, the breathtaking town of Alcalá del Júcar comes into view as you descend via hairpin turns. Its landmark castle (admission €2, under 8yr free; ⊙11am-2pm & 4-7pm), dating mostly from the 15th century, towers over the houses that spill down the steep bank of the river gorge. At the foot of the town there's a medieval bridge with Roman origins and a leafy meeting-and-greeting plaza. It's a good destination for young kids, with a large traffic-free area, and safe paddling in a bend of the river.

There are several well-priced hotels, including Hostal Rambla (☑967 47 40 64; www.hostalrambla.es; Paseo Los Robles 2; s/d incl breakfast €45/55; 🅿🤶) by the 'Roman' bridge. Rooms are compact, but it's friendly and well located, and there's a pleasant restaurant with a large terrace, specialising in chargrilled meats (mains €10 to €16) served with green peppers and potatoes.

La Asomada (☑652 182440; Calle de la Asomada 107; mains €7-13; ⊙dinner Fri, lunch & dinner Sat & Sun), at the top of the village, should be sought out by eco folks. Located in a cave and former bodega, owner Pilar Escusa uses organic produce and prepares delicious seasonal dishes. Reservations essential.

The small tourist office (☑967 47 30 90; www.turismocastillalamancha.com; ⊙10am-2pm daily, plus 4-7pm Sat & Sun) by the bridge has information about *casas rurales* (rural homes), cave accommodation and activities, including river trips and local walking trails. Several companies offer a full range of land and water excursions. Avenjúcar (☑967 47 41 34; www.avenjucar.com; Calle San Roque, Tolosa) is an operator that comes reader recommended and also has a most welcoming rural *hostal* (doubles €60) with great river views, 6km from Alcalá in Tolosa.

There are one to two buses daily except Sunday between Albacete and Alcalá (€5.80, 1½ hours).

WORTH A TRIP

THE BIRTH OF THE WORLD

For all those who think Castilla-La Mancha is flat and boring, head out from Riópar around 8km to the spectacular Nacimiento del Río Mundo (Source of the River Mundo; ⊙10am-dusk), signposted off the Siles road. From the car park, it's a short walk through the forest of mainly coniferous trees to the bottom of the falls; above towers an awesomely high concave cliff face. It's a steep climb to the second viewpoint above, but worth the effort. Water emerges from the rocks just above the platform, almost close enough to touch, in a dramatic drop of some 24m (spraying you liberally en route). The falls are surrounded by dense forest stretching to a rocky horizon.

SIERRA DE ALCARAZ

Stretching across the southern strip of Albacete province, the cool, green peaks of the Sierra de Alcaraz offer a great escape from the dusty plains around Albacete.

The gateway to the region, sleepy hilltop Alcaraz, has a Renaissance Plaza Mayor and a lattice of narrow cobbled streets. Nearby, a handsome, mainly 16th-century building houses the Mirador Sierra de Alcaraz (☑967 38 00 17; www.alcarazmirador.com; Calle Granada 1; d €47-69; 🅿). Located around a central courtyard, its rooms have beamed ceilings, carved wooden bedheads and heavy period-style curtains and furnishings. Two daily buses (€5.50; one on Saturday, none on Sunday) head here from Albacete.

The most scenic countryside is to be found along the CM412, particularly between Puerto de las Crucetas (elevation 1300m) and Elche de la Sierra. The largest choice of accommodation is in and around unattractive Riópar.

The region's standout place to stay is high up in the hills above the road 11km west of Riópar, beyond the Nacimiento del Río Mundo turn-off. Las Salegas del Maguillo (☑660 249692; www.lassalegasdelmaguillo.com; Ctra Riópar-Siles Km11; d €90, 4/6 person apt €150/210; 🅿🤶) is a complex built in modern rustic style, all dark wood and dressed stone, that includes a small hotel featuring pretty rooms with fireplace and wickerwork fans, a restaurant and self-catering houses.

It's all very attractive, and it's great for walkers and kids, but the three big highlights are the charming little swimming pool, the genuine warmth of the staff and the unforgettable sunset views from the superb balconies of the hotel rooms.

THE NORTHEAST

This region has a rich hinterland of craggy mountains and lush green valleys studded by unspoilt, pretty villages. It is also home to some of the country's most enchanting towns and *pueblos* (villages).

Cuenca

POP 56,700

Cuenca is one of Spain's most memorable cities, its old centre a World Heritage stage-set of evocative medieval buildings. Most emblematic are the *casas colgadas* (hanging houses), which cling like swallows' nests above the deep gorges that surround the town.

◉ Sights & Activities

Most of the sights are in the spectacular Old Town, on a hill between the gorges of Ríos Júcar and Huécar. Just wandering its narrow streets, tunnels and staircases, stopping every now and again to admire the majestic views (and catch your breath) is the chief pleasure of Cuenca. The new town spreads out at the base of the hill; this is where you'll find normal Cuenca life – the Old Town is a little museum-like and few locals live there.

TOP CHOICE **Museo de Arte**
Abstracto Español   MUSEUM

(Museum of Abstract Art; www.march.es/arte/cuenca; adult/child €3/free; ⊘11am-2pm & 4-6pm Tue-Fri, 11am-2pm & 4-8pm Sat, 11am-2.30pm Sun) This impressive contemporary art museum is one of several spaces devoted to modern art and sculpture, its galleries memorably occupying one of the *casas colgadas*. Begun as an attempt by Fernando Zóbel to unite the works of his fellow artists from the so-called Abstract Generation of the 1950s and '60s, the museum's constantly evolving displays include works by Eduardo Chillida, Antoni Tàpies and Manuel Millares. Don't miss the extraordinary gouache landscapes by Eusebio Sempere, which re-ally capture the colourful patterned plains of La Mancha, or Antonio Saura's crazy portraits of Brigitte Bardot and Philip II.

Casas Colgadas   HISTORIC BUILDINGS

The most striking element of medieval Cuenca, the *casas colgadas* jut out precariously over the steep defile of Río Huécar. Dating from the 14th century, the houses, with their layers of wooden balconies, seem to emerge from the rock as if an extension of the cliffs. For the best views of the *casas colgadas,* cross the **Puente de San Pablo** footbridge or walk to the **mirador** at the northernmost tip of the Old Town.

📷 **Ars Natura**   MUSEUM

(www.centroarsnatura.es; Calle Diego Ramírez de Villaescusa; adult/child €3/free; ⊘10am-2pm & 4-7pm Tue-Sat, 10am-2pm Sun; 🅿) This impressive environmental museum has several vast galleries with interactive exhibits ranging from local flora and fauna to basket-weaving video demonstrations. Climate change, local geology, environmental impact studies and overall sustainability are given the hands-on approach. All information is in Spanish, but there's enough here to keep nonspeakers interested, including a river-fish aquarium and an outdoor section with examples of different wetland environments and sustainable technologies. Bus 7 stops outside. Open until 8pm in summer.

Museo de Cuenca   MUSEUM

(Calle Obispo Valero 12; adult/child €1.20/free, Sat & Sun free; ⊘10am-2pm & 4-7pm Tue-Sat, 11am-2pm Sun) Exceptionally well laid out and well documented (in Spanish) exhibits range from the Bronze Age to the 18th century. Sala 7 is particularly awe-inspiring, with its original Roman statues, including Emperor Augustus, plus columns and pediments discovered at nearby Segóbriga and Valeria.

Espacio Torner   GALLERY

(www.espaciotorner.com; Calle de Hoz de Huécar, Iglesia San Pablo; adult/child €3/free; ⊘11am-2pm & 4-6pm Tue-Sat, 11am-2pm Sun) One of several Cuenca spaces placing contemporary art in historic buildings, this is set in a Gothic church with great views of the Old Town. It displays abstract paintings and sculptures by Gustavo Torner, one of several artists who made Cuenca their home in the 1960s. The soaring vaulted ceilings

Cuenca

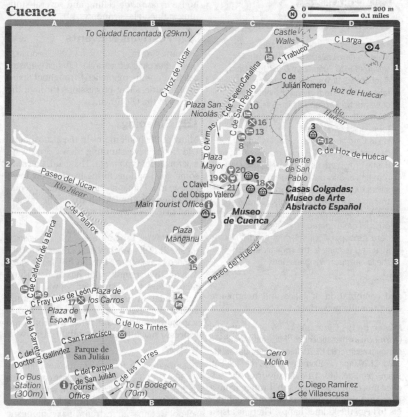

Cuenca

Top Sights

Casas Colgadas	C2
Museo de Arte Abstracto Español	C2
Museo de Cuenca	C2

Sights

1	Ars Natura	C4
2	Catedral	C2
3	Espacio Torner	D2
4	Mirador	D1
5	Museo de las Ciencias	C3
6	Museo Diocesano	C2

Sleeping

7	CH Victoria Alojamientos	A3
8	Convento del Giraldo	C2
9	Hostal Cánovas	A3
10	Hostal San Pedro	C1
11	Hostal Tabanqueta	C1
12	Parador de Cuenca	D2
13	Posada de San José	C2
14	Posada Huécar	B3

Eating

	Ars Natura	(see 1)
15	El Secreto	B3
16	Figón del Huécar	C2
17	La Bodeguilla de Basilio	A3
18	Mesón Casas Colgadas	C2
19	San Juan Plaza Mayor	C2

Drinking

20	Bar La Tinaja	C2
21	Lolita Lounge Bar	C2

WORTH A TRIP

VALERIA'S ROMAN RUINS

The fascinating archaeological site of Valeria (www.valeriaromana.es; admission free; ☉10.30am-2pm & 5.30-8.30pm) is located 34km south of Cuenca. It's fairly untouristed, giving the pleasure of wandering around a sizeable Roman town without the distraction of bus tours and school groups. The location is sublime, amid wild meadows and dramatic gorges. A ruined medieval castle crowns the hillside; below are the remains of a forum, as well as a basilica, four reservoirs, urban streets and the well-preserved remains of a vast extravagant fountain. There is also the original *casa colgada* (hanging house) here, its upper floor still clearly constructed to cling to the rock side, with the lower floors visible below.

and combination of space and height are exceptionally powerful.

Museo de las Ciencias MUSEUM
(www.jccm.es/museociencias; Plaza de la Merced; museum adult/child €1.20/free, planetarium adult/child €1.20/free; ☉10am-2pm & 4-7pm Tue-Sat, 10am-2pm Sun; ☷) This family-friendly science museum has displays that range from a time machine to plenty of interactive gadgets to keep the kiddies happy. There is also a **planetarium.**

Museo Diocesano MUSEUM
(Calle Obispo Valero 1; admission €2.50, incl cathedral €5; ☉11am-2pm & 4-6pm Tue-Sat, 11am-2pm Sun Nov-Mar, 10am-1pm & 4-7pm Tue-Sat, 10am-1pm Sun Apr-Oct) Better than the average museum of religious art in Spain, this has an excellent collection of Flemish tapestries, some fine Romanesque and Gothic sculpture, and a notable collection of paintings that includes two canvases by El Greco, one a particularly moving Christ carrying the cross.

Catedral CATHEDRAL
(Plaza Mayor; adult/child €3.80/2, incl Museo Diocesano & audioguide €5; ☉10am-1pm & 4-6pm, to 7pm Apr-Oct) Dominating the Plaza Mayor, Cuenca's cathedral was built on the site of the main mosque after the city's reconquest by Alfonso VIII in 1177. Highlights within include the Gothic tombs of the Montemayor family, an impressive sacristy, the chapter-

house *artesonado* ceiling and several stunning stained-glass windows.

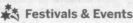

Festivals & Events

Semana Santa HOLY WEEK
(www.juntacofradiascuenca.es) Cuenca's Easter celebrations are renowned throughout Spain for the eerie, silent processions through the streets of the Old Town.

Sleeping

Many of the hotel rooms in the atmospheric Old Town have stunning views, so always ask for a room *con vista*. That said, there are some good options in the livelier new town below, too. Phone ahead for budget accommodations in the Old Town, as the owners tend to live elsewhere.

TOP CHOICE Hostal Tabanqueta HOSTAL €
(☎969 21 12 90; www.hostaltabanqueta.com; Calle Trabuco 13; d €60; ☷) Up the hill from Plaza Mayor, this friendly spot has free parking nearby and top-of-the-town views. The accommodation is excellent, with heating, stylish tiled bathrooms, attractive artwork, and hotel-standard amenities like toiletries, espresso machine and hospitality tray with pastries.

Posada de San José HISTORIC HOTEL €€
(☎969 21 13 00; www.posadasanjose.com; Ronda de Julián Romero 4; d from €82, s/d without bathroom €30/43) This 17th-century former choir school retains an extraordinary monastic charm with its labyrinth of rooms, eclectic artwork, uneven floors and original tiles. All rooms are different; cheaper ones are in former priests' cells, while more costly doubles combine homey comfort with old-world charm. Several have balconies with dramatic views of the gorge. There's a tapas restaurant and the owners also rent out tastefully furnished self-contained apartments.

Parador de Cuenca HISTORIC HOTEL €€€
(☎969 23 23 20; www.parador.es; Calle de Hoz de Huécar; s/d €138/173; ☷☀❄☲) This majestic former convent commands stunning views of the *casas colgadas*. The aesthetically revamped rooms have a luxury corporate feel, while the public areas are headily historic with giant tapestries and antiques.

Posada Huécar HOSTAL €
(☎969 21 42 01; www.posadahuecar.com; Paseo del Huécar 3; s/d €30/50; ☷@❄☷) Located

squarely between the old and new towns, this upbeat place has large rooms with terracotta tiles, rustic furnishings and river views. There are bicycles for rent (€4 for two hours). The young owners also run a successful Spanish-language school, so there are often foreign student groups staying. There's also free parking along the road outside.

CH Victoria Alojamientos HOSTAL €€
(☑620 782937; www.chvictorialojamientos.com; Calle Mateo Miguel Ayllón 2; s €40, d €80-95; P⑦) Blurring the lines between *hostal* and hotel, the rooms at this excellent new-town place offer every comfort, with stylish decoration, modern bathrooms, firm mattresses and plenty of thoughtful extras. Doubles are a fair bit cheaper low season.

Hostal San Pedro HOSTAL €
(☑628 407601, 969 23 45 43; www.hostalsanpedro. es; Calle de San Pedro 34; s/d €35/60; ⑦) In this excellently priced and positioned *hostal,* rooms have butter-coloured paintwork, wrought-iron bedheads and rustic wood furniture, and the bathrooms are shiny and modern. The owners live elsewhere, so call first.

Convento del Giraldo HOTEL €€
(☑969 23 27 00; www.hotelconventodelgiraldo. com; Calle de San Pedro 12; s/d €114/141; ✳@⑦) Just above the cathedral, this conversion of a 17th-century convent wins points for location and style, though there aren't too many original features left. Nevertheless, the attractive rooms feature dark wooden furniture, big bathrooms and great views from many of them. You can find good discounts online.

Hostal Cánovas HOSTAL €
(☑969 21 39 73; www.hostalcanovas.net; Calle Fray Luis de León 38; s/d €45/60; ✳) This upbeat and welcoming *hostal* in the new town has spacious rooms and a warm colour scheme.

✖ Eating

The Plaza Mayor (in the Old Town) and Plaza de España (new town) are the centres of their respective eating zones. There is a good choice in and surrounding both squares.

La Bodeguilla de Basilio TAPAS €
(Calle Fray Luis de León 3; raciones €10-13; ☺lunch & dinner Mon-Sat, lunch Sun) Arrive here with an appetite, as you're presented with a complimentary plate of tapas when you order a drink, and not just a slice of dried-up cheese – typical freebies are a combo of quail eggs, ham, fried potatoes, lettuce hearts and zucchinis (courgettes). Understandably, it gets packed out, so head to the restaurant at the back for specials like *patatas a lo pobre* (potatoes with onions, garlic and peppers) or lamb chops. The walls are covered with fascinating clutter, ranging from old pics of Cuenca to farming tools.

Ars Natura MODERN SPANISH €€€
(Manolo de la Osa; ☑969 21 95 12; www.restau rantearsnatura.com; Calle Río G ritos 5, Cerro Molina; mains €23-26, menus €38-76; ☺lunch & dinner Tue-Sat, lunch Sun) Celebrated chef Manuel de la Osa's second restaurant at Ars Natura showcases unique dishes using traditional local ingredients, like red partridge salad with butter beans and oyster mushrooms. The decor is suitably elegant. Reservations essential.

Mesón Casas Colgadas TRADITIONAL SPANISH €€
(☑969 22 35 52; Calle de los Canónigos 3; mains €14-25, menus €27) Housed in one of the *casas colgadas,* Cuenca's gourmet pride and joy fuses an amazing location with delicious traditional food on the menu, such as venison stew and the quaintly translated *boned little pork hands stew* (pig-trotter stew). Reservations are recommended.

El Secreto SPANISH €€
(www.elsecretocuenca.com; Calle de Alfonso VIII 81; mains €11-16; ☺lunch Mon & Tue, lunch & dinner Thu-Sun; ✍) Exuberant decor featuring painted tiles and a friendly laid-back attitude characterise this place, which has a pretty dining room with vistas behind a small front bar. There's a good selection of pastas and salads, and meat dishes include a tasty venison burger.

Figón del Huécar SPANISH €€€
(☑969 24 00 62; www.figondelhuecar.es; Calle de Julián Romero 6; mains €18-22; ☺lunch & dinner Mon-Sat, lunch Sun) With a romantic terrace offering spectacular views, this is a highlight of Old-Town eating. Roast suckling pig, stewed partridge, lamb stew and other Castilian specialities are presented and served with panache. The house used to be the home of Spanish singer José Luis Perales.

San Juan Plaza Mayor SPANISH €
(Plaza Mayor 5; mains €7-14; ☺lunch & dinner Tue-Sat, lunch Sun) This bright and buzzy tapas

bar on Plaza Mayor has fine cathedral views from its terrace and a good selection of tasty bar snacks. The dining room offers a broad range of cheap eats, including a wide selection of rice dishes for two, as well as salads and grilled meats. Simpler dishes are the way to go here. Service is scatty.

El Bodegón
SPANISH €

(Cerrillo de San Roque A1; mains €6-14; ⊙lunch & dinner Tue-Sun) Up a narrow lane in the new town, this sociable bar has a peaceful terrace and several indoor tables where you can watch your meat being expertly grilled on the wood stove in the corner. No frills; great value.

Drinking & Entertainment

Cuenca is a student town with lively nightlife. Calle San Francisco in the new town has an energetic row of terrace bars with a pre-clubbing party feel from around 9pm on weekends. There are several more sophisticated venues around Plaza Mayor. For later action, head for the disco-pubs on Calle del Doctor Galíndez, near Plaza de España.

Lolita Lounge Bar
BAR

(www.lolitaloungebar.es; Calle Clavel 7; ⊙11pm-4am Fri, 4pm-4am Sat, also Thu & Sun May-Sep) A slick minimalist bar with lots of steely metal and slate. Cocktails, a huge range of gins, imported beers and a good mix of music attract the high-heeled and slicked-back-hair set.

Bar La Tinaja
TAPAS BAR

(Calle del Obispo Valero 4; ⊙lunch & dinner Wed-Mon) Enjoying an ace position beside the cathedral, this place is typically crowded with crusty locals who come for the delicious (and free) tapas provided with every drink. The pasta dishes (€6) are good, too.

Information

There's a free internet terminal in the Museo de las Ciencias (p226).

Main tourist office (http://turismo.cuenca.es; Calle Alfonso VIII 2; ⊙9am-9pm Mon-Sat, to 2.30pm Sun) Helpful. Ask about visiting the medieval tunnels that honeycomb the Old Town and are under ongoing investigation.

Tourist office (☑969 23 58 15; Plaza Hispanidad; ⊙10am-2pm & 5-8pm Mon-Thu, 10am-8pm Fri-Sun, reduced hours Nov-Mar) Cuenca's second slightly smaller tourist office in the new town, open somewhat reduced hours on weekends in winter.

Getting There & Away

The train and bus stations are located almost across from each other, southwest of Calle de Fermín Caballero. Fast AVE trains use the Fernando Zóbel station, southwest of town. Bus 12 links it with the town centre.

There are up to nine buses daily to Madrid (€11.45, two hours) and regular services to other cities in Castilla-La Mancha as well as Valencia.

Numerous daily trains run to Madrid, ranging from slow *regionales* (trains operating within one region, usually stopping all stations; €12.25, three hours) to swift AVEs (€38.70, 55 mins). The other way, to Valencia, is a similar deal, with almost identical times and prices.

Getting Around

Local buses 1 and 2 do the circuit from the new town to Plaza Mayor (€0.75, every 30 minutes), stopping outside the train station. There's a large free car park on Calle Larga above the arch at the top of the Old Town.

Around Cuenca
SERRANÍA DE CUENCA

Spreading north and east of Cuenca, this is a heavily wooded and fertile zone of craggy mountains, sandstone gorges and

---

GOLD ON A PLATE

Saffron is one of the most sensuous spices in the world: its intense colour, aroma and delicacy are accentuated by a wealth of nuances. It's also among the most expensive spices – hardly surprising when you consider that it takes some 160,000 flowers to produce just 1kg of commercial saffron.

Spain leads the European saffron market, and La Mancha is the region where the flowers have been grown and cultivated since Moorish times, primarily around Cuenca and Albacete. Visit here in October and the surrounding fields are a sumptuous blanket of purple blooms.

Saffron is used as a culinary spice around the world. In Spain, it most famously appears in traditional paella.

green fields. Ríos Júcar and Huécar flow through the high hinterland, through landscapes well worth exploring with your own transport.

Head out from Cuenca 30km via the CM2105 to extraordinary Ciudad Encantada (adult/child €3/free; ⊙10am-sunset). Surrounded by pine woods, limestone rocks have been eroded into fantastical shapes by nature. The shaded 40-minute circuit around the open-air rock museum is great for breaking up a car journey. It's crowded on weekends.

The CM2105 continues north via the picturesque village of Uña, the crystal-clear waters of Embalse del Tobar and past the Reserva Natural de El Hosquillo, a protected park where reintroduced brown bears roam wild. Continue to the Nacimiento del Río Cuervo, a couple of small waterfalls from which Río Cuervo rises. From here you could loop around towards Beteta and the Hoz de Beteta gorge, encircled by lofty limestone crags and ridges.

Beteta has a charming porticoed Plaza Mayor with half-timbered buildings, and a crumbly hilltop castle. Lodging options in town include a couple of *casas rurales*. You can return to Cuenca via the CM210, a quiet rural route that passes several traditional villages, the source of Spain's trademark blue-bottled water, Solán de Cabras (with summer spa hotel), as well as Priego, a lovely valley town that dates from Roman times and has sights including medieval churches, Roman arches and Moorish towers.

If you're heading on to Sigüenza, track northeast from Beteta to Molina de Aragón, a pretty town utterly dominated by one of Spain's most spectacular castles, built by the Moors before being embellished after falling into Christian hands. It's regrettably not open to the public except by guided tour – call the tourist office on ☑949 83 20 98 or email turismo@molina-aragon.com to see if you can join a group.

ALARCÓN

One hundred kilometres or so south of Cuenca is the seductive medieval village of Alarcón. The approach is via a narrow road winding through three medieval defensive arches.

The most famous sight here is the triangular-based Islamic castle, now a sumptuous parador (Marqués de Villena; ☑969 33 03 15; www.parador.es; s/d incl breakfast €194/242; P✷☎), offering old-world charm and su-

premely comfortable rooms with exposed brick-and-stone walls, and plush fabrics and furnishings. Alternatively, Meson Don Julián (☑969 33 03 00; Plaza Autónomo 1; s/d €40/50; ✷☎), near the castle entrance, has pretty, rustic rooms with balconies and fridges, and a friendly bar-restaurant. The best restaurant in town is enchanting La Cabaña de Alarcón (Álvaro de Lara 21; mains €11-18; ⊙lunch & dinner Mon-Sat, lunch Sun), with its picture windows, dark-pink paintwork, contemporary artwork and well-priced, well-executed local dishes.

Stop at the tourist office (☑969 33 03 01; Calle Posadas 6; ⊙10am-2pm Tue-Sat) for a map of walks around the village and beyond. If it's closed, there are detailed signboards with maps nearby.

SEGÓBRIGA

These Roman ruins (adult/child €4/free; ⊙10am-9pm Tue-Sun Apr-Sep, 10am-6pm Tue-Sun Oct-Mar) may date as far back as the 5th century BC. The best-preserved structures are a Roman theatre and amphitheatre on the fringes of the ancient city, looking out over a valley. Other remains include the outlines of a Visigothic basilica and a section of the aqueduct, which helped keep the city green in what was otherwise a desert. A small museum (included in the price) has some striking exhibits.

The site is near Saelices, 2km south of the A3 motorway between Madrid and Albacete. From Cuenca, drive west 55km on the N400, then turn south on the CM202.

Guadalajara

POP 84,450

Despite its romantic name, Guadalajara is, disappointingly, a modern, somewhat

CASTILLA-LA MANCHA GUADALAJARA

scruffy city, of more historical than aesthetic interest. It's worth the easy half-day trip from Madrid or Sigüenza just for its fabulous palace.

Guadalajara (from the Arabic *wad al-hijaara*, meaning 'stony river') was, in its medieval Muslim heyday, the principal city of a large swathe of northern Spain under the green banner of Islam at a time when Madrid was no more than a military observation point. In 1085 Alfonso VI finally took Guadalajara as the Reconquista moved ponderously south. The city was repeatedly sacked during the War of the Spanish Succession (1702–13), the Napoleonic occupation and the Spanish Civil War.

The main remnant of Guadalajara's glory days is the fabulous Palacio de los Duques del Infantado (☑949 21 33 01; Plaza de los Caídos; admission free; ☉patio 9am-9.30pm Mon-Fri, 9am-2.30pm & 5-8pm Sat, 10am-2.30pm & 5-7pm Sun), where the Mendoza family held court. It's one of Spain's most striking buildings, with its elaborate studded flamboyant Gothic-Mudéjar facade and stunning patio, with carved heraldic lions and griffins above exuberant arches. It holds the local art museum, open shorter hours. The town's tourist office (☑949 21 16 26; www.turismocastillalamancha.com; Plaza de los Caídos 6; ☉9am-2pm & 4-7pm Mon-Fri, 9am-3pm & 4-6pm Sat, 10am-2pm Sun) is opposite the *palacio*.

A day trip isn't a day trip without a decent lunch or tapas stop, and a short walk via Plaza Mayor from the palace is El Figón (www.elfigon.com; Calle Bardales 7; raciones €6-11; ☉lunch Wed-Mon, dinner Wed-Sun; ☎), a gloriously traditional place decorated with antlers and serving good-value *raciones* (full-plate-size tapas serving) of typical Spanish fare. It's a Guadalajara classic.

There are regular fast trains from Madrid to Guadalajara, but the station is 2km north of town. The bus station (Calle del Dos de Mayo) is just a short walk from the *palacio* and has regular connections to Madrid (€4.24, 50 minutes) and Sigüenza (€6.80, 1½ hours).

Pastrana

POP 1080

Pastrana should not be missed. It's an unspoilt place with twisting cobbled streets flanked by honey-coloured stone buildings. Forty-two kilometres south of Guadalajara along the CM200, the heart and soul of the

place is the Plaza de la Hora, a large square dotted with acacias and fronted by the sturdy Palacio Ducal, a work of Alonso de Covarrubias. It is in Pastrana that the one-eyed princess of Éboli, Ana Mendoza de la Cerda, was confined in 1581 for a love affair with the Spanish king Felipe II's secretary. You can see the caged window of her 'cell', where she died 10 years later, and arrange a tour (Spanish only; €2) via the tourist office (☑949 37 06 72; www.pastrana.org; Plaza de la Hora 5; ☉10am-2pm & 4-7pm Mon-Fri, to 8pm Sat, 10am-2pm Sun).

Walk from the square along Calle Mayor and you'll soon reach the massive Iglesia de Nuestra Señora de la Asunción. Inside, the interesting little museum (Colegiata; adult/child €2.50/free; ☉11.30am-2pm & 4.30-7pm Tue-Sat, 1-2pm & 4.30-7pm Sun) contains the jewels of the princess, some exquisite 15th-century tapestries and even an El Greco.

Hotel Palaterna (☑949 37 01 27; www.hotelpalaterna.com; Plaza de los Cuatro Caños; s/d €50/65; ✲✺) is a pleasant modern hotel overlooking a small square complete with bubbling fountain. Rooms are painted in cool colours, contrasting with dark wood furniture. A block higher up the town, La Aljama (☑949 37 02 70; http://perso.wanadoo.es/laaljama; Calle Adolfo Martín Gamero 6; d €70-75) is an attractive and character-packed *casa rural* (village or farmstead accommodation) in a centuries-old building run with a friendly, laissez-faire attitude.

Pastrana has plenty of restaurants and bars, centred along Calle Mayor. Don't miss the locals' local, Casa Seco (Calle Mayor 36; tapas from €2), with all four walls, plus ceiling, papered with faded bullfighting posters. It's run by a wonderfully matriarchal lady who keeps the flat-cap clientele under control.

There's a daily bus each way between Guadalajara and Pastrana (1¼ hours).

Around Pastrana

Thirteen kilometres south of Pastrana, signposted off the Tarancón road (turn right just after passing the nuclear power plant), Recópolis (www.patrimoniohistoricoclm.es; Zorita de los Canes; adult/child €5/1; ☉10am-6pm mid-Sep–Apr, 10am-2pm & 5-9pm May–mid-Sep) is an intriguing ruin in a lovely situation above Río Tajo. The word Visigoth usually calls up images of horned-helmeted lager louts urinating on the dying embers of Roman civilisation, but it's not a fair portrayal of these skilled metalworkers and early Christian monarchs. After uniting most of the peninsula under his rule, King Leovigildo, whose capital was at Toledo, founded Recópolis in 578AD as a planned walled city named after his son Recaredo. You can see the royal palace complex, workshops and the main street, though later modifications by the Moors and others muddy the waters slightly. There's an interpretation centre and good information in English throughout. Admission includes a nature trail and entrance to the nearby ruined castle at Zorita de los Canes.

Sigüenza

POP 4950

Sleepy, historic and filled with the ghosts of a turbulent past, Sigüenza is well worth a detour. The town is built on a low hill cradled by Río Henares and boasts a castle, a cathedral and several excellent restaurants set among twisting lanes of medieval buildings. Start your ambling at the beautiful 16th-century Plaza Mayor.

◉ Sights

Catedral CATHEDRAL

(◷9.30am-2pm & 4-8pm Tue-Sat, noon-5.30pm Sun) Rising up from the heart of the Old Town is the city's centrepiece, the *catedral*. Begun as a Romanesque structure in 1130, work continued for four centuries as the church was expanded and adorned. The largely Gothic result is laced with elements of other styles, from plateresque through to Renaissance to Mudéjar. The church was heavily damaged during the civil war, but was subsequently rebuilt.

The dark interior has a broodingly ancient feel and some fine stained glass, including some magnificent rose windows, plus an impressive 15th-century altarpiece along the south wall. To enter the chapels, sacristy and Gothic cloister, you'll need to join a Spanish-language-only guided tour (per person €4; noon, 1pm, 4.30pm & 5.30pm Tuesday to Sunday). The highlights of the tour include the Capilla Mayor, home of the reclining marble statue of Don Martín Vázquez de Arce (the statue is named *El Doncel*), who died fighting the Muslims in the final stages of the Reconquista. Particularly beautiful is the Sacristía de las Cabezas, with a ceiling adorned with hundreds of

heads sculpted by Covarrubias. The Capilla del Espíritu Santo boasts a doorway combining plateresque, Mudéjar and Gothic styles; inside is a remarkable dome and an *Anunciación* by El Greco.

Museo Diocesano de Arte RELIGIOUS, ART

(admission €3; ◷11am-2pm & 4-7pm Tue-Sat, 11am-2pm Sun) Across the square from the cathedral, this well-presented museum has a variety of mediocre religious art from Sigüenza and the surrounding area, as well as some more interesting pieces, including an Immaculate Virgin hovering over Seville by Zurbarán, and some naïve wall paintings of the Last Judgement taken from a regional church. An Attic red-figure vase and a votive frog are more offbeat inclusions. Afternoon opening is 5pm to 8pm in summer.

Castillo CASTLE

Calle Mayor heads south up the hill from the cathedral to a magnificent-looking castle, which was originally built by the Romans and was, in turn, a Moorish *alcázar* (fortress), royal palace, asylum and army barracks. Virtually destroyed during the Spanish Civil War, it was subsequently rebuilt under Franco as a *parador*.

⌂ Sleeping

There are lots of accommodation options; nearly all are substantially cheaper midweek and during low season.

Parador de Sigüenza HISTORIC HOTEL €€€

(☎949 39 01 00; www.parador.es; Plaza del Castillo; s/d €129/161; ℗⁕⊛) Sigüenza's *parador* ably provides its guests with the usual combination of luxury, attentive service and period furnishings. It is set in the castle, which dates back to the 12th century, and overlooks the town. The magnificent courtyard is a wonderful place to pass the time. The rooms have castle-style windows so can be on the dark side: ask for one with a balcony to make the most of natural light and views.

El Doncel HOTEL €€

(☎949 39 00 01; www.eldoncel.com; Paseo de la Alameda 3; d €85; ⁕⊛) With earthy colours, lots of exposed stone, spot lighting, minibar, and marshmallow-soft duvets and pillows, this place is aimed squarely at couples on a romantic weekend away from Madrid. It's comfortable and attractive, and there's a good restaurant too. Prices drop substantially midweek.

Sigüenza

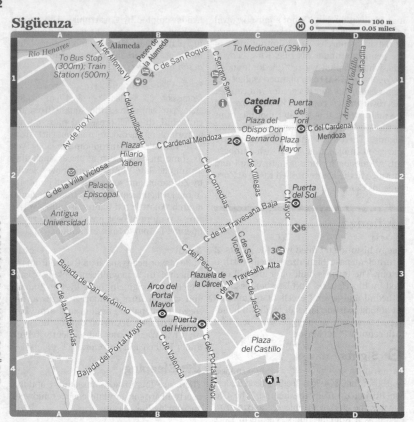

Sigüenza

Hospedería Porta Coeli   HOSTAL **€€**
(☎949 39 18 75; www.crusa.es; Calle Mayor 50; s/d
€57/75; ❄🏠) Housed in a sumptuous historic building, the university-owned Porta
Coeli has light tiles and pale paintwork that
provide a bright, fresh look to the good-sized
bedrooms. The combination of modern styling and ancient building works very well,
the location between castle and cathedral is
great, and breakfast is included. Prices halve
during low season.

Hostal Puerta Medina   HOSTAL **€€**
(☎949 39 15 65; www.puertamedina.es; Calle Serrano Sanz 17; s/d €50/67; 🏠) Tucked away in a
noble 18th-century building a block downhill from the cathedral, things look a little
rickety on your way in. Until you reach the

door, for this *hostal* offers a genuine welcome and bright, spacious, quiet rooms with plenty of original character. The affable owner puts on a good breakfast (included) with home-baked bread. Easy parking on this street. Much cheaper outside the high summer season.

🍴 Eating & Drinking

Sigüenza has heaps of restaurants, some of which open only on weekends to cater to the Madrid influx. Along the Alameda are several decent eating options.

TOP CHOICE Calle Mayor
SPANISH €€

(☎949 39 17 48; www.restaurantecallemayor.com; Calle Mayor 21; mains €12-18) A standout meal stop on the hill between the cathedral and castle. Traditional dishes like delicious roast goat or fried lamb's brains take their place alongside more elaborate creations. It offers excellent value for the quality on offer and a stylish but comfortable dining area to match. Service is correct if a little on the cold side.

Gurugú de la Plazuela
TAPAS €€

(www.gurugudelaplazuela.com; Plaza de la Cárcel; mushroom dishes €12-18; ☺lunch & dinner Thu-Sat, lunch Sun; ☑) Overlooking the atmospheric small Plaza de la Cárcel, the speciality of this historic tavern is mushrooms, lots of them, with some 16 varieties on the menu, prepared all sorts of ways. Other choices include a nice line in game dishes. There are regular art and photography exhibitions.

Taberna Seguntina
SPANISH €€

(www.latabernaseguntina.es; Calle Mayor 43; mains €14-20; ☺Thu-Tue) A swallow's swoop from the castle, this restaurant has a traditional menu that includes local classics like suckling pig, roasted lamb and pheasant.

Cafe-Bar Alameda
TAPAS BAR

(Paseo de la Alameda 2; raciones €6-10) Join the local card players at this down-home bar. Its counter groans with tempting tapas and *pinchos* (canapes), including *caracoles* (snails) and *orejas* (pig's ears) for the intrepid, as well as more-digestible, albeit still unusual, choices like tortilla stuffed with bacon and cheese.

ℹ Information

Tourist office (☎949 34 70 09; turismo@siguenza.es; Calle Serrano Sanz 9; ☺10am-2pm & 4-6pm Mon-Thu & Sat, 10am-2pm & 4-8pm Fri, 10am-2pm Sun) Just down the hill from the cathedral. Opens and closes an hour later in the afternoon in summer.

ℹ Getting There & Away

Buses are infrequent and mainly serve towns around Sigüenza, including Guadalajara. They stop on Avenida de Alfonso VI. Six daily regional trains go to Madrid's Chamartín station (€11.25, 1½ hours) via Guadalajara; some go on to Soria in the other direction.

Around Sigüenza

IMÓN
POP 40

This tiny gem of a hamlet, located 15km northwest of Sigüenza, has a surprising amount on offer, including sophisticated places to stay and eat (for weekending *madrileños*), a spa complex, and excellent walking and birdwatching potential.

Don't miss the salt-extraction pans a short stroll away along the Sigüenza road; with the crumbling buildings around them as a backdrop, there are some great photo opportunity here. For an easy walk, follow Don Quijote's path at the end of the main street (Calle Cervantes), heading north. The 4.5km pleasant stroll through fields leads to a 15th-century castle, **La Riba de Santiuste**, perched high on a rock above the semi-abandoned village of the same name. The castle is partly in ruins and is fascinating to explore.

Salinas de Imón (☎949 39 73 11; www.salinasdeimon.com; Real 49; r €92-146, ste €215; ✳☞☔) is housed in a mid-17th-century stone building. It has 13 rooms, restored with sensitive integrity, that retain a sense of history. There is nothing historic about the luxurious bathrooms, however. The garden is secluded and lovely, with lawns, a bower and a pool. Nearby, **La Botica** (☎949 39 74 15; www.laboticahotelrural.com; Calle Cervantes 40; d incl breakfast €130-151; ✳☞☔) is a former chemist's with stunningly romantic rooms with Jacuzzi and top facilities. Both places guarantee excellent hospitality, serve dinner, and have access to a modern spa complex located a few metres away (€30 per one-hour session). Call to book either place if arriving midweek outside the summer months.

ATIENZA
POP 440

Some 15km northwest of Imón lies Atienza, a charming walled medieval village crowned

CASTILLA-LA MANCHA AROUND SIGÜENZA

by yet another castle ruin. Wandering the streets here is utterly enchanting; this is one of Spain's most beautiful villages. The main half-timbered square and former 16th-century market place, Plaza del Trigo, is overlooked by the Renaissance Iglesia San Juan Bautista, which has an impressive organ and lavish gilt *retablo*. There are several more mostly Romanesque churches, three of which hold small museums (admission 1/3 museums €1.50/3; ⊙11.30am-2pm & 4-7pm mid-Jul–mid-Sep, Sat & Sun only mid-Sep–mid-Jul). One of these is devoted to the Caballada, a spectacular procession of horses on Corpus Christi.

The best place to stay is the **Antiguo Palacio de Atienza** (☑949 39 91 80; www. palaciodeatienza.com; Plaza de Agustín González 1; s €43, d €65-96; ❇🤖🔄), a former palace with handsome rooms featuring grey stone walls and beams. The variation in price relates to the size of the room and option of a hot tub. Balconies overlook the lawns and pool.

El Mirador (☑949 39 90 38; www.elmirador deatienza.com; Calle Barruelo; s/d/tw €24/36/45; ❇🤖), with spotless rooms that are a steal at this price, is a budget option in a modern whitewashed building offering great panoramic views over the fields below. The excellent restaurant (mains €11 to €20) shares the vistas and has creative dishes, as well as the standard *cordero* (lamb) and *cabrito* (kid).

A couple of buses leave early in the morning, bound for Guadalajara, Madrid and Sigüenza.

Barcelona

Includes »

Best Places to Eat

» Tickets (p291)
» Tapaç 24 (p290)
» Alkímia (p290)
» Koy Shunka (p287)
» Cal Pep (p288)

Best Places to Stay

» Hotel Neri (p283)
» Hotel Banys Orientals (p285)
» Hotel Praktik (p285)
» Casa Camper (p284)
» Hotel Constanza (p286)

Why Go?

Barcelona is a mix of sunny Mediterranean charm and European urban style, where dedicated hedonists and culture vultures feel equally at home. From Gothic to Gaudí, the city bursts with art and architecture; Catalan food is among the country's best; summer sun seekers fill the beaches in and beyond the city; and the bars and clubs heave year-round.

From its origins as a middle-ranking Roman town, of which vestiges can be seen today, Barcelona became a medieval trade juggernaut. Its old centre holds one of the greatest concentrations of Gothic architecture in Europe. Beyond this are some of the world's more bizarre buildings: surreal spectacles capped by Antoni Gaudí's La Sagrada Família.

Barcelona has been breaking ground in art, architecture and style since the late 19th century. From Picasso and Miró to the modern wonders of today, the racing heart of Barcelona has barely skipped a beat. Equally busy are the city's avant-garde chefs, who compete with old-time classics for the gourmet's attention.

When to Go
Barcelona

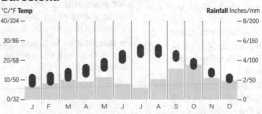

May Plaça del Fòrum rocks during Primavera Sound, a long weekend of outdoor concerts.

Jun Sónar, Europe's biggest celebration of electronic music, is held across the city.

Sep Festes de la Mercè is Barcelona's end-of-summer finale and biggest party.

DON'T MISS

No matter the season, taking a stroll – better yet, a bike ride – along Barcelona's revitalised waterfont makes a splendid complement to exploring medieval lanes and Modernista architecture. In the summer, open-air beach bars provide refreshing pit stops along the way.

Fast Facts

» Population: 1.62 million
» Greater metropolitan area: 636 sq km
» Average annual income (2009): €23,900
» Number of visitors (2010): 7.3 million

Best of What's Free

» Park Güell (p268)
» Església de Santa Maria del Mar (p252)
» Estadi Olímpic (p280)
» Castell de Montjuïc (p273)

Resources

» Barcelona Turisme (www.barcelonaturisme.com) Official tourism website.

» Barcelona (www.bcn.cat) Barcelona Town Hall, with links.

» Le Cool (http://lecool.com) What's-on guide.

» Barcelona Yellow (www.barcelonayellow.com) Links on everything from Gaudí to gourmet dining.

A Hidden Portrait at La Sagrada Família

Careful observation of the Passion Facade of Antoni Gaudí's masterpiece, La Sagrada Família (p257), will reveal a special tribute to the genius architect from sculptor Josep Subirachs. In a building dripping with symbology, some of it less than obvious to the uninitiated, this search is not too difficult a task. The central sculptural group (below Christ crucified) shows, from right to left, Christ bearing his cross, Veronica displaying the cloth with Christ's bloody image, a pair of soldiers and, watching it all, a man called the Evangelist. Subirachs used a rare photo of Gaudí, taken a couple of years before his death, as the model for the Evangelist's face.

MANIC MONDAYS

Many attractions shut their doors on Monday, but there are plenty of exceptions. Among the more enticing open attractions are Casa-Museu Gaudí (Park Güell), Gran Teatre del Liceu, Jardí Botànic, La Catedral, La Pedrera, La Sagrada Família, Mirador de Colom, MACBA (Museu d'Art Contemporani de Barcelona), Museu de la Xocolata, Museu del Futbol Club Barcelona, Museu del Modernisme Català, Museu Marítim, Palau de la Música Catalana and the Pavelló Mies van der Rohe.

Top Modernista Gems

» **La Sagrada Família** (p257) Antoni Gaudí's unfinished symphony is a soaring cathedral that people love or loathe. Work continues apace on this controversial project.

» **Palau de la Música Catalana** (p252) A gaudily sumptuous home for music to suit the most eclectic of tastes; a giddy example of Modernista fantasy.

» **La Pedrera** (p265) Gaudí's wavy corner apartment block, with an exquisite period apartment and crowned by a sci-fi roof, is one of the best examples of the star architect's work.

» **Casa Batlló** (p265) Possibly kookier than La Pedrera, it looks at first glance like some strange sea creature frozen into a building facade. Inside, it's all curls and swirls.

» **Hospital de la Santa Creu i de Sant Pau** (p267) Long one of the city's main hospitals, featuring 16 uniquely decorated pavilions.

History

It is thought that Barcelona may have been founded by the Carthaginians in about 230 BC, taking the surname of Hamilcar Barca, Hannibal's father. Roman Barcelona (known as Barcino) covered an area within today's Barri Gòtic and was overshadowed by Tarraco (Tarragona), 90km to the southwest.

In the wake of Muslim occupation and then Frankish domination, Guifré el Pilós (Wilfrid the Hairy) founded the house of the Comtes de Barcelona (Counts of Barcelona) in AD 878. In 1137 Count Ramon Berenguer IV married Petronilla, heiress of Aragón, creating a joint state and setting the scene for Catalonia's golden age. Jaume I (1213-76) wrenched the Balearic Islands and Valencia from the Muslims in the 1230s to '40s. Jaume I's son Pere II followed with Sicily in 1282.

The accession of the Aragonese noble Fernando to the throne in 1479 augured ill for Barcelona, and his marriage to Queen Isabel of Castilla more still. Catalonia effectively became a subordinate part of the Castilian state. After the War of the Spanish Succession (1702-13), Barcelona fell to the Bourbon king, Felipe V, in September 1714.

MODERNISME, ANARCHY & CIVIL WAR

The 19th century brought economic resurgence. Wine, cotton, cork and iron industries developed, as did urban working-class poverty and unrest. To ease the crush, Barcelona's medieval walls were demolished in 1854, and in 1869 work began on L'Eixample, an extension of the city beyond Plaça de Catalunya. The flourishing bourgeoisie paid for lavish buildings, many of them in the eclectic Modernisme style, whose leading exponent was Antoni Gaudí.

In 1937, a year into the Spanish Civil War, the Catalan communist party (PSUC; Partit Socialista Unificat de Catalunya) took control of the city after fratricidal street battles against anarchists and Trotskyists. George Orwell recorded the events in his classic *Homage to Catalonia*. Barcelona fell to Franco in 1939 and there followed a long period of repression.

FROM FRANCO TO THE PRESENT

Under Franco Barcelona received a flood of immigrants, chiefly from Andalucía. Some 750,000 people came to Barcelona in the '50s and '60s, and almost as many to the rest of Catalonia. Many lived in appalling conditions.

Three years after Franco's death in 1975, a new Spanish constitution created the autonomous community of Catalonia (Catalunya in Catalan; Cataluña in Castilian), with Barcelona as its capital. The 1992 Olympic Games put Barcelona on the map. Under the visionary leadership of popular Catalan Socialist mayor Pasqual Maragall, a burst of public works brought new life to Montjuïc and the once-shabby waterfront.

Flush with success after the Olympics makeover, Barcelona continued the revitalisation of formerly run-down neighbourhoods. El Raval, still dodgy in parts, has seen a host of building projects, from the opening of Richard Meier's cutting-edge Macba (Museu d'Art Contemporani de Barcelona) in 1995 to the new Filmoteca de Catalunya in 2012. Further west, the once-derelict industrial district of Poble Nou has been reinvented as 22@ (vint-i-dos arroba), a 200-hectare zone that is today a centre for technology and design. Innovative companies and futuristic architecture by the likes of Zaha Hadid, among others, continue to reshape the urban landscape of this ever-evolving city.

On other fronts, Catalonia continues to be a trendsetter for the rest of Spain. Barcelona's shared biking program Bicing, launched in 2007, has become a model for sustainable-transport initiatives, and the city continues to invest in green energy (particularly in its use of solar power and electric and hybrid vehicles).

Once a great kingdom unto its own, Catalonia has a long independent streak that sometimes puts it at odds with the rest of Spain. In 2012 the Catalan parliament banned bullfighting – making the region the first in mainland Spain to outlaw the sport. Some viewed the move as a Catalan-nationalist snub of an activity deeply rooted in Spanish culture.

◉ Sights

Barcelona could be divided up into thematic chunks. In Ciutat Vella (especially the Barri Gòtic and La Ribera) are clustered the bulk of the city's ancient and medieval splendours. Along with El Raval, on the other side of La Rambla, and Port Vell, where old Barcelona meets the sea, this is the core of the city's life, both by day and by night. Top attractions here include the Museu d'Història de Barcelona, La Catedral and the Museu Picasso.

L'Eixample is where the Modernistas went to town. Attractions here are more

Barcelona Highlights

1 Marvel at **La Sagrada Família** (p257), Antoni Gaudí's still-unfolding Modernista masterpiece

2 Stroll the narrow medieval lanes of the enchanting **Barri Gòtic** (p243)

3 See a concert in the extravagant concert hall of **Palau de la Música Catalana** (p297)

4 Join the riotous carnival at an FC Barça match in hallowed **Camp Nou** (p272)

5 Drink in the views from Gaudí's **Park Güell** (p268)

6 Dine and drink amid the architecturally rich streetscape of **L'Eixample** (p257)

7 Discover Pablo's early masterpieces inside the atmospheric **Museu Picasso** (p249)

8 Feast on fresh seafood, followed by a stroll along the boardwalk in **La Barceloneta** (p255)

9 Take in the nightlife of bohemian-loving **El Raval** (p248)

10 Explore **Montjuïc** (p272), home to Romanesque art, a brooding fort, Miró and beautiful gardens

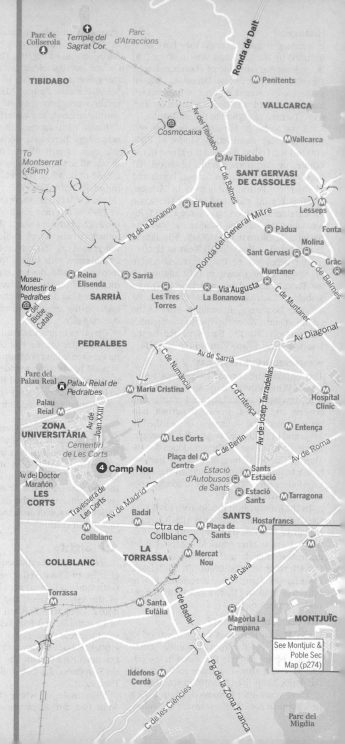

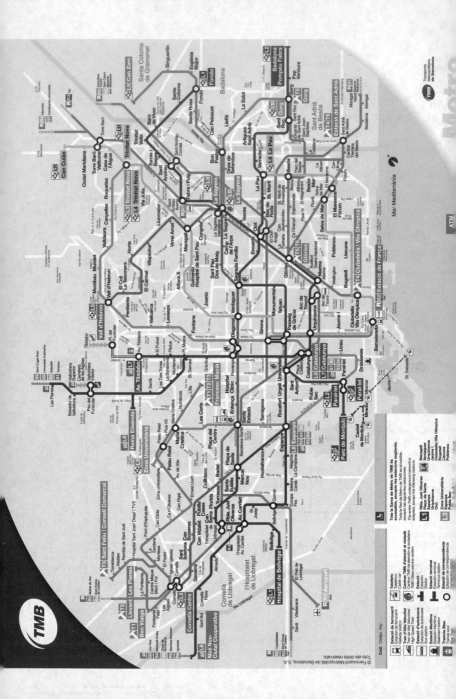

spread out. Passeig de Gràcia is a concentrated showcase for some of their most outlandish work, but La Sagrada Família, Gaudí's masterpiece, is a long walk (or short metro ride) from there.

Other areas of interest include the beaches and seafood restuarants of the working-class district of La Barceloneta. Montjuïc, with its gardens, museums, art galleries and Olympic Games sites, forms a microcosm on its own. Not to be missed are the Museu Nacional d'Art de Catalunya and the Fundació Joan Miró.

Gaudí's Park Güell is just beyond the area of Gràcia, whose narrow lanes and interlocking squares set the scene for much lively nightlife.

Futher out, you'll find the amusement park and church of high-up Tibidabo, the wooded hills of Parc de Collserola, FC Barcelona's Camp Nou football stadium and the peaceful haven of the Museu-Monestir de Pedralbes.

LA RAMBLA

Head to Spain's most famous street for that first taste of Barcelona's vibrant atmosphere.

Flanked by narrow traffic lanes and plane trees, the middle of La Rambla is a broad pedestrian boulevard, crowded every day until the wee hours with a cross section of *barcelonins* and out-of-towners. Dotted with cafes, restaurants, kiosks and news stands, and enlivened by buskers, pavement artists, mimes and living statues, La Rambla rarely allows a dull moment.

La Rambla gets its name from a seasonal stream (*raml* in Arabic) that once ran here. It was outside the city walls until the 14th century and was built up with monastic buildings and palaces in the 16th to 18th centuries. Unofficially La Rambla is divided into five sections, each with its own name.

La Rambla de Canaletes   STREET

(Ⓜ Catalunya) To the north, from Plaça de Catalunya, La Rambla de Canaletes is named after an inconspicuous fountain, whose drinking water (despite claims that anyone who drinks it will return to Barcelona) nowadays leaves much to be desired. Delirious football fans gather here to celebrate when the main home side, FC Barcelona, wins a cup or the league premiership. A block east along Carrer de la Canuda is Plaça de la Vila de Madrid, with a sunken garden where Roman tombs lie exposed in the Via Sepulcral Romana (Map p250; ☑ 93 256 21 00; www.museuhistoria.bcn. cat; Plaça de la Vila de Madrid; admission €2; ◷ 11am-2pm Tue-Fri, to 7pm Sat & Sun; Ⓜ Catalunya).

La Rambla dels Estudis   STREET

(Ⓜ Catalunya) La Rambla dels Estudis, from Carrer de la Canuda running south to Carrer de la Portaferrissa, is dotted with ice-cream and snack stands.

La Rambla de Sant Josep   STREET

(Ⓜ Liceu) From Carrer de la Portaferrissa to Plaça de la Boqueria, what is officially called La Rambla de Sant Josep (named after a now nonexistent monastery) is lined with flower stalls, which give it the alternative name La Rambla de les Flors.

The Palau de la Virreina is a grand 18th-century rococo mansion housing a municipal arts-and-entertainment information and

BARCELONA SIGHTS

FREE BARCELONA

Entry to some sights is free on occasion, most commonly on the first Sunday of the month. Other attractions are free on Sunday afternoons. Here are some sights that offer free admssion days:

» **Museu Picasso** (p249) Sundays 3pm to 8pm and all day on first Sunday of the month.

» **La Catedral** (p243) From 8am to 12.45pm and 5.15pm to 8pm Monday to Saturday.

» **Museu Barbier-Mueller d'Art Pre-Colombí** (p252) First Sunday of the month.

» **Museu d'Història de Barcelona** (p247) From 3pm to 8pm Sunday.

» **Museu d'Història de Catalunya** (p255) First Sunday of the month.

» **Museu Etnològic** (p278) First Sunday of the month.

» **Museu Marítim** (p251) From 3pm to 8pm Sunday.

» **Museu Nacional d'Art de Catalunya** (p273) First Sunday of the month.

» **Palau Güell** (p249) First Sunday of the month.

» **Palau Reial de Pedralbes** (p271) First Sunday of the month.

BARCELONA IN...

Two Days

Start with the **Barri Gòtic**. After a stroll along **La Rambla**, wade into the labyrinth to admire **La Catedral** and the **Museu d'Història de Barcelona** on historic Plaça del Rei. Cross Via Laietana into **La Ribera** for the city's most beautiful church, the **Església de Santa Maria del Mar**, and the nearby **Museu Picasso**. Round off with a meal and cocktails in the funky **El Born** area.

The following day, start with a walk through Gaudí's unique **Park Güell**, then head for his work in progress, **La Sagrada Família**. Afterwards, head to El Raval for dinner at the classic **Ca L'Isidre** followed by drinks at nearby **La Confitería**.

Four Days

Start the third day with another round of Gaudí, visiting **Casa Batlló** and **La Pedrera**, followed by beachside relaxation and seafood in **La Barceloneta**. Day four should be dedicated to **Montjuïc**, with its museums, galleries, fortress, gardens and Olympic stadium.

One Week

With three extra days, you can explore further, taking in **El Raval**, **Gràcia**, a game at **Camp Nou**, **Tibidabo** amusement park, and the rolling **Collserola** parklands. A tempting one-day excursion is **Montserrat**, Catalonia's 'sacred mountain'. Another option is to spend a day at the beach at **Sitges**.

ticket office, and an exhibition space. Next is the **Mercat de la Boqueria** (Map p250; ☎93 412 13 15; www.boqueria.info; La Rambla 91; ☉8am-8.30pm Mon-Sat; ⓂLiceu), one of the best-stocked and most colourful produce markets in Europe. Plaça de la Boqueria, where four side streets meet just north of Liceu metro station, is your chance to walk all over a Miró – the colourful **Mosaïc de Miró** (Map p244) in the pavement, with one tile signed by the artist.

La Rambla dels Caputxins STREET
(La Rambla del Centre; ⓂLiceu) La Rambla dels Caputxins, named after a now nonexistent monastery, runs from Plaça de la Boqueria to Carrer dels Escudellers. The latter street is named after the potters' guild, founded in the 13th century, whose members lived and worked here (their raw materials came principally from Sicily). On the western side of La Rambla is the **Gran Teatre del Liceu**. Further south on the eastern side of La Rambla dels Caputxins is the entrance to the palm-shaded **Plaça Reial**. Below this point, La Rambla gets seedier.

Gran Teatre del Liceu ARTS CENTRE
(Map p244; ☎93 485 99 14; www.liceubarcelona. com; La Rambla dels Caputxins 51-59; admission with/without guide €10/5; ☉guided tour 10am, unguided visits 11.30am, noon, 12.30pm & 1pm; ⓂLiceu) If you can't catch a night at the op-

era, you can still have a look around one of Europe's great opera houses, known to locals as the Liceu.

Built in 1847, the Liceu launched such Catalan stars as Josep (aka José) Carreras and Montserrat Caballé. Fire virtually destroyed it in 1994, but city authorities brought it back to life in 1999. You can take a 20-minute quick turn around the main public areas of the theatre or join a one-hour guided tour.

On the guided tour you are taken to the grand foyer, with its thick pillars and sumptuous chandeliers, and then up the marble staircase to the Saló dels Miralls (Hall of Mirrors). With mirrors, ceiling frescoes, fluted columns and high-and-mighty phrases in praise of the arts, it all exudes a typically neobaroque richness worthy of its 19th-century patrons. You are then led up to the 4th-floor stalls to admire the theatre itself. The tour also takes in a collection of Modernista art, El Cercle del Liceu.

La Rambla de Santa Mònica STREET
(ⓂDrassanes) The final stretch of La Rambla widens out to approach the **Mirador de Colom** overlooking Port Vell. La Rambla here is named after the Convent de Santa Mònica, which once stood on the western flank of the street and has since been converted into an art gallery and cultural centre, the

Centre d'Art Santa Mònica (Map p244; ☎93 567 11 10; www.artssantamonica.cat; La Rambla de Santa Mònica 7; admission free; ◎11am-9pm Tue-Fri, 3-8pm Sat; MDrassanes).

Museu de Cera MUSEUM
(Map p244; ☎93 317 26 49; www.museocerabcn. com; Passatge de la Banca 7; adult/child €15/9; ◎10am-10pm daily Jun-Sep, 10am-1.30pm & 4-7.30pm Mon-Fri, 11am-2pm & 4.30-8.30pm Sat, Sun & holidays Oct-May; MDrassanes) Inside this late-19th-century building, you can stand, sit and lounge about with 300 wax figures. Frankenstein is here, along with Luke Skywalker, Hitler and General Franco. Kids may get a kick out of the museum, but the price tag is steep for often poorly executed representations.

Mirador de Colom VIEWPOINT
(Map p244; ☎93 302 52 24; Plaça del Portal de la Pau; lift adult/child €4/3; ◎8.30am-8.30pm; MDrassanes) High above the swirl of traffic on the roundabout below, Columbus keeps permanent watch, pointing vaguely out to the Mediterranean. Built for the Universal Exhibition in 1888, the monument allows you to zip up 60m in the lift for bird's-eye views back up La Rambla and across the ports of Barcelona.

BARRI GÒTIC

Barcelona's 'Gothic Quarter', east of La Rambla, is a medieval warren of narrow, winding streets, quaint *places* (plazas), and grand mansions and monuments from the city's golden age. Many of its buildings date from the 15th century or earlier. The district is liberally seasoned with restaurants, cafes and bars, so relief from sightseeing is always close by.

TOP
CHOICE **La Catedral** CHURCH
(Map p244; ☎93 342 82 60; www.website.es/cate dralbcn; Plaça de la Seu; admission free, special visit €5, coro admission €2.20; ◎8am-12.45pm & 5.15-8pm Mon-Sat, special visit 1-5pm Mon-Sat, 2-5pm Sun & holidays; MJaume I) Approached from the broad Avinguda de la Catedral, Barcelona's central place of worship presents a magnificent image. The richly decorated main (northwest) facade, laced with gargoyles and the stone intricacies you would expect of northern European Gothic, sets it quite apart from other churches in Barcelona.

The facade was actually added in 1870 (and is receiving a serious round of restoration), although it is based on a 1408 design.

The rest of the building was built between 1298 and 1460.

The interior is a broad, soaring space divided into a central nave and two aisles by lines of elegant, slim pillars. The cathedral was one of the few churches in Barcelona spared by the anarchists in the civil war, so its ornamentation, never overly lavish, is intact.

In the first chapel on the right from the northwest entrance, the main Crucifixion figure above the altar is Sant Crist de Lepant. It is said Don Juan's flagship bore it into battle at Lepanto and that the figure acquired its odd stance by dodging an incoming cannonball. Further along this same wall, past the southwest transept, are the wooden coffins of Count Ramon Berenguer I and his wife Almodis, founders of the 11th-century Romanesque predecessor to the present cathedral.

The Choir, Crypt & Rooftop

In the middle of the central nave is the late-14th-century, exquisitely sculpted timber coro (choir stalls). The coats of arms on the stalls belong to members of the Barcelona chapter of the Order of the Golden Fleece.

A broad staircase before the main altar leads you down to the crypt, which contains the tomb of Santa Eulàlia, one of Barcelona's two patron saints. The reliefs on the alabaster sarcophagus recount some of her tortures and, along the top strip, the removal of her body to its present resting place.

For a bird's-eye view of medieval Barcelona, visit the cathedral's roof and tower by taking the lift (€2.20) from the Capella de les Animes del Purgatori near the northeast transept.

The Cloister & Around

From the southwest transept, exit by the partly Romanesque door (one of the few

BARCELONA SIGHTS

Barri Gòtic & La Rambla

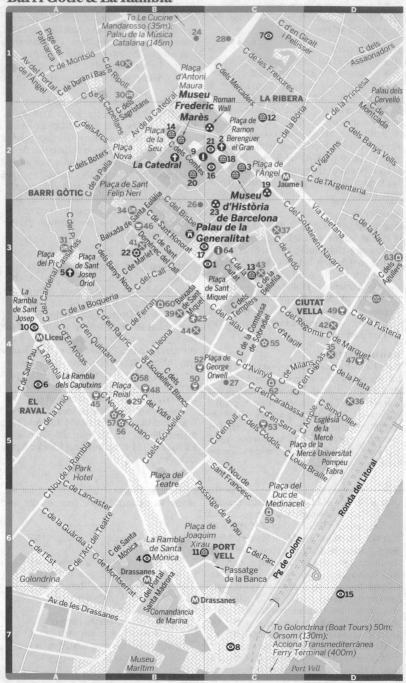

remnants of the present church's predecessor) to the leafy **claustre** (cloister), with its fountains and flock of 13 geese. The geese supposedly represent the age of Santa Eulàlia at the time of her martyrdom and have, generation after generation, been squawking here since medieval days. One of the cloister chapels commemorates 930 priests, monks and nuns martyred during the civil war.

Along the northern flank of the cloister you can enter the **Sala Capitular** (Chapter House; Map p244; admission €2; ☉10am-12.15pm & 5.15-7pm Mon-Sat, 10am-12.45pm & 5.15-7pm Sun). Although it's bathed in rich red carpet and graced with fine timber seating, the few artworks gathered here are of minor interest. Among them figures a Pietat by Bartolomeo Bermejo.

Visiting La Catedral

You may visit La Catedral in one of two ways. In the morning or afternoon, entrance is free and you can opt to visit any combination of the choir stalls, chapter house and roof. To visit all three areas, it costs less (and is less crowded) to enter for the so-called 'special visit' between 1pm and 5pm.

Col·legi de Arquitectes

Across Plaça Nova from La Catedral your eye may be caught by childlike scribblings on the facade of the Col·legi de Arquitectes (Architectural College). It is, in fact, a giant contribution by Picasso from 1962. Representing Mediterranean festivals, it was much ridiculed by the local press when it was unveiled.

Museu Diocesà MUSEUM
(Casa de la Pia Almoina; Map p244; ☎93 315 22 13; www.arqbcn.org; Avinguda de la Catedral 4; adult/child €6/3; ☉10am-2pm & 5-8pm Tue-Sat, 11am-2pm Sun; Ⓜ Jaume I) Housed in a medieval almshouse, the Diocesan Museum has a small exhibit on Gaudí (including a fascinating documentary on his life and philosophy) on the top floor. There's also a sparse collection of medieval religious art usually supplemented by a temporary exhibition or two.

Plaça de Sant Jaume SQUARE
(Map p244; Ⓜ Liceu or Jaume I) In the 2000 or so years since the Romans settled here, the area around this square (often remodelled), which started life as the forum, has been the focus of Barcelona's civic life. Facing each other across it are the **Palau de la Generalitat** (seat of Catalonia's regional government)

Barri Gòtic & La Rambla

on the north side and the *ajuntament* (town hall) to the south.

Palau de la Generalitat   PALACE
(Map p244; www.gencat.cat; Plaça de Sant Jaune; M Liceu or Jaume l) Founded in the early 15th century, the Palau de la Generalitat is open on limited occasions only (the second and fourth weekends of the month, plus open-door days). The most impressive of the ceremonial halls is the Saló de Sant Jordi, named after St George, the region's patron saint. At any time, however, you can admire the original Gothic main entrance on Car-

EL CALL

One of our favourite places in the *ciutat vella* to wander is El Call (pronounced 'kye'), which is the name of the medieval Jewish quarter that flourished here until a tragic pogrom in the 14th century. Today, its narrow lanes hide some surprising sites (including an ancient synagogue unearthed in the 1990s and the fragments of a women's bathhouse inside the basement of the cafe, Caelum). Some of the old town's most unusual shops are here – selling exquisite antiques, handmade leather products, even kosher wine. Its well-concealed dining rooms and candelit bars and cafes make a fine destination in the evening.

El Call (which probably derives from the Hebrew word '*kahal*', meaning 'community') is a tiny area, and a little tricky to find. The boundaries are roughly Carrer del Call, Carrer dels Banys Nous, Baixada de Santa Eulalia and Carrer de Sant Honorat.

rer del Bisbe. To join weekend visits, book on the website.

Ajuntament   ARCHITECTURE
(Map p244; ☑93 402 70 00; www.bcn.cat; Plaça de Sant Jaume; ◷10.30am-1.30pm Sun; MLiceu or Jaume I) Outside, the only feature of the *ajuntament* that's now worthy of note is the disused Gothic entrance on Carrer de la Ciutat. Inside, you can visit the **Saló de Cent**, a fine arched hall created in the 14th century (but since remodelled) for the medieval city council, the Consell de Cent. Guided visits start every 30 minutes; there's one tour in English (at 11am).

Museu d'Idees i Invents de Barcelona   MUSEUM
(Museum of Ideas & Inventions; Map p244; ☑93 332 79 30; www.mibamuseum.com; Carrer de la Ciutat 7; adult/child €7/5; ◷10am-7pm Tue-Sat, to 2pm Sun; MJaume I) The Museum of Ideas and Inventions has a fascinating collection of curiosities from the world of both brilliant and bizarre inventions: mops with microphones on the handle, wristbands that measure UV rays and eyeglasses adjustable to any prescription. There are also metal slides between floors (who needs stairs?) and some rather creatively configured toilets.

Plaça Reial   SQUARE
(Map p250; MLiceu) One of the most photogenic squares in Barcelona, the Plaça Reial is a delightful retreat from the traffic and pedestrian mobs on nearby La Rambla. Numerous eateries, bars and nightspots lie beneath the arcades of 19th-century neoclassical buildings, with a buzz of activity at all hours.

The lamp posts by the central fountain are Antoni Gaudí's first known works in the city.

FREE **Temple Romà d'August**   RUIN
(Map p244; Carrer del Paradis; ◷10am-8pm Tue-Sun; MJaume I) Near Plaça de Sant Jaume, you'll find four mighty columns – remnants of Barcelona's main Roman temple, built in the 1st century AD.

Plaça del Rei   SQUARE
(Map p244) A stone's throw east of the cathedral, Plaça del Rei is the courtyard of the former Palau Reial Major, the palace of the counts of Barcelona and monarchs of Aragón.

Museu d'Història de Barcelona   MUSEUM
(Map p244; ☑93 256 21 00; www.museuhistoria.bcn.cat; Plaça del Rei; adult/child €7/free, from 4pm 1st Sat of month & from 3pm Sun free; ◷10am-7pm Tue-Sat, 10am-8pm Sun; MJaume I) One of Barcelona's most fascinating museums takes you back through the centuries to the very foundations of Roman Barcino. You'll stroll over ruins of the old streets, sewers, laundries and wine- and fish-making factories that flourished here following the town's funding by Emperor Augustus around 10 BC.

Equally impressive is the building itself, which was once part of the Palau Reial Major (Grand Royal Palace) on Plaça del Rei (King's Sq, the former palace's courtyard), among the key locations of medieval princely power in Barcelona. Enter through Casa

TOP FIVE FOR ART LOVERS

» Museu Nacional d'Art de Catalunya (p273)

» Museu Picasso (p249)

» Fundació Joan Miró (p273)

» Macba (Museu d'Art Contemporani de Barcelona) (p249)

» Fundació Antoni Tàpies (p266)

Padellàs (Map p244), just south of Plaça del Rei. Casa Padellàs was built for a 16th-century noble family in Carrer dels Mercaders and moved here, stone by stone, in the 1930s. It has a courtyard typical of Barcelona's late-Gothic and baroque mansions, with a graceful external staircase up to the 1st floor. Today it leads to a restored Roman tower and a section of Roman wall (whose exterior faces Plaça Ramon de Berenguer el Gran), as well as a section of the house set aside for temporary exhibitions.

Below ground is a remarkable walk through about 4 sq km of excavated ruins, complete with sections of a Roman street, baths and shops, and remains of a Visigothic basilica.

You eventually emerge near the Saló del Tinell (Map p244), the banqueting hall of the royal palace and a fine example of Catalan Gothic (built 1359-70).

As you leave the *saló* you come to the 14th-century Capella Reial de Santa Àgata (Map p244), the palace chapel. Inside, all is bare except for the 15th-century altarpiece and the magnificent techumbre (decorated timber ceiling).

Head down the fan-shaped stairs into Plaça del Rei and look up to observe the Mirador del Rei Martí (Map p244) (lookout tower of King Martin), built in 1555, and offering splendid views over the old city.

FREE Palau del Lloctinent   HISTORIC SITE
(Map p244; Carrer dels Comtes; ⊙10am-7pm; MJaume I) This converted 16th-century palace has a peaceful courtyard, covered with an extraordinary sculpted ceiling made to resemble the upturned hull of a boat.

The *palau* was built in the 1550s as the residence of the Spanish viceroy of Catalonia and is now home to a royal archive dating back to the 12th century. The *palau* sometimes hosts exhibitions, often related in some way to the archives.

Museu Frederic Marès   MUSEUM
(Map p244; ☑93 256 35 00; www.museumares.bcn. es; Plaça de Sant Iu 5; admission €4.20, after 3pm Sun & 1st Sun of month free; ⊙10am-7pm Tue-Sat, 11am-8pm Sun; MJaume I) One of the wildest collections of historical curios lies inside this vast medieval complex. Frederic Marès i Deulovol (1893-1991) was a rich sculptor, traveller and obsessive collector. He amassed some impressive medieval Spanish sculptures, huge quantities of which are on display on the ground and 1st floors.

The top two floors hold a mind-boggling array of knick-knacks, from toy soldiers and cribs to scissors and 19th-century playing cards. A room that once served as Marès' study and library is now crammed with sculptures. The shady courtyard houses a pleasant summer cafe (Cafè de l'Estiu).

Roman Wall   RUIN
From Plaça del Rei it's worth a detour to see the two best surviving stretches of Barcelona's Roman walls. One is on the southeast side of Plaça de Ramon Berenguer el Gran, with the Capella Reial de Santa Àgata on top. The other is further south, by the north end of Carrer del Sots-tinent Navarro. They date from the 3rd and 4th centuries, when the Romans rebuilt their walls after the first attacks by Germanic tribes from the north.

Plaça de Sant Josep Oriol   SQUARE
(Map p250; MLiceu) This small plaza, ringed with tranquil cafes and restaurants, is one of the prettiest in the Barri Gòtic.

Looming over the square is the flank of the Església de Santa Maria del Pi (Map p244; ⊙9.30am-1pm & 5-8.30pm; MLiceu), a Gothic church built in the 14th to 16th centuries. The beautiful rose window above its entrance is claimed by some to be the world's biggest. The interior of the church was gutted when leftists ransacked it in the opening months of the civil war in 1936 and most of the stained glass is modern.

Sinagoga Major   SYNAGOGUE
(Map p244; ☑93 317 07 90; www.calldebarcelona. org; Carrer de Marlet 5; admission by suggested donation €2.50; ⊙10.30am-6.30pm Mon-Fri, to 2.30pm Sat & Sun; MLiceu) In the heart of El Call – Barcelona's medieval Jewish quarter – this was one of four synagogues in the medieval city.

Fragments of medieval and Roman-era walls remain in the small vaulted space that you enter from the street. Also remaining are tanners' wells installed in the 15th century. The second chamber has been spruced up for use as a synagogue. A remnant of late-Roman-era wall, given its orientation facing Jerusalem, has led some to speculate that there was a synagogue here even in Roman times.

EL RAVAL

West of La Rambla, Ciutat Vella spreads to Ronda de Sant Antoni, Ronda de Sant Pau and Avinguda del Paral·lel, which together trace the line of Barcelona's 14th-century walls. Known as El Raval, the area contains what remains of one of the city's slums, the dwindling but still seedy red-light zone and drug abusers' haunt of the Barri Xinès, at its south end. It's not nearly as tricky as it once was, but watch your pockets nonetheless.

TOP Macba   MUSEUM

(Museu d'Art Contemporani de Barcelona; Map p250; ☑93 412 08 10; www.macba.cat; Plaça dels Àngels 1; adult/concession €7.50/6; ☺11am-8pm Mon & Wed, to midnight Thu & Fri, 10am-8pm Sat, 10am-3pm Sun & holidays; ⓂUniversitat) Designed by Richard Meier and opened in 1995, the Macba has become the city's foremost contemporary-art centre, with captivating exhibitions for the serious art lover. The permanent collection is on the ground floor and dedicates itself to Spanish and Catalan art from the second half of the 20th century, with works by Antoni Tàpies, Joan Brossa and Miquel Barceló, among others. Temporary visiting exhibitions are almost always challenging and intriguing.

Centre de Cultura Contemporània de Barcelona   CULTURAL BUILDING

(CCCB; Map p250; ☑93 306 41 00; www.cccb.org; Carrer de Montalegre 5; 2 exhibitions adult/child under 16yr/senior & student €6/free/4.50, 1 exhibition €5/free/3, free Wed, 8-10pm Thu, 3-8pm Sun; ☺11am-8pm Tue, Wed & Fri-Sun, 11am-10pm Thu; ⓂUniversitat) In a converted 18th-century

hospice, CCCB is yet another architecturally daring place, with 4500 sq metres of exhibition space dedicated to an avant-garde-leaning program of exhibitions, film cycles and other cultural fare.

FREE Antic Hospital de la Santa Creu   HISTORIC BUILDING

(Map p250; ☑93 270 23 00; www.bnc.cat; Carrer de l'Hospital 56; ☺9am-8pm Mon-Fri, to 2pm Sat; ⓂLiceu) Behind the Mercat de la Boqueria stands what was, in the 15th century, the city's main hospital. The restored Antic Hospital de la Santa Creu (Former Holy Cross Hospital) today houses the Biblioteca de Catalunya (Catalonia's national library). Take a look inside to admire some fine Catalan Gothic construction. The adjacent Institut d'Estudis was, in the 17th century, a house of convalescence. The tile-decorated main cloister is well worth a peek if it's open. The former hospital's Gothic chapel, La Capella (Map p250; ☑93 442 71 71; www.bcn.cat/lacapella; admission free; ☺noon-2pm & 4-8pm Tue-Sat, 11am-2pm Sun & holidays; ⓂLiceu) is worth poking your nose into for the frequent temporary exhibitions.

Palau Güell   PALACE

(Map p250; ☑93 317 39 74; www.palauguell.cat; Carrer Nou de la Rambla 3-5; adult/reduced €10/8; ☺10am-8pm Apr-Sep, 10am-5.30pm Oct-Mar; ⓂDrassanes) Finally reopened in its entirety

BARCELONA SIGHTS

DON'T MISS

MUSEU PICASSO

Museu Picasso (Map p254; ☑93 256 30 00; www.museupicasso.bcn.es; Carrer de Montcada 15-23; adult/senior & child under 16yr/student €11/free/6, temporary exhibitions adult/senior & child under 16yr/student €6/free/2.90, 3-8pm Sun & 1st Sun of month free; ☺10am-8pm Tue-Sun & holidays; ⓂJaume I) Set in five contiguous medieval stone mansions, the celebrated Museu Picasso includes more than 3500 artworks from one of the giants of the art world. This collection is uniquely fascinating, concentrating on Picasso's formative years and several specific moments in his later life, but those interested primarily in cubism may not be satisfied.

A visit starts with sketches and oils from Picasso's earliest years in Málaga and La Coruña – around 1893–95. Some of his self-portraits and the portraits of his father, which date from 1896, are evidence enough of his precocious talent.

The enormous Ciència i Caritat (Science and Charity) showcases his masterful academic techniques of portraiture.

His first consciously themed adventure, the Blue Period, is well covered. His nocturnal blue-tinted views of Terrats de Barcelona (Roofs of Barcelona) and El Foll (The Madman) are cold and cheerless, yet somehow spectrally alive.

Among the later works, done in Cannes in 1957, Las Meninas is a complex technical series of studies on Diego Velázquez' masterpiece of the same name (which hangs in the Prado in Madrid).

El Raval

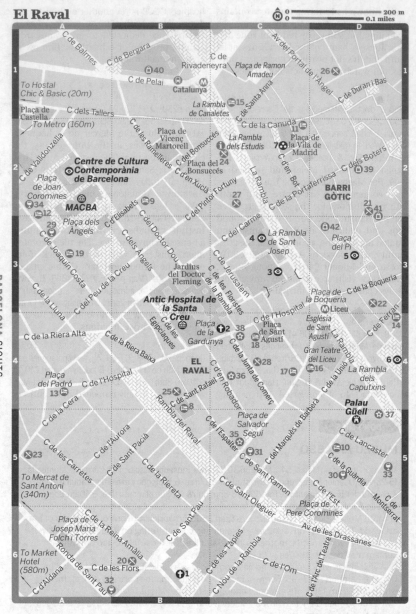

N 0 ――――――― 200 m
0 ――――――― 0.1 miles

in May 2010 after nearly 20 years under refurbishment, this is a magnificent example of the early days of Gaudí's fevered architectural imagination. Gaudí built the palace just off La Rambla in the late 1880s for his wealthy and faithful patron, the industrialist Eusebi Güell. Although a little sombre compared with some of his later whims, it is still a characteristic riot of styles (Gothic, Islamic, art nouveau) and materials. After the civil war, the police occupied it and tortured political prisoners in the basement.

El Raval

Up two floors are the main hall and its annexes; central to the structure is the magnificent music room with its rebuilt organ that is played during opening hours. The hall is a parabolic pyramid – each wall an arch stretching up three floors and coming together to form a dome. The family rooms are sometimes labyrinthine and dotted with piercings of light, or grand, stained-glass affairs. The roof is a mad tumult of tiled mosaics and fanciful design in the building's chimney pots.

Església de Sant Pau   CHURCH

(Map p250; Carrer de Sant Pau 101; ⊗cloister 10am-1pm & 4-7pm Mon-Sat; ▣Paral·lel) The best example of Romanesque architecture in the city is the dainty little cloister of this church. Set in a somewhat dusty garden, the 12th-century church also boasts some Visigothic sculptural detail on the main entrance.

Museu Marítim   MUSEUM

(Map p274; ☑93 342 99 20; www.mmb.cat; Avinguda de les Drassanes; adult/child under 7yr/senior & student €2.50/free/1.25, 3-8pm Sun free; ⊗10am-8pm; ▣Drassanes) The once mighty Reials Drassanes (Royal Shipyards) are now home to the Museu Marítim, a rare work of civil Gothic architectrue that was once the launch pad for medieval fleets. The permanent exhibit is currently closed while the museum remodels.

When it reopens, you'll be able to have a look at the museum's centrepiece, a full-sized replica (made in the 1970s) of Don Juan of Austria's flagship. A clever audio-visual display aboard the vessel brings to life the ghastly existence of the slaves, prisoners and volunteers (!) who, at full steam, could haul this vessel along at 9 knots.

Fishing vessels, old navigation charts, models and dioramas of the Barcelona

DON'T MISS

TOP FIVE MUSEUMS

» Cosmocaixa (p269)

» Museu Marítim (p251)

» Museu d'Història de Barcelona (p247)

» Museu Barbier-Mueller d'Art Pre-Colombí (p252)

» Museu d'Història de Catalunya (p255)

waterfront make up the rest of this engaging museum. Temporary exhibitions, usually maritime-related, are also held.

LA RIBERA
La Ribera is cut off from the Barri Gòtic by noisy Via Laietana, which was driven through the city in 1908. La Ribera, whose name refers to the waterfront that once lay much further inland, was the pumping commercial heart of medieval Barcelona. Its intriguing, narrow streets house major sights, and good bars and restaurants, mainly in El Born around Passeig del Born.

TOP CHOICE **Palau de la Música Catalana**   ARCHITECTURE
(☎902 475485; www.palaumusica.org; Carrer de Sant Francesc de Paula 2; adult/child/student & EU senior €15/free/€7.50; ⊗50min tours every 30 minutes 10am-6pm Easter week & Aug, 10am-3.30pm Sep-Jul; Urquinaona) This concert hall is a high point of Barcelona's Modernista architecture. It's not exactly a symphony, but more a series of crescendos in tile, brick, sculpted stone and stained glass. Built by Domènech i Montaner between 1905 and 1908 for the Orfeo Català musical society, it was conceived as a temple for the Catalan Renaixença (Renaissance).

The palace was built with the help of some of the best Catalan artisans of the time, in the cloister of the former Convent de Sant Francesc, and since 1990 it has undergone several major changes.

The *palau*, like a peacock, shows off much of its splendour on the outside. Take in the principal facade with its mosaics, floral capitals and the sculpture cluster representing Catalan popular music. Wander inside the foyer and restaurant areas to admire the spangled, tiled pillars. Best of all, however, is the richly colourful auditorium upstairs, with its ceiling of blue-and-gold stained glass and shimmering skylight that glows like a tiny sun. To see this, you'll need to join a guided tour or attend a concert.

Museu Barbier-Mueller d'Art Pre-Colombí   MUSEUM
(Map p254; ☎93 310 45 16; www.barbier-mueller. ch; Carrer de Montcada 14; adult/child under 16yr/ senior & student €3.50/free/1.70, 1st Sun of month free; ⊗11am-7pm Tue-Fri, 10am-7pm Sat, 10am-3pm Sun & holidays; Jaume I) The wonderfully illuminated artefacts inside the medieval Palau Nadal are part of the treasure trove of pre-Columbian art collected by Swiss businessman Josef Mueller (who died in 1977) and his son-in-law Jean-Paul Barbier, who directs the Musée Barbier-Mueller in Geneva. Together, the two museums form one of the most prestigious collections of such art in the world.

Disseny Hub   MUSEUM
(Map p254; ☎93 256 23 00; www.dhub-bcn.cat; Carrer de Montcada 12; adult/child under 16yr/senior & student €5/free/3, 3-8pm Sun free; ⊗11am-7pm Tue-Sat, to 8pm Sun, to 3pm holidays; Jaume I) The 13th-century Palau dels Marquesos de Llió is temporary home to part of the city's Disseny (Design) Hub collection of applied arts.

Often the exhibition on the ground floor is free, while the more extensive 1st-floor exhibition is what you pay for. Admission includes entry to this location as well as to the Palau Reial de Pedralbes (p271), which houses the permanent collection. Both will eventually move to a new building in Plaça de les Glòries Catalanes. The building's courtyard, with its cafe-restaurant, makes a delightful stop.

Carrer de Montcada   STREET
(Jaume I) This medieval high street is lined with impressive buildings that have been converted into museums and galleries. The 16th-century **Palau dels Cervelló** (Map p254) houses the prestigious Parisian Galeria Maeght (No 25). The baroque courtyard of the **Palau de Dalmases** (Map p254; ☎93 310 06 73; ⊗8pm-2am Tue-Sat, 6-10pm Sun; Jaume I) at No 20, has a small bar and restaurant, where you can often hear classical concerts and recitals.

Església de Santa Maria del Mar   CHURCH
(Map p254; ☎93 319 05 16; Plaça de Santa Maria del Mar; ⊗9am-1.30pm & 4.30-8pm; Jaume I) At the southwest end of Passeig del Born stands the apse of Barcelona's finest Catalan

Gothic church, Santa Maria del Mar (Our Lady of the Sea). Built in the 14th century with record-breaking speed for the time (it took just 54 years), the church is remarkable for its architectural harmony and simplicity.

Keep an eye out for music recitals, often baroque and classical.

Mercat de Santa Caterina   MARKET
(Map p244; ☑93 319 17 40; www.mercatsantacaterina.net; Avinguda de Francesc Cambó 16; ☉7.30am-2pm Mon, to 3.30pm Tue, Wed & Sat, to 8.30pm Thu & Fri; ⓜJaume I) This extraordinary-looking produce market, built in the 19th century and rebuilt in 2005, has a multicoloured ceramic roof that recalls a bit of Modernista whimsy.

Fragments from the 15th-century Monestir de Santa Caterina are on display in one corner.

Museu de la Xocolata   MUSEUM
(Map p254; ☑93 268 78 78; www.museuxocolata.cat; Plaça de Pons i Clerch; adult/child under 7yr/senior & student €4.30/free/3.65; ☉10am-7pm Mon-Sat, to 3pm Sun & holidays; ⓕ; ⓜJaume I) Inside the former Convent de Sant Agustí, this sweet-lover's haven traces the origins of chocolate, its arrival in Europe and the many myths and images associated with it. Kids and grown-ups can join guided tours or take part in chocolate-making and tasting sessions, especially on weekends. Under the Gothic arches of what remains of the convent's one-time cloister is a pleasant cafe-bar, the Bar del Convent (enter at Carrer del Comerç 36).

Arxiu Fotogràfic de Barcelona   GALLERY
(Map p254; ☑93 256 34 20; www.bcn.cat/arxiu/fotografic; Plaça de Pons i Clerch; admission free; ☉10am-7pm Mon-Sat; ⓜJaume I) Upstairs from the Museu de la Xocolata, the Arxiu Fotogràfic de Barcelona has modest photo exhibitions related to the city.

Museu del Rei de la Magia   MUSEUM
(Map p244; ☑93 319 73 93; www.elreydelamagia.com; Carrer de l'Oli 6; with/without show €12/5; ☉6-8pm Thu, with show 6pm Sat & noon Sun; ⓕ; ⓜJaume I) A timeless curio, this museum is the scene of magic shows, and is home to collections of arcane material dating back to the late 1800s. It's run by a magician couple who also have a magic shop on nearby Carrer de la Princesa.

Parc de la Ciutadella   PARK
(Map p256; Passeig de Picasso; ☉8am-6pm Nov-Feb, to 8pm Oct & Mar, to 9pm Apr-Sep; ⓜArc de Tri-

omf) Come for a stroll, a picnic, a visit to the zoo or to inspect Catalonia's regional parliament, but don't miss a visit to this, the most central green space near the old quarter.

After the War of the Spanish Succession, Felipe V razed a swathe of La Ribera to build a huge fortress (La Ciutadella), designed to keep watch over Barcelona. Much reviled as a symbol of the maligned Bourbon reign, the fort was demolished in 1869 and turned into a park; it later played a starring role in the Universal Exhibition of 1888.

The monumental cascada (Map p256) near the Passeig de Pujades park entrance is a dramatic combination of statuary, rugged rocks, greenery and thundering water. All of it perfectly artificial!

Northwest of the park, Passeig de Lluís Companys is capped by the Modernista Arc de Triomf (Passeig de Lluís Companys; ⓜArc de Triomf), with unusual, Islamic-style brickwork.

Parlament de Catalunya   NOTABLE BUILDING
(Map p256; www.parlament.cat; ☉guided tours 10am-1pm Sat, Sun & holidays) Southeast, in La Ciutadella's former arsenal, is the regional Parlament de Catalunya. Head up the sweeping Escala d'Honor (Stairway of Honour) and through several solemn halls to the Saló de Sessions, the semicircular auditorium where parliament sits. You can join free guided tours. It also opens on 11 September.

Zoo de Barcelona   ZOO
(Map p256; ☑902 457545; www.zoobarcelona.com; Passeig de Picasso & Carrer de Wellington; adult/child under 3yr/senior/child 3-12yr €17/free/8.90/10.20; ☉10am-7pm Jun-Sep, to 6pm mid-Mar–May & Oct, to 5pm Nov–mid-Mar; ⓕ;

ⓘ **MUSEUMS WITHIN A MUSEUM**

One combined ticket, which has no expiry date, can be used to visit all the components of the Museu d'Història de Barcelona. The main centre is the Plaça del Rei complex, where you can discover parts of Roman and medieval Barcelona. It also includes the Museu-Monestir de Pedralbes (p271), the Centre d'Interpretació in Park Güell (p268), the civil-war air-raid shelter, MUHBA Refugi 307 (p272) and the Via Sepulcral Romana (p241).

BARCELONA SIGHTS

La Ribera

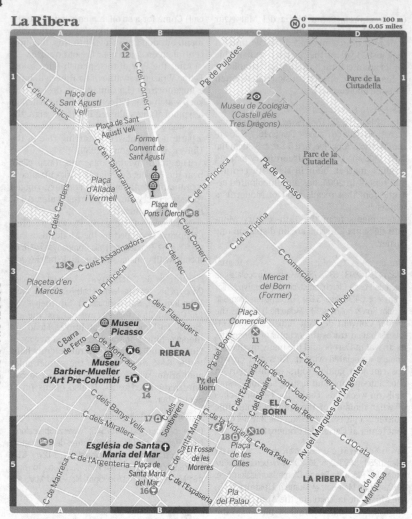

N ⊙ 0 ──────── 100 m
  0 ──────── 0.05 miles

(M) Barceloneta) The zoo is a great day out for kids, with 7500 critters that range from geckos to gorillas – there are more than 400 species, plus picnic areas dotted all around.

PORT VELL

Barcelona's old port at the bottom of La Rambla, to the west of La Barceloneta, was transformed in the 1990s to become a popular leisure zone.

Moll de la Fusta   PROMENADE
Northeast from the quay stretches the promenade Moll de la Fusta. Usually the **Pailebot de Santa Eulàlia** (Map p244; Moll de la Fusta; adult/child incl Museu Marítim €4/free; ⊙noon-7.30pm Tue-Fri, 10am-7pm Sat & Sun; (M)Drassanes), a fully functioning 1918 schooner restored by the Museu Marítim, is moored here for visits, although sometimes it's off on the high seas; admission is free with a Museu Marítim ticket.

Moll d'Espanya   PROMENADE
The heart of the redeveloped harbour is Moll d'Espanya, a former wharf linked to Moll de la Fusta by a wave-shaped footbridge, **Rambla de Mar**, which rotates to let boats enter the marina behind it. At the end of Moll d'Espanya is the glossy **Maremàgnum**

La Ribera

shopping and eating complex, but the major attraction is **L'Aquàrium** (Map p256; ☑93 221 74 74; www.aquariumbcn.com; Moll d'Espanya; adult/child €18/13, dive €300; ⊙9.30am-11pm Jul & Aug, to 9pm Sep-Jun, dive 9.30am-2pm Wed, Fri & Sat; Ⓜ Drassanes), with its 80m-long shark tunnel. Beyond L'Aquàrium is the big-screen **Imax cinema** (☑93 225 11 11; www.imaxportvell. com; Moll d'Espanya).

LA BARCELONETA & THE WATERFRONT

La Barceloneta, laid out in the 18th century and subsequently heavily overdeveloped, was once a factory workers' and fishermen's quarter. Today the smokestacks are gone (as are most of the fishing families), though an authentic, ungentrified air still permeates these narrow gridlike streets. You'll find some excellent seafood restaurants here and a few bohemianesque neighbourhood bars. Barceloneta meets the sea at the city's sparkling new waterfront, with a beachside promenade extending some 4.5km past artificial beaches, parks and new high-rises to El Fòrum.

Museu d'Història de Catalunya   MUSEUM
(Museum of Catalonian History; Map p256; ☑93 225 47 00; www.mhcat.net; Plaça de Pau Vila 3; adult/child permanent exhibition only €4/3, permanent & temporary exhibitions €5/4, 1st Sun of month free; ⊙10am-7pm Tue & Thu-Sat, to 8pm Wed, to 2.30pm Sun; Ⓜ Barceloneta) Spanning over 2000 years of Catalan history, this harbourfront museum takes you from the Stone Age through to the early 1980s, with dioramas, artefacts, videos, models and audio recordings helping to conjure up the past.

See how the Romans lived, listen to Arab poetry from the time of the Muslim occupation of the city, peer into the dwelling of a Dark Ages family in the Pyrenees and descend into a civil-war air-raid shelter. Afterwards, you can enjoy a meal with fine views at the first-rate rooftop restaurant and cafe.

Passeig Marítim de la Barceloneta   PROMENADE
(Ⓜ Barceloneta or Ciutadella Vila Olímpica) On La Barceloneta's seaward side are the first of Barcelona's **beaches**, which are popular on summer weekends. The pleasant Passeig Marítim de la Barceloneta, a 1.25km promenade from La Barceloneta to Port Olímpic, is a haunt for strollers, runners and cyclists.

Port Olímpic   MARINA
(Map p256; Ⓜ Ciutadella Vila Olímpica) A busy marina built for the Olympic sailing events, Port Olímpic is surrounded by bars and restaurants. An eye-catcher on the approach from La Barceloneta is Frank Gehry's giant copper *Peix* (Fish) sculpture. The area behind Port Olímpic, dominated by twin-tower blocks, is the former Vila Olímpica living quarters for the Olympic competitors, which were later sold off as apartments.

El Fòrum   NEIGHBOURHOOD
(☑93 356 10 50; Ⓜ El Maresme Fòrum) Where before there was wasteland, half-abandoned

La Barcelonета

N 0 ——————— 200 m
0 ——————— 0.1 miles

To Teatre Nacional de Catalunya (1.1km);
Els Encants Vells (1.6km)

25
To Razzmatazz
(1km)

C de Joan Miró

C de la Marina

C de Salvador Espriu

Av del Litoral

C de Wellington

C de Villena

1

2

3

Pg de Picasso

Ciutadella
Vila
Olímpica

C de Ramon Trias Fargas

To Xiringuito
D'Escribà (680m);
Base Nautica
Municipal (1.1km)

Torre
Mapfre

5

7
4
21
22
24

10

C de Trelawny

Av del Marquès de l'Argentera

Pg de Circumval·lació

Ronda del Litoral

C d'Ocata

C del Doctor Aiguader

C del Gasòmetre

Platja de la
Barceloneta

Barceloneta

Parc de la
Barceloneta

C de Balboa

C de Ginebra

C Pizarro

C Carbonell

Plaça
de Pau
Vila

19

12

15

C de la Maquinista

LA BARCELONETA

Pg Marítim de la Barceloneta

Museu
d'Història de
Catalunya

C de
Ballard

Plaça de
la Font

Plaça de la
Barceloneta

C de Sant
Carles

23

17

Plaça del
Poeta
Bosca

20

Platja
de Sant
Sebastià

Marina

C de l'Almirall Cervera

L'Aquàrium

16

14

C del Almirall
Aixada

C del Mar

11

C del Judici

8

Plaça
del
Mar

Pg de Joan de Borbó

Moll de Balears

Port
Vell

18

9

Platja
de Sant
Miquel

Pg Escullera

MEDITERRANEAN
SEA

13

Moll de la Barceloneta

Moll d'Espanya

1
2
3
6

A B C D

La Barceloneta

factories and a huge sewage-treatment plant in the city's northeast corner, there are now high-rise apartment blocks, luxury hotels, a marina (Port Fòrum), a shopping mall and a conference centre.

The most striking element is the eerily blue, triangular *2001: A Space Odyssey*–style Edifici Fòrum building by Swiss architects Herzog & de Meuron. The navy-blue raised facades look like sheer cliff faces, with angular crags cut into them as if by divine laser. Grand strips of mirror create fragmented reflections of the sky. Inside the Museu Blau (Blue Museum; ☑93 256 60 02; Parc del Fòrum; adult/child €6/2.70; ⊗10am-7pm Tue-Fri, to 8pm Sat & Sun; ⓂEl Maresme Fòrum) provides interactive displays on natural history.

L'EIXAMPLE

Stretching north, east and west of Plaça de Catalunya, L'Eixample (the Extension) was Barcelona's 19th-century answer to overcrowding in the medieval city.

Work on it began in 1869, following a design by Ildefons Cerdà, who specified a grid of wide streets with plazas that were formed by their cut-off corners. Cerdà also planned numerous public green spaces, but few survived the ensuing scramble for real estate.

The development of L'Eixample coincided with the city's Modernisme period and so it's home to many Modernista creations. Apart from La Sagrada Família, the principal ones are clustered on or near L'Eixample's main avenue, Passeig de Gràcia.

Along the area's grid of straight streets are the majority of the city's most expensive shops and hotels, plus a range of eateries, bars and clubs.

TOP
CHOICE **La Sagrada Família** CHURCH
(☑93 207 30 31; www.sagradafamilia.org; Carrer de Mallorca 401; adult/child under 10yr/senior & student €13/free/11; ⊗9am-8pm Apr-Sep, to 6pm Oct-Mar; ⓂSagrada Família) If you have time for only one sightseeing outing, this should be it. La Sagrada Família inspires awe by its sheer verticality, and in the manner of the medieval cathedrals it emulates, it's still under construction after more than 100 years. When completed, the highest tower will be more than half as high again as those that stand today.

Unfinished it may be, but it attracts nearly three million visitors a year. Pope Benedict XVI consecrated the church in a huge ceremony in 2010.

The Temple Expiatori de la Sagrada Família (Expiatory Temple of the Holy Family) was Gaudí's all-consuming obsession in the latter half of his life. He envisioned a temple 95m long and 60m wide, able to seat 13,000 people, with a central tower 170m high above the transept (representing Christ) and another 17 of 100m or more.

La Sagrada Família

A TIMELINE

1882 Francesc del Villar is commissioned to construct a neo-Gothic church.

1883 Antoni Gaudí takes over as chief architect, and plans a far more ambitious church to hold 13,000 faithful.

1926 Death of Gaudí; work continues under Domènec Sugrañes. Much of the **apse 1** and **Nativity Facade 2** is complete.

1930 Bell towers 3 of the Nativity Facade completed.

1936 Construction is interrupted by Spanish Civil War; anarchists destroy Gaudí's plans.

1939-40 Architect Francesc de Paula Quintana i Vidal restores the crypt and meticulously reassembles many of Gaudí's lost models, some of which can be seen in the **museum 4**.

1976 Completion of **Passion Facade 5**.

1986-2006 Sculptor Josep Subirachs adds sculptural details to the Passion Facade including the panels telling the story of Christ's last days, amid much criticism for employing a style far removed from what was thought typical of Gaudí.

2000 Central nave vault 6 completed.

2010 Church completely roofed over; Pope Benedict XVI consecrates the church; work begins on a high-speed rail tunnel that will pass beneath the church's **Glory Facade 7**.

2020-40 Projected completion date.

TOP TIPS

» **Light** The best light through the stained-glass windows of the Passion Facade bursts through into the heart of the church in the late afternoon

» **Time** Visit at opening time on weekdays to avoid the worst of the crowds

» **Views** Head up the Nativity Facade bell towers for the views, as long queues generally await at the Passion Facade towers

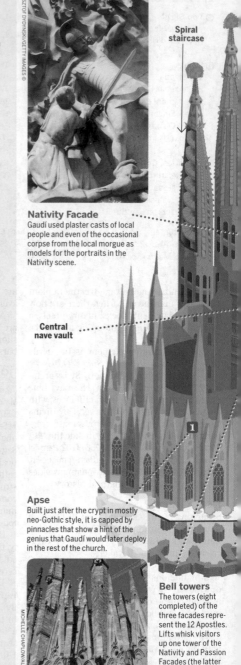

KRZYSZTOF DYDYNSKI/GETTY IMAGES ©

Spiral staircase

Nativity Facade
Gaudí used plaster casts of local people and even of the occasional corpse from the local morgue as models for the portraits in the Nativity scene.

Central nave vault

Apse
Built just after the crypt in mostly neo-Gothic style, it is capped by pinnacles that show a hint of the genius that Gaudí would later deploy in the rest of the church.

MICHELLE CHAPLOW/ALAMY ©

Bell towers
The towers (eight completed) of the three facades represent the 12 Apostles. Lifts whisk visitors up one tower of the Nativity and Passion Facades (the latter gets longer queues) for fine views.

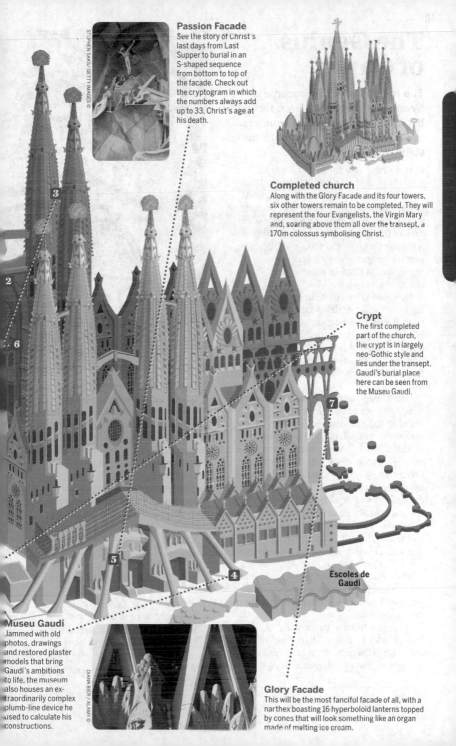

Passion Facade
See the story of Christ's last days from Last Supper to burial in an S-shaped sequence from bottom to top of the facade. Check out the cryptogram in which the numbers always add up to 33, Christ's age at his death.

Completed church
Along with the Glory Facade and its four towers, six other towers remain to be completed. They will represent the four Evangelists, the Virgin Mary and, soaring above them all over the transept, a 170m colossus symbolising Christ.

Crypt
The first completed part of the church, the crypt is in largely neo-Gothic style and lies under the transept. Gaudí's burial place here can be seen from the Museu Gaudí.

Escoles de Gaudí

Museu Gaudí
Jammed with old photos, drawings and restored plaster models that bring Gaudí's ambitions to life, the museum also houses an extraordinarily complex plumb-line device he used to calculate his constructions.

Glory Facade
This will be the most fanciful facade of all, with a narthex boasting 16 hyperboloid lanterns topped by cones that will look something like an organ made of melting ice cream.

STEPHEN SAKS/GETTY IMAGES ©

DIANA BIER/ALAMY ©

The Genius of Gaudí

The name Gaudí has become a byword for Barcelona and, through his unique architectural wonders, one of the principal magnets for visitors to the city.

Born in Reus and initially trained in metalwork, Antoni Gaudí i Cornet (1852–1926) personifies, and largely transcends, the Modernisme movement that brought a thunderclap of innovative greatness to turn-of-the-century Barcelona. Gaudí was a devout Catholic and Catalan nationalist, and his creations were a conscious expression of Catalan identity and, in some cases, of great piety.

He devoted much of the latter part of his life to what remains Barcelona's call sign: the unfinished Sagrada Família. His inspiration in the first instance was Gothic, but he also sought to emulate the harmony he observed in nature, eschewing the straight line and favouring curvaceous forms.

Gaudí used complex string models weighted with plumb lines to make his calculations. You can see examples in the upstairs mini-museum in La Pedrera.

The architect's work is an earthy appeal to sinewy movement, but often with a dreamlike or surreal quality. The private apartment house Casa Batlló is a fine example in which all appears a riot of the unnaturally natural – or the naturally unnatural. Not only are straight lines eliminated, but the lines between real and unreal, sober and dream-drunk, good sense and play are all blurred. Depending on how you look at the facade, you might see St George defeating a dragon, or a series of fleshless sea monsters straining out of the wall.

He seems to have particularly enjoyed himself with rooftops. At La Pedrera and Palau Güell, in particular, he created all sorts of fantastical, multicoloured tile figures as chimney pots, looking like anything from *Alice in Wonderland* mushrooms to *Star Wars* imperial troopers.

Much like his work in progress, La Sagrada Família, Gaudí's story is far from over. In March 2000 the Vatican decided to proceed with the examination of the case for canonising him, and pilgrims already stop by the crypt to pay him homage. One of the key sculptors at work on the church, the Japanese Etsuro Sotoo, converted to Catholicism because of his passion for Gaudí.

GAUDÍ'S BEST

» **La Sagrada Família** (p257), a symphony of religious devotion

» **La Pedrera** (p265), dubbed 'the Quarry' because of its flowing facade

» **Casa Batlló** (p265), a fairy-tale dragon

» **Park Güell** (p268), a park full of Modernista twists

» **Palau Güell** (p249), one of Gaudí's earliest commissions

---

Clockwise from top left
1. Casa Batlló (p265) 2. La Pedrera (p265) 3. Palau Güell (p249)

L'Eixample

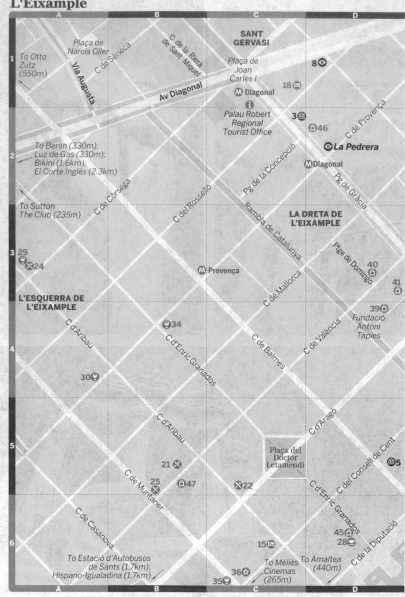

The completed sections and museum may be explored at leisure. Fifty-minute guided tours (€4) are offered. Alternatively, pick up an audio tour (€4), for which you need ID. Enter from Carrer de Sardenya and Carrer de la Marina. Once inside, €2.50 will get you into lifts that rise up inside towers in the Nativity and Passion Facades. Buy tickets online and go early to beat the crowds.

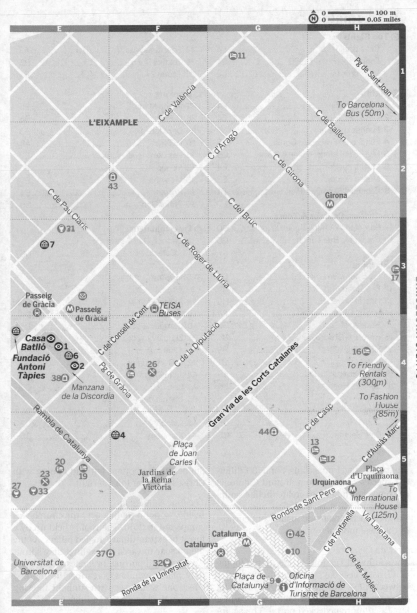

Nativity Facade

The Nativity Facade is the artistic pinnacle of the building, mostly created under Gaudí's personal supervision. The three-part portal portrays Christ's birth and childhood.

Three sections of the portal represent, from left to right, Hope, Charity and Faith. Among the forest of sculpture on the Charity portal you can see, low down, the manger surrounded by an ox, an ass, the shepherds and

L'Eixample

kings, and angel musicians. Some 30 different species of plant from around Catalonia are reproduced here; to create lifelike sculptures, Gaudí used real animals and people – and the occasional one made from corpses in the local morgue!

Passion Facade

The southwest Passion Facade, on the theme of Christ's last days and death, was built between 1954 and 1978 based on surviving drawings by Gaudí, with four towers and a large, sculpture-bedecked portal. The sculptor, Josep Subirachs, worked on its decoration from 1986 to 2006. He did not attempt to imitate Gaudí, rather producing angular, controversial images of his own. The main series of sculptures, on three levels, are in an S-shaped sequence, starting with the Last Supper at the bottom left and ending with Christ's burial at the top right.

The Interior & Apse

Inside, work on roofing over the church was completed in 2010. The roof is held up by a forest of extraordinary angled pillars. As the pillars soar towards the ceiling, they sprout a web of supporting branches, with carefully placed windows creating the mottled effect one would see with sunlight filtering through the branches of a thick forest.

Glory Facade

The Glory Facade is under construction and will, like the others, be crowned by four towers – the total of 12 representing the Twelve Apostles. Gaudí wanted it to be the most magnificent facade of the church. Further decoration will make the whole building a microcosmic symbol of the Christian church, with Christ represented by a massive 170m central tower above the transept, and the five remaining planned towers symbolising the Virgin Mary and the four evangelists.

Museu Gaudí

Open the same times as the church, the Museu Gaudí, below ground level, includes interesting material on Gaudí's life and other works, as well as models and photos of La Sagrada Família. A side hall leads to a viewing point above the simple crypt where Gaudí is buried.

Casa Batlló   ARCHITECTURE
(Map p262; ☎93 216 03 06; www.casabatllo.es; Passeig de Gràcia 43; adult/child under 7yr/student, child 7-18yr & senior €18.15/free/14.55; ⊙9am-8pm; ⓂPasseig de Gràcia) One of the strangest residential buildings in Europe, this is Gaudí at his hallucinogenic best. The facade, sprinkled with bits of blue, mauve and green tiles and studded with wave-shaped window frames and balconies, rises to an uneven blue-tiled roof with a solitary tower.

Locals know Casa Batlló variously as the *casa dels ossos* (house of bones) or *casa del drac* (house of the dragon). It's easy enough to see why. The balconies look like the bony jaws of some strange beast and the roof represents Sant Jordi (St George) and the dragon. Even the roof was built to look like the shape of an animal's back, with shiny scales – the 'spine' changes colour as you walk around. If you stare long enough at the building, it seems almost to be a living being.

Inside, Gaudí eschewed the straight line, and so the staircase wafts you up to the 1st (main) floor, where the salon looks on to Passeig de Gràcia. Everything swirls: the ceiling is twisted into a vortex around its sun-like lamp; the doors, window and skylights are dreamy waves of wood and coloured glass. Twisting, tiled chimney pots add a surreal touch to the roof.

FREE Casa Amatller   ARCHITECTURE
(Map p262; ☎93 487 72 17; www.amatller.org; Passeig de Gràcia 41; ⊙10am-8pm Mon-Sat, to 3pm Sun, guided tour in English noon Fri, in Catalan & Spanish noon Wed; ⓂPasseig de Gràcia) One of Puig i Cadafalch's most striking bits of Modernista fantasy, Casa Amatller combines Gothic window frames with a stepped gable borrowed from Dutch urban architecture. But the busts and reliefs of dragons, knights

APPLE OF DISCORD

Casa Batlló is the centrepiece of the so-called Manzana de la Discordia (Apple of Discord – in a play on words, *manzana* means both city block and apple), along with Casa Lleó Morera and Casa Amatller, on the western side of Passeig de Gràcia between Carrer del Consell de Cent and Carrer d'Aragó. All three buildings were completed between 1898 and 1906. According to Greek myth, the original Apple of Discord was tossed onto Mt Olympus by Eris (Discord) with orders that it be given to the most beautiful goddess, sparking jealousies that helped start the Trojan War

and other characters dripping off the main facade are pure caprice.

The pillared foyer and staircase lit by stained glass are like the inside of some romantic castle. Renovation due for completion in 2013 will see the 1st floor converted into a museum with period pieces, while the 2nd floor will house the Institut Amatller d'Art Hispanic (Amatller Institute of Hispanic Art).

Casa Lleó Morera   ARCHITECTURE
(Map p262; Passeig de Gràcia 35; ⓂPasseig de Gràcia) Domènech i Montaner's 1905 contribution to the Manzana de la Discordia has Modernista carving outside and a bright, tiled lobby with floral motifs.

Museu del Perfum   MUSEUM
(Map p262; ☎93 216 01 21; www.museudelperfum.com; Passeig de Gràcia 39; adult/student & senior €5/3; ⊙10.30am-1.30pm & 4.30-8pm Mon-Fri, 11am-2pm Sat; ⓂPasseig de Gràcia) Housed in the back of the Regia perfume store, this museum contains everything from ancient Egyptian and Roman (the latter mostly from the 1st to 3rd centuries AD) scent receptacles to classic eau-de-cologne bottles – all in all, some 5000 bottles of infinite shapes, sizes and histories.

La Pedrera   ARCHITECTURE
(Casa Milà; Map p262; ☎902 400973; www.fundaciocaixacatalunya.es; Carrer de Provença 261-265; adult/student/child €15/13.50/7.50; ⊙9am-8pm Mar-Oct, to 6.30pm Nov-Feb; ⓂDiagonal) This undulating beast is another madcap Gaudí masterpiece, built in 1905–10 as a combined

THE MODERNISTAS' MISSION

Antoni Gaudí (1852–1926), known above all for La Sagrada Família (p257), was just one, albeit the most imaginative, of a generation of inventive architects who left an indelible mark on Barcelona between 1880 and the 1920s. They were called the Modernistas.

The local offshoot of the Europe-wide phenomenon of art nouveau, Modernisme was characterised by its taste for sinuous, flowing lines and (for the time) adventurous combinations of materials like tile, glass, brick, iron and steel. But Barcelona's Modernistas were also inspired by an astonishing variety of other styles: Gothic and Islamic, Renaissance and Romanesque, Byzantine and baroque.

Gaudí and co were trying to create a specifically Catalan architecture, often looking back to Catalonia's medieval golden age for inspiration. It is no coincidence that Gaudí and the two other leading Modernista architects, Lluís Domènech i Montaner (1850–1923) and Josep Puig i Cadafalch (1867–1957), were prominent Catalan nationalists.

L'Eixample, where most of Barcelona's new building was happening at the time, is home to the bulk of the Modernistas' creations. Others in the city include Gaudí's Palau Güell (p249) and Park Güell (p268); Domènech i Montaner's Palau de la Música Catalana (p252), Castell dels Tres Dragons (Map p254) and the Hotel España restaurant (Map p250; ☑93 318 17 58; www.hotelespanya.com; Carrer de Sant Pau 9-11; s €100, d €125-155; ❋; Ⓜ Liceu); and Puig i Cadafalch's Els Quatre Gats restaurant (Map p250; ☑93 302 41 40; Carrer de Montsió 3; meals: €30-€40; ☺8am-2am; Ⓜ Urquinaona).

apartment and office block. Formally called Casa Milà, after the businessman who commissioned it, it is better known as La Pedrera (the Quarry) because of its uneven grey stone facade, which ripples around the corner of Carrer de Provença.

The top-floor apartment, attic and roof together make up the **Espai Gaudí** (Gaudí Space). The roof is the most extraordinary element, with its giant chimney pots looking like multicoloured medieval knights. One floor below, you can appreciate Gaudí's taste for parabolic arches in a modest **museum** dedicated to his work.

The next floor down is the **apartment** (El Pis de la Pedrera), an elegantly furnished home, done up in the style a well-to-do family might have enjoyed in the early 20th century. Sensuous curves and whimsical flourishes are present throughout.

On hot August evenings, La Pedrera usually stages a series of brief concerts on the roof.

Fundació Antoni Tàpies GALLERY
(Map p262; ☑93 487 03 15; www.fundaciotapies. org; Carrer d'Aragó 255; adult/child under 16yr €7/5.60; ☺10am-8pm Tue-Sun; Ⓜ Passeig de Gràcia) The Fundació Antoni Tàpies is both a pioneering Modernista building (completed in 1885) and the major collection of the leading 20th-century Catalan artist, Antoni Tàpies. A man known for his esoteric work, Tàpies died in 2012, leaving behind a pow-

erful range of paintings and a foundation intended to promote contemporary artists.

The building, designed by Domènech i Montaner, combines a brick-covered iron frame with Islamic-inspired decoration. Tàpies crowned it with the meanderings of his own mind, a work called *Núvol i Cadira* (Cloud and Chair) that spirals above the building like a storm.

Inside, the collection spans the arc of Tàpies' creations (with more than 800 works) and contributions from other contemporary artists. In the main exhibition area (level 1, upstairs) you can see an ever-changing selection of around 20 of Tàpies' works, from early self-portraits of the 1940s to grand items like *Jersei Negre* (Black Jumper; 2008). Level 2 hosts a small space for temporary exhibitions. Rotating exhibitions take place in the basement levels.

Museu del Modernisme Català MUSEUM
(Map p262; ☑93 272 28 96; www.mmcat.cat; Carrer de Balmes 48; adult/child under 5yr/child 5-16yr/ student €10/free/5/7; ☺10am-8pm Mon-Sat, to 3pm Sun; Ⓜ Passeig de Gràcia) Housed in a Modernista building, the ground floor seems like a big Modernista furniture showroom. Several items by Antoni Gaudí, including chairs from Casa Batlló and a mirror from Casa Calvet, are supplemented by items from his lesser-known contemporaries, including some typically whimsical, mock medieval pieces by Josep Puig i Cadafalch.

The basement, showing off Modernista traits like mosaic-coated pillars, bare brick vaults and metal columns, is lined with Modernista art, including paintings by Ramon Casas and Santiago Rusiñol, and statues by Josep Llimona and Eusebi Arnau.

FREE Palau del Baró Quadras   ARCHITECTURE
(Casa Asia; Map p262; ☑93 368 08 36; www.casaasia.es; Avinguda Diagonal 373; ⊗10am-8pm Tue-Sat, to 2pm Sun; ⓂDiagonal) Puig i Cadafalch designed Palau del Baró Quadras (built 1902–06) in an exuberant Gothic-inspired style. The main facade is its most intriguing, with a soaring, glassed-in gallery. If you take a closer look at the gargoyles and reliefs, the pair of toothy fish and the sword-wielding knight are clearly the same artistic signature as the architect behind Casa Amatller.

Decor inside is eclectic, but dominated by Middle Eastern and Oriental themes. The setting is appropriate for its occupant: Casa Asia is a cultural centre celebrating the relationship between Spain and the Asia-Pacific region. Visiting the varied temporary exhibitions (mostly on the 2nd floor) allows you to get a good look inside this intriguing building. Take in the views from the roof terrace.

Hospital de la Santa Creu
i de Sant Pau   ARCHITECTURE
(☑93 317 76 52; www.rutadelmodernisme.com; Carrer de Cartagena 167; guided tour adult/senior & student €10/5; ⊗tours 10am, 11am, noon & 1pm in English, others in Catalan, French & Spanish; ⓂHospital de Sant Pau) Domènech i Montaner outdid himself as architect and philanthropist with this Modernista masterpiece, long considered one of the city's most important hospitals. The complex, including 16 pavilions – together with the Palau de la Música Catalana, a joint World Heritage site – is lavishly decorated and each pavilion is unique.

The hospital facilities have been transferred to a new complex on the premises, freeing up the century-old structures, which are being restored to their former glory in a plan to convert the complex into an international centre on the Mediterranean.

Guided tours are the only way to get inside this unique site – but the building might one day open up for more regular visits.

Torre Agbar   ARCHITECTURE
(☑93 342 21 29; www.torreagbar.com; Avinguda Diagonal 225; ⓂGlòries) Barcelona's very own cucumber-shaped tower, Jean Nouvel's luminous Torre Agbar (which houses the city water company's headquarters), is the most daring addition to Barcelona's skyline since the first towers of La Sagrada Família went up. Completed in 2005, it shimmers at night in shades of midnight blue and lipstick red. Unfortunately, you can only enter the foyer on the ground floor, frequently used to host temporary exhibitions.

Fundación Francisco Godia   GALLERY
(Map p262; ☑93 272 31 80; www.fundacionfgodia.org; Carrer de la Diputació 250; adult/child under 5yr/student €6.50/free/3.50; ⊗10am-8pm Mon & Wed-Sun; ⓂPasseig de Gràcia) An intriguing mix of medieval art, ceramics and modern paintings make up this varied private collection.

Housed in Casa Garriga Nogués, this is a stunning, carefully restored Modernista residence originally built for a rich banking family by Enric Sagnier in 1902–05.

Museu Egipci   MUSEUM
(Map p262; ☑93 488 01 88; www.museuegipci.com; Carrer de València 284; adult/senior & student €11/8; ⊗10am-8pm Mon-Sat, to 2pm Sun; ⓂPasseig de Gràcia) Hotel magnate Jordi Clos has spent much of his life collecting ancient Egyptian artefacts, brought together in this private museum. It's divided into different thematic areas (the Pharaoh, religion, funerary practices, mummification, crafts etc) and boasts an interesting variety of exhibits.

Highlights include a fabulous golden ring from around the 7th century BC, ceramics and a bed made of wood and leather. On the rooftop terrace is a pleasant cafe.

Fundació Suñol   GALLERY
(Map p262; ☑93 496 10 32; www.fundaciosunol.org; Passeig de Gràcia 98; adult/concession €5/3; ⊗4-8pm Mon-Sat; ⓂDiagonal) Housing yet another of Barcelona's intriguing private collections,

---

DEADLY SERIOUS

Museu de Carrosses Fúnebres
(☑934 841920; www.cbsa.cat; Mare de Déu de Port 56-58; admission free; ⊗10am-1pm & 4-6pm Mon-Fri, 10am-1pm Sat, Sun & holidays) is probably the weirdest museum in town. This hearse museum is the place to come if you want to see how the great and good have been transported to their final resting places in Barcelona since the 18th century. Solemn, wigged mannequins and life-size model horses accompany a series of dark hearses.

the Fundació Suñol has a varied collection of mostly 20th-century art. Rotating exhibits offer anything from Man Ray's photography to sculptures by Alberto Giacometti and a hefty band of Spanish artists, including Picasso and Plensa.

GRÀCIA

Gràcia lies north of L'Eixample. Once a separate village and, in the 19th century, an industrial district famous for its Republican and liberal ideas, it became fashionable among radical and Bohemian types in the 1960s and '70s. Now more sedate and gentrified, it retains a slightly rebellious air (witness all the Catalan nationalist youth graffiti and the occasional surviving squat), a mixed-class population (with a high rate of students, both local and from abroad) and a very Catalan feel. Gràcia's interest lies in the atmosphere of its narrow streets, small plazas and its multitude of bars and restaurants.

The liveliest plazas are Plaça del Sol, Plaça de la Vila de Gràcia with its clock tower (a favourite meeting place) and Plaça de la Virreina with the 17th-century **Església de Sant Joan** (Map p268). Three blocks northeast of Plaça de la Vila de Gràcia, there's a big covered market, the **Mercat de l'Abaceria** (Map p262; Travessera de Gràcia 186; ⏰7am-2.30pm & 5.30-8pm Mon-Sat; Ⓜ Fontana). West of Gràcia's main street, Carrer Gran de Gràcia (from Fontana metro station, walk a block north to Carrer de les Carolines and turn left), seek out an early Gaudí house, the turreted, vaguely Mudéjar **Casa Vicens** (www.casavicens.es; Carrer de les Carolines 22; ⓇFGC Plaça Molina); it's not open to the public.

TOP CHOICE Park Güell   PARK
(☑93 413 24 00; Carrer d'Olot 7; admission free; ⏰10am-9pm Jun-Sep, 10am-8pm Apr, May & Oct, 10am-7pm Mar & Nov, 10am-6pm Dec-Feb; ☒24, Ⓜ Lesseps or Vallcarca) North of Gràcia and about 4km from Plaça de Catalunya, Park Güell is where Gaudí turned his hand to landscape gardening. It's a strange, enchanting place where his passion for natural forms really took flight – to the point where the artificial almost seems more natural than the natural.

Park Güell originated in 1900, when Count Eusebi Güell bought a tree-covered hillside (then outside Barcelona) and hired Gaudí to create a miniature city of houses for the wealthy in landscaped grounds. The project was a commercial flop and was abandoned in 1914 – but not before Gaudí

Gràcia

⊙ **Sights**
1 Església de Sant Joan...........................A1

⊟ **Sleeping**
2 Hotel Casa Fuster A4

⊗ **Eating**
3 Envalira A2
4 La Nena A2
5 O'Gràcia! A2
6 Sureny A2

⊙ **Drinking**
7 La Cigale B2
8 Le Journal A3
9 Musical Maria A3
10 Raïm B3
11 Sabor A Cuba A3

⊙ **Entertainment**
12 Verdi...A1
13 Verdi Park...A1

had created 3km of roads and walks, steps, a plaza and two gatehouses.

Pavelló de Consergeria

Just inside the main entrance on Carrer d'Olot, immediately recognisable by the two Hansel-and-Gretel gatehouses, is the park's newly refurbished Centre d'Interpretaciò, in the Pavelló de Consergeria, which is a typically curvaceous former porter's home that hosts a display on Gaudí's building methods and the history of the park. There are nice views from the top floor.

Sala Hipóstila

The steps up from the entrance, which is guarded by a mosaic dragon-lizard, lead to the Sala Hipóstila, a forest of 88 stone columns (some of them leaning at an angle), intended as a market. On top of the Sala Hipóstila is a broad open space; its highlight is the **Banc de Trencadís**, a tiled bench curving sinuously around its perimeter and designed by Gaudí's right-hand man, Josep Maria Jujol (1879–1949).

Casa-Museu Gaudí

The spired house to the right of Sala Hipóstila is the **Casa-Museu Gaudí** (www.casamuseu gaudi.org; adult/senior & student €5.50/4.50; ⊙10am-8pm), where Gaudí lived for most of his last 20 years (1906–26). It contains furniture by him and other memorabilia.

TIBIDABO

Tibidabo (512m) is the highest hill in the wooded range that forms the backdrop to Barcelona and is a good place for some fresh air and fine views. It gets its name from the devil, who, trying to tempt Christ, took him to a high place and said, in the Latin version: '*Haec omnia tibi dabo si cadens adoraberis me*' ('All this I will give you, if you will fall down and worship me').

Cosmocaixa   MUSEUM

(Museu de la Ciència; ☎93 212 60 50; www.funda cio.lacaixa.es; Carrer de Isaac Newton 26; adult/child €3/2; ⊙10am-8pm Tue-Sun; ☐60, ☐FGC Avinguda Tibidabo) Kids (and kids at heart) are fascinated by displays at this interactive science museum. The highlight is the re-creation of 1 sq km of Amazon rainforest (Bosc Inundat), complete with anacondas, poisonous frogs and caymans.

Other attractions explore the worlds of geology, outer space (via a planetarium), physics and living organisms.

Outside, there's a nice stroll through the extensive Plaça de la Ciència, whose modest garden flourishes with Mediterranean flora.

Parc d'Atraccions   AMUSEMENT PARK

(☎93 211 79 42; www.tibidabo.cat; Plaça de Tibidabo 3-4; adult/child €25.20/9; ⊙closed Jan-Feb) The reason most *barcelonins* come up to Tibidabo is for some thrills in this funfair, close to the top funicular station. In addition to high-speed rides and 4-D cinema, the park also has some old-fashioned classics such as the Museu d'Autòmats, with 50 automated puppets going as far back as 1880. Check the website for opening times.

BARCELONA SIGHTS

WORTH A TRIP

COLÒNIA GÜELL

Apart from La Sagrada Família, Gaudí's last big project was the creation of a utopian textile workers' complex, the **Colònia Güell** (☎93 630 58 07; www.coloniaguellbarcelona. com; Carrer de Claudi Güell 6; adult/student €8/6.60; ⊙10am-7pm Mon-Fri, to 3pm Sat & Sun; ☐FGC lines S4, S7, S8 or S33), built for his magnate patron Eusebi Güell outside Barcelona at Santa Coloma de Cervelló. Gaudí's main role was to erect the colony's church. Work began in 1908 but the idea fizzled eight years later and Gaudí only finished the crypt, which still serves as a working church.

This structure is a key to understanding what the master had in mind for his magnum opus, La Sagrada Família. The mostly brick-clad columns that support the ribbed vaults in the ceiling are inclined at all angles in much the way you might expect trees in a forest to lean. That effect was deliberate, but also grounded in physics. Gaudí worked out the angles so that their load would be transmitted from the ceiling to the earth without the help of extra buttressing.

Near the church spread the cute brick houses designed for the factory workers and still inhabited today. In a five-room display with audiovisual and interactive material, the history and life of the industrial colony and the story of Gaudí's church are told in colourful fashion.

GETTING TO TIBIDABO

Take one of the frequent Ferrocarrils de la Generalitat de Catalunya (FGC) trains to Avinguda de Tibidabo from Catalunya station in Plaça de Catalunya (€2, 10 minutes). Outside Avinguda de Tibidabo station, hop on the *tramvia blau* (one way/return €3/4.70, 15 minutes, every 15 or 30 minutes 10am to 6pm Saturdays, Sundays and holidays), Barcelona's last surviving old-style tram. It runs between fancy Modernista mansions – of particular note is Casa Roviralta, now home to a well-known grill restaurant, El Asador de Aranda (p291) – and Plaça del Doctor Andreu and has been doing so since 1901. When the tram isn't in operation, a bus serves the route (€1.40).

From Plaça del Doctor Andreu, the Tibidabo funicular railway climbs through the woods to Plaça de Tibidabo at the top of the hill (return €7.50, five minutes). Departures start at 10.15am and continue until shortly after the park's closing time.

An alternative is bus T2, the 'Tibibús', from Plaça de Catalunya to Plaça de Tibidabo (€2.80, 30 minutes). It runs every 30 to 50 minutes on Saturday, Sunday and holidays; purchase tickets on the bus. The last bus down leaves Tibidabo 30 minutes after the Parc d'Atraccions closes. You can also buy a combined ticket that includes the bus and entry to the Parc d'Atraccions (€25.20).

FREE **Temple del Sagrat Cor** CHURCH
(Church of the Sacred Heart; ☎93 417 56 86; Plaça de Tibidabo; admission free, lift €2; ☻8am-7pm, lift 10am-7pm) The Church of the Sacred Heart, looming above the top funicular station, is meant to be Barcelona's answer to Paris' Sacré-Cœur. The church, built from 1902 to 1961 in a mix of styles with some Modernista influence, is certainly as visible as its Parisian namesake, and even more vilified by aesthetes. It's actually two churches, one on top of the other. The top one is surmounted by a giant statue of Christ and has a lift to take you to the roof for the panoramic (and often wind-chilled) views.

Jardins del Laberint d'Horta GARDENS
(☎93 413 24 00; Passeig del Castanyers 1; adult/student €2.20/1.40, Wed & Sun free; ☻10am-sunset; ⊛; Ⓜ Mundet) Laid out in the twilight years of the 18th century, this carefully manicured park remained a private family idyll until the 1970s, when it was opened to the public.

The gardens take their name from a labyrinth in their centre, but other paths take you past a pleasant artificial lake (*estany*), waterfalls and a neoclassical pavilion.

To reach the gardens, take the right exit upstairs at Mundet Metro station; on emerging, turn right and then left along the main road (with football fields on your left) and then the first left uphill to the gardens (about five minutes).

COLLSEROLA

Parc de Collserola PARK
(☎93 280 35 52; www.parcnaturalcollserola.cat; Carretera de l'Església 92; ☻Centre d'Informació 9.30am-3pm, Can Coll 9.30am-3pm Sun & holidays, closed Jul & Aug; ☒FGC Peu del Funicular, Baixador de Vallvidrera) *Barcelonins* needing an escape from the city without heading too far into the countryside seek out this extensive, 8000-hectare park in the hills. It is a great place to hike and bike and bristles with eateries and snack bars.

Aside from nature, the principal point of interest is the sprawling **Museu-Casa Verdaguer** (☎93 204 78 05; www.museuhistoria.bcn.cat; Vil·la Joana, Carretera de l'Església 104; admission free; ☻10am-2pm Sat, Sun & holidays Sep-Jul), 100m from the Centre d'Informació (information centre) and a short walk from the train station. Catalonia's revered writer Jacint Verdaguer lived in this late-18th-century country house before his death in 1902.

Other highlights include a few country chapels, the ruins of a 14th-century castle (Castellciuro) in the west, various lookout points and, to the north, the 15th-century Can Coll – a grand farmhouse with environment-related exhibits.

Torre de Collserola LOOKOUT
(☎93 406 93 54; www.torredecollserola.com; Carretera de Vallvidrera al Tibidabo; adult/child €5/3; ☻noon-2pm & 3.15-8pm Wed-Sun Jul & Aug, noon-2pm & 3.15-6pm Sat, Sun & holidays Sep-Jun, closed Jan & Feb; ☒111, Funicular de Vallvidrera) Sir Norman Foster designed the 288m-high Torre de Collserola telecommunications tower, which was completed in 1992 and offers fine views over the city. A lift takes you up to the top.

PEDRALBES

A wealthy residential area north of the Zona Universitària, Pedralbes is named after the eponymous convent that is a key attraction in the area.

Palau Reial de Pedralbes   PALACE

(📞93 256 34 65; Avinguda Diagonal 686; all collections adult/student & senior €5/3, 1st Sunday of month & 3-6pm Sun free; ⏰museums 10am-6pm Tue-Sun, 10am-3pm holidays, park 10am-6pm daily; Ⓜ Palau Reial) Overlooking the elegant gardens of Parc del Palau Reial, this early-20th-century building belonged to the family of Eusebi Güell (Gaudí's patron) until they handed it over to the city in 1926 to serve as a royal residence. Today the palace houses three museums.

The Museu de Ceràmica (www.museuceramica.bcn.es) has a fine collection of Spanish ceramics from the 10th to 19th centuries, including work by Picasso and Miró.

The Museu de les Arts Decoratives (www.museuartsdecoratives.bcn.es) brings together an eclectic assortment of furnishings, ornaments and knick-knacks dating as far back as the Romanesque period.

The Museu Tèxtil i d'Indumentària (www.museutextil.bcn.es), on the 2nd floor, contains some 4000 items that range from 4th-century Coptic textiles to 20th-century local embroidery. The heart of the collection is the assortment of clothing from the 16th century to the 1930s.

Excluding the Museu de Ceràmica, these collections will form the bedrock of the new Disseny Hub (p252) museum that will eventually open at Plaça de les Glòries Catalanes.

Over by Avinguda de Pedralbes are the stables and porter's lodge designed by Gaudí for the Finca Güell, as the Güell estate here was called. Known also as the Pavellons Güell, they were built in the mid-1880s, when Gaudí was strongly impressed by Islamic architecture. Outside visiting hours, there is nothing to stop you admiring Gaudí's wrought-iron dragon gate from the exterior.

Museu-Monestir de Pedralbes   MONASTERY

(📞93 256 34 34; www.museuhistoria.bcn.cat; Baixada del Monestir 9; adult/child €7/5; ⏰10am-5pm Tue-Sat, to 8pm Sun; 🚆FGC Reina Elisenda, 🚌22, 63, 64 or 75) This peaceful old convent was first opened to the public in 1983 and is now a museum of monastic life. It stands at the top of Avinguda de Pedralbes in a residential area that was countryside until the 20th century, but which remains a divinely quiet corner of Barcelona.

The architectural highlight is the large, elegant, three-storey cloister, a jewel of Catalan Gothic, built in the early 14th century. Upstairs is a grand hall that was once the Dormidor (sleeping quarters), which today houses a modest collection of the monastery's art.

BARCELONA SIGHTS

BARCELONA FOR CHILDREN

There's plenty to interest kids, from street theatre on La Rambla to the beaches. Transport is good, many attractions are huddled fairly close together and children are generally welcome in restaurants and cafes.

An initial stroll along La Rambla is full of potential distractions and wonders, from the bird stands to the living statues and buskers. The **Museu de Cera** (Wax Museum) is a classic diversion.

At the bottom end of La Rambla, more options present themselves: a ride up to the top of the **Mirador a Colom** or seeing sharks at **L'Aquàrium**.

The **Teleferico del Puerto**, strung across the harbour between La Barceloneta and Montjuïc, is an irresistible ride. Or scare the willies out of them with hair-raising rides at Tibidabo's **Parc d'Atraccions** amusement park.

Of the city's museums, those most likely to capture children's imaginations as much as those of their adult companions are the **Museu Marítim**, the **Museu de la Xocolata** and the popular interactive **Cosmocaixa** science museum.

In the summer months, you will doubtless be rewarded by squeals of delight if you take the bairns to one of the city's **swimming pools** or the **beach**. In cooler weather, parks can be a good choice. A walk in the gardens of Montjuïc, including some exploration of **Castell De Montjuïc**, will appeal to everyone. Adults find the maze of the **Jardins del Laberint d'Horta** hard to work out, too. Another old favourite with most children is a visit to see the animals at the **Zoo de Barcelona**.

ROMANESQUE TREASURES IN THE MUSEU NACIONAL D'ART DE CATALUNYA

The Romanesque art section in the Museu Nacional d'Art de Catalunya (MNAC) constitutes one of Europe's greatest such collections and is an absolute must for lovers of medieval art – and an excellent place to learn about it for those who have had few previous opportunities. The collection consists mainly of 11th- and 12th-century murals, woodcarvings and altar frontals – painted, bas-relief wooden panels that were forerunners of the elaborate *retablos* (altarpieces) that adorned later churches. Gathered from decaying rural churches in northern Catalonia early last century, they are a surprising treasure of vivid colour, discrediting the idea that medieval churches were bereft of decoration. The two outstanding items are an image of Christ in Majesty, done around 1123 and taken from the apse of the Església de Sant Climent de Taüll in northwest Catalonia, and an apse image of the Virgin Mary and Christ Child from the nearby Església de Santa Maria de Taüll.

Camp Nou
STADIUM

(☎93 496 36 00; www.fcbarcelona.com; Carrer d'Aristides Maillol; adult/child €23/17; ⓧ10am-8pm Mon-Sat, to 2.30pm Sun; ⓜPalau Reial) Among Barcelona's most-visited attractions is the high-tech Camp Nou Experience, a multimedia museum exploring the lore of the city's legendary home team, FC Barcelona. Barça is one of Europe's top football clubs, and its museum is a hit with football fans the world over. The best bits of the museum are the photo section, the goal videos and the views out over the stadium.

Hi-tech multimedia displays project great moments in Barça history. Sound installations include the club's anthem and match-day sounds from the stadium.

Unless you see a game, the only way to visit Camp Nou is by purchasing a ticket to the Camp Nou Experience, which (available in seven languages) provides a look at the museum, followed by a self-guided tour of the stadium. The tour takes in the team's dressing rooms, heads out through the tunnel, onto the pitch and winds up in the presidential box. Set aside about 2½ hours for the whole visit.

EL POBLE SEC
Draped on the eastern slopes of Montjuïc down to Avinguda del Paral·lel, working-class El Poble Sec (the Dry Village) is short on sights but hides several interesting bars and eateries. Until the 1960s the avenue was the centre of Barcelona nightlife, crammed with theatres and cabarets. A handful of them survive and one, the Sala Apolo (p298), converted itself successfully into a club.

MUHBA Refugi 307
HISTORIC SITE

(Map p274; ☎93 256 21 22; www.museuhistoria. bcn.cat; Carrer Nou de la Rambla 169; admission incl tour €3; ⓧtours 11am-2pm Sat & Sun; ⓜParal·lel) Barcelona was the most heavily bombed city during the Spanish Civil War and had more than 1300 air-raid shelters. Local citizens started digging this one under a fold of Montjuïc in March 1937.

Half-hour tours (in Catalan or Spanish; book ahead for English or French) provide some fascinating insights into wartime Barcelona.

MONTJUÏC
Montjuïc, the hill overlooking the city centre from the southwest, is dotted with museums, soothing gardens and the main group of 1992 Olympic sites, along with a handful of theatres and clubs.

The name Montjuïc (Jewish Mountain) indicates there was once a Jewish cemetery, and possibly settlement, here. Montjuïc also has a darker history: its castle was used as a political prison and execution site by various governments, including the Republicans during the civil war and Franco thereafter.

The first main burst of building on Montjuïc came in the 1920s, when it was chosen as the stage for Barcelona's 1929 World Exhibition. The Estadi Olímpic, the Poble Espanyol and some museums all date from this time. Montjuïc got a facelift and more new buildings for the 1992 Olympics.

Abundant roads and paths, with occasional escalators, plus buses and a chairlift, allow you to visit Montjuïc's sights in any order you choose. The main attractions – the Museu Nacional d'Art de Catalunya, CaixaForum, the Poble Espanyol, the Pavelló Mies van der Rohe, the Fundació Joan Miró, the Estadi Olímpic and the views from the castle – make for a full couple of days' sightseeing.

Plaça d'Espanya
SQUARE

(Map p274) The approach to Montjuïc from Plaça d'Espanya gives you the full benefit of the landscaping on the hill's northern side and allows Montjuïc to unfold for you from the bottom up. On Plaça d'Espanya's northern side is the former Plaça de Braus Les Arenes bullring, built in 1900 and now a shopping centre, with rooftop promenade.

Behind Les Arenes is Parc Joan Miró, created in the 1980s, and worth a quick detour for Miró's giant, highly phallic sculpture *Dona i Ocell* (Woman and Bird) in the northwest corner.

Museu Nacional d'Art de Catalunya
MUSEUM

(MNAC; Map p274; ☑93 622 03 76; www.mnac. es; Mirador del Palau Nacional; adult/senior & child under 15yr/student €10/free/7, 1st Sun of month free; ☺10am-7pm Tue-Sat, 10am-2.30pm Sun & holidays, library 10am-6pm Mon-Fri, to 2.30pm Sat; ⓂEspanya) From across the city, the neobaroque silhouette of the Palau Nacional can be seen on the slopes of Montjuïc. Built for the 1929 World Exhibition and restored in 2005, it houses a vast collection of mostly Catalan art spanning the early Middle Ages to the early 20th century.

The highlight here is the Romanesque art section, considered the most important concentration of early medieval art in the world. Rescued from neglected country churches across northern Catalonia in the early 20th century, the collection consists of huge 11th- and 12th-century frescoes, woodcarvings and painted altar frontals.

The museum's Gothic art section also shines. Look out for pivotal works by Bernat Martorell and Jaume Huguet. As the Gothic collection draws to a close, two separate and equally eclectic private collections showcase an array of European works by Old Masters. Highlights are Fra Angelico's (1395–1455) *Madonna of Humility* and works by the Venetian Renaissance masters Veronese (1528–88), Titian (1490–1557) and Canaletto (1697–1768), along with those of Rubens (1577–1640) and even England's Gainsborough (1727–88); its grand finale being examples of work by Francisco de Goya (1746–1828).

Up on the next floor, after a series of rooms devoted to mostly minor works by a variety of 17th-century Spanish Old Masters, the collection turns to modern Catalan art. It is an uneven affair, but it is worth looking out for Modernista painters Ramon Casas and Santiago Rusiñol, as well as the recently deceased Antoni Tàpies.

Fundació Joan Miró
MUSEUM

(Map p274; www.bcn.fjmiro.es; Plaça de Neptu; adult/senior & child €10/7; ☺10am-8pm Tue, Wed, Fri & Sat, to 9.30pm Thu, to 2.30pm Sun & holidays; ☐50, 55, 193, ⓂParal·lel) Joan Miró, the city's best-known 20th-century artistic progeny, bequeathed this art foundation to his hometown in 1971. Its light-filled buildings, designed by close friend and architect Josep Lluís Sert (who also built Miró's Mallorca studios), are crammed with seminal works, from Miró's earliest timid sketches to paintings from his last years.

The foundation rests amid the greenery of Montjuïc and holds the greatest single collection of the artist's work, comprising some 220 of his paintings, 180 sculptures, some textiles and more than 8000 drawings spanning his entire life. Only a small portion is ever on display.

For a deeper understanding of the artist and his time, see the basement rooms containing Homenatge a Joan Miró (Homage to Joan Miró), featuring photos, a 15-minute video on his life and a series of works from some of his contemporaries, like Henry Moore, Antoni Tàpies, Fernand Léger and others.

FREE Castell de Montjuïc
FORTRESS, GARDENS

(Map p274; ☺9am-9pm Tue-Sun Apr-Sep, to 7pm Tue-Sun Oct-Mar; ☐193, Telefèric de Montjuïc (Castell de Montjuïc)) The forbidding Castell de Montjuïc (castle or fort) dominates the southeastern heights of Montjuïc. It dates, in its present form, to the late 17th and 18th centuries. For most of its dark history, it has been used to watch over the city and as a political prison and killing ground.

In the coming years, it is planned to establish an international peace centre in the castle, as well as a display on its history.

Around the seaward foot of the castle an airy walking track, the Camí del Mar, offers breezy views of city and sea.

FREE Jardins
GARDENS

Towards the foot of the fortress, above the main road to Tarragona, the Jardins de Mossèn Costa i Llobera (Map p274;

Montjuïc & Poble Sec

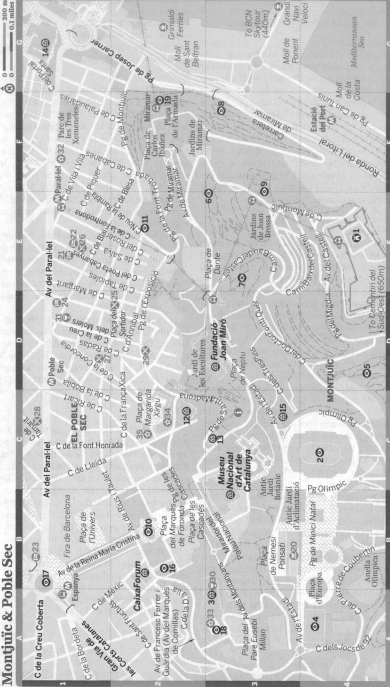

Montjuïc & Poble Sec

BARCELONA SIGHTS

⊙10am-sunset; Transbordador Aeri (Miramar)) have a good collection of tropical and desert plants – including a veritable forest of cacti. Near the Estació Parc Montjuïc (funicular station) are the ornamental **Jardins de Mossèn Cinto Verdaguer** (Map p274; ⊙10am-sunset; Funicular Parc de Monjuïc), full of beautiful bulbs and aquatic plants. East across the road are the landscaped **Jardins Joan Brossa** (Map p274; ⊙10am-sunset; Telefèric de Montjuïc (Mirador)), set on the site of a former amusement park. These gardens contain many Mediterranean species, from cypresses to pines and a few palms. From the **Jardins del Mirador** (Map p274; Telefèric de Montjuïc (Mirador)), opposite the Estació Mirador, you have fine views over the port of Barcelona.

Poble Espanyol CULTURAL CENTRE
(Map p274; www.poble-espanyol.com; Avinguda de Francesc Ferrer i Guàrdia; adult/child €9.50/5.60; ⊙9am-8pm Mon, to 2am Tue-Thu, to 4am Fri, to 5am Sat, to midnight Sun; ⊞; ⊟50, 61 or 193, ⓂEspanya) Welcome to Spain! All of it! This 'Spanish Village' is both a cheesy souvenir hunters' haunt and an intriguing scrapbook of Spanish architecture built for the Spanish crafts section of the 1929 World Exhibition. You can meander from Andalucía to the Balearic Islands in the space of a couple of hours, visiting surprisingly good copies of Spain's characteristic buildings.

You enter from beneath a towered medieval gate from Ávila. Inside, to the right, is an information office with free maps. Straight ahead from the gate is the Plaza Mayor (Town Square), surrounded with mainly Castilian and Aragonese buildings. It is sometimes the scene of summer concerts. Elsewhere you'll find an Andalucian *barrio,* a Basque street, Galician and Catalan quarters and even a Dominican monastery (at the eastern end). The buildings house dozens of restaurants, cafes, bars, craft shops and workshops (such as glassmakers), and some souvenir stores.

At night the restaurants, bars and especially the discos become a lively corner of Barcelona's nightlife.

Montjuïc

A ONE-DAY ITINERARY

Montjuïc, perhaps once the site of pre-Roman settlements, is today a hilltop green lung looking over city and sea. Interspersed across varied gardens are major art collections, a fortress, an Olympic stadium and more. A solid one-day itinerary can take in the key spots.

Alight at Espanya metro stop and make for **CaixaForum 1**, always host to three or four free top-class exhibitions. The nearby **Pavelló Mies van der Rohe 2** is an intriguing study in 1920s futurist housing by one of the 20th century's greatest architects. Uphill, the Romanesque art collection in the **Museu Nacional d'Art de Catalunya 3** is a must, and its restaurant is a pleasant lunch stop. Escalators lead further up the hill towards the **Estadi Olímpic 4**, scene of the 1992 Olympic Games. The road leads east to the **Fundació Joan Miró 5**, a shrine to the master surrealist's creativity. Contemplate ancient relics in the **Museu d'Arqueologia de Catalunya 6**, then have a break in the peaceful **Jardins de Mossèn Cinto Verdaguer 7**, the prettiest on the hill, before taking the cable car to the **Castell de Montjuïc 8**. If you pick the right day, you can round off with the gorgeously kitsch **La Font Màgica 9** sound and light show, followed by drinks and dancing in an open-air nightspot in **Poble Espanyol 10**.

TOP TIPS

» **Moving views** Ride the Transbordador Aeri from Barceloneta for a bird's eye approach to Montjuïc. Or take the Teleféric de Montjuïc cable car to the Castell for more aerial views.

» **Summer fun** The Castell de Montjuïc features outdoor summer cinema and concerts (see http://sala montjuic.org).

» **Beautiful bloomers** Bursting with colour and serenity, the Jardins de Mossèn Cinto Verdaguer are exquisitely laid out with bulbs, especially tulips, and aquatic flowers.

CaixaForum
This former factory and barracks designed by Josep Puig i Cadafalch is an outstanding work of Modernista architecture; like a Lego fantasy in brick.

Piscines Bernat Picornell

Olympic Needle

Poble Espanyol
Amid the rich variety of traditional Spanish architecture created in replica for the 1929 Barcelona World Exhibition, browse the art on show in the Fundació Fran Daurel.

Pavelló Mies van der Rohe
Admire the inventiveness of the great German architect Ludwig Mies van der Rohe in this recreation of his avant garde German pavillion for the 1929 World Exhibition.

La Font Màgica

Take a summer evening to behold the Magic Fountain come to life in a unique 15-minute sound and light performance, when the water glows like a cauldron of colour.

Museu Nacional d'Art de Catalunya

Make a beeline for the Romanesque art selection and the 12th-century polychrome image of Christ in majesty, which was recovered from the apse of a country chapel in northwest Catalonia.

9

3

6

Museu Etnològic

Teatre Grec

5

Museu Olímpic i de l'Esport

7

4

Estadi Olímpic

Jardí Botànic

8

Jardins de Mossèn Cinto Verdaguer

Castell de Montjuïc

Enjoy the sweeping views of the sea and city from atop this 17th-century fortress, once a political prison and long a symbol of oppression.

Fundació Joan Miró

Take in some of Joan Miró's giant canvases, and discover little-known works from his early years in the Sala Joan Prats and Sala Pilar Juncosa.

Museu d'Arqueologia de Catalunya

Seek out the Roman mosaic depicting the Three Graces, one of the most beautiful items in this museum, which was dedicated to the ancient past of Catalonia and neighbouring parts of Spain.

GETTING TO MONTJUÏC

You *could* walk from Ciutat Vella (the foot of La Rambla is 700m from the eastern end of Montjuïc). Escalators run up to the Palau Nacional from Avinguda de Rius i Taulet and Passeig de les Cascades. They continue as far as Avinguda de l'Estadi.

Bus

Several buses make their way up here, including buses 50, 55 and 61. Local bus 193 does a circle trip from Plaça d'Espanya to the castle.

Metro & Funicular

Take the metro (lines 2 and 3) to Paral·lel station and get on the **funicular railway** (⊘9am-10pm Apr-Oct, 9am-8pm Nov-Mar) from there to Estació Parc Montjuïc.

Telefèric de Montjuïc

From Estació Parc Montjuïc, this **cable car** (adult/child one way €6.80/5.20; ⊘10am-9pm) carries you to the Castell de Montjuïc via the *mirador* (lookout point).

Aeri del Port

To get to the mountain from the beach, take the **Aeri del Port** (Teleférico del Puerto; www. telefericodebarcelona.com; one way/return €10/15) (aerial cable car). It runs between Torre de Sant Sebastiá in La Barceloneta and the Miramar stop on Montjuïc.

FREE Fundació Fran Daurel   MUSEUM
(Map p274; www.fundaciofrandaurel.com; Avinguda Francesc Ferrer i Guàrdia 13; ⊘10am-7pm) The Fundació Fran Daurel (in Poble Espanyol) is an eclectic collection of 300 works of art, including sculptures, prints, ceramics and tapestries by modern artists ranging from Picasso and Miró to more contemporary figures, including Miquel Barceló. The foundation also has a sculpture garden, boasting 27 pieces, nearby the Fundació and within the grounds of Poble Espanyol (look for the Montblanc gate).

Font Màgica   FOUNTAIN
(Map p274; Avinguda de la Reina Maria Cristina; ⊘every 30min 7-9pm Fri & Sat Oct-late Jun, 9-11.30pm Thu-Sun late Jun-Sep; MEspanya) The main fountain of a series that sweeps up the hill from Avinguda de la Reina Maria Cristina to the grand facade of the Palau Nacional, Font Màgica comes alive with a 15-minute lights, water and music show repeated several times per evening.

Pavelló Mies van der Rohe   ARCHITECTURE
(Map p274; ☑93 423 40 16; www.miesbcn.com; Avinguda de Francesc Ferrer i Guàrdia; adult/child under 18yr/student €4.75/free/2.60; ⊘10am-8pm; MEspanya) Designed in 1929 by Ludwig Mies van der Rohe (1886–1969) as the Pavelló Alemany (German Pavilion) for the World Exhibition, it was removed after the show and reconstructed only in 1980, after the building had been consistently referred to as one of the key works of modern architecture.

There is a free English guided tour on Saturdays at 10am.

CaixaForum   GALLERY
(Map p274; www.fundacio.lacaixa.es; Avinguda de Francesc Ferrer i Guàrdia 6-8; adult/student & child €3/2, 1st Sunday of month free; ⊘10am-8pm Tue-Fri & Sun, to 10pm Sat; MEspanya) Set in a former factory and a Modernist gem designed by Puig i Cadafalch, the CaixaForum hosts some of the city's top art exhibitions. On occasion portions of La Caixa's own collection of 800 works of modern and contemporary art are also on display. Musical recitals are sometimes held in the museum, especially in the warmer months.

Museu Etnològic   MUSEUM
(Map p274; www.museuetnologic.bcn.cat; Passeig de Santa Madrona 16-22; adult/senior & student €3.50/1.75; ⊘noon-8pm Tue-Sat, 11am-3pm Sun; ☑55) The museum takes visitors on a whirlwind tour through some of Spain and the world's vibrant cultures. Highlights include the Pyrenees region in Catalonia (including traditional instruments and archive images of traditional dances) and Salamanca in central Spain, to look at now largely extinct rural societies. Further collections take in Japan, Morocco, Ethiopia, Australia, Papua New Guinea and the Americas.

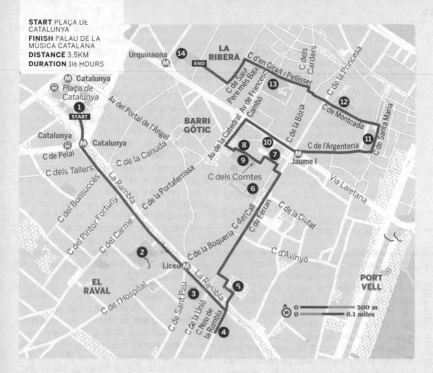

START PLAÇA DE
CATALUNYA
FINISH PALAU DE LA
MÚSICA CATALANA
DISTANCE 3.5KM
DURATION 1½ HOURS

Walking Tour
Old Town

❯ A great deal of what makes Barcelona fascinating is crowded into a relatively compact space, making an introductory strolling tour a great way to make the city's acquaintance. There's nothing wrong with following the crowds to start off with, so wander down La Rambla from ❶ **Plaça de Catalunya**. Along the way, sniff around the ❷ **Mercat de la Boqueria**, one of Europe's most colourful and well-stocked produce markets. Pop into the ❸ **Gran Teatre del Liceu**, the city's main opera house, and then visit one of Gaudí's earlier efforts, the ❹ **Palau Güell**. From here, cross La Rambla and busy ❺ **Plaça Reial** and make for ❻ **Plaça de Sant Jaume**, at the core of the Barri Gòtic and the political heart of the city for 2000 years. You can examine the city's Roman origins in the nearby ❼ **Museu d'Història de Barcelona**, which also leads you to a fine Catalan Gothic hall and medieval chapel. From the complex of buildings huddled around the museum and Plaça del Rei, you pass the ❽ **Museu Frederic Marès** en route

for the main facade of the ❾ **Catedral** – make time to spend inside and to head up to the roof for bird's-eye views of the medieval city. From there, make the loop down Vía Laietana to admire what remains of the ❿ **Roman walls**, and then branch off along Carrer de l'Argenteria (once home to Barcelona's silversmiths) to reach the splendid Gothic ⓫ **Església de Santa Maria del Mar**, a striking symbol of Catalan identity. Circle around it and up noble Carrer de Montcada, home to fine centuries-old mansions, several of which house museums – including the ⓬ **Museu Picasso**. Proceed north past the ⓭ **Mercat de Santa Caterina**, a daring 21st-century reincarnation of a grand 19th-century produce market on the site of a medieval monastery; and then dogleg on to the stunning Modernista ⓮ **Palau de la Música Catalana**, best visited for a performance of anything from flamenco to Portuguese fado.

Museu d'Arqueologia de Catalunya
MUSEUM

(MAC; Map p274; www.mac.cat; Passeig de Santa Madrona 39-41; adult/student €3/2.10; ☉9.30am-7pm Tue-Sat, 10am-2.30pm Sun; ☐55 or 193) This archaeology museum, housed in what was the Graphic Arts palace during the 1929 World Exhibition, covers Catalonia and cultures from elsewhere in Spain. Items range from copies of pre-Neanderthal skulls to lovely Carthaginian necklaces and jewel-studded Visigothic crosses.

There's good material on the Balearic Islands and Empúries, the Greek and Roman city on the Costa Brava. The most beautiful piece is a mosaic depicting *Les Tres Gràcies* (The Three Graces), unearthed near Plaça de Sant Jaume in the 18th century.

Anella Olímpica
OLYMPIC SITE

(☉8am-9pm Apr-Sep, 8am-7pm Oct-Mar) The 'Olympic Ring' is the group of sports installations where the main events of the 1992 Olympics were held. Westernmost is the **Institut Nacional d'Educació Física de Catalunya** (Inefc; Map p274), a kind of sports university, designed by one of Catalonia's best-known contemporary architects, Ricardo Bofill. Past a circular arena, Plaça d'Europa, with the Torre Calatrava telecommunications tower behind it, is the Piscines Bernat Picornell, where the swimming and diving events were held.

Estadi Olímpic
STADIUM

(Map p274; Avinguda de l'Estadi; ☉10am-8pm; ☐50, 61 or 193) The 65,000-seat Estadi Olímpic was the main stadium of Barcelona's Olympic Games. It was opened in 1929 and restored for 1992.

Museu Olímpic i de l'Esport
MUSEUM

(Map p274; www.museuolimpicbcn.com; Avinguda de l'Estadi 60; adult/student €4/2.50; ☉10am-8pm; ☐50, 61 or 193) The Museu Olímpic i de l'Esport is an information-packed inter-active museum dedicated to the history of sport and the Olympic Games. After picking up tickets, you wander down a ramp that snakes below ground level and is lined with displays on the history of sport, starting with the ancients.

Jardí Botànic
GARDENS

(Map p274; www.jardibotanic.bcn.es; Carrer del Doctor Font i Quer 2; adult/student €3.50/1.70; ☉10am-8pm; ☐50, 61 or 193) This botanical garden is dedicated to Mediterranean flora and has a collection of some 40,000 plants and 1500 species that thrive in areas with a climate similar to that of the Mediterranean, such as the Eastern Mediterranean, Spain, North Africa, Australia, California, Chile and South Africa.

Cementiri del Sud-Oest
CEMETERY

(☉8am-6pm; ☐193) On the hill to the south of the Anella Olímpica stretches this huge cemetery, the Cementiri del Sud-Oest or Cementiri Nou, which extends down the southern side of the hill. Opened in 1883, it's an odd combination of elaborate architect-designed tombs for rich families and small niches for the rest. It includes the graves of numerous Catalan artists and politicians.

Among the big names are Joan Miró, Carmen Amaya (the flamenco dance star from La Barceloneta), Lluís Companys (nationalist president of Catalonia executed by Franco's henchmen in 1940) and Ildefons Cerdà (who designed l'Eixample).

Transbordador Aeri
CABLE CAR

(Map p274; www.teleferidebarcelona.com; Av de Miramar, Jardins de Miramar; one way/return €10/15; ☉11am-7pm; ☐50 & 153) This cable car strung across the harbour to Montjuïc provides an eagle-eye view of the city. The cabins float between Miramar (Montjuïc) and Barceloneta. At the top of the Torre de Sant Sebastià is a spectacularly located restaurant, Torre d'Alta Mar.

🏃 Activities

Popular places for a run or a bike ride are in Montjuïc and in the Parc de Collserola (among the best trails there is the 9km-long Carretera de les Aigües): both are hilly but much less stressful than the rest of the city in terms of traffic. Another good place for a spin or a jog is along the esplanade from Barceloneta beach up to El Fòrum.

Base Nautica Municipal
SAILING, WINDSURFING

(☎93 221 04 32; www.basenautica.org; Avinguda de Litoral; ⓜPoblenou) Just back from Platja de la Mar Bella, the Base Nautica has classes in kayaking (€132 for 10 hours' tuition), windsurfing (€196 for 10 hours' tuition) and sailing (€229 for 12 hours' tuition).

Club Natació Atlètic-Barcelona
SWIMMING

(Map p256; www.cnab.cat; Plaça del Mar; adult/child €11.20/6.50; ☉7am-11pm Mon-Sat, 8am-8pm Sun; ☐17, 39, 57, 64, ⓜBarceloneta) This athletic club has one indoor and two outdoor pools, a gym and private beach access.

Golondrina BOAT TOUR
(☎93 442 31 06; www.lasgolondrinas.com; Moll de les Drassanes; adult/child €14.50/5.25; ☺Mar Nov; Ⓜ Drassanes) For a view of the harbour from the water, you can take a *golondrina* from in front of the Mirador a Colom. The 90-minute round trip takes you past Port Olímpic to El Fòrum and back. For a short jaunt around the port, sign up for a 35-minute excursion (€7/3 per adult/child).

Orsom CRUISE
(☎93 441 05 37; www.barcelona-orsom.com; Moll de les Drassanes; adult/child €14/11; ☺Apr-Oct; Ⓜ Drassanes) Aboard a large sailing catamaran, Orsom makes the 90-minute journey to the Fòrum and back. There are three or four departures per day, and the last is a jazz cruise, scheduled around sunset. The same company also runs daily speedboat tours (adult/child €12/8).

Piscines Bernat Picornell SWIMMING
(Map p274; www.picornell.cat; Avinguda de l'Estadi 30-38; adult/child €9.65/5.95; ☺6.45am-midnight Mon-Fri, 7am-9pm Sat, 7.30am-4pm Sun; ☐50, 61 or 193) Barcelona's official Olympic pool on Montjuïc has a gym, saunas and spa bath.

Poliesportiu Marítim SWIMMING
(Map p256; www.claror.cat; Passeig Marítim de la Barceloneta 33-35; general admission Mon-Fri €16, Sat, Sun & holidays €19; ☺7am-midnight Mon-Fri, 8am-9pm Sat, 8am-4pm Sun; Ⓜ Ciutadella Vila Olímpica) In addition to the small pool for lap swimming, there is a labyrinth of hot, warm and freezing-cold spa pools, along with thundering waterfalls for massage relief.

🥢 Courses

Barcelona is bristling with schools offering Spanish- and Catalan-language courses. You can learn lots more in Barcelona, too, such as salsa and sauces.

Cook and Taste COOKING COURSE
(Map p244; ☎93 302 13 20; www.cookandtaste. net; Carrer del Paradís 3; half-day workshop €65; Ⓜ Liceu) Learn to whip up a few tapas dishes, paella and a traditional Catalan dessert at this Spanish cookery school. It also offers a Boqueria market tour.

Alicianet DANCE COURSE
(Map p244; ☎670 267276; www.alicianet.net; Carrer de la Beates 2; Ⓜ Barceloneta) Alicianet offers various levels of flamenco instruction. One-off classes cost €25 per hour, or you can

enrol in courses (up to four hours a week, at €110 a month).

International House LANGUAGE COURSE
(☎93 268 45 11; www.ihes.com/bcn; Carrer de Trafalgar 14; Ⓜ Arc de Triomf) Intensive courses from around €410 for two weeks. Staff can also organise accommodation.

Universitat de Barcelona –
Catalan Courses LANGUAGE COURSE
(☎93 403 54 77; www.eh.ub.edu; Carrer de Melcior de Palau 140; Ⓜ Sants) Intensive courses (40 hours' tuition over periods ranging from two weeks to a month; €457) in Spanish are held year-round. Catalan courses are also available (80 hours' tuition for €400).

👉 Tours

A number of tour options present themselves if you want a hand getting around the sights.

Barcelona Walking Tours WALKING TOUR
(Map p262; ☎93 285 38 34; www.barcelonaturisme. com; Plaça de Catalunya 17-S; Ⓜ Catalunya) The Oficina d'Informació de Turisme de Barcelona organises guided walking tours, most lasting two hours and starting at the tourist office. One explores the Barri Gòtic (adult/child €14/5; ☺in English 9.30am daily, in Spanish & Catalan 11.30am Sat); another follows in the footsteps of Picasso (adult/child €20/7; ☺in

---

BICYCLE TOURS

Barcelona is awash with companies offering bicycle tours. Tours typically cost around €22, take two to four hours and generally stick to the old city, La Sagrada Família and the beaches. Operators include **Barcelona By Bike** (Map p256; ☎93 268 81 07; www. barcelonabybike.com; Carrer de la Marina 13; tours €22; Ⓜ Cuitadella/Vila Olimpica), whose meeting point is on Carrer de la Marina, near the casino at Port Olímpic; **BarcelonaBiking.com** (Map p244; ☎656 356300; www.barcelonabiking. com; Baixada de Sant Miquel 6; ☺10am-8pm; Ⓜ Jaume I or Liceu); **Bike Tours Barcelona** (Map p254; ☎93 268 21 05; www.bicicletabarcelona.com; Carrer de l'Esparteria 3; tour €22); and **Fat Tire Bike Tours** (Map p244; ☎93 301 36 12; http://fattirebiketours.com/barcelona; Carrer dels Escudellers 48; tours €22).

English 3pm Tue, Thu & Sun) and winds up at the Museu Picasso, entry to which is included in the price; and a third takes in the main jewels of Modernisme (adult/child €14/5; ☺in English 4pm Fri & Sat Oct-May, 6pm Fri & Sat Jun-Sep). Foodies can opt for a gourmet tour (adult/child €20/7; ☺in English 10am Fri & Sat, in Spanish & Catalan 10.30am Sat), learning about (and some tasting of) fine foodstuffs across the old city. Most tours last two hours and start at the tourist office. A whole range of other tours are offered – maritime Barcelona, literary tours, birdwatching, film locations, running excursions and more.

Runner Bean Tours
WALKING TOUR

(Map p244; ☎636 108776; www.runnerbeantours. com; ☺tours 11am year-round & 4.30pm Apr-Sep) Runner Bean Tours offers several daily thematic tours. It's a pay-what-you-wish tour, with a collection taken at the end for the guide. The Old City tour explores the Roman and medieval history of Barcleona, visiting highlights in the Ciutat Vella. The Gaudí tour takes in the great works of Modernista Barcelona. It involves two hops on the metro. Both depart from Plaça Reial.

Bus Turístic
BUS TOUR

(☎93 285 38 32; www.barcelonaturisme.com; day ticket adult/child €24/14; ☺9am-8pm) This hop-on, hop-off service covers three circuits (44 stops) linking virtually all the major tourist sights. Tourist offices, TMB transport authority offices and many hotels have leaflets explaining the system. Each of the two main circuits takes approximately two hours. The third circuit, from Port Olímpic to El Fòrum, runs from April to September and is less interesting.

Catalunya Bus Turístic
BUS TOUR

(Map p262; ☎93 285 38 32; www.catalunyabusturistic.com; Plaça de Catalunya) Routes include Girona and Figueres (€71); a Penedès wine and cava (sparkling wine) jaunt with three winery tours and lunch (€61); Montserrat and Colonia Güell (€59). All tours leave at 8.30am from late March to October from Plaça de Catalunya; tours arrive back between 4.30pm and 7.30pm. Save 10% by booking online.

Barcelona Scooter
DRIVING TOUR

(Map p256; ☎93 221 40 70; tour €50; ☺10.30am Sat, 3.30pm Thu) Run by Cooltra, Barcelona Scooter offers a three-hour tour by scooter around the city in conjunction with the city tourism office. Departure is from the Cooltra rental outlet (p303).

BCN Skytour
SCENIC FLIGHTS

(☎93 224 07 10; www.cathelicopters.com; Heliport, Passeig de l'Escullera; 5-min/35-min tour per person €50/300; ☺10am-7pm; ⓜDrassanes or Paral·lel) Ascend 800m up in a helicopter for an awe-inspiring view of the city. Longer tours take in the Montserrat Mountains. Take a taxi to the heliport.

Gocar
DRIVING TOUR

(Map p244; ☎902 301333; www.gocartours.es; Carrer de Freixures 23bis; per hr/day €35/99; ☺9am-9pm) These GPS-guided 'cars' (really two-seat, three-wheel mopeds) allow you to tour around town and listen to commentaries on major sights as you go.

My Favourite Things
TOUR

(☎637 265405; www.myft.net; tours €26-32) Offers tours (with no more than 10 participants) based on numerous themes: anything from design to food and rollerblading to sailing. Some of the more unusual activities cost more and times vary.

✨ Festivals & Events

Reis/Reyes
EPIPHANY

Epifanía (the Epiphany) on 6 January is also known as the Dia dels Reis Mags/Día de los Reyes Magos (Three Kings' Day). The night before, children delight in the Cavalcada dels Reis Mags (Parade of the Three Kings), a colourful parade of floats and music during which tonnes of sweets are thrown into the crowd of eager kids (and not a few adults!).

Festes de Santa Eulàlia
CITY FESTIVAL

(www.bcn.cat/santaeulalia) Around 12 February, this big winter fest celebrates Barcelona's first patron saint with a week of cultural events, from concerts to castellers (human-castle builders).

Dia de Sant Jordi
PATRON SAINT FESTIVAL

This is the day of Catalonia's patron saint (George) and also the Day of the Book: men give women a rose, women give men a book, publishers launch new titles. La Rambla and Plaça de Sant Jaume and other central city streets and squares are filled with book and flower stalls. Celebrated on 23 April.

Pride Barcelona
GAY PRIDE

(www.pridebarcelona.org) The Barcelona gay-pride festival is a week of celebrations held in late June or early July with a crammed program of culture and concerts, along with the gay-pride march.

Sónar
MUSIC

(www.sonar.es) Barcelona's celebration of electronic music is said to be Europe's biggest such event. Locations and dates change each year.

Primavera Sound
MUSIC

(www.primaverasound.com) For three days in late May or early June, the Auditori Fòrum and other locations around town become the combined stage for a host of international DJs and musicians.

Dia de Sant Joan
MIDSUMMER

This is a colourful midsummer celebration on 24 June with bonfires, even in the squares of L'Eixample, and fireworks marking the evening that precedes this holiday.

Festival del Grec
MUSIC, DANCE

(www.barcelonafestival.com) Held from late June to August, this festival involves music, dance and theatre at many locations across the city.

Festa Major de Gràcia
CITY FESTIVAL

(www.festamajordegracia.org) This is a madcap local festival held in Gràcia around 15 August, with wildly decorated streets, dancing and concerts.

Festes de la Mercè
CITY FESTIVAL

(www.bcn.cat/merce) The city's biggest party involves four days of concerts, dancing, *castellers*, fireworks, parades of gegatones (costumed giants) and *correfocs* – fireworks-spitting monsters and demons who run with the crowd. Held around 24 September.

🛏 Sleeping

Those looking for cheaper accommodation close to the action should check out the

Barri Gòtic and El Raval. Some good lower-end *pensiones* (small private hotels) are also scattered about L'Eixample. A range of boutique-style hotels with real charm in all categories has enriched the offerings in the past few years. Many midrange and top-end places are spread across L'Eixample, most of them in easy striking distance of the old town. Several fine hotels are located on the fringes of the busy El Born area of La Ribera and a there's a handful of options near the beaches at La Barceloneta.

LA RAMBLA

Hotel Continental
HOTEL €€

(Map p250; ☑93 301 25 70; www.hotelcontinental.com; La Rambla 138; s/d from €92/102; ❋🐱; ⓂCatalunya) Rooms at this old-fashioned hotel (where George Orwell stayed during the Spanish Civil War) are worn and rather spartan, but have romantic touches such as ceiling fans, brass bedsteads and frilly bedclothes. An extra €20 gets you a room with a small balcony overlooking La Rambla.

BARRI GÒTIC

TOP CHOICE Hotel Neri
DESIGN HOTEL €€€

(Map p244; ☑93 304 06 55; www.hotelneri.com; Carrer de Sant Sever 5; d from €270; ❋@🐱; ⓂLiceu) Occupying a beautifully adapted, centuries-old building this stunningly renovated medieval mansion has elegant rooms with designer fittings. There's a fantastic restaurant on the ground floor and a small roof deck for catching some rays.

Alberg Hostel Itaca
HOSTEL €

(Map p244; ☑93 301 97 51; www.itacahostel.com; Carrer de Ripoll 21; dm €11-26, d €60; @🐱; ⓂJaume I) A bright, quiet hostel near the Catedral, Itaca has spacious dorms (sleeping six, eight or 12 people), with parquet floors, spring colours and a couple of doubles with private

BARCELONA SLEEPING

LONGER-STAY ACCOMMODATION

An alternative accommodation option can be apartment rental. Typical short-term prices are around €80 to €100 for two people per night. An excellent option, with hundreds of listings is **Air BnB** (www.airbnb.com). In addition to full apartments, the site also lists rooms available, which can be a good way to meet locals and/or other travellers if you don't mind sharing common areas. Prices for a room range from €30 to €60 on average.

There are scores of rental services: **Aparteasy** (☑93 451 67 66; www.aparteasy.com; Carrer de Santa Tecla 3); **Feelathomebarcelona.com** (Map p250; ☑651 894141; www.feelathomebarcelona.com; Carrer Nou de la Rambla 15); **Barcelona On Line** (Map p262; ☑902 887017, 93 343 79 93; www.barcelona-on-line.es; Carrer de València 352); **Friendly Rentals** (☑93 268 80 51; www.friendlyrentals.com; Passatge de Sert 4) and **Rent a Flat in Barcelona** (☑93 342 73 00; www.rentaflatinbarcelona.com; Ronda del Guinardó 2).

bathroom. It also has a couple of nearby apartments for six people (€120 per night).

Hostal Campi
HOSTAL €

(Map p250; ☎93 301 35 45; www.hostalcampi.com; Carrer de la Canuda 4; d €70, s/d without bathroom €35/60; @🖪; ⓜCatalunya) The best rooms at this friendly, central *hostal* are doubtless the doubles with their own loos and showers. They are extremely roomy and bright, with attractive tile floors.

Hotel California
HOTEL €€

(Map p250; ☎93 317 77 66; www.hotelcaliforniabcn. com; Carrer d'en Rauric 14; s/d €70/120; ❄@🖪; ⓜLiceu) A classic, central, gay-friendly establishment, the California offers 31 simple but spotlessly kept rooms in light, neutral colours, with good-sized beds, plasma-screen TVs and a bustling breakfast room. Room service operates 24 hours.

El Jardí
HOTEL €€

(Map p244; ☎93 301 59 00; www.eljardi-barcelona. com; Plaça de Sant Josep Oriol 1; d €65-120; ❄🖪; ⓜLiceu) The best rooms in this attractively located spot are the doubles with balcony overlooking one of Barcelona's prettiest squares. The rest are lacklustre.

EL RAVAL

TOP CHOICE Casa Camper
DESIGN HOTEL €€€

(Map p250; ☎93 342 62 80; www.casacamper.com; Carrer d'Elisabets 11; s/d €240/270; ❄@; ⓜLiceu) Run by the well-known Mallorcan shoe people, the Casa Camper has an artfully designed foyer and spacious rooms.

Each is decorated in red, black and white and comes standard with Camper slippers and Vinçon furniture, where you can contemplate the hanging gardens outside your window.

Whotells
APARTMENT €€

(Map p250; ☎93 443 08 34; www.whotells.com; Carrer de Joaquín Costa 28; apt from €180; ❄@🖪; ⓜUniversitat) Decked out with Muji furniture and very comfortable, these apartments (which sleep up to six) give a sense of being a home away from home. Cook up a storm in the kitchen with products bought in the nearby La Boqueria market, or flop in front of the LCD TV. The owners have other apartment buildings in L'Eixample and La Barceloneta.

Hostal Chic & Basic
HOSTAL €€

(☎93 302 51 83; www.chicandbasic.com; Carrer de Tallers 82; s €80, d €103-124; ❄@; ⓜUniversitat) Aiming to live up to its name, this simple

but stylish guesthouse has lily-white rooms with plasma-screen TVs and iPod docks. The street can get noisy.

Hotel San Agustín
HOTEL €€

(Map p250; ☎93 318 16 58; www.hotelsa.com; Plaça de Sant Agustí 3; r from €80-180; ❄@🖪; ⓜLiceu) This former 18th-century monastery opened as a hotel in 1840, making it the city's oldest. The location is perfect – a quick stroll off La Rambla on a curious square. Rooms sparkle, and are mostly spacious and light-filled. Consider an attic double with sloping ceiling and bird's-eye views.

Hostal Gat Xino
HOSTAL €€

(Map p250; ☎93 324 88 33; www.gatrooms.es; Carrer de l'Hospital 149-155; s/d €80/115, ste with terrace €140; ❄@🖪; ⓜLiceu) A hostel for those who don't necessarily like hostels – it's chic, sleek and squeaky clean with its white and lime-green decor. All the rooms have bathrooms, while the suite is plush and has a wonderful terrace. The staff also run the slightly cheaper Hostal Gat Raval nearby.

Hostal Gat Raval
HOSTAL €€

(Map p250; ☎93 481 66 70; www.gataccommoda tion.com; Carrer de Joaquín Costa 44; s/d without bathroom €63/82; ❄@🖪; ⓜUniversitat) A hip 2nd-floor *hostal* located on a bar-lined lane.

Barceló Raval
DESIGN HOTEL €€

(Map p250; ☎93 320 14 90; www.barceloraval.com; Rambla del Raval 17-21; d €160-230; ❄@; ⓜLiceu) This oval-shaped designer hotel adds a dash of 21st-century style to rough-and-tumble Raval. Three classes of rooms come loaded with creature comforts (including iPod docks and Nespresso machines), while the rooftop terrace and stylish B-Lounge bar-restaurant are worth a visit even if you don't stay.

Hotel Peninsular
HOTEL €€

(Map p250; ☎93 302 31 38; www.hpeninsular. com; Carrer de Sant Pau 34; s/d €55/78; ❄@🖪; ⓜLiceu) An oasis on the edge of the slightly dicey Barri Xinès, this former convent has a plant-draped atrium and 60 simple but mostly spacious rooms.

LA RIBERA

Chic & Basic
DESIGN HOTEL €€

(Map p254; ☎93 295 46 52; www.chicandbasic. com; Carrer de la Princesa 50; s €96, d €132-192; ❄@; ⓜJaume I) This is a very cool hotel indeed, with its 31 spotlessly white rooms and fairy-lights curtains that change colour, adding an entirely new atmosphere to the space. Many beautiful old features of the original

CAMPING

The nearest campgrounds to Barcelona lie some way out of town. A couple are on the main coast road heading for Sitges.

Some 11km northeast of the city and only 200m from El Masnou train station (reached by *rodalies* trains from Catalunya station on Plaça de Catalunya), **Camping Masnou** (☑972 454175; www.campingmasnou.com; Camí Fabra 33; 2-person site with car €26-45, bungalows €46-70; ⊙year-round) offers some shade, is near the beach and is reasonable value.

Camping Tres Estrellas (☑93 633 06 37; www.camping3estrellas.com; 2-person site with car €29-36; ⊙mid-Mar–mid-Oct; P@≋) is one of several campgrounds located on a stretch of beach starting about 12km southwest of Barcelona. It has shops, restaurants, bars, several pools and laundry facilities. There's a play area for kids and a basketball court. It's a comparatively green spot under shady pines. Bus L95 runs from the corner of Ronda de la Universitat and Rambla de Catalunya.

building have been retained, such as the marble staircase. Chic & Basic also runs a *hostal* in El Raval.

Hotel Banys Orientals　BOUTIQUE HOTEL €€
(Map p254; ☑93 268 84 60; www.hotelbanysori entals.com; Carrer de l'Argenteria 37; s/d €88/105, ste €130; ❄@; MJaume I) Cool blues and aquamarines combine with dark-hued floors to lend this boutique hotel a quiet charm. All rooms, on the small side, look onto the street or back lanes. There are more spacious suites in two other nearby buildings.

Hostal Orleans　HOSTAL €
(Map p244; ☑93 319 73 82; www.hostalorleans. com; Avinguda del Marquès de l'Argentera 13; MBarceloneta) On the edge of the old quarter, this affable accommodation comprises large rooms (many with en suite), a cosy and tranquil living room with period touches, and an owner whose warm welcome is ample compensation for the three flights of stairs you must climb.

Pensió 2000　PENSIÓN €€
(☑93 310 74 66; www.pensio2000.com; Carrer de Sant Peremés Alt 6; s/d €60/80; @; MUrquinaona) This 1st-floor, family-run place is opposite the anything-but-simple Palau de la Música Catalana. Seven reasonably spacious doubles all have mosaic-tiled floors. Two have en suite bathroom. Eat breakfast in the little courtyard. From Urquinaona metro station, walk southeast along Via Laietana and turn left on Carrer de Sant Peremés.

PORT VELL & LA BARCELONETA

W Barcelona　LUXURY HOTEL €€€
(Map p256; ☑93 295 28 00; www.w-barcelona.com; Plaça de la Rosa dels Vents 1; r from €310; P❄@ ☎≋; ☐17, 39, 57 or 64, MBarceloneta) In an ad-

mirable location at the end of a beach, the spinnaker-shaped tower has stylish rooms and suites that are the last word in contemporary hotel chic. Guests can flit between gym, infinity pool (with bar) and spa. There's avant garde dining on the 2nd floor in Carles Abellán's Bravo restaurant and panoramic cocktail sipping in the top-floor Eclipse bar.

Hotel 54　HOTEL €€
(Map p256; ☑93 225 00 54; www.hotel54bar celoneta.com; Passeig de Joan de Borbó 54; s/d €140/150; ❄@☎; MBarceloneta) This place is all about location. Modern rooms, with dark tile floors and designer bathrooms are sought after for the marina and sunset views. Other rooms look out over the lanes of La Barceloneta. You can also sit on the roof terrace and enjoy the harbour views.

Hotel del Mar　HOTEL €€
(Map p244; ☑93 319 30 47; www.gargallo-hotels. com; Pla del Palau 19; s/d €113/130; ❄@☎; MBarceloneta) Strategically placed between Port Vell and El Born, Hotel del Mar has nicely designed rooms with dark tile floors and designer bathrooms. The best rooms have balconies with waterfront views.

Hotel Marina Folch　HOTEL €
(Map p256; ☑93 310 37 09; www.hotelmarinafol chbcn.com; Carrer del Mar 16; s/d/tr €45/65/85; ❄☎; MBarceloneta) A simple dig above a busy seafood restaurant, this family-run hotel has rooms of varying sizes and quality. The best are those with small balconies facing out towards the marina.

L'EIXAMPLE

Hotel Praktik　BOUTIQUE HOTEL €€
(Map p262; ☑93 343 66 90; www.hotelpraktikram bla.com; Rambla de Catalunya 27; r from €80-170;

❄@☎; MPasseig de Gràcia) This Modernista gem hides a gorgeous little boutique number. The 43 rooms have daring ceramic touches, spot lighting and contemporary art. There is a chilled reading area and deck-style lounge terrace.

Five Rooms
BOUTIQUE HOTEL €€
(Map p262; ✉93 342 78 80; www.thefiverooms. com; Carrer de Pau Claris 72; s/d from €115/135, apt from €175; ❄@☎; MUrquinaona) On the edge of L'Eixample, Five Rooms indeed has five rooms. Each is different, and features include broad, firm beds, stretches of exposed brick wall, restored mosaic tiles and minimalist decor.

Hotel Omm
DESIGN HOTEL €€€
(Map p262; ✉93 445 40 00; www.hotelomm.es; Carrer de Rosselló 265; d from €360; P❄@☎; MDiagonal) Design meets plain zany here, with a wild facade that would no doubt have appealed to Dalí. Light, clear tones dominate in the ultramodern rooms, of which there are several categories.

Hotel Constanza
BOUTIQUE HOTEL €€
(Map p262; ✉93 270 19 10; www.hotelconstanza. com; Carrer del Bruc 33; s/d €130/150; ❄@; MGirona or Urquinaona) This boutique beauty has stolen the hearts of many a visitor to Barcelona. Design touches abound, and little details like flowers in the bathroom add charm. The terrace is a nice spot to relax with views over the rooftops of L'Eixample.

Hostal Goya
HOSTAL €€
(Map p262; ✉93 302 25 65; www.hostalgoya.com; Carrer de Pau Claris 74; s €70, d €96-113; ❄; MPasseig de Gràcia) The Goya is a modestly priced gem on the chichi side of L'Eixample. Rooms have a light colour scheme that varies from room to room. Pricier doubles have a balcony.

Hotel Axel
HOTEL €€
(Map p262; ✉93 323 93 93; www.axelhotels. com; Carrer d'Aribau 33; r from €142; ❄@☎❄; MUniversitat) Fashion- and gay-friendly, the sleek-lined Axel offers modern touches in its designer rooms (and king-size beds in the doubles). Take a break in the rooftop pool, the Finnish sauna or the hot tub. Or sip a cocktail at the summertime Skybar.

Hotel D'Uxelles
HOTEL €€
(Map p262; ✉93 265 25 60; http://hostalduxelle shotelbarcelona.priorguest.com; Gran Vía de les Corts Catalanes 688; s/d €90/109; ❄@; MTetuan) A charming simplicity pervades the rooms, with wrought-iron bedsteads and flowing drapes. Some rooms have little terraces. Get a back room, as Gran Vía is quite noisy.

Fashion House
B&B €€
(✉637 904044; www.bcnfashionhouse.com; Carrer del Bruc 13; s/d/tr without bathroom €55/80/125; MUrquinaona) This typical, broad 1st-floor L'Eixample flat contains eight rooms of varying size done in tasteful style, with high ceilings, parquet floors and, in some cases, a little gallery onto the street. Bathrooms are located along the broad corridor, one for every two rooms.

Market Hotel
BOUTIQUE HOTEL €€
(✉93 325 12 05; www.forkandpillow.com; Passatge de Sant Antoni Abad 10; s €110, d €120-130, ste €145; ❄@; MSant Antoni) Attractively located in a renovated building along a narrow lane, this place has an air of simple chic. Room decor is a pleasing combination of white, dark nut browns, light timber and reds.

Hostal Oliva
HOSTAL €€
(Map p262; ✉93 488 01 62; www.hostaloliva.com; Passeig de Gràcia 32; d €85, s/d without bathroom €38/66; ❄☎; MPasseig de Gràcia) A picturesque antique lift wheezes its way up to this 4th-floor *hostal*, a terrific, reliable cheapie in one of the city's most expensive neighbourhoods. Some of the single rooms are barely big enough to fit a bed but the doubles are big enough, light and airy.

Somnio Hostel
HOSTEL €€
(Map p262; ✉93 272 53 08; www.somniohostels. com; Carrer de la Diputació 251; dm €25, d €87, s/d without bathroom €44/78; ❄@☎; MPasseig de Gràcia) A crisp, tranquil hostel with 10 rooms (all with a simple white and light-blue paint job), Somnio is nicely located in the thick of things in L'Eixample and a short walk from the old town.

GRÀCIA
Hotel Casa Fuster
DESIGN HOTEL €€€
(Map p268; ✉93 255 30 00, 902 202345; www.ho telcasafuster.com; Passeig de Gràcia 132; s/d from €300/330; P❄@☎❄; MDiagonal) This sumptuous Modernista mansion is one of Barcelona's most luxurious hotels. Standard rooms are plush, if small, and period details feature throughout. The rooftop terrace (with pool) offers great views, while the Café Vienés hosts some excellent jazz nights.

EL POBLE SEC
Hotel Gran Via
HOTEL €€
(Map p274; ✉93 318 19 00; www.nnhotels.es; Gran Vía de les Corts Catalánes 642; d from €132;

Ⓜ Passeig de Gràcia) This place oozes old-fashioned elegance and much of its 19th-century interior remains intact. Guest rooms have been comfortably tweaked, but the public areas, complete with antique furnishings, retain the grace of another age and there's a wonderful and relaxing courtyard.

Hostel Mambo Tango
HOSTEL €

(Map p274; ☑ 93 442 51 64; www.hostelmambotango.com; Carrer del Poeta Cabanyes 23; dm €26; @ 🛜; Ⓜ Paral·lel) A fun, international hostel to hang out in, the Mambo Tango has basic dorms (sleeping from six to 10 people) and a welcoming, somewhat chaotic atmosphere.

Hostal Oliveta
HOSTEL €

(Map p274; ☑ 93 329 23 16; Carrer del Poeta Cabanyes 18; s/d €40/60, without bathroom €30/50; Ⓜ Paral·lel) Six squeaky-clean little rooms huddle above a simple family eatery just off busy Avinguda del Paral·lel in Poble Sec. It's hard to argue with the prices and you get to live just beyond the tourist hubbub.

Melon District
HOSTEL €

(Map p274; ☑ 93 329 96 67; www.melondistrict.com; Avinguda del Paral·lel 101; s €55-65, d €60-70; 🅿 ❋ @ 🛜; Ⓜ Paral·lel) Erasmus folks and an international student set are attracted to this *hostal*-style spot, where whiter than white is the aesthetic of choice.

✕ Eating

Barcelona is something of a foodies' paradise, combining rich Catalan cooking traditions with a new wave of culinary wizards by chefs at the vanguard of *nueva cocina española*.

Traditional restaurants, often quite affordable, are scattered across the Barri Gòtic and El Raval, where you'll also find plenty of hip little places. The El Born area of La Ribera teems with eateries, ranging from high-end experimental to many atmospheric spots in historic buildings.

Barceloneta and the waterfront is famed for its seafood eateries, while Gràcia spreads a diverse range of tapas bars, inexpensive Middle Eastern and Greek joints and classic Spanish eateries.

Across the broad expanse of L'Eixample, the Zona Alta and further outlying districts, you'll find all sorts of places, from designer sushi bars and top-end dining rooms to festive old-world eateries. You need to know where you are going, however, as wandering about aimlessly and picking whatever

takes your fancy is not as feasible as in the old city.

Cartas (menus) may be in Catalan, Spanish or both; quite a few establishments also have foreign-language menus.

BARRI GÒTIC

TOP CHOICE Koy Shunka
JAPANESE €€€

(Map p244; ☑ 93 412 79 39; www.koyshunka.com; Carrer de Copons 7; multicourse menus €72-108; �)lunch Tue-Sun, dinner Tue-Sat; Ⓜ Urquinaona) Down a narrow lane north of the cathedral, Koy Shunka opens a portal to exquisite dishes from the East – mouth-watering sushi, sashimi, seared wagyu beef and flavour-rich seaweed salads are served alongside inventive cooked fusion dishes. Don't miss the house speciality of *toro* (tender tuna belly).

Pla
FUSION €€

(Map p244; ☑ 93 412 65 52; www.elpla.cat; Carrer de la Bellafila 5; mains €18-24; ☉dinner; ☑; Ⓜ Jaume I) One of Gòtic's long-standing favourites, Pla is a stylish, romantically lit medieval den that churns out temptations like oxtail braised in red wine, seared tuna with roasted aubergine, and 'Thai-style' monkfish.

La Vinateria dell Call
SPANISH €€

(Map p244; ☑ 93 302 60 92; http://lavinateriadelcall.com; Carrer de Sant Domènec del Call 9; small plates €7-11; ☉dinner; Ⓜ Jaume I) In a magical setting in the former Jewish quarter, this tiny jewel box of a restaurant serves up tasty Iberian dishes. Portions are small and made for sharing, and there's a good and affordable selection of wines.

Cafè de l'Acadèmia
CATALAN €€

(Map p244; ☑ 93 319 82 53; Carrer de Lledó 1; mains €13-17; ☉Mon-Fri; Ⓜ Jaume I) At lunchtime, local *ajuntament* (town hall) office workers pounce on the *menú del día* (for €14, or €10 at the bar) at this famous restaurant. In the evening it is rather more romantic, as low lighting emphasises the intimacy of the timber ceiling and wooden decor.

Can Culleretes
CATALAN €€

(Map p250; ☑ 93 317 30 22; Carrer Quintana 5; mains €8-14; ☉lunch & dinner Tue-Sat, lunch Sun; Ⓜ Liceu) Founded in 1786, Barcelona's oldest restaurant is still going strong, with tourists and locals flocking to enjoy its rambling interior, old-fashioned tile-filled decor, and enormous helpings of traditional Catalan food.

BARCELONA EATING

Bar Celta
GALICIAN €€

(Map p244; Carrer de la Mercè 16; tapas €3-6; ⊗noon-midnight Tue-Sun; ⓂDrassanes) This bright, rambunctious tapas bar specialises in *pulpo* (octopus) and other sea critters like *navajas* (razor clams). It does a good job: even the most demanding of Galician natives give this spot the thumbs up.

Agut
CATALAN €€

(Map p244; www.restaurantagut.com; Carrer d'en Gignàs 16; mains €16-25; ⊗lunch & dinner Tue-Sat, lunch Sun; ⓂDrassanes) Deep in the Gothic labyrinth lies this classic eatery. A series of cosy dining areas is connected by broad arches while, high up, the walls are tightly lined with artworks. There's art in what the kitchen serves up too, from the oak-grilled meat to a succulent variety of seafood offerings.

Cereria
VEGETARIAN €€

(Map p244; ✆93 301 85 10; Baixada de Sant Miquel 3; mains €9-16; ⊗dinner Mon-Sat; 🔊✍; Ⓜ Jaume I) Black-and-white marble floors, a smattering of old wooden tables and ramshackle displays of instruments (most made on site) lend a certain bohemian charm to this small vegetarian restaurant. The pizzas are delicious here and feature organic ingredients – as do the flavourful galettes, dessert crêpes and bountiful salads. Vegan options too.

Caelum
CAFE €

(Map p250; ✆93 302 69 93; Carrer de la Palla 8; snacks €2-4; ⊗10.30am-8.30pm Mon-Thu, 10.30am-11.30pm Fri & Sat, 11.30am-9pm Sun; ⓂLiceu) Sweets (such as the irresistible marzipan from Toledo) made by nuns in convents across the country make their way to this exquisite medieval space. There's also an atmospheric underground chamber where you can secret yourself for tea and pastries from 3.30pm to closing time.

Milk
BRUNCH €

(Map p244; www.milkbarcelona.com; Carrer d'en Gignàs 21; mains €9-10; ⊗10am-4pm & 6.30-11.30pm ; Ⓜ Jaume I) Known to many as a cool cocktail spot, the Irish-run Milk's key role for Barcelona night owls is providing morning-after brunches (served till 4pm).

EL RAVAL

TOP CHOICE Bar Pinotxo
TAPAS €€

(Map p250; Mercat de la Boqueria; meals €20; ⊗6am-5pm Mon-Sat Sep-Jul; ⓂLiceu) Arguably La Boqueria's best tapas bar sits among the half-dozen-or-so informal eateries within the market. The popular owner, Juanito,

might serve up chickpeas with a sweet sauce of pine nuts and raisins, soft baby squid with cannelini beans, or caramel sweet pork belly.

Ca L'Isidre
CATALAN €€€

(Map p250; ✆93 441 11 39; www.calisidre.com; Carrer de les Flors 12; mains €20-70; ⊗Mon-Sat, closed Easter & 3 weeks in Aug; ⓂParal·lel) Ca L'Isidre is an old-world gem. Try artichoke hearts stuffed with mushrooms and foie gras, tuna steak with a tomato coulis or lamb's brains with black butter.

Granja Viader
CAFE €

(Map p250; ✆93 318 34 86; www.granjaviader.cat; Carrer d'en Xuclà 4; ⊗9am-1.45pm & 5-8.45pm Tue-Sat, 5-8.45pm Mon; ⓂLiceu) For more than a century, people have flocked down this alley to get to the cups of homemade hot chocolate and whipped cream (ask for a *suis*) ladled out in this classic Catalan-style milk-bar-cum-deli.

Can Lluís
CATALAN €€€

(Map p250; Carrer de la Cera 49; meals €30-35; ⊗Mon-Sat Sep-Jul; ⓂSant Antoni) Three generations have kept this spick-and-span old-time classic in business since 1929. Expect fresh fish and seafood. The *llenguado* (sole) is oven cooked in whisky and raisins.

Casa Leopoldo
CATALAN €€

(Map p250; ✆93 441 30 14; www.casaleopoldo. com; Carrer de Sant Rafael 24; meals around €50; ⊗lunch & dinner Tue-Sat, lunch Sun Sep-Jul; ⓂLiceu) Several rambling dining areas in this 1920s classic have magnificent tiled walls and exposed-beam ceilings. The mostly seafood menu is extensive and the wine list strong. The €25 fixed menus – available most weekdays and occasional weeknights – offer good value.

Organic
VEGETARIAN €

(Map p250; www.antoniaorganickitchen.com; Carrer de la Junta de Comerç 11; mains €5-8; ⊗12.45pm-midnight; ✍; ⓂLiceu) Servings at this sprawling vegetarian spot are generous and imaginative. The set lunch costs €9.50 plus drinks.

LA RIBERA

TOP CHOICE Cal Pep
TAPAS €€

(Map p254; ✆93 310 79 61; www.calpep.com; Plaça de les Olles 8; mains €8-18; ⊗lunch Tue-Sat, dinner Mon-Fri Sep-Jul; ⓂBarceloneta) Ever-popular Cal Pep has queues around the square with people trying to get in. And if you want one of the five tables out the back, you'll need to call ahead. Most people are happy elbowing their way to the bar for some of the tastiest gourmet seafood tapas in town.

Casa Delfín   SPANISH €

(Map p254; Passeig del Born 36; mains €4-12; ☺noon-1am; Ⓜ Barceloneta) One of Barcelona's culinary delights, Casa Delfín is everything you dream of when you think of Catalan (and Mediterranean) cooking. Meaty monkfish roasted in white wine and garlic, mussels and clams with Catalan flatbread and many other dishes are all done to perfection.

Le Cucine Mandarosso   ITALIAN €

(☎932 69 07 80; www.lecucinemandarosso.com; Carrer Verdaguer i Callis 4; mains €8, lunch menu €10; ☺lunch & dinner; Ⓜ Urquinaona) This is Italian comfort food done to perfection. Combine an outstanding pasta dish with a green salad, and follow up with some homemade cakes (more can be had at Mandarosso Pastis, around the corner at Carrer del General Alvarez de Castro 5). The €10 lunch menu is exceptionally good value. Book in advance for dinner.

Pla de la Garsa   CATALAN €€

(Map p254; ☎933 15 24 13; www.pladelagarsa.com; Carrer dels Assaonadors 13; mains €10; ☺dinner; ✿; Ⓜ Jaume I) This 17th-century house, with its timber beams, anarchically scattered tables and soft ambient music make an enchanting setting for hearty Catalan cooking.

Centre Cultural Euskal Etxea   BASQUE €€€

(Map p244; ☎93 310 21 85; Placeta de Montcada 1; tapas €20-25, meals €35-40; ☺lunch & dinner Tue-Sat, lunch Sun; Ⓜ Jaume I) This Basque eatery is the real deal. Choose your *pintxos* (tapas), sip *txacoli* wine, and keep the toothpicks so the staff can tally up your bill at the end.

Comerç 24   INTERNATIONAL €€€

(Map p254; ☎93 319 21 02; www.carlesabellan. com; Carrer del Comerç 24; meals €50-60; ☺Tue-Sat; Ⓜ Barceloneta) The edgy black-red-yellow decor in the rear dining area lends this culinary cauldron a New York feel. Chef Carles Abellán whips up some eccentric dishes, inspired by everything from sushi to *crostini*. Plump for the tasting menu (€54) and leave it up to Abellán.

LA BARCELONETA & THE COAST

Can Majó   SEAFOOD €€

(Map p256; ☎93 221 54 55; Carrer del Almirall Aixada 23; mains €18-24; ☺lunch & dinner Tue-Sat, lunch Sun; ☐45, 57, 59, 64 or 157; Ⓜ Barceloneta) Virtually on the beach (with tables outside in sum-

mer), Can Majó has a long and steady reputation for fine seafood, particularly its rice dishes and bountiful *suquets* (fish stews).

Can Maño   SPANISH €

(Map p256; Carrer del Baluard 12; mains €8-12; ☺Mon-Sat; Ⓜ Barceloneta) It may look like a dive, but you'll need to be prepared to wait before being squeezed in at a packed table for a raucous night of *raciones* (posted on a board at the back) over a bottle of turbio – a cloudy white plonk. The seafood is abundant with first-rate squid, shrimp and fish served at rock-bottom prices.

Vaso de Oro   TAPAS €

(Map p256; Carrer de Balboa 6; tapas €5-9; ☺10am-midnight; Ⓜ Barceloneta) Always packed, this narrow bar gathers a festive, beer-swilling crowd who come for fantastic tapas.

La Cova Fumada   TAPAS €

(Map p256; ☎93 221 40 61; Carrer de Baluard 56; tapas €3-6; ☺9am-3.20pm Mon-Wed, 9am-3.20pm & 6-8.20pm Thu & Fri, 9am-1.20pm Sat; Ⓜ Barceloneta) This tiny, unsigned tapas spot always packs a crowd. The secret? Mouth-watering *pulpo*, *culamar*, *sardinias* and 15 or so other small plates cooked up to perfection in the small open kitchen near the door. The *bombas* (potato and ham croquettes served with alioli) and grilled *carxofes* (artichokes) are famous.

Xiringuito D'Escribà   SEAFOOD €€

(☎93 221 07 29; www.escriba.es; Ronda Litoral 42; mains €18-22; ☺lunch daily year-round, dinner Thu-Sat Apr-Sep; Ⓜ Llacuna) The clan that brought you Escribà sweets and pastries also operates one of Barcelona's most popular waterfront seafood eateries. You can also choose from a selection of Escribà pastries for dessert – worth the trip alone.

Can Ros   SEAFOOD €€

(Map p256; ☎93 221 45 79; Carrer del Almirall Aixada 7; mains €16-28; ☺Tue-Sun; ☐45, 57, 59, 64 or 157; Ⓜ Barceloneta) The guiding principle from this 1911 classic is straightforward: serve juicy fresh fish cooked with a light touch. Can Ros also does a rich *arròs a la marinera* (seafood rice), *fideuá* with shrimp and clams and a mixed seafood platter for two.

Torre d'Alta Mar   MEDITERRANEAN €€€

(Map p256; ☎93 221 00 07; www.torredealtamar. com; Torre de Sant Sebastià; mains around €30; ☺lunch & dinner Tue-Sat, dinner Sun & Mon; ☐17, 39, 57 or 64, Ⓜ Barceloneta) Head 75m skyward to the top of the Torre de Sant Sebastià and

SELF-CATERING

Shop in the Mercat de la Boqueria (Map p250; www.boqueria.info), one of the world's great produce markets, and complement with any other necessities from a local supermarket. Handy ones include Carrefour Express (Map p250; La Rambla dels Estudis 113; ⏰10am-10pm Mon-Sat; Ⓜ️Catalunya), near the northern end of La Rambla; and Superservis (Map p244; Carrer d'Avinyó 13; ⏰8.45am-2pm & 5-8.30pm Mon-Thu & Sat, 8.45am-8.30pm Fri; Ⓜ️Liceu) in the heart of Barri Gòtic.

take a ringside seat for magnificent city and waterfront views while dining on first-rate seafood.

L'EIXAMPLE

TOP CHOICE Tapaç 24   TAPAS €€

(Map p262; www.carlesabellan.com; Carrer de la Diputació 269; mains €10-20; ⏰9am-midnight Mon-Sat; Ⓜ️Passeig de Gràcia) Carles Abellán, master of Comerç 24 (p289) in La Ribera, runs this basement tapas haven known for its gourmet versions of old faves. Specials include the *bikini* (toasted ham and cheese sandwich – here the ham is cured and the truffle makes all the difference), a thick black *arròs negre de sípia* (squid-ink black rice) and, for dessert, *xocolata amb pa, sal i oli* (balls of chocolate in olive oil with a touch of salt and wafer).

Alkímia   CATALAN €€€

(📞93 207 61 15; www.alkimia.cat; Carrer de l'Indústria 79; set menu €38-84; ⏰lunch & dinner Mon-Fri Sep-Jul; Ⓜ️Verdaguer) Jordi Vila, a culinary alchemist, serves up refined Catalan dishes with a twist in this elegant, white-walled locale well off the tourist trail. Dishes such as his *arròs de nyore i safrà amb escamarlans de la costa* (saffron and sweet-chilli rice with crayfish) earned Vila his first Michelin star.

Can Kenji   JAPANESE €

(📞93 476 18 23; www.cankenji.com; Carrer del Rosselló 325; mains €6-12; ⏰1-3.30pm & 8.30-11.30pm Mon-Sat; Ⓜ️Verdaguer) If you want to go Japanese in Barcelona, this is the place. The understated little *izakaya* features Japanese dishes with a Mediterranean touch. Recent hits include sardine tempura with an auber-gine, miso and anchovy puree; and *tataki* (lightly grilled meat) of bonito (tuna) with *salmorejo* (a Córdoban cold tomato and bread soup).

Cinc Sentits   INTERNATIONAL €€

(Map p262; 📞93 323 94 90; www.cincsentits.com; Carrer d'Aribau 58; mains €10-20; ⏰lunch & dinner Tue-Sat ; Ⓜ️Passeig de Gràcia) The 'Five Senses' has earned rave reviews for its indulgent tasting menu (from €49 to €69), consisting of a series of small, experimental dishes. A key is the use of fresh local product, such as fish landed on the Costa Brava and top-quality suckling pig from Extremadura.

Amaltea   VEGETARIAN €

(www.amalteaygovinda.com; Carrer de la Diputació 164; mains €5; ⏰lunch & dinner Mon-Sat; 📷; Ⓜ️Urgell) The ceiling fresco of blue sky sets the scene in this popular vegetarian eatery. The weekday set lunch (€10.50) offers a series of dishes that change frequently with the seasons.

Cata 1.81   TAPAS €€

(Map p262; 📞93 323 68 18; www.cata181.com; Carrer de València 181; tapas €7-12; ⏰dinner Mon-Sat; Ⓜ️Passeig de Gràcia) A beautifully designed eatery, this is the place to come for fine wines and dainty gourmet dishes, such as *raviolis amb bacallà* (salt-cod dumplings) or *truita de patates i tòfona negre* (thick potato tortilla with a delicate trace of black truffle).

Taktika Berri   BASQUE, TAPAS €€

(Map p262; Carrer de València 169; mains €15; ⏰lunch & dinner Mon-Fri, lunch Sat; Ⓜ️Hospital Clínic) Get in early as the bar teems with punters from far and wide, anxious to wrap their mouths around some of the best Basque tapas in town. The hot morsels are all snapped up as they arrive from the kitchen; it's all over by about 10.30pm.

📷 Fastvínic   CAFE €

(Map p262; 📞93 487 32 41; www.fastvinic.com; Carrer de la Diputació 251; sandwiches €6-10; ⏰noon-midnight Mon-Sat; Ⓜ️Passeig de Gracia) A project in sustainability all round, this is slow food done fast, with ingredients, wine and building materials all sourced from Catalonia. It's all sandwiches on the menu, with some wonderful choices of roast beef, mustard and honey, or more adventurous crunchy suckling pig, banana chutney and coriander; there is also a self-service wine machine with quality Spanish choices.

Cosmo
CAFE €

(Map p262; www.galeriacosmo.com; Carrer d'Enric Granados 3; ⏰10am-10pm Mon-Thu, noon-2am Fri & Sat, noon-10pm Sun; 🛜; Ⓜ Universitat) Cosmo is a groovy space with psychedelic colouring in the tables and bar stools, high white walls out back for exhibitions and a nice selection of teas, pastries and snacks, all set on a pleasant pedestrian strip behind the university.

GRÀCIA

O'Gràcia!
MEDITERRANEAN €€

(Map p268; Plaça de la Revolució de Setembre de 1868 15; meals €10-12; ⏰Tue-Sat; Ⓜ Fontana) This is an especially popular lunch option, with the *menú del día* outstanding value at €10.50. The *arròs negre de sepia* (black rice with cuttlefish) makes a good first course, followed by a limited set of meat and fish options with vegetable sides.

Sureny
CATALAN €

(Map p268; ✆93 213 75 56; Plaça de la Revolució de Setembre de 1868; meals €8-10; ⏰Tue-Sun; Ⓜ Fontana) Appearances can be deceiving: the cooks in this unremarkable-looking corner restaurant dedicate themselves to producing gourmet tapas and *raciones*, ranging from exquisite *vieiras* (scallops) to a serving of *secreto ibérico*, a particular tasty cut of pork.

La Nena
CAFE, CHOCOLATE €

(Map p268; ✆93 285 14 76; Carrer de Ramon i Cajal 36; snacks €2-4; ⏰9am-2pm & 4-10pm Mon-Sat, 10am-10pm Sun & holidays; 🚼; Ⓜ Fontana) A French team has created this delightful chaotic, family-friendly space where neighbourhood regulars linger over rich hot chocolate (*suïssos*), fine desserts and savoury crêpes.

Botafumeiro
SEAFOOD €€

(✆93 218 42 30; www.botafumeiro.es; Carrer Gran de Gràcia 81; meals €15-25; ⏰1pm-1am; Ⓜ Fontana) It is hard not to mention this classic temple of Galician shellfish and other briny delights, long a magnet for VIPs visiting Barcelona. You can bring the price down by sharing a few *medias raciones* to taste a range of marine offerings or a *safata especial del Mar Cantàbric* (seafood platter) between two.

Envalira
CATALAN €

(Map p268; Plaça del Sol 13; meals €8; ⏰lunch & dinner Tue-Sat, lunch Sun; Ⓜ Fontana) Surrounded by cool hang-outs, you'd barely notice the modest entrance to this delicious relic. Head for the 1950s time-warp dining room out the

back for all sorts of seafood and rice dishes – from *arròs a la milanesa* (savoury rice dish with chicken, pork and a light cheese gratin) to *bullit de lluç* (slice of white hake boiled with herb-laced rice and clams).

TIBIDABO

El Asador de Aranda
SPANISH €€€

(✆93 417 01 15; www.asadordearanda.com; Avenida del Tibidabo 31; mains €20-22; ⏰closed Sun dinner; 🚃 Av Tibidabo) A great place for a meal after visiting Tibidabo, El Asador de Aranda is set in a striking Modernista building, complete with stained-glass windows, Moorish-style brick arches and elaborate ceilings. You'll find a fine assortment of tapas plates for sharing, though the speciality is the meat (roast lamb, spare ribs, beef), beautifully prepared in a wood oven.

MONTJUÏC & EL POBLE SEC

TOP CHOICE Tickets
SPANISH €€

(Map p274; www.ticketsbar.es, Avinguda del Paral·lel 164; tapas €4-12; Ⓜ Paral·lel) Tickets is the much-touted new venture created by rockstar chef Ferran Adrià (of the legendary El Bulli) and his brother Albert. It's a fairly flamboyant affair in terms of decor, playing with circus images and theatre lights, while the food has kept some of the El Bulli's whimsical molecular dishes; there's also a more serious seafood bar. Head to the bar 41° in back for imaginative cocktails. Reservations are tough. You can book a table online, two months in advance.

Quimet i Quimet
TAPAS €€

(Map p274; Carrer del Poeta Cabanyes 25; tapas €3-11; ⏰lunch & dinner Mon-Fri, noon-6pm Sat; Ⓜ Paral·lel) There's barely space to swing a calamari in this bottle-lined, standing-room-only place, but it is a treat for the palate. Look at all those gourmet tapas waiting for you! Let the folk behind the bar advise you, and order a drop of fine wine to go with the food.

Xemei
ITALIAN €€

(Map p274; ✆93 553 51 40; Passeig de l'Exposició 85; mains €10-20; ⏰Wed-Mon; Ⓜ Paral·lel) Xemei is a wonderful slice of Venice in Barcelona. To the accompaniment of gentle jazz, you might try an entrée of mixed *cicheti* (Venetian seafood tapas), followed with *bigoi in salsa veneziana* (thick spaghetti in an anchovy and onion sauce).

La Tomaquera
CATALAN €

(Map p274; ✆93 441 85 18; Carrer de Margarit 5; mains €7; ⏰lunch & dinner Tue-Sat; Ⓜ Poble Sec)

BARCELONA EATING

The waiters shout and rush about this classic, while carafes of wine are sloshed about the long wooden tables. You can't book, so it's first in, first seated. Try the house speciality of snails or go for hearty meat dishes. Cash only.

Taverna Can Margarit CATALAN €

(Map p274; Carrer de la Concòrdia 21; mains €8-10; ⊗dinner Mon-Sat; ⊠Poble Sec) Traditional Catalan cooking is the name of the game. Surrounded by aged wine barrels, take your place at old tables and benches and perhaps order the *conejo a la jumillana* (fried rabbit herbs).

Drinking

Barcelona's bars run the gamut from wood-panelled wine cellars to bright waterfront places and trendy cocktail lounges. Most are at their liveliest around midnight. Barcelona's clubs are spread a little more thinly than bars across the city. They tend to open from around midnight until 6am.

The old town is jammed with venues. One of the hippest areas is El Born, in the lower end of La Ribera, but there is an impressive scattering of bars across the lower half of the Barri Gòtic and in El Raval too. The last especially is home to some fine old drinking institutions as well as a new wave of funky, inner-city locales.

Elsewhere, a series of squares and some streets of Gràcia are loaded up with bars. In the broad expanse of L'Eixample you need to know where to go. The upper end of Carrer d'Aribau is the busiest area (late in the week), along with the area around its continuation northwest of Avinguda Diagonal.

Some useful sources of information on bars, clubs and gigs include **Barcelonarocks.com** (www.barcelonarocks.com), **Clubbingspain.com** (www.clubbingspain.com) and **LaNetro.com** (http://barcelona.lanetro.com).

BARRI GÒTIC

Oviso BAR

(Map p244; Carrer d'Arai 5; ⊗10am-2am; ⊠Liceu) Oviso is a budget-friendly restaurant by day, and bohemian drinking den by night, with a wildly mixed crowd and a rock-and-roll vibe amid a two-room fin-de-siecle interior that's plastered with curious murals.

Marula Cafè BAR

(Map p244; www.marulacafe.com; Carrer dels Escudellers 49; ⊗11pm-5am; ⊠Liceu) A fantastic funk find in the heart of the Barri Gòtic, Marula will transport you to the 1970s and the best in funk and soul. Occasionally the DJs slip in other tunes, from breakbeat to house. Samba and other Brazilian dance sounds also penetrate here.

Barcelona Pipa Club BAR

(Map p244; ✆93 302 47 32; www.bpipaclub.com; Plaça Reial 3; ⊗10pm-4am; ⊠Liceu) This pipe smokers' club is like an apartment, with all sorts of interconnecting rooms and knick-knacks. Buzz at the door and head two floors up.

Polaroid BAR

(Map p244; Carrer dels Còdols 29; ⊗7pm-2.30am; ⊠Drassanes) True to name, Polaroid is a blast from the VHS tapes and old film comic-book-covered tables and other kitschy design. It draws a fun, unpretentious crowd who come for cheep beer (€2 *cañas*), good mojitos and free popcorn.

La Cerveteca BAR

(Map p244; Carrer de Gignàs 25; ⊗4-10pm Mon-Thu, 1-11pm Fri & Sat, 1-10pm Sun; ⊠Jaume I) An unmissable stop for beer lovers, La Cerveteca serves an impressive variety of global craft brews and is great for an early evening pick-me-up.

Dusk LOUNGE

(Map p244; Carrer de la Mercè 23; ⊗6pm-2.30am; ⊠Drassanes) Tucked away on an atmospheric lane in the Gothic quarter, Irish-owned Dusk teeters between rowdy bar and intimate cocktail lounge. It has various rooms with low lighting, age-old stone walls and comfy couches framed by red curtains but also shows sports on a big-screen TV.

Karma CLUB

(Map p244; ✆93 302 56 80; www.karmadisco.com; Plaça Reial 10; ⊗midnight-5.30am Tue-Sun; ⊠Liceu) During the week, tiny Karma plays good, mainstream indie music, while on weekends the DJs spin anything from rock to disco.

Čaj Chai CAFE

(Map p244; ✆93 301 95 92; Carrer de Sant Domènec del Call 12; ⊗3-10pm Mon, 10.30am-10pm Tue-Sun; ⊠Jaume I) Inspired by Prague's bohemian tea rooms, this bright and buzzing cafe in the heart of the old Jewish quarter is a tea connoisseur's paradise. Čaj Chai stocks over 100 teas from China, India, Korea, Japan, Nepal, Morocco and beyond. It's a much-loved local haunt.

EL RAVAL

Bar la Concha
BAR

(Map p250; Carrer de la Guàrdia 14; ⊙5pm-3am; MDrassanes) La Concha used to be a largely gay and transvestite haunt, but anyone is welcome and bound to have fun – especially when the drag queens come out to play. The music ranges from *paso dobles* to Spanish retro pop.

La Confitería
BAR

(Map p250; Carrer de Sant Pau 128; ⊙11am-2am; MParal·lel) A quiet enough spot for a house *vermut* in the early evening, this mural-covered 19th-century classic (a former confectioner's shop) fills with theatregoers and local partiers later at night.

33|45
BAR

(Map p250; Carrer Joaquín Costa 4; ⊙10am-1:30am Mon-Thu, 10am-3am Fri & Sat, 10am-midnight Sun; MUniversitat) A super trendy cocktail bar on the nightlife-laden Joaquín Costa street, this place has excellent mojitos and a fashionable crowd. The main area has DJ music and lots of excited noise making, while the back room is scattered with sofas and armchairs for a post-dancing slump.

Negroni
COCKTAIL BAR

(Map p250; Carrer de Joaquin Costa 46; ⊙7pm-2am Mon-Thu, 7pm-3am Fri & Sat; MLiceu) This teeny cocktail bar with black and beige decor lures in a largely student set to try out the bar's cocktails, among them the flagship Negroni (equal parts Campari, gin and sweet vermouth).

Bar Marsella
BAR

(Map p250; Carrer de Sant Pau 65; ⊙10pm-2am Mon-Thu, 10pm-3am Fri & Sat; MLiceu) Hemingway used to slump over an *absenta* (absinthe) in this bar, which has been in business since 1820. It still specialises in absinthe, a drink to be treated with respect.

Moog
CLUB

(Map p250; www.masimas.com/moog; Carrer de l'Arc del Teatre 3; admission €10; ⊙midnight-5am; MDrassanes) This fun and minuscule club is a standing favourite with the downtown crowd. In the main dance area, DJs dish out house, techno and electro, while upstairs you can groove to indie and occasional classic-pop throwbacks.

LA RIBERA

El Xampanyet
WINE BAR

(Map p254; Carrer de Montcada 22; ⊙noon-4pm & 7-11pm Tue-Sat, noon-4pm Sun; MJaume I) Nothing has changed for decades in one of the city's best-known *cava* bars. Plant yourself at the bar or seek out a table against the decoratively tiled walls for a glass or three of *cava* and an assortment of tapas, such as the tangy *boquerons en vinagre* (white anchovies in vinegar).

Gimlet
COCKTAIL BAR

(Map p254; Carrer del Rec 24; cocktails €10; ⊙10pm-3am; MJaume I) White-jacketed bar staff with all the appropriate aplomb will whip you up a gimlet or any other classic cocktail. Barcelona cocktail guru Javier Muelas is behind this and several other cocktail bars around the city, so you can be sure of excellent drinks, some with a creative twist.

Mudanzas
BAR

(Map p244; ☑93 319 11 37; Carrer de la Vidrieria 15; ⊙10am-2.30am; MJaume I) This was one of the first bars to get things into gear in El Born and it still attracts a faithful crowd. It's a straightforward place for a beer, a chat and perhaps a sandwich.

La Vinya del Senyor
WINE BAR

(Map p254; Plaça de Santa Maria del Mar 5; ⊙noon-1am Tue-Sun; MJaume I) Relax on the *terrassa*, which lies in the shadow of Església de Santa Maria del Mar, or crowd inside at the tiny bar. The wine list is as long as *War and Peace*.

PORT VELL & LA BARCELONETA

The Barcelona beach scene warms up to dance sounds from Easter to early October. In addition to waterfront restaurants and bars (especially on and near Port Olímpic), a string of *chiringuitos* (rustic bars) sets up along the beaches. Most serve food and some turn into miniclubs on the sand from the afternoon until as late as 2am.

Xampanyeria Can Paixano
WINE BAR

(Map p244; ☑93 310 08 39; Carrer de la Reina Cristina 7; tapas €3-6; ⊙9am-10.30pm Mon-Sat, to 1pm Sun; MBarceloneta) This lofty old champagne bar has long run on a winning formula. The standard poison is bubbly rosé in elegant little glasses, combined with bite-sized *bocadillos* (filled rolls). This place is always jammed to the rafters.

CDLC
LOUNGE

(Map p256; www.cdlcbarcelona.com; Passeig Marítim de la Barceloneta 32; ⊙noon-3am; MCiutadella Vila Olímpica) This Asian-inspired lounge is ideal for a warm-up before heading to the nearby clubs. You can come for the food or wait until about midnight, when they roll up the tables and the DJs and dancers take full control.

Ké? BAR

(Map p256; Carrer del Baluard 54; ⊙11am-2am; MBarceloneta) An eclectic crowd hangs about this hippie-ish little bar near La Barceloneta's market. Pull up a padded 'keg chair' or grab a seat on one of the worn lounges in back.

Shôko LOUNGE

(Map p256; www.shoko.biz; Passeig Marítim de la Barceloneta 36; ⊙noon-3am Tue-Sun; MCiutadella Vila Olímpica) This stylish restaurant, club and beachfront bar brings in a touch of the Far East via potted bamboo, Japanese electro and Asian-Med fusion cuisine. Later Shôko transforms into deep-grooving nightspot with top DJs spinning for a glammy crowd.

Absenta BAR

(Map p256; Carrer de Sant Carles 36; MBarceloneta) Decorated with old paintings, vintage lamps and curious sculpture, this creative drinking den takes its liquor seriously. Stop in for absinthe or house-made vermouth.

Catwalk CLUB

(Map p256; ☑93 224 07 40; www.clubcatwalk.net; Carrer de Ramon Trias Fargas 2-4; admission €15-18; ⊙midnight-6am Thu-Sun; MCiutadella Vila Olímpica) A well-dressed crowd piles in here for good house music, occasionally mellowed down with more body-hugging electro, R&B, hip hop and funk. Alternatively, you can sink into a fat lounge for a quiet tipple and whisper. Popular local DJ Jekey leads the way most nights.

Razzmatazz CLUB

(☑93 320 82 00; www.salarazzmatazz.com; Carrer de Pamplona 88; admission €15-30; ⊙midnight-3.30am Thu, to 5.30am Fri & Sat; MMarina or Bogatell) A half-dozen blocks from Port Olímpic is this stalwart of Barcelona's club and concert scene, with five different clubs in one huge space.

Opium Mar CLUB

(Map p256; ☑902 267486; www.opiummar.com; Passeig Marítim de la Barceloneta 34; ⊙8pm-6am; MCiutadella Vila Olímpica) This seaside dance place has a spacious dance floor that attracts a mostly foreign crowd. It is best in summer, when you can spill onto a terrace overlooking the beach.

L'EIXAMPLE

There are three main concentrations for carousers in L'Eixample. The top end of Carrer d'Aribau and the area where it crosses Avinguda Diagonal attract a heterogeneous but mostly local crowd to its many bars and clubs. Carrer de Balmes is lined with clubs for a mostly teen 'n' 20s crowd. The city's gay-and-lesbian circuit is concentrated in 'Gaixample' around Carrer del Consell de Cent.

TOP CHOICE Monvínic WINE BAR

(Map p262; ☑932 72 61 87; www.monvinic.com; Carrer de la Diputació 249; ⊙wine bar 1.30-11.30pm, restaurant 1.30-3.30pm & 8.30-10.30pm; MPasseig de Gracia) One of Spain's best wine bars, Monvínic has a wine list with more than 3000 varieties (including 60 by the glass). At the back is a restaurant that specialises in Mediterranean cuisine, with ingredients sourced locally from Catalan farmers.

La Fira BAR

(Map p262; www.lafiraclub.com; Carrer de Provença 171; admission €8-12; ⊙10.30pm-3am Wed-Sat; ⑯FGC Provença) A designer bar with a difference. Wander in past distorting mirrors and ancient fairground attractions from Germany. Put in coins and listen to hens squawk. Speaking of squawking, the music swings wildly from whiffs of house through '90s hits to Spanish pop classics.

Les Gens Que J'Aime BAR

(Map p262; Carrer de València 286; ⊙6pm-2.30am Sun-Thu, to 3am Fri & Sat; MPasseig de Gràcia) This intimate basement relic of the 1960s follows a deceptively simple formula: chilled jazz music in the background, minimal lighting from vintage lamps and a cosy scattering of red velvet-backed lounges around tiny tables.

Berlin BAR

(Carrer de Muntaner 240; ⊙10am-2am Mon-Thu, to 3am Fri & Sat; MDiagonal or Hospital Clínic) Service can be harried but the location is excellent for starting an uptown night – either at outdoor tables on the footpath or in the designer lounges downstairs.

Dry Martini BAR

(Map p262; ☑93 217 50 72; www.drymartinibcn.com; Carrer d'Aribau 162-166; ⊙5pm-3am; MDiagonal) The house drink, taken at the bar or in one of the plush green leather lounges, is a safe bet, served in enormous glasses! Out the back is a restaurant, Speakeasy (Map p262; 93 217 50 80; www.drymartinibcn.com; Carrer d'Aribau 162-166; mains €10-15; ☺lunch & dinner Mon-Fri, dinner Sat Sep-Jul; MDiagonal).

Premier
BAR
(Map p262; Carrer de Provença 236; ☺6pm-2.30am Mon-Thu, to 3am Fri & Sat; FGC Provença) This funky little French-run spot has a small wine list and decent mojitos. Hug the bar, sink into a lounge or hide up on the mezzanine. Later in the evening, a DJ adds to the ambience.

Milano
COCKTAIL BAR
(Map p262; www.camparimilano.com; Ronda de la Universitat 35; ☺noon-2.30am; MCatalunya) You'll find happily imbibing crowds and a festive, anything-goes air at this vast downstairs cocktail den.

GRÀCIA

La Cigale
BAR
(Map p268; 93 457 58 23; http://poesialacigale. blogspot.co.uk; Carrer de Tordera 50; ☺6pm-2.30am Sun-Thu, 6pm-3am Fri & Sat; MJoanic) La Cigale is a civilised place for a cocktail (or two for €8 before 10pm), with occasional poetry readings. Prop up the zinc bar, sink into a secondhand lounge chair or head upstairs. Music is chilled and conversation is lively.

Raïm
BAR
(Map p268; www.raimbcn.com; Carrer del Progrés 48; ☺8pm-2.30am; MDiagonal) Dripping with nostalgia, Raïm is plastered with oversized mirrors and black-and-white photos from Cuba. A buzzing crowd comes for rum drinks and Caribbean tunes.

Le Journal
BAR
(Map p268; 93 218 04 13; Carrer de Francisco Giner 36; ☺6pm-2.30am Sun-Thu, 6pm-3am Fri & Sat; MFontana) Students love the conspiratorial air of this narrow basement bar, whose walls and ceiling are plastered with newspapers (hence the name).

Musical Maria
BAR
(Map p268; Carrer de Maria 5; ☺9pm-3am; MDiagonal) Those longing for rock 'n' roll crowd into this animated bar, listen to old hits and knock back bottles of Estrella.

Sabor A Cuba
BAR
(Map p268; Carrer de Francisco Giner 32; ☺10pm-2.30am Mon-Thu, 10pm-3am Fri & Sat; MDiagonal) A mixed crowd of Cubans and Caribbean fans come to drink mojitos and shake their stuff in this diminutive, good-humoured hang-out.

TIBIDABO & LA ZONA ALTA

Mirablau
BAR
(Plaça del Doctor Andreu; ☺11am-4.30am Sun-Thu, to 5am Fri & Sat; Avinguda Tibidabo then tramvia blau) Gaze out over the entire city from this privileged balcony restaurant on the way up to Tibidabo. Wander downstairs to join the folk in the tiny dance space. In summer you can step out onto the even smaller terrace for a breather.

Elephant
CLUB
(93 334 02 58; www.elephantbcn.com; Passeig dels Til·lers 1; ☺11.30am-4am Thu, to 5am Fri & Sat; P; MPalau Reial) Getting in here is like being invited to a private fantasy party in Beverly Hills. Models and wannabes mix with immaculately groomed lads who most certainly didn't come by taxi. There's a big tentlike dance space as well as a series of garden bars in summer.

Luz de Gas
CLUB
(93 209 77 11; www.luzdegas.com; Carrer de Muntaner 246; admission up to €20; ☺11.30pm-6am; MDiagonal, then 6, 7, 15, 27, 32, 33, 34, 58 or 64) Several nights a week this club, set in a grand former theatre, hosts a wide mix of concerts ranging through soul, country, salsa, rock, jazz and pop. It gets a little sweaty in the dedicated club room Sala B, which opens on Friday and Saturday nights only.

Otto Zutz
CLUB
(www.ottozutz.com; Carrer de Lincoln 15; admission €15; ☺midnight-6am Tue-Sat; FGC Gràcia) Beautiful people only need apply for entry to this three-floor dance den. Head downstairs for house, or upstairs for funk and soul. Friday and Saturday it's hip hop, R&B and funk on the ground floor and house on the 1st floor.

Sutton The Club
CLUB
(www.thesuttonclub.com; Carrer de Tuset 13; admission €15; ☺midnight-5am Wed & Thu, midnight-6am Fri & Sat, 10.30pm-4am Sun; MDiagonal) A classic disco with mainstream sounds, this place inevitably attracts just about everyone pouring in and out of the nearby bars at some stage of the evening. The people are mostly beautiful and the bouncers can be tough.

MONTJUÏC & EL POBLE SEC

Tinta Roja
BAR
(Map p274; Carrer de la Creu dels Molers 17; ☺8.30pm-2am Thu, to 3am Fri & Sat; MPoble Sec) A succession of nooks and crannies, dotted

with what could be a flea market's collection of furnishings and dimly lit in violets, reds and yellows, makes the 'Red Ink' an intimate spot for a drink and the occasional show in the back – with anything from actors to acrobats.

Terrazza CLUB
(Map p274; www.laterrrazza.com; Avinguda de Francesc Ferrer i Guàrdia; admission €10-20; ⊗midnight-5am Thu, to 6am Fri & Sat; MEspanya) One of the city's top summertime dance locations, Terrrazza attracts squadrons of the beautiful people for a full-on night of music and cocktails partly under the stars inside the Poble Espanyol complex.

☆ Entertainment

To keep up with what's on, pick up a copy of the weekly listings magazine *Guía del Ocio* (€1, www.guiadelocio.com) from news stands. Newspapers also have listings (with an extensive entertainment section on Fridays) and the Palau de la Virreina (Map p250) information office can clue you in to present and forthcoming events.

The easiest way to get hold of *entradas* (tickets) for most venues throughout the city is through the Caixa de Catalunya's Tel-Entrada (www.telentrada.com) service or Servi-Caixa (www.servicaixa.com). Another one to try for concerts is Ticketmaster (www.ticketmaster.es). There's a *venta de localidades* (ticket office) on the ground floor of the Plaça de Catalunya branch of **El Corte Inglés** and at some of its other branches around town; and at the **FNAC store** in the El Triangle shopping centre on the same square. You can also buy tickets through El Corte Inglés (www.elcorteingles.es) by phone and online (click on *entradas*).

You can purchase some half-price tickets in person no more than three hours before the start of the show you wish to see at the Palau de la Virreina. The system is known as Tiquet-3.

Cinemas

Foreign films, shown with subtitles and their original soundtrack, rather than dubbed, are marked VO (*versión original*) in movie listings. These cinemas show VO films.

TOP CHOICE **Filmoteca de Catalunya** CINEMA
(Map p250; ☎93 567 10 70; www.filmoteca.cat; Plaça Salvador Seguí 1-9 ; tickets from €2-4; ⊗8am-10pm; MLiceu) In a sleek new space that opened in 2012, the Filmoteca de Catalunya has two cinema screens that showcase innovative works, a film library, a bookshop, a cafe and ample exhibition space.

Méliès Cinemes CINEMA
(☎93 451 00 51; www.cinesmelies.net; Carrer de Villarroel 102; admission €3-5; MUrgell) A cosy cinema with two screens, the Méliès specialises in old classics from Hollywood and European cinema.

Renoir Floridablanca CINEMA
(☎93 426 33 37; www.cinesrenoir.com; Carrer de Floridablanca 135; MSant Antoni) With seven screens, this is one of a small chain of art-house cinemas in Spain showing quality flicks. It's located one block southwest of Ronda de Sant Antoni (take Carrer de Valldonzella).

Verdi CINEMA
(Map p268; ☎93 238 79 90; www.cines-verdi.com; Carrer de Verdi 32; MFontana) A popular movie house in the heart of Gràcia.

Verdi Park CINEMA
(Map p268; ☎93 238 79 90; www.cines-verdi.com; Carrer de Torrijos 49; MFontana) Sister to the Verdi, the Verdi Park is a block away and follows the same art-house philosophy.

Yelmo Cines Icària CINEMA
(Map p256; ☎93 221 75 85; www.yelmocines.es; Carrer de Salvador Espriu 61; MCiutadella Vila Olímpica) This vast cinema complex screens movies in the original language on 15 screens, making for plenty of choice.

Theatre

Theatre is almost always performed in Catalan or Spanish. For what's on, visit the information office at Palau de la Virreina, where you'll find leaflets and *Teatre BCN*, the monthly listings guide.

Teatre Lliure THEATRE
(Map p274; ☎93 289 27 70; www.teatrelliure.com; Plaça de Margarida Xirgu 1; tickets €13-26; ⊗box office 5-8pm; MEspanya) Housed in the magnificent former Palau de l'Agricultura building on Montjuïc and consisting of two modern spaces (Espai Lliure and Sala Fabià Puigserver), the 'Free Theatre' puts on a variety of quality drama, contemporary dance and music.

Teatre Mercat De Les Flors DANCE
(Map p274; ☎93 426 18 75; www.mercatflors.org; Carrer de Lleida 59; tickets €15-20; ⊗box office 11am-2pm & 4-7pm Mon-Fri & 1hr before show;

GAY & LESBIAN BARCELONA

Somewhat overshadowed by the beachy gay mecca of Sitges up the coast, Barcelona has a lively gay scene. Gay bars, clubs and cafes are mostly concentrated around the 'Gaixample', between Carrer de Muntaner and Carrer de Balmes, around Carrer del Consell de Cent.

For information, pick up a copy of **Shanguide** (www.shangay.com), available in many gay bars and shops. Other sources of info include www.60by80.com, www.barcelona gay.com and www.guiagaybarcelona.es.

Popular with a young, cruisy gay crowd, **Arena Madre** (Map p262; ☑93 487 83 42; www.arenadisco.com; Carrer de Balmes 32; admission €6-12; ☺12.30-5.30am; ⓂPasseig de Gràcia) is one of the top gay clubs in town. Keep an eye on Wednesday's drag shows. At **Dietrich Gay Teatro Café** (Map p262; ☑93 451 77 07; Carrer del Consell de Cent 255; ☺10.30pm-3am; ⓂUniversitat), it's show time at 1am, with at least one drag-queen gala per night at this cabaret-style locale dedicated to Marlene.

Metro (☑93 323 52 27; www.metrodiscobcn.com; Carrer de Sepúlveda 185; ☺1-5am Mon, midnight-5am Sun & Tue-Thu, midnight-6am Fri & Sat; ⓂUniversitat) attracts a casual crowd with its two dance floors, three bars and very dark room. A long-time favourite, and a great place to start off the night, is **Punto Bcn** (Map p262; ☑93 453 61 23; www.arenadis co.com; Carrer de Muntaner 63-65; ☺6pm-3am; ⓂUniversitat).

ⓂEspanya) Next door to the Teatre Lliure, and together with it known as the Ciutat de Teatre (Theatre City), this is a key venue for top local and international contemporary dance acts.

Teatre Nacional de Catalunya
PERFORMING ARTS

(☑93 306 57 00; www.tnc.cat; Plaça de les Arts 1; tickets €12-32; ☺box office 3-7pm Wed-Fri, 3-8.30pm Sat, 3-5pm Sun & 1hr before show; ⓂGlòries or Monumental) Ricard Bofill's ultra-neoclassical theatre, with its bright, airy foyer, hosts a wide range of performances, principally drama but occasionally dance and other performances.

Teatre Romea
THEATRE

(Map p250; ☑93 301 55 04; www.teatreromea.com; Carrer de l'Hospital 51; tickets €17-28; ☺box office 4.30pm until start of show Wed-Sun; ⓂLiceu) Deep in El Raval, this 19th-century theatre was resurrected at the end of the 1990s and is one of the city's key stages for quality drama.

Live Music

There's a good choice most nights of the week. Many venues double as bars and/or clubs. Starting time is rarely before 10pm. Admission charges range from nothing to €20 or more – the higher prices often include a drink. Note that some of the clubs previously mentioned, including Razzmatazz, Sala Apolo and Luz de Gas often stage concerts. Keep an eye on listings.

Big-name acts, either Spanish or from abroad, often perform at venues such as the 17,000-capacity Palau Sant Jordi on Montjuïc or the Teatre Mercat de les Flors.

TOP CHOICE Palau de la Música Catalana
LIVE MUSIC

(☑902 442882; www.palaumusica.org; Carrer de Sant Francesc de Paula 2; ☺box office 10am-9pm Mon-Sat; ⓂUrquinaona) A feast for the eyes, this Modernista delight is also the city's traditional venue for classical and choral music, along with the occasional flamenco, gospel or world-music group.

Jazz Sí Club
LIVE MUSIC

(☑93 329 00 20; www.tallerdemusics.com; Carrer de Requesens 2; admission €8, drink included; ☺6-11pm; ⓂSant Antoni) A cramped little bar run by the Taller de Músics (Musicians' Workshop) serves as the stage for a varied program of jazz through to some good flamenco (Friday nights). Thursday night is Cuban night, Sunday is rock and the rest are devoted to jazz and/or blues sessions. Concerts start around 9pm but arrive early to beat the crowds.

Harlem Jazz Club
LIVE MUSIC

(Map p244; ☑93 310 07 55; www.harlemjazzclub. es; Carrer de la Comtessa de Sobradiel 8; admission €6-15; ☺8pm-4am Tue-Thu & Sun, to 5am Fri & Sat; ⓂDrassanes) This narrow, old-town dive is one of the best spots in town for jazz – along with the occasional Latin, blues or African band.

Bikini — LIVE MUSIC

(☎93 322 08 00; www.bikinibcn.com; Avinguda Diagonal 547; admission €10-20; ⊙midnight-6am Wed-Sat; 🚇6, 7, 33, 34, 63, 67 or 68, ⒨Entença) This grand old star of the Barcelona nightlife hosts a wide range of sounds, from Latin and Brazilian beats to funk and 1980s disco. Performances generally start between 8pm and 10pm, with the club opening around midnight.

Jamboree — LIVE MUSIC

(Map p244; ☎93 319 17 89; www.masimas.com/jamboree; Plaça Reial 17; admission €8-13; ⊙8pm-6am; ⒨Liceu) Jamboree has headline jazz and blues acts, with two concerts most nights (at 8pm and 10pm). Afterwards, Jamboree morphs into a DJ-spinning club at midnight.

Robadors 23 — LIVE MUSIC

(Map p250; Carrer d'en Robador 23; admission €2-3; ⊙8pm-2am; ⒨Liceu) On what remains a classic dodgy El Raval street, this narrow little bar has made a name for itself with Wednesday night jazz jams, improvisational jazz on Mondays, flamenco on Fridays and Saturdays and DJs on other nights. Concerts start between 9pm and 10pm.

Sidecar Factory Club — LIVE MUSIC

(Map p244; ☎93 302 15 86; www.sidecarfactoryclub.com; Plaça Reial 7; admission €8-18; ⊙10pm-5am Mon-Sat; ⒨Liceu) With its entrance on Plaça Reial, you can come here for food or drinks before midnight, or descend into the red-tinged, brick-vaulted cellar for live music. Just about anything goes, from UK indie through to country punk, but rock and pop lead the way. Most shows start around 10pm.

Sala Apolo — LIVE MUSIC

(Map p274; ☎93 441 40 01; www.sala-apolo.com; Carrer Nou de la Rambla 113; admission €6-12; ⊙12.30-6am Fri & Sat, midnight-5am Sun-Thu; ⒨Paral·lel) This is a fine old theatre, with local and international bands earlier in the night and DJ-fueled club sounds as the evening wears on.

Sala Tarantos — FLAMENCO

(Map p244; ☎93 319 17 89; www.masimas.net; Plaça Reial 17; admission from €7; ⊙shows 8.30pm, 9.30pm & 10.30pm; ⒨Liceu) These days, Tarantos has become a mostly tourist-centric affair, with half-hour flamenco shows held three times a night.

Tablao Cordobés — FLAMENCO

(Map p250; ☎93 317 57 11; www.tablaocordobes.com; La Rambla 35; show €39, with dinner €62-70; ⊙shows 8.15pm, 10pm & 11.30pm; ⒨Liceu) This

tablao (flamenco club) is typical of its genre and has been in business since 1970. Generally, tourists book for the dinner and show, though you can skip the food and just come along for the performance (about 1¼ hours).

Tablao De Carmen — FLAMENCO

(Map p274; ☎93 325 68 95; www.tablaodecarmen.com; Carrer dels Arcs 9, Poble Espanyol; show only €35, with tapas/dinner €45/69; ⊙shows 7.30pm & 10pm Tue-Sun; ⒨Espanya) Named after the great Barcelona *bailaora* (flamenco dancer) Carmen Amaya, the set-up here is similar to that at the Tablao Cordobés, though it is somewhat larger and the pseudo-Andalucian decor has a colder, more modern look.

Gran Teatre del Liceu — THEATRE

(Map p244; ☎93 485 99 00; www.liceubarcelona.com; La Rambla dels Caputxins 51-59; ⊙box office 1.30-8pm Mon-Fri & 1hr before show Sat & Sun; ⒨Liceu) Barcelona's grand old opera house is one of the most technologically advanced theatres in the world. Tickets can cost anything from €8 for a cheap seat behind a pillar to €194 for a well-positioned night at the opera.

L'Auditori — CLASSICAL MUSIC

(☎93 247 93 00; www.auditori.org; Carrer de Lepant 150; admission €10-60; ⊙box office 3-9pm Mon-Sat; ⒨Monumental) Barcelona's modern home for music lovers, L'Auditori puts on plenty of orchestral, chamber, religious and other music.

Dance

The best chance you have of seeing people dancing the *sardana* (the Catalan folk dance) is at 6.30pm on Saturday or noon on Sunday in front of the Catedral. You can also see the dancers during some of the city's festivals.

Sport

Circuit de Catalunya — FORMULA ONE

(☎93 571 97 00; www.circuitcat.com) Formula One drivers come to Barcelona every April/May to rip around the track at Montmeló, about a 30-minute drive north of the city. A seat for the Grand Prix race can cost anything from €120 to €450. On race days, the Sagalés bus company runs buses to the track from Passeig de Sant Joan 52 (€9 return), between Carrer de la Diputació and Carrer del Consell de Cent.

 Shopping

All of Barcelona seems to be lined with unending ranks of fashion boutiques and design stores.

FC BARCELONA

Football in Barcelona has the aura of religion and for much of the city's population, support of FC Barcelona is an article of faith. FC Barcelona is traditionally associated with the Catalans and even Catalan nationalism. Pride is at all-time high these days, with FC Barça continually ranked among the world's best teams.

It all started in 1899 when, four years after English residents had first played the game here, Swiss Hans Gamper founded FC Barcelona (Barça). His choice of club colours, the blue and maroon of his hometown, Winterthur, has stuck. By 1910, FC Barcelona was the premier club in a rapidly growing league. Since the league got fully underway in 1928, Barça has emerged champion 21 times, second only to arch-rival Real Madrid (with 32 victories). Between them, the two have virtually monopolised the game.

For a pure adrenaline rush, try to see a match at the massive 99,000-seat Camp Nou (p272) (Europe's largest football arena). Tickets are available at Camp Nou, as well as by phone and online. You can also purchase them through the ServiCaixa ticketing service. Tickets cost anything from €35 to €200, depending on the seat and match. If you can't make a match, the high-tech Camp Nou museum is a worthwhile alternative – and must-see for football fans.

Mainstream fashion and design stores can be found on Plaça de Catalunya as it heads along Passeig de Gràcia, turning left into Avinguda Diagonal. From here as far as Plaça de la Reina Maria Cristina, the Diagonal is jammed with shopping options.

Fashion does not end in the chic streets of L'Eixample and Avinguda Diagonal. The El Born area in La Ribera, especially on and around Carrer del Rec, is awash with tiny boutiques, especially those purveying young, fun fashion. A bubbling fashion strip is the Barri Gòtic's Carrer d'Avinyó. For secondhand stuff, head for El Raval, especially Carrer de la Riera Baixa. Carrer de Verdi in Gràcia is good for alternative shops too.

The single best-known department store is **El Corte Inglés**, with branches at Plaça de Catalunya (Map p262; 902 400222; www.elcorteingles.es; Plaça de Catalunya 14; MCatalunya), Plaça de la Reina Maria Cristina (Avinguda Diagonal 617) and other locations around town. FNAC (Map p250; 93 344 18 00; www.fnac.es; Plaça de Catalunya 4; 10am-10pm Mon-Sat; MCatalunya), the French book, CD and electronics emporium, has a couple of branches around town. Bulevard Rosa (Map p262; 93 215 44 99; www.bulevardrosa.com; Passeig de Gràcia 53; 10.30am-9pm Mon-Sat; MPasseig de Gràcia) is one of the most interesting arcades, while the Maremagnum (Map p244; www.maremagnum.es; Moll d'Espanya 5; 10am-10pm; MDrassanes) shopping centre can be a diversion when wandering around Port Vell.

Winter sales officially start on or around 10 January and the summer equivalents on or around 5 July.

L'Arca de l'Àvia VINTAGE, CLOTHING
(Map p250; 93 302 15 98; Carrer dels Banys Nous 20; MLiceu) Grandma's chest is indeed full of extraordinary remembrances from the past, including 18th-century embroidered silk vests, elaborate silk kimonos and wedding dresses and shawls from the 1920s.

El Bulevard dels Antiquaris ANTIQUES
(Map p262; 93 215 44 99; www.bulevarddelsantiquaris.com; Passeig de Gràcia 55-57; 10.30am-8.30pm Mon-Sat; MPasseig de Gràcia) More than 70 stores (most are open from 11am to 2pm and from 5pm to 8.30pm) are gathered under one roof to offer the most varied selection of collector's pieces: old porcelain dolls, jewellery, Asian antique furniture, old French goods, and African and other ethnic art.

La Manual Alpargatera SHOES
(Map p244; 93 301 01 72; http://homepage.mac.com/manualp; Carrer d'Avinyó 7; MLiceu) Everyone from Salvador Dalí to Jean Paul Gaultier has ordered a pair of *espadrilles* (rope-soled canvas shoes or sandals) from this famous store, which is the birthplace of the iconic footwear.

Art Montfalcon ARTS & CRAFTS
(Map p250; 93 301 13 25; www.montfalcon.com; Carrer dels Boters 4; 10am-9pm; MLiceu) Beneath the overarching vaults of this Gothic cavern is spread an incredible range of gift ideas and art, including lots of Barcelona memorabilia, from ceramics to arty T-shirts.

EXPLORING BARCELONA'S MARKETS

The sprawling **Els Encants Vells** (Fira de Bellcaire; ☑93 246 30 30; www.encantsbcn.com; Plaça de les Glòries Catalanes; ☺7am-6pm Mon, Wed, Fri & Sat; MGlòries) is the city's principal flea market. There is an awful lot of junk, but you can turn up interesting items if you hunt around. The Barri Gòtic is enlivened by an **art and crafts market** (Plaça de Sant Josep Oriol; MLiceu) on Saturday and Sunday, the antiques **Mercat Gòtic** (Plaça Nova; MLiceu or Jaume I) on Thursday, and a **coin and stamp collectors' market** (Plaça Reial; MLiceu) on Sunday morning. Just beyond the western edge of El Raval, the punters at the **Mercat de Sant Antoni** (Carrer de Mallorca 157; ☺7am-8.30pm; MHospital Clínic) dedicate Sunday morning to old maps, stamps, books and cards.

Joan Murrià   FOOD
(Map p262; ☑93 215 57 89; www.murria.cat; Carrer de Roger de Llúria 85; MPasseig de Gràcia) Ramon Casas designed the century-old Modernista shopfront ads for this delicious delicatessen. For a century the gluttonous have trembled at this altar of speciality food goods from Catalonia and beyond.

Antonio Miró   FASHION
(Map p262; ☑93 487 06 70; www.antoniomiro.es; Carrer del Consell de Cent 349; ☺10am-8pm Mon-Sat; MPasseig de Gràcia) Antonio Miró is one of Barcelona's haute couture kings. Miró concentrates on light, natural fibres to produce smart, unpretentious men's and women's fashion.

Custo Barcelona   FASHION
(Map p254; ☑93 268 78 93; www.custo-barcelona.com; Plaça de les Olles 7; MJaume I) The dazzling colours and cut of anything from dinner jackets to hot pants here are for the uninhibited. Custo has five other stores around town.

Urbana   FASHION
(Map p244; ☑93 269 09 20; Carrer d'Avinyó 46; ☺11am-9pm Mon-Sat; MLiceu) Colourful, fun city clothes, shoes and accessories await boys and girls in this easy-going store with Basque Country origins.

Casa Gispert   FOOD
(Map p254; ☑93 319 75 35; www.casagispert.com; Carrer dels Sombrerers 23; MJaume I) The wonderful, atmospheric and wood-fronted Casa Gispert has been toasting nuts and selling all manner of dried fruit since 1851.

Vila Viniteca   DRINK
(Map p244; ☑902 327777; www.vilaviniteca.es; Carrer dels Agullers 7; ☺8.30am-8.30pm Mon-Sat; MJaume I) One of the best wine stores in Barcelona, this place has been searching out the best in local and imported wines since 1932.

At No 9 it has another store devoted to gourmet food products.

Xampany   DRINK
(Map p262; ☑610 845011; Carrer de València 200; ☺4.30-10pm Mon-Fri, 10am-2pm Sat; MPasseig de Gràcia) Since 1981, this 'Cathedral of Cava' has been a veritable Aladdin's cave of *cava*, with bottles of the stuff crammed high and into every possible chaotic corner of this dimly lit locale.

Vinçon   HOMEWARES
(Map p262; ☑93 215 60 50; www.vincon.com; Passeig de Gràcia 96; ☺10am-8.30pm Mon-Sat; MDiagonal) An icon of the Barcelona design scene, Vinçon has the slickest furniture and household goods, both local and imported. The building once belonged to the Modernista artist Ramon Casas.

Camper   SHOES
(Map p262; ☑93 215 63 90; www.camper.com; Carrer de València 249; MPasseig de Gràcia) What started as a modest Mallorcan family business has become a major name in shoe design across the globe. Camper footwear, from the eminently sensible to the stylishly fashionable, is known for reliability. It has stores all over town.

Laie   BOOKS
(Map p262; ☑93 318 17 39; www.laie.es; Carrer de Pau Claris 85; ☺10am-9pm Mon-Fri, 10.30am-9pm Sat; MCatalunya or Urquinaona) Laie has novels and books on architecture, art and film in English, French, Spanish and Catalan. It also has a great upstairs cafe.

Antinous   BOOKS
(Map p244; ☑93 301 90 70; www.antinouslibros.com; Carrer de Josep Anselm Clavé 6; MDrassanes) Gay and lesbian travellers may want to browse in this spacious and relaxed gay bookshop, which also has a modest cafe out the back.

ℹ Information

Emergency

Tourists who want to report thefts need to go to the Catalan police, known as the **Mossos d'Esquadra** (☑088; Carrer Nou de la Rambla 80; Ⓜ Paral.lel) or the **Guàrdia Urbana** (local police; ☑092; La Rambla 43; Ⓜ Liceu).

Ambulance (☑061)

EU standard emergency number (☑112)

Fire brigade (Bombers; ☑080, 085)

Policía Nacional (national police; ☑091)

Internet Access

A growing number of hotels, restaurants, cafes, bars and other public locations around the city offer wi-fi access.

Bornet (Carrer de Barra Ferro 3; per hr/10hr €2.80/20; ☺10am-11pm Mon-Fri, 2-11pm Sat, Sun & holidays; Ⓜ Jaume I) A cool little internet centre and art gallery.

Media

La Vanguardia and *El Periódico* are the main local Castilian-language dailies. *El País* includes a daily supplement devoted to Catalonia.

Medical Services

Call 010 to find the nearest late-opening duty pharmacy. There are also several 24-hour pharmacies scattered across town.

Farmàcia Castells Soler (Passeig de Gràcia 90; Ⓜ Diagonal)

Farmàcia Clapés (La Rambla 98; Ⓜ Liceu)

Farmàcia Torres (www.farmaciaabierta24h.com; Carrer d'Aribau 62; Ⓡ FGC Provença)

Hospital Clínic i Provincial (Carrer de Villarroel 170; Ⓜ Hospital Clínic)

Hospital Dos de Maig (Carrer del Dos de Maig 301; Ⓜ Sant Pau–Dos de Maig)

Money

Banks abound in Barcelona, many with ATMs, including several around Plaça de Catalunya, on La Rambla and on Plaça de Sant Jaume in the Barri Gòtic.

The foreign-exchange offices that you see along La Rambla and elsewhere are open for longer hours than banks but generally offer poorer rates. **Interchange** (☑93 342 73 11; Rambla dels Caputxins 74; ☺9am-11pm; Ⓜ Liceu) represents American Express and will cash Amex travellers cheques, replace lost cheques and provide cash advances on Amex cards.

Post

The **main post office** (Plaça d'Antoni López; ☺8.30am-9.30pm Mon-Fri, 8.30am-2pm Sat; Ⓜ Jaume I) is opposite the northeast end of Port Vell. There's a handy **branch** (Carrer d'Aragó 282; ☺8.30am-8.30pm Mon-Fri, 9.30am-1pm Sat; Ⓜ Passeig de Gràcia) just off Passeig de Gràcia.

Tourist Information

In addition to the following listed tourist offices, information booths operate at Estació Nord bus station, Plaça del Portal de la Pau and at the foot of the Mirador a Colom. At least three others are set up at various points around the city centre in summer.

Oficina d'Informació de Turisme de Barcelona has its **main branch** (☑93 285 38 34; www.barcelonaturisme.com; underground at Plaça de Catalunya 17-S; ☺8.30am-8.30pm; Ⓜ Catalunya) in Plaça de Catalunya. It concentrates on city information and can help book accommodation. The branch in the EU arrivals hall at **Aeroport del Prat** (Aeroport del Prat, terminals 1, 2B & 2A; ☺9am-9pm) has information on all of Catalonia; a smaller office at the international

ℹ DISCOUNTS

Students generally pay a little over half of adult admission prices, as do children aged under 12 years and senior citizens (aged 65 and over) with appropriate ID. Possession of a Bus Turístic ticket entitles you to discounts to some museums.

Articket (www.articketbcn.org) gives you admission to seven important art galleries for €30 and is valid for six months. The galleries are the Museu Picasso, Museu Nacional d'Art de Catalunya, Macba (Museu d'Art Contemporani de Barcelona), the Fundació Antoni Tàpies, the Centre de Cultura Contemporània de Barcelona, the Fundació Joan Miró and La Pedrera. You can buy the ticket at the museums or at the tourist offices on Plaça de Catalunya, Plaça de Sant Jaume and Sants train station.

Aficionados of Barcelona's Modernista heritage should consider the **Ruta del Modernisme pack** (www.rutadelmodernisme.com). For €12 you receive a guide to 115 Modernista buildings great and small, a map and discounts of up to 50% on the main Modernista sights in Barcelona, as well as some others around Catalonia. Pick it up at the tourist office at Plaça de Catalunya.

WARNING: KEEP AN EYE ON YOUR VALUABLES

Every year aggrieved readers write in with tales of woe from Barcelona. Petty crime and theft, with tourists as the prey of choice, are a problem, so you need to take a few common-sense precautions.

Thieves and pickpockets operate on airport trains and the metro, especially around stops popular with tourists (such as La Sagrada Família). The Old City (Ciutat Vella) is the pickpockets' and bag-snatchers' prime hunting ground. Take special care on and around La Rambla. Prostitutes working the lower (waterfront) end often do a double trade in wallet snatching.

arrivals hall opens the same hours. The branch at **Estació Sants** (☉8am-8pm; ⓂSants Estació) has limited city information. There's also a helpful branch in the **town hall** (Plaça Sant Jaume; Map p244; ☑93 285 38 32; Carrer de la Ciutat 2; ☉8.30am-8.30pm Mon-Fri, 9am-7pm Sat, 9am-2pm Sun & holidays; ⓂJaume I).

Centre Gestor del Parc de Montjuïc (Passeig de Santa Madrona 28; ☉10am-8pm) For information on Parc de Montjuïc, head for the Centre Gestor del Parc de Montjuïc in the Font del Gat building, a short walk off Passeig de Santa Madrona, east of the Museu Etnològic.

La Rambla information office (www.barce lonaturisme.com; La Rambla dels Estudis 115; ☉8.30am-8.30pm; ⓂLiceu)

Palau Robert regional tourist office (☑93 238 80 91, from outside Catalonia 902 400012; www.gencat.net/probert; Passeig de Gràcia 107; ☉10am-8pm Mon-Sat, 10am-2.30pm Sun) A host of material on Catalonia, audiovisual resources, a bookshop and a branch of Turisme Juvenil de Catalunya (for youth travel).

Travel Agencies

Halcón Viatges (☑902 091800; www.halcon viajes.com; Carrer de Pau Claris 108; ⓂPasseig de Gràcia) Reliable chain of travel agents that sometimes has good deals. This is one of many branches around town.

Orixà (☑93 487 00 22; www.orixa.com; Carrer d'Aragó 227; ⓂPasseig de Gràcia) A good local independent travel agent.

Websites

www.barcelonaturisme.com The city's official tourism website.

www.bcn.cat The City of Barcelona's municipal website, with many links.

www.lecool.com Subscribe for free to this site for weekly events listings.

www.rutadelmodernisme.com Routes, monuments and events related to Modernisme.

ⓘ Getting There & Away

Air

Aeroport del Prat (☑902 404704; www.aena. es) is 12km southwest of the centre at El Prat de Llobregat. Barcelona is a big international and domestic destination, with direct flights from North America, as well as many European cities.

Several budget airlines, including Ryanair, use Girona-Costa Brava airport, 11km south of Girona and about 80km north of Barcelona. Buses connect with Barcelona's Estació del Nord bus station.

Boat

BALEARIC ISLANDS

Regular passenger and vehicular ferries to/from the Balearic Islands, operated by **Acciona Trasmediterránea** (☑902 454645; www.tras mediterranea.es; ⓂDrassanes), dock along both sides of the Moll de Barcelona wharf in Port Vell.

ITALY

The Grimaldi group's **Grandi Navi Veloci** (☑in Italy 010 209 4591; www1.gnv.it; ⓂDrassanes) runs high-speed, luxury ferries three (sometimes more) days a week between Genoa and Barcelona. The journey takes 19 hours. Ticket prices vary wildly and depend on the season and how far in advance you purchase, but start at about €99 one way for an airline-style seat in summer. They can be bought online or at Acciona Trasmediterránea ticket windows. The same company runs a similar number of ferries between Barcelona and Tangiers, in Morocco (voyage time about 26 hours).

Grimaldi Ferries (☑902 531333, in Italy 081 496444; www.grimaldi-lines.com) operates similar services from Barcelona to Civitavecchia (near Rome; 20½ hours, six to seven times a week), Livorno (Tuscany; 19½ hours, three times a week) and Porto Torres (northwest Sardinia; 12 hours, daily). An economy-class airline-style seat costs from €45 in low season to €80 in high season on all routes.

Boats of both lines dock at Moll de Sant Bertran and all vessels take vehicles.

Bus

Long-distance buses for destinations throughout Spain leave from the **Estació del Nord** (☑902 260606; www.barcelonanord.com; Carrer d'Ali Bei 80; ⓂArc de Triomf). A plethora of companies operates services to different parts of the country, although many come under the umbrella of **Alsa** (☑902 422242; www.alsa.es). There are frequent services to Madrid, Valencia and Zaragoza (20 or more a day) and several daily departures to such distant destinations as Burgos, Santiago de Compostela and Seville.

Eurolines (www.eurolines.es), in conjunction with local carriers all over Europe, is the main international carrier. It runs services across Europe and to Morocco, departing from Estació del Nord and **Estació d'Autobusos de Sants** (Carrer de Viriat; Ⓜ Sants Estació), which is next to Estació Sants Barcelona. For information and tickets in Barcelona, contact Alsa. Another carrier is **Linebús** (www.linebus.com).

Within Catalonia, much of the Pyrenees and the entire Costa Brava are served only by buses, as train services are limited to important railheads such as Girona, Figueres, Lleida, Ripoll and Puigcerdà. If there is a train, take it – they're usually more convenient.

Various bus companies operate across the region, mostly from Estació del Nord.

Departures from Estació del Nord are listed in the table below (where frequencies vary, the lowest figure is usually for Sunday; fares quoted are the lowest available).

Alsina Graells (📞 902 422242; www.alsa.es) A subsidiary of Alsa, it runs buses from Barcelona to destinations west and northwest, such as Vielha, La Seu d'Urgell and Lleida.

Barcelona Bus (📞 902 130014; www.barcelonabus.com) Runs buses from Barcelona to Girona (and Girona–Costa Brava airport), Figueres, parts of the Costa Brava and northwest Catalonia.

Hispano-Igualadina (📞 902 292900; www.igualadina.net; Estació Sants & Plaça de la Reina Maria Cristina) Serves central and southern Catalonia.

Sarfa (📞 902 30 20 25; www.sarfa.com) The main operator on and around the Costa Brava.

TEISA (📞 93 215 35 66; www.teisa-bus.com; Carrer de Pau Claris 117; Ⓜ Passeig de Gràcia) Covers a large part of the eastern Catalan Pyrenees from Girona and Figueres. From Barce-

lona, buses head for Camprodon via Ripoll and Olot via Besalú.

Car & Motorcycle

Autopistas (tollways) head out of Barcelona in most directions, including the C31/C32 to the southern Costa Brava; the C32 to Sitges; the C16 to Manresa (with a turn-off for Montserrat); and the AP7 north to Girona, Figueres and France, and south to Tarragona and Valencia (turn off along the AP2 for Lleida, Zaragoza and Madrid). The toll-free alternatives, such as the A2 north to Girona, Figueres and France, and west to Lleida and beyond, or the A7 to Tarragona, tend to be busy and slow.

RENTAL

Avis, Europcar, Hertz and several other big companies have desks at the airport, Estació Sants train station and Estació del Nord bus terminus.

Avis (📞 902 110 275; www.avis.com; Carrer de Còrsega 293-295; Ⓜ Diagonal)

Cooltra (📞 93 221 40 70; www.cooltra.com; Passeig de Joan de Borbó 80-84; Ⓜ Barceloneta) You can rent scooters here for around €35 (plus insurance). It also organises scooter tours.

Europcar (📞 93 302 05 43; www.europcar.com; Gran Via de les Corts Catalanes 680; Ⓜ Girona)

Hertz (📞 93 419 61 56; www.hertz.com; Carrer del Viriat 45; Ⓜ Sants)

National/Atesa (📞 93 323 07 01; www.atesa.es; Carrer de Muntaner 45; Ⓜ Universitat)

Train

The main international and domestic station is **Estació Sants** (Plaça dels Països Catalans; Ⓜ Sants Estació), 2.5km west of La Rambla. Other stops on long-distance lines include Catalunya and Passeig de Gràcia. Information windows operate at Estació Sants and Passeig de Gràcia station. Sants station has a **consigna** (left-luggage lockers; ⏰ 5.30am-11pm), a tourist

BARCELONA GETTING THERE & AWAY

BUS DEPARTURES

DESTINATION	FREQUENCY (PER DAY)	DURATION (HR)	COST (ONE WAY, €)
Almería	4-5	11¼-14	66
Burgos	5-6	7½-8½	37
Granada	5-8	12½-14¼	73
Madrid	up to 16	7½-8	30
Seville	1-2	14¾	82
Valencia	up to 14	4-4½	27
Zaragoza	up to 22	3¾	15

TRAIN DEPARTURES

DESTINATION	FREQUENCY (PER DAY)	DURATION (HR)	COST (ONE WAY, €)
Alicante	up to 8	4¾-5½	52-57
Burgos	4	6-7	66-81
Valencia	up to 15	3-4½	36-45
Zaragoza	up to 35	1½-4¼	52-66

office, a telephone and fax office, currency-exchange booths and ATMs.

INTERNATIONAL

One or two daily services connect Montpellier in France with Estació Sants (€59 each way in *turista* class, 4½ hours). A couple of other slower services (with a change of train at Portbou) also make this run. All stop in Perpignan.

From Estació Sants, up to eight trains daily run to Cerbère (from €12, 2½ hours), on the French side of the border, from where you can pick up trains to Paris via Montpellier.

DOMESTIC

Eighteen high-speed Tren de Alta Velocidad Española (AVE) trains between Madrid and Barcelona run daily in each direction, nine of them in under three hours. A typical one-way price is €118. The line will eventually run right across Barcelona (via a controversial tunnel) and north to the French frontier. A new high-speed TGV from France connects Paris with Figueres (from €74, 5½ hours). Some other popular runs are listed in the table above (fares are a range of lowest fares depending on type of train).

ℹ Getting Around

The metro is the easiest way of getting around and reaches most places you're likely to visit (although not the airport). For some trips you need buses or FGC suburban trains. The tourist office gives out the comprehensive *Guia d'Autobusos Urbans de Barcelona*, which has a metro map and details all bus routes. See also the metro map on p240.

For public transport information, call ✆010.

To/From the Airport

The **A1 Aerobús** (✆93 415 60 20; one way €5.65) runs from Terminal 1 to Plaça de Catalunya via Plaça d'Espanya, Gran Via de les Corts Catalanes (on the corner of Carrer del Comte d'Urgell) and Plaça de la Universitat (every six to 15 minutes depending on the time of day; 35 minutes) from 6.10am to 1.05am. A2 Aerobús does the same run from Terminal 2, from 6am to 1am. You can buy tickets on the bus.

Renfe's R2 Nord train line runs between the airport and Passeig de Gràcia (via Estació Sants) in central Barcelona (about 35 minutes), before heading out of town. Tickets cost €3.60, unless you have a T-10 multitrip public-transport ticket. The service from the airport starts at 5.42am and ends at 11.38pm daily.

A taxi to/from the centre, about a half-hour ride depending on traffic, costs €25 to €30.

Sagalés (✆902 130014; www.sagales.com) runs the Barcelona Bus (p303) service between Girona airport and Estació del Nord bus station in Barcelona (one way/return €15/25, 70 minutes).

Car & Motorcycle

An effective one-way system makes traffic flow fairly smoothly, but you'll often find yourself flowing the way you don't want to go, unless you happen to have an adept navigator and a map that shows one-way streets.

Limited parking in the Ciutat Vella is virtually all for residents only, with some metered parking. The narrow streets of Gràcia are not much better. The broad boulevards of L'Eixample are divided into blue and green zones. For nonresidents they mean the same thing: limited meter parking. Fees vary but tend to hover around €3 per hour. Parking stations are also scattered all over L'Eixample, with a few in the old centre too. Prices vary from around €4 to €5 per hour.

Public Transport

BUS

The city transport authority, **Transports Metropolitans de Barcelona** (TMB; ✆010; www.tmb. net), runs buses along most city routes every few minutes from 5am or 6am to 10pm or 11pm. Many routes pass through Plaça de Catalunya and/or Plaça de la Universitat. After 11pm, a reduced network of yellow *nitbusos* (night buses) runs until 3am or 5am. All *nitbus* routes pass through Plaça de Catalunya and most run about every 30 to 45 minutes.

METRO & FGC

The TMB metro has seven numbered and colour-coded lines. It runs from 5am to midnight Sunday to Thursday and holidays, from 5am to

2am on Friday and days immediately preceding holidays, and 24 hours on Saturday. Line 2 has access for people with disabilities and a growing number of stations on other lines also have lifts.

Suburban trains run by the **Ferrocarrils de la Generalitat de Catalunya** (FGC; ☑93 205 15 15; www.fgc.net) include a couple of useful city lines. One heads north from Plaça de Catalunya. A branch of it will get you to Tibidabo and another within spitting distance of the Monestir de Pedralbes. Some trains along this line run beyond Barcelona to Sant Cugat, Sabadell and Terrassa. The other FGC line heads to Manresa from Plaça d'Espanya and is handy for the trip to Montserrat. These trains run from about 5am (with only one or two services before 6am) to 11pm or midnight (depending on the line) Sunday to Thursday, and from 5am to about 1am (or a little later, depending on the line and stop) on Friday and Saturday.

Three **tram** (☑902 193275; www.trambcn.com) lines run into the suburbs of greater Barcelona from Plaça de Francesc Macià and are of limited interest to visitors. Another line (T4) runs from behind the zoo near the Ciutadella Vila Olímpica metro stop to Sant Adrià via Fòrum. The T5 line runs from Glòries to Badalona. All standard transport passes are valid.

TICKETS & TARGETAS

The metro, FGC trains, *rodalies/cercanías* (Renfe-run local trains) and buses come under one zoned fare regime. Single-ride tickets on all standard transport within Zone 1 (which extends beyond the airport), except on Renfe trains, cost €2.

Targetes are multitrip transport tickets. They are sold at most city-centre metro stations. The prices given here are for travel in Zone 1. Children under four travel free.

Targeta T-10 (€9.25) Ten rides (each valid for 1¼ hours) on the metro, buses and FGC trains. You can change between metro, FGC, *rodalies* and buses.

Targeta T-DIA (€6.95) Unlimited travel on all transport for one day.

Targeta T-50/30 (€37) For 50 trips within 30 days.

Two-/Three-/Four-/Five-Day Tickets (€12.80/18.50/23.50/28) These provide unlimited travel on all transport except the Aerobús; buy them at metro stations and tourist offices.

T-Mes (€50) For unlimited use of all public transport for a month.

Taxi

Taxis charge €2.05 flag fall plus meter charges of €0.93 per kilometre (€1.18 from 8pm to 8am and all day on weekends). A further €3.10 is added for all trips to/from the airport, and €1 for luggage bigger than 55cm by 35cm by 35cm. The trip from Estació Sants to Plaça de Catalunya, about 3km, costs about €11. You can call a **taxi** (☑Fonotaxi 93 300 11 00, Radiotaxi 93 303 30 33, Radiotaxi BCN 93 225 00 00) or flag them down in the streets. The call-out charge is €3.40 (€4.20 at night and on weekends). In many taxis it is possible to pay with credit card.

Taxi Amic (☑93 420 80 88; www.taxi-amic -adaptat.com) is a special taxi service for people with disabilities or difficult situations (such as transport of big objects). Book at least 24 hours in advance if possible.

Catalonia

Includes »

Best Places to Eat

- » Mas Prades (p368)
- » El Celler de Can Roca (p319)
- » Arcs Restaurant (p364)
- » Mas Pau (p327)
- » eF & Gi (p358)

Best Places to Stay

- » Albergue Taüll (p345)
- » Cal Perello (p354)
- » Mirador de Siurana (p354)
- » Torre del Remei (p354)
- » Mas del Tancat (p368)

Why Go?

From metropolitan Barcelona spreads a land of such diversity that you could spend weeks discovering it. The stunning cove beaches of the Costa Brava are the jewel in the tourism crown, but for those who need more than a suntan, urban fun and Jewish history is to be found in the medieval city of Girona, while Figueres offers a shrine to Salvador Dalí in the form of its 'theatre-museum'.

For something utterly different head north to where the Pyrenees rise up to mighty 3000m peaks from a series of green and often remote valleys criss-crossed with numerous hiking trails.

And if that weren't enough, there are the flamingo-tinted wetlands of the Ebro delta, the Roman and Greek ruins of Tarragona and Empuriés, and mighty medieval monasteries and isolated hilltop villages scattered throughout.

Wherever you venture there is the undeniable sense that Catalonia (Catalunya in Catalan, Cataluña in Spanish) is different to the rest of Spain. It's a difference worth celebrating.

When to Go

Tarragona

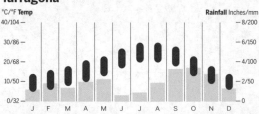

May Girona's in bloom during its flower festival and Costa Brava beaches are gorgeous.

Sep The Catalan Pyrenees are aflame in autumnal colours and the hiking is perfect.

Oct & Nov The museums and galleries of the Dalí circuit are at their quietest and best.

FRANCE

Vielha •

Pica d'Estates (3143m) ▲

ANDORRA LA VELLA ⊛

Llavorsi •

Puigcerdà •   • Llívia

Puig Neulós (1256m) ▲

Portlligat

④
Parc Nacional d'Aigüestortes i Estany de Sant Maurici

Bellver de Cerdanya •

Ribes de Freser •

Cadaqués

Roses

La Molina •   Beget •   **Figueres** ③

Riu Fluvià

Torroella de Mont

• Tremp

• Ripoll   • Olot

CATALONIA

Solsona •

Riu Ter   **Girona** ⑤

Begur ①

Tan

⑥ **Río Noguera Pallaresa**

• Ponts

Vic •

Palafrugell ①

Cardona •

Santa Coloma de Farners •

Pala

Riu Segre

• Balaguer

Manresa •

Sant Celoni •

Lloret de Mar

Sant F de Gui

• **Lleida**

Granollers •   A9

Blanes •

Tossa de Mar

Riu Segre

AP2

• Igualada   • Terrassa

• Mataró

• Premià de Mar

Reial Monestir ✚ de Santa Maria de Poblet

Vilafranca del Penedès •

⊚ **Barcelona**

TARRAGONA

Reus •

• Castelldefels

RUEL

Móra d'Ebre •

• Altafulla

⑤ Sitges

Vilanova i la Geltrú

Port Aventura •   **Tarragona**

MEDITERRANEAN

Riu Ebro

AP7

SEA

• Tortosa

Amposta •

⑦ Delta de l'Ebre

AP7

Sant Carles de la Ràpita

ASTELLÓN DE LA PLANA

Catalonia Highlights

① Chill out on Costa Brava coves and beaches near **Tossa de Mar** (p308), **Palafrugell** (p311) or **Begur** (p313)

② Discover the magical village of **Cadaqués** (p323) and nearby **Portlligat** (p323), haunted by the memory of Salvador Dalí

③ Contemplate the absurd with a visit to the **Teatre-Museu Dalí** (p326) in Figueres

④ Conquer the trails of the **Parc Nacional d'Aigüestortes i Estany de Sant Maurici** (p343)

⑤ Explore the flower-bedecked medieval city centre of **Girona** (p315)

⑥ Ride the rapids of **Río Noguera Pallaresa** (p341)

⑦ See the skies turn pink under flocks of flamingos in the **Delta de l'Ebre** (p366)

COSTA BRAVA

Stretching north from Blanes all the way to the French border, the Costa Brava ranks with the Costa Blanca and Costa del Sol as one of Spain's three great holiday coasts. Though for many it is synonymous with some occasionally awful concrete hotels and English breakfasts, the 'Rugged Coast' has some of the most spectacular stretches of sand and sea in all of Spain; its very ruggedness prevents excessive development.

Nestling in the hilly back country – green and covered in umbrella pine in the south; but barer and browner in the north – are charming stone villages, the towering monastery of St Pere de Rodes and Salvador Dalí's fantasy castle home at Púbol. A little further inland are the bigger towns of Girona, with its sizeable and strikingly well-preserved medieval centre, and Figueres, famous for its bizarre Teatre-Museu Dalí, the foremost of a series of sites associated with the famous eccentric surrealist artist Salvador Dalí.

The ruggedness of the Costa Brava continues under the sea, offering some of the best diving in Spain, with the protected islets off L'Estartit – Illes Medes – boasting probably the most diverse sea life along the Spanish coast.

❶ Getting There & Away

Direct buses from Barcelona go to most towns on or near the Costa Brava. From Girona and Figueres there are also fairly good bus services to the coast.

The train line between Barcelona and the coastal border town of Portbou runs inland, through Girona and Figueres.

In summer you could take an alternative approach to the southern Costa Brava from Barcelona by a combination of *rodalies* (local trains) and boat.

If driving, the AP7 *autopista* (tollway) and the NII highway both run from Barcelona via Girona and Figueres to the French border. The C32 *autopista* follows the NII up the coast as far as Blanes.

Tossa de Mar

POP 5920

Curving around a boat-speckled bay and guarded by a headland crowned with impressive defensive medieval walls and towers, Tossa de Mar is a picturesque village of crooked, narrow streets onto which tourism has tacked a larger, modern extension. In July and August it's hard to reach the water's edge without tripping over oily limbs, but out of high season it is still an enchanting place to visit.

Tossa was one of the first places on the Costa Brava to attract foreign visitors – a small colony of artists and writers gravitated towards what painter Marc Chagall dubbed 'Blue Paradise' in the 1930s – and was made famous by Ava Gardner in the 1950 film *Pandora and the Flying Dutchman*.

◎ Sights & Activities

Old Tossa
OLD TOWN

The deep-ochre, fairy-tale walls and towers on the pine-dotted headland, Mont Guardí, at the end of the main beach, were built between the 12th and 14th centuries. The area they girdle is known as the Vila Vella – or old town – full of steep little cobbled streets and picturesque whitewashed houses, garlanded with flowers. Mont Guardí is crowned with the Far de Tossa (lighthouse; adult/child €3/1.50; ⊙10am-10pm Tue-Sun mid-Jun–mid-Sep, shorter hours rest of year) Inside there is an imaginative 20-minute walk-through display on the history of lighthouses and life inside them. Next door is the groovy Bar Far de Tossa, overlooking the steep drop – perfect for an Ava Gardner cocktail. In August, concerts are held on various nights by the light of the lighthouse.

Beaches & Boats
BEACHES

The main town beach, golden Platja Gran, tends to be busy. Beyond the headland, at the end of Avinguda de Sant Ramon Penyafort, is the quieter and smaller Platja Mar Menuda, popular with divers. The best beaches, however, are found north and south along the coast, accessible only to those with their own transport, or energetic walkers (see the boxed text, p313).

In the period from Easter to September glass-bottomed boats (www.fondocristal. com; adult/5-12yr €14/9) run hourly or half-hourly (10am to 5pm, 20 minutes) to more tranquil beaches northeast of Platja Gran, such as Cala Giverola (a pleasant sandy cove with a couple of restaurants and bars).

Museu Municipal
MUSEUM

(Plaça de Roig i Soler 1; adult/child €3/free; ⊙10am-8pm Tue-Sat, 10am-2pm & 4-8pm Sun & Mon mid-Jun–mid-Sep, shorter hours rest of year) In the lower part of Vila Vella, the Museu Munici-

Costa Brava

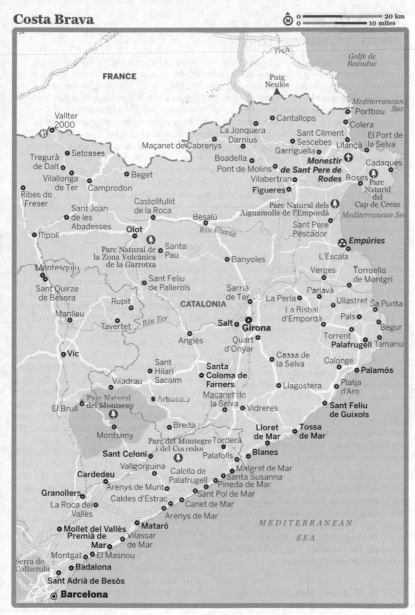

pal, set in the 14th- and 15th-century Palau del Batlle, has mosaics and other finds from a **Roman villa**, off Avinguda del Pelegrí, and Tossa-related art, including Chagall's *Celestial Violinist*.

🛏 Sleeping

Most accommodation is open from Semana Santa (Holy Week) to October, with only a handful of options outside those months.

WORTH A TRIP

MUSEU DEL MAR DE LLORET

Lloret de Mar may be a Costa Brava cliché, complete with rampaging neon-and-concrete development, bingo-playing pensioners and cheesy clubs, but it's worth a detour for this museum. The excellent Museu del Mar de Lloret (www.lloretdemar.org; Passeig Camprodon I Arrieta 1; admission €4; ☺10am-1pm & 4-8pm Mon-Sat, to 7pm Sun Jun-Aug, shorter hours rest of year) provides context for Lloret's metamorphosis from a fishing village to a major trade port to a holiday resort through its engrossing exhibits, such as the display of scale model boats and period furnishings. Until Charles III removed the ban on Catalonia's trade with the Americas in 1778, Lloret and its counterparts were simple fishing villages, but once trans-Atlantic trade took off, mass emigration followed and many Catalans went abroad to make their fortune in Latin America and the Caribbean in industries such as cotton and the slave trade. Some – such as the local Macía and Porés families – became fabulously wealthy and were afterwards referred to as *Americanos* or *indianos*, whereas those who came back as poor as when they'd left were teased for 'losing their suitcase in the strait'.

TOP CHOICE Hostal Cap d'Or   HOSTAL €€

(☎972 34 00 81; www.hotelcapdor.com; Passeig de la Vila Vella 1; s/d incl breakfast €63/103; ✳🛜) Rub up against the town's history in this family-run spot right in front of the walls. Rooms are lovingly decorated in sea-blues and whites and the best of them look straight onto the beach.

Hotel Diana   HOTEL €€€

(☎972 34 18 86; www.hotelesdante.com; Plaça d'Espanya 6; d incl breakfast €145, with sea views €170-180; ☺Apr-Nov; P✳🛜) Fronting Platja Gran, this artistic 1920s hotel has a Gaudí-built fireplace in the lounge and oozes Modernista decor and stained glass in the central covered courtyard. Half of the spacious, tiled rooms have beach views.

Hotel Hermes   HOTEL €

(☎972 34 02 96; www.hotelhermes-tossademar.com; Avenguda Ferrán Agulló 6; s/d €35/58; 🛜🖥) This pink concoction a block from the bus station has compact en suites with marble floors, presided over by a friendly *señora*. A bargain for the price, especially with the Jacuzzi on the roof thrown in.

Camping Cala Llevadó   CAMPGROUND €

(☎972 34 03 14; www.calallevado.com; sites per adult €12; ☺May-Sep; P@🖥) This ground stretches back from a cove 4km southwest of Tossa in the settlement of Santa Maria de Llorell. As well as its shady camping spots and prime location with steps leading down to a pretty beach, there are tennis courts, a pool, a restaurant, shops and bars. It also has four-person bungalows from €115.

🍴 Eating

Look out for a local speciality, *cim-i-tomba*, a hearty one-pot fish-and-vegetable stew, harking back to Tossa's fishing days. There are plenty of paella-and-sangria restaurant cliches, but a lot of good seafood as well.

TOP CHOICE La Cuina de Can Simon   CATALAN €€€

(☎972 34 12 69; Carrer del Portal 24; mains €30-50, taster menus €68-98; ☺lunch & dinner Wed-Sat & Mon, lunch Sun) Tossa's culinary star nestles by the old walls in a former fisherman's stone house and distinguishes itself by the most imaginative creations in town. Taking the *mar i muntanya* theme to its logical extreme, it presents you with pig trotters with sea cucumber as well as the more mainstream *fideuá* with rock fish. Even if you're not splurging on the gobstoppingly good taster menu, stop by for the chocolate soup.

Can Calav   SPANISH €

(Carrer Socors; tapas €6-7) The dangling bundles of dried chillies and farming apparel create a cosy rustic atmosphere in an appealing seafront location, and while the menu may not be the most original, everything – from the *calamares a la romana* to the *patatas bravas* – is executed perfectly.

❶ Information

Tourist information office (☎972 34 01 08; www.infotossa.com; Avinguda del Pelegrí 25; ☺9am-9pm Mon-Sat, 10am-2pm & 5-8pm Sun Jul & Aug, shorter hours rest of year) Next to the bus station.

ℹ️ Getting There & Away

From April to October, a couple of companies run boats several times daily between Blanes, Lloret de Mar and Tossa de Mar (one to 1½ hours) and beyond. Catch one of the *rodalies* from Barcelona's Catalunya station to Blanes, then transfer to the boat. Tickets are sold on the beach.

Sarfa (www.sarfa.com) runs to/from Barcelona's Estació del Nord (€12, 1¼ hours, up to 11 daily) via Lloret de Mar (€1.70). Buses to other destinations are infrequent. The bus station is next to the tourist office.

The C32 *autopista* connects Tossa to Barcelona, while the picturesque GI682 leads north to Sant Feliu de Guíxols.

Sant Feliu de Guíxols

POP 21,810

A snaking road hugs the spectacular ups and downs of the Costa Brava for the 23km from Tossa de Mar to Sant Feliu de Guíxols with – allegedly – a curve for each day of the year.

Sant Feliu itself has an attractive waterside promenade and a handful of curious leftovers from its long past, the most important being the so-called **Porta Ferrada** (Iron Gate): a wall and entrance, which is all that remains of a 10th-century monastery, the **Monestir de Sant Benet**. The gate lends its name to an annual music festival held here every July since 1962.

Just north along the coast is the village of **S'agaró**, each of its Modernista houses designed by Gaudí disciple Rafael Masó. Leave your wheels behind and take the Camí de Ronda to **Platja Sa Conca** – one of the most attractive beaches in the area.

Sarfa buses call in here from Barcelona (€14.70, 1½ hours, up to 12 daily), en route to Palafrugell.

Palafrugell & Around

Halfway up the coast from Barcelona to the French border begins one of the most beautiful stretches of the Costa Brava. The town of Palafrugell, 5km inland, is the main access point for a cluster of enticing beach spots. Calella de Palafrugell, Llafranc and Tamariu, one-time fishing villages squeezed into small bays, are three of the Costa Brava's most charming, low-key resorts.

Begur, 7km northeast of Palafrugell, is a curious, tight-knit, castle-topped village with a cluster of less-developed beaches nearby (some of them splendid). Inland, seek out charming Pals and Peratallada.

PALAFRUGELL

POP 22,820

Palafrugell is the main transport, shopping and service hub for the area. The C66 Palamós–Girona road passes through the western side of Palafrugell, a 10-minute walk from the main square, Plaça Nova. The **tourist office** (📞972 30 02 28; www.turisme palafrugell.org; Carrer del Carrilet 2; ⊗9am-9pm Mon-Sat, 10am-1pm Sun Jul & Aug, 10am-1pm & 5-8pm Mon-Sat, 10am-1pm Sun May, Jun & Sep, shorter hours rest of year) is beside the C66 Hwy. The **bus station** (Carrer de Torres Jonama 67-9) is a short walk from the tourist office. Sarfa buses run to Barcelona (€16.15, two hours, up to 16 daily) and Girona (€5.45, one hour, up to eight daily).

CALELLA DE PALAFRUGELL

POP 770

The low-slung buildings of Calella, the southernmost of Palafrugell's crown-jewel beaches, are strung Aegean-style around a bay of rocky points and small, pretty beaches, with a few fishing boats still hauled up on the sand. The seafront is lined with restaurants serving the fruits of the sea.

◉ Sights & Activities

In addition to lingering on one of the beaches, you can stroll along pretty coastal footpaths northeast to Llafranc (20 or 30 minutes), or south to Platja del Golfet beach, close to Cap Roig (about 40 minutes).

Jardí Botànic de Cap Roig　　GARDENS
(adult/child €6/free; ⊗9am-8pm Jun-Sep, to 6pm Oct-Mar) Atop Cap Roig, the Jardí Botánic de Cap Roig is a beautiful garden of 500 Mediterranean species, set around the early-20th-century castle-palace of Nikolai Voevodsky. He was a tsarist colonel with expensive tastes, who fell out of grace in his homeland after the Russian Revolution.

🎊 Festivals & Events

Cantada de havaneres　　MUSIC
Havaneres are melancholy Caribbean sea shanties that became popular among Costa Brava sailors in the 19th century, when Catalonia maintained busy links with Cuba. These folksy concerts are traditionally accompanied by the drinking of *cremat* – a rum, coffee, sugar, lemon and cinnamon concoction that you set alight briefly before quaffing. Held in August.

Festival Jadrins de Cap Roig   MUSIC

Excellent music festival held at the namesake gardens around mid-July to late August, with anything from rock to jazz and featuring big names, such as Leonard Cohen and Bob Dylan.

🛏 Sleeping & Eating

TOP CHOICE Hotel Mediterrani   BOUTIQUE HOTEL €€€
(☑972 61 45 00; www.hotelmediterrani.com; Francesc Estrabau 40; s €110, d €130-210; ☺mid-May–Sep; ▣❀🛜) Swish, arty rooms decked out in placid creams, with breathtaking views of a hidden sliver of sand and an aquamarine sea from some rooms, make this hotel, at the southern end of town, very hard to beat.

Camping Moby Dick   CAMPGROUND €
(☑972 61 43 07; www.campingmobydick.com; Carrer de la Costa Verde 16-28; sites per 2-person tent & car €25; ☺Apr-Sep; ▣🛉) Set in a pine-and-oak stand about 100m from the seaside, this camping ground is in an ideal location. It has tennis courts and offers the chance of diving and kayak excursions in the area.

La Gavina   CATALAN €€
(Carrer Gravina 7; meals €25-30; ☺dinner) Excellent family-run restaurant where the gifts of the sea are the star. It's hard to go wrong with grilled squid or fish so fresh it may as well have jumped out of the sea onto your plate.

La Croissanteria de Calella   ICE CREAM €
(Carrer Chopitea 3-5; ice cream €2; ☺10am-5pm) The main reason for stopping by here is the truly exceptional Sandro Desii ice cream (www.sandrodesii.com). The pistachio, canelo con café, or even the humble vanilla will leave you in raptures.

ℹ Information

Tourist office (☑972 61 44 75; www.visitpalafrugell.cat; Carrer de les Voltes 6; ☺10am-8pm Jul & Aug, shorter hours rest of year)

ℹ Getting There & Away

Buses from Palafrugell serve Calella and Llafranc (€1.40, four to 16 daily, 15 minutes).

LLAFRANC
POP 330

Barely 2km northeast of Calella de Palafrugell, and now merging with it along the roads back from the rocky coast between them, upmarket Llafranc has a smaller bay but a longer stretch of sand, cupped on either side by pine-dotted craggy coast.

From the Far de Sant Sebastiá (a lighthouse) and Ermita de Sant Sebastiá (a chapel now incorporated into a luxury hotel), up on Cap de Sant Sebastià (east of the town), there are tremendous views in both directions along the coast. It's a 40-minute walk up: follow the steps from the harbour and the road up to the right. There are walking paths joining Llafranc to Palafrugell and Tamariu (two hours).

🛏 Sleeping & Eating

Hostal Celimar   HOSTAL €€
(☑972 30 13 74; www.hostalcelimar.com; Carrer de Carudo 12-14; s/d €50/80) This sunset-yellow hostal is barely a stumble from the beach and offers bright rooms, with differing colour schemes from room to room, and spotless bathrooms. One of the best deals in town.

Hotel El Far   HOTEL €€€
(☑972 30 16 39; www.elfar.net; Far de Sant Sebastiá; d from €450; ▣❀🛜) A happy marriage of secluded clifftop luxury (each room has its own large balcony affording superb sea views) with surprisingly affordable seafood-based cuisine; the rice dishes and the fideuá are particularly good.

Chez Tomás   FRENCH €€
(☑972 30 62 15; Carrer de Lluís Marqués Carbó 2; mains €15-22; ☺dinner daily Jun-Sep, lunch & dinner Fri-Sun Oct-May) As the name hints, the food here has a French flavour. Its strength is the use of fresh market produce to come up with such dishes as filet de bou amb Torta de Casar trufada (sirloin steak with a truffle-infused serving of a creamy cheese from Extremadura).

ℹ Information

Tourist office (Passeig Cypsela; ☺10am-8pm Jul & Aug, shorter hours rest of year) A kiosk at the western end of the beach.

ℹ Getting There & Away

Buses from Palafrugell serve Llafranc via Calella (€1.40, 15 minutes, four to 16 daily).

TAMARIU
POP 275

Four kilometres north up the coast from Llafranc, quiet Tamariu is a small crescent-shaped cove surrounded by pine stands and other greenery. Its beach has some of the most translucent waters on Spain's Mediterranean coast.

🛏 Sleeping & Eating

Hotel Es Furió HOTEL €€€

(☎972 62 00 36; www.esfurio.com; Carrer del Foraió 5-7; s/d incl breakfast €82/144; ✸🤶) This one-time fishing family's house was converted into a hotel in 1934. Es Furió is set just back from the beach and has spacious, cheerfully decorated rooms, where pale oranges, aqua tints and other seaside hues hold sway.

Hotel Tamariu HOTEL €€€

(☎972 62 00 31; www.tamariu.com; Passeig del Mar 2; s/d incl breakfast €98/154; ✸🤶) A former fishermen's tavern, the Hotel Tamariu has marine-coloured rooms, stripy bedspreads and decent bathrooms.

Restaurant Royal SEAFOOD €€

(Paseo Royal 9; tapas €7, mains €12-18) The only restaurant on the seafront to offer tapas portions of its dishes. The place is consistently packed with happily masticating diners, the service is swift and friendly and the fried whitebait and *calamares a la romana* are super-fresh.

ℹ Information

Tourist office (☎972 62 01 93; Carrer de la Riera; ⏱10am-1pm & 5-8pm Mon-Sat, 10am-1pm Sun Jun-Sep)

ℹ Getting There & Away

Sarfa buses run to Palafrugell (€1.60, 15 minutes, three to four daily) from mid-June to mid-September only. Parking in the village is a nightmare in summer.

BEGUR
POP 4220

Attractive little Begur, 7km northeast of Palafrugell, is dotted with tempting little bars and cafes and topped by a castell (castle), which dates to the 10th century and towers above the hill village. It's in much the same state in which it was left by the Spanish troops who wrecked it to impede the advance of Napoleon's army in 1810. Jazz and classical musicians take the stage during the Festival de Música de Begur, between late July and late August.

There's a helpful tourist office (☎972 62 45 20; www.visitbegur.com; Avinguda del Onze de Setembre 7; ⏱9am-2pm & 4-9pm Mon-Fri, 10am-2pm Sat & Sun late Jun–mid-Sep, shorter hours rest of year).

A few steps towards the castle from the central church is Hotel Rosa (☎972 62 30 15; www.hotel-rosa.com; Carrer de Pi i Ralló 19; s/d from €84/109; ⏱Mar-Nov; ✸🤶), a little surprise package with well-kept, spacious rooms and bubbly staff. Its Fonda Caner (meals €35;

CATALONIA PALAFRUGELL & AROUND

¡VAMOS A LA PLAYA!

Away from the overdeveloped parts of Costa Brava, the 'rugged coast' boasts some of the prettiest coves and beaches in Spain.

The coast to the northeast and southwest of Tossa is dotted by rocky coves, some with charming little beaches. You can walk cross-country from Tossa to Cala Llevado and Cala d'En Carles beaches, 3km southwest, or the longer Platja de Llorell (3.5km away), or drive down to Platja de Llorell from the GI682. To the northeast, you can walk down from the GI682 to sandy coves such as Cala Pola (4km), Cala Giverola (5km), Cala Salions (8km) and Platja Vallpregona (11km).

Off the cliffside road that runs between Tossa and Feliu there are several enticing inlets and largely hidden beaches, where the water is emerald green. Easier ones to find include Cala Pola and Cala Giverola. About 7km further north, at Km 35.1, you'll find parking for the cliff-backed 800m-long naturist beach, Cala del Senyor Ramon.

Between Palamós and Begur there is a string of pretty beaches: Cap Roig, with its jutting, pine-covered headland, the secluded coves of Es Tramadiu and Ses Herbes near Aiguablava, Fornells, with its picturesque rocky beach and tiny harbour, the pebbled beach and azure waters of Sa Tuna, the rocky cove of Aiguafreda, backed by pine-covered hills and dotted with a few fishermen's boats, and the nudist beach of Isla Roja – named after the red cliff rising up from the sea – reachable from tranquil Sa Riera via a lovely coastal walk.

Finally, at the north end of the coast is the craggy, windswept Cap de Creus (p325); you won't find any golden sand here, but plenty of spots to watch the waves crash against the rock and contemplate in silence, as well as a rocky Cala Fredosa nudist area just to the south of the lighthouse.

These are just a few suggestions to whet your appetite; let us know what other beautiful spots you discover!

WORTH A TRIP

QUEEN OF THE CASTLE

Two kilometres away from the village of La Pera, just south of the C66 and 22km north-west of Palafrugell, the Castell de Púbol (www.salvador-dali.org; Plaça de Gala Dalí; adult/student & senior €8/5; ☉10am-8pm daily mid-Jun–mid-Sep, shorter hours rest of year) forms the southernmost point of northeast Catalonia's 'Salvador Dalí triangle', other elements of which include the Teatre-Museu Dalí (p326) in Figueres, and his home (p323) in Portlligat.

Having promised to make his wife, Gala – his muse and the love of his life – 'queen of the castle', in 1969 Dalí finally found the ideal residence to turn into Gala's refuge, since at the age of 76, she no longer desired Dalí's hectic lifestyle – a semi-dilapidated Gothic and Renaissance stronghold which includes a 14th-century church in the quiet village of Púbol.

The sombre castle, its stone walls covered with creepers, is almost the antithesis to the flamboyance of the Teatre-Museu Dalí or the Dalí's seaside home: Gala had it decorated exactly as she wished and received only whom she wished. Legend has it that Dalí himself had to apply for written permission to visit her here.

The interior reflects her tastes: her bedroom is simple and almost unadorned; the 'everlasting' flowers that she was so fond of prevail everywhere and a gallery upstairs showcases a splendid collection of dresses designed for her by the likes of Piere Cardin, Christian Dior and Elizabeth Arden. A slightly creepy mannequin, designed to look like Gala, sits with its back to the visitor.

Dalí touches nevertheless creep in: a radiator cover with radiators painted over the top, spindly-legged elephant statues in the exuberant garden, a see-through table with ostrich legs with a stuffed horse visible below, a melted clock on a coathanger in the guest room, and a stuffed giraffe staring at Gala's tomb in the crypt.

In the dining room you'll find a replica of *Cua d'oreneta I violoncels* (Swallow's Tail and Cellos) – Dalís last work, completed here in 1983 during the two years of mourning following Gala's death.

To get here, catch one of the frequent Palafrugell-bound buses from Girona (€2.50, 40 minutes), alight at the second La Pera stop along the C66 and walk the 2km to the castle, or else take a train from Girona to Flaça (12 to 15 minutes, hourly, €2.95) and then catch a taxi for the last 4km.

☉dinner Mon-Fri, lunch & dinner Sat & Sun) specialises in hearty Catalan dishes.

Sarfa buses run to Barcelona (€20, two to 2¼ hours, four daily) via Palafrugell and Girona (€6.10, 1½ hours, one daily on weekdays).

AROUND BEGUR

The sublime coastline around Begur, with its pocket-sized coves hemmed in by pine trees and subtropical flowers and lapped by azure water, is home to some of the most beautiful beaches in Spain, most of which, on account of their small size and difficult access, remain largely undeveloped. From Begur, attractive winding roads run down to the four main beaches – Aiguablava, Fornells, Sa Tuna and Aiguafreda, all minuscule coves and utterly heavenly – through aromatic pine tree groves. Southernmost Aiguablava is also reachable via a scenic hilly drive from Tamariu. All four beaches boast exclusive accommodation. A *bus platges* (beach bus) service runs from Plaça de Forgas in Begur between late June and mid-September.

PALS
POP 2725

About 6km inland from Begur (a five-minute ride on the Palafrugell bus, €1.60) is the pretty walled town of Pals. The main monument is the 15m Torre de les Hores (clock tower) but what makes the trip worthwhile is simply wandering around the uneven lanes and poking your nose into one medieval corner or another. From the Mirador del Pedró you can see northeast across the coastal plains to the sea, with the Illes Medes in the background. There are a number of *pensiones* and *casas rurales* (rural homes) in and around the town.

Sarfa buses run to Barcelona (€14.40, 2¼ hours, up to four daily on weekdays).

PERATALLADA
POP 150

The warm stone houses of Peratallada have made this village a favourite day trip for Catalans. Its beautifully preserved narrow streets, heavy stone arches, 12th-century Romanesque church as well as 11th-century castle-mansion (now a luxury hotel and restaurant) are supplemented by several places to stay, enticing restaurants and a sprinkling of low-key boutiques.

Hostal Miralluna (☑972 63 43 04; www. hostalmiralluna.com; Plaza del Olí 2; d incl breakfast from €180; ☺Mar-Nov; ✹☎) is a 17th-century village home, where the old stone-and-timber frame has been teamed with modern comforts to create an artistically rustic place to stay, its sumptuous rooms decorated in soothing whites and creams. An extra bonus is the exquisite hidden garden.

There are a number of other places to stay in the village, including some cheaper *casas rurales*.

Buses run to Begur (€2.65, two daily) and Girona (€3.90, one daily).

Girona

POP 95,720

A tight huddle of ancient arcaded houses, grand churches, climbing cobbled streets and medieval baths, and Catalonia's most extensive and best-preserved Call (medieval Jewish quarter), all enclosed by defensive walls and the lazy Río Onyar, constitute a powerful reason for visiting north Catalonia's largest city, Girona.

The Roman town of Gerunda lay on Vía Augusta, the highway from Rome to Cádiz. Taken from the Muslims by the Franks in AD 797, Girona became capital of one of Catalonia's most important counties, falling under the sway of Barcelona in the late 9th century. Its wealth in medieval times produced many fine Romanesque and Gothic buildings that have survived repeated attacks and sieges, which is today combined with fine examples of Modernisme, as well as lively nightlife and art and music festivals.

⦿ Sights

Museu d'Història dels Jueus de Girona   MUSEUM
(Carrer de la Força 8; adult/child €2/free; ☺10am-8pm Mon-Sat, 10am-2pm Sun Jul & Aug, shorter hours rest of year) Until 1492 Girona was home to Catalonia's second-most important medieval Jewish community (after Barcelona), and one of the finest Jewish quarters in the country. The Call (Catalan for 'ghetto'), was centred on the narrow Carrer de la Força for 600 years, until relentless persecution forced the Jews out of Spain. The restored Centre Bonstruc ça Porta, named after Jewish Girona's most illustrious figure – a 13th-century cabbalist philosopher and mystic – houses the excellent Museu d'Història dels Jueus de Girona, which shows genuine pride in Girona's Jewish heritage without shying away from the less salubrious aspects, such as persecution by the Inquisition and forced conversions. Other well-presented displays deal with Girona's Jewish contribution to medieval astronomy and medicine, the synagogue, everyday life and rituals in the Jewish community and the Jewish diaspora, and standout objects include funerary slabs and the original documents ordering the expulsion of Jews from Spain.

Catedral   CATHEDRAL
(www.catedraldegirona.org; Plaça de la Catedral; museum adult/child €5/1.20, Sun free; ☺10am-8pm) The billowing baroque facade of the cathedral seems even grander as it stands at the head of a majestic flight of 86 steps rising from Plaça de la Catedral. Though the beautiful Romanesque cloister dates back to the 12th century, most of the building has been repeatedly rebuilt and altered down the centuries, giving the cathedral the second-widest Gothic nave (23m) in Christendom. The cathedral's museum, through the door marked 'Claustre Tresor', contains numerous ecclesiastic treasures, including the masterly Romanesque *Tapís de la Creació* (Tapestry of the Creation) and a Mozarabic illuminated *Beatus* manuscript, dating from 975. The Creation tapestry (under restoration at the time of writing) shows God at the epicentre and in the circle

CATALONIA GIRONA

ⓘ MUSEUM PASS

The GironaMuseus card (www. gironamuseus.cat), covering the five Girona museums and also available at the tourist office, is the most economical way of visiting the city's museums. You pay the full entrance fee at the first museum you visit and then get a 50% discount at the remainder. It's valid for six months.

Girona

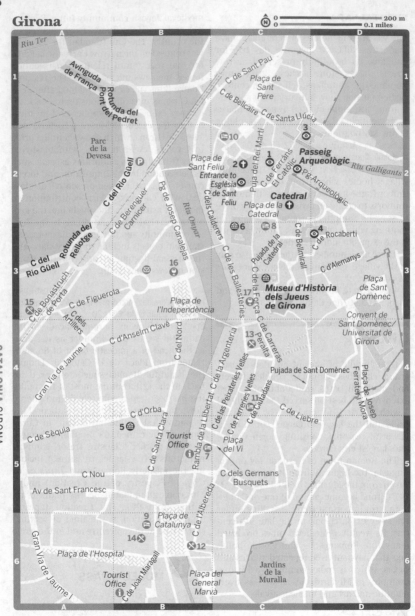

N 0 _____ 200 m
0 _____ 0.1 miles

Riu Ter

Avinguda de França

Rotunda del Pont del Pedret

C de Sant Pau

Plaça de Sant Pere

C de Bellcaire · C de Santa Llúcia

Parc de la Devesa

C del Rio Güell

Rotunda del Rellotge

C de Berenguer Carnicer

Pg de Josep Canalejas

Riu Onyar

Plaça de Sant Feliu
Entrance to Església de Sant Feliu

Puja del Rei Martí

C de Ferrans

Passeig Arqueològic

Riu Galligants

Pg Arqueològic

El Catòlic

Catedral

Plaça de la Catedral

C dels Calderers

C de les Ballesteries

C de Belmirall

C de Rocaberti

C d'Alemanys

C del Rio Güell

C de Bonastruch de Porta

C de Figuerola

C dels Artillers

Plaça de l'Independència

Pujada de la Catedral

C de la Força

Museu d'Història dels Jueus de Girona

Plaça de Sant Domènec

Convent de Sant Domènec/ Universitat de Girona

Gran Via de Jaume I

C d'Anselm Clavé

C del Nord

C de Carreras

Peralta

Pujada de Sant Domènec

Plaça de Josep Ferrater Móra

C de Sèquia

C d'Orba

C de Santa Clara

Rambla de la Llibertat

C de l'Argenteria

C de les Peixateries Velles

C de Ferreries Velles

C de Ciutadans

C de Llebre

Tourist Office

Plaça del Vi

C dels Germans Busquets

C Nou

Av de Sant Francesc

C de l'Albereda

Plaça de Catalunya

Plaça de l'Hospital

Gran Via de Jaume I

C de Joan Maragall

Tourist Office

Plaça del General Marvà

Jardins de la Muralla

---

around him the creation of Adam, Eve, the animals, the sky, light and darkness.

Passeig Arqueològic HISTORIC SITE
(⏱10am-8pm) A walk along Girona's medieval walls, also known as the Passeig de la Muralla, is a wonderful way to appreciate the city landscape from above. There are several points of access, the most popular being across the street from the Banys Àrabs, where steps lead up into some heavenly gardens where town and plants merge

Girona

into one organic masterpiece. The southernmost part of the wall ends right near Plaça Catalunya.

Museu d'Història de la Ciutat MUSEUM
(www.girona.cat; Carrer de la Força 27; adult/student/child €4/2/free; ⊙10am-2pm & 5-7pm Tue-Sat, 10am-2pm Sun & holidays) The engaging and well-presented City History Museum does Girona's long and impressive history justice, its displays covering everything from the city's Roman origins, through the siege of the city by Napoleonic troops to the *sardana* (Catalonia's national folk dance) tradition. A separate gallery houses cutting-edge temporary art and photography exhibits.

Museu d'Art ART
(www.museuart.com; Plaça de la Catedral 12; admission €2; ⊙10am-7pm Tue-Sat, 10am-2pm Sun & holidays) Next door to the cathedral, in the 12th-to-16th-century Palau Episcopal, the art museum collection consists of around 8500 pieces of art from the Girona region, ranging from Romanesque woodcarvings and stained-glass tables to Modernist sculptures by Olot-born Miquel Blay and early-20th-century paintings by Francesc Vayreda.

Banys Àrabs BATHHOUSE
(www.banysarabs.org; Carrer de Ferran Catòlic; adult/child €2/1; ⊙10am-7pm Mon-Sat Apr-Sep, 10am-2pm Sun & holidays, shorter hours rest of year) Although modelled on earlier Muslim and Roman bathhouses, the Banys Àrabs are a finely preserved 12th-century Christian affair in Romanesque style. This is the only public bathhouse discovered from medieval Christian Spain, where, in reaction to the Muslim obsession with water and cleanliness, washing almost came to be regarded as ungodly. The baths contain an *apodyterium* (changing room), followed by a *frigidarium* and *tepidarium* (with respectively cold and warm water) and a *caldarium* (a kind of sauna) heated by an underfloor furnace.

FREE **Església de Sant Feliu** CHURCH
(Plaça de Sant Feliu; ⊙9.30am-2pm & 4-7pm Mon-Sat, 10am-noon Sun) Girona's second great church is downhill from the cathedral. The 17th-century main facade, with its landmark single tower, is on Plaça de Sant Feliu, but the entrance is around the side. The nave has 13th-century Romanesque arches but 14th- to 16th-century Gothic upper levels and a baroque tower. The northernmost of the chapels is graced by a masterly Catalan Gothic sculpture, Aloi de Montbrai's alabaster *Crist Jacent* (Recumbent Christ).

Monestir de Sant Pere de Galligants MONASTERY
(www.mac.cat/cat/Seus/Girona; Carrer de Santa Llúcia; adult/senior & child €2.30/free; ⊙10.30am-1.30pm & 4-7pm Tue-Sat Jun-Sep, 10am-2pm Sun & holidays) This 11th- and 12th-century Romanesque Benedictine monastery has a lovely cloister, featuring otherworldly animals and mythical creatures on its pillars, and is home to the **Museu Arqueològic**, with exhibits that range from prehistoric to me-

CATALONIA GIRONA

dieval times, including Roman mosaics and medieval Jewish tombstones.

Museu del Cinema — MUSEUM

(www.museudelcinema.org; Carrer de Sèquia 1; adult/child €5/free; ⊙10am-8pm Jul & Aug, shorter hours & closed Mon rest of year) The Casa de les Aigües houses Spain's only cinema museum. The Tomás Mallol (Girona film director) collection includes not only displays tracing the history of cinema from the late-19th-century debut of the Lumiére brothers, but also a parade of hands-on items for indulging in shadow games, optical illusions and the like – it's a great experience for children.

🛏 Sleeping

Bed & Breakfast Bells Oficis — B&B €€

(☎972 22 81 70; www.bellsoficis.com; Carrer dels Germans Busquets 2; r incl breakfast €40-85; ✱🌐) Up the wobbly-winding staircase of a 19th-century building right in the heart of Girona you'll discover six very desirable rooms, lovingly restored by knowledgeable Javi and his wife. Some have unusual pebble art in the bathrooms, while others have views over the street. The biggest (€99) has ample room for four people.

Casa Cúndaro — BOUTIQUE HOTEL €€

(☎972 22 35 83; www.casacundaro.com; Pujada de la Catedral 9; d €60-80; 🌐) The understated exterior of this medieval Jewish house, run by a friendly family, hides five sumptuous rooms and four self-catering apartments – all combining original exposed stone walls with modern luxuries such as satellite TV. The location right next to the cathedral is either a boon or a bane, depending on whether you enjoy the sound of church bells.

COWER, BRIEF MORTALS

If you're in the area on Holy Thursday (Easter), stop by the town of Verges, 15km east of Girona. On that night, the dead (well, people dressed as skeletons) roam the streets, performing the macabre **Dansa de la Mort** (Dance of Death) and reminding spectators of the brevity of existence as part of a much bigger evening procession enacting Christ's way to Calvary.

Girona–Torroella buses pass through here.

Equity Point Hostel — HOSTEL €

(☎972 31 20 45; www.equity-point.com; Plaça de Catalunya 23; dm/d incl breakfast from €17/48; ✱@🌐) Part of an international network of hostels, this friendly, efficient place offers not just the cheapest night's kip in Girona but also a host of perks – from mounds of tourist info, guest kitchen and colourful lounge to rooftop terrace and spacious rooms equipped with lockers and card-key access. En suite dorms cost a couple of euros more.

Hotel Llegendes de Girona — HOTEL €€

(☎972 22 09 05; www.llegendeshotel.com; Portal de la Barca 4; d €123, 'Fountain of Lovers' room €288; ℗✱🌐) The rooms at this restored 18th-century building are supremely comfortable, with all manner of hi-tech gadgets, and the all-glass bathrooms have huge rain showers. This incongruous blend of modernity and antiquity includes a guide to tantric sex positions in each room; three of the rooms even have an 'Eros' sofa to try them out on.

Pensió Viladomat — PENSIÓN €

(☎972 20 31 76; www.pensioviladomat.com; Carrer dels Ciutadans 5; s/d without bathroom €23/40, d with bathroom €50) This is one of the nicest of the cheaper *pensiones* scattered about the southern end of the old town. It has eight simple but well-maintained rooms.

🍴 Eating

Restaurant Txalaka — BASQUE €€
TOP CHOICE

(☎972 22 59 75; Carrer Bonastruc de Porta 4; mains €17-23, pintxos €2.50-4; ⊙closed Sun) For sensational Basque cooking and *pintxos* (tapas) washed down with *txakoli* (the fizzy white wine from the Basque coast) poured from a great height, don't miss this popular local spot. Just load up your plate with the likes of garlic prawns, fresh anchovy *montaditos*, marinated wild mushrooms and octopus dusted in paprika, and pay according to the number of *montadito* sticks/dishes.

L'Alqueria — CATALAN €€

(☎972 22 18 82; www.restaurantalqueria.com; Carrer de la Ginesta 8; mains €18-22; ⊙lunch & dinner Wed-Sat, lunch Tue & Sun) This smart minimalist **arrocería** serves the finest *arrós negre* (rice cooked in cuttlefish ink) and *arrós a la Catalan* in the city, as well as around 20 other superbly executed rice dishes, includ-

COOKING UP A THREE-STAR STORM

Once a simple bar and grill clutching onto a rocky perch high above the bare Mediterranean beach of Cala Montjoi and accessible only by dirt track from Roses, 6km to the west, El Bulli (www.elbulli.com) held three Michelin stars and the title of 'Best Restaurant in the World' a record five times, thanks to star chef Ferran Adrià, the 'Dalí of gastronomy'. Though he closed El Bulli's doors in 2011, due to open the El Bulli Foundation – an academy for advanced cuisine – in 2014 instead, fear not, gourmets! Catalonia still has three three-star Michelin establishments, one of which was quick to slip into El Bulli's place.

El Celler de Can Roca (☏972 22 21 57; www.cellercanroca.com; Carrer Can Sunyer 48; 5/9 course menus €130/160; ☺lunch & dinner Tue-Sat), the second-best restaurant in the world as of 2012, located 2km west of central Girona in a refurbished country house, is run by three brothers – Joan, Josep and Jordi – who focus on 'emotional cuisine' through their ever-changing takes on Mediterranean dishes. The style is playful – how about a 'dry gambini' (with a prawn serving the olive role in a dry martini)? – and the five- and nine course tasting menus are reasonably priced.

Can Fabes (☏93 867 28 51; www.canfabes.com; Carrer de Sant Joan 6; meals €180, tasting menus plus wine €105-195; ☺lunch & dinner Wed-Sat, lunch Sun, closed Jan) has long attracted a steady stream of 'gastronauts' from Barcelona. Chef Santi Santamaria (the first Catalan chef ever to be awarded three Michelin stars) is a local boy who started up here in 1981. Dishes based on local, seasonal products (seafood landed at Blanes, for example) are at the core of his cooking, the flavours are clean and the presentation stylish without being pretentious.

Sant Pau (☏93 760 06 62; www.ruscalleda.com; Carrer Nou 10, Sant Pol de Mar; menus €146; ☺lunch & dinner Tue, Wed, Fri & Sat, dinner Thu, closed most of May & Nov), another foodie fave, is a beautifully presented mansion whose garden overlooks the Mediterranean. Carme Ruscalleda is the driving force, with Eastern touches, such as tempura, making an appearance on an otherwise Catalan menu.

ing paellas. Eat your heart out, Valencia! It's wise to book ahead for dinner.

+Cub
TAPAS €

(Plaça de Catalunya; 3 tapas €10.40; ☺lunch daily, dinner Mon-Sat; ☑) This über-central cafe is distinguished by the friendly service, innovative tapas – from black pudding with pistachio to salad with black fig sorbet – fresh fruit-juice combos, shakes and Girona's own La Moska microbrew, as well as numerous other beers from all over Spain.

Creperie Bretonne
CAFE €

(www.creperiebretonne.com; Cort Reial 14; crêpes €6-8; ☑☑) Your sweet or savoury crêpes are cooked to order inside a small bus and there are colour pencils and paper provided for kids or the artistically inclined. The lemon-and-sugar crêpe is a standout classic and the ice cream with the signature salted caramel is worth detouring for.

🍷 Drinking

Students make the nightlife here, so in summer things calm down. You can keep going until the wee hours near the river north of the old town, where you will find a string of bars along Carrer de Palafrugell and Ronda de Pedret.

Lola Cafe
BAR

(Carrer de la Força 7; ☺6pm-3am) Re-creating a sultry Latin night in the midst of medieval Girona with occasional live salsa and rumba, this bar really hits the spot if you happen to have a weakness for caipirinhas, mojitos and more.

Lapsus
BAR

(Plaça de l'Independència 10; ☺10am-3am) Popular with students and 30-somethings, this bar gets pretty rowdy whenever a big match is on. A good spot to alternate your beers and cocktails with tapas or even grab some breakfast.

ℹ Information

Tourist office (☏972 22 65 75; www.girona. cat/turisme; Rambla de la Llibertat 1; ☺8am-8pm Mon-Fri, 8am-2pm & 4-8pm Sat, 9am-2pm Sun)

Tourist office (www.girona.cat; Joan Maragall 2; ☺8am-8pm Mon-Fri, 8am-2pm & 4-8pm Sat, 9am-2pm Sun)

CATALONIA GIRONA

GIRONA'S JEWS

Jews settled in Girona in the 9th century, and lived by and large peacefully alongside their Christian neighbours (in fact, the synagogue was originally located next door to the cathedral), gaining in prosperity and contributing to fields as diverse as astronomy and medicine. In its heyday, the Jewish quarter (the Call) was known as 'the Mother City of Israel'. Little by little, though, and especially with the later crusades in the 12th and 13th centuries, the Jewish community became a ready target for racist attacks. The Call – a maze of tiny alleys, surrounded by a stone wall – went from refuge to ghetto as Jews were gradually confined to their tiny corner of the town. Things came to a head in 1391, when a mob broke into the ghetto, massacring 40 residents. Since the Jews were still under the king's protection, troops were sent in and the survivors were confined to the Galligants Tower 'for their own safety' for 17 weeks, only to find their houses and possessions destroyed upon emerging. In 1492 the Jewish community left Girona forever.

❶ Getting There & Away

Girona-Costa Brava airport (www.barcelona-girona-airport.com), Ryanair's Spanish hub, is located 11km south of the centre, with **Sagalés Barcelona Bus** (www.sagales.com) connecting it to Girona's main bus/train station (€2.60, 25 minutes, hourly), as well as Barcelona's Estació del Nord (€15/25 one way/return, 1¼ hours). A **taxi** (☑ 872 97 50 00) to central Girona costs around €22/25 day/night.

Teisa (www.teisa-bus.com) runs to Besalú (€3.55, 50 minutes, four to eight daily) and Olot (€6.50, 1¼ hours, up to eight daily), while **Sarfa** (www.sarfa.com) serves Cadaques (€5.50, 1¾ hours, two to three daily) via Roses (€3.70, 1¼ hours) and Tossa de Mar (€8.50, 55 minutes). The bus station is next to the train station.

Girona is on the train line between Barcelona (from €9.70, 1½ hours, up to 20 daily), Figueres (€4.80 to €14.10, 25 to 40 minutes, up to 16 daily) and Portbou (from €5.40, one hour, 13 daily), some crossing the border to Cerbère (France).

Torroella de Montgrí

POP 11,385

On the Riu Ter, about 30km northeast of Girona and 15km north of Palafrugell, the agreeable medieval town of Torroella de Montgrí is the funnel through which travellers to L'Estartit must pass and the site of the annual **Festival Internacional de Música** (www.festivaldetorroella.com) – a month-long feast of classical music held in the main plaza in July and August.

Overlooking the town from the top of the 300m limestone Montgrí hills to the north, the impressive **Castell de Montgrí** was built between 1294 and 1301 for King Jaume II, during his efforts to bring to heel the dis-obedient counts of Empúries, to the north. There's no road, and by foot it's a 40-minute climb from Torroella. Head north from Plaça del Lledoner along Carrer de Fátima, at the end of which is a sign pointing the way. **Ampsa** (www.ampsa.org) runs buses to L'Estartit (€1.40, 10 minutes, eight to 16 daily) and Girona (€2.80, one hour, up to eight daily), while Sarfa serves Barcelona (€20.45, 2¾ hours, three daily).

L'Escala

POP 10,550

Travel back millennia to the ancient Greco-Roman site of Empúries, set behind a near-virgin beach facing the Mediterranean. Its modern descendant, L'Escala, 11km north of Torroella de Montgrí, is a sunny and pleasant medium-sized resort on the often-windswept southern shore of the Golf de Roses. Birdwatchers flock to the Parc Natural dels Aiguamolls de l'Empordà, coastal wetlands that lie about 10km north of Empúries.

◎ Sights & Activities

TOP CHOICE **Empúries** RUINS

Empúries was probably the first, and certainly one of the most important, Greek trading posts on the Iberian Peninsula, though the site was originally founded by Phoenicans. Early Greek traders, pushing on from a trading post at Masilia (Marseille in France), set up shop around 600 BC at what is now the charming village of Sant Martí d'Empúries, then an island. Soon afterwards they founded a mainland colony, Emporion

CATALONIA TORROELLA DE MONTGRÍ

(Market), which remained an important trading centre, and conduit of Greek culture to the Iberians, for centuries.

In 218 BC Roman legions clanked ashore here to cut off Hannibal's supply lines in the Second Punic War. About 195 BC they set up a military camp and, by 100 BC, had added a town. A century later it had merged with the Greek one. Emporiae, as the place was then known, was abandoned in the late 3rd century AD, after raids by Germanic tribes. Later, an early Christian basilica and a cemetery stood on the site of the Greek town, before the whole place disappeared under the sands for a millennium until its excavation in the 20th century.

The windswept Greek town, its broken columns fingering the sky, lies in the lower part of the site, closer to the shore. Points of interest include the thick southern defensive walls, the site of the Asklepion (a shrine to the god of medicine) with a copy of his statue found here, and the Agora (town square), with remnants of the early Christian basilica and the Greek *stoa* (market complex), beside it.

A museum (www.mac.cat; adult/child €3/free; ⊙10am-8pm Easter & Jun Sep, to 6pm rest of yr) separating the Greek town from the larger Roman town on the upper part of the site, houses some stunning mosaics, statues and 2000-year-old drinking cups. Highlights of the Roman town include the mosaic floors of a 1st-century-BC house, the Forum and ancient walls. Outside the walls are the remains of an oval amphitheatre. A 2nd-century-AD bust in Carrara marble of the Roman god Bacchus was unearthed on the site in 2005.

Between March and October, on the last Sunday of the month, there are entertaining tours of the site led by 'Romans' who explain the functions of the different buildings (€4); book in advance.

🛏 Sleeping & Eating

L'Escala is famous for its *anchoas* (anchovies) and fresh fish. Numerous mid-priced eateries are scattered along the waterfront parade of Port d'en Perris. The town is split into two halves – the northern part is centred on the scrappy *nucli antic* (old town), more popular with Spanish tourists; the hotels listed here are in this part. The southern half – Riels – which spreads along a big sandy bay, lacks the character of the old town.

Hotel Empúries BOUTIQUE HOTEL €€€
(☑972 98 29 36; www.hostalempuries.com; Platja del Portitxol; d €195; P☀☎) A stylish hotel next to the Roman ruins and fronting a sandy splash of ocean. Some rooms are as sandy coloured as the beach and the mosaic bathrooms clearly take their inspiration from the ruins; the rooms in the new wing, with rain showers and enormous beds, are particularly comfortable and the two restaurants specialise in creative Mediterranean and seafood dishes using the freshest local produce.

Can Miquel HOTEL €€
(☑972 77 14 52; www.canmiquel.com; Platja de Montgró; d incl breakfast €119; P☀☎☒) A stone's throw from the beach, framed by jagged cliffs, the thoroughly modern rooms of this hotel are decked out in soothing neutral shades and the restaurant specialises in – you've guessed it! – fish.

TOP CHOICE **La Gruta** FUSION €€
(☑972 77 62 11; Carrer Enric Serra 15; 3-course menus €25; ⊙lunch Mon-Thu, lunch & dinner Fri & Sat) This innovative place with slick service is definitely one of the most interesting places to eat in town: as well as catch-of-the-day, you'll find such delights as pork spare ribs glazed with honey and cumin and bone marrow risotto with foie gras; the desserts are just as inventive.

ℹ Information

If you arrive by Sarfa bus, you'll alight on Avinguda Girona, just down the street from the **tourist office** (☑972 77 06 03; www.lescala.cat; Plaça de les Escoles 1; ⊙9am-8pm Mon-Sat, 10am-1pm Sun mid-Jun–mid-Sep, shorter hours rest of year). Empúries is 1km northwest of the town centre along the coast.

ℹ Getting There & Away

Sarfa has daily buses from Barcelona (€22, three hours, three daily), Girona (€6, one hour, five daily except Sunday) and Figueres (€6, one hour, six daily except Sunday).

Castelló d'Empúries

POP 12,885

This well-preserved ancient town was once the capital of Empúries, a medieval Catalan county that maintained a large degree of independence up to the 14th century. Today it makes a superb base for the nearby Parc

DIVING OFF THE COSTA BRAVA

L'Estartit (www.visitestartit.com), 6km east of Torroella de Montgrí, has a long, wide beach of fine sand but nothing over any other Costa Brava package resort – with the rather big exception of the Illes Medes! The group of rocky islets barely 1km offshore is home to some of the most abundant marine life on Spain's Mediterranean coast.

The shores and waters around these seven islets, rich in bird and marine life, have been protected since 1985 as a *reserva natural submarina*, which has brought a proliferation in their marine life and made them Spain's most popular destination for snorkellers and divers. The range of depths (down to 50m) and underwater cavities and tunnels around the seven islets contribute much to their attraction. On and around rocks near the surface are colourful algae and sponges, as well as octopuses, crabs and various fish. Below 10m or 15m, cavities and caves harbour lobsters, scorpion fish and large conger eels and groupers. Some groupers and perch may feed from the hand. With luck, you'll spot some huge wrasse. If you get down to the sea floor, you may see angler fish, thornback rays or marbled electric rays. Be aware that this area gets pretty busy with divers, especially on summer weekends.

The tourist office has lists of L'Estartit's scuba-diving outfits. If you're a qualified diver, a two-hour trip usually costs around €35 per person. Full gear rental can cost up to €55 a day and night dives are €40 to €45. If you're a novice, do an introductory dive for around €70 or a full, five-day PADI Open Water Diver course for around €420.

Hotel Les Illes (972 75 12 39; www.hotellesilles.com; Carrer de Les Illes 55; s/d incl breakfast €50/100, full board available; ❄️🐾) is a white, bright, family-friendly divers' hangout with its own dive shop and tidy rooms with balconies. For campers, Les Medes (972 75 18 05; www.campinglesmedes.com; Paratge Camp de l'Arbre; site per adult €18; ⏲️Dec-Oct; P 📶 ❄️ 🐾) is the best of the eight camping grounds in and around town. It's set in a leafy location about 800m from the seaside and has a sauna as well as three pools, with bike rental and even massages available.

Eateries serving mostly fresh seafood as well as standard Spanish fare are plentiful along the seafront.

L'Estartit is easily reachable by bus from Torroella de Montgrí.

Natural dels Aiguamolls de l'Empordá, as well as a number of wind-blown but peaceful beaches. Away from the feathered treats of the natural park, man-made beauty can be found in the town centre's Església de Santa Maria on Plaça de Jacint Verdaguer. It's a voluminous 13th- and 14th-century Gothic church with a sturdy Romanesque bell tower.

⊙ Sights & Activities

Parc Natural dels Aiguamolls de l'Empordá   BIRDWATCHING
(www.parcsdecatalunya.net; parking €2; ⊙El Cortalet information centre 9.30am-2pm & 4.30-7pm Apr-Oct, shorter hours rest of year) The remnants of the mighty marshes that once covered the whole coastal plain of the Golf de Roses are preserved in this natural park, which is a key site for migrating birds. Birdwatchers have spotted more than 100 species a day in the March–May and August–October migration periods, which bring big increases in the numbers of wading birds and even the occasional flamingo, bee eater, glossy ibis, spoonbill or rare black stork. In all, in the migratory periods more than 300 species pass through (some 90 nest here). There are usually enough birds around to make a visit worthwhile at any time of year.

There are two marked trails, leading to a 2km stretch of beach and several *aguaits* (hides) with saltwater-marsh views; the longer of the two takes five hours and is best cycled. From the top of the Observatori Senillosa, a former silo, you can observe the whole park. The paths are always open, but morning and evening are the best times for birds. The El Cortalet information centre is 1km east off the Sant Pere Pescador–Castelló d'Empúries road.

The nearest places to El Cortalet that can be reached by bus are Sant Pere Pescador, 6km south (served by four or five Sarfa buses daily from L'Escala and Figueres), and Castelló d'Empúries, 8km north.

🛏 Sleeping & Eating

There are a couple of great-value places to eat and drink in the town, as well as numerous *casas rurales* in the surrounding countryside and campsites aplenty in nearby Sant Pere Pescador.

TOP CHOICE **Hotel Casa Clara** HOTEL €€
(📞972 25 02 15; www.hotelcasaclara.com; Carrer de la Fruita 27; s/d €36/72; 🅿❄🛜) The 11 spacious, tiled rooms at this adorable little hotel all feature plenty of natural light, an individual colour scheme and very comfortable beds – some with wrought-iron bedsteads. The attached restaurant features a changing weekly menu of imaginative, beautifully executed dishes, such as courgette and hazelnut bake and sea bream with shitake mushrooms (two courses €17).

Hotel Canet HOTEL €€
(📞972 25 03 40; www.hotelcanet.com; Plaça del Joc de la Pilota 2; s/d from €65/81; 🅿❄🛜🏊) This modernised 17th-century mansion in the town centre has elegant rooms, low-slung stone arches and a sun deck. A soothing swimming pool glistens within the stone walls of the interior courtyard. The decent restaurant (mains around €17) offers Catalan fare cooked mainly from local produce.

ℹ Getting There & Away

Sarfa runs buses to Figueres (€1.40, 15 minutes, eight to 12 daily), Cadaqués (€3.90, 50 minutes, five to six daily) and Barcelona's Estació del Nord (€19.30, two hours, two daily).

Cadaqués & Around
POP 2900

If you have time for only one stop on the Costa Brava, make it Cadaqués. A whitewashed village around a rocky bay, its narrow, hilly streets perfect for wandering, it and the surrounding area have a special magic – a fusion of wind, sea, light and rock – that isn't dissipated even by the throngs of summer visitors.

A portion of that magic owes itself to Salvador Dalí, who spent family holidays in Cadaqués during his youth, and lived much of his later life at nearby Portlligat. Thanks to Dalí and other luminaries, such as his friend Federico García Lorca, Cadaqués pulled in a celebrity crowd for decades. One visit by the poet Paul Éluard and his Russian wife, Gala, in 1929 caused an earthquake in Dalí's life: he ran off to Paris with Gala (who was to become his lifelong obsession and, later, his wife) and joined the surrealist movement. In the 1950s the crowd he attracted was more jet-setting – Walt Disney, the Duke of Windsor and Greek shipowner Stavros Niarchos.

CATALONIA CADAQUÉS & AROUND

DON'T MISS

CASA MUSEU DALÍ

Located by a peaceful cove in Portlligat, a tiny fishing settlement a 1.25km walk from Cadaqués, the **Casa Museu Dalí** (📞972 25 10 15; www.salvador-dali.org; adult/child €11/free; ⏱by advance reservation only) – the lifelong residence of Salvador Dalí – started life as a mere fisherman's hut, was steadily altered and enlarged by Dalí, who lived here with his wife from 1930 to 1982, and is now a fascinating insight into the lives of the (pun intended!) surreal couple. If the Teatre-Museu Dalí is the mask that the showman presented to the world, then this is an intimate glimpse of his actual face. This splendid, bizarre whitewashed structure is a mishmash of cottages and sunny terraces, linked together by narrow labyrinthine corridors and containing an assortment of bizarre furnishings, each chosen with great care.

From the stuffed-bear umbrella/walking-stick holder in the entry hall and the stuffed swans in the library, to the moving easel in Dalí's study that allowed him to manipulate the canvas if he were working on a particularly large painting, the yellow everlasting flowers beloved by his wife and the mirror in the bedroom which allowed them to watch the sunrise, there's no end to little surprises. See what catches your eye. Some of the stranger touches include The Oval – the heart of the house built as a sanctuary for Gala; the – let's face it – penis-shaped swimming pool and labial sofa and the little tower topped with a giant egg, abristle with pitchforks.

Compulsory small-group tours are conducted by multilingual guides; booking ahead is essential.

THE COSTA BRAVA WAY

The 255km-long stretch of cliffs, coves, rocky promontories and pine groves that make up the signposted Costa Brava Way, stretching from Blanes to Colliure in France, unsurprisingly offers some of the best walks in Catalonia, ranging from gentle rambles to high-octane scrambles (or one long, demanding hike if you want to do the whole thing). For the most part, the trail follows the established GR92, but also includes a number of coastal deviations.

Choice walks include **Cadaqués to the Cap de Creus Lighthouse** (2½ hours), a relatively easy walk from the centre of Cadaqués that passes Portlligat before continuing along windswept, scrub-covered rocky ground past several isolated beaches before reaching the lighthouse. Another lovely route runs from **Aiguablava to Sa Riera** (four to five hours) via the Begur lighthouse; part of the way takes you along some spectacular pine-covered cliffs with grand views of the aquamarine waters breaking on the rocks below before descending to the coves of Sa Tuna and Aiguafreda, and finally emerging at the stunning Platja de Sa Riera.

For more information, grab a copy of *The Costa Brava Way* by Triangle Postals and see what other walks you discover!

In the 1970s Mick Jagger and Gabriel García Márquez popped by. Today the crowd is not quite as famous, and leans heavily to day-tripping French from across the border, but the enchantment of Cadaqués' atmosphere remains.

◎ Sights

Museu de Cadaqués   MUSEUM
(Carrer de Narcís Monturiol 15; adult/child €5/3.50; ⊙10am-1.30pm & 4-7pm Mon-Sat Apr-Jun, shorter hours rest of year) Dalí features strongly in the works of art displayed here, as do his contemporaries, also connected to Cadaques, such as Picasso.

⌂ Sleeping

Hostal Vehí   PENSIÓN €€
(☑972 25 84 70; www.hostalvehi.com; Carrer de l'Església 5; s/d without bathroom €30/55, d with bathroom €77; ⊛🛜) Near the church in the heart of the old town, this simple *pensión* with clean-as-a-whistle rooms, run by a friendly family, tends to be booked up for July and August. It's a pain to get to if you have a lot of luggage and the wi-fi policy is annoying, but it's easily the cheapest deal in town, and also about the best. Breakfast is €6 extra.

Hotel Llané Petit   HOTEL €€€
(☑972 25 10 20; www.llanepetit.com; Carrer del Dr Bartomeus 37; d with/without seaview €173/124; 🅿⊛🛜⚡) A four-storey place overlooking a pocket-sized cobbled beach, the hotel is perhaps not as 'petite' as all that (it has 35 rooms), but the location is splendid and most rooms have a generous balcony to sit on. Breakfast (€12) and parking (€10) cost extra.

L'Hostalet de Cadaqués   HOTEL €€
(☑972 25 82 06; www.hostaletcadaques.com; Carrer Miquel Rosset 13; d €70; ⊛🛜) The rooms in this hotel are tiny but exceptionally well kept, and hanging enticingly off the walls are pictures of the various beaches that you will shortly be swimming off if you're made of tough stuff. It can suffer a little from noise from the nearby bars.

✗ Eating & Drinking

The seafront is lined with fairly pricey seafood eateries. Cadaqués' signature dish is *suquet* – a hearty potato-based fish-and-shellfish stew that reflects the town's fishing roots. Carrer Miquel Rosset has many hole-in-the-wall bars that get jam-packed on sultry summer nights.

Es Baluard   SEAFOOD €€
(☑972 25 81 83; www.esbaluard-cadaques.net; Riba Nemesi Llorens; mains €16-22) The family that runs this old-school restaurant that's set into the old sea wall clearly worships at the throne of Poseidon, because the tastiest of his subjects wind up on your plate. Fish dishes drawing on local market produce, such as the *anchoas de Cadaqués* and *gambitas de Roses*, dominate the menu and you shouldn't shy away from the *crema catalana*, either.

Pilar CATALAN €€
(Carrer de la Miranda; mains €16-20; ⊙lunch & dinner Mon-Sat, lunch Sun) This compact, family-run place is where locals come for some of the best rice dishes and *fideuá* in town; the latter arrives crowned with rock lobster and other gifts of the sea.

Casa Nun SEAFOOD €
(📞972 25 88 56; Plaça del Port Ditxos 6; menus €22) Head for the cute upstairs dining area or take one of the few tables outside overlooking the port. Everything is prepared with care, and, you guessed it, seafood predominates.

L'Hostal BAR
(Passeig del Mar 8; ⊙10pm-5am Sun-Thu, 10pm-6am Fri & Sat) One evening in the 1970s, an effusive Dalí called this beachside bar the *lugar más bonito del mundo* (the most beautiful place on earth). Photos of the artist adorn the walls and live bands play most nights.

ℹ️ Information
Tourist office (📞972 25 83 15; Carrer del Cotxe 2; ⊙9am-9pm Mon-Sat, 10am-1pm & 5-8pm Sun late Jun–mid-Sep, shorter hours rest of year)

ℹ️ Getting There & Away
Sarfa buses connect Cadaqués to Barcelona (€23.70, 2¾ hours, two to five daily), Figueres (€5.30, one hour, three to seven daily) via Castelló d'Empúries, and Girona (€3.50, 1¾ hours, two to three daily).

CAP DE CREUS
Cap de Creus is the most easterly point of the Spanish mainland and is a place of sublime, rugged beauty, battered by the merciless tramontana wind and reachable by an 8km-long lonely road that winds its way through the moonscapes. The odd-shaped rocks, barren plateaux and deserted shorelines that litter Dalí's famous paintings were not just a product of his fertile imagination. This is the landscape the artist would draw inspiration from, described by him as a 'grandiose geological delirium'. See if you can find the huge rock that morphed into the subject of his painting *The Great Masturbator*.

With a steep, rocky coastline indented by dozens of turquoise-watered coves, it's an especially wonderful place to be at dawn or sunset. On top of the cape stand a lighthouse featuring a small museum (admission free; ⊙10am-7pm in summer, shorter hours rest of year) and the world's most unexpected curry

house (📞972 19 90 05; mains €15-19), where you get the likes of Khari ghost as well as local dishes and cheesecake. You can also sleep over in one of a handful of rooms; book ahead (particularly in summer) with Chris Little (📞972 19 90 05).

Cadaqués to the French Border

If you want to prolong the journey to France, El Port de la Selva and Llançá are pleasant, low-key beach resorts–cum–fishing towns. The former is backed by powerful mountains and filled with bobbing yachts, while the latter boasts a string of strands and coastal walking trails. From El Port de la Selva you can undertake a wild and woolly walk high along the rugged coast. The trail, which is awkward at some points, leads east to Cap de Creus. Portbou, on the French frontier, seems rather desolate and deserted, not least because a large chunk of its population fled when border control between Spain and France was abolished.

MONESTIR DE SANT PERE DE RODES
Combine all-encompassing views of a deep-blue Mediterranean and the (sometimes) snowy peaks of the nearby Pyrenees with a spectacular piece of Romanesque architecture and what you get is the Monestir de Sant Pere de Rodes (adult/under 7yr €5/free, Tue free; ⊙10am-7.30pm Tue-Sun Jun-Sep, 10am-5pm Tue-Sun Oct-May), which sits 500m up in the hills southwest of El Port de la Selva. Founded in the 8th century, it later became the most powerful monastery between Figueres and Perpignan in France. Looking at its mighty, brooding exterior, you're transported into the Middle Ages, though the effect is somewhat spoiled by the intensive restoration efforts which fail to blend in with the ruins. It's particularly enjoyable to admire the original stonework

THE WIND OF MADNESS
For several months of the year, the northern Costa Brava lies at the mercy of the fierce northern wind known as the tramontana. Its incessant howling is said to have a disturbing effect on the human psyche and to either make residents taciturn or drive them to madness.

MOVING ON?

For tips, recommendations and reviews, head to shop.lonelyplanet.com to purchase a downloadable PDF of the Languedoc-Roussillon chapter from Lonely Planet's *France* guide.

inside the great triple-naved, barrel-vaulted basilica, flanked by the square Torre de Sant Miquel bell tower, while ducking in and out of subterranean nooks and crannies will put gamers in mind of Assassin's Creed.

There are no public buses to the monastery, though it is reachable by road either from coastal El Port de la Selva or Vilajuíga, inland.

Figueres

POP 44,765

Twelve kilometres inland from the Golf de Roses, Figueres is a pleasant-enough town with an unmissable attraction: Salvador Dalí. Dalí was born in Figueres in 1904 and although his career took him to Madrid, Barcelona, Paris and the USA, he remained true to his roots. In the 1960s and '70s he created here the extraordinary Teatre-Museu Dalí – a monument to surrealism and a legacy that outshines any other Spanish artist, both in terms of popularity and sheer flamboyance. Whatever your feelings about this complex, egocentric man, this is worth every cent and minute you can spare.

◎ Sights

Teatre-Museu Dalí   MUSEUM
(www.salvador-dali.org; Plaça de Gala i Salvador Dalí 5; admission incl Dalí Joies & Museu de l'Empordá adult/child €12/free; ⊙9am-8pm Jul-Sep, 9.30am-6pm Mar-Jun & Oct, shorter hours rest of year) The first name that comes into your head when you lay your eyes on this red castle-like building, topped with the artist's trademark giant eggs and stylised Oscar-like statues and studded with plaster-covered croissants, is Dalí. An entirely appropriate final resting place for the master of surrealism, its entrance watched over by medieval suits of armour balancing baguettes on their heads, it has assured his immortality.

Between 1961 and 1974 Salvador Dalí converted Figueres' former municipal theatre, ruined by a fire at the end of the civil war in 1939, into the Teatre-Museu Dalí. 'Theatre-museum' is an apt label for this trip through the incredibly fertile imagination of one of the great showmen of the 20th century. It's full of surprises, tricks and illusions, and contains a substantial portion of Dalí's life's work, though you won't find his most famous pieces here: they are scattered around the world.

Even outside, the building aims to surprise, from the collection of bizarre sculptures outside the entrance, on Plaça de Gala i Salvador Dalí, to the pink wall along Pujada del Castell. The Torre Galatea, added in 1983, was where Dalí spent his final years.

Choice exhibits include **Taxi Plujós** (Rainy Taxi), composed of an early Cadillac, surmounted by statues. Put a coin in the slot and water washes all over the occupant of the car. The **Sala de Peixateries** (Fish Shop Room) holds a collection of Dalí oils, including the famous *Autoretrat Tou amb Tall de Bacon Fregit* (Soft Self-Portrait with Fried Bacon) and *Retrat de Picasso* (Portrait of Picasso). Beneath the former stage of the theatre is the crypt with Dalí's plain tomb, located at 'the spiritual centre of Europe' as Dalí modestly described it.

Gala – Dalí's wife and lifelong muse – is seen throughout – from the *Gala Mirando el Mar Mediterráneo* (Gala Looking at the Mediterranean Sea) on the 2nd level, which also appears to be a portrait of Abraham Lincoln from afar, to the classic *Leda Atómica* (Atomic Leda).

After you've seen the more notorious pieces, such as the famous **Mae West Room**, see if you can find a turtle with a gold coin balanced on its back, the nightmarish *El Cavall Feliç* (The Happy Horse), and the peepholes into a tiny mysterious room with a mirrored flamingo amidst fake plants.

A separate entrance (same ticket and times) leads into the Owen Cheatham collection of 37 jewels, designed by Dalí, called **Dalí Joies** (Dalí Jewels). Dalí did these on paper (his first commission was in 1941) and the jewellery was made by specialists in New York. Each piece, ranging from the disconcerting *Ull del Temps* (Eye of Time) through to the *Cor Reial* (Royal Heart), is unique.

Museu del Joguet   MUSEUM
(www.mjc.cat; Carrer de Sant Pere 1; adult/child €5.80/free; ⊙10am-7pm Mon-Sat, 11am-6pm Sun Jun-Sep, shorter hours rest of year) Spain's only toy museum has more than 3500 toys

ℹ VISITING THE TEATRE-MUSEU DALÍ

Given that the Teatre-Museu Dalí is the second-most-visited museum in Spain, it pays to visit it outside the weekends and public holidays, and if you're visiting it in spring or early summer, get here for opening time to avoid the worst of the crowds. In August the museum opens at night (admission €12, 10pm to 1am) for a maximum of 500 people (booking essential); ticket price includes a glass of *cava* (sparkling wine).

through the ages – from the earliest board games involving coloured stones and ball-in-a-cup (that timeless classic!) to intricate dolls' houses, 1920s dolls with the creepiest expressions you're ever likely to see, Dinky Toys, and Catalonia- and Valencia-made religious processions of tiny figures. Absolutely mesmerising, and not just for the kids!

Castell de Sant Ferran   CASTLE
(www.lesfortalesescatalanes.info; admission €6; ⊙10.30am-8pm Easter & Jul–mid-Sep, 10.30am-6pm mid-Sep–Oct & Apr-Jun, to 3pm rest of year) The impregnable-looking 18th-century fortress – the largest in Europe – has commanding views of the surrounding plain from a low hill 1km northwest of the centre. Built in 1750 to repel any French invaders and large enough to house 10,000 men, it nevertheless fell to their Gallic neighbours – both in 1794 and 1808. In the 20th century, after abandoning Barcelona, Spain's Republican government held its final meeting of the civil war (8 February 1939) in the dungeons. Take a peek inside the vast stables underneath the main buildings to get some idea of just how much cavalry the castle held during its heyday. The admission fee is for a tour of the interior of the fortress; more active tours, involving jeeps and boats, are to be booked in advance.

Museu de l'Empordá   MUSEUM
(www.museuemporda.org; La Rambla 2; adult/child €2/free; ⊙11am-8pm Tue-Sat, 11am-2pm Sun & holidays) This local museum combines Greek, Roman and medieval archaeological finds with a sizeable collection of art, mainly by Catalan artists, but there are also some works on loan from the Prado in Madrid. Admission is free with a Teatre-Museu Dalí ticket.

🛏 Sleeping & Eating

Most people treat Figueres as a day trip from Barcelona or the coast, but it's worth staying overnight if you want to beat the coachloads of tourists to the Dalí museum. The restaurants closest to the Teatre-Museu Dalí are overpriced, medicore tourist traps.

Hotel Durán   HOTEL €€
(☑972 50 12 50; www.hotelduran.com; Carrer de Lasauca 5; s/d from €74/89; P✳🛜) Staying at this mid-19th-century hotel is very much in keeping with the Dalí theme as he and his wife used to frequent the place themselves. The rooms are modern with forgettable soft beige, brown and white decor but the restaurant is like a royal banquet hall, with smooth service and and a fantasic €20 lunch menu which features such expertly prepared delights as seared tuna steak and rabbit loin.

Mas Pau   CATALAN €€€
(☑972 54 61 54; www.maspau.com; Avinyonet de Puigventós; meals €65-90; ⊙lunch & dinner Wed-Sat, dinner Tue, lunch Sun) Five kilometres southwest of Figueres along the road to Besalú, this enchanting 16th-century *masiu* (farmhouse), made of rough-hewn stone and set amid soothing gardens, is run by Toni and Xavier – both formerly of Ferran Adrià's El Bulli. This Michelin-starred restaurant offers a seasonal menu with an emphasis on fresh local ingredients; the pork trotter crackling stuffed with crayfish and acorn-fed duck with chestnuts are both inspired dishes.

El Motel   CATALAN €€
(☑972 50 05 62; www.elmotel.cat; Hotel Empordá, Avinguda Salvador Dalí I Doménech 170; tasting menus €35-55, s/d from €93/109; ⊙lunch & dinner) Jaume Subirós, the chef and owner of this restaurant, located inside the Hotel Empordá on a busy road 1km north of the centre, is widely hailed for making the transition from traditional Catalan home cooking to the polished, innovative restaurant it is today. Gourmets have been making pilgrimates here for decades for such dishes as sea urchins from Cadaqués, cod with truffle and calf's cheek in red wine. If you don't feel like going anywhere after your meal, there are moderately priced rooms at your disposal.

Sidrería Txot's   BASQUE €
(www.sidreriatxots.com; Av Salvadór Dalí 114; meals €12-20) Perch on a wooden seat and watch your Basque cider poured from on high

Salvador Dalí at Home

Born in Figueres, Salvador Dalí (1904–1989) was one of the leading lights of the surrealist movement. In addition to painting, Dalí, who had a larger-than-life presence, delved into the world of sculpture, film and photography.

Today Dalí's presence remains everywhere on the northern Costa Brava, but there are some places where his spirit runs extra thick and colourful.

Dalí's goal in creating the Teatre-Museu Dalí (p326) in Figueres was to express his 'desires, enigmas, obsessions and passions' for everyone to see.

Figueres may have been his home town but Dalí's favourite place in Catalonia was whitewashed Cadaqués (p323), and its tiny neighbour of Portlligat (p323), where he lived and painted for the better part of 50 years.

Towards the end of his life Dalí, with his muse (and wife), Gala, moved to the Castell de Púbol (p314), northeast of Girona, where Gala now lies in her crypt surrounded by giraffe-legged elephants.

DENNIS JOHNSON / GETTY IMAGES ©

RUAIRIDH STEWART / ZUMA PRESS / CORBIS ©

ESSENTIAL DALÍ

Dalí created more than 1500 works in his lifetime. Some of the best known are:

» **The Persistence of Memory** (1931) Dalí's most famous work features the images of melting clocks, which symbolise the irrelevance of time.

» **Crucifixion (Corpus Hypercubus)** (1954) Jesus crucified on a net of hyper-cubes whilst Dalí's wife, Gala, looks on.

» **The Sacrament of the Last Supper** (1955) A classic Christian scene re-enacted through the eyes of a surrealist.

Clockwise from top left
1. Dalí statue, Cadaqués (p323) **2. & 3.** Teatre-Museu Dalí, Figueres (p326) **4.** Gardens, Casa Museu Dalí (p323)

WHAT'S COOKING IN CATALONIA?

Cuina Catalana nudges Basque cuisine for the title of Spain's best, drawing ingredients from *mar i muntanya* (sea and mountain). It has come a long way since the medieval recipes for roast cat with garlic: its essence now lies in its sauces for meat and fish. There are five main types: *sofregit*, of fried onion, tomato and garlic; *samfaina*, *sofregit* plus red pepper and aubergine or zucchini (courgette); *picada*, based on ground almonds, usually with garlic, parsley, pine nuts or hazelnuts, and sometimes breadcrumbs; *aliolí*, garlic pounded with olive oil and egg yolk to make a mayonnaise; and *romesco*, an almond, tomato, olive oil, garlic and vinegar sauce, also used as a salad dressing.

Calçots, which are a type of long spring onion, are delicious as a starter with *romesco* sauce and are in season in late winter/early spring. This is when Catalans get together for a *calçotada*, the local version of a barbecue.

Catalans find it hard to understand why other people put mere butter on bread when *pa amb tomàquet*, bread slices rubbed with tomato, olive oil and garlic, is so easy.

Starters

» *escalivada* – red peppers and aubergines (sometimes with onions and tomatoes), grilled, peeled, sliced and served lukewarm dressed with olive oil, salt and garlic

» *esqueixada* – salad of shredded salted cod *(bacallá)* with tomato, red pepper, onion, white beans, olives, olive oil and vinegar

Main Dishes

» *arrós a la cassola* or *arrós a la catalana* – Catalan paella, cooked in an earthenware pot, without saffron

» *arrós negre* – rice cooked in cuttlefish ink, studded with cuttlefish bits

» *bacallá a la llauna* – salted cod baked in tomato, garlic, parsley, paprika and wine

» *botifarra amb mongetes* – pork sausage with fried white beans

» *cargols* – snails; a religion in parts of Catalonia, often eaten in stews

» *escudella* – a meat, sausage and vegetable stew

» *fideuá* – similar to paella, but using vermicelli noodles as the base, usually cooked with seafood

» *mandonguilles amb sipia* – meatballs with cuttlefish

» *sarsuela (zarzuela)* – mixed seafood cooked in *sofregit* with various seasonings

» *suquet* – a fish-and-potato hotpot, with generous clumps of both drenched in a tomato-based broth

Dessert

» *crema catalana* – Catalonia's take on *crème brûlée*

from the barrel (as it's supposed to be), then tuck into cured meats, cheeses and salads, as well as dishes such as chorizo in cider and L'Escala anchovies on toast.

ℹ Information

Tourist office (☏ 972 50 31 55; www.figueresciutat.com; Plaça del Sol; ⏲ 9am-8pm Mon-Sat, 10am-2pm Sun Jul-Sep, shorter hours rest of year)

ℹ Getting There & Away

Sarfa buses serve Castelló d'Empúries (€1.40, 15 minutes, 10 to 18 daily) and Cadaqués (€4.80, one hour, up to eight daily).

There are hourly train connections to Girona (€4, 30 minutes) and Barcelona (from €9.40, 1¾ hours) and to Portbou and the French border (€2 to €2.30, 25 minutes). There are also eight daily international trains to Cerbére, just over the border, daily links to Paris and thrice-weekly connections to Zurich and Milan.

Besalú

POP 2370

The tall, crooked 11th-century Pont Fortificat (Fortified Bridge) spread over Río Fluvià in medieval Besalú, with its two tower gates and heavy portcullis, is an arresting sight, leading you into the coiled maze of cobbled narrow streets (look up to see the chairs nailed to a wall along one of them) that make up the core of this delightfully well-preserved town. Following a succession of Roman, Visigothic and Muslim rulers, in the 10th and 11th centuries Besalú was the capital of an independent county that stretched as far west as Cerdanya before it came under Barcelona's control in 1111.

⊙ Sights

Miqvé and Around MUSEUM

(Baixada de Mikwe; guided tours €2.20) Besalú's thriving Jewish community fled the town in 1436 after relentless Christian persecution, leaving behind a miqvé – a 12th-century ritual bath – the only survivor of its kind in Spain. It sits down by the river inside a vaulted stone chamber, around which remnants of the ancient synagogue were unearthed in excavations in 2005. The *miqvé* itself was sealed when it was discovered in 1964, suggesting that those who left it behind were hoping to return. Access is by guided tour only (conducted twice daily, in Spanish and in Catalan); there are also guided tours of the bridge and the Romanesque Església de Sant Vicenç. Have a look at the 11th-century Romanesque church of the Monestir de Sant Pere, with an unusual ambulatory (walkway) behind the altar, and the 12th-century Romanesque Casa Cornellá.

Micromundi MUSEUM

(www.museuminiaturesbesalu.com; Plaça Prat de Sant Pere 15; adult/child €3.90/2.90; ⊙10am-7pm; 👪) This curious museum is dedicated to painstakingly painted miniatures and micro-miniatures that you can peer at through microscopes. The exhibits include the incredibly detailed representation of Pinocchio and Gepetto's workshop (inside a pistachio nut) and Anatoly Konenko's minute camels passing through the eye of a needle.

🛏 Sleeping & Eating

There are a couple of inexpensive *pensiones* in Besalú, including one right on the plaza.

Els Jardins de la Martana BOUTIQUE HOTEL €€

(☑972 59 00 09; www.lamartana.com; Carrer del Pont 2; s/d €90/120; P❄🏠) This is a charming mansion set on the out-of-town end of the grand old bridge. It has well-appointed rooms, with tiled floors, high ceilings and peaceful garden terraces. Most offer views from balconies across the bridge to the town.

Pont Vell CATALAN €€

(☑972 59 10 27; Pont Vell 26; meals €27-33; ⊙lunch & dinner Wed-Sun, lunch Mon, closed late Dec-late Jan & 1st week Jul) The views to the old bridge (after which the restaurant is named) are enough to tempt you to take a seat here, even without considering the wide-ranging, Michelin-approved menu full of locally sourced delights, such as rabbit with prunes.

❶ Information

Tourist office (☑972 59 12 40; www.besalu. cat; Plaça de la Llibertat 1; ⊙10am-2pm & 4-7pm, closed 1st week Jan) Book your guided tours of the *miqvé* and old town here.

❶ Getting There & Away

Buses run to Barcelona (1¾ hours, two daily), Olot (€3.40, 30 minutes, two daily), Figueres (€2.50, 30 minutes, four daily) and Girona (€3.50, 50 minutes, two daily).

The N260 road from Figueres to Olot meets the C66 from Girona at Besalú.

THE PYRENEES

The Pyrenees in Catalonia encompass some awesomely beautiful mountains and valleys. Above all, the Parc Nacional d'Aigüestortes i Estany de Sant Maurici, in the northwest, is a jewel-like area of lakes and dramatic peaks. The area's highest mountain, the Pica d'Estats (3143m), is reached by a spectacular hike (suitable only for experienced hikers) past glittering glacial lakes. On arrival at the top, you enjoy a privileged point with 360-degree views over France and Spain.

As well as the natural beauty of the mountains, and the obvious attractions of walking, skiing and other sports, the Catalan

THE CHANGING FORTUNES OF CATALONIA

Away from the big cities and Costa Brava, it feels as if you've entered a separate country. Virtually no Spanish is spoken and the red-and-yellow flag of Catalonia flutters from the balconies. Mention Catalonia to friends in Madrid and they screw up their faces; mention Madrid to Catalan friends and the reaction is often the same. Euphoria and despair generated by matches between Barcelona FC and Real Madrid reach fever pitch. The overall feeling, as expressed by an oft-encountered piece of graffiti, is that 'Catalonia is not Spain.'

Catalan identity is a multifaceted phenomenon, but Catalans are, more than anything else, united by the collective triumphs and shared grievances of the region's tumultuous past.

The Catalan golden age began in the early 12th century when Ramon Berenguer III, who already controlled Catalonia and parts of southern France, launched the region's first seagoing fleet. In 1137 his successor, Ramon Berenguer IV, was betrothed to the one-year-old heiress to the Aragonese throne, thereby giving Catalonia sufficient power to expand its empire out into the Mediterranean. By the end of the 13th century, Catalan rule extended to the Balearic Islands and Catalonia's seaborne trade brought fabulous riches.

But storm clouds were gathering; weakened by a decline in trade and foreign battles, Catalonia was vulnerable. And when Fernando became king of Aragón in 1479 and married Isabel, Queen of Castile, Catalonia became a province of Castile. Catalonia resented its new subordinate status but could do little to overturn it. After backing the losing side in the War of Spanish Succession (1702–13), Barcelona rose up against the Spanish crown whose armies besieged the city from March 1713 until 11 September 1714. The victorious Felipe V abolished Catalan self-rule, built a huge fort (the Ciutadella) to watch over the city, banned writing and teaching in the Catalan language, and farmed out Catalonia's colonies to other European powers.

Pyrenees and their foothills have a rich cultural heritage, notably the countless lovely Romanesque churches and monasteries, often tucked away in remote valleys. They are mainly the product of a time of prosperity and optimism in this region in the 11th and 12th centuries, after Catalonia had broken ties with France in 988 and as the Muslim threat from the south receded. You may find that some villagers are wary of outsiders as the hand of Franco's retribution reached deep into these rural parts after the civil war.

When looking for a place to kip, keep an eye out for *cases rurales* or *cases de pagés* (country houses converted into accommodation), usually set in old village houses and peppered across the Pyrenees. The annual *Guia d'Establiments de Turisme Rural* guide, published by the Generalitat (regional Catalan government), covers most of them.

Olot

POP 33,725 / ELEV 443M

Olot is the pleasant, somewhat-spread-out capital of the La Garrotxa province, with wide, tree-lined walkways (with the exception of its serpentine medieval heart) and plenty of options for rambling in the surrounding countryside, shaped by the ancient activity of the now well-dormant volcanoes of the nearby Parc Natural de la Zona Volcánica de la Garrotxa.

Four volcanoes stand sentry on the fringes of Olot. To continue your education in volcanoes head for Volcá Montsacopa, 500m north of the centre, or Volcá La Garrinada, 1km northeast of the centre, both of which are volcanic craters.

◉ Sights

Museu Comarcal de la Garrotxa MUSEUM
(Carrer de l'Hospici 8; adult/child €3/free; ⊗11am-2pm & 4-7pm Tue-Sat, 11am-2pm Sun & holidays Jul-Sep, shorter hours rest of year) In spite of not belching fire and brimstone for centuries, volcanos in the Garrotxa area seem to dominate everything – from art to food. This museum, in the same building as the tourist office – an atmospheric 18th-century hospital – covers Olot's growth and development as an early textile centre, though its star exhibit is the collection of works by local painters and sculptors (such as Iu Pascual i Rodés and Miguel Blay i Fabregues) who clearly drew inspiration from this volatile land.

Museu dels Volcans MUSEUM
(adult/child €3/free; ⊗11am-2pm & 4-7pm Tue-Sat, 10am-2pm Sun & holidays Jul-Sep, shorter hours rest of year) Found inside the pleasant

Trade again flourished from Barcelona in the centuries that followed, and by the late 19th and early 20th centuries there were growing calls for greater self-governance to go with the city's burgeoning economic power. However, after Spanish general Francisco Franco's victory in 1939, Catalan Francoists and the dictator's army shot in purges at least 35,000 people, most of whom were either anti-Franco or presumed to be so. Over time, the use of Catalan in public was banned, all street and town names were changed into Spanish, and *castellano* (Castilian) was the only permitted language in schools and the media. Franco's lieutenants remained in control of the city until his death in 1975 and the sense of grievance in Barcelona remains even to this day, more than three decades after self-government was restored in Catalonia in 1977. Catalan culture has been resurrected, however; you'll see this reflected in the reemergence of traditional festivals and dances, the prevalence of Catalan flags on many facades and the near-universal use of Catalan in public.

As there is no real sense of ethnic identity in Catalonia – over the centuries everybody has either passed through here or settled here – Catalans tend to make their language the key to identity: an active (or good passive) knowledge of Catalan is enough to make one a Catalan.

Whether one supports it or opposes it, the issue of independence from Spain has been very much at the forefront of Catalan politics for years, and the idea has been steadily gaining in popularity among the general populace. Repeated requests that Madrid grant Catalonia the same degree of fiscal autonomy as that of the Basque Country and Navarre have been denied, and in April 2012 Convergència i Unió (CiU) – the main party in Catalonia, a historically timid, centre-right coalition, which for decades has defended remaining part of Spain – has opted for eventual succession.

Jardí Botànic, a botanical garden of Olot-area flora, the Museu dels Volcans can teach you everything you ever wanted to know about volcanoes, such as their geological origins and the causes of earthquakes. The museum's interactive section will even let you experience the latter in a simulator! Other displays cover local flora, fauna and ecosystems.

Sleeping & Eating

TOP CHOICE **Can Blanc** CASA RURAL €€
(✆972 27 60 20; www.canblanc.es; Paratges de la Deu; s/d incl breakfast €61/100; P ❋ ❄ ⛲) This place, which fills the gap between a hotel and a *casa rural,* sits on the southwestern edge of Olot, surrounded by parkland. Rooms come in a range of styles from classic colours to the well and truly mismatched. The pleasing gardens and pool will put a smile on your face on hot summer days and a great breakfast is thrown in. Ask for the next-door La Deu Restaurant, as people are more likely to know this.

Torre Malagrida HOSTEL €
(✆972 26 42 00; www.xanascat.cat; Passeig de Barcelona 15; dm student & under 26yr/26yr & over €19/23; ⊗closed Aug) With stone lions guarding the entrance to this marble-columned early-20th-century Modernista building that's surrounded by gardens, it's hard to believe that this is actually a youth hostel. The unadorned dorms are comfortable without living up to the promise of the exterior; there are meals available, as well as bicycles for rent.

Les Cols CUINA VOLCÀNICA €€€
(✆972 26 92 09; www.lescols.com; Carretera de la Canya; meals €35-45; ⊗lunch & dinner Wed-Sat, lunch Sun) Set in a converted 19th century *masia,* Les Cols is about 4km north of central Olot. Inside, the decor has a 21st-century edge, with iron and glass walls, a chilled-out ambience and gourmet ambitions. Dishes with local products are prepared with a silken touch, from chicken and duck to wild boar.

La Deu Restaurant CUINA VOLCÀNICA €€
(✆972 26 10 04; www.ladeu.es; Carretera la Deu; menus from €12; ⊗lunch & dinner Mon-Sat, lunch Sun) Family-run restaurant going back to the 19th century and famous for its takes on the hearty *cuina volcànica.* Expect the likes of rabbit stewed with snails (much tastier than it sounds!) and *botifarra* sausage with haricot beans.

La Quinta Justa CUINA VOLCÀNICA €€
(✆972 27 12 09; www.laquintajusta.cat; Passeig de Barcelona 7; menus from €12; ⊗lunch & dinner)

CATALONIA OLOT

VOLCANIC CUISINE

In Olot and around, a dedicated group of chefs proudly carries on the cuina volcànica (www.cuinavolcanica.cat) culinary tradition, which stems from the exceptionally fertile volcanic soil, responsible for a bounty of locally grown produce that forms the base of this hearty cuisine. Ingredients include black radishes, wild mushrooms, emmer (white corn flour), Santa Pau beans, ratafia (walnut liquor with aromatic herbs) and *puimoc* (dry pork sausage).

Central, stylish restaurant serving such volcanic delights as *arròs crémos de ceps amb formatge* (rice with wild mushrooms and cheese) and *bistec de vedella amb escalivada* (beef steak with grilled vegetable salad).

❶ Information

Casal dels Volcans (☎972 26 62 02; www.turismegarrotxa.com; Jardí Botànic, Avinguda de Santa Coloma de Farners) Information about the Parc Natural de la Zona Volcànica de la Garrotxa.

Patronat Municipal de Turisme (☎972 26 01 41; http://areadepromocio.olot.cat; Carrer del Hospici 8; ⏱10am-2pm & 4-7pm Mon-Sat, 10am-2pm Sun mid-Jul–mid-Sep, shorter hours rest of year) Near the bus station; sells joint tickets to museums.

❶ Getting There & Away

Teisa (www.teisa-bus.com) runs buses to/from Barcelona (€15.70, two to 2¾ hours, up to seven daily) and Girona via Besalú (€6.90, 1½ hours, up to 15 daily). The easiest approach by car from Barcelona is by the AP7 and C63.

Parc Natural de la Zona Volcánica de la Garrotxa

The hills around Olot are volcanic in origin, making up the Parc Natural de la Zona Volcánica de la Garrotxa. Volcanic eruptions began here about 350,000 years ago but the last time was 11,500 years ago. The park completely surrounds Olot but the most interesting area is between Olot and the village of Santa Pau, 10km southeast.

In the park there are about 40 volcanic cones, up to 160m high and 1.5km wide. Together with the lush vegetation, a result of fertile soils and a damp climate, these create a landscape of verdant beauty. Between the woods are crop fields, a few hamlets and scattered old stone farmhouses.

The main park information office is the Casal dels Volcans in Olot, where you can collect helpful hiking maps and info on various trails.

The old part of Santa Pau village, perched on a rocky outcrop, contains a porticoed plaza, the Romanesque Església de Santa Maria and a locked-up baronial castle. The village itself, which, though very pretty, is a little bit too twee, has a couple of places to stay, including the great-value Can Menció (☎972 68 00 14; www.canmencio.com; Plaça Major 17; d €45), a cosy place on the main square. Camping Lava Ecològic (☎972 68 03 58; www.canmencio.com; Carretera Olot-Santa Pau, Km7; site per adult €9) is a good place to pitch a tent. Wild camping is banned in the Garrotxa district, which stretches from east of Besalú to west of Olot, and from the French border to south of Sant Feliu de Pallerols.

Several good marked walks, which you can complete in less than a day, allow you to explore the park with ease. There are numerous easy hikes to several of the cones from car parks near Olot, but to get the most out of the park, an overnight stay is recommended. Inquire at the park information offices about routes.

Ripoll

POP 10,910 / ELEV 691M

One of Spain's finest pieces of Romanesque art is to be found at the medieval heart of this otherwise somewhat shabby industrial town, split down the middle by the Riu Ter and surrounded by hills.

Thirty kilometres west of Olot, Ripoll can claim, with some justice, to be the birthplace of Catalonia; you'll find that all signs, menus and notices are exclusively in Catalan. In the 9th century it was the power base from which local strongman Guifré el Pilós (Wilfred the Hairy) succeeded in uniting several counties of the Frankish March along the southern side of the Pyrenees. Guifré went on to become the first Count (Comte) of Barcelona. To encourage repopulation of the Pyrenees valleys, he founded the Monestir de Santa Maria, the most powerful monastery of medieval Catalonia – and was buried there after death.

Tiny Ripoll has also had a greater impact on the rest of the world than you'd think. It was here, in 1027, that the *Pau i Treva de Deu* (Peace and Treaty of God) was promoted; one of its principles – the inviolability of refuge in a church – still stands today.

◉ Sights

Monestir de Santa Maria MONASTERY
(adult/child €3/1; ◎10am-1pm & 3-7pm Apr-Sep, to 6pm Oct-Mar) Founded in AD 879, the Monestir de Santa Maria was Catalonia's spiritual and cultural heart from the mid-10th to mid-11th centuries. A five-naved basilica was built, and adorned in about 1100 with a stone portal that's among some of the most splendid Romanesque art in Spain. Restored after two fires had left the basilica in ruins by 1885, its most interesting feature inside is the restored tomb of Guifré el Pilós.

A chart near the basilica's portal (in Catalan) helps to decipher the feast of sculpture: a medieval vision of the universe, from God the Creator, in the centre at the top, to the month-by-month scenes of daily rural life on the innermost pillars for the medieval illiterate.

⌂ Sleeping & Eating

Hostal Ripollés HOSTAL €
(☑972 70 02 15; www.hostaldelripolles.com; Palça Nova 11; s/d €30/46) One of only two lodging options in the town's medieval heart, this friendly family establishment consists of eight refurbished en-suite rooms with TV

above a restaurant mixing pizza and pasta with regional dishes.

El Crocus CATALAN €€
(☑972 70 54 57; www.restauranteelcrocus.com; Carrer Berenguer el Vell 4; menus €16.15, meals €25-40; ◎lunch daily, dinner Tue-Fri) Traditional Catalan dishes such as *crema de pésols* (pea soup), *mandonguilles* (meatballs) and a selection of *arroces* (rice dishes) await you just up the street from the cathedral.

ⓘ Information

Tourist office (☑972 70 23 51; www.ripoll. cat/turisme; Plaça del Abat Oliba; ◎9.30am-1.30pm & 4-7pm Mon-Sat, 10am-2pm Sun) Next door to the Monestir de Santa Maria.

ⓘ Getting There & Away

Daily *rodalies* trains (line R3) run to Barcelona via Vic (€7.30, two hours, 12 to 16 daily), Ribes de Freser (€1.80, 20 minutes, up to seven daily) and Puigcerdà (€3.65, 1¼ hours, seven daily).

Vall de Núria & Ribes de Freser

Around AD 700, the story goes, Sant Gil came from Nîmes in France to live in an isolated mountain valley 26km north of Ripoll, preaching the Gospel to shepherds. Before he fled Visigothic persecution four years later, Sant Gil hurriedly hid away a wooden Virgin-and-child image he had carved, a cross, his cooking pot and the bell he had used to summon the shepherds.

DRAGONS, GIANTS & BIG-HEADS

Fire and fireworks play a big part in many Spanish festivals, but Catalonia adds a special twist with the *correfoc* (fire-running), in which devil and dragon figures run through the streets spitting fireworks at the crowds.

Correfocs are often part of the *festa major*, a town or village's main annual festival, which usually takes place in July or August. Part of the *festa major* fun are the *sardana* (Catalonia's national folk dance) and *gegants*, splendidly attired 5m-high giants that parade through the streets or dance in the squares. Giants tend to come in male-and-female pairs, such as a medieval king and queen. Almost every town and village has its own pair, or up to six pairs, of giants. They're accompanied by grotesque 'dwarfs' (known as *capsgrossos*, or 'big-heads').

On La Nit de Sant Joan (23 June), big bonfires burn at crossroads and town squares in a combined midsummer and St John's Eve celebration, and fireworks explode all night. The supreme fire festival is the Patum in Berga, 30km west of Ripoll. An evening of dancing and fireworks-spitting angels, devils, mulelike monsters, dwarfs, giants and men covered in grass culminates in a mass frenzy of fire and smoke. Patum is thought to be named after the sound of the drum: 'pa-tum, pa-tum'; the 'real' Patum happens on Corpus Christi (the Thursday following the eighth Sunday after Easter Sunday).

WORTH A TRIP

MONESTIR DE SANT JOAN DE LES ABADESSES

Located in Sant Joan de les Abadesses, an attractive little town just northeast of Ripoll, the Monestir de Sant Joan de les Abadesses (Plaça de l'Abadessa; admission €3; ☉10am-7pm Jul & Aug, 10am-2pm & 4-7pm May, Jun & Sep, shorter hours rest of year) is a monastery founded by Guifré el Pilós, which began life as a nunnery – the nuns were expelled in 1017 for alleged licentious conduct. Its elegant 12th-century church contains the marvellous and somewhat unnerving Santíssim Misteri, a 13th-century polychrome woodcarving of the descent from the cross, composed of seven life-sized figures. Also remarkable is the Gothic retablo (alterpiece) of Santa Maria La Blanca, carved in alabaster. The attached museum charts the town's religious history through a formidable display of sacred art and artefacts. Teisa (www.teisa-bus.com) operates up to seven buses daily from Ripoll to Sant Joan de les Abadesses (€1.60, 15 minutes).

They stayed hidden until 1079, when an ox led some shepherds to the spot. The statuette, the Mare de Déu de Núria, became the patron of Pyrenean shepherds and Núria's future was assured. Today, Núria is a small ski resort and pilgrimage site, consisting of a single hotel-and-sanctuary combo, framed by snow-covered mountains and reachable only on foot or via the narrow-gauge rack-and-pinion railway (cremallera) that rises over 1000m on its 12km journey from Ribes de Freser, on the N152, 14km north of Ripoll. The cremallera has been operating since 1931, and the journey up the Gorges de Núria – the green, rocky valley of the thundering Riu Núria – is worth it for the scenery alone.

⊙ Sights

TOP CHOICE Santuari de la Mare de Déu PILGRIMAGE SITE

(www.valldenuria.com; ☉8.30am-6.30pm) Sant Gil would recoil in shock if he came back today. The sanctuary (1911) housing the Mare de Déu statuette sits incongruously in the centre of a building that looks like a penitentiary or a severe boarding school, but is, in fact, a hotel. The Mare de Déu de Núria sits behind a glass screen above the altar and is in the Romanesque style of the 12th century, so either Sant Gil was centuries ahead of his time or this isn't his work! The small chapel on the left contains a bell, a cross and a cooking pot (which all date from at least the 15th century). To have your prayer answered, put your head in the pot and ring the bell while you say it. Peek into the chapel with a stained-glass window depicting Sant Bernat, carrying a pair of skis and accompanied by a Bernese mountain dog – he's the

patron saint of skiers and hikers. Nearby is a small church (1615) with Sant Gil's symbols etched into the stone at the entrance.

☆ Activities

In winter, Núria is a small-scale ski resort (day lift pass €29.50) with 11 short runs catering to all abilities. There's also a separate area for kids, with tobogganing in winter and pony rides in summer.

Walkers should get Editorial Alpina's Puigmal map guide before coming to Núria. One of the best walks is the trail leading down through the gorge from Núria to Queralbs (2½ hours), and from the Vall de Núria, you can also cap several 2700m to 2900m peaks on the main Pyrenees ridge in about 2½ to four hours' walking (one way) for each. The most popular is Puigmal (2909m).

⊨ Sleeping & Eating

Wild camping is banned in the whole Ribes de Freser–Núria area.

NÚRIA

Hotel Vall de Núria HOTEL €€

(☎972 73 20 20; www.valldenuria.cat; half-board per person for 2 nights up to €190) The rather severe grey building surrounding the sanctuary has comfortable, if somewhat overpriced, rooms with bathroom and satellite TV, a cafeteria, a bar and two restaurants. In the exhibition hall you'll find entertaining displays on the history of the cremallera in four languages.

Alberg Pic de l'Àliga HOSTEL €

(☎972 73 20 48; www.xansacat.cat; dm student & under 26yr/26yr & over incl breakfast €22/27; ☉closed Oct-Dec) The youth hostel is in a spacious lodge in a stunning location at the top of the *telecabina* (cable car) leading up from the Hotel Vall de Núria. Dorm rooms sleep from four to 14. The cable car runs from 9am to 6pm daily (to 7pm mid-July to mid-September).

RIBES DE FRESER

TOP CHOICE Hotel Els Caçadors HOTEL €€
(☎972 72 70 06; www.hotelsderibes.com; Carrer de Balandrau 24; s/d from €40/80; ☞) A family-run business, this small hotel offers simple rooms with bathroom and TV. The buffet breakfast (€8) is grand – local cold meats, cheeses, juice, cereal and sweet pastries. The downstairs restaurant is one of the most popular places to eat in town and serves large portions of excellent Catalan dishes, such as rabbit with wild mushrooms. There's a filling lunch menu for €17.50; a three-course dinner for hotel guests is €15.

❶ Information

Núria's **tourist office** (☎972 73 20 20; www.valldenuria.com; ☒8.30am-5.45pm mid-Sep–mid-Jul, 8.30am-6.30pm mid-Jul–mid-Sep) is in the sanctuary.

❶ Getting There & Away

Transports Mir runs services between Ripoll and Ribes de Freser (€2.20, 25 minutes, one to two buses daily except Sunday).

Up to seven trains a day run to Ribes-Enllaç from Ripoll (€1.80, 20 minutes) and Barcelona (€8, 2¼ hours).

The **cremallera** (www.valldenuria.cat; one way/return adult €13.65/21.90, child €8.20/13.15) runs from Ribes de Freser to Núria via Queralbs six to 12 times a day (35 minutes), depending on the season. There are two stations in Ribes de Freser: Rebes-Enllaç, just south of town, with connecting trains to Barcelona, and the more centrally located Ribes-Vila.

Cerdanya

Cerdanya, along with French Cerdagne across the border, occupies a low-lying green basin between the higher reaches of the Pyrenees to the east and west. Although Cerdanya and Cerdagne, once a single Catalan county, were divided by the Treaty of the Pyrenees in 1659, Catalan is spoken on both sides of the border and Spain flows seamlessly into France. Cerdanya is particularly popular with hikers and mountain bikers in the summer and skiers in winter.

PUIGCERDÁ
POP 8800 / ELEV 1202M

Just 2km from the French border, Puigcerdá (puh-cher-*da*) dates back to the 12th century – not that you'd know it, since it lost most of its historical buildings during the civil war. The town's not much more than a way station, but it's a jolly one, teeming with hikers in summer and used as a base by skiers during the winter season. A dozen Spanish, Andorran and French ski resorts lie within 45km.

❍ Sights

Only the tower remains of the 17th-century **Església de Santa Maria** (Plaça de Santa Maria). The 13th-century Gothic **Església de Sant Domènec** (Passeig del 10 d'Abril) was also wrecked but later rebuilt. It contains 14th-century Gothic murals that somehow survived (opening times are erratic). The *estany* (lake) in the north of town is speckled with snow-white swans against a backdrop of equally snow-white mountains. It was created back in 1380 for irrigation and is surrounded by turn-of-the-20th-century summer houses, built by wealthy Barcelona families.

⬛ Sleeping

The town and the surrounding area is home to a number of hotels, *pensiones* and *casas rurales*.

Hospes Villa Paulita HISTORIC HOTEL €€€
(☎972 88 46 22; www.hospes.com; Avinguda Pons I Gasch 15; d incl breakfast from €138; ⓟ☞☒) The town's most luxurious option has sublime modern rooms in a rusty-red 19th-century manor house, some with views over the nearby snow-drenched peaks. A plethora of massages is available for après-ski relaxation and the food at the gourmet restaurant is akin to art.

Sant Marc CASA RURAL €€
(☎972 88 00 07; www.santmarc.es; Les Pereres, 1.5km from Puigcerdá; d €60-80; ⓟ☞☒) At

❶ HIKING IN CERDANYA

Walkers should get a hold of Editorial Alpina's *Cerdanya* map and guide booklet (scaled at 1:50,000). They are available from most bookshops around Catalonia and in some of the larger tourist offices.

CATALONIA CERDANYA

this *casa rural* just outside town, you are greeted by extensive tree-lined grounds and down-filled duvets on plush beds. The wood-floored rooms are spacious and decorated in soothing creams and the stone-walled restaurant specialises in dishes that make maximum use of local meats, cheeses and pretty much anything that grows in the area.

Cámping Stel
CAMPGROUND €

(☑972 88 23 61; www.stel.es; sites per 2-person tent & car €38.10; ☺Apr-Sep; P☂☖) Out along the road to Llívia, this is the only nearby camping option, and an action-packed one at that, with a pool, ping-pong hall, indoor climbing wall, basketball court and a football pitch.

☒ Eating

El Caliu
CATALAN €€

(www.elcaliu.com; Carrer Alfons Primer 1; menus from €12.50; ☺closed Wed) Seasonal dishes, such as meat with wild mushrooms and stewed pig's trotters with Cerdanya turnips, as well as year-round favourites such as chicken casseroled in beer, all make an appearance on the menu of this busy family-run spot, popular with locals.

El Pati de la Tieta
INTERNATIONAL €€€

(☑972 88 01 56; Carrer dels Ferrers 20; pizzas €12-15, meals €35-45; ☺daily in high season, Thu-Sun Jul-May) One of the best choices, this understated and mostly Mediterranean restaurant offers a creative range of dishes, like the succulent *broquetes de cangur i verdures* (kangaroo on a skewer with vegetables) and the less outlandish pizza and homemade pasta.

Bar Miamidos
SPANISH €€

(Plaça Herois 1; menus €11) Well-stocked bar with hams dangling from the ceiling and content diners tucking into plates of paella, grilled meats and platters of *jamón* (cured ham).

ⓘ Information

The bus and train stations are located at the foot of the hill.

A funicular takes you to Plaça de l'Ajuntament, off which is the **tourist office** (☑972 88 05 42; Carrer de Querol 1; ☺9.30am-1pm & 4-7pm Mon-Sat, 10am-1pm Sun Jun-Sep, closed Mon & Sun rest of year). There is also a helpful **regional tourist office** (☑972 14 06 65; Carretera Nacional 152; ☺10am-1pm & 4-7pm Mon-Sat, 10am-1pm Sun) on the main road into town if coming from Barcelona.

ⓘ Getting There & Away

Alsina Graells runs two to three daily buses from Barcelona (€19.20, three hours) via La Seu d'Urgell (€6, one hour).

From Barcelona, the C16 approaches Puigcerdá through the Túnel del Cadí. Puigerdá is also reachable via the picturesque N152 from Ribes de Freser. The main crossing into France is at Bourg-Madame, immediately east of Puigcerdá.

Trains run from Barcelona to Puigcerdà (€9.40, three hours, six daily) via Vic, Ripoll and Ribes de Freser and over the border to Latour-de-Carol in France (seven minutes, four to five daily), where they connect with trains from Toulouse or Paris.

LLÍVIA
POP 1665 / ELEV 1224M

Six kilometres northeast of Puigcerdá, across flat farmland, Llívia is a piece of Spain within France. Under the 1659 Treaty of the Pyrenees, Spain ceded 33 villages to France, but Llívia was a 'town' and so, together with the 13 sq km of its municipality, remained a Spanish possession.

You might expect Llívia to feel more French than Spanish, but as soon as you enter the town there's absolutely no mistaking where the town's loyalties lie. This is most notable in the early evening or on a Sunday, when the surrounding French villages are library-quiet and Llívia is boisterous with life.

Llívia's sights lie in its tiny medieval nucleus, near the top of the town. The Museu Municipal (Carrer dels Forns 4), featuring what's claimed to be Europe's oldest pharmacy, was due to reopen by the end of 2012. The 15th-century Gothic Església de Mara de Déu dels Àngels, just above the museum (get the key from the tourist office), is particularly lively during the music festival in August, held in and around the church. From the church you can walk up to the ruined Castell de Llívia where, during the short-lived period of Islamic dominion in the Pyrenees, the Muslim governor Manussa enjoyed a secret dalliance with Lampégia, daughter of the Duke of Aquitaine (or so legend has it).

Plaça Major is the best spot to sample local cuisine; the pick of the restaurants is Restaurant Can Ventura (☑972 89 61 78; Plaça Major 1; menus €25; ☺Wed-Sun), a ramshackle building dating from 1791. The food is delightful – traditional Catalan fare, such as slow-cooked local lamb.

Two or three buses a day run from Puigcerdá train station to Llívia.

LA MOLINA & MASELLA

These ski resorts lie either side of Tosa d'Alp (2537m), 15km south of Puigcerdá, and are linked by the Alp 2500 lift. The two resorts have a combined total of 117 runs (day lift pass for the whole area €40) of all grades at altitudes of 1600m to 2537m. Rental equipment and ski schools are available at both resorts (www.lamolina.com) and La Molina is better for beginners. In the summer, La Molina caters to adrenaline junkies with its mountain-bike park, quad biking and more.

⨖ Sleeping

Many skiers choose to stay in Puigcerdá or further afield, but there are any number of resort-style hotels around the village – all of which are booked solid through the ski season.

Hotel Adserá   HOTEL €€
(☏972 89 20 01; www.hoteladsera.com; La Molina; d from €65; P🛎🎿🖥) This beautifully located mountain hotel makes a great base not just for hitting the slopes but also for snow mobiling, dog sledding and ice skating in winter and mountain biking, canyoning and hot-air ballooning in summer.

Alberg Mare de Déu de les Neus   HOSTEL €
(☏972 89 20 12; www.xanascat.cat; dm student & under 26yr/26yr & over €22/27; ⊗closed mid-Oct–Nov & 1 week mid-Apr; P@) At the bottom part of La Molina, near the train station, this handy youth hostel is far and away the cheapest place to stay. Rooms range from doubles to eight-bed dorms and there are cooking facilities for guests.

❶ Getting There & Away

In the ski season there's a sporadic bus service from Puigcerdá. The easiest driving route from Barcelona is by the C58 toll road and the C16 through the Túnel del Cadí.

Serra del Cadí

The N260 runs west along the wide Riu Segre valley from Puigcerdà to La Seu d'Urgell, with the Pyrenees climbing northwards towards Andorra, and the craggy pre-Pyrenees range of the Serra del Cadí rising steep and high along the southern flank. The range's most spectacular peak is Pedraforca ('stone pitchfork'; 2497m), with the most challenging rock climbing in Catalonia, while the main Cadí range, part of Parc Natural Cadí-Moixeró, offers some excellent mountain walking for those suitably equipped and experienced. There is a number of staffed refuges in the park for serious multiday hikes. To travel around the area it's best to have your own wheels, as bus services are scarce.

◉ Sights

The villages used as jumping-off points for exploring the area are strung along the picturesque B400, which runs west from the Barcelona-bound C16 from Puigcerdá to La Seu d'Urgell on the C14. First up is little Saldes, sitting in the shadow of the Pedraforca and a popular base for hikes. The pretty stone village of Gósol, 6km further west, is topped by the ruins of an 11th-century castle.

A road west from Gósol climbs the 1625m Coll de Josa pass, then descends past the picturesque hamlet of Josa del Cadí, a smattering of stone houses cluttered around a stone church perched atop a lush green hill. Next up is Tuixén (1206m), another attractive village on a small hill. From Tuixén, scenic paved roads lead northwest to La Seu d'Urgell (36km) and south to Sant Llorenç de Morunys (28km), which is on a beautiful cross-country road from Berga to Organyá.

⚐ Activities

Rock Climbing

Popular with rock climbers, the two separate rocky peaks of Pedraforca – the northern Pollegó Superior (2497m) and the southern Pollegó Inferior (2400m) – are divided by a saddle called L'Enforcadura. The northern face, rising near-vertically for 600m, has some classic rock climbs; the southern has a wall that sends alpinists into raptures.

Hiking

From Refugi Lluís Estasen – a 1½ hour hike from Saldes – you can reach the Pollegó Superior summit in about three strenuous hours – either southward from the refuge, then up the middle of the fork from the southeast side (a path from Saldes joins this route); or westward up to the Collada del Verdet, then south and east to the summit. The latter route has some hairy precipices and requires a good head for heights. It's not suitable for coming down: you must use the first route.

¿PARLES CATALÁ?

Get out of Barcelona and away from Costa Brava's beaches and you'll find that Catalá (Catalan) is all around you: the menus and street signs are in Catalan and it's pretty much the only language spoken in the villages. Written Catalan resembles both Spanish and French; its roots are in Latin and it's an Occitano-Romance language, stemming from medieval Provençal. It is spoken by 9.5 million people, making it a far more widely spoken language than, say, Norwegian or Bulgarian. Catalan is spoken in Catalonia (both Spanish and French), Andorra, the Balearic Islands, Valencia, Sicily and part of Spain's Murcia province.

Though Catalan was severely suppressed under Franco, with books destroyed and the language banned from schools, since his death it has made quite a comeback and far more foreign-language authors are being translated into Catalan than into English.

🛌 Sleeping

SALDES & AROUND

There are at least four **camping grounds** along the B400 between the C16 and Saldes, some open year-round. In Saldes you'll find a handful of *pensiones* and a larger hotel.

Refugi Lluís Estasen   REFUGE €
(☑608 31 53 12; dm €15; ☑daily Jun-Sep, Sat, Sun & holidays rest of year) Run by the FEEC and located near the Mirador de Gresolet, this *refugi* offers 87 places, meals and a warden in summer. In winter it has about 30 places. When the place is full you can sleep outside, but not in a tent. Reserve well ahead in summer.

GÓSOL & TUIXÉN

You'll find a handful of *casas rurales* in both villages, although some are rented out only on weekends or for a week at a time in summer. Reserve in advance as the villages are packed on weekends.

Cal Farragetes   CASA RURAL €
(☑973 37 00 34; www.calfarragetes.com; Carrer del Coll 7; d per person €25; Ⓟ☎) This is a big, friendly stone place that's set over two floors around a sprawling courtyard. A country village house, it has smallish but immaculate rooms featuring iron bedsteads and wood panelling.

ℹ Information

The Parc Natural del Cadí-Moixeró's main **Centre d'Informació** (☑938 24 41 51; Carrer de la Vinya 1; ☑9am-1pm & 4-7pm Mon-Sat, 9am-1pm Sun Jun-Sep, shorter hours rest of year) is in **Bagá**, a quiet village on the C16; pick up maps of the park and info on mountain refuges here.

ℹ Getting There & Around

You need your own vehicle to reach Saldes, Gósol or Tuixén.

La Seu d'Urgell

POP 13,010 / ELEV 691M

The lively valley town of La Seu d'Urgell (la *se*-u dur-*zhey*) is Spain's gateway to Andorra, 10km to the north. La Seu has an attractive medieval centre, watched over by an admirable medieval cathedral. When the Franks evicted the Muslims from this part of the Pyrenees, in the early 9th century, they made La Seu a bishopric and capital of the counts of Urgell. It has been an important market and cathedral town since the 11th century.

◉ Sights

Catedral de Santa Maria   CATHEDRAL
(adult/child €3/free; ☑10am-1pm & 4-7pm Mon-Sat, 10am-1pm Sun Jun-Sep, shorter hours rest of year) On the southern side of Plaça dels Oms, the 12th-century Catedral de Santa Maria & Museu Diocesá is one of Catalonia's outstanding Romanesque buildings, despite various attempts at remodelling. It's one of more than 100 Romanesque churches lining what has come to be known as the Ruta Románica, from Perpignan (France) to the Urgell district.

The fine western facade, through which you enter, is decorated in typical Lombard style. The inside is dark and plain but still impressive, with five apses, some murals in the southern transept, and a 13th-century Virgin-and-child sculpture in the central apse.

From next to the cathedral you can enter its **Museu Diocesá**, a superb museum that encompasses the fine cloister, its pillars held up by monkeys, gargoyles and harpies, and the 12th-century Romanesque **Església de Sant Miquel**, pleasantly free of adornment, as well as some medieval Pyrenean church murals, sculptures and altarpieces.

Sleeping & Eating

Casa Rural

La Vall del Cadí   CASA RURAL €
(☑973 35 03 90; www.valldelcadi.com; Carretera de Tuixén; s €30, d €45-55; P❋☎) Barely a 1km walk south of the centre and across the Segre River, you are in another, protected, bucolic world in this stone country house on a working family-run farm (and it smells as such!). The cosy rooms, with terracotta floors, iron bedsteads and, in some cases, timber ceiling beams, have a nice winter detail – floor heating. Some rooms share bathrooms. The extensive breakfast (€7) features regional cured meats and cheeses and *pa amb tomaquet* (bread smeared with fresh tomato).

Hotel Andria   HISTORIC HOTEL €€
(☑973 35 03 00; www.hotelandria.com; Passeig Joan Brudieu 24; s/d incl breakfast from €86/98; P☎) Easily the best town-centre option, this hotel, with its old knick-knacks on the walls and high, plant-bedecked arches and shady gardens, actually feels more like some old English colonial retreat in an Indian hill station than just another hotel in an Andorran border town.

Restaurant Les Tres Portes   SPANISH €€
(Carrer de Joan Garriga i Massó 7; meals €33-38; ☺Thu-Sun) This is a homely spot, where you can chow down on mixed Spanish cuisine in the peaceful garden. Inside, the decor is bright but warm, with orange walls and yellow-and-red table linen. The imaginative menu will sate carnovores and pescaterians alike, with the *mitjana de cavall amb alls* (horsemeat prepared in garlic) and the duck burger with foie gras being the more inspired items.

Cal Pacho   CATALAN €€
(Carrer Font 11; meals €20-30; ☺lunch & dinner Tue-Sat, lunch Sun) The menu at this small, rustic spot is Catalan through and through, with such firm favourites as the *mandonguilles amb sépia* (meatballs with squid). If you're driving, you might want to steer clear of the potent *torta de whiskey*.

Ignasi   FRENCH €
(☑973 35 49 49; Carrer de Capdevila 17; mains €5-9; ☺Mon-Sat) Popular crêperie, with plenty of sweet and savoury fillings on the menu.

ℹ Information

Tourist office (☑973 35 15 11; www.turisme seu.com; Carrer Major 8; ☺9am-7pm Mon-Fri, 10am-2pm & 4-7pm Sat, 10am-2pm Sun Jul & Aug, 10am-2pm & 4-6pm Mon-Sat Sep-Jun) Ultra-helpful office across the street from the cathedral has a leaflet on historical walks.

ℹ Getting There & Away

The bus station is on the northern edge of the old town. **ALSA** (www.alsa.es) runs buses to Barcelona (€26.40, 3½ hours, three to five daily), Puigcerdá (€6.70, one hour, three daily) and Lleida (€16.75, 2½ hours, one daily).

The N260 Hwy heads 6km southwest to Adrall, then turns off west over the hills to Sort. The C14 carries on south to Lleida, threading the towering Tresponts gorge about 13km beyond Adrall.

Vall de la Noguera Pallaresa

The Riu Noguera Pallaresa, running south through a dramatic valley about 50km west of La Seu d'Urgell, is Spain's best-known white-water river. The main centres for white-water sports are the town of Sort and the villages of Rialp and Llavorsí. You'll find companies that can take you rafting, hydrospeeding, canoeing and kayaking or canyoning, climbing, mountain biking, horse riding and ponting (bungee jumping from bridges).

🏃 Activities

The Riu Noguera Pallaresa's grade-4 drops (on a scale of 1 to 6) attract a constant stream of white-water fans between April

ℹ **CATALONIA'S PARKS & RESERVES**

Catalonia boasts 17 parks, nature reserves, a marine reserve and areas of special interest. For a complete run-down on all of them, check out www. parcsdecatalunya.net, which is full of useful background information.

THROW AWAY YOUR GUIDEBOOK!

As beautiful and dramatic as Vall de la Noguera Pallaresa and Val d'Aran are, they can certainly feel rather overrun in summertime by rafters and hikers, respectively. If you're looking for solitude and adventure off the beaten track, there is plenty more beguiling nature to be found north of the valley. Why not take the B-roads up into the hills northeast of Llavorsí and Esterri d'Àneu, or else north of Vielha, leading to some remote and, in parts, tough mountain-walking country along and across the Andorran and French borders. From Llavorsí you can take the L504 into the Vall de Cardós, visiting villages such as Lladrós, Lladorre and Tavascan, or brave the tough road to the Estany de Certascan – an enormous crystal-blue glacial lake. Or take the other fork into the Vall Ferrera, seek out the prettiest highland hamlets among the likes of Araós, Alins and Àreu and tackle scores of beautiful mountain walks, such as the ascent of the Pica d'Estats (3143m), the highest peak in Catalonia. Esterri d'Àneu is another good starting point for back-road exploration, the twisting C147 leading up into the Vall d'Isil, passing the tiny villages Borén, Isil and ending at the utterly remote, half-abandoned Alós d'Isil.

From Vielha, the serpentine drive up to the French border is a real delight, with delightful Romanesque churches and rambling narrow lanes in sleepy, charming villages such as Arrós, Vilamós and Bossóst, plenty of walking trails leading off into the tall forbidding mountains of the Aragonese Pyrenees, and campsites for dedicated hikers.

and August. It's usually at its best in May and June.

The best stretch is the 14km or so from Llavorsí to Rialp, on which the standard raft outing lasts one to two hours and costs around €35 per person for two hours, or around €80 for longer trips. Longer rides to Sort and beyond will cost more, and Sort is the jumping-off point for the river's tougher grade-4 rapids.

In Llavorsí, Yeti Emotions (☎973 62 22 01; www.yetiemotions.com; Carrer de Borda Era d'Alfons) organises high-grade trips, for experienced rafters only, further upstream. It can also take you hiking, abseiling and on winter husky-sledge rides! Other recommended Llavorsí operators include Roc Roi (☎973 62 20 35; www.rocroi.com; Plaça Nostra Sra De Biuse 8), with horseback riding also on the menu, and Rafting Llavorsí (☎973 62 21 58; www.raftingllavorsi.com; Camí de Riberies), which can also take you kayaking (€80 for two days' instruction).

Bring your own swimming costume, towel and a change of clothes; other equipment provided.

🛏 Sleeping & Eating

Llavorsí is the most pleasant base, much more of a mountain village than Rialp or Sort.

Hostal Noguera   HOSTAL €
(☎973 62 20 12; www.hostalnoguera.com; Carretera Vall d'Aran; s/d €40/54; 🕿🔲) This stone building, on the southern edge of the village, has pleasant rooms overlooking the river. The downstairs restaurant specialises in regional cuisine and the fresh local fish is particularly good (lunch menu €18).

Camping Aigües Braves   CAMPGROUND €
(☎973 62 21 53; www.campingaiguesbraves.com; site per 1-person tent/per 2-person tent & car €11/20.40; ☉May-Sep; 🅿🔲) About 1km north of Llavorsí proper, this pleasant riverside camping ground has a pool, a bar and a minimarket.

Camping Riberies   CAMPGROUND €
(☎973 62 21 51; www.campingriberies.cat; Camí de Riberies, just east of Llavorsí; site per 1-person tent/ per 2-person tent & car €10.60/15.90; ☉mid-Jun–mid-Sep; 🅿🔲) A decent, fully equipped camping ground with numerous activities on offer.

❶ Information

The main **tourist office** (☎973 62 10 02; www.pallarssobira.cat; Camí de la Cabanera; ☉9am-8pm Mon-Fri, 10am-2pm & 3-8pm Sat, 10am-1pm Sun Jul & Aug, 9am-3pm Mon-Thu, 9am-3pm & 4-6.30pm Fri, 10am-2.30pm Sat Sep-Jun) for the area is in Sort, with helpful info on the region and rafting operators.

❶ Getting There & Away

ALSA runs daily buses from Barcelona to Llavorsí via Sort and Rialp (€34, five hours).

Parc Nacional d'Aigüestortes i Estany de Sant Maurici & Around

Catalonia's only national park (http://red deparquesnacionales.mma.es/parques, www.gencat.cat/parcs/aiguestortes) extends 20km east to west, and only 9km from north to south. But the rugged terrain within this small area positively sparkles with more than 400 lakes and countless streams and waterfalls, combined with a backdrop of pine and fir forests, and open bush and grassland, bedecked with wild flowers in spring, to create a wilderness of rare splendour.

Created by glacial action over two million years, the park is essentially two east–west valleys at 1600m to 2000m altitude lined by jagged 2600m to 2900m peaks of granite and slate.

The national park, whose boundaries cover 141 sq km, lies at the core of a wider wilderness area. The outer limit is known as the *zona periférica* and includes some magnificent high country to the north and south. The total area covered is 408 sq km and is monitored by park rangers.

The main approaches are via the village of Espot, 4km east of the park's eastern boundary and 8km away from the huge Estany de Sant Maurici lake, and Vall de Boí, part of its western sector.

◉ Sights

Romanesque Churches   CHURCHES
(www.vallboi.cat; admission €1.50 each or €6 for all 6 churches; ⊙10am-2pm & 4-7pm, Santa Maria de Taüll 10am-8pm) The Vall de Boí, southwest of the park, is dotted with some of Catalonia's loveliest little Romanesque churches.

Parc Nacional d'Aigüestortes i Estany de Sant Maurici

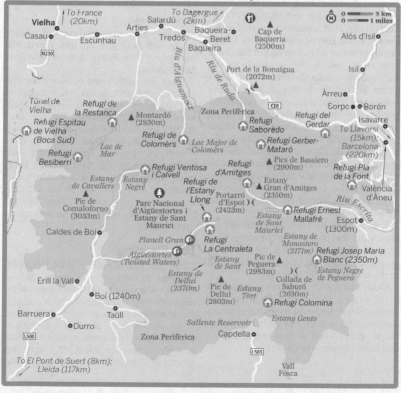

THE CASE OF THE MISSING PAINTINGS

If you visit the Romanesque churches in Vall de Boí and around, you'll find them free of adornment. That wasn't always the case: they used to sport beautiful 12th- and 13th-century frescoes, such as the rather severe Christ from the Sant Climent church in Taüll; but when art nouveau came into being, those frescoes suddenly became ultrafashionable and there was a real danger that foreigners would swoop in and make off with these works of art (in fact, some had). To prevent the frescoes from being spirited away abroad, they were instead painstakingly removed and brought down to the Museu Nacional d'Art de Catalunya (p273) in Montjuïc, Barcelona, where they reside still.

These unadorned stone structures sitting in the crisp alpine air, constructed between the 11th and 14th centuries were declared a Unesco World Heritage site in 2000. Two of the finest are at Taüll, 3km east of Boí. **Sant Climent de Taüll**, at the entrance to the village, with its slender six-storey bell tower, is a gem, not only for its elegant, simple lines but also for the art that once graced its interior (see the boxed text above). The central apse contains a copy of a famous 1123 mural that now resides in Barcelona's Museu Nacional d'Art de Catalunya. At the church's centre is a *Pantocrator* (Christ figure), whose rich Mozarabic-influenced colours, and expressive but superhuman features, have become a virtual emblem of Catalan Romanesque art.

Santa Maria de Taüll, up in the old village centre and possessing a five-storey tower, is also well represented in the Barcelona museum but lacks the in situ copies that add to the interest of Sant Climent.

Other worthwhile Romanesque churches in the area are **Sant Joan** (at Boí), **Sant Feliu** (Barruera), **Nativitat** (Durro) and **Santa Eulália** (Erill la Vall). The latter has a slender six-storey tower to rival Sant Climent's and slopes upwards to the altar.

Activities

The park is criss-crossed by plenty of paths, ranging from well marked to unmarked, enabling you to pick suitable routes.

East–West Traverse

You can walk right across the park in one day. The full Espot–Boí (or vice versa) walk is about 25km and takes nine hours, but you can shorten this by using Jeep-taxis to/from Estany de Sant Maurici or Aigüestortes (3km downstream from Estany Llong) or both. Espot (1300m) to Estany de Sant Maurici (1950m) is 8km (two hours). A path then climbs to the Portarró d'Espot pass (2423m), where there are fine views over both of the park's main valleys. From the pass you descend to Estany Llong and Aigüestortes (1820m; about 3½ hours from Estany de Sant Maurici). Then you have around 3.5km to the park entrance, 4km to the L500 and 2.5km south to Boí (1240m) – a total of about three hours. If attempting this route make sure you have the relevant maps and a compass as well as suitable clothing for a high mountain trek.

Shorter Walks

Numerous good walks of three to five hours' return will take you up into spectacular side valleys from Estany de Sant Maurici or Aigüestortes.

From the eastern end of Estany de Sant Maurici, one path heads south 2.5km up the Monastero valley to **Estany de Monastero** (2171m), passing Els Encantats on the left. Another goes 3km northwest up by Estany de Ratero to **Estany Gran d'Amitges** (2350m). From **Planell Gran** (1850m), 1km up the Sant Nicolau valley from Aigüestortes, a path climbs 2.5km southeast to **Estany de Dellui** (2370m). You can descend to **Estany Llong** (3km); it takes about four hours from Aigüestortes to Estany Llong.

🛏 Sleeping

There are four similarly priced camping grounds in and around Espot. Serious walkers will want to take advantage of the network of six *refugis* in the park and nine more inside the *zona periférica*. They tend to be staffed from early or mid-June to September and for some weeks in the first half of the year for skiers. At other times several of them leave a section open where you can stay overnight; if you are unsure, call ahead or ask at the park information offices. Most charge €15 per person to stay overnight and must be booked in advance, particularly in summer. See www.feec.org for more information.

The villages of Espot, Boí and Taüll have a range of accommodation options. There are *hostales* and *cases de pagés* in Barruera, El Pont de Suert, Capdella and La Torre de Capdella.

ESPOT

Casa Palmira CASA RURAL €
(☎973 62 40 72; www.pensiopalmira.com; d incl breakfast €60; 📶) This friendly, family-run place with immaculate rooms on a cobbled street just off the main square is a traveller favourite. It is one of three country homestays here, all of which charge about the same.

Camping Vorapark CAMPGROUND €
(☎973 62 41 08; www.voraparc.com; Prat del Vedat; site per adult €14; ⏲Apr-Sep; P) This campground is the best in Espot, around 1.5km out of town towards the park entrance. It has a pleasant swimming pool, as well as a pool hall, a bar and a minimarket.

TAÜLL

Three kilometres uphill from Boí, Taüll is by far the most picturesque place to stay on the west side of the park. It has over a dozen hotels and *pensiones*, either in the village itself or in the surrounding area. There's also a small ski resort higher up in the valley, though its future is currently uncertain.

CHARIOTS OF FIRE

So, you think you're a fit hiker? Think you can do the circular 55km trek between nine of the park's *refugis* (mountain shelters)? Do we hear a yes? In that case, can you do it...in one day? The ultra-gruelling **Carros de Foc** (Chariots of Fire; www.carrosdefoc.cat), invented in 1987, requires you to battle the capricious weather and the altitude as well as the terrain, getting your documents stamped at each *refugi* as you go along. The Sky Runner race takes place on the 29th and 30th of July and the currect record stands at nine hours and 32 minutes.

TOP CHOICE **Albergue Taüll** HOSTEL €
(☎973 69 62 52; www.alberguetaull.com; Avenida Feixanes 5-7; dm/d incl breakfast €23/46; P📶) The brainchild of transplanted Arizonian Tony, this is everything a hostel should be: the large beds feature orthopaedic matresses, there's underfloor heating for those crisp mornings and a large map of the park in the common area to help you plan your hikes. Families are welcome and Tony's on hand to give advice. At the time this book went to print, the hostel was hoping to have a hot tub (from which to look down on Taüll below) up and running in early 2013.

Pensión Santa Maria BOUTIQUE HOTEL €€
(☎973 69 61 70; www.taull.com; Plaça Cap del Riu 3; d incl breakfast from €110; P📶) Through a shady entrance a grand stone archway leads into the quiet courtyard of this rambling country haven with rose-draped balcony, run by congenial hosts. The rooms are tastefully furnished and the building, all stonework with a timber-and-slate roof, oozes timeless character.

Camping Taüll CAMPGROUND €
(☎973 69 61 74; www.campingtaull.com; site per person €5.50, cabins from €80; P) Attractive cluster of fully equipped wooden cabins (some with shared bathrooms) by the stream. Campers can pitch their tents here and make use of the facilities.

Eating

Throughout the area many places close midweek and in the low season.

TOP CHOICE **Sedona** INTERNATIONAL €
(☎973 69 62 52; Les Feixes 2; meals €20-25) A varied menu of Catalan and international dishes (including the most humongous, juicy Arizona burgers!), longer opening hours than anywhere else in the village and use of locally grown organic produce puts this friendly spot ahead of the competition. The bar's a good place to haunt, après-ski or après-hiking, too.

Restaurant Juquim CATALAN €
(☎973 62 40 09; Plaća San Martí 1; meals €22-28; ⏲daily Jun–mid-Oct, Wed-Mon mid-Oct–May) This classic on Espot's main square has a varied menu concentrating largely on hearty country fare, with generous winter servings of *olla pallaresa* (steaming hotpot) or *civet de senglar* (wild boar stew).

TONY CAPANNA: RESTAURATEUR/OWNER OF ALBERGUE TAÜLL, VALL DE BOÍ

Best Hike The Marmot Trail – a round trip of 3½ hours – which begins next to the impressive Cavallers dam and passes a series of waterfalls. The hike ends at the Estany Negré (Black Lake), which is close to this trail's first *refugi*, Ventosa i Calvell; you spend a half-day amongst the beautiful mountains with breathtaking views of the Vall de Boí. There is also a nice three-hour trail from Taüll that takes in the entire valley and passes through the four villages along the way – Boí, Duro, Barrerra, Boí again, and back to Taüll.

Hiking Tip If you want to stay in the *refugis* (mountain shelters) in the national park, they are more comfortable in May, June, September and October than in July and August, when there are 70 people sleeping in the same room.

Favourite Time of Year It's a tough one! In spring the valley is at its greenest, and the rivers are running the fastest from the snowmelt; in autumn the colours are at their best, and both spring and autumn are a great time for hiking as there are not too many visitors.

ℹ Information

There are national park information offices in **Espot** (📞973 62 40 36; Carrer de Sant Maurici 5, Espot; ⏰9am-1pm & 3.30-6.45pm Jun-Sep) and **Boí** (📞973 69 61 89; Carrer de les Graieres 2, Boí; ⏰9am-2pm & 3.30-6pm Jul & Aug, closed Sun rest of year). The best map of the park is produced by **Editorial Alpina** (www.editorialalpina.com).

PARK RULES Private vehicles cannot enter the park. Wild camping is not allowed, nor (sadly!) is swimming or other 'aquatic activities' in the lakes and rivers. Hunting, fishing, mushroom picking and just about every other kind of potentially harmful activity are banned.

ℹ Getting There & Away

Daily ALSA buses from Barcelona, Lleida and La Pobla de Segur to Esterri d'Àneu stop at the Espot turn-off on the C13. From there it's an 8km uphill walk to Espot. Buses to La Pobla de Segur (€28.10, three to 4½ hours, up to three daily) run year-round. From July to mid-September a connecting bus runs daily from La Pobla de Segur to El Pont de Suert and from there to Barruera and the Boí turn-off (1km short of Boí).

ℹ Getting Around

The closest you can get to the eastern side of the park is a car park 4km west of Espot. There are more or less continuous Jeep-taxi services between Espot and Estany de Sant Maurici, and between Boí and Aigüestortes, saving you, respectively, 8km and 10km. The return fare for either trip is €10 per person and the services

run from outside the park information offices in Espot and Boí (8am to 7pm July to September, other months 9am to 6pm).

Val d'Aran

POP 10,210

It wasn't all that long ago that the verdant Val d'Aran, Catalonia's northernmost outpost, was one of the remotest parts of Spain and its only connection to the outside world was via a small pass leading into France. All this changed with the opening of a tunnel connecting the valley's capital, Vielha, with the rest of the country in the 1950s, which led to a surge of tourism development. Despite all this, though, the valley feels like a secret world of cloud-scraping mountain peaks and tumbling valley slopes dotted with hill villages, many with exquisite little Romanesque churches. From Aran's pretty side valleys, walkers can go over the mountains in any direction, notably southward to the Parc Nacional d'Aigüestortes i Estany de Sant Maurici.

Thanks in part to its geography, Aran's native language is not Catalan but Aranese *(aranés)*, which is a dialect of Occitan or the *langue d'oc*, the old Romance language of southern France.

Despite this northward orientation, Aran has been tied politically to Catalonia since 1175, when Alfonso II took it under his protection to forestall the designs of rival counts on both sides of the Pyrenees. A major hiccup came with the Napoleonic occupation from 1810 to 1815.

ℹ Getting There & Away

Alsina Graells buses run between Barcelona and Vielha (€34.20, 5½ hours, two daily) via Lleida (€13.70, three hours).

The N230 from Lleida and El Pont de Suert reaches Aran through the 5.25km Túnel de Vielha. From the Vall de la Noguera Pallaresa, the C28 crosses the Port de la Bonaigua pass (2072m) into Naut Aran, meeting the N230 Hwy at Vielha.

VIELHA
POP 5710 / ELEV 974M

Vielha is Aran's junction capital, a sprawl of holiday housing and apartments straggled along the valley and creeping up the sides, crowded with skiers in winter. The tiny centre retains some charm in the form of the Església de Sant Miquéu, which houses some notable medieval artwork, namely the 12th-century *Crist de Mijaran*. The **Muséu dera Val D'Aran** (Carrer Major 11; adult/child €2/1; ⊙10am-1pm & 5-8pm Tue-Sat, 11am-2pm Sun), housed in a turreted and somewhat decaying old mansion, covers Aranese history through a series of black-and-white photos and period furnishings.

🛏 Sleeping & Eating

High season is Christmas to New Year, Easter and other peak holiday periods: high

MAPS & GUIDES

Editorial Alpina's map guides are adequate, although they don't show every single trail. *Sant Maurici – Els Encantats* covers the eastern half of the Parc Nacional d'Aigüestortes i Estany de Sant Maurici and its approaches; *Vall de Boí* covers the western half and its approaches; *Montsent de Pallars* covers the northern Vall Fosca; and *Val d'Aran*, naturally, covers the Val d'Aran. A better map of the whole area is the Institut Cartogràfic de Catalunya's *Parc Nacional d'Aigüestortes i Estany de Sant Maurici*, scaled at 1:25,000 – but even this isn't perfect.

Lonely Planet's newly updated *Hiking in Spain* guide gives detailed route descriptions of several walks in and around the park.

summer (July to August) and the ski season (January to February). The local speciality is *olla aranesa* (a hearty hotpot).

TOP CHOICE Hotel Ço de Pierra HOTEL €€
(☎973 64 13 34; www.hotelpierra.com; Carrèr Major 26; s/d €52/66) In Betrén, a timeless village tacked on to the eastern end of Vielha's sprawl, this gorgeous place respects the stone-and-slate pattern of traditional housing and its 10 rooms combine stone, timber and terracotta for warmth.

Hotel El Ciervo BOUTIQUE HOTEL €€
(☎973 64 01 65; www.hotelelciervo.net; Plaça de Sant Orenç 3; s/d €60/85; ⊙closed Jun & Nov; 🛜🅿🐕) With an exterior covered in paintings of trees and forest creatures, it's clear that this hotel is a departure from the mundane ski chalet norm, and the interior, with each room varying in style and feel, doesn't disappoint.

Restaurant Gustavo (Era Móla) FRENCH €€
(☎973 64 24 19; Carrèr de Marrèc 14; meals €30-35; ⊙dinner Mon, Tue, Thu & Fri, lunch & dinner Sat & Sun) This is easily the best restaurant in town. Expect carefully prepared local cooking with a heavy French hand (you can't get more French than potted duck, ie rillettes) and savour the *solomillo de cerdo al Calvados* (pork fillet bathed in Calvados).

ℹ Information
Tourist office (☎973 64 01 10; www.visitvaldaran.com; Carrèr de Sarriulèra 10; ⊙9am-9pm)

ARTIES
POP 490 / ELEV 1143M

Six kilometres east of Vielha, this village on the southern side of the highway sits astride the confluence of the Garona and Valarties rivers. Among its cheerful stone houses is the Romanesque Església de Santa Maria, with its three-storey belfry and triple apse.

🛏 Sleeping

Aside from the two options listed here, almost all other accommodation in the village closes up in May/June and October/November.

Casa Irene HOTEL €€€
(☎973 64 43 64; www.hotelcasairene.com; d €187; 🅿❄🛜) Expect exposed wooden beams, marble bathrooms and colourful throws on the king-sized beds at this luxurious property. The suites come with own hot tubs and there a plethora of on-site muscle soothers,

OUT & ABOUT IN THE PYRENEES

The Catalan Pyrenees provide magnificent walking and trekking. You can undertake strolls of a few hours, or day walks that can be strung together into treks of several days. Nearly all can be done without camping gear, with nights spent in villages or *refugis* (mountain shelters).

Most of the *refugis* are run by two Barcelona mountain clubs, the **Federació d'Entitats Excursionistes de Catalunya** (FEEC; www.feec.org) and the **Centre Excursionista de Catalunya** (CEC; www.cec.cat), which also provide info on trails. A night in a *refugi* costs around €12.50 to €18. Normally FEEC *refugis* allow you to cook; CEC ones don't. Moderately priced meals (around €15 to €17) are often available.

The coast-to-coast **GR11 long-distance trail network** traverses the entire Pyrenees from Cap de Creus on the Costa Brava to Hondarribia on the Bay of Biscay. Its route across Catalonia goes by way of La Jonquera, Albanyá, Beget, Setcases, the Vall de Núria, Planoles, Puigcerdá, Andorra, south of Pica d'Estats (3143m), over to the Parc Nacional d'Aigüestortes i Estany de Sant Maurici, then on to the southern flank of the Val d'Aran and into Aragón. The tougher **HRP (Haute Radonnée Pyrénéenne)**, recommended for experienced trekkers only, passes through part of the Parc Nacional d'Aigüestortes I Estany de sant Maurici, taking you higher up into the mountains and crossing the Spanish–French border several times.

The season for walking in the high Pyrenees is from late June to early October. Always be prepared for fast-changing conditions, no matter when you go.

Local advice from tourist offices, park rangers, mountain *refugis* and other walkers is invaluable. Dedicated hiking maps and guidebooks are essential. Lonely Planet's *Hiking in Spain* contains numerous options in the Catalan Pyrenees.

There's boundless scope for **climbing** – Pedraforca in the Serra del Cadí offers some of the most exciting ascents.

from the Turkish hammam to sauna and jacuzzi. The menu at the gourmet restaurant runs the gamut from Catalan pig's trotters with wild mushrooms to oysters au gratin.

Hotel Edelmeiss HOTEL €€
(☑973 64 09 02; s/d incl breakfast €60/100; P🅿🛜) There's nothing remotely fancy about this small, family-run hotel, but much of the electricity comes from the solar panels outside and breakfast is served in the Boísterous downstairs bar – a meeting point for the whole local community.

SALARDÚ
POP 460 / ELEV 1267M

Three kilometres east of Arties, Salardú's nucleus of old houses and narrow streets has largely resisted the temptation to sprawl. In the apse of the village's 12th- and 13th-century Sant Andreu church, you can admire the 13th-century *Crist de Salardú* crucifixion carving. The nicest restaurant in the village, **Refugi Rosta**, houses an entertaining private **PyrenMuseu** (adult €5; ☺10.30am-1pm & 5.30-8pm) covering the history of tourism in Val d'Aran, with a glass of

wine included in the price to enhance your enjoyment.

The town is a handy base for the Baqueira-Beret ski resort, 4km from here.

🛏 Sleeping

In May/June and October/November absolutely everything in and around Salardú goes into hibernation.

Hotel Seixes HOTEL €€
(☑973 64 54 06; www.seixes.com; Bagergue, 2km north of Salardú; s/d hotel incl breakfast €47/67, hostel €41/55; ☺hotel May-Oct, hostel late Jul-late Aug; P🛜) This hikers' favourite has spacious and comfortable rooms, some of which have huge views over the valley and surrounding peaks; the hostel rooms are marginally more spartan. While you're tucking into a hearty buffet breakfast the staff will fill you in on all the local trekking routes.

Alberg Era Garona HOSTEL €
(☑973 64 52 71; www.tojuaran.com; Carretera de Vielha; r per person €26; P🛜) Fairly utilitarian-looking youth hostel, with four-bedded ensuite dorms and an outdoor climbing wall.

BAQUEIRA-BERET

Baqueira, 3km east of Salardú, and Beret, 8km north of Baqueira, form Catalonia's premier ski resort (www.baqueira.es; day lift pass €45), favoured by the Spanish royal family, no less! Its good lift system gives access to 72 varied pistes totalling 104km (larger than most other Spanish resorts), amid fine scenery at between 1500m and 2510m.

There's nowhere cheap to stay in Baqueira, and nowhere at all in Beret. Many skiers stay down the valley in Salardú, Arties or Vielha. Out of season everything is closed.

CENTRAL CATALONIA

Away from the beaches and mountains is a host of little-visited gems splashed across the Catalan hinterland. About halfway between Barcelona and the Pyrenees lies the graceful town of Vic, with its grand Plaça Major. Northwest of the capital you can strike out for Montserrat, with its mountain shrine, Cardona, with its windy castle complex, and Solsona, en route to Lleida. An alternative route to Lleida takes you further south through the Conca de Barberà, which is dotted with majestic medieval monasteries.

Vic

POP 38,960

With its enchanting old quarter crammed with Roman remnants, medieval leftovers, a grand Gothic cloister, an excellent art museum, some hectic markets and a glut of superb restaurants, Vic is one of Catalonia's gems. Despite its resolutely Catalan political outlook, the town is very multicultural. Vic makes for a great day trip from Barcelona, but it's better to stay a little longer and wallow in the town's atmosphere.

◎ Sights

Old Town   OLD TOWN

Plaça Major, the largest of Catalonia's central squares, is lined with medieval, baroque and Modernista mansions. It's still the site of the huge twice-weekly market (Tuesday and Saturday mornings) flogging fresh local fruit, veg and the town's famous *llonganisa* sausages. This market has provided the square with an alternative name, Plaça del Mercadal. Around it swirl the narrow serpentine streets of medieval Vic, lined by mansions, churches, chapels and an undeniably sunny southern atmosphere.

Catedral de Sant Pere   CATHEDRAL

(Plaça de la Catedral; adult/child €2/free; ☉10am-1pm & 4-7pm) The Catedral de Sant Pere is a neoclassical Goliath with a rather gloomy interior, flanked by a Romanesque bell tower. Inside, the dark, square-based pillars are lightened by murals depicting biblical scenes by Josep Maria Sert (he had to do them twice because the first set was destroyed by fire in 1936). The highlights of a visit are the Romanesque crypt, the treasury rooms and a wander through the stone lacework splendour of the Gothic cloister. Entrance to the cathedral itself is free – the listed prices and times apply to the cloisters, treasury room and crypt.

Museu Episcopal   MUSEUM

(www.museuepiscopalvic.com; Plaça del Bisbe Oliba 3; adult/child over 10yr €7/3.50; ☉10am-7pm Tue-Sat, 10am-2pm Sun Apr-Sep, shorter hours rest of year) This museum holds a marvellous collection of Romanesque and Gothic art, second only to the Museu Nacional d'Art de Catalunya collection in Barcelona. The Romanesque collection depicts some wonderfully gory images – from saints being beheaded or tortured to the Archangel Michael spearing a devil through his jaw, as well as the vivid *Davallament*, a scene depicting the taking down of Christ from the cross. The Gothic collection contains works by such key figures as Lluís Borrassá and Jaume Huguet.

✯✯ Festivals & Events

Vic has a packed festival calendar.

Mercat de Ram   EASTER MARKET

In the week running up to Palm Sunday, Plaça Major hosts the Mercat del Ram (Palm Market, a tradition that goes back to AD 875), selling palms and laurels. The Mercat del Ram is also the excuse for a major gastronomic fiesta, with the Rambla del Carme and Rambla de Passeig along the northern border of the old town filling with stalls selling cured meats, cheeses, *coca* (Easter cake) and other fantastic regional produce.

Fira d'Antiguitats de Vic   ANTIQUE FAIR

(www.fav.cat) The trade fair grounds host one of Spain's biggest annual antiques markets for a week over mid- to late August.

Mercat de Música Viva   MUSIC
(www.mmvv.net) The town hosts the Mercat de Música Viva, a big if somewhat chaotic event, over several days in September in which Catalan, national and foreign acts of various schools of Latin rock and pop and jazz get together to jam.

🛏 Sleeping & Eating

The town is known for its disproportionate density of high-quality restaurants.

Estadió del Nord   HOTEL €
(☑93 516 62 92; www.estaciodelnord.com; Plaça del Estadió 4; s/d €50/60; ℗🛜) The 14 refurbished rooms of this little boutique hotel, well located on the 1st floor of the 1910 train station, are decked out in soothing creams and whites and overseen by a friendly family.

TOP CHOICE La Taula   CATALAN €€
(☑93 886 32 29; Plaça de Don Miguel de Clariana 4; menus from €18; ☉daily Jul & Aug, Tue-Sat & lunch only Sun Oct-Jun, closed Feb) In a town that bristles with superlative eateries, this one stands out as a bright star of traditional cooking, with fair prices and no pretensions (and considered by locals as one of the best in town).

El Jardinet   CATALAN €€
(☑93 886 28 77; www.eljardinetdevic.com; Carrer de Corretgers 8; menus from €16; ☉lunch & dinner Tue-Sat) Within a spare interior, livened up with the odd modern art piece and made larger with mirrors, you can expect classic Catalan cooking such as *botifarra* with peas. Gets very busy at lunchtime.

ℹ Information

Tourist office (☑93 886 20 91; www.victur isme.cat; Carrer de la Ciutat 4; ☉10am-2pm & 4-8pm Mon-Sat, 10.30am-1.30pm Sun)

ℹ Getting There & Away

Regular *rodalies* (line R3) run from Barcelona (€5.80, up to 1½ hours).

Montserrat

Montserrat (Serrated Mountain), 50km northwest of Barcelona, is a 1236m-high mountain of strangely rounded rock pillars, shaped by wind, rain and frost from a conglomeration of limestone, pebbles and sand that once lay under the sea (or else by baby angels, depending on whom you talk to). With the historic Benedictine Monestir de Montserrat, one of Catalonia's most important shrines, cradled at 725m on its side, it's the most popular outing from Barcelona. From the mountain, on a clear day, you can see as far as the Pyrenees. Its caves and many mountain paths make for spectacular rambles, reachable by funiculars.

The *cremallera* chugs up the mountainside, arriving just below the monastery, next to the cable-car station. From there, the main road curves (past a snack bar, cafeteria, information office and the Espai Audiovisual) up to the right, passing the blocks of Cel·les Abat Marcel, to enter Plaça de Santa Maria, at the centre of the monastery complex.

The monastery throngs with day trippers, so it's well worth staying overnight to enjoy the stillness and the silence of this remarkable place and to commune in peace with La Moreneta before the first tour buses pull up.

◉ Sights & Activities

Monestir de Montserrat   MONASTERY
(www.abadiamontserrat.net; ☉9am-6pm) The monastery – the second-most-important pilgrimage centre in Spain after Santiago de Compostela – was founded in 1025 to commemorate a vision of the Virgin on the mountain, seen by – you've guessed it – shepherds, after which the Black Virgin icon, allegedly carved by St Luke and hidden by St Peter in the mountains, was discovered thanks to said vision. Wrecked by Napoleon's troops in 1811, then abandoned as a result of anticlerical legislation in the 1830s, the monastery was rebuilt from 1858. Today a community of about 80 monks lives here. Pilgrims come from far and wide to venerate the Virgen de Montserrat, affectionately known as La Moreneta ('the little brown one' or 'the Black Madonna'), a 12th-century Romanesque dark wooden sculpture of a regal-looking Mary with an elongated nose, holding the infant Jesus and a globe which pilgrims come to touch; she has been Catalonia's patron since 1881 and her blessing is particularly sought by newly married couples.

Museu de Montserrat   MUSEUM
(Plaça de Santa Maria; adult/student €6.50/5.50; ☉10am-6pm) The two-part Museu de Montserrat has an excellent collection, ranging from an Egyptian mummy and Gothic altarpieces to art by El Greco, Monet, Degas and Picasso, as well as modern art and

THE MONASTERIES ROUTE

The verdant oasis of La Conca de Barberá lies 30km west of Vilafranca del Penedès. Vineyards and woods succeed one another across rolling green hills, studded with the occasional medieval village and a trio of grand Cistercian monasteries (a combined ticket to all three is available for €9) along the so-called Ruta del Cister (Cistercian Route) . With your own vehicle, it is possible to extend a Penedès wineries excursion to some of these magnificent sights.

Following the AP-7 freeway southwest from Vilafranca, take the AP-2 fork about 18km west, then exit 11 north for the medieval Reial Monestir de Santes Creus (Royal Monastery of the Holy Crosses; Plaça de Jaume el Just; adult/senior & student €4.50/ free, guided visit extra €2.20; ☺10am-6pm Jun-Sep, 10am-5pm Oct-May). Cistercian monks moved in here in 1168 and from then on the monastery developed as a major centre of learning and a launch pad for the repopulation of the surrounding territory. Behind the Romanesque and Gothic facade lies a glorious 14th-century sandstone cloister, austere chapter house and royal apartments where the comtes-reis (count-kings; rulers of the joint state of Catalonia and Aragón) often stayed when they popped by during Holy Week. The church, begun in the 12th century, is a lofty Gothic structure in the French tradition and there is evidence of Moorish influence in the shape of a cloister full of orange trees.

Back on the AP-2, travel another 22km to the medieval town of Montblanc, still surrounded by its defensive walls, and then L'Espluga de Francolí, beyond which you continue 3km to the fortified Reial Monestir de Santa Maria de Poblet (Royal Monastery of St Mary of Poblet; www.poblet.cat; adult/student €6/3.50; ☺10am-12.40pm & 3-5.55pm Mon-Sat, 10am-12.25pm & 3-5.25pm Sun & holidays mid-Mar–mid Oct, shorter hours rest of year), the jewel in the crown of the Conca de Barberà and a Unesco World Heritage site. Founded by Cistercian monks from southern France in 1151, it became Catalonia's most powerful monastery (it is said to be the largest Cistercian monastery in the world) and the burial place of many of its rulers. Poblet was sacked in 1835 by marauding peasants as payback for the monks' abuse of their feudal powers, which included imprisonment and torture. A community of Cistercian monks moved back in after the Spanish Civil War and did much to restore the monastery to its former glory. High points include the mostly Gothic main cloister and the alabaster sculptural treasures of the Panteón de los Reyes (Kings' Pantheon). The raised alabaster sarcophagi contain eight Catalan kings, such greats as Jaume I (the conqueror of Mallorca and Valencia) and Pere III. Entry is by guided tour only, since monks are resident here once more.

Swinging away north from Montblanc (take the C-14 and then branch west along the LP-2335), country roads guide you up through tough countryside into the low hills of the Serra del Tallat and towards the Reial Monestir de Santa Maria de Vallbona de les Monges (Royal Monastery of St Mary of Vallbona of the Nuns; ☎973 33 02 66; adult/child €3.50/2; ☺10.30am-1.30pm & 4.30-6.45pm Tue-Sat, noon-1.30pm & 4.30-6.45pm Sun & holidays Mar-Oct, shorter hours rest of year). It was founded in the 12th century and is where a dozen monges (nuns) still live and pray. You will be taken on a guided tour, probably in Catalan. The monastery has undergone years of restoration, which has finally cleared up most of the remaining scars of civil war damage and the church marks the clear transition between Romanesque and Gothic architecture.

some fantastic 14th-century Russian icons (look for the Last Judgement with detailed punishments awaiting sinners). In a hall separate from the rest of the exhibits, the Espai Audiovisual (adult/senior & student €2/1.50; ☺9am to 6pm), free with Museu de Montserrat entry, is a walk-through multimedia space (with images and sounds) that illustrates the daily life and activities of the monks and the history and spirituality of the monastery.

Basilica CHURCH
(admission €5; ☺7.30am-8pm) From Plaça de Santa Maria you enter the courtyard of the 16th-century Renaissance basilica,

the monastery's church. The basilica's facade, with its carvings of Christ and the 12 Apostles, dates from 1901, despite its 16th-century plateresque style. The stairs to the narrow Cambril de la Mare de Déu (☉7-10.30am & noon-6.30pm), housing La Moreneta, are just to the right of the main basilica entrance; the best times to visit her are early in the morning or during the choir performance.

On your way out, have a look in the room across the courtyard from the basilica entrance, filled with gifts and thank-you messages to the Montserrat Virgin from people who give her the credit for all manner of happy events. The souvenirs range from plaster casts and motorcycle helmets to wedding dresses; Barcelona FC dedicate their victories to her.

Santa Cova   CHAPEL
To see the chapel on the spot where the holy image of the Virgin was discovered, you can take the Funicular de Santa Cova (one way/return €2/3.20; ☉every 20min 10am-5.30pm), or else it's an easy walk down, followed by a stroll along a precipitous mountain path which offers some fabulous views of the valley below.

Montserrat Mountain   MOUNTAIN
You can explore the mountain above the monastery on a web of paths leading to some of the peaks and to 13 empty and rather dilapidated hermitages. The Funicular de Sant Joan (one way/return €5.05/8; ☉every 20min 10am-6.50pm, closed Jan & Feb) will carry you up the first 250m from the monastery. If you prefer to walk, the road past the funicular's bottom station leads to its top station in about one hour (3km).

From the top station, it's a 20-minute stroll (it's signposted) to the Sant Joan chapel, which provides fine westward views. More exciting is the one-hour walk northwest, along a path marked with some blobs of yellow paint, to Montserrat's highest peak, Sant Jeroni, from where there's an awesome sheer drop on the north face. The walk takes you across the upper part of the mountain, and you get a close-up experience of some of the weird rock pillars. Many of these have names: on your way to Sant Jeroni look over to the right for La Prenyada (the Pregnant Woman), La Mòmia (the Mummy), L'Elefant (the Elephant) and El Cap de Mort (the Death's Head).

🛏 Sleeping & Eating

Hotel Abat Cisneros   HOTEL €€
(📞93 877 77 01; s/d €60/104; P✳🍴) The only hotel in the monastery complex has modern, comfortable rooms, some of which look over Plaça de Santa Maria. It has a good restaurant serving imaginative Catalonian dishes (meals €36).

Cafeteria   FAST FOOD €
(meals €15-20; ☉ noon-4pm) Self-service spot where you can grab a sandwich or more substantial mains – *calamares a la romana*, meatballs, burgers – the usual suspects.

☆ Entertainment

Montserrat Boys Choir   CHORAL MUSIC
(www.escolania.cat; ☉performances 1pm Mon-Fri, noon Sun late Aug-late Jun) Escolania, reckoned to be Europe's oldest music school, has the Montserrat Boys Choir, which sings in the basilica daily, their clear voices echoing inside the stone walls the way they have done since the 13th century. It is a rare (albeit brief) treat as the choir does not often perform outside Montserrat; they tend to sing *Virolai*, written by Catalonia's national poet Jacint Verdaguer. The 40 to 50 *escolanets*, aged between 10 and 14, go to boarding school at Montserrat and must endure a two-year selection process to join the choir. See the website for latest performance times.

❶ Information

Information office (📞93 877 77 01; www.montserratvisita.com; ☉9am-5.45pm Mon-Fri, to 6.45pm Sat & Sun) Located in the monastery, this has information on the complex and walking trails.

❶ Getting There & Away

Take the C16 from Barcelona, then the C58 shortly after Terrassa, followed by the C55 to Monistrol de Montserrat. Leave the car at the free car park at Monistrol Vila and take the *cremallera* up to the top.

The R5 line trains operated by **FGC** (www.fgc. net) run hourly from Plaça d'Espanya station, starting at 8.36am (52 to 56 minutes). They connect with the **cable car** (📞93 835 00 05; www.aeridemontserrat.com; one way/return €5/7.90; ☉9.40am-7pm Mar-Oct, 10.10am-5.45pm Mon-Sat, 10.10am-6.45pm Sun & holidays Nov-Feb, 17 minutes) at the Montserrat Aeri stop and the **cremallera** (📞902 312020; www.cremallerademontserrat.com; one way/return €6/9; ☉5 minutes) at the following stop, Monistrol de Montserrat.

Cardona

POP 5200

Long before arrival, you spy in the distance the outline of the impregnable 18th-century fortress high above Cardona, which itself lies next to the Muntanya de Sal (Salt Mountain). Until 1990 the salt mine was an important source of income; tours of its salty interior are available for those who are not claustrophobic.

The castle – follow the signs uphill to the Parador Ducs de Cardona (www.parador.es), a lovely place to stay overnight – was built over an older predecessor. The single most remarkable element of the buildings is the lofty and spare Romanesque Església de Sant Vicenç (adult/child €3/2; ⊙10am-1pm & 3-6pm Tue-Sun Jun-Sep, shorter hours rest of year). The bare stone walls were once covered in bright frescoes, some of which can be contemplated in the Museu Nacional d'Art de Catalunya in Barcelona.

Cardona is served by ALSA buses from Barcelona (€14, two hours, two to four daily), Manresa (€4.90, one hour, three to four daily) and Solsona (€2.70, 25 minutes, two to four daily).

Solsona

POP 9300

They call the people of Solsona *matarucs* (donkey killers), which seems an odd tag until you hear what the townsfolk's favourite festive activity used to be. Every February the high point of Solsona's Carnaval fun was the hoisting of a donkey, by the neck, up the town bell tower (Torre de les Hores). The donkey, scared to death, not unreasonably, would defecate and urinate on its way up, much to the delight of the drink-addled crowd below. To be hit by a glob of either substance was considered good fortune. Nowadays the donkey is a water-spraying fake. The *festa major* in September is another fun fest (see the boxed text, p335).

The Catedral de Santa Maria (Plaça de la Catedral; admission free; ⊙10am-1pm & 4-8pm) boasts Romanesque apses, a Gothic nave, a pretty cloister, a tiny 12th-century Virgin carved of black stone, and the ghosts of a lot of pissed-off donkeys. Behind the cathedral is the neoclassical Palau Episcopal (Plaça del Palau; adult/senior & child €3/2; ⊙10am-1pm & 4.30-7pm Tue-Sat, 10am-2pm Sun May-Sep, shorter hours rest of year). Built in the 18th century, it houses a considerable collection of medieval art gathered from churches in the surrounding district.

Solsona is served by two to four daily buses from Barcelona (€17.10, two to 2½ hours) via Cardona.

Lleida

POP 138,420

The hot, dry inland provincial capital Lleida has forever been squeezed by Spain on one side and France on other like a nut in a vice. It is the place where the battle lines were drawn throughout Catalonia's turbulent history: Lleida has had the misfortune of backing the losing side in just about every battle and much of the old town was reduced to rubble when Lleida was overrun by Spanish forces in 1714. The conquerors duly built a citadel to protect their new acquisitions, only for it to be sacked by the French in 1812. However, the mighty fortress-church on top of the hill in the town centre – Lleida's major historical landmark – is one of the most spectacular in Spain and is in itself reason enough to visit. There's a noticeable African migrant presence in the lively streets; they are drawn by the intensive fruit-picking seasons in the orchards spread

---

GETTING HIGH IN CATALONIA

Montsec, a hilly range 65km north of Lleida, is the main stage for hanggliders and microlights in Catalonia. It is also a popular area for walking, caving and climbing. The focal point is the village of Àger, and there are a halfdozen take-off points, including one at the Sant Alís peak (1678m), the highest in the range. Voláger (☎973 32 02 30; www.volager.com; Camí de Castellnou), based in Bellpuig, offers hang-gliding courses here and provides all the equipment. You can go hang-gliding with the school for a day (€80), while a full six-day course comes to €700.

Globubolg (☎689 97 22 02; www.globubolg.com) offer something less intensive but equally spectacular – hot-air balloon flights over parts of Catalonia, including a crossing of the Pyrenees at an altitude of a whopping 4000m; flights start from €160 per person.

HOUSE IN THE COUNTRY

Though Catalonia's cities and towns have their share of luxury and style, some of the region's most attractive lodgings are found in tiny villages in the countryside. Here are three choices to get you started; let us know what other magnificent options you discover!

Mirador de Siurana (📞977 82 14 72; www.miradordesiurana.com; Carretera Cornudella a Suirana, Km 7, Priorat; d from €130; 🅿️❄️🛜♨️) On a clifftop in the emerging wine region of Priorat, northwest of Tarragona, this revamped 1960s mansion is a bona fide romantic getaway. The spacious, bright rooms are individually decorated in neutral shades with warm accents, most with sweeping views of the valley below, and there are wine-tasting excursions to the nearby vineyards for connoisseurs.

Cal Perello (📞696 12 85 77; www.calperello.cat; Gracia 4, l'Ametlla de Segarra; s/d incl breakfast €50/80; 🛜) In a tiny village in the countryside east of Lleida, welcoming David and Eva run a restored 16th-century farmhouse, complete with cats wandering in and out of the cavernous dining room, antique furniture in guest rooms and horses for guests to ride. Full board is available, the food is hearty Catalan and the owners make you feel like part of the family. Multiday horseback-riding excursions and vineyard visits can be arranged; book in advance.

Torre del Remei (📞972 14 01 82; www.torredelremei.com; Camí Reial; d from €325; 🅿️❄️🛜♨️) Near the Pyrenees village of Bolvir, this tastefully decorated Modernista mansion (which during the civil war was requisitioned as a school and later as a hospital by the Republican government) sits majestically amid tranquil gardens, and is a full-blown romantic dream fit for a king and queen. The rooms, exquisitely furnished and each one different, are superb and the dining is equally tempting, the chef working wonders with local seasonal ingredients (though the pleasure doesn't come cheap).

across the plain around Lleida and many hope to stay and better their lives.

◉ Sights

TOP CHOICE La Seu Vella CATHEDRAL
(www.turoseuvella.cat; adult/child €3/free, recinte admission free; ⊙10am-7.30pm Tue-Sat, 10am-3pm Sun May-Sep, shorter hourrs rest of year) Lleida's 'old cathedral', La Seu Vella, enclosed within a recinte (compound) of defensive castle walls erected between the 12th and 19th centuries, towers above the city from its commanding hilltop location.

The main entrance to the recinte is from Carrer de Monterey on its western side, but during the cathedral's opening hours you can use the extraordinarily ugly ascensor (€0.20) from above Plaça de Sant Joan.

The cathedral was built in sandy-coloured stone in the 13th to 15th centuries on the site of a former mosque (Lleida was under Islamic control from AD 719 to 1149). It's a masterpiece of the Transitional style – with sturdy Romanesque pillars, Gothic vaults and arches hinting at Arabic inspiration – although it only recently recovered from 241 years' use as a barracks, which began as Felipe V's punishment for the city's opposition in the War of the Spanish Succession.

A 70m octagonal bell tower rises at the southwest end of the beautiful cloisters, the windows of which are laced with exceptional Gothic tracery; lined with a veritable forest of slender columns with carved capitals, the cloisters give a wonderful feeling of space and light.

Above the cathedral are the remains of the Islamic fortress and residence of the Muslim governors, known as the Castell del Rei or La Suda, and there are sweeping views of the Urgell Plain from the castle walls.

FREE Centre d'Art Contemporani La Panera GALLERY
(www.lapanera.cat; Plaça de la Panera 2; ⊙10am-2pm & 5-8pm Tue-Sat, 11am-2pm Sun & holidays Jun-Sep, shorter hours rest of year) Though the building housing it is centuries old – a medieval pantry, in fact – the art it houses is thoroughly contemporary. The constantly changing exhibitions – paintings, sculpture, installations and more – give you a chance to see some of the brightest new talent – both local and international.

Museu de Lleida
MUSEUM

(www.museudelleida.cat; Carrer de Sant Crist 1; adult/child €4/free; ⊙10am-2pm & 4-8pm Tue-Sat, 10am-2pm Sun Jun-Sep, hours rest of yea) This swish museum brings under one roof collections of artefacts that reach back to the Stone Age, pass through a handful of Roman remains and medieval art and on to the 19th century. Entrance is free on the first Tuesday of the month.

FREE Museu d'Art Jaume Morera
GALLERY

(☑973 70 04 19; Carrer Major 31; ⊙11am-2pm & 5-8pm Tue-Sat, 11am-2pm Sun) This impressive collection of Catalan art focuses particularly on work by Lleida-associated artists, such as the surrealist sculptures by Leandre Cristòfol, with excellent temporary photography exhibitions held here as well.

FREE Dipòsit del Pla de l'Aigua
HISTORIC SITE

(Carrer de Múrcia 10; ⊙11am-2pm Sat, Sun & holidays) Lleida's 18th-century engineering wonder long stored and supplied the city's drinking water via five public fountains. With 25 imposing stone pillars, it could hold nine million litres of water. No wonder they called it the Water Cathedral!

🛏 Sleeping & Eating

Lleida's light tourist traffic means few lodging options. Lleida is also Catalonia's snail (cargol)-eating capital: so many cargols are swallowed during the annual **Aplec del Cargol** (Snail Festival), held on a Sunday in early May, that some have to be imported.

Hotel Real
HOTEL €

(☑973 23 94 05; www.hotelrealleida.com; Avinguda de Blondel 22; s/d from €49/51; P❋🐾) A modern mid-rise place, business-oriented Hotel Real overlooks the river near the train and bus stations. The rooms are bright and clean; the better ones have generous balconies and all come with TV. Avoid street-facing rooms, though, as there's no soundproofing.

Alberg Sant Anastasi
HOSTEL €

(☑973 26 60 99; www.xanacat.cat; Rambla d'Aragó 11; dm from €18; ❋🐾) Central, efficiently run youth hostel with a plethora of perks and four-bed dorms. Over 30s are penalised by €4.

TOP CHOICE L'estel de la Mercè
CATALAN €€

(☑973 28 80 08; www.lesteldelamerce.com; Carrer Templers 19; menus from €35; ⊙lunch & dinner Wed-Sat, lunch Mon & Tue) This prolific mother-and-son team draws on its international experience to create beautiful fusion dishes using fresh seasonal produce. Feast on the likes of fig 'carpaccio' with foie gras, *risotto de bogavante* (lobster risotto) and cod loin with *butifarra negra* (black pudding) and finish off with strawberries flambéed with pepper.

El Celler del Roser
CATALAN €

(Carrer dels Cavallers 24; menus from €11.80; ⊙lunch & dinner Mon-Sat) This friendly local favourite specialises in slithery snail dishes (from €12.50), along with eight possible permutations of its award-winning *bacallá* (cod; from €18.40).

❶ Information

Centre d'Informació i Reserves (☑973 70 04 02; www.turismolleida.com; Carrer Major 31; ⊙10am-2pm & 4-7pm Mon-Sat, 10am-2pm Sun & holidays) Helpful Turisme de Lleida provides information about the city.

❶ Getting There & Away

From the bus station on Plaça de Sant Joan (20 minutes west of the train station along Avinguda de Blondel), daily services include Barcelona (€20, two to three hours, up to 14 daily); Vielha (€13, 2¾ hours, four to five daily); La Seu d'Urgell (€17, three hours, two daily); Poblet (€7.80, 1¼ hours, three daily except Sunday); and Tarragona (€18, two hours, three daily).

Up to 34 trains, ranging from slow regionals (3½ hours) to the high-speed AVE, run daily to/from Barcelona via Reus/Tarragona or Valls, taking from 58 minutes in the new Avant-class trains to 3¼ hours. Fares range from €11.90 to €47. AVE trains proceed to Madrid via Zaragoza (€80, 2¼ hours, nine daily).

COSTA DAURADA & AROUND

South of Barcelona stretches the Costa Daurada (Golden Coast), a series of mostly quiet resorts with unending broad beaches along a mainly flat coast, capped by the delta of the mighty Riu Ebre, which protrudes 20km out into the Mediterranean. Along the way is the lively gay-friendly beach town of Sitges, followed by the old Roman capital of Tarragona, and the modern extravaganza of Port Aventura – Catalonia's answer to EuroDisney. Inland lies Penedés, Catalonia's prime wine country.

Sitges

POP 28,620

Just 35km along the coast from Barcelona, this fishing-village-turned-pumping-beach-resort town has been a favourite with upper-class Barcelonians since the late 19th century, as well as a key location for the burgeoning Modernisme movement which paved the way for the likes of Picasso. The happy masses have been flooding in since

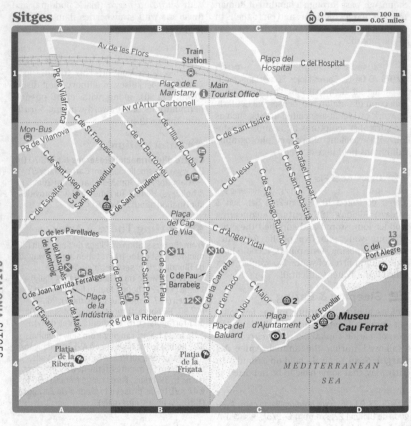

Sitges

◎ Top Sights
Museu Cau Ferrat D3

◎ Sights
1 Església de Sant Bartomeu i
Santa Tecla C4
2 Fundació Stämpfli Museu d'Art
Contemporani C3
3 Museu Maricel del Mar D4
4 Museu Romàntic A2

🛏 Sleeping
5 Hostal Bonaire B3

6 Hotel de la Renaixença B2
7 Hotel Romàntic B2
8 Parrots Hotel A3

🍴 Eating
9 Amor de Pintxo A3
10 eF & Gi C3
11 El Pou B3
12 La Nansa B3

🍷 Drinking
13 Bar Voramar D3

the 1960s – from day-tripping shoppers and clubbers to honeymooners and weekending families. A famous gay destination, in July and August Sitges turns into one big beach party with a nightlife to rival Ibiza; the beaches are long and sandy, the tapas bars prolific and the Carnaval bacchanalian.

◉ Sights & Activities

Beaches   BEACHES
The main beach is flanked by the attractive seafront Passeig Maritim, dotted with *chiringuitos* (beachside bars) and divided into nine sections with different names by a series of breakwaters. The Sant Sebastià, Balmins and D'aiguadolç beaches run east of the headland that's crowded with museums and graced by the striking Església de Sant Dartomeu i Santa Tecla. Though Bassa Rodona used to be the unofficial 'gay beach', gay sunbathers are now spread out pretty evenly, while Balmins is the sheltered bay favoured by nudists.

Museu Romàntic   MUSEUM
(Carrer de Sant Gaudenci 1; adult/student €3.50/2; ⊙9.30am-2pm & 4-/pm Tue-Sat, 10am-3pm Sun) Housed in late-18th-century Can Llopis mansion, the Museu Romàntic re-creates with its furnishings and dioramas the lifestyle of a 19th-century Catalan landowning family, the likes of which would often have made their money in dubious businesses, such as cotton raising using slave labour in South America, and were commonly dubbed Americanos or Indianos. Some of the odder objects include a porcelain violin, four-poster crib and a cross between a mini-piano and accordion. Upstairs is an entertaining collection of several hundred antique dolls, some downright creepy, some with haughty, petulant expressions and impossibly tiny waists.

Fundació Stämpfli Museu d'Art Contemporani   GALLERY
(www.fundacio-stampfli.org; Plaça Ajuntament; adult €3.50; ⊙9.30am-2pm & 4-7pm Fri & Sat, 10am-3pm Sun) This excellent new art gallery opened in late 2010, with a focus on 20th-century art from the 1960s onwards. The striking paintings and sculptures by artists from all over the world, spread throughout the two renovated historical buildings, include works by Richard 'Buddy' di Rosa, Oliver Mosset and Takis.

Museu Cau Ferrat   MUSEUM
(Carrer de Fonollar) Built in the 1890s as a house-cum-studio by artist Santiago Rusiñol – a pioneer of the Modernista movement who organised three groundbreaking art festivals in Sitges in the late 19th century – this whitewashed mansion is full of his own art and that of his contemporaries, including his friend Picasso, as well as a couple of El Grecos. The interior, with its exquisitely tiled walls and lofty arches, is enchanting. Under renovation at the time of writing, the museum was due to reopen by the end of 2012.

Museu Maricel del Mar   MUSEUM
(Carrer de Fonollar) With Catalan art, sculpture and handicrafts from the Middle Ages to the 20th century; due to reopen by the end of 2012.

✲ Festivals & Events

Carnaval   CARNIVAL
(www.sitges.com/carnaval) Carnaval in Sitges is a week-long booze-soaked riot made just for the extroverted and exhibitionist, complete with masked balls and capped by extravagant gay parades held on the Sunday and the Tuesday night, featuring flamboyantly dressed drag queens, giant sound systems and a wild all-night party with bars staying open until dawn. Held in February/March; dates change from year to year.

Festa Major   TOWN FESTIVAL
The town's Festa Major (Major Festival), held over six days fin mid-August in honour of Sitges' patron saint, features a huge fireworks display on the 23rd as well as numerous processions, *sardanes* (traditional dances) and fire-breathing beasts.

International Film Festival   FILM
(http://sitgesfilmfestival.com) Early October is a particular treat for fantasy-film buffs, as Sitges' International Film Festival is the best fantasy-film festival in the world.

🛏 Sleeping

Sitges has around 50 hotels and *hostales,* but many close from around October to April, then are full in July and August, when prices are at their highest and booking is advisable. Many are gay-friendly without being exclusively so. Gay travellers looking for accommodation in Sitges can try Throb (www.throb.co.uk). Amazingly, there's still no youth hostel.

CATALONIA SITGES

Hotel Romàntic
BOUTIQUE HOTEL €€

(☎93 894 83 75; www.hotelromantic.com; Carrer de Sant Isidre 33; s/d from €70/100; ❋) These three adjoining 19th-century villas are presented in sensuous Modernista style, with a leafy dining courtyard and friendly service, though the rooms are smallish and could do with sprucing up. Just around the corner is its charming sister hotel, **Hotel La Renaixença** (☎93 894 06 43; www.hotelromantic.com; Carrer d'Illa de Cuba 45; s/d from €70/100), which is actually better value.

Parrots Hotel
HOTEL €€

(☎93 894 13 50; www.parrots-group.com; Calle Joán Tarrida 16; s/d from €96/106; ❋🛜) It's hard to miss this bright-blue gay hotel; the thoroughly modern rooms come with cable TV and air-con (a godsend in summer), there are balconies for people-watching and a sauna to get steamy in.

Hostal Bonaire
PENSIÓN €€

(☎93 894 53 26; www.bonairehostalsitges.com; Carrer de Bonaire 31; d €65) Barely a stumble from the beach and with all sorts of fairly simple but perfectly comfortable rooms, this is a decent family-run budget option. Some rooms have balconies and all have their own bathroom. The singles, however, are very poky.

 Eating

A couple of local specialities to watch out for are *arròs a la sitgetana* (a brothy rice dish with meat and seafood) and *xató* (a green salad with cod, tuna, anchovies and olives with dressing containing garlic, almonds, hazelnuts, chilli pepper and more).

El Pou
TAPAS €€

(www.elpoudesitges.com; Carrer de Sant Pau 5; meals €30; ⊙lunch & dinner Wed-Mon) The tiny Wagyu beef burgers at this friendly gourmet tapas place are an absolute delight, and the rest doesn't lag far behind; the traditional *patatas bravas* sit alongside the likes of *mojama* (salted dried tuna) with almonds, fried aubergine and *xató*; the presentation delights the eye as much as the flavours delight the palate. We're in raptures and salivating in anticipation of our next visit.

eF & Gi
INTERNATIONAL €€

(www.efgirestaurant.com; Carrer Major 33; meals €35-50; ⊙dinner Tue-Sat mid-Jan–mid-Dec) Fabio and Greg (eF & Gi) are not afraid to experiment and the results are startlingly good: the mostly Mediterranean menu, with touches of Asian inspiration, throws out such delights as chargrilled beef infused with lemongrass and kaffir lime and tuna loin encrusted with peanuts and kalamata olives with mango chutney. Don't skip the dessert, either.

Amor de Pintxo
TAPAS €

(Carrer del Marquès de Montroig 8; meals €10; ⊙lunch & dinner Fri-Tue, lunch Wed Jan-Nov) This tapas bar certainly shows its love of the *pintxo*, its selection of delectable morsels ranging from the classis *jamón Serrano* sandwiches and stuffed peppers to tiny ceramic flying pans filled with chips and topped with a fried quail's egg. Five *pintxos* and a *caña* of beer go for €9.50.

La Nansa
SEAFOOD €€

(www.restaurantlanansa.com; Carrer de la Carreta 24; meals €37; ⊙lunch & dinner Thu-Mon, lunch only Wed, closed Jan) Cast just back from the town's waterfront and up a little lane in a fine old house is this seafood specialist, appropriately named after a fishing net. It does a great line in paella and other rice dishes, including a local speciality, *arròs a la sitgetana*.

🍷 Drinking & Entertainment

Much of Sitges' nightlife happens on one short pedestrian strip packed with humanity right through the night in summer: Carrer 1er de Maig aka Calle del Pecado (Sin Street), Plaça de la Indústria and Carrer del Marquès de Montroig, all in a short line off the seafront, though most bars shut by around 3.30am. All-night revellers are drawn to the clubs just outside of town.

L'Atlàntida Club
CLUB

(www.clubatlantida.com; Platja de Les Coves; ⊙Fri & Sat plus 2 more nights per week Jun-Sep) On hot summer nights, partygoers pack the large open-air dance floor at this Ibizaesque big mama of a beachside nightclub, about 3.5km west of the centre. A shuttle bus runs here from Platja de Sant Sebastià on those nights it's open.

Sweet Pachá Club
CLUB

(www.sweetpacha.com; Avinguda Port d'Aiguadolç 9) The white leather seats are perfect for a pause in between cocktail-fuelled sessions on the dance floor and there's a decent seafood restaurant for those wanting a quieter night. It's located just back from the Aiguadolç marina, 1.2km east along the coast from the Museu Maricel del Mar.

Bar Voramar   BAR
(www.pub-voramar.com; Carrer del Port Alegre 55)
On Platja de Sant Sebastià, Bar Voramar is
a 1960s throwback decked out like a ship
playing flamenco, jazz and more. Live music
some nights.

Pachá   CLUB
(www.pachasitges.com; Carrer de Sant Dídac,
Vallpineda; ⊗Fri & Sat) Guest DJ talent and
pumping bass heat up the two huge dance
floors at Sitges' original megaclub.

ⓘ Information

Main tourist office (☏93 894 42 51, www.
sitgestur.cat; Plaça de E Maristany 2; ⊗10am-
2pm & 4-6.30pm Mon-Sat, 10am-2pm Sun)

ⓘ Getting There & Away

A direct bus run by **Mon-Bus** (www.monbus.
cat) goes to Barcelona airport from Passeig de
Vilanova in Sitges.

From about 6am to 10pm four R2 *rodalies*
trains an hour run to Barcelona's Passeig de Gràcia and Estació Sants (€3.60, 27 to 46 minutes).

The best road from Barcelona to Sitges is the
C32 tollway.

Penedès Wine Country

Some of Spain's finest wines come from the
Penedès plains southwest of Barcelona. Most
of the grapes grown in Catalonia are native
to Spain and include the white *macabeo,
garnacha* and *xarel lo* (for white wines),
and the black *garnacha, monastrell* and
ull de llebre (hare's eye) red varieties. Foreign varieties (such as chardonnay, riesling,
chenin blanc, cabernet sauvignon, merlot
and pinot noir) are also widespread.

Sant Sadurní d'Anoia, located about a
half-hour train ride west of Barcelona, is
the capital of *cava*, a sparkling white wine
strongly reminiscent of champagne, though
less expensive and very popular in the United States, among other countries. Vilafranca
del Penedès, 12km further down the track, is
an attractive historical town and the heart
of the Penedès Denominación de Origen
(DO; Denomination of Origin) region, which
produces noteworthy light whites and some
reasonable reds, though nothing as famous
as Rioja.

What's the difference between *cava* and
champagne? Once you've tasted both, you
may be hard-pressed to tell the difference.
In fact, up until the 1980s, *cava* was known

as Catalan champagne, until prevented from
calling it such by the French Champagne
district, which did not – as some feared –
amount to disaster, but has instead allowed
the *cava* trade to grow and develop its own
identity, giving its French counterpart a run
for its money. '*Cava*' is Spanish for 'wine
cellar', but in this part of the country, it has
come to mean its contents.

SANT SADURNÍ D'ANOIA
POP 12,345

One hundred or so wineries around Sant
Sadurní produce 140 million bottles of *cava*
a year – something like 85% of the entire
national output. *Cava* is made by the same
method as French Champagne. If you happen to be in town in October, you may catch
the Mostra de Caves i Gastronomia, a
cava- and food-tasting fest.

VILAFRANCA DEL PENEDÈS
POP 39,225

Vilafranca is larger and more interesting
than Sant Sadurní, with appealing narrow
streets lined with medieval mansions. The
mainly Gothic Basílica de Santa Maria
(Plaça de Jaume I) stands at the heart of the
old town. Begun in 1285, it has been much
restored. There are sunset visits to the bell
tower in summer, complete with a glass of
cava; arrange at the tourist office.

The basílica faces the Museu de les Cultures del Vi de Catalunya (www.vinseum.
cat; Plaça de Jaume I 5; admission €5; ⊗10am-7pm
Tue-Sat, 10am-2pm Sun & holidays Jun Aug, shorter
hours rest of year) across Plaça de Jaume I.
Housed in a fine Gothic building, a combination of museums here covers local archaeology, art, geology and bird life, along with
an excellent section on wine.

A statue on Plaça de Jaume I pays tribute
to Vilafranca's famous *castellers,* who do
their thing during Vilafranca's lively Festa
Major (main annual festival) at the end of
August.

⌕ Tours

TOP CHOICE El Molí Tours   CYCLING, WINERY TOUR
(☏93 897 22 07; www.elmolitours.com; Torreles de
Foix) This highly recommended tour company, headed by the indomitable Paddy,
arranges all manner of tours of the wine
country – from luxury gourmet day tours
(€295) to numerous cycling options, which
as half-/full-day guided bike tours which
include lunch and *cava* sampling (€75/125),

IN SEARCH OF THE PERFECT TIPPLE

It's easier to get around the wine country if you have your own wheels, though several companies run tours of the wineries from Barcelona (which might be a better option, especially if you're intent on some serious wine sampling). Visitors are welcome to tour several of the region's wineries, though advance booking is essential in most places, as many wineries only open their doors to the public at limited times. The more enthusiastic ones will show you how wines and/or *cava* are made and finish off with a glass or two. Tours generally last about 1½ hours and some may only be in Catalan and/or Spanish. This list should get you started:

Codorníu (☎93 891 33 42; www.codorniu.es; Avinguda de Jaume Codorníu; ☺9am-5pm Mon-Fri, 9am-1pm Sat, Sun & holidays) The headquarters of Codorníu – Freixenet's biggest rival – are in a beautiful Modernista cellar at the entry to Sant Sadurní d'Anoia when coming by road from Barcelona. Manuel Raventós, head of this firm back in 1872, was the first Spaniard to be successful in producing sparkling wine by the Champagne method.

Freixenet (☎93 891 70 96; www.freixenet.com; Carrer de Joan Sala 2; adult/child 9-17yr €6.30/3.60; ☺1½hr tours 10am-1pm & 3-4.30pm Mon-Thu, 10am-1pm Fri-Sun) The biggest *cava*-producing company in the world, with an easily accessible cellar next to the Sant Sadurní train station. Visits include a tour of its 1920s cellar, a spin on the tourist train around the property and samples of its best *cava*. English, French and German spoken.

Giró Ribot (☎93 897 40 50; www.giroribot.es; Finca el Pont; tours per person €6; ☺9am-5pm Mon-Fri, 10am-2pm Sat & Sun) The magnificent farm buildings ooze centuries of tradition. These vintners use mostly local grape varieties to produce a limited range of fine *cava* and wines (including muscat). The times given are for the shop. To visit the cellars, call ahead.

Jean León (☎93 899 55 12; www.jeanleon.com; Pago Jean León; tours per person €6.50; ☺9.30am-5pm Mon-Fri, 9.30am-1pm Sat, Sun & holidays) Born in Santander as Ceferino Carrión in 1928, Jean León uses cabernet sauvignon and other grape types imported from prestigious vineyards in France to create a unique name in wines. Visits must be booked; English, French and German spoken.

Torres (☎93 817 74 87; www.torres.es; tours per person €6.50; ☺9am-5pm Mon-Sat, 9am-1pm Sun & holidays) About 3km northwest of Vilafranca on the BP-2121 near Pacs del Penedès, Torres' El Maset winery is home to the area's premier winemaker. The Torres family tradition dates from the 17th century, but the family company, in its present form, was founded in 1870; it revolutionised Spanish winemaking in the 1960s by introducing new temperature-controlled, stainless-steel technology and French grape varieties. Torres produces an array of reds and whites of all qualities, using many grape varieties, including chardonnay, sauvignon blanc, merlot, cabernet sauvignon, pinot noir and local ones such as *parellada*, *garnacha* and *tempranillo*.

If you taste buds are still not sated, you can search www.dopenedes.es and www.eno turismealtpenedes.net for more wine-tourism suggestions.

and EcoSubirats half-day bike tours (€30; weekends only).

Cellar Tours WINERY TOUR
(☎91 143 65 43; www.cellartours.com) One-week all-inclusive or tailor-made luxury tours of the top wineries in Penedés, as well as other parts of Catalonia and Spain. Prices depend on the number of people on the tour and style of accommodation.

Catalunya Bus Turístic WINERY TOUR
(www.catalunyabusturistic.com; Plaça de Catalunya; €61; ☺Mon, Wed, Fri & Sun) Day tours which include visits to three bodegas, cheese and wine matching and tapas.

✗ Eating

While there is no need to stay in Vilafranca, eating is another story altogether. **Cal Ton** (www.restaurantcalton.com; Carrer Casal 8; meals €50; ☺lunch & dinner Wed-Sat, lunch Tue & Sun, closed Easter and most of Aug) is one of several enticing options in town. Hidden away down a narrow side street, Cal Ton has crisp, modern decor and offers inventive Mediterranean cuisine with a touch of oriental influence – all washed down with local wines.

ⓘ Information

Tourist office (☎93 818 12 54; www.turisme vilafranca.com; Carrer de la Cort 14; ⊙4-7pm Mon, 9am-1pm & 4-7pm Tue-Sat, 10am-1pm Sun) Can provide tips on visiting some of the smaller wineries in the area.

ⓘ Getting There & Away

Up to three *rodalies* trains per hour run from Estació Sants Barcelona to Sant Sadurní (€3.20, 45 minutes) and Vilafranca (€3.90, 55 minutes). By car, take the AP7 and follow the exit signs.

Tarragona

POP 140,180

The eternally sunny port city of Tarragona is a fascinating mix of Mediterranean beach life, Roman history and medieval alleyways. Easily Catalonia's most important Roman site, Tarragona's number-one attraction is its seaside-facing Roman amphitheatre. The town's medieval heart is one of the most beautifully designed in Spain, its maze of narrow cobbled streets encircled by steep walls and crowned with a splendid cathedral and its sandstone buildings seemingly suffused with golden light. Add into the mix plenty of tempting food options and an array of bars heaving into the wee hours and you get the most exciting urban centre in southern Catalonia.

History

Tarragona was first occupied by the Romans, who called it Tàrraco, in 218 BC; prior to that the area was first settled by Iberians, followed by Carthagians. Scipio launched his successful military endeavours from here and in 27 BC Augustus made it the capital of his new Tarraconensis province (roughly all modern Spain) and stayed until 25 BC, directing campaigns in Cantabria and Asturias. During its Roman heyday Tarragona was home to over 200,000 people (more than its current population) and, though abandoned when the Muslims arrived in AD 714, the city was reborn as the seat of a Christian archbishopric in 1089. Today, the city's lovely old quarter, studded with a wealth of Roman ruins, offsets the unprettyness of Catalonia's second-largest port.

◉ Sights

The tourist office dishes out three handy booklets detailing routes around the city taking in Roman, medieval and Modernista sites.

Museu d'Història de Tarragona RUINS
(MHT; www.museutgn.com; adult/child per site €3/ free, all MHT sites €10/free; ⊙9am-9pm daily Easter-Sep, shorter hours rest of year) The 'museum' title is somewhat misleading, as this is in fact four separate Roman sites (which since 2000 together have constituted a Unesco World Heritage site), including the museum.

Start exploring with the **Pretori i Circ Romans** (Plaça del Rei), which includes part of the vaults of the Roman circus, where chariot races were once held, ending at the Pretori tower on Plaça de Rei. The circus, 300m long, stretched from here to beyond Plaça de la Font to the west. Nearby Plaça del Fòrum was the location of the provincial forum and political heart of Tarraconensis province.

Near the beach is the crown jewel of Tarragona's Roman sites, the well-preserved **Amfiteatre Romà** (Plaça d'Arce Ochotorena; ⊙9am-9pm Tue-Sat, 9am-3pm Sun Easter-Sep, 9am-5pm Tue-Sat, 10am-3pm Sun & holidays Oct-Easter), where gladiators battled either each other or wild animals to the death. In its arena are the remains of 6th- and 12th-century churches built to commemorate the martyrdom of the Christian bishop Fructuosus and two deacons, who, they say, were burnt alive here in AD 259. Much of amphitheatre was picked to bits, the stone used to build the port, so what you see now is a partial reconstruction.

The northwest half of **Fòrum Romà** (Carrer del Cardenal Cervantes) was occupied by a judicial basilica (where legal disputes were settled), from where the rest of the forum stretched downhill to the southwest. Linked to the site by a footbridge is another excavated area, which includes a stretch of Roman street. The discovery in 2006 of remains of the foundations of a temple to Jupiter, Juno and Minerva (the major triumvirate of gods at the time of the Roman republic) suggests the forum was much bigger and more important than had previously been assumed.

TARRAGO!NA CARD

The 48-hour **Tarrago!na Card** (€15), available from the tourist office and various hotels, gives you free access to all of the city's museums and free travel on local buses, as well as discounts in select restaurants and shops.

CATALONIA TARRAGONA

Tarragona

200 m
0.1 miles

To Camping Las Palmeras (400m)

Mediterranean Sea

Catedral
Museu Diocesà
Entrance to Catedral
Cloister
Catedral

C de Sant Pau
C de les Coques
C de Sant Llorenç
C Granada
Pg de Sant Antoni
C del Nou Patriarca
Plaça del Fòrum

Pla de Palau
Pla de la Seu

C de la Civaderia
C Major
C Ruidecòls
C Cuirateries
C de la Nau

Plaça del Rei

Pretori i Circ Romans
Museu Nacional Arqueològic de Tarragona
Via Augusta
Tourist Information Kiosk

Plaça d'Arce Ochotorena
Balcó Bus to Beaches

Platja del Miracle

Pg Marítim Rafael de Casanovas

Amfiteatre Romà

Pg de les Palmeres

To Train Station (300m)

Camp de Mart

Tourist Information Kiosk

Av de Maria Cristina

Via de l'Imperi Romà

C Cavallers
C de Sant Domènec

Plaça de la Font

Rambla Vella

C Portalet
C de Sant Agustí
C de Girona

C Roger de Llúria

C d'Adrià

Av de Catalunya

C d'Assalt
C Comte de Rius
C d'August

Tourist Information Kiosk

C de Pin i Soler

C d'Estanislau Figueres

Av de Pau Casals

C de Rovira i Virgili

Rambla Nova

Regional Tourist Office

Plaça de Corsini

C del Governador González

C Reding
C de la Unió

Forum Romà

C del Cardenal Cervantes

C de Soler II

Av de Ramon i Cajal

To Necròpolis Paleocristians (1km)

Av Prat de la Riba

Plaça Ponent

To El Varadero (400m)

Tarragona

Museu Nacional Arqueològic de Tarragona   MUSEUM
(www.mnat.es; Plaça del Rei 5; adult/child €3.50/free; ⊙10am-8pm Tue-Sat, 10am-2pm Sun & holidays Jun-Sep, shorter hours rest of year) This excellent museum does justice to the cultural and material wealth of Roman Tarraco. Well-laid-out exhibits include part of the Roman city walls, frescoes, sculpture and pottery. The mosaic collection traces the changing trends from the simple black-and-white designs to complex full-colour creations; a highlight is the large, almost complete *Mosaic de Peixos de la Pineda*, showing fish and sea creatures. In the section on everyday arts you can admire ancient fertility aids, including an outsized stone penis, symbol of the god Priapus.

Necrópolis Paleocristians   RUINS
(www.mnat.cat; Avinguda de Ramón i Cajal 80; adult/child €2.40/free; ⊙9am-8.30pm Tue-Sat, 10am-2pm Sun Jun-Sep, shorter hours rest of year) Only found in 1923 during the construction of the tobacco factory, this vast Roman-Christian city of the dead consists of over 2000 elaborate tombs. It's estimated that this burial ground on Passeig de la Independéncia, on the western edge of town, was used from the 3rd century AD, thus attesting to Rome's conversion to Christianity. While you can only look at the tombs through the fence, the museum features curious funereal objects and sarcophagi. Entry is free if you have already purchased a ticket to the Museu Nacional Arqueològic de Tarragona.

Catedral   CATHEDRAL
(Pla de la Seu; adult/child €4/1.40; ⊙10am-7pm Mon-Sat Junmid-Oct, shorter hours rest of year) Sitting grandly at the top of the old town, Tarragona's cathedral has been undergoing a major facelift for some time (although it's scheduled to be finished in 2012), though the cloisters and museum alone are a worth a peek. Built on the site of a Roman temple, the length of its construction (from 1171 to 1331) has endowed it with both Romanesque and Gothic features, as typified by the main facade on Pla de la Seu, and its fortress-like exterior betrays fears of the Moors.

The cloister has Gothic vaulting and Romanesque carved capitals, one of which shows rats conducting what they imagine to be a cat's funeral...until the cat comes back to life! It's a lesson about passions seemingly lying dormant until they reveal themselves.

The rooms off the cloister house the **Museu Diocesá**, with an extensive collection extending from Roman hairpins to some lovely 12th- to 14th-century polychrome woodcarvings of a breastfeeding Virgin.

The interior of the cathedral, over 100m long, is Romanesque at the northeastern end and Gothic at the southwest. The arm of St Thecla, Tarragona's patron saint, is normally kept in the **Capella de Santa Thecla** on the southeastern side, while the marble main **altar** was carved in the 13th century with scenes from the life of St Thecla.

Pont del Diable   RUIN
The so-called Devil's Bridge is actually the **Aqüeducte de les Ferreres**, a marvel left by the Romans and an irrigation engineer's wet dream. Its most intact section sits 4km away from the centre, in the leafy rough just off the AP7 freeway, which leads into Tarragona. It is a fine stretch of a two-tiered aqueduct (217m long and 27m high); in its glory days, it delivered water to over 200,000 people from the Riu Gayo, 32km away. Bus 5 to Sant Salvador from Plaça Imperial de Tàrraco, running every 20 minutes until 10.45pm,

CATALONIA TARRAGONA

will take you to the vicinity, or park in one of the lay-bys marked on either side of the AP7, just outside the freeway toll gates.

Passeig Arqueològic Muralles HISTORIC SITE
(admission €3; ⏰9am-9pm Tue-Sat, 9am-3pm Sun Easter-Oct, shorter hours rest of year) The Passeig Arqueològic is a peaceful walk around part of the perimeter of the old town between two lines of city walls; the inner ones are mainly Roman and date back to the 3rd century BC, while the outer ones were put up by the British in 1709 during the War of the Spanish Succession. Prepare to be awed by the vast gateways built by the Iberians and clamber up onto the battlements from the doorway to the right of the entrance for all-encompassing views of the city. The walk starts from the Portal del Roser on Avenida Catalunya.

🛏 Sleeping

Hotel Plaça de la Font HOTEL €€
(📞977 24 61 34; www.hotelpdelafont.com; Plaça de la Font 26; s/d €55/70; ❄) Simple, spic-and-span rooms overlooking a bustling terrace in a you-can't-get-more-central-than-this location, right on the popular Plaça de la Font. If there's no room at the inn, the sister **Hostal La Noria** (📞977 23 87 17; Plaça de la Font 53; s/d €30/48), also on the plaza, has a selection of compact, spartan singles and doubles.

Hotel Lauria HOTEL €€
(📞977 23 67 12; www.hotel-lauria.com; Rambla Nova 20; s/d from €49/69; 🅿❄🛜🏊) In the newer part of town, a five-minute walk from the medieval part, this smart hotel of-fers modern rooms with welcome splashes of colour and large bathrooms and a small swimming pool. The rooms at the back are less exposed to the noise from the *rambla*.

Camping Las Palmeras CAMPGROUND €
(📞977 20 80 81; www.laspalmeras.com; sites per 2-person tent & car €40-50, tent €11; 🅿🛜🏊) This cheerful camping ground lies 3km north-east of Tarragona; perks include a big pool amidst leafy parkland just back from the beach and untouched coastal woodland nearby. Windsurfing and kitesurfing classes are also on offer.

🍴 Eating

The quintessential Tarragona seafood experience can be had in **Serrallo**, the town's fishing port. About a dozen bars and restaurants here sell the day's catch, and on summer weekends in particular the place is packed.

Arcs Restaurant MEDITERRANEAN €€
(📞977 21 80 40; www.restaurantarcs.com; Carrer Misser Sitges 13; menus €23; ⏰lunch & dinner Tue-Sat) Inside a medieval cavern with bright splashes of colour in the form of contemporary art, you are served some wonderful takes on Mediterranean dishes – from *tartar de atún* (tuna carpaccio) and the inspired pumpkin soup with *morcilla* (black pudding) and goat's cheese to the most intense *salmorejo* (a thicker, more savoury gazpacho) outside Andalucía.

WORTH A TRIP

REUS – THE BIRTHPLACE OF GAUDÍ

The compact city of Reus, 14km west of Tarragona, beckons art nouveau aficionados with its collection of handsome Modernista mansions; the **tourist office** (📞972 30 02 28; www.turismepalafrugell.org; Carrer del Carrilet 2; ⏰9am-9pm Mon-Sat, 10am-1pm Sun Jul-Aug, shorter hours rest of year) can provide a map guiding you to the 30-odd buildings which make up the Ruta de Modernisme and can also organise guided visits (sometimes in English and French) to some of the most interesting of these houses, for which you need to book in advance.

Though Antoni Gaudí was born here in 1852, there are no Gaudí buildings in the city, though the superb **Gaudí Centre** (www.gaudicentre.com; Plaça del Mercadal; adult/child under 7/senior €7/free/4; ⏰10am-8pm Mon-Sat, 11am-2pm Sun Jun-Sep, shorter hours rest of year; ♿) gives you a thorough introduction to the man and his work – from his designs to his influence on architecture around the world – through its engaging audiovisual, sensory and hands-on displays; its prize possession is the only surviving handwritten Gaudí notebook.

Regular trains connect Reus with Tarragona (€2.50, 15 to 20 minutes).

CATALUNYA'S HUMAN CASTLES

One of the strangest things you'll see in Catalonia are *castells*, or human 'castles' – a sport which originated in Valls, near Tarragona, in the 18th century and which has spread to other parts of Catalonia since. It involves teams of *castellers* standing on each other's shoulders with a death-defying child scrambling up the side of the human tower to perch precariously at the top as the final touch before the whole structure gracefully disassembles itself; the highest 'tower' so far has been 10 stories tall. Don't try this at home! For the most spectacular *castells*, pay a visit to Tarragona's Festival de Santa Tecla in mid-September.

Aq
CATALAN €€
(☎977 21 59 54; www.aq-restaurant.com; Carrer de les Coques 7; menus from €18; ⊙lunch & dinner Tue-Sat) This is a bubbly designer haunt with stark colour contrasts (black, lemon and cream linen), slick lines and intriguing plays on traditional cooking, such as *ventresca de tonyina amb ceba caramelitzada, tomáquet, formatge de cabra i olives* (tuna belly meat with caramelised onion, tomato, goat's cheese and olives).

El Palau del Baró
CATALAN €€
(☎977 24 14 64; Carrer de Santa Anna 3; meals €35-45, menus €15-18; ⊙lunch & dinner Tue-Sat, lunch Sun) The Baron's Palace provides a romantic, sumptuous 18th-century mansion setting. Dishes are served with aplomb, and range from paella and *arròs negre* to the likes of the sublime grilled *llom de tonyina fresca* (seared tuna steak).

El Varadero
SEAFOOD €
(Carrer de Trafalgar 13; raciones €7-9; ⊙lunch & dinner) This informal spot has locals lining up for the simple, mouth-wateringly delicious seafood dishes, which might include *tigres* (stuffed, breaded and fried mussels), *ostrón* (fat oyster) and *cigalas a la plancha* (grilled crayfish).

🍷 Drinking & Entertainment

The bars and clubs along the waterfront at the Port Esportiu (marina), and in some of the streets in front of the train station, such

as along Carrer de la Pau del Protectorat, are the main concentration of nightlife. Soho (Calle de San Martín 49); at the marina, spins a chilled-out jazzy selection of tunes, while Groove Bar (Carrer del Cardenál Cervantes 4) plays a good mix of funk, soul and more, with frequent guest DJ appearances.

El Candil
BAR, CAFE
(Plaça de la Font 13; hot chocolate €3; ⊙11am-3pm & 5pm-midnight) Over 30 different hot chocolate combinations on the menu at this cave-like cafe-bar, as well as a good selection of beers and *cava* for its nocturnal transformation into a cellar bar.

❶ Information
Tourist office (☎977 25 07 95; www.tarragonaturisme.es; Carrer Major 39; ⊙10am-9pm Mon-Sat, 10am-2pm Sun Jul-Sep, shorter hours rest of year) Good place for booking guided tours of the city.

❶ Getting There & Away
The bus station is 1.5km northwest of the old town along Rambla Nova, at Plaça Imperial Tarraco. Destinations include Barcelona (€8.10, 1½ hours, 16 daily), Lleida (€10.70, 1¾ hours, five daily) and Valencia (€20.20, 3½ hours, seven daily).

The local train station is a 10-minute walk along the waterfront to the old town while the faster AVE trains arrive at the swanky Camp de Tarragona station, a 15-minute taxi ride from the centre. Departures include Barcelona (€15.90 to €35.10, 35 minutes to 1½ hours, every 30 minutes); Lleida (€7 to €22, 25 minutes to 1¾ hours, 12 daily) and Valencia (€20.30 to €37.30, two to 3½ hours, 13 daily).

Port Aventura

One of Spain's most popular amusement parks, as well as Europe's largest, Port Aventura (www.portaventura.com; adult/child €44/38; ⊙10am-7pm Jul & Aug, shorter hours rest of year) lies 7km west of Tarragona. The park has plenty of spine-tingling rides and other attractions, including 'fun' rides such as the Furius Baco (in which they claim you experience the fastest acceleration of any ride in the world).

The complex also includes Caribe Aquatic Park (adult/child & senior €22/20; ⊙10am-7pm Jul & Aug, shorter hours rest of year), a water-world with ominously named wet rides, such as the Triángulo de las Bermudas

THE BATTLE FOR CATALONIA

The Spanish Civil War may only have lasted three years (1936–39) but its scars linger well into the present and you'll be hard-pressed to find a family in Catalonia, or indeed Spain, which hasn't been affected by the conflict. The largest battle of the war was fought in the Ebro Valley, leading to the destruction of the town of Corbera, and a crushing defeat of the Republicans, with a loss of around 100,000 soldiers on the losing side alone.

North of Tortosa along the C12 and then the C43 lies the town of Gandesa, home to the recently restored Centre d'Estudis de la Batalla de l'Ebre (www.usuaris.tinet. cat/cebe/; Avinguda Catalunya 3-5, Ap C4; entry by donation; ⊙3.15-5.45pm Tue, 10am-1pm & 3.15-5.45 Wed-Fri, 10.30-2pm & 3.15-8pm Sat, 10.30am-2pm Sun), an excellent museum which presents a balanced account of the civil war and the decisive battle in the Ebro Valley through a host of artefacts, photographs and interactive maps. The moving video interviews with those who lived through the horrors of the war are a recent development; the 'pact of forgetfulness' after Franco's death in 1975 meant that the victims of the dictatorship continued to endure past abuses in silence until the last few years in a country where there has not been any formal postwar reconciliation.

and Barracudas, which include some fear-inducing water slides.

Trains run to Port Aventura's own station, about a 1km walk from the site, several times a day from Tarragona (€2.20 to €12.10, seven minutes) and Barcelona (from €9.20 to €20.60, around 1½ hours). By road, take exit 35 from the AP7, or the N340 from Tarragona.

Tortosa

POP 34,430

Towering over this somewhat dusty inland town is a castle complex built by the Muslims when Tortosa, which was first settled by Iberian tribes more than 2000 years ago, was on the front line between the medieval Christian and Muslim Spain. The old town, concentrated at the western end of the city, north of the Ebro, is watched over by the imposing Castell de la Suda, where a small medieval Arab cemetery has been unearthed and in whose grounds there now stands a splurge-worthy parador (☏977 44 44 50; www.parador.es; d from €100; P❄☷☕) for those who wish to stay in luxurious medieval surroundings. The Gothic Catedral de Santa Maria (Carrer Portal del Palau; ⊙10am-1.30pm & 4.30-7pm Mon-Sat, 12.30-2pm Sun) dates back to 1347 and contains a pleasant cloister and some baroque additions.

More recently, Tortosa was also on the front line between Nationalists and Republicans during the civil war and the site of an epic battle which wrecked much of its medieval centre and cost over 35,000 lives – the loss commemorated by a metal monument in the centre of the river flowing through the town.

The tourist office (☏977 44 20 05; www.tortosaturisme.com; Jardins del Príncep; ⊙10am-1.30pm & 4.30-7.30pm Tue-Sat, 11am-1.30pm Sun May-Sep, shorter hours rest of year) is inside the lovely Jardins del Príncep (adult/child €3/2; ⊙same hours as tourist office), which is filled with sculptures and shady trees and makes a perfect place for a stroll (although the slopes are pretty steep!).

Hostal Virginia (☏977 44 41 86; www.hotelvirginia.net; Avinguda de la Generalitat 139; s/d €24/42) is a cheerful, central stop, with modern, bright rooms boasting good-sized beds and cool tile floors. For food you could do worse than tuck into one of the lunch menús (€14) at the Restaurant Los Banys (Pare Cirera 5) or at the parador.

The train and bus stations are opposite each other on Ronda dels Docs. It's easiest to get here by train from Tarragona (€7.10, 1¼ hours).

Delta de L'Ebre

The delta of the Río Ebre, formed by silt brought down by the river, sticks out 20km into the Mediterranean near Catalonia's southern border. Dotted with reedy lagoons and fringed by dune-backed beaches, this completely flat and exposed wetland, with Parc Natural Delta de l'Ebre comprising 77 sq km, is northern Spain's most important water-bird habitat. The migration season (October and November) sees the bird population peak, with an average of 53,000 ducks and 15,000 coots, but they are also numerous in winter and spring: 10% of all water birds wintering on the Iberian Peninsula choose to park themselves here.

Even if you're not a twitcher, a visit here is worthwhile for the surreal landscapes alone. Tiny whitewashed farmhouses seem to float on tiny islands among green and brown paddy fields – responsible for most of Catalonia's rice – which stretch to the horizon. It's completely unlike anywhere else in Catalonia.

The town of Deltebre straggles along the northern bank of the river at the centre of the delta and makes for a good starting point, facing Sant Jaume d'Enveja across the river and connected to other villages in the delta by a network of roads.

◉ Sights & Activities

Birdwatching
BIRDWATCHING

Early morning and evening are the best times for birdwatching, and good areas include L'Encanyissada and La Tancada lagoons and Punta de la Banya, all in the south of the delta. L'Encanyissada has two observation towers and La Tancada one (others are marked on a map you can pick up at the Centre d'Informació). La Tancada and Punta de la Banya are generally the best places to see the greater flamingos, the delta's most spectacular birds. Almost 2000 of the birds nest here, and since 1992 the delta has been one of only five places in Europe where they reproduce. Punta de la Banya is joined to the delta by a 5km sand spit with the long, sandy, and often windy and rubbish-splattered Platja de l'Eucaliptus at its northern end.

Ecomuseu
MUSEUM

(Carrer de Martí Buera 22; admission €1.50; ⊙10am-2pm & 3-7pm Mon-Sat, 10am-2pm Sun May-Sep, shorter hours rest of year) A fantastic introduction to the strange world of the delta, this museum walks you through the traditional trades, such as fishing and rice cultivation, while the extensive garden shows off a vast array of local plants and the aquarium – the museum's highlight – puts the spotlight on the delta's freshwater denizens, which include what looks like the missing link between a fish and an amphibian.

Boat Trips
BOAT TOUR

Several companies based in Deltebre run identical daily tourist boat trips (€10 per person, 1½ hours) to the mouths of the Ebro and the delta's tip. The frequency of departures depends on the season (and whether or not there are enough takers).

In El Poblenou del Delta, visit Mas de la Cuixota (✆977 26 12 25; http://ebre.info/cuixota; Partida de l'Encanyissada). It rents out binoculars for birdwatching and runs organised trips along the delta canals in traditional, pole-propelled barques de perxar (shallow-bottom boats).

Cycling
CYCLING

Cycling is an excellent way of exploring the delta, with recommended bike routes (pick up brochures at the tourist information centre) ranging from 7km to 43km. The 26km Lagoon Route is particularly good for birdwatchers, while the 7km Family Route takes in several viewpoints along the river, as well as the rice paddies around Riumar – the coastal village at the delta's easternmost point. Bicycles can be rented both at Deltebre and Riumar.

🛏 Sleeping & Eating

Several camping grounds are scattered about Deltebre and Riumar, 10km east of Deltebre, along with a sprinkling of low-key hotels and a fair few casas rurales in

TAKING THE BULLS BY THE HORNS

Many Catalans advertise their loathing of bullfighting (or loathing of Spanish traditions!) – and indeed that loathing became official from 2012 when Catalonia banned bullfighting altogether – but some may not be aware that in the southern corner of their region, locals have indulged in their own summer bovine torment. In Amposta and neighbouring towns, people celebrate bous capllaçats and bous embolats, the former a kind of tug-of-war between a bull with ropes tied to its horns and townsfolk, the latter involving bulls running around with flaming torches attached to their horns. Denounced by animal rights groups, they are allowed by the Catalan government, which recognises the right to hold these events because of their long history and the fact that the bulls are not killed.

the countryside. All the main villages offer simple eating options (and some gourmet ones!); one of the regional specialities is delta rice with wild duck.

TOP CHOICE Mas del Tancat
CASA RURAL €

(☑656 90 10 14; www.ebreguia.com/masdeltancat; Camí dels Panissos; d €60; P✳🛜) A converted historic farmhouse, Mas del Tancat has just five rooms with iron bedsteads, terracotta floors and a warm welcome. Sitting by the waters of the delta, with farm animals wandering through the grounds, it is a tranquil escape and excellent home-cooked dinners are available on request. It's between the town of Ampara and the village of Sant Jaume d'Enveja; call ahead for directions.

Camping Riumar
CAMPGROUND €

(☑636 05 68 80; www.camping-riumar.com; Riumar; site per 2-person tent €12.50; P🏊) Large, lively campsite near the water, with a plethora of facilities and cute chalet-style four-/six-person bungalows available for those who don't wish to rough it. Swimming pool, billiards and table football keep you entertained and there's a shop and restaurant on site, too.

TOP CHOICE Mas Prades
CATALAN €€

(☑977 05 90 84; Carretera T-340, Km 8; menus €30) Gourmets come all the way down from Barcelona to this revamped country house to sample its superb delta cuisine. The five-course gut-busting lunch *menú* is great value for money and allows you to sample the tiny tender local mussels and baby squid, as well as the classic *arrós d'anec al foc de llenya* (delta rice with wild duck), finishing off with the sublime *crema catalana*.

Casa Núri
SEAFOOD €€

(☑977 48 01 28; Final Goles de Ebre, Riumar; meals €35-45, menus €15-18; ⊙10am-10pm) Locals fill this waterfront place, thanks to its reputation for superb local seafood and rice dishes. Try the signature *arroz á banda* (seafood rice).

❶ Information

The main **Centre d'Informació** (☑977 48 96 79; Carrer de Martí Buera 22; ⊙10am-2pm & 3-7pm Mon-Sat, 10am-2pm Sun May-Sep, shorter hours rest of year) is combined with the Ecomuseu (p367). Pick up maps of the region and brochures on cycle routes here. The Editorial Alpina map E-50 is particularly helpful.

❶ Getting There & Away

The delta is easiest to get to and around with your own wheels.

Aragón

Why Go?

Landlocked and little-known, Aragón is one of Spain's most surprising regions. It's in Aragón that the Pyrenees take on an epic quality, from shapely peaks to deep, deep valleys where quiet rivers meander through forests and past small hamlets that seem unchanged by the passing of time. Stone-built *pueblos* (villages) such as these are an Aragonese speciality: all across Aragón, you'll find numerous candidates for the title of Spain's most beautiful village. Connections to the past also overflow from the cities, whether in Mudéjar Teruel or in Zaragoza, a city bursting with sound and fury yet replete with soaring monuments to Roman, Islamic and Christian Spain. There are also world-class activities – hiking, canyoning and skiing – for those eager to explore the region under their own steam. But Aragón's calling card is its sense of timelessness, the sort of place where Old Spain lives and breathes.

Best Places to Eat

» Tiempo de Ensueño (p404)
» La Tasca de Ana (p385)
» Restaurante El Duende (p389)
» Restaurante Callizo (p390)
» La Cocina del Principal (p381)

Best Places to Stay

» Casa de San Martín (p389)
» Hotel los Siete Reyes (p390)
» Parador de Sos del Rey Católico (p380)
» La Casa del Tío Americano (p403)
» Hotel Barosse (p385)

When to Go
Zaragoza

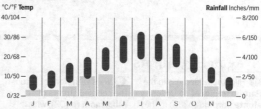

Feb Teruel's Fiesta Medieval returns you to the Middle Ages.

Mid-Jun–early Sep The best time to hike the high country of the Aragonese Pyrenees.

Oct Zaragoza's Fiestas del Pilar combine the sacred with the city's famed love of revelry.

Aragón Highlights

1 Hike the wilderness in the **Parque Nacional de Ordesa y Monte Perdido** (p386) in the Pyrenees

2 Return to the medieval past in the stone-built villages of **Aínsa** (p389) and **Sos del Rey Católico** (p380) in the foothills of the Pyrenees

3 Walk with wonder through the cobbled streets of **Albarracín** (p402), with its epic reminders of the Islamic past

4 Hit the buzzing streets and bars of **Zaragoza** (p371) by night and visit its glorious monuments by day

5 Savour the Mudéjar architecture and wafer-thin perfection of the best *jamón* (ham) from **Teruel** (p399)

6 Go quietly through the beautiful Pyrenean valleys of **Echo** (p381) and **Ansó** (p382)

7 Plunge down the canyons any way you can in **Alquézar** (p394)

ZARAGOZA

POP 674,730

Zaragoza (Saragossa) rocks and rolls. The feisty citizens of this great city, on the banks of the mighty Río Ebro, make up over half of Aragón's population and they live a fairly hectic lifestyle with great tapas bars and raucous nightlife. But Zaragoza is so much more than just a city that loves to live the good life: it also has a host of historical sights spanning all the great civilisations that have left their indelible mark on the Spanish soul.

History

The Romans founded Caesaraugusta (from which 'Zaragoza' is derived – listen to its pronunciation and you'll see what we mean) in 14 BC. As many as 25,000 people migrated to the city whose river traffic brought the known world to the banks of Río Ebro. The city prospered for almost three centuries, but its subsequent decline was confirmed in 472 when the city was overrun by the Visigoths. In Islamic times Zaragoza was capital of the Upper March, one of Al-Andalus' frontier territories. In 1118 it fell to Alfonso I 'El Batallador' (The Battler), ruler of the expanding Christian kingdom of Aragón, and immediately became its capital. In the centuries that followed, Zaragoza grew to become one of inland Spain's most important economic and cultural hubs and a city popular with Catholic pilgrims. It is now Spain's fifth-largest city.

Sights

The great eras of the city's colourful history – Roman, Islamic and Christian – all left enduring monuments in Zaragoza.

CHRISTIAN ZARAGOZA

FREE Basílica de Nuestra Señora del Pilar CHURCH

(Plaza del Pilar; lift admission €2; 7am-8.30pm, lift 10am-1.30pm & 4-6.30pm Tue-Sun) Brace yourself for the saintly and the solemn in this great baroque cavern of Catholicism. The faithful believe that it was here on 2 January AD 40 that Santiago (St James the Apostle) saw the Virgin Mary descend atop a marble *pilar* (pillar). A chapel was built around the remaining *pilar*, followed by a series of ever-more-grandiose churches, culminating in the enormous basilica that you see today. Originally designed in 1681 by Felipe Sánchez y Herrera, it was greatly modified in the 18th century by the heavier hand of Ventura Rodríguez. The exterior is another story altogether, its splendid main dome lording over a flurry of 10 mini-domes, each encased in chunky blue, green, yellow and white tiles, creating a muscular Byzantine effect.

The legendary **pilar** is hidden in the Capilla Santa, inside the east end of the basilica. A tiny oval-shaped portion of the *pilar* is exposed on the chapel's outer west side. A steady stream of people line up to brush lips with its polished and seamed cheek, which even popes have air-kissed. Parents also line up from 1.30pm to 2pm and from 6.30pm to 7.30pm to have their babies blessed next to the Virgin. More than the architecture, these symbols of the sacred, and the devotion they inspire in the faithful, are what makes this cathedral special.

Hung from the northeast column of the Capilla Santa are two wickedly slim shells that were lobbed at the church during the civil war. They failed to explode. A miracle, said the faithful; typical Czech munitions, said the more cynical.

The basilica's finest artwork is a 16th-century alabaster altarpiece by Damián Forment. It stands at the outer west wall of the choir. Goya painted *La reina de los mártires* (Mary, Queen of Martyrs) in a cupola above the north aisle, outside the Sacristía de la Virgen.

A **lift** whisks you most of the way up the north tower (Torre Pilar) from where you climb to a superb viewpoint over the domes and downtown Zaragoza.

La Seo CHURCH

(Catedral de San Salvador; Plaza de la Seo; admission €4; 10am-6pm Tue-Fri, 10am-2pm & 3-6pm Sat, 10-11.30am & 2.30-6pm Sun Jun-Sep) Dominating the eastern end of Plaza del Pilar is the Catedral de San Salvador, more popularly known as La Seo. Built between the 12th and 17th centuries, it displays a fabulous spread of architectural styles from Romanesque to baroque – it's Zaragoza's finest example of Christian architecture. It stands on the site of Islamic Zaragoza's main mosque

> **BOOKING ARAGÓN**
>
> The website www.visitaragon.es is a good resource if you want to plan your trip around Aragón without having to make the bookings yourself.

Zaragoza

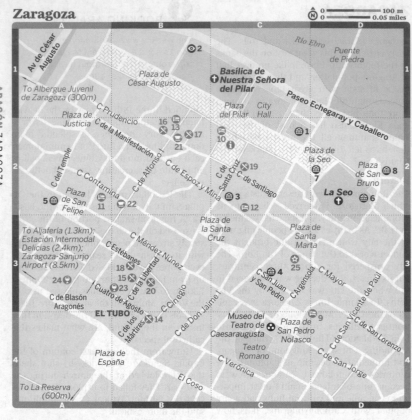

Zaragoza

(which in turn stood upon the temple of the Roman forum). The northwest facade is a Mudéjar masterpiece, deploying classic dark brickwork and colourful ceramic decoration in eye-pleasing geometric patterns. All the chapels are framed by beautiful stonework and ring the changes from the eerie solemnity of the Capilla de San Marcos to the glorious Renaissance facade of the central Christ Chapel and the exquisite 15th-century high altarpiece in polychrome alabaster.

The admission price includes entry to La Seo's **Museo de Tapices** (Plaza de la Sao; admission €2; ⊗10am-8.30pm Tue-Sun Jun-Sep, shorter hours rest of year), an impressive collection of 14th- to 17th-century Flemish and French tapestries.

Iglesia de San Pablo   CHURCH
(cnr Calles de San Pablo & Miguel do Ara; ⊗9am-1pm) This pretty church (200m west of Avenida de César Augusto) has a delicate 14th-century Mudéjar tower and an early-16th-century *retablo* (altarpiece) by Damián Forment.

ROMAN ZARAGOZA

The four museums dedicated to Zaragoza's Roman past form part of what's known as the Ruta de Caesaraugusta; a combined ticket costs €7.

Museo del Foro de Caesaraugusta   MUSEUM
(Plaza de la Seo 2; admission €2.50; ⊗9am-8.30pm Tue-Sat, 10am-2pm Sun Jun-Sep, shorter hours rest of year) The trapezoidal building on Plaza de la Seo is the entrance to an excellent reconstruction of part of Roman Caesaraugusta's forum, now well below ground level. The remains of porticoes, shops, a great *cloaca* (sewer) system, and a limited collection of artefacts from the 1st century AD are on display. An interesting audiovisual show, presented on the hour in Spanish, breathes life into it all, and audio guides in English (€2) are available.

Museo del Teatro de Caesaraugusta   RUIN, MUSEUM
(Calle de San Jorge 12; admission €3.50; ⊗9am-8.30pm Tue-Sat, to 1.30pm Sun) Discovered during the excavation of a building site in 1972, the ruins of Zaragoza's Teatro Romano (Roman theatre) are the focus of this interesting museum. The theatre once seated 6000 spectators, and great efforts have been made to help visitors reconstruct the edifice's former splendour, including evening projections of a virtual performance on the stage; get there early to ensure a place. The exhibit culminates in a boardwalk tour through the theatre itself. The theatre is visible from the surrounding streets.

Other Roman Remains   RUIN, MUSEUM
Just across Plaza de San Bruno from La Seo is the absorbing **Museo del Puerto Fluvial** (Plaza de San Bruno 8; adult/concession €3/2, 1st Sun of month free; ⊗9am-8.30pm Tue-Sat, 9am-1.30pm Sun), which displays the Roman city's river-port installations. There's a quaint but enjoyable audiovisual program every half-hour. The **Museo de las Termas Públicas** (Calle San Juan y San Pedro 3-7; adult/concession €3/2, 1st Sun of month free; ⊗9am-8.30pm Tue-Sat, 9am-1.30pm Sun) houses the old Roman baths.

ISLAMIC ZARAGOZA

Aljafería   PALACE
(Calle de los Diputados; adult/under 12yr €3/free, Sun free; ⊗10am-2pm Sat-Wed, 4.30-8pm Mon-Wed, Fri & Sat Jul & Aug, shorter hours rest of year) The Aljafería is Spain's finest Islamic-era edifice outside Andalucia. It's not in the league of Granada's Alhambra or Córdoba's Mezquita, but it's a glorious monument nonetheless.

The Aljafería was built as a pleasure palace for Zaragoza's Islamic rulers, chiefly in the 11th century. After the city passed into Christian hands in 1118, Zaragoza's Christian rulers made alterations. In the 1490s the Reyes Católicos (Catholic Monarchs), Fernando and Isabel, tacked on their own palace, whereafter the Aljafería fell into decay. Twentieth-century restorations brought the building back to life, and in 1987 Aragón's regional parliament, the Cortes de Aragón, was established here.

Inside the main gate, cross the rather dull introductory courtyard into a second, the **Patio de Santa Isabel**, once the central courtyard of the Islamic palace. Here you're confronted by the delicate interwoven arches typical of the geometric mastery of Islamic architecture. Opening off the stunning northern porch is a small, octagonal **oratorio** (prayer room), with a magnificent horseshoe-arched doorway leading into its mihrab (prayer niche indicating the direction of Mecca). The finely chiselled floral motifs, Arabic inscriptions from the Quran and a pleasingly simple cupola are fine examples of Islamic art.

Moving upstairs, you pass through rooms of the Palacio Mudéjar, added by Christian rulers in the 12th to 14th centuries, then to the Catholic Monarchs' palace, which, as though by way of riposte to the Islamic finery below, contains some exquisite Mudéjar coffered ceilings, especially in the lavish Salón del Trono (Throne Room).

Spanish-language guided tours lasting 50 minutes run throughout the day and are included in the admission price; they generally start half past the hour.

OTHER SIGHTS

FREE **Museo Camón Aznar** MUSEUM
(Museo Ibercaja; Calle de Espoz y Mina 23; ⊙10am-1.45pm & 5-8.45pm Tue-Sat, 10am-1.45pm Sun) This collection of Spanish art through the ages is dominated by an extraordinary series of etchings by Goya (on the 2nd floor), one of the premier such collections in existence. You'll also find paintings by other luminaries (including Ribera and Zurbarán), which spread over the three storeys of the Palacio de los Pardo, a Renaissance mansion. But it's the Goyas that will really take your breath away.

FREE **La Lonja** HISTORIC BUILDING
(Plaza del Pilar; ⊙10am-1.30pm & 5-8.30pm Tue-Sat, 10am-1.30pm Sun) Now an exhibition hall, this finely proportioned Renaissance-style building, the second building east of the basilica, was constructed in the 16th century as a trading exchange. The coloured medallions on its exterior depict kings of Aragón, but the soaring columns rising to an extraordinary ceiling are the standout features. La Lonja has a full calendar of temporary exhibitions.

FREE **Museo de Zaragoza** MUSEUM
(Plaza de los Sitios 6; ⊙10am-1.45pm & 5-7.45pm Tue-Sat, 10am-1.45pm Sun) Devoted to archaeology and fine arts, the city museum displays artefacts from prehistoric to Islamic times, with some exceptional mosaics from Roman Caesaraugusta. The upper floor contains 15 paintings by Goya and more than two dozen of his etchings. It's 400m south of the Teatro Romano.

FREE **Patio de la Infanta** GALLERY
(Calle San Ignacio de Loyola 16; ⊙9am-1.30pm & 6-8.30pm Mon-Thu, 9am-1.30pm & 6-10.30pm Fri, 11am-1.30pm & 6-10.30pm Sat, 11am-1.30pm Sun) This exhibition space houses the Ibercaja bank's collection of paintings, including Goyas, which are displayed in a lovely plateresque (15th- and 16th-century Spanish baroque) courtyard. It's 600m south of Plaza de España.

Museo de Pablo Gargallo GALLERY
(Plaza de San Felipe 3; adult/concession €4/3; ⊙9am-8.30pm Tue-Sat, to 1.30pm Sun) Within the wonderfully restored 17th-century Palacio Argillo is a representative display of sculptures by Pablo Gargallo (1881–1934), probably Aragón's most gifted artistic son after Goya.

✦✦ Festivals & Events

Cincomarzada LOCAL FIESTA
Every 5 March, locals commemorate the 1838 ousting of Carlist troops by a feisty populace. Thousands head for Parque Tío Jorge, north of the Ebro, for concerts, games, grilled sausages and wine.

Fiestas del Pilar RELIGIOUS
Zaragoza's biggest event is a week of full-on celebrations (religious and otherwise) peaking on 12 October, the Día de Nuestra Señora del Pilar.

🛏 Sleeping

TOP CHOICE **Sabinas** APARTMENT €€
(☎976 20 47 10; www.sabinas.es; Calle de Alfonso I 43; d/apt €50/75; ❄🐾) These apartments are a terrific option, with a contemporary-style kitchen and sitting room, and an address just a few steps off Plaza del Pilar. The bathrooms are lovely and the price is extraordi-

---

GOYA IN ARAGÓN

Francisco José de Goya y Lucientes, better known as the master painter Goya, was born in Aragón and his work can be seen all over his native region.

» Casa Natal de Goya (p378), Fuendetodos

» Museo del Grabado de Goya (p378), Fuendetodos

» Ermita de la Fuente (p378), Muel

» Museo Camón Aznar, Zaragoza

» Museo de Zaragoza, Zaragoza

» Basílica de Nuestra Señora del Pilar (p371), Zaragoza

» Museo de Huesca (p396), Huesca

narily good considering the location and size of the rooms. It also has standard doubles with a microwave. The star performer is the Bayeu Attic, a two-bedroom apartment with fabulous Pilar views. Reception is at Hotel Sauce, around the corner.

Hotel Las Torres HOTEL €€
(☎976 39 42 50; www.hotellastorres.com; Plaza del Pilar 11; s/d incl breakfast from €75/85; 🕸🌐) The rooms are designer cool with dazzling white furnishings and daring wallpaper in the public spaces; they're not averse to the odd chandelier in the midst of all this modern chic. The bathrooms have hydromassage showers, and the views of the square and basilica from the balconies attached to most rooms are simply stunning. It also has a spa in the basement. Our only complaint? Two years after it opened, the fittings in some of the rooms are already showing considerable wear and tear.

Hostal el Descanso HOSTAL €
(☎976 29 17 41; www.hostaleldescanso.es; Calle de San Lorenzo 2; s/d without bathroom €18/30; 🌐) This welcoming family-run place combines a terrific location overlooking a pretty plaza near the Roman theatre with simple, bright rooms with comfortable mattresses. It adds up to one of the best budget choices in town.

Hotel Sauce HOTEL €
(☎976 20 50 50; www.hotelsauce.com; Calle de Espoz y Mina 33; s/d €53.50/58; 🕸🌐) This small hotel has good rooms with a mix of styles from traditional and cosy to modern and classy. Bookings are advisable. Breakfast costs €8.

Albergue Juvenil de Zaragoza HOSTEL €
(Zaragoza Hostel; ☎976 28 20 43; www.albergue zaragoza.com; Calle de los Predicadores 70; dm incl breakfast from €16, s/d €20/40; @) This excellent hostel has modern facilities to go with

the lovely original architectural features in the basement bar. Free breakfast, internet access and lockers are among the highlights. There is live music on most Thursday to Sunday nights.

Hotel Río Arga HOTEL €€
(☎976 39 90 65; www.hotelrioarga.es; Calle Contamina 20; s/d from €40/45; 🕸🌐) In a quiet location, yet ideal for all central needs, Río Arga offers comfy rooms. Most of them have been renovated, and have flat-screen TVs and a modern look.

✗ Eating

The tangle of lanes in El Tubo, immediately north of Plaza de España, is home to one of Spain's richest gatherings of tapas bars.

Casa Pascualillo TAPAS €
(Calle de la Libertad 5; mains €5-14; ☉lunch & dinner Tue-Sat, lunch Sun) When *Metropoli*, the respected weekend magazine of *El Mundo* newspaper, set out to find the best 50 tapas bars in Spain a few years back, it's no surprise that Casa Pascualillo made the final cut. The bar groans under the weight of enticing tapas varieties, the house speciality is El Pascualillo, a 'small' *bocadillo* (filled roll) of *jamón*, mushrooms and onion. There's also a more formal restaurant attached.

Mery Limón Gastrobar INTERNATIONAL €€
(www.merylimon.com; Calle de Santiago 30; mains €6-14, menú del día €15) This terrific little bar has an unusual menu divided into three parts – Italian, New York and Mediterranean. But what really stands out is the *menú del día* (daily set menu), which combines seven small dishes from the cutting edge of Spanish gastronomy and wines to go with them. You'd pay at least double this for the same deal in Barcelona.

WHAT'S COOKING IN ARAGÓN?

The kitchens and tables of Aragón are, like so many in inland Spain, dominated by meat. That's not to say you won't find fish, seafood and other Spanish staples. It's just that the *aragoneses* (people from Aragón) really get excited when offered *jamón de Teruel* (cured ham from Teruel province), *jarretes* (hock of ham or shanks) and, above all, *ternasco* (suckling lamb, usually served as a steak or ribs with potatoes). The latter is so beloved that there's even a website devoted to the dish (www.iloveternascodearagon. com) with recipes and general adulation. Other popular dishes include *conejo a la montañesa* (rabbit mountain-style), *migas* (breadcrumbs, usually cooked with cured meats), *cardo* (cardoons) and *caracoles* (snails). Aragón also has five recognised wine-growing regions, the best known of which is Somontano.

Taberna Doña Casta
TAPAS €€

(Calle Estébanes 6; ⊙Tue-Sun) If you like your tapas without too many frills, this enduringly popular and informal *taberna* (tavern) could become your culinary home in Zaragoza. The bottle of wine and six tapas for €23 is a terrific way to meet all your gastronomic needs at a reasonable price. Its specialities are *croquetas* (croquettes) and egg-based dishes.

Casa Lac
TAPAS €€

(☑976 29 90 25; Calle de los Mártires 12; 3 tapas €6.50-8, mains from €12; ⊙Wed-Mon) The grand old lady of the Zaragoza dining scene, Casa Lac's upstairs restaurant pays homage to the 19th century (it opened in 1825) with its refined decor and impeccable service. The kitchen for the downstairs tapas bar has recently had a change of direction, however, and it's an exciting one – avant-garde tapas and a creative *menú gastronómico* (€25).

La Miguería
TAPAS €

(Calle Estébanes 4; migas €5-10, raciones €6-19; ⊙Mon-Sat) Who would have thought you could do so much with *migas* (breadcrumbs)... La Miguería serves this filling Aragonese quick-fix food in more than a dozen varieties, including drenched in olive oil, and topped with sardines and foie gras. It opens at 7.30pm, which may help those struggling to cope with late Spanish dinner-times.

El Rincón de Aragón
ARAGONESE €€

(☑976 20 11 63; Calle de Santiago 3-5; mains €10-20) The decor here is basic and the food stripped down to its essence, but the dishes are top-notch and ideal for finding out why people get excited about Aragonese cooking. One house speciality is the *ternasco asado con patatas a la pobre* (roasted lamb ribs with 'poor man's potatoes'). If you're feeling hungry, this and other local dishes usually appear on the four-course *menú Aragonés* (€19.90), which is a great order. The restaurant is in the covered lane between Calle de Santiago and Plaza del Pilar.

La Reserva
MODERN SPANISH €€

(☑976 22 50 80; Calle de Cádiz 10; tapas from €3, mains €14-20) Vying for attention with numerous international restaurants along Calle de Cádiz, La Reserva is always full and deservedly so. It serves tapas, *raciones* (large tapas servings), rice dishes (minimum two people), warm salads and some good-sized mains. It's all very creative and contemporary, and the atmosphere informal. To get here, head south from Plaza de España for about 200m and turn right into Calle de Cádiz.

Churrería la Fama
CHURROS €

(chocolate with 4 churros €3.10; ⊙8am-1pm & 5-9.30pm) La Fama, off Calle de Alfonso I, is a good spot for *churros* (long, deep-fried doughnuts) and chocolate; if you've been out all night, being here when it opens is a great way to begin (or end) your day.

🍷 Drinking

Calle del Temple, southwest of Plaza del Pilar, is the spiritual home of Zaragoza's roaring nightlife. This is where the city's considerable student population heads out to drink and there are more bars lined up along this street than anywhere else in Aragón – they're all pretty much the same, so follow the noise, stick your head in the door and take your pick. It's the sort of street that you can wander down as late as 11pm and wonder if the action has moved elsewhere – no, it hasn't arrived yet and doesn't really get going until well after midnight.

Café Botanico
CAFE

(Calle de Santiago 5; ⊙9am-1pm Tue & Wed, 9am-2am Thu & Fri, 10am-2am Sat, 10am-11pm Sun, 9am-2pm Mon) Opened in October 2011, Café Botanico combines a florist (think plenty of greenery, including fragrant herbs) and a cafe serving great coffee, a tea menu and a handful of snacks and cakes. It has a real buzz about it, there's contemporary art in the basement and the tables are almost always full regardless of the hour.

Gran Café de Zaragoza
CAFE

(Calle de Alfonso I 25; ⊙8.30am-10pm Sun-Thu, 9-2.30am Fri & Sat) This Zaragoza institution evokes the grand old cafes of Spain's past with a gold-plated facade and an old-style civility in the service. That said, it's a place to be seen by young and old alike and the elegant salon is a good place for morning (or any-time-of-day) coffee.

Rock & Blues Café
MUSIC BAR

(Cuatro de Agosto 5-9; ⊙3pm-2.30am, later on weekends) Rock 'n' roll paraphernalia, paying homage to the likes of Jimi Hendrix, sets the tone for the music and style of this long-standing favourite. There's live pop, rock or blues most Thursdays at 10pm.

ⓘ ZARAGOZA – CHEAP & EASY

More information on the following options is available from any of the tourist offices.

Zaragoza Card (☑976 20 12 00; www.zaragozacard.com; 24/48/72hr €15/20/24) Free entry to all sights, travel on the Tourist Bus and discounts on hotels, restaurants and car hire.

Tourist Bus (Bus Turístico; ☑976 20 12 00; www.zaragozaturismo.es; adult/child/concession under 5 €7.50/free/4.50) Hop-on, hop-off sightseeing bus that does two 75-minute city circuits daily in summer, and less frequently the rest of the year.

Guided Tours (www.zaragozaturismo.es; tours €5.30-13; ⊙10am & 11am Sat & Sun, daily Jul-Aug) A selection of gastronomic, cultural and architectural walking tours. Book through the tourist office.

BiziZaragoza (☑902 319931; www.bizizaragoza.com; 3-day card €5) Public bicycle hire from numerous pick-up and drop-off points around town; first 30 minutes are free and there's a maximum of two hours (€2).

Zen Gong Café LOUNGE
(www.cafegong.com; Calle de Alfonso I 13; ⊙7am-2am Sun-Thu, 8am-4.30am Fri & Sat; ☎) This place wouldn't look out of place in Madrid or Barcelona, with stylish decor, weird-and-wonderful lighting and a breadth of atmospheres, from breakfast cafe to lunchtime wine bar and then a venue for pop, house and even drag acts by night.

☆ Entertainment

La Casa del Loco LIVE MUSIC
(www.lacasadelloco.com; Calle Mayor 10-12; live music free-€20; ⊙9pm-5.30am Thu-Sat) Hugely popular, especially when there's a live band playing. It's mostly rock with a mixed young-retro crowd. After the bands go home, DJs ensure that things stay lively until late.

Oasis CLUB
(☑976 43 95 34; www.oasisclubteatro.com; Calle de Boggiero 28; admission from €8; ⊙midnight-6am Fri & Sat) A few streets west of the old centre, Oasis began life long ago as a variety theatre. It's currently going strong as a club

with good techno-house spun by SantiB, but with a bit of 'anything goes'.

ⓘ Information

Municipal tourist office (☑976 20 12 00; www.zaragozaturismo.es; Plaza del Pilar; ⊙9am-9pm mid-Jun–mid-Oct, 10am-8pm mid-Oct–mid-Jun) Has branch offices around town, including the train station.

Oficina de Turismo de Aragón (www.turismodearagon.com; Avenida de César Augusto 25; ⊙9am-2pm & 5-8pm Mon-Fri, from 10am Sat & Sun) Around 500m southwest along Av de César Augusto from the western end of Plaza de César Augusto.

ⓘ Getting There & Away

Air

The **Zaragoza-Sanjurjo airport** (☑976 71 23 00), 8.5km west of the city centre, has direct **Ryanair** (www.ryanair.com) flights to/from London (Stansted), Brussels (Charleroi), Paris (Beauvais), Milan (Bergamo), Lanzarote and Seville. **Iberia** (www.iberia.es) and **Air Europa** (www.aireuropa.com) also operate a small number of domestic and international routes.

Bus

Dozens of bus lines fan out across Spain from the bus station attached to the Estación Intermodal Delicias train station. The following companies are the more useful ones:
Alosa (☑902 210700; www.alosa.es) Up to eight buses to/from Huesca (€7.30, one hour) and Jaca (€14.50, 2½ hours).
ALSA (☑902 422242; www.alsa.es) Frequent daily buses to/from Madrid (from €15.29, 3¾ hours) and Barcelona (€14.49, 3¾ hours).

Train

Zaragoza's futuristic, if rather impersonal, **Estación Intermodal Delicias** (Calle Rioja 33) is connected by almost hourly high-speed AVE services to Madrid (€60.10, 1¼ hours) and Barcelona (€65.80, from 1½ hours). There are also services to Valencia (€29.80, 4½ hours), Huesca (from €7.90, one hour), Jaca (€12.25, 3½ hours) and Teruel (€16.55, 2¼ hours).

ⓘ Getting Around

Airport Buses (☑902 360065; €1.70) run to/from Paseo María Agustín 7 – which crosses Avenida de César Augusto around 500m southwest of Plaza de España – via the bus/train station every half-hour (every hour on Sunday).

Buses 34 and 51 travel between the city centre and the Estación Intermodal Delicias; the former travels along the Avenida de César Augusto.

SKIING ARAGÓN

Aragón is one of Spain's premier ski destinations. Following are the major ski stations:

Candanchú (☑974 37 31 94; www.candanchu.com) Around 42km of widely varied pistes, 28km north of Jaca.

Astún (☑974 37 30 88; www.astun.com) Also 42km of pistes, mostly for experienced skiers, 3km east of Candanchú.

Panticosa (☑974 48 72 48; www.panticosa-loslagos.com) At the confluence of two pretty valleys, the runs aren't Aragón's most challenging, though the 2km-long Mazaranuala run is an exception; accessible from the A136 north of Sabiñago.

Formigal (www.formigal.com) A regular host for ski competitions, Formigal has 57km of ski runs and 22 lifts; accessible from the A136 north of Sabiñago.

Cerler & Ampriu (www.cerler.com) Cerler sits at 1500m, 6km southeast of Benasque; while Ampriu is at 1900m, 8km beyond Cerler. Together they boast 45 runs totalling 52km.

A new tram line was being built through the centre of town at the time of writing.

SOUTH OF ZARAGOZA

The A23 south towards Teruel passes through **Campo de Cariñena**, one of Aragón's premier wine regions. Just off the motorway, the **Ermita de la Fuente** (Avenida Virgen de la Fuenta; admission free; ⊙9am-8pm daily) in **Muel** has some fine paintings of saints by the young Goya. If you take the slower but more tranquil N234 to **Cariñena**, **bodegas** (wine cellars) line the main road, and in Cariñena there's a good **Museo del Vino** (Wine Museum; Camino de la Platera 7; admission €2.50; ⊙10am-2pm & 4-6pm, closed Sun afternoon & Mon).

Some 23km east of Cariñena along the A220 lies the small village of **Fuendetodos**, where Francisco José de Goya y Lucientes (Goya) began his days in 1746. The **Casa Natal de Goya** (www.fundacionfuendetodosgoya. org; Calle Zuloaga 3; incl Museo del Grabado de Goya €3; ⊙11am-2pm & 4-7pm Tue-Sun) stayed in his family until the early 20th century, when renowned artist Ignacio Zuloaga bought it. Down the road, the **Museo del Grabado de Goya** (incl Casa Natal de Goya €3; ⊙11am-2pm & 4-7pm Tue-Sun) contains an important collection of the artist's engravings. Up to four buses daily head to Fuendetodos (€6.75, one hour) from Zaragoza's bus station.

A further 18km east, the twin towns of **Belchite** are an eloquent reminder of the destruction wrought in the Spanish Civil War. The ruins of the old town, which have been replaced by an adjacent new village, stand as a silent memorial to a brutal tug of war for possession of Aragón between Republican and Nationalist forces during the war. There are regular buses (€5, 45 minutes, three times daily) from Zaragoza.

WEST OF ZARAGOZA

Tarazona

POP 11,120

The quiet, serpentine streets of Tarazona's old town are an evocative reminder of the layout of a medieval Spanish town. It has more than enough monuments to warrant a stop.

◉ Sights

A signposted walking route takes you around the twisting cobbled ways of the medieval 'high part' of town, north of Río Queiles, and meandering through these laneways is the undoubted highlight of Tarazona. Focal points for your wanderings include the extravagant facade of the **Ayuntamiento** and the slender Mudéjar tower of the **Iglesia de Santa María Magdalena**. There are splendid views from the church steps, and the **Palacio Episcopal** (Bishop's Palace), next door, was a fortified Islamic palace. Tarazona's medieval *judería* (Jewish quarter) is also exceptionally well preserved. Throughout, the high balconied projections of the 'hanging houses' are remarkable.

In the lower town Tarazona's **cathedral** is a fetching concoction of Romanesque,

Gothic, Mudéjar and Renaissance styles; it's currently closed to the public. Nearby, the octagonal Plaza de Toros Vieja (Old Bullring) is made up of 32 houses, built in the 1790s and complete with ringside window seats.

🛏 Sleeping & Eating

Hostal Santa Agueda   HOSTAL €€
(☑976 64 00 54; www.santaagueda.com; Calle Visconti 26; s/d incl breakfast from €34/49; ✳🛜) Just off Plaza San Francisco, this 200-year-old home has lovely rooms with wooden beams and a charming proprietor. The little breakfast room is a glorious shrine to Raquel Meller, Aragón's queen of popular song during the early 20th century. Street-facing rooms cost the most and some have a sofa.

Hotel Condes de Visconti   HOTEL €€
(☑976 64 19 08; www.condesdevisconti.com, Calle Visconti 15; d €90; P✳@) Beautiful rooms, mostly with colourful individual decor, plus a preserved Renaissance patio, make this 16th-century former palace a fine stopover. It also has a cafe and good old-fashioned service.

El Patio   TAPAS €
(Calle de Marrodán 16; mains €7.50-15; ◷10am-midnight) A local favourite, this tapas bar, behind the back wall of the Hostal Palacete de los Arcedianos, has loads of small dishes lined up along the bar.

ℹ Information

Tourist office (☑976 64 00 74; www.tarazona. es; Plaza San Francisco 1; ◷9am-1.30pm & 4.30-7pm Mon-Fri, 10am-1.30pm & 4.30-7pm Sat & Sun) Organises Spanish-language guided tours of the city (one-/two-hour tours €3/5; 5pm Saturday, noon Sunday).

ℹ Getting There & Away

Up to seven **Therpasa** (☑976 64 11 00; www. therpasa.es) buses run daily to/from Zaragoza's Estación Intermodal Delicias (€6.88, 1¼ hours) and Soria (€5.38, one hour).

Monasterio de Piedra

This one-time Cistercian monastery (☑902 196052; www.monasteriopiedra.com; park & monastery adult/child €13.50/10, monastery adult €8; ◷park 9am-8pm, monastery 10.15am-1.15pm & 3-7pm), 28km southwest of Calatayud, dates from the 13th century but was abandoned in the 1830s. Subsequent owners laid out the ground as a formal wooded park full of caves and waterfalls, the latter fed by Río Piedra. It's a wonderful place to spend a day with kids, although it can get overrun on summer weekends. Incorporated into the complex is the Hotel Monasterio de Piedra (☑976 84 90 11; www.monasteriopiedra.com; r from €93; ✳).

On Tuesday, Thursday, Saturday and Sunday (or daily in summer), Automóviles Zaragoza runs a 9am bus from Zaragoza to the monastery (€13.75, 2½ hours) via Calatayud, returning at 5pm.

THE NORTH (THE PYRENEES)

Leaving behind Zaragoza's parched flatlands, a hint of green tinges the landscape and there's a growing anticipation of very big mountains somewhere up ahead. And they are big. The Aragonese Pyrenees boast several peaks well over the 3000m mark and they're among the most dramatic and rewarding on the Spanish side of the range. Viewed from the south their crenellated ridges fill the northern horizon wherever you turn and their valleys offer magnificent scenery, stunning stone-built villages, several decent ski resorts and great walking.

🏃 Activities

Some 6000km of trails, both long-distance (Grandes Recorridos; GR) and short-distance (Pequeños Recorridos; PR), are marked all across Aragón. The coast-to-coast GR11 traverses the most spectacular Aragón Pyrenees.

The optimum time for walking is mid-June to early September, though the more popular parks and paths can become crowded in midsummer. The weather can be unpredictable at any time of the year, so walkers should be prepared for extreme conditions at all times.

Dotted throughout the mountains are several mountain *refugios* (refuges). Some are staffed and serve meals, while others are empty shacks providing shelter only. At holiday times staffed *refugios* are often full, so unless you've booked ahead, be prepared to camp. The Federación Aragonesa de Montañismo (FAM; p853) in Zaragoza can provide information, and a FAM card will get you substantial discounts on *refugio* stays. To make reservations in *refugios* and *albergues* (refuges), try www.alberguesy refugiosdearagon.com.

The Aragonese publisher Prames produces the best maps for walkers.

Sos del Rey Católico

POP 670 / ELEV 625M

If Sos del Rey Católico (or simply Sos to its friends) were in Tuscany, it would be a world-famous hill town. It's one of Aragón's most beautiful villages and its old medieval town is a glorious maze of twisting, cobbled lanes that wriggle between dark stone houses with deeply overhung eaves.

Sos has historical significance to go with its beauty: half of one of the most formidable double acts in history, Fernando II of Aragón, was born here in 1452. He and his wife, Isabel I of Castilla, became known as the Reyes Católicos (Catholic Monarchs). Together they conquered the last Islamic kingdom of Granada and united Spain.

◉ Sights

Iglesia de San Esteban　　　CHURCH
(admission €1; ◷10am-1pm & 3.30-5.30pm) The Gothic Iglesia de San Esteban, with a weathered Romanesque portal, has a deliciously gloomy crypt with wonderful medieval frescos.

Casa Palacio de Seda　　HISTORIC BUILDING
(adult/child €2.60/1.50, incl tour of village €4/2; ◷10am-2pm & 4-8pm) Fernando is said to have been born in this building in 1452. It's an impressive noble mansion, which now contains an interpretative centre, with fine exhibits on the history of Sos and the life of the king. The tourist office, housed in the same building, runs guided tours of the building.

Castillo de la Peña Feliciano　　RUIN
The 12th-century watchtower is all that remains of the castle that once guarded the frontier between the two Christian king-

---

MOVING ON?

For tips, recommendations and reviews, head to shop.lonelyplanet.com to purchase a downloadable PDF of The Pyrenees chapter from Lonely Planet's *France* guide.

---

doms of Aragón and Navarra. From the base of the tower there are fabulous views in all directions.

Ayuntamiento　　NOTABLE BUILDING
Lording it over the central Plaza de la Villa, the Renaissance-era town hall is one of the grandest public buildings in Sos.

🛏 Sleeping & Eating

Parador de Sos del Rey Católico　　HOTEL €€
(✆948 88 80 11; www.parador.es; Calle Arquitecto Sainz de Vicuña 1; r €142; ◷closed Jan–mid-Feb; P🅿❄🛜) A place that might just have pleased Los Reyes themselves, this grand building blends in perfectly with the stone buildings of Sos. Rooms have terracotta-tiled floors and some have lovely views out over the village or surrounding plains. The service is faultless and there's a terrific restaurant (set menus €32) serving a changing menu of regional specialities.

El Peirón Hotel　　HOTEL €€
(✆948 88 82 83; www.elpeiron.com; Calle Mayor 24; s/d/ste incl breakfast from €70/80/130; ❄🛜) El Peirón occupies a lovely 17th-century Sos house and the rooms have exposed stone walls and are tastefully designed without being overdone; the bathrooms have hydromassage showers.

Ruta del Tiempo　　HOTEL €€
(✆948 88 82 95; www.rutadeltiempo.es; Calle Larraldía 1; s incl breakfast €50, d incl breakfast €70-108; ❄🛜) This charming family-run place, next to the central Plaza de la Villa, has rooms on the 1st floor themed around three Aragonese kings, while the four 2nd-floor rooms have decorations dedicated to four different continents. They're all good but 'Asia' and 'Africa' are the largest and best rooms.

Albergue Juvenil　　HOSTEL €
(✆948 88 84 80; www.alberguedesos.com; Calle de las Encinas; dm under/over 26yr €15/17.50) Enjoy life in a restored medieval tower in superb modern conditions at this excellent hostel that has bright, stylish decor. Meals (€6.50) are also served.

As Bruixas　　GUESTHOUSE €€
(✆948 88 84 15; www.asbruixas.com; Calle Mayor 25; d/ste €60/70; ❄🛜) Named 'The Witches' by its charming management, this terrific place has three rooms offering a refreshing blend of vivid style and comfort, with plump

mattresses, gleaming bathtubs and bohemi an objects fished out of thrift shops. Its similarly postmodern dining room (mains €12 to €15) offers Aragonese cuisine that gives traditional ingredients a fresh twist.

Hostal las Coronas
HOSTAL €€

(☑948 88 84 08; www.hostallascoronas.com; Calle Pons Sorolla 2; s/d from €56/70) Run by the friendly Fernando, this *hostal* has attractive rooms with the barest hints of character and those with balconies overlooking the plaza are lovely. The downstairs bar serves *bocadillos* (€5 to €7), tapas (€2 to €6) and *raciones* (from €7).

La Cocina del Principal
ARAGONESE €€

(☑948 88 83 48; Calle Mayor 17; mains €14-17.50; ☺Tue-Sat, lunch Sun) Outside of the hotel restaurants, this is the best restaurant in town, with carefully prepared local cooking that changes with the seasons, including snails and *jarretes* (hock of ham or shanks). Reservations recommended.

🛍 Shopping

Morrico Fino
FOOD

(Calle Mayor 14; ☺10am-1.30pm & 5-8pm) Tiny shops selling regional food products (especially wines, cheeses and cured meats) are found hidden in Sos' lanes, and this place is a fine example of the genre.

❶ Information

Tourist office (☑948 88 85 24; Plaza Hispanidad; ☺10am-2pm & 4-8pm) Housed in the Casa Palacio de Sada, the tourist office runs twice-daily guided tours (one/two hours €2.60/4) of the village on weekends.

❶ Getting There & Away

A **Gómez** (☑976 67 55 29) bus departs from Zaragoza (1½ hours, €9.75) for Sos at 7pm Monday to Friday. It returns from Sos at 7am.

Around Sos del Rey Católico

From just north of Sos, the engaging A1601 begins its 34km-long snaking journey west and then northwest en route to the N240. It passes the pretty villages of Navardún and Urriés, before climbing over the Sierra de Peña Musera and down to the gorgeous abandoned village of Ruesta. The final stretch traverses past some unusual rock formations and wheat fields with fine views of the hilltop village of Milanos away to the east.

Valles de Echo & Ansó

The verdant Echo and Ansó valleys are mountain magic at its best, beginning with gentle climbs through the valleys and the accumulating charms of old stone villages punctuating slopes of dense mixed woods of beech, pine, rowan, elm and hazel. As the valleys narrow to the north, 2000m-plus peaks rise triumphantly at their heads. Go quietly through these beautiful valleys; they encourage a gentle touch.

A bus to Jaca leaves Ansó at 6.30am, Siresa at 6.53am and Echo at 7am, Monday to Saturday, returning from Jaca at 6.50pm. A good road links Ansó and Echo, a distance of about 12km.

ECHO (HECHO)
POP 630 / ELEV 833M

Lovely Echo, the biggest village in the valley, is an attractive warren of solid stone houses with steep roofs and flower-decked balconies.

◉ Sights

The helpful tourist office also contains the small **Museo de Arte Contemporáneo**, a basement art gallery of changing exhibitions. Alongside is the **Museo de Escultura al Aire Libre**, a hillside sculpture park. At the heart of the village is the endearing **Museo Etnológico Casa Mazo**, with a terrific display of photographs of villagers from the 1920s and 1930s.

🛏 Sleeping & Eating

Casa Blasquico
RURAL HOTEL €

(☑974 37 50 07; www.casablasquico.es; Plaza de la Fuente 1; d €40-53, tr €65; ☺closed 1st half Sep) The best place to stay in town, the charming Casa Blasquico has six rooms with a mix of wooden and wrought-iron furnishings. Breakfast costs €6.

Camping Valle de Hecho
CAMPGROUND

(☑974 37 53 61; www.campinghecho.com; sites per adult/tent/car €4.29/4.29/4.29; 🛜🏊) South of town, this campground is well kept and has an outstanding range of facilities, from a wi-fi zone to a small supermarket and a picturesque setting.

Restaurante Gaby　　　ARAGONESE

(☑974 37 50 07; www.casablasquico.es; Plaza de la Fuente 1; mains €9-19) This much-lauded restaurant, downstairs in Casa Blasquico, is a delightful place to eat with an intimate wood-beamed dining room and an extensive wine list that includes 17 local wines; specialities include *ensalada de perdiz* (pheasant salad), *crepes de setas* (wild mushroom crepes) and *conejo a la casera* (home-style rabbit).

❶ Information

Tourist office (☑974 37 55 05; www.valledehecho.net; Carretera Oza; ◷10am-1.30pm & 5.30-7pm Fri & Sat, 10am-1pm Sun)

SIRESA & AROUND
POP 130 / ELEV 850M

A couple of kilometres north of Echo, Siresa is another charming village, although on a smaller scale. The beautiful 11th-century **Iglesia de San Pedro** (admission €1.50; ◷11am-1pm & 5-7pm, closed Wed afternoon) is the town's centrepiece; it originally comprised part of one of Aragón's earliest monasteries.

🛏 Sleeping & Eating

Hotel Usón　　　RURAL HOTEL

(☑974 37 53 58; www.hoteluson.com; s incl breakfast €40-50, d €53-58, apt €65-125; ◷Easter-Oct; ℗) There's perfect peace in fabulous surroundings at the outstanding Hotel Usón, high in the Echo valley, 5km north of Siresa on the road to the Selva de Oza. Peace extends to the absence of TVs. The restaurant offers excellent home-cooked meals.

Hotel Castillo d'Acher　　　HOTEL

(☑974 37 53 13; www.castillodacher.com; Plaza Mayor; d €40, without bathroom €65) This hotel has a pleasant mix of rooms, some rather old-fashioned, others pine-clad and modern. It also has *casas rurales* (village accommodation; doubles €28). The big in-house restaurant does a good *menú del día* (€14).

Albergue Siresa　　　HOSTEL

(☑tel/fax 974 37 53 85; www.alberguesiresa.com; Calle Reclusa; dm incl breakfast €15, sheets €2.50) This cheerful hostel provides bunk-and-breakfast accommodation in clean conditions, with other meals available. It also rents out mountain bikes (€12 per day).

SELVA DE OZA

This top end of the Valle de Echo is particularly beautiful, the road running parallel to Río Aragón Subordán as it bubbles its way through thick woodlands. Around 7km beyond Siresa, the road squeezes through the Boca del Infierno (Hell's Mouth), while about 14km from Siresa the paved road ends, shortly after it connects with the GR11 path en route between Candanchú and Zuriza. At least half a dozen mountain peaks sit in an arc to the north for strenuous day ascents.

ANSÓ
POP 480 / ELEV 860M

Ansó takes you even further into a world of high places and harmony. The rough-hewn stone houses here are in grey stone, with red-tiled roofs. Some walls are whitewashed, making a pleasing chequerboard pattern. Forested slopes climb ever upwards from where Ansó straggles along a low escarpment above a partly covered streambed. A grid of narrow streets surrounds the main square, Plaza Mayor.

🛏 Sleeping & Eating

Posada Magoria　　　RURAL HOTEL

(☑974 37 00 49; http://posadamagoria.com; Calle Milagros 32; d €55-60; ☎) Adjoining the rough-walled church, the delightful Posada Magoria is crammed with character and lovingly kept by a family with lots of local knowledge. The kitchen *comedor* (dining room) serves up an excellent €12 *menú* of organically sourced vegetarian dishes; vegans are catered for too.

Casa Baretón　　　HOSTAL

(☑974 37 01 38; www.casabareton.com; Calle Pascual Altemir 16; s/d €35/49) At Casa Baretón, the craftsman owner of this lovingly restored stone house has retained a number of old features to add to the comfort and charm of the rooms.

Bar Zuriza　　　TAPAS €

(Calle Mayor 71) Near the top end of the village, this bar serves decent tapas.

❶ Information

Tourist office (☑974 37 02 25; Plaza Mayor; ◷10am-2pm & 5-8pm Jul & Aug, weekends only Sep-Jun) Offers free guided tours of the village.

VALLE DE ZURIZA

This narrow valley, which runs for 15km north of Ansó, follows the Río Jeral and leads high into remote Pyrenean corners where raptors circle high above and there's a good chance of seeing chamois. Where the paved road ends, wonderful walking trails such as the GR11 take over.

TICKETS & PARKING

Tickets to the two monasteries and to an audiovisual presentation on the Kingdom of Aragón are sold only at the Monasterio Nuevo. Tickets for one/two/three of these sights cost €7/8.50/11 for adults; students and seniors pay €6/7/9; while children between six and 14 pay €4/4.50/6.

Except in winter, the only permissible parking is up the hill at the Monasterio Nuevo, from where a semiregular bus shuttles down to the Monasterio Viejo and back. In winter you may be able to park around 200m down the hill from the Monasterio Viejo.

MONASTERIO DE SAN JUAN DE LA PEÑA

High in a mountain eyrie, 21km southwest of Jaca, Monasterio de San Juan de la Peña is Aragón's most fascinating monastery. Gateway to the monastery is Santa Cruz de la Serós, a pretty village 4km south of the N240.

From Santa Cruz, a winding road climbs the Sierra de la Peña 7km to the stunning Monasterio Viejo (Old Monastery; www.monasteriosanjuan.com; ⊙10am-8pm mid-Jul–Aug, shorter hours rest of year), tucked under an overhanging lip of rock at a bend in the road.

The rock shelter where the Monasterio Viejo is built, perhaps used by Christian hermits as early as the 8th century, became a monastery in the 10th century, when the Mozarabic lower church was constructed. The monastery emerged as the early spiritual and organisational centre of the medieval kingdom of Aragón. The highlight is the Romanesque **cloister**, with marvellous carved 12th- and 13th-century capitals depicting Genesis and the life of Christ. The first three kings of Aragón – Ramiro I (1036–64), Sancho Ramírez (1064–94) and Pedro I (1094–1104) – are among those buried here.

A fire in 1675 led the monks to abandon the old monastery and build a new one in brick further up the hill: Monasterio Nuevo (New Monastery; ⊙10am-8pm mid-Jul–Aug, shorter hours rest of year). It has a large visitors centre as well as the Monastery Interpretation Centre, which documents the archaeological history of the site; and the Kingdom of Aragón Interpretation Centre, devoted to the kings of Aragón.

Unless you've got a specialist interest, most visitors will be satisfied with the Monasterio Viejo.

🛏 Sleeping & Eating

Hostelería Santa Cruz HOSTAL €
(☑974 36 19 75; www.santacruzdelaseros.com; Calle Ordana; s/d from €50.50/62.50; 🖸) Near the church in Santa Cruz de la Serós, this is a beautiful place with friendly service and lovely rooms. Its restaurant serves a good *menú del día* (€12).

Hospedería Monasterio San Juan de la Peña HISTORIC HOTEL €€
(☑974 37 44 22; www.hospederiasdearagon.oc; d from €64; 🅿🖸🖺) Part of the Monasterio Nuevo, this recently opened four-star hotel has supremely comfortable rooms, a spa complex and good restaurant. It's wheelchair accessible.

❶ Getting There & Away

There's no public transport to the monastery. For walkers, a stiff 4km marked path (the GR65.3.2) leads up from Santa Cruz to the Monasterio Viejo. With an ascent of 350m, it takes about 1½ hours.

Jaca

POP 13,300 / ELEV 820M

A gateway to the western valleys of the Aragonese Pyrenees and an agreeable place in its own right, Jaca has a pretty old town dotted with remnants of its past as the capital of the nascent 11th-century Aragón kingdom. These include an unusual fortress and a sturdy cathedral, while the town also has some great places to eat. On winter weekends, après-ski funsters provide a lively soundtrack.

◉ Sights & Activities

Cathedral CATHEDRAL
(Plaza de la Catedral; ⊙11.30am-1.30pm & 4.15-8pm) Jaca's 11th-century cathedral is a formidable building, its imposing facade typical of the sturdy stone architecture of northern Aragón. It was once more gracefully French Romanesque in style, but a Gothic overhaul in the 16th century bequeathed a hybrid look. The interior retains some fine features, in particular the side chapel dedicated to Santa Orosia, the city's patron saint, whose martyrdom is depicted in a series of mysterious murals.

Jaca

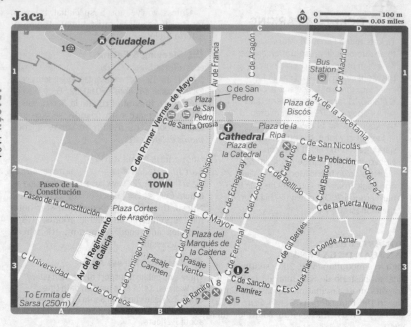

Jaca

◎ Top Sights
Cathedral	C2
Ciudadela	A1

◎ Sights
1 Museo de Miniaturas Militares	A1
2 Torre del Reloj	C3

◉ Sleeping
3 Hostal París	B1
4 Hotel Mur	B1

✖ Eating
5 Crepería El Bretón	C3
6 La Casa del Arco	C2
7 La Tasca de Ana	B3
8 Restaurante El Portón	C3

Ciudadela FORTRESS

(Citadel; www.ciudadeladejaca.es; adult/concession €10/5; ⏱11am-2pm & 5-8pm Tue-Sun, last tickets sold at 1pm & 7pm) The star-shaped, 16th-century citadel is Spain's only extant pentagonal fortress (the one in Pamplona is not complete) and one of only two in Europe. It now houses an army academy, but visits are permitted, with 40-minute guided tours (in English, Spanish or French). In the citadel the **Museo de Miniaturas Militares** (Museum of Military Miniatures; www.museomini aturasjaca.es) is an extraordinary collection of models and dioramas of battles ancient and otherwise, with more than 32,000 toy soldiers on show. Deer graze in the moat surrounding the citadel.

Old Town HISTORIC SITE

There are some lovely old buildings in the streets of the *casco historico* (old city) that fans out south of the cathedral, including the 15th-century **Torre del Reloj** (clock tower; Plaza del Marqués de la Cadena) and the charming little **Ermita de Sarsa** (Avenida Oroel).

⚜ Festivals & Events

Festividad del Primer Viernes de Mayo MEDIEVAL

To see displays of medieval archery, visit on the first Friday of May, when Jaca celebrates a Christian victory over the Muslims in 760.

Fiesta de Santa Orosia RELIGIOUS
Jaca puts on its party gear for the week-long Fiesta de Santa Orosia, which revolves around the saint's day of 25 June.

Festival Folklórico de los Pirineos FOLKLORE
The Festival Folklórico de los Pirineos, in late July and early August, offers 1½ weeks of international music, dance, crafts and theatre. It's held on odd-numbered years.

🛏 Sleeping

It's worth booking ahead at weekends throughout the year, during the skiing season, and in July and August.

TOP CHOICE Hotel Barosse BOUTIQUE HOTEL €€
(974 36 05 82; www.barosse.com; s incl breakfast €72-136, d incl breakfast €115-170; ❋❀❦) In the quiet hamlet of Barós, 2km south of Jaca, Hotel Barosse has six individually styled rooms with lovely attention to detail, from exposed stone walls, high ceilings and splashes of colour to fine bathroom packages of goodies. There's a reading room, garden, an on-site jacuzzi and sauna, and fine views of the Pyrenees. Best of all, José and Gustavo are wonderful hosts. It's easily the best choice in the area. If you don't have your own vehicle, a taxi will cost at least €10 from the town centre.

Hostal París HOSTAL €
(974 36 10 20; www.hostalparisjaca.com; Plaza de San Pedro 5; s/d without bathroom from €30/40; ❦) Close to the cathedral, this friendly, central option has spotless, ample-sized rooms and smart shared bathrooms (seven bathrooms for 20 rooms) that you'd swear were recently renovated. Many rooms overlook the square.

Hotel Mur HOTEL €€
(974 36 01 00; www.hotelmur.com; Calle de Santa Orosia 1; s/d incl breakfast from €50/60; ❦) A pleasantly rambling place, this long-established hotel provides comfort and light-filled rooms, some of which have views towards the citadel; those without exterior windows can be claustrophobic.

🍴 Eating

TOP CHOICE La Tasca de Ana TAPAS €
(Calle de Ramiro I 3; tapas from €3; 7-11.30pm Mon-Fri, 12.30-3.30pm & 7-11.30pm Sat & Sun; ❦) One of Aragón's best tapas bars, La Tasca de Ana has tempting options lined up along the bar, more choices cooked to order and a carefully chosen list of local wines. Check out its 'tapas mas solicitados' (most popular orders) listed on the blackboard. When we were there, the 'Rodolfito' (prawn in sauce) had been top of the list for years, but there's so much here to get excited about. We especially like the toast with goat's cheese and blueberries.

La Casa del Arco VEGETARIAN €
(974 36 44 48; www.lacasadelarco.blogspot.com; Calle de San Nicolás 4; mains €5-10; ❦) A haven of imaginative vegetarian food and with a delightfully alternative ambience, La Casa del Arco is terrific. There's a range of set menus and downstairs is a nice little bar, the Tetaría el Arco, which stages occasional music sessions and other events.

Restaurante El Portón ARAGONESE €€
(974 35 58 54; Plaza del Marqués de la Cadena 1; mains €15-28) Located in a little tree-shaded plaza, this classy venue serves haute-cuisine versions of Aragonese fare. Foie gras is something of a speciality – try the bison stuffed with foie. Reservations are a must. Highly recommended.

Crepería El Bretón CREPERIE €
(974 35 63 76; Calle de Ferrenal 3; mains €7-12; Tue-Sun) Serving sweet and salty crêpes that are faithful to old Brittany recipes, this intimate French-run place is a fine alternative to Spanish cooking. It also serves salads, tapas, Brittany cider and an excellent *menú Bretón* for €10.50.

ℹ Information

Tourist office (974 36 00 98; Plaza de San Pedro 11-13; 9am-1.30pm & 4.30-7.30pm Mon-Sat)

ℹ Getting There & Away

Regular **Alosa** (www.alosa.es) buses go to Huesca (€7.15, 1¼ hours) and Zaragoza (€14.50, 2¼ hours) most days, and one goes to Pamplona (€7.45, 1¾ hours) from the central **bus station** (974 35 50 60; Plaza de Biscós).

Around Jaca

VALLE DE TENA

From the regional centre of Biescas, north of Sabiñánigo, the A136 climbs gently towards the French border.

Leading deep into the mountains, a narrow road up the Valle de Tena runs 8km past the ski resort of Panticosa to the **Panticosa Resort** (☏974 48 71 61; www.panticosa.com), a stunning complex that includes the four-star **Hotel Continental** (s/d from €133/150); three restaurants including the sophisticated **Restaurante del Lago** (meals from €65); bars; a casino; and the **Balneario** (☏974 48 71 61; www.balneariodepanticosa.com; baths/massages from €21/40; ⊙11am-midnight), a luxurious spa complex recently remodelled by star architect Rafael Moneo. The setting is stunning, alongside a lake in an enclosed valley high in the Pyrenees.

Returning to the main A136, **Sallent de Gállego**, 3.5km north of the Panticosa turn-off, is a lovely stone village with a bubbling brook running through it.

From Jaca, one or two daily buses wind over to Panticosa and Formigal (€5.75, two hours). The N260 leaves the valley at Biescas and follows a pretty route to Torla and Aínsa.

Parque Nacional de Ordesa y Monte Perdido

This is where the Spanish Pyrenees really take your breath away. At the heart of it all is a dragon's back of limestone peaks skirting the French border, with a southeastward spur that includes Monte Perdido (3348m), the third-highest peak in the Pyrenees. Deep valleys slice down from the high ground. Most were carved by glaciers and at their heads lie bowl-like glacial *circos* (cirques) backed by spectacular curtain walls of rock. Chief among the valleys are Pineta (east), Escuaín (southeast), Bellos (south), Ordesa (southwest), Bujaruelo (west) and Gavarnie (north, in France).

🏃 Activities

Ordesa Taxi   DRIVING TOUR
(☏630 418918; www.ordesamiradores.es; Calle Fatas; adult/child €30/20; ⊙departures 10am & 4pm

Parque Nacional de Ordesa y Monte Perdido

THE NATIONAL PARK IN A NUTSHELL

Access Towns

The main entry point into the park is Torla, 3km south of the southwest corner of the national park.

From Escalona, 11km north of Aínsa on the A138, a minor paved road heads north-west across to Sarvisé. This road crosses the park's southern tip, with a narrow, sinuous section winding up the dramatic Bellos valley and giving access to walks in the spectacular Cañón de Añisclo (the upper reaches of the Bellos valley).

From Bielsa a 12km paved road runs up the Valle de Pineta in the park's northeastern corner.

Park Access

Private vehicles may not drive from Torla to Pradera de Ordesa during Easter week and July to mid-September. During these periods a shuttle bus (one way/return €3/4.50) runs between Torla's Centro de Visitantes and Pradera de Ordesa. A maximum of 1800 people are allowed in this sector of the park at any one time, although this number is rarely reached.

During the same periods, a one-way system is enforced on part of the Escalona–Sarvisé road. From the Puyarruego turn-off, 2km out of Escalona, to a point about 1km after the road diverges from the Bellos valley, only northwestward traffic is allowed. Southeastward traffic uses an alternative, more southerly road.

Information Centres

Bielsa (☎974 50 10 43; ⊙9am-2pm & 3.15-6pm daily Apr-Oct, weekends only Nov-Mar)

Centro de Visitantes de Tella (☎974 48 64 72; ⊙9am-2pm & 3.15-6pm daily Apr-Oct, weekends only Nov-Mar)

Centro de Visitantes de Torla (☎974 48 64 72; ⊙9am-2pm & 4-7pm)

Escalona (☎974 50 51 31; ⊙9am-2pm & 3.15-6pm daily Apr-Oct, weekends only Nov-Mar)

Maps

Ordesa y Monte Perdido Parque Nacional (1:25,000), published by the Ministerio de Fomento in 2000, costs around €7 and comes with a booklet detailing 20 walks. It's available in Torla shops.

If you're keen to traverse the park along the GR11, look for the strip maps *Senda Pyrenaica*, produced by Prames. Another good reference is the guidebook *Through the Spanish Pyrenees: GR11 – A Trekking Guidebook* by Paul Lucia and available from Cicerone Press (www.cicerone.co.uk).

Rules & Regulations

Bivouacing is allowed only above certain altitudes (1800m to 2500m, depending on the sector); ask at one of the information centres for details. Swimming in rivers or lakes, mountain biking, fishing and fires are banned.

Apr-Sep) This company takes you along an otherwise-inaccessible road just outside the park boundary. With stops at five lookouts during the four-hour excursion, it's a great way to take in some of the park's scenery.

Compañía Guías de Torla HIKING, ADVENTURE SPORTS
(☎616 706821; Calle Ruata) This Torla-based guide association can organise canyon-ing or rafting activities for visitors, or simply provide a guide for trekking excursions through the park.

Agua y Nieve ADVENTURE SPORTS
(☎620 973091; www.aguaynieve.com) This is another Torla-based operator that can take you climbing, skiing and rafting among other outdoors pursuits.

HIKING ROUTES

For a range of walking options in the park, pick up a copy of the *Senderos* maps and route descriptions for the four sectors (Ordesa, Añisclo, Escuaín and Pineta) from any of the information offices. They include maps and route descriptions for the following trails:

» **Circo de Soaso** A classic day walk that follows the Valle de Ordesa to Circo de Soaso, a rocky balcony with the Cola de Caballo (Horsetail) waterfall as its centrepiece.

» **Refugio de Góriz & Monte Perdido** Fit walkers can climb a series of steep switch-backs (part of the GR11) to Circo de Soaso and up to the Refugio de Góriz, at 2200m. From there, Monte Perdido is a serious undertaking that requires mountaineering skills, crampons and ice axes.

» **Faja Racón, Circo de Cotatuero & Faja Canarellos** This walk takes you along spectacular high-level paths on the north flank of the Valle de Ordesa.

» **Brecha de Rolando** The cool-headed may climb part of the wall of the Circo de Cotatuero by the Clavijas de Cotatuero, a set of 32 iron pegs hammered into the rock. From here you are about 2½ hours' march from the Brecha de Rolando (Roldán; 2807m), a dramatic, breezy gap in the mountain wall on the French frontier.

» **Puerto de Bujaruelo** The GR11 describes a 6km arc up the very pretty Valle de Bujaruelo to San Nicolás de Bujaruelo. From there an east–northeast path leads in about three hours (with a 950m ascent) up to the Puerto de Bujaruelo on the border with France.

» **Southern Gorges** The Cañón de Añisclo is a gaping wound in the earth's fabric. Energetic walkers can start from the Refugio de Góriz and descend the gorge from the north, from where numerous trails fan out into the mountains. The Gargantas de Escuaín is a smaller-scale but still-dramatic gorge on Río Yaga, further east.

» **Balcón de Pineta** This challenging hike begins close to the Parador Nacional de Bielsa and, after the waterfalls of the Cascadas del Cinca, climbs via a series of steep switchbacks up to the 'Pineta Balcony' for stunning glacier and mountain views.

Torla

POP 330

Torla is a lovely Alpine-style village of stone houses with slate roofs, although it does get overrun in July and August. Most people use Torla as a gateway to the national park, but the setting is also delightful, the houses clustered above Río Ara with a backdrop of the national park's mountains. In your ramblings around town, make for the 13th-century Iglesia de San Salvador; there are fine views from the small park on the church's northern side.

🛏 Sleeping

Hotel Villa de Torla　　　　HOTEL €€
(☎974 48 61 56; www.hotelvilladetorla.com; Plaza de Aragón 1; s €35-45, d €52-69; ☺mid-Mar–Dec; ☒) The rooms here are tidy – some are spacious and stylish, others have floral bedspreads and look a little tired. But the undoubted highlight is the swimming pool and the bar terrace, from where there are lovely views.

Hotel Villa Russell　　　　HOTEL €€
(☎974 48 67 70; www.hotelvillarussell.com; Calle de Capuvita; s €57-80, d €80-114; ℗🖳) Villa Russell has rooms that won't win a style contest, but they're enormous and come with sofas, microwave and hydromassage showers. On-site parking costs €6 and there's a jaccuzzi and sauna.

Hotel Ballarín　　　　HOTEL, HOSTEL €
(☎974 48 61 55; www.pirineosguiadeservicios.com/hotelballarin; Calle de Capuvita 11; s €32-42, d €40-50; 🖳) This place is well kept with superb views from the top rooms, but the welcome could be warmer. The owners also run the similarly well-tended Hostal Alto Aragón (☎974 48 61 72; Calle de Capuvita; s €30-32, d €38-48), a few doors down.

Refugio Lucien Briet · REFUGE €

(☎974 48 62 21; www.refugiolucienbriet.com; Calle de Francia; dm/d €10/40) This is a French-managed refuge-style place in the village.

✗ Eating

Most of the listed accommodation have restaurants with *menús* from €12 to €17.

Restaurante el Duende · ARAGONESE €€

(☎974 48 60 32; www.elduenderestaurante.com; Calle de la Iglesia; mains €14.60-20.55) This charming place is the best of many restaurants in town, with fine local cuisine, an extensive menu and eclectic decor in a lovely 19th-century building. Our favourite dish is duck tenderloin in apple cream and wine sauce.

ℹ Getting There & Away

One daily bus operated by **Alosa** (☎902 21 07 00; www.alosa.es) connects Torla to Aínsa (€3.25, one hour) and Sabiñánigo (€3.25, one hour). In July and August one daily bus makes the Sabiñánigo–Sarvisé (but not Aínsa) run.

Around Torla

VALLE DE BUJARUELO
North of Torla and shadowing the eastern boundary of the park, the pretty Valle de Bujaruelo is another good base.

🛏 Sleeping

Camping Valle de Bujaruelo · CAMPGROUND

(☎974 48 63 48; www.campingvalledebujaruelo.com; per person/tent/car €4.50/4.50/4.50, r €40-62; ☺Easter–mid-Oct) This campsite, 3.5km up the Valle de Bujaruelo, features a refuge with bunks, a restaurant and a supermarket. The setting's lovely and the facilities are well maintained.

Mesón de Bujaruelo · REFUGE

(☎974 48 64 12; www.mesondebujaruelo.com; dm/d incl breakfast €18.50/52, half-board per person €31.50-39.50) This old hostelry provides bunks and meals in a pretty location by the Puerto de Bujaruelo. Accommodation is too-cool-for-style mountain basics, but it's all about location here.

TORLA TO AÍNSA
The N260 from Torla to Aínsa runs for 44km through the lovely foothills of the Pyrenees. At around the halfway point, watch for the lookout over the Río Ara to the evocative ruins of Jánovas, a village abandoned in the 1950s.

🛏 Sleeping

Casa de San Martín · HISTORIC HOTEL €€€

(☎974 50 31 05; www.casadesanmartin.com; s/d from €129.60/162) Every now and then we find ourselves in a really special place. Along a dirt track 5km off the main Torla–Aínsa road (take the sign for San Martín de la Solana), Casa de San Martín is a stunning rural retreat. The handsome stone house has been beautifully renovated and the rooms are temples to good taste without being overdone. Mario and Evaldo are engaging but discreet hosts, the attention to detail is faultless, meals (set menus €37.50) are exceptional and the setting is tranquil and picturesque.

Aínsa

POP 2230

The beautiful hilltop village of medieval Aínsa (L'Aínsa in the local dialect), which stands above the modern town of the same name, is one of Aragón's gems, a stunning village hewn from uneven stone. From its perch, you'll have commanding panoramic views of the mountains, particularly the great rock bastion of La Peña Montañesa.

◉ Sights

Simply wander down through the village along either Calle de Santa Cruz or Calle Mayor, pausing in the handful of artsy shops en route; note the drain pipes carved into the shape of gargoyles.

Iglesia de Santa María · CHURCH

(belfry admission €1; ☺belfry 11am-1.30pm & 4-7pm Sat & Sun, longer hours Jul & Aug) The restored Romanesque Iglesia de Santa María, rising above the northeastern corner of Plaza Mayor, lights up when you pop €1 into a box, with five minutes of Gregorian chants thrown in. The crypt and Gothic cloister are charming; climb the belfry for glorious views of the mountains to the north and over the terracotta rooftops of the old town.

Museo de Oficios y Artes Tradicionales · MUSEUM

(admission €2.40; ☺10.30am-2pm & 5.30-9.30pm Fri-Sun) Down on Plaza de San Salvador, this interesting museum has exhibits on local culture in one of the best-preserved old buildings in Aínsa.

Castle
CASTLE

The castle and fortifications off the western end of the Plaza de San Salvador mostly date from the 1600s, though the main tower is 11th century; there are some reasonable views from the wall. It contains a fascinating ecomuseum (admission €4; ⊙11am-2pm Wed-Fri, 10am-2pm & 4-7pm Sat & Sun Easter-Oct) on Pyrenean fauna (the focus is on the endangered lammergeier, with some caged birds of prey out the back) and the Espacio del Geoparque de Sobrarbe (www.geoparquepirineos.com; admission free; ⊙10am-2pm & 4-7pm) with displays on the region's intriguing geology, as well as good views from the tower.

🎉 Festivals & Events

Festival Internacional de Música
MUSIC

(www.festivalcastillodeainsa.com) In July, Aínsa hosts this monthlong festival with predominantly Spanish and a few international music acts in the castle grounds.

🛏 Sleeping

Hotel los Siete Reyes
HOTEL €€

(☎974 50 06 81; www.lossietereyes.com; Plaza Mayor; d €70-129; ❄ 🛜) Set in one of the most charming stone buildings overlooking Plaza Mayor, this temple of style has stunning bathrooms, polished floorboards, exposed stone walls, flat-screen TVs and some lovely period detail wedded to a contemporary designer look. The attic rooms are enormous, but all are spacious and some have lovely mountain views, while others look out over the Plaza Mayor. Simply outstanding.

Albergue Mora de Nuei
HOSTEL €

(☎974 51 06 14; www.alberguemoradenuei.com; Calle del Portal de Abajo 2; dm €15-17, d incl breakfast €50-60; 🛜) At the lower end of the old town, facing onto Plaza de San Salvador, this fine place is one of Aragón's best hostels. Rooms are colourful, there's a roof terrace, an atmospheric basement bar, good food, and a semiregular calendar of live music and other cultural events. Highly recommended.

Hotel los Arcos
HOTEL €€

(☎974 50 00 16; www.hotellosarcosainsa.com; Plaza Mayor 23; d from €80; ❄ 🛜) In a fine position on Plaza Mayor, this lovely hotel has supremely comfortable rooms with canopied beds and good-sized bathrooms. It doesn't quite scale the dizzy heights of its neighbour, Hotel los Siete Reyes, but it's still a wonderful place.

Posada Real
RURAL HOTEL €€

(☎974 50 09 77; www.posadareal.com; Plaza Mayor 6; d from €70; ❄) A tastefully renovated noble mansion, this *posada* has large rooms and exposed wooden beams; some rooms have four-poster beds and/or good views. It's a few steps down off Plaza Mayor.

🍴 Eating

Restaurante Callizo
MODERN SPANISH €€

(☎974 50 03 85; http://restcallizo.restaurantesok.com; Plaza Mayor; set menus €25-42; ⊙closed Mon & dinner Sun) This place is definitely something special, cleverly combining traditional cuisine with gastronomic innovation on its constantly changing menu. The set menus are gastronomic journeys of the highest order; it also offers a (pricey) children's menu.

Bodegón de Mallacán
ARAGONESE €€

(www.posadareal.com; Plaza Mayor 6; mains €13-20) One of the most popular places on Plaza Mayor, with an extensive wine cellar, traditional local cooking and a number of pretty dining rooms. The duck in raspberry sauce is outstanding, but there's much to turn the head here. If you can't choose, try the 'Typical Aragón Menu' (€18).

L'Alfil
TAPAS €

(Calle Traversa; raciones €5.80-18.50; ⊙Thu-Tue) This pretty little cafe-bar, with floral accompaniment to its outside tables, is in a side street along from the church. It has a whole heap of *raciones* that are more creative than you'll find elsewhere, from ostrich chorizo, snails and deer sausage to wild-boar pâté and cured duck. It also serves good local wines.

WORTH A TRIP

SPAIN'S OLDEST MONASTERY

Around 5km northeast of Aínsa, the quiet and uniformly stone-built hamlet of El Pueyo de Araguás is home to the Monasterio de San Victorián; although it was much modified in the 16th century, its Romanesque origins ensure that it can lay claim to being the oldest monastery in Spain. Also in the village, the Casas Coronas from 1519 are among the oldest in the region.

Bodegas del Sobrarbe   ARAGONESE €€

(www.bodegasdelsobrarbe.com; Plaza Mayor 2; mains €15-22) This fine restaurant off the southeastern corner of Plaza Mayor offers meaty Aragonese fare with a few fish dishes. The wild boar with plum and green-apple purée is superb.

Shopping

Sabores de Pueblo   FOOD, WINE

(www.saboresdepueblo.com; Plaza Mayor 15; 10am-2pm & 3.30-8pm) Fronting onto the northeastern corner of Plaza Mayor, this gourmet food shop has tempting wines, cheeses and other local goodies.

Information

Municipal tourist office (974 50 07 67; www.ainsasobrarbe.net; Avenida Pirenáica 1; 9am-9pm) Inconveniently in the new town down the hill, but with an outpost in the Museo de Oficios y Artes Tradicionales.

Regional tourist office (974 50 05 12; www.turismosobrarbe.com; Plaza del Castillo 1, Torre Nordeste; 10am-2pm & 4-7pm) Extremely helpful; within the castle walls.

Getting There & Away

Alosa (902 21 07 00; www.alosa.es) runs daily buses to/from Barbastro (€5.40, one hour) and Torla (€4, one hour).

Benasque

POP 2240 / ELEV 1140M

Aragón's northeastern corner is crammed with the highest and shapeliest peaks in the Pyrenees, and Benasque (Benás in the local dialect) is perfectly sited to serve as gateway to the high valleys. Even in midsummer these epic mountains can be capped with snow and ice. The area, much of which is protected as the **Parque Natural Posets-Maladeta**, offers walkers almost limitless options and climbers a wide choice of peaks. Northeast of Benasque, the Pyrenees' highest peak, the Pico de Aneto (3404m), towers above the massif.

Sleeping

During the ski season most offer packages with *media pensión* (half-board).

Hotel Aneto   HOTEL €€

(974 55 10 61; www.hotelesvalero.com; Avenida de Francia 4; d incl breakfast from €104,) A cut above the usual lodge-style accommodation that is a Benasque speciality, Hotel Aneto

OUTFITTERS IN BENASQUE

Plenty of outfitters offer guides and instruction for climbing, skiing and other activities; most sell or hire out clothing and equipment for the hills.

Barrabés (www.barrabes.com; Avenida de Francia; 10.30am-1.30pm & 4.30-9pm)

Compañia de Guías Valle de Benasque (www.guiasbenasque.com; Avenida Luchón 19)

opened in 2008 with hardwood floors and a contemporary designer look.

Hotel Avenida   HOTEL €€

(974 55 11 26; www.h-avenida.com; Avenida de los Tilos 14; s/d from €55/70) Rooms here are handsomely furnished and the service is friendly. A restaurant is attached, and there are cheaper room rates for longer stays.

Camping Aneto   CAMPGROUND €

(974 55 11 41; www.campinganeto.com; per person/tent/car €6.50/6.50/6.50) The closest camping ground to town (3.5km away), Aneto is well equipped and has a shop and laundry.

Eating & Drinking

The best places are along Avenida de los Tilos and its continuation, Calle Mayor.

Taberna del Ixarso   TAPAS €

(Calle Mayor 12; mains €7-15) Meaty tapas such as chorizo and *salchichón* (sausage) help the drinks go down at this lively little bar, where local aficionados happily mix with tourists.

La Buhardilla   CREPERIE €

(www.labuhardilla.eu; Calle Mayor; mains €8-14) A plush crêperie at the heart of the old town, 'the attic's' sleek modern decor is softened by a big, open fire for chilly Pyrenean evenings. Sweet and savoury crêpes and fondues are what it's all about.

Restaurante el Fogaril   ARAGONESE €€

(974 55 16 12; Calle Mayor 5; mains €12-22) Treat yourself at this elegant country dining room, which serves outstanding Aragonese fare. Its specialities are young venison and stuffed partridge, *cozal* (small deer) and freshwater fish, all superbly prepared and presented.

Villages of Aragón

Few regions can rival Aragón for its spread of charming villages. Most are built in the sturdy stone typical of the region, with terracotta and slate roofs. And their setting – against a backdrop of Pyrenean peaks or hidden in isolated corners of the south – is as beguiling as the architecture.

Albarracín

1 One of Spain's most beautiful villages, Albarracín (p402) combines time-worn streets in shades of ochre with a dramatic setting. The views from the castle or the precipitous walls high on a ridge will stay with you long after you leave.

Aínsa

2 There's no more beautifully preserved village (p389) in Aragón after the sun sets, the crowds go home and silence reigns. Its stunning laneways, porticoed Plaza Mayor and views of the Pyrenees from the village's hilltop perch are simply wonderful.

Alquézar

3 A centre for canyoning and other high-octane pursuits, Alquézar's (p394) alter ego is a tranquil village that, from above, resembles a Tuscan hill town.

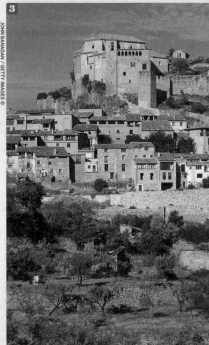

Sos del Rey Católico

4 Uniformly cobblestoned streets, the whiff of Spanish legend and a perch high above the madding crowd make Sos (p380) a memorable stop en route to or from the Pyrenees.

Daroca

5 Just when you think Aragón's southern badlands have little to offer, Daroca (p398) embraces you within its walls that encircle the town high on the ridgelines.

Clockwise from top left
1. Albarracín (p402) 2. Aínsa (p389) 3. Alquézar (p394)

ⓘ Information

Tourist office (☑974 55 12 89; www.turismo benasque.com; Calle San Sebastián 5; ⊙9.30am-1pm & 4.30-8pm)

ⓘ Getting There & Away

Two buses operate Monday to Saturday, and one runs on Sunday, from Huesca to Benasque (€12.25, 2½ hours) and back.

If you're driving, the approach from the south suddenly jumps out at you as the A139/N260 plunges through the Congosto de Ventamillo, a narrow defile carved by the crystalline Río Ésera. There's not much quarter given by traffic in either direction.

Around Benasque

South of Benasque, the village of Castejón de Sos is a paragliding centre with accommodation. For more information, try www. parapentepirineos.com and www.volaren castejon.com.

VALLE DE VALLIBIERNA

This valley runs southeast up from the A139 about 5.5km north of Benasque. Take the track towards Camping Ixeia; the track leaves the A139 just before the Puente de San Jaime (or Chaime) bridge, 3km from Benasque. You're now on the GR11 coast-to-coast trail, which after a couple more kilometres diverges into Valle de Vallibierna.

GR11 TO BIELSA

Westbound, the GR11 leaves the A139 just after the Puente de San Jaime. It's an easy three-hour walk (600m ascent) up the Valle de Estós to Refugio de Estós (☑974 34 45 15; dm adult/under 14yr €16.10/8.50), which is 1890m above sea level. It's a good 115-bunk refuge (dinner €15) attended year-round.

A further five hours brings you – via the 2592m Puerto de Gistaín (or Chistau) and some superb views of the Posets massif – to the excellent Refugio de Biadós (☑974 34 16 13; dm €11). Viadós is a base for climbs on Posets (3369m), a serious undertaking that requires mountaineering skills and equipment, and has potential altitude effects. The GR11 continues some six hours west to the hamlet of Parzán in the Bielsa valley, before heading into the Parque Nacional de Ordesa y Monte Perdido.

Autocares Bergua (☑974 50 00 18; www. autocaresbergua.com) runs a bus from Bielsa to Aínsa at 6.45am Monday, Wednesday and Friday (daily in July and August).

UPPER ÉSERA VALLEY & MALADETA MASSIF

North of Benasque, the A139 continues paved for about 12km. About 10km from Benasque, a side road leads 6km east along the pretty upper Ésera valley, ending at La Besurta, with a hut selling drinks and some food.

Hospital de Benasque (☑974 55 20 12; www.llanosdelhospital.com; s/d incl breakfast from €80/100; 🅿@🛜), a little under halfway from the A139 to La Besurta, is a large mountain lodge in a beautiful location, surrounded by handsome peaks. There's a bar, restaurant, spa and wellness centre and a variety of accommodation ranging from bunks to semi-luxurious rooms.

An exacting trail from Llanos del Hospital, the ski station adjacent to the Hospital de Benasque, heads northeast and upwards to Peña Blanca, and from there winds steeply up to the 2445m Portillón de Benasque pass on the French frontier. You could return via the Puerto de la Picada, another pass to the east – or another 3½ hours north down past the Boums del Port lakes to the French town of Bagnères-de-Luchon.

South of La Besurta is the great Maladeta massif, a superb challenge for experienced climbers. This forbidding line of icy peaks, with glaciers suspended from the higher crests, culminates in Pico de Aneto (3404m), the highest peak in the Pyrenees.

Refugio de la Renclusa (☑974 34 46 46; dm €16.10) is a 40-minute walk from La Besurta and stands 2140m above sea level. It's staffed and serves meals from about June to mid-October and weekends from March to June. Experienced and properly equipped climbers can reach the top of Aneto from here in a minimum of five hours.

The massif offers other peaks, including Maladeta (3308m). From La Besurta or La Renclusa, walkers can follow paths southeast beneath the Maladeta massif, leading into Catalonia.

Alquézar

POP 300 / ELEV 670M

Picturesque Alquézar, 23km northwest of Barbastro, would be worth visiting for its own sake – it's one of Aragón's more handsome villages. But Alquézar also means canyoning (descenso de barrancos), which involves following canyons downstream by whatever means available – walking, abseiling, jumping, swimming, even diving.

Sights

Colegiata de Santa María CASTLE, MONASTERY
(admission €2.50; ⊙11am-1.30pm & 4-6pm Wed-
Mon) Alquézar is crowned by this large castle-
monastery. Originally built as an *alcázar*
(fortress) by the Arabs in the 9th century,
it was conquered around 1060 by Sancho
Ramírez, who established an Augustinian monastery here in 1099. Remnants are
still visible. The columns within its delicate
cloister are crowned by perfectly preserved
carved capitals depicting biblical scenes,
and the walls are covered with spellbinding
murals. On the upper level is a museum of
sacred art. Visits are by guided tour only. The
door is locked while tours are in progress, so
simply wait for the next tour.

Activities

The main canyoning season is mid-June to
mid-September and prices, which vary depending on the number of people and the
graded difficulty of the trip, generally include
gear, guide and insurance; check the websites
of the various companies for details. Most of
the agencies also offer rafting, trekking, rock
climbing and other activities. **Avalancha**
(⊋974 31 82 99; www.avalancha.org; Calle Arrabal),
Guías Boira (⊋974 31 89 74; www.guiasboira.
com; Calle Arrabal) and **Vertientes** (⊋974 31 83
54; www.vertientesaventura.com; Calle San Gregorio
5) are all recommended places, lined up in a
row at the entrance to the village.

Sleeping

Hotel Maribel BOUTIQUE HOTEL €€€
(⊋974 31 89 79; www.hotelmaribel.es; Calle Arrabal;
d incl breakfast from €130; ❄🔊) This boutique
hotel has plenty of charm and, while the decor won't be to everyone's taste (following a
wine theme and ranging from gorgeous to
vaguely kitsch), every room is supremely
comfortable. If there's no-one at reception,
try the nearby Restaurante Casa Gervasio.

Hotel Villa de Alquézar HOTEL €€
(⊋974 31 84 16; www.villadealquezar.com; Calle
Pedro Arenal Cavero 12; d incl breakfast & parking
€69-110; P🔊) This is a lovely place with plenty of style in its large rooms; several rooms
have great views and there are period touches
throughout. The most expensive rooms on
the top floor are large and have wonderful
covered balconies – they're perfect for watching the sun set over town while nursing a
bottle of Somontano wine.

WORTH A TRIP

SIERRA DE GUARA

North of Alquézar, the A2205 road
to Aínsa via Colungo and Arcusa is a
delightful drive through pre-Pyrenean
canyon country in the Sierra de Guara.
There are some fine lookouts. Our
favourite is the spectacular **Mirador
del Vero** (also signposted as Barranca
de Portiarcha) – watch for Egyptian
vultures, imperial eagles and lammer-
geiers circling high overhead.

Albergue Rural de Guara REFUGE €
(⊋974 31 83 96; www.alberguerruraldeguara.com;
Calle Pilaseras; dm €14) This cheerfully run
albergue (refuge) is perched up above the
village with fine views from the surrounds.
Breakfast is €5.50 and staff can also arrange
picnic lunches (€8).

Eating

Restaurants line up along the *mirador*
(lookout) section of Calle Arrabal and you
could pretty much take your pick with
menús for €11 to €15.

Restaurante Casa Gervasio ARAGONESE €€
(⊋974 31 82 82; Calle Pedro Arnal Cavero; 4-course
set menu €25) With a menu that has barely
changed in three decades, this place up
in the old town is possibly Alquézar's best
restaurant, with an excellent *menu degustación* – cured meats and lamb ribs are
typical of what you'll encounter.

Information

Tourist office (⊋974 31 89 40; www.alquezar.
org; Calle Arrabal; ⊙9.30am-1.30pm & 4.30-
8pm daily Jun-Oct, Sat, Sun & festivals only
Nov-May) Runs guided tours (€3.50) three
times daily in summer and can arrange audio
guides (€4).

Getting There & Away

There's a daily bus to Alquézar from Barbastro
(€2) Monday to Saturday. Check with the tourist
office for times – it doubles as the local school
bus and times change during holidays.

Huesca

POP 52,440

Huesca is a provincial capital in more than
name, a town that shutters down during the
afternoon hours and stirs back into life in

DON'T MISS

SOMONTANO WINE REGION

Somontano won the coveted Denominación de Origen (DO) status in 1984 and it has since become Aragón's most prestigious wine-growing region. Centred around Barbastro, Somontano's more-than 30 vineyards produce reds, whites and rosés from 13 different types of foreign and local grape varieties (including chardonnay, cabernet sauvignon, syrah and pinot noir), often blending local grapes such as parreleta (a red grape indigenous to the Somontano region) with foreign varieties. Some of the better-known Somontano labels include Enate and Viñas del Vero.

The **tourist office** (☑974 30 83 50; turismo@barbastro.org; Avenida de la Merced 64; ☺10am-2pm & 4.30-7.30pm Tue-Sat Sep-Jun, daily Jul & Aug) in Barbastro has brochures in Spanish, English and French outlining the various bodegas (wineries) that can be visited for sales, tours and/or tastings. Always ring ahead to arrange a time; the tourist office will help you make the calls if you turn up in person.

Part of the same complex as the tourist office, the **Espacio de Vino** is an interpretation centre devoted to Somontano wines with audiovisual displays, interactive grape-aroma displays and occasional wine tastings (per person €10). Attached to the tourist office is also a wine shop. Both places keep the same hours as the tourist office.

Another excellent resource is the website www.rutadelvinosomontano.com, which maps out possible wine itineraries through the region. The website also has details of the Bus del Vino Somontano, a monthly all-day bus tour of selected bodegas from Zaragoza/Huesca (€28/26).

the evenings. That said, its old centre retains considerable appeal, it has excellent accommodation and its location in north-central Aragón can serve as a launch pad for the Aragonese high country.

◉ Sights

Catedral CATHEDRAL
(Plaza de la Catedral; admission €3; ☺10.30am-2pm & 4-8pm Mon-Fri, 10.30am-2pm Sat) Huesca's venerable Gothic cathedral is one of Aragón's great surprises. The richly carved main portal dates from 1300, the attached **Museo Diocesano** contains some extraordinary frescos and painted altarpieces, and the stately interior features an astonishing, 16th-century alabaster *retablo* by Damián Forment that betrays a mix of Gothic and Renaissance styles. Some of the chapels are also richly decorated. To appreciate it all, consider putting a euro in the slot on the column next to the Capilla de los Santos and the whole place will light up for five minutes. To round off your visit, climb the 180 steps of the **bell tower** for 360-degree views all the way to the Pyrenees.

FREE **Museo de Huesca** MUSEUM
(Plaza Universidad 1; ☺10am-2pm & 5-8pm Tue-Sat, 10am-2pm Sun) The octagonal city museum contains a well-displayed collection (labels in Spanish only) covering the archaeology

and art of Huesca province, including eight works by Goya (room 7).

Iglesia de San Pedro El Viejo CHURCH
(Plaza de San Pedro; adult/concession €2.50/1.50; ☺10am-1.30pm & 4-7.30pm, closed afternoons Oct-May) The church of San Pedro is 12th-century Romanesque and its small cloister is adorned with 38 beautifully carved Romanesque capitals.

🛏 Sleeping

TOP CHOICE **La Posada de la Luna** BOUTIQUE HOTEL €€€
(☑974 24 08 57; www.posadadelaluna.com; Calle Joaquin Costa 10; s/d €61/69; P❈🖤) Our favourite hotel in Huesca, this lovely boutique place incorporates some original features of old Huesca architecture with a whimsical but contemporary feel, designer bathrooms and hydromassage showers. It's a comfortable, charming place.

Hostal Un Punto Chic HOSTAL
(☑974 24 17 74; www.unpuntochic.com; Calle Joaquín Costa 20; s €39-49, d €49-59; ❈🖤) This stunningly renovated hostal is brought to you by the owners of La Posada de la Luna (which is where you'll find reception, a few doors down the road) and they've created one of Aragón's best *hostales*. There are slick furnishings and cutting-edge decoration

(photos take up entire walls), and some of the more expensive rooms have an exercise machine or a massage chair. Best of all, the hotel-quality place comes at the price of a *hostal*.

Hostal Lizana/Hostal Lizana 2 HOSTAL €
(☑974 22 07 76; www.hostal-lizana.com; Plaza de Lizana 6; s €24-38, d €36-56, tr €50-64; P✽☎) Facing each other across a pleasant little plaza are these two worthwhile places, both with simple but large rooms. The rooms in Lizana 2 are newer and you've got a better chance of a balcony room here. The family has been in the *hostal* business for 50 years and it shows in the friendly welcome and nice touches such as in-room fridges and hairdryers.

 Eating

Hervi ARAGONESE €€
(☑974 24 03 33; Calle Santa Paciencia 2; mains €9-20; ⊙closed Thu; ☑) A hugely popular lunchtime scene, Hervi offers a *menú del día* where the servings are enormous and, unusually for Aragón, there's a range of vegetarian options in the extensive menu. We enjoyed the breast of duck with pâté and mushroom sauce.

Taberna de Lillas
Pastia ARAGONESE, FUSION €€
(☑974 21 16 91; www.lillaspastia.es; Plaza de Navarra 4; mains €18-27, set menus €35-55) Dress up just a little for this classy eatery in the town's old casino. The food is excellent, with a gastronome's touch in both presentation and taste. Meat and fish are recurring themes (such the *manitas con cigala* – pig's trotters with prawns), there are special desserts that change daily, and service is attentive.

ℹ Information

Tourist office (☑974 29 21 70; www.huesca turismo.com; Plaza López Allué 1; ⊙9am-2pm & 4-8pm) Runs daily guided tours of the historic centre (adult/concession €2/1) from mid-June until mid-September, and vintage bus tours (adult/child/concession under 12yr €5/free/2.50) during the same period to the Castillo de Loarre, Los Mallos and the Sierra de la Guara.

ℹ Getting There & Away

Alosa (☑974 21 07 00; www.alosa.es) runs numerous daily buses to/from Zaragoza (€7.30, 1¼ hours), Jaca (€7.15, 1¼ hours), Barbastro (from €4.25, 50 minutes), Lleida (Lérida; €10.05, 2½

hours) and Barcelona (from €15.80, four hours), and a twice-daily service to Benasque (€12.25, 2¾ hours).

Nine trains a day run to/from Zaragoza (from €5.90, one hour), including two high-speed AVE services (€15.70, 40 minutes). There are also AVE services to/from Madrid (€62.90, 2¼ hours, one daily), as well as services to Teruel (€23.15, 3¼ hours, one daily), Valencia (€36.40, 5¾ hours, one daily) and Jaca (€7.65, 2¼ hours).

Around Huesca

LOARRE

The evocative Castillo de Loarre (www.castil lodeloarre.com; admission with/without tour €4.80/3.30; ⊙10am-2pm & 4-8pm) broods above the southern plains across which Islamic raiders once rode. Raised in the 11th century by Sancho III of Navarra and Sancho Ramírez of Aragón, its resemblance to a crusader castle has considerable resonance with those times. There's a labyrinth of dungeons and tunnels, and two towers offering magnificent views.

The castle is a 5km drive or a 2km, one-hour, uphill walk by the PR-HU105 footpath, from the village of Loarre, 35km northwest of Huesca.

Camping Castillo de Loarre (☑974 38 27 22; www.campingloarre.com; per person/tent/car €4/4/4; @) is a good site located halfway between the village and the castle. Hospedería de Loarre (☑974 38 27 06; www.hospe deriadeloarre.com; Plaza Miguel Moya; s/d incl breakfast from €63/78; ✽@) is a charming, small hotel occupying a converted 16th-century mansion on Loarre village square. Its restaurant offers medium-priced to expensive meals and the hotel is wheelchair accessible.

Daily buses run to Loarre village from Huesca (€2.62, 40 minutes) Monday to Saturday.

LOS MALLOS

After a rather unexciting patch along the Huesca–Pamplona road, you come to a dramatic area along Río Gállego north of Ayerbe. On the eastern bank, huge rock towers known as Los Mallos (Mallets) rise up – they wouldn't look out of place in the Grand Canyon and are popular with serious rock climbers. For a closer look, head for Riglos.

THE SOUTH

Don't be deceived by the monotony of the vast sweeps of countryside immediately

DANCING IN THE DESERT

The rural town of Fraga in the relentless flatlands between Zaragoza and the Mediterranean coast is the unlikely locale for Florida 135 (www.f135.com; Calle Sotet 2; admission €13; ⏰from 11.30pm Sat), the temple of Spanish techno. The windowless 3000-sq-metre graffiti-strewn space is the most recent incarnation of a dance hall that's been going since 1942. Busloads of clubbers arrive for the club's main Saturday-night sessions. In mid-July, Fraga hosts the Monegros Desert Festival (www.monegrosfestival.com; festival pass €70), formerly called the Groove Parade, attracting dozens of Spanish and internationally renowned DJs and bands.

south of Zaragoza. Head further south or southeast and the landscape takes on a certain drama and shelters some of inland Spain's most intriguing towns and villages.

Daroca

POP 2310

Daroca is one of southern Aragón's best-kept secrets, a sleepy medieval town, one-time Islamic stronghold and, later, a Christian fortress town in the early medieval wars against Castilla. Its well-preserved old quarter is laden with historic references and the crumbling old city walls encircle the hilltops; the walls once boasted 114 military towers. Coming from north or south, you slip quietly down off the N234 and enter Calle Mayor, the cobbled main street, through monumental gates and into another world.

Sights & Activities

Iglesia Colegiata de Santa María   CHURCH
(⏰11am-1pm & 5.30-7pm) The pretty Plaza de España, at the top of the village, is dominated by this ornate Romanesque Mudéjar Renaissance-style church, which boasts a lavish interior and organ. The 16th-century Gothic Puerta del Perdón rounds out the church's impressive portfolio of European architectural styles. Overall, it's one of Daroca's most appealing (and unexpected) gems.

Iglesia de San Miguel   CHURCH
Up the hill west of the town centre, this 12th-century church is an austerely beau-

tiful masterpiece of Romanesque architecture, but its greatest treasures are the Gothic frescos within. Sadly, the church is kept closed, except for guided tours run by the tourist office or for concerts during the town's festivals.

Guided Walks   WALKING TOURS
(guided tours €3; ⏰guided tours 11am & 4.30pm Tue-Sun) The best of the self-guided walks offered by the tourist office is the 45-minute Ruta Monumental, which gives a wonderful feel for the town and is well signposted. The other is the two-hour Ruta del Castillo y Las Murallas, a far more strenuous undertaking that climbs up to and follows the walls; the reward is magnificent views over Daroca. The tourist office also organises guided tours of the town, each lasting around an hour – these are well worth taking, not least because they give you access to the stunning Iglesia de San Miguel as well as other sites that are otherwise off limits to casual visitors.

Festivals & Events

Feria Medieval   MEDIEVAL
The best time to be in Daroca is during the last week of July, when Calle Mayor is closed to traffic, locals don their medieval finery and concerts mark the Medieval Festival.

Festival Internacional de Música Antigua   MEDIEVAL
In the first two weeks of August, Daroca hosts the International Festival of Medieval Music with courses and concerts in the two main churches.

Sleeping & Eating

Hotel Cien Balcones   HOTEL €€
(☏976 54 50 71; www.cienbalcones.com; Calle Mayor 88; s/d incl breakfast from €56/72; P🅿✳🛜) This stylish three-star hotel puts many four-star hotels to shame with large, designer rooms, modern bathrooms and strong colour schemes throughout. There's an excellent restaurant (mains from €9) and a cafe that serves up cheap raciones, bocadillos and pizza.

La Posada del Almudí   HOTEL €€
(☏976 80 06 06; www.posadadelalmudi.es; Calle Grajera 5; s/d/q incl breakfast €45/65/120; ✳🛜) A one-time 16th-century palace, this lovely old place has a charming personal touch. The rooms in the main building have been lovingly restored and are comfortable, although the larger duplexes with balcony are

the nicest. Across the lane it also has a range of supermodern, smallish but comfortable rooms. The attached restaurant (set menu €12; mains €15-18) offers good traditional cuisine; unusually its three-course meal is available in the evenings as well.

Apartamentos Melihah APARTMENT
(☑976 80 01 94; www.melihah.com; Calle Mayor 76; apt €75-120; ✶🛜) If you would like a little more space than you'll find in your average hotel, the apartments here have a lounge and kitchen area and provide a good base if you're planning on spending more than a night exploring southern Aragón. Some rooms have exposed wooden beams and stone walls; others sport bright colours.

❶ Information

Tourist office (☑976 80 01 29; Calle Mayor 44; ◷10am-2pm & 4-8pm)

❶ Getting There & Away

Buses stop outside the Mesón Félix bar, at Calle Mayor 104. Four daily buses run to Zaragoza (€10.11, three hours) and Teruel (€5.45, two hours), Monday to Saturday.

Laguna de Gallocanta

Some 20km south of Daroca, this is Spain's largest natural lake, with an area of about 15 sq km (though it can almost dry up in summer). It's a winter home for tens of thousands of cranes, as well as many other waterfowl – more than 260 bird species have been recorded here. The cranes arrive in mid-October and leave for the return flight to their breeding grounds in Scandinavia in March. Unpaved tracks of 36km in total encircle the lake, passing en route a series of hides and observation points; the tracks can be driven in normal vehicles except after heavy rain. Take binoculars.

🛏 Sleeping & Eating

Allucant HOSTAL €
(www.allucant.com; Calle San Vicente; d with/without bathroom from €30/45) Serious twitchers will feel right at home at this simple but well-run birdwatching base in the village of Gallocanta. Meals (€9 to €12) and picnic lunches (€7) can be arranged.

❶ Information

Centro de Interpretación – Bello (◷10am-2pm & 3-6pm Sat & Sun, daily Oct & Feb) Information and exhibitions, along the Tornos–Bello road near the southeast corner of the lake.

Teruel

POP 35,290 / ELEV 917M

One of Spain's most attractive provincial cities, compact Teruel is an open-air museum of ornate Mudéjar monuments. But this is very much a living museum where the streets are filled with life – a reflection of a city reasserting itself with cultural attitude. For decades, Teruel had something of an image problem and an air of neglect, a place seemingly left behind by modern Spain's mainstream renaissance – '¡Teruel existe!' (Teruel exists!) is still an oft-heard, only partly tongue-in-cheek refrain. But the city has pulled itself up by its boot-straps and it's well worth seeing what all the fuss is about. Be warned, though – in winter Teruel can be one of the coldest places in Spain, so come prepared.

◉ Sights & Activities

Most of Teruel's sights are close to Plaza del Torico (the name derived from a statue of what could be Spain's smallest bull), a lively focus of city life.

Cathedral CATHEDRAL
(Plaza de la Catedral; adult/child €3/2; ◷11am-2pm & 4-8pm) Teruel's cathedral is a rich example of the Mudéjar imagination at work with its kaleidoscopic brickwork and colourful ceramic tiles. The superb 13th-century bell tower has hints of the Romanesque in its detail. Inside, the astounding Mudéjar ceiling of the nave is covered with paintings that add up to a medieval cosmography – from musical instruments and hunting scenes to coats of arms and Christ's crucifixion. Other highlights include the 16th-century wooden *retablo mayor* and the extraordinary 15th-century Gothic *retablo* in the Capilla de la Coronación.

Fundación Amantes MUSEUM, CHURCH
(www.amantesdeteruel.es; Calle Matías Abad 3; Mausoleo/Iglesia de San Pedro & Torre de San Pedro €4/7, combined ticket €9; ◷10am-2pm & 4-8pm Sep-Jul, 10am-8pm Aug) The somewhat curious **Mausoleo de los Amantes** (Mausoleum of the Lovers) pulls out the stops on the city's famous legend of Isabel and Juan Diego. Here they lie in modern alabaster tombs, sculpted by Juan de Ávalos, with their heads tilted endearingly towards each other. Around this centrepiece has been shaped a

Teruel

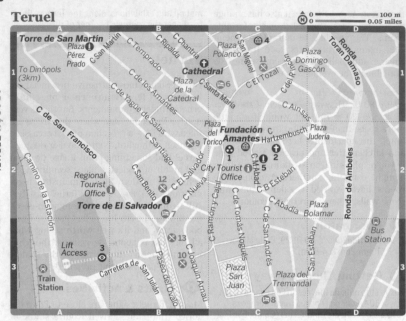

Teruel

remarkable audiovisual exhibition, featuring music and theatre. It skates very close to glorious kitsch, but is entirely persuasive.

Attached to the complex is the 14th-century **Iglesia de San Pedro**, with a stunning ceiling, baroque high altar and simple cloisters, as well as the **Torre de San Pedro** (Torre Mudéjar) with fine views over Teruel.

Torre de El Salvador   TOWER, MUSEUM
(www.teruelmudejar.com; Calle El Salvador; adult/concession €2.50/1.80; ⏰10am-2pm & 4-8pm) The most impressive of Teruel's Mudéjar towers is the Torre de El Salvador, an early-

14th-century extravaganza of brick and ceramics built around an older Islamic minaret. You climb the narrow stairways and passageways, and along the way you'll find exhibits on Mudéjar art and architecture. The views from the summit are Teruel's best.

Torre de San Martín   TOWER
(Calle San Martín) Although you can't climb it, Torre de San Martín, the northwestern gate of the old city, is almost as beautiful as the Torre de El Salvador. It was finished in 1316 and was incorporated into the city's walls in the 16th century.

FREE **Museo Provincial** MUSEUM
(Plaza Polanco; ⊙10am-2pm & 4-7pm Tue-Fri, 10am-2pm Sat & Sun) Teruel's Museo Provincial is housed in the 16th-century Casa de la Comunidad, a fine work of Renaissance architecture. The archaeological sections are a highlight, and there are changing exhibitions of contemporary art.

Aljibe Fondero RUIN
(Calle Ramón y Cajal; adult/concession €1.20/0.80; ⊙10am-2pm & 4-8pm) Off the southeastern corner of Plaza del Torico is the entrance to the Aljibe, an interesting 14th-century underground water-storage facility. In addition to showcasing the remnants of the cisterns, there are good Spanish-language audiovisual presentations on medieval Teruel.

La Escalinata STAIRCASE
The grand staircase that connects the Paseo del Óvalo on the old city's fringe to the train station, La Escalinata is a masterpiece of neo-Mudéjar monumental architecture. First built in 1920, it was painstakingly restored in the first years of the 21st century. Along with the redesigned Paseo del Óvalo, La Escalinata has won numerous awards for urban redesign. There's a lift back up to the Paseo.

Dinópolis AMUSEMENT PARK
(www.dinopolis.com; adult/child €24/19; ⊙10am-8pm, ticket office closes 6pm) It's fun for all at this large, modern dinosaur theme park. It's 3km southwest of the town centre, well signposted just off the Valencia road. There's the train through time, 3D and 4D animations and an excellent museum among other attractions. When things are busy, you could spend as much time in queues as in the actual attractions.

✯✯ Festivals & Events

Fiesta Medieval MEDIEVAL
On the weekend closest to 14 February, Teruel's inhabitants (and visitors from elsewhere) don medieval dress for the Fiesta Medieval. There are medieval markets and food stalls, but the centrepiece is the re-enactment of the Diego and Isabel legend.

Feria del Ángel LOCAL FIESTA
The **Día de San Cristóbal** (St Christopher's Day; 10 July) is the hub of the weeklong Feria del Ángel, which commemorates Teruel's founding.

🛏 Sleeping

TOP CHOICE **Hotel el Mudayyan** HOTEL €€
(☑978 62 30 42; www.elmudayyan.com; Calle Nueva 18; s €55-70, d €70-90; ❋⊛) Easily the most character-filled of Teruel's hotels, El Mudayyan has lovely rooms with polished wood floors, wooden beams and a charming interior design that's different in every room. It also has a *tetería* (teahouse) in the basement and a curious subterranean passage that dates back to earliest Teruel.

Hostal Aragón HOSTAL €
(☑978 60 13 87; www.hostalaragon.org; Calle Santa María 4; s with/without bathroom €26/22, d €45/30) An unassuming place on a narrow side street with well-kept wood-panelled rooms, Hostal Aragón drops its prices by a few euros midweek. We recommend booking at weekends and on holidays.

Hotel Plaza Boulevard HOTEL €€
(☑978 60 86 55; www.plazaboulevardhotel.com; Plaza del Tremandal 3; s/d from €49/89; ❋⊛) Probably the pick of Teruel's other midrange hotels, Hotel Plaza Boulevard has a good

---

THE LOVERS OF TERUEL

In the early 13th century Juan Diego de Marcilla and Isabel de Segura fell in love, but, in the manner of other star-crossed historical lovers, there was a catch: Isabel was the only daughter of a wealthy family, while poor old Juan Diego was, well, poor. Juan Diego convinced Isabel's reluctant father to postpone plans for Isabel's marriage to someone more appropriate for five years, during which time Juan Diego would seek his fortune. Not waiting a second longer than the five years, Isabel's father married off his daughter in 1217, only for Juan Diego to return, triumphant, immediately after the wedding. He begged Isabel for a kiss, which she refused, condemning Juan Diego to die of a broken heart. A final twist saw Isabel attend the funeral in mourning, whereupon she gave Juan Diego the kiss he had craved in life. Isabel promptly died and the two lovers were buried together.

location just off Plaza San Juan and comfortable modern rooms.

Eating

Landlocked Teruel is utterly devoted to meat eating and promotes its local *jamón* and other *embutidos* (cured meats) with enthusiasm. One local speciality you'll find everywhere is *las delicias de Teruel* (local *jamón* with toasted bread and fresh tomato).

Mesón Óvalo   ARAGONESE €€
(☑978 61 82 35; Paseo del Óvalo 8; mains €14-19; ☺lunch & dinner Tue-Sat, lunch Sun) There's a strong emphasis on regional Aragonese cuisine at this pleasant place, with meat and game dishes to the fore. One fine local speciality is *jarretes* (hock of lamb stewed with wild mushrooms, a dish that dates back to the period when Muslims ruled this part of Spain).

La Torre de Salvador   ARAGONESE €€
(☑978 61 73 76; Calle El Salvador; meals €11-19, set menu €20; ☺Tue-Sun) Right opposite the Torre de El Salvador, this smart restaurant raises the stakes with its nouveau cuisine Aragonese, with subtle dishes riffing on traditional themes, but plenty of local staples for those eager to get to the heart of Aragonese cooking. Think duck served in a sauce of sparkling wine, wild mushrooms and raisins.

Bar Gregory   TAPAS €
(Paseo del Óvalo 6; mains €6-13; ☺closed Tue) The pick of the tapas bars lined up along Paseo del Óvalo, this place has all the local staples, outdoor tables at which to enjoy them and good service.

La Taberna de Rokelin   TAPAS €
(Calle El Tozal 33; tapa/ración of ham €3.50/16) One of Teruel's most celebrated bars dedicated to *jamón*.

¡Aqui Teruel!   TAPAS €
(Calle de Yagüe de Salas 4; tapa/ración €3.50/11) This temple to *jamón* also offers better-than-average kids' menus.

ⓘ Information

City tourist office (☑978 62 41 05; Plaza de los Amantes 6; ☺10am-2pm & 4-8pm Sep-Jul, 10am-8pm Aug) Ask here for audio guides (€2) to the old town.

Regional tourist office (☑978 64 14 61; Calle de San Francisco 1; ☺9am-2pm & 4.45-7.45pm) Information about the wider Aragón region.

ⓘ Getting There & Away

From Teruel's **bus station** (☑978 61 07 89; www.estacionbus-teruel.com), there are regular buses to/from Zaragoza (€12.11, two to three hours), Valencia (€11.15, 2¼ hours) and Madrid (€22, 4½ hours).

Teruel is on the railway between Zaragoza (€16.55, two hours) and Valencia (€14.90, 2½ hours).

Albarracín

POP 1100 / ELEV 1180M

Albarracín, 38km west of Teruel, is one of Spain's most beautiful villages. It takes time to get here, but it's worth it for the marvellous sense of timelessness that not even the modern onslaught of summer coach tours can erase. Ragged fortress walls rise up the surrounding slopes and the town's streets retain their mazelike charm, with centuries-old buildings leaning over them.

Built on a steep, rocky outcrop and surrounded by a deep valley carved out by a meander of Río Guadalaviar, Albarracín was, from 1012 to 1104, the seat of a tiny Islamic state ruled by the Berber Banu Razin dynasty with links to Córdoba. From 1170 to 1285 it was an independent Christian kingdom sandwiched between Castilla and Aragón.

⊙ Sights

If you're staying overnight in the village, ask your hotel for *el bono*, which entitles you to small discounts at most sights and some tours.

Muralla   CITY WALL
Albarracín's highest point, the Torre del Andador (Walkway Tower) dates from the 9th century; the surrounding walls are more recent and date from the 11th or 12th century. It's a stiff climb to the summit, but worth every gasp for the views down over the town. For a different perspective, a path leads for 1km west along the hillside from the walls to the Ermita del Carmen, a small hermitage with more fabulous views.

Castle   CASTLE
(Castillo; admission €2.50; ☺guided tours 11am, noon, 1pm, 4.30pm & 5pm Sat-Mon, 1pm & 5.30pm Tue-Fri) Crowning the old town above the cathedral near the southern end of town, this fascinating castle, with 11 towers and an area of 3600 sq metres, dates from the 9th century when Albarracín was an important

Islamic military post. In private hands until 2005, the archaeological digs have revealed fascinating insights into the town's history. All is explained on the hour-long Spanish-language tour (buy your tickets at the Museo de Albarracín); contact the Centro de Información to arrange English-language tours. The views from the ramparts are superb.

Museo de Albarracín   MUSEUM
(Calle San Juan; admission €2.50; ⊙10.30am-1pm & 4.30-6pm Mon-Fri, 10.30am-2pm & 4.30-7.30pm Sat & Sun) In the old city hospital, this interesting museum is devoted to the town's Islamic heritage, with numerous finds from the archaeological digs in the castle. Opposite the museum's entrance, the 17th-century **Ermita de San Juan** was built on the site of Albarracín's former synagogue.

Cathedral   CATHEDRAL
With its cupola typical of the Spanish Levant, Albarracín's cathedral is one of the signature monuments of the village skyline; within, it has an elaborate gilded altarpiece. It was closed for restoration when we visited, with no clue as to its expected reopening.

Museo Diocesano   MUSEUM
(admission €2.50; ⊙10.30am-2pm & 4.30-6.30pm Mon-Fri, to 7.30pm Sat & Sun) The Palacio Episcopal (Bishop's Palace), backing onto the cathedral, houses a rich collection of religious art and is a cut above your average church museum. The 15th- to 17th-century tapestries in particular stand out, as does a strange glass salt-holder in the shape of a fish...

Museo de Juguetes   MUSEUM
(www.museodejuguetes.com; Calle Medio 2; adult/child €3/1.50; ⊙11am-2pm & 4-7pm Tue-Sat, 11am-2pm Sun Apr-Oct, weekends only Nov-Mar) Albarracín's toy museum is a fascinating journey through the historical world of toys – the kids will love it. It's down the hill, around 500m east of the tourist office.

🞜 Tours

El Andador   WALKING TOUR
(☑978 70 03 81; www.elandador.es; Calle de la Catedral 4; tours €3.50) El Andador organises 1½-hour walks through Albarracín two to six times daily.

Centro de Información   WALKING TOUR
(☑978 70 40 35; http://fundacionsantamariade albarracin.com; Calle de la Catedral; tours €3.50) Organises 1½-hour guided walks three to four times daily.

🛏 Sleeping

TOP
CHOICE La Casa del Tío
Americano   HOTEL €€
(☑978 71 01 25; www.lacasadeltioamericano.com; Calle Los Palacios 9; s/d incl breakfast €80/100; ☜) A wonderful small hotel, 'The House of

---

LUIS BUÑUEL & THE DRUMS OF CALANDA

Film-maker Luis Buñuel (1900–83) is one of Aragón's more curious cultural exports. This friend of Salvador Dalí was born in Calanda, 15km southwest of the regional centre of Alcañiz in Aragón's southeast, and his earliest memories were of the drums of Calanda.

In the centuries-old ritual of the film director's birthplace, Good Friday noon marks the *rompida de la hora* (breaking of the hour). At that moment thousands commence banging on *tambores* (snare drums) and *bombos* (bass drums), together producing a thunderous din. The ceremony goes on for 24 hours, only ceasing for the passage of the standard Easter processions.

'The drums, that amazing, resounding, cosmic phenomenon that brushes the collective subconscious, causes the earth to tremble beneath our feet,' Buñuel recalls in his memoir, *Mi último suspiro* (My Last Sigh). 'One has only to place his hand on the wall of a house to feel the vibrations... Anyone who manages to fall asleep, lulled by the banging, awakes with a start when the sound trails off. At dawn, the drum skins are stained with blood: hands bleed after so much banging. And these are the rough hands of peasants.'

This clamour worked its way into Buñuel's dreams and nightmares, and eventually into his surreal films; the drums left their imprint, along with a taste for ritual, costumes and disguises.

Buñuel's life and work are celebrated in the **Centro Buñuel Calanda** (☑978 84 65 24; www.cbcvirtual.com; Calle Mayor 48; adult/concession €3.50/2.50; ⊙10.30am-1.30pm & 4-8pm Tue-Sun) in Calanda.

the American Uncle' boasts brightly painted rooms, some with exposed stone walls and special views, and friendly, impeccable service from fine hosts Angelines and José Miguel. The views of the village from the breakfast terrace (and from rooms 2 and 3) are magnificent. A welcoming glass of champagne is a lovely touch, and the bathroom goodies are unusually generous. Not surprisingly, they get plenty of repeat visitors.

Posada del Adarve HOTEL €
(☎978 70 03 04; www.posadadeladarve.com; Calle Portal de Molina 23; s €35, d €50-75; @☎) A lovingly restored Albarracín town house near the Portal de Molina (Molina Gateway), this lovely little place has beautifully decorated rooms, friendly service and a wonderfully intimate feel.

Casa de Santiago HOTEL €€
(☎978 70 03 16; www.casadesantiago.net; Subida a las Torres 11; d/ste €70/95; ☎) A beautiful place, with lots of exposed wood and tiled floors, and charming service to go with it, the Casa lies at the heart of the old town a few steps up from Plaza Mayor. You step off the street into an immediate comfort zone.

La Casona del Ajimez HOTEL €€
(☎978 71 03 21; www.casonadelajimez.com; Calle de San Juan 2; d €76; ☎) Like other lovingly restored Albarracín small hotels, this place has warm and charming decor, and fine views from some rooms. It's at the southern end of town, near the cathedral.

Hotel Arabia HOTEL €€
(☎978 71 02 12; www.hotelarabia.es; Calle Bernardo Zapater 2; s €40-55, d €60-78, apt €89-122; ☎) Down the hill and inhabiting a 17th-century convent, Hotel Arabia has good rooms and enormous apartments with terrific views.

Hostal Los Palacios HOSTAL €
(☎978 70 03 27; www.montepalacios.com; Calle Los Palacios 21; s/d €28/45) This charming place has spotless rooms, some with balconies and gorgeous views. It's about 250m from Plaza Mayor, starting along Calle de Santiago and exiting through Portal de Molina.

Camping Ciudad de Albarracín CAMPGROUND €
(☎978 71 01 97; www.campingalbarracin.com; per person/tent/car €4/4/4; ⊙Apr-Oct) Pleasant, small and shaded, the camping ground is 2km from the heart of Albarracín, off the Bezas road.

 Eating

Tapas, *raciones* and hearty meals are available at all of the bars around town, with a particularly high concentration in the streets around the Plaza Mayor. Casa de Santiago hotel also has a good restaurant.

 Tiempo de Ensueño MODERN SPANISH €€
(☎978 70 40 70; www.tiempodeensuenyo.com; Calle Palacios 1B; menus €41, mains €19-25) Every now and then, you stumble upon something special. This high-class restaurant has a sleek, light-filled dining room, attentive but discreet service, and food that you'll remember long after you've left. Spanish nouvelle cuisine in all its innovative guises makes an appearance here with a changing menu, as well as a book-length wine list, mineral-water menu, choice of olive oils, welcome cocktail and, above all, exquisite tastes. There's a tempting *menu degustación* as well as à la carte choices. If you're staying in the village, you may be entitled to a 10% discount.

La Taberna TAPAS €
(Plaza Mayor 6; mains €5-15) A bustling bar right on Plaza Mayor, La Taberna does decent food (try the *delicias de Teruel* – local *jamón* with bread and tomato). The food's fairly similar to what you'll get elsewhere, but it wins our vote over others nearby because it rarely has the TV turned on...

 Drinking

El Molino del Gato BAR
(www.elgato.arrakis.es; Calle San Antonio 4; ⊙3pm-3am Thu-Tue Sep-Jun, noon-3am Jul & Aug) Just behind the tourist office, down the hill from the old town, this outstanding bar is the place to drink in Albarracín. Built around a 15th-century mill, it has water gushing beneath a glass panel in the floor, and the outdoor tables next to the water are fine places to nurse a drink; there are more than 25 types of beer. It also hosts regular contemporary art exhibitions, and José Miguel (better known as 'El Gato') is a welcoming host.

Shopping

Sierra de Albarracín FOOD
(www.quesodealbarracin.es; ⊙10am-2pm & 4-7pm Mon-Fri, to 8pm Sat & Sun) You'll see the respected local cheeses labelled as Sierra de

EL MAESTRAZGO

El Maestrazgo, a medieval knightly domain of wonderfully isolated valleys and rocky hills, spills over from Valencia province. Cantavieja, northeast of Teruel along the A226, is a dramatically sited ridge-top town that was reputedly founded by Hannibal and later became a seat of the Knights Templar. The best-preserved (and partly restored) part of town is the porticoed Plaza Cristo Rey. If you're heading for Morella in the Valencian Maestrazgo, the A226 north-east of Cantavieja will take you, snaking down past ragged cliffs and then via Mirambel, a fine example of a gently decaying, walled medieval town. One Monday-to-Friday bus runs from Teruel to Cantavieja (€8.75, 1½ hours).

Around Albarracín

The hills around Albarracín conceal some intriguing examples of prehistoric rock art, some of which date back 7000 years. In addition to animal representations (livestock, horses), there are some exceptional human figures.

To get here, follow the signs from the tourist office to '*pinturas rupestres*' (rock paintings). The main car park (with a picnic area and children's play area) is 4.5km further on, and well-signposted walking trails of between 2.3 and 3km (45 minutes to 1¼ hours) lead out into the hills. Three of the trails leave from here, and a fourth leaves from another car park around 700m back down the road towards Albarracín. Our favourite trail is the 2.5km Sendero del Arrastradero, which takes you to the iconic Abrigo del Arquero de los Callejones (a perfectly rendered human archer seemingly caught in flight) among other drawings and a lookout.

ROMAN AQUEDUCT

The road between Gea de Albarracín and Albarracín (18km) is shadowed by traces of an ancient Roman aqueduct. Signs point to the most accessible sections, and there's a new Centro de Interpretación that was about to open in Gea Albarracín soon after we were there.

BRONCHALES

Teruel's *jamón* is widely respected throughout Spain, and Jamones Bronchales (☑978 70 13 13; www.jamonesbronchales.com; admission free; ☉10am-2pm & 5-8pm Mon-Sat), in the village of Bronchales, 29km northwest of Albarracín, runs tours of its drying operations and shows how the *jamón* is prepared. A minimum of 15 are usually required to make up a tour, but they might show you around if things are quiet. You can also buy the end product here.

Albarracín in small shops all over the village, but why not go straight to the source? The owner's shop is around 3km from the tourist office on the road out of town to Gea de Albarracín, and has the full range of sheep and goat's cheese, including a sheep's cheese that won the gold medal at the World Cheese Awards in 2010. You can try most varieties before you buy.

ℹ Information

Centro de Información (☑978 70 40 35; Calle de la Catedral; ☉10am-2pm & 4-6.30pm Mon-Fri, to 7.30pm Sat & Sun) Excellent, privately run information office high in the old town.

Tourist office (☑978 71 02 62; Calle San Antonio; ☉10am-2pm & 4-7pm Mon-Sat, to 8pm Sun)

ℹ Getting There & Away

Buses travel once daily between Teruel and Albarracín (€3.40, 45 minutes).

Basque Country, Navarra & La Rioja

Best Places to Eat

» Arzak (p434)

» La Cuchara de San Telmo (p432)

» Rio-Oja (p416)

» Mesón las Migas (p452)

» Querida María Restaurante (p440)

Best Places to Stay

» Pensión Bellas Artes (p430)

» Palacio Guendulain (p444)

» Hospederia Las Pedrolas (p458)

» La Casa de los Arquillos (p440)

» Casa Rural Legado de Ugarte (p462)

Why Go?

The jade hills and drizzle-filled skies of this pocket of Spain are quite a contrast to the popular image of the country. The Basques, the people who inhabit this corner, also consider themselves different. They claim to be the oldest Europeans and to speak the original European language. Whether or not this is actually the case remains unproven, but what is beyond doubt is that they live in a land of exceptional beauty and diversity. There are mountains watched over by almost-forgotten gods, cultural museums and art galleries, street parties a million people strong, and arguably the best food in Spain.

Leave the rugged north behind and feel the temperature rise as you hit the open, classically Spanish plains south of Pamplona. Here you enter the world of Navarra and La Rioja. It's a region awash with glorious wine, sunburst colours, dreamy landscapes, medieval monasteries and enticing wine towns.

When to Go
Bilbao

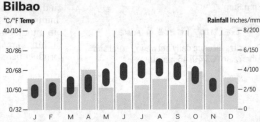

May–Jun Beat the crowds to the art galleries of Bilbao and the *pintxo* bars of San Sebastián.

6–14 Jul Get caught up in the chaos of Pamplona's renowned Sanfermines festival.

Sep Hike the high passes of the Navarran Pyrenees and relish the autumnal colours.

BASQUE COUNTRY

No matter where you've just come from, be it the hot, southern plains of Spain or gentle and pristine France, the Basque Country is different. Known to Basques as Euskadi or Euskal Herria ('the land of Basque Speakers') and called El Pais Vasco in Spanish,

this is where mountain peaks reach for the sky and sublime rocky coves are battered by mighty Atlantic swells. It's a place that demands exploration beyond the delightful and cosmopolitan main cities of Bilbao, Vitoria and San Sebastián. You travel through the Basque Country always curious, and always rewarded.

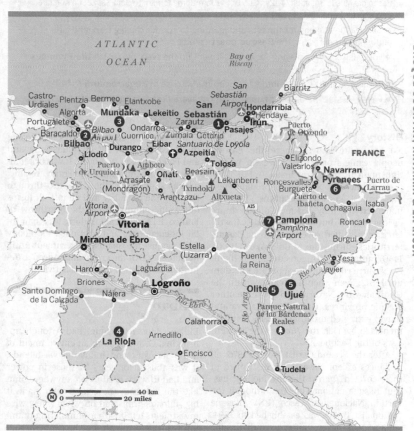

Basque Country, Navarra & La Rioja Highlights

❶ Play on a perfect beach, gorge on fabulous *pintxos* (Basque tapas), dance all night and dream of staying forever in stylish **San Sebastián** (p425), the food capital of the planet

❷ Wish that you too could paint like a genius in the galleries of **Bilbao** (p408)

❸ Get barrelled in the surf at **Mundaka** (p421) and re-create the Guggenheim in sand-castle form on a beautiful Basque beach

❹ Learn the secrets of a good drop in the museums and vineyards of **La Rioja** (p454)

❺ Roll back the years in the medieval fortress towns

of **Olite** (p451) and **Ujué** (p452)

❻ Climb mist-shrouded slopes haunted by witches and vultures in the **Navarran Pyrenees** (p448)

❼ Pretend you're Hemingway during the Sanfermines week of debauchery in **Pamplona** (p442)

TOP PICKS FOR KIDS

With all those tiring outdoor activities, the Basque Country, Navarra and La Rioja are great places for children. In no particular order, here are our top picks:

» Hunting for dinosaurs in **Enciso** (p457).

» Playing dungeons and dragons in the castles of **Olite** (p451) and **Javier** (p447).

» Gawping at Nemo and Jaws in San Sebastián's aquarium (www.aquariumss.com; Paseo del Muelle 34; adult/4-12yr €12/6; ☺10am-8pm Mon-Fri, to 9pm Sat & Sun Apr-Jun & Sep, shorter hours rest of year).

» Sandcastle building for the tots and learning to surf for the big boys and girls almost anywhere along the **Basque coast** (p421).

» For older children, playing Jack and Jill went up the (very big) hill in **the Pyrenees** (p448).

» Turning your little sister into a frog with the witches of **Zugarramurdi** (p449).

» Fiesta, fiesta! The daylight hours of almost every fiesta are tailor-made for children.

History

No one quite knows where the Basque people came from (they have no migration myth in their oral history), but their presence here is believed to predate even the earliest known migrations. The Romans left the hilly Basque Country more or less to itself, but the expansionist Castilian crown gained sovereignty over Basque territories during the Middle Ages (1000–1450), although with considerable difficulty; Navarra constituted a separate kingdom until 1512. Even when they came within the Castilian orbit, Navarra and the three other Basque provinces (Guipúzcoa, Vizcaya and Álava) extracted broad autonomy arrangements, known as the *fueros* (the ancient laws of the Basques).

After the Second Carlist War in 1876, all provinces except Navarra were stripped of their coveted *fueros,* thereby fuelling nascent Basque nationalism. Yet, although the Partido Nacionalista Vasco (PNV; Basque Nationalist Party) was established in 1894, support was never uniform as all Basque provinces included a considerable Castilian contingent.

When the Republican government in Madrid proposed the possibility of home rule (self-government) to the Basques in 1936, both Guipúzcoa and Vizcaya took up the offer. When the Spanish Civil War erupted, conservative rural Navarra and Álava supported Franco, while Vizcaya and Guipúzcoa sided with the Republicans, a decision they paid a high price for in the four decades that followed.

It was during the Franco days that Euskadi Ta Askatasuna (ETA; Basque Homeland and Freedom) was first born. It was originally set up to fight against the Franco regime, which suppressed the Basques through banning the language and almost all forms of Basque culture. After the overthrow of Franco, ETA called for nothing less than total independence and continued its bloody fight against the Spanish government until, in October 2011, the group announced a 'definitive cessation of its armed activity'.

Bilbao

POP 354,200

Bilbao (Bilbo in Basque) had a tough upbringing. Growing up in an environment of heavy industry and industrial wastelands, it was abused for years by those in power and had to work hard to get anywhere. But, like the kid from the estates who made it big, Bilbao's graft paid off when a few wise investments left it with a shimmering titanium fish called the Museo Guggenheim and a horde of arty groupies around the world.

The Botxo (Hole), as it's fondly known to its inhabitants, has now matured into its role of major European art centre. However, in doing so, it hasn't gone all toffee-nosed and forgotten its past: at heart it remains a hard-working and, physically, rather ugly town, but it's one that has real character. It's this down-to-earth soul, rather than its plethora of art galleries, that is the real attraction of the vital, exciting and cultured city of Bilbao.

History

Bilbao was granted the title of *villa* (city-state) in 1300 and medieval *bilbaínos* went about their business in the bustle of Las Siete Calles, the original seven streets of the old town, and down on the wharves. The conquest of the Americas stimulated trade and Basque fishers, merchants and settlers soon built strong links to cities such as Boston. By the late 19th century the smokestacks of steelworks, shipbuilding yards and chemical plants dominated the area's skyline.

From the Carlist Wars through to the Spanish Civil War, Bilbao was always considered the greatest prize in the north, largely for its industrial value. Franco took the city in the spring of 1937 and reprisals against Basque nationalists were massive and long lasting. Yet during the Franco era, the city prospered as it fed Spanish industrial needs. This was followed by the seemingly terminal economic decline that has been so dynamically reversed in recent years.

◉ Sights

Museo Guggenheim   GALLERY

(www.guggenheim-bilbao.es; Avenida Abandoibarra 2; adult/child €13/free; ☉10am-8pm, closed Mon Sep-Jun) Opened in September 1997, Bilbao's Museo Guggenheim lifted modern architecture and Bilbao into the 21st century – with sensation. It boosted the city's already inspired regeneration, stimulated further development and placed Bilbao firmly in the world art and tourism spotlight.

Some might say, probably quite rightly, that structure overwhelms function here and that the Guggenheim is more famous for its architecture than its content. But Canadian architect Frank Gehry's inspired use of flowing canopies, cliffs, promontories, ship shapes, towers and flying fins is irresistible.

Like all great architects, Gehry designed the Guggenheim with historical and geographical contexts in mind. The site was an industrial wasteland, part of Bilbao's wretched and decaying warehouse district on the banks of Ría de Bilbao. The city's historical industries of shipbuilding and fishing reflected Gehry's own interests, not least his engagement with industrial materials in previous works. The gleaming titanium tiles that sheathe most of the building like giant herring scales are said to have been inspired by the architect's childhood fascination with fish.

Other artists have added their touch to the Guggenheim as well. Lying between the glass buttresses of the central atrium and River Nerviòn is a simple pool of water that emits at intervals a mist 'sculpture' by Fuyiko Nakaya. Nearby on the riverbank is a sculpture by Louise Bourgeois, a skeletal canopy representing a spider, entitled Maman, said to symbolise a protective embrace. In the open area to the west of the museum, a fountain sculpture randômly fires off jets of water into the air and youngsters leap to and fro across it. Whilst on the Alameda Mazarredo, on the city side of the museum, is Jeff Koons' kitsch whimsy Puppy, a 12m-tall Highland terrier made up of thousands of begonias. Bilbao has hung on to 'El Poop', who was supposed to be a passing attraction as part of a world tour. With the fond, deprecating humour of citizens of all tough cities, *bilbaínos* will tell you that El Poop came first – and then they had to build a kennel behind it.

Heading inside, the interior of the Guggenheim is purposefully vast. The cathedral-like atrium is more than 45m high. Light pours in through the glass cliffs. Permanent exhibits fill the ground floor and include such wonders as mazes of metal and phrases of light reaching for the skies.

For most people, though, it is the temporary exhibitions that are the main attraction (check the website for upcoming shows). During 2012, these included Cristina García Rodero's fantastic surrealist photographs, British artist David Hockney's landscape paintings and the work of 1960s artist Claes Oldenburg, considered one of the father figures of pop art.

Admission prices vary depending on special exhibitions and time of year. The prices we have quoted are the maxiunm (and most common); the last ticket sales are half an hour before closing. Free guided tours in Spanish take place at 11am and 5pm; sign up half an hour before at the information desk. Tours can be conducted in other languages but you must ask at the information

---

ℹ ARTEAN PASS

The Artean Pass is a joint ticket for the Guggenheim and the Museo de Bellas Artes (p410) which, at €13.50 for adults, offers significant savings. It's available from either museum.

Bilbao

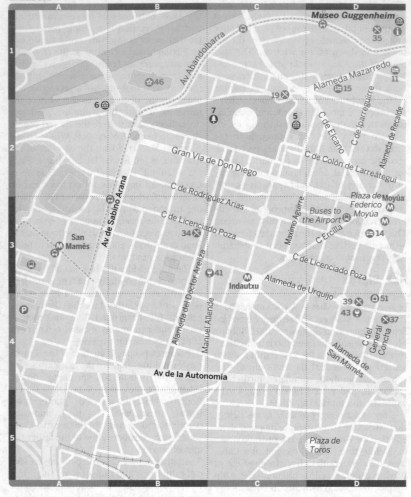

desk beforehand. Groups are limited to 20, so get there early. It's also possible to organise private group tours with advance request in Spanish, English, French and German, among others. The museum is equipped with specially adapted magnetic loop PDA video guides for those with hearing impairments. Excellent self-guided audio tours in various languages are free with admission and there is a special children's audio guide. Entry queues can be horrendous, with wet summer days and Easter almost guaranteeing you a wait of over an hour. The museum is wheelchair-accessible.

Museo de Bellas Artes GALLERY
(Fine Arts Museum; www.museobilbao.com; Plaza del Museo 2; adult/child €6/free, free Wed; ◷10am-8pm Tue-Sun) A mere five minutes from Museo Guggenheim is Bilbao's Museo de Bellas Artes. More than just a complement to the Guggenheim, it often seems to actually exceed its more famous cousin for content.

The museum houses a compelling collection that includes everything from Gothic sculptures to 20th-century pop art. There are three main subcollections: classical art, with works by Murillo, Zurbarán, El Greco, Goya and van Dyck; contemporary art, fea-

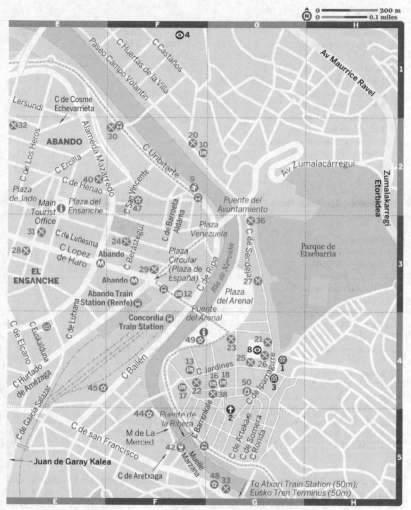

turing works by Gauguin, Francis Bacon and Anthony Caro; and Basque art, with works of the great sculptors Jorge de Oteiza and Eduardo Chillida, and strong paintings by the likes of Ignacio Zuloaga and Juan de Echevarria.

As with the Guggenheim, it's the temporary exhibitions (see website for upcoming exhibitions) that are the real hit though. Antonio López's exhibition of works in 2012 was the most popular the museum has ever staged, with over 209,000 visitors.

A useful audio guide costs €1. The museum is wheelchair accessible.

Casco Viejo   OLD TOWN

The compact Casco Viejo, Bilbao's atmospheric old quarter, is full of charming streets, boisterous bars and plenty of quirky and independent shops. At the heart of the Casco are Bilbao's original seven streets, Las Siete Calles, which date from the 1400s.

The 14th-century Gothic **Catedral de Santiago** (Plaza de Santiago; ⊙10am-1pm & 4-7pm Tue-Sat, 10.30am-1.30pm Sun) has a splendid Renaissance portico and pretty little cloister. Further north, the 19th-century arcaded **Plaza Nueva** is a rewarding *pintxo* (Basque tapas) haunt. There's a lively

Bilbao

Sunday-morning **flea market** here, which is full of secondhand book and record stalls, and pet 'shops' selling chirpy birds (some kept in old-fashioned wooden cages), fluffy mice and tiny baby terrapins. Elsewhere in the market children and adults alike swap and barter football cards and old stamps from countries you've never heard of; in between weave street performers and waiters with trays piled high. Note that the market is much more subdued in winter. A sweeter-smelling **flower market** takes place on Sunday mornings in the nearby **Plaza del Arenal**.

Euskal Museoa   MUSEUM
(Museo Vasco; www.euskal-museoa.org; Plaza Miguel Unamuno 4; adult/child €3/free, free Thu; ◷11am-5pm Tue-Sat, 11am-2pm Sun) This mu-

seum is probably the most complete museum of Basque culture and history in all of Spain. The story kicks off back in the days of prehistory and from this murky period the displays bound rapidly through to the modern age.

The main problem with the museum is that, unless you speak Spanish (or perhaps you studied Euskara at school?), it's all a little meaningless as there are no English or French translations.

The museum is housed in a fine old building, at the centre of which is a peaceful cloister that was part of an original 17th-century Jesuit college. In the cloister is the **Mikeldi Idol**, a powerful pre-Christian, possibly Iron Age, symbolic figure.

The museum is wheelchair-accessible.

Museo Marítimo Ría de Bilbao MUSEUM
(www.museomaritimobilbao.org; Muelle Ramón de la Sota 1; adult/child €5/free; ⊙10am-8pm Tue-Sun, to 6pm weekdays in winter) This space-age maritime museum, appropriately sited down on the waterfront, uses bright and well-thought-out displays to bring the watery depths of Bilbao and Basque maritime history to life. There's an outdoor section where children (and nautically inclined grown-ups) can clamber about a range of boats pretending to be pirates and sailors.

Arkeologi Museo MUSEUM
(Archaeological Museum; Calzadas de Mallona 2; adult/child €3/free, free Fri; ⊙10am-2pm & 4-7.30pm Tue-Sat, 10.30am-2pm Sun; ▣) Through the use of numerous flashing lights, beeping things and a fair few spearheads and old pots, this museum reinforces the point that the inhabitants of this corner of Spain have lived here for a very long time indeed. Labelling is in Spanish and Basque only.

Parque de Doña Casilda de Iturrizar PARK
Floating on waves of peace and quiet just beyond the Museo de Bellas Artes is another work of fine art – the Parque de Doña Casilda de Iturrizar. The centrepiece of this whimsical park is the large pond filled with ornamental ducks and other waterfowl.

Funicular de Artxanda FUNICULAR
(Artxanda Funicular Train; Plaza Funicular; adult/child €0.90/0.28; ⊙7.15am-10pm Mon-Sat, 8.15am-10pm Sun) Bilbao is a city hemmed by hills and mountains into a tight valley. For a breathtaking view over the city, the valley it sits in and the wild Basque mountains beyond, take a trip on the funicular railway that has creaked and moaned its way up the steep slope to the summit of Artxanda for nearly a century.

★✦ Festivals & Events

Bilbao has a packed festival calendar. The following are just the big daddies.

Carnaval CARNIVAL
Carnaval is celebrated with vigour in Bilbao in February.

Blues Music Festival MUSIC
In Getxo, 25km north of Bilbao, in June.

Bilbao BBK Live MUSIC
(www.bilbaobbklive.com) Bilbao's biggest musical event is Bilbao BBK Live, which takes place over three days in early July.

International Jazz Festival MUSIC
(www.jazzeuskadi.com) In Getxo for a week in July.

Semana Grande CULTURAL
Bilbao's grandest fiesta begins on the first Saturday after 15 August. It has a full program of cultural events over 10 days.

Folk Music Festival FOLK MUSIC
In the seaside suburb of Getxo in September.

▭ Sleeping

Bilbao, like the Basque Country in general, is increasingly popular and it can be very hard to find decent accommodation (especially at weekends). You would be wise to book as far ahead as possible. The Bilbao tourism authority has a very useful reservations department (☎902 877 298; www.bilbaoreservas.com).

BASQUE COUNTRY, NAVARRA & LA RIOJA BILBAO

CITY TOURS

There are a number of different city tours available. Some are general-interest tours others focus on specific aspects of the city such as architecture or food. The following are recommended.

Bilbao tourist office (p418) Organises 1½-hour walking tours (€4.50; 10am & noon Saturday and Sunday) covering either the old town or the architecture of the newer parts of town.

Bilboats (☎946 424 157; www.bilboats.com; adult/child from € 10/6) Runs boat cruises along the Nervión several times a day.

Bilbao Greeters (www.bilbaogreeters.com) One of the more original, and interesting, ways to see the city and get to know a local, is through the voluntary Bilbao Greeters organisation. Essentially a local person gives you a free tour of the city showing you their favourite sights, places to hang out and, of course, pintxo (Basque tapas) bars. You need to reserve through the website at least a fortnight in advance.

Walking Tour
Architecture & River Views

❯ One of the pleasures of a visit to Bilbao is just walking around admiring its crazy mix of architectural styles and the riverside walkways.

Start at the Baroque **❶ Teatro Arriaga**, on the edge of the Casco Vieja, which was built in 1890. Follow the river through the **❷ Plaza del Arenal** and pass by the grand **❸ ayuntamiento** (town hall), dating from the late 19th century. Continue upriver along the Paseo Campo Volantin, which is lined with buildings covering a range of styles. Cross over the **❹ Puente Zubizuri** (Zubizuri bridge); this wave-like construction was designed by Santiago Calatrava and is the most striking bridge in the city.

Arriving on the other side of the river turn right and carry on up the waterfront towards the most famous building in the city, the **❺ Museo Guggenheim**. It's hard to unhinge your eyes from the Guggenheim, but do be sure to check out the spider-like **❻ Maman** and **❼ Puppy**, the sweetest-smelling dog you ever did see.

Continue walking along the river past numerous sculptures. On your left is the **❽ Iberdrola tower**, a glass office block which, at 165m is the tallest building in the region. Eventually you arrive at the modern **❾ Euskalduna Palace**. Turn left and enjoy the stroll through the whimsical **❿ Parque de Doña Casilda de Iturrizar**, pass by the **⓫ Museo de Bellas Artes** and head down Calle de Elcano to **⓬ Plaza de Federico Moyúa**, which marks the centre of the new town. This square is lined by impressive buildings including, on your right, the **⓭ Palacio de Chávarri** and, opposite, the oh-so-grand **⓮ Hotel Carlton**. Turn down Calle Ercilla, then right down Alameda Mazarredo until you come to the pretty **⓯ Jardines Albia**, overlooked by the 16th-century church **⓰ Iglesia San Vicente Mátir**. Cut down to Calle López de Haro and, passing the art-nouveau facade of the **⓱ FEVE train station**, cross the Puente del Arenal to arrive back at the start of the walk.

Pensión Iturrienea Ostatua
BOUTIQUE HOTEL €€

(☎944 16 15 00; www.iturrieneaostatua.com; Calle de Santa María 14; r €50-70; ⊛) Easily the most eccentric hotel in Bilbao, it's part farmyard, part old-fashioned toyshop, and a work of art in its own right. The nine rooms here are so full of character that there'll be barely enough room for your own! There's a lovely breakfast area, with baby beds and chairs and lots of toys, it's family friendly. If you do stay here, remember: whatever else you do, for goodness' sake don't let the sheep escape.

Hostal Begoña
BOUTIQUE HOTEL €

(☎944 23 01 34; www.hostalbegona.com; Calle de la Amistad 2; s/d from €50/55; @⊛) The owners of this outstanding place don't need voguish labels for their very stylish and individual creation. Begoña speaks for itself with colourful rooms decorated with modern artworks, all with funky tiled bathrooms and wrought-iron beds. The common areas have mountains of books, traveller information and a rack of computers for internet usage.

It's probably the best hotel in the city in which to meet other travellers. There's a car park nearby.

Barceló Nervión
HOTEL €

(☎944 45 47 00; www.barcelonervion.com; Paseo Campo Volantin 11; s/d from €51/55; P⊛@⊛) OK, it's a chain hotel and, yes, whilst the rooms are cheap, they do charge over the odds for everything else. But let's be fair: hotels of this quality don't come much cheaper than this. The rooms are smart, comfortable and spacious and they'll throw in a baby cot for no extra charge. The location, on the riverfront and equidistant to the old town and the Guggenheim, is ideal.

Gran Hotel Domine
DESIGN HOTEL €€€

(☎944 25 33 00; www.granhoteldominebilbao.com; Alameda Mazarredo 61; r from €132; P⊛@⊛) Designer chic all the way, from the Javier Mariscal interiors to the Phillipe Starck and Arne Jacobsen fittings – and that's just in the loos. This stellar showpiece of the Silken chain has views of the Guggenheim from some of its pricier rooms, a giant column of rounded beach stones reaching for the heavens and a water feature filled with plates and glasses.

Yes, it's a little different! Booking online beforehand can lead to big discounts.

Pensión Gurea
PENSIÓN €

(☎944 16 32 99; www.hostalgurea.com; Calle de Bidebarrieta 14; s €40-45, d €60-65; ⊛) It's a family affair at this jolly *pensión,* where husband and wife run around trying to please you, and the kids just run around (don't worry: they're not noisy – normally!). It's well organised, with large rooms and an immensely friendly welcome. Add it all up and you get what is easily one of the best deals in the old town.

Hotel Carlton
HISTORIC HOTEL €€€

(☎944 16 22 00; www.hotelcarlton.es; Plaza de Frederico Moyúa 2; s/d €237/298; P⊛@⊛) Style, class and sophistication: the reception area is overpoweringly ornate and the trend continues into the rooms, which are simply stunning. When James Bond came to Bilbao in *The World is Not Enough,* you can be absolutely sure that this is where he'd have stayed. Book online in advance for occasional discounts of well over 50%.

Miró Hotel
DESIGN HOTEL €€€

(☎946 61 18 80; www.mirohotelbilbao.com; Alameda Mazarredo 77; s/d from €105/120; ⊛@⊛) This stunning hotel facing Bilbao's most famous designer building has common areas filled with modern photographic art and rooms that are of a slick, minimalist city style. All up it's a perfect fit with arty Bilbao.

Hotel Bilbao Jardines
BOUTIQUE HOTEL €€

(☎944 79 42 10; www.hotelbilbaojardines.com; Calle Jardines 9; s/d from €55/65; ⊛⊛) A welcome change from Casco Viejo's dusty facades, the Jardines has fresh, green decor and rooms that lap up light like a sunbathing lizard. Good value for money.

Pensión Ladero
PENSIÓN €

(☎944 15 09 32; Calle Lotería 1; s/d without bathroom €25/35) The no-fuss rooms here (all with shared bathrooms) are as cheap as Bilbao gets and represent good bang for your buck. You could probably get sponsored for clambering up the zillion-odd steps to the 4th storey where this *pensión* is located. Rooms cannot be reserved in advance.

Camping Sopelana
CAMPGROUND €

(☎946 76 19 81; www.campingsopelana.com; sites for 2 people & car €29.90; ⊛) This exposed site has a swimming pool and is within easy walking distance of Sopelana beach. It's on the metro line, 15km from Bilbao.

✕ Eating

In the world of trade and commerce, the Basques are an outward-looking lot, but when it comes to food they refuse to believe that any other people could possibly match their culinary skills (and they may well have a point). This means that eating out in Bilbao is generally a choice of Basque, Basque or Basque food. Still, life could be worse and there are some terrific places to eat.

The porticoed Plaza Nueva is a good spot for coffee and people watching, especially in summer.

Rio-Oja   BASQUE €
(✆944 15 08 71; Calle de Perro 4; mains €8-11) An institution that shouldn't be missed. It specialises in light Basque seafood and heavy inland fare, but to most foreigners the snails, sheep brains or squid floating in pools of its own ink are the makings of a culinary adventure story they'll be recounting for years. Don't worry, though: it really does taste much better than it sounds.

Mina Restaurante   BASQUE €€€
(✆944 79 59 38; www.restaurantemina.es; Muelle Marzana; tasting menu from €61) Offering unexpected sophistication and fine dining in an otherwise fairly grimy neighbourhood, this riverside, and appropriately fish-based, restaurant has been making waves in the Bilbao culinary world, with some critics citing it as the new *número uno* of Basque cooking. Reservations are essential.

Nerua   BASQUE €€€
(✆944 00 04 30; www.nerua.com; tasting menu €80; ⊙closed Mon & Jan–mid-Feb) The Guggenheim's modernist, chic restaurant, Nerua, is under the direction of super chef Josean Martínez Alija. Needless to say, the *nueva cocina vasca* (Basque nouvelle cuisine) is breathtaking – even the olives are vintage classics: all come from 1000-year-old olive trees! Reservations are essential. If the gourmet restaurant is too extravagant for you, try **El Goog's** bistro, which has set menus from €18.

Larruzz Bilbao   MEDITERRANEAN €€
(✆944 23 08 20; www.larruzzbilbao.com; Calle Uribitarte 24; mains €14-18) Set on the banks of the Nervión, this incredibly popular restaurant (book ahead) has a polished business exterior, but a stone-cottage country interior. Its real speciality is paella, but it also serves various meaty Mediterranean dishes.

Ristorante Passerela   ITALIAN €€
(✆944 44 03 46; Alameda de Urquijo 30; menú del día €12.50, mains €10-14) Opened in 1980 this is one of the oldest, and best regarded, Italian restaurants in Bilbao. In proper Italian style you order a plate of fresh pasta to start and then follow up with a meat or fish course, followed by a sticky Sicilian dessert. After which you'll probably get busy making plans for a holiday in Italy.

Zortziko Restaurante   BASQUE €€€
(✆944 23 97 43; Alameda Mazarredo 17; menus from €60; ⊙Tue-Sat; ✔) Michelin-starred chef Daniel García presents immaculate modern Basque cuisine in a formal 1920s-style French dining room. The highly inventive menu changes frequently but can include such delicacies as citrus soup or mussel cannelloni. If the food excites your taste buds that much, then sign up for one of his occasional cooking courses.

Abaroa   BASQUE €€
(✆944 13 20 51; www.abaroa.net; Paseo del Campo de Volantin 13; mains €8-15, menú del día €12.99) This intimate and brightly furnished restaurant is a big name with locals. It specialises in hearty countryside fare, but with a twist of today. The result is that black pudding and a bowl of beans have never been so well presented or tasted so good. There is a second, equally good branch on **Plaza del Museo**.

Casa Victor Montes   BASQUE €€
(✆944 15 70 67; www.victormontesbilbao.com; Plaza Nueva 8; mains €15) Part bar, part shop, part restaurant, total work of art, the Victor Montes is quite touristy but locals also appreciate its over-the-top decoration, its good food and the 1000 or so bottles of wine lined up behind the bar. If you're stopping by for a full meal, book in advance and savour the house special, *bacalao* (dried cod).

Restaurante Vegetariano   VEGETARIAN €€
(Alameda de Urquijo 33; mains €8-12; ⊙lunch Mon-Sat; ✔) Full of beans, this little place is one of the Basque Country's all-too-rare vegetarian restaurants. It has crispy fresh salads, imaginative quiches and lots of bean-based meals. There's an excellent noticeboard covering everything and anything alternative taking place in the city.

Drinking

In the Casco Viejo, around Calles Barrenkale, Ronda and de Somera, there are plenty of

PINTXO BARS IN BILBAO

Although it lacks San Sebastián's stellar reputation for *pintxos* (Basque tapas), prices are generally slightly lower here and the quality is about equal. There are literally hundreds of *pintxo* bars throughout Bilbao, but the Plaza Nueva on the edge of the Casco Viejo offers especially rich pickings, as do Calle de Perro and Calle Jardines. Some of the city's long-time standouts (all charge from around €2.50 per *pintxo*):

Bar Gure Toki (Plaza Nueva 12) With a subtle but simple line in creative *pintxos*.

Café-Bar Bilbao (Plaza Nueva 6) Cool blue southern tile work and warm northern atmosphere.

Casa Victor Montes As well known for its *pintxos* as its full meals.

Sorginzulo (Plaza Nueva 12) A matchbox-sized bar with an exemplary spread of *pintxos*. The house special is calamari but it's only served on weekends.

Berton Sasibil (Calle Jardines 8) Here you can watch informative films on the crafting of the same superb *pintxos* that you're munching on.

Claudio: La Feria del Jamón (Calle Esperanza 9-18) A creaky old place full of ancient furnishings. As you'll guess from the name and the dozens of legs of ham hanging from the ceiling, it's all about pigs here.

Don't restrict your search for the perfect *pintxo* to the Casco Viejo: the El Ensanche area also has some good options. Some of the best are **El Globo** (Calle de Diputación 8), an unassuming but popular bar with favourites such as *txangurro gratinado* (spider crab); **Los Candiles** (Calle de Diputación 1), a narrow, low-key little bar, with some subtle *pintxos* filled with the taste of the sea; and **Mugi** (Licenciado Poza 55), which is one of the best regarded *pintxo* bars in town. It can get so busy that you might have to stand outside.

terrific hole-in-the-wall, no-nonsense bars with a generally youngish crowd.

Across the river, in the web of streets around Muelle Marzana and Bilbao la Vieja, are scores of little bars and clubs. This is gritty Bilbao as it used to be in the days before the arty makeover. It's both a Basque heartland and the centre of the city's ethnic community. The many bars around here are normally welcoming, but one or two can be a bit seedy. It's not a great idea for a woman to walk here alone at night. Of the many bars in this neighbourhood, one very pleasant one for a sundowner over the river is **Marzana 16** (Calle de Marzana 16); its sandwiches are also worthy of praise.

Twiggy Bar BAR
(Alameda de Urquijo 37; ☺1pm-2am daily) Retro psychedelio! Happy post-hippie place with a cheerful mix of '60s kitsch for lovely people. Serves cheap snacks during the day.

Kamin Bar BAR
(Manuel Allende 8; ☺6.30pm-2.30am daily) Laid-back listening in rosy light among the Bilbao cognoscenti. The music trails sweetly through everything from rock and pop to alternative and fresh new sounds on the

Basque scene. To get there head down Calle Ercilla from Plaza de Federico Moyua, turn right onto Alameda de Urquijo and it's three blocks down on the left.

☆ Entertainment

There are plenty of clubs and live venues in Bilbao, and the vibe is friendly and generally easy-going. Venues' websites usually have details of upcoming gigs.

Bilbao offers regular performances of dance, opera and drama at the city's principal theatre and the Kafe Antzokia. Check the theatre websites for current information.

TOP CHOICE **Kafe Antzokia** LIVE MUSIC
(www.kafeantzokia.com; Calle San Vicente 2) This is the vibrant heart of contemporary Basque Bilbao, featuring international rock bands, blues and reggae, but also the cream of Basque rock-pop. Weekend concerts run from 10pm to 1am, followed by DJs until 5am. Cover charge for concerts can range from about €12 upwards. During the day it's a cafe, restaurant and cultural centre all rolled into one and has frequent exciting events on.

BASQUE COUNTRY, NAVARRA & LA RIOJA BILBAO

BASQUE COUNTRY, NAVARRA & LA RIOJA BILBAO

BILBAO CAFES

Bilbao has some classic cafes in which to enjoy a caffeine shot and a sweet snack. Styles range from frusty and old fashioned to modern and flash. Here's our pick of the crop.

Café Iruña (www.cafesdebilbao.net; cnr Calles de Colón de Larreátegui & Berástegui) Ornate Moorish style and a century of gossip are the defining characteristics of this grande old dame. It's the perfect place to indulge in a bit of people-watching.

Café Boulevard (Calle del Arenal 3) A Bilbao institution since 1871, this is a classic dusty art-deco cafe with old-fashioned service and waiters who certainly don't smile. Bring a work of highbrow literature, sip a strong black coffee and enjoy the classiest cafe in town.

La Granja (www.cafesdebilbao.net; Plaza Circular 3) With its claret-red furnishings and polished wooden bar top, this place, which first opened its doors in 1926, is another of Bilbao's old time-warp cafes.

Opila (Calle de Sendeja 4) Fantastic patisserie and cafe. Downstairs is all art-deco furnishings and glass display cabinets and upstairs is way more up to the moment.

Mami Lou Cupcake (Calle Barraincua 7; ⊘9am-8.30pm Mon-Sat) Relive your childhood at this cute little cafe with 1950s deco and colourful homemade cupcakes.

Teatro Arriaga THEATRE
(www.teatroarriaga.com; Plaza Arriaga) The baroque facade of this venue commands the open spaces of El Arenal between the Casco Viejo and the river. It stages theatrical performances and classical-music concerts.

Euskalduna Palace LIVE MUSIC
(www.euskalduna.net; Avenida Abandoibarra) About 600m downriver from the Guggenheim is another modernist gem, built on the riverbank in a style that echoes the great shipbuilding works of the 19th century. The Euskalduna houses the Bilbao Symphony Orchestra and the Basque Symphony Orchestra.

Conjunto Vacío CLUB
(Muelle de La Merced 4; admission Fri & Sat from €5) House is the spin here and there's a very style-conscious, confident, young, mixed gay-and-straight crowd. Admission price depends on the night and the event.

Le Club CLUB
(www.leclub.es; Muelle Marzana 4; admission €10) Three floors to twist, gyrate and then relax on. The 1st floor has rock and '80s pop, the 2nd has dance music and the 3rd is the chill-out lounge.

El Balcón de la Lola CLUB
(Calle Bailén 10; admission Fri & Sat €10) One of Bilbao's most popular mixed gay-and-straight clubs, this is the place to come if you're looking for hip industrial decor and

a packed Saturday-night disco. It's located under the railway lines.

 Shopping

The old town is full of quirky fashion shops.

Elkar Megadenda BOOKS
(Calle de Iparragirre 26) Basque publications are strongly represented here. It also stocks books in Spanish and a few in English, and there's an excellent map and travel section. There are a couple of other branches in the city.

Tintas Books BOOKS
(Calle del Generál Concha 10) Broad selection of novels (including some in foreign languages), travel books, Lonely Planet guides, road maps and topographical maps for trekkers.

 Information

Emergency
Policía Municipal (✆944 20 50 00; Calle de Luís Briñas 14)

Internet Access & Telephone
Locutomo Lazarnet Centre (Calle de Sendeja 5; per hr €3.60; ⊘10.30am-1am Mon-Fri, 11am-1am Sat & Sun) Also has cheap international phone rates.

Tourist Information
Tourist office (✆944 79 57 60) airport (✆944 71 03 01; airport; ⊘9am-9pm Mon-Sat, 9am-3pm Sun); Guggenheim (Alameda Mazarredo 66; ⊘10am-7pm Mon-Sat, 10am-6pm Sun,

shorter hours Sep-Jun); main office (Plaza del Ensanche 11; ⊘9am-2pm & 4-7.30pm Mon-Fri); Teatro Arriaga (Plaza Arriaga; ⊘9.30am-2pm & 4-7.30pm daily) Bilbao's friendly tourist-office staffers are extremely helpful, well informed and, above all, enthusiastic about their city. At all offices ask for the free bimonthly *Bilbao Guía,* with its entertainment listings plus tips on restaurants, bars and nightlife.

ℹ Getting There & Away

Air

Bilbao's **airport** (☏902 40 47 04; www.aena.es) is near Sondika, to the northeast of the city. A number of European flag carriers serve the city and, of the budget airlines, **EasyJet** (www.easyjet.com) and **Vueling** (www.vueling.com) cover the widest range of destinations.

Bus

Bilbao's main bus station, **Termibus** (San Mamés), is west of the centre. There are regular services to the following destinations:

DESTINATION	FARE (€)	DURATION (HR)
Barcelona	43.81	7-8
Biarritz (France)	18.85	3
Logroño	12.80	2¾
Madrid	28.45	4¾
Oñati	6.05	1¼
Pamplona	13.75	2¾
San Sebastián	10.10	1
Santander	from 7.02	1¼
Vitoria	5.80	1½

Bizkaibus travels to destinations throughout the rural Basque Country, including coastal communities such as Lekeitio (€3.20) and Bermeo (€2.35).

Train

The Abando train station is just across the river from Plaza Arriaga and the Casco Viejo. There are frequent trains to the following destinations:

DESTINATION	FARE (€)	DURATION (HR)
Barcelona	64.80	6¾
Burgos	22.70	3
Madrid	from 50.50	5
Valladolid	from 31.10	4

Next door is the Concordia train station, with its handsome art-nouveau facade of wrought iron and tiles. It is used by the **FEVE** (www.feve.es) private rail company for running trains west into Cantabria. There are three daily trains to

Santander (from €8.25, three hours) where you can change for stations in Asturias.

The Atxuri train station is about 1km upriver from Casco Viejo. From here, **Eusko Tren/Ferrocarril Vasco** (www.euskotren.es) operates services every half-hour to the following:

DESTINATION	FARE (€)	DURATION (HR)
Bermeo	3	1½
Guernica	3	1
Mundaka	3	1½

Hourly **Eusko Tren** (www.euskotren.es) trains go to San Sebastián (€5.30, 2¾ hours) via Durango, Zumaia and Zarautz, but the bus is much quicker.

ℹ Getting Around

To/From the Airport

The **airport bus** (Bizkaibus A3247; €1.30, 30 minutes) departs from a stand on the extreme right as you leave arrivals. It runs through the northwestern section of the city, passing the Museo Guggenheim, stopping at Plaza de Federico Moyúa and terminating at the Termibus (bus station). It runs from the airport every 20 to 30 minutes from 6.20am to midnight. There is also a direct hourly bus from the airport to San Sebastián (€15.70, 1¼ hours). It runs from 7.45am to 11.45pm.

Taxis from the airport to the Casco Viejo cost about €24.

Metro

There are metro stations at all the main focal points of El Ensanche and at Casco Viejo. Tickets start at €1.45. The metro runs to the north coast from a number of stations on both sides of the river and makes it easy to get to the beaches closest to Bilbao.

TRAVEL PASSES

The **Bilbaocard** (1-/2-/3-day pass €6/10/12) entitles the user to reduced rates on all city transport as well as reductions at many of the sights. It can be purchased from any of the tourist offices. **Creditrans** give significant discounts on the metro, tram and city-bus network. They are available in €5, €10 and €15 denominations from all metro and tram stations.

WORTH A TRIP

PUENTE COLGANTE

A worthwhile stop en route to the beaches is the Unesco World Heritage–listed Puente Colgante, designed by Alberto Palacio, a disciple of Gustave Eiffel (he of Parisian tower fame). Opening in 1893, it was the world's first transporter bridge and links the suburbs of Getxo and Portugalete. A platform, suspended from the actual bridge high above, is loaded with up to six cars plus foot passengers; it then glides silently over Río Nervión to the other bank. Rides cost €0.30 one way per person. You can also take a lift up to the superstructure at 46m (€5) and walk across the river and back for some great views (not for those prone to vertigo). Another choice is to cross the river by small ferry boat (€0.30). The nearest metro stop from Bilbao is Areeta or Portugalete (both €1.45).

Tram

Bilbao's Eusko Tren tramline is a boon to locals and visitors alike. It runs to and fro between Basurtu, in the southwest of the city, and the Atxuri train station. Stops include the Termibus station, the Guggenheim and Teatro Arriaga by the Casco Viejo. Tickets cost €1.40 and need to be validated in the machine next to the ticket dispenser before boarding.

Around Bilbao

BEACHES

Two reasonable beaches for swimming are Azkorri and Sopelana. The latter is the most consistent surf beach in the area. Better beaches can be found east of Plentzia. Also good is the sheltered beach at Gorliz, which has a pretty lighthouse and some fine views from the Astondo end of the beach. There are well-signposted tracks for walkers.

GUERNICA
POP 15,600

Guernica (Basque: Gernika) is a state of mind. At a glance it seems no more than a modern and ugly country town. Apparently, prior to the morning of 26 April 1937, Guernica wasn't quite so ugly, but the horrifying events of that day meant that the town was later reconstructed as fast as possible with little regard for aesthetics. Franco, who'd been having some problems with the Basques, decided to teach them a lesson by calling in his buddy Hitler. On that fateful morning planes from Hitler's Condor Legion flew backwards and forwards over the town demonstrating their newfound concept of saturation bombing. In the space of a few hours, the town was destroyed and many people were left dead or injured. Exactly how many people were killed remains very hard to quantify with figures ranging

from a couple of hundred to well over 1000. The Museo de la Paz de Gernika claims that around 250 civilians were killed and several hundred injured. What makes the bombings even more shocking is that it wasn't the first time this had happened. Just days earlier, the nearby town of Durango suffered a similar fate, but that time the world had simply not believed what it was being told.

Franco chose Guernica for his 'lesson' because of its symbolic value to the Basques. It's the ancient seat of Basque democracy and the site at which the Basque parliament met beneath the branches of a sacred oak tree from medieval times until 1876. Today the original oak is nothing but a stump, but the Tree of Guernica lives on in the form of a young oak tree.

The tragedy of Guernica gained international resonance with Picasso's iconic painting *Guernica*, which has come to symbolise the violence of the 20th century. A copy of the painting now hangs in the entrance hall of the UN headquarters in New York, while the original hangs in the Centro de Arte Reina Sofía (p79) in Madrid.

⊙ Sights

Museo de la Paz de Gernika   MUSEUM
(Guernica Peace Museum; www.peacemuseum guernica.org; Plaza Foru 1; adult/child €5/2; ⊙10am-2pm & 4-7pm Tue-Sat, 10am-2pm Sun) Guernica's seminal experience is a visit to the museum, where audiovisual displays calmly reveal the horror of war and hatred, both in the Basque Country and around the world. Display panels are in Castilian and Basque, but translations are available. The museum is wheelchair accessible. A couple of blocks north, on Calle Allende Salazar, is a ceramic-tile version of Picasso's *Guernica*.

Euskal Herriko Museoa MUSEUM
(Calle Allende Salazar; adult/child €3/1.50; ☺10am-2pm & 4-7pm Tue-Sat, 10.30am-2.30pm & 4 7.30pm Sun) Housed in the 18th-century Palacio de Montefuerte, this museum contains a comprehensive exhibition on Basque history and culture, with fine old maps, engravings and a range of other documents and portraits. The museum is wheelchair-accessible.

Parque de los Pueblos de Europa PARK, MONUMENT
The pleasant Parque de los Pueblos de Europa contains a couple of typically curvaceous sculptures by Henry Moore and other works by Eduardo Chillida. The park leads to the attractive Casa de Juntas, where the provincial government has met since 1979. Nearby is the famous Tree of Guernica, sheltered by a neoclassical gazebo.

🛏 Sleeping & Eating
The accommodation situation in Guernica is in a pretty sorry state and most people sensibly visit as a day trip from Bilbao. There are several simple restaurants and bars scattered around the main square and surrounding streets.

ℹ Information
Tourist office (☎946 25 58 92; www.gernika -lumo.org; Artekalea 8; ☺10am-2pm & 4-7pm Mon-Sat, 10am-2pm Sun) This helpful office has friendly multilingual staff.

ℹ Getting There & Away
Guernica is an easy day trip from Bilbao by ET/FV train from Atxuri train station (€2.80, one hour). Trains run every half-hour.

MUNDAKA
POP 1800
Universally regarded as the home of the best wave in Europe, Mundaka is a name of legend for surfers across the world. The wave breaks on a perfectly tapering sandbar formed by the outflow of the Río Urdaibai and, on a good day, offers heavy, barrelling lefts that can reel off for hundreds of metres. Fantastic for experienced surfers, Mundaka is absolutely not a place for novices to take to the waves.

Despite all the focus being on the waves, Mundaka has done a sterling job of not turning itself into just another 'hey dude' surf town and remains a resolutely Basque port with a pretty main square and harbour area. There's a small tourist office (☎946 17 72 01;

www.mundaka.org; Calle Kepa Deuna; ☺10.30am-1.30pm & 4-7pm Mon-Sat, 11am-2pm Sun).

Those wishing to stay and practise their tube-riding skills should pull in at the Hotel Atalaya (☎946 17 70 00; www.atalayahotel.es; Kalea Itxaropena 1; s/d €88/110; P ✿), which is in a lovely old building near the waterfront and has clean and reliable rooms – although, like everywhere in Mundaka, it's a little overpriced. If nights under canvas are more your thing, then Camping Portuondo (☎946 87 77 01; www.campingportuondo.com; sites per person/tent €8/15.30, bungalows from €100.70; ✿✿), just to the south of town, should fit the bill. It has pleasant terraced grounds, a pool and a restaurant, but gets overrun in the summer.

Buses and ET/FV trains between Bilbao and Bermeo stop here.

BERMEO
POP 17,000
Located just a few minutes to the north of Mundaka and on the open coast proper, this tough fishing port is refreshingly down to earth and hasn't lost its soul to tourism. Though there are no beaches here, it's an enjoyable place to while away a few hours watching the boats bustle in and out of the harbour.

There's a small tourist office (☎946 17 91 54; www.bermeo.org; Lamera; ☺10am-8pm Mon-Sat, 10am-2pm & 4-7pm Sun) on the waterfront. The absorbing Museo del Pescador (Plaza Torrontero 1; adult/child €3/1.50; ☺10am-2pm & 4-7pm Tue-Sat, 10am-2 15pm Sun), in the handsome 15th-century Torre Ercilla, is steeply uphill from the tourist office.

A few kilometres beyond Bermeo, the Ermita de San Juan de Gaztelugatxe stands on an islet that is connected to the mainland by a bridge. It also has two natural arches on its seaward side. Built by the Knights Templars in the 10th century, it has also served as a handy shelter for shipwrecked sailors.

Half-hourly buses and ET/FV trains run from Bermeo to Bilbao (€2.40, 1¼ hours).

The Central Basque Coast
The coast road from Bilbao to San Sebastián is a glorious journey past spectacular seascapes, with cove after cove stretching east and verdant fields suddenly ending where cliffs plunge into the sea. Casas rurales (village or farmstead accommodation) and camping grounds are plentiful and well signposted.

Basque Culture

The Basques are different. They have inhabited their corner of Spain and France seemingly forever. Whilst many aspects of their unique culture are hidden from prying eyes, the following are visible to any visitor.

Pelota

The national sport of the Basque country is *pelote basque,* and every village in the region has its own court – normally backing up against the village church. Pelota originates from an ancient game called *jeu de paume* from which modern tennis also stems. Pelota can be played in several different ways: bare-handed, with small wooden rackets, or – the version best known internationally – with a long hand-basket called *chistera,* with which the player can throw the ball at speeds of up to 300km/h. It's possible to see pelota matches throughout the region during summer.

Lauburu

The most visible symbol of Basque culture is *lauburu,* the Basque cross. The meaning of this ancient symbol is lost in the mists of time – some say it represents the four old regions of the Basque Country, others that it represents spirit, life, consciousness and form – but today most people regard it as a symbol of prosperity, hence its appearance in modern jewellery and above house doors. It is also used to signify life and death, and therefore commonly found on old headstones.

Traditional Basque Games

Basque sports aren't just limited to pelota: there's also log cutting, stone lifting, bale tossing and tug of war. Most stemmed from the day-to-day activities of the region's farmers and fishermen. Although

Clockwise from top left
1. Log cutting 2. Watching pelota 3. Folk dancers in traditional dress

technology has replaced the need to use most of these skills on a daily basis, the sports are kept alive at numerous fiestas.

Bulls & Fiestas

Although almost every town, village and city has its annual fiesta week, none are as famous (or perhaps infamous) as Sanfermines with its legendary *encierro* (running of the bulls) in Pamplona. But how did the madness first begin? The purpose of the *encierro* was to transfer bulls from the corrals where they would have spent the night to the bullring where they would fight. Sometime in the 14th century someone worked out that the quickest and 'easiest' way to do this was to chase the bulls out of the corrals and into the ring. One thing led to another and the *encierro* went from being merely a way of moving bulls around to the full-blown carnage of Pamplona's Sanfermines.

Traditional Dress

The daylight hours of most Basque festivals are a good time to see traditional Basque dress and dance. It's said that there are around 400 different Basque dances, many of which have their own special kind of dress.

Basque Language

Victor Hugo described the Basque language as a 'country', and it would be a rare Basque who'd disagree with him. The language, known as *euskara*, is the oldest in Europe and has no known connection to any Indo-European languages. Its earliest written elements are considered to be inscriptions dating from the 3rd century AD, found in 2006 at an archaeological site near Vitoria. Suppressed by Franco, Basque was subsequently recognised as one of Spain's official languages, and it has become the language of choice – and of identity – among a growing number of young Basques.

ELANTXOBE
POP 444

The tiny hamlet of Elantxobe, with its colourful houses clasping like geckos to an almost sheer cliff face, is undeniably one of the most attractive spots along the entire coast. The difficulty of building here, and the lack of a beach, has meant that it has been saved from the worst of tourist-related development. Public-transport fans will be so excited by Elantxobe that the earth really will move for them – the streets are so narrow that buses don't have space to turn around, so the road spins around for them! See the Lekeitio section for bus connections.

LEKEITIO
POP 7300

Bustling Lekeitio has an attractive old core centred on the unnaturally large and slightly out-of-place-looking late-Gothic Iglesia de Santa María de la Asunción.

For most visitors, it's the two beaches that are the main draw. The one just east of the river, with a small rocky mound of an island just offshore, is one of the finest beaches in the Basque Country.

The 'highlight' of Lekeitio's annual Fiesta de San Antolín (5 Sep) involves a tug of war with a goose (nowadays they use a pre-killed goose).

Accommodation is scarce and pricey, but the tourist office (946 84 40 17; Plaza Independencia) can point you in the direction of private rooms. Otherwise the Aisia Lekeitio (946 84 26 55; www.aisiahoteles.com; Avenida Santa Elena; s/d €98/144;), which includes a thalassotherapy centre, is the pick of the crop.

Bizkaibus A3513 (€3.20) leaves from Calle Hurtado de Amézaga, by Bilbao's Abando train station, about eight times a day (except Sunday) and goes via Guernica and Elantxobe. Fairly regular buses also run from Lekeitio to San Sebastián.

ZUMAIA
POP 8800

First impressions of Zumaia are not great, but struggle through the industrial zone that hems the town and you'll find an attractive centre. For beach lovers, further rewards await in the form of the Playa de Izturun, wedged in among slate cliffs, and the Playa de Santiago, a more traditional strand of soft sand a couple of kilometres east of the town centre.

For weary heads you'll find a couple of casas rurales in the hills behind Playa de Santiago. Of these, Karakas (943 86 17 36; www.nekatur.net/karakas; r/apt €48.60/108), 1km inland and with gorgeous views over lush green fields down to the sea, has cheerful rooms and offers great value. It's on a working farm, which will doubtless keep any kids in tow happy.

GETARIA & ZARAUTZ
POP 2525/22.000

The attractive medieval fishing settlement of Getaria is a world away from nearby cosmopolitan San Sebastián and is a much better place to get a feel for coastal Basque culture. The old village tilts gently downhill to a baby-sized harbour, at the end of which is a forested island known as El Ratón (the Mouse), on account of its similarity to a mouse (this similarity is easiest to see after several strong drinks!).

It might have been this giant mouse that first encouraged the town's most famous son, the sailor Juan Sebastián Elcano, to take to the ocean waves. His adventures eventually culminated in him becoming the first man to sail around the world, after the captain of his ship, Magellan, died halfway through the endeavour.

Getaria has a short but very pleasant beach next to the town's busy harbour, which is almost totally sheltered from all but the heaviest Atlantic swells. Its safe bathing makes it an ideal family beach. If you're more a culture vulture than a bronzed god or goddess, get your kicks at the new Cristóbal Balenciaga Museoa (www.cristobalbalenciagamuseoa.com; adult/child €8/free; 10am-8pm Tue-Sun). Local boy Cristóbal became one of the big names in fashion design in the 1950s and '60s and this impressive museum showcases some of his best works.

Just a couple of kilometres further east, along a coastal road that battles with cliffs, ocean waves and several cavelike tunnels, is Zarautz, which consists of a 2.5km-long soft sand beach backed by a largely modern strip of tower blocks. The town is a popular resort for Spaniards and in the summer it has a lively atmosphere with plenty of places to eat, drink and stay. The beach, which is one of the longest in the Basque Country, has some of the most consistent surfing conditions in the area and a number of surf schools will help you 'hang ten'.

Despite Zarautz's more energetic atmosphere, there's little doubt that Getaria actually makes for the more attractive base.

For accommodation in Getaria, try one of the following. **Getariano Pentsioa** (☑943 14 05 67; www.pensiongetariano.es; Calle Herrieta 3; s €40-50, d €55-70; 🛜) is a charming, mellow yellow building with flower-filled balconies and comfortable rooms. The **Hotel Itxas-Gain** (☑943 14 10 35; www.hotelitxasgain. com; Roke Devnal; s €50, d €65-125; 🛜) is a very good deal and has a mixture of room types: some have little balconies and whirlpool baths that overlook the whirlpool-like ocean. Weather permitting, breakfast (€6) is served in the peaceful gardens. In Zarautz, campers will find **Gran Camping Zarautz** (☑943 83 12 38; www.grancampingzarautz.com; sites for 2 people, tent & car €23.40; 🛜), which has memorable views off the cliffs, at the far eastern end of town.

For food we're willing to bet money on the fact that you won't be able walk past one of Getaria's harbour-front **restaurants**, where the days catch is barbequed up on open fires, without feeling hungry. Wash your lunch down with a glass of crisp, locally produced *txakoli* (white wine).

San Sebastián

POP 183,300

It's said that nothing is impossible. This is wrong. It's impossible to lay eyes on San Sebastián (Basque: Donostia) and not fall madly in love. This stunning city is everything that grimy Bilbao is not: cool, svelte and flirtatious by night, charming and well mannered by day. Best of all is the summer fun on the beach. For it's setting, form and attitude, Playa de la Concha is the equal of any city beach in Europe. Then there's Playa de Gros (also known as Playa de la Zurriola), with its surfers and sultry beach goers. As the sun falls on another sweltering summer's day, you'll sit back with a drink and an artistic *pintxo* and realise that, yes, you too are in love with sexy San Sebastián.

San Sebastián has three main centres of action. The lively Parte Vieja (old town) lies across the neck of Monte Urgull, the bay's eastern headland, and is where the most popular *pintxo* bars and many of the cheap lodgings are to be found. South of the Parte Vieja is the commercial and shopping district, the Centro Romántico, its handsome grid of late-19th-century buildings extend-

ing from behind Playa de la Concha to the banks of Río Urumea. On the east side of the river is the district of Gros, a pleasant enclave that, with its relaxed ambience and the surfing beach of Playa de Gros, makes a cheerful alternative to the honeypots on the west side of the river.

History

San Sebastián was for centuries little more than a fishing village, but by 1180 it was granted self-governing status by the king dom of Navarra, for which the bay was the principal outlet to the sea. Whale and cod fishing were the main occupations, along with the export of Castilian products to European ports and then to the Americas. After years of knockabout trans-European conflicts that included the razing of the city by Anglo-Portuguese forces during the Peninsular War, San Sebastián was hoisted into 19th-century stardom as a fashionable watering hole by Spanish royalty dodging the searing heat of the southern *meseta* (tableland). By the close of the century, the city had been given a superb belle-époque makeover that has left a legacy of elegant art-nouveau buildings and beachfront swagger.

After WWII the city's popularity sagged, but it's now undergoing a major revival and its overall style and excitement are giving it a growing reputation as a major venue for international cultural and commercial events. The beachfront area now contains some of the most expensive properties in Spain and the city is firmly entrenched on the Spanish tourist trail, which gives it a highly international feel.

In 2016 it will share the title of European City of Culture with the Polish city of Wrocław.

◎ Sights

Beaches & Isla de Santa Clara   BEACH
Fulfilling almost every idea of how a perfect city beach should be formed, **Playa de**

San Sebastián

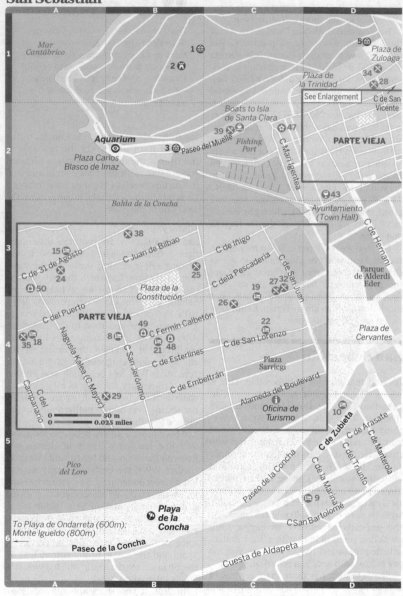

Mar Cantábrico

1

2

3

Aquarium

Plaza Carlos
Blasco de Imaz

Boats to Isla de Santa Clara

39

47

Paseo del Muelle

Fishing Port

Plaza de Zuloaga

34 28

Plaza de la Trinidad

See Enlargement

C de San Vicente

PARTE VIEJA

C Mari Gentea

43

Bahía de la Concha

Ayuntamiento
(Town Hall)

C de Hernani

Parque de Alderdi Eder

Plaza de Cervantes

38

15

24

C de 31 de Agosto

50

C del Puerto

PARTE VIEJA

8

Nagusia Kalea (C. Mayor)

35 18

C del Campanario

29

49

C Fermín Calbetón

21 48

C de San Jerónimo

C de Esterlines

C de Embeltrán

C Juan de Bilbao

Plaza de la Constitución

25

C de Íñigo

C de la Pescadería

19

26

22

C de San Juan

27 32

C de San Lorenzo

Plaza Sarriegi

Alameda del Boulevard

Oficina de Turismo

0 ___ 50 m
0 ___ 0.025 miles

Plaza de Cervantes

10

C de Zubieta

C de Arasate

C del Triunfo

C de Manterola

Pico del Loro

Paseo de la Concha

C de la Marina

9

C San Bartolomé

Playa de la Concha

*To Playa de Ondarreta (600m);
Monte Igueldo (800m)*

Paseo de la Concha

Cuesta de Aldapeta

la Concha and its westerly extension, Playa de Ondarreta, are easily among the best city beaches in Europe. Throughout the long summer months a fiesta atmosphere prevails, with thousands of tanned and toned bodies spread across the sands. The swimming is al-most always safe. The Isla de Santa Clara, about 700m from the beach, is accessible by glass-bottom boats (to the island €3.80, tour the bay €6) that run every half-hour from June to September from the fishing port. At low tide the island gains its own tiny beach.

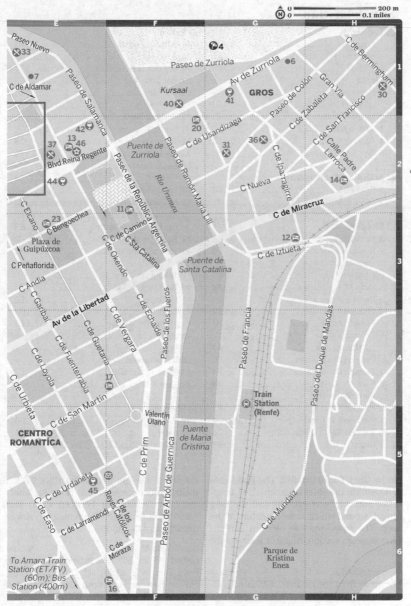

Less popular, but just as showy, **Playa de Gros** (Playa de la Zurriola), east of Río Urumea, is the city's main surf beach. Though swimming here is more dangerous than at Playa de la Concha, it has more of a local vibe.

Aquarium AQUARIUM
(www.aquariumss.com; Plaza Carlos Blasco de Imaz 1; adult/child €12/6; ⊙10am-8pm Mon-Fri, 10am-9pm Sat & Sun) In the city's excellent aquarium you'll fear for your life as huge sharks bear down on you and be tripped

San Sebastián

out by fancy fluoro jellyfish. The highlights of a visit are the cinema-screen-sized deep-ocean and coral-reef exhibits and the long tunnel, around which swim monsters of the deep. The aquarium also contains a maritime museum section. Allow at least 1½ for a visit.

Monte Igueldo FUNICULAR
The views from the summit of Monte Iguel-do, just west of town, will make you feel like a circling hawk staring over the vast panorama of the Bahía de la Concha and the surrounding coastline and mountains. The best way to get there is via the old-world **funicular railway** (return adult/child €2.80/2.10; ☺10am-10pm) to the **Parque de Atracciones** (www.monteigueldo.es; admission €1.90; ☺11am-9.30pm), a slightly tacky mini theme park at the top of the hill. Individual rides (which include roller coasters, boat rides, carousels and pony rides) cost between €1.80 and €2.50 extra. Trains on the funicular railway depart every 15 minutes.

San Telmo Museoa MUSEUM
(☎943 48 15 80; www.santelmomuseoa.com; Plaza Zuloaga 1; adult/child €5/free, Tue free; ☺10am-8pm Tue-Sun) Both the oldest and newest museum in the Basque Country, the San Telmo museum has existed since 1902 – sort of. It was actually closed for many years but after major renovation work it has recently reopened and is now a museum of Basque culture and society. The displays range from historical artefacts to the squiggly lines of modern art and all the pieces are supposed to reflect Basque cul-

ture and society in some way or another. In reality, though, for most people the collection is a bit haphazard and the connections between the pieces vague. Labelling is in Spanish and Basque, with free audio guides available in other languages.

Monte Urgull CASTLE, MUSEUM

You can walk to the top of Monte Urgull, topped by low castle walls and a grand statue of Christ, by taking a path from Plaza de Zuloaga or from behind the aquarium. The views are breathtaking. The castle houses the well-presented **Mirando a San Sebastián** (admission free; ⊙10am-2pm & 3-5.30pm), a small museum focusing on the city's history.

Museo Naval MUSEUM

(www.untzimuseoa.net; Paseo del Muelle 24; adult/child €1.20/free; ⊙10am-1.30pm & 4-7.30pm Tue-Sat, 11am-2pm Sun) This museum turns the pages of Basque seafaring and naval history. It's best appreciated by those with at least basic Spanish-language skills.

🎓 Courses & Tours

The tourist office runs a whole array of different city tours (including a running tour!) starting at €10.

Pintxo.Sanse COOKING COURSE

(☏902 44 34 42; www.sansebastianreservas.com; course €120) The food of San Sebastián is of a legendary status and it's those little parcels of delight, *pintxos*, that really set hearts aflutter. Just imagine how impressed your friends back home would be if the next time you throw a dinner party you whip out a few San Sebastián–style *pintxos*. In association with the tourist office, Pintxo. Sanse runs personalised three-hour courses (in Spanish, English and French) in creating your own culinary masterpiece.

San Sebastián Food TOUR, COOKING COURSE

(☏634 759 503; www.sansebastianfood.com) The highly recommended San Sebastián Food runs an array of *pintxo* tasting tours (from €75) and cookery courses (from €135) in and around the city, as well as wine tastings (from €25) and day-long wine-tasting tours to La Rioja (€225).

Sabores de San Sebastián TOUR

(Flavours of San Sebastián; ☏902 44 34 42; www.sansebastianreservas.com; tour €18; ⊙11.30am Tue & Thu Jul & Aug) The tourist office runs the Sabores de San Sebastián, a two-hour tour

(in Spanish and English, French tours are available on request) of some of the city's *pintxo* haunts. Tours are also held with less frequency outside of high season – contact the tourist office for dates.

Pukas SURFING

(www.pukassurf.com; Paseo de Zurriola 24; ⊙10am-1.30pm & 4-8pm Mon-Sat) Playa de Gros, with its generally mellow and easy waves, is a good place for learners to get to grips with surfing. Aspiring surfer wannabes should drop by Pukas, where surf lessons, and board and wetsuit hire are available. Prices vary depending on group size and lesson length, but start at €59 for a weekend course comprising a 1½-hour lesson each day.

🎊 Festivals & Events

San Sebastián has a busy festival calendar. The main events are:

Festividad de San Sebastián CITY FESTIVAL

On 20 January, this is the city's main winter knees-up.

Carnaval CARNIVAL

In mid-February, Carnaval is a big event, but nearby Tolosa goes even more berserk.

Heineken Jazzaldia JAZZ

(www.heinekenjazzaldia.com) Big-name acts converge in July for San Sebastián's jazz festival.

Semana Grande SUMMER FESTIVAL

In mid-August, Semana Grande is the big summer festival.

Regatta de Traineras ROWING

The Regatta de Traineras, a boat race in which local teams of rowers race out to sea, takes place on the first two Sundays in September.

Film Festival FILM

(www.sansebastianfestival.com) Since 1957, this world-renowned, two-week film festival has been an annual fixture in the second half of September.

🛏 Sleeping

Accommodation standards in San Sebastián are generally good, but prices are high and availability in high season is very tight. In fact, with the city's increasing popularity, many of the better places are booked up for July and August months in advance. If you do turn up without a booking, head to the

THE ART OF EATING PINTXOS

Just rolling the word *pintxo* around your tongue defines the essence of this cheerful, cheeky little slice of Basque cuisine. The perfect *pintxo* should have exquisite taste, texture and appearance and should be savoured in two elegant bites. The Basque version of a tapa, the *pintxo* transcends the commonplace by the sheer panache of its culinary campiness. In San Sebastián especially, Basque chefs have refined the *pintxo* to an art form.

Many *pintxos* are bedded on small pieces of bread or on tiny half-baguettes, upon which towering creations are constructed, often melded with flavoursome mayonnaise and then pinned in place by large toothpicks. Some bars specialise in seafood, with much use of marinated anchovies, prawns and strips of squid, all topped with anything from chopped crab to pâté. Others deal in pepper or mushroom delicacies, or simply offer a mix of everything. And the choice isn't normally limited to what's on the bar top in front of you: many of the best *pintxos* are the hot ones you need to order. These are normally chalked up on a blackboard on the wall somewhere.

Locals tend to just eat one or two of the house specials at each bar before moving on somewhere else. When it comes to ordering, tell the barman what you want first and never just help yourself to a *pintxo* off the counter!

tourist office, which keeps a list of available rooms.

Pensión Bellas Artes
BOUTIQUE HOTEL €€
(☑943 47 49 05; www.pension-bellasartes.com; Calle de Urbieta 64; s €69-89, d €89-109; 🛜) To call this magnificent place a mere *pensión* is to do it something of a disservice. Its rooms (some with glassed-in balconies), with their exposed stone walls and excellent bathrooms, should be the envy of many a more-expensive hotel.

It also has to be the friendliest hotel in town – Leira, the owner (who speaks excellent English), and her mother are absolute treasures who will do all they can to help you get the most out of your visit, including drawing maps pointing you to all their favourite hidden corners of the city.

Pensión Aida
BOUTIQUE HOTEL €€
(☑943 32 78 00; www.pensionesconencanto.com; Calle de Iztueta 9; s €60, d €82-88, studios €130-150; ✳@🛜) The owners of this excellent *pensión* read the rule book on what makes a good hotel and have complied exactly. The rooms are bright and bold, full of exposed stone and everything smells fresh and clean. The communal area, stuffed with soft sofas and mountains of information, is a big plus. If you've been on a shopping spree and need more space then take one of its handful of very slick studios (which come with kitchenettes). For our money, we'd say this one is very hard to beat.

Pensión Amaiur Ostatua
BOUTIQUE HOTEL €€
(☑943 42 96 54; www.pensionamaiur.com; Calle de 31 de Agosto 44; s €45, d €54-65; @🛜) Sprawling over several floors of an old town house, this excellent *pensión* was closed for renovations at the time of research (it has since reopened) but prior to this, its rooms – many of which shared bathrooms – were small but had a lot of thought put into them and all were strikingly different. The best ones are those that overlook the main street, where you can sit on a little balcony and be completely enveloped in blushing red flowers. There's a kitchen for guest use.

Pensión Edorta
BOUTIQUE HOTEL €
(☑943 42 37 73; www.pensionedorta.com; Calle del Puerto 15; r €80-90, r without bathroom €60-70; 🛜) A fine *pensión* with rooms that are all tarted up in brash modern colours, but with a salute to the past in the stone walls and ceilings. It's very well cared for and well situated.

Pensión Altair
PENSIÓN €€
(☑943 29 31 33; www.pension-altair.com; Calle Padre Larroca 3; s/d €60/86; ✳@🛜) This *pensión* is in a beautifully restored town house, with unusual church-worthy arched windows and modern, minimalist rooms that are a world away from the fusty decor of the old-town *pensiones*. Reception is closed between 1.30pm and 5pm.

Pensión Kursaal
BOUTIQUE HOTEL €€
(☑943 29 26 66; www.pensionesconencanto.com; Calle de Peña y Goñi 2; d €83-89; ✳@🛜) With

a rattling 1930s style lift and massive, wall-sized photos this excellent place, full of light and colour, is a real mix of the old and the new. The majestic rooms have a suitably refined edge, all of which help it feel more like a proper hotel than a *pensión*. It's virtually on Playa de Gros.

Pensión Donostiarra
PENSIÓN €€

(☑943 42 61 67; www.pensiondonostiarra.com; Calle de San Martín 6; s €64-66, d €89-98; ⑨) This *pensión*, with its imposing old-fashioned stairway and clanking lift, is a charmer. Most rooms are plush sky-blue affairs and some have wonderful stained-glass doors leading onto little balconies, but a few of them are a little plain so get there early to bag a good one.

Pensión San Fermín
PENSIÓN €

(☑943 42 54 91; dormirendonosti@hotmail.com; Calle Fermín Calbetón 23; d €60-80; @⑨) Shiny and new, this place has small, modern rooms which, unusually, all contain bunk beds (with a double bed on the downstairs and a single up above), which makes it ideal for families or arguing couples! The checkout time is very early for Spain: 10am.

Hotel Maria Cristina
HISTORIC HOTEL €€€

(☑943 43 76 00; www.starwoodhotels.com; Paseo de la República Argentina 4; s/d from €245/322; P❋@⑨) In case you're wondering what sort of hotels Lonely Planet authors normally stay in, the absolutely impeccable Maria Cristina, with its huge and luxurious rooms, is not one of them. However, don't be downhearted, because instead of hanging out with us, you'll get to mix with royalty and Hollywood stars. Yes, we know, it's disappointing.

Pensión Aldamar
HOTEL €€

(☑943 43 01 43; www.pensionaldamar.com; Calle de Aldamar 2; s €93, d from € €108-118; ❋⑨) Recently renovated this smart *pensión* is run on lines more akin to a hotel and offers superb white, modern rooms with stone walls, some of which have little balconies from which to watch the theatre of street life below. It's a big step in quality from many of the other old-town *pensións*.

Hostal Alemana
BOUTIQUE HOTEL €€

(☑943 46 25 44; www.hostalalemana.com; Calle de San Martín 53; r €115; P⑨) With a great location just a sandy footstep from the beach, this smart hotel has opted for the white, minimalist look, countered with stylish B&W photos, all of which works very well and makes the rooms light and airy. Parking is €12.50 per day.

Hotel de Londres e Inglaterra
HISTORIC HOTEL €€€

(☑943 44 07 70; www.hlondres.com; Calle de Zubieta 2; r from €169; P❋⑨) Queen Isabel II set the tone for this hotel well over a century ago and things have stayed pretty regal ever since. It oozes class and some rooms have stunning views over Playa de la Concha.

Urban House
HOSTEL €

(☑943 42 81 51; www.enjoyou.com; Plaza Gipuzkoa 2; dm €18-20, r from €35; ⑨) This busy party house, where summer fun rules supreme, is one of the longest-running hostels in town. It's close to all the action and the young, very Anglophone staff (so Anglophone that some don't speak any Spanish) will ensure you have a good time. They also organise a variety of city tours and surf lessons. The hostel also manages the bookings for several cheap and basic places elsewhere in the old town – so if the main building is full, the staff can always find you a bed elsewhere.

Pensión Izar Bat
PENSIÓN €€

(☑943 42 15 73; www.pensionizarbat.com; Calle Fermín Calbetón; d €60-70; ⑨) This sparkly, well-priced venture has rooms covered in disco glitter paint, flaming orange walls and colour-clashing bedspreads. All rooms come with small private bathrooms and have good double glazing to protect from noise from the street below.

Hospedaje Irune
PENSIÓN €€

(☑943 42 57 43; www.hospedajepensionirune.com; Calle San Jerónimo 17; s €47-52, d €69-75; ❋⑨) This cheerful place, with rooms that gather lots of sunlight and have good soundproofing, is a great deal. Some rooms have little balconies and all have attached bathrooms, which is rare in this price category.

Pensión Santa Clara
PENSIÓN €€

(☑943 43 12 03; www.pensionsantaclara.com; Calle de San Lorenzo 6; d €75; @⑨) This cheerful *pensión* has just a handful of small, rainbow-bright rooms and the owner is a mine of information. Santa Clara's so central that the smell of *pintxos* will virtually permeate your sleep. There's also a useful book-swap service. It's popular so book ahead.

Camping Igueldo
CAMPGROUND €

(☑943 21 45 02; www.campingigueldo.com; Paseo del Padra Orkolaga 69; sites for 2 people, car & tent

PINTXO BARS IN SAN SEBASTIÁN

No other city in Spain has made such a culture out of the creation, and consumption, of *pintxos* (tapas) and for many people the overriding memory of their stay in San Sebastián will be that of late nights in the *pintxo* bars.

Be sure to learn a little more about what *pintxos* are and the etiquette behind ordering and eating them before hitting the bars (see the boxed text, p430).

The following *pintxo* bars all charge between €2.50 to €3.50 for one *pintxo*. Not so bad if you just take one, but is one ever enough?

La Cuchara de San Telmo (Calle de 31 de Agosto 28) This unfussy, hidden-away (and hard to find) bar offers miniature *nueva cocina vasca* (Basque nouvelle cuisine) from a supremely creative kitchen. Unlike many San Sebastián bars this one doesn't have any *pintxos* laid out on the bar top; instead you must order from the blackboard menu behind the counter. Don't miss delights such as *carrílera de ternera al vino tinto* (calf cheeks in red wine), with meat so tender it starts to dissolve almost before it's past your lips.

Bar Borda Berri (Calle Fermín Cabetón 12) You won't find any *pintxos* sprawled across the bar counter at this outstanding little bar, which many locals swear blind is now the best in the city. Instead you must order them freshly made from the blackboard menu behind the bar. The bar staff are happy to offer advice on the day's best choice, but otherwise the house specials are pigs' ears and delicious calf cheeks.

Bergara Bar (General Artetxe 8) The neighbourhood of Gros is a growing powerhouse in the battle of the *pintxos* and many locals now prefer to take their nibbles here and leave the old town to the tourists. The Bergara Bar, which sits on the edge of a busy square, is one of the most highly regarded *pintxo* bars in Gros and has a mouth-watering array of delights piled onto the bar counter as well as others chalked up onto the board. There are several other really good bars in the vicinity.

Astelena (Calle de Iñigo 1) The *pintxos* draped across the counter in this bar, tucked into the corner of Plaza de la Constitución, stand out as some of the best in the city. Many of them are a fusion of Basque and Asian inspirations, but the best of all are perhaps the foie-gras-based treats. The great positioning means that prices are slightly elevated.

Bar Goiz-Argi (Calle de Fermín Calbetón 4) *Gambas a la plancha* (prawns cooked on a hotplate) are the house speciality. Sounds simple, we know, but never have we tasted prawns cooked quite as perfectly as this.

La Mejíllonera (Calle del Puerto 15) If you thought mussels only came with garlic sauce, come here to discover mussels (from €3.50) by the thousand in all their glorious forms. Mussels not for you? Opt for the calamari and *patatas bravas* (fried potatoes with a spicy tomato and mayo sauce). We promise you won't regret it.

Bar Nagusía (Nagusía Kalea 4) This bar, reminiscent of old San Sebastián, has a counter that moans under the weight of its *pintxos*. You'll be moaning after a few as well – in sheer pleasure.

Bodega Donostiarra (Calle de Peña y Goñl 13; ⊘closed Sun) The stone walls, pot plants and window ornaments give this place a real old-fashioned French bistro look, but at the same time it feels very up to date and modern. Although initial impressions make you think the food would be very high class, it's actually best regarded for humble *jamón*, chorizo and tortilla. It also has a long wine list (and an attached wine shop).

Bar Martinez (Calle 31 de Agosto 13) This small bar, with dusty bottles of wine stacked up, has won awards for its *morros de bacalao* (delicate slices of cod balanced atop a piece of bread) and is one of the more character-laden places to dip into some *pintxos*.

A Fuego Negro (Calle 31 de Agosto 31) This is something a little bit different for San Sebastián. There's none of the traditional Spanish bar look here; instead everything is bang up to date. It has an impressive *pintxo* list with creations as modern as the setting.

or caravan €33.20; P@🛜) This well-organised, tree-shaded camping ground, 5km west of the city, is served by bus 16 from Alameda del Boulevard (€1.45, 30 minutes).

 Eating

With 14 Michelin stars (including three restaurants with the coveted three stars) for a population of 183,000, San Sebastián stands

atop a pedestal as one of the culinary capitals of the planet. As if that alone weren't enough, the city is overflowing with bars – almost all of which have bar tops weighed down under a mountain of tapas (known as *pintxos* here) that almost every Spaniard will (sometimes grudgingly) tell you are the best in country. These statistics alone make San Sebastián's CV look pretty impressive. But it's not just us who thinks this: a raft of the world's best chefs, including such luminaries as Catalan super chef Ferran Adrià, have said that San Sebastián is quite possibly the best place on the entire planet to eat.

Bodegón Alejandro   SEAFOOD €€

(📞943 42 71 58; Calle de Fermín Calbetón 4; menú del día from €23, mains €15-18; ⊙closed Mon & dinner Sun) This highly regarded restaurant, which has a pleasant casual style, has a menu from which you can select such succulent treats as tripe with veal cheeks, baby tomatoes stuffed with squid or just plain old baked lobster. Oh, what choices!

Restaurante
Ni Neu   CONTEMPORARY BASQUE €€€

(📞943 00 31 62; www.restaurantenineu.com; Avenida de Zurriola 1; menus €18-38) The former Michelin-starred Kursaal has been rebranded as the Restaurante Ni Neu and, although the old chef and his star have gone, the food quality remains much the same with plenty of light, fluffy and utterly modern dishes that leave you hoping never to eat boring old-fashioned meat and two veg again! Throw in a spectacular setting, inside the Kursaal Centre, with a view straight over Playa de Gros and bargain-priced meals, and you get a place that's hard to beat.

Restaurante Alberto   SEAFOOD €

(📞943 42 88 84; Calle de 31 de Agosto 19; menus €15; ⊙closed Tue) A charming old seafood restaurant with a fishmonger-style window display of the day's catch. It's small and friendly and the pocket-sized dining room feels like it was once someone's living room. The food is earthy (well, salty) and good and the service swift.

Kaskazuri   SEAFOOD €€

(📞943 42 08 94; Paseo de Salamanca 14; menú del día €18) Upmarket Basque seafood is all the rage in this flash restaurant, which is built on a raised platform allowing views of the former home of your dinner. It cooks up a storm with the €18 *menú del día*.

Restaurante Mariñela   SEAFOOD €€

(📞943 42 73 83; Paseo del Muelle; mains €10-18) You pay for the fabulous harbour-front setting, but the location guarantees that the fish is so fresh it may well flop back off your plate and swim away. There are several similar neighbouring places.

La Zurri   BASQUE €

(📞943 29 38 86; Calle de Zabaleta 10; menus €10.80) Over the water in Gros, this ever-popular locals' seafood restaurant has a menu as long as a conger eel and all of it is consistently good. It doesn't accept credit cards.

Mercado de la Bretxa   MARKET €

On the east side of the Parte Vieja, Mercado de la Bretxa has an underground Lidl supermarket.

🍷 Drinking & Entertainment

It would be hard to imagine a town with more bars than San Sebastián. Most of the city's bars mutate through the day from calm morning-coffee hang-outs to *pintxo*-laden delights, before finally finishing up as noisy bars full of writhing, sweaty bodies. Nights in San Sebastián start late and go on until well into the wee hours.

Museo del Whisky   BAR

(Alameda Boulevard 5) Appropriately named, this Irish/Scottish-style bar is full of bottles of Scotland's finest (3000 bottles to be exact) as well as a museum's worth of whisky related knick-knacks – old bottles, tacky mugs and glasses and a nice, dusty, museum-like atmosphere.

Dioni's   GAY

(Calle Ijentea 2) More a spot for a black coffee in the early hours, this relaxed and very gay-friendly place has an '80s cocktail-bar ambience and is the perfect spot in which to watch the Eurovision Song Contest.

Bar Ondarra   BAR

(Avenida de Zurriola 16) Head over to Gros for this terrific bar that's just across the road from the beach. There's a great chilled-out mixed crowd and, in the rockin' downstairs bar, every kind of sound gets aired.

Be Bop   BAR, CLUB

(Paseo de Salamanca 3) This long-standing bar has recently reinvented itself and is now a snazzy jazz bar with occasional live performances. It attracts a slightly older crowd than some of the old town bars.

THREE SHINING STARS

The Basque Country seems to be engaged in an eternal battle with Catalonia for the title of the best foodie region in Spain and, just like in Catalonia, the Basque Country is home to an impressive number of restaurants that have been awarded a coveted three Michelin stars, as well as many more with one or two stars. All the three-star places are in and around San Sebastián.

Arzak (☎943 27 84 65; www.arzak.info; Avenida Alcalde Jose Elosegui 273; meals around €175; ☺closed Sun-Mon & Nov & late Jun) Acclaimed chef Juan Mari Arzak takes some beating when it comes to *nueva cocina vasca* (Basque nouvelle cuisine) and his restaurant is, not surprisingly, considered one of the best places to eat in Spain. Arzak is now assisted by his daughter Elena and they never cease to innovate. Reservations, well in advance, are obligatory. The restaurant is about 1.5km east of San Sebastián.

Martín Berasategui Restaurant (☎943 36 64 71; www.martinberasategui.com; Calle Loidi 4, Lasarte-Oria; meals around €120; ☺closed Mon, Tue, dinner Sun & Dec–mid-Jan) This superlative restaurant, about 9km southwest of San Sebastián, is considered by foodies to be one of the best restaurants in the world. The chef, Martín Berasategui, doesn't approach cooking in the same way as the rest of us. He approaches it as a science and the results are tastes you never knew existed. Reserve well ahead.

Akelaŕe (☎943 31 12 09; www.akelarre.net; Paseo Padre Orcolaga 56; tasting menu €145; ☺closed Mon, Tue, dinner Sun & Dec–mid-Jan) This is where chef Pedro Subijana creates cuisine that is a feast to all five senses (and possibly a few senses we haven't yet named!). As with most of the region's top *nueva cocina vasca* restaurants, the emphasis here is on using fresh, local produce and turning it into something totally unexpected. It's in the suburb of Igeldo just west of the city.

Splash BAR
(Sánchez Toca 1) A brash, modern bar with outdoor seating and strong beats inside.

Altxerri Jazz Bar LIVE MUSIC
(www.altxerri.com; Blvd Reina Regente 2) This jazz and blues temple has regular live gigs by local and international stars. Jamming sessions take over on nights with no gig and there's an in-house art gallery.

Etxe Kalte JAZZ
(Calle Mari Igentea) A very-late-night jazz haunt near the harbour, it sometimes throws open its doors to all kinds of dance-music styles.

 Shopping

The Parte Vieja is awash with small independent boutiques, whilst the Centro Romantíca has all your brand-name and chain-store favourites.

Elkar BOOKS
(Calle de Fermín Calbetón 30) For a huge range of travel books and guides (including lots of Lonely Planet guides), maps and hiking books in English, Spanish and French, try this specialist travel bookshop. Almost opposite it is a bigger mainstream **branch** dealing in Spanish- and Basque-language books.

Kukuxumusu CLOTHING
(Nagusía Kalea 15) The funkiest and best-known Basque clothing label has a whole wardrobe of original T-shirts and other clothing awaiting you here.

ℹ Information

Oficina de Turismo (☎943 48 11 66; www.sansebastianturismo.com; Alameda del Boulevard 8; ☺9.30am-1.30pm & 3.30-7pm Mon-Thu, 10am-7pm Fri & Sat, 10am-2pm Sun) This friendly office offers comprehensive information on the city and the Basque Country in general.

Zarranet (Calle de San Lorenzo 6; per hr €2; ☺10.30am-2.30pm & 4-9pm Mon-Sat, 4-9pm Sun) One of a handful of places that offer internet access.

ℹ Getting There & Away

Air

The city's **airport** (☎902 404704; www.aena.es) is 22km out of town, near Hondarribia. There are regular flights to Madrid and Barcelona and occasional charters to other major European cities. Biarritz, just over the border in France, is served by Ryanair and EasyJet, among various other budget airlines, and is generally much cheaper to fly into.

Bus

The main bus station is a 20-minute walk south of the Parte Vieja, between Plaza de Pío XII and the river. Local buses 28 and 26 connects the bus station with Alameda del Boulevard (€1.40, 10 minutes). For a few years now there has been talk of the bus station moving to a new location on Paseo de Francia, next to the train station. At the time of research there was some confusion about when, and if, this would actually happen but it seems that the project is temporarily on hold.

There are daily bus services to the following:

DESTINATION	FARE (€)	DURATION (HR)
Biarritz (France)	6.60	1¼
Bilbao	10.10	1
Bilbao airport	15.70	1¼
Madrid	from 33.60	5-6
Pamplona	7.29	1
Vitoria	10.10	1½

Train

The main **Renfe train station** (Paseo de Francia) is just across Río Urumea, on a line linking Paris to Madrid. There are several services daily to Madrid (from €54.20, five hours) and two to Barcelona (from €63.30, six hours).

For France you must first go to the Spanish/French border town of Irún (or sometimes they go as far as Hendaye; €2.20, 25 minutes), which is also served by **Eusko Tren/Ferrocarril Vasco** (www.euskotren.es) on a railway line nicknamed 'El Topo' (the Mole) and change there. Trains depart every half-hour from Amara train station, about 1km south of the city centre, and also stop in Pasajes (€1.50, 12 minutes) and Irún/Hendaye (€1.70, 25 minutes). Another ET/FV railway line heads west to Bilbao via Zarautz, Zumaia and Durango, but it's painfully slow (like quarter-of-a-day slow), so the bus is a much better plan.

❶ Getting Around

Buses to Hondarribia (€2.10, 45 minutes) and the airport (€2.10, 45 minutes) depart from Plaza de Guipúzcoa.

MOVING ON?

For tips, recommendations and reviews, head to shop.lonelyplanet.com to purchase a downloadable PDF of The French Basque Country chapter from Lonely Planet's *France* guide.

East of San Sebastián

PASAJES
POP 16,100

Pasajes (Basque: Pasaia), where Río Oiartzun meets the Atlantic, is the largest port in the province of Guipúzcoa. The main street and the area immediately around the central square are lined with pretty houses and colourful balconies, and are well worth a half-day's exploration. Highlights are the great seafood restaurants and the spectacular entrance to the port, through a keyhole-like split in the cliff face – it's even more impressive when a huge container ship passes through it.

Nowadays Pasajes is virtually a suburb of San Sebastián and there are numerous buses plying the route between them. For a much more enjoyable way of getting there though you can walk over the cliffs from San Sebastián. The walk takes about 2½ to three hours and passes through patches of forest, past the occasional idyllic beach and strange rock formations covered in seabirds and then descends to Pasajes, which you reach by taking the small ferry boat over the inlet. The tourist office in San Sebastián can supply route details, or get hold of Lonely Planet's *Hiking in Spain*.

HONDARRIBIA
POP 16,100

Lethargic Hondarribia (Castilian: Fuenterrabía), staring across the estuary to France, has a heavy Gallic fragrance and a charming Casco Antiguo (Old City), which makes it an excellent first or last port of call.

You enter the *casco* through an archway at the top of Calle San Compostela to reach the pretty Plaza de Gipuzkoa. Head straight on to Calle San Nicolás and go left to reach the bigger Plaza de Armas and the Gothic Iglesia de Santa María de la Asunción.

For La Marina, head the other way from the archway. This is Hondarribia's most picturesque quarter. Its main street, Calle San Pedro, is flanked by typical fishermen's houses, with facades painted bright green or blue and wooden balconies gaily decorated with flower boxes.

There are several places to stay, ranging from a campsite with right royal views to a castle converted into a luxury *parador* (state-owned hotel), and a number of great places to eat.

South of San Sebastián

The hills rising to the south between San Sebastián and Bilbao offer a number of appealing towns. There are plenty of *nekazal turismoas* (*casas rurales*; family homes in rural areas with rooms to rent).

SANTUARIO DE LOYOLA

Just outside Azpeitia (12km south of the A8 motorway along the GI631) lies the portentous Santuario de Loyola (www.santuario deloyola.org; house adult/child €2/free; ⊙10am-noon & 4-7pm, house 10am-1.30pm & 3.30-7pm Mon-Sat, 10am-1pm Sun), dedicated to St Ignatius, the founder of the Jesuit order. From the outside the dark, sooty basilica, laden with grey marble and plenty of carved ornamentation, is monstrous rather than attractive. Inside, however, is much brighter, and smaller, than you'd expect. The house, where the saint was born in 1490 is preserved in one of the two wings of the sanctuary and there's a small museum. Weekends are the most interesting times to come, as the sanctuary fills up with pilgrims.

Sitting so close to the basilica that you can probably overhear people's whispered prayers, you might expect the Hotel Arrupe (☎943 02 50 26; www.hotelarrupe.org; s/d incl breakfast €57/85; P🛜) to be overpriced, but in fact its modern rooms (with very cramped bathrooms) are something of a bargain.

OÑATI

POP 10,800

With a flurry of magnificent architecture and a number of interesting sites scattered through the surrounding green hills, the small, and resolutely Basque, town of Oñati is a great place to get to know the rural Basque heartland.

There are daily buses to/from San Sebastián, Vitoria and Bilbao.

The tourist office (☎943 78 34 53; Calle San Juan 14; ⊙10am-2pm & 3.30-7.30pm Mon-Fri, 10am-2pm & 4.30-6.30pm Sat, 10am-2pm Sun) is just opposite the Universidad de Sancti Spiritus.

◉ Sights

Universidad de Sancti Spiritus

HISTORIC BUILDING

Oñati's number-one attraction is the Renaissance treasure of the Universidad de Sancti Spiritus. Built in the 16th century, it was the first university in the Basque Country and, until its closure in 1902, alumni here were schooled in philosophy, law and medicine.

Today it's been taken over as local council offices, but you can still enter the Mudéjar courtyard (⊙9am-2.30pm Mon & Wed, 9am-1pm & 3-4.30pm Tue & Thu, 9am-2pm Fri) and admire its plateresque facade. The tourist office can organise guided tours (from €10) with 24 hours' notice. Although it's something of a hassle organising this in advance, it's well worth doing because you get a much more in-depth look at the building (as well as other sites throughout the town). Near the Universidad and also well worth a peek is the Iglesia de San Miguel, a late-Gothic confection whose cloister was built over the river. The church faces onto the main square, Foruen Enparantza, dominated by the eye-catching baroque ayuntamiento (town hall). At the opposite end of town is the Bidaurreta Monastery. Founded in 1510, it contains a beautiful baroque altarpiece.

⊨ Sleeping

Oñati doesn't get a lot of tourists staying overnight, a fact that is reflected by the relative dearth of accommodation.

TXOKO

Peek through the keyholes of enough Basque doors and eventually you'll come across an unusual sight: a large room full of men, and only men, seated around a table bending under the weight of food and drink. This is *Txoko* (Basque Gastronomic Society) and it is an almost exclusively male preserve. The men who come here (who often wouldn't be seen dead in the kitchen at home) are normally highly accomplished amateur chefs who take turns cooking their own speciality for the critical consumption of the other members. It's often said that the best Basque food is to be found at the *Txoko*. Recently a few women have started to enter the *Txoko*, but only as guests and even then they are never allowed into the kitchen when the cooking is in process in case they distract the men. Women are, however, let into the kitchen afterwards – to do the washing up!

THE THUNDER GODDESS

It's said that one of the numerous caves on the slopes of the wild hills around Oñati is the home of Mari, the pre-Christian goddess of the Basques, who is said to control the weather. If you get lost while out walking, just shout out her name three times and she'll appear in the skies above you to guide you in the right direction. If, however, you stumble upon her cave home, then leave as fast as possible because she'll get very angry and, trust us, you really don't want to see what an angry Basque goddess looks like!

Arregi CASA RURAL €
(📞943 78 36 57, 943 78 08 24; www.nekatur.net/arregi; Garagaltza 21; s/d €32/44; 🅿🛇) This is a splendid agritourism home 2km south of town. The nicely restored farmhouse sits in a green valley full of brown cows with big eyelashes, and has sheer views of bold mountainsides. The rooms themselves are spacious and nicely decorated, and there's a kitchen for guest use and a sitting room with a big log fire.

Ongí Hotela HOTEL €
(📞943 71 82 85; www.hotelongi.com; Calle Zaharra 19; incl breakfast s €30-40, d €42-54; ☒🛇) A central place with sparkling-clean rooms and a warm welcome.

SANTUARIO DE ARANTZAZU & ARRIKRUTZ CAVES

About 10km south of Oñati you'll find the love-it-or-loathe-it pilgrimage site of **Santuario de Arantzazu** (www.arantzazukosantutegia.org), a fabulous conflation of piety with avant-garde art. The sanctuary was built in the 1950s on the site where, in 1468, a shepherd found a statue of the Virgin under a hawthorn bush – on which the sanctuary's design is supposed to be based. The overwhelming impression of the building is of spiky towers and hollow halls guarded by 14 strange-looking, chiselled apostles and, in the crypt, a devil-red Christ – all of which caused a bit of a headache for the Vatican.

The road up and the setting are worth the trip in themselves, and the whole area lends itself to excellent walking – the Oñati tourist office has information on routes. If you do go for a walk around here, be a little careful – there's more to these spectacular hills than meets the eye (see the boxed text, left).

There's a cavern system a couple of kilometres back down the road towards Oñati. The **Arrikrutz caves** (adult/child €8/4; ⏰10am-2pm & 3-7pm Tue-Sun) have numerous slow-growing stalagmites and stalactites.

Vitoria

POP 235,600 / ELEV 512M

Vitoria (Basque: Gasteiz) has a habit of falling off the radar, yet it's actually the capital of not just the southern Basque province of Álava (Basque: Araba) but also the entire Basque Country. Maybe it was given this honour precisely because it is so forgotten, but, if that's the case, then prepare for a surprise. With an art gallery whose contents frequently supersede those of the more famous Bilbao galleries, a delightful old quarter, dozens of great *pintxo* bars and restaurants, a large student contingent and a friendly local population, you have the makings of a perfect city!

History

Vitoria's name may well derive from the Basque word *beturia*, meaning height, a reference to the hill on which the old town stands. It was so named by the Visigoths. Sancho VI of Navarra settled things by founding a 'New Vitoria' in the 12th century. Thereafter, Vitoria bounced to and fro between the Castilian and Navarran crowns. The economic advances of the late 19th century triggered Vitoria's expansion, which carried over into the 20th century. The city's historic and well-preserved nature made it a good choice for capital of the Basque autonomous government in 1981. The University of the Basque Country also has its base here.

⊙ Sights

At the base of Vitoria's medieval Casco Viejo is the delightful Plaza de la Virgen Blanca. It's lorded over by the 14th-century **Iglesia de San Miguel** (Plaza de la Virgen Blanca), whose statue of the Virgen Blanca, the city's patron saint, lends its name to the plaza below.

The 14th-century **Iglesia de San Pedro** (Calle Herrería) is the city's oldest church and has a fabulous Gothic frontispiece on its eastern facade.

Vitoria has no shortage of museums (free admission; ⏰10am-2pm & 4-6.30pm Tue-Fri, 10am-2pm Sat, 11am-2pm Sun) in which you

Vitoria

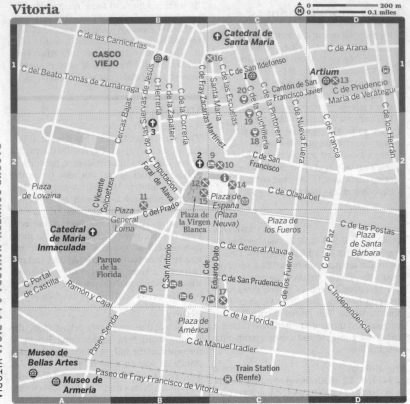

Vitoria

◎ Top Sights

◎ Sights

◎ Sleeping

◎ Eating

◎ Drinking

can enrich yourself with knowledge about dinosaur bones, knights in armour, bits of old pottery and playing cards. In all of these signage is in Spanish and Basque only.

Artium
TOP CHOICE

GALLERY

(www.artium.org; Calle de Francia 24; adult/child €6/free; ☉11am-2pm & 5-8pm Tue-Thu, 11am-2pm & 4-9pm Fri-Sun, closed Sep) Unlike some famous Basque art galleries, Vitoria's palace of modern art, the Artium, doesn't need to dress to impress. It knows it's what's on the inside that really counts. It is daring, eccentric and challenging in a way other museums could never get away with.

The large subterranean galleries are filled with engrossing works by Basque, Spanish and international artists, displaying some fairly intense modernist work. For example, at the time of research, the collection included exhibitions featuring children's drawings depicting suicide and a grainy, and very bloody, video of a woman having her hymen sewn back up to make her a 'virgin' again. Yes, this is art designed to shock. Guided tours, in Spanish, run several times a day. After digesting the art, it's worth digesting some food at the much-praised Cube Café (menú del día €15), inside the museum. The gallery is wheelchair-accessible.

Catedral de Santa María
CATHEDRAL

(✆945 255 135; www.catedralvitoria.com; tours €8; ☉10am-2pm & 4-7pm) At the summit of the old town and dominating its skyline is the medieval Catedral de Santa María. For a number of years the cathedral has been undergoing a lengthy, but much-praised, restoration project.

There are excellent guided tours that give an insight into the excitement of restoration and discovery and give you a taste not just of the past and future of the cathedral but of the city as a whole – the restoration work has unearthed all manner of interesting signs into Vitoria's past. Technically you must book a tour in advance either by telephone or via the website, but in reality on quiet days it's often possible to just turn up and join the next tour.

The word on the street is that the restoration work will be completed during the lifetime of this book so it's possible that the guided tours might be very different by the time you get here.

Museo de Bellas Artes
FREE

GALLERY

(Paseo de Fray Francisco de Vitoria; ☉10am-2pm & 4-6.30pm Tue-Fri, 10am-2pm & 5-8pm Sat, 11am-2pm Sun & holidays) Housed in an astoundingly ornate building, the absorbing Museo de Bellas Artes has Basque paintings and sculpture from the 18th and 19th centuries. The works of local son Fernando de Amaríca are given good space and reflect an engaging romanticism that manages to mix drama with great warmth of colour and composition.

Catedral de María Inmaculada
CATHEDRAL

(Cadena y Eleta) Vitoria's cathedral might look old but in fact it only dates from the early 1970s. There are some impressive, fairly adventurous stained-glass windows and a neck-stretching high nave. More interesting, though, is the attached Museo Diocosano de Arte Sacro (adult/child €3/free; ☉11am-2pm & 4-6.30pm Tue-Fri, 11am-2pm Sat & Sun), which contains some early Christian stone carvings and Basque crosses, detailed paintings of biblical scenes and a glittering ensemble of crucifixes and ceremonial crosses – all of which come from the Basque Country.

Museo de Armería
MUSEUM

(Paseo de Fray Francisco de Vitoria) Any damsels in distress reading this ought to head to this museum where your knight in shining armour awaits. This collection of armour through the ages is surprisingly absorbing and begs the question of how on earth gallant men wearing all this lot even managed to move let alone rescue damsels from the clutches of fire-breathing dragons.

Museo de Ciencias Naturales
MUSEUM

(Calle de las Siervas de Jesús 24) Inside this museum is a dazzling collection of minerals. You can also marvel at a mantis caught in amber, learn about the local wildlife and stare slack-jawed at a dinosaur jaw.

Bibat
MUSEUM

(Calle de la Cuchillería/Aiztogile Kalea 54) The Museo de Arqueología and the Museo Fournier de Naipes (Card Museum; ✆945 18 19 20; Calle de la Cuchillería 54) are combined into one museum known as Bibat. The Museo de Arqueología has giant TV screens that bring the dim and distant past to life. The eccentric Museo Fournier de Naipes has an impressive collection of historic presses and playing cards, including some of the oldest European decks.

🎉 Festivals & Events

Azkena Rock Festival
MUSIC

(www.azkenarockfestival.com) A fairly new gig is the Azkena Rock Festival held in mid-June. In 2012 headliners included Ozzy Osbourne and The Darkness.

Jazz Festival
JAZZ

(www.jazzvitoria.com) A jazz festival is held in mid-July that attracts numerous big national and international acts.

Fiestas de la Virgen Blanca
CITY FESTIVAL

The calm sophistication of Vitoria takes a back seat during the boisterous Fiestas de la Virgen Blanca, held from 4 to 9 August, with a range of fireworks, bullfights, concerts and street dancing. All of this is preceded by the symbolic descent of Celedón, a Basque effigy that flies down on strings from the Iglesia de San Miguel into the plaza below.

🛏 Sleeping

TOP CHOICE La Casa de los Arquillos
B&B €€

(945 15 12 59; www.lacasadelosarquillos.com; Paseo Los Arquillos 1; d incl breakfast €79; 📶) This B&B is the most exciting accommodation in Vitoria. Located inside a beautiful old building in a prime location above the main square, the eight immaculate rooms take their young and funky inspiration from the artwork in the Artium. Every room is individually decorated in a highly original style – one has tape measures above the bed and another has a doll sprouting limbs from its head! A hearty breakfast is thrown in.

The reception is supposedly manned from 8am to 9pm but our experience has always been very different, therefore it's best to call in advance and let them know what time you're arriving.

Hotel Dato
HOTEL €

(945 14 72 30; www.hoteldato.com; Calle de Eduardo Dato 28; s/d €38.66/54.88; 📶) It's hard to know if the extravagant art-deco style, full of semi-naked nymphs, Roman pots and frilly fittings is kitsch or classy (though we'd probably have to go with the first one). Either way it works well and the whole ensemble produces an exceptionally good-value and memorable hotel. Hotel Dato's annexe is the **Hotel Dato 28** on a parallel street.

Hotel Almoneda
HOTEL €€

(945 15 40 84; www.hotelalmoneda.com; Calle de la Florida 7; s/d incl breakfast €63/105; 📶) This confident hotel has recently been given a makeover and the rooms, which are as bright and cheery as a sunny summer morning, have creaky, polished wooden floors and beds as soft as a cloud, but the bathrooms are cramped to the extreme.

Hotel América
HOTEL €

(945 13 05 06; Calle de la Florida 11; s/d €45/65; 📶) Functional, user-friendly rooms that get the job done but that's really about all. The receptionist is often hanging out over the road, so you might have to wait a minute or two for him to turn up.

🍴 Eating

Alright, so it can never match San Sebastián's stellar range of *pintxos* but all the same Vitoria has a thriving, and highly competitive, local *pintxos* scene all of its own and unlike in that other Basque town each *pintxo* is a very affordable €1 to €2.

Of the numerous restaurants and *pintxo* bars lining Plaza de España, the current pick of the bunch are the **Bar Deportivo Alaves** (945 23 39 11; Plaza de Espana 13; pintxos €1-2; ⏰8am-1am daily) and **Noventa y Siete** (945 149 387; Plaza Virgen Blanca; pintxos €1-2; ⏰8am-1am daily) for their *pintxos,* and **Izartza** (945 235 533; Plaza de España 5; pintxos €1-2; ⏰closed Sun), which is one of the more sophisticated *pintxo* bars in town and with a quality of food and wine that matches its upmarket reputation.

TOP CHOICE Querida María
Restaurante
MODERN BASQUE €€

(Plaza de Santa María; mains €12-18, menus €18) Facing the cathedral in the prettiest part of the old town, this is an informal and stylish poppy-red restaurant. For the price, the food is absolutely magnificent. The menu focuses on classic Basque dishes but most have been given a light touch of the unexpected. And when it comes to dessert, if the waitress tells you the apple tart is good then listen to her – she knows what she's talking about!

Usokari
TAPAS €

(Calle de Eduardo Dato 25; pintxos €1.50) Of the ample selection of excellent *pintxo* bars in Vitoria, this discreet and modern bar, in the new town, is generally considered one of the best. Its range of *pintxos* is quite small (and they tend to run out quite early on) but the owners know all about the expression 'It's quality not quantity that counts'. An equally impressive wine selection accompanies the nibbles.

Arkupe
BASQUE €€
(☑945 23 00 80; Calle Mateo Benigno de Moraza 13; menus €25-41, mains from €18) For divine and very creative Basque cooking, check out this place. The rough wood exterior belies a formal and slightly chic atmosphere that's given a slightly playful edge by the butterflies and flowers on the menu cards. There's an extensive wine list, with all the offerings racked up against the back wall. Reserve in advance.

Asador Sagartoki
SIDRERÍA €€
(Calle del Prado 18; menus €10.50-50, mains €18; ⊙10am-midnight) A marvellous *sidrería* (cider house) that has one of the most creative menus around and an atmosphere to go with it. The dining room stretches way beyond the busy front bar and the *pintxos* are sublime award winners. Marvel as the bar staff, arms flailing like birds wings, orchestrate jets of cider from the big barrels to the glasses in their outstretched hands; then try it yourself in the restaurant. Like most *sidrerias,* this is a place to come with friends.

🍸 Drinking

There's a strong politico-arty vibe in the Casco Viejo, where a lively student cadre keeps things swerving with creative street posters and action. The main action is at Calle de la Cuchillería/Aiztogile and neighbouring Cantón de San Francísco Javier, both of which are packed with messy bars such as Gora (☑945 12 14 52; Cantón de San Francisco Javier) and El Parral (Calle Cantón San Francisco Javier 4). El 7 (Calle de la Cuchillería/Aiztogile) is another very popular bar that attracts a whole range of age groups. There is a heavy Basque nationalist atmosphere in some bars.

ℹ Information

Tourist office (☑945 16 15 98; www.vitoria -gasteiz.org/turismo; Plaza de España 1; ⊙10am-8pm) In the central square of the old town.

ℹ Getting There & Away

Vitoria's **airport** (☑945 16 35 91) is at Foronda, about 9km northwest of the city, with connections to Madrid and Barcelona. There are car-hire offices and an ATM at the airport. Taxis to town cost €20/25 during the day/night.

There are car parks by the train station, by the Artium and just east of the cathedral.

Vitoria's **bus station** (Calle de los Herrán) has regular services to these destinations:

DESTINATION	FARE (€)	DURATION (HR)
Barcelona	39.74	7
Bilbao	5.95	1¼
Madrid	25.34	4½
Pamplona	8.30	1¾
San Sebastián	10.10	1¼

Trains go to the following places:

DESTINATION	FARE (€)	DURATION (HR)	FREQUENCY
Barcelona	from 59.30	5	1 daily
Madrid	from 46.10	4-6	5 daily
Pamplona	5.65	1	4 daily
San Sebastián	from 13.35	1¾	up to 10 daily

NAVARRA

Several Spains intersect in Navarra (Basque: Nafarroa). The soft greens and bracing climate of the Navarran Pyrenees lie like a cool compress across the sun-struck brow of the south, which is all stark plains, cereal crops and vineyards, sliced by high sierras with cockscombs of raw limestone. Navarra is also pilgrim territory: for centuries the faithful have used the pass at Roncesvalles to cross from France on their way to Santiago de Compostela (p511).

Navarra was historically the heartland of the Basques, but dynastic struggles and trimming due to reactionary politics, including Francoism, has left it as a semi-autonomous province, with the north being Basque by nature while the south leans towards Castilian Spain. The centre hangs somewhere in between and Navarra seems intrinsically uncommitted to the vision of a Basque future.

The Navarran capital, Pamplona, tends to grab the headlines with its world-famous running of the bulls, but the region's real charm is in its peppering of small towns and villages that seem to melt in with the landscape.

Pamplona

POP 195,800 / ELEV 456M

Senses are heightened in Pamplona (Basque: Iruña), capital of the fiercely independent Kingdom of Navarra, alert constantly to the fearful sound of thundering bulls clattering like tanks down cobbled streets and causing mayhem and bloodshed all the way. Of course, visit outside the eight days in July when the legendary festival of Sanfermines takes over the minds and souls of a million people and the closest you'll come to a bloodthirsty bull is in a photograph. For

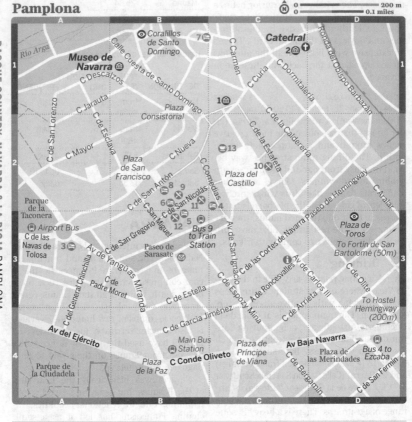

Pamplona

those who do dare venture here outside fiesta time, despite the overriding feeling that you're the only one who missed the party, you will find Pamplona a fascinating place. And for those of you who come during fiesta week? Welcome to one of the biggest and most famous festivals in the world – if you hadn't drunk so much, it would have been a week you would remember forever!

History

The Romans called the city Pompaelo, after its founder Pompey the Great. They were succeeded by the Visigoths and then, briefly, by the Muslims. Navarra has been a melting pot of dynastic, political and cultural aspirations and tensions ever since Charlemagne rampaged across the Pyrenees from France in 778. The city achieved great things under Sancho III in the 11th century and its position on the Camino de Santiago ensured its prosperity. Twentieth-century affluence saw an expansion of the city.

◉ Sights

Catedral   CATHEDRAL

(Calle Dormitalería; guided tour per adult/child €5/ free; ⊘10am-6pm Mon-Sat) Pamplona's main cathedral stands on a rise just inside the city ramparts amid a dark thicket of narrow streets. The cathedral is a late-medieval Gothic gem spoiled only by its rather dull neoclassical facade, an 18th-century appendage. The vast interior reveals some fine artefacts, including a silver-plated Virgin and the splendid 15th-century tomb of Carlos III of Navarra and his wife Doña Leonor. The real joy is the Gothic **cloister**, where there is marvellous delicacy in the stonework.

The **Museo Diocesano** occupies the former refectory and kitchen, and houses an assortment of religious art, including some fine Gothic woodcarvings. The cathedral itself is open daily for free entry outside the above stated hours, but you can't access the cloisters or museum.

Museo de Navarra   MUSEUM

(www.cfnavarra.es/cultura/museo; Calle Cuesta de Santo Domingo 47; adult €2, free Sat afternoon & Sun; ⊘9.30am-2pm & 5-7pm Tue-Sat, 11am-2pm Sun) Housed in a former medieval hospital, this superb museum has an eclectic collection of archaeological finds (including a number of fantastic Roman mosaics unearthed mainly in southern Navarra), as well as a selection of art, including Goya's *Marqués de San Adrián*. Labelling is in

Spanish only but foreign translation leaflets are available.

Ciudadela & Parks   FORTRESS, PARK

(Avenida del Ejército) The walls and bulwarks of the grand fortified citadel, the star-shaped Ciudadela, lurk amid the verdant grass and trees in what is now a charming park, the portal to three more parks that unfold to the north and lend the city a beautiful green escape.

Museo Oteiza   MUSEUM

(www.museooteiza.org; Calle de la Cuesta 7, Alzuza; adult €4, free Fri; ⊘11am-7pm Tue-Sat, 11am-3pm Sun) Around 9km northeast of Pamplona in the town of Alzuza, this impressive museum contains almost 3000 pieces by the renowned Navarran sculptor Jorge Oteiza. As well as his workshop, this beautifully designed gallery incorporates the artist's former home in a lovely rural setting.

Three buses a day run to Alzuza from Pamplona's bus station. If you're driving, Alzuza is signposted north off the NA150, just east of Huarte.

Fortín de San Bartolomé   CITY WALLS

(www.murallasdepamplona.com; Calle Arrieta; adult/child €3/1.50; ⊘11am-2pm & 5-8pm Tue-Sun) Bring the past of Pamplona to life through the story of the old town walls. After you've enriched yourself with knowledge, work up an appetite for lunch by walking the 5km circumference of the walls.

🛏 Sleeping

During Sanfermines, hotels raise their rates mercilessly – all quadruple their usual rack rates and many increase them fivefold – and it can be near impossible to get a room without reserving between six months and a year in advance. If you can't get a room, then it's possible to sleep in almost any park in the city (watch your belongings!) or you may just find that a patch of rubbish-strewn pavement suddenly looks like a very inviting bed! The tourist office also maintains a list of private houses with rooms to rent during this period and touts hang around the bus and train stations offering rooms. With numerous 'San Fermín' buses travelling up from all nearby Spanish and French cities, it's actually not a bad idea to stay in a different town altogether and catch a ride on the party buses. Ask local tourist offices for details of departure times and costs.

THE RUNNING OF THE BULLS

Liberated, obsessive or plain mad is how you might describe aficionados (and there are many) who regularly take part in Pamplona's Sanfermines (Fiesta de San Fermín), a non-stop cacophony of music, dance, fireworks and processions – and the small matter of running alongside a handful of agitated, horn-tossing *toros* (bulls) – that takes place from 6 to 14 July each year.

The bullrun is said to have originally developed way back in the 14th century as a way of herding bulls into market, with the seller running alongside the bulls to speed up their movement into the marketplace. In later times the same technique was used to transport bulls from the corrals to the bullring, and essentially that is still the case today. *El encierro*, the running of the bulls from their corrals to the bullring for the afternoon bullfight, takes place in Pamplona every morning during Sanfermines. Six bulls are let loose from the Coralillos de Santo Domingo to charge across the square of the same name. They continue up the street, veering onto Calle de los Mercaderes from Plaza Consistorial, then sweep right onto Calle de la Estafeta for the final charge to the ring. Devotees, known as *mozos* (the brave or foolish, depending on your point of view), race madly with the bulls, aiming to keep close – but not too close. The total course is some 825m long and lasts little more than three minutes.

Participants enter the course before 7.30am from Plaza de Santo Domingo. At 8am two rockets are fired: the first announces that the bulls have been released from the corrals; the second lets participants know they're all out and running. The first danger point is where Calle de los Mercaderes leads into Calle de la Estafeta. Here many of the bulls skid into the barriers because of their headlong speed on the turn. They can become isolated from the herd and are then always dangerous. A very treacherous stretch comes towards the end, where Calle de la Estafeta slopes down into the final turn to Plaza de Toros. A third rocket goes off when all the bulls have made it to the ring, and a final one when they have been rounded up in the stalls.

Those who prefer to be spectators rather than action men (and we use the word 'men' on purpose here as, technically, women are forbidden from running, although an increasing number are doing it anyway) bag their spot along the route early. A space doesn't mean an uninterrupted view because a second 'security' fence stands between the spectators and

At any other time of year Pamplona is packed with good-value accommodation and it's rarely worth booking ahead. The following prices are for high season but not during Sanfermines.

TOP CHOICE **Palacio Guendulain** HISTORIC HOTEL €€€
(☑948 22 55 22; www.palacioguendulain.com; Calle Zapatería 53; d incl breakfast from €133.92; P❋☎) To call this stunning hotel, inside the converted former home of the viceroy of New Granada, sumptuous is an understatement. On arrival, you're greeted by a museum-piece 17th-century carriage decked in gold, and a collection of classic cars lies scattered about the courtyard under the watchful eye of the viceroy's private chapel. The rooms contain *Princess and the Pea*–soft beds, enormous showers and regal armchairs.

Hostel Hemingway HOSTEL €
(☑948 98 38 84; www.hostelhemingway.com; Calle Amaya 26; dm €19-22, s/d from €22/42; @)

Bright, funky colours predominate at this well-run hostel a few minutes' walk from the old town. The dorms have four to six beds and share three bathrooms. There's a TV lounge and a kitchen for guest use. We don't have to tell you what a party it would be staying here during Sanfermines. It's just off Avenida de Carlos III.

Hotel Puerta del Camino BOUTIQUE HOTEL €€
(☑948 22 66 88; www.hotelpuertadelcamino.com; Calle Dos de Mayo 4; s/d from €89/95; P❋☎) A very stylish hotel inside a converted convent (clearly the nuns appreciated the finer things in life!) beside the northern gates to the old city. The functional rooms have clean, modern lines and it's positioned in one of the prettier, and quieter, parts of town. Some rooms have views across the intricate city walls and beyond to the soaring Pyrenees.

runners, blocking much of the view (only police, medical staff and other authorised people can enter the space between the two fences). Some people rent a space on one of the house balconies overlooking the course. Others watch the runners and bulls race out of the entrance tunnel and into the bullring by buying a ticket for a seat in the ring. Whichever the vantage point, it's all over in a few blurred seconds.

Each evening a traditional bullfight is held. Sanfermines winds up at midnight on 14 July with a candlelit procession, known as the Pobre de Mí (Poor Me), which starts from Plaza Consistorial.

Concern has grown about the high numbers of people taking part in recent *encierros*. Since records began in 1924, 16 people have died during Pamplona's bullrun. Many of those who run are full of bravado (and/or drink) and have little idea of what they're doing. The 2004 fiesta was considered to be one of the most dangerous in recent years, with dozens of injuries, but no deaths. For the 2005 fiesta, the authorities used a special antislip paint on the streets to cut down on bull skid, but there seemed to be just as many falls and there were several injuries, including four gorings. The 2008 event was also quite an eventful one, with 45 serious injuries (four of them due to gorings), and in 2009 a man was gored to death after a bull became separated from the rest of the herd. The 2012 run was one of the safest in years, with only four minor gorings. For dedicated *encierro* news, check out www.sanfermin.com.

You can live out a virtual-reality version of the *encierros* at the new Museo del Encierro (www.museoencierro.com; Calle Mercaderes 17; adult/child €8/free; ⊙10am-2pm & 4-8pm Mon-Fri, 11am-8pm Sat-Sun). A visit guides you through the history and culture of the *encierro* and San Fermín in general, after which you can don the special glasses and step (or rather run) straight into the middle of a hectic bullrun in a 3-D film. There are plenty of other interactive displays, and children will have a great time.

Animal-rights groups oppose bullrunning as a cruel tradition, and the participating bulls will almost certainly all be killed in the afternoon bullfight. The PETA-organised anti-bullfighting demonstration, the Running of the Nudes, takes place two days before the first bullrun.

Hostal Arriazu
HOTEL €

(☑948 21 02 02; www.hostalarriazu.com; Calle Comedias 14; s/d €51/60; 🛜) Falling somewhere between a budget *pensión* and a midrange hotel, there is superb value to be found in this former theatre. The rooms are pleasingly old-fashioned and smell of wood polish and the bathrooms are as good as you'll like. There's a nice plant-packed glassed-in courtyard and a communal lounge area. Breakfast is €7 extra.

Habitaciones Mendi
PENSIÓN €

(☑948 22 52 97; www.pensionmendi.es; Calle de las Navas de Tolosa 9; s/d €30/40; 🛜) Full of the spirits of Pamplona past, this charming little guesthouse is a real find. Creaky, wobbly, wooden staircases and equally creaky, chintzy rooms make it just like being at your gran's, and the woman running it will cluck over you as if she were your gran.

Hotel Castillo de Javier
BOUTIQUE HOTEL €€

(☑948 20 30 40; www.hotelcastillodejavier.com; Calle de San Nicolás 50; s/d from €45/63; ❇🛜) On a street of cheap digs, this slick hotel shows a touch of class. The reception area is modern through and through, and the rooms are typical of a business-class hotel. Ask to see a few first as some are much more spacious than others.

Hostal Bearan
PENSIÓN €

(☑948 22 34 28; Calle de San Nicolás 25; s/d €38/50) There's real value to be found here, particularly if you bag one of the larger rooms which are spacious enough for them to have squeezed a sofa in. Sofa or not, make sure you ask for a room away from the noisy street.

Ezcaba
CAMPGROUND €

(☑948 33 03 15; www.campingezcaba.com; sites per person/tent/car €5.75/6.20/5.75; P🛜❇👶) On the banks of Río Ulzama, about 7km to the north on the N121, this is Pamplona's nearest camping ground. Bus 4 runs four times daily (more during Sanfermines) from Plaza de las Merindades by the BBVA bank. Prices double during Sanfermines.

Eating

Baserri
BASQUE €

(☎948 22 20 21; Calle de San Nicolás 32; menú del día €14) This place has won enough *pintxo* awards that we could fill this entire book listing them. In fact, it's staggering to know that so many food awards actually exist! As you'd expect from such a certificate-studded bar, the *pintxos* and full meals are superb.

Casa Otaño
BASQUE €€

(☎948 22 50 95; Calle de San Nicolás 5; mains €15-18) A little pricier than many on this street but worth the extra. Its formal atmosphere is eased by the dazzling array of pink and red flowers spilling off the balcony. Great dishes range from the locally caught trout to heavenly duck dishes. The €17.50 *menú del día* is good value.

Sarasate
VEGETARIAN €€

(☎948 22 57 27; Calle de San Nicolás 21; mains €10-15; ☑) This bright, uncluttered vegetarian restaurant on the 1st floor offers excellent veggie dishes and gluten-free options. The quality is undoubted. It's well worth getting stuck into one of its €14 *menús del día*.

Bodegón Sarria
BASQUE €

(☎948 22 77 13; Calle de la Estafeta 50-52; mains €8-15; ☑) This eternal favourite of the Pamplona foodie scene has had something of a facelift recently but, whether you opt just to graze on *pintxos* or delve into a full meal, the food remains the same hearty old-fashioned local fare that has led to it gaining such a loyal following for so many years. On Tuesdays and Thursdays *pintxos* are a bargain €2.

🍷 Drinking & Entertainment

Pamplona's resident student population ensures a lively after-dark scene year-round. There's a strong Basque vibe in the bars around Calle Carmen and Calle de la Caldería and up towards the cathedral. The area opposite the bullring on Paseo de Hemingway is also home to a few more bars and clubs. Larger nightclubs are found a walk or short taxi ride south and west of the old city centre, in the direction of the university. Doors at these places are usually open after 11pm Thursday to Saturday and the cover charge tends to be around €8 to €12, depending on the night.

Café Iruña
CAFE

(Plaza del Castillo 44) Opened on the eve of Sanfermines in 1888, Café Iruña's dominant position, powerful sense of history and frilly belle-époque decor make this by far the most famous and popular watering hole in the city. As well as caffeine and alcohol, it also has a good range of *pintxos* and light meals.

ℹ Information

Tourist office (☎848 42 04 20; www.turismo. navarra.es; Avenida Roncesvalles 4; ☺9am-7pm Mon-Fri, 10am-2pm & 4-7pm Sat, 10am-2pm Sun) This extremely well-organised office, just opposite the statue of the bulls in the new town, has plenty of information about the city and Navarra. There are a couple of summer-only tourist info booths scattered throughout the city.

ℹ Getting There & Away

Air
Pamplona's **airport** (☎948 16 87 00), about 7km south of the city, has regular flights to Madrid and Barcelona. Bus 16 (€1.20) travels between the city (from the bus station and Calle de las Navas de Tolosa) and the suburb of Noáia, from where it's about a 200m walk to the airport. A taxi costs about €15.

Bus
From the **main bus station** (Calle Conde Oliveto 8), buses leave for most towns throughout Navarra, although service is restricted on Sunday.

Regular bus services travel to these places:

DESTINATION	FARE (€)	DURATION (HR)
Bilbao	14.15	2
Logroño	8.38	1¾
San Sebastián	7.29	1
Vitoria	7.58-8.35	1¼-2

Regional destinations include these towns:

DESTINATION	FARE (€)	DURATION (HR)	FREQUENCY
Estella	4.13	1	10 daily
Olite	3.51	¾	16 daily

Train
Pamplona's train station is linked to the city centre by bus 9 from Paseo de Sarasate every 15 minutes. Tickets are also sold at the **Renfe**

agency (Calle de Estella 8; ⊘9am-1.30pm & 4.30-7.30pm Mon-Fri, 9am-1pm Sat).

Trains run to/from the following places:

DESTINATION	FARE (€)	DURATION (HR)	FREQUENCY
Madrid	57.90	3	4 daily
San Sebastián	from 21.20	2	2 daily
Tudela	from 19.20	1	5 daily
Vitoria	5.65	1	4 daily

North of Pamplona

SIERRA DE ARALAR

One of Navarra's many natural parks, the scenic Sierra de Aralar offers pleasant walking. There's not much to Lekunberri, the area's main town, except a gaggle of solid Basque farmhouses in the old quarter and an ever-growing estate of soulless modern housing beyond. The tourist office (✆948 50 72 04; oit.lekunberri@cfnavarra.es; Calle de Plazaola 21, Lekunberri) here is very helpful and can advise on the numerous fantastic walks the area offers.

Most buses between Pamplona and San Sebastián stop in Lekunberri, but you'll need your own vehicle to explore the sierra.

◉ Sights

Santuario de San Miguel de Aralar CHURCH (⊘10am-2pm & 4-8pm Jun-Sep) For most people, the main reason for visiting Lekunberri is to travel the bendy back road NA1510, which leads southwest through a tasty tapestry of mixed deciduous and evergreen forests to culminate (after 21km) at the austere and very bleak 9th-century Santuario de San Miguel de Aralar, which lies in the shadow of Monte Altxueta (1343m).

Despite its attractive naves and 800-year-old altarpiece, it isn't the sort of place you'd want to visit on a moonless night. There are some spectacular views down onto the plains to the south.

🛏 Sleeping & Eating

Hotel Ayestarán HISTORIC HOTEL €€ (✆948 50 41 27; www.hotelayestaran.com; Calle de Aralar 27, Lekunberri; d €91; 🅿🛜🏊) Sleep with the memory of Hemingway at this beautiful hotel where the writer stayed en route to the Pamplona party. A signed photograph of him standing outside the hotel hangs on the wall. The attached restaurant is equally superb (*menú del día* €16).

SIERRA DE ANDIA

Looking south from the Santuario de San Miguel de Aralar, it's impossible to miss the tempting massif rising up off the plains. This is the Sierra de Andia, and it, too, offers wonderful walking opportunities. To get there, take the very narrow, vertigo-inducing dirt road leading south from the *sanctuario* (do not attempt to drive this route in icy, foggy or very wet conditions) and then join the NA120, which runs, eventually, on to Estella via a laborious clamber up onto the sierra. The sheer mountainsides keep vultures and eagles hanging like mobiles on the thermals, and the limestone heights are a chaos of karst caves that once provided a home to witches. Once up on the plateau, things calm down considerably and you'll find a number of wild walks clearly signposted from the first car park you pass.

East of Pamplona

JAVIER

POP 80 / ELEV 448M

Tiny Javier (Xavier), 11km northeast of Sangüesa, is a quiet rural village set in gentle green countryside. It's utterly dominated by a childhood-fantasy castle that is so perfectly preserved you half expect the drawbridge to come crashing down and a knight in armour to gallop out on a white steed. As well as being an inspiration for fairy-tale dreams, this is also the birthplace of the patron saint of Navarra, San Francisco Xavier, who was born in the village in 1506. Xavier spent much of his life travelling, preaching, teaching and healing in Asia. Today his body lies in a miraculous state of preservation in a cathedral in Goa, India. The Castillo de Javier (admission €2.50; ⊘10am-1.30pm & 3.30-6.30pm) houses a small museum dedicated to the life of the saint.

If you want to stay, the red-brick, ivy-clad Hotel Xabier (✆948 88 40 06; www.hotelxabier.com; s €55-67, d €88; 🅿🛜) has small rooms, from which you can peer out of your window on a moonlit night and look for ghosts flitting around the castle keep.

MONASTERIO DE LEYRE

Totally swamped with visitors on public holidays, the Monasterio de Leyre (adult/child €2.70/free; ⊘10.15am-2pm & 3.30-7pm Mon-Fri, 10.15am-2pm & 4-7pm Sat & Sun Mar-Nov) is in an attractive setting in the shadow of the Sierra de Leyre, about 4km from Yesa on the N240. The early Romanesque crypt has a three-nave structure with a low roof and the 12th-century main portal of the church is a fine example of Romanesque artistry.

Look down from the monastery, towards the main road, and you won't fail to notice the Embalse de Yesa, an enormous expanse of water that is perfect for swimming.

The Pyrenees

Awash in greens and often concealed in mists, the rolling hills, ribboned cliffs, clammy forests and snow-plastered mountains that make up the Navarran Pyrenees are a playground for outdoor enthusiasts and pilgrims on the Camino de Santiago. Despite being firmly Basque in history, culture and outlook, there is something of a different feeling to the tiny towns and villages that hug these slopes. Perhaps it's their proximity to France, but in general they seem somehow more prim and proper than many of the lowland towns. This only adds to the charm of exploring what are, without doubt, some of the most delightful and least exploited mountains in Europe.

Trekkers and skiers should be thoroughly equipped at any time of the year and should note emergency numbers in case of difficulties: ☑112 in Navarra and ☑17 in Aquitaine (France).

VALLE DEL BAZTÁN
This is rural Basque Country at its most typical, a landscape of splotchy reds and greens.

THE CAMINO IN NAVARRA & LA RIOJA

At the gates of Spain, Navarra is the first Spanish leg of the journey to Santiago de Compostela for walkers on the Camino Francés route. The opening section, which crosses over the Pyrenees, is also one of the most spectacular parts of the entire Camino.

Roncesvalles to Pamplona

Just north of Roncesvalles at Puerto de Ibañeta, the Camino dramatically enters Spain and drops down to Roncesvalles. Dominated by its great, imposing abbey, Roncesvalles admirably sets the tone for this extraordinary route. Inside the heavily restored 13th-century Gothic church, you'll find the first statue of Santiago dressed as a pilgrim (with scallop shells and staff).

Pamplona became an official stop along the Camino in the 11th century, cementing its prosperity. Just inside the cathedral's bland neoclassical facade are the pure, soaring lines of the 14th-century Gothic interior.

Pamplona to Logroño & Beyond

Heading west out of Pamplona via Zariquiegui and the Sierra del Perdón, pilgrims reach Puente la Reina, where the Camino Aragonés, coming from the east, joins up with the Camino Francés.

Estella, the next stop, contains exceptional monumental Romanesque architecture: the outstanding portal of the Iglesia de San Miguel; the cloister of the Iglesia de San Pedro de la Rúa; and the Palacio de los Reyes de Navarra.

Outside Estella, evergreen oaks and vineyards fill undulating landscapes until a long, barren stretch leads through the sleepy towns of Los Arcos, Sansol and Torres del Río. In hillside Torres you'll find another remarkably intact eight-sided Romanesque chapel, the Iglesia del Santo Sepulcro.

The great Río Ebro marks the entrance to Logroño and explains its wealth and size. The dour Gothic Iglesia de Santiago houses a large Renaissance altarpiece depicting unusual scenes from the saint's life, including run-ins with the wicked necromancer Hermogenes.

Nájera literally grew out of the town's red cliff wall when King Ramiro discovered a miraculous statue of the Virgin in one of the cliff's caves in the 11th century.

Santo Domingo de la Calzada is one of the road's most captivating places. It is named for its energetic 11th-century founder, Santo Domingo, who cleared forests, built roadways, a bridge, a pilgrim's hospice and a church, and performed many wondrous miracles depicted masterfully in Hispano-Flemish paintings in the cathedral.

Camino in Navarra & La Rioja

Minor roads take you in and out of charming little villages, such as **Arraioz**, known for the fortified Casa Jaureguizar; and **Ziga**, with its 16th-century church.

Just beyond Irurita on the N121B is the valley's biggest town, **Elizondo**, given a distinctly urban air by its tall half-timbered buildings. It's a good base for exploring the area. There's accommodation at the **Antxitónea Hostal** (☑948 58 18 07; www.antxitonea.com; Calle Braulio Iriarte 16; d from €74; ☏), which has plain rooms with flower-coated balconies. The attached restaurant is worth frequenting.

Beyond Elizondo, the NA2600 road meanders dreamily about picturesque farms, villages and hills before climbing sharply to the French border pass of **Puerto de Izpegui**, where the world becomes a spectacular collision of crags, peaks and valleys. At the pass, you can stop for a short, sharp hike up to the top of **Mt Izpegui**. You'll find a good number of *casas rurales* throughout the area.

The N121B continues northwards to the Puerto de Otxondo and the border crossing into France at Dantxarinea. Just before the border, a minor road veers west to the almost overly pretty village of **Zugarramurdi**, home to the decidedly less pretty **Cuevas de Las Brujas** (adult/child €3.50/2; ⊙11am-8pm). These caves were once, according to the Inquisition, the scene of evil debauchery. Having established this, the perverse masters of the Inquisition promptly tortured and burned scores of alleged witches. Playing on the flying-broomstick theme is the **Museo de las Brujas** (adult/child €4.50/2; ⊙11am-6.30pm Wed-Fri, 11am-7pm Sat & Sun), a fascinating dip into the mysterious cauldron of witchcraft in the Pyrenees.

Zugarramurdi has lots of *casas rurales*.

TO FRANCE VIA RONCESVALLES

As you bear northeast out of Pamplona on the N135 and ascend into the Pyrenees, the yellows, browns and olive greens of lower Navarra begin to give way to more-luxuriant vegetation before the mountains thunder up to great Pyrenean heights. It would be fair to say that this route, which follows the Camino de Santiago, is, in comparison to some mountain areas, more culturally than physically attractive.

BURGUETE

The main road runs tightly between neat, whitewashed houses with bare cornerstones at Burguete (Basque: Auritz), lending a more sober French air to things. Despite lacking the history, it actually makes a better night's halt than nearby Roncesvalles.

There are a sprinkling of *casas rurales* in the surrounding area. In the village itself you'll find **Don Jauregui de Burguete** (☑948 76 00 31; www.donjaureguideburguete.com; Calle de San Nicolás 32; d from €49.68), which has bright, youthful rooms and an excellent attached restaurant. The **Hotel Loizu** (☑948 76 00 08; www.hotelloizu.com; Calle de San Nicolás 13; s/d €63/89; ⊙Apr-Dec; 🅿🅯), has comfortable, mellow-coloured rooms; the ones on the upper floors have attractive beams and exposed stone walls. Campers will be happy at **Camping Urrobi** (☑948 76 02 00; www.campingurrobi.com; sites per person/tent/car €5.15/5.15/5.15, dm €10.30; ⊙Apr-Oct; ☏), a few kilometres south of town. It also has a 42-bed hostel.

RONCESVALLES

History hangs heavily in the air of Roncesvalles (Basque: Orreaga). Legend has it that it was here that the armies of Charlemagne were defeated and Roland, commander of Charlemagne's rearguard, was killed by Basque tribes in 778. This is an event celebrated in the epic 11th-century poem *Chanson de Roland* (Song of Roland) and a battle still talked about by today's Basques. In addition to violence and bloodshed, though, Roncesvalles has long been a key point on the road to Santiago de Compostela and today Camino pilgrims continue to give thanks at the famous monastery for a successful crossing of the Pyrenees, one of the hardest parts of the Camino de Santiago.

The main event here is the monastery complex (admission €4.20; ☉10am-2pm & 3.30-7pm), which contains a number of different buildings of interest. The 13th-century Gothic Real Colegiata de Santa María (admission free; ☉9am-8.30pm), houses a much-revered, silver-covered statue of the Virgin beneath a modernist-looking canopy worthy of Frank Gehry. Also of interest is the cloister, which contains the tomb of King Sancho VII (El Fuerte) of Navarra, the apparently 2.25m-tall victor in the Battle of Las Navas de Tolosa, fought against the Muslims in 1212. Nearby is the 12th-century Capilla de Sancti Spiritus.

If you just can't walk another step, you'll find a couple of places in town to stay, including the Hostal Casa Sabina (☏948 76 00 12; www.casasabina.es; s/tw €40/50), where the rooms have twin beds only – possibly to stop any hanky-panky so close to a monastery? The bar and restaurant get more lively than the bedrooms. The Casa de Beneficiados (☏948 76 01 05; www.casadebeneficiados.com; d €70; ☏) is an 18th-century monks' residence converted to a comfortable and utterly modern hotel. Another option, with simple rooms and gentle country charm, is La Posada (☏948 76 02 25; www.laposadaderon cesvalles.com; s/d €50/55), which has a fine restaurant with a *menú del día* for €16.

THE ROADS TO OCHAGAVÍA

Happy wanderers on wheels can drift around a network of quiet country roads, with pretty villages along the way, in the area east of the main Roncesvalles road. A couple of kilometres south of Burguete, the NA140 branches off east to Garralda. Push on to Arive, a charming hamlet, from where you could continue east to the Valle del Salazar, or go south along Río Irati past the fine Romanesque church near Nagore. Another option is to take a loop northeast through the beautiful Bosque de Irati forest, with its thousands of beech trees that turn the slopes a flaming orange every autumn and invite exploration on foot. Eventually this route will link you up with the Valle del Salazar at Ochagavía. If you stick to the NA140 between Arive and Ochagavía, Abaurregaina and Jaurrieta are particularly picturesque. Most villages along the route have *casas rurales*.

OCHAGAVÍA

This charming Pyrenean town lying astride narrow Río Zatoya sets itself quite apart from the villages further south. Grey stone, slate and cobblestones dominate the old centre, which straddles a bubbling stream crossed by a pleasant medieval bridge. The town's sober dignity is reinforced by the looming presence of the Iglesia de San Juan Evangelista.

This is a popular base for walkers and even skiers, so there are plenty of *casas rurales*. Camping Osate (☏948 89 01 84; www.campingosate.net; sites per person/tent/car €5/4.50/4.70) also has two-person cabins from €43 and a hostel. The Hostal Auñamendi (☏948 89 01 89; www.hostalauniamendi.com; d €81; ☏) on the main square is the only official hotel in town.

To reach France, take the NA140 northeast from Ochagavía into the Sierra de Abodi and cross at the Puerto de Larrau (1585m), a majestically bleak pass.

VALLE DEL RONCAL

Navarra's most spectacular mountain area is around Roncal and this easternmost valley is an alternative route for leaving or entering the Navarran Pyrenees. For details of *casas rurales* in the valley, visit Roncal-Salazar (www.roncal-salazar.com).

BURGUI

The gateway to this part of the Pyrenees is Burgui – an enchanting huddle of stone houses built beside a clear, gushing stream (the Río Esca) bursting with frogs and fish and crossed via a humpbacked Roman bridge. Hostal El Almadiero (☏948 47 70 86; www.almadiero.com; Plaza Mayor; d incl half-board €128.60; ☉closed Mon-Thur Nov-Mar), in the heart of the village, has bright and colourful rooms with 19th-century bathrooms (though with mod cons like hot water and flushing toilets!). In high season rooms are on a half-board-only basis; the food is very good.

RONCAL

The largest centre along this road, though still firmly a village, Roncal is a place of cobblestone alleyways that twist and turn between dark stone houses and meander down to a river full of trout. Roncal is renowned for its Queso de Roncal, a sheep's-milk cheese that's sold in the village.

Across the river, on the southern exit from Roncal, is Hostal Zaltua (948 47 50 08; www.zaltua.com; Calle de Castillo 23; d €50), which has cute rooms, some with river views. Outside the high season, it's closed on Sundays.

ISABA

Lording it over the other villages in the valley, lofty Isaba, lying above the confluence of Ríos Belagua and Uztárroz, is another popular base for walkers and skiers. The closest reliable cross-country skiing is about 12km away in Belagua.

There are plenty of sleeping places, but many are block-booked during the skiing season. A character-infused option is the Hostal Onki Xin (948 89 33 20; www.onkixin. com; d €55), in a converted traditional house with fancily painted rooms and lots of wrinkly old wood and open stone walls. Camping Asolaze (948 89 30 34; www.campingasolaze. com; sites per person/tent/car €5/4.50/4.75, dm €12.50) is at Km 6 on the road to France. It also has hostel-style accommodation.

The tourist office (948 89 32 51; www. valled}eroncal.es; 10am-2pm & 4-8pm Mon-Sat, 10am-2pm Sun) can advise on skiing and hiking.

South of Pamplona

Take the A15 south of Pamplona and you only have to drive for 15 minutes before you will enter an entirely new world. Within the space of just a few kilometres, the deep greens that you will have grown to love in the Basque regions and northern Navarra vanish and are replaced with a lighter and more Mediterranean ochre. As the sunlight becomes more dazzling (and more commonly seen!), the shark's-teeth hills of the north flatten into tranquil lowland plains, while the wet forests become scorched vineyards and olive groves, and even the people

change – they're more gregarious and, as the graffiti ascertains, often fiercely anti-Basque. For the traveller it feels as though you are finally arriving in the Spain of the clichés.

OLITE

POP 3440 / ELEV 365M

Bursting off the pages of a fairy tale, the turrets and spires of Olite are filled with stories of kings and queens, brave knights and beautiful princesses. Though it might seem a little hard to believe today, this insignificant, honey-coloured village was once the home of the royal families of Navarra and the walled old quarter is crowded with their memories.

Founded by the Romans (parts of the town wall date back to Roman times), Olite first attracted the attention of royalty in 1276 but didn't really take off until it caught the fancy of King Carlos III (Carlos the Noble) in the 15th century who embarked on a series of daring building projects.

◉ Sights

Palacio Real CASTLE
(Castillo de Olite; www.palaciorealdeolite.com; adult/child €3.50/2; 10am 8pm) It's Carlos that we must thank for the exceptional Palacio Real, which towers over the village. Back in Carlos' day, the inhabitants of the castle included not just princes and jesters but also lions, giraffes and other exotic pets, as well as Babylon-inspired hanging gardens. Today, though the princesses and lionesses are sadly missing, some of the hanging gardens remain.

Integrated into the castle is the Iglesia de Santa María la Real, which has a superbly detailed Gothic portal. There are guided

---

WORTH A TRIP

LAGUNA DE PITILLAS

The lakes and marshes that make up the Laguna de Pitillas are one of the top birding sites in Navarra – a region already renowned for its variety of feathered friends. Now a protected Ramsar wetland site of international importance, the Laguna de Pitillas provides a home for around 160 permanent and migratory species, including marsh harriers, great bitterns and even ospreys. To get there, take the N121 south of Olite and then turn off down the NA5330.

tours of the church; check with the tourist office for times.

Museo de la Viña y el Vino de Navarra · MUSEUM

(☑948 74 12 73; Plaza de los Teobaldos 10; adult/child €3.50/2; ⏱10am-2pm & 4-7pm Mon-Sat, 10am-2pm Sun) Don't miss this museum, which is a fascinating journey through wine and wine culture. Everything is well labelled and laid out and some fascinating facts are revealed. For instance, did you know that Noah (the one of the Ark fame) was apparently the first human ever to get drunk?

Galerías Subterráneas · MUSEUM

(Plaza Carlos III; adult/child €1.50/1; ⏱11am-1pm Tue-Fri, 11am-2pm & 4.30-7pm Sat, Sun & public holidays) These underground galleries, whose origin and use remain something of a mystery, contain a small museum explaining the town's medieval life (in Spanish). These basically illustrate that if you had blue blood or were rich then life was one jolly round of wine, food and things that your mother wouldn't approve of and, if you weren't, well, life sucked.

🛏 Sleeping & Eating

Hotel el Juglar · BOUTIQUE HOTEL €€

(☑948 74 18 55; www.merindaddeolitehoteles.com; Rúa Romana 39; s €90-100, d €105-115; [P][❄][🐾][⛤]) A few minutes' walk into the new suburbs, this is the best deal in town. The handful of rooms are all slightly different from one another – some have big round whirlpool baths, some old-fashioned stone baths, and others elaborate walk-in showers. All have four-poster beds and lots of fancy decorations, and there's a pool to cool off in on a hot summer day.

Hostal Rural Villa Vieja · BOUTIQUE HOTEL €€

(☑948 74 17 00; www.hostalvillavieja.com; Calle Villaveija 11; s €62, d €70-88; [🐾]) Doing away with all the twee old-world decoration that is so common elsewhere in Olite, the slick rooms in this hotel stick firmly with the 21st century thanks to the ample use of bright colours and pop art.

Principe de Viana · HISTORIC HOTEL €€€

(☑948 74 00 00; www.parador.es; Plaza de los Teobaldos 2; r incl breakfast from €140; [❄][🐾][@]) Situated in a wing of the castle (though some of the cheaper rooms are in a newer extension), this offering from the Parador chain is in a sumptuous, atmospheric class of its own. Though there might be good rooms

available elsewhere in town for considerably fewer euros, they don't come with a castle attached.

Hotel Merindad de Olite · HISTORIC HOTEL €€

(☑948 74 07 35; www.merindaddeolitehoteles.com; Rúa de la Judería 11; s €58-68, d €68-78; [❄][🐾]) Built almost into the old town walls, this charming place has small but comfortable rooms and masses of period style. Get in fast because it fills quickly.

❶ Information

Olite has a friendly and helpful **tourist office** (☑948 74 17 03; Plaza de los Teobaldos 10; ⏱10am-2pm & 4-7pm Mon-Sat, 10am-2pm Sun), in the same building as the wine museum.

❶ Getting There & Away

Up to nine buses a day run between Olite and Pamplona (€3.51, 50 minutes).

UJUÉ

Balancing atop a hill criss-crossed with terraced fields, the tiny village of Ujué, some 18km east of Olite and overlooking the plains of southern Navarra, is a perfect example of a fortified medieval village. Today the almost immaculately preserved village is sleepy and pretty, with steep, narrow streets tumbling down the hillside, but what gives it something special is the hybrid **Iglesia de Santa María**, a fortified church of mixed Romanesque-Gothic style. The church contains a rare statue of the Black Virgin, which is said to have been discovered by a shepherd who was led to the statue by a dove. In addition to the Virgin, the church also contains the heart of Carlos II.

The village plays host to a fascinating *romería* (pilgrimage) on the first Sunday after St Mark's Day (25 April), when hundreds of people walk through the night from Tudela to celebrate Mass in the village church.

Unfortunately, there is no formal accommodation in the village, but it makes a great lunch stop. **Mesón las Migas** (☑948 73 90 44; Calle Jesús Echauri; mains €12-18, menú del día €26; ⏱Fri-Sun), which serves traditional south Navarran food, is the best place to eat delights such as hunks of meat cooked over an open wood fire, but the house special is *migas de pastor* (fried breadcrumbs with herbs and chorizo).

The 12th-century **Monasterio de la Oliva** (☑948 72 50 06; guided tours €2; ⏱9am-12.30pm & 3.30-6pm Mon-Sat, 9-11.30am & 4-6pm Sun), 2km from Carcastillo, was founded by Cis-

ⓘ WALKING

There are numerous walking trails of mixed lengths and difficulties in the Pyrenees. It's even possible to follow high-altitude trails across the entire breadth of the range in around 45 days. If you are intending to do some proper walking, then keep in mind that the weather up here changes alarmingly fast. Even in August, a beautiful morning can quickly slide into an afternoon of violent storms. For even fairly moderate exploration, a two-season sleeping bag and all-weather gear are essential – even in summer.

Finding a suitable place to begin hiking can be a little confusing and, without a dedicated guidebook, a decent map and a compass, the most rewarding walks will elude you. Fortunately we can help you out here, too, with Lonely Planet's *Hiking in Spain* guide, which includes a number of walks in the Navarran Pyrenees and elsewhere in the Basque regions. Otherwise, almost every newsagent, bookshop and tourist office in the region has a full stock of locally produced hiking guides, but they are all in Spanish or French only and to understand the routes they describe you must speak one of these languages to a high level. Some of the shorter and more popular walks are more clearly signposted and accessible without knowledge of Spanish or French; otherwise tourist offices can sometimes supply basic maps of short walks.

We have not attempted to describe any walking routes here and have focused instead on mountain areas and villages accessible to visitors with their own car.

Further information (in Spanish) on these wonderful mountains can be obtained from the Federación Navarra de Deportes de Montaña y Escalada (☎in Pamplona 948 22 46 83, in San Sebastián 943 47 42 79; www.fedme.es).

tercian monks and is still functioning as a community. Its austere church gives onto a peaceful Gothic cloister. The monks are dressed in exotic white hooded robes.

PARQUE NATURAL DE LAS BÁRDENAS REALES

In a region largely dominated by wet mountain slopes, the last thing you'd expect to find is a sunburnt desert, but, in the Parque Natural de las Bárdenas Reales, a desert is exactly what you'll find. Established as a natural park in 1999 and as a UN Biosphere Reserve in 2000, the Bárdenas Reales is a desiccated landscape of blank tabletop hills, open gravel plains and snakelike gorges covering over 410 sq km of southeastern Navarra. As well as spectacular scenery, the park plays host to numerous birds and animals, including the great bustard, golden eagles, Egyptian and griffon vultures, numerous reptiles, mountain cats and wild boar. This may look like an almost pristine wilderness, but it is, in fact, totally artificial. Where now there is desert there was once forest, but man, being quite dumb, chopped it all down, let his livestock eat all the lower growth and suddenly found himself living in a desert. There are a couple of dirt motor tracks and numerous hiking and cycling trails, all of which are only vaguely signposted. The tourist offices in Olite and Tudela are the best

places to pick up reliable information and maps.

West of Pamplona

PUENTE LA REINA
POP 2670 / ELEV 421M

The spectacular six-arched medieval bridge at Puente la Reina (Basque: Gares), 22km southwest of Pamplona on the A12, throngs with the ghosts of a multitude of pilgrims. Their first stop here was at the late-Romanesque Iglesia del Crucifijo, erected by the Knights Templars and still containing one of the finest Gothic crucifixes in existence.

ESTELLA
POP 14,251 / ELEV 483M

Estella (Basque: Lizarra) was known as 'La Bella' in medieval times because of the splendour of its monuments and buildings, and though the old dear has lost some of its beauty to modern suburbs, it's not without charms. During the 11th century, Estella became a main reception point for the growing flood of pilgrims along the Camino de Santiago (see the boxed text, p448). Today most visitors are continuing that same plodding tradition.

The 12th-century Iglesia de San Pedro de la Rúa is the most important monument in Estella. Its cloisters are a fine example of Romanesque sculpture whilst its 18th-century porch has a vaguely Arab influence. The Palacio de los Reyes (www.museogusta vodemaeztu.com; Calle de San Nicolás 2; admission free; ⊙9.30am-1pm Tue-Fri, 11am-2pm Sat-Sun) is a rare example of Romanesque civil construction. It houses an intriguing collection of paintings by Gustavo de Maeztu y Whitney (1887-1947), who was of Cuban-English parentage but emphatically Basque in upbringing and identity. Landscapes, portraits and full-bodied nudes reflect Maeztu's engaging sensual romanticism. Across the river and overlooking the town is the Iglesia de San Miguel, with a fine Romanesque north door.

From the last Friday in July, Estella hosts a week-long feria (fair) with its own encierro (running of the bulls).

The Hotel Yerri (☎948 54 60 34; www.hotel yerri.es; Avenida de Yerri 35; s €45, d €62-67; P ⊛) is a large place a few minutes' walk from the old centre with comfortable, though not terribly interesting, rooms.

The town's flashiest rooms are to be found in the new Chapitel Hospedería (☎948 55 10 90; www.hospederiachapitel.com; s/d from €70/90; ⊛); although the rooms themselves here are the last word in comfort (in a sterile business kind of way) the bathrooms seem to be very much an afterthought.

On the main square, Astarriaga Asador (Plaza de Los Fueros 12; mains €10-15) is a very popular restaurant with Galicia-bound pilgrims on account of its energy-enhancing steak selections – some are almost the size of a cow.

About 10 buses leave from the bus station (Plaza Coronación) for Pamplona (€4.13, one hour) Monday to Friday, and six on Saturday and Sunday.

AROUND ESTELLA

The countryside around Estella is littered with monasteries. One of the best is the Monasterio de Irache (admission free; ⊙10am-1.15pm & 4-7pm Wed-Sun, closed 1-17 Jan), 3km southwest of Estella, near Ayegui. This ancient Benedictine monastery has a lovely 16th-century plateresque cloister and its Puerta Especiosa is decorated with delicate sculptures.

About 10km north of Estella, near Abárzuza, is the Monasterio de Iranzu (www.monasterio-iranzu.com; admission by donation; ⊙10am-2pm & 4-8pm). Originally founded way back in the 11th century, but recently restored, this sandy-coloured monastery with beautiful cloisters is so calm and tranquil that it could inspire religious meditation in Lucifer himself.

From this monastery a pleasing, and well-signed, short walk (1¼ hours return) leads to the Cañón del Río Iranzu, a narrow defile in the rock.

LA RIOJA

Get out the *copas* (glasses) for La Rioja and some of the best red wines produced in the country. Wine goes well with the region's ochre earth and vast blue skies, which seem far more Mediterranean than the Basque greens further north. In fact, it's hard not to feel as if you're in a different country altogether. The bulk of the vineyards line Río Ebro around the town of Haro, but extend into neighbouring Navarra and the Basque province of Álava. This diverse region offers more than just the pleasures of the grape, though, and a few days here can see you mixing it up in lively towns and quiet pilgrim churches, and even hunting for the remains of giant reptiles.

Logroño

POP 153,000

Logroño doesn't feel the need to be loud and brash. Instead it's a stately town with a heart of tree-studded squares, narrow streets and hidden corners. There are few monuments here, but there is a monumentally good selection of *pintxos* (tapas) bars. In fact, Logroño is quickly gaining a culinary reputation to rival anywhere in Spain. All up this is the sort of place that you cannot help but feel contented in – and it's not just the wine.

⊙ Sights

A stroll around the old town and down to the river is a pleasant diversion. The Museo de La Rioja (Plaza San Agustin) has been undergoing renovation for the past five years and when we enquired at the tourist office as to when it might reopen we were told '20-blah- blah'. It's worth popping past to see if we've yet reached the year 20-blah-bah. See also the boxed text, p448.

Catedral de Santa María
de la Redonda   CATHEDRAL
(Calle de Portales; ⊙8am-1pm & 6-8.45pm Mon-Sat, 9am-2pm & 6.30-8.45pm Sun) The Catedral

Logroño

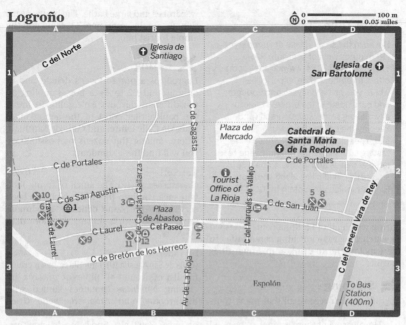

Logroño

◎ Top Sights

◎ Sights

⬚ Sleeping

◎ Eating

◎ Shopping

de Santa María de la Redonda started life as a Gothic church before maturing into a full-blown cathedral in the 16th century. Inside you'll find it a little dark and overpowering. Outside it seems lighter and friendlier, thanks, no doubt, to the huge square in which it proudly sits.

Iglesia de San Bartolomé   CHURCH
(Calle de Rodríguez Paterna) The impressive main entrance to the 13th-century Iglesia de San Bartolomé has a splendid portico of deeply receding borders and an expressive collection of statuary.

🎊 Festivals & Events

Actual   CULTURE
A program of cultural, musical and artistic events that takes place through the first week of January.

Feast of San Bernabé   FEAST DAY
The Feast of San Bernabé is held on 11 June and commemorates the French siege of Logroño in 1521.

Fiesta de San Mateo   GRAPE HARVEST
Logroño's week-long Fiesta de San Mateo starts on the Saturday before 21 September and doubles as a harvest festival,

RIOJA TREK

Based in the small village of Fuenmayor (10 minutes west of Logroño) **Rioja Trek** (☎941 58 73 54; www.riojatrek.com) offers three-hour wine 'experiences' where you visit a vineyard and bodega and participate in the process of actually making some wine yourself (and keeping the bottle afterwards). The same people also run well-priced wine-tasting courses, family-friendly wine related activities and, as the name would suggest, guided hikes along some of La Rioja's fabulous mountain trails.

during which all of La Rioja comes to town to watch the grape-crushing ceremonies in the Espolón and to drink ample quantities of wine.

🛏 Sleeping

Logroño doesn't receive all that many tourists and this shows in the relative lack of hotels. However, what there is tends to be good value. Aside from those listed below, Logroño is also home to a number of comfortable but sterile business-class hotels, most of which are scattered around the fringes of the new town.

Hotel Marqués de Vallejo   DESIGN HOTEL €€
(☎941 24 83 33; www.hotelmarquesdevallejo.com; Calle del Marqués de Vallejo 8; s/d €76/97; P❈🐾🛜) From the driftwood art and photographic flashlights in the communal spaces to the lollipops and raunchy red pouffes in the rooms, a huge amount of thought and effort has gone into the design of this stylish, modern and very well-priced hotel.

Hostal Niza   PENSIÓN €
(☎941 20 60 44; www.hostalniza.com; Calle de Capitán Gallarza 13; s/d from €40/60; 🛜) The communal areas of this smart *pensión* are so extravagantly multicoloured it's like being trapped inside a packet of mixed sweets. The rooms are simple, good value and all have tea- and coffee-making facilities. Right in the heart of the action.

Hostal La Numantina   PENSIÓN €
(☎941 25 14 11; www.hostalnumantina.com; Calle de Sagasta 4; s/d from €36/59; 🛜) This professional operation caters perfectly to the traveller's needs. The rooms are comfortable and homely, and some have crazy patterned

wardrobes and large baths. The best aspects, though, are the communal TV room and the ample tourist info.

🍴 Eating

Logroño is a *pintxo* lover's delight and at only around €2 to €4 a pop, sampling all the different flavours isn't going to break the bank either. Most of the action takes place on Calle Laurel and Calle de San Juan, where, among the dozens of possibilities, you will find these standouts.

Bar Soriano   TAPAS €
(Travesía de Laurel 2) The smell of frying food will suck you into this bar, which has been serving up the same delicious mushroom tapa, topped with a shrimp, for more than 30 years.

La Taberna de Baco   TAPAS €
(Calle de San Agustín 10) This place has a cracking list of around 40 different *pintxos*, including *bombitas* (potatoes stuffed with mushrooms) and *rabas de pollo* (fried chicken slices marinated in spices and lemon juice). You'll also find some delicious casseroles and salads.

La Fontana   TAPAS €
(Calle del Laurel 16) Another stellar *pintxo* bar with a welcoming atmosphere. This one's speciality is *sepia fontana*. And when you order this what emerges from the kitchen? A pile of egg, mushroom, aubergine and foie-gras. The octopus isn't bad either.

Bar Vinissimo   TAPAS €
(Calle de San Juan 23; ☺closed Wed & Thu lunch) The speciality of this cramped little local's bar is fresh foie gras cooked on the *plancha* (a type of hotplate widely used for cooking on in Spain).

Bar Charly   TAPAS €
(Travesía de Laurel 4; ☺dinner) Renowned for its *pimientos rellenos* (spicy red peppers stuffed full of meat), it's open in the evenings only.

La Taberna del Laurel   TAPAS €
(Calle Laurel 7) The speciality at La Taberna del Laurel is *patatas bravas* (potatoes in a spicy tomato sauce). They're not just good: they're damn near divine.

Bar A Tu Gusto   TAPAS €
(Calle de San Juan 21; ☺closed Wed) This place serves delicious shellfish and calamari in an

Andalucian-flavoured bar and has an impressive wine list.

Shopping

Vinos El Peso WINE SHOP
(Calle el Peso 1; ⊙9am-9pm Mon-Fri, 9am-4pm Sat, 9am-2pm Sun) There are countless wine outlets in town, but this one is excellent.

❶ Information

There are post offices in Calle Lobete or Calle Pérez Galdós.

Tourist office of La Rioja (☑941 29 12 60; www.larlojaturlsmo.com; Calle de Portales 50; ⊙10am-2pm & 4-7pm Mon-Fri, 10am-2pm & 5-8pm Sat, 10am-2pm & 5-7pm Sun)

❶ Getting There & Away

If you arrive at the train or bus station, first head up Avenida de España and then Calle del General Vara de Rey until you reach the Espolón, a large, park-like square lavished with plane trees (and with an underground car park). The Casco Viejo starts just to the north.

Buses bounce off to the following:

DESTINATION	FARE (€)	DURATION (HR)
Bilbao	12.80	2¾
Burgos	7.43	2¼
Haro	3.26	1
Pamplona	8.38	1-1¾
Santo Domingo de la Calzada	3.05	45 min

By train, Logroño is regularly connected to the following:

DESTINATION	FARE (€)	DURATION (HR)
Bilbao	21.90	2½
Burgos	14.90-35	1¾
Madrid	58.30	3¼
Zaragoza	14.90-36	2½

South of Logroño

For those with their own transport, heading south for Soria leads through some stunning countryside. One route, which takes in shades of the Arab world and reminders of the prehistoric, heads southeast of Logroño on the N232 past the large town of Calahorra with the twisted, bendy streets of an old quarter straight out of North Africa. From here head southwest, via Arnedo, to perfect Arnedillo.

ARNEDILLO & AROUND

The delightful spa village of Arnedillo, surrounded by slowly eroding hills, terraced in olive groves and watched over by circling hawks and vultures, is an ideal place to spend a peaceful day or two walking and dinosaur hunting. Just beyond Arnedillo is the hamlet of Peroblasco, confidently perched in a defensive posture on the crown of a hill and well worth a wander.

◉ Sights

Dinosaur Museums MUSEUM
Never mind dodging crazy truck drivers: if you had been driving around these parts some 120 million years ago, it would have been crazy tyrannosauruses that you would have been dodging. Perhaps a little disappointingly, the dinosaurs are long gone, but, if you know where to look, you can still find clues to their passing.

In the small and pretty hill village of Enciso, 10km or so further down the road from Arnedillo, dinosaur fever reaches a peak at the excellent Centro Paleontológico de Enciso (adult/child €4/2; ⊙11am-2pm & 5-8pm), where both children and children at heart will enjoy checking their stats against those of a brontosaurus. Displays are in Spanish only.

Also in Enciso is the newly opened El Barranco Perdido (www.barrancoperdido.com; adult/child €23/17; ⊙11am-8pm), a dino theme park containing a museum, various climbing frames, zip-wire slides and an outdoor swimming pool complex surrounded by dinosaur 'skeletons'. The highlight though is the chance to see some real life dinosaur footprints scattered across former mudflats (now rock slopes) in the surrounding countryside.

Further dinosaur footprints can be found throughout the region – get hold of a map indicating sites from either the Centro Paleontológico de Enciso or any nearby tourist office.

Eagle Observation BIRDWATCHING
Just outside Arnedillo is a small observation hide from where you can watch the region's booted eagles at their nesting sites via closed-circuit television. Booted eagles are the smallest member of the eagle family nesting in Europe and their acrobatics, as they dart in and around the cliff faces of Arnedillo, would put most fighter pilot jets to shame. Access to the observation post is by appointment through Arnedillo tourist office (p458).

Sleeping & Eating

For accommodation, the tourist office can supply details of nearby *casas rurales*. The following are all to be found in Arendillo.

TOP CHOICE Hospederia Las Pedrolas
CASA RURAL €€

(☎941 39 44 01; www.laspedrolas.com; Plaza Felix Merino 16; s/d incl breakfast €70/95; ❀) In Arnedillo centre this is an immaculately restored house full of tasteful furnishings and crooked roof beams. Comfortable rooms splashed in glaring whitewash leave you feeling as if you're sleeping inside a Mr Whippy ice cream and it's run with the kind of care and service you'd normally expect of a five-star hotel.

Casa Rural La Fuente
CASA RURAL €

(☎941 39 41 38; www.lafuentedearnedillo.com; r from €45) At this funky *casa rural*, you get an art-stuffed room, kitchen use and a primitive sitting room.

Bodega la Petra
NAVARRAN €

(☎941 39 40 23; mains €10-15) You won't have failed to notice the now largely disused cave houses burrowed deeply into the sunburst red gorges throughout this area. Well, in this welcoming, village-centre restaurant, you finally get the chance to take a look inside one of these caves and live out any caveman fantasies you might be harbouring. In addition, you can get a meal that's probably much better than any a caveman got to eat.

❶ Information

Tourist office (☎941 39 42 26; www.valcidacos.es; Calle Amancio Gonzáez 2; ◷10am-2pm & 4.30-7pm Mon-Sat, 10.30am-2pm Sun)

West of Logroño

NÁJERA
POP 8100 / ELEV 506M

The main attraction of this otherwise unexciting town is the Gothic Monasterio de Santa María la Real (admission €3; ◷10am-1pm & 4-7pm Tue-Sat, 10am-12.30pm & 4-6pm Sun), in particular its fragile-looking, early-16th-century cloisters. Buses between Logroño and Santo Domingo de la Calzada stop in Nájera.

SAN MILLÁN DE COGOLLA
POP 270 / ELEV 733M

About 16km southwest of Nájera, in the hamlet of San Millán de Cogolla, are two remarkable monasteries, which between them helped give birth to the Castilian language. On account of their linguistic heritage and artistic beauty they have been recognised by Unesco as World Heritage sites.

The Monasterio de Yuso (www.monasteriodeyuso.org; adult/child €5/2; ◷10am-1.30pm & 4-6.30pm Tue-Sun), sometimes presumptuously called El Escorial de La Rioja, contains numerous treasures in its museum. You can only visit as part of a guided tour (in Spanish only; non-Spanish speakers will be given an information sheet in English and French). Tours last 50 minutes and run every half-hour or so. In August it's also open on Mondays.

A short distance away is the Monasterio de Suso (admission €3; ◷9.30am-1.30pm & 3.30-6.30pm Tue-Sun). Built above the caves where San Millán once lived, it was consecrated in the 10th century. It's believed that in the 13th century a monk named Gonzalo de Berceo wrote the first Castilian words here. Again, it can only be visited on a guided tour. Tickets, which must be bought in advance and include a short bus ride up to the monastery, can be reserved by calling ☎941 37 30 82 or can be picked up at the very helpful **tourist office** at the Monasterio de Yuso. Maps detailing short walks in the region can also be obtained at the tourist office.

SANTO DOMINGO DE LA CALZADA
POP 6260 / ELEV 630M

Santo Domingo is small-town Spain at its very best. A large number of the inhabitants continue to live in the partially walled old quarter, a labyrinth of medieval streets where the past is alive and the sense of community is strong. It's the kind of place where you can be certain that the baker knows all his customers by name and that everyone will turn up for María's christening. Santiago-bound pilgrims have long been a part of the fabric of this town and that tradition continues to this day, with most visitors being foot-weary pilgrims. All this helps to make Santo Domingo one of the most enjoyable places in La Rioja.

The morose, monumental cathedral and its attached museum (adult/child €3/1.50, free Sun; ◷10am-7.30pm Mon-Fri, 10am-7.10pm Sat, 10am-12.20pm & 2-7.10pm Sun) glitter with the gold that attests to the great wealth the Camino has bestowed on otherwise backwater towns (see the boxed text, p448). The cathedral's most eccentric feature is the Disneyesque white rooster and hen that forage in a glass-fronted cage opposite the entrance to the crypt (look up!). These two celebrate a long-standing legend, the *Miracle of the Rooster,* which tells of a young man who was unfairly executed only to recover miraculously, while the broiled cock and hen on the plate of his judge suddenly leapt up and chickened off, fully fledged.

The **Hostal R Pedro** (☎941 34 11 60; www. hostalpedroprimero.es; Calle San Roque 9; s/d €48/59; ☞) is a carefully renovated town house with small, but superb-value rooms with wooden roof beams and entirely modern bathrooms. If your idea of a religious-run hotel includes lumpy beds, 5am prayers and severe sisters, then forget it, because the **Hospedería Sta Teresita** (☎941 34 07 00; www.cister-lacalzada.com; Calle Pinar 2; s/d €38/55; ☞) is much more about elevators, swipe cards and comfortable rooms. There are two state-run *paradors* in town. The swishest is the **Parador Santo Domingo** (☎941 34 03 00; www.parador.es; Plaza del Santo 3; r from €100; P☞), which is the antithesis of the town's general air of piety. Occupying a 12th-century former hospital, opposite the cathedral, this palatial hotel offers anything but a frugal medieval-like existence. Just on the edge of the old town is the **Parador Santo Domingo Bernado de Fresneda** (☎941 34 11 50; www.parador.es; Plaza de San Francisco 1;

r from €100; P☞), which occupies a former convent and pilgrim hostel. It's a slightly toned-down version of its big brother, but you certainly wouldn't describe it as a hostel anymore.

There are a few lacklustre cafes and bars in the modern centre of town by the bus stop, and some posher, but not necessarily better ones near the cathedral.

Buses run to Logroño (€3.05, one hour via Nájera, up to 13 daily on weekdays, fewer on weekends).

Wine Region

La Rioja wine rolls on and off the tongue with ease, by name as well as by taste. All wine fanciers know the famous wines of La Rioja, where the vine has been cultivated since Roman times. The region is classic vine country and vineyards cover the hinterland of Río Ebro. On the river's north bank, the region is part of the Basque Country and is known as La Rioja Alavesa.

HARO
POP 11,500 / ELEV 426M

Despite its fame in the wine world, there's not much of a heady bouquet to Haro, the capital of La Rioja's wine-producing region. But the town has a cheerful pace and the

---

IN SEARCH OF THE FINEST DROP

La Rioja is as much about serious wine drinking as it is holidaying. Well, there's a downside to everything!

Searching for the finest drop should be conducted only after proper training, so we recommend you begin at one or all of the region's wine museums. In Navarra, there is the exceptional Museo de la Viña y el Vino de Navarra (p452) in Olite. In La Rioja proper is Haro's Museo del Vino (p460), Villa Lucia (p460) in Laguardia and, finally, the big daddy of them all, Dinastía Vivanco (p461).

After all that history, you'll be needing a drink. What will it be? Wine categories in La Rioja are termed Young, Crianza, Reserva and Gran Reserva. Young wines are in their first or second year and are inevitably a touch 'fresh'. Crianzas must have matured into their third year and have spent at least one year in the cask, followed by a few months resting in the bottle. Reservas pay homage to the best vintages and must mature for at least three full years in cask and bottle, with at least one year in the cask. Gran Reservas depend on the very best vintages and are matured for at least two years in the cask followed by three years in the bottle. These are the 'velvet' wines.

Experts have developed a classification system for the years in which the wine was particularly good. Five stars (the maximum) were awarded in 1982, 1994, 1995, 2001, 2004, 2005 and 2010. Four-star years include 1981, 1987, 1991, 1996, 1998, 2006, 2007, 2008 and 2009.

The tourist offices in Haro, Laguardia and Logroño have lists of bodegas that can be visited throughout the region, although it usually requires ringing in advance to arrange a time.

THE NEW GUGGENHEIM(S)

'If Bilbao has one, we want one too', scream the villages of rural La Rioja. Impressed by the effect El Goog had on Bilbao's international standing and apparently unconcerned by the size and wealth difference between the big industrial city and their small farming communities, two villages have got themselves a Guggenheim lookalike.

When the owner of the Bodegas Marqués de Riscal, in the village of Elciego, decided he wanted to create something special, he certainly didn't hold back. The result is the spectacular Frank Gehry–designed Hotel Marqués de Riscal (945 18 08 80; www. starwoodhotels.com/luxury; r from €304;). Costing around €85 million to construct and now managed by the Starwood chain, the building is a flamboyant wave of multicoloured titanium sheets that stands in utter contrast to the creaky old village behind it. Like the Guggenheim, this building is having a radical effect on the surrounding countryside and has led to more tourists, more jobs, more wine sales and more money appearing in the hands of locals. Casual visitors are not, however, welcome at the hotel. If you want a closer look, you have three options. The easiest is to join one of the bodega's wine tours (945 18 08 88; www.marquesderiscal.com; tour €10) – it's necessary to book in advance. You won't get inside the building, but you will get to see its exterior from some distance. A much closer look can be obtained by reserving a table at one of the two superb in-house restaurants; the Michelin-approved Restaurante Marqués de Riscal (945 18 08 80; menus from €70; closed Sun & Jan) or the Bistró 1860 (945 18 08 80; menus €55). But for the most intimate look at the building, you'll need to reserve a room for the night, but be prepared to part with some serious cash!

But what one Riojan bodega can do, another can do better and just a couple of kilometres to the north of Laguardia are the Bodegas Ysios (www.ysios.com; Camino de la Hoya, Laguarida). Designed by Santiago Calatrava as a 'temple dedicated to wine', it's wave-like roof made of aluminium and cedar wood matches the flow of the rocky mountains behind it. However, it looks its best at night when pools of light flow out of it. Daily tours (945 60 06 40; per person €6) of the bodega are by appointment only.

There are several other, somewhat less architecturally challenging, wine cellars around Laguarida that can be visited, often with advance notice only – contact the tourist office in Laguardia for details. Bodegas Palacio (945 60 01 51; www.bodegaspalacio.com; Carretera de Elciego; tour €5), only 1km from Laguardia on the Elciego road, is one of the most receptive to visitors. Its tours run several times daily Monday to Saturday in Spanish, English and German. Reservations are not essential but are a good idea (especially out of season). The same bodega also runs excellent wine courses. The beginners' wine-tasting course (€30) runs monthly throughout the year except August and January. Advance reservations are essential. It also does an advanced course (€40; minimum 10 people), but these only run when requested in advance. There's also a hotel (945 62 11 95; d €85;) attached to the complex, but compared to options in Laguardia, it lacks character.

Also just outside Laguardia is the Centro Temático del Vino Villa Lucia (945 60 00 32; www.villa-lucia.com; Carretera de Logroño; tour €5.50; 11am-6.30pm Tue-Fri, 10.15am-6.30pm Sat, 11am-12.30pm Sun), a new wine museum and shop selling high-quality wine from a variety of small, local producers. Museum visits are by guided tour only and finish with a 3-D film.

It's worth noting that buried under the houses of Laguardia are numerous small wine bodegas, some of which are open to the public. Ask at the tourist office for details.

compact old quarter, leading off Plaza de la Paz, has some intriguing alleyways with bars and wine shops aplenty.

Sights & Activities

Museo del Vino — MUSEUM

(Estacíon Enológica; 941 31 05 47; www.vinodel rioja.org; Avenida Breton de los Herreros 4; adult/child €3/free, wine-tasting courses €15; 10am-2.30pm & 3.30-6pm Fri & Sat, 10am-2pm Sun, wine-tasting courses 11.30am Sat & Sun) Haro's wine interpretation centre, near the bus station, houses a detailed display on how wine is made and has helpful information in Spanish, French and English. Wine-tasting courses are also held here. Places are limited so reserve in advance.

Bodegas Muga
WINERY

(🏛941 30 60 60; www.bodegasmuga.com; winetasting tour €6) Just after the railway bridge on the way out of town, this bodega gives daily guided tours and tastings in Spanish and, although technically you should book in advance in high season, you can often just turn up and tack onto the back of a tour. For an English-language tour, it's essential to book several days ahead.

🎆 Festivals & Events

Batalla del Vino WINE FESTIVAL

On 29 June the otherwise mild-mannered citizens of Haro go temporarily berserk during the Batalla del Vino (Wine Battle), squirting and chucking wine all over each other in the name of San Juan, San Felices and San Pedro. Plenty of it goes down the right way, too.

🛏 Sleeping & Eating

There are plenty of cafes and bars around Plaza de la Paz and the surrounding streets.

Casa de Legarda CASA RURAL €€

(🏛605 600646; www.mesonchomin.com/casa; Calle Real 11; r €48-70; P🅿🛜) In the small village of Briñas, 4km northeast of Haro, this gorgeous *casa rural* is housed inside a honeycoloured building dating back to 1634. Whilst the common areas are smothered in equally old-fashioned style, the room decoration is all bright theatrical paint jobs that are very much up to date. There's a minimum stay of three nights in August.

Los Agustinos HISTORIC HOTEL €€

(🏛941 31 13 08; www.aranzazu-hoteles.com; Calle San Augustín 2; r from €100, restaurant mains €12; P🅿🛜) History hangs in the air of this luxurious hotel. The rooms are lovely although they've possibly gone a little overboard on the flowery bedspreads, but it's the stunning covered courtyard of this former monastery that steals the show. The attached **restaurant**, with its fabulous setting, is highly recommended.

Hotel Arrope HOTEL €€

(🏛941 30 40 25; www.hotelarrope.com; Calle Vega 31; s/d from €65/81; 🅿🛜) This new towncentre hotel has a young and cool attitude, which is quite unexpected in conservative Haro. Closer inspection reveals that the furnishings and fittings are quite plasticky. The attached bar-cafe is a very pleasant place for a drink and some tapas.

Hostal La Peña PENSIÓN €

(🏛941 31 00 22; Calle La Vega 1; d from €35) Just off Plaza de la Paz is this family-run, slightly oldfashioned place tiled in bold blue and white.

Restaurante Beethoven I & II NAVARRAN €

(Calle de Santo Tomás 5 & 10; menus from €16) The best places to fill hungry tummies in Haro are these two restaurants facing each other across the narrow street. Number II is more formal, but both offer excellent La Riojan cuisine, all of it complemented by the very best local wines.

ℹ Information

Tourist office (🏛941 30 33 66; Plaza de Florentino Rodríguez; ⊙10am-2pm & 4.30-7.30pm Mon-Sat, 10am-2pm Sun Jul-Sep, 10am-2pm Mon-Fri, 10am-2pm & 4-6pm Sat Oct-Jun) A couple of hundred metres along the road from Plaza de la Paz, it has plenty of excellent information, including a list of wineries open to the public.

ℹ Getting There & Away

Regular trains connect Haro with Logroño (€5 to €14.20, 40 minutes). Buses additionally serve Logroño , Vitoria, Bilbao, Santo Domingo de la Calzada and Laguardia.

BRIONES
POP 900 / ELEV 501M

One man's dream has put the small, obscenely quaint village of Briones firmly on the Spanish wine and tourism map. The sunset-gold village crawls gently up a hillside and offers commanding views over the surrounding vine-carpeted plains. It's on these plains where you will find the fantastic **Dinastía Vivanco** (Museo de la Cultura del Vino; www.dinastiavivanco.com; adult/child €7.50/free; ⊙10am-6pm Tue-Thu & Sun, 10am-8pm Fri & Sat). This space-age museum is the creation of Pedro Vivanco Paracuello. As he relates in the introductory film, he wanted to leave a legacy to the land that has provided for his family for generations. This museum is that legacy and it truly is an incredible one. There can be few more advanced private museums in the country. Over several floors and numerous rooms, you will learn all about the history and culture of wine and the various processes that go into its production. All of this is done through interesting displays brought to life with the latest in computer technology. The treasures on display include Picasso-designed wine jugs; Roman and Byzantine mosaics; gold-draped, wine-inspired religious artefacts; and the world's largest corkscrew collection – and yes, they do have some in the shape of amusingly large penises. At the end of the tour, you can enjoy some wine tasting and, by booking in advance, you can join a tour of the winery (€6.50 or €12 including museum entry; in Spanish only).

The village itself is also worth exploring, with the 16th-century Iglesia de Santa María de la Asunción, which contains a magnificent organ, an equally impressive altar, and a side chapel painted from head to toe with the great and good of the local Christian world. At the far end of the village are the battered remains of an 11th-century castle, which now hide a small garden.

The only place to rest wine-heavy heads is Los Calaos de Briones (941 32 21 31; www.loscalaosdebriones.com; Calle San Juan 13; r €58), which has four delicious rooms brushed up in subtle colour schemes. Some have suitably romantic four-posters. The attached restaurant, in an old wine cellar, is stuffed with excellent locally inspired cuisine (mains €14 to €17).

The village is several kilometres southeast of Haro and a couple of buses a day trundle out here.

LAGUARDIA
POP 1490 / ELEV 557M

It's easy to spin back the wheels of time in the medieval fortress town of Laguardia, or the 'Guard of Navarra' as it was once appropriately known, sitting proudly on its rocky hilltop. The walled old quarter, which makes up most of the town, is virtually traffic-free and is a sheer joy to wander around. As well as memories of long-lost yesterdays, the town further entices visitors with its wine-producing present.

◉ Sights

Maybe the most impressive feature of the town is the castle-like Puerta de San Juan, one of the most stunning city gates in Spain. Equally impressive is the Iglesia de Santa María de los Reyes (guided tours €2), which has a breathtaking late-14th-century Gothic doorway thronged with beautiful sculptures of the disciples and other motifs. If the church doors are locked, pop down to the tourist office where you can get a key.

It is also possible to visit some of the many bodegas in the area (including some in the old town itself), as well as a wine museum; see the boxed text, p460.

🛏 Sleeping & Eating

Laguardia has only a few places to stay, so, if you are determined to stay here, it may be wise to book ahead, especially at weekends and during holidays.

TOP CHOICE Casa Rural
Legado de Ugarte   CASA RURAL €€
(945 60 01 14; www.legadodeugarte.com; Calle Mayor 17; r incl breakfast €75;) This is one that you're going to either love or hate – we love it. Inside a tenderly renovated house in the heart of the old town, the entrance and reception have more of the same old-world flavour you'll be starting to get bored of, but the bright and very comfortable rooms are an arresting mix of purple, silver and gold pomp. If that sounds a little too much, it also has a more classic blue-and-white room. The gregarious host is charming. There isn't always someone around so it's worth calling ahead to let them know you're coming.

Posada Mayor de Migueloa   HISTORIC HOTEL €€
(945 62 11 75; www.mayordemigueloa.com; Calle Mayor 20; s/d €96/121;) For the ultimate in gracious La Rioja living, this old mansion-hotel is irresistible. Couples will be delighted to know that guests are supplied with a full range of massage oils and instructions on how to use them! The in-house restaurant, which is open to non-guests, is superb and offers original twists on local cuisine with meals starting at about €20. Under the hotel is a small wine bodega.

Hospedería de los
Parajes   HISTORIC HOTEL €€€
(945 62 11 30; www.hospederiadelosparajes.com; Calle Mayor 46-48; r from €140;) Extraordinarily plush rooms that combine a bit of today with a dollop of yesteryear. The beds are divinely comfortably and the showers have rustic stone floors and the service is top-notch.

ℹ Information
Tourist office (945 60 08 45; www.laguardia-alava.com; Calle Mayor 52; 10am-2pm & 4-7pm Mon-Fri, 10am-2pm & 5-7pm Sat, 10.45am-2pm Sun) Has a list of bodegas that can be visited in the local area.

ℹ Getting There & Away
Six slow daily buses connecting Vitoria and Logroño pass through Laguardia.

Cantabria & Asturias

Includes »

Best Places to Eat

» El Molín de la Pedrera (p501)

» Restaurante Cares (p503)

» La Conveniente (p469)

» días desur (p469)

» Real Balneario de Salinas (p491)

Best Places to Stay

» Hotel del Oso (p506)

» La Posada de Babel (p490)

» Posada de Cucayo (p505)

» Posada del Valle (p499)

» La Casona de Amandi (p488)

Why Go?

You can traverse either of these two regions from north to south in little more than an hour. But don't. The coastline is a sequence of sheer cliffs, beautiful beaches and small fishing ports. Behind it, gorgeously green river valleys dotted with stone-built villages rise to the 2000m-plus mountain wall of the Cordillera Cantábrica, which reaches majestic heights in the Picos de Europa. The beauty is endless and ever-changing. The damp climate makes sure you'll eat and drink well too: quality meat, local cheeses, and cider from Asturias' apple orchards are on offer, as well as the fruits of the sea. And travellers with a feel for history will be in their element: early humans painted some of the world's most wonderful prehistoric art at Altamira and elsewhere, and it was at Covadonga in Asturias that the seed of the Spanish nation first sprouted 1300 years ago.

When to Go
Oviedo

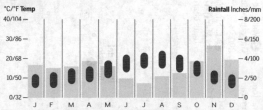

May, Jun & Sep Temperatures up, rainfall and prices down, crowds away – best time for most reasons.

Aug Descenso Internacional del Sella – canoe mania from Arriondas to Ribadesella.

Late Aug Join thousands of tipplers at Gijón's Fiesta de la Sidra Natural (Natural Cider Festival).

Cantabria & Asturias Highlights

① Marvel at the prehistoric artistic genius of **Altamira** (p475), Puente Viesgo's **Cuevas de El Castillo** (p470) and Ribadesella's **Cueva de Tito Bustillo** (p488)

② Walk the dramatic **Garganta del Cares** (p503) gorge

③ Let medieval **Santillana del Mar** (p473) bewitch you with its charms

④ Ride the scary **Teleférico de Fuente Dé** (p506) to the superb heights of the Picos de Europa

⑤ Delight in the grace of Oviedo's **pre-Romanesque buildings** (p480)

⑥ Sidle up for cider in Asturias' convivial **sidrerías** (cider bars; p482)

⑦ Bathe at spectacular, secluded **Playa del Silencio** (p491) or **Playa de Toribia** (p489)

⑧ Cycle the **Senda del Oso** (p493) and meet its bears

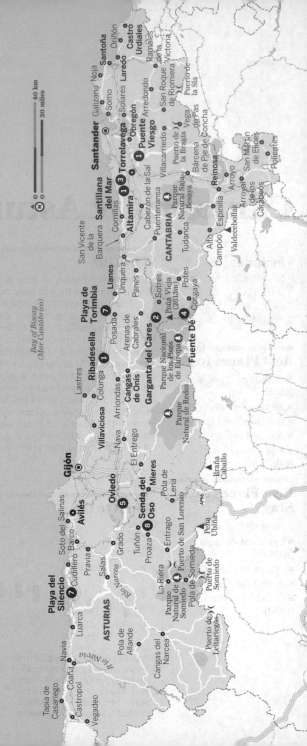

CANTABRIA

It's no wonder both Romans and Visigoths had a hard time subduing the Cantabrian clans. The lushness of the vegetation belies the complexity of much of Cantabria's terrain, which is sliced up by deep, multi-branched mountain valleys connected only by steep passes. For the modern traveller, Cantabria offers a little of everything. Some pretty beaches make summer seaside days quite possible (unreliable weather permitting), while the inland valleys, sprinkled with quiet towns and villages, arc a feast for the eyes, whether you choose to drive the country roads or walk the trails. The rugged ranges culminate in the west in the abrupt mountain walls of the Picos de Europa.

The capital, Santander, provides a slice of urban seaside life with bustling bodegas and beaches. Santillana del Mar and Comillas entice with their medieval and Modernista trappings. The prehistoric art of the Cuevas de Altamira, El Castillo and Covalanas is some of the very best in the world.

The Romans finally carried the day against the proud Cantabrians and pacified the area by around 19 BC. The Visigoths only managed to secure the area shortly before they were themselves eclipsed by the Moors in AD 711, after which Cantabria quickly became part of the nascent Christian Kingdom of Asturias. In later centuries, Cantabria was long regarded simply as Castilla's gateway to the Bay of Biscay, before becoming a separate region under Spain's 1978 constitution. Cantabrians are known as *montañeses* because Castilians thought of them as hailing from the mountains of the Cordillera Cantábrica.

Santander

POP 138,900

The belle-époque elegance of El Sardinero apart, modern Santander is not the most beautiful of cities. A huge fire raged through the centre back in 1941, leaving little that's old or quaint. But Cantabria's capital makes the most of its setting along the northern side of the handsome Bahía de Santander, and it's a lively place to spend a day or two, with good city beaches, a heaving bar and restaurant scene, and a few cultural attractions to leaven the mix. It's a very popular summer holiday resort for Spanish tourists.

ⓘ CANTABRIA WEBSITES

» **www.turismodecantabria.com**
Comprehensive official site.

» **www.culturadecantabria.com**
Good source on caves, museums and cultural events.

» **www.clubcalidadcantabriainfinita .es** Around 100 top-quality, characterful places to stay and eat.

» **www.turismoruralcantabria.com**
Over 200 country-home lodgings, many of them beautifully restored.

The parklands of the Península de la Magdalena mark the eastern end of the bay. North of the peninsula, Playa del Sardinero, the main beach, faces the open sea.

History

Founded by the Romans as Portus Victoriae (Victory Harbour) in 21 BC, Santander prospered as a trading and fishing port from the 12th century, and emerged as Cantabria's main city in the 18th century. Its heyday came in the early 20th century when King Alfonso XIII made a habit of spending summer here and turned Santander, especially the Sardinero area, into a fashionable seaside resort.

◉ Sights & Activities

Península de la Magdalena   PARK
(⊘8am-10pm) These parklands are perfect for a stroll and popular with picnickers. Kids will enjoy the seals and penguins and the little train that choo-choos around the headland. The peninsula is crowned by the **Palacio de la Magdalena**, an eclectic pile built between 1908 and 1912 as a gift from the city to the royal family, which used it every summer until 1930.

Beaches   BEACH, SURFING
Playa de los Peligros, **Playa de la Magdalena** and **Playa de Bikinis**, the bay beaches on the Bahía de Santander 1.5km to 2.5km east of the city centre, are more protected than the glorious 1.25km sweep of ocean-facing **Playa del Sardinero**. Surfers emerge in force along Sardinero when the waves are right, mainly in autumn and winter, when they can reach 1.5m. Sardinero is backed by some of Santander's most expensive real estate, including emblematic early-20th-century piles such as the **Gran**

Santander

Scale: 200 m / 0.1 miles

Map labels:

C de Tetuán

C de Juan de la Cosa

C Castelar

C de Andrés del Río

C de Casimiro Sainz

C de San Emeterio

C de Bonifaz

C de la Peña Herbosa

13

C Gándara

15

C de Hernán Cortés

Paseo de Menéndez Pelayo

C del Sol

C de Vallicierbo

C de Santa Lucía

C de Lope de Vega

C del Río de la Pila

C de Gómez Oreña

14 19

17

C de Daoíz y Velarde

4

12

5

C General Mola

Paseo de Pereda

18

1

Paseo de Pereda

Estación Marítima
Los Reginas (Ferries to
Playas del Puntal & Somo)

Oficina de Turismo
Municipal

C de Marcelino
Sanz de Sautuola

C de Bailén

C del Arrabal

Oficina de
Turismo de
Cantabria

C del Río de la Pila

11

Plaza Alfonso XIII

Paseo de Pereda

Jardines
de Pereda

Av de Alfonso XIII

10

Estación
Marítima
(Ferries to UK)

C de Rualasal

7

C de Juan de Herrera

Buses to
Sardinero

Plaza de
Obispo
Eguino y Trecu

C de
Somorrostro

Catedral de
la Asunción

C de Antonio López

C de Guevara

8

C de Méndez
Núñez

C de Calvo Sotelo

9

16

Callejón de la Barca

C Navas
de Tolosa

C de Cisneros

C de Cubo

6
3

Museo de Arte
Moderno y
Contemporáneo

Av de Calvo Sotelo

To Airport (5km);
Somo (20km);
Puente Viesgo (28km);
Santillana del Mar (28km)

C de Cádiz

Bus
Station

C de Rodríguez

C de Cervantes

2

C de Rubio

C de Burgos

C Alta

Train Station
(Renfe)

Train Station
(FEVE)

To Jardín
Secreto
(110m)

Puerto
Chico

Bahía de
Santander

To Museo Marítimo
del Cantábrico (845m);
Península de la
Magdalena (2km);
Bay Beaches (2.1km);
Playa del Sardinero (2.1km)

To Playa de Puntal (2.5km);
Playa del Somo (5km)

Santander

◉ Top Sights

◉ Sights

◉ Sleeping

◉ Eating

◉ Entertainment

Casino. Buses 1, 2 and 3 (€1.20) run to Sardinero from Avenida de Calvo Sotelo beside the main post office.

Playa del Puntal, a finger of sand jutting out from the southern side of the bay roughly opposite Playa de la Magdalena, is idyllic on calm days (but beware the currents). Weather permitting, passenger ferries (€3.80 return) sail there about every 30 minutes from 10.30am to 7.45pm, June to late September, from the **Estación Marítima Los Reginas** (www.losreginas.com; Paseo Marítimo).

From the same station there is a year-round ferry (one way/return €2.50/4.50, every 30 or 60 minutes from 9.30am to 7.30pm) to **Playa de Somo**, just beyond Playa del Puntal. Somo has another sandy beach with, usually, bigger surf than Sardinero. You'll find several surf shops: board/wetsuit rental costs around €15/10 per half-day. Somo's **Escuela Cántabra de Surf** (☑942 51 06 15; www.escuelacantabradesurf.com; Calle Cabo Mayor, Somo; per person 2hr group class incl board & wetsuit €30; ☺daily mid-Mar–mid-Nov), one of several Santander surf schools, has been doing the job for two decades and gives classes in English, Spanish or Italian.

Catedral de la Asunción   CATHEDRAL
(Plaza del Obispo José Eguino y Trecu; ☺upper church 10am-1pm & 4.30-7pm, Iglesia del Santísimo Cristo 8am-1pm & 4-8pm) Santander's cathedral is composed of two Gothic churches, one above the other. The 14th-century **upper church**, off which is a 15th-century cloister, was extensively rebuilt after a 1941

fire. In the lower, 13th-century **Iglesia del Santísimo Cristo**, glass panels reveal excavated bits of Roman Santander under the floor. Displayed nearby are silver vessels containing the skulls of the early Christian martyrs San Emeterio and San Celedonio, Santander's patron saints.

Jardines & Paseo de Pereda   PARK, PROMENADE
The pretty Jardines de Pereda (Pereda's Gardens) are named after the Cantabrian writer José María de Pereda, whose seminal work, *Escenas Montañesas,* is illustrated in bronze and stone here. You can't miss the 1875 **Banco Santander** building, with the arch in the middle, across the street. The Santander is now one of the world's biggest banks, so the architectural grandiloquence is not entirely misplaced.

The bayfront promenade fronting the Jardines de Pereda continues east to the Puerto Chico (Little Port) marina. Half the city seems to stroll here on summer evenings. Both Paseo de Pereda and Calle Castelar, opposite Puerto Chico, are dotted with appealing cafes and lined with grand buildings characterised by their glassed-in balconies.

Plazas   SQUARE
The streets of central Santander open out in several interesting plazas. The stately **Plaza Porticada**, surrounded by 64 porticoes, was created after the disastrous fire of 1941. A short walk east are the more spacious **Plaza de Pombo** and lively **Plaza de Cañadío**, which brims with bars and can

get quite boisterous at night. To the west, **Plaza La Esperanza**, behind the city hall, is home to the **Mercado La Esperanza** (Plaza la Esperanza; ⊘8am-2pm Mon-Sat), a colourful, bustling market with masses of fish and seafood downstairs, and meat and cheese upstairs.

Museo Marítimo del Cantábrico MUSEUM (www.museosdecantabria.com; Calle de San Martín de Bajamar; adult/child €6/4; ⊘10am-7.30pm, closed Mon Oct-Apr) If seafaring is your thing, visit the maritime museum near the bay beaches. The four floors cover all facets of Cantabria's relationship with the sea, and include an aquarium. The maritime history section is perhaps the most interesting, dealing with, for example, the Roman port of Portus Victoriae. The 60-tonne whale skeleton is a star attraction.

FREE **Museo de Arte Moderno y Contemporáneo** MUSEUM (MAS; ☏942 20 31 20; Calle de Rubio 6; ⊘10.30am-1pm & 6-9pm Tue-Sat, 11am-1.30pm Sun) Santander's extensive art museum offers a large, eclectic collection spanning the 16th to 21st centuries. Much of it is secondary Spanish art, though you'll find the odd curio such as Goya's portrait of King Fernando VII, and the contemporary layout of some sections brings out intriguing connections between contrasting works. In an equally portentous building next door is the **Biblioteca de Menéndez Pelayo** (☏942 23 45 34; admission free; ⊘9-11.30am Mon-Fri), a vast old library built in 1915 to house the 41,500 books bequeathed to the city by local teacher, philosopher and poet Marcelino Menéndez Pelayo (1856–1912). Behind the library stands his family home, the **Casa Museo de Menéndez Pelayo** (☏942 23 44 93; ⊘10.30am-1pm & 6.30-8pm Mon-Fri, 10.30am-1pm Sat).

✵ Festivals & Events

Semana Grande (www.semanagrandesantander.com) is Santander's big summer fiesta, a week of fun around 25 July. In mid-July the **Baños de Ola** is several days of events at Playa del Sardinero commemorating the arrival of the first sea-bathing tourists there in the 19th century. Right through summer, the Palacio de la Magdalena hosts the **Universidad Internacional Menéndez Pelayo** (www.uimp.es), a global get-together for specialists in all sorts of disciplines. The **Festival Internacional de Santander**

(www.festivalsantander.com) musical season, throughout August, offers everything from jazz to opera.

🛏 Sleeping

The city centre, where most of the action is, has options in all price ranges. There are also some good midrange and top-end digs over by Playa del Sardinero, though some of these close from about October to mid-May. Most rates dip sharply outside the high season, which is typically July and August.

Jardín Secreto BOUTIQUE HOTEL €€ (☏942 07 07 14; www.jardinsecretosantander.com; Calle de Cisneros 37; s/d €60/75; ⊛) This is a charming little six-room world of its own in a two-centuries-old house close to the city centre. It's run by an engaging brother-and-sister team, and designed by their mother in a comfortable contemporary style with silvers, greys and some exposed stone and wood. A tiny back garden gives the place its name. No breakfast, but free coffee and cakes.

Hotel Las Brisas BOUTIQUE HOTEL €€ (☏942 27 50 11; www.hotellasbrisas-santander.com; Calle La Braña 14; s/d incl breakfast €80/110; ⊘closed mid-Dec–end Jan; @⊛) Almost as much gallery as hotel, Las Brisas is a three-storey belle-époque Sardinero villa decked with art and crafts from guests and the family and travels of its genial host Jesús. The 13 comfy rooms feature coffee- and tea-makers and newly updated bathrooms with huge shower heads. Some enjoy beach views, as does the front terrace. For longer stays consider its nearby apartments.

Hotel Bahía HOTEL €€€ (☏942 20 50 00; www.hotelbahiasantander.es; Avenida de Alfonso XIII 6; s/d €160/240; 🅿❋@⊛) Central Santander's top hotel, opposite the UK ferry port, offers large, very comfortable rooms with thick carpets and solid wood furnishings. Many have sea views. The hotel sports an elegant restaurant and spacious, tastefully outfitted common areas.

Hostel BBB HOSTEL € (☏942 22 78 17; www.hostelsantander.com; 1st fl, Calle de Méndez Núñez 6; dm incl breakfast €21; ⊛) Cosy, colourful dorms, high standards of cleanliness and a friendly, helpful welcome make this hostel a top budget choice. The bright common area overlooks an open plaza and the bay.

WHAT'S COOKING IN CANTABRIA?

Cantabria's eating traditions vary considerably from the coast to the interior. Santander is perhaps the best place for fresh seafood, while the rivers inland are the source of trout and salmon. The classic regional dish is *cocido montañés*, a hearty stew of white beans, cabbage, potato, chorizo, black pudding and sometimes port. Cantabria's green cattle pastures yield not only good beef but also an array of tasty cheeses: lovers of ultra-tangy cheese should seek *queso picón* (from a mix of cow's, sheep's and goat's milk), made in the Picos de Europa villages of Tresviso and Bejes. *Embutidos* (sausages) and *cecinas* (dried meats) made from venison and wild boar are other local favourites.

Plaza Pombo B&B
B&B €€

(☎942 21 29 50; www.plazapombo.com; 3rd fl, Calle de Hernán Cortés 25; r with/without bathroom incl breakfast €80/62; ⚲) A long-established *pensión* recently modernised by keen new owners. The high-ceilinged rooms have a light and airy feel and comfortable beds, and some boast balconies overlooking Plaza de Pombo,

Hostal La Mexicana
HOSTAL €

(☎942 22 23 50; www.hostallamexicana.com; Calle de Juan de Herrera 3; s/d €46/64; ⚲) A very well-kept and well-run 38-room *hostal* (budget hotel) on a mostly traffic-free shopping street. Rooms have a solid, old-fashioned style.

Hotel Central
HOTEL €€€

(☎942 22 24 00; www.elcentral.com; Calle General Mola 5; s/d €101/156; ✳@⚲) Worth considering from mid-September to June, when rates are slashed. It's centrally located, not far from the main transport terminals, and the rooms are clean and comfortable, though smallish.

✖ Eating

Central Santander throngs with great food options. You can push in for a few scrumptious snacks in a tapas bar, dig into hearty local food in a no-nonsense bodega or head upmarket in any number of restaurants. And do sample the beloved local Regma ice cream, sold in immense scoops at several kiosks around town.

TOP CHOICE La Conveniente
TAPAS, TABLAS €€

(Calle de Gómez Oreña 9; raciones & tablas €5-20; ⏱from 7pm Mon-Sat) This cavernous bodega has high stone walls, wooden pillars and beams, and more wine bottles than you may ever have seen in one place. Squeeze into the tramlike enclosure at the front or line up for a seat in the cave-like back room (or just snack at the bar). The food offerings are fairly straightforward – *tablas* (platters) of cheese, *embutidos* (sausages), ham, pâtés – and servings are generous.

días desur
SPANISH, INTERNATIONAL €€

(Calle de Hernán Cortés 47; tapas €1.25-3, mains €10-15; ⏱8am-1.30am; ⚲) The white brick walls, black-and-white photos and space to sit and converse augur something out of the ordinary, and the tapas meet that challenge with a mix of Cantabrian, Andalucian and international flavours. Try a mini chicken tikka masala brochette or an Ivory Coast spicy lamb roll, along with one of the lyrically described wines. The upper level has a restaurant with similarly inventive dishes and a tempting €13 set lunch.

Cañadío
CONTEMPORARY CANTABRIAN €€€

(☎942 31 41 49; www.restaurantecanadio.com; Calle de Gómez Oreña 15; mains €19-26; ⏱Mon-Sat) A tastefully contemporary place with art on the red walls, fine linen and timber floors, Cañadío offers creative cooking with local inspiration. Hake is prepared every which way. Or you can join the crowds in the front bar for ultra-tempting tapas.

El Machichaco
SEAFOOD, BREAKFAST €€

(Calle de Calderón de la Barca 9; mains €11-25; ⏱breakfast, lunch & dinner) A welcoming and good-value seafood spot convenient to all transport terminals and the city centre. Go for tapas such as the Santander speciality *rabas* (deep-fried squid or potato strips) or heartier choices such as baked fish of the day with crunchy potatoes. It's also good for breakfast – even eggs, bacon and potatoes.

Mesón Rampalay
TAPAS, RACIONES €€

(www.meson-rampalay-santander.com; Calle de Daoíz y Velarde 9; tapas €1.35-2.20, raciones €6-18; ⏱Wed-Mon) The packed Rampalay has a particularly tempting array of tapas, from sirloin in wine to eggs scrambled with prawns and asparagus.

CANTABRIA & ASTURIAS SANTANDER

Bar Del Puerto SEAFOOD €€€
(☎942 21 30 01; www.bardelpuerto.com; Calle de Hernán Cortés 63; mains €18-42; ⓧlunch Tue-Sun, dinner Tue-Sat) With its grand windows looking out towards the Puerto Chico waterfront, the upstairs restaurant here is a perfect spot for top-class seafood. It offers a huge choice: fish of the day is never a bad selection, and you might try something *a la gabardina* (deep-fried in batter, literally 'in a raincoat'). The €45 lunch and dinner menu makes some of the decisions for you.

 Drinking

Plaza de Cañadío is home to several *bares de copas,* where you can enjoy an outdoor beer as well as cocktails, spirits and wine. At Pub Blues (Calle de Gómez Oreña 15; ⓧ7pm-3am) you might encounter live jazz/rock/blues from about 9.30pm. This and several similar establishments along Calles de Daoíz y Velarde and Hernán Cortés generally go on well after midnight.

The neighbourhood of Calle de Santa Lucía, Calle del Sol and Calle del Río de la Pila teems with a more bohemian bevy of bars, most staying open until 3am or 4am. Wander around and you'll probably run across a couple with music and atmosphere to your liking.

 Information

Oficina de Turismo Municipal (☎942 20 30 00; www.ayto-santander.es; Jardines de Pereda; ⓧ9am-9pm) A branch office in El Sardinero, opposite Plaza de Italia, operates in summer.

Oficina de Turismo de Cantabria (☎901 11 11 12, 942 31 07 08; www.turismodecantabria. com; Calle de Hernán Cortés 4; ⓧ9am-9pm) Inside the Mercado del Este.

 Getting There & Around

Air

The airport is 5km south of town at Parayas. Buses run to/from Santander bus station (€1.60) about every half-hour, 6.30am to 10.30pm (fewer on weekends).

Iberia (www.iberia.com) Madrid several times daily.

Ryanair (www.ryanair.com) London (Stansted), Dublin, Madrid, Barcelona, Brussels (Charleroi), Frankfurt (Hahn), Málaga, Milan (Bergamo), Paris (Beauvais-Tillé), Rome (Ciampino), Seville and Valencia.

Vueling (www.vueling.com) Barcelona from about late June to late October.

Boat

Brittany Ferries (www.brittany-ferries.co.uk) Two weekly car ferries from Portsmouth, UK (24 hours), and one from Plymouth, UK (20 hours). Fares can vary enormously: a two-week return trip for two adults and a car, with two-berth interior cabins, booked in April, might cost UK£1000 for July/August travel or UK£550 for October, from either UK port.

Bus

Transporte de Cantabria (www.transportede cantabria.es) is a useful source for schedules.

ALSA (www.alsa.es) is the major company operating from the **bus station** (☎942 21 19 95; Calle Navas de Tolosa), with services to many Cantabrian and other destinations including the following:

Bilbao (€6.23 to €13.88, 1¼ to two hours, 22 or more daily)

Madrid (€29.14 to €45.22, 5¼ to 6¼ hours, eight daily)

Oviedo (€11.81 to €25.40, 2¼ to 3¼ hours, eight or more daily)

San Sebastián (€12.46 to €26.94, 2½ to four hours, eight or more daily)

Train

There are two train stations, next door to each other on Calle de Rodríguez:

FEVE (☎942 20 95 22; www.feve.es; Calle de Rodríguez) Two daily trains to San Vicente de la Barquera, Llanes, Ribadesella, Arriondas and Oviedo (€15, 4½ hours); three to Bilbao (€8.25, 2¾ hours).

Renfe (www.renfe.com; Calle de Rodríguez) Two or three long-distance trains daily to Madrid (€49.40, 4½ hours) via Palencia and Valladolid; two daily regional trains as far as Valladolid (€17.10, four hours).

Around Santander

CUEVAS DE MONTE CASTILLO

The valley town of Puente Viesgo, 25km south of Santander, lies at the foot of the conical Monte Castillo. About 2km up this hill are the Cuevas de Monte Castillo, a series of caves frequented by humans since 150,000 years ago. Four caves are World Heritage–listed for their top-rank cave art and two of these, the Cuevas de El Castillo y Las Monedas (☎942 59 84 25; http://cue vas.culturadecantabria.com; per cave adult/child €3/1.50; ⓧ9.30am-2.30pm & 3.30-7.30pm Tue-Sun, shorter hours & closed Tue mid-Sep–mid-Jun), are open for guided visits (45 minutes each). El Castillo is the more spectacular: here, you penetrate 760m into the cave where the art is almost as breathtaking as Altamira's. The 275 paintings and engravings of deer, bison, horses, goats, aurochs, mammoths, handprints and mysterious symbols date from 26,000 to 11,000 BC – and unlike what you see at Altamira, these are the genuine article rather than a replica. Las Monedas has less art (animals painted in black outline, from around 10,000 BC) but also contains an astounding array of stalactites and stalagmites. Booking ahead by phone or online is highly advisable, especially for El Castillo. After the caves you could take a half-hour trot up Monte Castillo, where you will find the minor remains of a medieval castle.

Four or more daily buses run to Puente Viesgo from Santander (€2.15, 40 minutes).

PARQUE DE LA NATURALEZA CABÁRCENO

This open-air zoo (☑942 56 37 36; www.parque dccabarceno.com; adult/child €21/13; ☉9.30am-6pm; [P][⛟]), 17km south of Santander, is a curious but successful experiment, a free-range home for everything from rhinos to wallabies and gorillas to dromedaries, on the site of former open-cut mines. You need a car to tour its 20km of roadways. Access is from Obregón on the CA262.

LANGRE

The wild beaches of Langre are backed by cliffs topped with green fields. Most people head for Langre Grande, although adjacent Langre Pequeña is more protected. Like the less spectacular Somo and Loredo beaches to its west, Langre often has surfable waves. It's about a 25km drive from Santander: round the bay to Somo, then east on the CA141 for a couple of kilometres, then turn left to Langre.

Eastern Cantabria

The 95km stretch of coast between Santander and Bilbao offers citizens of both cities several seaside boltholes. While the towns are less appealing than those on Cantabria's western coast, some of the beaches are top-drawer.

SANTOÑA
POP 11,160

The fishing port of Santoña is famed for its anchovies, which are bottled or tinned here with olive oil to preserve them. Santoña is dominated by two fortresses, the Fuerte de San Martín and, further east,

the abandoned Fuerte de San Carlos. You can take a pleasant walk around both, or take the shuttle ferry (€1.70) across the estuary to the western end of Laredo beach. Or head off for a hike in the Parque Cultural Monte Buciero, which occupies the hill-cum-headland rising northeast of the town. Otherwise, go north along the C141 to Playa Berria, a magnificent sweep of sand and surf on the open sea, linked to Santoña by frequent buses (€1.40). Here, Hotel Juan de la Cosa (☑942 66 12 38; www.hoteljuandela-cosa.com; s €91, d €91-132; ☉closed mid-Dec–end Jan; [P][✳][@][🛜][🏊]) may be in an unsympathetic-looking building, but about two-thirds of its spacious, blue-hued rooms have beach views. It has a good restaurant with a seafood emphasis, too.

Thirteen buses run Monday to Saturday (six on Sunday) to Santoña from Santander (€4, one hour). From July to September there's also a half-hourly passenger ferry to central Laredo (€3).

LAREDO
POP 11,470

Laredo's long, sandy beach, across the bay from Santoña, is backed by ugly 20th-century blocks. But at the east end of town the cobbled streets of the old Puebla Vieja slope down from the impressive 13th-century Iglesia de Santa María, with the remains of the Fuerte del Rastrillar on La Atalaya hill above. The Puebla Vieja has a lively food and drinks scene: for tasty creative tapas and *ractones*, such as *lubina con cilantro y tallarines de calamares* (sea bass with coriander and squid noodles), head to Somera (Rua Mayor 17-19; tapas €1.50-3; ☉closed 5 Nov-6 Dec & Mon Sep-Jun).

Plenty of buses from Santander (€3.95, 40 minutes) call in here.

PLAYAS DE ORIÑÓN & SONABIA

The broad sandy strip of Playa de Oriñón, just off the *autovía* (toll-free highway) 14km east of Laredo, is set deep behind protective headlands, making the water calm and *comparatively* warm. The settlement here is made up of drab holiday flats and caravan parks. Continue 1.7km past Oriñón to the smaller but wilder Playa de Sonabia, set in a rock-lined inlet beneath high crags from which a colony of huge griffon vultures circles the skies above you. An up-and-down 10km walking trail links Oriñón with Laredo via Playa de Sonabia and the even more isolated Playa de San Julián.

WORTH A TRIP

CANTABRIA'S EASTERN VALLEYS

Rich in unspoiled rural splendour, the little-visited valleys of eastern Cantabria are ripe for exploration. The following route could be taken after a visit to the Cuevas de Monte Castillo.

From El Soto, just off the N623 shortly south of Puente Viesgo, take the CA270 and CA262 southeast towards Vega de Pas, the 'capital' of the Valles Pasiegos (the Pas, Pisueña and Miera valleys; www.vallespasiegos.org), one of Cantabria's most traditional rural areas. The views from the Puerto de la Braguía pass are stunning. From Vega de Pas continue southeast into Castilla y León, before turning north again near Las Nieves to follow the BU571 up over the Puerto de la Sía pass towards Arredondo in Cantabria's southeastern Alto Asón district (www.citason.com). The road is full of switchbacks, has a couple of mountain passes and takes you past the 50m waterfall that constitutes the Nacimiento (Source) del Río Asón.

Alto Asón claims more than half of the 9000 known caves in Cantabria, and from Arredondo you can go east to Ramales de la Victoria, a valley town with two outstanding visitable caves. The Cueva de Cullalvera (☑942 59 84 25; http://cuevas.cultura decantabria.com; adult/child €3/1.50; ⊙9.30am-2.30pm & 3.30-6.30pm Tue-Sun, closed Tue mid-Sep–mid-Jun) is an impressively vast cavity with some signs of prehistoric art. The Cueva de Covalanas (☑942 59 84 25; cuevas.culturadecantabria.com; adult/child €3/1.50; ⊙9.30am-2.30pm & 3.30-6.30pm Tue-Sun, closed Tue mid-Sep–mid-Jun), 3km up the N629 south from Ramales, then 650m up a footpath, is World Heritage–listed for its numerous excellent animal paintings from around 18,000 BC, done in an unusual dot-painting technique. Guided visits to either cave last 45 minutes and it's advisable to book ahead by phone or online.

South of Ramales the N629 climbs to the panoramic Alto de los Tornos lookout at 920m, before continuing towards Burgos in Castilla y León.

CASTRO URDIALES
POP 25.600

The haughty Gothic jumble that is the Iglesia de Santa María de la Asunción (⊙10am-1.30pm & 4-7.30pm Tue-Sun) stands out above the harbour and the tangle of narrow lanes which make up the medieval centre of Castro Urdiales. The church shares its little headland with the ruins of the town's old defensive bastion, now supporting a lighthouse.

Of Castro's two beaches, the northern Playa de Ostende is the more attractive. Find out about other beaches in the area at the tourist office (☑942 87 15 12; Parque Amestoy; ⊙9.30am-1.30pm & 4-7pm), on the seafront.

🛏 Sleeping & Eating

Several inexpensive places to stay are scattered about the old town centre, but you'll find top digs at Hotel Las Rocas (☑942 86 04 00; www.lasrocashotel.com; Calle Flavióbriga 1; s/d €108/135; 🅿❄🛜) just behind Playa de Brazomar. The contemporary-style rooms are adorned with a touch of colourful art and most have large glassed-in galleries and beach views.

Traditional fare, such as *sopa de pescado* (fish soup) and *pudín de cabracho* (scorpion-fish pâté), abounds in *mesones* (old-style eateries) and *tabernas* (taverns) along Calle de la Mar and Calle de Ardigales, and on Plaza del Ayuntamiento in front of the fishing boats.

❶ Getting There & Away

ALSA (Calle de Leonardo Rucabado 42) runs at least nine buses daily to Santander (€5.95, one hour). Buses to Bilbao (€2.88, 45 minutes) go every half-hour until 10pm, making various stops including at La Barrera flower shop at Calle La Ronda 52, half a block from the seafront.

Southern Cantabria

Fine panoramas of high peaks and deep river valleys flanked by patchwork quilts of green await the traveller penetrating the Cantabrian interior. Every imaginable shade of green seems to have been employed to set this stage, strewn with warm stone villages and held together by a network of narrow country roads.

REINOSA
POP 10.200 / ELEV 851M

Southern Cantabria's main town is an unexceptional place, but its Oficina de Turismo (☏942 75 52 15; http://turismoreinosa.es; Avenida del Puente de Carlos III 23; ⊗9.30am-2.30pm & 5-8pm Mon-Fri, 9.30am-2.30pm Sat & Sun, closed Sun Oct-Jun) can inform you about plenty of curiosities nearby. These include the Colegiata de San Pedro in Cervatos, 5km south, one of Cantabria's finest Romanesque churches, with rare erotic carvings on its corbels, and the remains of Cantabria's most significant Roman town, Julióbriga (☏626 325927; adult/child €3/1.50; ⊗9.30am-2.30pm & 3.30-6.30pm Tue-Sun; ℗), at Retortillo, 5km east. The guided visit at Julióbriga includes the Museo Domus, a full-scale recreation of a Roman house.

Reinosa has a half-dozen sleeping options. Set in a charmingly restored, century-old Modernista building, Villa Rosa (☏902 93 03 74; www.villarosa.com; Calle de los Héroes de la Guardia Civil 4; d incl breakfast €92; @🖭) looks more like something you'd expect in central Europe. Most of the 12 very comfy rooms have an inviting period feel as well as good, up-to-date installations. It's handily close to the train and bus stations.

Eight Renfe *cercanías* (suburban trains; €4.20, 1¾ hours) and at least six buses (€6.05, 1¼ hours) head from Santander to Reinosa daily. A few daily trains and buses head south to Palencia, Valladolid, Salamanca and Madrid.

Western Cantabria

SANTILLANA DEL MAR
POP 1060

They say this is the city of the three lies, since it is not holy *(santi)*, flat *(llana)* or by the sea *(del mar)*! Some good-looking liar! This medieval jewel is in such a perfect state of preservation, with its bright cobbled streets and tanned stone and brick buildings huddling in a muddle of centuries of history, that it seems too good to be true. Surely it's a film set! Well, no. People still live here, passing their precious houses down from generation to generation.

Strict town planning rules were first introduced back in 1575, and today they include the stipulation that only residents or guests in hotels with garages may bring vehicles into the old heart of town. Other hotel guests may drive to unload luggage and must then return to the car park at the town entrance.

Santillana is a bijou in its own right, but also makes an obvious base for visiting nearby Altamira.

◎ Sights

Colegiata de Santa Juliana   CHURCH
(admission €3; ⊗10am-1.30pm & 4-7.30pm Tue-Sun) A stroll along Santillana's cobbled main street, past solemn nobles' houses from the 15th to 18th centuries, leads you to this lovely 12th-century Romanesque ex-monastery. The big drawcard is the cloister, a formidable storehouse of Romanesque handiwork, with the capitals of its columns carved into a huge variety of figures. The monastery originally grew up around the relics of Santa Juliana, a 3rd-century Christian martyr from Turkey (and the real source of the name Santillana), whose sepulchre stands in the centre of the church.

Museo de Tortura   MUSEUM
(Calle del Escultor Jesús Otero 1; adult/student/child €3.60/2.40/free; ⊗10am-9pm) This exhibition displays more than 70 grim instruments of torture and capital punishment used by the Inquisition and elsewhere in Europe. You may not want to bring kids in here even though their entry is free!

🛏 Sleeping

There are dozens of places to stay, many of them in atmospheric historic buildings converted for your comfort and pleasure. They are scattered about the old part of town, around Campo del Revolgo south of the main road, and along the roads towards Altamira, Comillas and Santander. Rates at most places dip sharply outside August. Some close for varying periods in winter.

Casa del Organista   HOTEL €€
(☏942 84 03 52; www.casadelorganista.com; Calle de Los Hornos 4; s/d €77/93; ⊗closed late Dec–mid-Jan; ℗@🖭) The 14 rooms at this elegant 18th-century house, once home to the *colegiata*'s organist, are particularly attractive, with plush rugs, antique furniture and plenty of exposed heavy beams and stonework. Some have balconies looking across fields towards the *colegiata*. The welcome is warm and helpful, and an excellent breakfast costs €5.75. There are three or four similarly styled places up the street.

CANTABRIA & ASTURIAS WESTERN CANTABRIA

WORTH A TRIP

ALONG THE RÍO EBRO

Spain's most voluminous river, the Ebro, rises at Fontibre about 6km west of Reinosa, fills the Embalse del Ebro reservoir to the east, and then meanders south and east into Castilla y León. Its course is strung with some fascinating and picturesque stops. You can follow it on the GR-99 long-distance footpath or on minor roads out of Reinosa.

Head first east along the CA730 (visiting Roman Julióbriga en route if you like) to Arroyo, where you turn south and follow signs to the Monasterio de Montesclaros, which has a fine site overlooking the Ebro valley and a history going back to at least the 12th century. From here follow the CA741 down to Arroyal de los Carabeos, then head south on the CA272 to a roundabout where it meets the CA273. Nine kilometres west on the CA273 is the remarkable Iglesia Rupestre de Santa María de Valverde. This beautiful, multi-arched church, hewn from the living rock, is the most impressive of several *iglesias rupestres* (rock-cut churches) in this area, dating from probably the 7th to 10th centuries, the early days of Christianity in the region. Santa María church itself is often locked but you can get the key from the nearest house across the road. Next to the church, the Centro de Interpretación del Rupestre (☑626 325927, 616 849251; adult/child €3/1.50; ⊙9.30am-2.30pm & 3.30-6.30pm Tue-Sun, by appointment only Tue-Fri mid-Sep–mid-Jun; ℙ) tells the story of the area's curious rock-church phenomenon through photos, maps, video and multimedia – well worth a visit even if you don't understand Spanish – and can provide plenty of information on the area. From here head back east and continue to the area's biggest village, Polientes, which has a bank, petrol station (self-service with credit cards only) and four places to stay, of which the pick is Posada El Cuartelillo Viejo (☑942 77 61 51; www.elcuartelilloviejo.com; Carretera General 31; r incl breakfast €45-58).

East of Polientes you'll find the best of the area's other rock-cut churches. Those at Arroyuelos and Presillas de Bricia are both two-level affairs: ask for keys at the nearest house in each case. Across the Ebro from Arroyuelos, San Martín de Elines is well worth a detour for its lovely Romanesque church (key available at the priest's house). The small but wonderfully sited El Tobazo cave-church is part of a small group of caves towards the top of the Ebro gorge east of Arroyuelos. To find it cross the bridge into Villaescusa del Ebro, turn immediately left and follow the track for 900m to a grassy clearing on the right. From here you have a 700m uphill walk, starting from the far corner of the clearing. A beautiful waterfall (appearing as a moss-covered, cave-pocked cliff after prolonged dry weather) comes into view about halfway up, with the cave-church just above it to the right.

From Villaescusa the CA275 continues along the Ebro gorge to picturesque Orbaneja del Castillo in Castilla y León.

Hotel Siglo XVIII HOTEL €€
(☑942 84 02 10; www.hotelsigloxviii.com; Calle de Revolgo 38; s/d €65/85; ℙ⊛✿) This stone mansion, although quite new, is faithful to Santillana's style and is one of the better deals here. Surrounded by a garden and green fields 400m south of the main road, its 16 rooms are all exterior and inviting, with antique-style furniture. Access to a pool at these prices is a bonus.

Casa del Marqués HISTORIC HOTEL €€€
(☑942 81 88 88; www.turismosantillanadelmar.com; Calle del Cantón 24; r €169; ⊙early Mar-early Dec; ℙ⊛@�) Feel like the lord or lady of the manor in this 15th-century Gothic mansion,

once home to the Marqués de Santillana. Exposed timber beams, thick stone walls and cool terracotta floors contribute to the atmosphere of the 15 all-different rooms. The owners are proud of their banister, 700 years old and made from a single tree.

Posada Santa Juliana HOSTAL €€
(☑942 84 01 06; www.santillanadelmar.com; Calle Carrera 19; r incl breakfast €65; ⊙Apr-Oct) A short walk in from the main road, this is a charming medieval house with six smallish but tastefully restored doubles with creaking timber floors and wooden furniture. Inquire with the friendly folk at Los Nobles restaurant opposite.

Posada de la Abadía GUESTHOUSE €

(☑942 84 03 04; www.posadadelabadia.com; Calle de Revolgo 26; s/d €48/59; P◉) A small family-run place in a traditional Cantabrian-style house, 200m south of the main road. It's clean and friendly, and the 10 pretty, if not exactly inspired, rooms all have a bathtub.

✗ Eating

Santillana has many humdrum eateries catering to the passing tourist trade, and you should be able to get a full meal at most for around €20 to €25. A few options stand out from the crowd, however.

Restaurante Gran Duque CANTABRIAN €€

(www.granduque.com; Calle del Escultor Jesús Otero 5; mains €10-19; ⊘closed Sun dinner & Jan) The food is high-quality local fare and what sets it apart is the setting, a grand stone house with noble trappings and nice decorative touches such as the exposed brick and beams. There is a reasonable balance of surf or turf options including *mariscadas* (seafood feasts) for two at €65 or €98.

Casa Uzquiza CANTABRIAN €€

(www.casauzquiza.com; Calle del Escultor Jesús Otero 5; mains €9-18; ⊘closed Feb & Tue Sep-May) This two-floor restaurant with some garden tables offers many of the usual local suspects, such as *cocido montañés,* but also surprises with an elegant touch, such as *lomos de bacalao en pil-pil de erizo* (soft steamed cod drenched in a thick yellow sea urchin sauce). The *menú de picoteo cántabro* (€40 for two) is an interesting selection of regional specialities.

❶ Information

Tourist office (☑942 81 88 12; Calle del Escultor Jesús Otero 20; ⊘9am-9pm) Located at the main car park.

❶ Getting There & Away

Autobuses La Cantábrica (☑942 72 08 22) Runs three or more daily buses from Santander to Santillana (€2.45, 40 minutes), and on to Comillas and San Vicente de la Barquera. They stop by Campo del Revolgo.

ALTAMIRA

Spain's finest prehistoric art, the wonderful paintings of bison, horses and other animals in the Cueva de Altamira, 2km southwest of Santillana del Mar, was discovered in 1879 by Cantabrian historian and scientist Marcelino Sanz de Sautuola and his eight-year-old daughter María Justina. By 2002 Altamira had attracted so many visitors that the cave

was closed to prevent deterioration of the art, but a replica cave in the museum here now enables everyone to appreciate the inspired, 14,500-year-old paintings.

TOP CHOICE **Museo de Altamira** MUSEUM

(museodealtamira.mcu.es; adult/child, EU senior or student €3/free, Sun & from 2.30pm Sat free; ⊘9.30am-8pm Tue-Sat, to 3pm Sun & holidays; P) The museum's highlight is the Neocueva, a dazzling, full-sized re-creation of the real cave's most interesting chamber, the Sala de Polícromos (Polychrome Hall). Other excellent displays, in English and Spanish, cover prehistoric humanity and cave art around the world, from Altamira to Australia.

The museum is very popular (around 270,000 visitors a year) so it's a good idea to reserve tickets in advance, especially for Easter week, July, August and September. You can do so with a Visa or MasterCard by phone to ☑902 242424 or online via the Altamira website – although, oddly enough, the final stages for online payment are available in Spanish only. Advance tickets cost €3 for everybody, children, students and seniors included, and are not available for Saturday afternoon or Sunday. Same-day tickets are sold only at the museum ticket office. With all tickets you are assigned an exact time for entering the Neocueva. During busy periods this might involve a wait of several hours if you have not reserved in advance.

Those without vehicles must walk or take a taxi to Altamira from Santillana del Mar.

COMILLAS

POP 1940

Sixteen kilometres west from Santillana through verdant countryside, Comillas has a golden beach and a tiny fishing port, but there is more: a pleasant, cobbled old centre, and hilltops crowned by some of the most original buildings in Cantabria. For the latter, Comillas is indebted to the first Marqués de Comillas, who was born here as plain Antonio López, made a fortune in Cuba as a tobacco planter, shipowner, banker and slave trader, and then returned to commission leading Catalan Modernista architects to jazz up his home town in the late 19th century. This in turn attracted other bourgeoisie to construct quirky mansions here.

◉ Sights

Capricho de Gaudí ARCHITECTURE

(www.elcaprichodegaudi.com; Barrio de Sobrellano; adult/child €5/2.50; ⊘10.30am-2pm & 3-9pm)

Antoni Gaudí left few reminders of his genius beyond Catalonia, but of those that he did, the 1885 Gaudí Caprice in Comillas is easily the most flamboyant. The brick building, originally a summer playpad for the Marqués de Comillas' sister-in-law's brother, is liberally striped on the outside with ceramic bands of alternating sunflowers and green leaves. Its interior is comparatively restrained but still has quirky touches like *artesonado* ceilings (patterns of timber beams inset with decorative panels). It's worth watching the video in the greenhouse/conservatory before you go round the rest of the interior.

Palacio de Sobrellano   MANSION
(☑942 72 03 39; admission €3; ☺9.40am-2.30pm & 3.30-6.20pm Tue-Sun) In hillside parklands stands the Marqués de Comillas' wonderful neo-Gothic Palacio de Sobrellano. With this building, Modernista architect Joan Martorell truly managed to out-Gothic real Gothic. Martorell also designed the marquis' ornate family tomb, the **Capilla Panteón de Sobrellano** (admission €3; ☺9.40am-2.30pm & 3.30-6.20 Tue-Sun), next door. Visits to both buildings are by guided tour.

Town Centre   SQUARE.
Comillas' compact medieval centre is built around several cobbled plazas, with a vernacular architecture of solid sandstone houses with wooden balconies or glassed-in galleries. The main church, the **Iglesia de San Cristóbal**, was constructed in the 17th century from the townspeople's own pockets after they took umbrage at the Duque de Infantado's retinue refusing to share a pew with common folk in the old church.

Seminario Mayor   ARCHITECTURE
(Calle de Manuel Noriega; adult/child €3/free, car €2; ☺10am-1pm & 5-8pm, closed afternoons Oct-Jun; ℗) Modernista architects Joan Martorell and Lluís Domènech i Montaner both had a hand in this large, elaborate, former seminary, with Domènech i Montaner contributing its medieval flavour. It's now an international Spanish-language-and-culture study centre, the **Centro Internacional de Estudios Superiores de Español** (www.fundacioncomillas.es). Visits inside the building are guided; you can visit the grounds for free (unless you take a car in).

Cemetery   CEMETERY
Comillas' old parish church, in ruins, now forms part of a cemetery down towards the beach. It's topped by a white marble guardian angel statue by Jose Llimona, and has a distinctly spooky aura when floodlit at night.

🛏 Sleeping

Hotel Marina de Campíos   BOUTIQUE HOTEL €€
(☑942 72 27 54; www.marinadecampios.com; Calle del General Piélagos 14; r incl breakfast €110-150; ☺closed Mon-Thu mid-Sep–Jun; ❇@⏾) This 19th-century house, a few steps from the central plaza, Corro de Campíos, has been revamped into a stylish contemporary hotel with 19 all-different rooms, sporting bold design and in many cases curtained beds. There's a lovely inner patio, with the piano bar opening on to it.

Hostal Esmeralda   HOSTAL €€
(☑942 72 00 97; www.hostalesmeralda.com; Calle de Antonio López 7; s/d €60/80; ⏾) A short distance east of the town centre, Esmeralda is a handsomely restored 1874 stone building with large, old-fashioned but comfy rooms, good beds, lots of character and dashes of colourful decor. It's well looked after and well run by the fourth generation of the family that built it. Rates dive outside August.

🍴 Eating

Plenty of restaurants and cafes around the central squares provide straightforward seafood and meat *raciones* (large tapas servings; €7 to €16), menus (€12 to €15) and *platos combinados* (meat-and-three-veg dishes; €7 to €8).

Restaurante Gurea   CANTABRIAN, BASQUE €
(Calle Ignacio Fernández de Castro 11; mains €8-10; ☺closed Mon Oct-May) This elegant restaurant, hidden in a small street a few blocks from the town centre, dishes up Basque and Cantabrian fare. The €50 menu for two, available for lunch or dinner, is a good bet.

Restaurante Filipinas   SPANISH €
(Calle de los Arzobispos 12; raciones & mains €7-15; ☺8am-1am) Restaurante Filipinas has a strong local flavour, decked with black-and-white photos of old Comillas.

❶ Information

Tourist office (☑942 72 25 91; www.comillas.es; Plaza de Joaquín del Piélago; ☺9am-2pm & 4-6pm Mon-Sat, 9am-2pm Sun) In the town hall building.

❶ Getting There & Away

Comillas is served by the same buses as Santillana del Mar (€3.70, one hour from Santander).

The main stop is on Calle del Marqués de Comil las, close to the town centre.

SAN VICENTE DE LA BARQUERA & AROUND
POP (SAN VICENTE) 3370

The last town on the Cantabrian coast before you enter Asturias, San Vicente de la Barquera sits handsomely on a point of land between two long inlets. The eastern one, the estuary of the Río Escudo, is spanned by the long, low-slung, 15th-century Puente de la Maza. San Vicente was one of the Cuatro Villas de la Costa, a federation of four dominant medieval ports that was converted into the province of Cantabria in 1779 (the others were Santander, Laredo and Castro Urdiales). The long beaches east of town make San Vicente quite a busy spot in summer. The tourist office (☏942 71 07 97; www.san vicentedelabarquera.org; Avenida del Generalísimo 20; ☉10am-1.30pm & 4.30-7pm Mon-Sat, 10am-2pm Sun) doubles as an agent for *casas rurales* in the area.

◉ Sights & Activities

The old part of town includes the 13th-century Castillo del Rey (adult/child €1.40/0.70; ☉10.30am-1.30pm & 4-7pm Tue Sun), but its outstanding monument is the Iglesia de Nuestra Señora de los Ángeles (admission €1.50; ☉10am-1pm & 4.30-8.30pm Mon-Sat, 10am-1pm & 5-7pm Sun). Although Gothic, this sports a pair of impressive Romanesque doorways. Inside, the lifelike statue of 16th-century Inquisitor Antonio del Corro (reclining on one elbow, reading) is deemed the best piece of Renaissance funerary art in Spain.

Along the coast east of town, Playa El Rosal and Playa de Merón are basically one broad, golden strand 4km long. Merón gets some surf and you should heed the warning flags at these beaches: red means don't swim, yellow means take care.

A popular outing inland is to El Soplao (☏902 82 02 82; www.elsoplao.es; adult/senior, student & child €11/8.50; ☉10am-9pm, closed Mon Oct-Jun; P), an extensive cave system full of stalactites and stalagmites, that before 1979 was a lead and zinc mine. The one-hour visit travels 400m into the cave in a mine train then continues a little further on foot. Telephone reservations are advised. A separate adventure tour going 3km into the caves (€32, 2½ hours) opens up an extraordinary subterranean world. It's about a 30km drive southwest of San Vicente: turn east off the CA181 at Rábago and climb 7km.

🛏 Sleeping & Eating

Hotel Luzón   HOTEL €€
(☏942 71 00 50; www.hotelluzon.net; Avenida Miramar 1; s/d €45/70; 🛜) The centrally positioned Luzón is a stately looking, century-old town house still possessing an air of older times with its high ceilings and quiet drawing rooms. Rooms are plain and simple but most have a sense of space, and many have broad views over town and water.

Hotel Azul de Galimar   HOTEL €€
(☏942 71 50 20; www.hotelazuldegalimar.es; Camino Alto Santiago 11; s/d €80/105; P🛜) This modern hotel is set in an excellent elevated position on the east side of town and has just 16 bright, appealing rooms. Many of them have balconies or terraces overlooking the Escudo estuary. There's a nice bright breakfast room and a small lawned garden. It's signposted from the Puente de la Maza.

El Pescador   SEAFOOD €€
(Avenida del Generalísimo 26; raciones €6-15; ☉closed Tue & Mon dinner Sep-May) The liveliest of the mainly seafood-dominated restaurants lining Avenida del Generalísimo, leading off the central Plaza de José Antonio. Stand around in the good-natured bar area knocking back tapas, or make your way through to the dining area overlooking the estuary.

❶ Getting There & Away

BUS San Vicente's bus station (Avenida Miramar), near the Puente de la Maza, is served by at least eight daily buses to Santander (€4.80, 1¼ hours, some via Comillas and Santillana del Mar), five to Oviedo (€8.52, two hours, some via Llanes, Ribadesella and Arriondas) and two to Potes (€3.50, 1¼ hours).

TRAIN Two slower FEVE trains stop daily en route between Santander and Oviedo.

ASTURIAS

'Ser español es un orgullo', the saying goes, 'ser asturiano es un título'. 'If being Spanish is a matter of pride, to be Asturian is a title', or so some of the locals would have you think. Asturias, they claim, is the real Spain; the rest is simply *tierra de reconquista* (reconquered land). Like neighbouring Galicia, Asturias was Celtic territory before the Romans arrived (and is bagpipe territory today!). It's also the sole patch of Spain never completely conquered by the Muslims. A Visigothic chieftain, Pelayo, warded them off in the Battle of Covadonga in AD 722, laying the foundations of the Kingdom of Asturias from which modern Spain grew.

Asturias has many similarities with neighbouring Cantabria and its scenic beauty is, if anything, even greater. The coast is a little wilder and more dramatic, and strung with even more beaches (more than 600, it's said), always with rolling green countryside behind. Inland, the mountains are generally higher, the valleys deeper (though equally green) and the villages a mite more rustic. Much of the Picos de Europa are on Asturian territory. For the architecture buff, Asturias is the land of the pre-Romanesque – modest but unique survivors from early medieval times. The region's cultured capital, Oviedo, is both historic and contemporary. Asturias also has its gritty industrial side. The Oviedo–Gijón–Avilés triangle is the heart of industrial Asturias and mines still operate in various spots, especially in the southwest.

The Reconquista's southward progress left Asturias increasingly a backwater. As a concession, Juan I of Castilla y León made Asturias a *principado* (principality) in 1388, and to this day the heir to the Spanish throne holds the title Príncipe de Asturias (Prince of Asturias). Awards handed out by the prince to personalities of distinction in Oviedo's Teatro Campoamor every October are Spain's equivalent of the Nobel prizes.

Oviedo

POP 210,000 / ELEV 232M

The compact but characterful and historic *casco antiguo* (old town) of Asturias' civilised capital is agreeably offset by elegant parks and modern shopping streets to its west and north. Out on the periphery, the hum and heave of factories is a strong reminder that Oviedo is a key producer of textiles, weapons and food.

History

When Asturian king Alfonso II El Casto (the Chaste; AD 791–842) defeated a Muslim detachment that had practically razed the settlement of Oviedo, he was sufficiently impressed by the site to rebuild and expand it, and move his court there from Pravia. Oviedo remained the Asturian kingdom's capital until 910, when León replaced it and the kingdom became the Kingdom of León. Oviedo's university was founded around 1600, and industry took off in the 19th century. The 1934 miners' revolt and a nasty siege in the first months of the Spanish Civil War led to the destruction of much of the Old Town.

◉ Sights

Catedral de San Salvador   CATHEDRAL

The cathedral's origins lie in the Cámara Santa, a pre-Romanesque chapel built by Alfonso II to house holy relics. The chapel is now a small part of a bigger complex that was built piecemeal over many years, chiefly in Gothic and baroque styles between the 13th and 18th centuries.

In the northwest corner of the Capilla del Rey Casto, a baroque chapel entered from the cathedral's north transept, the **Panteón Real** is believed to hold the tombs of most of the Asturian monarchs, including Alfonso II himself.

You enter the Cámara Santa, cloister and museum from the southern transept. The **Cámara Santa** (admission €2, incl museum & cloister €3.50, Thu afternoon free; ⊙10am-2.30pm & 4-8pm Mon-Fri, to 6pm Sat) contains some key symbols of medieval Spanish Christianity, including two jewel-encrusted gold crosses: Alfonso II presented the central Cruz de los Ángeles (Cross of the Angels) to the cathedral in 808, and it's still Oviedo's city emblem. A century later Alfonso III donated the Cruz de la Victoria (Cross of Victory), which in turn became the sign of Asturias. Behind the Cruz de los Ángeles is the Santo Sudario, a cloth said to have covered Christ's face. These items are viewed from the Sala Apostolar, whose remarkable Romanesque sculptures of the 12 apostles are in the style of Maestro Mateo, creator of Santiago de Compostela's Pórtico de la Gloria. Turning to leave, you'll see three heads sculpted from a single block of stone above the doorway. This strikingly simple work depicts, from left to right, the Virgin Mary, Christ and St John on Calvary. Their bodies were originally painted on the wall below.

Oviedo

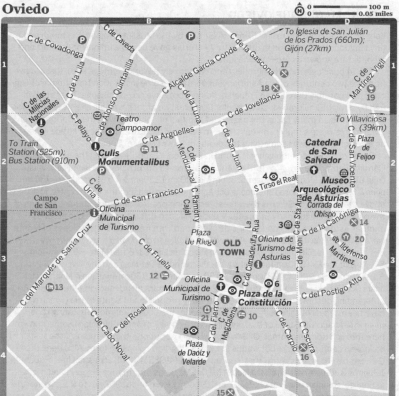

Oviedo

CANTABRIA & ASTURIAS OVIEDO

PRE-ROMANESQUE OVIEDO

Largely cut off from the rest of Christian Europe by the Muslim invasion, the tough and tiny kingdom that emerged in 8th-century Asturias gave rise to a unique style of art and architecture known as pre-Romanesque.

The 14 buildings, mostly churches (and collectively a World Heritage site), that survive from the two centuries of the Asturian kingdom take some inspiration from Roman, Visigothic and possibly Carolingian French buildings, but have no real siblings. They are typified by straight-line profiles, semicircular Roman-style arches, and a triple-naved plan for the churches. In many cases the bases and capitals of columns, with their Corinthian or floral motifs, were simply cannibalised from earlier structures. The use of lattice windows as a design effect owes something to developments in Muslim Spain.

Some of the best of the genre is found in and near Oviedo, including the cathedral's Cámara Santa. The Iglesia de San Julián de los Prados (Iglesia de Santullano; adult/child €1.20/0.60, Mon free; ☺10am-12.30pm Mon, 10am-12.30pm & 4-5.30pm Tue-Fri, 9.30am-noon & 3.30-5pm Sat, closed afternoons Oct-Apr), 1km northeast of the town centre, just above the highway to Gijón, is the largest remaining pre-Romanesque church, and one of the oldest, built in the early 9th century under Alfonso II. It is flanked by two porches – another Asturian touch – and the inside is covered with frescoes. On the slopes of Monte Naranco, 3km northwest of central Oviedo, the tall, narrow Palacio de Santa María del Naranco (adult/child incl Iglesia de San Miguel de Lillo €3/2, free Mon; ☺9.30am-1pm & 3.30-7pm Tue-Sat, 9.30am-1pm Sun & Mon, shorter hours Oct-Mar) and the Iglesia de San Miguel de Lillo (☺9.30am-1pm & 3.30-7pm Tue-Sat, 9.30am-1pm Sun & Mon, shorter hours Oct-Mar) were built by Ramiro I (842–50), and mark an advance in Asturian art. An outstanding decorative feature of the beautifully proportioned Santa María (which may have been a royal hunting lodge) is the *sogueado*, the sculptural motif imitating rope used in its columns. Some of the medallions are copies of ancient Iranian motifs, known here through Roman contact. Of San Miguel, only about one-third remains – the rest collapsed centuries ago – but what's left has a singularly pleasing form. Also here, the Centro de Interpretación de Prerrománico (☎985 11 49 01; admission free; ☺10am-1.30pm & 3.30-6pm or later, closed Mon & Tue Oct-May) has informative displays and models in English, Spanish and French. Take bus 10, hourly from about 9.10am to 9.10pm, northwest from a stop on Calle de Uría near the train station.

Visits to San Julián, Santa María and San Miguel are guided (in Spanish) except on Monday.

The cloister is pure 14th-century Gothic, rare enough in Asturias. The pre-Romanesque Torre Vieja (Old Tower), from the late 9th century, rises above its northwestern corner (best viewed from the street Tránsito de Santa Bárbara).

FREE Museo Arqueológico
de Asturias   MUSEUM
(www.museoarqueologicodeasturias.com; Calle de San Vicente 3; ☺9.30am-8pm Wed-Fri, 9.30am-2pm & 5-8pm Sat, 9.30am-3pm Sun) Reopened in 2011 after an eight-year modernisation job, Asturias' archaeological museum makes the most of the region's archaeological riches through video as well as informative displays of artefacts. Subject matter ranges from prehistoric cave art to *castro* (pre-Roman fortified village) culture, Roman times and the medieval Kingdom of Astu-

rias. Explanatory matter is in Spanish but staff will lend you a guide booklet in English or French.

FREE Museo de Bellas
Artes de Asturias   MUSEUM
(www.museobbaa.com; Calle de Santa Ana 1; ☺10.30am-2pm & 4.30-8.30pm Tue-Sat, 10.30am-2.30pm Sun) The Fine Arts Museum, housed in two of Oviedo's finest urban palaces, has a large and rewarding collection including paintings by Spanish and European greats such as Goya, Zurbarán, Picasso, Titian and Brueghel the Elder, and plenty by Asturians, such as Evaristo Valle.

Plazas & Statues   SQUARE, MONUMENT
A chief pleasure of Oviedo is exploring the Old Town's nooks and crannies. Plaza de Alfonso II, in front of the cathedral, and

neighbouring **Plaza de Porlier** are fronted by elegant mansions from the 17th and 18th centuries. **Plaza de la Constitución** occupies a barely perceptible rise close to the heart of old Oviedo, capped at one end by the **Iglesia de San Isidoro**, and lined by the 17th-century **ayuntamiento** (town hall). Past the colourful **Mercado El Fontán** food market, arcaded **Plaza Fontán** is equipped with a couple of *sidrerías* (cider bars) and has passages leading in under the pretty houses from surrounding streets.

Other little squares include **Plaza de Trascorrales** and **Plaza del Paraguas**. The latter got its name from its inverted umbrella design, which once accommodated an open-air market. Today it sports a big concrete umbrella to protect people from the elements.

Wandering around central Oviedo, you'll run into an array of striking modern open-air sculptures, such as Eduardo Úrculo's **Culis Monumentalibus** (a pair of legs topped by a pair of large buttocks) on Calle Pelayo, and a **statue of Woody Allen** (minus glasses, which some vandal has removed) on Calle de las Milicias Nacionales. Allen expressed a particular affection for Oviedo when filming here for his 2008 flick *Vicky Cristina Barcelona*.

✯ Festivals & Events

Oviedo's biggest fiesta is that of **San Mateo**, celebrated in the third week of September and climaxing around 21 September.

🛌 Sleeping

There's only one place to stay actually in the Old Town, but a reasonable range of places is scattered around its periphery.

Hotel Fruela   HOTEL €€
(☑985 20 81 20; www.hotelfruela.com; Calle de Fruela 3; r €72-79; P❄🐾) With a pleasing contemporary style and a touch of original art, plus professional yet friendly service, the 28-room Fruela achieves a cosy, almost intimate feel and is easily the top midrange option in central Oviedo. Breakfast, some original tapas and other meals are available in its cafe-restaurant. Its new sister hotel across the street, the Princesa Munia, will be worth checking out too.

Hotel Campoamor   HOTEL €€
(☑985 21 07 80; www.hotelcampoamoroviedo.com; Calle de Argüelles 23; s/d €99/105; ❄@🐾) The new rooms in this medium-size hotel are in very contemporary style with contrasting colours, enormous shower heads, and leather sofas and bedheads. The older ones are a bit more classical, but either type amounts to a good comfortable choice. Service is both professional and welcoming, there's a good restaurant, and the location opposite the Teatro Campoamor is handy for everything.

Barceló Oviedo Cervantes   HOTEL €€
(☑985 25 50 00; www.barcelo.com; Calle de Cervantes 13; r €130; P❄@🐾) Comprising a revamped century-old mansion and two modern smoked-glass wings, the 72-room Barceló is just a couple of blocks northwest of the central Campo de San Francisco. Impeccably contemporary style runs right through it, from the lobby bar with its glassed-in terrace to the spacious, luxurious rooms and their glass-partitioned bathrooms and rain-effect showers.

Hotel de la Reconquista   HOTEL €€
(☑985 24 11 00; www.hoteldelareconquista.com; Calle de Gil de Jaz 16; r €119-163; P❄@🐾) The city's fanciest lodgings, two blocks northwest of the central Campo de San Francisco, started life as an 18th-century hospice and are built around several patios. The somewhat formal rooms come in different shapes and sizes, with timber furniture, floor-to-ceiling windows, and gentle ochre-and-white colour schemes. Spanish royalty and other luminaries lodge here during the annual Príncipe de Asturias prizes jamboree each October.

Hotel Santa Cruz   HOTEL €€
(☑985 22 37 11; www.santacruzoviedo.com; Calle del Marqués de Santa Cruz 6; s/d €54/70; P🐾) With well-sized, spotless rooms and a central location, this small hotel amounts to decent value, even though only two rooms (22 and 23) overlook the lovely big green park across the street.

Hostal Arcos   HOSTAL €
(☑985 21 47 73; www.hostal-arcos.com; Calle de Magdalena 3; s/d €35/55; 🐾) The only lodging actually in the Old Town is a modern brick building with a friendly welcome and 10 simple, clean rooms, all quite cheery and colourful.

🍴 Eating

Oviedo's *sidrería* rules include getting good grub at reasonable prices. To sample the experience head for Calle de la Gascona, which is lined with boisterous *sidrerías*, most serving *raciones* from €8 to €18. Two or three of these constitute a full meal. Elsewhere, Oviedo also boasts some of northern Spain's most sophisticated eateries.

Tierra Astur   SIDRERÍA €€

(✆985 20 25 02; www.tierra-astur.com; Calle de la Gascona 1; mains €9-21) A particularly atmospheric *sidrería*-restaurant, Tierra Astur is famed for its grilled meats and prize-winning cider. Folks queue for tables, or give up and settle for tapas at the bar. Some just buy typical local products in the shop area to the right and go home. Platters of Asturian sausage, cheese or ham are a good starter option.

La Corrada del Obispo   ASTURIAN €€

(✆985 22 00 48; Calle de la Canóniga 18; mains €16-24; ⊙closed Mon & dinner Sun) Modern decor combines with the exposed stone walls of this 18th-century house to provide a welcoming setting for fine local cooking. It offers a tempting variety of fish and meat dishes, including game such as wild boar and venison when they're in season. You might be able to snare a table in the upstairs gallery. Woody Allen shot some scenes for *Vicky Cristina Barcelona* here.

Sidrería El Pigüeña   SIDRERÍA, SEAFOOD €€

(Calle de la Gascona 2; mains €15-25; ⊙Thu-Tue; 🖭) A boisterous Gascona *sidrería* and restaurant, the Pigüeña is jammed most nights, especially weekends, with a broad mix of locals, from labourers to lovers, hoeing into seafood and *rollitos de verdura con marisco* (seafood-stuffed vegetable tubes), and slurping bottles of cider. Let the waiters serve the cider though!

🍷 Bocamar   SEAFOOD €€€

(✆985 23 70 92; www.bocamar.es; Calle del Marqués de Pidal 20; mains €18-27; ⊙closed Sun dinner) With a decidedly maritime air, this is probably the best seafood restaurant in town, where all items (fresh from the sea to the north) are prepared with a lightness of touch that makes all the difference. Tempting offerings include wild turbot *(rodaballo salvaje)* and brochette of anglerfish *(pixín)*, prawns and vegies. It's 200m north of Campo de San Francisco.

Sidrería El Fartuquín   ASTURIAN €€

(www.restauranteelfartuquin.es; Calle del Carpio 19; mains €11-20; ⊙closed Sun) The Fartuquín's busy little dining room offers an excellent range of Asturian meat, fish and seafood, and its good-value €14 set menu, including wine, is available for dinner as well as lunch Monday to Friday. Locals pack into the front bar for tapas in the evenings.

La Puerta Nueva   SPANISH €€

(✆985 22 52 27; Calle de Leopoldo Alas 2; mains €14-26; ⊙lunch & dinner Fri & Sat, lunch Sun) Despite its limited opening times, this is a gourmet experience worth seeking out. The market-based menu mixes northern Spanish with Mediterranean cuisine in a welcoming atmosphere, and the €33 set menu (including wine) is probably the best option.

🍷 Drinking & Entertainment

For *sidrerías* head to Calle de la Gascona *(el bulevar de la sidra)*. The Old Town's narrow pedestrian streets are thronged with people having a great time inside and outside dozens of bars on weekends. The main axis is

---

SAMPLING CIDER

Ancient documents show that Asturians were sipping cider as far back as the 8th century! The region churns out 80% of Spanish cider: anything up to 30 million litres a year, depending on the apple harvest. Apples are reaped in autumn and crushed to a pulp (about three-quarters of which winds up as apple juice). The cider is fermented in *pipes* (barrels) kept in *llagares* (the places where the cider is made) over winter. It takes about 800kg of apples to fill a 450L *pipa*, which makes 600 bottles.

Traditionally, the *pipes* were transported to *chigres* (cider taverns) and punters would be served direct from the *pipa*. The *chigre* is dying out, though, and most cider now comes in bottles in *sidrerías* (cider bars), often with food. The cider is served *escanciada*, that is, poured from a bottle held high overhead into a glass held low. This gives it some fizz. Such a shot of cider, about one-fifth of a glass, is known as a *culete* or *culín* and should be knocked back in one (leaving a tiny bit in the bottom of the glass) before the fizz fizzles out.

The main cider-producing region is east of Oviedo: find out more at **Comarca de la Sidra** (www.lacomarcadelasidra.com).

Calle de Mon, with wall-to-wall bars, and its extension, the slightly less manic Calle Oscura. During the week, these bars are generally open 11pm to 3.30am and can be quiet. On Friday and Saturday they mostly stay open until 5.30am and are jammed. For bars with live music, head to Calle de Martínez Vigil, where you might hear anything from blues to Celtic music to Spanish indie rock to Beatles covers, starting any time from 8pm to 11pm.

Ca Beleño MUSIC BAR
(www.facebook.com/cabeleno; Calle de Martínez Vigil 4; ☺from 5pm) This small pub is a well-established venue for Celtic music, whether of Asturian, Galician or Irish extraction. It usually has live groups or jams from 10pm on Thursday.

Salsipuedes CLUB
(www.salsipuedes.es; Calle de Ildefonso Martínez 7; ☺midnight-5am Sun-Thu, midnight-7.30am Fri & Sat; ☏) The place to go if you're looking to party on around 3am, blue-lit Salsipuedes has several bars and dance floors on three levels of an Old-Town house.

ⓘ Information

Oficina de Turismo de Asturias (☏902 30 02 02; www.infoasturias.com; Calle de Cimadevilla 4; ☺10am-7pm Mon-Sat year-round, 10am-5pm Sun Jul & Aug)

Oficina Municipal de Turismo (ayto-oviedo.es) Bus Station (☏985 11 70 50; Calle de Pepe Cosmen; ☺9.30am-2pm & 4.30-7.30pm Jul-Sep); Campo de San Francisco (☏985 22 75 86; Calle del Marqués de Santa Cruz 1; ☺9.30am-2pm & 4.30-7.30pm); Old Town (☏984 08 60 60; Plaza de la Constitución 4; ☺9.30am-7.30pm)

ⓘ Getting There & Around
Air
The **Aeropuerto de Asturias** (☏902 40 47 04) is at Santiago del Monte, 47km northwest of Oviedo and 40km west of Gijón. Buses run hourly to/from Oviedo's bus station (€7.50, 45 minutes).

Airlines and destinations:

Air Berlin (www.airberlin.com) Destinations in Germany, via Palma de Mallorca.

easyJet (www.easyjet.com) London (Stansted), Geneva and Lisbon.

Iberia (www.iberia.com) Madrid and Valencia.

Ryanair (www.ryanair.com) Barcelona and Madrid.

Volotea (www.volotea.com) Málaga.

Vueling Airlines (www.vueling.com) Barcelona.

Bus
From the **bus station** (☏902 49 99 49; www.estaciondeautobusesdeoviedo.com; Avenida de Pepe Cosmen), 700m north of the central Campo de San Francisco park, direct services head up the motorway to Gijón (€2.25, 30 minutes) every 10 or 15 minutes from 6.30am to 10.30pm. Other daily buses head to destinations in Asturias, Galicia, Cantabria and elsewhere, including the following:

Cangas de Onís (€6.50, 1½ hours, seven or more daily)

Madrid (€30.62 to €53.08, 5¼ to 6½ hours, 18 or more daily)

Ribadesella (€7.45, 1¼ to 1¾ hours, seven or more daily)

Santander (€11.81 to €25.40, 2¼ to 3¼ hours, eight or more daily)

Santiago de Compostela (€27.63 to €40.75, 4¾ to 7¼ hours, six daily)

Train
One **train station** (Avenida de Santander; ☏) serves both train companies, Renfe and FEVE, the latter located on the upper level. Destinations of **Renfe** (www.renfe.com) include León (€8.20 to €19.60, two to three hours, five or more trains daily), Madrid (€50.90, five to 5¾ hours, three or four daily) and Barcelona (€98.20, 11 hours, one overnight). For Gijón, Renfe *cercanías* (€2.85, 33 minutes) go up to three times hourly until 10.45pm.

FEVE (☏985 98 23 81; www.feve.es) runs two to four daily trains to Arriondas (€4.75, 1½ hours), Ribadesella (€6.15, two hours) and Llanes (€7.90, 2½ hours), with two continuing to Santander (€15, 4¾ hours). Westbound, FEVE has three direct trains daily to Cudillero (€3.05, 1¼ hours), and two to Luarca (€6.85, 2¼ hours), which continue into Galicia as far as Ferrol.

Around Oviedo
EL ENTREGO
Asturias has a proud mining history, an industry that promoted the arrival of the railways and metal industries. You can plunge into that history at the **Museo de la Minería y de la Industria** (☏985 66 31 33; www.mumi.es; Calle El Trabanquín; adult/child €5.50/2.50; ☺10am-8pm Tue-Sun; ℗) in El Entrego, 25km east of Oviedo. The displays, full-scale machinery models, and a replica of a mine-shaft and tunnel, bring to life the tough story of mining. Hourly Renfe *cercanías* from Oviedo run to El Entrego (€2.20, 40 minutes).

Gijón

POP 264,000

Bigger, grittier and gutsier than Oviedo, Gijón (khi-*hon*) produces iron, steel and chemicals, and is the main loading terminal for Asturian coal. But Gijón has emerged like a phoenix from its industrial roots, having given itself a facelift with pedestrianised streets, parks, seafront walks and cultural attractions. It's a party and beach town too, and in summer puts on a vast entertainment program.

⊙ Sights & Activities

Cimadevilla   OLD TOWN

The ancient core of Gijón is concentrated on the headland known as Cimadevilla. At the top of this, the grassy Parque del Cerro Santa Catalina contains an early-20th-century gun battery, a mock sailing ship for small kids to scramble around, and the Elogio del Horizonte, a brutal concrete sculpture by Basque artist Eduardo Chillida that has become a symbol of the city.

Wrapped around the landward side of Cimadevilla is an enticing web of narrow lanes and small squares. Plaza de Jovellanos is dominated by the home of Gijón's most celebrated scion, the 18th-century Enlightenment politician Gaspar Melchor de Jovellanos. It is now the Museo Casa Natal de Jovellanos (☎985 34 63 13; http://museos.gijon. es; Plaza de Jovellanos 2; admission free; ☺10am-2pm & 5-7.30pm Tue-Sun). A section of Gijón's Roman walls and towers has been reconstructed stretching west from the plaza.

To the east, underneath Campo Valdés, are the town's Termas Romanas (Roman Baths; ☎985 18 51 51; museos.gijon.es; adult/senior & stu-dent/child €2.50/1.40/free, Sun free; ☺10am-2pm & 5-7.30pm Tue-Sun), constructed in the 1st to 4th centuries AD. West of Campo Valdés opens the harmonious, porticoed Plaza Mayor.

Museo del Ferrocarril de Asturias   MUSEUM

(☎985 30 85 75; http://museos.gijon.es; Plaza de la Estación del Norte; adult/senior & student/child €2.50/1.40/free, Sun free; ☺10am-7pm Tue-Sun; ☑) Gijón's excellent railway museum explores the important role of trains in Asturian history, with 50 locomotives and carriages, and plenty of railway paraphernalia. You can even take a short train ride around its interior. It's housed in the 19th-century Renfe train station, a few minutes' walk west of the city centre.

Acuario   AQUARIUM

(☎958 18 52 20; http://acuario.gijon.com; adult/senior & student/child €12/8/6; ☺10am-7pm or later; ☑) On Playa de Poniente, a few minutes' walk west along the seafront from the city centre, this singular aquarium houses 4000 specimens, from otters to sharks and penguins, in 50 tanks ranging over 11 separate underwater environments, from tropical oceans to the Bay of Biscay and an Asturian river.

Muséu del Pueblu d'Asturies   MUSEUM

(☎985 18 29 60; http://museos.gijon.es; Paseo del Dr Fleming 877; adult/senior & student/child €2.50/1.40/free, free Sun; ☺10am-7pm Tue-Sun; ☑) This museum, located 2km east of the city centre, is devoted to traditional Asturian culture, with several typical buildings in its grounds, including grain stores, houses, a bowling alley and some quirky shepherds' shelters. There are also exhibits of bagpipes, cooking, carriages and more. Take bus 1 (€1.20) from Calle de Pedro Duro just north of Plaza del Humedal.

Beaches   BEACH

Playa de San Lorenzo is a surprisingly good, clean city beach, but virtually disappears when the tide comes in. Playa de Poniente, west of the Puerto Deportivo (marina), has imported sand and is much broader.

✯✯ Festivals & Events

Throughout summer Gijón finds some excuse for a fiesta almost every week, from the Semana Negra (Black Week) literature and arts festival in July to the Fiesta de la Sidra Natural (Natural Cider Festival) in

---

WORTH A TRIP

PARQUE NATURAL DE REDES

Drivers looking for a treat should head southeast from El Entrego along the AS117 up the Nalón valley towards the 1490m Puerto de la Tarna pass on the Castilla y León border. The latter part of the route is a paradise of green, crossing the Parque Natural de Redes, with plenty of walking routes, a range of accommodation, and a Centro de Interpretación (☎985 60 80 22; www.parquenaturalderedes.es; ☺10am-2pm & 4-8pm; ☑) at Campo de Caso.

Gijón

Gijón

◎ Top Sights

Plaza de Jovellanos	C1
Plaza Mayor	C2
Termas Romanas	D1

◎ Sights

1	Museo Casa Natal de Jovellanos	C1
2	Playa de Poniente	A3
3	Playa de San Lorenzo	D3
4	Roman Walls	C1

🛏 Sleeping

5	Hotel Alcomar	D3
6	Hotel Asturias	C2
7	Hotel Hernán Cortés	C4
8	Hotel Pasaje	C2
9	La Casona de Jovellanos	C1

✖ Eating

10	Casa Zabala	C1
	La Galana	(see 6)
11	Restaurante Sidrería Ataulfo	D4

🍷 Drinking

12	Café Dam	D3

✪ Entertainment

13	Ca Beleño	A3
14	La Bodeguita del Medio	A3

late August, which includes an annual attempt on the world record number of people simultaneously pouring cider (7294 in 2011). The biggest fiesta of all is **Semana Grande** (the first two weeks of August). Varied musical programs and plenty of partying accompany all of these events.

WHAT'S COOKING IN ASTURIAS?

The most traditional Asturian food is simple peasant fare. Best known is *fabada asturiana*, a hearty bean dish jazzed up with meat and sausage. *Cachopo* (breaded veal stuffed with ham, cheese and vegetables) is a carnivore's dream, with vegetables to boot! As in Cantabria, there is a wealth of fresh seafood and good meat, while the rivers provide trout, salmon and eels.

The region is also famed for its cheeses, especially the powerful bluey-green *queso de Cabrales* from the foothills of the Picos de Europa. The basic raw material of Cabrales is untreated cow's-milk cheese, sometimes mixed with small quantities of goat's and/or sheep's milk. The cheese is matured in mountain caves and is strong, and very pungent, stuff – but surprisingly moreish.

🛏 Sleeping

Getting a room in August can be a challenge, so try to book ahead. Prices tumble outside summer, and you can often obtain better rates in advance or online.

Hotel Pasaje   HOTEL €€
(☎985 34 49 15; www.hotelpasaje.es; Calle del Marqués de San Esteban 3; s/d €65/110; ☎) A pleasant, friendly, family-run, small hotel with good, clean, bright rooms, many enjoying sea views. It's conveniently and centrally located facing the Puerto Deportivo (marina) and has its own cafe.

Hotel Alcomar   HOTEL €€
(☎985 35 70 11; www.hotelalcomar.com; Calle de Cabrales 24; s/d incl breakfast €91/130; ❋☎) In a prime position facing Playa de San Lorenzo, the Alcomar provides friendly service and a small touch of class. Rooms are neat if not inspired, with walnut furnishings and mini-chandeliers. Those in the newer section are larger and air-conditioned. Add €20 for a sea-view room between late July and early September.

Hotel Asturias   HOTEL €€
(☎985 35 06 00; www.hotelasturiasgijon.es; Plaza Mayor 11; s/d incl breakfast €92/130; ❋☎) The Asturias' rooms are plain but spacious and quite comfy, and some have sea glimpses. The location is ultra-central, overlooking Cimadevilla's main square.

Hotel Hernán Cortés   HOTEL €€
(☎985 34 60 00; www.hotelhernancortes.es; Calle de Fernández Vallín 5; s/d from €85/110; ❋@☎) This medium-sized hotel offers polished, personal service and large, very comfy, classical-style rooms with solid wood furnishings and marble bathroom fittings.

La Casona de Jovellanos   HOTEL €€
(☎985 34 20 24; www.lacasonadejovellanos.com; Plaza de Jovellanos 1; s/d €60/75; P☎) One of only two hotels in the old heart of town, the Casona de Jovellanos stands on one of Cimadevilla's nicest squares. It's a refurbished 18th-century house with straightforward but attractive wood-floored rooms, and a lively cider tavern downstairs.

✗ Eating

The most atmospheric area is Cimadevilla, though the newer part of the city centre also offers many options.

Casa Zabala   SEAFOOD €€€
(☎985 34 17 31; Calle del Vizconde de Campo Grande 2; mains €18-25; ⊗closed Mon & dinner Sun) Nestled among the many estimable *sidrerías* around Cimadevilla, Casa Zabala is good for seafood and fish of a more sophisticated ilk than you generally encounter hereabouts. The old-time looks have been maintained, and it's not everywhere you'll be served sea bass with wild-mushroom risotto.

Restaurante Ciudadela   ASTURIAN €€
(www.restauranteciudadela.com; Calle de Capua 7; mains & raciones €9-24; ⊗closed Mon & dinner Sun) Like many Gijón eateries, the Ciudadela has a front bar where you can nibble tapas and a dining room at the back. In this case there is also a unique cave-like basement dining area that attempts to re-create a Castilian bodega of yesteryear. The carefully prepared dishes range over the best of Asturian offerings, some with a creative touch, from *pucheros* (casserole/stews) to seafood to excellent meat and game dishes. It's half a block off Playa de San Lorenzo, just southeast of the Jardines del Naútico.

**Restaurante Sidrería
Ataulfo** SEAFOOD, SIDRERÍA €€€
(Calle de Cabrales 29; mains €15-40; ⊘closed Mon & dinner Sun) A good, fairly informal place for quality fresh fish and shellfish. For its speciality *arroz con bugre* (rice with a type of lobster; minimum two orders) it's best to order beforehand.

Casa Gerardo ASTURIAN €€€
(✆985 88 77 97; www.marcosmoran.com; Carretera AS19, Prendes; mains €22-28; ⊘lunch Tue-Sun, dinner Sat & Sun) About 12km west of Gijón, this stone-fronted house with a semi-rustic ambience has been serving good local cooking since 1882. Five generations of the Morán family have refined their art to the point of snagging a Michelin star. The fish and shellfish are delectable. To best sample their combination of tradition and innovation go for one of the set menus (€50 to €80).

La Galana SIDRERÍA €€
(Plaza Mayor 10; mains & raciones €15-24) The front bar is a boisterous *sidrería* where you can nibble on tapas (€4 to €7) to accompany the torrents of cider that bar staff pour into your glass. Up a few steps at the back is a spacious sit-down dining room. Fish is the strong suit but you could also try one of its rice dishes or a *sartén de la abuela* (grandma's frying pan) of eggs, chorizo sausage, peppers and potatoes.

🍷 Drinking & Entertainment

Normal bars shut by 1.30am Sunday to Thursday and 3.30am on weekends. Those licensed to have bands and DJs (many fall into this category) can remain open two hours more. Clubs disgorge their punters at 7.30am. The folks here really are deprived!

The *sidrerías* in Cimadevilla and around town are a fun way to start the night (and inject some food), and further up in Cimadevilla a student/teenage music-bar scene flourishes around Plaza Corrada and down Calle de la Vicaría. The Naútico area near Playa de San Lorenzo harbours a whole assortment of locales from funky little cocktail and music bars to large nightclubs: Amsterdam-inspired Café Dam (Calle de San Agustín 14; ⊘5.30pm-1am Sun-Thu, 5.30pm-close Fri & Sat; 🎵) is a gallery, chill bar and a great den for varied live music and DJs from midnight on Friday and Saturday.

A more mature crowd descends on the string of bars and clubs in the Fomento area near Playa de Poniente, ranging from salsa den La Bodeguita del Medio (✆985 35 21 46; Calle de Rodríguez San Pedro 43; ⊘from 8pm) to Ca Beleño (✆984 29 22 53; http://cabeleno. com; Calle de Rodríguez San Pedro 39; ⊘5pm-1am or later; 🎵), a jazz and Celtic-music bar.

ℹ️ Information

Gijón Turismo (✆985 34 17 71; www.gijon.info; Espigón Central de Fomento; ⊘10am-8pm) The main tourist offfice, on a pier of the Puerto Deportivo, is very helpful and full of information; summer information booths open at Playa de San Lorenzo and elsewhere.

ℹ️ Getting There & Around

Boat

The French **LD Lines** (ldlines.com) makes three weekly sailings from Saint-Nazaire in northwest France to Gijón and back. Fares for the 15 hour crossing vary with season and demand: a July return trip for two adults and a car, booked in April, could cost less than €400 or more than €700. The ferries dock at Puerto de El Musel, 6km west of Gijón centre.

Bus

Buses fan out across Asturias and beyond from the **ALSA bus station** (✆902 42 22 42; www. alsa.es; Calle de Magnus Blikstad), including to Asturias airport (€7.50, 35 minutes, hourly 6am to 8pm, plus 10pm), Oviedo (€2.15, 30 minutes, every 10 to 20 minutes from 7am to 10.30pm) and Santander (€13.52 to €27.96, 2¾ to 3¾ hours, nine or more daily).

Train

All trains use the temporary **Estación Sanz Crespo** (Calle de Sanz Crespo), 1km west of the city centre, while work on underground lines into the centre proceeds. **Renfe** (✆902 32 03 20; www. renfe.com) has several daily trains to León and Madrid, as well as *cercanías* to Oviedo (€2.85, 33 minutes) up to three times hourly. **FEVE** (✆985 98 23 81; www.feve.es) runs direct *cercanías* to Cudillero (€3.05, 1¾ hours, five to 12 daily). For most FEVE destinations you must change at Pravia or Oviedo. City buses 5 and 16 (€1.20) link the station with the city centre.

East Coast

Mostly Spanish holidaymakers seek out a summer spot on the beaches and coves along the coast east of Gijón, backed by the Picos de Europa, which rise only 15km inland.

CANTABRIA & ASTURIAS EAST COAST

VILLAVICIOSA & AROUND

POP (VILLAVICIOSA) 6300

Apart from the Romanesque Iglesia de Santa María, Villaviciosa's pretty little centre is mostly a child of the 18th century. The town rivals Nava as Asturias' cider capital and at **El Gaitero** (☎985 89 01 00; www.gaitero.com; bodegas/museum free/€1.50; ⏲10am-1.15pm & 4-6.15pm Mon-Fri, 10am-1.15pm Sat mid-Jun–mid-Sep, 10am-12.30pm & 4-6.30pm Thu-Sun mid-Sep–mid-Jun; P), on the N632 1km from the centre, you can tour both the company's cider-brewing bodegas and its museum.

The surrounding area is sprinkled with often diminutive and ancient churches. Don't miss the **Iglesia de San Salvador de Valdediós** (☎985 89 23 24; admission €1.50; ⏲11am-1pm & 4.30-7pm Tue-Sun, closed afternoons Oct-Mar), about 9km southwest, in a beautiful valley off the AS267 to Pola de Siero. This triple-naved pre-Romanesque church was built in AD 893 as part of a palace complex for Alfonso III.

The broad golden sands of 1km-long **Playa de Rodiles** front the sea at the mouth of the Ría de Villaviciosa, 11km north of town. Surfers might catch a wave here in late summer.

Colunga, 18km east of Villaviciosa, is home to the popular **Museo del Jurásico de Asturias** (MUJA; www.museojurasicoasturias.com; Rasa de San Telmo; adult/senior & child €7/4.60, Wed free; ⏲10.30am-8pm, shorter hours & closed Mon & Tue Sep-Jun; P 👪), which takes us through 185 million years of prehistory with dinosaur footprints, fossils and bones (which are plentiful along this part of the Asturian coast), and 20 giant dinosaur replicas. The pair of mating tyrannosaurus is over 12m high. Of several sandy beaches on this stretch of coast, one of the less busy in summer is 770m-long **Playa de Caravia**, backed by green slopes, near Prado.

Villaviciosa has plenty of *sidrerías*, a few restaurants, and a dozen hotels and *pensiones* (small private hotels). But the most attractive lodgings in the area are at British-run **La Casona de Amandi** (☎985 89 01 30; www.lacasonadeamandi.com; Calle de San Juan 6, Amandi; s/d incl breakfast €90/100; P 📶 👪), a beautiful, large, 19th-century farmhouse in Amandi, 1.5km south of town. Rooms, all of which ooze their own character and vary in size, contain some original furnishings. From mid-July to mid-September dinner is available and in decent weather it's nice to eat it outside in the ample lawned gardens.

ℹ Getting There & Away

ALSA provides nine or more buses daily to Oviedo (€3.95, 35 minutes to one hour) and Ribadesella (€3.60, 35 minutes to one hour), and 13 or more to Gijón (€2.70, 30 minutes to 1¼ hours).

RIBADESELLA

POP 3020

Unless you've booked in advance, it's best to stay away from Ribadesella on the first weekend of August, when the place goes mad for the **Descenso Internacional del Sella** (www.descensodelsella.com), a canoeing festival. Otherwise, Ribadesella is a low-key fishing town and resort. Its two halves, split by Río Sella's estuary, are joined by a long, low bridge. The western half has a good, expansive beach, Playa de Santa Marina, while the older part of town and fishing harbour are on the eastern side.

Sights

TOP CHOICE **Cueva de Tito Bustillo** CAVE

(☎902 30 66 00, reservations 985 86 12 55; www.centrodearterupestredetitobustillo.com; adult/senior, student & child incl Centro de Arte Rupestre €7.10/5.10, Wed free; ⏲10.15am-5pm Wed-Sun mid-Mar–Oct; P) To see some of Spain's best cave art, including superb horse paintings probably done around 13,000 to 12,000 BC, plan a visit to this World Heritage–listed cave, a short distance south of the western end of the Sella bridge. Daily visitor numbers are limited so reservations by telephone are essential. The 45-minute visit (guided in Spanish) includes some slippery stretches, and children under seven years are not admitted. Even if you miss the cave itself, the **Centro de Arte Rupestre Tito Bustillo** (adult/senior, student & child €5.20/3.10, Wed free; ⏲10am-8pm Jul & Aug, 10am-2.30pm & 3.30-6pm or 7pm Sep-Jun), 200m along the road, is well worth a visit for its displays, video and replicas. Visits to **La Cuevona**, a separate, impressively large cave (though without art), are free with the Centro de Arte Rupestre ticket: nine groups of 20 are taken in each day when the Centro is open (reservations advisable).

Sleeping

Rates everywhere decline dramatically outside the August peak season.

Hotel Ribadesella Playa HOTEL €€

(☎985 86 07 15; www.hotelribadesellaplaya.com; Calle de Ricardo Cangas 3; s incl breakfast €90, d incl breakfast €110-120; P 📶) Most hotels are in the western part of town and this one fronts Playa de Santa Marina in a quaint turreted 1900s mansion. Rooms are nice and tasteful in blues and greens, with carpets and full-length mirrored wardrobes. Depending on business, it may close from about November to February.

Villa Rosario HISTORIC HOTEL €€€
(☎985 86 00 90; www.hotelvillarosario.com; Calle de Dionisio Ruisánchez 6; r incl breakfast with/without sea view €270/215; [P][✴][@][☎]) This luxurious Playa de la Marina seafront hotel is a classic century-old *casa de indianos* (mansion built by a returned emigrant from Latin America or the Caribbean), eclectically styled with materials from marble to steel to cherry wood, though the rooms are contemporary with a nod to minimalism. Try to ensure a room in the original *palacete* rather than the new section across the street, which is equally comfortable but less stylish.

Hotel Covadonga HOTEL €
(☎985 86 01 11; www.hotelcovadongaribadesella.com; Calle de Manuel Caso de la Villa 6; r €60-75; [☎]) About 100m back from the port in the older part of town, the Covadonga is a step back in time, full of character and generally booked in August.

✖ Eating

The busy waterfront *sidrerías* on the eastern side of the river are a good bet for seafood.

Casa Gaspar ASTURIAN €€
(Calle de López Muñiz 6; dishes €9-20; ⊘Fri-Wed) For a change from seafood you could opt for grilled meats, *revueltos* (scrambled-egg dishes) or other *raciones*, and cider in copious quantities, at Casa Gaspar, in the heart of the Old Town. On summer nights it gets rollickingly busy.

❶ Information

Tourist office (☎985 86 00 38; www.ribadesella.es; Paseo Princesa Letizia; ⊘10am-9pm, shorter hours & closed Mon mid-Sep–Jun) At the eastern end of the Sella bridge.

❶ Getting There & Away

BUS The **bus station** (☎985 86 13 03; Avenida del Palacio Valdés) is about 300m south of the Sella bridge. Destinations include Oviedo (€7.45, one to 1¾ hours, 10 or more daily), Gijón (€6.35, 1½ hours, six to nine daily), Llanes (€2.55, 30 to 40 minutes, eight or more daily) and Santander (€7.52, 1½ or 2½ hours, two daily).

TRAIN FEVE trains run at least three times daily to Llanes, Arriondas and Oviedo, and twice to Santander.

RIBADESELLA TO LLANES

More than 20 sandy beaches and pretty coves await discovery between Ribadesella and Llanes by those with transport and time. About 12km short of Llanes, **Playa de San Antolín** is a vast, unprotected beach where surfers might pick up the odd wave.

Playa de Torimbia, a beautiful golden crescent bounded by rocky headlands and a bowl of green hills, is truly spectacular. Turn off the AS263 at Posada to reach Niembro (2km), from where it's a further 2km to the beach. You have to walk the last kilometre or so, which keeps the crowds down too. **Playa de Toranda**, only 500m from Niembro and backed by fields and a forested headland, is also pretty nice. **Hotel La Portilla** (☎985 40 78 42; hotellaportilla.blogspot.com.es; s/d incl breakfast €80/120; [✴]) is a dull grey-stone building but has a pleasant modern interior and is a short stroll from Playa de Toranda.

LLANES
POP 5370

Inhabited since ancient times, Llanes was for a long period an independent-minded town and whaling port with its own charter awarded by Alfonso IX of León in 1206. Today, with a small medieval core and bustling harbour, it's one of northern Spain's more popular holiday destinations – a handy base for the Asturias coast, with the Picos de Europa close at hand.

Strewn alongside the far end of the pier like a set of children's blocks are the **Cubes of Memory**, painter Agustín Ibarrola's playful public artwork using the port's breakwater as his canvas. **La Basílica**, the town's main, mostly Gothic church, was begun in 1240 and is worth a quick inspection if you find it open. Of the three town beaches, **Playa de Toró** to the east, its limpid waters dotted with jutting pillars of rock, is easily the best.

The **tourist office** (☎985 40 01 64; www.llanes.com; Calle de Posada Herrera 15; ⊘10am-2pm & 5-9pm, shorter hours & closed Sun afternoon mid-Sep–mid-Jun) is in La Torre, a tower left over from Llanes' 13th-century defences, and staff can tell you about plenty of good walking routes in the area, including the E9 coastal path that passes through here on its journey from Russia to Portugal.

🛏 Sleeping & Eating

Llanes and its surrounding area have plenty of accommodation, but from June to mid-September booking is virtually essential, especially in the town itself.

TOP CHOICE **La Posada de Babel** RURAL HOTEL €€
(📞985 40 25 25; www.laposadadebabel.com; s/d €84/120; ⊗closed mid-Dec–Mar; 🅿🖾) In La Pereda, 4km south of Llanes centre, this unique spot combines attractive contemporary architecture and design with lovely, large lawns and a relaxed yet civilised vibe. Its owners were inspired to create it during extended travels in Asia. The 12 rooms are installed in four contrasting buildings, including one in a typical Asturian *hórreo* (grain store) on stone stilts. The kitchen emphasises market-fresh fish and organic vegetables and beef from nearby farms.

Pensión La Guía PENSIÓN €€
(📞985 40 25 77; www.pensionlaguia.com; Plaza de Parres Sobrino 1; s/d €40/65; 🖾) This spick-and-span budget spot, in a 300-year-old house, is a charming web of dark timber beams and terracotta floors; the rooms are plain but bright, with glassed-in balconies overlooking a central plaza.

Restaurante Siete Puertas SEAFOOD €€€
(Calle de Manuel Cué 7; mains €18-30, menus €22-30; ⊗closed Mon) Plenty of lively *marisquerías* (seafood eateries) and *sidrerías* line Calles Mayor and Manuel Cué, so stoking up on sea critters and washing them down with cascades of cider is an easy task. The Siete Puertas is a cut above the average, with neat white tablecloths, efficient service and well-prepared dishes. Fish and home-made desserts are its strong suits.

❶ Getting There & Away

Four daily ALSA buses head to Gijón (€8.17, 1¾ to two hours), six to Santander (€5.58, 1¼ to two hours) and at least 12 to Oviedo (€9.95, 1¼ to 2¼ hours). Three or four FEVE trains come here daily from Oviedo, Arriondas and Ribadesella, two of them continuing to Santander.

EAST OF LLANES

The 350m-long Playa La Ballota is a particularly attractive beach a few kilometres east of Llanes, hemmed in by green cliffs and accessible by dirt track from the Cué–Andrín road.

From Puertas de Vidiago, 6km east of Llanes on the N634, signs past the church lead you 2km to Los Bufones de Arenillas,

a dozen geyser-style jets of seawater which are pumped up through holes in the earth by the pressure of seawater. When heavy seas are running, some jets can spurt 20m high and are quite a spectacle (and it's dangerous to get too close). With calm seas, you'll just hear an eerie sound of air and water whooshing through the tunnels below.

Playa de la Franca, further towards Cantabria, is another nice beach and has a summer campground. Two kilometres from Pimiango (past a spectacular coastal lookout), the World Heritage–listed Cueva del Pindal (📞608 175284; adult/senior & child €3/1.50; ⊗10am-2pm & 3.30-4.30pm Wed-Sun) contains 31 Palaeolithic paintings and engravings of animals, including rare depictions of a mammoth and a fish. It's not in the same league as the Altamira or Tito Bustillo caves, but with its setting among wooded sea-cliffs and with a 16th-century chapel, ruined Romanesque monastery and interpretation centre nearby, it's an appealing visit. Reserve cave visits by phone; a maximum of eight groups of 25 can enter each day.

West Coast

The cliffs of Cabo Peñas, 20km northwest of Gijón, mark the start of the western half of Asturias' coast as well as its most northerly and highest (almost 100m) points.

AVILÉS
POP 78,500

This old estuary port makes for an attractive couple of hours' strolling. The central Plaza de España is fronted by two elegant 17th-century buildings, one of which houses the town hall. Attractive colonnaded old streets like Calles Ferrería, San Francisco and Galiana radiate out from the plaza. But the key symbol of today's Avilés is the Centro Cultural Internacional Avilés (CCIA, Centro Niemeyer; 📞902 30 66 00; www.cciaviles.com; admission free; ⊗10am-10pm Sun-Thu, 10am-midnight Fri & Sat), whose bold contemporary structures rise just across a colourful footbridge from the old centre. The CCIA was designed by Brazilian architect Oscar Niemeyer (the creator of Brasilia) as a gift to Asturias and as a cultural nexus between the Iberian Peninsula and Latin America. It stages music, dance, theatre, film and art by international performers. The broad deck on which it stands affords views of the river, the port, the city opposite and assorted industrial installations behind – and it is a favourite with local skaters. With its futuristic lines the centre is also a statement of Avilés' regeneration from declining industrial city towards a cleaner, more tech- and culture-based future.

You'll find everything up to a five-star historic-building hotel among Avilés' hotels and *pensiones*. **Hotel Don Pedro** (☑985 51 22 88; www.hdonpedro.com; Calle de La Fruta 22; s/d €81/103; @☎) has attractive, comfy rooms with exposed stone or brick, and rugs on wooden floors.

Central streets such as San Francisco and Galiana, and Plaza de Carbayedo at the end of Galiana, have plenty of good eating options including the 'gastronomic tavern' **Llamber** (Calle Galiana 30; raciones €8-16; ☺closed Mon evening & Tue; ☑), with some original concoctions such as octopus *au gratin* with smoked cheese. But serious food lovers should make for Salinas, a coastal suburb, and the **Real Balneario de Salinas** (☑985 51 86 13; www.realbalneario.com; Avenida de Juan Sitges 3; mains €25-40; ☺closed Mon, dinner Sun & early Jan-early Feb). Opened as a bathing centre right on the beach by King Alfonso XIII in 1916, it's a top restaurant today, particularly strong on fish (you can choose from a variety of traditional or 'new concept' preparations) and shellfish – plus some very tempting desserts! Afterwards (or before) take a walk along to the rocky cape La Peñona.

Avilés' helpful **tourist office** (☑985 54 43 25; Calle de Ruiz Gómez 21; ☺10am-8pm) can give you a good map. ALSA buses run frequently to Oviedo (€2.35, 30 to 60 minutes) and Gijón (€2.20, 30 minutes). FEVE trains head to both cities too.

CUDILLERO
POP 1580

Cudillero is the most picturesque fishing village on the Asturian coast, and it knows it. The houses, painted in varying pastel shades, cascade down to a tiny port on a narrow inlet. Despite its touristy feel, Cudillero is cute and remains reasonably relaxed, even in mid-August when almost every room in town is occupied.

The main activity in town is watching the fishing boats come in (between 5pm and 8pm) and unload their catch, then sampling fish, molluscs and urchins at the *sidrerías*. You can also head along well-made paths to several lookouts, including **La Garita La Atalaya** perched high above the harbour.

The coast around here is an appealing sequence of cliffs and beaches. The nearest beach is the fine, sandy **Playa de Aguilar**, a 3km drive or walk east.

[TOP CHOICE] **Playa del Silencio**   BEACH
This is one of Spain's most beautiful beaches: a long sandy cove backed by a natural rock amphitheatre. It's 15km west of Cudillero: head to Castañeras on the N632 and follow the signs. The last 500m down to the beach is on foot.

🛏 Sleeping & Eating
Accommodation in Cudillero itself is limited, especially during the low season, when some places shut down. The cheaper places are back up the main street, away from the port. Plenty of hotels, *casas de aldea* (village houses), *pensiones* and apartments are scattered around the countryside within a few kilometres. There's no shortage of eateries down towards the port. A meal with drinks is likely to cost you €25 to €35 in most places.

La Casona de Pío   HOTEL €€
(☑985 59 15 12; www.lacasonadepio.com; Calle del Ríofrío; s/d €73/92; ☺closed 10 Jan-10 Feb; ☎) Just back from the port area is this charming hotel in a 200-year-old stone building, featuring 11 very comfortable rooms with a rustic touch and hydromassage baths, and a good restaurant serving a terrific €7 breakfast.

Hotel Casa Prendes   HOTEL €€
(☑985 59 15 00; www.hotelprendes.com; Calle San José 4; r €89; ☎) A nicely maintained hotel near the harbour with nine stone-walled rooms. Rates drop dramatically outside August. The owners rent apartments close by.

El Faro   SEAFOOD €€
(Calle del Ríofrío; mains €12-22; ☺closed Wed) An attractive eatery hidden one street back from the port. Stone, timber and blue decor create a welcoming atmosphere in which to dig into fish of the day or an *arroz caldoso* (seafood and rice stew).

ℹ Information
Tourist office (☑985 59 13 77; www.cudillero .org; Plaza del Oeste; ☺10am-8pm, shorter hours & closed Sun afternoon Oct-May) Located by the port, which is also the only place to park.

ℹ Getting There & Away
From the bus station, at the top of the hill 800m from the port, three or more daily buses go to Gijón (€5.15, 1¼ hours) and six or more to Avilés (€2.95, 45 minutes), where you can connect for

Oviedo. The FEVE train station is 1km further inland: trains to Gijón (€3.05, 1¾ to two hours) run about hourly until 6pm (fewer on weekends); for Oviedo (€3.05, 1¼ to two hours) you must usually change at Pravia.

LUARCA
POP 5280

Marginally less picturesque than Cudillero, Luarca has a similar setting in a deep valley running down to a larger harbour full of small fishing boats. It's a base for some good nearby beaches. Find your way up to the town's Atalaya lookout, with its small church, surprisingly elaborate cemetery and dramatic coastal views. Luarca's mariners' guild met for centuries at the nearby Mesa de Mareantes, where the town's history is now told in colourful tiles. Out near the end of the harbour, the Centro del Calamar Gigante (www.cepesma.org; Paseo del Muelle 25; adult/child €4/3; ⊙10am-2pm & 4-8pm Tue-Sun) displays several giant squids and all sorts of other monsters from the deep that were washed up on Asturian beaches, all preserved in a mixture of water and alcohol. It's run by Cepesma, a marine environmentalist organisation.

Sandy, 600m-long Playa de Cueva, 7km east of Luarca on the old coast road (N634), is one of the best beaches in the district, with cliffs, caves, a river and occasional decent surf. Five kilometres further on, Cabo Busto will give you some sense of the Asturian coast's wildness as waves crash onto the jagged, rocky cliffs. West of Luarca, Playa de Barayo is part of a protected natural reserve, with a good sandy beach in a pretty bay at the mouth of a river winding through wetlands and dunes. Turn off the N634 11km from central Luarca on to the NV2 towards Puerto de Vega, then after 800m turn right towards Vigo (1.5km), from where the beach is signposted. From the car park, the beach is accessible by a well-marked 30-minute nature hike.

🛏 Sleeping & Eating

At least seven hotels and *hostales* are on or just off the central Plaza de Alfonso X, including three cheapies in Calle Crucero. Seafood eateries dot the waterfront.

Hotel La Colmena   HOTEL €€
(☎985 64 02 78; www.lacolmena.com; Calle de Uría 2; s/d €45/65; ☜) Rooms are better and more comfortable than the dour exterior facing Plaza de Alfonso X suggests. It has some nice touches, such as the dark par-

quet floors, high ceilings and tall windows, though the showers are a bit of a squeeze.

Hotel 3 Cabos   RURAL HOTEL €€
(☎985 92 42 52; http://hotelrural3cabos.com; Carretera de El Vallín, Km4; s incl breakfast €95, d incl breakfast €105-125; P@☜🐾) A lovely recent conversion of a 120-year-old farmhouse, 3 Cabos enjoys fabulous panoramas from its elevated site a few kilometres inland, and provides six well-designed, well-equipped rooms with stone walls, original timber beams, wide, comfy beds and good-sized bathrooms. There's a lovely panoramic bar-restaurant area for breakfast and dinner (mains €16 to €20, with a focus on fresh local fish and meat), and a grassy garden with play area. Take the El Vallín turning off the N634 about 4km southwest of central Luarca and go 4.5km – it's well signed.

Hotel Villa La Argentina   HISTORIC HOTEL €€
(☎985 64 01 02; www.villalaargentina.com; Parque de la Barreda, Villar; r €98-108, ste €138, apt €152-162; ⊙closed early Jan–mid-Mar; P@☜🐾) This 1899 *casa de indianos* is one of approximately 20 such elaborate mansions in the Villar district about 1.5km southeast (uphill) from Luarca, all built by local folk who made fortunes in Latin America. It's now a comfy 12-room hotel amid lovely gardens, and drips with belle époque elegance. Antique furniture brings warmth to the rooms, with their high ceilings, chandeliers and understated decoration, and staff are welcoming.

🍴 Restaurante Sport   SEAFOOD €€€
(Calle de Rivero 9; mains €17-30; ⊙closed Wed dinner mid-Sep–mid-Jun) This seafood restaurant, facing the river a few steps back from the harbour, has been pleasing customers with its local fish and shellfish since the early 1950s. Slurp a half-dozen oysters (€9) as a starter. The *rollo de bonito al estilo de Luarca* (delicious patties of northern tuna mixed with vegetables and drowned in fresh tomato sauce) is a traditional local dish. *Percebes* (goose barnacles), a northwest-Spain delicacy, are sold at €7 per 100g when available. Anything '*del pincho*' has been caught with a rod and line.

❶ Information
Tourist office (☎985 64 00 83; www.turismo luarcavaldes.com; Calle de los Caleros 11; ⊙10.30am-2pm & 4.30-8pm Mon-Sat, 11am-2pm & 5-7pm Sun, shorter hours & closed Sun afternoon & Mon Oct-Jun) Facing the central Plaza de Alfonso X.

❶ Getting There & Away

At least four daily ALSA buses run east to Oviedo (€9.20, 1¼ to two hours) and west to Ribadeo (€6.45, 1½ hours) in Galicia. Two daily services head to Santiago de Compostela (€19.70, four or five hours). The FEVE train station is 800m south of the town centre. Two trains run daily east to Cudillero and Oviedo, and west to Ribadeo and as far as Ferrol (Galicia).

COAÑA & RÍO NAVIA

The small town of Coaña lies about 4km inland of the port of Navia, west of Luarca. A couple of kilometres beyond is the Castro de Coaña (☑985 97 84 01; adult/senior & child €3/1.50, Wed free; ☺10.30am-5pm Wed-Sun), one of the best-preserved Celtic settlements in northern Spain and well worth visiting.

From the *castro* a road snakes its way high above the cobalt-blue Río Navia across classic Asturian countryside – meadows alternating with rocky precipices – to Lugo in Galicia, crossing some of Galicia's least-visited and wildest territory around the town of Fonsagrada.

Inland Western Asturias

There's some gorgeous country in southwest Asturias. Even just driving through on alternative routes into Castilla y León can be rewarding, such as the AS228 via the 1587m Puerto Ventana, the AS227 via the beautiful 1486m Puerto de Somiedo or the AS213 via the 1525m Puerto de Leitariegos.

SENDA DEL OSO

The Senda del Oso (Path of the Bear) is a 20km cycling and walking track along the course of a former mine railway between the villages of Tuñón and Entrago, southwest of Oviedo. With easy gradients, it runs through increasingly spectacular valley scenery into deep, narrow canyons, with several bridges and tunnels. It also offers the high probability of seeing Cantabrian brown bears in a large enclosure, and it's a fun outing with (or without) children. A recently opened branch track southeast to Santa Marina in the Valle de Quirós has increased the total rideable track to 36km. There are many *casas rurales* and village hotels in the area, and a good source of further information (including on numerous walking trails) is www.caminrealdelamesa.es.

You can rent mountain or city bikes for €9 to €12 per day at four places along the route, typically open daily in July and August, and on Saturday and Sunday in April, May, June, September and October:

Centro BTT Valle del Oso (☑659 209383, 985 76 11 77; www.vallesdeloso.es; ⚤) At Tuñón.

Deporventura (☑666 557630, 985 24 52 67; www.deporventura.es; ⚤) At the Área Recreativa Buyera, beside the AS228 road about 5km south of Tuñó.

La Cabaña del Oso Goloso (☑985 76 10 29; http://osogoloso.blogspot.com.es; ⚤) At Proaza, 2km south of the Área Recreativa Buyera.

TeverAstur (☑608 2324628; www.descenso delasenda.com; ⚤) At Entrago.

It's advisable to reserve bikes one or two days ahead. All of the outfits we've listed offer assorted options such as baby seats, trailers for small children, electric bikes or Segways. Some also offer activities like caving, canyoning and guided mountain-bike trips elsewhere in the area. One option with TeverAstur is a one-way ride from Entrago to Tuñón, with a drive back to Entrago afterwards, so that you only do the route in the downhill direction (Entrago is 380m higher than Tuñón).

About 5.5km south of Tuñón (or a 1.1km walk from the Área Recreativa Buyera), the Senda del Oso reaches the Cercado Osero, a 40,000-sq-metre hillside compound for Paca and Tola, two female bears orphaned as cubs by a hunter in 1992. Since 2008 they have spent much of their time in a second enclosure just below the path at the same spot, joined by a male bear, Furaco, from Cantabria's Parque de la Naturaleza Cabárceno. Hopes that baby bears might ensue were abandoned in 2011, but for the time being the three bears were staying on in the lower enclosure, where they are usually easily visible in daytime. Paca and Tola may eventually be returned to their original upper compound, where in the past they were fed around noon daily (outside their December-to-February hibernation) at a spot beside the path, attracting crowds of spectators.

The Casa del Oso (☑985 96 30 60; www. osodeasturias.es; admission free; ☺10am-2pm & 4-6pm) in Proaza is the headquarters of the Fundación Oso de Asturias which runs the Paca-Tola project, and has exhibits on Spanish brown bears.

Four kilometres south of Entrago, the Parque de la Prehistoria (☑902 306600; www.parquedelaprehistoria.es; Hwy AS228; adult/

THERE'S A BEAR IN THERE

The wild mountain area of southwest Asturias and northwestern Castilla y León, including Parque Natural de Somiedo, is the main stronghold of Spain's biggest animal, the brown bear (oso pardo). Bear numbers in the Cordillera Cantábrica have climbed to around 200 from as low as 70 in the mid-1990s, including a smaller population in a separate easterly area straddling southeast Asturias, southwest Cantabria and northern Castilla y León. Killing bears has been illegal in Spain since 1973 but only since the 1990s have concerted plans for bear recovery been carried out. The year 2011 saw a record 52 new cubs in the western area. Experts are further heartened by the fact that there has been at least one recent case of interbreeding between the western and eastern groups.

This lumbering beast can reach 250kg and live 25 to 30 years, and has traditionally been disliked by farmers even though it is almost entirely vegetarian. Public support has played a big part in its recent recovery in the Cordillera Cantábrica, and owes a lot to the celebrated bears of Asturias' Senda del Oso. Experts warn that the bear is not yet completely out of the woods – illegal snares set for wild boar and poisoned bait put out for wolves continue to pose threats, as do forest fires, new roads and ski stations, which reduce the bears' habitat and mobility.

There are also 25 to 30 brown bears in the Pyrenees, moving between Spain, France and Andorra. Numbers there have increased from single figures in the past decade thanks to animals introduced from Slovenia. The last autochthonous Pyrenean female was shot by a French hunter in 2004.

Pola de Somiedo's Centro de Interpretación 'Somiedo y El Oso' (609 515156; adult/senior & child €2/1; 11am-2pm & 5-9pm Wed-Sun mid-Jun–mid-Sep;) is a good place to bone up on bear facts. It's run by the Fundación Oso Pardo (985 76 34 06; www.fundacionosopardo.org), which also organises bear-themed hikes (half-/full day adult €11/19, child €3/6) in the Somiedo park, which has around 80 bears. The walks are not specifically aimed at spotting bears, though you might get lucky. The Fundación's website has some terrific bear video, by the way.

senior & child €5.90/3.50; 10am-2.30pm & 3-6pm Wed-Fri, 10.30am-2.30pm & 4-7pm Sat & Sun, open daily Jul & Aug, closed mid-Jan–mid-Feb, closed Mon-Wed Dec–mid-Jan & 2nd half Feb; P) provides an excellent introduction to Spanish and European cave art and is well worth a visit. It includes replicas of Asturias' World Heritage–listed Tito Bustillo and Candamo caves and France's Niaux cave, and has a very good museum-gallery that explains much of the what, when, who, how and why of Europe's Palaeolithic cave art phenomenon.

Getting There & Away
Transportes Bimenes (985 46 58 78) runs three or four daily buses from Oviedo's ALSA bus station to Tuñón, Proaza and Entrago (one hour), terminating at San Martín, 1km beyond Entrago and 3km before the Parque de la Prehistoria.

PARQUE NATURAL DE SOMIEDO
If you fancy exploring beautiful mountain country that few foreigners reach, head for this 292-sq-km Unesco-listed biosphere reserve on the northern flank of the Cordillera Cantábrica. Composed chiefly of five valleys descending from the Cordillera's 2000m-plus heights, the park combines thick woodlands, dramatic rocky mountains and high pastures dotted with brañas, groups of (now largely abandoned) thatched herders' shelters (cabanas de teito). It's also a chief stronghold of Spain's bear population.

Each of the valleys has a number of marked walking trails, which you can find out about at the park's excellent Oficina de Información (Information Centre; 985 76 37 58; www.parquenaturalsomiedo.es; 10am-2pm & 4-7pm Tue-Sun, shorter hours Sep-May, closed Mon & Tue Sep-Oct & Apr-May, closed Mon-Fri Nov-Mar) in the village of Pola de Somiedo. Pola also has a bank, ATM and supermarket.

One of the best (and most popular) walking areas is the Valle del Lago, whose upper reaches contain glacial lakes and high summer pastures. You must leave vehicles in Valle del Lago village, a wonderful 8km drive southeast of Pola de Somiedo that winds and climbs to about 1300m. Other good walks include the La Peral–Villar de Vildas route in the upper Pigüeña valley, which passes one of the largest and best-preserved *brañas,* La Pornacal, and the ascent of the park's highest peak, Cornón (2194m).

🛏 Sleeping & Eating

Pola de Somiedo has around 15 places to stay and there are several more in Valle del Lago village.

Palacio de Florez Estrada HISTORIC HOTEL €€
(☑985 76 37 09; www.florezestrada.com; s/d incl breakfast €80/110; ☉closed mid-Dec–mid-Mar; P🐾🛜🍴) A gorgeous olde-worlde riverside mansion in lovely gardens just off the road to Valle del Lago, on the east side of Pola de Somiedo.

Auriz APARTMENT €€
(☑619 320007; www.auriz.es; apt for 2/4/6 people €70/120/160; P🛜🍴) Six excellent, modern, two-floor, three-bedroom apartments with kitchen and wood-burning stoves, beside a trout stream just off the road to Valle del Lago, on the east side of Pola de Somiedo.

Hotel Castillo del Alba HOTEL €€
(☑985 76 39 96; www.hotelcastillodelalba.es; Calle de Florez Estrada; s/d incl breakfast €60/76; ☉closed late Jan-early Mar; 🛜🍴) Welcoming 15-room hotel in Pola de Somiedo with appealing, contemporary-style rooms and two emblematic bear statues at the door. If you have children along, ask for one of the rooms with a sofa bed that neatly converts into a pair of bunks. There's also a decent restaurant (mains €10 to €20).

Braña La Code CABIN €€
(☑985 76 37 76; www.lacode.es; cabins for 1 or 2 €80, each extra person €15; P) This quirky spot in Valle del Lago village offers accommodation in *cabanas de teito,* built with traditional materials but with more comfort than the real thing (including kitchenettes and bathrooms)! Book ahead for July or August. Adjoining is the agreeably rustic Camping Lagos de Somiedo (☑985 76 37 76; www.campinglagosdesomiedo.com; sites per 2 people, car & tent €22.68; ☉Easter-Sep; P). The two share a bar-restaurant serving simple meals.

❶ Getting There & Away

An ALSA bus departs Oviedo bus station for Pola de Somiedo (€8, two hours) at 5pm Monday to Friday and 10am on weekends, returning from Pola at 6.30am (5.45pm on weekends).

From the Senda del Oso area, with your own wheels, you can approach Somiedo by the spectacular AS265 west from San Martín to La Riera, via the Puerto de San Lorenzo pass (1347m,

often snowed under in winter). At the pass the road crosses the Camín Real de la Mesa, an ancient track linking Astorga (Castilla y León) with the Asturian coast, that is now a long-distance footpath, the GR-101.

PICOS DE EUROPA

These jagged, deeply fissured mountains straddling southeast Asturias, southwest Cantabria and northern Castilla y León amount to some of the finest walking country, and some of the most spectacular country of any kind, in Spain. The Picos comprise three limestone massifs: the eastern Macizo Andara, with a summit of 2444m; the western Macizo El Cornión, rising to 2596m; and the particularly rocky Macizo Central or Macizo Los Urrieles, reaching 2048m. The 647 sq km Parque Nacional de los Picos de Europa covers all three massifs.

Virtually deserted in winter, the area bursts with visitors in August, when you should always try to book ahead, whether you are heading for a hotel or a mountain refuge. July is not far behind. June and September are more tranquil and just as likely to be sunny as August.

❶ Information

The national park has four main information centres:

Centro de Información Casa Dago (☑985 84 86 14; Avenida de Covadonga 43, Cangas de Onís; ☉8.30am-2.30pm Mon-Fri, 9am-2pm & 4-7pm Sat, closed Sat mid-Sep–Jun)

Centro de Visitantes Pedro Pidal (☉10am-6pm mid-Mar–mid-Dec) At the Lagos de Covadonga.

Centro de Visitantes Sotama (☑942 73 05 55; ☉9am-8pm Jul-Sep, 9am-6pm Oct-Jun) On the N621 in Tama, 2km north of Potes.

Oficina de Información Posada de Valdeón (☑987 74 05 49; El Ferial, Posada de Valdeón;

WARNING

Picos weather is notoriously changeable, and mist, rain, cold and snow are common problems. When the summer sun shines, you need protection from that too. Higher up, few trails are marked and water sources are rare. Paying insufficient attention to these details has cost several lives over the years.

Picos de Europa

The mountains of the Cordillera Cantábrica, striding east–west along the southern boundaries of Cantabria and Asturias, reach their greatest, and most spectacular, heights in the subrange called the Picos de Europa.

Rising up only 15km from the Bay of Biscay, and stretching little more than 40km from east to west and 25km north to south, the Picos still encompass enough awesome mountain and gorge scenery to make them arguably the finest hill-walking country in Spain. They offer plentiful short and long outings for striders of all levels, plus lots of scope for climbers and cavers, too.

The Picos' three limestone massifs are divided by deep valleys, running north–south. One of them, the stunning Garganta del Cares (Cares Gorge), forms the most popular mountain walk in the country. Elsewhere you can ramble past high-level lakes and across alpine meadows dotted with grazing cattle, peer over kilometre-high precipices, and traverse rocky wildernesses while spotting chamois skipping around dramatic crags. At the heart of the Picos rises the iconic El Naranjo de Bulnes, a huge tower of rock that presents a classic challenge for serious climbers.

However, the Picos are not just about energetic outdoor pursuits. You can enjoy them without moving a foot (almost). A couple of roads, a cable car and a funicular railway all climb to some very spectacular places.

Right
1. Garganta del Cares (Cares Gorge; p503) 2. El Naranjo de Bulnes (Pico Urriello; p504)

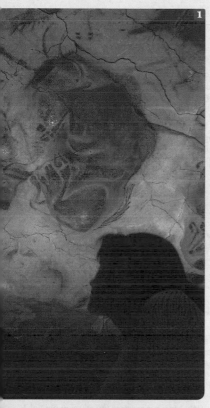

Cave Art

Humanity's first accomplished art was painted, drawn and engraved on the walls of European caves by Palaeolithic (Old Stone Age) hunter-gatherers between about 35,000 and 10,000 BC. The greatest concentration of this art, and its greatest artistic heights, are found in northern Spain and southern France.

Most of the images depict wild animals such as horses, deer, bison, wild boar and mammoths. In the best examples the fluidity of the drawing, the skilful employment of colour and relief, and the lifelike animal representations, attain the level of artistic genius. Getting a close-up view of this work, created by hunter-gatherers living an arduous existence during the last Ice Age – probably as some form of homage or worship – is truly awe-inspiring.

The world-famous bison and other beasts of the Cueva de Altamira (p475), now viewable in replica form only, have been on the World Heritage List since 1985, and in 2008 a further 17 Palaeolithic art caves in northern Spain were added to the list. In addition to Altamira, any of the following will be a highlight of your trip:

» **Cueva de Tito Bustillo** (p488)
» **Cueva de El Castillo** (p470)
» **Cueva de Covalanas** (boxed text, p472)

Also well worth a visit is Asturias' Parque de la Prehistoria (p493), which has three spectacular replica caves and an excellent museum.

For more on cave art check out http://cuevas.culturadecantabria.com and www.infoasturias.com.

Left
1. Museo de Altamira (p475) **2.** Cueva de El Castillo (p470)

Picos de Europa

⊘9am-5pm Jul–mid-Sep, 8am-2.30pm Mon-Fri mid-Sep–Jun)

Other information points open at strategic places around the national park from 1 July to 15 September and during major national holidays. Local tourist offices provide information too.

Cangas de Onís and Potes are the best places to buy outdoor equipment. Wild camping is not permitted within the national park except for overnight bivouacking above 1600m.

Websites worth checking out:

www.liebanaypicosdeeuropa.com For the eastern Picos.

www.picosdeeuropa.com

www.reddeparquesnacionales.mma.es The official national parks site.

Maps

The best maps of the Picos, sold in shops in Cangas de Onís, Potes and elsewhere for €4 to €5 each, are Adrados Ediciones' *Picos de Europa* (1:80,000), *Picos de Europa Macizos Central y Oriental* (1:25,000) and *Picos de Europa Macizo Occidental* (1:25,000).

① Getting There & Around

The main access towns for the Picos are Cangas de Onís in the northwest, Arenas de Cabrales in the central north, Potes in the southeast and Posada de Valdeón in the south. Paved roads

lead from Cangas southeast up to Covadonga and the Lagos de Covadonga; from Arenas south up to Poncebos then east up to Sotres and Tresviso; from Potes west to Fuente Dé, and from Posada de Valdeón north to Caín. This last is extremely narrow in parts.

Only a few bus services (mostly summer only) will get you into the hills from the access towns. An alternative to buses is taxis.

Bus & Train

Details of these services change from time to time, but their broad outlines are fairly reliable.

Cangas de Onís to Arenas de Cabrales & Potes Two or three buses daily run between Cangas and Arenas (€2.75, 35 minutes). To get from the northwest side of the Picos around to Potes, you must take a bus from Arriondas to Panes via Ribadesella, then one from Panes to Potes at noon or 6.45pm Monday to Friday, and 12.45pm or 5pm Saturday and Sunday.

Cangas de Onís to Covadonga & Lagos de Covadonga Three or more ALSA buses daily run from Cangas to Covadonga (€1.45, 15 minutes). To avoid traffic chaos from late July to early September and during some other major holidays, private vehicles cannot drive up from Covadonga to the Lagos de Covadonga from about 10am to 7pm. During these times a shuttle bus service (day ticket adult/child €7.50/3.50) operates to Covadonga and the lakes from four car parks (per vehicle €2) in

Cangas de Onís and along the road between there and Covadonga. Private vehicles *can* drive up to the lakes before 10am or after 7pm and, once up, can drive down any time.

Cangas de Onís to Oseja de Sajambre One bus a day, Monday to Friday from early September to late June only, links these two spots (€2.95, one hour).

León to Caín Monday to Friday you can get from León to Posada de Valdeón and Caín (€12.10, four hours) with a change of buses in Riaño. Take the 5.30pm bus from León. To return, again with a change in Riaño, there are buses from Caín at 3pm daily and 6.15am Monday to Friday. Schedules are changeable, so do double-check.

Oviedo to Arriondas & Cangas de Onís From Oviedo, ALSA runs at least seven buses daily to Arriondas (€5.80, one to 1¼ hours) and Cangas de Onís (€6.50, 1½ hours). Arriondas is on the FEVE railway between Oviedo, Ribadesella, Llanes and Santander.

Ribadesella & Llanes to Arriondas & Arenas de Cabrales Arriondas is linked with the two coastal towns by three or more buses (€1.70, 25 minutes from Ribadesella; €4.20, one hour from Llanes) and three or four FEVE trains daily. Two buses daily, Monday to Friday only, link Arenas with Llanes (€3.15, one hour, or €5.95, two hours).

Santander to Eastern Picos From Santander, **Autobuses Palomera** (☑942 88 06 11; www. autobusespalomera.com) travels via San Vicente de la Barquera and Panes to Potes (€7.75, 2½ hours), and returns, two to four times daily. A connecting service between Potes and Espinama (€1.40, 30 minutes) runs once or twice daily Monday to Friday, and in July and August it's usually extended to Fuente Dé (50 minutes from Potes), with up to three daily services.

Taxi

As well as regular taxis that stick to the better roads, such as **Taxitur** (☑689 143881; www .taxitur.com) in Cangas, there are 4WD taxi services that can manage some of the mountain tracks. Several of these offer 4WD day trips in the Picos for typically €50 per person. A regular taxi costs €28 from Cangas de Onís to the Lagos de Covadonga, about €20 from Arenas de Cabrales to Sotres, or Potes to Fuente Dé, and about €80 from Caín to Cangas de Onís or Potes.

Western Picos

ARRIONDAS

POP 2600 / ELEV 85M

The ordinary little town of Arriondas is the starting point for highly popular and fun canoe trips down the pretty Río Sella to various end points between Toraño and Llovio (7km to 16km). A dozen agencies in town will rent you a canoe, paddle, life jacket and waterproof container, show you how to paddle and bring you back to Arriondas at the end. This stretch of the Sella has a few entertaining minor rapids, but it's not a serious white-water affair, and anyone from about eight years old can enjoy the outing. The standard charge, including a picnic lunch, is €25 per person. Starting time is normally from 11am to 1pm. Bring a change of clothes. Agencies in Cangas de Onís and nearby coastal towns offer much the same deal, including transport to Arriondas and return.

Arriondas is mayhem on the first weekend in August when tens of thousands of people converge for the Descenso Internacional del Sella (p488), an international canoeing event that sees around 1500 serious canoeists starting off downriver to Ribadesella at noon on the Saturday, followed by many more fun paddlers later in the day.

🛏 Sleeping & Eating

TOP CHOICE **Posada del Valle** RURAL HOTEL €€
(☑985 84 11 57; www.posadadelvalle.com; r €64-77; ⊙Apr-Oct; 🅿🛜🍴) This remarkable place, in a beautiful valley setting 3km north of town, just past Collía village, is not only a charming rural retreat and a wonderful base for walkers, but also a multifaceted sustainable-living experience. The hotel, run by a British family, has its own organic farm, managed partly for wildflower conservation (there are over 350 flower species). About 35% of food served is home grown and all meals have a vegetarian option. The 12 rooms all have valley views, and design and decor emphasise local art and artisanry. Self-guided walking information is provided for the Picos de Europa and Asturias coast as well as the local area. Also on offer are various courses and workshops, including organic vegetarian cooking, felt-making, landscape 'walkshops' and Sense Experience (transformative learning for sustainable living).

Hotel La Estrada HOTEL €
(☑985 84 07 67; www.laestradahotel.com; Calle Inocencio del Valle 1; s/d incl breakfast €60/80; ⊙mid-Mar–Oct; 🛜) This bright and comfortable modern place in *indiano* style, a few steps off the main street, Avenida de Europa, is the most attractive option in the town itself.

El Corral del Indianu
CONTEMPORARY ASTURIAN €€€

(☑985 84 10 72; www.elcorraldelindianu.com; Avenida de Europa 14; mains €20-30; ⊙closed Sun & Wed dinner, Thu) The most original place for a feed, with a lovely garden for summertime meals. Inside, the decor is startling, with bare stone and contemporary art. If you're not up for the highly creative (and extensive) €75 tasting menu, you might start with oysters and follow up with a wild-boar-and-vegetables casserole.

CANGAS DE ONÍS
POP 4600 / ELEV 84M

Good King Pelayo, after his victory at Covadonga, moved about 12km down the hill to settle the base of his nascent Asturian kingdom at Cangas in AD 722. Cangas' big moment in history lasted 70 years or so, until the capital was moved to Pravia. Its second boom time arrived in the late 20th century with the invasion of Picos de Europa tourists. In August, especially, the largely modern and rather drab town is bursting with trekkers, campers and holidaymakers.

◉ Sights

Puente Romano
BRIDGE

Arching like a cat in fright, the so-called Roman Bridge that spans the Río Sella was actually built in the 13th century, but is no less beautiful for the mistaken identity. From it hangs a copy of the Cruz de la Victoria, the symbol of Asturias that resides in Oviedo's cathedral.

Capilla de Santa Cruz
CHAPEL

(Avenida Contranquil; admission €1; ⊙10am-1pm & 3-6.30pm Wed-Sun, reduced hours mid-Sep–mid-Jun) This tiny chapel was built in 1943 to replace an 8th-century predecessor (erected by Pelayo's son Favila) that was destroyed during the Spanish Civil War. The 1940s rebuilders discovered that the mound the chapel sits on was an artificial one containing a megalithic tomb 6000 years old, which can now be seen beneath the chapel's floor. Visits are guided in Spanish.

☆ Activities

Many agencies, including Los Cauces (☑985 94 73 18; www.loscauces.com; Avenida Covadonga 6) and the ubiquitous Cangas Aventura (☑985 84 92 61; www.cangasaventura. com; Avenida de Covadonga 17), offer a range of activities, including canoeing down the Río Sella from Arriondas (€25 per person), horse riding (per one/two hours €18/30), canyoning (€40 for three hours) and caving (€22 to €25 for two to 2½ hours).

🛌 Sleeping

Cangas has loads of hotels and a few *pensiones*, many of which almost halve their high-season rates from about mid-September to June. There are plenty more places, including numerous *casas rurales*, in nearby villages such as Soto de Cangas, Mestas de Con and Benia de Onís, all along the road towards Arenas de Cabrales.

Hotel Nochendi
HOTEL €€

(☑985 84 95 13; www.hotelnochendi.com; Calle de Constantino González 4; r €100; 🐾) Occupying one floor of an apartment block beside the Río Güeña, this is a lovely surprise and easy to feel at home in. The spacious, bright, white rooms feature spot lighting, hanging lamps and a touch of modern art, and most have river views.

Parador de Cangas de Onís
HISTORIC HOTEL €€€

(☑985 84 94 02; www.parador.es; s/d incl breakfast €133/166; P✳🐾) Cangas' *parador* (luxurious state-owned hotel) stands by the Río Sella in Villanueva, 3km northwest of Cangas towards Arriondas. The main building was originally a monastery, built between the 12th and 18th centuries: some rooms are former monks' cells (suitably upgraded!). Check the website for offers. The adjoining monastery church, the Iglesia de San Pedro, is embellished with very unusual medieval carvings depicting sins and the story of the early Asturian king Favila's death.

Hotel Puente Romano
HOTEL €€

(☑985 85 94 59; www.hotelimperion.com/puente romano; Calle del Puente Romano; r €75; ⊙closed mid-Oct–Easter; P🐾) An 1880s Asturian mansion, much remodelled inside but still with a good deal of original stone and wood, this is one of Cangas' more characterful hotels. Rooms are attractive and good-sized, and those on the 1st and 2nd floors are bright.

Hostal de Fermín
HOSTAL €

(☑676 015377, 985 94 75 62; www.casafermin.net; Paseo de Contranquil 3; d incl breakfast €64, apt for 4 €97; P🐾) This brick structure on the northern edge of town has bright, clean, simple rooms, five good, recently created apartments, and a popular summer *sidrería*. From the bus station, just walk 300m along the road to the right.

✗ Eating

TOP CHOICE El Molín de la
Pedrera   CONTEMPORARY ASTURIAN €€
(☑985 84 91 09; www.elmolin.com; Calle del Río
Güeña 2; dishes €9-21; ☺closed Tue dinner, Wed)
This stone-and-brick-walled, family-run eatery wins with both its traditional Asturian
dishes like *fabada* or *tortos de maíz* (maize
cakes) and more creative efforts like the
starter of filo pastry with Cabrales cheese
and hazelnuts, or the delicious home-made
desserts. The meat dishes are generally excellent, and welcoming service and good
wines complete a top dining experience

Los Arcos   ASTURIAN €€
(☑985 84 92 77; Avenida Covadonga 17; mains
€17-36) Entered through a cider bar on the
main street, Los Arcos offers a few expensive gourmet items such as young veal with
'ecological micro-vegetables', but pulls a lot
of its punters in with its excellent-value €15
set menu, available for dinner and lunch.

❶ Information

Tourist office (☑985 84 80 05; www.cangas
deonis.com; Avenida de Covadonga 1; ☺9am-
9pm)

COVADONGA
POP 70 / ELEV 260M

The importance of Covadonga, 12km southeast of Cangas de Onís, lies in what it represents rather than what it is. Somewhere
hereabouts, in approximately AD 722, the
Muslims received their first defeat in Spain,
at the hands of the Visigothic nobleman
Pelayo – an event considered to be the beginning of the 800-year Reconquista.

The place is an object of pilgrimage, for
in a cave here, the Santa Cueva, the Virgin
supposedly appeared to Pelayo's warriors before the battle. On weekends and in summer
long queues of the faithful and curious line
up to enter the cave, now with a chapel installed. The Fuente de Siete Caños spring,
by the pool below the cave, supposedly ensures marriage within one year to women
who drink from it.

Landslides destroyed much of Covadonga in the 19th century and the main
church, the Basílica de Covadonga, is a
neo-Romanesque affair built between 1877
and 1901. Nearby is the extensive Museo
de Covadonga (☑985 84 60 96; adult/senior
& child €2.50/1.50; ☺10.30am-2pm & 4-6.30pm
Wed-Mon), devoted to Covadonga history and
gifts from the faithful.

LAGOS DE COVADONGA

Don't let summer crowds deter you from
continuing 10km uphill past Covadonga to
these two beautiful twin lakes. Most of the
trippers don't get past patting a few cows'
noses near the lakes, so walking here is as
nice as anywhere else in the Picos. At peak
visitor periods the road to the lakes is closed
to private vehicles, but a shuttle bus runs
from Cangas de Onís.

Lago de Enol is the first lake you reach,
with the main car park just past it. It's linked
to Lago de la Ercina, 1km away, not only by
the paved road but also by a footpath via the
Centro de Visitantes Pedro Pidal (☺10am-
6pm mid-Mar–mid-Dec), which has displays on
Picos flora and fauna. There are rustic restaurants near both lakes, closed in winter.

When mist descends, the lakes, surrounded by the green pasture and bald rock that
characterise this part of the Picos, take on an
eerie appearance.

WALKS FROM THE LAKES

A marked circuit walk, the Ruta de los Lagos (PR-PNPE2; about 2½ hours), takes in
the two lakes, the visitors centre and an old
mine, the Minas de Buferrera. About 400m
south of Lago de Enol, the route passes the
Refugio Vega de Enol (☑622 203897, 985
94 28 28; www.elrefugiovegadeenol.com; dm €10;
☺year-round), whose 10 bunks are the nearest accommodation to the lakes. It has hot
showers, serves basic meals (€6 to €8), and
is reachable by vehicle.

Two other relatively easy trails will take
you a bit further afield. The PR-PNPE4 leads
about 5km southeast from Lago de la Ercina, with an ascent of 600m, to the Vega de
Ario, where the Refugio Vega de Ario (Refugio Marqués de Villaviciosa; ☑656 843095, 984 09
20 00; www.refugiovegadeario.es; dm €12; ☺Jun-
Oct; ☏) has bunks for 34 people, plus meal
service. The reward for about 2½ hours'
effort in getting there is magnificent views
across the Garganta del Cares to the Picos'
Macizo Central.

The PR-PNPE5 takes you roughly south
from Lago de Enol to the 68-place Refugio
de Vegarredonda (☑626 343366, 985 92 29
52; www.vegarredonda.com; dm €12; ☺Mar-Nov),
with meal service, and on to the Mirador
de Ordiales, a lookout point over a 1km
sheer drop into the Valle de Angón. It's
about a 3½-hour walk each way – relatively
easy along a mule track as far as the *refugio*, then a little more challenging on up to
the mirador. Track conditions permitting,

PICOS WILDLIFE

Although a few wolves survive in the Picos and the odd brown bear might wander through, far more common is the *rebeco* (chamois), some 6000 of which skip around the rocks and steep slopes. Deer, badgers, wild boar, squirrels and martens, in various quantities, inhabit wooded areas.

Eagles, hawks and other raptors soar in the Picos' skies. Keep your eyes peeled for the majestic *águila real* (golden eagle) and the huge scavenging *buitre leonado* (griffon vulture). Choughs, with their unmistakable caws, accompany walkers at high altitudes.

drivers can save about 40 minutes by driving as far as the Pandecarmen car park, 2km from Lago de Enol.

SOUTH FROM CANGAS DE ONÍS

The N625 south from Cangas de Onís follows the Río Sella upstream through one of the most extraordinary defiles in Europe. The road through the **Desfiladero de los Beyos** gorge is a remarkable feat of engineering. Towards the southern end of the defile, you cross from Asturias into Castilla y León. About 6km later a left turn leads 4km north to the pretty hamlet of **Soto de Sajambre**, a good base for hikers with a handful of sleeping options. Walks from here include La Senda del Arcediano (GR-201), a very scenic trip of five or six hours north to Amieva, manageable by most walkers, and a more difficult trail east to Posada de Valdeón.

Central Picos

A star attraction of the Picos' central massif is the gorge that divides it from the western Macizo El Cornión. The popular Garganta del Cares (Cares Gorge) trail can be busy in summer, but the walk is always an exciting experience. This part of the Picos also has plenty of less heavily tramped paths and climbing challenges. Arenas de Cabrales is a popular base with a lot of accommodation, but Poncebos, Sotres, Bulnes and Caín also have sleeping options.

ARENAS DE CABRALES
POP 830 / ELEV 135M

Arenas lies at the confluence of the bubbling Ríos Cares and Casaño, 30km east of Cangas de Onís. The busy main road is lined with hotels, restaurants and bars, and just off it lies a little tangle of quiet squares and back lanes. You can learn all about the fine smelly Cabrales cheese at Arenas' **Museu del Quesu** (Cueva del Cabrales; ☑985 84 67 02; www.fundacioncabrales.com; adult/child €4.50/3; ⏱10am-2pm & 4-8pm, reduced hours Oct-Mar), a cheese-cave museum 500m from the centre on the Poncebos road, with 45-minute guided visits in Spanish.

Buses stop in front of the **tourist office** (☑660 405774; www.cabralesturismo.com; ⏱4-9pm Tue-Sat, 10am-2pm Sun, closed Sun-Thu mid-Sep–Jun), in the middle of town opposite the junction of the Poncebos road.

🛏 Sleeping & Eating

The large number of places to stay and eat here keeps prices healthily competitive.

Hotel Rural El Torrejón　　　HOTEL €
(☑985 84 64 11; www.eltorrejon.com; s/d incl breakfast €35/57; ⏱closed mid-Dec–mid-Jan; 🅿🛜) This friendly, family-run country house welcomes the weary traveller with tastefully decorated rooms in a rural style and some original colour schemes. It's good value and the setting is idyllic, beside the Río Casaño a couple of minutes' walk from the village centre.

Hotel Rural El Ardinal　　　HOTEL €€
(☑985 84 64 34; www.ardinal.com; Barriu del Riu; r €65; ⏱closed Jan & Feb; 🅿🛜) In a lovely tranquil spot with good views, this small, cosy hotel offers rooms with a cottagey feel (plenty of wood, wrought iron and flowery prints) and a warm sitting room-cum-bar with a fireplace. It's on the north edge of Arenas, 400m up a lane opposite the central Restaurante Cares.

Hostal Naturaleza　　　PENSIÓN €
(☑985 84 64 87; s/d incl breakfast €25/40; 🅿🛜) About 600m along the road to Poncebos, this quiet little house has a series of smallish but well-scrubbed rooms.

Camping Naranjo de Bulnes　CAMPGROUND €
(☑985 84 65 78; campingnaranjobulnes@yahoo.es; sites per 2 people, car & tent €25; ⏱closed Nov-mid-Mar; 🅿) A large and efficiently run camping ground in a riverside chestnut grove, 1.5km along the Panes road.

TOP CHOICE Restaurante Cares ASTURIAN €€

(☑985 84 66 28; mains €14-22, menus €15; ☺closed Mon Oct-May) Beside the Poncebos junction on the main road, this is one of the best-value restaurants for miles around. It does a great-value *menú de noche* in addition to a *menú del día*, as well as *platos combinados* and à la carte fish and meat dishes. Dig into a hearty *cachopo* (veal steak stuffed with ham and cheese) and finish with *delicias de limón* (between lemon mousse and yoghurt).

GARGANTA DEL CARES

Ten kilometres of well-maintained path (the PR-PNPE3) high above the Río Cares between Poncebos and Caín constitute, perhaps unfortunately, the most popular mountain walk in Spain; in August the experience can be akin to London's Oxford St on a Saturday morning. But the walk is still a spectacular and at times vertiginous excursion along the gorge separating two of the Picos' three massifs. If you're feeling fit (or need to get back to your car), it's quite possible to walk the whole 10km and return in one (somewhat tiring) day's outing; it takes six to seven hours plus stops. A number of agencies in Picos towns will transport you to either end of the walk and pick you up at the other end, usually for €35 to €50 per person.

PONCEBOS

Poncebos, a tiny straggle of buildings at the northern end of the Cares gorge, is set amid already spectacular scenery. A side-road uphill from here leads 1.5km to the hamlet of Camarmeña, where there's a lookout with views to El Naranjo de Bulnes in the Macizo Central.

Poncebos' eight-room Hotel Garganta del Cares (☑985 84 64 63; www.hotelgarganta delcares.com; Calle de Poncebos; s/d incl breakfast €38/62; ☺closed Dec & Jan; P🛜) offers the beds and meals (*menú del día* €10) that are the closest to the Garganta del Cares trail. Rooms are simple, clean and comfy, with twin beds. The slightly fancier Hotel Mirador de Cabrales (☑985 84 66 73; www.arcea hoteles.com; r €85; ☺closed approx mid-Sep–Easter; P) stands next door.

GARGANTA DEL CARES WALK

By doing the walk from north to south, you save the best till last. Follow the 'Ruta de Cares' sign pointing uphill about 700m along the road from the top end of Poncebos. The beginning involves a steady climb in the wide and mostly bare early stages of the gorge. After about 3km you'll reach some abandoned houses. A little further and you're over the highest point of the walk. You should encounter a couple of drink stands along the way (the stuff is transported by horse).

As you approach the regional boundary with Castilla y León, the gorge becomes narrower and its walls thick with vegetation, creating greater contrast with the alpine heights above. The last stages of the walk are possibly the prettiest, and as you descend nearer the valley floor, you pass through a series of low, wet tunnels to emerge at the end of the gorge among the meadows of Caín.

CAÍN

If you're coming from the south, the trailhead of the Cares walk is at the hamlet of Caín, where the narrow (and picturesque) road from Posada de Valdeón comes to an end. There's a handful of simple places to stay – Hostal La Ruta (☑987 74 27 02; r €50; 🛜), with clean, reasonable-sized rooms, is closest to the gorge and one of the best – plus several restaurants offering very similar lunch menus for €11. More lodgings are in the villages south of Caín, including Cordiñanes and the rather drab Posada de Valdeón.

BULNES

POP 22 / ELEV 647M

The hamlet of Bulnes, inaccessible by road, sits high up a side-valley off the Cares Gorge, south of Poncebos. You can get there by a quite strenuous uphill walk of about two hours or by riding the Funicular de Bulnes (☑985 84 68 00; one way/return adult €16.80/21.10, child €4.10/6.40; ☺10am-8pm Easter & mid-Jun–mid-Sep, 10am-12.30pm & 2-6pm rest of year; ♿), a tunnel railway that climbs steeply for 2km up inside the mountain from its lower station just below Poncebos. The funicular makes the seven-minute trip every half-hour in both directions.

Bulnes is divided into two parts, the upper Barrio del Castillo and the lower La Villa. All amenities are in La Villa, including an attractive six-room *casa rural*, La Casa del Chiflón (☑608 181581, 985 84 59 43; www.casa delchiflon.com; s/d/tr incl breakfast €45/60/75; ☺closed mid Oct–Easter; 🛜), and Bar Bulnes (☑985 84 59 34; raciones €4-11; ☺10am-8pm Easter & Jul-Sep, 10am-6pm rest of year, closed Mon-Fri Jan & Feb), with good home cooking.

You can also approach Bulnes from the east by walking about one hour down from the Collado de Pandébano.

SOTRES
POP 130 / ELEV 1045M

A side road heads up 11km from Poncebos to Sotres, the highest village in the Picos and the starting point for a number of good walks. There are half a dozen places to stay, most with their own restaurants.

Casa Cipriano (☑985 94 50 24; www. casacipriano.com; s/d €30/45; ◴closed Jan; 🤶) is a long-time haunt of mountain aficionados. Aside from 14 simple but cheerful rooms, it offers a professional mountain-and-caving guide service and a simple restaurant.

Hotel Peña Castil (☑985 94 50 49; www. hotelpenacastil.com; s/d incl breakfast €40/60; 🤶) has 10 smallish but impeccable rooms in a renovated stone house. They have graciously tiled floors and half-stone walls, and some have perky balconies.

WALKS AROUND SOTRES

A popular route goes east to the village of Tresviso and on down to Urdón, on the Potes–Panes road. As far as Tresviso (10km) it's a paved road, but the final 7km is a dramatic walking trail, the Ruta de Tresviso (PR-PNPE30), snaking 850m down to the Desfiladero de la Hermida gorge. Doing this in the upward direction, starting from Urdón, is at least as popular.

Many walkers head west from Sotres to the Collado de Pandébano, one to 1½ hours' walk away on the far side of the Duje valley. At Pandébano the 2519m rock finger called El Naranjo de Bulnes (Pico Urriello) comes into view – an emblem of the Picos de Europa and a classic challenge for climbers. Few walkers can resist the temptation to get even closer to El Naranjo. From Pandébano it's about three hours, with 700m of ascent, up the PR-PNPE21 trail to the Vega de Urriello, at the foot of the mountain. Here the 96-bunk Refugio Vega de Urriello (☑650 780381, 985 92 52 00; www.fempa.net; dm €12; ◴mid-Mar–mid-Dec) is attended, with meal service, nine months of the year.

Otherwise, you can descend for about an hour west from Pandébano to Bulnes.

Eastern Picos

The AS114 east from Cangas and Arenas meets the N621, running south from the coast, at the humdrum town of Panes. South of Panes, the N621 to Potes follows the Río Deva upstream through the impressive Desfiladero de la Hermida gorge. You cross into Cantabria at Urdón, 2km before the hamlet of La Hermida, which has a couple of *pensiones*.

LEBEÑA

About 8.5km south of La Hermida, 600m east off the N621, stands the fascinating little Iglesia de Santa María de Lebeña (admission €1; ◴10am-1.30pm & 4-7.30pm Tue-Sun; 🅿), built in the 9th or 10th century. The horseshoe arches in the church are a telltale sign of its Mozarabic style – rarely seen this far north in Spain. The floral motifs on the columns are Visigothic, while below the main *retablo* (altarpiece) stands a Celtic stone engraving. They say the yew tree outside (finally reduced to a sad stump by a storm in 2007) was planted 1000 years ago.

POTES
POP 1470 / ELEV 291M

Overrun in peak periods, but with some charm in the old town centre, Potes is a popular staging post on the southeastern edge of the Picos, with the Macizo Andara rising close at hand. Potes is effectively the 'capital' of Liébana, a beautifully verdant valley area lying between the Picos and the main spine of the Cordillera Cantábrica. The heart of town is a cluster of bridges, towers and quaint back streets restored in traditional slate, wood and red tile after considerable damage during the civil war. Beside the medieval San Cayetano bridge, the squat Torre del Infantado (◴10am-2pm & 4-6pm Mon-Fri) is now the town hall, with an amazingly modern interior inside its 15th-century shell.

Monasterio de Santo Toribio de Liébana
MONASTERY

(http://santotoribiodeliebana.com; admission free; ◴10am-2pm & 4-7pm; 🅿) Christian refugees, fleeing from Muslim-occupied Spain to Liébana in the 8th century, brought with them the Lígnum Crucis, purportedly the single biggest chunk of Christ's cross and featuring the hole made by the nail that passed through Christ's left hand. The holy relic has been housed ever since in the Santo Toribio Monastery, 3km west of Potes, and is an extraordinary magnet for the faithful. It's kept inside a crucifix of gold-plated silver in a lavish 18th-century baroque chapel off the monastery's austere Gothic church.

POTES TO POSADA DE VALDEÓN

Drivers will be well rewarded by a trip around the southern approaches to the Picos, and there are a couple of great places to stay off the N621 as it winds through verdant Liébana not far south of Potes. They provide info on local walks and make good bases for the eastern and southern Picos.

A turn 5km from Potes leads 4.5km up to the pretty hamlet of Tudes, where you'll find English-owned **La Casa de las Chimeneas** (☑942 73 63 00; www.lacasadelaschimeneas. es; 2-bedroom apt per week late Jul-Aug €945-1050, rest of year per night €80-125; [P][🕏][✲][🏐]), an old farmstead converted into eight very comfy, well equipped and characterful apartments. Most are on two or three levels. Enjoy the curved infinity pool, fabulous views, and drinks and light meals in the equally original **Taberna del Inglés** (⊙closed Mon-Thu Nov-Apr) across the street.

Posada de Cucayo (☑942 73 62 46; www.laposadadecucayo.com; s incl breakfast €45-51, d incl breakfast €56-65; ⊙closed mid-Jan–mid-Feb; [P][🕏]) sits over 900m high in little **Cucayo** village, at the top of a lovely 12km drive up from the crossroads hamlet of La Vega de Liébana. Around you are scarred mountain peaks and green fields below. Eleven of the 12 spacious, tasteful rooms at this marvellous little family-run hotel enjoy sweeping views. The farm next door provides a lot of the meat, eggs or vegetables you'll eat in their good-value restaurant, and you can help milk the cows if you truly want a taste of rural bliss!

From La Vega de Liébana, the N621 southwest rises to the **Puerto de San Glorio** pass (1609m), where you enter Castilla y León. In clear weather the 2km detour to the panoramic **Mirador de Llesba** is very worthwhile. The N621 drops down quickly on the Castilian side of the frontier. From **Portilla de la Reina**, take a narrow and pretty country road northwest across the **Puerto de Pandetrave** (1562m) to Santa María de Valdeón and **Posada de Valdeón**, where you are at the southern gateway to the Picos.

Head of the monastery in the latter half of the 8th century was Beato de Liébana, celebrated around medieval Europe for his beautifully illustrated *Commentary on the Apocalypse*. Copies of this tome were distributed throughout Europe and came to be known as Beatos. Around 25 survive today, but the original was lost.

You can drive 500m past the monastery to the tiny **Ermita de San Miguel**, a chapel with great valley and Picos views.

🛏 Sleeping, Eating & Drinking

Potes' dozen or so places to stay are mostly simple, straightforward places.

Casa Cayo HOSTAL €
(☑942 73 01 50; www.casacayo.com; Calle Cántabra 6; s/d €35/45; 🕏) This is the best value in Potes, with helpful service and attractive, comfy, wood-beamed rooms. Ask for room 206, 207 or 305 if you'd like to look down on the burbling river below. You can eat well in the restaurant (mains €7 to €17), which has particularly good meat such as *solomillo* (sirloin) with blue Tresviso cheese or the local speciality *lechazo asado* (roast young lamb or kid).

Hotel Picos de Valdecoro HOTEL €€
(☑942 73 00 25; hotelvaldecoro@hotmail.com; Calle Roscabado; s/d incl breakfast €48/75; [P][🕏]) For slightly more than Potes' typical comfort levels, try this 43-room hotel 500m north of the town centre. The ample, pleasingly uncluttered rooms are all exterior. Those in the rear half have a more old-fashioned style but are still clean and comfy. The sign on the road frontage says Restaurante Paco Wences, which is the hotel's restaurant.

Bar Los Camachos BAR
(Plaza Llano; ⊙9am-midnight) For a drop of real local flavour, duck into this shabby but friendly establishment for a shot or two of the *orujo* – a potent liquor made from grape pressings that is found throughout northwest Spain and is something of a Potes speciality. The family makes several varieties, including one flavoured with honey from their own bees.

ℹ Information

Tourist office (☑942 73 81 26; Plaza de la Independencia; ⊙10am-2pm & 3.30-6pm) In the deconsecrated Iglesia de San Vicente, a nice example of rustic 14th-century Gothic architecture (with an exhibition hall).

POTES TO FUENTE DÉ

The CA185 from Potes to Fuente Dé is a beautiful 23km trip, and is dotted with several hotels, *hostales* and campgrounds. At San Pelayo, 5km from Potes, Posada San Pelayo (☎942 73 32 10; www.posadasanpelayo. com; s/d €65/81; P🛜📶) is a friendly, family-run *casa rural,* of recent construction but in traditional country style. Its spacious rooms come in cheerful colours, and there are ample common areas and a lovely garden with great mountain views.

Hotel del Oso (☎942 73 30 18; www.hotel deloso.com; s/d €68/85; ⊗closed Jan–mid-Feb; P🛜📶) in Cosgaya, 13km southwest of Potes, comprises majestic twin stone houses facing each other across the Río Deva and the road. Spacious rooms with timber floors and finishings are very inviting, the restaurant (mains €10 to €22, menu €23) is one of the area's best, with top-quality meat and desserts, and there's a lovely big outdoor pool.

FUENTE DÉ & THE TELEFÉRICO

At 1078m, Fuente Dé lies at the foot of the stark southern wall of the Macizo Central. In four minutes the dramatic Teleférico de Fuente Dé (☎942 73 66 10; www.cantur.com; adult/child return €15.50/6; ⊗9am-8pm Easter & Jul–mid-Sep, 10am-6pm rest of year, closed early Jan–mid-Feb) cable car whisks people 753m up to the top of that wall, from where walkers and climbers can make their way deeper into the central massif.

Be warned that during the high season (especially August) you can wait an hour or more for a place in the cable car, going up or down.

🏃 Activities

It's a 3.5km walk from the top of the *teleférico* to the Hotel Áliva, where you can get refreshments. From the hotel two 4WD tracks descend into the valley that separates the central massif from its eastern cousin. The first winds its way 7km south down to Espinama on the CA185 (about 2½ hours' walking); the other heads north to Sotres via Vegas de Sotres (about two hours' walking).

Other possibilities for the suitably prepared include making your way across the massif to El Naranjo de Bulnes or climbing Peña Vieja (2613m). These require proper equipment and experience – Peña Vieja has claimed more lives than any other mountain in the Picos. Less exacting is the PR-PNPE23, a route of about 5.5km northwest from the *teleférico,* passing below Peña Vieja to the foot of the Horcados Rojos crags, with an ascent of 500m. It takes about 4½ hours there and back.

🛏 Sleeping & Eating

Hotel Rebeco　　　　　　　　　　HOTEL €€
(☎942 73 66 01; www.hotelrebeco.com; s/d incl breakfast €54/70; P🛜📶) Many of the 30 rooms in this handsome stone lodge at Fuente Dé have mountain views, and 11 (most with rear view) include loft levels suitable for kids. It has a good, reasonably priced restaurant and you can't help but admire owner Conchi Cuesta's tapestries!

Hotel Áliva　　　　　　　　　　HOTEL €€
(☎942 73 09 99; www.cantur.com; s/d €47.50/75.75; ⊗mid-Jun–mid-Oct) Set 1700m high, this 27-room mountain lodge features a cafe and restaurant as well as a sun deck. It's linked by 4WD tracks to the top of the *teleférico* (which is operated by the same company, Cantur) and to Espinama and Sotres. Packages including transport are offered.

Santiago de Compostela & Galicia

Best Places to Eat

» La Casa de las 5 Puertas (p536)

» O Fragón (p521)

» Restaurante Bitadorna (p542)

» Hotel Orillamar (p530)

» La Taberna de Rotilio (p537)

Best Places to Stay

» Casa de Trillo (p521)

» Hotel Herbeira (p529)

» Parador de Santo Estevo (p547)

» Hotel Rústico Ínsula Finisterrae (p521)

» Nagari (p539)

Why Go?

Galicia's spiritual, cultural and official capital is Santiago de Compostela, the destination of tens of thousands of pilgrims who set out every year on the famous Camino de Santiago. This magical medieval city still has a palpable aura of the Middle Ages.

But Galicia, a unique region with its own language and distinctive culture, is much more than Santiago. The wild coastline is frayed up and down its 1200km length by majestic *rías* (inlets or estuaries), and strung with cliffs, sandy beaches, islands and fishing ports that bring in indisputably the best seafood in Spain. Then there's the interior, a labyrinth of valleys and hills, green as Ireland and dotted with half-forgotten, stone-built villages, twisting country lanes and aged monasteries. Galicia isn't all lost in the past either. Buzzing cities like A Coruña, Vigo and Lugo are contemporary cultural and commercial hubs with nocturnal lives as heady as anywhere in the country.

When to Go
Santiago de Compostela

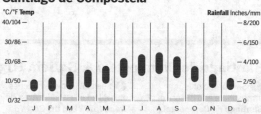

Jun & Sep No peak-season crowds or prices but (hopefully) decent weather.

Jul Dance a jig at the Festival Ortigueira, Spain's biggest Celtic music festival.

24 Jul Spectacular fireworks end Santiago de Compostela's celebration for the Día de Santiago.

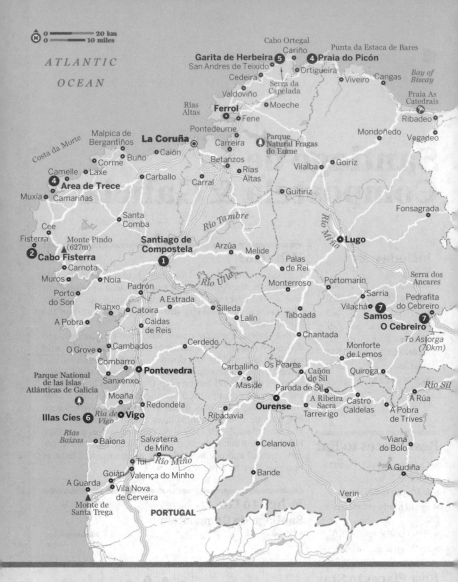

Santiago de Compostela & Galicia Highlights

1 Savour the unique atmosphere and history of **Santiago de Compostela** (p509)

2 Gaze towards America at Spain's 'Land's End', **Cabo Fisterra** (p520)

3 Feast on freshly caught **seafood**, anywhere near the coast

4 Seek out remote beaches on rugged coasts, like **Area de Trece** (p522) on the Costa da Morte or the Rías Altas' **Praia do Picón** (p530)

5 Stand atop southern Europe's highest sea cliffs at the **Garita de Herbeira** (p529)

6 Sail out to the pristine beaches and walking trails of the spectacular, traffic-free **Illas Cíes** (p540)

7 Follow the Camino de Santiago down from the heights of **O Cebreiro** (p546) to the monastery at **Samos** (p546)

History

EARLY CIVILISATIONS

Early Galicians built many dolmens (megalithic tombs) and Iron Age *castros* (protected settlements of circular stone huts). Many such monuments can be visited today. Most Galicians say the *castro*-builders were Celts, though sceptics claim that supposed Celtic origins are an invention by romantic Galician nationalists.

The Romans pacified 'Gallaecia' (which also included what's now northern Portugal) in the 1st century BC, founding cities like Lucus Augusti (Lugo). The Germanic Suevi conquered the region in AD 409, before the Visigoths asserted control in the 580s.

MIDDLE AGES

After the Muslim invasion in 711, the Iberian Peninsula's sole surviving Christian kingdom, Asturias, soon drew Galicia into its ambit. Galicia remained within the Asturian kingdom and its successors, León and Castilla, thereafter, apart from brief independent spells in the 10th and 11th centuries.

The area's big event in medieval times was the 'rediscovery' of the grave of Santiago Apóstol (St James the Apostle) in about 814, at what would become Santiago de Compostela. The site grew into a rallying symbol for the Christian Reconquista of Spain, and pilgrims from all over Europe began trekking to Santiago, which came to rival Rome and even Jerusalem as a pilgrimage site.

But by the time the Reconquista was completed in 1492, Galicia had become an impoverished backwater, where Spain's centralist-minded Catholic Monarchs, Isabel and Fernando, had already begun to supplant the local tongue and traditions with Castilian culture.

MODERN GALICIA

The Rexurdimento, an awakening of Galician national consciousness, surfaced late in the 19th century, but then suffered a 40-year interruption during the Franco era. In the 19th and 20th centuries, hundreds of thousands of impoverished Galicians departed on transatlantic ships in search of a better life in Latin America.

Things looked up after democracy returned to Spain in the 1970s. Galicia today is an important fishing, shipbuilding and agricultural region and has more ports than any other region of the EU. The labyrinthine coastline, incidentally, serves as a major

European entry point for South American cocaine.

Thanks to their distinctive culture and history of isolation from the centre, most Galicians today see their region as somewhat apart from the rest of Spain, though only a tiny minority want independence.

Language

Most Galicians speak both Spanish (Castilian) and the separate Galician language (Galego or, in Castilian, Gallego). Galician is a Romance language that is close to Portuguese and slightly less so to Castilian. In this chapter we use the place names you're most likely to encounter during your travels. By and large, these are Galician.

Santiago de Compostela

POP 79,000 / ELEV 260M

Locals say the arcaded, stone streets of Santiago de Compostela are at their most beautiful in the rain, when the old city glistens. Most would agree, however, that it's hard to catch the Galician capital in a bad pose. Whether you're wandering the medieval streets of the old city, nibbling on tapas in the taverns, or gazing down at the rooftops from atop the cathedral, Santiago seduces.

The faithful believe that Santiago Apóstol (St James the Apostle) preached in Galicia and, after his death in Palestine, was brought back by stone boat and buried here. The tomb was supposedly rediscovered in about 814 by a religious hermit following a guiding star (hence, it's thought, 'Compostela' – from the Latin *campus stellae*, field of the star). The Asturian king Alfonso II had a church erected above the holy remains, pilgrims began flocking to it and by the

Santiago de Compostela

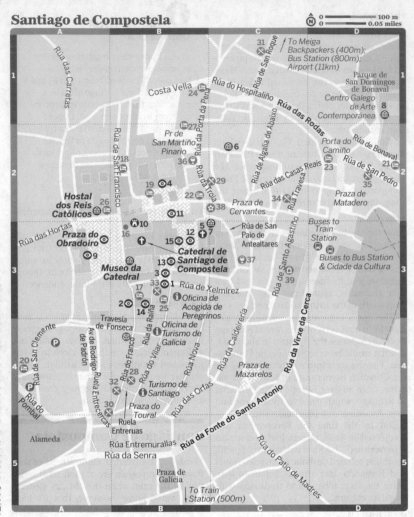

11th century the pilgrimage was becoming a major European phenomenon, bringing a flood of funds into the city. Bishop Gelmírez obtained archbishopric status for Santiago in 1100 and added numerous churches in the 12th century. The following few centuries, however, were marked by squabbling between rival nobles, and Santiago gradually slipped into the background.

Only since the 1980s, as capital of the autonomous region of Galicia and a rediscovered tourist and pilgrimage destination, has the city been revitalised. Today an average of 150,000 pilgrims and countless thousands of other visitors make the journey here each year. The biggest numbers hit the city in July and August, but Santiago has a festive atmosphere throughout the warmer half of the year. If you'd like to enjoy the place less than jam-packed, May, June and September are good months to come. For more on the Camino de Santiago pilgrim trail, see p45.

Praza de Galicia marks the boundary between the Old Town and the Ensanche (Extension), the 20th-century shopping and residential area to its south.

Santiago de Compostela

◎ Sights

Among Santiago's greatest pleasures are simply wandering its arcaded streets and drifting in and out of the tapas bars along Rúas Franco and Raíña.

Catedral de Santiago de Compostela CATHEDRAL

(www.catedraldesantiago.es; Praza do Obradoiro; ◎7am-9pm) The grand heart of Santiago, the cathedral soars above the city centre in a splendid jumble of moss-covered spires and statues. Built piecemeal over several centuries, its beauty is a mix of Romanesque with baroque and Gothic flourishes. What you see today is actually the fourth church to stand on this spot. The bulk of it was built between 1075 and 1211, in Romanesque style, with a traditional Latin-cross layout and three naves. Much of the 'bunting' (the domes, statues and endless trimmings) came later. The lavish baroque facade facing Praza do Obradoiro was erected in the 18th century partly to protect the original Romanesque entrance, the Pórtico de la Gloria.

The Obradoiro facade is also the cathedral's main entrance, but owing to restoration work inside, it is likely to be closed until at least 2014. In the meantime, most people enter through the south door on Praza das Praterías (beneath the only facade that conserves its original Romanesque structure).

The artistically unparalleled Pórtico de la Gloria (Galician: Porta da Gloria), just inside the Obradoiro entrance, features 200 Romanesque sculptures by Maestro Mateo, who was placed in charge of the cathedral-building program in the late 12th century. The exact meaning of all these detailed and inspired sculptures is much debated, but they add up to a comprehensive review of major figures from the Bible, with the Old Testament on the left (looking from the Obradoiro doorway), the New Testament on the right, and glory and resurrection depicted in the central archway. The restoration work

ℹ TURGALICIA

Galicia's official tourism website, www.turgalicia.es, is an encyclopedic reference for visitors, available in nine languages. It includes an online booking service for many of the region's attractive rural accommodation options.

means, unfortunately, that you may well find the portico partly shrouded in scaffolding.

The main figure in the portico's central archway is a throned, resurrected Christ, surrounded by the four Evangelists plus angels and symbols of Jesus' passion. In an arc above are the 24 musicians said in Revelations to sit around the heavenly throne. Below Christ's feet is Santiago, and below him Hercules (holding open the mouths of two lions). On the other side of the central pillar is Maestro Mateo. For centuries, tradition called for visitors to bump heads with the maestro to acquire some of his genius. But countless knocks led to Mateo's notably flat nose, and he is now blocked off behind a metal barrier. Another tradition called for a brief prayer as visitors placed their fingers in the five holes above Hercules' head, created by the repetition of this very act by millions of faithful over the centuries. Hercules too is now blocked off.

The large, remarkably lifelike figures on the right-hand pillars of the portico are apostles, while those on the left-hand pillars are Old Testament prophets. The very bright smile on the prophet Daniel's face is, in popular belief, reckoned to be caused by the tightly dressed figure of Queen Esther opposite him. Local lore also has it that Esther's stone breasts were originally much larger, but were filed down on orders of a disapproving bishop – to which cheeky townspeople responded by inventing Galicia's cone-shaped *tetilla* (nipple) cheese in Esther's honour.

Towards the far (west) end of the cathedral's main nave, to the right of the fantastically elaborate, churrigueresque **Altar Mayor** (Main Altar), a small staircase leads up to a 13th-century **statue of Santiago**, which the faithful queue up to kiss or embrace. From here you emerge on the left side, then descend some steps to contemplate the **Cripta Apostólica**, which we are assured is Santiago's tomb. Behind the Altar Mayor is the **Puerta Santa** (Holy Door; Praza das Praterías), which opens onto Praza da Quintana and is cracked open only in holy years (next in 2021).

A special pilgrims' Mass is usually celebrated at noon daily, with other Masses usually at 9.30am or 10am daily, 1.15pm Sunday, 6pm Saturday and Sunday, and 7.30pm daily. Touristic visits are not allowed during these services.

Cathedral Rooftop Tour

(☑ 981 55 29 85; www.catedraldesantiago.es; tours per person €10; ⊙ 10am-2pm & 4-8pm) For unforgettable bird's-eye views of the cathedral interior, and of the city from the cathedral roof, take the rooftop tour, which starts in the **Pazo de Xelmírez** to the left of the cathedral's Obradoiro facade. This is also the only way to visit the Pazo de Xelmírez itself, dating from 1120, where the main banquet hall is adorned with exquisite little wall busts depicting feasters, musicians, kings and jugglers. The tours are popular, so go beforehand to reserve a time slot. Tours are given in English if there is enough demand, and the guides provide a good insight into Santiago's history.

Museo da Catedral   MUSEUM

(www.catedraldesantiago.es; Praza do Obradoiro; adult/child/student & pilgrim €5/free/3; ⊙ 10am-2pm & 4-8pm, closed Sun afternoon) The Cathedral Museum, entered to the right of the cathedral's Obradoiro facade, spreads over four floors and includes the cathedral's large, 16th-century, Gothic/plateresque cloister. You'll see a sizeable section of Maestro Mateo's original carved stone choir (destroyed in 1603 but recently pieced back together), an impressive collection of religious art (including the *botafumeiros*, in the 2nd-floor library), the lavishly decorated 18th-century *sala capitular* (chapter house) and, off the cloister, the Panteón de Reyes, with tombs of medieval León's kings.

Around the Cathedral   SQUARE

The cathedral is surrounded by handsome plazas that invite you to wander through them. The grand **Praza do Obradoiro** (Workshop Plaza) earned its name from the stonemasons' workshops set up there while the cathedral was being built. It's free of both traffic and cafes and has a unique atmosphere. At its northern end, the Renaissance **Hostal dos Reis Católicos** (admission €3; ⊙ noon-2pm & 4-6pm Sun-Fri) was built in the early 16th century by order of the Catholic Monarchs, Isabel and Fernando, as a refuge for pilgrims and a symbol of the crown's power in this ecclesiastical city. Today it shelters well-off travellers instead, as a *parador* (luxurious state owned hotel), but its four courtyards and some other areas are open to visitors. Along the western side of Praza do Obradoiro is the elegant 18th-century Pazo de Raxoi (Praza do Obradoiro), now the city hall.

South of the cathedral, stop in cafe-lined Praza de Fonseca to look into the Colexio de Fonseca (admission free; ⊙11am-2pm & 5-8.30pm Tue-Sat, 11am-2pm Sun) with a beautiful Renaissance courtyard; it was the original seat of Santiago's university (founded in 1495).

Around the corner, Praza das Praterías (Silversmiths' Square) is marked by the Fuente de los Caballos fountain (1829), with the cathedral's south facade at the top of the steps. Curiously, the Casa do Cabildo, on the lower side of the square, is no more than a 3m-deep facade, erected in 1758 to embellish the plaza.

Following the cathedral walls, you enter Praza da Quintana, lined by the long, stark wall of the Mosteiro de San Paio de Antealtares (Praza da Quintana), founded by Alfonso II for Benedictine monks to look after Santiago's relics. Inside its entrance at the top of the plaza steps, the Museo de Arte Sacra (Vía Sacra 5; admission €1.50; ⊙10.30am-1.30pm & 4-7pm Mon-Sat, 4-7pm Sun) contains the original altar raised over the Santiago relics.

The cathedral walls continue northwards to Praza da Inmaculada, where pilgrims arriving in Santiago via the Camino Francés (French Route) first set eyes on the cathedral. Opposite looms the huge Benedictine Mosteiro de San Martiño Pinario (Praza da Inmaculada), an austere baroque seminary.

Museo do Pobo Galego   MUSEUM
(Galician Folk Museum; www.museodopobo.es; Rúa San Domingos de Bonaval; adult/senior & student/child €3/1/free, Sun free; ⊙10am-2pm & 4-8pm Tue-Sat, 11am-2pm Sun) A short walk northeast of the Old Town, the former Convento de San Domingo de Bonaval houses large and interesting exhibits on Galician life and arts ranging from fishing boats and bagpipes to traditional costumes and crafts.

Cidade da
Cultura de Galicia   CULTURAL CENTRE
(City of Culture of Galicia; www.cidadedacultura.org; ⊙8am-11pm, building interiors 10am-2pm & 4-8pm, museum closed Mon; P) This vast prestige project is taking shape atop Monte Gaiás, a hill about 1.5km southeast of the Old Town, to the designs of American Peter Eisenman. You can't help thinking that when Bilbao got its Guggenheim, and Valencia its Ciudad de las Artes y las Ciencias, Santiago decided it had to follow suit. The first sections, the Library and Archive of Galicia, opened in 2011 after 10 years of building, delays and administrative rethinks. The concept is full of symbolism – the overall shape resembles a giant stone wave sliced into sections and is intended to be vaguely similar to a conch shell (symbol of the Camino de Santiago), while the passageways between the buildings are meant to recall the streets trodden by pilgrims arriving in Santiago. A walk around the existing buildings and spaces is worth an hour or two of your time. Free guided tours in Spanish are given at 12.30pm and 6.30pm daily except Monday. The Museo de Galicia, opened in 2012, added a new venue for events and exhibitions including assorted concerts (the museum has no permanent collection). The other three main buildings, including art and performing-arts centres, are still to be completed. You can reach the City of Culture on bus 9 (hourly Monday to Friday until 10.35pm and Saturday until 1.35pm) or bus C11 (5.35pm and 8.05pm Saturday and four times on Sunday), northbound from a stop opposite the market on Rúa da Virxe da Cerca.

THE BOTAFUMEIRO

The use of a large censer or *botafumeiro* (loosely 'smoke spitter') in Santiago's cathedral dates from the 13th century, a time when covering up the odours of road-weary pilgrims who slept and cooked inside the cathedral was more than a mere ceremonial act. Today the cathedral has two *botafumeiros*, one made in 1851 of silver-plated brass, the other a 1971 silver replica, which is the more commonly swung. When not in action, they're kept in the Museo da Catedral. Each weighs up to 100kg when filled with coal and incense, and reaches a speed of 68km/h as it swings high over the centre of the cathedral, reaching an angle of 82 degrees from vertical. The *botafumeiro* has fallen only twice, in 1499 and 1622. These days it only swings on certain feast days or if a pilgrimage group donates €300.

FREE **Museo das Peregrinacións** MUSEUM
(www.mdperegrinacions.com; Rúa de San Miguel 4; ⊙10am-8pm Tue-Fri, 10.30am-1.30pm & 5-8pm Sat, 10.30am-1.30pm Sun) Eight rooms explore the Camino de Santiago phenomenon over the centuries.

👉 Tours

Turismo de Santiago (p519) offers a range of two-hour walking tours in English and/ or Spanish that give a fascinating glimpse into the stories behind Santiago's old stone walls. From April to September, a general Old Town tour in English (€10) starts from Praza das Praterías at 4pm Thursday to Saturday and noon on Sunday.

✨ Festivals & Events

Día de Santiago FIREWORKS
(Feast of Saint James; ⊙25 July) The Día de Santiago is simultaneously Galicia's 'national' day. Ten days of festivities surround this celebration, peaking in a spectacular fireworks at the cathedral on 24 July.

🛏 Sleeping

From *hostales* (budget hotels) and hostels to chic hotels, Santiago has hundreds of lodgings at all price levels. Even so, the best-value places may fill up weeks ahead in summer, especially July and August. Book ahead if you can. High season lasts longer here than elsewhere in Galicia, so you'll be lucky to get any discounts between Easter and October.

Hotel Costa Vella BOUTIQUE HOTEL €€
(☑981 56 95 30; www.costavella.com; Rúa da Porta da Pena 17; s €59, d €81-97; ✴🖢) The tranquil, thoughtfully designed rooms (some with glassed-in galleries), friendly welcome and lovely garden cafe make this a wonderful option. Even if you don't stay, it's an ideal spot for breakfast or coffee.

Hotel Casas Reais BOUTIQUE HOTEL €€
(☑981 55 57 09; www.casasreais.es; Rúa das Casas Reais 29; d incl breakfast €90; ✴🖢) The 11 bright, contemporary rooms here are originally and discreetly themed after different real or pop-culture monarchs. White linen, mirrors and galleries all help to maximise light and this is undoubtedly one of the most attractive of Santiago's recent wave of new hotels in old buildings.

Casa-Hotel As Artes BOUTIQUE HOTEL €€
(☑981 55 52 54; www.asartes.com; Travesía de Dos Puertas 2; r €95-105; @🖢) On a quiet street close to the cathedral, As Artes' seven lovely stone-walled rooms exude a romantic rustic air. Breakfast (€10.80) is served in a homey dining room overlooking the street.

Hotel Rúa Villar HOTEL €€
(☑981 51 98 58; www.hotelruavillar.com; Rúa do Vilar 8-10; s €85, d €105-140; ✴🖢) Rúa Villar is in an artfully restored 18th-century building whose upstairs focal point is a central sitting area capped with a splendid stained-glass skylight. Service is attentive and the 16 rooms, with soft beds, are cosy and inviting, if not spacious. Original work by first-rank modern Spanish artists adorns the walls, and the classy restaurant (mains €12 to €22, menus €16) specialises in daily fresh seafood.

Hotel Carrís Casa de la Troya HOTEL €€
(☑981 55 58 79; www.carrishoteles.com; Rúa da Troia 5; r €90-119; ✴@🖢) Contemporary rooms in a sort of cubist white-and-brown concept, combined with exposed white-and-stone walls, make for attractive lodgings in this efficiently run, centrally located little hotel. It has a tapas bar downstairs and buffet breakfast is available for €8.

Barbantes Libredón HOSTAL €€
(☑981 57 65 20; www.libredonbarbantes.com; Praza de Fonseca; s €48, d €58-68; 🖢) This is actually two *hostales* under the same management on opposite sides of the same lively little square, almost next to the cathedral. Rooms in both are simple but bright and fresh-feeling. The Barbantes, on the south side of the square, has a touch more contemporary pizzazz. Bathrooms are a bit cramped and there are no lifts. Reception for both is in the Libredón, on the north side of the square.

Hotel Bonaval HOTEL €€
(☑981558883; www.hotelbonaval.com; Rúa Bonaval 2-4; s/d €98/118; ✴@🖢) A recently converted 18th-century house, on a quiet street on the fringe of the Old Town, the Bonaval has rooms that are cosier and less spartan in style than in some comparable establishments. Service is professional and friendly, and you can breakfast in the nice little garden.

Parador Hostal dos Reis Católicos   HISTORIC HOTEL €€€
(☏981 58 22 00; www.parador.es; Praza do Obradoiro 1; s/d incl breakfast from €224/280; P❄🕾) Opened in 1509 as a pilgrims' hostel, and with a claim to be the world's oldest hotel, this palatial *parador* is Santiago's top hotel, with regal (if rather staid) rooms. If you're not staying, stop in for a look round (p512) and coffee and cakes at the elegant cafe, or a meal in one of the restaurants (mains €20 to €35).

Pensión da Estrela   PENSIÓN €
(☏981 57 69 24; www.pensiondaestrela.com; Praza de San Martíño Pinario 5; r €60; 🕾) There are just six smallish rooms here but they're bright, colourful and clean, and four of them overlook a quiet plaza. The welcome is warm, with nice touches like neatly rolled towels and a bag of sweets, and there's a small kitchen with free tea and coffee.

Meiga Backpackers   HOSTEL €
(☏981 57 08 46; www.meiga-backpackers.es; Rúa dos Basquiños 67; dm incl breakfast €17-18; @🕾) Clean, colourful, friendly, and handily placed between the bus station and city centre, Meiga has spacious bunk dorms, a good kitchen, bright lounge and a long garden. It's the top choice if you're on the budget backpacking trail. The owners also run **Pensión La Bruja** (☏981 59 64 01; www.meiga-backpackers.es; Rúa da República del Salvador 32; d €32-36; 🕾), 400m southwest of Praza de Galicia in the new town, which is similar in style, with another good kitchen, but has double and triple rooms instead of dorms.

Hospedería Seminario Mayor   MONASTERY €
(☏981 56 02 82; www.sanmartinpinario.eu; Praza da Inmaculada 3; s/d €50/60; 🕾) This establishment offers the rare experience of staying inside a Benedictine monastery (San Martiño Pinario), one wing of which has been upgraded as a hotel. With over 100 rooms, it often has vacancies when other places don't. The rooms are spartan in decor, with massively thick walls, but have comfy beds with wrought-iron bedheads, and glassed-in showers. Common areas are attractively decorated and meals are available in large *comedores* (dining rooms).

Hostal Alameda   HOSTAL €
(☏981 58 81 00; www.alameda32.com; Rúa de San Clemente 32; s/d €35/55, without bathroom €26/42; 🕾) Great value, with good-sized, recently decorated rooms, this well-kept *hostal*, run by a friendly family, sits opposite the Alameda park on the edge of the Old Town.

✖ Eating

Central Santiago is packed with eateries, especially along Rúa do Franco (named for the French, not the dictator) and parallel Rúa da Raíña. Most do their job pretty well. Rúa da Troia is another fruitful grazing ground.

CRACKIN' GOOD CRUSTACEANS

Galician seafood is plentiful, fresh, and may well be the best you have ever tasted. The region's signature dish is *pulpo á galega*, tender slices of octopus tentacle sprinkled with olive oil and paprika (*pulpo á feira* has chunks of potato added). Shellfish fans will delight over the variety of *ameixas* (clams), *mexillons* (mussels), *vieiras* and *zamburiñas* (both types of scallop), *berberechos* (cockles), *navajas* (razor clams) and the tiny, much-prized goose barnacles known as *percebes*, which bear a disconcerting resemblance to fingernails. Other delicacies include various crabs, from little *nécoras* and *santiaguiños* to huge *centollos* (spider crabs) and the enormous *buey del mar* ('ox of the sea'). Also keep an eye open for the *bogavante* or *lubrigante*, a large, lobsterlike creature with two enormous claws. Shellfish are often priced by weight and are not generally cheap: the most expensive can go for over €100 per kg. Around 250g is a typical main-course-size serving.

Amid the shellfish fever, don't forget that many Galician restaurants also serve market-fresh fish and top-class meat from the lush inland pastures. The Galician *chuletón* (a giant beef chop) is almost as famed among Spaniards as Galician seafood.

While mussels, oysters and some fish are farmed, most crabs are caught wild. Look for '*salvaje*' (wild) or '*del pincho*' (rod-caught) on menus to identify nonfarmed fish. Locals claim that both octopus and *centollos* are best in months containing the letter 'r' (the same months in Spanish as in English!).

Santiago de Compostela

Built on the belief that the apostle St James the Greater (Santiago in Spanish) lies buried here, Santiago de Compostela became one of medieval Christendom's three most important pilgrimage centres, along with Jerusalem and Rome.

The faithful flocked from all over Europe along the various Caminos de Santiago (Santiago Routes) for contact with the sacred relics and the salvation this could bring. In his guise as Santiago Matamoros (St James the Moor-Slayer), the saint became the patron and inspiration of the Christian Reconquista of Spain. A magnificent stone cathedral was built over the burial site, and the flood of money the pilgrims brought to Santiago helped create a magnificent stone city around the cathedral.

The pilgrimage faded in importance after the 13th century but the cathedral and city remained, a centre of learning and Catholic culture in a remote corner of northwest Spain. With the amazing revival of the Camino since the 1990s, Santiago is again abuzz with the chatter of many tongues, while its ancient stone streets and buildings retain their medieval aura. It's also a 21st-century university town, with an equally buzzing contemporary cultural and entertainment scene. There's no place quite like it.

ESSENTIAL SANTIAGO

» **Cathedral** (p511)

» **Praza do Obradoiro** (p512)

» **Museo da Catedral** (p512)

» **Feasting on Galician seafood** (p515)

» **Celtic Music at Casa das Crechas** (p519)

Right

1. Praza das Praterías (p513) 2. Pórtico de la Gloria, Catedral de Santiago de Compostela (p511)

The Coast of Galicia

Deeply indented by over a dozen long estuaries, Galicia's coastline twists and turns for 1200km over a straight-line distance of little more than 350km. Along the way it encompasses hundreds of mainly sandy beaches, awesome cliffs, dozens of islands and a succession of fishing ports large and tiny.

Cabo Fisterra

1 Spain's 'Land's End' (p520), this dramatic, lighthouse-topped, rocky cape juts into the Atlantic on the beautiful, remote Costa da Morte. There's nothing between here and America except the ocean.

Illas Cíes

2 Part of Galicia's Islas Atlánticas national park, the three Cíes islands (p540) in the mouth of the Ría de Vigo combine spectacular cliffs and lookouts with pristine beaches. They're traffic-free, and the only accommodation is a summer campground.

Torre de Hércules

3 A Coruña's lighthouse (p523) has an 18th-century shell but the interior is pure Roman, placed on a windy headland in the 1st century AD to mark the edge of the civilised world for legions sailing north to Brittany.

On the Beach

4 You needn't go far to find a spectacular strand. Galicia's 772 beaches range from long, open sands where Atlantic surf rolls in, eg Praia da Mar de Fora (p521), to isolated coves like Area de Trece (p522) and dramatic rocky scenery such as Praia As Catedrais (p531).

Fruits of the Sea

5 Galicia's ocean-fresh seafood (p515), from *pulpo á galega* (tender, spicy octopus slices) to melt-in-the-mouth *lubiña* (sea bass), is a reason in itself to come here. In any coastal town or village (and many inland) you can get a meal to remember.

Left
1. Scallops 2. View from Torre de Hércules (p523)

Don't leave Santiago without trying a *tarta de Santiago,* the city's famed almond cake.

O Curro da Parra
CONTEMPORARY GALICIAN €€
(www.ocurrodaparra.com; Rúa do Curro da Parra 7; tapas €5-8, mains €14-20; ⊙closed Mon) With a neat little stone-walled dining room upstairs and a narrow tapas and wine bar below, this relative newcomer serves up a broad range of thoughtfully created, market-fresh fare. You might go for rod-caught fish in almond and wild-mushroom sauce, or pork cheeks with pumpkin-and-orange purée. On weekday lunchtimes it serves a great-value €11 *menú mercado* (market menu).

Bierzo de Enxebre
LEONESE €€
(www.bierzoenxebre.es; Rúa da Troia 10; raciones €8-14; ⊙closed Tue) The cuisine at this busy and atmospheric spot is that of El Bierzo, a rural area of northwest Castilla y León, meaning excellent grilled and cured meats, but also cheeses, pies and vegetables. There are two small, stone-walled, wood-beamed dining rooms and the outside tables are highly popular.

Mesón Ó 42
GALICIAN €€
(www.restauranteo42.com; Rúa do Franco 42; raciones €6-14, mains €16-19; ⊙closed Sun evening) With favourite local *raciones* (large tapas servings) like empanadas (pies), shellfish, octopus and tortillas, as well as fish, meat and rice dishes, this popular place stands out from the crowd with well-prepared food and good service. You can opt for the rustic front bar or nicely skylit rear dining room.

La Bodeguilla de San Roque
SPANISH €€
(☏981 56 43 79; www.labodeguilladesanroque. com/; Rúa de San Roque 13; raciones & mains €5-16) Just northeast of the Old Town, this busy two-storey restaurant-cum-wine-bar serves a range of excellent dishes, from salads and scrambled eggs to grilled monkfish with prawns, Galician beef sirloin in port, or plates of cheeses, sausages or ham.

El Pasaje
SEAFOOD €€
(☏981 55 70 81; Rúa do Franco 54; mains €15-23; ⊙closed dinner Sun) A classic spot offering melt-in-your-mouth Galician fish, shellfish and steaks. A series of intimate dining rooms scattered over several floors ensures a tranquil setting.

O Beiro
TAPAS, RACIONES €
(Rúa da Raíña 3; raciones €5-10; ⊙closed Sun night & Mon approx Oct-Mar) The house speciality is *tablas* (trays) of delectable cheeses and sausages, but there are plenty of other *raciones* and tapas at this friendly two-level wine bar. It also offers a terrific range of Galician wines and the fiery local grape-based liquors *orujo* and *aguardiente.*

A Taberna do Bispo
TAPAS €
(☏981 58 60 45; Rúa do Franco 37; tapas & raciones €1.50-8; ⊙closed Mon) Tantalising tapas are arrayed along the bar's length, Basque-style, and you can order all sorts of goodies, like a *timbal de vieiras* (scallops with potatoes, wild mushrooms, shellfish and port) or *montaditos* (small open sandwiches) of *solomillo* (pork sirloin) with bacon, cheese and dates.

Restaurante Ó Dezaseis
GALICIAN €€
(☏981 56 48 80; www.dezaseis.com; Rúa de San Pedro 16; mains €12-15; ⊙closed Sun) Wood-beam ceilings and exposed stone walls give an invitingly rustic air to this cellar eatery just outside the Old Town. It's a hearty rather than gourmet experience but has a good atmosphere and is very popular with locals of all types, tucking into specialities like *lacón con grelos* (ham with greens), grilled octopus or entrecôte steak, or the good-value Monday-to-Friday lunch menu (€12).

🍷 Drinking & Entertainment

On summer evenings every streetside nook in the Old Town is filled with people relaxing over tapas and drinks. The liveliest bar area lies east of Praza da Quintana, especially along Rúa de San Paio de Antealtares. Santiago's large student population comes out in full force approaching midnight, Thursday to Saturday. Later people gravitate towards clubs along Rúas da República Arxentina and Nova de Abaixo, in the new town.

A busy agenda of concerts, theatre and exhibitions goes on year-round. Pick up a program at Turismo de Santiago or find the cultural guide on its website.

Borriquita de Belém
MUSIC BAR
(borriquitadebelem.blogspot.com.es; Rúa de San Paio de Antealtares 22; ⊙from 9pm) The inviting, tightly packed 'Little Donkey' serves mojitos and wine from the barrel and has live jazz, flamenco, reggae or Latin music from around 11pm several nights a week.

Atlántico
BAR
(☏981 57 73 96; Rúa da Fonte de San Miguel 9; ⊙5.30pm-3am or later) This multilevel bar pulls in a hip 20s and 30s clientele, with cocktails and music ranging from Cajun blues to Spanish indie.

TOP CHOICE Casa das Crechas LIVE MUSIC
(www.casadascrechas.com; Vía Sacra 3; ⊙from 6pm) There's no better place for Celtic music. Head to the tightly packed downstairs bar from 10.30pm most Tuesdays, Wednesdays and Thursdays for jam sessions (admission €1) or concerts (€4 to €8).

🛍 Shopping

The Old Town is full of enticing boutiques and shops purveying jewellery (including pieces made from Santiago's traditional jet), books, art, Galician wine and *tetilla* cheese, and Galician crafts such as Camariñas lace and Sargadelos pottery. The Mercado de Abastos (www.mercadodeabastosdesantiago.com; Rúa das Ameas; ⊙7am-3pm Mon-Sat) food market is always a lively scene, with fresh produce from the seas and countryside, and plenty of spots for a bite or drink around it.

ℹ Information

Hospital Clínico Universitario (☑981 95 00 00; chusantiago.sergas.es; Travesa da Choupana) Southwest of the Old Town; emergency service.
Oficina de Acogida de Peregrinos (Pilgrims' Reception Office; ☑981 56 88 46; www. peregrinossantiago.es; Rúa do Vilar 3; ⊙9am-9pm) People who have covered at least the last 100km of the Camino de Santiago on foot or horseback, or the last 200km by bicycle, with spiritual or religious motives, can obtain their 'Compostela' certificate to prove it here.

Oficina de Turismo de Galicia (www.turgalicia. es; Rúa do Vilar 30-32; ⊙10am-8pm Mon-Fri, 11am-2pm & 5-7pm Sat, 11am-2pm Sun) The scoop on all things Galicia as well as on the Camino de Santiago.
Turismo de Santiago (☑981 55 51 29; www. santiagoturismo.com; Rúa do Vilar 63; ⊙9am-9pm, to 7pm Nov-Mar) The efficient main municipal tourist office.

ℹ Getting There & Away

Air

Santiago's **Lavacolla airport** (☑981 54 75 00; www.aena.es) is 11km east of the city. Airlines:
Air Berlin (www.airberlin.com) Germany via Palma de Mallorca.
Aer Lingus (www.aerlingus.com) Dublin.
easyJet (www.easyjet.com) Geneva.
Iberia (www.iberia.com) Madrid, Barcelona, Bilbao.
Ryanair (www.ryanair.com) Barcelona, Frankfurt (Hahn), London (Stansted), Madrid, Málaga, Milan (Bergamo), Valencia.
Volotea (www.volotea.com) Venice.
Vueling Airlines (www.vueling.com) Barcelona, Paris .

Bus

The **bus station** (☑981 54 24 16; www.tussa. org; Praza de Camilo Díaz Baliño; 🚲) is about a 20-minute walk northeast of the city centre.

Castromil-Monbus runs to A Coruña (€6, 50 to 90 minutes, 15 or more daily), Pontevedra (€5.85, 50 to 90 minutes, 14 or more daily),

GALICIA BUS & TRAIN COMPANIES

Main bus companies in Galicia:
ALSA (☑902 42 22 42; www.alsa.es)
Arriva (☑902 27 74 82; www.arriva.es)
ATSA (☑986 61 02 55)
Aucasa (☑981 58 88 11)
Autna (www.autna.com)
Autocares Vázquez (☑981 14 84 70; www.autocaresvazquez.net)
Autores & Avanza (www.avanzabus.com)
Castromil-Monbus (☑902 29 29 00; www.monbus.es)
Empresa Freire (☑981 58 81 11; www.empresafreire.com)
Hefesl (☑981 87 36 43)
Rialsa (☑981 37 20 01)

Most trains are run by Renfe (☑902 32 03 20; www.renfe.com), but a second company, FEVE (☑981 37 04 01; www.feve.es), operates a line running east from Ferrol to Ribadeo and on across Asturias and Cantabria to Bilbao.
   All the above websites give timetable information and in some cases online ticketing.

Ourense (€9, 1½ to two hours, four or more daily) and many other places in Galicia. Empresa Freire heads to Lugo (€8.50, two hours, five or more daily).

ALSA operates further afield, including to Oviedo (€27.63, 5¼ to 8¾ hours, five or more daily), Santander (€46 to €66, eight to 10 hours, three daily), León (€27.91, six hours, one daily), Madrid (€44.13 to €63.45, 7¾ to 10 hours, seven or more daily), Porto (€30, 4¼ hours) and Lisbon (€50, 9¾ hours).

Further daily services head to the Costa da Morte and Rías Baixas.

Train

The **train station** (☎ 981 59 18 59; Rúa do Hórreo) is about a 15-minute walk south from the Old Town. Regional trains run roughly every hour up and down the coast, linking Santiago with Vigo (€8.55 to €10.20, 1½ to 1¾ hours), Pontevedra (€5.65 to €6.75, one hour) and A Coruña (€5.65 to €6.75, 35 minutes). A daytime Talgo and an overnight Trenhotel head to Madrid (€50.60 to €53.60, 6¼ to 9½ hours).

❶ Getting Around

Santiago is walkable, although it's a bit of a hike from the train and bus stations to the city centre. Private vehicles are barred from the Old Town from about 10am to dusk for most of the summer. Underground car parks around its fringes generally charge about €16 per 24 hours.

Up to 37 Empresa Freire buses (€3, 35 minutes) run daily between Lavacolla airport and Rúa do Doutor Teixeiro, in the new town southwest of Praza de Galicia, via the bus station. Taxis charge around €20.

City bus 6 runs every 20 to 30 minutes from Rúa do Hórreo near the train station to Rúa da Virxe da Cerca on the eastern edge of the Old Town. Bus 5 runs every 15 to 30 minutes between the bus station, Rúa da Virxe da Cerca and Praza de Galicia. Tickets cost €1.

COSTA DA MORTE

Rocky headlands, winding inlets, small fishing towns, narrow coves, wide sweeping bays and many a remote, sandy beach – this is the eerily beautiful 'Coast of Death'. For some the most enchanting part of Galicia, this relatively isolated and unspoilt shore runs from Muros, at the mouth of the Ría de Muros, around to Caión, just before A Coruña. It's a coast of legends, like the one about villagers who put out lamps to lure passing ships on to deadly rocks. Despite its many lighthouses, this treacherous coast has certainly seen a lot of shipwrecks, and the

idyllic landscape can undergo a rapid transformation when ocean mists blow in.

One of the appealing rural hotels could be just the ticket as a base for exploring the region. Many are listed at the useful www. turismocostadamorte.com.

Public transport is limited and a car makes it far easier to get about. The area's sinuous highways aren't the easiest to navigate, but it's a marvellous area to get lost in.

Muros & Carnota

The Costa da Morte starts just past Muros, long an important port for Santiago de Compostela. At Monte Louro, the coast turns north and you immediately encounter a series of long, sweeping, sandy beaches facing the open Atlantic, most notably the spectacular 7km curve of Praia de Carnota. Carnota's most protected sections are at its south end, signposted (all with separate names) from Lira village. Carnota village is renowned as home to Galicia's largest *hórreo* (traditional stone grain store) – 34.5m long and built in the 18th century. Caldebarcos, at the north end of the Carnota bay, and O Pindo, a few kilometres further on, are starting points for walking routes in the amazingly eroded granite hills above the coast here. O Pindo has a trio of *pensiones* (small private hotels) with restaurants on the main road. From there the road continues around the beautiful Ría de Corcubión towards Fisterra.

Fisterra & Around

POP (FISTERRA) 2950

Cabo Fisterra (Cabo Finisterre in Castilian) is the western edge of Spain, at least in popular imagination. The real westernmost point is Cabo de la Nave, 5km north, but that doesn't keep throngs of people from heading out to this beautiful, windswept cape (Km 0 of the 86km Fisterra variant of the Camino de Santiago). Pilgrims ending their journeys here ritually burn smelly socks, T-shirts etc on the rocks just past the lighthouse.

The cape is a 3.5km drive past the town of Fisterra. On the edge of town you pass the 12th-century Igrexa de Santa María das Areas. Some 600m past the church, a track up to the right to Monte Facho and Monte de San Guillerme provides a more challenging but more tranquil alternative walking route to the cape. The area was once a site of pagan fertility rites, and they say childless couples used to come up here to improve their chances of conception.

Fisterra itself is a fishing port and popular tourist destination, with a picturesque harbour. The spectacular beach Praia da Mar de Fora, over on the ocean side of the promontory, is reachable via an 800m walk. For a view of Cabo Fisterra from the ocean, take a one-hour cruise with Cruceros Fisterra (☑607 198095; www.crucerosfisterra.com; adult/child €15/7.50). It travels about four times daily.

Sleeping & Eating

There are a dozen or so places to stay, and the harbourfront is full of seafood eateries.

TOP CHOICE Hotel Rústico

Ínsula Finisterrae   RURAL HOTEL €€
(☑981 71 22 11; www.insulafinisterrae.com; Lugar da Insua 76; r incl breakfast €79-109; P⊗≋) The best place to stay is this characterful, cosy, well-run, converted farmhouse at the top of town, 700m from the harbour. The spacious, sunny rooms have brass beds, fresh white linen and stone walls, and some have fantastic views.

Hostal Mariquito   HOSTAL €
(☑981 74 00 44; www.hostalmariquito.es; Rúa de Santa Catalina 44; s/d €30/42; @) Spacious, clean rooms (though some saggy beds) just above the waterfront.

TOP CHOICE O Fragón   CONTEMPORARY GALICIAN €€
(☑659 077320; Praza da Cerca 8; menus €20; ⊗closed dinner Sun-Thu Oct-Mar) Neat O Fragón prepares original and tasty dishes from locally available ingredients. The *menú gastronómico*, available for lunch and dinner, is a diverse feast that includes fish, shellfish and meat dishes and a starter and dessert (drinks are extra). It's just round the corner past the main restaurant strip.

O Centolo   SEAFOOD €€
(www.centolo.com; Paseo del Puerto; mains €17-24; ⊗breakfast, lunch & dinner, closed mid-Dec–mid-Feb;⊗) A cut above most other harbourfront eateries, the Centolo provides well-prepared fish and shellfish, with good, friendly service in two big-windowed dining rooms.

ⓘ Getting There & Away

Monbus runs three to five daily buses to/from Santiago de Compostela (€12.50, two to 2½ hours) via Noia, Muros and Carnota. Autocares Vázquez runs up to five buses to/from A Coruña (€13.30, two hours). You may be able to reach Muxía and Camariñas with a transfer at Cee, but schedules are changeable.

Muxía & Around
POP (MUXÍA) 1600

The route north from Fisterra to Muxía passes along enchanting lanes through thick woodlands; along the way is a nice detour to Cabo Touriñán, a very picturesque spot for a breezy walk. Just south of Muxía, Praia de Lourido is an unspoilt stretch of sand in a sheltered bay perfect for a sunny day.

Muxía itself is a photogenic little fishing port with a handful of cosy bars. Follow the 'Santuario da Barca' signs to reach one of Galicia's most beloved pilgrimage points, Punta da Barca. Here the baroque Santuario da Virxe da Barca marks the spot where (legend attests) the Virgin Mary arrived in a stone boat and appeared to Santiago (St James) while he was preaching here. Two of the rocks strewn before the chapel are, supposedly, the boat's sail and tiller.

Casa de Trillo (☑981 72 77 78; www.casadetrillo.com; s €56-74, d €70-92, apt for 2 €95, all incl breakfast; ⊗closed 10 Jan-10 Feb; P@⊗) offers plenty of charm, deep in typically Galician countryside about 8km south of Muxía, at Santa Mariña. This hospitable 16th-century manor house has a lot of history, lovely gardens, cosy rooms and home-grown food. It's a great base for exploring the area.

In Baiuca, just outside Muxía on the Santiago road, you can get a fabulous seafood meal and a good bed at Tira da Barca (☑981 74 23 23; www.tiradabarca.com; mains €12-22, menus €20-42; ⊗restaurant closed Tue approx Jul-Sep, closed Sun-Fri dinner rest of year; P⊗), a seven-room hotel (rooms €60) with a restaurant that draws people from far and wide for top-quality shellfish and rod-caught sea bass.

Heading on from Muxía towards Camariñas, take the road via the inviting Praia do Lago, the *hórreo*-studded hamlet Leis and the riverside village of Cereixo.

One to three daily buses link Muxía with Cee, Camariñas and A Coruña (with Autocares Vázquez) and Santiago (with Hefesl).

Camariñas & Around
POP (CAMARIÑAS) 2800

The fishing village of Camariñas is known for its women's traditional lacework. Several shops specialise in lace and there's an interesting Museo do Encaixe (Lace Museum;

Praza Insuela; admission €2; ⊙11am-2pm & 5-8pm Tue-Sun) in front of the town hall.

The best spot to lay your head is Hotel Puerto Arnela (⌨981 70 54 77; puertoarnela.net; Plaza del Carmen 20; d incl breakfast €55; 🖥), facing the harbour. A stone manor house with delightful country-style rooms, it also has a decent restaurant (mains €6 to €15; closed Sunday) serving good, uncomplicated shellfish, fish and meat.

Camariñas has at least one daily bus service to/from A Coruña, Muxía and Cee (with Autocares Vázquez), and Santiago (with Aucasa).

The rugged coast between Camariñas and Camelle is one of the most beautiful stretches of the Costa da Morte. You can walk, bike or drive the coastal road (part paved, part smooth dirt/gravel) from Camariñas northwest to the Cabo Vilán lighthouse (5km), then northeast and east to Camelle, a further 22km. The road winds past secluded beaches like Area de Trece, across windswept hillsides and past weathered rock formations, and there are many places to stop along the way, such as the Ceminterio dos Ingleses (English Cemetery), the sad burial ground from an 1890 British shipwreck.

The sleepy fishing village of Camelle has no special charm, but it does have the Museo do Alemán, a (now sadly unkempt) open-air sculpture garden made by 'Man', an eccentric long-time German resident, from rocks and ocean bric-a-brac beside the end of the pier. Praia de Traba, a little-frequented 2.5km stretch of sand with dunes and a lagoon, is a nice 4km walk east along the coast. A Molinera (⌨981 71 03 28; Rúa Principal 79; apt €42; 🖥) in Camelle has four good-value apartments for up to four people: ask for the owner, Lola, along the street at Rúa Principal 44.

Laxe & Around

POP (LAXE) 1850

A sweeping bay beach runs right along the lively waterfront of Laxe, and the 15th-century Gothic church of Santa María da Atalaia stands guard over the harbour.

Hostal Bahía (⌨630 160317, 981 72 83 04; www.bahialaxe.com; Avenida Besugueira 24; s €42, d €50-70; 🖥), 150m up past Santa María church, has good-value rooms of assorted sizes in shades of orange and yellow, most with sea views. Owner Manolo is only too keen to supply ideas and information on places to go on the Costa da Morte. Call at his Cafe Bar Bahía (Rúa Rosalia de Castro 9) as you enter Laxe. Playa de Laxe Hotel (⌨981 73 90 00; www.playadelaxe.com; Avenida Cesáreo Pondal 27; s €76, d €86-108; ⊙closed early Jan-late Feb; P🖥@🖥), just off the beach towards the south end of town, is modern, spick and span, comfortable and bland. Best views are from the seven top-floor 'special' rooms.

There are several inviting places for tapas, raciones and drinks along the main waterfront street, Rúa Rosalía de Castro. Best for a meal is Mesón O Salvavidas (Avenida Cesáreo Pondal 27; mains €12-27; 🖥), with tempting grilled seafood and meats, right next door to the Playa de Laxe Hotel.

Much of this area's appeal lies beyond its towns. Laxe's tourist office (⌨981 70 69 65; Avenida Cesáreo Pondal 26; ⊙11am-2pm & 5.30-8.30pm Tue-Sun, closed Thu afternoon) has information on walks in the area, including a coastal walk west to Praia de Traba via the surf beach Praia de Soesto. For a fascinating archaeological outing, drive inland past Canduas, then 2.4km south on the AC430 to find the turn-off to the Castro A Cidá de Borneiro, a pre-Roman castro amid thick woodlands. One kilometre further on the AC430, turn right to the Dolmen de Dombate (1km), a large 3700 BC megalithic tomb newly encased in a protective pavilion. A full-size replica, which (unlike the real thing) you'll be able to go inside, was due to be ready in the visitors centre by 2013.

Laxe is linked to A Coruña by two or more daily Vázquez buses (€8.45 to €10.20, 1¾ to 2½ hours). There's at least one daily service to Muxía.

A CORUÑA & THE RÍAS ALTAS

In few places do land and sea meet in such abrupt beauty. The untamed beaches, towering cliffs and powerful waves of the Rías Altas (the eastern half of Galicia's north coast) are certainly more dramatic than the landscapes of the Rías Baixas. They're also far less touristic, and make an ideal destination for travellers yearning to get off the heavily beaten path. Add in the allure of cultured, maritime A Coruña and the lively little towns further along the shores, and you'll wonder why more visitors don't journey north.

A Coruña

POP 219,000

A Coruña (La Coruña in Castilian) is a port city and a beachy hot spot; a busy commercial centre and a cultural enclave; a historic city and a modern metropolis with a buzzing nightlife – all in all, an intriguing place to discover.

Britain looms large on A Coruña's horizon. In 1588 the ill-fated Spanish Armada weighed anchor here. The following year Sir Francis Drake tried to occupy the city but was seen off by María Pita, a heroine whose name lives on in the city's main square. In 1809 a British army sent to help Spain resist the invading French was forced into a Dunkirk-style evacuation here, losing its leader Sir John Moore in the process. In the 19th and 20th centuries, A Coruña's port was the gateway through which hundreds of thousands of Galician emigrants left for new lives in the Americas. Today this is Galicia's wealthiest provincial capital.

Central A Coruña lies along a northeast-pointing isthmus with the port on its southeast side and the main beaches on the northwest. A mushroom-shaped headland extends 2km north from the isthmus, with a wonderful broad pedestrian walkway circling its entire perimeter.

◉ Sights & Activities

Torre de Hércules　　　　　　　LIGHTHOUSE
(www.torredeherculesacoruna.com; Avenida de Navarra; adult/senior & child €3/1.50, Mon free; ☺10am-8.45pm Sun-Thu, to 11.45pm Fri & Sat, earlier closing Sep-Jun; ℗) A city symbol that achieved Unesco World Heritage status in 2009, the 'Tower of Hercules' sits near the windy northern tip of the city. Legend attributes its construction to one of the labours of Hercules, but it was actually the Romans who built a lighthouse here in the 1st century AD – a beacon on the edge of the civilised world. The 50m-high, square stone tower we see today was erected in 1790, but inside, apart from the staircase and cupola, it is original Roman. Climb the 234 steps for views of the city, coast and intriguing sculptures of the surrounding Parque Escultórico (Sculpture Park).

To get here, take bus 3 or 5 from Paseo de la Dársena near Plaza de María Pita.

Ciudad Vieja　　　　　　　　　OLD CITY
Shady plazas, charming old churches, hilly cobbled lanes and a good smattering of cafes and bars fill A Coruña's compact old city, making it an enjoyable place for a stroll. Start from the stately Plaza de María Pita, rimmed with cafes and dominated by the early-20th-century Ayuntamiento (Town Hall) and a monument to the eponymous heroine.

The 12th-century Iglesia de Santiago (Calle de Santiago), with three Romanesque apses backing on to pretty little Plaza de la Constitución, is the city's oldest church. A short walk through the labyrinth brings you to the Xardín de San Carlos (Calle de San Francisco), where the British General Sir John Moore (killed in the nearby Battle of Elviña in 1809) lies buried. Charles Wolfe's famous poem on Moore's burial is inscribed on a plaque. Across the street, the Museo Militar (℡981 20 53 00; Plaza de Carlos I; ☺10am-2pm & 4-7pm Mon-Sat, 10am-2pm Sun) showcases a surprising assembly of military hardware and software from the 18th to 20th centuries.

Standing proud at the entrance to the port, the 16th-century Castillo de San Antón houses the Museo Arqueológico (℡981 18 98 50; Paseo Marítimo; ☺10am-9pm Tue-Sat, to 3pm Sun), an interesting collection on the area's prehistoric and Roman times.

On your way back to the centre, stop by the Plaza del Humor, decked with caricatures of famous laughter-makers from Cervantes to the Pink Panther.

Monte de San Pedro　　　　　　PARK
(℗🚌) This hilltop park 2km northwest of the city centre provides exceptional views over the city and coast, and contains the Cúpula Atlántica (admission €2; ☺11.30am-7.30pm Tue-Sun, to 9pm Sat), an observation dome with displays on A Coruña and its history, plus a maze, cafe, restaurant and two very large 1920s guns. Part of the fun is getting up there by the Ascensor Panorámico (Panoramic Lift; one way €3; ☺11.30am-7.30pm Tue-Sun, to 9pm Sat; ℗), a large glass ball which slowly ascends the steep hillside from Avenida San Roque at quarter to and quarter past the hour (it comes down on the hour and half-hour). You can reach the foot of the *ascensor* by car or foot along the road/footpath starting from the west end of Playa de Riazor.

Museo de Belas Artes　　　　　MUSEUM
(℡881 881700; http://museobelasartescoruna. xunta.es; Calle de Zalaeta; admission €2.40, Sat afternoon & Sun free; ☺10am-8pm Tue-Fri, 10am-2pm & 4.30-8pm Sat, 10am-2pm Sun) Works by

A Coruña

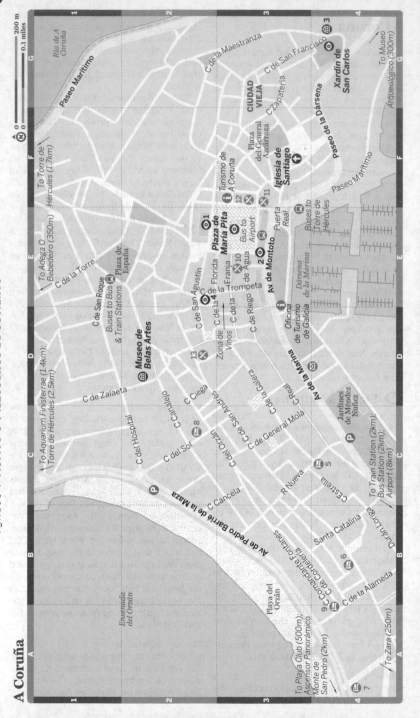

N 0 — 200 m
0 — 0.1 miles

Ría de A Coruña

Paseo Marítimo

To Torre de Hércules (1.7km)

To Adega O Bebedeiro (350m)

To Aquarium Finisterrae (1.4km); Torre de Hércules (2.5km)

C de la Maestranza

C de San Francisco

CIUDAD VIEJA

C Zapatería

Xardín de San Carlos

To Museo Arqueológico (300m)

Paseo de la Dársena

Paseo Marítimo

Plaza del General Azcárraga

Iglesia de Santiago

Turismo de A Coruña

Plaza de María Pita

Buses to Airport

Puerta Real

Buses to Torre de Hércules

Dársena de la Marina

C de la Torre

Plaza de España

C de San Roque

Buses to Bus & Train Stations

Museo de Belas Artes

C de San Agustín

C de Florida

C de la Franja

Av de Montoto

C de Riego de Agua

C de la Trompeta

Oficina de Turismo de Galicia

C de Zalaeta

C de San Andrés

C Ciega

Zona de Vinos

C de la

C del Orzán

C del Hospital

C Canalejo

C de la Galera

C Real

C de General Mola

Jardines de Méndez Núñez

C del Sol

R Nueva

C Estrella

To Train Station (2km); Bus Station (2km); Airport (8km)

Av de Pedro Barrié de la Maza

C Cancela

Durán Loriga

Santa Catalina

C Comandante Fontanes

C de Comandante Barja

Ensenada del Orzán

Playa del Orzán

To Playa Club (500m); Ascensor Panorámico; Monte de San Pedro (2km)

To Zara (250m)

C de la Alameda

Av de la Marina

A Coruña

masters like Goya, Rubens and Sorolla, and a fine collection of 19th-century Galician Sargadelos ceramics, are among the highlights of the sleek fine-arts museum.

Galerías   ARCHITECTURE
The expanse of classic late-19th-century Galician *galerías* (glassed-in balconies) fronting Avenidas de Montoto and de la Marina is an emblematic A Coruña sight and the origin of its label 'the city of glass'.

Aquarium Finisterrae   AQUARIUM
(☑981 18 98 42; http://mc2coruna.org/aquarium; Paseo Marítimo 34; adult/senior & child €10/4; ⊙10am-9pm, shorter hours Sep-Jun; ⛴) Kids love the seal colony and the underwater Nautilus room (surrounded by sharks and 50 other fish species) at this aquarium, on the city's northern headland.

Beaches   BEACH
A Coruña's city beach is a glorious, 1.4km-long, protected sweep of sand. Named Playa del Orzán at its east end and Playa de Riazor at the west, it gets busy in summer.

🛏 Sleeping

Central lodging options are mostly straitjacket business hotels or modest *hostales,* but a few places escape the mould. Prices dip outside August.

Hotel Sol   HOTEL €€
(☑981 21 03 62; www.hotelsolcoruna.com; Calle del Sol 10; r €76; ⓟ@⛲) A friendly, family-run place with eight stylish, modernised rooms and 30 older but still comfortable ones, the Sol is a good deal. Parking is free. The street can get noisy on weekend nights, so request an inside room if you bed down early.

Hotel Riazor   HOTEL €€
(☑981 25 34 00; www.riazorhotel.com; Avenida de Pedro Barrié de la Maza 29; r €63-109; ✴⛲) Overlooking Riazor beach, this 12-storey hotel has 174 attractive, bright, well-equipped rooms, and a good-value cafe and restaurant. Some rooms have fabulous beach views, though interior rooms can be larger.

Hotel Zenit Coruña   HOTEL €€
(☑981 21 84 84; www.zenithoteles.com; Calle Comandante Fontanes 19; r €110-130; ⓟ✴@⛲) The sunny, stylishly minimalist, all-exterior rooms have glass wardrobe doors and washbasins, tasteful modern art, marble bathrooms and a menu of pillows, and there's a creative but not overpriced restaurant. Just a block from Playa del Orzán.

Hotel Nido   HOTEL €
(☑981 21 32 01; www.hotel-nido-coruna.com; Calle de San Andrés 146; s/d €40/60; ⛲) Welcoming and clean, the modest-looking Nido offers 47 well-kept, medium-size rooms and is an excellent budget choice. It's well located, well run and has a good little cafe for breakfast. Rooms facing the busy street have double glazing.

Hostal La Provinciana   HOSTAL €
(☑981 22 04 00; www.laprovinciana.net; Rúa Nueva 9; s/d €45/58; @⛲) The 20 all-exterior rooms here are bright and squeaky clean, with generous-sized bathrooms and hardwood floors. The style is retro frilly, and the staff amiable.

🍴 Eating

For tapas, *raciones,* wine and cheap lunch menus, hit the Zona de Vinos – the narrow lanes west of Plaza de María Pita, especially Calle de la Franja. Here you'll find plenty of straightforward, lively *mesones* (old-style eateries) and *tabernas* (taverns), such as the octopus specialist **Mesón do Pulpo** (Calle de la Franja 9; ☉closed Sun). It serves up *raciones* of seafood (€5 to €15), grilled meats and fish, as well as two-person *mariscadas* (shellfish platters) and *parrilladas* (fish mixed grills) for €40 plus.

Taberna Da Penela
GALICIAN €€
(☎981 20 19 69; www.lapenela.com; Plaza de María Pita 9; mains €9-19; ☉closed Mon) Get tasty Galician favourites like octopus, *caldo gallego* (a soup of beans, cabbage, potatoes and bits of meat), monkfish and roast veal at this popular plazaside spot. It does a great *tortilla de Betanzos* (a gooey potato omelette), too, and has a long wine list.

Tapa Negra
CONTEMPORARY TAPAS €
(Calle de Barrera 32; tapas €1.80-2.90, raciones €9-14.50; ☉closed Mon) Stone walls and black, white and red decor bespeak something different, and this popular spot delivers with tasty combinations like *filloa de mariscos* (seafood crepe) and *fajita árabe* (spicy chicken in pita bread).

Pablo Gallego Restaurante
CONTEMPORARY GALICIAN €€€
(☎981 20 88 88; www.pablogallegorestauracion.com; Plaza de María Pita 11; mains €14-50; ☉closed Sun) The classiest choice on the main square, this serene, stone-walled dining room does 21st-century updates on traditional Galician ingredients. Try goose-barnacle croquettes, steamed seabass with algae and sea urchins, or straightforward grilled wild turbot.

Adega O Bebedeiro
GALICIAN €€
(☎981 21 06 09; www.adegaobebedeiro.com; Calle de Ángel Rebollo 34; mains €11-24; ☉closed dinner Sun) It's in a humble street 500m northwest of Plaza de España and it looks a dump from outside, but the inside is rustically neat with stone walls and a conversation-inspiring assortment of Galician bric-a-brac. The food is classic home-style cooking with a few inventive touches, like scallop-stuffed sea bass in puff pastry, or Galician entrecôte with grated goat's cheese, all in generous quantities. Packed on weekends.

Drinking & Entertainment

At night, A Coruña buzzes with taverns, bars and clubs. Before midnight, navigate the Zona de Vinos or head to Plaza de María Pita for low-key drinks and people-watching.

Dozens of pubs and music bars on Calle del Sol, Calle de Canalejo and other streets behind Playa del Orzán party on from around midnight till 3am or 4am on weekends.

Playa Club
CLUB
(www.playaclub.net; Playa de Riazor; admission incl 1 drink €4.50-7; ☉sessions from 3am Thu-Sat) As the pubs close, the clubs start to fill. This ever-popular beachside spot with three different zones boasts views across the bay and a dance-inducing musical mix of alternative pop, funk, soul-jazz, disco and electronica.

Information

Oficina de Turismo de Galicia (☎981 22 18 22; Dársena de la Marina; ☉10am-2pm & 4-7pm Mon-Fri, 11am-2pm & 5-7pm Sat, 11am-2pm Sun) Regional tourist office.

Turismo de A Coruña (☎981 92 30 93; www.turismocoruna.com; Plaza de María Pita 6; ☉9am-8.30pm Mon-Fri, 10am-2pm & 4-8pm Sat, 10am-3pm Sun) The main city tourist office.

Getting There & Away

Air

From A Coruña's **Alvedro airport** (☎981 18 72 00), 8km south of the city centre, Iberia and easyJet fly daily to Madrid; Vueling Airlines flies to London (Heathrow) and Barcelona; and **TAP Portugal** (www.flytap.com) flies to Lisbon.

THE FIRST ZARA

Fashion fans might like to make the pilgrimage to the original Zara (cnr Calle de Juan Flórez & Avenida de Arteixo; ☉10am-2pm & 5-9pm Mon-Sat), in A Coruña's main shopping area at the southwest end of the central isthmus. Opened in 1975, it today looks much like the other 1200-plus Zara boutiques around the world. This was the small beginning for the mega-successful Inditex group, which has since launched Pull&Bear, Bershka, Stradivarius and other international brands, and is the world's biggest clothing retailer, but still has its headquarters in Arteixo on A Coruña's outskirts. Inditex founder Amancio Ortega was rated the world's fifth-richest man by *Forbes* magazine in 2012, with a net worth of US$37.5 billion.

Bus

From the **bus station** (☎981 18 43 35; Calle de Caballeros), 2km south of the city centre, Castromil-Monbus heads south to Santiago de Compostela (€6, one to 1½ hours, 13 or more daily) and beyond. Arriva serves Ferrol, the Rías Altas, Lugo and Ourense; Autocares Vázquez serves the Costa da Morte; and ALSA heads to Madrid (€42.60 to €63.71, 6¾ to nine hours, seven or more daily) and towns along Spain's north coast.

Train

The **train station** (Plaza de San Cristóbal) is 2km south of the city centre. Renfe heads south about hourly to Santiago de Compostela (€6.75, 40 minutes), Pontevedra (€14.75, 1½ hours) and Vigo (€16.60, two to 2½ hours). Four daily trains head to Lugo (€16.10, 1½ hours), five to León (€36, 6¼ hours) and two to Madrid (€53 to €56, seven to 10 hours). Trains along Spain's north coast are operated by FEVE and start from Ferrol, which is served by four or five daily Renfe trains (€5, 1¼ hours) from A Coruña.

🛈 Getting Around

Buses (€1.25) run every half-hour (hourly on Saturdays and Sundays) from about 7.15am to 9.45pm between the airport and Puerta Real in the city centre.

Local bus 5 runs from the train station to Avenida de la Marina in the city centre, and back to the station from Plaza de España. Buses 1, 1A and 4 run from the bus station to various places in the city centre. Going out to the bus station, take bus 1A from Puerta Real or bus 4 from Plaza de España. Rides cost €1.20.

Rías Altas

If you're seeking dramatic scenery, look no further than the Rías Altas. Here, towering forests open to views of sheer sea cliffs, sweeping beaches and vivid green fields studded with farmhouses. Add in medieval towns like Betanzos and Pontedeume, a scattering of quaint fishing ports, and the constant roar of the Atlantic, and it's easy to argue that the Rías Altas form Galicia's most beautiful area.

BETANZOS
POP 10,700

The medieval town of Betanzos straddles the Ríos Mendo and Mandeo, which meet here to flow north into the Ría de Betanzos. Once a thriving port rivalling A Coruña, Betanzos has a well-preserved Old Town and is renowned for its welcoming taverns with local wines and good food.

◉ Sights

Praza dos Irmáns García Navelra   SQUARE

The sprawling main square is named after two local brothers who made a fortune in Argentina then returned to do good works in Betanzos in the late 19th century. Around 50,000 people cram into the square at midnight on 16 August to witness the release of an enormous paper hot-air balloon in the Fiesta de San Roque.

Museo das Mariñas   MUSEUM

(☎981 77 19 46; adult/child €1.20/free; ⊙10am-2pm & 4-8pm Mon-Fri, 10.30am-1pm Sat) Just around the corner from the main square, this museum, housed in a 16th-century convent, peers into traditional Galician life with exhibits ranging from the mundane (old coffee mugs) to the culturally significant (typical costumes), plus archaeology and art.

Old Town   CHURCHES

Take Rúa Castro up into the oldest part of town. Praza da Constitución is flanked by a couple of appealing cafes along with the Romanesque/Gothic Igrexa de Santiago. A short stroll northeast, two beautiful Gothic churches, Santa Maria do Azougue and San Francisco, stand almost side by side. The latter is full of fine stone carving, including many sepulchres of 14th- and 15th-century Galician nobility – notably that of Fernán Pérez de Andrade 'O Boo' (The Good), the powerful local lord who had all three of these medieval churches built. O Boo's sepulchre rests on a stone bear and boar (the latter being the Andrade family emblem). Spot the Galician bagpiper amid the Last Judgement carvings above the altar.

🍽 Sleeping & Eating

Hotel Garelos (☎981 77 59 30; www.hotel garelos.com; Calle Alfonso IX 8; s/d €65/86; ❈🖤), 150m down from Praza dos Irmáns Garcia Naviera, has spick-and-span rooms with parquet floors and marble bathrooms, plus 60 attractive original watercolours.

A string of cafes flanks the main square. Amid the sidewalk tables dart two narrow alleyways, Venela Campo and Travesia do Progreso. The taverns down here are popular for drinks, tapas (€1.50 to €2.50) and *raciones* (€5 to €12). Be sure to try *tortilla de Betanzos*, a gooey potato omelette for which the town is famed. The terrific €16 *menú del día* (daily set menu) at O Pote (www.meson opote.com; Travesia do Progreso 9) includes the said tortilla.

DON'T MISS

TOP FIVE BEACHES

Of the 772 beaches along Galicia's 1200km of coastline, these five stand out from the crowd.

» Illas Cíes (p540) for strolling.

» Praia da Mar de Fora (p521) for sunsets.

» Area de Trece (p522) for seclusion.

» Praia As Catedrais (p531) for stellar picnics.

» Praia do Picón (p530) for stunning scenery.

ℹ Information

Tourist office (📞981 77 66 66; www.betanzos. es; Praza da Galicia 1; ⊙10am-2pm Tue-Sun, 4.30-7.30pm Wed-Fri, closed Sun Oct-May) On an extension of Praza dos Irmáns García Naveira.

ℹ Getting There & Away

BUS Arriva buses to/from A Coruña (€2, 40 minutes, at least hourly 8am to 10pm) stop in Praza dos Irmáns García Naveira. Four or more Arriva buses head to Pontedeume (€2.05, 30 minutes) and a few to Ferrol, Lugo, Viveiro and Ribadeo.

TRAIN Betanzos Cidade train station is northwest of the town centre, across the Río Mendo. Four to six trains go daily to/from A Coruña (€3.40, 40 minutes) and Pontedeume (€1.50, 15 minutes).

PONTEDEUME
POP 4600

This hillside town overlooks the Eume estuary, where fishing boats bob. The Old Town is an appealing combination of handsome galleried houses, narrow cobbled streets and occasional open plazas, liberally sprinkled with taverns and tapas bars. Several parallel narrow streets climb up from the main road; the central one is the porticoed Rúa Real.

Pontedeume has a few *hostales,* such as the clean and friendly Hostal Allegue (📞981 43 00 35; Calle del Chafaris 1; r €40; 🛜), but the area's most enticing sleeping options are rural hotels like the Casa do Castelo de Andrade (📞981 43 38 39; www.casteloandrade. com; Lugar Castelo de Andrade; d Aug €85-105, other months €60-85; ⊙closed mid-Dec–Feb; 🅿), 7km southeast of town and close to the Parque Natural Fragas do Eume. It's a pretty stone farmhouse in enormous grounds, with 10 immaculate olde-worlde-style rooms.

A fine place to eat in town is Restaurante Luis (Calle San Agustín 12; mains €7-17; ⊙closed dinner Sun), with a full range of Galician hunger-killers from fried squid to a 400g *chuletón* (giant beef chop).

PARQUE NATURAL FRAGAS DO EUME

East of Pontedeume, the 91-sq-km Parque Natural Fragas do Eume runs up the valley of the Río Eume, home to Europe's best-preserved Atlantic coastal forest, with mixed deciduous woodlands and several species of rare relict ferns that have survived here for many millions of years. The Centro de Interpretación (📞981 43 25 28; ⊙10am-2pm & 4-8pm, closed afternoons Mon-Fri approx mid-Sep–mid-Jun) is 6km from Pontedeume on the Caaveiro road (no public transport comes here). Next door, Restaurante Andarubel (📞981 43 39 69; www.andarubel.com; mains €8-21; ⊙closed Mon Easter-Jun & Sep, closed Mon-Fri Oct-Easter) is a good lunch spot, and from Easter to about September rents bikes for €5/8/12 per one/two/four hours. You can cycle or drive a paved road along the thickly forested, fairly flat (but steep-sided) valley for 7.5km to a stone footbridge, from where a 500m path leads up to the Mosteiro de Caaveiro. This monastery dates back to the 9th century and occupies a lovely, scenic outcrop among the woods. Walkers can cross to a footpath on the bank opposite the road for the final 5km to the monastery. Over Easter and from mid-June to the end of September, the road from the Centro de Interpretación is closed to cars, but is covered by a half-hourly free bus.

This is the only part of the park most visitors see, though there are several walking trails further east (the Centro de Interpretación has leaflets in Spanish). A second visitors centre, near the Mosteiro de Monfero on the south side of the park, may open by 2014.

Eumeturismo (www.eumeturismo.org) is a useful web source on the area.

CEDEIRA & AROUND
POP (CEDEIRA) 4750

Heading north, the coast is studded with small maritime towns and pretty beaches worth exploring. The Rías Altas' largest hub is the naval port of Ferrol, 17km north of Pontedeume. It's the western terminus of the FEVE railway from the Basque Country and was the birthplace of General Franco, but it has little to detain you. Continuing north, you reach Valdoviño, with the beautiful Praia Frouxeira. Just beyond Valdoviño,

Praia de Roda at Pantín has a great right-hander for surfers and hosts a world surfing championship in September.

Some 38km from Ferrol is the fishing port and very low-key resort of Cedeira. The cute, little Old Town, with narrow streets and white houses, sits on the west bank of the Río Condomiñas, while popular **Praia da Magdalena** fronts the modern, eastern side of town. Around the headland to the south is the more appealing **Praia de Vilarrube**, a protected dunes and wetlands area.

For a nice hour or two's stroll, walk ocean-ward along the waterfront to the fishing port, climb up beside the old fort above it and then walk out onto the headland overlooking the mouth of the Ría de Cedeira. The rocky coast around here produces rich harvests of *percebes* (goose barnacles), a much-coveted delicacy.

Sleeping & Eating

Cedeira has a fair supply of *hostales* and small hotels, but two places in Cordobelas, just off the main road 1km before Cedeira as you approach from the south, stand out. The town is full of bars and cafes, especially around the river mouth and just east of it on Praza Sagrado Corazón.

Hotel Herbeira TOP CHOICE HOTEL €€
(☎981 49 21 67; www.hotelherbeira.com; Cordobelas; s/d €92/108; ☺closed 22 Dec-12 Jan; P❄@🅿🛜❄♿) As sleek as Galicia gets, this family-run hotel boasts 16 contemporary rooms with glassed-in galleries and stunning views over the *ría* (estuary). There's a beautiful pool at the front and and a nice, bright cafe for breakfast.

Hospedería Cordobelas COUNTRY HOUSE €€
(☎981 48 06 07; www.cordobelas.com; Rúa Cordobelas 29; s/d €60/76; ☺closed mid-Dec–mid-Jan; P🛜) This really charming stone-built property comprises four converted century-old village houses with comfortable, spacious, rustic-style rooms, and a fabulous garden.

Mesón Muiño Kilowatio TAPAS, RACIONES €€
(Rúa do Mariñeiro 9; raciones €8-16; ☺closed Mon-Thu approx Nov-Mar) This tiny bar packs 'em in for generous servings of squid, pork *solomillo* (sirloin), *marraxo* (a type of shark), *raxo* and *zorza* (types of chopped grilled pork) and other Galician delights.

Information
Tourist office (☎981 48 00 00; Avenida de Castelao 18; ☺10.30am-2pm & 5-8pm Mon-Fri,

11am-2pm Sat) On the main road in the new part of town.

Getting There & Away
By bus from the south, you'll need to change in Ferrol, from where Rialsa runs up to seven buses daily to Cedeira (€2.85, 45 minutes). Arriva runs one or two daily buses, Monday to Friday, from Cedeira to Cariño (€2.70, 50 minutes). For points further east, take a Cariño bus as far as Campo do Hospital, where Viveiro bound buses pass through at 1.20pm and (except Sunday) 6.05pm.

CABO ORTEGAL & AROUND
The wild, rugged coastline for which the Rías Altas are famous begins above Cedeira. If you have your own car (and, even better, time for some walks), Galicia's northwestern corner is a captivating place to explore, with lush forests, vertigo-inducing cliffs, stunning oceanscapes and horses roaming free over the hills.

Busloads of tourists descend on **San Andrés de Teixido** (12km past Cedeira), a jumble of stone houses renowned as a sanctuary of relics of St Andrew. Head on up the winding CP2205 across the Serra da Capelada towards Cariño for incredible views. Six kilometres beyond San Andrés is the must-see **Garita de Herbeira** lookout, 600m above sea level. This is the best place to be wowed over southern Europe's highest sea cliffs.

Four kilometres north of the workaday town of **Cariño** looms the mother of Spanish capes, **Cabo Ortegal**, where the Atlantic Ocean meets the Bay of Biscay. Great stone shafts drop sheer into the ocean from such a height that the waves crashing on the rocks below seem pitifully benign. **Os Tres Aguillóns**, three islets, provide a home to hundreds of marine birds, like yellow-leg seagulls and storm petrels. With binoculars, you may spot dolphins or whales near the cape.

There are some lovely walks out here. On the road from Cariño, stop at the first mirador to take the 1.6km cliff-top trail to the **San Xiao de Trebo** chapel (about 30 minutes). This well-marked path traverses a forest, crosses the Río Soutullo and affords grand views. From the chapel you can continue along the road to Cabo Ortegal (1.5km).

Rural hotels are the way to go in the area. Charming **Muíño das Cañotas** (☎981 42 01 81; www.muinodascanotas.com; A Ortigueira 10; r incl breakfast €65-80; P🛜), in a pretty little valley 200m off the main DP6121, 2km south

PIPERS & FIDDLERS

Galician folk music has much in common with other Celtic traditions in Brittany, Ireland and Scotland, and the sounds of the *gaita* (bagpipe), violin, *bombo* (a big drum) and accordion-like *zanfona* provide the soundtrack to many events. Several Celtic music festivals liven up the summer months. The biggest and best is the Festival Ortigueira (www.festivaldeortigueira.com) at Ortigueira in the Rías Altas in July. Other festivals worth seeking out include the Festival Intercéltico do Morrazo in Moaña (Ría de Vigo) and the Festa da Carballeira (www.festadacarballeira.com) in Zas (Costa da Morte) – both are held on the last weekend of July or the first weekend of August.

Leading *gaiteros* (bagpipers) and other folkies are popular heroes in Galicia. If you fancy tuning into this soulful, quintessentially Galician cultural genre, look out for gigs by pipers Carlos Núñez, Xosé Manuel Budiño, Susana Seivane, piper/singer Mercedes Peón, singer Uxía, or groups Luar Na Lubre, Berrogüetto or Milladoiro.

of Cariño, has five beautiful rooms in a converted 14th-century watermill.

CARIÑO TO VIVEIRO

From Cariño, the road south heads round the Ría de Ortigueira to the fishing port of Ortigueira. Further on, a short detour off the AC862 leads to the small but lovely Praia de Santo António in Porto de Espasante. For a chillout base overlooking this beach, book in at Hotel Orillamar (981 40 80 14; www.hotelorillamar.com; s/d incl breakfast €55/80; P@) with rooms recently remodelled in original silvers and greys, and its own seawater seafood nursery, which helps make its panoramic restaurant (mains €12 to €35) one of the best in the Rías Altas.

Between here and the Bares peninsula to the east, the coast is strung with some of the most dramatic and least-known beaches in Spain, at the foot of the spectacular Acantilados de Loiba cliffs. Easiest to reach is Praia do Picón: take the signposted turning at Km 63 of the AC862, and follow the DP6104 to Picón village, where a sharp left turn leads to a small picnic area, from which a path with a wooden handrail heads down to the beach. Loiba FEVE station is 2km from the beach

O Barqueiro, on the Ría del Barqueiro, is a storybook Galician fishing village where slate-roofed, white houses cascade down to the port. A few *pensiones* and restaurants overlook the harbour. There's little to do but stroll along the coast and watch the day's catch come in. A few daily FEVE trains and Arriva buses on Ferrol–Viveiro routes serve the town.

For an even quieter base, push north up the Bares peninsula to Porto de Bares, little more than a beach with a few boats bellyup in the sand. For a treat, book a room in the signalling-station-turned-contemporary-hotel Semáforo de Bares (981 41 71 47, 699 943584; www.hotelsemaforodebares.com; r €65-101, ste €151; P), with six rooms (the best are quite indulgent), sitting 3km above the village on a panoramic hilltop. Restaurante La Marina (mains €15-25) does great seafood paellas (€20 to €30).

The Bares peninsula has several good walking trails. From the lighthouse near its tip, a 500m trail follows the spine of a rock outcrop to the Punta da Estaca de Bares – Spain's most northerly point, with awe-inspiring cliffs and fabulous panoramas.

VIVEIRO
POP 7400

This town at the mouth of the Río Landro has a well-preserved historic quarter of stone buildings and stone-paved streets, where outward appearances haven't changed a great deal since Viveiro was rebuilt after a 1540 fire. It's famous for its elaborate Easter-week celebrations, when the town fills with processions and decorations. Check out the Gothic Igrexa de Santiago, where the Easter images are kept, and the 13th-century Romanesque Igrexa de Santa María do Campo – and the bizarre Gruta de Lourdes behind the latter, festooned with plastic limbs and dolls.

Sleeping & Eating

Hotel Ego   HOTEL €€€
(982 56 09 87; www.hotelego.es; Playa de Area; r €108-162; P@) This excellent modern hotel is 4km north of town on the Ribadeo road, overlooking Playa de Area beach. Most of the 45 rooms have sea views and balconies, and they're kitted out with comfy beds, modern art and well-equipped bathrooms.

The adjoining Restaurante Nito (mains €15-40, 4-course menu €30) is one of the coast's best eateries, providing quality meals overlooking the beach.

Hotel Vila
HOTEL €

(☎982 56 13 31; www.hotel-vila.es; Avenida Nicolás Cora Montenegro 57; s/d €32/53.50; ☎) Just down from FEVE's Viveiro Apeadero station, this well-kept one-star hotel has bright, yellow-walled rooms and up-to-date furnishings. Manager Magdalena speaks fluent English.

O' Asador
SPANISH €€

(☎982 56 06 88; www.oasador.com; Rúa Melitón Cortiñas 15; mains €12-25) In town, you can eat good fish, steak or salads at frilly O' Asador.

❶ Getting There & Away

FEVE trains between Ferrol and Oviedo stop here, and a few Arriva buses fan out to Lugo and along the Rías Altas as far as A Coruña and Ribadeo, though there are none to Ribadeo on weekends.

RIBADEO
POP 6600

This lively port town on the Ría de Ribadeo, which separates Galicia from Asturias, is a sun-seeker magnet in summer. The Old Town is an attractive mix of maritime charm and eclectic 20th-century architecture. For sea and sand you'll have to head out of town, but you won't be disappointed with the spectacular beaches, especially Praia As Catedrais (Cathedrals Beach), 10km west. This 1.5km sandy stretch is home to awesome Gothic-looking rock arches, creations best seen at low tide.

This area has plenty of camping grounds, beachy *hostales* and appealing hotels. One of the best is Hotel Rolle (☎982 12 06 70; www.hotelrolle.com; Rúa de Ingeniero Schulz 6; r incl breakfast €90; ❋@☎), just two blocks from Praza de España, with spacious, attractive rooms in a rustically modern style, with plenty of exposed stone and wood, and good, up-to-date bathrooms. The owner is keen to tell you about things to see and do in the area. Not quite so central, the Casona de Lazurtegui (☎982 12 00 97; hotelcasona.com; Rúa Julio Lazurtegui 26-28; d €81-103; P❋@☎) is a recently restored townhouse with very comfortable, contemporary tasteful rooms.

Just up from the leisure port, you can get fine seafood, grilled meats and egg dishes in the cosy upstairs dining room or informal downstairs tavern at Solana (www.lasolana restaurante.com; Rúa de Antonio Otero 41; mains €14-28; ☎lunch & dinner daily).

Get the scoop on everything else at the tourist office (☎982 12 86 89; www.ribadeo.org; Praza de España 7; ☎9am-2pm Tue-Fri, 11am-2pm Sat, 4-7pm Mon-Sat).

Multistop FEVE trains operate to/from Oviedo (€11.40, 3½ hours, two daily) and Ferrol (€10.35, three hours, four daily). Four or more daily buses head to Luarca, Oviedo, Lugo and (except weekends) Viveiro, and two go daily to Santiago de Compostela.

RÍAS BAIXAS

Wide beaches and relatively calm, warm waters have made the Rías Baixas (Rías Bajas in Castilian) Galicia's best-known tourist area. It boasts way more towns, villages, hotels, rental apartments and restaurants than other stretches of the Galician coast, which obscures some of its natural beauty. Still, the mix of pretty villages, sandy beaches and good eating options keep most people happy. Throw in the Illas Cíes, lovely old Pontevedra and bustling Vigo, and you have a tempting travel cocktail.

The following sections start at the inland end of each *ría* and work outwards, but if you have a vehicle and plenty of time you could simply follow the coast around from one *ría* to the next. That would be some 250km from Muros to Nigrán – a straight-line distance of just 72km!

It's a great idea to book accommodation ahead for the second half of July or August. At other times room prices often dip dramatically. There's lots of information about the area, including links to rural hotels, at www.riasbaixas.depo.es.

Ría de Muros y Noia

NOIA
POP 8450

This beachless town was Santiago de Compostela's de facto port for centuries. Now the crooked streets of its historic centre make a pleasing place for a stroll. Two must-see monuments are the Gothic Igrexa de San Martiño (☎8.30am-noon & 4.30-9pm), dominating Praza do Tapal, and the Igrexa de Santa María A Nova (Carreiriña do Escultor Ferreiro; ☎10.30am-1.30pm & 4-6pm, closed Sat & Sun afternoon). Both are classics of the Galician so-called sailors' Gothic style, typified by a single very wide nave. San Martiño's

Rías Baixas

western facade is adorned with wonderful sculptures of the apostles, Christ and archangels. Santa María contains a curious collection of tombstones of members of medieval guilds, many showing tools of their trades such as an anchor or butchers' knives.

Noia has a lively tapas scene. Just north of the Igrexa de San Martiño, **Tasca Típica** (Rúa Cantón 15; raciones €5-14) is a dark, stone-walled tavern in the stables of the 14th-century Pazo Dacosta. It's great for drinks, snacks or even a sit-down meal in the candle-lit dining room.

SOUTH SHORE

The coast here isn't completely unspoilt, but it's pleasantly low-key. In **Porto do Son**, a busy port, a small beach and diminutive Old Town jumble together by the *ría*, and you'll find several good tapas bars and informal restaurants. **Hotel Villa del Son** (981 85 30 49; www.hotelvilladelson.es; Rúa de Trincherpe

11; s €40, d €48-69;) has tidy rooms with cool tile floors, bright bathrooms and cheery country-cottage-type decor.

Two kilometres past Porto do Son you'll reach the turn-off for the spectacular **Castro de Baroña** prehistoric settlement. Park by the cafe and take the rocky path down to the ruins. Galicia's ancients sure knew how to choose real estate: the settlement is poised majestically on a wind-blasted headland overlooking the crashing waves of the Atlantic. Stretching south from the *castro*, **Praia Area Longa** is the first of a small string of surfing beaches down this side of the *ría*.

Drivers can continue to the **Dolmen de Axeitos**, a well-preserved megalithic monument, signposted between Xuño and Ribeira, or **Corrubedo** at the tip of the peninsula, with beaches either side of town and a few relaxed bars around its small harbour.

Ría de Arousa

PADRÓN
POP 3050

As the story goes, this is where Santiago's corpse landed in Galicia in its stone boat. Today Padrón is best known for its tiny green peppers, *pimientos de padrón,* which were imported from Mexico by 16th-century Franciscan friars and are now grown all around town. When fried up and sprinkled with coarse salt, they're one of Spain's favourite tapas. Just beware of the odd very spicy one.

Padrón produced both Galicia's 'national poet' Rosalía de Castro (1837–85) and Nobel Prize–winning novelist Camilo José Cela (1916–2002). The poet's pretty stone house, opposite the train station, is now the **Casa-Museo Rosalía de Castro** (www.rosaliadecastro.org; A Matanza; admission €1.50; 10am-2pm & 4-8pm Tue-Sat, 10am-1.30pm Sun); Cela's life and work is extensively documented at the **Fundación Camilo José Cela** (www.fundacioncela.com; adult/senior & student €8/5; 10am-2pm & 4-8pm Mon-Fri, closed Fri afternoon Sep-Jun), in Iria Flavia, 1km north of central Padrón, with hourly guided visits.

A Casa dos Martínez (981 81 05 77; http://elblogdeacasadosmartinez.blogspot.com.es; Rúa Longa 7; menus €27; 2-3.30pm Tue-Sun, 9.30-11pm Fri & Sat), on a pedestrian street in the old heart of town, serves up great creative *cocina de mercado* (with meat, seafood, vegies and other market-fresh ingredients).

Castromil buses run several times daily from Padrón to Santiago de Compostela (€1.90, 30 minutes) and Pontevedra (€3.80, one hour), and a few travel daily to Cambados and O Grove.

CAMBADOS
POP 6900

The capital of the Albariño wine country, famed for its fruity whites, Cambados is a pretty little *ría*-side town founded by the Visigoths, with a compact core of old streets lined by stone architecture.

○ Sights & Activities

You can visit and taste at wineries in and around town (more than 30 can be visited in the district), and the Fiesta del Albariño fills Cambados on the first Sunday of August and the four preceding days.

Though better-known wineries lie outside Cambados itself, the most accessible are two small ones in the handsome, 17th-century Pazo de Fefiñáns, on broad Praza de Fefiñáns at the northern end of town: Bodegas del Palacio de Fefiñanes (www.fefinanes.com; with/without tasting €4/2; ⊙10am-2pm & 4-8pm Mon-Sat) and Gil Armada (http://bodegagil armada.wordpress.com; with/without tasting €4/2; ⊙10am-2pm & 5-8pm Mon-Sat).

It's best to call ahead for out-of-town wineries to ensure visits are available. Galicia's best-known winery, Martín Códax (www. martincodax.com; Rúa Burgáns 91; incl tasting €3; ⊙11am-1pm & 5-7pm Mon-Fri), is in Vilariño, only a short drive from Cambados: 45-minute tours are available hourly. You can get more details on Rías Baixas wine routes at Cambados' tourist office, or at Expo Salnés (Paseo da Calzada; admission free; ⊙10am-2pm & 5-8pm Mon-Fri, 11am-2pm Sat), which has displays on local architecture, archaeology and wine, or at www.rutadel vinoriasbaixas.com.

Cambados has museums (joint admission adult/senior & child €3.10/1.55; ⊙10am-2pm & 5-8pm Tue-Sat, 10am-2pm Sun), three of them covering wine, fishing and local culture and one preserving a quaint old tide-operated cereal mill.

🛏 Sleeping & Eating

One lovely sleeping option is Pazo A Capitana (☑986 52 05 13; www.pazoacapitana.com; Rúa Sabugueiro 46; d €91; ⊙closed mid-Dec–mid-Jan; P❈🄟), a 17th-century country house on the edge of town with stately rooms, expansive gardens and an on-site winery. Another is Hotel Real Ribadomar (☑986 52 44 04; www.hotelrealribadomar.com; Rúa Real 8; r incl breakfast €60-95; ❈🄟), a charmingly renovated central townhouse with pretty, wallpapered rooms, fresh white linen on comfy beds, and gleaming, up-to-date bathrooms.

Pedestrian-friendly Rúa Príncipe, Rúa Real and Praza de Fefiñáns have plenty of rather touristy eateries and some characterful bars like Bar Laya (Praza de Fefiñáns), which makes its own wine. For something more upscale, head to family-run Restaurante Ribadomar (www.ribadomar.es; Rúa Valle Inclán 17; mains €10-20; ⊙closed Tue dinner & Sun, Sep-late Jul), where you can get a great traditional Galician meal with dishes such as sole with scallops or *chuletón de ternera* (giant beef chop), amid original paintings and sculptures.

❶ Information

Tourist office (☑986 52 07 86; www.camba dos.es; Praza do Concello; ⊙10am-2pm & 5-8pm, closed Sun afternoon & Mon Oct-Easter) Helpful office a few steps from the bus station.

SANTIAGO DE COMPOSTELA & GALICIA RÍA DE AROUSA

GALICIAN WINES

There's no better accompaniment to Galician food than one of Galicia's wines, which have a character all of their own. Best known is the fruity white Albariño, named after its grape and constituting 99% of wine in the Rías Baixas Denominación de Origen (DO), located near Galicia's southwestern coast and along the lower Río Miño. Albariño's popularity has, to some palates, yielded wines that are too sweet and fruity. A good traditional Albariño should have the aroma of a green apple and a slightly sour taste.

The Ribeiro DO, from the Ribadavia area in southern Galicia, produces further good whites, mostly from the Treixadura grape. The Ribeira Sacra DO in the southeast yields rich reds from Mencía grapes often grown on that region's amazingly steep hillsides. Don't confuse either Ribeiro or Ribeira Sacra with Ribera del Duero, a Castilla y León DO producing good reds that also often appear on Galician wine lists!

❶ Getting There & Away

Several daily buses head to/from Santiago de Compostela, Pontevedra and O Grove.

O GROVE
POP 7400

More than two dozen sandy beaches have made this seaside town and the relatively unspoilt peninsula surrounding it a buzzing summer destination.

◉ Sights & Activities

Dune-backed Praia A Lanzada sweeps a spectacular 2.3km along the west side of the isthmus leading to the peninsula: it's enticingly natural, but not exactly deserted, as the mammoth car park attests.

Approaching O Grove proper, you could cross the bridge to Illa A Toxa (Castilian: Isla La Toja), a manicured island known for its golf course, expensive holiday homes, upmarket hotels and the Capilla de las Conchas, a chapel completely plastered with scallop shells.

In fine weather from April to November, several companies depart from O Grove harbour on 75-minute ría cruises (incl mussel tasting adult/child €13/6), chiefly to look at the *bateas* – platforms where shellfish are cultivated. An interesting summer destination is Illa de Sálvora, one of the small islands that make up Galicia's Islas Atlánticas national park. Sálvora has a mainly rocky coast, a lighthouse, an abandoned village, and an old fish-salting-plant-cum-mansion. Daily four-hour trips (adult/child €20/10) from July to mid-September with Cruceros do Ulla (☎986 73 18 18; www.crucerosdoulla.com) or Cruceros Rías Baixas (www.crucerosrias baixas.com) include a guided walk and a little beach time.

To learn more about Galician marine life, visit the Acuario de O Grove (www.acua riodeogrove.com; adult/senior & child €12/10; ⊙10.30am-2pm & 3.30-7pm Mon-Fri, 10.30-8pm Sat & Sun, closed Mon-Fri Nov-Mar; ⊕) at Punta Moreiras, where some 100 mostly Galician species, including several types of shark, are showcased.

Marked walking trails ramble around the western part of the O Grove peninsula. For wonderful views, and birdwatching, head up to the Mirador A Siradella, sitting 159m high, above the town.

⌂ Sleeping & Eating

Nine camping grounds are scattered around the west side of the peninsula. There are plenty of hotels in town: Hotel La Noyesa

(☎986 73 09 23; www.hotelnoyesa.com; Plaza de Arriba 4; s/d incl breakfast €76/86; ⊙closed mid-Dec–mid-Jan; 🅿❄🛜) is 150m inland from the main car park on Praza do Corgo. It offers spacious, bright and clean rooms. Across the street Hotel Noyesa Plaza, with a more contemporary touch, is part of the same business with the same prices. They may require a three-night minimum at peak periods.

O Grove is famous for its shellfish and in mid-October it stages the Festa do Marisco shellfish festival. Of the slew of seafood eateries facing the seafront, a superior option is El Crisol (Rúa do Hospital 12; mains €13-20; ⊙closed Mon lunch). Tables are set with fresh flowers and napkins folded like bishops' mitres, service is efficient and friendly, the fish is market fresh, the €25 menu is generous and the cheesecake is a great way to round it off.

❶ Information

Tourist office (☎986 73 14 15; www.turismo grove.es; Praza do Corgo; ⊙10am-3pm Mon, 10am-8pm Tue-Sat, 11am-2pm Sun) Near the fishing harbour, market and main car park, in the heart of O Grove.

❶ Getting There & Away

The bus station (☎986 73 03 55; Rúa Beira-mar) is by the port. Monbus runs at least nine buses daily to Pontevedra (€3.90, one hour) via Sanxenxo, and three to Santiago de Compostela (€6.60, 2¼ hours) via Cambados.

Pontevedra
POP 61,400

Galicia's smallest provincial capital may have a story-book old quarter, but it's no sleepy museum city. The interlocking lanes and plazas of the compact centre are abuzz with shops, markets, cafes and tapas bars. In the 16th century Pontevedra was the biggest city in Galicia and an important port. Columbus's flagship, the *Santa María*, was built here. Today it's an inviting riverside city that combines history, culture and style into a lively base for exploring the Rías Baixas.

◉ Sights

Pontevedra's pedestrianised historic centre was once enclosed behind medieval walls, though remnants are scarce. More than a dozen plazas dot the old quarter – the liveliest are Prazas da Verdura, do Teucro, da Leña and da Ferrería.

At the southeastern edge of the Old Town, you can't miss the distinctive curved facade

Pontevedra

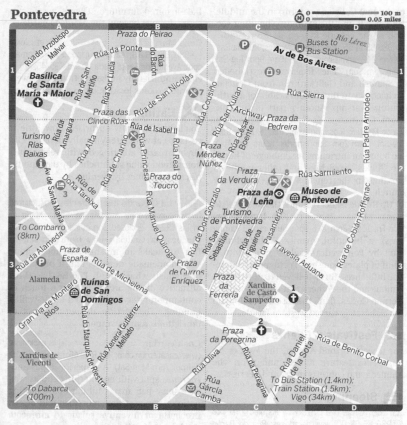

Pontevedra

of the **Santuario da Virxe Peregrina** (Praza da Peregrina), an almost circular 18th-century caprice with a distinctly Portuguese flavour. Set back from broad Praza da Ferrería is the 14th-century **Igrexa de San Francisco**, said to have been founded by St Francis of Assisi on pilgrimage to Santiago de Compostela.

Head down Rúa da Pasantería to **Praza da Leña**, an enchanting nook, partly colonnaded and with a *cruceiro* (stone crucifix; a traditional Galician art form) in the middle. Here you'll find the main, two-building section of the eclectic Museo de Pontevedra (☑986 85 14 55; www.museo.depo.es; Rúa da Pasantería 2-12; admission free; ☺10am-9pm Tue-Sat, 11am-2pm Sun). The displays here (labelled in Spanish and Galician) run from Galician archaeology to the captain's cabin of a 19th-century warship. Another part of the museum, the Ruínas de San Domingos (Gran Vía de Montero Ríos; admission free; ☺10am-9pm Tue-Sat, 11am-2pm Sun, shorter hours Oct-Apr), harbours an intriguing assemblage of heraldic shields, sepulchres and other medieval carvings in the remains of a 14th-century church.

Up Rúa de Isabel II stands the Basílica de Santa María a Maior (☺10am-1pm & 5-9pm Mon-Fri, 10am-2pm & 6-9pm Sun, except during Mass), a beautiful, mainly Gothic church built by Pontevedra's sailors' guild with a whiff of plateresque and Portuguese Manueline influences. Busts believed to portray Columbus and that other great empire-builder, Hernán Cortés, flank the rosette window on the elaborately carved western facade.

✺ Festivals & Events

For a week in mid-August, the Festas da Peregrina feature a big funfair on the Alameda and concerts in Praza da Ferrería.

🛏 Sleeping

Parador Casa del Barón HISTORIC HOTEL €€€
(☑986 85 58 00; www.parador.es; Rúa do Barón 19; s/d incl breakfast €133/166; P☀🛜) A refurbished 17th-century palace, this elegant hotel is equipped with antique-style furniture and historic art, and has a lovely little garden.

Hotel Rúas HOTEL €€
(☑986 84 64 16; www.hotelruas.net; Rúa de Figueroa 35; s/d €48/70; ☀@🛜) The rooms are attractive, with shiny wooden floors, unfussy furnishings and large bathrooms, and many have nice plaza views, but some are starting to need a lick of refurbishment. The lively restaurant does a very good set lunch for €12 Monday to Friday.

Dabarca HOTEL €€
(☑986 86 97 23; www.hoteldabarca.com; Calle Palamios 2; s/d €101/107; P☀🛜🍴) Run like a hotel but offering spacious apartments instead of standard rooms, this pleasant spot is ideal for families. Apartments are fitted with a kitchenette, washing machine and beige,

Ikea-inspired furniture. There's a cafe upstairs. It's just beyond the Alameda gardens.

Casa Maruja PENSIÓN €
(☑986 85 49 01; casamarujapontevedra@gmail.com; Avenida de Santa María 12; s/d €35/45; 🛜) A clean and friendly budget option with several bright rooms looking on to a quiet plaza.

✺ Eating

You'll be pleasantly surprised how little it costs to eat well here. Virtually all of the Old Town's plazas are ringed with restaurants doing good-value set lunches by day and tapas and raciones by evening.

TOP CHOICE La Casa de las 5 Puertas GALICIAN €€
(www.5puertas.com; Avenida de Santa María 8; mains €12-16; ☺closed Sun dinner) Serving up the best of Galician fare from ría-caught fish to steaks in mushroom sauce, along with homemade desserts and a big choice of Spanish wines, the 5 Puertas has three attractive dining areas sporting a touch of contemporary style, in an old stone-walled building. The tortilla de patatas (potato omelette) is a prizewinner!

Casa Verdún TAPAS, RACIONES €
(www.casaverdun.com; Rúa Real 46; raciones €7-16; ☺from 7pm Mon-Sat) A superior tapas-and-raciones spot with an interior patio as well as a busy bar area. Multifarious tempting options range from monkfish-and-prawn brochette or inventive salads to entrecôte steak in Arzúa cheese.

O Rianxo GALICIAN €
(Praza da Leña 6; mains €7-11) One of several good places on attractive Praza da Leña, O Rianxo serves top local favourites like merluza del pincho a la gallega (rod-caught hake in a piquant potato-and-onion sauce) or revuelto de lacón y grelos (eggs scrambled with ham and greens), either out on the square or in the upstairs dining room.

Bar 5 Calles TAPAS, RACIONES €
(Praza das Cinco Rúas; raciones €3-6) Sit at the solid wooden tables here for drinks and all sorts of very Galician, very good snacks, such as octopus, cockle pie or calamares a la romana (squid fried in egg and flour), freshly sizzled up in the busy kitchen.

🍷 Drinking & Entertainment

It's hard to find a barless street in the Old Town. For coffee, laid-back drinks and people-watching, you have several atmospheric squares to choose from, like Prazas da Verdura, do Teucro or da Leña, or the tapas bars along Rúa Real. From there you can head to the pocket of bars on Rúa do Barón and then, for some heftier *marcha* (action), up the road to the thumping music bars of Rúa de Charino.

ⓘ Information

Turismo de Pontevedra (☑986 09 08 90; www.visit-pontevedra.com; Praza da Verdura; ⊙9.30am-2pm & 4.30-8.30pm Mon-Sat, 10am-2pm Sun) The helpful city tourist office has a convenient central location.

Turismo Rías Baixas (☑986 84 26 90; www.riasbaixas.depo.es; Praza de Santa María; ⊙9am-9pm Mon-Fri, 10am-2.30pm & 4.30-8pm Sat & Sun) Information on the entire Pontevedra province.

ⓘ Getting There & Around

The **bus station** (☑986 85 24 08; www.autobusespontevedra.com; Rúa da Estación) is about 1.5km southeast of the town centre. Castromil-Monbus goes at least 17 times daily to Vigo (€2.50, 30 minutes), 12 times to Santiago (€5.70, one hour) and six times to Ourense (€10.45, two hours). Buses also run to Sanxenxo, O Grove, Cambados, Tui, Lugo and far-off cities like Madrid.

Pontevedra's **train station** (☑986 85 13 13), across the street from the bus station, is on the Vigo–Santiago de Compostela line, with almost hourly services to those cities and A Coruña.

City buses run between the bus station and Avenida de Bos Aires, on the north edge of the Old Town, every half-hour.

Ría de Pontevedra

COMBARRO
POP 1300

Near Pontevedra on the *ría's* north shore, the postcard-perfect old quarter of Combarro unfurls around a tidy bay and looks like it was plucked straight out of the Middle Ages. With a jumble of seaside *hórreos,* crooked lanes (some of them hewn directly out of the rock bed) dotted with *cruceiros,* and a smattering of waterside restaurants, this is some people's favourite stop in the Rías Baixas. It can get extremely busy in high summer, though.

The main activity here is eating: savour excellent fish, rice and meat dishes and cheaper *raciones* at spots like Taberna O

Peirao (Rúa do Mar 6; mains €12-21), featuring a waterside terrace among the *hórreos.*

Monbus buses between Pontevedra and Sanxenxo stop at Combarro.

SANXENXO
POP 2350

Sanxenxo (Sangenjo in Castilian) has been dubbed the 'Marbella of Galicia' and, though almost deserted for half the year, it does have a thing or two in common with Spain's Mediterranean resorts in the summer season: a busy leisure port, some good beaches, a long buzzing waterfront, and streets packed with eateries and tourist accommodation. The tourism here is almost exclusively Spanish.

Praia de Silgar is a fine, sandy and busy beach. Beyond Sanxenxo, the road towards O Grove parallels the wave-battered shore at the tip of the *ría,* although sand-and-sea views are limited because of the nonstop parade of hotels, *hostales* and general tourism sprawl.

Stylish and comfortable Hotel Rotilio (☑986 72 02 00; www.hotelrotilio.com; Avenida do Porto 7; s/d €75/120; ⊙closed mid-Dec–mid-Jan; ❋☞), now run by the third generation of the same family, overlooks both Praia de Silgar and the marina. The 39 rooms, all with sea views, are bright and pretty, with unusual silk paintings by local fine-arts students. Its restaurant, La Taberna de Rotilio (mains €15-27; ⊙closed Sun night & Mon Sep-Jun, Tue-Thu nights Nov-Mar), serves up terrific Galician seafood and meat with a creative touch, and also has an innovative downstairs '*gastroteca*', where you can enjoy tasty smaller creations like spider-crab cannelloni or vegetable crêpes with a glass or two of good Albariño. Portonovo, 2km west, has many tapas bars and seafood eateries.

There's a tourist office (☑986 72 02 85; www.sanxenxo.es; Porto Juan Carlos I; ⊙10am-2pm & 4-8.30pm, closed Sun & Mon mid-Oct–mid-Jun), plus a large car park, in the shiny marina development in front of Hotel Rotilio.

Buses between Pontevedra and O Grove (over 20 a day in summer) stop in Sanxenxo.

SOUTH SHORE

Zip past the sprawl surrounding Marín to discover the quiet appeal of the *ría's* southern shore, where you can stop at beaches like wide Praia de Lapamán or in maritime towns like Bueu, with its lovely waterfront. Venture past the fishing hamlet of Beluso towards Cabo de Udra, where the jagged shoreline has a backdrop of the Illa de Ons

ILLA DE ONS

In summer you can hop on a boat out to vehicle-free Illa de Ons, part of the Islas Atlánticas national park, with its sandy beaches, cliffs, ruins, walking trails and rich bird life. Campers wanting to pitch at the island's camping area (free of charge) must make reservations beforehand online at www.iatlanticas.es.

Weather permitting, Naviera Mar de Ons (www.mardeons.com) and Cruceros Rías Baixas (www.cruceros riasbaixas.com) sail to Illa de Ons several times daily from Sanxenxo and Portonovo, from late June to late September (round trip adult/child €14/7).

and there are several secluded (though not secret) beaches, such as clear-watered Praia Mourisca.

Ría de Vigo

The AP9 motorway's Puente de Rande suspension bridge brings the northern shore of the *ría* into easy reach of Vigo city. At the far tip of the *ría,* the peaceful village of Hío draws visitors for a look at Galicia's most famous *cruceiro*, a small but elaborate cross standing outside the San Andrés de Hío church. Sculpted during the 19th century from a single block of stone, its delicate, detailed carvings narrate key passages of Christian teaching, from Adam and Eve to the taking down of Christ from the cross.

Numerous sandy beaches are signposted in the area. About 2.5km north of Hío by paved road is the tranquil, sandy Praia Areabrava.

Continue west through the hamlet of Donón to windswept Cabo de Home, a rocky cape with walking trails, three lighthouses, views of the Illas Cíes, and a sandy beach (Playa de Melide) on its southeast side. The partly excavated Iron Age *castro* of Berobriga sits atop panoramic Monte Facho nearby.

Near the famous *cruceiro* at Hío, the friendly, sparkling clean Hotel Doade (☑986 32 83 02; www.hoteldoade.com; Bajada Praia de Arneles 1; s €45-70, d €70-90, incl breakfast; ☺closed Nov; P☀️☎️) has spacious rooms with fresh, white linen, and a restaurant (mains €10-30;

☺closed Nov & dinner Mon & Tue) specialising in *ría*-fresh seafood, with baked fish the speciality.

Vigo

POP 205,000

Depending on where you aim your viewfinder, Vigo is a historic and cultured city or a gritty industrial port. Home to Europe's largest fishing fleet, this is an axis of trade and commerce in northern Spain. Yet its centre is walkable and compact and full of intriguing nooks, and it's the main gateway to the beautiful Illas Cíes.

Vigo began to overtake Baiona as a major port in the Middle Ages but its major growth was in the 20th century, when its population multiplied 15-fold. Today it's a port of call for many cruise ships.

The Casco Vello (Old Town) climbs uphill from the port; the heart of the modern town spreads east from here, between Rúa do Príncipe and the waterfront, with Praza de Compostela a welcome green space in its midst.

◉ Sights & Activities

Casco Vello   OLD TOWN
At the heart of the Old Town's jumbled lanes is the elegant Praza da Constitución, a perfect spot for a drink. Head down Rúa dos Cesteiros, with its quaint wicker shops, and you'll come upon the Igrexa de Santa María, built in 1816 – long after its Romanesque predecessor had been burnt down by Sir Francis Drake.

Parque do Castro   PARK
Directly south (and uphill) of the Old Town you can wander in the verdant Parque do Castro, where you can inspect the partly reconstructed Castro de Vigo (admission free; ☺11am-1pm & 5-7pm Wed-Sun), which dates back to the 3rd century BC, and poke around the hilltop **Castelo do Castro**, which formed part of Vigo's defences built under Felipe IV.

Museo do Mar   MUSEUM
(www.museodomar.com; Avenida Atlántida 160; adult/child €3/1.50, aquarium €2/1; ☺11am-2pm & 5-8pm Tue-Fri, 11am-9pm Sat & Sun, shorter hours mid-Sep–mid-Jun; P♿) On the coast 4km west of central Vigo, the reasonably interesting Sea Museum highlights Galicia's relationship with the sea, encompassing among oth-

cr things a small aquarium and a torpedo-launching buoy installed in the Ría de Vigo in 1898 against a possible US attack. Several buses run from the city centre, including the C15C, about hourly from Porta do Sol.

Praia de Samil
BEACH

A long swath of sandy beaches stretches southwest of the city. Best is Praia de Samil (1.2km long), beginning about 5km from the city centre. It's backed by a long promenade and has great views of the Illas Cíes.

FREE Museo de Arte Contemporánea de Vigo
MUSEUM

(Marco; www.marcovigo.com; Rúa do Príncipe 54; ⊙11am-2.30pm & 5-8pm Tue-Sat, 11am-2.30pm Sun) Vigo has a reputation as an art centre, with several top-line museums and galleries to prove it. The Contemporary Art Museum is the prime venue for exhibitions ranging from painting and sculpture to fashion and design.

🛏 Sleeping

Nagari
LUXURY HOTEL €€

(☑986 21 11 11; www.granhotelnagari.com; Praza de Compostela 21; s/d incl breakfast from €102/113; P❋☗☞❄) Luxurious new Nagari has a welcome personal feel to its contemporary design and service. State-of-the-art rooms boast giant-headed showers, remote-controlled colour-changing lighting, coffee-makers and big-screen TVs that connect to the internet. Nagari also has a spa, two good eateries, and a rooftop heated pool and terrace with fabulous views.

Hotel América
HOTEL €€

(☑986 43 89 22; www.hotelamerica-vigo.com; Rúa de Pablo Morillo 6; s/d incl breakfast €76/85; P❋@☞) The América gets a big tick for its stylish contemporary feel (well-equipped, spacious rooms; tasteful modern art; elegantly muted colour schemes; friendly, efficient staff and quiet side-street location near the waterfront. The breakfast is a good buffet-style affair, served on the roof terrace in summer.

Hotel Puerta Gamboa
HOTEL €€

(☑986 22 86 74; www.hotelpuertagamboa.com; Rúa Gamboa 12; s/d incl breakfast €65/85; ❋☞) A recent remodelling of a 19th-century stone townhouse, the Puerta Gamboa provides a friendly welcome and 11 attractive rooms with wood floors, flowery bedspreads and good bathrooms.

Hotel Náutico
HOTEL €

(☑986 12 24 40; www.hotelnautico.net; Rúa de Luis Taboada 28; s/d incl breakfast €37/48; ☞) With clean, crisp style and a pleasant nautical look, this contemporary budget hotel near the Praza de Compostela park is a solid bet. Rooms are small but cosy.

🍴 Eating

Rúa Pescadería, in the lower part of the Old Town, is a short block jammed with people tucking into fresh seafood. From 9.30am until 3.30pm you can buy oysters for €12 per dozen from the *ostreras* (shuckers) at the west end of the street. Sit down to eat them with a drink at one of the neighbouring restaurants. Oysters and Albariño wine are Vigo's traditional Sunday-morning hangover cure.

For tapas bars and informal cafes, head to the narrow lanes and pretty plazas of the Old Town, especially around Praza da Constitución.

Taverna da Curuxa
CONTEMPORARY GALICIAN €€

(☑986 43 88 57; Rúa dos Cesteiros 7; menus €8.50, mains €10-12; ⊙closed Sun & Mon nights, Tue) This delightful stone tavern just off Praza da Constitución mixes the traditional and contemporary in decor and menu. Try Galician favourites like *arroces* (rice dishes) and fish *cazolas* (casseroles), or opt for a creative salad or seafood tapas. It has a great atmosphere, and the lunch menu is a terrific deal. Worth booking for dinner.

Casa Esperanza
GALICIAN €€

(Rúa de Luis Taboada 28; mains €15-24; ⊙closed Sun & 2nd half of Aug) Serving up traditional, fresh Galician fare since 1949, stone-walled Esperanza is equally great for meats (with or without cheese sauces) or any type of fish prepared almost any way you desire.

La Trastienda del Cuatro
GALICIAN, FUSION €€

(www.latrastiendadelcuatro.com; Rúa de Pablo Morillo 4; tapas €3-15, mains €11-21; ⊙lunch & dinner) The Trastienda, just off the Praza de Compostela park, has a lively front bar with high tables where you can sample tapas and wine, and a quieter, stone-walled restaurant area behind. The creative fare ranges from chicken supreme on toast to sushi, tempura, pasta and rice dishes.

🍷 Drinking & Entertainment

Vigo's nightlife is hopping. Start off slow at one of several enticing cafe-bars around Praza da Constitución in the Old Town, or Praza de Compostela or Rúa de Montero Ríos (opposite the waterfront) to the east. **Estrella de Galicia** (Praza de Compostela 17; ⊗9am-late) has Galicia's favourite beer (Estrella) sitting in big copper vats, and plenty to eat as well. From around 10pm to 1am, the bars along Rúa de Rosalía de Castro further east, such as Jamaica, with cocktails and tropical ambience, or the packed pub Van Gogh Café, are at their peak.

The real *zona de marcha*, from around midnight, is the Churruca district about 1km southeast of the Old Town. You might start at the retro lounge-style **Black Ball** (Rúa de Churruca 8), run by Silvia Superstar of 1990s punk band The Killer Barbies, then stop into **La Fábrica de Chocolate Club** (Rúa de Rogelio Abalde 22), which hosts two or three live bands or guest DJs weekly. Especially bohemian haunts are found along Rúa dos Irmandiños and Rúa de Iglesia Espondas.

Faro de Vigo newspaper and free booklet *Go!* have what's-on listings.

❶ Information

Oficina Municipal de Información Turística (☑986 22 47 57; www.turismodevigo.org; Estación Marítima de Ría, Rúa Cánovas del Castillo 3; ⊗9am-9pm) In the same building as the Illas Cíes ferry offices.

❶ Getting There & Away

Air

Vigo's Peinador airport, 9km east of the city centre, has direct flights to/from London Heathrow (by Vueling Airlines), Paris (Air France), Madrid (Iberia and Air Europa) and Barcelona (Iberia and Vueling).

Bus

The **bus station** (☑986 37 34 11; Avenida de Madrid 57) is 2km southeast of the Old Town. Castromil-Monbus makes several trips daily to all major Galician cities, including Pontevedra (€2.50, 30 minutes), Santiago de Compostela (€8, 1½ hours) and Ourense (€9, 1½ hours), and the coastal resorts. Autores heads to Madrid (€40 to €55, 7¼ to nine hours, at least six daily); Autna runs at least twice daily to/from Porto, Portugal (€12, 2½ hours), with connections there for Lisbon.

Train

Vigo-Guixar station, about 800m east of the Old Town, is being used for all Renfe services while the main train station is under reconstruction. Trains run about hourly to Pontevedra (€3.40, 30 minutes) and Santiago de Compostela (€10.20, 1½ to two hours), eight times daily to

Ourense (€11.35 to €19.70, 1½ to 2½ hours) and twice daily to Madrid and Barcelona.

❶ Getting Around

Vitrasa (☑986 29 16 00; www.vitrasa.es) runs city buses (€1.22 per ride). Bus C9A runs between the central Porta do Sol and the airport; buses C2 and C4C link Porta do Sol and the bus station.

Illas Cíes

The Illas Cíes, three spectacular islands that form a beautiful bird sanctuary and are home to some of Galicia's most privileged beaches, are a 45-minute ferry ride from Vigo. Sitting 14km offshore, this small archipelago is the main attraction of the **Parque Nacional de las Islas Atlánticas de Galicia** (www.iatlanticas.es), a national park that also includes the Ons, Sálvora and Cortegada archipelagos further north.

The three Cíes islands (Illa de Monteagudo and Illa do Faro, which are joined by a sandy isthmus, and the southern Illa do San Martiño) form a 6km breakwater that protects Vigo and its *ría* from the Atlantic's fury. This is an ideal spot for swimming and lolling on pristine beaches, birdwatching, or walking trails along the shores and up to spectacular high lookouts.

You can only visit the Illas Cíes during Semana Santa (Holy Week), on weekends from then to the end of May, and daily from June to a variable date in September. To stay overnight you must camp at **Camping Islas Cíes** (☑986 68 76 30; www.campingislascies.com; sites per person €10, 2-person tent rental per night €46 with 2-night minimum), and for camping from June to September you must book in advance, either online or at the **camping office** (☑986 43 83 58; Estación Marítima de Ría; ⊗8.30am-1.30pm & 3.30-7pm Jun-Sep) in the Illas Cíes ferry terminal in Vigo. The camping ground has a restaurant and supermarket, and a capacity of about 800 people – often filled in August.

Boats to the islands (round trip adult/child €18.50/6) are run, weather permitting, by three companies. **Naviera Mar de Ons** (☑986 22 52 72; www.mardeons.com) organises up to eight trips daily from Vigo, four from Cangas, and five (July and August only) from Baiona. **Cruceros Rías Baixas** (www.crucerosriasbaixas.com) runs up to three daily trips from Vigo. **Nabia Naviera** (www.piratasdenabia.com) does three daily trips from Vigo.

SANTIAGO DE COMPOSTELA & GALICIA ILLAS CÍES

THE SOUTHWEST

From Vigo, the PO552 Hwy runs southwest along the *ría* to Baiona, then dives south, skimming a rocky coast that, while beautiful, has resisted excessive tourism development because it has fewer sandy beaches.

Baiona

POP 3000

Crowned with a spectacular seaside fortress, Baiona (Bayona in Castilian) is a popular resort that balances coast and culture. Its shining moment came on 1 March 1493, when one of Columbus' small fleet, the *Pinta,* stopped in for supplies, bearing the remarkable news that the explorer had made it to the (West) Indies. Today you can visit a replica of the Pinta (admission €1; ⊙10am-8pm; 🐕) in Baiona's harbour.

A tangle of inviting lanes, with a handful of 16th- and 17th-century houses and chapels, makes up Baiona's casco histórico (historic centre).

You can't miss the pine-covered promontory Monte Boi, dominated by the Fortaleza de Monterreal (pedestrian/car €1/5; ⊙10am-10pm). The fortress, erected between the 11th and 17th centuries, is protected by a 3km circle of walls, and an enticing 40-minute walking trail loops the promontory's rocky shoreline, which is broken up by a few small beaches. Also within the precinct today is a *parador* — have a drink on its cafe terrace, with fabulous views across the bay.

Four kilometres east of the town centre is the magnificent sweep of Praia América at Nigrán.

🛏 Sleeping & Eating

Many of Baiona's hotels are clustered near the harbour-front road, and the cobbled lanes of the old centre are full of restaurants, tapas bars and watering holes.

Hotel Anunciada　　　　　HOTEL **€€**
(📞986 35 60 18; www.hotel-anunciada.com; Rúa Elduayen 16; s €48, d €65-86; 🖥) The Anunciada is a well-run hotel with some inviting, contemporary-style rooms which offer bay views, and other smaller rooms, also pleasant, with flowery prints.

Parador de Baiona　　　LUXURY HOTEL **€€€**
(📞986 35 50 00; www.parador.es; s/d incl breakfast €196/238; 🅿❄🖥🏊) This privileged *para-*

dor stands in the centre of Monte Boi. The grandiose rooms boast canopied beds and wonderful views, while the sophisticated restaurant (mains €15 to €30) offers a sampling of local specialities like sea bass with razor clams in *grelos* (greens) sauce.

Jaqueyvi　　　　　　　RESTAURANT **€€**
(Rúa do Reloxo 2; mains €8-21; ⊙closed mid-Jan–mid-Feb) A fine choice, with some tables out on its pedestrian street, it does excellent grilled meats as well as all the Galician seafood favourites.

❶ Information

Tourist office (📞986 68 70 67; www.baiona. org; Paseo da Ribeira; ⊙10am-2pm & 4-8pm) On the approach to the Monte Boi promontory.

❶ Getting There & Away

ATSA buses run to and from Vigo (€2.35) every 30 or 60 minutes till 9pm, but just a couple a day go south to A Guarda.

A Guarda

POP 6250

A fishing port just north of where the Río Miño spills into the Atlantic, A Guarda (La Guardia in Castilian) has a pretty harbour and some good seafood restaurants, but its big draw is beautiful Monte de Santa Trega (admission in vehicle per person Tue-Sun Feb-Dec €0.80, other times free), whose summit is a 4km drive or 45-minute trail walk up from town. On the way up, poke around the top Iron Age Castro de Santa Trega. At the top of the mount, you'll find a 16th-century chapel, an interesting small archaeological museum (admission free; ⊙10am-8pm Tue-Sun) on *castro* culture, a couple of cafes and cheesy souvenir stalls, the odd tour bus – and majestic panoramas up the Miño, across to Portugal and out over the Atlantic.

It's also nice to take the 3km walking path south from A Guarda's harbour along the coast to the heads of the Miño.

A real treat, Hotel Convento de San Benito (📞986 61 11 66; www.hotelsanbenito.es; Praza de San Bieito; s €57, d €83-104; 🅿❄🖥) is housed in a 16th-century convent down by the harbour. Its 33 elegant rooms are romantic and individually decorated, with period furniture and original architectural elements like exposed stone walls.

A Guarda is famed for its *arroz con bogavante* (rice with lobster), and more than a dozen eateries are lined up in front of the harbour.

Restaurante Bitadorna (☑986 61 19 70; www.bitadorna.com; Rúa do Porto 30; mains €18-23, menus €55-78; ☺closed Sun & Mon nights), slightly more upscale than most of its neighbours, prepares both traditional and creative treatments of whatever fish and shellfish come in fresh from the local fishing boats. A good plan is to go for one of its daily menus of up to five courses including wine.

ATSA buses run to/from Vigo (€5.55, 80 minutes) approximately half-hourly until 7pm (fewer on weekends). Most go via Tui, but a few go via Baiona. A **ferry** (car & driver €2.75, passenger €0.80; ☺hourly 9.30am-10.30pm, to 8.30pm Sep-Jun) crosses the Miño from Camposancos, 2km south of A Guarda, to Caminha, Portugal.

Tui
POP 6100

Sitting above the broad Río Miño, the border town of Tui (Tuy in Castilian) draws Portuguese and Spanish day trippers with its lively cafe scene, tightly packed medieval centre and magnificent cathedral. Just across the Gustave Eiffel–designed bridge is Portugal's equally appealing Valença.

◎ Sights

The highlight of the Old Town is the fortress-like **Catedral de Santa María** (admission €2, Sun free; ☺9am-2pm & 4-8pm), which reigns over Praza de San Fernando. Begun in the 12th century, it reflects a stoic Romanesque style in most of its construction, although the ornate main portal is considered the earliest work of Gothic sculpture in the Iberian Peninsula. You can visit the main nave and chapels for free, but it's well worth the ticket price to see the lovely Gothic cloister, the 15th-century tower, the gardens with views over the river, and the **Museo Diocesano** (☺10am-1.30pm & 4-8pm Easter–mid-Oct, closed Mon-Thu to end May), across the street, with its archaeology and art collection.

⌂ Sleeping & Eating

There are several inviting places to eat near the cathedral. On Friday to Sunday nights, Entrefornos and other quaint cobbled streets in the Old Town are the scene of some major partying.

O Novo Cabalo Furado HOSTAL €
(☑986 60 44 45; www.cabalofurado.com; Rúa Seijas 3; s/d/apt €35/60/75; ☎) In the heart of the Old Town, the rooms and apartments at this superior *hostal* are simple but inviting, with all-wood furnishings and sparkling bathrooms.

O Novo Cabalo Furado GALICIAN €€
(Plaza do Concello; tapas €5.50-9, mains €10-20; ☺closed Sun night & Mon, Sun lunch Jul & Sep) A couple of doors from the cathedral, this restaurant has a semiformal dining room and a fairly casual front bar, and is very strong on fish, shellfish and heaping plates of lamb chops – but also tapas delicacies like quail eggs with *chistorra* suasage.

ⓘ Information

Municipal tourist kiosk (☑677 418405; www.concellodetui.org; Paseo de Calvo Sotelo; ☺10am-7.30pm Easter–mid-Dec)

ⓘ Getting There & Away

ATSA buses to both Vigo and A Guarda (both €3, 40 minutes, approximately half-hourly) stop on Paseo de Calvo Sotelo, opposite Librería Byblos. Service is reduced on weekends.

THE EAST

Although often overshadowed by Galicia's glorious coastline and the better-known attractions of Santiago de Compostela, eastern Galicia is a treasure trove of enticing provincial cities, spectacular landscapes and old-fashioned rural enclaves. Every valley is another world and this is perfect territory for travellers who like digging out their own gems.

Ourense
POP 101,000

Galicia's third-largest city has a spruced-up labyrinth of a historic quarter, a lively tapas scene and tempting thermal baths. An oddly beguiling place, Ourense (Orense in Castilian) first came into its own as a Castilian trading centre in the 11th century and has a long ecclesiastical history.

The broad Río Miño runs east–west across the city, crossed by several bridges, including the medieval Ponte Vella (sometimes inaccurately called the Ponte Romana). The central area, including the compact Old Town, rises to the south of the river.

Sights & Activities

OLD TOWN

The Old Town unfolds around the 12th-century Catedral de San Martiño (Rúa de Juan de Austria; ⊙11.30am-1.30pm & 4-7.30pm Mon-Sat, 4.30-7.30pm Sun), whose artistic highlight is the gilded Santo Cristo chapel, inside the northern entrance. At the west end of the dark interior is the Pórtico do Paraíso, a coloured (and less inspired) Gothic copy of Santiago de Compostela's Pórtico de la Gloria.

Around the cathedral is a maze of narrow streets and small plazas begging to be explored. Intriguing churches like the concave-facaded, baroque Santa Eufemia and the 12th-century Trinidade dot the centre. The largest square is sloping Praza Maior, rimmed by cafes and with the Casa do Concello (City Hall) at its foot.

THERMAL POOLS

Ourense's original raison d'être was the hot springs, As Burgas (Rúa As Burgas), a short walk southwest of the central Praza Maior; gushing out 67°C waters with therapeutic properties, they have been used since Roman times. People still fill containers with steaming water from spouts at the foot of the plaza here. Above is a recently spruced-up thermal pool, the Piscina Termal As Burgas (http://burgas.gpazos.es; admission €3; ⊙9am-12.30pm & 6-11pm Tue-Sun), for which tickets are sold at Ourense's municipal tourist office.

More enticing for taking a dip are the hot pools along a nicely landscaped 4km stretch of the north bank of the Miño. Here, four sets of open-air pools are free and open 24 hours daily, and there are also two privately run sets of partly indoor pools. Closest to the centre are the A Chavasqueira open pools, on the riverbank, and Termas Chavasqueira (www.termaschavasqueira.com; admission €5; ⊙9am-1am Tue-Thu, 6pm-3am Fri & Sat, 9am-11.30pm Sun), with four hot pools and one cold one, plus two saunas and a cafe. You can walk to these from the Old Town in 20 to 30 minutes, but it's a further 3km to 3.5km to the other pools. Or take the Tren das Termas (tickets €0.80; ⊙hourly 10am-1pm & 4-8pm, reduced frequency approx Oct-May), a minitrain from Praza Maior that goes to all the pools.

Take swimming gear, a towel and flip-flops (thongs) to any of the pools, and remember that their waters are hot and mineral-laden, so don't spend more than about 10 minutes in them without a break.

Sleeping

Central hotel choices are limited but there are a couple of good options.

Hotel Cardenal Quevedo HOTEL €€
(☎988 37 55 23; www.carrishoteles.com; Rúa Cardenal Quevedo 28; r €70-80, ste €90-110; P❄@⊛) New in 2012, this hotel in a small Galician chain is aimed at both leisure and business travellers. It provides bright and pleasing rooms with contemporary lines, and amiable, professional service, and is just a 600m walk north from the heart of the Old Town.

Hotel Irixo HOTEL €
(☎988 25 46 20; www.hotelirixo.es; Rúa dos Irmans Villar 15; s/d €37/53; ⊛) On a small Old Town square, the Irixo provides simple but neat, contemporary and clean rooms, though only a few look out on the street. Singles can be tight but have ample bathrooms.

Eating

Ir de tapeo ('going for tapas') is a way of life in Ourense, and central streets like Fornos, Paz, Lepanto, Viriato, San Miguel and Praza do Ferro brim with taverns where having to push and shove your way to the bar is seen as a sign of quality. Tapas begin at €1 and are nearly always washed down with a glass of local wine.

Mesón Porta da Aira TAPAS, RACIONES €
(Rúa dos Fornos 2; tapas €2-7, dishes €9-24; ⊙closed Sun night, Mon & 2nd half of Sep) This tiny eatery has locals flocking in for the generous platters of *huevos rotos:* lightly fried eggs over a bed of thinly sliced potatoes, to which you can add various sausages and meats.

Restaurante San Miguel GALICIAN €€
(www.restaurante-sanmiguel.com; Rúa San Miguel 12; mains €12-24, menus €33; ⊙closed Jan) Specialising in seafood (as the gurgling lobster tanks attest), this is the kind of place where bow-tied waiters sweep breadcrumbs off the table and even the water is served in goblets. There's also a good selection of Galician meats.

Arco da Vella TAPAS, RACIONES €
(Rúa dos Fornos 9; tapas €1.20-3, raciones €3-9; ⊙7pm-midnight) A classic down-to-earth Old Town tapas bar with rapid service and an ambience a bit like a garage. It's known for its *chipirones* (cuttlefish) and wonderful runny *tortilla* (omelette).

Drinking & Entertainment

Ourense is packed with intimate pubs and tapas bars that easily make the transition into night-time. Stroll the streets around the cathedral for a host of options. For live music, try Praza Eufemia, where Miudiño (Rúa de Arcediagos 13; ⏱3pm-3.30am) sometimes hosts Celtic musicians, and Café Latino (Praza Eufemia 7; ⏱7.30am-3.30am) has a fabulous corner stage for jazz and other styles.

❶ Information

Oficina Municipal de Turismo (☑988 36 60 64; www.turismodeourense.com; Calle Isabel La Católica 2; ⏱9am-2pm & 4-8pm Mon-Fri, 11am-2pm Sat & Sun) A very helpful place underneath the Xardinillos Padre Feijóo park, just off pedestrianised Rúa do Paseo.

❶ Getting There & Away

BUS From Ourense's **bus station** (☑988 21 60 27; Carretera de Vigo 1), 2km northwest of the city centre, Monbus runs to Santiago (€9, two hours, four or more daily), Vigo (€10, 1½ hours, nine or more daily), Lugo (€8, 1¾ hours, two or more daily) and elsewhere. Avanza journeys to Madrid (€34 to €48, six to seven hours, five or more daily).

TRAIN The **train station** (Rúa de Eulogio Gómez Franqueira) is 500m north of the Río Miño. Renfe runs to Santiago (€9.15 to €19.50, 1¾ to two hours, eight or more daily), Vigo (€11.35 to €19.70, two hours, eight daily), León (€26 to €48, four hours, four daily), Madrid (€44.30, 5½ to 7½ hours, two daily) and elsewhere.

❶ Getting Around

Local buses 1, 3 and 6A (€0.80) run between the train station and the central Parque de San Lázaro. Buses 6A, 6B and 12 connect the bus station with Parque San Lázaro.

Ribadavia & Around

POP (RIBADAVIA) 3300

The headquarters of the Ribeiro Denominación de Origen (DO), which produces some of Galicia's best white wines, Ribadavia sits on the Río Avia in a verdant valley. Its little historic centre is an enticing maze of narrow stone streets lined with heavy stone arcades and broken up by diminutive plazas; within this area in medieval times was Galicia's largest Jewish quarter.

◉ Sights & Activities

Above the tourist office (☑988 47 12 75; www.ribadavia.travel; Praza Maior 7; ⏱9.30am-2.30pm & 4-8pm, closed Sun afternoon), in the former mansion of the Counts of Ribadavia on the lovely main square, is the Centro de Información Xudía de Galicia (Praza Maior 7; admission €2; ⏱9am-1.30pm & 4-8pm, closed Sun afternoon), with exhibits, in Galician, on the Jews of Galicia.

The heart of the medieval Barrio Xudío (Jewish Quarter) was Rúa Merelles Caulla, running from Praza Maior to Praza Madalena. The Museo Etnolóxico (Rúa Santiago 10; admission free; ⏱10am-2.30pm & 4-8pm Tue-Fri, 11am-2.30pm Sat & Sun), with its Galician folk-history collection, is worth a look, too – it's next to the Romanesque Igrexa de Santiago. You can also wander round the large, chiefly 15th-century Castelo do Sarmento (Rúa Progreso; admission €2), one of Galicia's biggest medieval castles: tickets are sold at the tourist office.

Several wineries in the area are open for visits, usually charging around €3. You can ask the tourist office to call and arrange a visit for you. In early July Ribadavia stages Galicia's biggest wine festival, the Feria del Vino del Ribeiro. For more information on the Ribeiro wine area, check www.rutadelvinoribeiro.com.

Relax with a stroll along the 5km riverside path that runs by the Ríos Avia and Miño: you can access it by steps down from Praza Buxán, next to Praza Madalena.

⏢ Sleeping & Eating

Hostal Plaza (☑988 47 05 76; www.hostalplazaribadavia.com; Praza Maior 15; s/d €27.50/37.50; 🖧) has 12 simple but neat and well-kept rooms.

There are several wonderful rural hotels in the area. A 10-minute drive east of Ribadavia is the Casal de Armán (☑699 060464; www.casaldearman.net; O Cotiño, San Andrés; r incl breakfast €75-90; 🅿🖧), a dignified country house with six cosy rooms overlooking the countryside, a rustic-chic restaurant (meals €30-45; ⏱closed Mon & dinner Sun-Thu Nov-May) serving good traditional Galician fare, and a winery (☑638 043335; incl tasting €5; ⏱visits by reservation 1, 6 & 8pm Tue-Sun, closed 20 Sep-31 Oct) too. Viña Meín (☑617 326385; www.vinamein.com; Meín, San Clodio; d incl breakfast €65; ⏱closed mid-Dec–Jan; 🅿🖧🍽), in a beautiful part of the Avia valley about 10km north of town, is a delightful country guesthouse and winery (☑617 326248; visits free; ⏱9am-1pm & 4-7pm Mon-Fri, by reservation), run by a friendly family.

In town, Praza Maior is ringed by cafes and restaurants, such as Restaurante Plaza (Praza Maior 15; menus €10, mains €6-12; ☺breakfast, lunch & dinner), which serves straightforward fish, meat and shellfish in generous quantities.

❶ Getting There & Away

At least three buses and four trains run daily to Ourense and Vigo from stations in the east of town, just over the Río Avia.

Ribeira Sacra & Cañón do Sil

Northeast of Ourense, along the Ríos Sil and Miño, unfolds the unique natural beauty and cultural heritage of the Ribeira Sacra (Sacred Riverbank), so called because of the abundance of monasteries in the area. From the 6th century or even earlier, Christian hermits and monks were drawn to this remote but beautiful and fertile area, and at least 18 monasteries grew up here in medieval times. The area is poorly served by public transport, but if you have a vehicle, a good map and an explorer inside you, it makes for a marvellous road trip. The following sections outline a possible day or two-day route through the area, focusing on the magnificent Cañón do Sil (Sil Canyon), surrounded by steep hills and dense woodlands. For more information, see www.ribeirasacra.org.

OURENSE TO PARADA DE SIL

Leave Ourense by Avenida de Buenos Aires, which feeds into the OU536 Hwy. At Tarreirigo, 500m past the Km 15 post, turn left on to the OU0509 and follow lanes meandering through the forests to the Mosteiro de San Pedro de Rocas (4km). Founded in AD 573, this enchanting mini-monastery consists chiefly of three cave chapels carved into the rock of the hillside. You can just about make out the only known Romanesque world map painted on a wall of the left-hand chapel. Next door is a Centro de Interpretación (admission free; ☺10.30am-1.45pm & 4-7.45pm Tue-Sun), whose displays on the Ribeira Sacra are worthwhile even if you don't understand Spanish or Galician. You can also take a beautiful walk round the Camiño Real (PR-G4), a 9km circuit that loops through this area of dense woods and rocky crags.

Back on the OU0509, continue to Luintra then head east following signs to the mammoth Mosteiro & Parador de Santo Estevo. This monastery dates to the 12th century, after pilgrims started arriving to pray at the tombs of nine bishops who had retreated to this isolated spot in preceding centuries. It has three magnificent cloisters (one Romanesque/Gothic, two Renaissance), an originally Romanesque church and an 18th-century baroque facade. Abandoned in the 19th century, it was reopened as a *parador* hotel in 2004. Nonguests are free to wander round the main monumental parts and eat in the cafe or restaurant.

Continue east along the OU0508 to Loureiro. Here, a scenic and sinuous road leads 4km down to the Embarcadoiro de Santo Estevo on the Río Sil at the foot of the canyon, where you can take a 1½ hour river cruise (adult €11.50-14, senior & child €8.50-12) with Viajes Pardo (☎902 21 51 00; www.riosil.com) or Hemisferios (☎902 10 04 03; www.hemisferios.es). Schedules vary, but between them the two companies make at least two trips daily except Monday from Easter to mid-October, and several sailings daily in July and August.

The river canyon is perhaps even more beautiful from above. Continue along the OU0508 as it winds through moss-drenched forests and along a ridge high above the gorge to Parada de Sil, which has a handful of *casas rurales* (country-house lodgings). Here, a side road leads 4km down to the Mosteiro de Santa Cristina de Ribas de Sil, a small medieval monastery with a 12th-century Romanesque church, hidden romantically among trees above the canyon. The spectacular Balcón de Madrid lookout is 1km from the village, and the well-signed PR-G98 walking trail from Parada heads to the monastery via the lookout.

CASTRO CALDELAS & AROUND
POP (CASTRO CALDELAS) 700

From Parada de Sil the country road continues east as the OU0605, passing waterfalls, impossibly steep vineyards, time-lost stone villages and occasional jaw-dropping vistas of the gorge below. At a crossroads with multiple signposts after 17km, go left along the OU0606 to A Teixeira, then follow the signs to Castro Caldelas. This delightful village with the requisite cobblestone streets, glassed-in Galician balconies and well-tended flower boxes is a good spot to spend the night. Explore the old quarter at the top of the village, crowned by the 16th-century Igrexa de Santa Isabel and a 14th-century castle, which affords great views from its tower. The well-informed Centro Comarcal (☎988 20 46 30; ⏰10am-2pm & 5-8pm), just outside the castle, can tell you anything you want to know about the district.

From Castro Caldelas, the OU903 winds down to the Sil Canyon. River cruises (☎982 26 01 96; www.lugoterra.com; adult/senior & child €9/5) of 1¾ hours from the bridge here go at least twice daily year-round, ex-

cept Monday and Tuesday from about October to May. The road becomes the LU903 as it climbs the north side of the gorge, cutting across some of the almost vertical vineyards that characterise the area. At quaint Doade, a few kilometres up the hill towards Monforte de Lemos, you can visit and taste at the Regina Viarum (☎619 009777; www.reginaviarum.es; ⏰10am-2pm & 4-8pm, closed Mon & Tue Oct-Mar) and Adega Algueira (☎982 15 22 38; www.adegaalgueira.com) wineries. It's best to call ahead; both places have restaurants too.

CAMINOS OF GALICIA

All of the Caminos de Santiago converge in Galicia, their shared goal. About 80% of pilgrims arrive by the Camino Francés, breasting the hills on the border of Castilla y León, then striding west for the final 154km across welcome green countryside to Santiago de Compostela. But plenty also reach Santiago by the Camino Portugués (crossing the border at Tui), Camino Inglés (from A Coruña or Ferrol) or Camino Primitivo (from Oviedo via Lugo).

Tiny O Cebreiro, where the Camino Francés enters Galicia, is 1300m above sea level and marks the top of the route's longest, hardest climb. Several *pallozas* (circular, thatched dwellings known in rural Galicia since pre-Roman times) are dotted among its stone houses. About half the buildings here are bars (many doing cheap *menús del día;* daily set menus) or pilgrims' hostels: the nicest accommodation is the five-room Hotel O Cebreiro (☎982 36 71 82; www.hotelcebreiro.com; r €40-60).

In Triacastela, 19km downhill from O Cebreiro, the Camino divides, with both paths reuniting later in Sarria. The more attractive option is the longer (25km) southern route via Samos, a lovely village built around the very fine Benedictine Mosteiro de Samos (www.abadiadesamos.com; tours €3; ⏰tours about every 30min 10am-12.30pm Mon-Sat, 12.45-1.30pm Sun, 4.30-6.30pm daily). This monastery has two beautiful big cloisters (one Gothic, with distinctly unmonastic Greek nymphs adorning its fountain, the other neoclassical and filled with roses). Upstairs are four walls of murals detailing St Benedict's life, painted in the 1950s after a horrendous fire that burned almost everything in the monastery. Samos has several refuges and *hostales* (budget hotels), but much nicer is the Casa de Díaz (☎982 54 70 70; www.casadediaz.com; d €39-69; P🅿🛰🌊), an 18th-century farmhouse turned rural hotel at Vilachá, 3.5km beyond Samos.

People undertaking just the last 100km of the Camino usually start in Sarria, which has a nice *casco antiguo* (old town) on the hill above its charmless centre. The Camino winds through village after village, across forests and fields, then descends steeply to Portomarín, above the Río Miño. Further on, the stretch from Palas de Rei to Melide follows some lovely rural lanes. From Melide, 53km remain through woodlands, villages, countryside and, at the end, city streets. The Camino approaches the centre of Santiago de Compostela along Rúa de San Pedro and arrives in Praza da Inmaculada on the northern side of the cathedral. Most pilgrims take a few more steps down through an archway to emerge on magnificent Praza do Obradoiro, in front of the cathedral's famous western facade.

If you're touring Galicia rather than pilgriming it, the 30km from O Cebreiro to Samos make a marvellous side trip. Drivers entering Galicia along the A6 from Astorga can turn off into Pedrafita do Cebreiro, then follow the LU633 4km south to O Cebreiro. The road from there to Samos winds down through green countryside with great long-distance views, frequently criss-crossing the Camino.

At 5pm Monday to Friday and 1.45pm Saturday, a bus departs Lugo bus station for Pedrafita do Cebreiro (€9.55, two hours) via Sarria, Samos and O Cebreiro. The return service starts from Pedrafita at 6.45am Monday to Saturday.

Camino in Galicia

MONFORTE DE LEMOS

POP 16,700

The historic crossroads town of Monforte de Lemos is neither as compact nor as pristine as other stops on the route. The **Centro do Viño da Ribeira Sacra** (982 10 53 03; www.centrovino-ribeirasacra.com; Rúa Comercio 6; tour incl glass of wine €3; ⊙11am-2.30pm & 5-9pm, closed 9 Jan-11 Feb & Sun afternoon & Mon Oct-Jun) has displays on the region's wine, culture and history, which are brought to life in enjoyable 45-minute guided visits, usually scheduled for noon, 1pm, 6pm and 7pm: call the day before for English or French. The centre doubles as Monforte's tourist office and has a nice cafe and lots of Ribeira Sacra wine for sale. Rising above the town centre is the **Monte de San Vicente**, where the **Pazo Condal**, formerly the residence of the counts of Lemos, is now a parador hotel. Flanking the *pazo* are the Renaissance church facade of the **Mosteiro de San Vicente** and the medieval **Torre da Homenaxe**, the last vestige of the counts' castle.

🛏 Sleeping & Eating

TOP CHOICE / **Parador de Santo Estevo** HISTORIC HOTEL €€€
(988 01 01 10; www.parador.es; Nogueira de Ramuín; s/d €148/185; P❋🛜) The Ribeira Sacra's best-known monastery is also an indulgent hotel with all the comforts, including a good spa, and a wonderful setting above the river canyon overlooked by many of the rooms.

Casa Grande de Cristosende RURAL HOTEL €
(988 20 75 29; www.casagrandecristosende.es; Cristosende; r €49-79; 🛜) A charming 500-year-old manor house in the village of Cristosende, between Parada de Sil and A Teixeira, this rural hotel has seven large, inviting rooms with modern furnishings but an almost monastic simplicity. The restaurant (menus €16) serves hearty Galician fare.

Pousada Vicente Risco HOSTAL €
(988 20 33 60; www.pousadavicenterisco.com; Rúa Grande 4, Castro Caldelas; s/d incl breakfast €38/48; 🛜) One of three charming lodgings in the old upper part of Castro Caldelas, this quaint place has eight well-kept rooms in a classic country style, with small chandeliers and big bathrooms. The restaurant-cum-bar (menus €10 to €12) serves terrific home-style meals and is also a hang-out for local chaps who get very excited about their card games.

Hotel Puente Romano HOTEL €
(982 41 11 67; www.hpuenteromano.com; Paseo do Malecón, Monforte de Lemos; s/d €30/43; 🛜) This modest Monforte hotel overlooks the 16th-century Ponte Vella (Old Bridge) on the Río Cabe, and has 33 bright, clean, good-sized rooms. Neighbouring **Hostal Puente Romano** (s/d €18/28), under the same management, has mostly smaller rooms, all with river views, for very reasonable rates.

Restaurante O Grelo GALICIAN €€
(982 40 47 01; Campo de la Virgen, Monforte de Lemos; mains €12-21; ⊙lunch & dinner) A rustic stone building on the road that climbs Monforte's Monte de San Vicente, character-filled O Grelo specialises in grilled meats, game dishes like venison with chestnuts,

and other Galician favourites like *lacón con grelos*.

ⓘ Getting There & Away

From Monforte, the wide N120 Hwy zips back to Ourense. Monbus buses (€5, one hour, three daily) and Renfe trains (€4.75 to €21.90, 45 minutes, five or more daily) link the two places. A few buses head from Monforte to Lugo, Santiago de Compostela and León. Trains between León and Vigo also stop here.

Castro Caldelas has a Monbus service to and from Ourense (€5.10, 1¼ hours) twice daily Monday to Friday and once on Sunday, and a bus to Monforte de Lemos (€2.60, 45 minutes) at 10.30am Monday, Wednesday, Thursday and Friday (returning at 2pm).

Lugo

POP 89,500 / ELEV 475M

The grand Roman walls encircling old Lugo are considered the world's best preserved and are the number-one reason visitors land here. Yet within the fortress is a beautifully preserved labyrinth of streets and squares, most of them traffic-free and ideal for strolling. Established as Lucus Augusti over an ancient *castro* in 15 BC, Lugo was a major town of Roman Gallaecia and today is a quiet but very engaging city. The main plazas and most interesting streets, plus the large cathedral, are mostly concentrated in the southwest quarter of the old city.

◉ Sights

Roman Walls   WALLS

The path running right round the top of the World Heritage–listed Roman walls is to Lugo what a maritime promenade is to a seaside resort: a place to jog, take an evening stroll, see and be seen. The walls make a 2.2km loop around the old city, rise 15m high and are studded with 85 stout towers. First erected in the 3rd century, they didn't save Lugo from being taken by the Suevi in 460 or the Muslims 300 years later. Until well into the 19th century tolls were charged to bring goods into the walled city, and its gates were closed at night.

The **Centro de Interpretación de la Muralla** (Praza do Campo 11; adult/senior, student & child €3/1.50; ◔10.30am-2pm & 4.30-8pm), a block north of Lugo's cathedral, gives interesting background on the Roman walls, with three videos and free audioguides, all available in English.

Catedral de Santa María   CATHEDRAL

(Praza Pío XII; ◔8am-9pm) The cathedral, inspired by Santiago's, was begun in 1129, though work continued for centuries, yielding an aesthetic mix with dashes of styles ranging from Romanesque (as in the transepts) to neoclassical (the main facade). It's a serene building that merits a close look. The superb original main altarpiece, carved with scenes from the life of Christ by Cornelis de Holanda in the 1530s, now stands in two parts in the two transepts. Behind the high altar, an ultra-ornate baroque chapel surrounds the beautiful Gothic image of *Nosa Señora dos Ollos Grandes* (Our Lady of the Big Eyes), Lugo's Christian patroness. Outside, just above the north doorway, the sculpture of Christ in majesty is one of Spain's finest pieces of Romanesque stone carving.

FREE Museo Provincial   MUSEUM

(www.museolugo.org; Praza da Soidade; ◔10am-2pm & 4.30-8.30pm Mon-Sat, 11am-2pm Sun, closed Sat afternoon & Sun Jul & Aug) Lugo's museum includes what remains of the Convento de San Francisco – a Gothic cloister and the convent kitchen and refectory. It's one of Galicia's best and biggest museums, with collections ranging from pre-Roman gold jewellery and Roman mosaics to Galician Sargadelos ceramics and art from the 15th to 20th centuries.

🛏 Sleeping

Orbán e Sangro   BOUTIQUE HOTEL €€

(☏982 24 02 17; www.pazodeorban.es; Travesía do Miño; r €86-140; ✳🐾🛜) The 12 rooms of this welcoming hotel, in an 18th-century mansion just inside the city walls, are regal, with rich linen, antique furnishings, designer bathrooms and huge 2.15m beds. It has its own tavern in a highly original early-20th-century style.

Hotel Méndez Núñez   HOTEL €€

(☏982 23 07 11; www.hotelmendeznunez.com; Rúa da Raíña 1; r €70; ✳🅿🛜) This century-old hotel, recently completely remodelled, offers bright, spacious quarters, gleaming bathrooms and good views from some rooms.

Pensión San Roque   PENSIÓN €

(☏982 22 27 00; Plaza de Comandante Manso 11; s/d incl breakfast €27.54/38.85) Just outside the Roman walls and convenient to the bus station, well-run San Roque provides bare but clean and modern rooms, all with windows.

Cable internet is available in some rooms. There are at least three other *pensiones* or *hostales* within 100m.

✕ Eating

Rúa da Cruz, Rúa Nova and Praza do Campo, north of the cathedral, are packed with tempting restaurants and tapas bars. Many of the latter offer two free tapas with a drink: one will be offered to you on a plate, and you have to try to pick the other from a list recited by bar staff at high speed.

A Nosa Terra   TAPAS, RACIONES €
(Rúa Nova 8; raciones €5-18) An inviting classic on the Rúa Nova tapas trail, with a long by-the-glass wine list. Stand in the narrow bar area or sit at tables in the back for *raciones* of *pulpo á galega* (tender slices of octopus sprinkled with olive oil and paprika) or *lacón con grelos*.

Mesón de Alberto   GALICIAN €€
(☑982 22 83 10; www.mesondealberto.com; Rúa da Cruz 4; tapas menus €15, mains €16-29; ☉closed Sun, dinner Tue) Alberto serves well-prepared traditional meat, fish and shellfish – meals in the dining room upstairs, tapas downstairs. The tapas tasting menu is a good bet.

Restaurante España CONTEMPORARY GALICIAN €€
(www.nove.biz/ga/espana; Rúa do Teatro 10; tapas €4-9, mains €14-26; ☉closed Mon, dinner Sun; ☎) Two brothers have successfully updated a 50-year-old family business at this spot just inside the walls. Downstairs is a lilac and silvery-grey 'gastrobar' with snacks like fish or vegetable tempura; the restaurant upstairs has an open kitchen concocting delicious updates on traditional Galician fare – seabass *pil-pil*, partridge pancakes, beef sirloin with truffles...

☘ Drinking & Entertainment

Weekend nights, things get lively in the old city. Start with tapas and drinks along Rúa Nova, Praza do Campo or Rúa da Cruz, north of the cathedral, then hit the music bars around the cathedral if you're in the mood for partying on.

By contrast, low-key jazz, classical or easy-listening music makes the old-timey **Café del Centro** (Praza Maior 9; ☉7am 2am) a chilled-out hangout from 11.30pm on Friday and Saturday.

ℹ Information

These two offices are a stone's throw apart, just north of the cathedral.
Oficina de Turismo de Galicia (☑982 23 13 61; Rúa do Miño 12; ☉10am-2pm & 4-7pm Mon-Sat)
Oficina Municipal de Turismo (☑982 25 16 58; www.lugoturismo.com; Praza do Campo 11; ☉10.30am-2pm & 4.30-8pm) In the Centro de Interpretación de la Muralla.

ℹ Getting There & Away

BUS From the **bus station** (☑982 22 39 85; Praza da Constitución), Empresa Freire runs to Santiago de Compostela (€8.50, 1½ to two hours, six or more daily), and Arriva heads to A Coruña (€9.80, 1¼ to two hours, six or more daily). Several daily buses head to Monforte de Lemos, Ourense, Pontevedra, Vigo, Viveiro, Ribadeo and Ponferrada. ALSA serves León and Madrid, and Asturias and beyond.

TRAIN Four or more daily Renfe trains head to A Coruña (€8.50 to €16.10, 1¾ hours) and Monforte de Lemos (€5.10 to €15, one hour). One overnight train, except Saturday, goes to Madrid (€52, nine hours).

Valencia & Murcia

Best Places to Eat

» Delicat (p564)
» Seu-Xerea (p564)
» Appetite (p565)
» Canela y Clavo (p591)
» La Tartana (p603)

Best Places to Stay

» Caro Hotel (p562)
» Cases Noves (p592)
» Chill Art Jardín Botánico (p562)
» Hotel Huerto del Cura (p594)
» Hostal Les Monges Palace (p587)

Why Go?

Every year millions of tourists descend on Valencia and Murcia and while it's true that parts of the coast have been horrendously over-developed (Hello Benidorm!), much of this sun-scorched region remains wholly Spanish.

Valencia city exudes confidence. Its nightlife, quality museums, great restaurants and the stunning contemporary architecture of the City of Arts & Sciences make this an utterly addictive city.

So many visitors confine themselves to the coastal playgrounds, but rent a car, leaving behind the hedonism of the thin coastal strip and you'll savour the region's rich interior where mountains buckle, castles crown hilltops and villages – many dating back to Muslim times – slumber on.

To really leave the tourist hordes behind get busy exploring the delightful region of Murcia with its busy capital, Murcia City; home to a splendid cathedral and superb tapas bars, and the ancient port of Cartagena, which is excavating its past to reveal a rich classical heritage.

When to Go
Valencia City

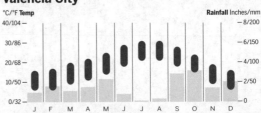

15–19 Mar Las Fallas, Valencia City's wild spring festival, brings some two million visitors to town.

22–24 Apr At Alcoy's Moros y Cristianos fiesta, warriors engage in mock battle.

Sep Get into the historical spirit of Cartagena during the annual Carthagineses y Romanos festival.

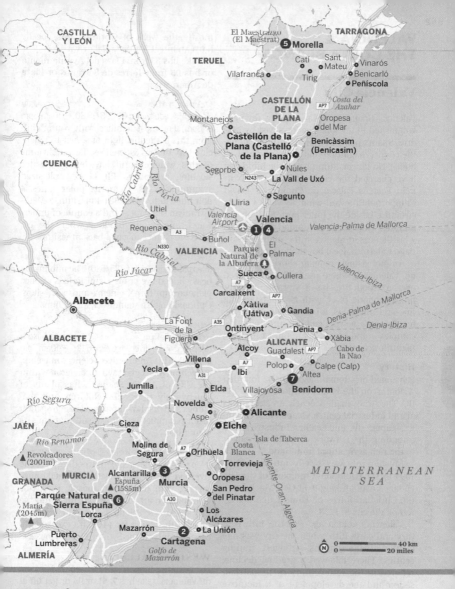

Valencia & Murcia Highlights

① Fling fireworks and suffer serious sleep deprivation at **Las Fallas** (p562), Europe's wildest spring festival

② Explore Cartagena's fascinating **Roman and Carthaginian sites** (p601)

③ Sip a drink at sundown in **Murcia's** (p595) Plaza del Cardenal Belluga overlooked by the magnificent cathedral

④ Gasp at the daring architecture of the **Ciudad de las Artes y las Ciencias** (p557) in Valencia City

⑤ Savour your first glimpse of the medieval fortress town of **Morella** (p574) from afar

⑥ Lace up those hiking boots and explore the unspoilt beauty of the **Parque Natural de Sierra Espuña** (p606)

⑦ Tuck into a fried English breakfast and soak up the character of **Benidorm** (p582), the ultimate mass-tourism resort

VALENCIA & THE COSTA BLANCA

Valencia City

POP 815,000

Valencia, Spain's third-largest city, for ages languished in the long shadows cast by Madrid, Spain's political capital, and Barcelona, the country's cultural and economic powerhouse. No longer. Stunning public buildings have changed the city's skyline – Sir Norman Foster's Palacio de Congresos, David Chipperfield's award-winning Veles i Vents structure beside the inner port, and, on the grandest scale of all, the Ciudad de las Artes y las Ciencas, designed in the main by Santiago Calatrava, local boy made good.

An increasingly popular short-break venue, Valencia is where paella first simmered over a wood fire. It's a vibrant, friendly, mildly chaotic place with two outstanding fine-arts museums, an accessible old quarter, Europe's newest cultural and scientific complex – and one of Spain's most exciting nightlife scenes.

History

Pensioned-off Roman legionaries founded 'Valentia' on the banks of Río Turia in 138 BC. The Arabs made Valencia an agricultural and industrial centre, establishing ceramics, paper, silk and leather industries and extending the network of irrigation canals in the rich agricultural hinterland.

Muslim rule was briefly interrupted in 1094 by the triumphant rampage of the legendary Castilian knight El Cid. Much later, the Christian forces of Jaime I definitively retook the city in 1238.

Valencia's golden age was the 15th century and early 16th, when the city was one of the Mediterranean's strongest trading centres. There followed a gradual decline, relieved in the 19th century by industrialisation and the development of a lucrative citrus trade to northern Europe.

◉ Sights & Activities

CIUDAD DE LAS ARTES Y LAS CIENCIAS

The aesthetically stunning City of Arts & Sciences (✐reservations or book online 902 10 00 31; www.cac.es; combined ticket for Oceanogràfic, Hemisfèric & Museo de las Ciencias adult/child €32.90/25) occupies a massive 350,000-sqmetre swathe of the old Turia riverbed. It's

mostly the work of world-famous, locally born architect Santiago Calatrava.

Take bus 35 from Plaza del Ayuntamiento or bus 95 from Torres de Serranos or Plaza de América.

Oceanogràfic   AQUARIUM
(Map p554; adult/child €24.90/18.80; ⊘10am-6pm or 8pm) For most families with young children this is the highlight of a visit to Valencia's City of Arts & Sciences. The aquariums of this watery world have enough water sloshing around to fill 15 Olympic-sized swimming pools. There are polar zones, a dolphinarium, a Red Sea aquarium, a Mediterranean seascape – and a couple of underwater tunnels, one 70m long, where the fish have the chance to gawp back at visitors.

Hemisfèric   IMAX CINEMA
(Map p554; adult/child €7.85/6.10) The unblinking heavy-lidded eye of the Hemisfèric is at once planetarium, IMAX cinema and laser show. Optional English soundtrack for all films.

Museo de las Ciencias Príncipe Felipe   SCIENCE MUSEUM
(Map p554; adult/child €7.85/6.10; ⊘10am-7pm or 9pm) This interactive science museum, stretching like a giant whale skeleton within the City of Arts & Sciences, has plenty of touchy-feely things for children and machines and displays for all ages. Each section has a pamphlet in English summarising its contents.

Palau de les Arts Reina Sofía   ARTS CENTRE
(Map p554; www.lesarts.com) Brooding over the riverbed like a giant beetle, its shell shimmering with translucent mosaic tiles, this ultramodern arts complex, grafted onto the City of Arts & Sciences, has four auditoriums. With seating for 4400, it's exceeded in capacity only by the Sydney Opera House.

WESTERN VALENCIA

For both the Bioparc and Museo de Historia de Valencia, take bus 7, 81 or 95 or get off at the Nou d'Octubre metro stop.

Bioparc   ZOO
(Map p554; www.bioparcvalencia.es; Avenida Pio Baroja 3; adult/child €24/17; ⊘10am-dusk) 'Zoo' is far too old-fashioned and inept a term for this wonderful, innovative, ecofriendly and gently educational space where wild animals apparently (fear not: only apparently) roam free as you wander from savannah to equatorial Africa and Madagascar, where large-eyed lemurs gambol around your ankles.

CREEPING CATALAN

More and more town halls are re-placing street signs in Spanish with the Valenciano/Catalan equivalent. While the difference between the two versions is often minimal, this can sometimes be confusing for visitors. Occasionally we use the Valenciano form where it's clearly the dominant one. But since Spanish is the version every local understands and the majority uses, we've elected to stick with it in most cases.

Museo de Historia de Valencia   MUSEUM
(Map p554; Calle Valencia 42; adult/child €2/1; ⊙10am-7pm Tue-Sat, 10am-3pm Sun) This museum, very hands-on and with plenty of film and video, plots more than 2000 years of the city's history. Ask to borrow the museum's informative folder in English.

PLAZA DE LA VIRGEN & AROUND
Busy Plaza de la Virgen, ringed by cafes and imposing public buildings, was once the forum of Roman Valencia, the axis where its main north–south and east–west highways met.

Central Fountain   FOUNTAIN
The handsome reclining figure in Plaza de la Virgen's central fountain represents Río Turia, while the eight maidens with their gushing pots symbolise the main irrigation canals flowing from it.

Catedral   CATHEDRAL
(Map p558; Plaza de la Virgen; adult/child incl audio guide €4.50/3; ⊙10am-4.45pm or 5.45pm Mon-Sat, 2-4.45pm Sun) Valencia's cathedral is a microcosm of the city's architectural history: the Puerta del Palau on the eastern side is pure Romanesque; the dome, tower and Puerta de los Apóstoles on Plaza de la Virgen are Gothic; the presbytery and main entrance on Plaza de la Reina are resplendently baroque.

Don't miss the rich, recently revealed Italianate frescoes above the main altarpiece. In the flamboyant Gothic Capilla del Santo Cáliz, right of the main entrance, is what's claimed to be the Holy Grail, the chalice from which Christ sipped during the Last Supper. The next chapel north, La Capilla de San Francisco de Borja, has a pair of particularly sensitive Goyas.

Left of the main portal is the entrance to the Miguelete bell tower (Map p558; adult/child €2/1; ⊙10am-7pm or 7.30pm). Climb the 207 steps of its spiral staircase for terrific 360-degree city-and-skyline views.

As for over 1000 years, the Tribunal de las Aguas (Water Court) meets every Thursday exactly at noon outside the cathedral's Puerta de los Apóstoles. Here, Europe's oldest legal institution settles local farmers' irrigation disputes in Valenciano, the regional language.

La Almoina   ARCHAEOLOGICAL SITE
(Map p558; adult/child €2/1, with guided tour €2.50; ⊙10am-7pm Tue-Sat, 10am-3pm Sun) Beneath the square just to the east of Valencia's cathedral, the archaeological remains of the kernel of Roman, Visigoth and Islamic Valencia shimmer through a water-covered glass canopy. Explore this underground area at your own pace or pay a mere €0.50 extra for a 30-minute guided tour.

Cripta de la Cárcel de San Vicente Mártir   CHURCH
(Map p558; ☎96 208 45 73; Plaza del Arzobispo 1; adult/child €2/1; ⊙10am-7pm Tue-Sat, 10am-3pm Sun) The crypt of this Visigoth chapel, reputedly used as a prison for the 4th-century martyr San Vicente, isn't particularly memorable in itself. What's really worthwhile is the multimedia show that presents Valencia's history and the saint's life and death. Reserve by phone or on the spot and ask for a showing in English.

Nuestra Señora de los Desamparados   CHURCH
(Map p558; Plaza de la Virgen; ⊙7am-2pm & 4.30-9pm) Above the altar is a highly venerated statue of the Virgin, patron of Valencia. If you come after hours or during Mass, peer in through the grilles, worn smooth over the years by thousands of supplicants, on the southern, cathedral side.

Palau de la Generalitat   PALACE
(Map p558; Plaza de la Virgen) This handsome 15th-century Gothic palace, much amended over the years, is the seat of government for the Valencia region. Its symmetry is recent: the original renaissance tower received its twin only in the 1950s.

PLAZA DEL MERCADO
Facing each other across Plaza del Mercado are two emblematic buildings, each a masterpiece of its era.

Valencia City

Beniferri Ⓜ

La Safor

New Valencia CF Football Stadium

C Dr Nicasio Benlloch

Ⓜ Garbi

Av Juan XXII

Ⓜ Benicalap

Trànsits Ⓜ

Av Dr. Peset Aleixandre

C de San Pancracio

Marxalenes

Parque de Marxalenes

C Reus

Ⓜ Reus

Av General Aviles

Av Campanar

C Padre Ferris

Av Buriassot

C de Llano de Zaídia

Av Maestro Rodrigo

Av de Pío XII

Ⓜ Campanar-La Fe

C Joaquín Ballester

C de Blanquerías

Bioparc 🐾

Valle de la Ballestera

Bus Station

Av Menéndez Pidal

See Valencia City Central Map (p558)

Av de Tirso de Molina

Ⓜ Turia

3

C de Turia

Paseo de la Pechina

11

🚰 10

Parque de Cabecera

Puente 9 de Octubre

C Castan Tobenas

Av Perez Galdos

C de Juan Llorens

C de Gabriel Miró

C de Quart

C de Lepanto

12

C Valencia

🏛 8

C Brasil

C Sta Cruz de Tenerife

C de Calixto III

C Ángel Guimerà

28

Ángel Guimerà Ⓜ

Av del Cid

C Linares

C Enguera

C de Buen Orden

C San José de Calasanz

Plaza de España Ⓜ

C Musico Ayllón

C José María Mortes Lerma

C Tres Forques

Av Salavert

C Cuenca

C de Jesús

C Albacete

Estación Joaquín Sorolla 🚆

Av Tres Cruces

C Archiduque Carlos

C Fontanares

C Beato Nicolás Factor

27

Jesús Ⓜ

C San Vicente Mártir

Av Tres Cruces

Ⓜ Patraix

C Venezuela

Av Giorgeta

Ⓜ Hospital

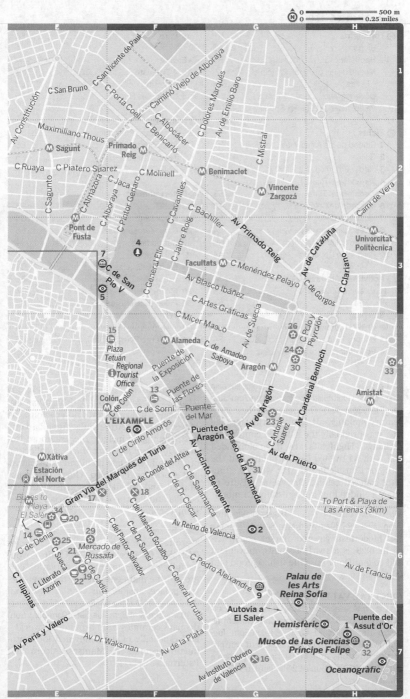

Valencia City

La Lonja   HISTORIC BUILDING

(Map p558; adult/child €2/1; ☺10am-7pm Tue-Sat, 10am-3pm Sun) This splendid late-15th-century building, a Unesco World Heritage site, was originally the silk and commodity exchange. Highlights are the colonnaded hall with its twisted Gothic pillars and the 1st-floor Consulado del Mar with its stunning coffered ceiling. Browse at leisure or enjoy a guided tour in English for €1 more.

Mercado Central   MARKET, ARCHITECTURE

(Map p558; ☺7.30am-3pm Mon-Sat) Valencia's vast Modernista covered market, constructed in 1928, is a swirl of smells, movement and colour. Don't miss the fish, seafood and offal annexe.

CENTRAL VALENCIA

Instituto Valenciano de Arte Moderno   ART

(IVAM; Map p558; www.ivam.es; Calle Guillem de Castro 118; adult/child €2/1; ☺10am-8pm Tue-Sun) IVAM ('ee-bam') hosts excellent temporary exhibitions and houses an impressive permanent collection of 20th-century Spanish art.

FREE **Museo de Bellas Artes**   MUSEUM

(Map p554; Calle San Pío V 9; ☺10am-7pm Tue-Sun, 11am-5pm Mon) Bright and spacious, the Museo de Bellas Artes ranks among Spain's best. Highlights include the grandiose Roman *Mosaic of the Nine Muses,* a collection of magnificent late-medieval altarpieces, and works by El Greco, Goya, Velázquez, Murillo and Ribalta, plus artists such as Sorolla and Pinazo of the Valencian Impressionist school.

**Palacio del
Marqués de Dos Aguas**   PALACE

(Map p558; Calle Poeta Querol 2) A pair of wonderfully extravagant rococo caryatids curl around the main entrance of this over-the-top palace. Inside, the **Museo Nacional de Cerámica** (Map p558; adult/child €3/free; ☺10am-2pm & 4-8pm Tue-Sat, 10am-2pm Sun) displays ceramics from around the world – and especially of the renowned local production centres of Manises, Alcora and Paterna.

Torres de Serranos GATE, ARCHITECTURE
(Map p558; Plaza de los Fueros; adult/child €2/1; ⊙10am-7pm Tue-Sat, 10am-3pm Sun) Once the main exit to Barcelona and the north, the imposing 14th-century Torres de Serranos overlook the former bed of Río Turia. Together with the Torres de Quart, they are all that remain of Valencia's old city walls. Climb to the top for a great overview of the Barrio del Carmen and riverbed.

Torres de Quart GATE, ARCHITECTURE
(Map p558; Calle Guillem de Castro; adult/child €2/1; ⊙10am-7pm Tue-Sat, 10am-3pm Sun) You can clamber to the top of the 15th-century Torres de Quart, which face towards Madrid and the setting sun. Up high, notice the pockmarks caused by French cannonballs during the 19th-century Napoleonic invasion.

Estación del Norte NOTABLE BUILDING
(Map p558; Calle Xàtiva) Trains first chugged into this richly adorned Modernista terminal in 1917. Its main foyer is decorated with ceramic mosaics and murals – and mosaic 'bon voyage' wishes in major European languages.

Museo del Patriarca GALLERY
(Map p558; Calle la Nave 1; admission €2; ⊙11am 1.30pm) This bijou gallery is a must if you're interested in ecclesiastical art. It's particularly strong on Spanish and Flemish Renaissance painting, with several canvases by Juan de Juanes, Ribalta and El Greco.

FREE **Museo de Etnología** MUSEUM
(Map p558; Calle de Corona 36; ⊙10am-8pm Tue-Sun) This fascinating folk museum displays photographs, artefacts and household items from both city and region. It shares premises (usually called La Beneficencia) with Museo de Prehistoria (Map p558), a history museum that covers the region's more remote past.

Museo Fallero MUSEUM
(Map p554; Plaza Monteolivete 4; adult/child €2/1; ⊙10am-7pm Tue-Sat, 10am-3pm Sun) Each Fallas festival, only one of the thousands of *ninots*, figurines that pose at the base of each *falla* (huge statues of papier mâché and polystyrene), is saved from the flames by popular vote. Those reprieved over the years are displayed here.

Mercado de Colón MARKET
(Map p554; www.mercadocolon.es; Calle de Cirilo Amorós) This magnificent Modernista building, now colonised by boutiques and cafes, was formerly a market, built in 1916 to serve the rising bourgeoisie of the new suburb of L'Eixample.

Plaza Redonda SQUARE
(Map p558) Again trim and smart after an elaborate makeover, this small, circular space – which was once the abattoir of Valencia's Mercado Central – is ringed by stalls selling bits and bobs, buttons and bows, clothes and locally made crafts and ceramics.

FREE **Museo Taurino** MUSEUM
(Map p558; Pasaje de Doctor Serra 10; ⊙10am-8pm Tue-Sun) This small museum, right beside Plaza de Toros, holds a collection of bullfighting memorabilia, just the place for

VALENCIA & MURCIA VALENCIA CITY

VALENCIA FOR CHILDREN

Beaches, of course. The nearest is the combined beach of Malvarrosa and Las Arenas (the latter meaning 'sand'), a shortish bus or tram ride from Valencia's centre. The **high-speed tram** itself is fun: feel the G-force as it surges along.

The other great playground, year-round, is the diverted Río Turia's former 9km riverbed. Of its formal playgrounds, the giant **Gulliver** (Map p554; Jardines del Turia; admission free; ⊙10am-8pm Sep-Jun, 10am-2pm & 5-9pm Jul & Aug; ▣19, 95), in the Jardines del Turia, just asks to be clambered all over.

The Jardín Botánico (p560) is altogether more peaceful; mind the cacti and feral cats, play hide-and-seek among the trees, and keep an eye out for frogs in the fountain.

Of the **Ciudad de las Artes y las Ciencias** (p552) diversions, the Oceanogràfic, with more than 45,000 aquatic beasts and plants, has something for all ages. The science museum, reasonably documented in English, is more for over 12 year olds (we've seen primary-school kids innocently and casually wrecking the hands-on exhibits), while the IMAX cinema offers thrills for all. The fun is far from free, however, so do research the range of family and combined tickets, available online.

Valencia City Central

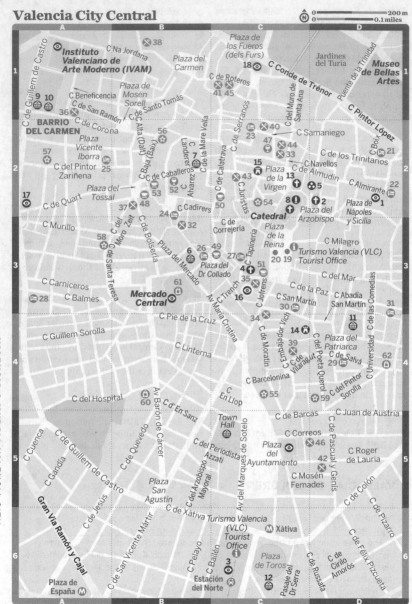

those who get their kicks from men in sequins and tights. After visiting the museum, you're allowed to strut a while in the sand of the bullring and dream.

L'Iber (Museo de Soldaditos de Plomo)

MUSEUM

(Map p558; www.museoliber.org; Calle de Caballeros 22; adult/child €4/2.80; ⊗11am-2pm & 4-7pm Wed-Sun) With more than 85,000 pieces, L'Iber

Valencia City Central

claims to be the world's largest collection of toy soldiers. The 4.7m x 2.8m set piece of the Battle of Almansa (1707) has 9000 combatants, while cases teem with battalions and regiments of toy soldiers.

FREE **Baños del Almirante** BATHHOUSE
(Map p558; Calle Baños del Almirante 3-5; ⊙10am-1.30pm & 6-7.30pm Tue-Sat, 10am-1.30pm Sun)

These Arab-style baths, constructed in 1313, functioned continuously as public bathing facilities until 1959. Visits take place every half-hour with an excellent audiovisual presentation, followed by a short guided tour.

Iglesia de Santa Catalina CHURCH
(Map p558; Plaza Lope de Vega) The striking 18th-century baroque belfry is one of Valencia's best-known landmarks.

FUN FOR FREE

The following museums and sites, normally paying, don't charge visitors on Saturday and Sunday.

» La Lonja (p556)
» Museo Fallero (p557)
» Museo de Historia de Valencia (p553)
» La Almoina (p553)
» Torres de Serranos (p557)
» Torres de Quart (p557)
» Cripta de la Cárcel de San Vicente Mártir (p553)
» Museo Nacional de Cerámica (p556)

Entry is free to IVAM every Sunday.

Town Hall   MUSEUM
(Plaza del Ayuntamiento 1; ☉9am-2pm) Valencia's handsome neoclassical *ayuntamiento* (town hall) dominates the square that takes its name. Within is the **Museo Histórico Municipal**, a repository of items important to the city's identity, such as the sword that Jaime I is reputed to have brandished when defeating the Muslim occupiers, and a fascinating 1704 map of Valencia, drafted by Padre Tosca. Enter via the door just south of the main steps.

Main Post Office   NOTABLE BUILDING
(✆90 212 32 12; Plaza del Ayuntamiento 24; ☉8.30am-8.30pm Mon-Fri, 9.30am-2pm Sat) Drop into Correos, Valencia's neoclassical main post office, to admire its spaciousness and superb stained-glass ceiling. The winged angels and sculpted train on its roof could perhaps get letters more swiftly to their destination than today's service. Let children pop postcards into the mouths of the two resplendent lion letter boxes on Calle de Correos.

PARKS & GARDENS

Jardines del Turia   GARDENS
(Map p554) Stretching the length of Río Turia's former course, this 9km-long lung of green is a mix of playing fields, cycling, jogging and walking paths, lawns and playgrounds. See Lilliputian kids scrambling over a magnificent, ever-patient **Gulliver** east of the Palau de la Música.

Jardín Botánico   GARDENS
(Map p554; http://www.jardibotanic.org; Calle de Quart 80; adult/child €2/1; ☉10am-dusk) Established in 1802, this was Spain's first botanic garden. With mature trees and plants, an extensive cactus garden and a wary colony of feral cats, it's a shady, tranquil place to relax.

Jardines del Real   PARK
(Map p554) Reaching down to the riverbed are the Royal Gardens, a lovely spot for a stroll, with a small aviary. Once the grounds of a palace, they're usually called Los Viveros.

Parque de Cabecera   PARK
(Map p554; Paseo de la Pechina) This public park at the western extremity of the riverbed has a mini lake where you can hire swan-shaped pedalos. Climb the man-made hillock for a special panorama of Valencia.

BEACHES

At the coastal end of the tram line, **Playa de la Malvarrosa** runs into **Playa de las Arenas**. Each is bordered by the **Paseo Marítimo** promenade and a string of restaurants and cafes. One block back, lively bars and discos thump out the beat in summer.

Playa El Salér, 10km south, is backed by shady pine woods. Yellow **Autocares Herca** (✆96 349 12 50; www.autocaresherca.com) buses run between Valencia and Perelló hourly (half-hourly in summer), calling by El Salér village. They stop (look for the Herca sign) at the junction of Gran Vía de las Germanias and Calle de Sueca, beside Plaza de Cánovas and in front of the Ciudad de las Artes y Las Ciencias.

☞ Tours

Carriage Rides   CARRIAGE RIDES
(Map p558) Hire a horse-drawn carriage in Plaza de la Reina and clip-clop around the Centro Histórico, lording it over the pedestrians below. A 40-minute trip costs €30 for up to five passengers.

Valencia Guías   TOUR
(Map p554; ✆96 385 17 40; www.valenciaguias. com; Paseo de la Pechina 32) Daily three-hour guided bicycle tours in English (€25 including rental and snack; minimum two persons). Also two-hour walking tours in Spanish and English (adult/child €15/free), leaving the Plaza de la Reina tourist office at 10am each Saturday.

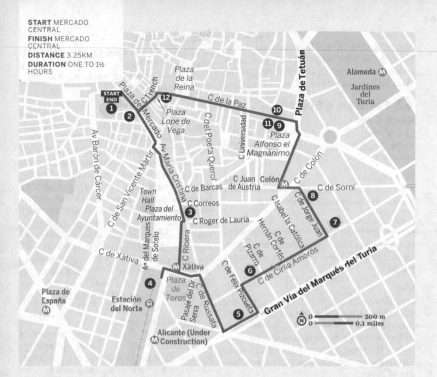

START MERCADO CENTRAL
FINISH MERCADO CENTRAL
DISTANCE 3.25KM
DURATION ONE TO 1½ HOURS

Walking Tour
Modernisme Meander

❯ This walk takes in Valencia's main Modernista (art nouveau) buildings.

After sniffing around ❶ **Mercado Central** take in the elaborate stucco facade of ❷ **Calle Ramilletes**, on the corner where it meets Plaza del Mercado. Follow Avenida María Cristina to Plaza del Ayuntamiento, site of the resplendent ❸ **central post office**. Drop in and look up to savour its magnificent leaded-glass dome. Valencia's biggest concentration of flower stalls fringes this open square, where the strictly neoclassical town hall stares across at its Modernista rival.

At the end of Calle Ribera, detour briefly to ❹ **Estación del Norte**, with its Modernista booking area of dark wood, and adjacent hall with its elaborate tilework. Take Calle de Russafa, then turn left for ❺ **Casa Ortega** (Gran Vía 9), with its ornate floral decoration and balcony, supported by a pair of handsome caryatids. Go left along Calle de Félix Pizcueta, then take the first right onto Calle de Cirilo Amorós. From here onwards, lift your gaze above the modern, ground-floor

shops to appreciate each building's original structure. Pause by ❻ **Casa Ferrer** (No 29), garlanded with stucco roses and ceramic tiling. Continue northwards to the resplendent ❼ **Mercado de Colón**, a chic spot for a drink stop, then head west to ❽ **Casa del Dragón** (Calle de Jorge Juan 3), named for its dragon motifs.

Cross Calle de Colón, turn right along Calle Poeta Quintana and pass the mounted statue of a haughty King Jaime I to join Calle de la Paz. Back in the 19th century, ❾ **Hotel Vincci Palace** was known as the Palace Hotel, in its time Valencia's finest. Both it and ❿ **No 31**, opposite, have elaborate, decorated miradors (corner balconies), while ⓫ **Red Nest Hostel** (No 36) has delicate, leafy iron railings.

At the end of Calle de la Paz, continue straight – maybe calling in for an *horchata* (sugary drink made from tiger nuts) at ⓬ **Horchatería Santa Catalina**. Then, at Plaza Lope de Vega, turn left into Calle Trench to return to the Mercado Central.

Art Valencia
WALKING TOUR

(Map p558; ☎96 310 61 93; www.artvalencia.com)
Two-hour walking tours (€13.50) in English
and Spanish departing 11am Friday from the
Plaza de la Reina tourist office.

✯✯ Festivals & Events

March & April

Las Fallas
PARADES, FIREWORKS

Valencia City's wild spring festival. See the
boxed text, p567.

Semana Santa
HOLY WEEK

Elaborate Easter Holy Week processions in
the seaside district of La Malvarrosa.

Fiesta de San Vicente Ferrer
PARADES, THEATRE

Colourful parades and miracle plays performed around town on the Sunday after
Easter.

May

Fiesta de la Virgen
RELIGIOUS

The effigy of the Virgen de los Desamparados (Valencia's patron saint), hemmed in
by fervent believers struggling to touch her,
makes the short journey across Plaza de la
Virgen to the cathedral on the second Sunday of May.

Danza Valencia
DANCE

Strictly contemporary dancing by Spanish
and international dance troupes during two
weeks spanning late April and early May.

June

Corpus Christi
RELIGIOUS

Celebrated with an elaborate procession
and mystery plays on the ninth Sunday after
Easter.

Día de San Juan
BONFIRES

On the night of 23 June, *valencianos* in
their thousands celebrate Midsummer's Day,
the longest day of the year, with bonfires on
the beach.

July

Feria de Julio
FIESTA

Performing arts, brass-band competitions,
bullfights, fireworks and a 'battle of the
flowers' in the second half of July.

October

Día de la Comunidad
LOCAL FIESTA

Commemorates every 9 October the city's
1238 liberation from the Arabs.

🛏 Sleeping

As Valencia is a business centre, big hotels
struggle to fill rooms outside the working
week. Most offer fat weekend and high-
summer discounts.

TOP CHOICE Caro Hotel
HOTEL €€€

(Map p558; ☎96 305 90 00; www.carohotel.com;
Calle Almirante 14; r €140-200; ❋☎) This spanking new hotel, housed in a sumptuous 19th-
century mansion, sits atop some 2000 years
of Valencian history. Its recent restoration
has revealed a hefty hunk of the Arab wall,
Roman column bases and Gothic arches.
Each room is furnished in soothing dark
shades and is unique in design. Bathrooms
have sensuous, circular bathtubs, bathrobes
and sexy Bulgari toiletries. For that very
special occasion, reserve the 1st-floor grand
suite (€500), once the ballroom. Savour, too,
its equally new restaurant, Alma del Temple (Map p558; mains €12-19; ⊙Tue-Sun).

TOP CHOICE Chill Art Jardín Botánico
BOUTIQUE HOTEL €€

(Map p554; ☎96 315 40 12; www.hoteljardinbota
nico.com; Calle Doctor Peset Cervera 6; s/d from
€85/90; ❋☎) Welcoming and megacool, this
intimate – only 16 rooms – hotel is furnished
with great flair. Candles flicker in the lounge
and each bedroom has original artwork.
You'll understand why the Instituto Valenciano de Arte Moderno (IVAM), an easy
walk away, regularly selects it as a venue for
its guests.

Ad Hoc Monumental
HOTEL €€

(Map p558; ☎96 391 91 40; www.adhochoteles.
com; Calle Boix 4; s €65-101, d €76-125; ❋☎)
Friendly Ad Hoc offers comfort and charm
deep within the old quarter and also runs
a splendid small restaurant (dinner Monday
to Saturday). The late-19th-century building
has been restored to its former splendour
with great sensitivity, revealing original ceil-

APARTMENTS

For independence and your own accommodation, from one night to a long
stay, consult these websites:

» www.roomsdeluxe.com

» www.valenciaflats.com

» www.accommodation-valencia.com

HOSTELS

Valencia has plenty of cheerful, modern, great-value hostels.

Center Valencia (Map p558; ☎96 391 49 15; www.center-valencia.com; Calle Samaniego 18)

Hilux Hostal (Map p558; ☎96 391 46 91; www.feetuphostels.com; Calle Cadirers 11)

Hôme Backpackers (Map p558; ☎96 391 37 97; www.homehostelsvalencia.com; Calle Santa Cristina)

Hôme Youth Hostel (Map p558; ☎96 391 62 29; www.homehostelsvalencia.com; Calle Lonja 4)

Indigo Youth Hostel (Map p558; ☎96 315 39 88; www.indigohostel.com; Calle Guillem de Castro 64)

Purple Nest Hostel (Map p554; ☎96 353 25 61; www.nesthostelsvalencia.com; Plaza Tetuan 5)

Red Nest Hostel (Map p558; ☎96 342 71 68; www.nesthostelsvalencia.com; Calle Paz 36)

---

ings, mellow brickwork and solid wooden beams.

Petit Palace Bristol
BOUTIQUE HOTEL €€

(Map p558; ☎96 394 51 00; www.hthotels.com; Calle Abadía San Martín 3; r €60-130; ❀@🖳) Hip and minimalist, this boutique hotel, a comprehensively made-over 19th-century mansion, retains the best of its past and does a particularly scrumptious buffet breakfast. Invest €15 extra for one of the superior top-floor doubles, with a broad wooden terrace giving panoramic views over the city. Free bikes for guests.

Petit Palace Germanías
BOUTIQUE HOTEL €€

(Map p554; ☎96 351 36 38; www.hthotels.com; Calle de Sueca 14; r €65-120; ❀@🖳) This attractive boutique hotel, younger sister to Petit Palace Bristol and just that little bit further from the city centre, has similar facilities, to which it adds its own seductive charms. Guests can borrow bikes for free.

Neptuno
HOTEL €€

(☎96 356 77 77; www.neptunohotel-valencia.com; Paseo de Neptuno 2; s/d from €126/130; ❀🖳) Neptuno, ultramodern and ultracool, overlooks the leisure port and beach of Las Arenas. It's ideal for mixing cultural tourism with a little beach frolicking. The hotel restaurant, Tridente, is one of Valencia's finest.

Hospes Palau de la Mar
HOTEL €€€

(Map p554; ☎96 316 28 84; www.hospes.es; Calle Navarro Reverter 14; s from €111, d €123-173; ❀🖳) Created by the merging of two elegant 19th-century mansions (plus 18 very similar modern rooms surrounding a tranquil internal garden), this boutique hotel, all black, white, soft fuscous and beige, is cool and contemporary. There's a sauna, Jacuzzi – and a pool scarcely bigger than your bathtub.

Hostal Antigua Morellana
HOSTAL €

(Map p558; ☎96 391 57 73; www.hostalam.com; Calle En Bou 2; s €45-55, d €55-65; ❀) The friendly, family-run 18-room Hostal Antigua Morellana is tucked away near the Mercado Central. It occupies a renovated 18th-century *posada* (where wealthier merchants bringing their produce to the nearby food market would spend the night) and has cosy, good-sized rooms, most with balconies.

Pensión París
PENSIÓN €

(Map p558; ☎96 352 67 66; www.pensionparis.com; 1st & 3rd fl, Calle de Salvá 12; s €23, d €34-42) Welcoming, with spotless rooms – most with shared bathrooms, some with private facilities – this family-run option on a quiet street is the antithesis of the crowded, pack-'em-in hostel.

Acta Atarazanas
HOTEL €€

(☎96 320 30 10; www.hotelatarazanas.com; Plaza Tribunal de las Aguas 5; r from €65; ❀🖳) The cream walls and fabrics of each bedroom contrast with the dark, stained woodwork. Sybaritic bathrooms have deep tubs with hydromassage and the broad shower head is as big as a discus. Handy for both beach and port, its breezy rooftop terrace offers a magnificent wraparound view of sea and city.

✕ Eating

Valencia is the capital of La Huerta, a fertile coastal agricultural plain that supplies the city with delightfully fresh fruit and

VALENCIA & MURCIA VALENCIA CITY

vegetables. With more than 1700 restaurants, it seriously spoils you for choice.

CENTRO HISTÓRICO

TOP CHOICE **Delicat** TAPAS, FUSION €
(Map p558; ☑96 392 33 57; seudelicat@hotmail.es; Calle Conde Almodóvar 4; mains €4-11, menus €12; ☉Tue-Sun) At this particularly friendly, intimate option (there are only nine tables, plus the terrace in summer), Catina, up front, and her partner, Paco, on full view in the kitchen, offer an unbeatable value five-course menu of samplers for lunch and a range of truly innovative tapas anytime.

TOP CHOICE **Seu-Xerea** FUSION, MEDITERRANEAN €€
(Map p558; ☑96 392 40 00; www.seuxerea.com; Calle Conde Almodóvar 4; mains around €20, menus €19-45; ☉Tue-Sat) Recently renovated, this welcoming restaurant is favourably quoted in almost every English-language press article about Valencia City. The creative, regularly changing, rock-reliable à la carte menu features dishes both international and deep rooted in Spain. Wines, selected by the owner, a qualified sommelier, are uniformly excellent.

Vuelve Carolina MEDITERRANEAN €€
(Map p558; ☑96 321 86 86; www.vuelvecarolina.com; Calle Correos 8; mains €12-16, menus €30; ☉Mon-Sat) This new, popular place (reservations are essential) could be a ship's hull. Walls, the bar and just about everything are of stripped pine, subtly lit. The crockery, with plates shaped like fretted leaves and oval glasses, also speaks style. The cuisine is correspondingly original with subtle, creative dishes such as a starter of thick, creamy yoghurt enfolding a single, succulent mussel.

Carosel MEDITERRANEAN €
(Map p558; ☑96 113 28 73; www.carosel.es; Calle Taula de Canvis 6; mains €6-10, menus €15-18; ☉lunch & dinner Tue-Sat, lunch Sun) Jordi and his partner, Carol, run this delightful small restaurant. After a trio of tasty lunchtime starters, attractively presented on a single platter, comes a rice dish of just the right consistency, then a choice of rich desserts. The evening menu follows the same pattern but with more of all. Warmly recommended.

Tap MEDITERRANEAN, TAPAS €
(Map p558; ☑96 391 26 27; www.enotecaeltap.com; Calle de Roteros 9; mains €6-11, menus €12; ☉lunch & dinner Tue-Sat, dinner Mon) Tap is a recent addition to the Barrio del Carmen's rich selection of small, characterful restaurants. Run by Michele and Edu, together with René, who sweats it out in the kitchen, it's excellent value. Tapas are original and delightfully prepared, and there's a carefully selected choice of both wines and boutique beers.

La Pilareta TAPAS €
(Map p558; ☑96 391 04 97; Calle del Moro Zeit 13; meals around €15; ☉noon-midnight) Cramped, earthy La Pilareta (also known as Bar Pilar) is great for hearty tapas and *clóchinas* (small, juicy local mussels), available between May and August. For the rest of the year it serves *mejillones,* altogether fatter if less tasty. Ask for an *entero*, a platterful in a spicy broth that you scoop up with a spare shell. At the bar, etiquette demands that you dump your empty shells in the plastic trough at your feet.

Mattilda MEDITERRANEAN €€
(Map p558; ☑96 382 31 68; Calle de Roteros 21; menus €11-13, mains €11-17; ☉lunch Mon & Tue, lunch & dinner Wed-Sat) The decor is stylish, modern and unpretentious – just like Francisco Borell and his cheery young team, who offer friendly service, an imaginative à la carte selection and a particularly good-value lunch menu.

Ginger Loft Café BAR, CAFE €
(Map p558; ☑96 352 32 43; www.thegingerloft.com; Calle de Vitoria 4; mains €7-12.50, menus €12.75; ☉lunch & dinner Tue-Sat, brunch Sun) Mike from Scotland and his Peruvian-Japanese partner, Santiago, run this delightful small cafe. Select wines are all from the Valencia region. There's a pageful of sexy cocktails and just about the largest selection of gins you've ever seen. Snack from their great selection of Spanish hams and cheeses, or choose a dish from the international range of mains.

La Tastaolletes VEGETARIAN €
(Map p558; ☑96 392 18 62; www.latastaolletes.com; Calle de Salvador Giner 6; tapas & salads €5-9.50, mains €9.50-12; ☉lunch & dinner Tue-Sat, lunch Sun; ☑) La Tastaolletes does a creative range of vegetarian tapas and mains. Pleasantly informal, it does good, wholesome food created from quality prime ingredients. Salads are large and leafy and desserts (indulge in the cheesecake with stewed fruits) are a dream.

Palacio de la Bellota SEAFOOD €€€
(Map p558; ☑96 351 49 94; www.palaciodelabellota.es; Calle de Mosén Femades 7; menus €46-55;

WHAT'S COOKING IN VALENCIA?

Arroz (rice) underwrites much of Valencian cuisine – such as paella, first simmered here and exported to the world. For a more original experience, try alternatives such as *arroz a banda* (simmered in a fish stock); *arroz negro* (with squid, including its ink); or *arroz al horno* (baked in the oven). For *fideuá*, Valencian cooks simply substitute noodles for rice.

Other regional specialities include *horchata*, an opaque sugary drink made from pressed *chufas* (tiger nuts), into which you dip large finger-shaped buns called – no sniggering, now! – *fartons*. Finally, despite its name, *Agua de Valencia* couldn't be further from water. The local take on Buck's Fizz, it mixes *cava* (sparkling Champagne-method wine), orange juice, gin and vodka.

⊙Mon-Sat) Palacio de la Bellota is one of a clutch of upmarket seafood restaurants flanking this pedestrianised street. Shell-fish are hauled fresh from the Mediterranean and the fish selection is also excellent. There's ham as well, legs of it dangling like chorus girls' thighs from the ceiling. Eat inside or on its street terrace.

La Lluna
VEGETARIAN €

(Map p558; ☎96 392 21 46; Calle de San Ramón 23; meals around €15; ⊙Mon-Sat; 🖋) Friendly and full of regulars, with walls of clashing tilework, La Lluna has been serving quality, reasonably priced vegetarian fare (including a superb-value four-course lunch menu at €7.70) for over 25 years.

La Utielana
VALENCIAN €€

(Map p558; ☎96 352 94 14; Plaza Picadero dos Aguas 3; menus €10, mains €15; ⊙lunch & dinner Mon-Fri, lunch Sat) Tucked away off Calle Prócida and not easy to track down, La Utielana well merits a minute or two of sleuthing. Very Valencian, it packs in the crowds, drawn by the wholesome fare and exceptional value for money. Arrive early as it doesn't take reservations – if you have to wait, grab a numbered ticket from the dispenser.

Las Cuevas
TAPAS €

(Map p558; ☎96 391 71 96; Plaza Cisneros 2; tapas €4.50-10; ⊙lunch & dinner Mon-Fri, dinner Sat) Aptly named, 'The Caves' is vast and full of nooks and crannies. Its bar groans with a huge range of freshly made tapas.

Pepita Pulgarcita
TAPAS €

(Map p558; ☎96 391 46 08; Calle de Caballeros 19; tapas €5.50-9.50; ⊙lunch & dinner Thu-Sun, dinner Mon-Wed) With wines stacked high behind the bar and subtle, inventive tapas, tastefully presented, tiny Pepita Pulgarcita is great for a snack, meal or simply a *copa*.

EASTERN VALENCIA

New restaurants and cafes sprout up almost monthly in the up-and-coming *barrio* (district) of Russafa and beyond.

TOP CHOICE / Appetite
INTERNATIONAL FUSION €€

(Map p554; ☎96 110 56 60; www.appetite.es; Calle Salvador Abril 7; 6/8-course menus €26/32; ⊙dinner Thu-Mon plus lunch Sat & Sun) 'Multicultural cuisine' is how Bonnie from Australia and her partner, Arantxa, as Valencian as they come, describe their fusion delights with their Asian slant, reflecting Bonnie's Singaporean origins. Sit back and let her compose your menu for you. Each dish is freshly prepared, delightfully presented and enticingly described in excellent English by Arantxa.

TOP CHOICE A Tu Gusto
MEDITERRANEAN €€

(Map p554; ☎96 322 70 26; www.atugusto.com; cnr Avenida Instituto Obrero & Calle Escritor Rafael Ferreres; mains €14-20, menus €10-36; ⊙lunch & dinner Wed-Sat, lunch Sun & Tue) At this strictly contemporary place, the decor is sleek, all pistachio and pitch black but for the gleaming white bar. Salvador Furió, the powerhouse in the kitchen, has worked with some of Spain's finest chefs. His cuisine is modern, creative and attractively presented, and portions are generous.

Coloniales Huerta
SPANISH, TAPAS €€

(Map p554; ☎96 334 80 09; www.colonialeshuerta.com; Calle del Maestro Gozalbo 13; meals around €25, menus €16-25; ⊙lunch & dinner Tue-Sat, lunch Sun) Recently established Coloniales Huerta occupies what was until its recent closure a classic Valencian delicatessen (indeed, one wing of the restaurant still sells the finest of foodstuffs). Imaginatively converted, it retains an air of benign clutter and unhurried pace. Wines are at shop prices with the addition of a very reasonable €4 corkage charge.

LAS ARENAS

On weekends locals in their hundreds head for Las Arenas, just north of the port, where a long line of restaurants overlooking the beach all serve up authentic paella in a three-course meal costing around €20.

Tridente
FUSION €€

(☎96 356 77 77; Paseo de Neptuno 2; mains €16, menus €29-49; ☺lunch & dinner Mon-Sat, lunch Sun) Begin with an aperitif on the broad beachfront terrace of Tridente, restaurant of Neptuno hotel, then move inside, where filtered sunlight bathes its soothing cream decor. There's an ample à la carte selection but you won't find details of the day's menus in front of you – they're delivered orally by the maître d', who speaks good English. Dishes, with their combinations of colours and blending of sweet and savoury, are delightfully presented and portions are generous.

Lonja del Pescado
SEAFOOD €

(☎96 355 35 35; Calle de Eugenia Viñes 243; meals around €20; ☺lunch Sat & Sun, dinner Tue-Sun Mar-Oct, lunch Sat & Sun, dinner Fri & Sat Nov-Feb) One block back from the beach at Malvarrosa, this busy, informal place in what's little more than an adorned tin shack offers unbeatable value for fresh fish. Grab an order form as you enter and fill it in at your table.

La Pepica
SEAFOOD €€

(☎96 371 03 66; Paseo de Neptuno 6-8; meals around €25; ☺lunch & dinner Mon-Sat, lunch Sun) More expensive than its many beach-side competitors, La Pepica, run by the same family for more than a century, is renowned for its rice dishes and seafood. Here, Ernest Hemingway, among other luminaries, once strutted. Between courses, browse through the photos and tributes that plaster the walls.

Drinking

The Barrio del Carmen has both the grungiest and grooviest collection of bars. On weekends, Calle de Caballeros, the main street, seethes with punters seeking *la marcha* (the action). Up-and-coming Russafa these days threatens to rival the Carmen for nightlife, while the university area, especially around Avenidas de Aragón and Blasco Ibáñez, has enough bars and *discotecas* to keep you busy beyond sunrise. In summer the port area and Malvarrosa leap to life.

CENTRO HISTÓRICO

TOP CHOICE Sant Jaume
CAFE, BAR

(Map p558; Plaza del Tossal) At this converted pharmacy, you can still see the old potion bottles and jars ranged behind the counter. Its 1st floor is all quiet crannies and poky passageways.

Cafe-Bar Negrito
CAFE, BAR

(Map p558; Plaza del Negrito) El Negrito's large terrace trumps the cramped interior. It occupies the whole of the square and traditionally attracts a more left-wing, intellectual clientele.

Café Lisboa
CAFE, BAR

(Map p558; Plaza del Doctor Collado 9) This lively, student-oriented bar has a large, street-side terrace. The bulletin board is a palimpsest of small ads for apartment shares and language tuition.

Café Infanta
CAFE, BAR

(Map p558; Plaza del Tossal) The interior is a clutter of cinema memorabilia, while its external terrace, beside the busy square, is great for people-watching.

Johnny Maracas
BAR

(Map p558; 39 Calle de Caballeros) This suave salsa place, beating to Latino rhythms, attracts Valencia's beautiful people and is great for a drink or dance. Not least of its charms are the fish tanks on the bar.

Café de las Horas
COCKTAIL BAR

(Map p558; Calle Conde de Almodóvar 1) Offers high baroque, tapestries, music of all genres, candelabras, bouquets of fresh flowers and a long list of exotic cocktails.

RUSSAFA

You're spoilt for choice in the edgy, on-the-rise *barrio* of Russafa.

As befits this up-and-coming, Boho district, there are a couple of great cafes-cum-

---

SAMPLING HORCHATA

Two great traditional places to sample *horchata* in the heart of town are **Horchatería de Santa Catalina** (Map p558; ☎96 391 23 79; Plaza Santa Catalina 6; ☺8am-9pm) and **Horchatería el Siglo** (Map p558; Plaza Santa Catalina), facing each other in eternal rivalry on Plaza Santa Catalina.

LAS FALLAS

The exuberant, anarchic swirl of Las Fallas de San José (www.fallas.es) – fireworks, music, festive bonfires and all-night partying – is a must if you're visiting Spain in mid-March.

The *fallas* themselves are huge sculptures of papier mâché on wood (with, increasingly, environmentally damaging polystyrene), built by teams of local artists. Despite Spain's deep economic recession, in 2012 the combined cost of their construction was well over €8 million. Each neighbourhood sponsors its own *falla*, and when the town wakes after the *plantà* (overnight construction of the *fallas*) on the morning of 16 March, more than 350 have sprung up. Reaching up to 15m in height, with the most expensive costing €400,000 in 2012, these grotesque, colourful effigies satirise celebrities, current affairs and local customs.

Around-the-clock festivities include street parties, paella-cooking competitions, parades, open-air concerts, bullfights and free firework displays. Valencia considers itself the pyrotechnic capital of the world and each day at 2pm from 1 to 19 March a *mascletà* (over five minutes of deafening thumps and explosions) shakes the window panes of Plaza del Ayuntamiento.

After midnight on the final day each *falla* goes up in flames – backed by yet more fireworks.

bookshops-cum-cultural centres. Each promotes concerts, runs films and workshops, welcomes outsiders, and is family-friendly and welcoming.

Backstage Russafa
DAR

(Map p554; Calle Literato Azorin 1) Backstage is popular with theatre folk and hangers-on – hence the name, decor and theatrical lighting. Big-band music throbs in the background, cocktails are shaken with histrionic panache, and even the toilets are labelled (oh dear me, yes) *actores* and *actrices*.

Tula
CAFE, BAR

(Map p554; www.tulacafe.es; cnr Calles de Cádiz & Literato Azorín) Tula was among the very first of the spruce, modern Russafa bars. A friendly spot, it remains a relaxed, welcoming, laid-back place for a drink or snack, whether in the brightly coloured interior or on its streetside terrace.

Slaughterhouse
CAFE, BAR

(Map p554; www.slaughterhouse.es; Calle de Denia 22) Once a butcher's shop (hence its title, also inspired by the Kurt Vonnegut novel of the same name), Slaughterhouse abounds in books (even in the toilets), new, old, for sale and simply for browsing. There's a limited menu, where every dish has a literary reference (we couldn't resist its toothsome Arena de Chocolate Willy Wonka).

Ubik Café
CAFE, BAR

(Map p554; http://ubikcafe.blogspot.com.es; Calle Literato Azorín 13) This child-friendly cafe, bar and bookshop is a comfy place to lounge and browse. It has a short, well-selected list of wines and serves cheese and cold-meat platters, salads and plenty of Italian specialities.

☆ Entertainment

La Turia is a detailed weekly guide in Spanish on sale at kiosks and newsagents. *24-7 Valencia* and *In VLC* are free monthlies. Both are available in tourist offices and selected bars and clubs.

Most clubs have admission prices (€8 to €20), so keep an eye out for discounted passes, carried by many local bars.

Dance Clubs & Discotecas

Terraza Umbracle
LOUNGE

(Map p554; ⊙midnight-8am Thu–Sat May–mid-Oct) At the southern end of the Umbracle walkway within the City of Arts & Sciences, this a cool, sophisticated spot to spend a hot summer night. Catch the evening breeze under the stars on the terrace, then drop below to Mya, a top-of-the-line club with an awesome sound system that's open year-round. Admission (€15) covers both venues.

Radio City
CLUB

(Map p558; www.radiocityvalencia.es; Calle de Santa Teresa 19; ⊙11pm-3.30am) Almost as much mini-cultural centre as club, Radio City, always seething, pulls in the punters with activities including cinema, flamenco and dancing to an eclectic mix. Pick up a flyer here for its younger sister, Music Box, also

VALENCIA & MURCIA VALENCIA CITY

in the Centro Histórico, which stays open until dawn.

Music Box
CLUB

(Map p558; Calle del Pintor Zariñena 16; ⊙midnight-7am Tue-Sat) The music here is eclectic with something for everyone. Entry is free except after 3am on Friday and Saturday, when there's a €10 admission.

Xtra Lrge Playground
BAR, CLUB

(Map p554; cnr Gran Vía de las Germanias & Calle de Cádiz; ⊙midnight-4am Thu-Sat) Spread over 600 sq metres, this recently opened venue merits its name. All soft pastel colours on brute metal and concrete, it offers live DJs, and is already popular with Valencia's movers and shakers. Sip something special at the Spanglishly named Gintonería-Coktelería, then dance away until late.

Mosquito
MUSIC BAR

(Map p554; Calle Polo y Peyrolón 11) DJs at this tiny box of a place dispense an eclectic mix of sounds. However many shots you knock back, you'll know you're in the right place by the giant papier mâché mosquito hovering above the circular bar.

Dub Club
CLUB

(Map p554; Calle Jesús 91; ⊙10pm-6am Thu-Sun) 'We play music not noise' is the slogan of this funky dive, with its long, narrow bar giving onto a packed dance floor. And it indeed offers great music and great variety, including, depending upon the night, live jazz jamming, reggae, dub, drum 'n' bass, funk, breakbeat and more.

Excuse Me?
CLUB

(Map p554; www.excusemeclub.org; Calle de Tomasos 14; ⊙midnight-7.30am Fri & Sat) At decidedly retro Excuse Me?, in the heart of Russafa, divide your time between its two retro rooms, where indie, punk and soul plays upstairs, while down below there's a wider variety of sounds. Arrive before 3am and you'll squeeze in for free.

La 3
CLUB

(cnr Avenida del Puerto & Calle del Padre Porta; ⊙1-7am Fri & Sat) At this megacomplex near the port, you get three clubs in one (hence the name), each with its own dance floor, throbbing mainly to indie-electronic, electroclash and nu-disco. Your entry ticket lets you roam from one floor to another and there are often live bands.

Calcatta
CLUB, PUB

(Map p558; www.calcatta.es; Calle Reloj Viejo 4; ⊙2-7am Fri & Sat) For drinks, get your card punched at this long-established club, housed in a 17th-century mansion. Its three floors overlook the interior patio and dance floor.

Caribbean's
DANCE, BAR

(Map p554; Calle de Bélgica 5; ⊙Tue-Sat) Drinks (try the mojitos) are decently priced at this small, below-ground and usually jam-packed dance bar that blends house, hip-hop and R&B. Wednesday night is student night.

Live Music

Black Note
JAZZ

(Map p554; http://blacknoteclub.com; Calle Polo y Peyrolón 15; ⊙from 11.30pm) Valencia City's most active jazz venue, Black Note has live music daily except Sunday and good canned jazz. Admission, including first drink, ranges from free to €15, depending on who's grooving.

Café Mercedes Jazz
JAZZ

(Map p554; www.cafemercedes.es; Calle de Sueca 27; ⊙10pm-3.30am Thu-Sun) This attractive contemporary cafe offers the best from the local jazz scene. Entry is free to jam sessions and less than €10 when a recognised combo's billed.

Jimmy Glass
JAZZ

(Map p558; www.jimmyglassjazz.net; Calle Baja 28) Playing jazz from the owner's vast CD collection, Jimmy Glass also sometimes has live performances. It's just what a jazz bar should be – dim and serving jumbo measures of high-octane cocktails.

Wah Wah
CLUB

(Map p554; www.wahwahclub.es; Calle Campoamor 52; ⊙10pm-3am Thu-Sat) For many clubbers, Wah Wah remains Valencia's hottest venue for live music, especially underground and international indie.

El Loco
LIVE MUSIC

(Map p554; www.lococlub.org; Calle Erudito Orellena 12; ⊙from 10.30pm) This popular, long-established venue puts on groups and solo acts, usually between Thursday and Saturday. Entry, depending upon the band of the day, is €5 to €15.

Football

Valencia Club de Fútbol (www.valenciacf.com) is the city's major football team.

Valencia's other professional club, Levante (www.levanteud.com), a minnow by comparison, bounces in and out of La Liga, the Spanish first division. Do take in a game – these guys, on a high as we write, need all the support they can get.

Cinemas

Filmoteca CINEMA
(Map p558; www.ivac-lafilmoteca.es; Plaza del Ayuntamiento; admission €1.50) This cinema, on the 4th floor of the Teatro Rialto building, screens undubbed classic and art-house films – and hasn't raised its admission price in over 25 years!

Babel CINEMA
(Map p554; www.cinesalbatrosbabel.com; Calle Vicente Sancho Tello 10) Multiscreen Babel shows exclusively undubbed films and runs a pleasant cafe. Admission prices are lower on Monday.

Theatre & Opera

Teatro Principal THEATRE
(Map p558; ☑96 353 92 00; Calle de Barcas 15) Valencia's main venue for theatre.

Palau de la Música CONCERT HALL
(Map p554; ☑96 337 50 20; www.palaudevalencia.com; Paseo de la Alameda 30) Hosts mainly classical music recitals.

Palau de les Arts Reina Sofía OPERA
(☑902 20 23 83; www.lesarts.com; Autovía a El Saler) A spectacular arts venue offering mostly opera.

🛍 Shopping

Librería Patagonia BOOKS
(Map p558; www.libreriapatagonia.com; Calle de Hospital 1) Excellent travel bookshop and travel agency with some guides in English and lots of Lonely Planet titles.

Mercado Central MARKET, FOOD
(Map p558; Plaza del Mercado; ⊗7.30am-3pm Mon-Sat) A visit to Valencia's magnificent covered central market is a must, even if you only browse.

Valencia Club de Fútbol Shop SOUVENIRS
(Map p558; Calle del Pintor Sorolla 24) Souvenirs, scarfs, woolly hats and many a memento more for the city's major football club.

ℹ Information

Call ☑902 12 32 12 throughout the region for tourist information (at premium rates).

The best of several online guides to the city are www.thisisvalencia.com and www.valenciacityguide.com.

Regional tourist office (☑96 398 64 22; www.comunitatvalenciana.com; Calle de la Paz 48; ⊗9am-8pm Mon-Sat, 10am-2pm Sun) A fount of information about the Valencia region.

Turismo Valencia (VLC) tourist office (☑96 315 39 31; www.turisvalencia.es; Plaza de la Reina 19; ⊗9am-7pm Mon-Sat, 10am-2pm Sun) Has several other branches around town, including the train station and airport arrivals area.

ℹ Getting There & Away

Air

Valencia's **Aeropuerto de Manises** (☑96 159 85 00) is 10km west of the city centre along the A3, towards Madrid. It's served by metro lines 3 and 5.

Budget flights serve major European destinations such as Paris, Milan, Geneva, Amsterdam and Brussels. The following airlines fly to/from Ireland and the UK:

EasyJet London (Gatwick)

Ryanair Year-round: London (Stansted). Summer only: Bristol, Dublin, East Midlands, Manchester.

Boat

Acciona Trasmediterránea (www.acciona-trasmediterranea.es) operates car and passenger ferries to Ibiza, Mallorca and Menorca.

Bus

Valencia's **bus station** (☑96 346 62 66) is beside the riverbed on Avenida Menéndez Pidal. Bus 8 connects it to Plaza del Ayuntamiento.

Avanza (www.avanzabus.com) operates hourly bus services to/from Madrid (€27.50 to €34.50, four hours).

ALSA (www.alsa.es) has up to 10 daily buses to/from Barcelona (€27 to €32, 4½ hours) and over 10 to Alicante (around €19, 2½ hours), most passing by Benidorm (€15.20, 1¾ hours).

Train

From Valencia's Estación del Norte, major destinations include the following:

DESTINATION	PRICE (€)	DURATION (HR)	FREQUENCY
Alicante	17-29	1¾	10
Barcelona	40-44	3-3½	at least 12
Madrid	63-80	1¾	up to 15

ℹ Getting Around

Valencia has an integrated bus, tram and metro network.

LA TOMATINA

Buñol? It'll make you see red.

The last or penultimate Wednesday in August (the date varies) marks Spain's messiest festival. Held in Buñol, 40km west of Valencia City, La Tomatina is a tomato-throwing orgy that attracts more than 40,000 visitors to a town of just 9000 inhabitants.

At precisely 11am, over 100 tonnes of squishy tomatoes are tipped from trucks to the waiting crowd. For precisely one hour everyone joins in a cheerful, anarchic tomato battle. After being pounded with pulp, expect to be sluiced down with hoses by the local fire brigade.

Don't forget a set of fresh clothes and perhaps a pair of goggles to protect the eyes. For more background, visit www.latomatina.es.

Tourist offices of Turismo Valencia (VLC) sell the **Valencia Tourist Card** (€15/20/25 per one/two/three days), entitling you to free urban travel and discounts at participating sights, shops and restaurants.

To/From the Airport

Metro lines 3 and 5 connect the airport, central Valencia and the port. A taxi into the city centre costs around €17 (there's a supplement of €2.50 above the metered fee for journeys originating at the airport).

Bicycle Hire

Do You Bike (☑96 315 55 51; www.doyoubike.com; Calle Mar 14)

Orange Bikes (☑96 391 75 51; www.orangebikes.net; Calle Editor Manuel Aguilar 1)

Solution Bike (☑96 110 36 95; www.solutionbike.com; Calle Embajador Vich 11)

Valencia Guías (☑96 385 17 40; www.valenciaguias.com; Calle Tapinería 13 & Paseo de la Pechina 32)

Car & Motorcycle

Street parking is a pain. There are large underground car parks beneath Plazas de la Reina and Alfonso el Magnánimo and, biggest of all, near the train station, covering the area between Calle Xàtiva and the Gran Vía.

Reliable local car-rental companies are usually substantially less expensive than the multinationals. Those operating from Valencia airport include the following:

Javea Cars (☑96 579 33 00; www.javeacars.com)

Solmar (☑96 646 10 00; www.solmar.es)

Victoria Cars (☑96 583 02 54; www.victoriacars.com)

Public Transport

Most buses run until about 10pm, with seven night services continuing until around 1am. Buy a **Bonobús Plus**, a touch-sensitive, rechargeable card (€9.50 for 10 journeys), sold at major metro stations, most tobacconists and some newspaper kiosks or pay as you go on (€1.50).

The high-speed tram is a pleasant way to get to the beach and port. Pick it up at Pont de Fusta or where it intersects with the metro at Benimaclet.

Metro (www.metrovalencia.es) lines cross town and serve the outer suburbs. The closest stations to the city centre are Ángel Guimerá, Xàtiva (for the train station), Colón and Pont de Fusta.

Taxi

Call **Radio-Taxi** (☑96 370 33 33) or **Valencia Taxi** (☑96 357 13 13).

Around Valencia City

LA ALBUFERA

About 15km south of Valencia, La Albufera is a huge freshwater lagoon separated from the sea by La Devesa, a narrow strip of sand dunes and pine forests. The lake and its shores are a breeding ground and sanctuary for migrating and indigenous birds. Keen birdwatchers flock to the Parque Natural de la Albufera, where around 90 species regularly nest while more than 250 others use it as a staging post on their migrations.

Sunsets can be spectacular. You can take a boat trip out on the lagoon, joining the local fisherfolk, who use flat-bottomed boats and nets to harvest fish and eels from the shallow waters.

Surrounded by rice fields, La Albufera was the birthplace of paella. Every second house in the villages of El Palmar and El Perellonet is a restaurant, often run by ex- or part-time fisherfolk and serving paella and other rice and seafood dishes.

Autocares Herca buses for Playa El Salér are also good for La Albufera, and go on to either El Palmar (minimum five daily) or El Perello (hourly or half-hourly), further down the coast.

SAGUNTO
POP 70,600

You come to Sagunto (Valenciano: Sagunt), 25km north of Valencia, primarily to enjoy the spectacular panorama of the town, coast and green sea of orange groves from its hilltop castle complex. It's usually visited as a day or half-day excursion from Valencia.

Sagunto was once a thriving Iberian community (called – infelicitously, with hindsight – Arse) that traded with Greeks and Phoenicians. In 219 BC Hannibal besieged and destroyed the town, sparking the Second Punic War between Carthage and Rome. Rome won, named the town Saguntum and set about rebuilding it.

From the train station, an uphill walk brings you first to the over-restored Roman theatre. Higher up, the stone walls of the castle complex (admission free; ⊙10am-dusk Tue-Sat, 10am-2pm Sun) girdle the hilltop for almost 1km. Mostly in ruins, its seven rambling sections each speak of a different period in Sagunto's long history.

There are frequent trains running between Valencia and Sagunto (one way/return €3.05/4.80).

Costa del Azahar

All along the Costa del Azahar (Orange Blossom Coast) spread citrus groves, from whose headily scented flowers the region takes its name. The busy, developed – not always harmoniously – seaside resorts are enticing if you're after sun and sand. By contrast, the high hinterland, especially the wild, sparsely populated lands of the Maestrazgo, offer great walking solitude and hearty mountain cooking.

BENICÀSSIM
POP 18,100

Benicàssim, scarcely a couple of blocks wide, stretches for 6km along the coast. It has been a popular resort since the 19th century, when wealthy Valencian families built summer residences here. Today over 75% of summer visitors are Spanish and many people from Madrid, Valencia and nearby Castellón own summer apartments.

⊙ Sights & Activities

Those 6km of broad beach are the main attraction. Bordering the promenade at the northeastern end are Las Villas, exuberant, sometimes frivolous holiday homes built by wealthy *valencianos* at the end of the 19th century and into the 20th. Ask for the tourist office leaflet, *The Las Villas Path*.

WORTH A TRIP

REQUENA

Requena, 65km west of Valencia, grew rich from silk; at one time it had about 800 active looms, making this tiny town Spain's fourth-biggest producer. Today it's primarily wine and livestock country, producing robust reds, sparkling *cavas* (sparkling wines), rich sausages and spicy meats. From its heart rears La Villa, the medieval nucleus, with its twisting streets and blind alleys.

Two venues for wine lovers are Museo del Vino (Calle Somera; adult/child €4/3; ⊙11am-2pm Wed-Sun), a wine museum within the handsome 15th-century Palacio del Cid, and Ferevin (Cuesta de las Carnicerías; ⊙11am-2pm Tue-Sun plus 5-7pm Sat), a showroom for local wine producers. Signing, alas, is only in Spanish.

Within the intestines of Plaza Albornoz is a network of interlinked cellars, once used as storerooms and, during strife, hideouts. Guided visits (adult/child €4/3; ⊙3-6 times daily Tue-Sun) meet outside No 6. Ask at the tourist office for times.

The tourist office (☑96 230 38 51; www.requena.es; Calle García Montés; ⊙9.30am-2pm Tue-Sun plus 4-7pm Sat & Sun) is below the main entrance to the Old Town. Ask for the English version of its *Sensaciones por Descubrir*, a helpful guide to La Villa.

Requena is right beside the Valencia–Madrid motorway. Up to 12 buses (€4.75, one hour) and seven trains (one way/return €4.65/7.25, 1½ hours) run daily to/from Valencia.

TOP CHOICE **Desierto de las Palmas** HILL

The twisting, climbing CV147 leads after about 6km to this inland range – cooler than the coast, on occasion misty – with a Carmelite monastery (1697) and first-class restaurant at its heart. Nowadays a nature reserve and far from desert (for the monks it meant a place for mystic withdrawal), it's a green, outdoor activities area. From **Monte Bartolo** (728m), its highest point, there are staggering views. The tourist office hands out an excellent booklet listing a range of different walks in the hills.

Time your visit to coincide with lunch at Restaurante Desierto de las Palmas.

Aquarama AMUSEMENT PARK

(www.aquarama.net; adult/child half-day €14/10, day €21/15; ⌚11am-7pm mid-Jun–early Sep) This vast water park is just south of town, off the N340.

Festivals & Events

Festival Internacional de Benicàssim MUSIC

(FIB; www.fiberfib.com) Usually held in mid-July, fans by the tens of thousands gather for this annual four-day festival, one of Europe's major outdoor music festivals. Top acts in 2012 included Bob Dylan and The Stone Roses.

Sleeping

Benicàssim's five camping grounds are all within walking distance of the beaches.

Hotel Benicàssim BOUTIQUE HOTEL €€

(☎620 56 98 48; www.hotelbenicassim.net; Calle San Antonio 13; s/d €55/80; @📶) Full of summertime colour and flair, this is a superb new boutique hotel. The rooms have massive raised beds and showers with pebble floors. The common areas are adorned in pop art, pictures of French street scenes (it's French-American run), Spanish movie posters and a giant old clock. Oh, and there's a glamorous bikini-clad beach babe standing guard outside. It's on the edge of the town centre. There have been a few complaints regarding the pre-paying of rooms via the internet.

Hotel Voramar HOTEL €€

(☎964 30 01 50; www.voramar.net; Paseo Marítimo Pilar Coloma 1; s €81, d €94-145, incl breakfast ; P❄📶) Venerable (it's been run by the same family for four generations) and blooded in battle (it functioned as a hospital in the Spanish Civil War), the Voramar has more character than most of Benicàssim's modern upstarts. It's spectacularly located right at the very northern edge of the beach. The restaurant, where the cuisine is first class, has large windows overlooking the sea.

Camping Azahar CAMPGROUND €

(☎96 430 31 96; www.campingazahar.es; sites per 2 people/tent/car from €18.80; ⌚year-round; 📶🏊) Extensive sites are shaded by mature mulberry trees. There's a restaurant, a large pool, and toilet blocks that are kept scrupulously clean.

Eating

Plenty of economical restaurants line Calles de Santo Tomás and Castellón, the Old Town's main street.

Restaurante Desierto de las Palmas RESTAURANT €€

(☎964 30 09 47; www.restaurantedesierto.com; mains €15-24; ⌚lunch & dinner daily Jun-Sep, lunch Wed-Mon Oct-May) Families flock from miles around to this popular venue, famed for its rice and seafood dishes, in the hills behind Benicàssim. Lively, noisy and very Spanish, it sits on a spur close to the Carmelite monastery and offers heart-stopping views from its broad windows.

Torreón RESTAURANT €€

(☎964 30 03 42; Avenida Ferrandis Salvador 2; mains €12-15) Overlooking the 16th-century Torre San Vicente watchtower that gives this cafe-restaurant its name, this is a great spot to catch the sea breezes while nibbling on a snack, sipping a drink or tucking into a full meal. If you're dining, book in advance to enjoy a place on the smaller, less crowded of its two terraces.

Information

Main tourist office (☎964 30 01 02; www.turismobenicassim.com; Calle Santo Tomás 74; ⌚9am-2pm & 4-7pm) One kilometre inland in the Old Town.

Getting There & Away

Buses run every half-hour (every 15 minutes in summer) to Castellón de la Plana, from where train connections are much more plentiful.

PEÑÍSCOLA

POP 8090

Peñíscola's Old Town, all cobbled streets and whitewashed houses, huddles within stone walls that protect the rocky promontory jutting into the sea. It's pretty as a postcard – and just as commercial, with ranks of souvenir and ceramics shops (one prominent item: a pot with a – oh dear – stiff penis for a spout, a pun that doesn't even work in Spanish). By contrast, the high-rises sprouting northwards along the coast are mostly leaden and charmless. But the **Paseo Marítimo** promenade makes pleasant walking, and the beach, which extends as far as neighbouring Benicarló, is superb, sandy and over 5km long.

Sights & Activities

Castle   CASTLE
(adult/child €3.50/free; ⊙9.30am-5.30pm or 9.30pm) The rambling 14th-century castle was built by the Knights Templar on Arab foundations and later became home to Pedro de Luna ('Papa Luna', the deposed Pope Benedict XIII). There are various exhibits relating to the history of the castle and town.

Sierra de Irta   NATURE PARK
To escape the summer crowds, seek solitude in the Sierra de Irta. Running south from Peñíscola, it's both nature park and protected marine reserve. It's also one of the very last unspoilt stretches of Valencian coastline, best explored on foot or by mountain bike. You can attack the full 26km of the circular PR V-194 trail or slip in one or more shorter loops. Ask at the tourist office for its free *Paths Through Irta* brochure.

Sleeping & Eating

Chiki Bar Restaurante   PENSIÓN €
(☑605 280295; Calle Mayor 3-5; r €40-50) High in the Old Town, Chiki Bar has, in addition to its engaging name, seven spotless, modern rooms with views. You might want your earplugs since the nearby parish church chimes tinnily, on the hour, every hour. From March to October, it runs an attractive restaurant (mains from €9; closed Tuesday) with a great-value three-course menu (€11). Hours are unreliable, so ring in advance.

Hostería del Mar   HOTEL €€
(☑964 48 06 00; www.hosteriadelmar.net; Avenida Papa Luna 18; s €71-100, d €101-133; ❄@☎☂) Once, this four-star, family-owned place was the only hotel along the promenade. And it still preserves more character than most of its undistinguished multistorey neighbours. Nearly all rooms have balconies overlooking the beach and there's even a casino, should you fancy your chances of recovering your room cost.

Hotel-Restaurante Simó   HOTEL €€
(☑964 48 06 20; www.hotelrestaurante-simo.com; Calle Porteta 5; s €40-55, d €55-75; ⊙closed Jan)

At the base of the castle pile and right beside the sea (on a stormy winter day it must be virtually in the sea!), the Simó has a restaurant (mains €13 to €25) with magnificent views across the bay. Seven of its nine simple, unfussy and relatively spacious rooms enjoy an equally impressive vista.

Hogar del Pescador   SEAFOOD €€
(☑964 48 95 88; Plaza Lonja Vieja; fish from €10, menú del día from €10) Squatting below the Old Town walls this popular fisherfolk's restaurant is great value for everything from the sea. A lunch time *menú del día* typically starts with something along the lines of tiny, fried fish before moving onto a hearty paella-style main course.

Information
Main tourist office (☑964 48 02 08; www.peniscola.es; ⊙9am-8pm Mon-Fri, 10am-1pm & 4.30-8pm Sat & Sun) At the southern end of Paseo Marítimo. Pick up its free descriptive booklet, *The Old City*.

Getting There & Around
Year-round, local buses run at least half-hourly between Peñíscola, Benicarló and Vinaròs. From July to mid-September there's an hourly run to Peñíscola/Benicarló train station.

El Maestrazgo

Straddling northwestern Valencia and southeast Aragón, El Maestrazgo (El Maestrat in Valenciano) is a mountainous land, a world away from the coastal fleshpots. Here ancient *pueblos* (villages) huddle on rocky outcrops and ridges. One such place, Sant Mateu, was chosen in the 14th century by the maestro (hence the name El Maestrazgo) of the Montesa order of knights as his seat of power.

The Maestrazgo is great, wild, on-your-own trekking territory. *La Tinença de Benifassà* and *Els Ports*, two excellent 1:30,000 maps, designed for walkers and available from the Morella tourist office among other outlets, cover most of the area. Also, get hold of Lonely Planet's *Hiking in Spain* for detailed route descriptions of a number of walks in this region.

SANT MATEU
POP 2200 / ELEV 325M

A drive 5km south from the N232 along the CV132 brings you to Sant Mateu, once capital of the Maestrazgo. Its solid mansions and elaborate facades recall the town's more illustrious past and former wealth, based upon the wool trade.

A moment or so's strolling distance from the colonnaded Plaza Mayor, ringed with cafe terraces, are four small municipal museums (each adult/child €1.50/free): the Museo Paleontológico (Arrabal de Barcelona 23; ☺10am-2pm & 4-7pm Tue-Sun), which as its name suggests is all about the giant, scary reptiles that long ago hunted in these hills; the Museo Arciprestal (Calle Santo Domingo; ☺guided tours noon Tue-Fri, 11am, noon, 1pm, 4.15pm & 5.15pm Sat, 11am & 1.15pm Sun), which is a museum of religious art (inside the Iglesia Arciprestal – visits are by guided tour only, in Spanish); the Museo les Presons (Calle La Cort 28; ☺10am-2pm & 4-7pm Tue-Sun), in the former jail (you might need to get the key from the house at Calle La Cort 32); and Museo Histórico Municipal (☺10am-2pm Tue-Fri), entered via the tourist office.

Radiating from the village are three signed circular walking trails of between 2½ and five hours that lead through the surrounding hills. Ask for the free tourist office pamphlet *Senderos de Sant Mateu* (in Spanish).

Family-run (see the photos of its three generations around the tiled dining room), Hotel-Restaurante La Perdi (☎964 41 60 82; laperdicb@hotmail.com; Calle Historiador Betí 9; s/d €20/40) is a bargain with five plain, comfortable rooms and a restaurant (mains €6-14.50) that does an equally good value *menú del día* (€12.50).

Follow signs from Plaza Mayor to the Ermita de la Mare de Déu dels Àngels, perched on a rocky hillside, a 2.5km drive or a considerably shorter walk away. A monastery until the Spanish Civil War (take a peep at its over-the-top baroque chapel), today it's the quality Restaurante dels Àngels (☎626 525219; menus €21; ☺lunch Wed-Sun, dinner Sat), offering incomparable views of the surrounding plain and fairly incomparable food.

Sant Mateu's tourist office (☎964 41 66 58; www.santmateu.com; Calle Historiador Betí 13; ☺10am-2pm & 4-6pm Tue-Sat, 10am-2pm Sun) is just off Plaza Mayor, in Palacio Borrull, a stalwart 15th-century building.

ℹ Getting There & Away

Weekdays, **Autos Mediterráneo** (☎964 22 00 54) buses link Sant Mateu with the following destinations:

Castellón €4.80, 1½ hours, three daily
Morella €3, 45 minutes, two daily
Vinaròs €2.50, 35 minutes, four daily

On Saturday, one service runs from Castellón to Morella via Sant Mateu. The bus stop is in Plaza Llaurador, 100m east of Hotel Restaurante Montesa.

AROUND SANT MATEU

Museo de Valltorta (☎964 33 60 10; ☺10am-2pm & 4-7pm or 5-8pm Tue-Sun), located 10km southwest of Sant Mateu in Tirig, is a well-illustrated museum. It presents the Maestrazgo's rich heritage of rock paintings, which are recognised as a Unesco World Heritage treasure. From here guided walks to the clifftop overhangs and much-faded paintings leave four times daily.

MORELLA

POP 2800 / ELEV 1000M

Bitingly cold in winter and refreshingly cool in summer, Morella is the Maestrazgo's principal town. This outstanding example of a medieval fortress town is perched on a hilltop, crowned by a castle and girdled by an intact rampart wall over 2km long. It's the ancient capital of Els Ports, the 'Mountain Passes', a rugged region offering some outstanding scenic drives and strenuous cycling excursions, plus excellent possibilities for walkers.

☉ Sights & Activities

Morella is a pleasantly confusing, compact jumble of narrow streets, alleys and steep steps. Its main street, running between Puerta San Miguel and Puerta de los Estudios, is bordered by shops selling mountain honey, perfumes, cheeses, pickles, pâtés, skeins of sausages and fat hams.

On the outskirts of town stretch the arches of a handsome 13th-century aqueduct. You can also get a guards'-eye view of the town by climbing up onto the city walls and into a guard tower. Ask at the tourist office for the key.

Castle   CASTLE
(adult/child €3/1.50; ☺11am-5pm or 7pm) Though badly knocked about, Morella's castle well merits the strenuous ascent to savour breathtaking views of the town and surrounding countryside. At its base is the bare church and cloister of the Convento de San Francisco, which is destined to become a *parador* (luxurious state-owned hotel, many of them in historic buildings) during the lifetime of this book.

Basílica de Santa María la Mayor   CHURCH
(Plaza Arciprestal; ☺11am-2pm & 4-6pm or 7pm, closed Mon Sep-Jul & Sun pm mid-Nov–mid-Mar)

This imposing Gothic basilica has two elaborately sculpted doorways on its southern facade. A richly carved polychrome stone staircase leads to the overhead choir, while cherubs clamber and peek all over the gilded altarpiece. Its ecclesiastical treasure is kept within the Museo Arciprestal (admission €1.50).

Museo Tiempo de Dinosaurios   MUSEUM
(adult/child €2/1.50; ⊙11am-2pm & 4-6pm or 7pm Tue-Sun) Opposite the tourist office, this museum, which is full of dinosaur bones and fossils, is one for children, children at heart and cavemen. The Maestrazgo's remote hills have been a treasure trove for palaeontologists. The museum film is in Spanish only.

Museo del Sexenni   MUSEUM
(adult/child €2/1.50, city walls adult/child €1.50/free) In the former Church of Sant Nicolau, this museum displays models, photos and items associated with the Sexenni, Morella's major fiesta. It's only open on demand, which you should do through the tourist office.

✹ Festivals & Events

Sexenni   TOWN FESTIVAL
Morella's major festival is the Sexenni, held during August every six years without interruption since 1673 (the next is in 2018) in honour of the town's patron, the Virgen de Vallivana. Visit the Museo del Sexenni to get the flavour of this major celebration with its tonnes of confetti and elaborate compositions in crêpe paper.

Festival de Música Barroca   MUSIC
Held annually in August, this baroque-music festival stars the Basílica de Santa María la Mayor's huge organ.

🛏 Sleeping & Eating

Hotel del Pastor   HOTEL €€
(☑964 16 02 49; www.hoteldelpastor.com; Calle San Julián 12; s/d incl breakfast €55/73; 🐾) This is an excellent deal, with slightly old-fashioned rooms spread over four floors (there's no lift but that's the only downside of this option). Rooms are traditionally furnished and come in warm ochre colours with plenty of polished wood. Bathrooms all have marble washstands and bathtub and large mirrors.

Hotel El Cid   HOTEL €
(☑964 16 01 25; www.hotelelcidmorella.com; Puerta San Mateu 3; s/d €35/59; 🐾) Beside the ramparts and above its popular bar and restaurant, Hotel El Cid has slick, white modern rooms (rooms 204 and 304, at the same price, have a small salon attached). Most have balconies, offering magnificent views over the ramparts and down into the valley below.

Hotel Rey Don Jaime   HOTEL €€
(☑964 16 09 11; www.reydonjaimemorella.com; Calle Juan Giner 6; s/d incl breakfast €76/102; 🅿🐾) This place has the prime spot just next to the main entrance to the Old Town, with comfortable rooms and good service, but for the price it rather lacks character. Parking is available for €10.

⬆ TOP
CHOICE Daluan   CONTEMPORARY, FUSION €€
(☑964 16 00 71; www.daluan.es; Callejón Cárcel 4; mains €12-15, lunch menus €14, menus €26-36; ⊙lunch Sun-Wed, lunch & dinner Fri & Sat) Run by Avelino Ramón, a cookery teacher by trade, and his wife, Jovita, Daluan's small interior is satisfyingly contemporary. Its terrace, beside a quiet alley, is equally relaxing. Expect friendly service and a hugely creative menu that changes regularly with the seasons.

Mesón del Pastor   TRADITIONAL SPANISH €€
(☑964 16 02 49; www.hoteldelpastor.com; Cuesta Jovaní 5-7; mains €10-14, menus €14-24; ⊙lunch Thu-Tue, dinner Sat) Within the dining room, bedecked with the restaurant's trophies and diplomas, it's all about robust mountain cuisine: thick gruels in winter, rabbit, juicy sausages, partridge, wild boar and goat. It's located a short walk from the hotel of the same name.

❶ Information

The **tourist office** (☑964 17 30 32; www.morellaturistica.com; Plaza San Miguel 3; ⊙10am-2pm & 4-6pm or 7pm Mon-Sat, 10am-2pm Sun daily Apr-Oct, closed Mon Nov-Mar) is just behind Torres de San Miguel, twin 14th-century towers flanking the main entrance gate.

❶ Getting There & Around

Morella is best reached via Castellón, which has good train connections. Two daily weekday buses (€9, 2¼ hours) and one Saturday service with Autos Mediterráneo run to/from Castellón's train station.

VILAFRANCA
POP 2500

Vilafranca, like Morella 36km to its north, grew rich from wool. Sheep no longer graze in such numbers but their legacy lives on in the estimated 1000km of drystone walls that stripe and criss-cross the land. Stone for walls, sheep pens, huts and houses are all illustrated in the excellent Museo de

Space-Age Splendour

Rising from the former riverbed and extending over 2km, the giant structures of the Ciudad de las Artes y las Ciencias (City of Arts & Sciences; p552) define contemporary Valencia.

Oceanogràfic

1 Fish and marine animals from the seven seas live within this watery world, the largest of its kind in Europe. Watch the fish watching you as you walk its underwater tunnels.

Hemisfèric

2 Seen from outside, the daringly designed Hemisfèric broods like a huge, heavy-lidded eye over the shallow lake that laps around it. Inside, it's both IMAX cinema and planetarium.

Palau de les Arts

3 Darth Vader's helmet? A giant extra-terrestrial carapace? Perhaps a supine armadillo? Or simply the world's largest opera auditorium, Sydney's excepted. Shimmering with *trencadís* – bright, white slivers of broken-tile mosaic – it broods over the former riverbed.

Restaurante Submarino

4 For a great gastronomic experience in original surroundings, drop down beneath wide mock-lilypads to where, instead of wallpaper, more than 1000 silvery bream slowly gyrate around you, mournfully eyeing your plate and their erstwhile brothers and sisters.

L'Umbracle

5 Diaphanous, feathery arches, albeit in concrete, recall the ribs of a palm frond and curve above this 320m-long walkway. In summer Valencia's most beautiful people will sip cocktails here before dropping to the *discoteca* beneath.

Clockwise from top left
1. Palau de les Arts Reina Sofía, designed by Santiago Calatrava and Félix Candela (p552) 2. L'Umbracle 3. Oceanogràfic (p552)

Pedra en Sec (Dry Stone Museum; ☑964 44 14 32; ☉10am-1.30pm & 4-7pm Thu-Sat, 10.30am-1.30pm Sun). Documentation is only in Valenciano but it's a very visual experience.

Call by the tourist office, just opposite, which holds the museum keys. Then, to stretch your legs and consolidate the museum experience, enjoy one of three one-hour country walks, supported by the tourist office's audio guide in English.

Costa Blanca

The long stripe of the Costa Blanca (White Coast) is one of Europe's most heavily visited areas. If you're after a secluded midsummer beach, stay away – or head inland to enjoy traditional villages and towns that have scarcely heard the word tourism. Then again, if you're looking for a lively social scene, good beaches and a suntan...

It isn't all concrete and package deals. Although the original fishing villages have long been engulfed by the sprawl of resorts, a few Old Town kernels, such as those of Xàbia (Jávea) and Altea, still survive.

In July and August it can be tough finding accommodation if you haven't booked. Out of season, those places remaining open usually charge far less than in high summer.

Most buses linking Valencia and Alicante head down the motorway, making a stop in Benidorm. A few, however, call by other intervening coastal towns. A smart new tram plies the scenic route between Alicante and Denia. Renfe trains connect Valencia with Gandia.

GANDIA
POP 78,700

Gandia, 67km south of Valencia, is a tale of two cities. The main town, once home to a branch of the Borja dynasty (more familiar as the infamous Borgias), is a prosperous commercial centre with a lively atmosphere. The other side of the coin is the fun-in-the-sun beach town a short drive away.

◉ Sights & Activities

Palacio Ducal de los Borja   PALACE
(www.palauducal.com; Calle Duc Alfons el Vell 1; guided tour adult/child €6/5; ☉10am-2pm & 4-8pm Mon-Sat, 10am-2pm Sun) Gandia's magnificent palace was the 15th-century home of Duque Francisco de Borja. Highlights include its finely carved *artesonado* ceilings and rich ceramic work – look out for the vivid *mapa universal* floor composition.

Forty-five-minute guided tours in Spanish (tours in English are available for groups of 10 or more with advance booking), with an accompanying leaflet in English, leave every hour.

Playa de Gandia   BEACH
Four kilometres away on the coast, Playa de Gandia is a long, broad beach of fine sand, groomed daily by a fleet of tractors. It's a popular and predominantly Spanish resort with a good summer and weekend scene.

🛏 Sleeping & Eating

Eating choices abound in Paseo Marítimo Neptuno. Most places offer just cheap and cheerful holiday food that won't win any food-quality awards. You'll also find a few longer-established places at the western end of the port and along Calle Verge.

Hotel Riviera   HOTEL €€
(☑96 284 50 42; www.hotelesrh.com; Paseo Marítimo Neptuno 28; half-board per person €62; ✱@☎🏊) This is one of Gandia's oldest seaside hotels, but the rooms are up-to-date and luxurious in a way that is unexpected for a three-star hotel.

Hostal El Nido   GUESTHOUSE €€
(☑96 284 46 40; www.hostalelnido.com; Calle Alcoy 22; s €35-50, d €45-69; ☎) This homey place is the mirror opposite of all the giant resort hotels that line the beach and the rooms are as cheerful as the owners. It's a block back from the beach. Between June and September it also runs a small bar for guests.

Restaurante Coronada   SEAFOOD €€
(☑96 284 18 21; Paseo Marítimo Neptuno 72; mains €8-15) Standing out from the seafront masses this place offers good-quality, tasty and well-presented seafood and rice-based dishes. On sunny Sundays it's packed with families coming down from Valencia City for the day.

🍷 Drinking

There's great summer and weekend nightlife at Playa de Gandia, with bars clustered around Plaza del Castell, barely 300m inland from the beach. Otherwise head straight to the complex on the corner of Carrer Legazpi and Carrer Navegant (look out for the naff glow in the dark, plastic palm trees), two blocks from the beach, where you'll find a bunch of bars and clubs, such as La Dolce Vita, 625 and Bacarra, all of which are cut from much the same mould.

ℹ️ Information

Playa de Gandia tourist office (📞96 284 24 07; www.gandiaturismo.com; Paseo de Neptuna 45; ⏰9.30am-8.30pm Mon-Sat, 9.30am-1.30pm Sun)

Town tourist office (📞96 287 77 88; ⏰9.30am-2.30pm & 4-8pm Mon-Fri, 9.30am-1.30pm Sat) Opposite the bus and train station.

ℹ️ Getting There & Around

Trains run between Gandia and Valencia (€4.40, one hour) every 30 minutes (hourly on weekends). The combined bus and train station is opposite the town tourist office. Stopping beside the office, La Marina Gandiense buses for Playa de Gandia run every 20 minutes.

DENIA
POP 44,730

Denia, the Comunidad Valenciana's major passenger port (it has the shortest sea crossings to the Balearic Islands), is a cheery place that lives for more than just tourism. The Old Town snuggles up against a small hill mounted by a tumbledown castle and the town's streets buzz with life. The beaches of La Marina, to its north, are good and sandy, while southwards the fretted coastline of Las Rotas and beyond offers less-frequented rocky coves.

◉ Sights & Activities

Castle   CASTLE
(adult/child incl Museo Arqueològic de Denia €3/1; ⏰10am-1.30pm & 5-8.30pm) From Plaza de la Constitución, steps lead up to the ruins of Denia's castle from where there's a great overview of the town and coast. The castle grounds contain the Museo Arqueològic de Denia; a collection of pot shards illustrating the town's long history. Signage is in Spanish only. Outside high summer the castle closes at dusk.

Mundo Marino   BOAT TOUR
(www.mundomarino.es) To catch the sea breezes, sign on with Mundo Marino, which runs a whole array of different boat trips (from €15) including 'mini cruises' to/from Xàbia, Calpe and Altea.

🛏️ Sleeping

Hotel Chamarel   TOP CHOICE   BOUTIQUE HOTEL €€
(📞96 643 50 07; www.hotelchamarel.com; Calle Cavallers 13; r incl breakfast €85; ❄️📶) This delightful hotel, tastefully furnished in period style by a pair of seasoned travellers, occupies an attractive 19th-century bourgeois mansion. Its 15 rooms surround a tranquil, plant-shaded internal patio. The vast internal salon with its correspondingly large marble-topped bar is equally relaxing. The whole place is a capacious gallery for the paintings of artist and owner Mila Vidallach, whose canvases decorate bedrooms and public areas. Ask for room 201, under the eaves, oriental in mood and positively breathing feng shui. Parking is €12.

Posada del Mar   HOTEL €€€
(📞96 643 29 66; www.laposadadelmar.com; Plaza Drassanes 2; s €145-165, d €160-180, incl breakfast; 🅿️❄️@📶) This sensitively renovated hotel occupies a 13th-century building that last functioned as Denia's customs house. Each of its 25 rooms is individually decorated with a nautical theme and light streams through large windows that overlook the harbour. It's debatable whether the room quality justifies the high prices, though. Parking is €16.

Hotel Fontanella   HOTEL €
(📞96 578 49 60; www.hotelfontanella.es; Calle Fontanella 18; s €50-60, d €60-70, incl breakfast; ❄️📶) On a quiet street, a block back from the port, this is a recently renovated, colourful pop-art hotel that offers good value for money. The rooms might be small but they've been laid out in such a way as to make the most of the available space. There's a decent bar downstairs.

El Raset   HOTEL €€
(📞96 578 65 64; www.hotelelraset.com; Bellavista 1; s/d incl breakfast €112/137; ❄️@📶) Modern designer hotel overlooking the port with spotlight-lit rooms, colourful bedspreads and art on the walls. Run by a friendly and helpful chap.

🍴 Eating

There's a clutch of tempting restaurants, catering for all pockets, along harbour-facing Explanada Cervantes and Calle Bellavista, extending to Plaza del Raset. Many began life as simple bars for the fisherfolk from the old fish market, just across the road. Pedestrianised Calle Lepanto, which extends westwards from Hotel Chamarel, is flanked by tempting tapas bars.

Sal de Mar   MODERN SPANISH €€
(📞96 642 77 66; menus €20-40, mains €17-23; ⏰Wed-Mon) The gourmet restaurant of hotel Posada del Mar is a splendid option, whether you choose to dine or simply *tapear* (eat tapas), either in its intimate interior or on the summertime terrace.

El Raset
SPANISH, SEAFOOD €€

(📞96 578 50 40; Calle Bellavista 7; menus €22, mains €17-24) Eat on the wide terrace or within the cool, air-conditioned interior of El Raset, reputed for its rice dishes. Its excellent four-course lunch menu includes, as starters, a variety of tapas such as baby cannelloni stuffed with seafood. Dishes are attractively presented and service is genial and helpful.

Asador del Puerto
GRILL €€

(📞96 642 34 82; Plaza del Raset 10-11; menus €27-38.50, mains €19-24) This is an excellent choice for either meat, roasted in a wood-fired oven, or fish dishes. Try the *cochinillo* (suckling pig), crispy on the outside, juicy within and roasted to a turn.

❶ Information

The **tourist office** (📞96 642 23 67; www.denia. net; Calle Manuel Lattur 1; ☉10am-1.30pm & 5-8.30pm) is near the waterfront. Both the train station and ferry terminal are close by.

❶ Getting There & Away

BOAT For the Balearic Islands, **Balearia Lines** (📞902 16 01 80; www.balearia.com) runs ferries to/from Mallorca and Ibiza.

TRAIN From Denia's station, hourly trains follow the scenic route southwards to Benidorm, connecting with the tram for Alicante. For Valencia you need to go to Gandia first and take a train from there.

XÀBIA
POP 32.470

With a third of its resident population and over two-thirds of its annual visitors non-Spanish (every second shop seems to be an estate agent/realtor), Xàbia (Jávea in Spanish) isn't the best place to meet the locals. That said, it's a gentle, family-oriented place that has largely (but not totally!) resisted the high-rise tourist developments that blight so much of the Costa Blanca's coast. In fact, early in the season, when the sun shines but the masses have yet to arrive, we'd say that Xàbia is by far the most pleasant of the area's beach resorts.

Xàbia comes in three flavours: the small Old Town 2km inland; El Puerto (the port), directly east of the Old Town; and the beach zone of El Arenal, a couple of kilometres south of the harbour.

🏃 Activities

In addition to fun in the sun on El Arenal's broad beach, the Old Town, with its quiet plazas and boutique shops, well merits a wander.

The tourist office carries a pack titled *Xàbia: Nature Areas Network*, containing five brochures, each describing a waymarked route in the area, including an ascent of Montgó, the craggy mountain that looms over the town. Year-round, the tourist office leads free guided walks at least twice weekly; for details, see its leaflet, *Rutas Senderismo*.

🛏 Sleeping

Hotel Miramar
HOTEL €€

(📞96 579 01 00; www.hotelmiramar.com.es; Plaza Almirante Bastarreche 12; s/d €42/72; ❇🐾) You'll be that close to the sea that you might want to sleep in your swimming things in this family-run hotel, right beside the port. Its 26 rooms, eight with balcony, are cosy; those overlooking the bay carry a €15 supplement. There's a bar and restaurant, too.

Pensión la Marina
PENSIÓN €

(📞96 579 31 39; www.lamarinapension.com; Avenida Marina Española 8; r €40-75; 🐾) This small, English-owned place has eight rooms plus a couple of family options, all with ceiling fans and smile-inducing decorations. Its huge plus is its position, right beside the pedestrianised seafront promenade. For dinner, go no further than the pizzeria below, and enjoy your 20% discount as a client of the *pensión*.

Parador de Jávea
PARADOR €€€

(📞96 579 02 00; www.paradores.es; Avenida del Mediterráneo 233; d €279) Architecturally, Xàbia's boxy, once-modern *parador* is unexciting but it enjoys a magnificent site, on a headland overlooking the bay of El Arenal, and has all the usual *parador* comforts.

🍴 Eating & Drinking

The Old Town has several enticing tapas bars, while restaurants and bars flank Avenida de la Marina Española, the pedestrianised promenade south of the port. In El Arenal, cafes and restaurants hug the rim of beachside Paseo Marítimo.

La Renda
VALENCIAN €€

(Santisimo Cristo del mar 12; meals per person €9-12) There's more than you think to a paella, and this well-priced but classy place has 14 different variations on that Valencian classic. The house special, though, is *arroz de renda* (creamy rice with snails). For most dishes a minimum of two people are required.

El Posito
MEDITERRANEAN €€

(📞96 579 30 63; Plaza Almirante Bastarreche 11; menus €14, meals around €25) Sharing with the port tourist office what was once the fishermen's social centre, this pretty blue-and-white building is a class above most waterfront restaurants and has some unusual items on the menu (seaweed noodles anyone?). El Posito does an excellent-value menu, makes a relaxing drinks stop, and has a good range of tapas and sandwiches.

Bar Imperial TAPAS €
(☑96 646 11 81; Plaza de Baix 2; mains €8-10) In the Old Town, full of old-fashioned Spanish atmosphere (think old men in flat caps playing cards) and well worth a visit, serving tapas and full meals.

La Rebotica TAPAS €
(☑96 646 13 18; Calle San Bartolomeo 6; mains €8-10) At La Rebotica, inland and in the Old Town, you can either tuck into a full meal or nibble on tapas.

El Tropezón VALENCIAN €€
(☑96 579 13 16; Calle Tossal de Dalt 3; mains €10-15) Intimate, rectangular and within a typical renovated town house, this relatively new arrival with its bare stone walls and beams specialises in regional cuisine.

❶ Information
Tourist offices (www.xabia.org; ☯9am-1.30pm & 4-7.30pm or 4.30-8pm Mon-Fri, 10am-1.30pm Sat) El Arenal (☑96 646 06 05; Carretera Cabo de la Nao, El Arenal); Old Town (☑96 579 43 56; Plaza de la Iglesia, Old Town); Port (☑96 579 07 36; Plaza Almirante Bastareche 11, Port; ☯also Sat afternoon & Sun morning).

❶ Getting There & Around
At least six buses run daily to both Valencia (€10.90) and Alicante (€9.25). They stop on Avenida Óndara, at Rotonda del Olivo, with a large olive tree at its heart.

You can rent a cycle at **Xàbia's Bike Centre** (www.xabiasbike.com; Avenida Lepanto 21; per day €9) in the port area.

CALPE
POP 29.650
The Gibraltaresque Peñon de Ifach, a giant molar protruding from the sea, rears up from the seaside resort of Calpe (Calp in Valenciano).

Two large bays sprawl either side of the Peñon: Playa Arenal on the southern side is backed by the Old Town, while Playa Levante (also known as Playa la Fossa), to the north, is pretty much wall-to-wall super-sized tourist developments with little to offer independent travellers (except the beach, which is glorious).

From the Peñon's Aula de Naturaleza (Nature Centre), a fairly strenuous walking trail – allow 2½ hours for the round trip – climbs towards the 332m-high summit, offering great seascapes from its end point. In July and August walkers depart every 15 minutes in batches of 20, so you may have a short wait.

Less strenuous nature awaits you at the small Parque Natural las Salinas, a sheet of water just behind the town, which is often full of gulls, waders and other water birds, as well as a few flamingos.

🛏 Sleeping
Hostal Terra de Mar BOUTIQUE HOTEL €€
(☑629 665124; www.hostalterrademar.com; Calle Justicia 31; s/d incl breakfast €95/130; ❄🤶) At this highly original, and artistic, hotel you're greeted by a giant mural of bangled hands, from which rose petals flutter. Each floor has its own style (climb the stairs and you can travel from Japan to Morocco to Africa and Paris). The low-season tariff for its 12 rooms (single/double with breakfast €45/55 October to May) is an excellent deal – the high-season prices less so. It's very popular so book ahead.

Pensión Centrica PENSIÓN €
(☑96 583 55 28; mjpiffet@hotmail.com; Plaza de Ifach 5; s/d €13/30) This French-run place just off Avenida Gabriel Miró has 13 well-maintained rooms with ceiling fans and shared bathrooms. Look out for the giant iguana...

🍴 Eating
There are plenty of restaurants and bars around Plaza de la Constitución and along main Avenida de Gabriel Miró, plus a cluster of good fish places down by the port as well as many typically overpriced tourist restaurants and All-Day English Breakfast joints.

Los Zapatos MODERN EUROPEAN €€
(☑96 583 15 07; www.restauranteloszapatos.com; Calle Santa María 7; menus €17, mains €14.50-23; ☯Thu-Mon) Highly recommended, this German-run restaurant has a short, specialised à la carte menu and a carefully selected wine list of mainly Spanish vintages. In season it does a tempting *menú caza y pescado* (hunting and fish menu) with wild boar and fish of the day.

La Cambra SPANISH €€
(☑96 583 06 05; Calle Delfín 2; mains €15-21; ☯lunch Mon-Thu, lunch & dinner Fri & Sat) All antique

SUPERLATIVE BENIDORM

» In 2009 Benidorm registered nearly 10 million overnight stays.

» Around five million visitors arrive every year, including well over a million Brits.

» Its 127 hotels (let's not even consider the apartment blocks) provide nearly 40,000 beds. In Europe, only London and Paris can claim more hotels.

» There's a full 6km of sandy beach.

wood and tiles, traditional La Cambra specialises in rice dishes (around €12) and also has a rich à la carte selection of Basque and Valencian dishes.

🛍 Shopping

Librería Europa   BOOKSHOP
(www.libreria-europa-calpe.com; Calle Oscar Esplá 2) Superb, old-fashioned-style bookshop where the (English) owner will happily chat for hours about literature, travel and books in general. It has an excellent stock of titles in English and other European languages as well as plenty of Lonely Planet titles.

ℹ Information

Main tourist office (🖉96 583 85 32; www.calpe.es; Plaza del Mosquit; ⏱9am-6pm Mon-Fri, 9am-2pm Sat) In the Old Town.

ℹ Getting There & Away

BUS Connects Calpe with both Alicante (€6.55, 1½ hours, 10 daily) and Valencia (€12.30, 3½ hours, five daily). The **bus station** (Avenida de la Generalitat Valenciana) is just off the ring road.

TRAIN Trams travel daily northwards to Denia (€2.25, 40 minutes) and south to Benidorm (€2, 30 minutes), connecting with trams for Alicante.

ALTEA
POP 24,060

Altea, separated from Benidorm only by the thick wedge of the Sierra Helada, could be a couple of moons away. Altogether quieter, its beaches are mostly of pebbles. The modern part, extending along the coast, is a bog-standard coastal resort. By contrast, the whitewashed Old Town, perched on a hilltop overlooking the sea, is just about the prettiest *pueblo* in all of the Comunidad Valenciana.

Aparthotel & Restaurante Venus Albir (🖉96 686 48 20; www.venusalbir.com; Albir-Alfaz

del Pi, Plaza Venus; d €47-90, tr €63-120; ❋🛜🐾), in Albir, a continuation of Altea southwards, is an ecofriendly hotel. It has 24 comfortable apartments with mini-kitchen and balcony and you can indulge in a variety of healthy, de-stressing activities. At its restaurant (mains €13.50 to €23), open to all, ingredients are strictly organic.

Off Plaza de la Iglesia in Altea's Old Town, and especially down Calle Major, there's a profusion of cute little restaurants, many open for dinner only, except in high summer.

Altea's **tourist office** (🖉96 584 41 14; Calle San Pedro 9; ⏱10am-2pm & 5-7.30pm or 8pm Mon-Fri, 10am-1pm Sat) is on the beachfront.

BENIDORM
POP 72,060

It's easy to be snobbish about Benidorm and write it off as the worst possible example of the ugly side of mass tourism and, yes, you'd be right; Benidorm long ago sold its birthright to mass package tourism. But yet, though violated most summer nights by louts from northern Europe, and the fact that Spanish culture has been utterly drowned under an onslaught of English bars and fried breakfasts, and it would be very hard to describe the endless tower-block hotels (including some of the tallest tower blocks in Europe) as attractive, Benidorm does have one thing going for it that many other Costa Blanca beach resorts lack. It has character in abundance. It just might not be the sort of character you came to Spain for! Still, if you haven't been to Benidorm, you can hardly say you've been to the Spanish Mediterranean.

Oh, and there's another plus point for Benidorm. The foreshore is magnificent as the twin sweeps of Playa del Levante and the longer Playa del Poniente meet beneath Plaza del Castillo, where the land juts into the bay like a ship's prow.

In winter half of all visitors are over 60, mostly from northern Europe. During summer Benidorm is for all ages.

◉ Sights & Activities

Terra Mítica   AMUSEMENT PARK
(Mythical Land; www.terramiticapark.com; adult/child €35/25; ⏱10am-8pm mid-Mar–Sep) Everything is bigger and brasher in Benidorm, so it should come as no surprise to learn that this is Spain's biggest theme park. A fun day out, especially if you're with children, it's Mediterranean (well, kind of) in theme, with plenty of scary rides, street entertainment,

and areas devoted to ancient Egypt, Greece, Rome, Iberia and the islands. Opening days are complex, so check its website outside high season.

Terra Natura & Aqua Natura   ZOO
(www.terranatura.com; adult/child €25/20, water park supplement €8; ⊙10am-dusk, water park Jun–mid-Sep) Over 1500 animals live in habitats approximating their natural environment at this theme park. There's also a great **water park** and the chance to swim with sea lions.

Aqualandia   AMUSEMENT PARK
(www.aqualandia.net; adult/child €20.50/16.50; ⊙10am-dusk mid-May–mid-Oct) Aqualandia is Europe's largest water park. Beside it is **Mundomar** (✆96 586 01 00; www.mundomar. es; adult/child €18.50/16.50; ⊙10am-dusk), a marine and animal park with parrots, dolphins, sea lions, even bats. Each park (combined ticket adult/child €38/28) is worth a full day.

Excursiones Marítimas
Benidorm   BOAT TOUR
(www.excursionesmaritimasbenidorm.es) Runs hourly boats (adult/child return €12.50/10) to the Isla de Benidorm, a cruise up the coast to Calpe (adult/child €22.50/15) as well as a full-day outing to the island of Tabarca (p589).

Sierra Helada   WALKING
Should Benidorm's frenetic pace get you down, pick up a free copy of *Routes Across Sierra Helada* from the tourist office and stride out into the hills of the Sierra Helada, just north of Rincón de Loix, for superb bay views.

🛏 Sleeping

TOP CHOICE Villa Venecia   BOUTIQUE HOTEL €€€
(✆96 585 54 66; www.hotelvillavenecia.com; Plaza San Jaime 1; s €144-176, d €288-352; ❋❋🖥❄) Up high opposite the Old Town's church and lording it over the seething beach crowds below, this plush five-star hotel has it all. Each of the 25 rooms has plunging sea views, an ultramodern bathtub, power showers and large flat-screen TV. As you lounge beside its puddle of a rooftop pool, perhaps after a session in the spa and wellness centre (one of whose treatments is called Eternal Youth – if this is really true, then we'd say the otherwise high rates are well worthwhile!), you could be nautical miles away from Benidorm. Its bar and excellent Llum de Mar restaurantare open to allcomers.

Hotel Fetiche   BOUTIQUE HOTEL €
(✆96 618 32 46; www.fetichebenidorm.com; Calle Paseo de la Carretera 11; s/d €30/60; ❋❄) This is a welcome new addition to the Benidorm hotel scene. It's all white walls, arty B&W photos and bright pop-art furnishings. It's on a quiet side street just on the edge of the Old Town.

Hotel La Santa Faz   HOTEL €€
(✆96 585 40 63; www.santafazhotel.com; Calle Santa Faç 18; s €50-60, d €100-120; ⊙May-Oct; ❋❄) This long-established hotel, sandwiched between two streets in the Old Town, is friendly and full of character. All rooms have a balcony, and there's a well-stocked bar and a billiard table.

Hotel Colón   HOTEL €€
(✆96 585 04 12; www.hotelcolon.net; Paseo de Colón 3; s €50-60, d €100-120; ⊙Apr-Oct; ❋❄) Conveniently positioned where the Old Town meets Playa del Poniente, the Colón, with rooms as blue as the sea, is great value outside the high season. Half-board is only €4 more than B&B, though don't expect fine cuisine. West-facing rooms have great views of Playa del Poniente.

Hotel Iris   HOTEL €
(✆96 586 52 51; www.iris-hotel.net; Calle Palma 47; s/d €30/60; ❋@) Here's a friendly English-run budget choice on a fairly quiet street. Rooms that don't have air-con come with fans and most have a small balcony, too. There's a cosy ground-floor bar with an internet terminal. If it's good enough for the mayor of Benidorm, who has been known to sleep here during the town's fiesta, it's good enough for you...!

Gran Hotel Bali   HOTEL €€
(✆96 681 52 00; www.granhotelbali.com; Calle Luis Prendes; s/d incl breakfast from €95/130; ❋@❄🏊) This mammoth complex, 186m high and as much space-age village as hotel, is Europe's tallest. Like a massive silver knife

---

ℹ ACCOMMODATION DISCOUNTS

Almost everyone's on a package deal in Benidorm, so accommodation can be expensive for the independent traveller. Book online through **Benidorm Spotlight** (www.benidorm-spotlight.com) for significant discounts.

VALENCIA & MURCIA COSTA BLANCA

cleaving the sky, its vastness isn't to everyone's taste but, with 23 lifts (have fun riding one of the two external ones), 776 rooms and a pair of restaurants that can accommodate up to 1000 diners, it's superlative in many senses.

✗ Eating

In general Benidorm isn't renowned for fine dining, but if you know where to look (which you now do), there are a few places serving decent Spanish fare. And, if you don't want to eat Spanish, well yeah the rumours you've heard are true; there are a fair few sausage and chips and English breakfast kind of places. Oh yes, there are certainly a few of them!

TOP CHOICE La Cava Aragonesa TAPAS €€
(☎restaurant 96 680 12 06; Plaza de la Constitución; restaurant menus €10-13, mains €10-18) What a magnificent selection of tapas, fat canapés and 20 different plates of cold cuts, all arrayed before you at the bar and labelled in both Spanish and English! In fact, this place almost feels Spanish (not that you come to Benidorm for Spain). Next door is its sit-down restaurant, where you can select from 20 different wooden platters of mixed foods – and more than 600 varieties of wine.

Llum de Mar MEDITERRANEAN €€
(☎96 585 54 66; Plaza San Jaime 1; rice dishes €12.50-15.50, mains €18-22) Light of the Sea, restaurant of Villa Venecia hotel and open to all, is an intimate place. With a capacity for scarcely 30 (reservations essential), it offers splendid à la carte fare while a vast seascape spreads before you through its large picture windows.

Restaurante Marisquería Club Náutico MEDITERRANEAN €€
(☎96 585 54 25; Paseo de Colón; menus €24-50, mains €10-19) At this elegant restaurant beside the port, you can pick at tapas by the bar or have a full meal on the large terrace – where you can also simply enjoy a drink and the view over Benidorm's small port.

Casa de la Portuguesa MEDITERRANEAN €€
(☎96 585 89 58; Calle San Vicente 39; mains €10-16) With its tables spilling onto the narrow street in summer, this restaurant, a favourite of Benidorm's movers and shakers, is nevertheless very reasonably priced. It's family-run and it owes its reputation to its great rice dishes, fresh fish and, yes, a few

THE CHOCOLATE FACTORY

Even if your name's not Charlie and though you may be over 12 years old, you'll enjoy a tour of the Museo de Chocolate (Chocolate Museum; www. valor.es; Calle Pianista Gonzalo Soriano 13; admission free; ◷10am-1pm & 4-7pm Mon-Fri, 10am-1pm Sat) in Villajoyosa, 14km south of Benidorm. This showcase of Valor, Spain's largest chocolate-making company, displays everything related to cocoa, chocolate and the transformation of one to another, has a gallery of sculptures in – yes – chocolate, and includes a visit to the factory and shop, where you'll need all your willpower to resist such sweet temptation. Guided visits on the hour, every hour.

Portuguese classics such as goat or *bacalahu* (cod).

La Rana SPANISH €€
(☎96 586 81 20; Costero del Barco 6; mains €5.50-17.50) One of Benidorm's oldest restaurants (that aged cash register must have rung up the very first bills), The Frog (see the hundreds of model frogs, large and small, in a glass case) is family-run and something of a time warp, with the feel of a generation ago. It serves authentic Spanish cuisine, using the freshest of ingredients plucked from the giant fridge before you. Tucked away up a cobbled alley, it's well worth tracking down.

☿ Drinking & Entertainment

There are literally hundreds upon hundreds of bars in Benidorm. All have a slightly different style and feel but it's generally a style that is loud and brash. The Old Town is the centre of Benidorm's thriving gay scene and there are numerous gay bars here.

For a slightly more noted for subtlety, park yourself on a stool at Fratelli (Calle Doctor Orts Llorca; ◷1pm-5am), a cool designer cocktail place that styles itself 'Bar Fashion'.

At the western end of Playa del Levante, music spills out from three beachside bars (open 10am to 5pm) that each have mega *discotecas* on Avenida de la Comunidad Valenciana on the outskirts of town. Their *discotecas* and other similar giants open daily in July and August, and on weekends year-round. Back on the beach, Ku (www.

kubenidorm.es), with its reproduction Hindu and Buddhist statues, plays the oriental card and has a cool rear chill-out zone. At its near neighbour **KM** (www.kmdisco.com), the music's eclectic until 6pm, when it's strictly house. Next door to KM, **Beach Club Penelope** (www.penelopebeach.com) is a small sibling of the Penelope brand, found all over Europe.

❶ Information

Main tourist office (☑96 585 13 11; www.beni dorm.org; Avenida Martínez Alejos 16; ☺9am-9pm Mon-Fri, 10am-5pm Sat, 10am-2pm Sun) Also kiosks at the bus station, on Avenida de Europa and in Rincón de Loix.

❶ Getting There & Away

BUS From Benidorm's bus station (served by local bus 41 and 47), **ALSA** (www.alsa.es) runs to the following destinations:

Alicante €4.10 to €8.05, one hour, frequent

Alicante airport €8.20, 50 minutes, hourly

Valencia €15.05 to €15.40, 1¾ hours to three hours, 12 daily

TRAIN Trams run to Alicante (€5.70, one hour, every 30 minutes).

ALICANTE
POP 334,300

Thanks to the nearby airport and proximity to a large number of major beach-resort towns, Alicante (Alacant in Valenciano) has been tarred with something of a tacky package-tour reputation. In reality, though, this is a dynamic, attractive provincial city that lives for much more than just tourism. Around Catedral de San Nicolás are the narrow streets of El Barrio, the historic quarter. Try to fit in at least one overnight stay to experience its frenetic – and unmistakably Spanish – nightlife.

◎ Sights & Activities

FREE **Castillo de Santa Bárbara**   CASTLE
(lift €2.40 return; ☺10am-10pm, until 8pm Oct-Mar, lift 10am-8pm) There are sweeping views over the city from this large 16th-century castle, which houses the **Museo de la Ciudad de Alicante** (MUSA; ☺10am-2.30pm & 4-8pm), a new museum recounting the history of the city. It's a sweaty walk up the hill to the castle, but there's a **lift**, reached by a footbridge opposite Playa del Postiguet, that rises through the bowels of the mountain to the summit. To return, it's a pleasant, and much less sweaty, walk through Parque de

la Ereta via Calle San Rafael to Plaza del Carmen.

FREE **Museo de Arte Contemporáneo de Alicante**   MUSEUM
(MACA; Plaza Santa María 3) This splendid museum, inside the 17th-century Casa de la Asegurada, has an excellent collection of 20th-century Spanish art, including works by Dalí, Miró, Chillida, Sempere, Tàpies and Picasso.

Museo Arqueológico Provincial   MUSEUM
(MARQ; www.marqalicante.com; Plaza Doctor Gómez Ulla; adult/child €3/free; ☺11am-2pm & 6pm-midnight Tue-Sat, 11am-2pm Sun Jul & Aug, 10am-7pm Tue-Sat, 10am-2pm Sun Sep-Jun) Very visual and high-tech, this museum well merits a visit, even though there's little information in English. It's an easy walk from the city centre or hop on bus 2, 6, 9, 20 or 23.

FREE **Museu de Fogueres**   MUSEUM
(Museo de las Hogueras; Rambla de Méndez Núñez 29; ☺10am-2pm & 5-8pm or 6-9pm Tue-Sat, 10am-2pm Sun) In addition to a wealth of photographs, costumes and *ninots* (small effigies saved from the flames), it has a great audiovisual presentation of what the Fiesta de Sant Joan, all fire and partying, means to *alicantinos*.

FREE **Museo de Bellas Artes Gravina**   ART
(Mubag; Calle Gravina 13-15; ☺10am-9pm Tue-Sat, 11am-3pm Sun) Alicante's fine-arts museum, with canvases from the Middle Ages to the 1920s, is within the Palacio de Gravina, a stalwart 18th-century mansion. The setting and presentation are terrific – perhaps more so than the paintings themselves.

Basílica de Santa María   CHURCH
(Plaza Santa María; ☺10.30am-noon & 6-7.30pm) The flamboyant, 18th-century facade and ornate, gilded altarpiece both contrast with the nave's Gothic simplicity.

Beaches   BEACH
Immediately north of the port is the sandy beach of **Playa del Postiguet**. **Playa de San Juan**, easily reached by the tram, is larger and usually less crowded.

Kon Tiki   BOAT TOUR
(☑96 521 63 96) Makes the 45-minute boat trip (€12 to €39 depending on type of trip) to the popular island of Tabarca (p589).

VALENCIA & MURCIA COSTA BLANCA

Alicante

200 m
0.1 miles

MEDITERRANEAN SEA

To A7 (9km); Playa de San Juan (22km); Benidorm (45km)

Av Juan Bautista Lafora

paseo de Gomiz

Playa del Postiguet

Castillo de Santa Bárbara ⓚ 血 4

2

Parque de la Ereta

C de Villavieja

Plaza Arquitecto M.López

Museo de Bellas Artes Gravina (MUBAG) ●

血 1

Plaza Santa María

C de Toledo

血 3

⊗ 6

C Maldonado

C Monges

C de Jorge Juan

C Gravina

Buses to Airport

Buses to San Juan

⊗ 10

Santísima Faz

Plaza de Faz

Plaza Municipal

Puerta del Mar

17 ⊗

Calle San Nicolás

EL BARRIO

Catedral de San Nicolás

☩ 9

C de San Nicolás

Tourist Office

C de Rafael Altamira

To Compañía Haddock (120m); Port Rell (140m); Coyote Ugly (230m)

Plaza del Carmen

Plaza San Rafael del Carmen

C de los Labradores

C San Isidro

15 血

C de San Cristóbal

Rambla de Méndez Núñez

14

Plaza de Elche

Portal de Elche

C de Bilbao

C de San Fernando

Paseo del Conde Vallellano

Museu de Fogueres ● 血

⊗ 7

8 ⊗

Regional Tourist Office

C de Bailén

16 ●

Plaza de Gabriel Miró

Boats to Tabarca

Paseo de España

Plaza de España

Paseo Explanada de

C San Ildefonso

Av de la Constitución

C de los Castaños

C del Teatro

Plaza Nueva

C de Gerona

C del Barón de Finestrat

C de San Francisco

C Valdés

⊗ 12

C de Lanuza

C de Capitán Segarra

Covered Market

C de Poeta Quintana

11 ⊗

Av Alfonso X El Sabio

C de Médico Pascual Pérez

C de Jerusalén

C Canalejas

C de Pablo Iglesias

C de Ángel Lozano

Plaza de Calvo Sotelo

C del Pintor

C del Pintor Casanova

To Bus Station (175m)

C Belando

C de Álvarez Sereix

Av del Doctor Gadea

C de Alemania

C del Portugal

C Segura

血 5

Plaza de los Luceros

C de General O'Donnell

Av Maisonnave

C del Morell

Arquitecto Lorenzo

13 ⊗

Av de General Marva

Av Estación

To Train Station (600m)

Alicante

🎊 Festivals & Events

Fiesta de Sant Joan   MIDSUMMER

Alicante's major festival is the Fiesta de Sant Joan, spread either side of 24 June, the longest day, when the city stages its own version of Las Fallas, with fireworks and satirical effigies (Valenciano: *fogueres*; Spanish: *hogueras*) going up in smoke all over town.

🛏 Sleeping

TOP CHOICE Hostal Les Monges Palace HOSTAL €

(☎96 521 50 46; www.lesmonges.es; Calle San Agustín 4; s €37-45, d €53-60; ❈@☎) This agreeably quirky place is a treasure with its winding corridors, tiles, mosaics and antique furniture. Each room is individually decorated and reception couldn't be more welcoming. To pamper yourself, choose one of the two rooms with sauna and Jacuzzi (€100). Look out for the small Dalí original beside the reception. Private parking is available.

Guest House   HOSTAL €

(☎650 718353; www.guesthousealicante.com; Calle Segura 20; s/d/apt €40/50/90; P❈☎) Here's a magnificent budget choice. Each of the eight large, tastefully decorated rooms differs: some have exposed stone walls and others are painted in shocking lime green, daffodil yellow or deep-sea blue. All have a safe, full-sized fridge and free beverage-making facilities. There are also a couple of well-equipped apartments. The only drawback is that it's a bit far from all the action. Parking is €15.

Pensión Alicante San Nicolás GUESTHOUSE €

(☎96 521 70 39; www.alicantesanicolas.com; Calle San Nicolás 14; s €30, d €40-45; ❈☎) This small, central and family-run guesthouse is so brightly painted that you might just need to wear sunglasses before stepping inside. All rooms come with tea- and coffee-making facilities and tiny bathrooms. One room has its own kitchen.

Hostal La Milagrosa   HOSTAL €

(☎96 521 69 18; www.hostallamilagrosa.com; Calle de la Villavieja 8; s/d incl breakfast €35/50, without bathroom & incl breakfast €25/40 , ❈@☎) The Miracle, which feels a bit like a youth hostel, is in fact an excellent-value budget choice, with simple rooms, a small guest kitchen, washing machine and roof terrace. It's a good place to meet other backpackers. It also has three apartments (€60) that can sleep up to six (per extra person €20).

Hotel Amérigo   HOTEL €€€

(☎96 514 65 70; www.hospes.es; Calle de Rafael Altamira 7; r from €150; ❈@☎❈) Within an old Dominican convent, this glorious five-star choice harmoniously blends the traditional and ultramodern. Savour the cuisine in Monastrell, its gourmet restaurant, enjoy the views from the rooftop pool, itself a work of art, or build up a sweat in the fitness area – if you can tear yourself away from the comfort of your stunningly designed room.

VALENCIA & MURCIA COSTA BLANCA

✗ Eating

TOP CHOICE Piripi VALENCIAN €€

(☎965 22 79 40; Avenida Oscar Esplá 30; mains €12-26) This highly regarded restaurant is strong on rice, seafood and fish, which arrives fresh and daily from the wholesale markets of Denia and Santa Pola. There's a huge variety of tapas (we counted 10 different cylinders of salami and sausage arranged on the bar and one of the jovial team of waiters is engaged constantly in cutting near-transparent slices of prime quality ham). There's a *valenciano* speciality that changes daily. It's a short walk west of the city centre.

El Trellat MODERN SPANISH €

(☎965 20 62 75; Calle de Capitán Segarra 19; lunch menus €10, dinner menus €10-25; ⊘lunch Mon-Thu, lunch & dinner Fri & Sat) Beside the covered market, this small, friendly place does exceptionally creative, flexible menus: first course is a serve-yourself buffet, then an ample choice of inventive mains. For dessert, trust Manuel, the chef/owner; he previously worked in Alicante's premier cake shop.

One One MEDITERRANEAN €€

(☎96 520 63 99; Calle Valdés 9; meals around €25; ⊘Tue-Sat, closed mid-Aug–mid-Sep) It's easier if you speak a little Spanish at this wonderfully eccentric place (pronounced 'on-eh, on-eh') with its faithful following of regulars but a touch of bravado will get you by (just ask your ebullient host about his travels to Peru). It's a true bistro, the walls scarcely visible for photos and posters, and there's no menu. Just listen carefully as Bartólome intones...

Tabulé VEGETARIAN €

(☎96 513 34 45; Avenida Pérez Galdós 52; menus €12-18; ⊘lunch daily, dinner Wed-Sat; ✍) Service is swift and friendly at this fairly upmarket vegetarian restaurant, where you take what's on offer on one of the day's different menus, which includes a drink and coffee. You won't repeat yourself; it's original, inventive and changes weekly.

Cantina Villahelmy FUSION €€

(Calle Mayor 37; mains €8-17; ⊘lunch & dinner Tue-Sat, lunch Sun) One wall's rough stone, another bright orange and blood red, and it's luridly painted with skeletons, creepy-crawlies and a frieze of classical figures. Intimate, funky and popular, the Villahelmy has lots of funky snacks, excellent salads and a menu that features dishes from couscous to octopus and a fair helping of rice-based dishes.

🍷 Drinking

Wet your night-time whistle in some of the wall-to-wall bars of the historic quarter, around Catedral de San Nicolás. Early opener **Desdén Café Bar** (Calle de los Labradores 22) is a friendly place to kick off the evening, while **Desafinado** (Santo Tomas 6) is a heaving dance bar with DJs that also offers good jazz. An easy walk away, **Z Klub** (Calle Coloma; ⊘Tue-Sun) blasts out house music. Don't turn up before 3am unless you want to dance alone.

Alternatively, head for the sea. Paseo del Puerto, tranquil by day, is a double-decker line of bars, cafes and night-time discos, while Semiramis, a short ferry hop across the harbour's waters, competes for your attention. Coyote Ugly has a sign outside reading 'Welcome to the Jungle' and that about sums it up nicely. A couple of doors away is Levante, an equally neon-lit pulsating bar, next door to that is Compañía Haddock and, on the floor above, Port Rell, which brings up the back end of this fearsome foursome.

☆ Entertainment

Casino CASINO

(Calle Levante 3; ⊘4pm-4am Mon-Sat) Looking like a neon-lit electric butterfly at night, Alicante's brashest attraction offers plenty of opportunities to fritter away your holiday money.

❶ Information

Municipal tourist office (www.alicantetur ismo.com) Branches at the train station and at Calle Portugal 17 just to the west of the city centre, and on Paseo Explanada de España 1, right in the city centre.

Regional tourist office (☎96 520 00 00; Rambla de Méndez Núñez 23; ⊘9am-8pm Mon-Sat, 10am-2pm Sun)

❶ Getting There & Away

AIR Alicante's El Altet airport, gateway to the Costa Blanca, is around 12km southwest of the city centre. It's served by budget airlines, charters and scheduled flights from all over Europe.

BUS From the bus station destinations include the following:

DESTINATION	PRICE (€)	DURATION (HR)	FREQUENCY
Benidorm	4.10	1	frequent
Murcia	5.63	1	at least 7 daily
Valencia	19	2½	at least 10 daily

Destinations from the main **Renfe Estación de Madrid** (Avenida de Salamanca) include the following:

Barcelona €57, five hours, eight daily

Madrid €60.20, 3¼ hours, seven daily

Murcia €7.90 to €17.70, 1¼ hours, hourly; some travel via Orihuela and Elche

Valencia €14.05 to €29.60, 1½ to two hours, 10 to 11 daily; some travel via Villena and Xàtiva

TRAIN For timetables and other information on the city's (and region-wide) tram/train service, see the **TRAM** (www.fgvalicante.com) website. The Tram line 1 to Benidorm (€5.70, one hour, every 30 minutes) takes a coastal route that's scenically stunning at times. It continues onto Denia. Catch it from the Mercado stop beside the covered market or from Puerto Plaza del Mar, changing at La Isleta or Lucentum.

❶ Getting Around

BUS Bus C-6 (€2.70, 30 minutes, every 20 minutes) runs between Plaza Puerta del Mar and the airport, passing by the north side of the bus station. Special 'resort buses' also run direct from the airport to resort towns up and down the coast.

CAR There are numerous car-rental offices at the airport.

ISLA DE TABARCA

A trip to Tabarca, around 20km south of Alicante as the seagull flies, makes for a pleasant day trip – as much for the boat ride itself as for the island, which heaves with tourists in summer. Pack your towel and snorkel mask. Most of the waters that lap this small island, 1800m long and 400m wide at its broadest point, are protected and no-go areas. But fish don't understand such boundaries and you'll enjoy some great underwater viewing in permitted areas.

In summer, daily boats visit the island from Alicante, Benidorm and Torrevieja, and there are less-regular sailings year-round.

TORREVIEJA

POP 102,140

Torrevieja, set on a wide coastal plain between two lagoons, one pink, one emerald, is a through-and-through resort town. There is also a very large, mainly British, expat population. The beaches are good and in summer the nightlife fairly busy, but the town itself has no real soul or character. Sea-salt production remains an important element of its economy.

◉ Sights & Activities

FREE **Museo del Mar y de la Sal**   MUSEUM

(Sea & Salt Museum; Calle Patricio Pérez 10; ⊙10am-2pm & 4-9pm Tue-Sat, 10am-2pm Sun) An appealing clutter of mementoes and bric-a-brac, this museum helps you appreciate why salt still means so much to *torreviejenses*. At the time of research the museum was in the process of being relocated to a nearby site overlooking the port.

FREE **Centro de Interpretación de la Industria Salinera**   MUSEUM

(Avenida de la Estación; ⊙8.30am-2pm Mon-Fri) This centre delves into the crusty world of salt extraction. Located in Torrevieja's former train station, its contents and information are displayed in a fun and light-hearted way.

FREE **Museo Flotante**   MUSEUM

(⊙5-10pm Wed-Sun Jun-Sep, 9am-2pm Oct-May) The 'floating museum' is something of a misnomer as it's based inside a submarine and therefore would be better called the '20,000 Leagues Under the Sea' museum. Sadly, nowadays it stays firmly above the waves. There's an old customs boat nearby that you can also explore.

Vía Verde   WALKING, CYCLING

The Vía Verde is a 6km-long walking and cycling track that follows an old train line, down which the last train steamed over 50 years ago. Running beside the lagoon and through the salt pans, it makes for a great half-day outing.

Day Trip to Tabarca   BOAT TOUR

(www.maritimastorrevieja.com; return trip adult €22, child 5-10yr €10; ⊙Tue-Thu & Sat) Just to the south of the tourist office is a large parking area and the jetty from which boats of Marítimas Torrevieja leave for day trips to the island of Tabarca.

🛏 Sleeping

Considering how touristy Torrevieja is, there's surprisingly little in the way of hotel-style accommodation (and even less for backpackers). Most people are here on a package with prebooked self-catering rooms in apartment blocks.

Hotel Fontana Plaza   BUSINESS HOTEL €€

(☎96 692 89 25; www.hotelfontanaplaza.com; Calle Rambla Juan Mateo 19; s/d €70/80; 🅿❄@)

Brand-new at the time of research, this is a classic white minimalist-style business-class hotel. The rates are surprisingly low, and it has a great location in the town centre and just back from the beach.

Cabo Cervera
RESORT €€

(☑96 692 17 11; www.hotelcabocervera.com; Carretera Torrevieja a La Mata s/n; s/d €62.80/125.60; P✿@≋) This is a full-on package-tour-style hotel but the spacious rooms, which come with little lounges and terraces, polished service and range of facilities make it a decent option for the night. You'll need to book way in advance in high summer. It's around 4km north of town overlooking the sea.

Hotel Madrid
HOTEL €€

(☑96 571 13 50; www.ansahotel.com; Calle Villa Madrid 15; s/d incl breakfast €58/88; ✿@🛜≋) The Madrid is a friendly, family-run option with 40 comfortable rooms, one equipped for travellers with disabilities. There's also a top-floor Jacuzzi and, just across the road, the hotel's swimming pool. It's a long old hike from the town centre though, but fortunately it has bikes available for rent.

✗ Eating

Plenty of restaurants around the waterfront offer cheap meals and international menus, though the quality is generally low. On Plaza Isabel II, park yourself on a patio and enjoy great grilled fresh fish.

Rincón de Capis
VALENCIAN €€

(☑96 570 85 00; Calle San Gabriel 5; mains €10-15, menú del día €13; ⊙closed Tue) Four siblings and a couple of in-laws run this splendid choice, where you can eat à la carte in the very *torreviejense* decor upstairs, enjoy the bar lunch menu or treat yourself to their creative eight-course *menú de degustación* (€50, or €60 with wines to match).

Mesón de la Costa
MEDITERRANEAN €€

(☑96 670 35 98; www.elmesondelacosta.com; Calle Ramón y Cajal 23; meals €20) Hams (and the odd bull's head) dangle from the ceiling of this low-beamed house of plenty. Greeting you as you enter are salvers and tureens of chicken, snails, grilled vegetables and fresh seafood on ice, and a cornucopia of fruit lies behind the glass doors of the refrigerator. Set one block back from the promenade, it's an authentically, enticingly Spanish restaurant that prides itself on the prime quality of its raw materials.

❶ Information

The **main tourist office** (☑96 570 34 33; Plaza de Capdepont; ⊙8.30am-8.30pm Mon-Fri, 10am-2pm Sat) is near the waterfront.

❶ Getting There & Away

From the **bus station** (Calle Antonio Machado), Autocares Costa Azul runs around a dozen buses daily (less on weekends) to Cartagena (€4.20, 1½ hours) and Alicante (€3.65, one hour).

Inland from the Costa Blanca

The borderline between the holiday *costa* and the interior is, perhaps appropriately, a motorway. Venture away from the Med, west of the AP7, to find yourself in a different, truly Spanish world. By far the easiest way to explore this hinterland is with your own transport.

XÀTIVA
POP 29,470

Xàtiva (Spanish: Játiva) makes an easy and rewarding 50km day trip from Valencia. It has a small historic quarter and a mighty castle strung along the crest of the Serra Vernissa, at the base of which the town snuggles.

The Muslims established Europe's first paper-manufacturing plant in Xàtiva, which is also famous as the birthplace of the Borgia Popes Calixtus III and Alexander VI. The town's glory days ended in 1707 when Felipe V's troops torched most of the town.

◉ Sights & Activities

What's interesting lies south and uphill from the Alameda. Ask at the tourist office for its English-language brochure *Xàtiva: Monumental Town*.

TOP CHOICE Castle
CASTLE

(adult/child €2.40/1.20; ⊙10am-6pm or 7pm Tue-Sun) Xàtiva's castle, which clasps to the summit of a double-peaked hill overlooking the Old Town, is arguably the most evocative and interesting in all of the Valencia region. If you think its big today, imagine what it must have looked like 300 years ago when it was even larger. Sadly, an earthquake in 1748 badly damaged it and it never really recovered. Today, behind its crumbling battlements you'll find a mixture of flower gardens (for a lunch with a view bring a picnic), tumbledown turrets, towers and other buildings, and an excellent museum on medieval life which recounts things like how to build a castle and how best to kill your enemies and lay siege to their towns using 17th-century weapons of mass destruction.

The walk up to the castle is a long one, but the views are sensational. On the way up, on your left is the 18th-century **Ermita de San José** and, to the right, the lovely Romanesque **Iglesia de Sant Feliu** (1269), Xàtiva's oldest church. You'll also pass by the very battered remains of part of the old Muslim town. If the walk is too much, hop aboard the little tourist train (€4 return) that heads up from the tourist office at 12.30pm and 5.30pm (4.30pm mid-September to mid-June) or call a taxi (296 227 16 81) and stride back down.

Museo del Almudín   MUSEUM
(Calle Correlgería 46; adult/child €2.20/1.10; ⊙9.30am-2.30pm Tue-Fri, 10am-2.30pm Sat & Sun, mornings only mid-Jun–mid-Sep) In this museum items of most interest, including a couple of fine portraits by Ribera, are up on the penultimate floor. You can't miss the portrait of Felipe V, hung upside down in retribution for his torching of the town.

🛏 Sleeping & Eating

Hostería Mont Sant   RURAL HOTEL €€
(296 227 50 81; www.mont-sant.com; s/d from €85/90; P❋🛜🛟) On the road to the castle, sitting charmingly amid extensive groves of palms and oranges, this place feels as if it's way out in the countryside rather than just a few minutes' walk from town. Stay in the main building, once a farm, or in one of the spacious modern wooden cabins. There's a

splendid restaurant, divided into intimate crannies.

La Maga Rooms   CASA RURAL €
(296 228 82 92; www.grupolamaga.com; Calle Almas 56-57; r €48-90; ❋🛜) Dare we say it, but from the outside this whitewashed guesthouse, on the road to the castle, looks a little run-down and nondescript, but oh how appearances can deceive. Inside, this Old Town house has been converted with flair and style into a series of startlingly white rooms with a dollop of big-city attitude.

TOP CHOICE ▸ **Canela y Clavo**   MEDITERRANEAN €€
(296 228 24 26; www.canelayclavo.com; Alameda Jaume I 64; mains €11-19) Staffed by black-clad waiters, this contemporary place stands out among the restaurants bordering Xàtiva's broad, tree-lined main avenue. It does particularly creative mains, an excellent-value four-course lunch menu (€16) and an equally innovative range of tapas, to be nibbled in its bright, modern bar. It's just a few doors down from the tourist office.

Casa la Abuela   MEDITERRANEAN €€
(296 228 10 85; Calle de la Reina 17; mains €12-19, menus from €21) Renowned for its rice dishes, 'Grandmother's House' is equally strong on meat options. It's more formal than you might imagine granny's house to be.

❶ Information
Tourist office (296 227 33 46; www.xativaturismo.com; Alameda Jaime I 50; ⊙10am-2.30pm Tue-Sun mid-Jun–mid-Sep, 10am-1.30pm & 4-6pm Tue-Fri, 10am-1.30pm

---

MOROS Y CRISTIANOS

More than 80 towns and villages in the south of Valencia hold their own **Fiesta de Moros y Cristianos** (Moors and Christians festival) to celebrate the Reconquista, the region's liberation from Muslim rule.

Biggest and best known is Alcoy's (22 to 24 April), when hundreds of locals dress up in elaborate traditional costumes representing different 'factions' – Muslim and Christian soldiers, slaves, guild groups, town criers, heralds, bands – and march through the streets in colourful processions with mock battles.

Processions converge upon Alcoy's main square and its huge, temporary wooden fortress. It's an exhilarating spectacle of sights and sounds: soldiers in shining armour, white-cloaked Muslim warriors bearing scimitars and shields, turban-topped Arabs, scantily clad wenches, brass bands, exploding blunderbusses, firework displays and confetti showering down on the crowds.

Each town has its own variation on the format, steeped in traditions that allude to the events of the Reconquista. So, for example, Villena's festival (5 to 9 September) features midnight parades, while La Vila Joiosa (24 to 31 July), near Benidorm, re-enacts the landing of Muslim ships on the beaches.

Sat & Sun rest of year) On the Alameda, Xàtiva's shady main avenue.

❶ Getting There & Away

The train is by far your best bet. Frequent regional trains connect Xàtiva with Valencia (€3.60, 40 minutes, half-hourly) and most Valencia–Madrid trains stop here too; though these are much more expensive. You can also reach Alicante (€10.50 to €11.95, 1¼ hours, six daily) from here.

VILLENA
POP 34,970

Villena, on the N330 between Alicante and Albacete, is the most attractive of the towns along the corridor of the Val de Vinalopó.

Plaza de Santiago is at the heart of its old quarter. Within the imposing 16th-century **Palacio Municipal** (Plaza de Santiago 2) is Villena's **Museo Arqueológico** (admission free; ⊗10am-2pm Tue-Fri, 11am-2pm Sat & Sun). Pride of its collection are 60 gold artefacts weighing over 10kg, dating from around 1000 BC and found by chance in an old riverbed. Perched high above the town, the 12th-century **Castillo de la Atalaya** is splendidly lit at night. Free guided visits, in Spanish with English summary, take place three times each morning, Tuesday to Sunday.

Hotel Restaurante Salvadora (☑96 580 09 50; www.hotelsalvadora.com; cnr Calles Luis García & Jacinto Benavente; s/d from €43/55; ❋ 🛜) is the town's sole hotel, featuring simple, clean, well-priced rooms, a popular bar with a great range of tapas, and a gourmet **restaurant** (mains €8-15, 4-course menú degustación €25) that does a mean *triguico picao* (€6.50), the local speciality – a thick gruel of wheat, beans, pork and turnip. It's on the main road running through the town.

The **tourist office** (☑96 615 02 36; www.turismovillena.com; Plaza de Santiago 5; ⊗9am-2pm Mon-Fri, 10.30am-1.30pm Sat & Sun) is on the main square.

ALCOY
POP 61,090 / ELEV 565M

The industrial town of Alcoy (Alcoi in Valenciano), 54km north of Alicante, makes the most of its heritage and well merits your passing by. Ask at the tourist office for its brochure *Modernism in Alcoy* and explore its fine Modernista buildings.

Begin your visit with **Explora** (Calle Tints; adult/child €3/1.50; ⊗10am-2pm & 4-7pm Tue-Sat, 11am-2pm Sun), a high-tech presentation of Alcoy from prehistoric times to the industrial age with additional sections on Modernisme and Moros and Cristianos fiestas (see the boxed text, p591).

Between 22 and 24 April, the town holds its rumbustious **Moros y Cristianos** festival. To get a feel for this exuberant fiesta, visit the **Museo Alcoyano de la Fiesta** (Calle Sant Miquel 60-62; adult/child €3/1.50; ⊗10am-2pm & 4-7pm Tue-Sat, 11am-2pm Sun) with its posters, musical instruments, resplendent costumes and a stirring, noisily evocative 20-minute film of the action.

The ultramodern **Hotel AC Ciutat d'Alcoi** (☑96 533 36 06; www.ac-hotels.com; Calle Colón 1; r from €65-107; 🅿❋@🛜) was once an electricity substation, though you'd never believe it. The black and chestnut brown of the bedroom furnishings contrast pleasingly with crisp white sheets. Parking is €10.80 and you have to pay for internet access.

Alcoy's **tourist office** (☑96 553 71 55; www.alcoiturisme.com; Plaça de España 14; ⊗10am-2pm & 4-6pm Mon-Fri, 11am-2pm Sat & Sun) is right in the heart of the Old Town.

GUADALEST
POP 240

You'll be far from the first to discover the village of Guadalest; nowadays coaches, heading up from the Costa Blanca resorts, disgorge more than two million visitors every year. But get there early, or stay around after the last bus has pulled out, and the place will be almost your own.

Crowds come because Guadalest, reached by a natural tunnel and overlooked by the **Castillo de San José** (adult/child €3/free; ⊗10am-2pm & 3-6pm Sun-Fri, 11am-2pm & 3-6pm Sat), is indeed very pretty, and it's a joy to stroll through a traffic-free village. There's not actually much left of the miniature castle, perched in Never Never Land style atop a needle of rock, but the views are stunning. To reach the castle you must pass through the **Orduña House**, a beautiful village house with its original 18th-century furnishings. Entrance to the house is included with the castle entrance ticket.

There are half a dozen or so other museums, including the completely bonkers **Museo de Saleros y Pimenteros** (www.museodesalerosypimenteros.es; adult/child €3/free; ⊗10.30am-7.30pm), which is a museum of salt and pepper pots. Its sheer quirkiness makes it worth visiting!

If you want to stay the night, there is one option that is worth travelling a very long way for. **Cases Noves** (☑676 01 01 71, 965 88 53 09; www.casesnoves.es; s €50-80, d €90-125, incl breakfast; ✳@🛜) is a *casa rural* (village or farmstead accommodation) run by local lass Sofia and her husband, Toni, but put simply they've taken the B&B thing to a whole new level and made a place to stay and eat that is close to perfect. The thoughtfully designed bedrooms all have power showers, a safe, DVD player and fresh flowers. You can also relax in the reading room, the TV room with over 300 feature films, or the adjacent music room with just as many CDs. In winter, toast your toes by the open fireplace. In summer, savour the gorgeous terrace with its views of the distant sea and the village illuminated at night. The owners know the area intimately and readily give advice on local sights and the splendid opportunities for hill walking and cycling (they'll rent you a bike, too). But the real clincher for this place is the food. When we ate here we assumed that Sofia was a highly trained chef, but in fact it turned out that she is just very talented and imaginative. The three-course evening meals (€20) are fantastic, but if you can time your arrival to coincide with the 10-course Saturday-evening affair (€25) – fabulous, absolutely fabulous!

ELCHE
POP 230,350
Precisely 23km southwest of Alicante, Elche (Elx in Valenciano) is split by the channelled trickle of Río Vinalopó. It's a Unesco World Heritage site twice over: for the *Misteri d'Elx*, its annual mystery play, and for its extensive palm groves, Europe's largest, plant-ed by the Phoenecians and extended by the Arabs. Islamic irrigation systems converted the region into a rich agricultural producer that still offers citrus fruit, figs, almonds, dates and 85% of Spain's pomegranates.

◉ **Sights & Activities**
Around 200,000 palm trees, some shaggy and in need of a haircut, most trim and clipped, each with a lifespan of some 250 years, make the heart of this busy industrial town a veritable oasis. A signed 2.5km walking trail (ask at the tourist office for its leaflet *Historic Palm Groves Route*) leads from the Museu del Palmerar through the groves.

TOP CHOICE **Huerto del Cura** GARDENS
(Porta de la Morera 49; adult/child €5/2, audio guide €2; ⊙10am-sunset) In the Islamic world, a garden is considered a form of Paradise. Elche's Islamic past and culture couldn't therefore be any more obvious than in these privately owned gardens where man and nature have joined forces to produce something that truly approaches the Islamic ideal. The highlights are the water features and the cactus gardens. It's opposite the hotel of the same name.

Museo Arqueológico y de Historia de Elche MUSEUM
(MAHE; Diagonal del Palau 7; adult/child €3/free; ⊙10am-1.30pm & 4.30-8pm Tue-Sat, 10.30am-1.30pm Sun) This museum is a superb introduction to the town's long and eventful history. Everything is particularly well

MISTERI D'ELX

The *Misteri d'Elx*, a two-act lyric drama dating from the Middle Ages, is performed annually in Elche's Basílica de Santa María.

One distant day, according to legend, a casket was washed up on Elche's Mediterranean shore. Inside were a statue of the Virgin and the *Consueta*, the music and libretto of a mystery play describing Our Lady's death, assumption into heaven and coronation.

The story tells how the Virgin, realising that death is near, asks God to allow her to see the Apostles one last time. They arrive one by one from distant lands and, in their company, she dies at peace. Once received into paradise, she is crowned Queen of Heaven and Earth to swelling music, the ringing of bells, cheers all round and – hey, we're in the Valencia region – spectacular fireworks.

The mystery's two acts, *La Vespra* (the eve of her death) and *La Festa* (the celebration of her assumption and coronation), are performed in Valenciano by the people of Elche themselves on 14 and 15 August respectively (with public rehearsals on the three previous days).

You can see a multimedia presentation – complete with virtual Apostle – in the Museu de la Festa (Carrer Major de la Vila 25; adult/child €3/free; ⊙10am-1.30pm & 4.30-8pm Tue-Sat, 10am-1pm Sun), about a block west of the basilica. The show lasts 35 minutes and is repeated several times daily, with optional English commentary.

displayed and labelled, and it occupies both a purpose-built building and the town's castle.

Museu del Palmerar
MUSEUM

(Porta de la Morera 12; adult/child €1/free; ☉10am-1.30pm & 4.30-8pm Tue-Sat, 10.30am-1.30pm Sun) In a former farmhouse, this museum is all about the date palm and the intricate blanched, woven fronds used throughout Spain in Palm Sunday rites. Wander through the delightful adjacent palm grove and orchard with its gurgling irrigation channels and typical fruit trees of the *huerta* (garden).

Baños Árabes
BATHHOUSE

(Arab Baths; ☑96 545 28 87; Passeig de les Eres de Santa Lucía 13; adult/child €1/free; ☉10am-1.30pm & 4.30-8pm Tue-Sat, 10.30am-1.30pm Sun) At these 12th-century baths you can also watch an enjoyable audiovisual presentation with optional English soundtrack. Free entry on Sundays.

Basílica de Santa María
CHURCH

(tower adult/child €2/1; ☉7am-1pm & 5.30-9pm, tower 11am-6pm or 7pm) This vast baroque church is used for performances of the *Misteri d'Elx*. Climb up its tower for a sweeping, pigeon's-eye view over the palms.

Alcúdia
ARCHAEOLOGICAL SITE

The well-documented site is 3.5km south of the town centre. Here was unearthed the *Dama de Elche,* a masterpiece of Iberian art that's now in Madrid's Museo Arqueológico Nacional collection. Visit the site's excellent **Museo Arqueológico** (www.laalcudia.ua.es; adult/child €3/free; ☉10am-5pm or 8pm Tue-Sat, 10am-3pm Sun). The museum displays the rich findings from a settlement that was occupied continuously from Neolithic to late-Visigoth times. There's wheelchair access to the site.

🛏 SLEEPING

Hotel Huerto del Cura
BOUTIQUE HOTEL €€

(☑96 661 00 11; www.huertodelcura.com; Porta de la Morera 14; r incl breakfast from €111; P❋@☀) This is a sublime hotel, with stylish white rooms and antique wooden furnishings. The accommodation is in trim bungalows within lush, palm-shaded gardens. It's a family-friendly place with a playground, large pool and babysitting service. Complete the cosseting at Elche's longest-standing luxury hotel by dining in **Els Capellans**, its renowned restaurant. Parking is €12. It has another, slightly less stately property nearby, **Hotel Jardín Milenio** (☑966 61 20 33; www.hotelm ilenio.com; Calle Curtidors 17; r incl breakfast from €86; P❋@☎☀).

🍴 EATING

Carrer Mare de Déu del Carmé (Calle Nuestra Señora del Carmen) has a cluster of cheap and cheerful eateries. On summer evenings almost the whole length of this short street is set with tables.

WORTH A TRIP

ORIHUELA

Beside the Río Segura and flush with the base of a barren mountain of rock, the historical heart of Orihuela, with its Gothic, Renaissance and, especially, baroque buildings, well merits a short detour.

The following buildings are particularly worth looking out for:

Convento de Santo Domingo (Calle Adolfo Claravana; ☉9.30am-1.30pm & 4-7pm or 5-8pm Tue-Sat, 10am-2pm Sun) A 16th-century convent with two fine Renaissance cloisters and a refectory clad in 18th-century tilework.

Catedral de San Salvador (Calle Doctor Sarget; ☉10.30am-2pm & 4-6.30pm Tue-Fri, 10.30am-2pm Sat) One of the town's splendid ecclesiastical buildings is this 14th-century Catalan Gothic cathedral, with its three finely carved portals and a lovely little cloister.

Iglesia de las Santas Justa y Rufina (Plaza Salesas 1; ☉10.30am-2pm & 4-6.30pm Tue-Fri, 10.30am-2pm Sat) Worth admiring is the church's Renaissance facade and its Gothic tower graced with gargoyles.

Also noteworthy are the mainly 14th-century **Iglesia de Santiago Apóstol** (Plaza de Santiago 2), and, crowning the mountain, the ruins of a **castle** originally constructed by the Muslims.

Restaurante Dátil de Oro   MEDITERRANEAN €€
(✆96 545 34 15; www.datildeoro.com; mains €12-20, menus €16-25) Within the municipal park, the Golden Date is a vast emporium to eating that can accommodate almost 800 diners. Even so, the cuisine is far from institutional and it's one of the best places in town to sample local dishes, such as *arroz con costra* (rice with a crusty egg topping); also date flan and even date ice cream.

El Granaíno   SPANISH €€
(✆96 666 40 80; Calle Josep María Buck 40; mains around €18; ☺Mon-Sat) The tiled exterior of this long-established favourite hints at the classic, quintessentially Spanish cuisine of this family-run restaurant.

Restaurante Ganivet   SPANISH €
(Calle Fatxo 1; mains around €8-10, menú del día €12) Near the cathedral, and with tables set out in the sunny plaza, this is a good bet for a filling, bargain-priced lunch of traditional local fare.

❶ Information
The **tourist office** (✆96 665 81 95; www.turis medelx.com; ☺9am-7pm Mon-Fri, 10am-7pm Sat, 10am-2pm Sun) is at the southeast corner of Parque Municipal (Town Park).

❶ Getting There & Around
Train and bus stations are beside each other on Avenida de la Libertad (also called Avenida del Ferrocarril).

From the bus station, destinations include the following:

Alicante €1.90, 35 minutes, every half-hour
Murcia €3.95, 45 minutes, four to six daily
Valencia €11.75, 2½ hours, four to six daily

Elche is on the Alicante–Murcia train line. About 20 trains daily rattle through, bound for Alicante (€2.10) or Murcia (€2.95) via Orihuela (€2.10).

MURCIA

Murcia City
POP 434,000

Officially twinned with Miami, Murcia is the antithesis of the city of vice; it's a laid-back provincial capital that comes alive during the weekend *paseo* (stroll). Bypassed by most tourists and treated as a country cousin by too many Spaniards, the city nevertheless more than merits a visit.

In AD 825 Muslims moved into the former Roman colony and renamed it 'Mursiya'. The town was reconquered in 1243 by Alfonso X of Castilla y León and it's said his shrivelled heart is preserved within the cathedral's altar. Enriched by silk and agriculture, the city was at its grandest in the 18th century, from when the cathedral's magnificent baroque facade dates.

Looted by Napoleonic troops in 1810, and then overcome by plague and cholera, the city fell into decline. A century later, during the Spanish Civil War, Murcia was the scene of bitter fighting and many churches were destroyed. Thankfully, the cathedral survived.

◉ Sights

TOP
CHOICE **Real Casino de Murcia**   HISTORICAL BUILDING
(www.casinodemurcia.com; Calle Trapería 18; admission €5; ☺11.30am-9pm) Murcia's resplendent casino first opened as a gentlemen's club in 1847. Painstakingly restored to its original glory, it was reopened by King Juan Carlos in November 2009. The building is a fabulous combination of historical design and opulence, providing an evocative glimpse of bygone aristocratic grandeur. Beyond the decorative facade are a dazzling Moorish-style patio; a classic English-style library with 20,000 books, some dating from the 17th century; a magnificent ballroom with glittering chandeliers; and a compelling *to cador* (ladies powder room) with a ceiling fresco of cherubs, angels and an alarming winged woman in flames. There is also the neoclassical *Patio Pompeyano* and the classic wood-panelled *sala de billar* (billiards room).

Catedral de Santa María   CATHEDRAL
(Plaza del Cardinal Belluga; ☺7am-1pm & 6-8pm Jul & Aug, 7am-1pm & 5-8pm Sep-Jun) Murcia's cathedral was built in 1394 on the site of a mosque. The initial Gothic architecture was given a playful baroque facelift in 1748. The 15th-century Capilla de los Vélez is a highlight; the chapel's flutes and curls resemble piped icing. The **Museo de la Catedral** (admission free; ☺9am-2pm Tue-Sat, 10am-1pm Sun Jul & Aug, 10am-1pm & 5-8pm Tue-Sat, 10am-1pm Sun Sep-Jun) displays religious artefacts, but is most striking for the excavations on display: the remains of an 11th-century Moorish dwelling and of a small *mezquita* (mosque), visible below a glass walkway.

VALENCIA & MURCIA MURCIA CITY

Murcia City

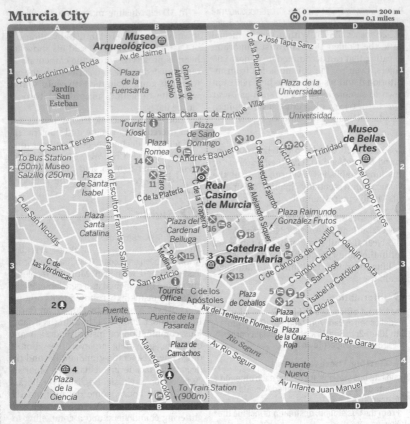

Murcia City

FREE Museo de Bellas Artes   GALLERY
(Calle del Obispo Frutos 12; ⊙10am-2pm Tue-Fri, 11am-2pm Sat & Sun Jul & Aug, 10am-2pm & 5-8pm Tue-Fri, 11am-2pm & 5-8pm Sat, 11am-2pm Sun Sep-Jun) An inviting, light gallery devoted to Spanish artists. The 2nd-floor Siglo de Oro gallery includes canvases by Murillo, Zurbarán and 'Lo Spagnoletto', José (Jusepe) de Ribera. For a break from all that religious piety, don't miss the superbly kitsch dazzle of glamorous *señoritas* on the 3rd floor.

Museo Salzillo   MUSEUM
(www.museosalzillo.es; Plaza de San Agustín 1-3; admission €5; ⊙10am-2pm Mon-Sat Jul & Aug, 10am-5pm Tue-Sat, 10am-2pm Sun Sep-Jun) Located in the baroque chapel of Ermita de Jesús and devoted to Murcian sculptor Francisco Salzillo (1707–83). The highlights are his exquisite *pasos* (figures carried in Semana Santa processions) and carved-wood nativity figurines. To get here head west from Gran Vía del Escultor Francsico Salzillo along Calle Santa Teresa.

Museo de la Ciencia y del Agua   MUSEUM
(Plaza de la Ciencia 1; adult/child €1.20/free; ⊙10am-2pm & 5-8pm Tue-Sat, 11am-2pm Sun; ⊞) Beside the river and one for the children. Although everything's in Spanish, this small hands-on science museum has plenty of buttons to press and knobs to twirl, plus fish tanks and a small planetarium.

FREE Museo Arqueológico   MUSEUM
(www.museoarqueologicomurcia.com; Avenida Alfonso X El Sabio 7; ⊙10am-2pm Tue-Fri, 11am-2pm Sat & Sun Jul & Aug, 10am-2pm & 5-8pm Tue-Fri, 11am-2pm & 5-8pm Sat, 11am-2pm Sun Sep-Jun) Has exceptionally well-laid-out and documented exhibits spread over two floors that start with Palaeolithic times and include audiovisual displays.

✦✦ Festivals & Events

Semana Santa   HOLY WEEK
The city's Easter processions rival Lorca's in their fervour.

Bando de la Huerta   SPRING FESTIVAL
Two days after Easter Sunday, the mood changes as the city celebrates this annual spring festival with parades, food stalls, folklore and carafe-fulls of fiesta spirit.

🛏 Sleeping

The range of accommodation in Murcia is fairly limited but prices are very low.

ℹ TOURIST TICKETS & INFORMATION

The tourist office has a handy service to save money and time: Puerto de Culturas (www.cartagenapuertodecultu ras.com) offers four different combined tickets (€11 to €20) covering Murcia's sights and tours. Tickets are available at each venue or at the tourist office.

Arco de San Juan   HISTORIC HOTEL €€
(☎968 21 04 55; www.arcosanjuan.com; Plaza de Ceballos 10; s/d €45/90; P🅿❄🛜) In a former 18th-century palace this hotel hints at its palatial past with a massive 5m-high original door and some hefty repro columns. The rooms are classic and comfortable, with hardwood details and classy fabrics, but they don't live up to the four stars the hotel's been awarded. Parking costs €16.

Hotel Casa Emilio   HOTEL €
(☎988 22 06 31; www.hotelcasaemilio.com; Alameda de Colón 9; s/d €45/50; P❄🛜) Across from Jardin Floridablanca, near the river, this well-maintained hotel is run by a helpful chap and has spacious, brightly lit rooms and good firm mattresses. Parking costs €11 and in-room wi-fi costs €1 per 24 hours.

Hotel Rincón de Pepe   BUSINESS HOTEL €€
(☎968 21 22 39; www.nh-hotels.com; Calle de los Apóstoles 34; r from €55; P❄@🛜) Acres of marble lobby greet guests at this corporate-style hotel. Rooms have glossy parquet floors and large luxurious bathrooms. The hotel restaurant promises a gourmet dining experience. There's a small casino here as well. Wi-fi is €10 per 24 hours.

Cathedral Hostel   HOSTEL €
(☎968 93 00 07; www.thecathedralhostel.com; Calle Trapería; dm incl breakfast €16; ⊙reception 10am-2pm & 5-10pm; ❄🛜) Murcia has never really been on the Spanish backpacker trail (or any other kind of trail for that matter), but even so the city now has its first dedicated backpacker hostel. It's clean, friendly, English speaking and perfectly located. The *azuleo*-tiled rooms contain bunk beds (quite a few per room) and there's a communal kitchen and common bathrooms. Staff can organise tours and a range of activities throughout the area. But remember there are a lot of beds crammed into each room...

VALENCIA & MURCIA MURCIA CITY

Hotel Hispano II
HOTEL €

(☑968 21 61 52; www.hotelhispano.net; Calle Radio Murcia 3; s/d incl breakfast from €43/54; P❊@🛜) Hotel Hispano II has sturdy old-fashioned rooms that really could be livened up a little, and it's clearly run as something of an afterthought to the highly regarded restaurant. Overlooking all that, you will get a peaceful and comfortable night's stay here. Parking is €13.

 Eating

Murcia has some outstanding restaurants. For the highest concentration, head for Plaza San Juan and Plaza Romea. Tapas bars are prolific around Plaza de las Flores and Plaza Santa Catalina.

Figón de Alfaro
TAPAS €

(Calle Alfaro 7; meals €12-15; ☽lunch & dinner Mon-Sat) Popular with all ages and budgets, Figón de Alfaro offers a chaotic bar area or a more sedate interconnecting dining room. Choose from full meals, a range of juicy *montaditos* (minirolls) or innovative one-offs such as *pastel de berejena con salsa de calabacín* (eggplant pie with a zucchini sauce).

La Parranda
MEDITERRANEAN €€

(Calle San José 1; meals €15-20; ☽lunch & dinner Thu-Tue) There are two branches of this restaurant. The *taberna* on Calle San José has an upbeat contemporary vibe with its light wood-panelled dining space and menu of traditional and modern tapas, *raciones* (large tapas servings) and more substantial meals. In a hurry? Go for the *brocheta de langostinas* (prawn skewer). In not so much of a hurry…follow this with a creamy panacotta. Its sister La Parranda restaurant is sit-uated on the nearby foodie square, Plaza San Juan, and is notable for having a great pile of delicious-looking fresh vegetables stacked up outside.

Los Zagales
TRADITIONAL SPANISH €

(Calle Polo Medina 4; meals €10-15) Lying within confessional distance of the cathedral, Los Zagales dishes up superb, inexpensive tapas, *raciones, platos combinados* (mixed platters), homemade desserts (and homemade chips). This is where the locals eat, so you may have to wait for a table. It's worth it.

Restaurante Real Casino de Murcia
CONTEMPORARY MURCIAN €€€

(☑968 22 28 09; Calle Trapería 18, Real Casino de Murcia; menus €28-45) For the ultimate in utterly refined dining, book a table in the Salon de Té of the Real Casino de Murcia. Despite the over-the-top 1920s setting the cuisine is a thoroughly modern take on Murcian classics and is as wonderful as the surrounds. It's wise to book ahead and look sharp.

Restaurante Hispano
MODERN SPANISH €€

(Calle Arquitecto Cerdán; raciones €7, meals €20-25; ☽lunch & dinner Mon-Sat, lunch Sun) The warm and inviting bar area has inventive *raciones*, such as baby broad beans sautéed with artichokes and onion. The smarter restaurant beyond, which is highly regarded by locals, serves more traditional dishes.

Los Arroces del Romea
SPANISH €€

(Plaza Romea; meals €20-25; ☑) Watch the speciality paella-style rice dishes being prepared in cartwheel-sized pans over the flames while you munch on circular *murciano* bread drizzled with olive oil. There are five rice dishes to choose from, including vegetarian. The setting, in front of the peachy-pink Teatro de Romea, is delightful.

Alborado
MODERN €€

(Calle Andrés Baquero 15; meals €20-25) This is a very discreet restaurant that you could easily pass by thinking it was merely another so-so place to eat, but in fact, this is actually one of the most talked-about restaurants in town. And with good reason! Its dishes are gourmet variations on traditional specialities and it also has a small but impressive tapas list.

Las Cadenas
MURCIAN €€

(☑968 22 09 24; Calle de los Apóstoles 10; meals €20-28; ☽Mon-Sat) Has an elegant dress for

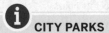

ℹ CITY PARKS

If you are visiting during midsummer, escape the blazing heat by visiting one of Murcia's lovely parks. The classic, small but beautiful **Jardín Flori-dablanca** has several magnificent banyan trees distinctive for their massive spread of thick woody roots, as well as jacarandas, Cyprus trees, palms, rose bushes and shady benches, plenty of them, for contemplating the view. A larger park and botanical garden, **Murcia Parque** lies just west of the Puente del Malecón footbridge and is similarly replete with leafy splendour.

GO THE TAPAS ROUTE

Murcia is excellent for tapas with plenty of variety, generous portions and a considerable vegetarian choice for non-carnivorous folk. Most of the restaurants listed in this chapter are fronted by tapas bars or serve *raciones* (large/full-plate-size tapas serving; literally 'rations'), which are great for sharing. Overall, Murciano tapas are more inventive than the norm and reflect the province's comprehensive agriculture with their use of fresh seasonal ingredients.

dinner feel and a traditional menu. Reservations recommended

 Drinking & Entertainment

Most through-the-night-life buzzes around the university. There are some vibrant bars and clubs here, including Sala Revolver (Calle Victorio), with its emphasis on Latin and Spanish rock. But, before you get that far through the night, kick things off at the Lemon Club Cafe (Calle Simon Garcia 4; ⊙5pm-late), which isn't really a cafe at all and nowhere near as wholesome as its name suggests, but is instead a bubbly bar full of bubbly students getting bubbly at the start of a long night (which will probably be quite bubbly as well). Nearby, Fitzpatrick (Plaza Cetina; ⊙3pm-3am) has a suitably blarney atmosphere and all the predictable ales on tap.

 Information

The regional tourist authority website is www.murciaturistica.es.

Locutorio Viajacom (Plaza de Camachos; per hr €1; ⊙10am-2pm & 4.30-10pm) Internet access.

Tourist kiosk (Calle de Santa Clara; ⊙10am-2pm & 5-8pm Mon-Sat, 10am-2pm Sun) Only open in summer.

Tourist office (☑968 35 87 49; www.murcia ciudad.com; Plaza del Cardenal Belluga; ⊙10am-2pm & 5-9pm Mon-Sat, 10am-2pm Sun)

 Getting There & Away

AIR Murcia's San Javier airport is situated beside the Mar Menor, closer to Cartagena than Murcia City. Connections to the UK include the following:
easyjet (www.easyjet.com) London (Gatwick), Birmingham, Bristol and Newcastle

Jet2.com (www.jet2.com) Blackpool, Edinburgh, Leeds, Manchester and Newcastle
Ryanair (www.ryanair.com) London (Luton and Stansted), Dublin, Leeds, Glasgow, East Midlands and Liverpool

BUS At least 10 buses run daily to both Cartagena (€3.95, one hour) and Lorca (€5.35, 1½ hours).
TRAIN Up to five trains travel daily to/from Madrid (€44.60, 4¼ hours). Hourly trains operate to/from Lorca (€15.60, one hour).

 Getting Around

From the bus station, take bus 3 into town; from the train station, hop aboard bus 9 or 39.

There's a handy car park at Jardín San Esteban, north of the city centre.

A taxi between the airport and Murcia City costs around €40.

Around Murcia City

The Murcia region offers a tantalising choice of landscapes and sights, ranging from the chill-out beaches of the Costa Cálida to the medieval magic of its towns and a wealth of reminders of the Roman Empire. To appreciate fully the unspoiled hinterland, you will need your own wheels.

CARTAGENA
POP 211,000

This is a city that feels old. Stand on the battlements of the castle that overlooks this city and you can literally see layer upon layer of history spread below you. There is the wharf where Phoenician traders docked their ships; there is the street where Roman legionnaires marched; there is the plaza that once housed a mosque where Islamic Spain prayed to Allah; there are the hills over which came the armies of the Christian Reconquista; there are the factories of the industrial age; and there, just below you, are the swirly decorations and pastel colours of yesterday's Modernista buildings.

Tourists have traditionally given Cartagena a miss, but this is starting to change. As archaeologists continue to strip back more and more of the town's old quarter to reveal a long-buried (and fascinating) Roman and Carthaginian heritage, the city is finally starting to get the recognition it deserves as one of the most historically and culturally fascinating places on the east coast of Spain.

VALENCIA & MURCIA AROUND MURCIA CITY

Cartagena

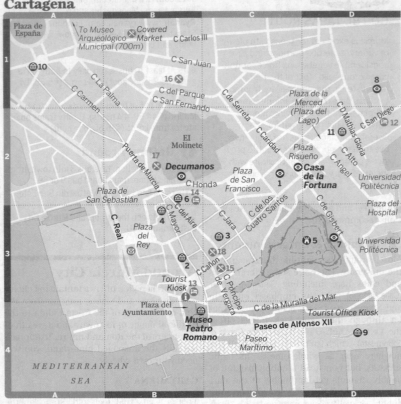

VALENCIA & MURCIA CARTAGENA

Cartagena

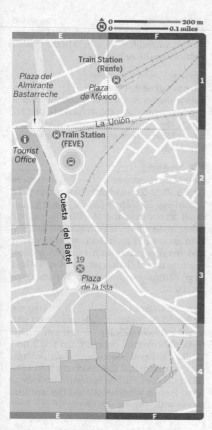

Train Station
(Renfe)

Plaza del
Almirante
Bastarreche

Plaza
de México

La Unión

Train Station
(FEVE)

Tourist
Office

Cuesta del Batel

19

Plaza
de la Isla

200 m
0.1 miles

History

In 223 BC Hasdrubal marched his invading
army into the Iberian settlement of Mastia,
renaming it Carthago Nova. The town prospered during Roman occupation and, under Muslim rule, became the independent
emirate of Cartajana. The Arabs improved
agriculture and established the town's reputation for building warships before being
expelled by the Catholics in 1242. The defensive walls were raised in the 18th century.
Although the city was badly bombed in the
civil war, industry and the population flourished during the 1950s and '60s.

Sights & Activities

TOP
CHOICE Museo Teatro Romano   MUSEUM
(Plaza del Ayuntamiento 9; adult/child €6/3;
⊙10am-8pm Tue-Sat, 10am-2pm Sun) The city's
finest museum was designed by Pritzker
Prize–winning architect Rafael Moneo. The
tour transports visitors from the initial mu-

seum on Plaza del Ayuntamiento, via escalators and an underground passage beneath
the ruined cathedral, to the magnificent, recently restored Roman theatre dating from
the 1st century BC. The tour and layout of
the museum is designed to reflect Cartagena's fascinating layers of urban history
and includes Roman statues and artefacts,
excavated from the site, as well as the cathedral's crypt and remains of an original
Moorish dwelling. Explanatory plaques are
in Spanish and English.

Roman Cartagena   ARCHAEOLOGICAL SITES
Other Roman sites include the Augusteum
(Calle Caballero; adult/child €2.50/free; ⊙4-
7.30pm Tue-Sun), which has an exhibition on
the Roman Forum. The Decumanos (Calle
Honda; adult/child €2/free; ⊙10am-2.30pm Tue-
Sun) has evocative remains of one of the
town's main Roman streets linking the port
with the forum, and including an arcade
and thermal baths. The Casa de la Fortuna
(Plaza Risueño; adult/child €2.50/free; ⊙10am-
2.30pm Tue-Sun) consists of fascinating remains of an aristocratic Roman villa dating
back to the 2nd and 3rd centuries, complete with murals and mosaics, and part
of an excavated road. Finally, the Muralla
Púnica (Calle de San Diego; adult/child €3.50/
free; ⊙10am-2.30pm & 4-7.30pm), built around
a section of the old Punic wall, concentrates
on the town's Carthaginian and Roman legacy. It also contains the tumbledown walls
of a 16th-century hermitage complete with
burial tombs filled with human bones.

Modernista Cartagena   ARCHITECTURE
Cartagena is rich in Modernista buildings;
several of the best now house banks (no
surprise there). Particularly magnificent
are Casa Cervantes (Calle Mayor 11); Casa
Llagostera (Calle Mayor 25); the zinc-domed
Gran Hotel (Calle del Aire); the strawberries-
and-cream confection of Casa Clares (Calle
del Aire 4); and the splendid Palacio Aguirre
(Plaza de la Merced), now an exhibition space
for modern art (known as Muram).

Castillo de la Concepción   CASTLE
(admission €1) For a sweeping panoramic
view, stride up to Castillo de la Concepción,
or hop on the lift. Within the castle's gardens, decorated by strutting peacocks, the
Centro de Interpretación de la Historia
de Cartagena (adult/child €3.75/free; ⊙10am-
2.30pm & 4-8.30pm) offers a mid-tech potted
history of Cartagena through the centuries

MUSEUM PASS

Visiting all the different archaeological sites and museums in Cartagena can work out quite expensive. Fortunately help is at hand in the form of a variety of passes (admission to four/five/six museums adult €12/15/18, child €9/11.25/13.50) that provide cheaper admission. Passes are available from the tourist office or the sites themselves. The Museo Teatro Romano counts as two museum entries.

via audio screens and a 10-minute film (in English and Spanish).

Museo Nacional de Arqueología Subacuática MUSEUM

(http://museoarqua.mcu.es; Paseo del Muelle Alfonso XII 22; adult/child €3/free; ⏰10am-9pm Tue-Thu, 10am-10pm Fri & Sat, 10am-3pm Sun) This futuristic new museum delves into the depths of a fairly futuristic science – underwater archaeology. It starts off by explaining the work of underwater archeologists and then sails on into the maritime history and culture of the Mediterranean. There's lots of old pots, flashy lights, buttons to press, films to watch and the remains of a Phonecian trading ship to marvel over. Free entry on Saturday afternoon and all day Sunday.

FREE Museo Arqueológico Municipal MUSEUM

(Calle Ramón y Cajal 45; ⏰10am-2pm & 5-8pm Tue-Fri, 11am-2pm Sat & Sun) Built above a late-Roman cemetery with a rich display of Carthaginian, Roman, Visigoth and Islamic artefacts. To get here, head northwest of the city centre, via Calle La Palma.

FREE Museo Naval MUSEUM

(Calle Menéndez Pelayo 8; ⏰10am-1.30pm Tue-Sun; 🚼) Has a great collection of naval maps and charts, plus replicas of boats big and small. Located northwest of the city centre via Calle Real.

☆☆ Festivals & Events

Semana Santa HOLY WEEK

During Holy Week Cartagena's haunting processions are as elaborate as anything Andalucía can offer.

La Mar de Músicas WORLD MUSIC

Bringing the best of world music to Cartagena, this annual festival is held in the castle's auditorium throughout July.

Carthagineses y Romanos HISTORICAL

(www.cartaginesesyromanos.es) For 10 days during the second half of September, locals play war games in a colourful fiesta that re-enacts the battles between rival Carthaginian and Roman occupiers during the second Punic War.

🛌 Sleeping

Hotel Los Habaneros HOTEL €€

(📞968 50 52 50; www.hotelhabaneros.com; Calle de San Diego 60; s/d from €50/60; 🅿❄@🛜) Located across from the Muralla Púnica, this shiny modern hotel is a straight-out bargain, with good-sized rooms decorated in cream and burgundy and with excellent service. Features include hairdryers, satellite TV and large bathtubs with showers. Parking costs €10.60.

Pensión Oriente HOTEL €

(📞968 50 24 69; 2nd fl, Calle Jara 27; s/d with shared bathroom €25/34) Go through a fantastically colourful doorway and you'll find 12 old-fashioned rooms with high ceilings, dark furniture and fans. A couple also have fridges and/or curling balconies with shuttered French windows. All but the spacious room with private bathroom (€38) have shared bathrooms.

Hotel NH Cartagena HOTEL €€

(📞968 12 09 08; www.nh-hotels.com; Calle Real 2; d €86; 🅿❄@🛜) Occupying the former port offices, the bland concrete facade jars somewhat with its neoclassical town-hall neighbour. The rooms are NH formula (modern and stylish); however, the upper floors have bay views and there are little extras such as electric kettles.

🍴 Eating

There are plenty of bars and restaurants around Plaza del Ayuntamiento and the side streets off Calle Mayor. Cartagena has a handy covered market (Calle Carlos III; ⏰7am-2pm Mon-Sat) that is good for self-caterers.

TOP CHOICE Techos Bajos SEAFOOD €€

(Santa Lucía; meals around €15; ⏰lunch Tue-Sun, dinner Fri & Sat) Locals absolutely flood this large, no-frills kind of place at lunchtime and if you sit back, under the warm Mediterranean sunshine, with a plate of tiny fried cuttlefish and a cold glass of white wine, it's easy to see why everyone comes here. Yes, the fresh-off-the-boat seafood is simple and superlative.

La Tartana   TAPAS €
(Puerta de Murcia 14; tapas €1.50, raciones €4-8) In a charming Modernista building on this wide pedestrian shopping street, this is the best place in town to come for tapas, *montaditos* and *raciones*. The selection includes classy numbers such as triangles of fried cheese with raspberry sauce. Typically packed with gossiping locals, La Tartana's atmosphere and service are tops.

La Tapería   TAPAS €€
(Calle del Parque 2; tapas €2, raciones €6-14) This intimate little place, on the edge of the old town, is built into the arches that surround Plaza Juan XXIII and offers quality tapas in an upmarket setting. There are a couple of other places nearby and the whole area is a good place to be in the early evening as locals pour onto the streets.

La Tagliatella   ITALIAN €€
(Calle Cañón 4; pizzas €11, pasta €13; ⊙lunch & dinner Tue-Sat, lunch Mon; 🗷) A step up from other Italian restaurants in the area, this is a welcoming eatery, good for sharing pizza and pasta with sauces including lobster and cream, and pesto with walnuts and Gorgonzola. The pizzas are crispy based with robust toppings.

Rincón Gallego   SEAFOOD €€
(Calle Cañón 13; meals €15-25; ⊙Mon-Sat) The extensive menu of fish dishes at this earthy local place includes several ways of preparing the speciality – octopus – including the deliciously simple grilled octopus with fresh lemons.

❶ Information
Tourist kiosk (Plaza del Ayuntamiento 1; ⊙10am-2pm & 5-7pm Mon-Fri, 10am-1.30pm Sat, 10.30am-1.30pm Sun)
Tourist office (☑968 50 64 83; www.cartagena.es; Calle San Diego 25; ⊙10am-2.30pm & 4-7.30pm Tue-Sun) Plenty of excellent information.

❶ Getting There & Away
BUS Buses run eight times daily to Alicante (€7.25, two hours), and 10 times to Murcia (€3.95, one hour) and to La Manga (€3.45 to €4.25, one hour).

TAXI A taxi to or from San Javier airport costs approximately €40.
TRAIN For Renfe train destinations, change in Murcia (€4.85, 50 minutes, four to seven daily). Beware: take the local train as the Talgo express alternative costs a hefty €16. Local FEVE trains make the short run to Los Nietos (€2.25, 30 minutes, every 40 minutes) on the Mar Menor.

Costa Cálida
With more than 300 days of annual sunshine and an average temperature of 18°C, the Hot Coast is aptly named.

MAR MENOR
The Mar Menor is a 170-sq-km saltwater lagoon. Its waters are a good 5°C warmer than the open sea and excellent for water sports, including jet-skiing, kayaking and waterskiing. Check the Sports category on the comprehensive www.marmenor.net website for more information. The lagoon is separated from the sea by La Manga (The Sleeve), a 22km sliver of land overdeveloped with close-packed high-rise accommodation; the world would lose little if it one day cut loose and drifted away.

Cabo de Palos, at the peninsula's southern limit, has a small harbour filled with pleasure boats and is surrounded by low-rise restaurants and holiday apartments. The waters around the tiny offshore (and protected) Islas Hormigas (Ant Islands) are great for scuba diving. Atura-Sub (www.aturasub.com; La Bocana 28) offers dives, including all equipment, from €60. The office is staffed sporadically; book through the website.

At the northern end of the lagoon, Lo Pagán is a mellow, low-rise resort with a

---

FREE MUD TREATMENTS

In Lo Pagán there is the added attraction (for some) of natural mud treatments. Head north of the promenade where a 2km walkway juts out into the lagoon, with a number of short wooden jetties. Have a dip on the west side of the path and coat yourself in mud. Be careful: *el lodo*, the squelchy, inky goo, retains the heat. Let it dry, wash it off, then to really tone yourself up take a dip in the saltwater lagoon opposite. Great fun and therapeutic, too, given the mud's high salt and iodine content.

long promenade, pleasant beach, and plenty of bars and restaurants.

Just east of Lo Pagán lie the Salinas de San Pedro (salt pans), where you can follow a well-signposted *senda verde* (footpath). This relatively easy walk of just over 4km passes by several lagoons favoured by flocks of pink flamingos trawling for small fry.

GOLFO DE MAZARRÓN

The rugged coast west of Cartagena is fretted with small coves and unspoilt beaches, best reached by car. Inland, where agricultural business prevails, the shimmering silver lakes turn out to be entire valleys sheathed in plastic where vegetables are force-grown in greenhouses for local and export markets.

If speed matters, take the AP7 toll motorway. Otherwise, opt for the more picturesque N332, which swoops and snakes through the coastal mountains. Both bring you to Puerto de Mazarrón, a bustling, likeable resort with shops and restaurants. Head west of the centre for the best beaches. At Playa La Ermita, the Centro de Buceo del Sureste (www.buceosureste.com; Calle Plaza del Mar 14) offers dives from €50. Five kilometres further west, the pleasant resort of Bolnuevo has surreal sandstone-sculptured rocks that eroded over millions of years: the Gredos de Bolnuevo (Bolnuevo Rocks). It's also unfairly well endowed with beaches. The Calas Nudistas, just beyond the village, are a series of beautiful undeveloped coves and, yes, that name does mean that most people will be in the nuddy and, no, sadly, most of the bodies on display are not as beautiful as the beaches. If you prefer your bathing with a modicum of decency, the main beach in the village, a long, sandy ribbon, will do very nicely indeed. Otherwise there's not much else to the village, just a few cafes, bars and places to stay. One of the best places for a meal is the reputable seafood restaurant, La Siesta (meals €20-25; ☺Fri-Wed).

CUT-PRICE CAVIAR

A local variant of caviar (*huevas de mújol*) is produced on the Mar Menor. It's available in jars in most local supermarkets at a very reasonable price compared to the real thing, but tastes surprisingly authentic – and good.

ÁGUILAS

Continuing on another 30km you come to low-key Águilas and its stunning beaches. The town has a slow vibe compared to some of the Valencian resorts and is popular with Spaniards and elderly English. The attractive town beaches are divided from each other by a low headland topped by a castle. The real interest, though, are the so-called Las Cuatro Calas a few kilometres south of town. These four desert coves are largely unmolested by tourist development (though that in no way means that they are undiscovered – they get very busy in summer) and have shimmering waters which merge into desert rock and are about as perfect as you'll find on the Spanish Med coast.

🛏 Sleeping & Eating

Hotel Madrid HOTEL €
(☎968 41 11 09; Plaza de Robles Vives 4; r €50-60; ❄) Welcome to a world of twee seaside resort hotels circa 1970. The Madrid is a real throwback to a (perhaps fortunately) bygone tourism age. It's friendly and the rooms are functional, if not a little dull. It's next to the port.

Hotel Carlos III HOTEL €
(☎968 41 16 50; Calle Rey Carlos III 22; r €50-60; ❄🖾) One block back from the beach, this is a dated seaside hotel that has a certain charm if you're in the right mood.

Bar Restaurante El Puerto SEAFOOD €€
(Plaza de Robles Vives 3; mains €10-13; ❄) Guess what's on the menu of this colourful, little portside restaurant? OK, you don't have to be Einstein to get this one. Seafood, lots of it and always good.

ⓘ Information

Tourist office (☎968 49 31 73; Plaza de Robles Vives; ☺9am-2pm & 5-7pm Mon-Sat, 10am-2pm Sun)

ⓘ Getting There & Around

Buses go to Lorca (€5.35, 1½ hours).

Lorca

POP 92,870 / ELEV 330M

The market town of Lorca has long been known for its pretty Old Town crowned by a 13th-century castle and for hosting one of Spain's most flamboyant Semana Santa (Holy Week) celebrations.

◉ Sights

Semana Santa Museums
MUSEUMS

Peculiar to Lorca are two small museums exhibiting the magnificent Semana Santa costumes (see the boxed text, p606). Some cloaks are up to 5m in length and all are elaborately hand-embroidered in silk, depicting colourful religious and historical scenes. The Museo de Bordados del Paso Azul (Calle Nogalte 7; adult/child €3/free; ☉10am-2pm & 5-7.30pm Tue-Sat, 10am-2pm Sun) competes in splendour with the Museo de Bordados del Paso Blanco (Calle Santo Domingo 8; adult/child €3/free; ☉10am-2pm & 5-7.30pm Tue-Sat, 10am-2pm Sun), annexed to the church of Santo Domingo.

Plaza de España
ARCHITECTURE

The highlight of the Old Town is a group of splendid baroque buildings around Plaza de España, including the Pósito, a 16th-century former granary; the 18th-century Casa del Corregidor; and the town hall. Lording over the square is the golden limestone Colegiata de San Patricio, a church with a handsome baroque facade and predominantly Renaissance interior. Although it looks good from the outside, it did suffer earthquake damage and is currently closed to the public.

La Fortaleza del Sol
CASTLE

(adult/child €8/free; ☉10.30am-6.30pm Tue-Sun, closed Jan-Mar; ♦) The town's castle has been transformed into a veritable theme park. La Fortaleza del Sol offers dioramas, actors in costume and various gadgetry. While children will probably enjoy all the jollity, adults may ponder the days when visiting the castle was a less contrived, more contemplative experience. Two of the castle towers were damaged in the earthquake, but the castle remains open to the public.

Museo Arqueológico
MUSEUM

(Plaza de Juan Moreno; adult/child €2/free; ☉10am-2pm & 5-7.30pm Tue-Sat, 10am-2pm Sun) Lorca's Museo Arqueológico, set in the grand 16th-century Casa de los Salazar, provides an insight into the city's ancient history, which dates back to the mid-Palaeolithic period.

Casa de Guevara
PALACE

(Calle Lope Gisbert) Sadly the wonderful baroque facade of the 17th-century Casa de Guevara suffered serious damage in the earthquake and is currently closed to the public.

LORCA EARTHQUAKE

On 11 May 2011 a magnitude 5.2 earthquake struck the Lorca area at a depth of just 1km. The quake left nine people dead, many injured and homeless, and caused significant damage to the town; with the Old Town being particularly badly affected. Spain sits on a fault line and everyday the country experiences numerous minor shakes (so minor you can't feel them). This one, though, was the worst earthquake to hit Spain in over 50 years. At the time of research much rebuilding was still taking place and many of the former buildings of tourist interest remained closed to the public.

The town is still well worth visiting (and the locals are desperate for tourists to return), but sadly it will take some years to return the old quarter to its former glory.

🛏 Sleeping

Jardines de Lorca
HOTEL €

(☎968 47 05 99; www.sercotelhoteles.com; Alameda de Rafael Méndez; s/d €55/60; P⊛@🖤🛜) If you're normally travelling on a budget, Lorca is the sort of place where it's worth shelling out a little bit more and getting a whole lot more, and the Jardines de Lorca is exactly what you should be aiming for. It has slick, corporate-style rooms with excellent facilities, including a spa.

Hotel Alameda
HOTEL €

(☎968 40 66 00; www.hotel-alameda.com; 1st fl, Calle Musso Valiente 8; s €35-45, d €60; P⊛🛜) Look beyond its location in the ugly tower-block building, and the insipid marble-chip flooring and dated floral fabrics, as the rooms here are large and fair value, and the hotel is excellently located. Add a zero to the price during Easter week, in return for front-row seats. Some rooms catch a lot of road noise.

Pensión del Carmen
HOTEL €

(☎968 46 64 59; Rincón de los Valientes 3; s/d €20/40; ⊛) A great budget choice. Cheerful and family-run, Carmen has seven doubles and seven singles, all spotless. You'll find it in a tiny square just off Calle Nogalte.

ADDING COLOUR TO SEMANA SANTA

In Lorca you'll find issues are clearly blue and white – the colours of the two major brotherhoods that have competed every year since 1855 to see who can stage the most lavish Semana Santa display.

Lorca's Easter parades beat to a different rhythm, distinct from the slow, sombre processions elsewhere in Murcia. While still deeply reverential, they're full of colour and vitality, mixing Old and New Testament legend with the Passion story.

If you hail from Lorca, you're passionately Blanco (White) or Azul (Blue). Each brotherhood has a statue of the Virgin (one draped in a blue mantle, the other in white, naturally), a banner and a spectacular museum. The result of this intense and mostly genial year-round rivalry is just about the most dramatic Semana Santa you'll see anywhere in Spain.

❶ Information

Centro de Visitantes (Visitors Centre; ☎968 47 74 37; www.lorcatallerdeltiempo.com; Convento de la Merced Puerto de San Ginés s/n; ◷9.30am-2pm & 4-7pm Tue-Sun) Located in a former convent and has a multimedia exhibition (adult/child €3/free) illustrating Lorca's long history.

Tourist office (☎968 44 19 14; www.lorca turismo.es; Convento de la Merced Puerto de San Ginés s/n; ◷9.30am-8.30pm Mon-Fri, 10am-3pm Sat, 10am-3pm Sun) Currently housed in the Centro de Visitantes after its Old Town offices were destroyed in the earthquake. It may change location during the lifetime of this book.

❶ Getting There & Around

Hourly buses (€5.35, 1½ hours) and trains (€15.60, one hour) run between Lorca and Murcia.

There's a large underground **car park** (Plaza Colón) 200m west of the tourist office.

Parque Natural de Sierra Espuña

The Sierra Espuña, a 40-minute drive southwest of Murcia towards Lorca, is an island of pine forest rising high into the sky above an ocean of heat and dust down below. Sitting just north of the N340, the natural park that protects this fragile and beautiful environment has more than 250 sq km of unspoilt highlands covered with trails and popular with walkers and climbers.

Limestone formations tower above the sprawling forests. In the northwest of the park are 26 *pozos de la nieve* (ice houses) where, until the arrival of industrial refrigeration, snow was compressed into ice, then taken to nearby towns in summer.

Access to the park is best via Alhama de Murcia. Visit the informative Ricardo Codorniu Visitors Centre (www.sierraespuna. com; ◷10am-2pm & 5-7pm Mon-Sat, 10am-2pm Sun) located in a traditional country house in the heart of the park.

The village of El Berro makes for a great base for the sierra. It has a couple of restaurants and the friendly Camping Sierra Espuña (☎968 66 80 38; www.campingsierra espuna.com; sites per person/tent/car €4, bungalows for 2-6 people €50-90; ☎⚟), with superb facilities, including barbecue pits, swimming pool, minigolf and cafeteria. For something altogether more luxurious you can't beat the Bajo el Cejo (☎968 66 80 32; www. bajoelcejo.com; s/d €86/97; P✳☎⚟). This delicious countryside hideaway is located inside a converted watermill and is absolutely dripping in style and glamour. The 13 rooms are superb but it's the swimming pool and the setting, overlooking the lemon groves and a deep valley, that are the real stars of the show. There's an excellent in-house restaurant. Reception is shut from 2pm to 5pm.

Another base for the sierra, and for northern Murcia in general, is the town of Mula, although you certainly need your own wheels to get from here to the heights of the hills. The town is a web of old streets squashed up against a pinnacle of dry rock topped by the very battered (and currently closed) remnants of a castle. From a distance the

ARTISTIC CENTRE IN FORMER CANNERY

Art is not a new concept in these parts where the rich cultural heritage ranges from the Neolithic cave paintings found in Cueva de los Letreros (just over the Andalucía border near Vélez Rubio) to Cartagena's stunning Roman mosaics. Located in the tiny village of Ceutí, La Conservera Centro de Arte Contemporáneo (http://laconservera.org; admission free; ☺4-8pm Tue-Fri, 11am-8pm Sat & Sun), 24km northwest of Murcia, opened in May 2009 as an artistic centre showcasing well-known international contemporary artists and sculptors whose work shares a common concept. The exhibition centre is housed in a converted cannery stripped of machinery. The result is vast spaces covering 4800 sq metres, ideal for these spacious, light-filled galleries.

town actually looks like it's dropped straight out of a Middle Eastern fairy tale. Excellent accommodation is available at El Molino de Felipe (☎968 66 20 13; www.hospederiaruralmo linodefelipe.es; r €40-85, apt €130-230; P❋☎✦). This is another peaceful rural retreat set among the citrus groves in a still-working mill. It has several beautifully equipped and spacious apartments and a couple of stylish rooms. Your breakfast bread will be fresh from the mill. It's about 4km out of town. Follow the road signs to the castle until you see it signposted.

Mallorca, Menorca & Ibiza

Includes »

Best Places to Eat

» Mesón El Gallo (p631)

» Simply Fosh (p615)

» La Paloma (p650)

» Comidas Bar San Juan (p644)

Best Places to Stay

» Hotel Palacio Ca Sa Galesa (p614)

» Cas Ferrer Nou Hotel (p623)

» S'Hotel des Puig (p619)

» Agroturismo Atzaro (p649)

» Casa Alberti (p627)

Why Go?

'Come to savour the splendid walking and cycling of the Tramontana and my northern coast', Mallorca will exhort. Menorca will cite her profusion of prehistoric sites and the forts her conquerors built and left behind. Unless she's still sleeping off her latest excess, in-your-face Ibiza will brag of her megaclubs, boutiques and oh-so-cool vibes. Tiny Formentera, for her part, will pipe up to remind you of her traffic-light country roads and white sands.

All four will protest vigorously and rightfully that they suffer from a bad press. 'Yes', the two big sisters will ruefully confess, 'patches have their share of mass tourism at its worst'. 'But', all four will chorus, 'you must meet us halfway'. So, take advantage of the islands' good public-transport system or hire a car to seek out an infinity of small coves, fishing villages, sandy beaches, endless olive and almond groves and citrus orchards.

When to Go
Palma de Mallorca

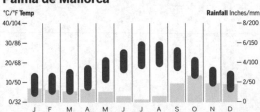

Mar & Apr Spring flowers brush your boots as you walk Mallorca's Serra de Tramuntana.

Jun–Sep Beach by day, clubbing through the night, raving round the Ibiza clock.

Jul & Aug Torch-lit re-enactments at Maó's Castell San Felipe on Menorca.

ℹ Getting There & Around

Air

In summer, masses of charter and regular flights converge on Palma de Mallorca and Ibiza from all over Europe. Major operators from the Spanish mainland include **Iberia** (www.iberia.es), **Air Europa** (www.aireuropa.com), **Air Berlin** (www.airberlin.com) and **Vueling** (www.vueling.com).

Tariffs for inter-island flights, with a flying time of less than 30 minutes, vary hugely. A trip from Palma de Mallorca to Maó or Ibiza costs anything from €50 to €170.

Boat

Compare prices and look for deals at **Direct Ferries** (www.directferries.es). Here are the main operators:

Acciona Trasmediterránea (☏902 454 645; www.trasmediterranea.es)

Baleària (☏902 160 180; www.balearia.com)

Iscomar (☏902 119 128; www.iscomar.com)

The following serve the Balearic Islands. Ferry routes to the mainland:

Formentera To/from Denia (Baleària).

Ibiza (Ibiza City) To/from Barcelona (Acciona Trasmediterránea, Baleària), Valencia (Acciona Trasmediterránea).

Ibiza (Sant Antoni) To/from Denia and Barcelona (Baleària), Valencia (Baleària).

Mallorca (Palma de Mallorca) To/from Barcelona and Valencia (Acciona Trasmediterránea, Baleària), Denia (Baleària).

Menorca (Maó) To/from Barcelona and Valencia (Acciona Trasmediterránea, Baleària).

Inter-island ferry routes:

Ibiza (Ibiza City) To/from Palma de Mallorca (Acciona Trasmediterránea, Baleària).

Mallorca (Palma de Mallorca) To/from Ibiza City (Acciona Trasmediterránea and Baleària) and Maó (Acciona Trasmediterránea, Baleària).

Mallorca (Port d'Alcúdia) To/from Ciutadella (Iscomar, Baleària).

Mallorca, Menorca & Ibiza Highlights

❶ Admire the Gothic splendour of the cathedral in **Palma de Mallorca** (p610)

❷ Take a hike in Mallorca's **Serra de Tramuntana** (p617)

❸ Join the party that sets the Mediterranean on fire in the amazing clubs of **Ibiza** (p640)

❹ Chill out on one of Formentera's breathtaking beaches such as **Cala Saona** (p653)

❺ Enjoy scented strolls in villages like **Fornalutx** (p621) in Mallorca's northwest

❻ Gasp at the turquoise hues of the sea around the promontory of **Cap de Formentor** (p623)

❼ Peer into prehistory at Naveta des Tudons and the other ancient monuments around **Ciutadella** (p631)

❽ Slip into Menorca's limpid waters at **Cala en Turqueta** (p639)

WEBSITES

Consult these pan-Balearics websites:

» **www.illesbalears.es** Official tourism website for all the islands.

» **www.platgesdebalears.com** The low-down on every beach.

» **www.balearsculturaltour.com** Handicrafts, cultural events, scenic splendours and more.

Menorca (Ciutadella) To/from Port d'Alcúdia (Iscomar).

Menorca (Maó) To/from Palma de Mallorca (Acciona Trasmediterránea, Baleària).

MALLORCA

In 1950 the first charter flight landed on a small airstrip on Mallorca, which, at 3620 sq km, is the largest of the Balearic Islands, and ever since then the island has earned itself a reputation as a place of package-tour excess and insensitive overdevelopment. However, when questioned, it often turns out that many of the island's most vocal detractors have never actually stepped foot on Mallorca and are merely rolling out time-worn clichés. Yes, there are areas that examplify the worst of mass tourism and yes, the local population of some 845,000 people (around half of whom live in the capital, Palma de Mallorca) are swamped by an annual 10 million visitors, but most of the island remains surprisingly undamaged by tourism and is often breathtakingly beautiful, amazingly diverse and highly cultured.

Palma de Mallorca (or, simply, Palma), the island's capital, is an energetic city filled with art galleries, fabulous resturants and some good places to stay. The south and east coasts are the home of crystal white-sand beaches and shimmering blue waters that'll leave you gasping at their beauty. But it's the northwest that most defies the clichés of Mallorca. Here the Serra de Tramuntana mountain range, matted with olive groves, pine forests and ochre villages, tumbles almost sheer into a sapphire-coloured Mediterranean. These mountains offer some of the best hiking and cycling in Spain with numerous walking trails from short family-friendly strolls to a multi-day trans-island traverse criss-crossing the range.

Getting Around

BOAT Palma and the major resorts and beaches around the island are connected by boat tours and water-taxi services. Most feature in the tourist-office brochure, *Excursions En Barca*, available in English.

BUS Most of the island is accessible by bus from Palma. All buses depart from or near the **bus station** (971 177 777; www.estaciondeauto buses.es/mallorca; Avinguda de Joan March 27, Carrer d'Eusebi Estada). For information, contact **Transport de les Illes Balears** (TIB; 971 17 77 77; http://tib.caib.es).

CAR & MOTORCYCLE You can rent cars and bikes, and often scooters too, in even the smallest resort. Palma alone has over 30 agencies. The big league has representatives at the airport and along Passeig Marítim, along with several cheaper companies. One of the best deals is **Hasso** (902 203 012; www.hasso-rentacar. com).

TAXI You can get around the island by taxi, but it's costly. Prices are posted at central points in many towns. You're looking at around €100 from the airport to Cala Ratjada or €35 to €40 from Palma to Sóller.

TRAIN Two train lines run from Plaça d'Espanya in Palma de Mallorca. The popular, old train runs to Sóller and is a pretty ride. A standard train line runs inland to Inca where the line splits with a branch to Sa Pobla and another to Manacor.

Palma de Mallorca

POP 869,070

Palma de Mallorca is the archipelago's only true city. Its old quarter is an enchanting blend of tree-lined boulevards and cobbled laneways, Gothic churches and baroque palaces, and private patios and designer bars.

Sights

CENTRAL PALMA DE MALLORCA

Central Palma is known especially for the elegant courtyards, called *patis,* of its many noble houses and mansions. Most are in

MALLORCA WEBSITES

» **www.infomamallorca.net** Official Mallorca tourism website.

» **www.abc-mallorca.com** Privately run and in the know.

» **www.mallorcahotelguide.com** Website of the Mallorca hoteliers' association.

Mallorca

private hands, but you can often peek into a *pati* through its wrought-iron grill.

Catedral
CATHEDRAL

(La Seu; ☑902 022 445, 971 723 130; www.catedral demallorca.org; Carrer del Palau Reial 9; adult/child €6/free; ⊙10am-6.15pm Mon-Fri, 10am-2.15pm Sat) Palma's vast cathedral is often likened to a huge ship moored at the city's edge. Construction on what had been the site of the main mosque started in 1300 but wasn't completed until 1601. This awesome structure is predominantly Gothic, apart from the main facade (replaced after an earthquake in 1851) and parts of the interior (renovated in Modernista style by Antoni Gaudí at the beginning of the 20th century).

Entry is via a small, three-room museum, which holds a collection of religious artwork and precious gold and silver effects. The cathedral's interior is stunning, with ranks of slender columns supporting the soaring ceiling and framing three levels of elaborate stained-glass windows. The front altar's centrepiece, a light, twisting wrought-iron sculpture suspended from the ceiling, is one of Gaudí's more eccentric creations. For once, however, Gaudí is upstaged by the island's top contemporary artist, Miquel Barceló, who reworked the Capella del Santíssim i Sant Pere, at the head of the south aisle, in a dream-fantasy, swirling ceramic rendition of the miracle of the loaves and fishes.

Palau de l'Almudaina
PALACE

(Carrer del Palau Reial; adult/child €9/4, audio guide €4, guided tour €6; ⊙10am-5.45pm Mon-Fri, to 1.15pm Sat) Originally an Islamic fort, this mighty construction was converted into a residence for the Mallorcan monarchs at the end of the 13th century. It is still occasionally used for official functions when King Juan Carlos is in town. At other times you can wander through a series of cavernous and austere stone-walled rooms, a chapel, with

Palma de Mallorca

Palma de Mallorca

a rare Romanesque entrance that contains the supposed bones of St Anna and, upstairs, royal apartments adorned with Flemish tapestries and period furniture.

Museu Diocesà
MUSEUM

(☑971 723 860; www.bisbatdemallorca.com; Carrer del Mirador 5; adult/child €3/free; ☺10am-2pm Mon-Sat) From the cathedral's exit, walk around the east end to the Palau Episcopal (bishop's residence) and, within it, to this rich collection. After the cathedral's seething crowds, it's a tranquil and fascinating excursion into Mallorca's Christian art history. Items, garnered from all over the island, are particularly well displayed and illuminated.

Es Baluard
MUSEUM

(Museu d'Art Modern i Contemporani; www.es baluard.org; Porta de Santa Catalina 10; adult/child €6/free, temporary exhibitions €4, free entry Tue; ☺10am-8pm Tue-Sat, 10am-3pm Sun) This 21st-century concrete complex nests within Palma's grand Renaissance-era seaward fortifications. A playful game of light, surfaces and perspective, it makes the perfect framework for the works within. These start with Catalan and other landscape artists at work in Mallorca in the 19th and 20th centuries and continue with a revolving display of 20th-century greats – you might see works by anyone from Oskar Kokoschka to Amedeo Modigliani. The views from the ramparts and cafe are splendid.

Palau March
MUSEUM

(Carrer de Palau Reial 18; adult/child €4.50/free; ☺10am-6.30pm Mon-Fri, to 2pm Sat) This house, palatial by any definition, was one of several residences of the phenomenally wealthy March family. Sculptures by 20th-century greats, such as Henry Moore, Auguste Rodin, Barbara Hepworth and Eduardo Chillida, grace the outdoor terrace. Within is a vast 18th-century Neapolitan nativity scene, alive with expressive folk figures, and a set of Salvador Dalí prints.

FREE Museu d'Art Espanyol Contemporani
MUSEUM

(Museu Fundació Juan March; www.march.es/arte/palma; Carrer de Sant Miquel 11; ☺10am-6.30pm Mon-Fri, 10.30am-2pm Sat) On permanent display within this 18th-century mansion are some 70 pieces held by the Fundación Juan March. Together they constitute a veritable who's who of mostly 20th-century artists, including Picasso, Miró, Juan Gris (of cubism fame), Dalí and the sculptor Julio González.

Can Marquès
HISTORIC BUILDING

(☑971 716 247; www.canmarquescontemporaneo.net; Carrer de Ca'n Angluda 2A; ☺10am-3pm Mon-Fri) This exquisitely furnished mansion, the only one of its kind in Palma open to visitors, retains elements dating to the 14th century. It gives a fascinating insight into how the well-to-do lived around the turn of the 20th century. The building shows elements of Gothic, baroque and even Modernista influences.

Basílica de Sant Francesc
CHURCH

(☑971 712 695; Plaça de Sant Francesc 7; admission €1.50; ☺9.30am-12.30pm & 3.30-6pm Mon-Sat, 9.30am-12.30pm Sun) One of Palma's oldest churches, Basílica de Sant Francesc was begun in 1281 in Gothic style; its baroque facade was added in 1700. You enter by the beautiful, two-tiered, trapezoidal cloister. Inside is the tomb of, and monument to, the 13th-century scholar Ramon Llull.

Casa-Museu Joaquim Torrents Lladó
GALLERY

(☑971 729 835; www.jtorrentsllado.com; Carrer de la Portella 9; adult/child €4/2.50; ☺11am-7pm Tue-Fri, 10am-2pm Sat) Once home of the eponymous Catalan artist (1946–93), this is another fine mansion, with a timber gallery overlooking a courtyard. Displaying many of his works, it has been largely preserved as he left it.

Banys Àrabs
BATHHOUSE

(☑971 721 549; Carrer de Serra 7; adult/child €2/free; ☺9.30am-8pm) These modest remains of Arab baths are one of the few reminders of Muslim domination of the island. All that survives are two small underground chambers, one with a domed ceiling supported by a dozen columns, with some of the capitals recycled from demolished Roman buildings.

The baths are set in one of Old Palma's prettiest gardens, where you can sit and relax.

WESTERN PALMA

Castell de Bellver
CASTLE

(Bellver Castle; ☑971 730 657; Carrer de Camilo José Cela 17; adult/child €2.50/free, Sun & public holidays free; ☺10am-7pm Tue-Sun) South of the Poble Espanyol, this unusual, circular 14th-century castle (with a unique round tower) is set atop a pleasant park. It's the setting for a July classical-music festival.

Fundació Pilar i Joan Miró   GALLERY

(📞971 701 420; http://miro.palma.cat; Carrer de Saridakis 29; adult/child €6/free; ◷10am-7pm Tue-Sat, 10am-3pm Sun; 🚌 3 from Plaça Espanya, 6 from Plaça de la Reina) On Cala Major (about 4km southwest of the city centre), this museum is housed in a modern complex on the site of Joan Miró's former studios. On show is a rotating collection of the works stored here at the time of his death.

🛏 Sleeping

There *are* budget places around but, in general, you'll be paying rather more if you want an alternative to unexceptional but good-value package-tour hotels.

TOP CHOICE Hotel Dalt Murada   HISTORIC HOTEL €€€

(📞971 425 300; www.daltmurada.com; Carrer de l'Almudaina 6A; s/d incl breakfast €177/210; ✳🔊; 🖥2) Gathered around a medieval courtyard, this carefully restored old town house, which dates from 1500, has 14 rooms and is a gorgeous option, with antique furnishings (including chandeliers and canopied beds) and art work. The decidedly 21st-century penthouse suite has incomparable views of the cathedral. Rates drop dramatically from those quoted above out of season.

TOP CHOICE Hotel Palacio
Ca Sa Galesa   HISTORIC HOTEL €€€

(📞971 715 400; www.palaciocasagalesa.com; Carrer del Miramar 8; s/d incl breakfast from €256/329; ✳@🔊✉; 🖥2) Lord and Lady (insert name here), welcome to your little place in the city. We are sure you'll enjoy your stay. This fabulouslly ornate 16th-century mansion is possibly the most extravagent hotel in Mallorca. Rooms and public spaces are rammed with antiques, there's a libary filled with tomes on art, bathrooms contain free-standing tubs and there's enough stained glass to make the cathedral jealous.

DON'T MISS

MALLORCA'S TOP BEACHES

» Platja de Formentor (p623)
» Cala Llombards (p625)
» Cala Sant Vicenç (p623)
» Cala Deià (p619)
» Sa Calobra (p622)

Hotel Santa Clara   BOUTIQUE HOTEL €€€

(📞971 72 92 31; www.santaclarahotel.es; Carrer de Sant Alonso 16; s/d from €122/168; ✳@🔊) Boutique meets antique in this historic mansion, converted with respect, where subdued greys, steely silvers and cream blend harmoniously with the warm stone walls, ample spaces and high ceilings of the original structure. There's a small, decked roof terrace, ideal for a sunbathe or a sundowner, and a spa with free facilities for guests. Service can, however, be rather abrupt.

Misión de San Miguel   BOUTIQUE HOTEL €€

(📞971 214 848; www.urhotels.com; Carrer de Can Maçanet 1; r from €139; ✳@🔊) This 32-room boutique hotel is an astounding deal with excellent prices and stylish designer rooms; it does the little things well with firm mattresses and rain showers, although some rooms open onto public areas and can be a little noisy. Service is friendly and professional.

Hotel San Lorenzo   HISTORIC HOTEL €€€

(📞971 728 200; www.hotelsanlorenzo.com; Carrer de Sant Llorenç 14; s €145-185, d €155-195, ste from €235; ✳🔊✉) Tucked away inside the old quarter, this hotel is in a beautifully restored 17th-century building. It has a fragrant Mallorcan courtyard, its own bar, a rooftop terrace with cathedral views and a lovely small garden with swimming pool. Rooms come in a range of styles, from antique wooden furniture and tiled bathrooms to bright-blue rooms with Mallorcan fabrics.

Central Palma Youth Hostel   HOSTEL €

(📞971 10 12 15; www.centralpalma.com; Plaça de Quadrado 2; dm €25; ◷reception manned 8-10am & 1-4pm; ✳@🔊) This brand-new privately run youth hostel offers the cheapest city-centre accommodation and has smart four-bed dorms decorated in gaudy computer graphics. There's an in-house bar-restaurant and plenty of traveller-related advice and facilities.

Hotel Palau Sa Font   HOTEL €€€

(📞971 712 277; www.palausafont.com; Carrer dels Apuntadors 38; s incl breakfast €85-112, d incl breakfast €145-245; ✳@🔊✉; 🖥1, 6, 15) Tucked away on a quiet side street, this former 16th-century palace offers 19 rooms, bright-pink walls and the *Mona Lisa* as a slippery serpent. Yes, they've opted for the eye catching look! Even so it's a little overpriced.

FINDING A BED

The Balearics in high summer (roughly, late June to mid-September) can be incredibly busy. Palma de Mallorca alone turns around some 40 inbound and outbound flights a day. Most of the millions of visitors have pre-booked package accommodation and the strain on local infrastructure can make it tricky for the independent traveller. Book at least the first couple of nights around this time to avoid an uncomfortable start. In July and August hotel prices are at their highest. In most places you can expect to pay considerably less in quieter times. Check hotel websites for special offers and promotions.

Eating

Plenty of eateries and bars cater to Palma's visitors in the maze of streets between Plaça de la Reina and the port. The seaside Es Molinar area around Es Portixol has cheerful seafood eateries and laid-back bars.

 Simply Fosh   INTERNATIONAL €€

(971 72 01 14; www.simplyfosh.com; Carrer de la Missió 7a; mains €18-26, dinner menus €48; ⊗Mon-Sat) Lovingly prepared Mediterranean grub with a special touch is the order of the day in the convent refectory, one of the home kitchens of Michelin-starred chef Marc Fosh. The range of set menus is a wonderful way to sample high-quality cooking at a reasonable price, but there are also à la carte choices.

There's a three-course lunchtime *menú del día* (€19.50) as well as a five-course *menú degustación* (tasting menu; €48).

Misa Braseria   BRASSERIE €€€

(971 595 301; www.misabraseria.com; Carrer de Can Maçanet 1; mains €16-20, menus from €17; ⊗1-3.30pm & 7.30-10.30pm Mon-Sat) The latest addition to Marc Fosh's ever-expanding restaurant empire, this attractive place consists of a basement restaurant adorned with famous restaurant menus on the walls, or offers lunchtime dining upstairs in its modern patio. The food is slickly presented and tastes are typically fresh with dishes that change weekly and with the seasons. The *menú del día* (€17) is outstanding.

Celler Pagés   MALLORCAN €€

(971 72 60 36; Calle de Felip Bauzà 2; mains €9-15, menú del día €19.50; ⊗closed Sun) This fuss-free family-run restaurant is actually located down below ground level in the cellars of an old town house. Drawing in a steady stream of locals the cuisine here is all about traditonal Mallorcan dishes all served up with a little extra pazzazz that helps to make this one of the best-regarded restaurants in the city. Reservations are a good idea.

La Bodeguilla   SPANISH €€

(971 71 82 74; www.la-bodeguilla.com; Carrer de Sant Jaume 3; mains €17.50-19.50; ⊗Mon-Sat) This gourmet restaurant does creative interpretations of dishes from across Spain; try the *cochinillo* (suckling pig) from Segovia or the *lechazo* (young lamb, baked Córdoba-style in rosemary). Also on offer is an enticing range of tapas – the marinated cubes of salmon with dill chutney caught our eye.

Bon Lloc   VEGETARIAN €

(971 71 86 17; www.bonllocrestaurant.com; Carrer de Sant Feliu 7; menus €13.50; ⊗lunch Mon-Sat; ⏦) This 100% vegetarian place is light, open and airy with a casual but classy atmosphere. All produce is organic and you're in assured hands here – this was Palma's first vegetarian restaurant and there are no agonising decisions, just a satisfying, take-it-or-leave-it four-course *menú*. It's hugely popular, so do ring to reserve.

Ca'n Eduardo   SEAFOOD €€€

(971 721 182; www.caneduardo.com; 3rd fl, Travesía Contramuelle, Es Mollet; mains €23-29; ⊗1-11.30pm) What better place to sample fish than here, right above the fish market? With it's refined contemporary decor it's not really the normal kind of port-side, salt-of-the-earth fishermen's restaurant, but Ca'n Eduardo has been in business since the 1940s and has a loyal clientele. Black-vested waiters serve up grilled fish and seafood and some fantastic rice dishes (minimum of two) – the *arroz bogavante* (lobster rice) is a favourite.

Drinking & Entertainment

The old quarter is the city's most vibrant nightlife zone. Particularly along the narrow streets between Plaça de la Reina and Plaça de la Drassana, you'll find an enormous selection of bars, pubs and bodegas. Look around the Santa Catalina (especially

FANCY FOOTWORK

Mallorca is better known for its shoe-making tradition (especially with the international success of the Camper company), but Menorca, too, has long had its share of cobblers. The best-loved local product is the *avarca* (*abarca* in Spanish), a loose, comfortable slip-on sandal that covers the front of the foot and straps around the heel. Sometimes with soles fashioned from recycled car tyres, they make great summer shoes. Shops sell them all over the island (and indeed all over the Balearics).

Carrer de Sant Magí) and Es Molinar districts too. About 2km west of the old quarter, along and behind Passeig Marítim (aka Avinguda de Gabriel Roca), is a concentration of taverns, girlie bars and clubs. According to a much-flouted law, bars should shut by 1am Sunday to Thursday, and 3am Friday and Saturday.

S'Arenal and Magaluf, the seaside resorts east and west of Palma respectively, are full of bars and discos filled to bursting with mainly package tourists. Magaluf in particular has gained an infamous reputation for the behaviour of its mainly young British clientele.

Vamos 365 (www.vamos-mallorca.com), a monthly freebie, has its finger on Palma's night-time pulse.

Puro Beach   BAR
(☑971 744 744; www.purobeach.com; ☺11am-1am May-Sep) This laid-back, sunset chill lounge carries more than a hint of Ibiza with a tapering outdoor promontory over the water and an all-white bar that's perfect for sunset cocktails, DJ sessions and fusion-food escapes. Blend in with the monochrome decor and wear white, emphasising your designer tan. It is just a two-minute walk east of Cala Estancia (itself just east of Ca'n Pastilla).

Ca'n Joan de S'Aigo   CAFE
(Carrer de Can Sanç 10; ☺8am-9pm Wed-Mon) Dating from 1700, this is *the* place for a hot chocolate in what can only be described as an antique-filled milk bar. The house speciality is *quart,* a feather-soft sponge cake that children love, with almond-flavoured ice cream.

Abaco   BAR
(www.bar-abaco.com; Carrer de Sant Joan 1; ☺from 8pm) Behind a set of ancient timber doors is this extraordinary bar. Inhabiting the restored patio of an old Mallorcan house, Abaco is filled with ornate candelabra, elaborate floral arrangements, cascading towers of fresh fruit, and bizarre artworks. It hovers between extravagant and kitsch, but the effect is overwhelming whatever your opinion. Paying this much for a cocktail is an outrage, but one might just be worth it here. Oh, and non-drinking customers – no photos please!

Jazz Voyeur Club   MUSIC BAR
(☑971 905 292; www.jazzvoyeurfestival.com; Carrer dels Apuntadors 5; admission free; ☺from 9.30pm daily Apr-Oct, closed Sun & Mon Nov-Mar) A tiny club no bigger than most people's living rooms, Voyeur hosts live bands nightly for much of the year – jazz is the focus, but you'll also hear flamenco, blues, funk and the occasional jam session. Red candles burn on the tables and a few plush chairs are scattered about – get here early if you want to grab one. In autumn it hosts a fine jazz festival.

El Garito   LIVE MUSIC
(☑971 736 912; www.garitocafe.com; Dàrsena de Can Barberà; ☺7pm-4.30am) DJs and live performers, doing anything from hip-hop to nu jazz and disco classics to electro beats, heat up the scene from around 10pm. Admission is generally free, but you're expected to buy a drink.

ℹ Information

Airport tourist office (☑971 789 556; Aeroport de Palma; ☺8am-8pm Mon-Sat, 8am-4pm Sun) Tourist information.

Consell de Mallorca tourist office (☑971 17 39 90; www.infomallorca.net; Plaça de la Reina 2; ☺8am-8pm Mon-Fri, 9am-2pm Sat) Covers the whole island. For cultural and sporting events, consult *On Anar,* its free quarterly 'what's happening' guide with a version in English.

Main municipal tourist office (☑902 102 365; www.imtur.es; Casal Solleric, Passeig d'es Born 27; ☺9am-8pm) Also has a branch in the train station.

Visit Palma (www.visit-palma.com) Palma's hotel association's website.

ℹ Getting Around

Sant Joan airport is about 10km east of Palma. There are trains and buses to other parts of the island.

TO/FROM THE AIRPORT Bus 1 (€2.50) runs every 15 minutes between Sant Joan airport and Plaça d'Espanya in central Palma and on to the ferry terminal. A taxi costs €17 to €20.

BUS There's an extensive local bus service around Palma and its bay suburbs with **EMT** (☑971214444; www.emtpalma.es). Single-trip tickets cost €1.50 or you can buy a 10-trip card for €10. For the beaches at S'Arenal, take bus 15 from Plaça d'Espanya.

TAXI For a taxi, call ☑971 75 54 40.

Southwest Coast

A freeway skirts around the Badia de Palma towards Mallorca's southwest coast. Along the way you'll pass the resorts of Cala Major, Ses Illetes (lovely little beaches), Palma Nova and Magaluf (nice long beaches and mass British tourism), all basically a continuation of Palma's urban sprawl. From Andratx (worth a stop for a taste of an inland Mallorca town, especially busy in the early evening when people sit around for drinks at terraces on Plaça d'Espanya and Plaça des Pou), two turn-offs lead down to the coast: one goes to Port d'Andratx, and the other to the seaside hamlet of Sant Elm, which is surorunded by leafy hills, has a pretty (but busy) sandy beach and the possibility of boat tours to the nearby, uninhabited, Illa Sa Dragonera with its good walking trails.

PORT D'ANDRATX

Port d'Andratx spreads around low hills surrounding a narrow bay, where yachties hang out. A couple of dive schools are based here.

Yes, the rooms themselves might be a bit dowdy, but the Hostal-Residencia Catalina Vera (☑971 671 918; www.hostalcatalinavera. es; Carrer Isaac Peral 63; s/d €55/75; P🐾) has a garden full of cactuses and a dining room crammed with knick-knacks, including church-worthy religious paintings, ancient pots pulled off the seabed and walls lined with hundreds of plates and this gives it real character.

A couple of blocks inland from the waterfront, Restaurante La Gallega (☑971 671 338; Carrer Isaac Peral 52; mains €13-25, menú del día €15.50; ☺1.30-11pm Tue-Sun, closed Nov) is a popular local seafood restaurant overlooked by many visitors, enticed by the pricier waterfront alternatives.

Northwest Coast & Serra de Tramuntana

Dominated by the rugged Serra de Tramuntana range, Mallorca's northwest coast is the Mediterranean before mass tourism. There are no sandy beach resorts here, but there are steep, forest shrouded cliffs and mountain slopes which tumble down towards a handful of idyllic coves with luminous blue waters. The few towns and villages are built largely of local stone and blend harmoniously into Mother Nature's dreamy canvas. The mountainous interior is much loved by walkers for its stirring landscapes of pine forests, olive groves and spring wild flowers. Beautiful in summer, it's a peaceful, virtually year-round destination for walkers.

The main road through the mountains (the Ma10) runs roughly parallel to the coast between Andratx and Pollença. It's a stunning, scenic drive and a hugely popular cycling route, especially during spring, when the muted mountain backdrop of browns, greys and greens is splashed with the bright colours of yellow wattles, bloodred poppies and garish cycling vests. There are plenty of well-sited *miradors* (viewpoints) to punctuate your trip.

ℹ️ BUSSING AROUND THE NORTHWEST

Between April and October, two daily buses leave Ca'n Picafort and Port de Sóller simultaneously at 9am and 3pm. Though very few passengers make the whole journey, the service is particularly popular with walkers. The following list shows the duration of the bus trip between each stop:

» **Port de Sóller–Sóller** 10 minutes

» **Sóller–Monasteri de Lluc** one hour

» **Monasteri de Lluc–Cala Sant Vicenç** 30 minutes

» **Cala Sant Vicenç–Port de Pollença** 15 minutes

» **Port de Pollença–Alcúdia** 15 minutes

» **Alcúdia–Port d'Alcúdia** 15 minutes

» **Port d'Alcúdia–Ca'n Picafort** 30 minutes

RENTING A FARMHOUSE IN PARADISE

Renting apartments, studios, bungalows and villas has long been a popular way to stay on the islands. Rural accommodation, often in stylishly transformed tranquil country retreats (almost always with a pool), has become especially popular. Mallorca leads the way with some truly beautiful, bucolic options. A great deal more can be found in Lonely Planet's *Mallorca*. Otherwise, these websites will get you started:

» www.fincas4you.com

» www.fincasinmallorca.com

» www.mallorca.co.uk

» www.rusticrent.com

» www.topfincas.com

ESTELLENCS
POP 390

Estellencs is a pretty village of stone buildings scattered around rolling hills below the **Puig Galatzó** (1025m) peak. It's a popular base for walkers and cyclists. A rugged walk of about 1km leads down to a cove with crystal-clear water and a cute little boat ramp.

The higgledy-piggledy, stone **Petit Hotel Sa Plana** ([☎]971 618 666; www.saplana.com; Carrer de Eusebi Pascual; s incl breakfast €75, d incl breakfast from €95; [☉]mid-Jan–Nov; [❄][含][⛱]), with its tousled garden and six rustic farmhouse rooms, is as gorgeous as the village it sits in. It's family-owned and particularly welcoming.

BANYALBUFAR
POP 600

Delightful Banyalbufar melds into the mountain slopes high above the coast. Surrounded by steep, stone-walled farming terraces carved into the hillside, the village has a cluster of bars and cafes, plus several hotels.

The four guest rooms of charming stone **Ca Madò Paula** ([☎]971 148 717; www.camadopaula.com; Carrer de la Constitució 11; d incl breakfast €99-120; [❄][@][含]) are pleasingly decorated with stone walls and a few antique touches. Downstairs is an excellent restaurant (mains around €17) and a stylishly retro bar.

Ferreted away at the top end of the village in a 15th-century building, the **Hotel Son Borguny** ([☎]971 14 87 06; www.sonborguny.com; Calle Borguny 1; d incl breakfast from €95; [❄][含]) has rooms that all differ from one another – some are painted a bright sky-blue and others have stone walls behind the beds. All, however, come with bundles of charm and some very happy staff.

The Palma–Estellencs bus passes through Banyalbufar four to nine times daily.

VALLDEMOSSA
POP 2000

Valldemossa is an attractive blend of tree-lined streets, old stone houses and impressive new villas. The ailing composer Frédéric Chopin and his lover, writer George Sand, spent their 'winter of discontent' here in 1838–39.

◉ Sights & Activities

Real Cartuja de Valldemossa MONASTERY (adult/child €8.50/4; [☉]9.30am-6.30pm Mon-Sat, 10am-1pm Sun) The monastery is a beautiful building surrounded by gorgeous gardens which enjoys fine views. Jaume II had a palace built on the site in 1310. After it was abandoned, the Carthusian order took over and converted it into a monastery, which, in 1399, was greatly expanded.

A series of cells shows how the monks (bound by an oath of silence they could break only for half an hour per week in the library) lived. Following the rules of the order, just 13 monks lived in this cavernous place.

Frédéric Chopin and George Sand stayed in this grand monastery, which had been turned into rental accommodation after its monks were expelled in 1835. Their stay wasn't entirely happy and Sand later wrote *Un Hiver à Mallorque* (A Winter in Mallorca), which, if nothing else, made her perennially unpopular with Mallorcans.

Tour buses arrive in droves to visit the monastery. In the couple's former quarters are Chopin's piano (which, due to shipping delays, arrived only three weeks before their departure), his death mask and several original manuscripts. Entry includes a 15-minute piano recital (up to eight times daily) and entry to the adjacent 14th-century **Palau del Rei Sanxo** and local **museum**.

Costa Nord CULTURAL CENTRE ([☎]971 612 425; www.costanord.es; Avinguda de Palma 6; adult/child €7.50/free; [☉]9am-8pm daily May-Oct, 9am-5pm Mon-Sat & 9am-1pm Sun Nov-Apr) The brainchild of part-time Valldemossa resident and Hollywood actor Michael

Douglas, Costa Nord describes itself as a 'cultural centre' and begins well with a 15-minute portrayal of the history of Valldemossa, narrated by Douglas himself. The subsequent virtual trip aboard *Nixe,* the 19th-century yacht of Austrian Archduke Luis Salvador, who owned much of western Mallorca, will be of less interest to most.

Camino del Archiduque   WALK
Stretch those legs by walking around 12.5km of this circular route from Valldemossa that offers dizzyingly spectacular coastal views and seascapes.

Port de Valldemossa   WALK, DRIVE
From Valldemossa, a tortuous 7km road leads down to this rocky cove with a dozen or so buildings.

⌂ Sleeping & Eating

TOP
**CHOICE Es Petit Hotel
de Valldemossa**   BOUTIQUE HOTEL €€
(📞971 612 479; www.espetithotel-valldemossa.com; Carrer d'Uetam 1; r incl breakfast €127-172; ✳@🛜) This friendly family home (the owners still live here) has been converted into an enticing boutique hotel. In the shady garden and on the terrace with a countryside view where humanity scarcely intrudes, you could be an island away from the flow of Cartuja visitors that streams by the front door.

The rooms themselves have strong primary colours and high ceilings, while five of the eight them have gorgeous valley views.

Restaurant Es Port   SEAFOOD €€
(📞971 616 194; mains €12.80-23.50; ⊙10am-6pm Sep-May, 10am-10pm Jun-Aug) Seafood is the mainstay here, as you'd expect, and it all somehow tastes better out on the 1st-floor terrace on a midsummer's evening. Rice dishes steal the show, as does the mixed seafood platter (€23.50), while the *calamares al ajillo con patatas* (cuttlefish cooked with potato cubes and lightly spiced) is perfectly prepared.

❶ Getting There & Away
Bus 210 from Palma to Valldemossa runs five to 12 times daily.

DEIÀ
POP 750
Deià is perhaps Mallorca's most famous village. Its setting is idyllic, with a cluster of stone buildings cowering beneath steep hill-sides terraced with vegetable gardens, vineyards and fruit orchards.

Such beauty has always been a drawcard and Deià was once second home to an international colony of writers, actors and musicians. The most famous member was the English writer Robert Graves, who died here in 1985 and is buried in the town's hillside cemetery.

◉ Sights & Activities

Casa Robert Graves   HISTORIC BUILDING
(Ca N'Alluny; 📞971 636 185; www.lacasaderobertgraves.com; Carretera Deià-Sóller; adult/child €7/3.50; ⊙10am-5pm Mon-Fri, 10am-3pm Sat) A five-minute walk out along the road to Sóller, Casa Robert Graves is a fascinating tribute to the writer who moved to Deià in 1929 and had his house built here three years later. It's a well presented insight into his life; on show you'll find period furnishings, audiovisual displays and various items and books that belonged to Graves himself. Afterwards enjoy exploring the gardens.

Cala Deià   BEACH
This shingled beach is a popular swimming spot with a couple of busy summertime bar-restaurants. The steep walking track from town takes about half an hour. You can also drive down (3km from central Deià), but competition for a parking spot (€5 for the day) can be intense.

Parish Church   CHURCH
The village's steep cobbled lanes lead to the parish church, which has an attached museum.

Deià Coastal Path   WALK
Some fine walks criss-cross the area, such as this gentle path to the pleasant hamlet of Lluc Alcari (three hours return). Another nearby option is the old mule trail between Deià and Sóller (two hours each way).

⌂ Sleeping

TOP
CHOICE S'Hotel des Puig   HISTORIC HOTEL €€€
(📞971 639 409; www.hoteldespuig.com; Carrer des Puig 4; s €95, d €150-160; ⊙Feb-Nov; ✳🛜❄) The eight rooms of this gem in the middle of the old town reflect a muted modern taste within ancient stone walls. Out the back are secrets impossible to divine from the street, such as the pool and lovely terrace. The 'House on the Hill' has appeared in a number of books about Mallorca, and even in a Robert Graves short story. All up this is

---

WORTH A TRIP

A SLOW CHUG NORTH TO SÓLLER

A delightful journey into the past is also a pleasing way to head north from Palma de Mallorca for Sóller. Since 1912, a narrow-gauge train with timber-panelled carriages has trundled along this winding 27km route from Plaça de l'Estació (one way/return €12.50/19.50, 1¼ hours, up to seven times daily). You pass through ever-changing countryside that becomes dramatic in the north as it crosses the Serra de Alfàbia, offering fabulous views over Sóller and the sea on the final descent into town.

one of the most exceptional small hotels in north Mallorca.

Hotel Costa d'Or HOTEL €€€
(☎971 639 025; www.hoposa.com; Lluc Alcari; s/d incl breakfast from €88/158; ☺Apr–Oct; P❋☎☎) This secluded spot offers designer rooms in a stone building that backs on to woods high above the Mediterranean. Whilst the rooms themselves lack some of the intimacy of the smaller, family-run hotels, this place, perched high above a sea of liquid lapis lazauli and surrounded by pine trees and squeaking cicadas, will quickly make you realise you've come about as close to paradise as you can get.

Hostal Miramar HOTEL €€
(☎971 63 90 84; www.pensionmiramar.com; Carrer de Ca'n Oliver; r incl breakfast €91, without bathroom €75; ☺Mar–mid-Nov; P) Hidden within the lush vegetation above the main road and with views across to Deià's hillside church and the sea beyond, this 19th-century stone house with gardens is a shady retreat with nine rooms. The rooms with shared bathrooms have the best views; others look onto the garden. It's a short, sharp climb above the town.

✗ Eating

Restaurant Juame MALLORCAN €€€
(☎971 63 90 29; www.restaurantejuame-deia.com; Avinguda del Arxiduc Lluís Salvador 22; mains €20-25; ☺closed Mon; ❋) This is the kind of restaurant we like. Family-run and exceptionally friendly with a relaxed, easygoing vibe but simply superb gourmet Mallorcan dishes

incorporating the very best local produce. It's a little more expensive than some of the other options in the village but it's worth every euro.

Sebastian INTERNATIONAL €€€
(☎971 639 417; Carrer de Felip Bauzà 2; mains €26-30; ☺7.30-10.30pm Thu-Tue Mar–mid-Nov; ❋) With its bare stone walls and crisp white linen, Sebastian offers a refined dining environment. The menu is short and subtle with three fish mains and three meat choices, each enhanced with a delicate sauce or purée. On offer when we were there was pan-fried breast of pigeon with rhubarb and aged balsamic, but the menu changes with the seasons.

El Barrigón de Xelini TAPAS €
(Avinguda del Arxiduc Lluís Salvador 19; meals €20; ☺Tue-Sun) You never quite know what to expect here, but tapas, more than 50 kinds drawn from all over Spain, are at the core. It has a penchant for mains of lamb too, including the delicious lamb stuffed with spinich. On summer weekends, there's live jazz.

❶ Information
Deià Mallorca (www.deia.info) Check out this website for information about the town.

SÓLLER
POP 13,950

The shady ochre town of Sóller is set amid citrus orchards in a broad valley. Behind it rise the stone walls of the Serra de Tramuntana. It makes a fine base for exploration of the northwest, whether on foot or by vehicle.

The main square, Plaça de la Constitució, is 100m downhill from the train station, (the forecourt of the station also hosts a couple of intriguing art exhibitions). Around the square are bars and restaurants, the town hall and the large, mainly baroque Església de San Bartolomé (Plaça de la Constitució; admission free; ☺11am-1.15pm & 3-5.15pm Mon-Thu, 11am-1.15pm Fri & Sat, noon-1pm Sun). Its Modernista facade was designed by a student of Antoni Gaudí, who is also responsible for the even more strikingly Modernista frontage of the Banco de Sóller (nowadays Banco de Santander), right beside the church. A busy market takes place in this square on Saturday mornings.

A 1km stroll west of the square leads to the Jardí Botànic (www.jardibotanicdesoller. org; adult/child €5/free; ☺10am-6pm Tue-Sat, 10am-2pm Sun), a peaceful botanical garden that showcases flowers and other plants native to the islands. In spring and summer herpetologists will be delighted to hear that the garden's water features are positively bubbling with snakes and frogs – we saw around eight snakes in a few minutes during our last visit. Non-herpetologists will be equally delighted to hear that said snakes are totally harmless.

Do jump aboard one of Sóller's open-sided, vintage wooden trams (€5), which rattle 2km down to Port de Sóller on the coast. They depart from the train station every 30 minutes between 7am and 8.30pm.

The Sóller area has plenty of boutique hotels in historic buildings and country houses; many are listed on www.sollernet. com. With just six rooms, the 19th-century Ca'n Isabel (☑971 638 097; www.canisabel.com; Carrer de d'Isabel II 13; s €99.50-131.50, d €124.50-156.50; ☉mid-Feb–mid-Nov; ✻@⊛) is a gracefully decorated hideaway, with a fine garden out the back. The owners have retained the period style impeccably. The best (and dearest) of the rooms come with their own delightful terrace.

In a palacial building in the centre of town l'Avenida Hotel (☑971 634075; www. avenida-hotel.com; Gran Vía 9; d incl breakfast from €245; ✻⊛⊛) combines the best of the 1920s with the striking art and style of today and is a seriously plush place to rest up. As good as the rooms are though, it's the courtyard pool that really steals the limelight. There's a minimum stay of three nights in high season. Right beside the train station, family-run Hotel El Guía (☑971 63 02 27; www.soller net.com/elguia; Carrer del Castanyer 2; s/d incl

breakfast €55/89; ✻⊛) has a polished old-fashioned reception area, present gardens and is a good place to meet fellow walkers. Its simple rooms feature timber trims and modern bathrooms and prices drop the longer you stay.

In an atmospheric former cart workshop, Ca's Carreter (☑971 63 51 33; Carrer del Cetre 9; meals €30-35, mains €13-17; ☉lunch & dinner Tue-Sat, lunch Sun) is a welcoming spot that serves unpretentious Mallorcan cooking, including fresh local fish and other mainly regional ingredients. The lamb casserole with honey, salmon with Sóller oranges, and zucchini stuffed with fish and spinach particularly caught our eye. It's a short pleasant walk northwest of the centre.

Sóller's tourist office (☑971 638 008; www.viu-soller.com; Plaça d'Espanya; ☉9.45am-2pm & 3.15-5pm Mon-Fri, 9.15am-1pm Sat Mar-Oct, 9.30am-3pm Mon-Sat Nov-Feb) is in an old train carriage beside the station. For planning walks around and beyond the Sóller basin, pick up the tourist office's pamphlet *Sóller Bon Dia Senderismo*. Lonely Planet's *Walking in Spain* describes three splendid day walks that set out from the village.

BINIARAIX & FORNALUTX

From Sóller it's a pleasant 2km drive, pedal or stroll through narrow laneways up to the hamlet of Biniaraix. From there, a classic walk ascends the Barranc de Biniaraix, following part of the old pilgrim route from Sóller to the Monestir de Lluc.

Climbing northwards, the narrow, twisting scenic road climbs to Fornalutx, through terraced citrus groves.

Fornalutx is a pretty village of distinctive stone houses with green shutters, colourful flower boxes and well-kept gardens, many now owned by expats.

Fornalutx Petit Hotel (☑971 631 997; www.fornalutxpetithotel.com; Carrer de l'Alba 22; s €89-123, d €161.50-184; ☉mid-Feb–mid-Nov; ✻@⊛⊛), a tastefully converted former convent just below the main square, is as much art gallery as boutique hotel. Each of the eight rooms is named after a contemporary Mallorcan painter and displays their canvases, all of which are for sale.

Ca'n Reus (☑971 631 174; www.canreushotel. com; Carrer de l'Alba 26; s €100, d €120-150, ste €170; ℗✻@⊛⊛) is tempting for a romantic escape. The British-owned country mansion was built by a certain Mr Reus, who got rich on the orange trade with France. The rooms are all quite different and all have views;

each is stunning and has restrained antique furnishings and exposed stonework, with plenty of light throughout. Children under five are not welcome.

SA CALOBRA

The 12km road between the Ma10 and the small port of Sa Calobra is a spectacular drive. Carved through weird mountainous rock formations, it skirts narrow ridges and twists down to the coast in an endless series of hairpin bends. You won't be alone in Sa Calobra. Armies of buses and fleets of pleasure boats disgorge battalion after battalion of visitors. A short trail through a rock tunnel leads to a small cove with some fabulous but often-crowded swimming spots and, upstream, a spectacular river gorge, the Torrent de Pareis.

Boats make spectacular excursions beneath the cliffs from Port de Sóller to Sa Calobra, some calling by Cala Tuent.

MONESTIR DE LLUC

Legend has it that, some time in the 13th century, a shepherd boy and a monk stumbled across a small statue of the Virgin Mary beside a stream and took it to the parish church. The next day, it had vanished and reappeared on the stream bank. After this happened twice more, the villagers got the message and built a chapel to shelter the sacred statue where it was originally found.

A monastery, Monestir de Lluc (☑971 871 525; www.lluc.net; Plaça dels Peregrins; monastery & gardens free, museum €4; ◷8.30am-8pm, museum 10am-1.30pm & 2.30-5pm, gardens 10am-1pm & 3-6pm), was established shortly thereafter. Since then thousands of pilgrims come every year to pay homage to the statue of the Virgin of Lluc, known as *La Moreneta* (The Little Dark One). If you're lucky you might hear *Els Blauets*, the famed boys' choir, singing. Founded nearly 500 years ago, they're called The Blues for the colour of their cassocks.

The present monastery is a huge, austere complex, dating from the 18th century. Off the central courtyard is the entrance to the Basílica de la Mare de Déu; the statue of the Virgin is in the ambulatory behind its main altar. There's also a museum of local archaeological finds and a modest art collection.

POLLENÇA

POP 17,260

Offering an attractive old quarter and easy beach and mountain access, the pleasant sun-baked town of Pollença makes an excellent base for this corner of Mallorca.

The devout climb up Calvari (Calvary), 365 stone steps leading to a hilltop chapel. The views from the top are well worth the effort. Central Plaça Major is a good place to relax; its cafes and restaurants have broad terraces.

If you're around on 2 August and notice a bunch of wild buccaneers disembarking, don't worry. It's just Pollença enjoying its Festes de la Patrona, celebrating the whupping of Muslim invaders back in 1550.

A 1.5km road, best attacked on foot, ascends south of the town up to the former monastery of Santuari de la Mare de Déu des Puig (☑971 184 132; per person €22), from where you can enjoy a superb wraparound panorama. If you like the place, you can stay in one of the monks' former cells. Rooms are basic but hey, what do you expect?

The best place in town to sleep is Hotel Desbrull (☑971 535 055; www.desbrull.com; Carrer del Marqués Desbrull 7; s/d incl breakfast from €80/90; ✳❡), which has six pleasantly fresh if coquettishly small doubles in a modernised stone house. White dominates the decor in rooms and bathrooms, offset with strong splashes of colour. It's run by a friendly brother-sister combination.

The cooking is assured at the Scottish-run La Font del Gall (☑971 530 396; lafontdelgall@

RUTA DE PEDRA EN SEC

A week's walk would see you traverse the Serra de Tramuntana from Port d'Andratx to Pollença, mostly following old mule trails that are often cobbled. You'd be following the partially completed 271km GR221 long-distance trail, aka the Ruta de Pedra en Sec (Dry Stone Route). Currently some 162km of the route is completed and open. The 'dry stone' refers to an age-old building method throughout the island. In the mountains you'd see farming terraces, houses, walls and more built of stone without mortar. Eventually the signed trail will have eight stages, with a *refugi* (mountain hostel) waiting for you at the end of each day. For a detailed guide to the route so far, pick up *GR221: Mallorca's Dry Stone Way* by Charles Davis. Also check out www.conselldemallorca. net/mediambient/pedra.

hotmail.com; Carrer del Monti-Sion 4; menú del día €14.50, mains €8-15; ⊙11.30am-3pm & 6.30-10pm Sun-Fri Mar-Oct) which promises fresh contemporary cuisine. Our favourite dish: the crisp, slow-roasted pork belly.

CALA SANT VICENÇ

A series of four jewel-like coves with water so limpid you feel you could see to the centre of the world, this is a tranquil resort in a magnificent setting. OK, 'resort' paints something of a grim picture. The reality is that this place is very low-key indeed and outside the main holiday season you'll pretty much have the place to yourself.

Set back from the road between Cala Molins and Cala Carbo, Hostal los Pinos (☎971 531 210; www.hostal-lospinos.com; Urbanització Can Botana; s incl breakfast €42-46, d incl breakfast €74-88; ⊙May–mid-Oct; P❀❁) has two gleaming white villas sitting on a leafy hillside. Superior doubles have partial sea views, plus separate sleeping and lounge areas and balconies. It's relaxed and peaceful, yet only a short walk from the beachside action.

CAP DE FORMENTOR

A splendid drive leads from Port de Pollença out high along this rocky promontory. Stop at the Mirador de Sa Creueta (232m), 3km out of Port de Pollença, for a dramatic view. Midway along the promontory is the historic Hotel Formentor, a jewel of pre-WWII days, and the nearby shady strand of Platja de Formentor (aka Platja del Pi). Another spectacular 11km brings you to the lighthouse on the cape that marks Mallorca's northernmost tip. A few kilometres short of the lighthouse two trails lead from a dirt car park down to the splendid beaches of Cala Figuera on the northern flank and Cala Murta on the southern side. Cala Figuera is the bleaker and wilder of the two whilst Cala Murta is reached after a 20-minute stroll through the pine forests. Neither have any kind of tourist infrastructure but both have mesmerising blue waters.

Badia d'Alcúdia

The long beaches of this bay fringe Mallorca's northeast coast, its broad sweeps of sand stretching from Port d'Alcúdia to Ca'n Picafort.

ALCÚDIA
POP 19,100

Wedged between the Badia de Pollença and Badia d'Alcúdia, the pretty walled, old town of Alcúdia was once a Roman settlement. Remnants of the Roman theatre survive and the old town is still partly protected by largely rebuilt medieval walls (parts of which you can stroll along). The highlight of the faded Roman ruins of Pollentia (☎971 897 102; Avinguda dels Prínceps d'Espanya; adult/student & senior incl museum €3/2; ⊙9.30am-8.30pm Tue-Sat, 10am-3pm Sun May-Sep, 10am-3.30pm Tue-Fri, 10am-1.30pm Sat & Sun Oct-Apr), just outside the ramparts, is the small theatre. Alcúdia makes a great base for this corner of the island.

The Cas Ferrer Nou Hotel (☎971 89 75 42; www.nouhotelet.com; Calle Pou Nou 1; s/d incl breakfast €95/125, ❀❁) is a fabulous six-room boutique hotel inside an old town house. Soft scented rose petals are scattered across the bed sheets, there are big, thick pillows, exposed stone walls and a flat-screen TV and DVD player in each room (with DVDs) and the free bottle of wine is a nice touch. Outside there's a sunny central courtyard and pretty bougainvillea plants clambering up the walls.

Fonda Llabres (☎971 545 000; www.fondallabres.com; Plaça de sa Constitució 6; d €45-55, s/d without bathroom €35/45; ❁) offers cheap yet comfortable beds. It occupies a pair of buildings (one was the former telephone exchange) in the heart of the village.

Bus 351 from Palma (€4.60, one hour) calls at Alcúdia hourly.

PORT D'ALCÚDIA

A lovely stretch of sand arcs southwards from the large harbour, from where boat trips leave daily to destinations such as Platja de Formentor. Nearby Cap des Pinar is a pretty peninsula that lends itself to cycling and hiking.

Parc Natural de S'Albufera, a protected wetland just south of Port d'Alcúdia, is a birdwatchers' paradise, where more than 300 species have been spotted. Leaving the main Ma12, it's a pleasant 1km canalside and duckboard walk to the visitors centre. From here you can follow signed walks ranging in length from 750m to 11.5km, each with hides and observation platforms. You must obtain a (free) visitors permit from the information centre before starting your walk.

The tidy and friendly Hostal Vista Alegre (971 547 347; www.hvista-alegre.com; Passeig Marítim 10; s €30, d €40-50; ✹@) sits on the waterfront and offers bright and breezy rooms that are as good a value as you'll find. Air-con costs €3 extra.

East Coast

Many of the fine beaches along Mallorca's east coast have succumbed to the ravages of mass tourism. Beside much of its northern half stretches a series of concrete jungles that rivals the worst excesses of the Costa del Sol on the Spanish mainland. Further south the coastline is corrugated with a series of smaller coves and ports, saving it from the same fate.

ARTÀ
POP 7400

Watching over the graceful inland town of Artà is a 14th-century hilltop fortress and Santuari de Sant Salvador (Via Crucis; ☻8am-8pm Apr-Oct, 8am-6pm Nov-Mar), from where you have a wonderful panorama across the rooftops, countryside and out to sea. A much-restored 4000-sq-metre complex, it boasts all the elements of a medieval fortress, down to the stone turrets ringing the top and the metre-thick walls.

On the coast, 11km southeast of Artà at the limit of the Ma4042, the Coves d'Artà (971 841 293; www.cuevasdearta.com; adult/child €11/free; ☻10am-6pm), sunken into the cliffs, are a less-visited rival to Porto Cristo's Coves del Drac. Tours of the caves leave every 30 minutes.

Hotel Casal d'Artà (971 829 163; www.casaldarta.de; Carrer de Rafael Blanes 19; s incl breakfast €55-69, d incl breakfast €91; ✹☎) is a wonderful old mansion in the heart of town. The 'arta' in the name is very appropriate as photographs and paintings covering everything from the Spanish Civil War to pop art and stern-faced portraits, smother every bit of available wall space. Beside reception is a small self-service honesty bar (drop your money in the piggy bank). Ask for room 4 or 8; both have sybaritic baths sunken into a tiny alcove.

An appealing mix of old and new, the Bar Parisien (971 835 440; cafeparisien@hotmail.com; Carrer de la Ciutat 18; mains €11-19; ☻10am-midnight Mon-Sat) draws a sophisticated crowd to this stylish restaurant, famed for its fresh market cuisine. The white-wicker-chair look and modern art on

the walls give it a casual but classy feel and the food is excellent – try the *cordero con ciruelas* (lamb with plums), *tumbet* (Mallorcan ratatouille) or fresh fish on display as you enter.

PORTOCOLOM

A tranquil village set on a generous harbour, Portocolom has managed to resist the tourist onslaught with dignity. Within a couple of kilometres are some fine beaches, such as the immaculate cove of Cala Marçal.

Right on the waterfront, Hostal Porto Colom (971 825 323; www.hostalportocolom.com; Carrer d'en Cristòfol Colom 5; s/d incl breakfast €63/96; ✹) has breezy rooms with big beds and colourful, sunny decor. Downstairs, there's a cool restaurant and lounge bar.

Buses 490 and 491 run to/from Palma via Felanitx (€5.50, 1¾ hours, eight daily).

CALA D'OR TO CALA MONDRAGÓ

Once a quaint fishing village, Cala d'Or is now an overblown big-dollar resort. Its sleek marina is lined with glistening megayachts and blindingly whitewashed villas crowd the surrounding hills.

Immediately south of Cala d'Or (and virtually joined to it by urban sprawl) is the smaller and more tranquil Portopetro. Centred on a boat-lined inlet and surrounded by residential estates, it has a cluster of harbourside bars and restaurants, and a couple of small beaches nearby.

Two kilometres south of Portopetro are the three cove beaches of Cala Mondragó. Put simply this is what you came to Mallorca for. Each of the coves is more spectacular than the last and even the first is pretty breathtaking. Development ranges from a hotel or two and a couple of beach shacks and deck chairs on the main beach to nothing but sparkling white sand on the others. The whole area is protected and people not staying in one of the hotels must park in the car park up above the beaches and walk from there.

Hotel Playa Mondragó (971 657 752; www.playamondrago.com; Cala Mondragó; s/d incl breakfast from €47/84; ☻Easter-Oct; P✹☎☎) is barely 50m back from the most accessible beach. It's a tranquil option, where the better rooms have balconies and fine sea views. There's a swimming pool but why you'd choose to swim in this rather than in the luminious blue sea is one of the great mysteries of the world.

CALA FIGUERA

The fisherfolk here really still fish, threading their way down the winding inlet before dawn, while tourists sleep off the previous night's food and drink. What has probably kept the place in one piece is the fact that the nearest beach, pretty Cala Santanyí, is a few kilometres drive southwest.

Nicer still is Cala Llombards, which you can walk to (scaling endless stairs) in about 30 minutes from Cala Santanyí or drive to via Santanyí (follow signs to Llombards, then Cala Llombards).

Perched on a bluff at the edge of the resort, the pleasant two-star Hotel Villa Sirena (☑971 645 303; www.hotelvillasirena. com; Carrer de la Verge del Carme 37; s/d €61/80, 2-person apt €83, 4-person apt €132; ☺hotel Apr-Oct, apt year-round; ❄❄) has enviable views of the sea. Rooms aren't fancy, but extras like a breezy seaside terrace make this a great choice. The well-priced apartments across the road are ideal if you're settling in for a longer stay.

Bus 502 makes the trip from Palma (€6.50, 1¾ hours) via Colònia de Sant Jordi twice a day.

MENORCA

Menorca (population 92,000) is the least overrun and most tranquil of the Balearic Islands. In 1993 Unesco declared it a Biosphere Reserve, aiming to preserve environmental areas, such as the Parc Natural S'Albufera d'es Grau wetlands, and the island's unique archaeological sites.

Its 216km coastline is fretted with relatively untouched beaches, coves and ravines. Inland, criss-crossing its fields and green, rolling hills are an estimated 70,000km of dry stone walls.

Some say the island owes much to Franco for not being overrun with tourist development. While neighbouring Mallorca went over to the Nationalists almost at the outset of the civil war, Menorca resisted. Franco later 'rewarded' Mallorca with a construction free-for-all and penalised Menorca by blocking development.

The second-largest and northernmost of the Balearics, Menorca has a wetter climate and is usually a few degrees cooler than the other islands. Particularly in the low season, the 'windy island' is buffeted by *tramuntana* winds from the north.

ⓘ MENORCA WEBSITES

» **www.menorca.es** Official Menorca tourism website.

» **www.visitmenorca.com** Website of the hoteliers' association.

» **www.menorcamonumental.net** Excellent presentation of Menorca's monuments and historical sites.

» **www.tmsa.es** Bus timetables throughout the island.

ⓘ Getting Around

TO & FROM THE AIRPORT Bus 10 (€1.80) runs between Menorca's airport, 7km southwest of Maó, and the city's bus station every half-hour. A taxi costs around €15.

BUS You can get to most destinations from Maó, but, with a few exceptions, services are infrequent and sluggish.

CAR & MOTORCYCLE Daily hire costs €35 to €45 for a modest sedan. All the big operators have representatives at the airport. In Maó, try the following:

Autos Mahon Rent (☑971 36 56 66; www. autosmahonrent.com; Moll de Llevant 35-36) Rents out bikes (€15 per day), scooters and cars.

Autos Valls (☑971 59 45 91; www.autosvalls. com; Plaça d'Espanya 13)

Maó

POP 29,250

The British have invaded Menorca four times (if you count the latest, modest campaign that began with the first charter flight from London in 1953). As a result Maó (Mahón in Spanish), the capital, is an unusual blend of Anglo and Spanish characteristics.

The British made it the capital of Menorca in 1713 and the influence of their almost-100-year presence (the island reverted to Spanish rule in 1802) is still evident in the town's architecture, traditions and culture. Maó's harbour, a full 5km long, is the second-largest natural haven in the world after Pearl Harbour. This strategic shelter, where Mediterranean seaways crossed, led to its possession and repossession by the Spanish, French and British. The town is built atop the cliffs that line the harbour's southern shore. Although some older buildings still remain, the majority of the architecture is in the restrained 18th-century Georgian style (note the sash windows and, as the

Menorca

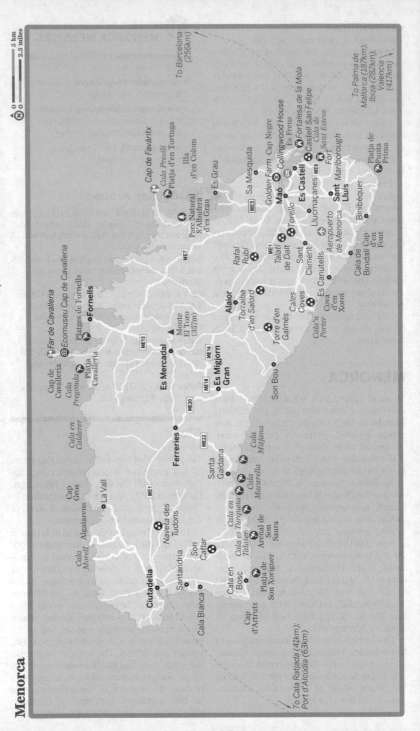

0 ——— 5 km
0 ——— 2.5 miles

To Barcelona (256km)

To Palma de Mallorca (187km); Ibiza (282km); Valencia (417km)

Cap de Favàritx
Cala Presili
Platja d'en Tortuga
Illa d'en Colom
Es Grau
Parc Natural S'Albufera d'es Grau
Sa Mesquida
Golden Farm Cap Negre
Es Freus
Fortalesa de la Mola
Castell San Felipe
Cala de Sant Esteve
Fort de Sant Esteve
Collingwood House
Maó
Es Castell
Sant Lluís
Platja de Punta Prima
Llucmaçanes
Aeropuerto de Menorca
Cala de Binidalí Cap d'en Font
Binibèquer
Es Canutells
Cova d'en Xoroi
Sant Climent
Talatí de Dalt
Rafal Rubí
Torelló
Cala'n Porter
Cales Coves
Torre d'en Galmés
Torralba d'en Salord
Alaior
Monte El Toro (357m)
Fornells
Platges de Fornells
Far de Cavalleria
Ecomuseu Cap de Cavalleria
Cap de Cavalleria
Cala Pregonda
Platja Cavalleria
Cala en Calderer
Cala Morell
Cap Gros
Algaiarens
La Vall
Son Catlar
Naveta des Tudons
Ciutadella
Santandria
Cala Blanca
Cap d'Artrutx
Cala en Bosc
Platja de Son Xoriguer
Arenal de Son Saura
Cala es Turqueta
Cala en Turqueta
Cala Macarella
Cala Mitjana
Santa Galdana
Ferreries
Es Mercadal
Es Migjorn Gran
Son Bou

ME1 ME5 ME6 ME7 ME15 ME16 ME18 ME20 ME22

To Cala Ratjada (41km); Port d'Alcúdia (63km)

Menorcans say to this day, *boínders* – bow windows).

◉ Sights & Activities

Maó's main plaza is the large Plaça de s'Esplanada, originally a parade ground, laid out by the British.

The narrow streets to the east are Maó's oldest. The Arc de Sant Roc (Carrer de Sant Roc, Old Quarter), a 16th-century archway straddling Carrer de Sant Roc, is the only remaining relic of the medieval walls that once surrounded the old city.

The Església de Santa Maria la Major (Plaça de la Constitució), further east, was completed in 1287 but rebuilt during the 18th century. Rearing above the east end is a massive organ, built in Barcelona and shipped across in 1810. At the northern end of Plaça de la Constitució is the neoclassical ajuntament (town hall), which also houses Maó's main **tourist office**.

Plaça d'Espanya
SQUARE

Just above Plaça d'Espanya is the Mercat Claustre del Carme (Plaça d'Espanya; ⊘Mon-Sat), where former church cloisters have been imaginatively converted into a buzzing market and shopping centre. Upstairs, enjoy temporary art exhibitions and the modest Museu Hernández Sanz Hernández Mora (☑971 35 05 97; admission free; ⊘10am-1pm Mon-Sat), devoted to Menorcan themes, illustrated by artworks, maps and decorative items dating back to the 18th century. In the square itself, explore the pungent fish market (⊘8am-1pm Tue-Sat), housed in an attractive olive-green wooden building.

Museu de Menorca
MUSEUM

(Plaça de Sant Francesc; adult/child €2.40/free; ⊘10am-2pm & 6-8.30pm Tue-Sat, 10am-2pm Sun) This 15th-century former Franciscan monastery has been in its time a nautical school, a public library, a high school and a children's home. Well documented and presented in Catalan, Spanish and English, its collection covers the earliest history of the island, Roman, Byzantine and Islamic Menorca, and includes paintings, some fascinating early maps and other material from more recent times, too.

FREE Xoriguer Gin Distillery
DISTILLERY

(www.xoriguer.es; Moll de Ponent 93; ⊘8am-7pm Mon-Fri, 9am-1pm Sat) At this showroom, you can taste and buy the distinctively aromatic Menorcan gin. From the range of sample liqueurs, try a shot of camomile-based Hierbas de Menorca, Palo with its bitter gentian flavour or Calent, cinnamon-scented and traditionally served hot.

Harbour Cruises
BOAT TOUR

A cluster of operators does one-hour glass-bottomed boat cruises (adult/child €11/5) around the harbour. The underwater perspective, enjoyable for its own sake, is outclassed by the stunning views of both banks.

Beaches
BEACH

The closest decent beaches to the capital are Es Grau, 10km to the north, and Platja de Punta Prima, 8km to the south. Both are connected to Maó by local bus.

🛏 Sleeping

To sleep steeped in history, stay at Collingwood House (see the boxed text, p631), the former residence of British Admiral Collingwood, Lord Nelson's right hand man.

TOP CHOICE Casa Alberti
HISTORIC HOTEL €€€

(☑971 35 42 10; www.casalberti.com; Carrer d'Isabel II 9; s/d incl breakfast €130/160; ⊘Easter-Oct) Climb the central stairs with striking wrought-iron banisters to your vast room with white walls and whitest-of-white sheets. Each of the six bedrooms within this 18th-century mansion is furnished with traditional items, while bathrooms are designer cool and contemporary. There's an intimate dinner-only Japanese restaurant (reservations essential). Rates drop substantially outside high season.

Hostal-Residencia La Isla
HOSTAL €

(☑971 36 64 92; www.hostal-laisla.com; Carrer de Santa Caterina 4; s/d incl breakfast €35/60; ❈🐾)

MAYONNAISE

Menorcans claim to have given the world the name 'mayonnaise', arguing that the term is derived from *salsa mahonesa*, meaning 'sauce of Mahón (Maó)'. The French, too, claim it as their own, but the islanders argue that it was originally brought to the mainland by the troops of the Duc de Richelieu after they defeated the British in 1756. A plausible story (in fact, it's widely used all around the northern Mediterranean), but perhaps best taken with a small pinch of salt – like the best mayonnaise.

Maó

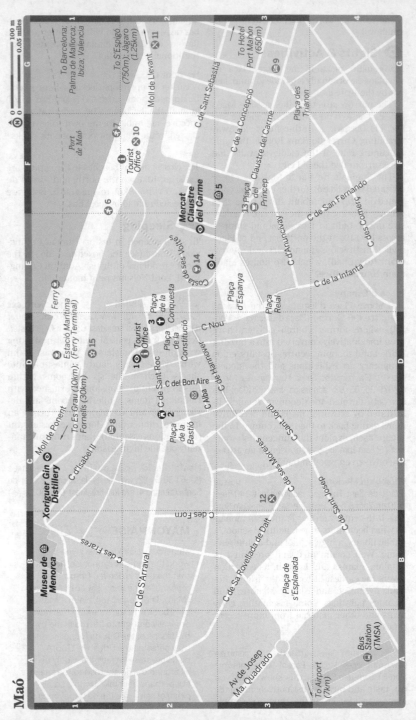

0 — 100 m
0 — 0.05 miles

To Barcelona; Palma de Mallorca; Ibiza; Valencia

Port de Maó

To S'Espigó (750m); Jàgaro (1.25km)

Moll de Llevant

C de Sant Sebastià

To Hotel Port Mahón (650m)

C de la Concepció

Plaça des Trianon

Tourist Office

Mercat Claustre del Carme

Plaça del Claustre del Carme

C de San Fernando

C des Comerç

C d'Anunciaváy

C de la Infanta

Costa de ses Voltes

Plaça d'Espanya

Plaça Reial

Ferry

Estació Marítima (Ferry Terminal)

Plaça de la Conquesta

C Nou

Tourist Office

Plaça de la Constitució

C de Sant Roc

C del Bon Aire

C de Harinover

C Alba

C des Moreres

C Sant Jordi

Moll de Ponent

To Es Grau (10km); Fornells (30km)

Xoriguer Gin Distillery

C d'Isabel II

Plaça de la Bastió

C des Forn

Museu de Menorca

C des Frares

C de S'Arraval

C de Sa Rovellada de Dalt

Plaça de s'Esplanada

C de Sant Josep

Av de Josep Ma. Quadrado

To Airport (7km)

Bus Station (TMSA)

Maó

MALLORCA, MENORCA & IBIZA MAÓ

This large, family-run *hostal* is excellent value. Its small rooms all come with their own bathroom and all have air-con. The decor is uninspiring, but the folks are friendly and run a bustling workers' bar-restaurant downstairs.

Hotel Port Mahón   HOTEL €€€
(☎971 36 26 00; www.sethotels.com; Avinguda del Port de Maó; s/d from €137/200; ❀⑧❀) This fine four-star hotel, built in traditional colonial style, has 73 nicely turned-out rooms, a pool and a pleasant garden with plenty of green. Rooms with balcony offer a grand view over the harbour. Decor varies from room to room and rates vary enormously from season to season.

✗ Eating

You're almost guaranteed to eat well at any of the harbourside fish restaurants. Also worth investigating are many waterfront eateries in Cales Fonts, just 3km away in Es Castell.

TOP CHOICE Jàgaro   SEAFOOD €€€
(☎971 36 23 90; Moll de Llevant 334; menus €14-46) Jàgaro, last in the long line of eateries fronting the harbour, is good enough for royalty (see the photos of the Crown Prince and Princess, who've preceded you here, at the entrance). The fish, hauled from the restaurant's own boat and varying according to the catch of the day, couldn't be fresher, while the more adventurous can begin with *ortiga de mar* (sea anemone) or *morena mansa* (sea cucumber).

La Minerva   SEAFOOD €€€
(☎971 35 19 95; www.restaurantelaminerva.com; Moll de Llevant 87; mains €10.50-42) Dine in the air-conditioned interior, with its tastefully nautical theme (no cheap swags of net or glass marker balls here), or, more romantically, on its pontoon, moored to the quayside. Perhaps prop yourself at the bar to savour the quite exceptional value (€10) choice of five tapas, picked from a list as long as a ship's yardarm and helped down by a couple of matching wines. Its €20 *menú,* offered at both lunch and dinner, is a special bargain.

Ses Forquilles   SPANISH €€
(☎971 35 27 11; www.sesforquilles.com; Carrer de Sa Rovellada de Dalt 20; tapas €2-7.50, mains €9-19.50; ⊘lunch & dinner Mon & Thu-Sat, lunch only Tue & Wed) At 'The Forks' (look for the four forks announcing its presence on the door) is run by a friendly young team. With its warm ox blood-coloured walls, it offers an ever-changing, seasonally dependent range of fishy and meat mains, plus creative tapas and *montaditos* (mini open sandwiches).

S'Espigó   SEAFOOD €€€
(☎971 36 99 09; www.sespigo.com; Moll de Llevant 267; fish mains €21-28; ⊘lunch & dinner Tue-Sat, lunch Sun) Among the long line of restaurants that offer delicacies pulled from the seas that surround Menorca, S'Espigó stands out. A brisk walk along the quayside will work up an appetite for dishes that are based upon what's hauled from the Mediterranean the previous day.

MENORCAN GIN

Although no document attests this, local lore has it that gin was first distilled on the island in the 18th century to slake the thirst of British and Dutch soldiers. You can drink it the usual way, long with tonic. Or do as the Menorcans do and ask for a *gin con limonada* (called locally a *pomada*), a shot of gin in a small glass, topped up with real lemonade. If you like your drink strong, order a *saliveta* (literally 'little spit') for a shot of neat gin, graced with a green olive.

El Varadero
SPANISH €€

(☑971 35 20 74; Moll de Llevant 4; mains €13-17; ☺Easter-Nov) With such a splendid vista from the harbourside terrace, it must be tempting to simply sit on your laurels. But El Varadero doesn't. There's a range of tempting rice dishes and a short, select choice of fish and meat mains. If a full meal is too much, drop by for a tapa or two with a glass of wine and savour the view.

Drinking & Entertainment

Nightlife in Maó is low-key compared with Mallorca or Ibiza. Most of the action is on the waterfront.

Mirador Café
MUSIC BAR

(www.miradorcafe.com; Plaça d'Espanya 2; ☺10am-2am Mon-Sat) Inside this small, popular music bar, your host's collection of exotic masks leers down at you. Best of all, take a ringside seat outside and drink in the port views with your beer. The cafe's beside a short cul-de-sac at the top of Costa de ses Voltes.

Ars Café
CAFE, RESTAURANT

(www.arscafe.info; Plaça del Príncep 12; menus €15, mains €7-12; ☺Mon-Sat) Arty and boho at the edges (despite the suave, ultramodern toilets, with their vast, full-length mirrors), this is a friendly, relaxing place to drink or eat. For maximum atmosphere, choose the front, main bar – except after midnight on Friday and Saturday, when you need to head down to the cellar bar, with its DJ and live music.

Akelarre
JAZZ

(www.akelarrejazz.es; Moll de Ponent 41-43; ☺3pm-4am) Akelarre is the best of a short strip of music and cocktail bars opposite the Estación Marítimo. Ambient and jazz dance music trill during the wee hours in this place, made welcoming by the warm, stone interior. There's sometimes live music.

Information

There are tourist offices in **town** (☑971 36 37 90; Plaça de Sa Constitució 22; ☺10am-1.30pm & 5.30-8.30pm Mon-Fri, 10am-2pm Sat), at the **airport** (☺8.30am-9.30pm Mon-Fri, 8.30am-4pm Sat & Sun) and at the **port** (Moll de Llevant 2; ☺8am-8.15pm Wed-Sun, 8am-2.45pm Mon & Tue). Opening hours from November to April are much reduced.

Getting There & Around

TMSA (www.tmsa.es) runs buses between Maó and Ciutadella (€4.75, 1¼ hours, at least hourly) calling by Alaior, Es Mercadal and Ferreries; there is also a regular service to south-coast beaches.

Five **Autos Fornells** (www.autosfornells.com) buses run daily between Maó and Fornells (50 minutes).

In winter, these services drop or are much reduced.

The Interior – Maó to Ciutadella

The Me1, Menorca's main road connecting Maó and Ciutadella, runs east–west, passing by Alaior, Es Mercadal and Ferreries. Along the way smaller roads branch off towards the beaches and resorts of the north and south coasts.

Many of Menorca's most significant archaeological sites are signposted off the main road.

ES MERCADAL

Es Mercadal, one of the oldest villages on the island (a market has been held here since at least 1300), is at the turn-off north for Fornells.

Restaurant N'Aguedet (☑971 37 53 91; Carrer de Lepanto 30; mains €11-25.50) prides itself, with reason, on its authentic, classic Menorcan cooking such as the melt-in-your-mouth *lechón* (suckling pig) or *conejo con cebolla y alcaparras* (rabbit with onion and capers).

FERRERIES

Ferreries is renowned for its cheese, shoes and leather goods. At its Saturday morning **market** (Plaça Espanya; ☺9am-1pm Sat), stallholders sell fresh produce, along with traditional Menorcan crafts, and there's folk dancing in high season. The turn-off to the resort of Santa Galdana is just west of town.

The beautiful, 200-year-old rambling whitewashed house and pretty garden at Mesón El Gallo (☑971 37 30 39; www.meson elgallo.com; mains €9-21; ☺Tue-Sun, reduced hours Feb-Apr) merit a visit for their own sake. Enjoy meat dishes, grilled just as you wish them, on the vine-clad terrace or in the rustic interior with its beams and terracotta floor. From Ferrerics, head down the Santa Galdana turn-off for 1.5km.

Ciutadella

POP 29,150

Founded by Carthaginians and known to the Muslims as Medina Minurqa, Ciutadella was almost destroyed following the 1558 Turkish invasion and much of the city was subsequently rebuilt in the 17th century. It was Menorca's capital until the British arrived in the early 18th century.

Known as Vella i Bella ('Old and Beautiful'), Ciutadella is an attractive, distinctly Spanish city with a picturesque port and an engaging old quarter. Its character is quite distinct from that of Maó, and its historic centre is far more appealing.

FORTS & MANSIONS

Great Britain occupied Menorca principally to gain possession of Maó's deep natural harbour. It built Fort Marlborough (adult/child €3/1.80; ☺9.30am-7pm Tue-Sat, 9.30am-2.30pm Sun Easter–mid-Dec) to defend the sound and protect Castell San Filipe, which it had also overrun. Most of the fortress is excavated into the rock beside the charming emerald-green inlet, Cala de Sant Esteve (2.5km beyond Es Castell – known historically as Georgetown to the Brits). A short video sets the historical background to a walk through the tunnels, enlivened by figurines, explosions and a well-produced recorded commentary (including an English version). From the central hillock there's a fine view of Cala de Sant Esteve, the scant above-ground remains of Castell San Felipe and, to the south, the circular Torre d'en Penjat (Torre Stuart).

Across the inlet, Castell San Felipe (☑971 36 21 00; www.museomilitarmenorca.com; adult/child €5/free), originally constructed in the 16th century, became, under British control, one of the largest fortresses in Europe. Its labyrinth of underground tunnels has remained more or less intact. Occasional guided visits are possible – call or check the website for latest times (usually once or twice a week). Night-time torchlit tours (adult/child €20/10; ☺8.30pm-11pm mid-Jun–mid-Sep), complete with actors playing soldiers and the acrid whiff of gunpowder, take you into the bowels of this once-mighty fortress.

To immerse yourself more fully in the area's British colonial past, stop at Collingwood House (☑971 36 27 00; www.hoteldelalmirante.com; Hotel del Almirante; s/d incl breakfast €85/110; ☎☒), once the residence of Admiral Cuthbert Collingwood, Nelson's fellow commander-at-sea. It's now a charming hotel, replete with maritime reminiscences, pool, terrace, bar and wonderful views over the harbour from its tiled restaurant. With its heavy carpets, dark-timber doors and furniture, and countless paintings and sketches of great vessels and their commanders, you could almost be in a minor museum. If you stay, ask for a room in the main, historic building. The hotel is located on the main road about halfway between Maó and Es Castell.

In the 19th century Queen Isabel II ordered the construction of the extensive Fortalesa de la Mola (www.fortalesalamola.com; adult/child €7/free, audio guide €3; ☺10am-8pm), built between 1848 and 1875, which sprawls over the promontory of the same name on the northern shore of the bay. It's about a 12km drive from Maó. Ramble through galleries, gun emplacements and barracks. The only way here is by car, unless you want to call a water taxi (☑616 428891; return per person €10, minimum two passengers). It will pick up at various points in Maó and Es Castell and makes for a scenic journey in its own right.

On the way back towards Maó, you'll notice a rose-coloured stately home surrounded by gardens. At Golden Farm (Granja Dorada; ☺closed to the public), they say, Nelson and his lover Lady Hamilton enjoyed a tryst in 1799.

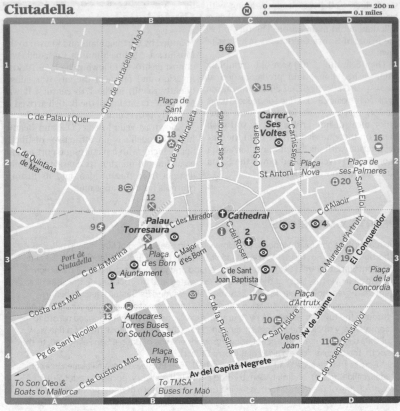

Ciutadella

Ciutadella

⊙ Sights

The glory of central Ciutadella is that it's almost entirely traffic-free.

Plaça d'es Born
SQUARE

Around Ciutadella's main square you will find gracious 19th-century buildings, including the ajuntament (town hall) and Palau Torresaura. The obelisk at the centre was raised to commemorate those townsfolk who died trying to ward off the Turks on 9 July 1558. For the finest view of the port and the town's remaining bastions and bulwarks, sneak behind the town hall and up to the Bastió d'Es Governador (⊙9am-2pm Mon-Fri). Nearby Plaça dels Pins, more relaxed and shaded by mature pine trees, has a children's playground and exercise trail.

Old Ciutadella
HISTORIC NEIGHBOURHOOD

The narrow cobbled lanes and streets between Plaça d'es Born and Plaça de ses Palmeres (Plaça d'Alfons III) hold plenty of interest, with simple whitewashed buildings abutting ornate churches and elegant palaces. Attractively arcaded Carrer ses Voltes (The Arches) is lined with smart shops, restaurants and bars. The town's small fish market (Plaça de la Llibertat; ⊙7am-1pm Tue-Sat) is in a pleasing Modernista tiled building, constructed in 1895.

Cathedral & Churches
ARCHITECTURE

The 14th-century cathedral (☑971 38 07 39; Plaça de la Catedral; ⊙10.30am-1.30pm & 4-7pm Mon-Sat) was built in Catalan Gothic style (although with a baroque facade) on the site of Medina Minurqa's central mosque.

Old Ciutadella also has a pair of fine baroque 17th-century churches. Església del Roser (Carrer del Roser) is now used as an occasional exhibition gallery. Església dels Socors (Carrer del Seminari 9) is home to the Museu Diocesà (adult/child €3/free; ⊙10.30am-1.30pm Tue-Sat May-Oct), a fine little museum, secular as much as religious. Opening hours can be irregular.

Noble Mansions
ARCHITECTURE

Noble mansions, such as Palau Martorell (Carrer del Santíssim 7) and Palau Saura (Carrer del Santíssim 2), are used for temporary exhibitions. Even if you can't get inside, their facades impress. Unhelpfully, neither bears a sign.

Museu Municipal
MUSEUM

(Bastió de sa Font; adult/child €2.50/free; ⊙10am-2pm & 6-9pm Tue-Sat May-Sep, morning only Oct-Apr) The single, vaulted gallery of the town museum has a small display of Talayotic, Roman and Islamic finds from the area. Ask to borrow its comprehensive documentation in English.

Castell de Sant Nicolau
TOWER

(Plaça del Almirante Ferragut) West of the town centre, this stout little 17th-century watchtower stands guard at the southern head of the port entrance. Views over the waters to Mallorca and southwards along the coast are stunning.

🏃 Activities

Menorca Blava
BOAT TOUR

(www.menorcablava.com; adult/child €42/21) Runs boat trips to the beaches of the southern coast, departing at 10am, returning at 5pm and including a paella lunch.

Diving Centre Ciutadella
DIVING

(☑971 38 60 30; www.menorcatech.com; Plaça de Sant Joan 10; per dive €48; ⊙May-Oct) One of three dive centres in and around Ciutadella, it's handily located in the port.

🛏 Sleeping

Hotel Sant Ignasi
COUNTRY HOUSE €€€

(☑971 38 55 75; www.santignasi.com; Carretera de Cala Morell; s/d incl breakfast €180/285; 🕸🤶🏊) This venerable 18th-century mansion, planted solidly in grounds shaded by mature wild olive trees, is in open country, a mere 3km outside Ciutadella. Each of the 20 serene rooms has its own individual style and there's a first-class restaurant. Prices more than halve over winter months. From the Cala Morell road, take a narrow lane signed 'Hotel Rural' for 1.6km.

Hotel Gèminis
HOTEL €€

(☑971 38 46 44; www.hotelgeminismenorca.com; Carrer de Josepa Rossinyol 4; s incl breakfast €31-56, d incl breakfast €45-92; ⊙April–mid-October; 🕸🤶🏊) A friendly, stylish two-star place, this graceful, three-storey, rose-and-white lodging offers comfortable if somewhat neutral rooms just a short walk away from the city centre. The best rooms have a sizeable balcony.

Hostal-Residencia Oasis
PENSIÓN €

(☑971 38 21 97; www.hostaloasismenorca.es; Carrer de Sant Isidre 33; r €34-64) Run by a delightful

MALLORCA, MENORCA & IBIZA CIUTADELLA

WORTH A TRIP

PEDRERES DE S'HOSTAL

You'll get butterflies simply gazing down into the depths of these vast stone quarries (www.lithica.es; Camí Vell; adult/child €4/free; ⊙9.30am-2.30pm & 4.30pm-sunset Mon-Sat, 9.30am-2.30pm Sun), on the outskirts of Ciutadella and exploited until 1994. The bleached *marés*, a variety of sandstone, has historically been Menorca's main building material. Over decades, powerful machines gouged out huge hollow, inverted cubes. In these deep pits with their superb acoustics, concerts are sometimes organised. In an earlier age, human muscle and sinew hacked away the rock, leaving bizarre shapes and formations. Here, in the older quarry, where nature has resumed possession, Lithica, the association of volunteers that has recovered this monument to human endeavour, maintains a botanical garden of endemic Menorcan species and a charming medieval garden with a fountain at its heart.

Allow at least 45 minutes to ramble through the quarries, which are off the old road to Maó. Take the Ronda Sur ring road to the Puerta del Mar roundabout with its large rectangular sculpture. They're well signed from here.

elderly couple, this quiet place is close to the heart of the old quarter. Rooms, mostly with bathroom, are set beside a spacious garden courtyard. Their furnishings, though still trim, are from deep into the last century.

✗ Eating

Ciutadella's small port teems with restaurants and cafes, many of which are set in the old city walls or carved out of the cliffs that line the waterfront.

Cas Ferrer de sa Font　　MENORCAN €€
(☑971 48 07 84; www.casferrer.com; Carrer del Portal de sa Font 16; mains €15-20; ⊙Tue-Sun) Nowhere on the island will you find more authentic Menorcan cuisine based upon meats and vegetables from the owner's organic farm. Dine on the delightful interior patio of this charming 18th-century building or inside, below beams and soft curves, in what was once a blacksmith's forge.

C'an Bep　　SPANISH €€€
(☑971 48 78 15; www.canbep.com; Passeig Sant Nicolau 4; menus €15, mains €14-26; ⊙Mon-Sat) Dine at the marble-topped bar, where locals congregate to chat, or in the smart rear restaurant. Like the port-side restaurants below it, C'an Bep offers plenty of fresh fish dishes, including *cap roig*, a delicious Balearic Islands' speciality that off-puttingly translates as 'sea scorpion'.

Cas Cònsol　　TAPAS, MEDITERRANEAN €€
(☑971 48 46 54; Plaça des Born 17; menus €13.50, mains €13-18; ⊙Tue-Sun) Occupying a substantial building that was once the French consulate, Cas Cònsol harmoniously blends the modern and minimalist within a historic setting. It serves a wide range of tapas and creative mains such as quail with apple sauce and raisins. From the small wedge of terrace, there are great views of the harbour below.

Café Balear　　SEAFOOD €€€
(☑971 38 00 05; www.cafe-balear.com; Plaça de Sant Joan 15; menus €18.50, meals €30-35; ⊙Tue-Sun) Sometimes the old-timers are the best. Set apart from the town's more frenetic restaurant activity, this remains one of Ciutadella's classic seafood stops. You can eat outside on the quayside while tucking into local prawns, *navajas* (razor shells) or fresh fish, caught from Café Balear's own boat.

🍷 Drinking & Entertainment

The bulk of the town's nightlife is concentrated along the waterfront and, in particular, around both sides of Plaça de Sant Joan.

Es Molí　　CAFE, BAR
(Plaça de ses Palmeres) Sit among the arches, pillars and mellow stonework of the interior, where the core of the old *molí* (windmill) still juts from its heart. Or, if you don't mind the traffic, plant yourself on the terrace for a fine prospect of the little square.

La Margarete　　BAR
(Carrer de Sant Joan Baptista 6; ⊙10pm-3.30am) Tucked away down a side street, this is a stylish option. The interior is slick with a modern, arty decor. On warmer nights, enjoy its pleasant cropped lawn.

Jazzbah LIVE MUSIC
(Plaça de San Joan 3; admission €10; ⊙11pm-5am)
This venue, dug deep into the cliff face, is
worth watching for its live concerts, happening house nights and chill-out sessions.

🔒 Shopping

Ciutadella has two great, long-established
delicatessens.

El Paladar FOOD
(www.elpaladar.es; Camí de Maó) Penetrate deep
into this boutique for wines, pickles, pâtés
and ripe local cheeses. Plenty of pig products too: the owner was recently the Spanish
ham-slicing champion.

Ca Na Fayas FOOD
(www.canafayas.es; Carrer Murada d'Artrutx 32 &
Avinguda do Jaume I El Conqueridor 47) This richly scented gourmet emporium has entrances
on two streets. Whole cheeses, shelf upon
shelf of them, fill the shop window.

ℹ Information

Tourist office (☑971 38 26 93; Plaça de la
Catedral 5; ⊙10am-1.30pm & 5.30-8.30pm
Mon-Fri, 10am-2pm Sat)

ℹ Getting There & Away

Ferries for Mallorca (Port d'Alcúdia and Cala
Ratjada) leave from Son Oleo, just south of town.

TMSA (www.tmsa.es) buses serve the coast
south of Ciutadella as far as Son Xoriguer, departing from Plaça dels Pins.

ℹ Getting Around

Autos Ciutadella (☑971 48 00 24; www.
autosciutadella.com; Avinguda del Capità
Negrete 49bis) Local car-rental agency offering
competitive prices.

Velos Joan (☑971 38 15 76; www.velosjoan.
com; Carrer de Sant Isidre 30) Bike rental (€10
per day).

North Coast

Menorca's north coast is rugged and rocky,
punctured by small, scenic coves. It's less
developed than the south and, with your
own transport and a bit of footwork, you'll
discover some of the Balearics' best off-the-
beaten-track beaches.

ES GRAU

This spruce, whitewashed hamlet sits beside
an open bay. You can rent a kayak or bike
from Menorca en Kayak (☑669 097977; www.

menorcaenkayak.com; ⊙Easter-Oct) and explore
the Parc Natural S'Albufera d'es Grau from
sea or land. The beach's shallow waters are
ideal for young families.

Bar Es Moll (Carrer d'es Pescadors 17; meals
€15-20; ⊙Apr-Oct) is a basic place with plastic
tables and chairs that serves tapas and portions of fresh sardines, mussels and prawns.
Its charm is its position, above the jetty
where local fishing boats dock.

PARC NATURAL S'ALBUFERA D'ES GRAU

Inland from Es Grau and separated from
the coast by a barrier of high sand dunes
is S'Albufera, the largest freshwater lagoon
in the Balearics. Home to many species of
wetland birds, it's also an important stopover for migrating species. The lagoon and
its shores form the 'nucleus zone' of Menorca's Biosphere Reserve, a natural park
protected from the threat of development.
Borrow a pair of binoculars from the park's
information office (⊙9am-3pm) which
is 1km off the Me5, Es Grau road. Guided
by an explanatory pamphlet (€1), you can
follow from here two easy, signed trails (a
third leads from Es Grau), each lasting under an hour.

CAP DE FAVÁRITX

The drive up to this narrow rocky cape
at the northern extremity of the park is a
treat. The last leg is across a lunar landscape of black slate. At the end of the road
(on the way, ignore the *propriedad pri-
vada* – private property – sign; it's public
access), a lighthouse stands watch. South
of the cape stretch some fine remote sandy
bays and beaches, including Cala Presili
and Platja d'en Tortuga, both accessible
only on foot.

CAP DE CAVALLERIA & AROUND

At a roundabout 3km south of Fornells, follow signs for Far de Cavalleria, to reach a
parking area after 7km. From here a walk of
less than 10 minutes brings you to the stunning little double-crescent, golden beach of
Platja Cavalleria.

Ecomuseu Cap de Cavalleria (www.
ecomuseudecavalleria.com; adult/child €3/free;
⊙10am-7pm or 8.30pm Apr-Oct) is a small, private museum 1km north of Platja Cavalleria's car park. Panels and videos illustrate
the north coast, its fauna, the lighthouse,
ancient inhabitants and Roman occupation. Borrow the booklet with full English
translations of the captions. The museum's

HOLGER LEUE / GETTY IMAGES ©

LONELY PLANET / GETTY IMAGES ©

1. D'Alt Vila, Ibiza City (p641)

D'Alt Vila's 16th-century walls were raised by Felipe II; the town is a Unesco World Heritage site.

2. Cala Sant Vicenç (p623)

A tranquil resort with a magnificent setting in a series of four jewel-like coves.

3. Castell de Bellver (p613)

An unusual, circular 14th-century castle (with a unique round tower) set atop a pleasant park.

4. Palma de Mallorca (p610)
Mallorca's only true city contains an enchanting blend of tree-lined boulevards, Gothic churches and designer bars.

5. Menorca's prehistoric sites (p638)
Taulas (horseshoe-shaped sanctuaries with tall T-shaped pillars at their heart) are unique to Menorca.

HOLGER LEUE/GETTY IMAGES ©

WORTH A TRIP

MENORCA'S PREHISTORIC MYSTERIES

As long ago as 2000 BC, the islanders were constructing sturdy stone edifices. Many of the most significant sites are open to the public. In winter, sites are unattended and can be visited freely (and free of charge).

The monuments are linked to three main periods: the Pre-Talayotic (or cave era) from 2000 BC to 1300 BC; the Talayotic (Bronze Age) from 1300 BC to 800 BC; and the Post-Talayotic (Iron Age) from 800 BC to around 100 BC. Similarly, there are three general types of structures: *navetas*, *talayots* and *taulas*.

Navetas, built from large rocks in the shape of upturned boat hulls, are thought to have been used as tombs or meeting places – perhaps both. *Talayots*, large stone mounds found all over the island (and elsewhere in the Balearics), were used as watch-towers or to exert power over the surrounding region. Unique to Menorca, *taulas* are horseshoe-shaped sanctuaries with tall T-shaped pillars at their heart. These could have been used as sacrificial altars, but nobody is sure how such enormous stone slabs were moved or what they signify.

South of Ciutadella (from the *ronda* – ring road – follow the road for Cala Macarella and after 2.8km veer right), Son Catlar (admission free; ⊘10am-sunset) is the largest Talayotic settlement in the Balearic Islands. Its five *talayots* and the remains of its dwellings cover around 6 hectares. East of Ciutadella (on the Me1, near the Km 40 road marker), the Naveta des Tudons (adult/child €2/1.20; ⊘9am-8pm Tue-Sun, 9.30am-3pm Mon) is a stone burial chamber constructed around 1000 BC.

From Maó, all the following sites are well signed from the Me1 highway to Ciutadella.

At the Talayotic settlement of Talatí de Dalt (adult/child €4/free; ⊘10am-sunset), 3km west of Maó, the roots of wild olive trees force apart the weathered stones of the large central *talayot*. There's also a particularly well-preserved *taula*.

About 4km further along on the north side of the road, a walk across the fields brings you to Rafal Rubí, a pair of well-preserved burial *navetas*.

Take a left turn from the Me1 after 5km more for Torralba d'en Salord (adult/child €3.50/free; ⊘10am-8pm Mon-Sat), another Talayotic settlement whose outstanding feature is an impressive *taula*.

If you only visit one Talayotic site, let it be Torre d'en Galmés (adult/child €3/1.80; ⊘9.30am-8pm Tue-Sat, 9.30am-3pm Sun, free roaming Mon). Stop by the small information centre, which has an instructive 10-minute video presentation, then wander at will over the site with its three hilltop *talayots*, rambling circular dwellings, deep underground storage chambers and sophisticated water-collection system.

Further south on the coast at Cales Coves, some 90 caves dug into the coastal cliffs were apparently used for ritual burials. Nearby, the large Cova d'en Xoroi (☎971 37 72 36; www.covadenxoroi.com; Cala'n Porter; adult/child €7.50/4; ⊘11.30am-10pm Jun-Sep) can be visited as a sight by day or club by night.

Les 7 Rutes is a detailed multilingual map showing every feature of the peninsula.

A further spectacular 2km drive north brings you to the tip of Cap de Cavalleria, abrupt cliffs, Far de Cavalleria (Spain's oldest lighthouse) and a series of crumbling civil war Republican gun emplacements.

FORNELLS
POP 950

This picturesque whitewashed village is on a large, shallow bay popular with windsurfers. Fornells is renowned for its waterfront seafood restaurants, most of which serve up the local, decidedly pricey speciality, *caldereta de llagosta* (lobster stew).

◉ Sights & Activities

The sheltered, unruffled waters of the long slim bay are ideal for novice windsurfers. Wind Fornells (☎971 18 81 50; www.windfornells.com; ⊘May–mid-Oct) rents out boards and offers courses at all levels from mid-May to October.

FREE Castell Sant Antoni   FORTRESS
'Castle' is a grand word for this insensitively 'restored' fort with its excess of crude

concrete. All the same, it's worth a brief visit. You can browse around at will and learn about the history of Fornells from the well-documented informative panels.

Dia Complert WATER SPORTS
(☎609 670996; www.diacomplert.com; Passeig Marítim 40; ☺Apr-Oct) This is your one-stop shop for most things maritime such as diving, guided kayak outings, mountain-bike sorties and speedboat trips along the coast. It also rents out bikes and kayaks.

Catamaran Kayak Charter WATER SPORTS
(☎626 486426; www.katayak.net; Passeig Marítim 69; ☺Apr-Oct) This outfit runs four-hour catamaran (adult/child €60/35) trips and also hires out kayaks and bicycles.

🛏 Sleeping & Eating

A pair of friendly, family-run bar-*hostales* with pools sit side by side on Plaça S'Algaret. Except for July and August (when rooms cost €90 to €100), they offer exceptional value – as do their popular bar and restaurant.

Hostal La Palma HOSTAL €
(☎971 37 66 34; www.hostallapalma.com; s/d incl breakfast €25/50; ☺Easter-Oct; ❄@≋) Behind this busy bar-restaurant are cheerful rooms with bathrooms, balconies and views of the surrounding countryside. Singles aren't available in August.

Hostal S'Algaret HOSTAL €
(☎971 37 65 52; www.hostal-salgaret.com; s/d €35/60; ☺May-Sep; ❄@≋) In business since the 1950s, this pleasant, simple *hostal* offers crisp, clean rooms with balconies and a warm welcome.

Es Port SEAFOOD €€
(☎971 37 64 03; Passeig Marítim 5; menus €15.50, mains €10-21; ☺Sat-Thu Easter-Oct) The fish and other seafood are the freshest here – unsurprisingly since Es Port has its own boat and lobster pots. Like most of its neighbours, it does *caldereta de llagosta* (€65), but less financial outlay goes into a sizzling *paella de llomanto* (lobster paella; €35).

S'Ancora SEAFOOD €€
(☎971 37 66 70; Passeig Marítim 7-8; menus €17, mains €12-20) 'The Anchor' with dark-brown wicker chairs on the terrace and olive-green decor within, offers all the fruits of the sea, attractively presented. For that special seaside gastronomic experience, indulge in its *menú estrella* ('star menu'; €50).

South Coast

Menorca's southern flank tends to have the better beaches – and thus the greater concentration of development. The jagged coastline is occasionally interrupted by a small inlet with a sandy beach, backed by a cluster of gleaming-white villas, largely small-scale and in the Moorish Mediterranean style. The Camí de Cavalls is mostly flat along Menorca's southern shores and makes for splendid, undemanding walking.

CIUTADELLA TO SON BOU

The rugged coastline south of Ciutadella gives way to a couple of smallish beaches at the resorts of Santandria and Cala Blanca. On the island's southwest corner looms the large resort of Cala en Bosc, a busy boating and diving centre. Not far east are the popular beaches of Platja de Son Xoriguer, connected to Ciutadella by frequent buses.

Between Son Xoriguer and Santa Galdana lie some of the island's least-accessible coves. A narrow country road leads south of Ciutadella (follow the 'Platjes' sign from the *ronda* – ring road) and then forks twice to (almost) reach the unspoiled beaches (from west to east) of Arenal de Son Saura, Cala Es Talaier, the especially lovely little Cala en Turqueta and Cala Macarella.

For Cala Macarella, for instance, you arrive at a car park, then walk 15 minutes to the beach (which has a restaurant). The walk between Cala Macarella and Cala en Turqueta takes an hour.

Southwest of Ferreries is Santa Galdana, settled around its lovely horseshoe-shaped

---

WORTH A TRIP

CAMÍ DE CAVALLS

This signed walking trail, the GR223, revives an 18th-century defensive route that linked coastal watchtowers, fortresses and artillery batteries. Well signed (look for the horseshoe symbol), it snakes around the coastline for 184km, with occasional forays inland and can be walked in easy sections. Most stretches are attackable by mountain bike, too. Ask for details at tourist offices or buy *Camí de Cavalls Guidebook: 20 Routes to Discover Menorca* (€21).

bay, marred by three monster hotels. The Camí de Cavalls leads west through pine trees to Cala Macarella (30 minutes) and eastwards to Cala Mitjana (20 to 30 minutes), another enticing strand that's also accessible by road.

The resort of Son Bou, southwest of Alaior, boasts the island's longest beach and most depressing development. Just beyond the beach's eastern limit are the remains of a 5th-century Christian basilica.

SOUTH OF MAÓ

The coast south of Maó is more intensively developed.

Sant Lluís, a bright, white, grid-pattern inland town, was built by the French during their brief occupation of the island between 1756 and 1763. It's well worth a short stop to visit the Molí de Dalt (☎971 15 10 84; adult/child €1.20/0.60; ☉10am-2pm Mon-Sat), a restored windmill, constructed during the French era. Within it, there's a small museum of rural implements and tools.

Just outside Sant Lluís, adults-only Hotel Biniarroca (☎971 15 00 59; www.biniarroca.com; r incl breakfast €170-275; ☉May–mid-Oct; 🛜🏊) is a cosy, welcoming, rambling rural retreat. Furnished for comfort and ease, it's run with panache by a pair of British lady artists and designers. Beyond their lovely garden, at once formal and pleasantly rumpled, ducks and geese peck and sheep graze. The reputed gourmet restaurant (☉dinner only) is open to all comers. Rates are much lower outside high summer.

Platja de Punta Prima is a small holiday resort with a pleasant 200m-long beach. Although it's protected by the low expanse of offshore Illa de l'Aire, distinguished by the thin pencil of its lighthouse, the waves still roll in gently and enticingly. Regular buses run here from Maó.

Westwards along the coast, Binibèquer (aka Binibeca) has all the appearance of a charming old fishing village; in fact, it was designed as a single unit and constructed in the early 1970s. Gleaming white and something of a tourist beehive, the curious houses, tight alleys and narrow cove with its transparent water are delightful, whatever their genesis.

At Menorca's largest winery, Bodegas Binifadet (☎971 15 07 15; www.binifadet. com; ☉10am-8pm Easter-Oct), you can amble around the vineyards at your own pace and sip a sample on its terrace or join a 30-minute tour (€7) that includes a tasting of its wines, grape jelly and tangy Menorcan goat cheese. It's just outside San Lluís, on the signed road to Sa Castell.

IBIZA

For many, Ibiza (Eivissa in Catalan) means endless partying in Mediterranean macroclubs. There is, however, another side to the island. The Greeks called Ibiza and Formentera the Islas Pitiusas (Islands of Pine Trees), and about half the island (especially the comparatively unspoilt northeast) remains covered by these thick woods. Alongside hardy pines, the most common crops are olives, figs and almonds and, away from the main resorts and towns, the island has a gentle rural charm.

In 1956 the island boasted 12 cars and in the 1960s the first hippies from mainland Europe began to discover its idyllic beaches. A mixed World Heritage site because of Ibiza City's architecture and the island's rich sea life, Ibiza soon latched on to the money-spinner of bulk tourism. Today the resident populace of 117,700 watches on as millions (more than four million passengers annually pass through its airport) visit S'Illa Blanca (The White Island) each year.

Birthplace of the rave, Ibiza has some of Spain's most (in)famous clubs and plenty of bars. But coastal walking trails, woods and quiet (if not deserted) beaches will allow you to elude Ministry of Sound–style madness, too.

❶ Getting Around

TO/FROM THE AIRPORT Bus 10 from Ibiza City every 20 minutes; during the summer months bus 9 goes to the airport from Sant Antoni every 1½ hours and bus 24 from Es Canar via Santa Eulària every two hours. Out of season you will have to go to Ibiza City first.

BUS Fares don't exceed €4 for the longest journey. Online, check out www.eivissabus.info.

Ibiza City

POP 49,390

Ibiza's capital is a vivacious, enchanting town with a captivating whitewashed old quarter topped by a cathedral. It's also a focal point for some of the island's best nightlife.

Ibiza

Sights

D'ALT VILA & AROUND

From Sa Penya wander up into D'Alt Vila, the old walled town (and a Unesco World Heritage site). The Romans were the first to fortify this hilltop. The existing walls were raised by Felipe II in the 16th century to protect against invasion by French and Turkish forces.

Ramparts   WALLS

A ramp leads from Plaça de Sa Font in Sa Penya up to the Portal de ses Taules gateway, the main entrance. Above it hangs a commemorative plaque bearing Felipe II's coat of arms and an inscription recording the 1585 completion date of the fortification – seven artillery bastions joined by thick protective walls up to 22m in height. You can walk the entire perimeter of these impressive Renaissance-era walls, designed to withstand heavy artillery, and enjoy great views along the way.

Catedral   CATHEDRAL

(⊘9.30am-1.30pm & 5-8pm) Ibiza's cathedral elegantly combines several styles: the original 14th-century structure is Catalan Gothic but the sacristy was added in 1592 and a major baroque renovation took place in the 18th century. Inside, the Museu Diocesà

(admission €1.50; ⊘9.30am-1.30pm Tue-Sun, closed Dec-Feb) contains centuries of religious art.

Bastions   FORTIFIED TOWERS

(⊘10am-2pm & 6-9pm Tue-Sat, 10am-2pm Sun) In the Baluard de Sant Jaume, an exhibition of military paraphernalia includes soldiers' cuirasses that you can try for size (and weight!) and cannonballs to heave. An exhibition within the Baluard de Sant Pere, the next bastion northwards, demonstrates the

---

ℹ️ IBIZA WEBSITES

» **www.ibiza.travel** Official Ibiza tourism website.

» **www.eivissaweb.com** Multilingual Ibiza search engine.

» **www.ibiza-online.com** Another general search engine.

» **www.ibizahotelsguide.com** Official website of Ibiza's hoteliers' association.

» **www.ibizaholidays.com, www.ibiza -spotlight.com** Good for accommodation and general island information.

» **www.ibizaruralvillas.com** For rural villas and houses.

Ibiza City

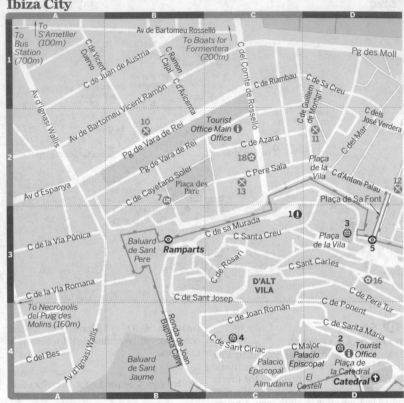

Ibiza City

FREE **Necròpolis del Puig des Molins** BURIAL GROUND

(Carrer de la Via Romana 31; ⊙10am-2pm & 6-8pm Tue-Sat, 10am-2pm Sun) The earliest tombs within this ancient burial ground date from the 7th century BC and Phoenician times. Follow the path around and peer into the burial caverns, oriented north to south, cut deep into the hill. You can descend into one interlocking series of these *hypogea* (burial caverns).

The site museum displays finds such as amulets and terracotta figurines discovered within the more than 3000 tombs that honeycomb the hillside. Both museum and site were closed for restoration works at the time of writing.

FREE **Museu d'Art Contemporani** MUSEUM

(Ronda de Narcís Puget; ⊙10am-1.30pm & 4-6pm Tue-Fri, 10am-1.30pm Sat & Sun) Its normal home is within an 18th-century powder store and armoury. While it undergoes lengthy refurbishing, elements of the collection are on show in the **Casa Consistorial** (Town Hall) on Plaça d'Espanya.

FREE **Museu Puget** MUSEUM

(✆971 39 21 47; Carrer de Sant Ciriac 18; ⊙10am-1.30pm & 5-8pm Tue-Fri, 10am-1.30pm Sat & Sun) A historic mansion with typical late-Gothic courtyard and stairs to the upper floor houses 130 paintings by Ibizan artist Narcís Puget Viñas (1874–1960) and his son, Narcís Puget Riquer (1916–83).

SA PENYA

There's always something going on portside. People-watchers will be right at home – this pocket must have one of the highest concentrations of exhibitionists and freaks in Spain.

Sa Penya bursts with funky and trashy **clothing boutiques**. The so-called **hippie markets**, street stalls along Carrer d'Enmig and the adjoining streets, sell everything under the sun, but don't let the 'hippy' bit of the name make you think that everything is being sold by people with a hatred of money and capitalist greed. Quite the opposite – you'll find that the prices are sky-high!

tricks of artillery warfare and how to mount a cannon and has an audiovisual illustration of how the city walls were constructed.

Centre d'Interpretació Madina Yasiba MUSEUM

(Carrer Major 2; adult/child €2/1.50; ⊙10am-2pm & 6-9pm Tue-Sat, 10am-2pm Sun) This small display replicates the medieval Muslim city of Madina Yabisa (Ibiza City) prior to the island's fall to Christian forces in 1235. Artefacts, audiovisuals and maps help transport you to those times. The centre is housed in what was, from the 16th century, the Casa de la Cúria (law courts). Parts of its walls were the original Islamic-era defensive walls. Much of the display was inspired by excavations done along Carrer de Santa Maria in the early 2000s.

DON'T MISS

IBIZA'S TOP BEACHES

» Cala Benirràs (p649)

» Cala Mastella (p648)

» Cala de Boix (p648)

» Cala Xarraca (p648)

» Cala Codolars (p651)

🛏 Sleeping

Hotel Mirador de Dalt Vila BOUTIQUE HOTEL €€€

(📞971 30 30 45; www.hotelmiradoribiza.com; Plaça d'Espanya 4; s €310, d from €480 Aug, s €250, d from €390 Jul & Sep; ☺Easter-Dec; ✳@🛜🛝) This rose-hued mansion is the Fajarnés family home. The 13 stunningly renovated rooms are delightfully furnished. At every turn, public areas display paintings and exquisite objets d'art, all from the family's private collection. The spa-pool has a counter-current swim jet for the active and the restaurant is a gourmet's delight.

Hotel La Ventana HISTORIC HOTEL €€€

(📞971 30 35 37; www.laventanaibiza.com; Carrer de Sa Carossa 13; d from €165; ✳🛜) This charming 15th-century mansion is set on a little tree-shaded square in the old town. Some rooms come with stylish four-poster beds and mosquito nets. The rooftop terrace, trim gardens and restaurant are welcome extras. Prices drop massively out of season.

Hostal Parque HOTEL €€

(📞971 30 13 58; www.hostalparque.com; Carrer de Vicent Cuervo 3; s €70-90, d €130-190; ✳🛜) The rooms here are small, but otherwise what you get are the basics done very well indeed, and it manages to be modern and cool without being Ibiza over the top. Rarely for central Ibiza City, there's decent double glazing so noise shouldn't be too much of an issue. The best doubles overlook pleasant Plaça des Parc and the downstairs cafe is a very popular place for a drink or a meal.

Hostal La Marina HOTEL €€

(📞971 31 01 72; www.hostal-lamarina.com; Carrer de Barcelona 7; r €75-170; ✳) Looking onto both the waterfront and bar-lined Carrer de Barcelona, this mid-19th-century building has rooms that are as flamboyant and colourful as an Ibizan club night. A handful of singles and some doubles look onto the street (with the predictable noise problem), but you can opt for pricier doubles and attics with terraces and panoramic port and/or town views. The same people run other lodging options along the street.

✖ Eating

TOP CHOICE **Comidas Bar San Juan** MEDITERRANEAN €

(Carrer de Guillem de Montgrí 8; meals €15-20; ☺Mon-Sat) Ibiza fashionistas? What are they all about then? This family-run operation, with two small dining rooms, harks back to the days before Ibiza became a byword for glam. It offers outstanding value, with fish dishes for around €10 and many small mains for €6 or less. It doesn't take reservations, so arrive early and expect to have other people sat at the same table as you.

Restaurant of Hotel Mirador de Dalt Vila MEDITERRANEAN €€€

(📞971 30 30 45; Plaça d'Espanya 4; menus €45, mains €26-30; ☺Easter-Dec) At this intimate – do reserve – restaurant with its painted barrel ceiling and original canvases around the walls, you'll dine magnificently. Service is discreet yet friendly, and dishes are creative, colourful and delightfully presented. Allow time to sip an *aperitivo* in the equally cosy bar; at your feet is an underfloor display of antiquities recovered from the sea.

Ca n'Alfredo IBIZAN €€€

(📞971 31 12 74; Passeig de Vara de Rei 16; menus €30, mains €18-30; ☺lunch & dinner Tue-Sat, lunch Sun) Locals have been flocking to Alfredo's since 1934. It's great place for the freshest of seafood and other island cuisine that's so good it's essential to book. Try the *filetes de gallo de San Pedro en salsa de almendras* (John Dory fillets in almond sauce).

S'Ametller IBIZAN €€

(📞971 31 17 80; www.restaurantsametller.com; Carrer de Pere Francesc 12; menus from €22, meals €35-40; ☺lunch Mon-Wed, lunch & dinner Thu, Fri & Sat) The 'Almond Tree' offers local cooking based upon fresh market produce. The daily *menú* (for dessert, choose the house *flaó,* a mint-flavoured variant on cheesecake and a Balearic Islands speciality) is inventive and superb value. As an indication of its credentials, S'Ametller also offers cookery courses – including one that imparts the secrets of that *flaó.*

La Brasa
GRILL €€

(⌨971 30 12 02; Carrer Pere Sala 3; mains €18-25) La Brasa's forte is its quality fish and meat, sizzled over charcoal. Another strong feature is its garden, shaded by vines, palms and banana trees and adorned with bursts of bougainvillea.

Croissant Show
CAFE €

(⌨971 31 76 65; Plaça de la Constitució; ⊘6am-11pm) Opposite the food market, this is where *everyone* goes for an impressive range of pastries and other post-partying breakfast goodies. It is quite a scene all on its own.

🍷 Drinking & Entertainment

Sa Penya is the nightlife centre. Dozens of bars keep the port area jumping from sunset until the early hours. Alternatively, various bars at Platja d'en Bossa combine sounds, sand and sea with sangria and other tipples. After they wind down, you can continue at one of the island's world-famous nightclubs.

Discobus (www.discobus.es; per person €3; ⊘midnight-6am Jun-Sep) runs around the major discos, bars and hotels in Ibiza City, Platja d'en Bossa, Sant Rafel, Es Canar, Santa Eulària and Sant Antoni.

Bars & Clubs

Carrer de Barcelona, which runs parallel with the harbour, is lined with high-energy bars. Most have tall tables on the street and pump out loud music. Touts do their damnedest to 'invite' passers-by to join them for a drink, sometimes with the lure of discounted passes to the clubs. All open nightly from early evening until 3am or 4am May to September. Those along Carrer de Garijo Cipriano are a little less in your face.

KM5
BAR

(www.km5-lounge.com; Carretera de Sant Josep, Km5.6; ⊘8pm-4am May-Sep) This bar, named after its highway location, is where you go to glam it up. Head out of town towards Sant Josep and dance in the gardens as you gear up for the clubs. Lounging is the second major activity and there are plenty of pillows strewn about the tents.

Teatro Pereira
MUSIC BAR

(www.teatropereyra.com; Carrer del Comte de Rosselló 3; ⊘8am-4am) Away from the waterfront hubbub, this hugely atmospheric time warp of a place, which is all stained wood and iron girders, was once the foyer of the long-abandoned 1893 theatre at its rear. It's packed most nights with a more eclectic crowd than the standard preclubbing bunch, and it offers nightly live-music sessions. By day, it's a stylish place for a drink or snack.

Lola's Club
BAR

(C Alfonso XII 10; ⊘1-6am) Anyone who remembers Ibiza in the '80s will have fond memories of Lola's Club, one of the first on the island. It's still a hip miniclub, nowadays with a gay leaning. Right beside it, Lolita (⊘7pm-3am), a sparky little terrace in its own right, is a great spot for a drink before climbing the stairs to join her bigger sister.

Bora Bora Beach Club
BAR

(www.boraborabrazil.com; ⊘noon-4am May-Sep) At Platja d'en Bossa, about 2km from the old town, this is *the* place – a long beachside bar where sun and fun worshippers work off hangovers and prepare new ones. Entry's free and the ambience is chilled, with low-key club sounds wafting over the sand. From midnight, everyone crowds inside. It's off Carrer del Fumarell.

Gay & Lesbian Venues

The gay scene is based towards the east end of Sa Penya, particularly along the far end of Carrer de la Mare de Déu and around Carrer de Santa Llúcia. Many of the big clubs have special gay nights. Check out www.gayibiza.net.

Angelo
GAY

(www.angeloibiza.com; Carrer de Santa Llúcia 12) In the shadow of the old city walls, Angelo is a busy gay bar with several levels. The atmosphere is relaxed and heteros wind up here too. Nearby are a handful of other gay-leaning bars, such as the slicker Soap (Carrer de Santa Llúcia 12).

Anfora
GAY

(www.disco-anfora.com; Carrer Sant Carles 7; admission €12-17; ⊘May-Oct) Seemingly dug out of walls of rock, this is probably the best-known gay dance haunt high up D'Alt Vila.

ℹ️ Information

The **tourist office** (⌨971 39 92 32; www.eivissa.es; Plaça de la Catedral; ⊘10am-2pm & 6-9pm Mon-Sat, 10am-2pm Sun) in the old town loans free audio guides to the city; bring your passport or identity document. There is also an **island-wide office** (www.ibiza.travel; Passeig de Vara de Rei 1; ⊘9am-8pm Mon-Fri, to 7pm Sat).

CLUBBING ON IBIZA

From late May to the end of September, the west of the island is one big, continuous dance party from sunset to sunrise and back again. Entrepreneurs have built an amazing collection of clubs here – huge, throbbing temples to which thousands of disciples flock to pay homage to the gods of hedonism. In 2011 the International Dance Music Awards quoted four Ibiza clubs – Amnesia, Pacha, Space and Privilege – among their worldwide top eight.

The major clubs operate nightly from around 1am to 6am. Each has something different to offer. Theme nights, fancy-dress parties and foam parties are regular features. Some places go a step or two further, with go-go girls (and boys), striptease acts and even live sex as the (ahem) climax.

Entertainment Ibiza-style doesn't come cheaply. Admission can cost anything from €25 to €60 (mixed drinks and cocktails then go for around €10 to €15). If you hang out around the right bars in Sa Penya, you might score a flier that entitles you to discounted admission handed out by sometimes scantily clad club promoters and touts – if they think you've got the look.

Space (www.space-ibiza.es; admission €29-60; ⊙Jun–mid-Oct) In Platja d'en Bossa, aptly named Space, which can pack in as many as 40 DJs and up to 12,000 clubbers, is considered one of the world's best night clubs. Action here starts mid-afternoon and regular daytime boats make the trip between Platja d'en Bossa and Ibiza City (€6 return).

Pacha (www.pacha.com; admission €23-57; ⊙nightly Jun-Sep, Fri & Sat Oct-May) In business on the northern side of Ibiza City's port since 1973, Pacha has 15 bars (!) and various dance spaces that can hold 3000 people. The main dance floor, a sea of colour, mirror balls and veils draped from the ceiling, heaves to deep techno. On the terrace, sounds are more gentle and relaxing.

Amnesia (www.amnesia.es; admission €40-65; ⊙early Jun-Sep) Four kilometres out on the road to Sant Rafel, it has a sound system that seems to give your body a massage. A huge glasshouse-like internal terrace, filled with palms and bars, surrounds the central dance area with a seething mass of mostly tireless 20-something dancers. It gets heated in here, so every now and then icy air is pumped through.

Es Paradis (www.esparadis.com; Carrer de Salvador Espriu 2, Sant Antoni; admission €15-33; ⊙mid-May–Sep) This club boasts an amazing sound system, fountains and an outdoor feel (there's no roof, but then it doesn't rain in summer anyway). It's one of the prettiest of the macro-clubs, with loads of marble, a glass pyramid and plenty of greenery. Queues can be enormous, so get there early. Es Paradis is known for its water parties, when the dance floor is flooded.

Privilege (www.privilegeibiza.com; admission around €40) Five kilometres along the road to Sant Rafel, this club, with its 20 bars, interior pool and capacity for 10,000 clubbers, claims to be one of the world's largest. The main domed dance temple is an enormous, pulsating area, where the DJ's cabin is suspended above the pool.

ⓘ Getting There & Away

AIR Ibiza's airport (Aeroport d'Eivissa), just 7km southwest of Ibiza City, receives direct flights from mainland Spanish cities and a host of UK and other European centres.

BOAT Formentera ferries leave from a separate terminal 300m north of the centre.

Aquabus (www.aquabusferryboats.com; one way/return €3.50/6) Hourly ferries to/from Playa d'en Bossa and Figueretes, May to October.

Cruceros Santa Eulària (www.ferrysanta eulalia.com) Boats to Cala Llonga (adult/child €12/6), Ibiza City (adult/child €16/8) and Formentera Island (adult/child €32/17), May to October.

BUS Buses to other parts of the island depart from the new bus station on Avenida de la Pau, northwest of the town centre.

ⓘ Getting Around

Bus 10 (€3.35, every 20 minutes) runs from the airport to the central port area via Platja d'en Bossa. A taxi costs about €15.

East Coast

A busy highway (C733) speeds you north out of Ibiza City towards Santa Eulària d'es Riu on the east coast. More scenic is the slower coastal road via Cala Llonga, which winds through low hills and olive groves, with detours along the way to several beaches. To follow it, take the turn-off to Jesús a couple of kilometres northwest of Ibiza City.

Cala Llonga is set on an attractive bay with high rocky cliffs sheltering a lovely sandy beach, but the town itself is blighted by high-rise hotels.

SANTA EULÀRIA D'ES RIU
POP 31,300

Ibiza's third-largest town is a bustling place, with a couple of child-friendly, gently sloping beaches, a large harbour and plenty of 20th-century tourist-resort architecture.

⊙ Sights

The hillock of Puig de Missa, a world away from the beaches, is the core of the original town. As well as the pleasant 16th-century church, the Església de Santa Eulària, you'll find the Museu Barrau (⊙10am-2pm Tue-Sat), a white house with blue shutters dedicated to local artist Laureà Barrau; and the Museu Etnogràfic (⊘971 33 28 45; adult/child €3/free; ⊙10am-2pm Mon-Sat, 11am-1.30pm Sun), which displays farming and household instruments.

⊨ Sleeping & Eating

Modern hotels and apartments crowd the Santa Eulària beachfront. You'll find a cluster of affordable *hostales* a couple of blocks inland.

Most restaurants and cafes along the beachfront are tacky and overpriced. Four blocks back, there are several decent eateries along Carrer de Sant Vicent.

Ca's Català   HOTEL €€
(⊘971 33 10 06; www.cascatala.com; Carrer del Sol; s €55, d €80-118; ✵⊛⊡) This cheerful British-run option has the feel of a private villa. The majority of its 12 particularly large rooms overlook a garden courtyard and pool with bar. Most bedrooms have ceiling fans and a few come with air-con. Doubles, all with four-poster bed, are in attractive, gleaming white. It's very close to the bus station.

Hostal-Residencia Sa Rota   HOSTAL €€
(⊘971 33 00 22; www.ibiza-hotels.com/sarota; s/d from €43/63; ✵⊛) A good-value *hostal*, open

year-round, this place features bright, generous rooms (the doubles in particular), with modern bath or shower. The downstairs cafe has a relaxing outdoor extension with an ivy-shaded pergola.

El Naranjo   SEAFOOD €€
(⊘971 33 03 24; Carrer de Sant Josep 31; menus €10, mains €19-23; ⊙Tue-Sun) Enjoy fish, always fresh and cooked to retain all its juices, in the shady garden of 'The Orange Tree'. This very Spanish gourmet option is especially popular with locals seeking somewhere special.

☆ Entertainment

Guarana   CLUB
(www.guaranaibiza.com; Passeig Marítim; ⊙8pm-6am May-Oct) By the marina, this is a cool club away from the Ibiza–Sant Rafel–Sant Antoni circuit. There's live music on Sunday evenings.

ⓘ Information

Tourist office (⊘971 33 07 28; www.santa eulariadesriu.com; Carrer Marià Riquer Wallis 4; ⊙9.30am-1.30pm & 5-7.30pm Mon-Fri, 10am-1pm Sat) Just off the main street. There are also a couple of summer-only information booths.

ⓘ Getting There & Away

Regular buses connect Santa Eulària with Ibiza City, Sant Antoni and the northern beaches.

SANTA EULÀRIA D'ES RIU TO S'AIGUA BLANCA

⊙ Sights & Activities

Sant Carles de Peralta   VILLAGE
This sleepy village sits on the main road northwest of Santa Eulària. Just outside the village, at Km12, is the Las Dalias alternative market (www.lasdalias.es; ⊙10am-8pm Sat & 8pm-1.30am Mon Jun Sep, 8pm-1.30am Tue Jul-Sep, 8pm-1am Sun Aug).

Cala Llenya & Cala Mastella   BEACH

A side road leads to Cala Llenya, a pleasant little pine-fringed cove with a deep, sandy beach, and the even tinier, just as pretty, Cala Mastella, which outside high season you could have totally to yourself. At the latter, scramble around the rocks at the eastern end along a much-crumbled concrete path to reach one of Ibiza's most authentic restaurants.

Cala de Boix, Es Figueral & S'Aigua Blanca   BEACH

The road to Cala Mastella continues a couple of kilometres to the curl of Cala de Boix and its tempting waters.

Back on the main road, the next turn-off leads to the low-key resort area of Es Figueral, with a golden-sand beach and turquoise water. A little further on, a turn-off takes you to the still-lovelier beaches of S'Aigua Blanca, where clothing is optional.

On weekends and from July to August, all these beaches can be very, very busy.

🛏 Sleeping & Eating

Hostal Restaurante Es Alocs   HOTEL €€

(🖂971 33 50 79; www.hostalalocs.com; Platja Es Figueral; s/d €40/65; ⊘May-Oct; 🅿🛜) This very friendly choice sits right on the beach at Platja Es Figueral. Rooms occupy two floors and most have a small fridge and balcony. The bar-restaurant has a wonderful terrace, deeply shaded with tangled juniper and chaste trees.

Hostal Cala Boix   HOSTAL €€

(🖂971 33 52 24; www.hostalcalaboix.com; Cala Boix; d €60-80; ⊘May-Oct; 🅿) Set uphill and back from Cala Boix, this option couldn't be further from the Ibiza madness. All rooms have a balcony and many have sea views. At S'Arribiada, its hearty resturant, Thursday is barbeque day, while each Tuesday fresh sardines sizzle on the grill.

Es Bigotes   SEAFOOD €€

(Cala Mastella; meals €25; ⊘lunch Easter-Oct) Offering *bullit de peix* (whatever fish was caught that morning simmered with herbs, mixed vegetables and potatoes in a huge vat), followed by *arròs caldós* (saffron rice cooked in the broth of the *bullit de peix*), this simple shack is known far and wide. Finish off with *café de caleta* (coffee prepared with lemon zest, cinnamon and flamed brandy). No phone, no reservations; in July and August, you need to turn up in person at least the day before to book a spot.

During other months, arrival by 1pm should get you a table. To arrive by car, take the last turning left before Cala Mastella.

Bar Anita   BAR €

(Sant Carles de Peralta; mains €8-16) A timeless tavern opposite the village church of Sant Carles de Peralta, this restaurant and bar has been attracting all sorts from around the island for decades. They come to enjoy pizza, pasta and a hearty meal – or simply to drink and chat.

CALA SANT VICENT

The package-tour resort of Cala Sant Vicent extends around the shores of a protected bay on the northeast coast. Its long stretch of sandy beach is backed by a string of modern midrise hotels. A 2.5km drive northwards winds through a leafy residential area high up to **Punta Grossa**, with spectacular views over the coast and east out to sea.

North Coast & Interior

The north of Ibiza has some of the island's most attractive landscapes. Its winding back roads, coastal hills and inland mountains are popular with both walkers and cyclists.

PORTINATX

Portinatx is the north coast's major tourist resort. Busy, yes, but a good spot for families and positively underpopulated when set against the megaresorts around Ibiza town. Its three adjoining beaches – S'Arenal Petit, S'Arenal Gran and Platja Es Port – are each beautiful but often crowded.

Cala Xarraca, west of Portinatx, is a picturesque, partly protected bay with a rocky shoreline and dark-sand beach. Development is limited to a solitary bar-restaurant and a couple of private houses.

SANT MIQUEL DE BALANSAT & AROUND

One of the largest inland villages, Sant Miquel is overlooked by its shimmering white, box-like 14th-century church (⊘9.30am-1.30pm & 4.30-7.30pm Tue-Fri, 9.30am-12.30pm Sat). The restored early-17th-century frescoes in the Capella de Benirràs are a swirl of flowers and twisting vines. Each Thursday from June to September, there's traditional island dancing on the pretty patio at 6.15pm.

The fine beaches of the busy resort of Port de Sant Miquel are dominated by the huge concrete honeycomb of Hotel Club San Miguel. In this attractive, deep-sunk

DON'T MISS

IBIZA'S RURAL ACCOMMODATION

Only a few decades ago the main economy in northern Ibiza was farming. Today, though, the money generated by tourism far outweighs that of tilling the land and many former farms have been converted into rural hotels.

If you're used to the humble, but normally excellent value, *casas rurales* of the mainland then you're in for a bit of a shock in Ibiza where pretty much all the rural accommodation falls very much into the luxury category, and most have a price tag to match. Even so, if you want to completely hide away from the stresses of modern, urban life, then the following should do the job nicely.

Ca Sa Vilda Marge (☎971 33 32 34; www.casavildamarge.com; Carretera de Portinatx; s/d incl breakfast €119/139; P🅿️❄️🛜🎿🅿️) This small, French-run rural guesthouse is a super deal; the rooms are in a modern countryhouse style, a fantastic breakfast is thrown in and the gardens, which have a pool tucked away in the corner, are pleasing to the eye. Despite all these plus points though, it's the owners who really make it stand out – bubbly and attentive they are determined to make sure their guests enjoy their stay. it's located 2km off the main C733 towards Portinatx.

Agroturismo Atzaro (☎971 33 88 38; www.atzaro.com; Carretera Sant Joan de Labritja & Sant Llorenç de Balàfia km 15; d from €370; P❄️🛜🎿) Combining Japanese zen with tribal Africa and farmhouse Ibiza, this is a luxurious rural bolthole. In addition to stunning rooms, pool and gardens there's a well-regarded restaurant. Of all the rural accomodation in Ibiza, this one Is probably the most plush.

Can Gall (☎971 33 70 31; www.agrocangall.com; r incl breakfast €225-265; ⊗closed Dec; ❄️🛜🎿) A few kilometres north from Sant Llorenç de Balàfia along the C733, a signed turn-off just after Km 17 leads to Can Gall, once a farmhouse and nowadays a tranquil rural paradise set amid citrus groves. The nine bedrooms are each a delight to linger in, but tear yourself away to wallow in the infinity pool or savour the breeze from its chillout terrace.

Can Planells (☎971 33 49 24; www.canplanells.com; Carrer de Venda Rubió 2; d incl breakfast from €200; ❄️🛜🎿) The country mansion of Can Planells, just 1.5km outside Sant Miquel on the road to Sant Mateu d'Aubarca, exudes relaxed rural luxury in its handful of tastefully arranged doubles and suites. The best suites have private terraces, and the house is set amid delightful gardens and fruit-tree groves.

Can Curreu (☎971 33 52 80; www.cancurreu.com; Carretera de Sant Carles Km 12; d incl breakfast from €275; ❄️🛜🎿) Above terracing of almond and other fruit trees and amid close-clipped lawns bordered by a kaleidoscope of roses, this much-modified Ibizan farmstead has 17 exquisitely decorated and furnished rooms. Room rates include access to the relaxing spa with its multiple facilities. Signed 'Casa Rural', the hotel's a short drive through fields from the Km 12 marker, 1.5km south of Sant Carles.

Can Talaias (☎971 33 57 42; www.hotelcantalaias.com; San Carlos ctra Cala Boix; d from €168; ⊗Apr-Oct; 🛜) Follow the signs up the dirt track for a good couple of kilometres and finally, after much bumping and bouncing, you come to this beautiful converted farmhouse perched atop a hill surrounded by pine forests and with views out over the sea. Appropriately a stay here is all about peace and quiet and relaxing in the gardens and beside the beautiful pool. Rooms are comfortable but undeniably a little overpriced even for Ibiza. It's between Sant Carlos de Peralta and Cala Boix.

bay, you can waterski, canoe and hire snorkelling gear to explore the rocky shoreline.

A turn-off to the right just before Port de Sant Miquel takes you around a headland to the Cova de Can Marçà (☎971 33 47 76; www.covadecanmarsa.com; adult/child €9/5; ⊗10.30am-7.30pm), underground caverns spectacularly lit by coloured lights. Tours in various languages take around 30 to 40 minutes. After resurfacing, pause for a drink on its terrace and savour the panorama of sheer cliffs and deep blue water.

Beyond the caves, an unsealed road continues 4km around the coast to the unspoiled bay of Cala Benirràs (with less bump and bounce, a sealed road from the Sant Joan–Sant Miquel road brings you there too), with high, forested cliffs and a couple of bar-restaurants that back onto the beach. At dusk on Sunday you may well encounter hippies with bongos banging out a greeting to the sunset, something they have been doing for decades.

SANT LLORENÇ DE BALÀFIA & AROUND

Overlooking this quiet hamlet is a brilliant-white Ibizan, 18th-century fortress-church, from when attacks by Moorish pirates were the scourge of the island. From Sant Llorenç head 500m east to the C733 road and turn north. Take a lane off the C733 beside the restaurant Balafía to reach the minuscule, once-fortified hamlet of Balàfia, with two towers, flowers and lots of *privado* signs around its half-dozen houses – but don't let these deter you from exploring its couple of lanes.

La Paloma (☑971 32 55 43; Sant Llorenç; mains €16-26; ☺dinner Tue-Sun mid-Mar–Nov) located in Sant Llorenç, 100m downhill from the church, is an ecofriendly option. It offers creative Mediterranean, especially Italian, cuisine (hams and salamis come fresh from Tuscany) and sources vegetables from its own kitchen garden.

Below La Paloma, Paloma Café (meals €15-20; ☺9am-4pm Mon-Sat; 🖉🖬) is a delightful, laid-back place where you can snack on anything from quiche to carrot cake in the shade of its overgrown terrace. Much of its produce is organic and locally sourced and the friendly young team will do you a picnic basket on request.

SANTA GERTRUDIS DE FRUITERA

If you blinked at the wrong time, you might miss tiny Santa Gertrudis, south of Sant Miquel. Clustered around the central, pedestrianised Plaça de l'Església, you'll find art-and-craft galleries, antique and bric-a-brac shops, plus several good bars, especially Bar Costa (Plaça de l'Església 11), with original paintings plastered on every wall of its cavernous interior.

How does your waistline like the sound of a foie-gras crème brûlée? For gourmet dining under the orange trees of its terrace, the Restaurant la Plaza (☑971 19 70 75; Plaça de l'Església 15; mains €16-21) can't be beaten.

West Coast

SANT ANTONI DE PORTMANY
POP 21,850

Sant Antoni (San Antonio in Spanish), widely known as 'San An', is about as Spanish as bangers and mash. It's the perfect destination if you've come in search of booze-ups, brawls and hangovers. The bulk of punters are young and from the UK.

About the only sight in town is the pretty, mainly 17th-century Església de Sant Antoni (Plaça de l'Església), a couple of blocks in from the marina.

Not far north of Sant Antoni are several undeveloped beaches, such as Cala Salada, a wide bay with sandy shores backed by pine forest. Closer to Sant Antoni are the pretty inlet beaches of Cala Gració and Cala Gracioneta, separated by a small rocky promontory.

🛏 Sleeping & Eating

Hostal la Torre   HOTEL €€

(☑971 34 22 71; www.hostallatorre.com; s incl breakfast €75, d incl breakfast €100-130; ☺Easter-Oct; ❄🖬🏵) Though barely 2km north of Sant Antoni on the headland of Cap Negret, it's a world away from the town's bustle. Sea views from the bar-restaurant terrace are magnificent – even more so from the upper area, exclusive to hotel guests. The 18 rooms are plain and all up it adds up to a realtively peaceful stay in San Antoni – the question is though; did you come here for peace and quiet?

Villa Mercedes   FUSION €€

(☑971 34 85 43; www.villamercedesibiza.com; Molls dels Pescadors; mains €13.50-23; ☺7pm-3am; 🖉) This traditional Ibizan bourgeois mansion stands out among the sometimes horrendous muddle of Sant Antoni. It looks over the marina and offers eclectic cooking, from wok-fried vegetables through rice and noodle dishes to the local catch of the day.

🍸 Drinking

From the port, head for the small rock-and-sand strip on the north shore to join hundreds of others for sunset drinks at a string of chilled bars. All serve food too.

Café del Mar (www.cafedelmarmusic.com; ☺4pm-1am) is an Ibiza institution that celebrated its 30th anniversary in 2010. Other options include Mint (www.mintloungeibiza. com), Café Mambo (www.cafemamboibiza.com; ☺1pm-2am) and Savannah (www.savannahibiza.com; ☺2pm-2am).

WHAT'S COOKING IN THE BALEARIC ISLANDS?

Fish and seafood are the lead items in many a Balearic kitchen. In the marshlands of S'Albufera, in eastern Mallorca, rice and eels are traditional mainstays. The former is used in many dishes, while the latter mostly pop up in *espinagada*, an eel-and-spinach pie. Valldemossa is famous for its versions of *coca*, a pizza-like snack that you will find around the islands, particularly around Mallorca. One of the local specialities is the potato version, *coca de patata*. Menorca is especially known for its cheeses and *caldereta de llagosta*, a juicy lobster stew. A favourite in Ibiza is *frito de pulpo* (a baked dish of octopus, potatoes, paprika and herbs). Another is *bullit de peix*, a fresh fish and potato stew.

The interior of Mallorca is serious wine country, with two Denominación de Orígen (DO) areas, Binissalem and Pla i Llevant (roughly the southeast sector of the island). Limited quantities of wine (some very good) are also made in Menorca, Ibiza and Formentera (try the whites here).

They face stiff competition from another set of stylish lounge bars about 300m further north along the pedestrian walkway. Places such as **Sun Sea Bar**, **Golden Buddha** and **Kanya Beach** all have pools and attract plenty of punters. Between June and September, once the sun goes down, all turn up the rhythmic heat and pound on until late.

Around the other side of the bay at Cala de Bou, you can eat, drink and soak up the final rays of the day at **Kumharas** (www.kumharas.org; Carrer de Lugo 2). Sunday night is best, with live performances (especially fire dancers). Look for the Rodeo Vaca Loca sign on the main road and turn down Carrer de Lugo towards the sea.

① Information
Tourist office (☑971 34 33 63; Passeig de Ses Fonts; ⊙9.30am-8.30pm Mon-Fri, 9.30am-1pm Sat & Sun) Beside the harbour.

① Getting There & Away
BOAT Cruceros Portmany (www.crucerosportmany.com; adult/child €9/4.50) boats depart around every half-hour to Cala Bassa (20 minutes) and Cala Compte (30 minutes).

BUS To Ibiza City (40 minutes), bus 3 runs every 15 to 30 minutes. Bus 7 (eight daily June to October) serves Cala Bassa.

CALA BASSA TO CALA D'HORT
Heading west and south from Sant Antoni, you'll come to the popular bay of Cala Bassa. Walk in beyond the rocks to this lovely, sandy horseshoe bay. The next few coves around the coast hide some extremely pretty beaches including **Cala Compte**, with its translucent water, and tiny **Cala Codolars**. All are accessible by local bus and/or boat from Sant Antoni. Further south, **Cala Vedella** is a modest resort, with a fine beach in the centre of town.

A gorgeous drive through scented pine trees brings you to the bijou bay of **Cala d'Hort**, overlooked by the towering mass of the islet of **Es Vedrà**. The water here is an inviting shade of blue and the beach is a long arc of sand sprinkled with pebbles and rocks. Sip a drink, ideally at sunset, on the terrace of **El Carmen** (☑971 18 74 49; paella from €21 per person minimum 2 people; ⊙mid-Mar–Oct). This friendly bar-restaurant-hotel, from where you tumble onto the beach, is also renowned for its seafood, in particular for its paellas, and every summer weekend sees a mass of locals tucking in.

FORMENTERA

A short boat ride south of Ibiza, Formentera is a tiny island (it's less than 20km across from east to west and has a population of just 9500) with a gentle and bewitching beauty. It also happens to have some of the best beaches you're ever likely to lounge about on. Of course, being so close to Ibiza means that you won't be the first to fall under the island's spell and it can get crowded in midsummer, but most of the time it is still possible to find yourself a strip of sand out of sight and earshot of others.

Formentera's predominantly flat landscape is rugged and, at times, bleak. The coast is alternately fringed with jagged cliffs and beaches backed by low dunes. A handful of farmers scrape a living from the land in the centre and east, but elsewhere the island is a patchwork of pine plantations, sun-bleached salt beds, low stone walls and mostly untilled fields.

Formentera

◉ Sights & Activities

Formentera is an island for sitting and being rather than doing, and apart from walking, cycling and lying on beaches, activities are limited. Points of interest include a series of crumbling stone watchtowers along the coastline, traces of a ruined Roman fortress (Fortificació Romà) on the south coast, and 40 minor archaeological sites (most signposted in distinctive pink off the main roads).

Divers could approach Diving Center Formentera (☑971 32 11 68; www.blue-adventure.com; Calle Almadrava 67-71, La Savina; dive with rental gear from €45), one of a handful of island dive centres. Wet4Fun (☑609 766084; www.wet4fun.com; ☺Apr-Nov), with its main base in Es Pujols, offers the chance to learn windsurfing and kitesurfing, as well as sailing, canoeing and kayaking.

PARQUE NATURAL DE SES SALINES
The Ses Salines nature park, a protected area, begins just north of Estany Pudent (the aptly named 'Smelly Lake'). It extends along the slim finger of land that pokes northwards towards Ibiza and across the narrow intervening strait to also embrace Ses Salines, the salt pans of Ibiza's southern tip. Platja de Llevant and Platja de ses Illetes,

a pair of beautiful strips of white sand, line the promontory. A 3km partly dirt road (toll for cars/motorbikes €4/2) heads north from the La Savina–Es Pujols road.

A 4km walking trail leads from the La Savina–Es Pujols road to the far end of the promontory, from where you could wade across the narrow strait to Illa s'Espalmador, a tiny uninhabited islet with beautiful, quiet beaches (especially S'Alga, on the southeast side) and mud baths. Be careful when wading out – you can easily be caught by incoming tides. The Barca Bahia boat runs up to three times daily from La Savina ferry port to the island, calling at Platja de ses Illetes.

SANT FRANCESC XAVIER
Formentera's capital and biggest population centre, Sant Francesc Xavier is an attractive whitewashed village, with some good cafes overlooking small, sunny plazas. The town's older buildings include a 14th-century chapel, an 18th-century fortress and the Museu Etnològic (☑971 32 26 70; Carrer de Jaume I 17; admission free; ☺10am-2pm & 5-7pm Mon-Fri, 10am-2pm Sat), a modest ethnological museum illustrating Formentera's agricultural and fishing heritage.

CALA SAONA

Delectable Cala Saona, which is on the road south of Sant Francesc Xavier, a third of the way to Cap de Barbaria, is pretty much perfect. The water is a gaudy, luminous blue and the sand so white that looking at it stings the eyes. In our opinion this is one of, if not THE, best beach on the Spanish Med. Fortunately there's not a lot of development here, bar one big out-of-place hotel and a couple of laid-back beach shacks serving fried fish and good vibes in the summer.

CAP DE BARBARIA

A narrow scaled road heads south out of the capital through stone-walled farmlands to Cap de Barbaria, the island's southernmost point. It's a pleasant ride to the lonely white lighthouse at the road's end, although there's little to do once you get there, except gaze out to sea. From the *far* (lighthouse) a 10-minute walk eastwards along a track leads to the Torre d'es Cap de Barbaria, an 18th-century watchtower.

ES PUJOLS

Once a sleepy fishing village, Es Pujols has been transformed by tourism and is now the closest Formentera comes to a proper beach resort, but in comparison to those just over the channel in Ibiza that's not very close at all! Rows of sun-bleached timber boat shelters still line the beachfront, overshadowed by modern hotels, apartments and restaurants. If the beaches are too crowded for your liking, more-secluded options lie within easy striking distance (keep walking northwest towards Platja de Llevant).

On the main road east of Sant Ferran just beyond Km 6, turn right at the Spar supermarket for the Cova d'en Xeroni (☑971 32 82 14; adult/child €4/2.50; ☺10am-1.30pm & 5-8pm Mon-Sat May-Oct). This underground cavern rich in stalactites and stalagmites was revealed in 1975 when the landowner was digging a well. It's a one-man band, so treat opening times with a grain of salt. How many visits are organised each day (the most likely times are 1pm and 6pm) depends on demand and whether or not the discoverer's son is around.

PLATJA DE MIGJORN

East of Sant Ferran towards Es Caló, a series of bumpy tracks leads from the main road to the south-coast beaches, known collectively as Platja de Migjorn. The best are at the eastern end around Es Arenals. Most of these beach settlements are no more than a handful of houses and apartments, a couple of bar-restaurants and the odd *hostal*.

EASTERN END

The fishing settlement of Es Caló is on a tiny rocky cove ringed by faded timber boat shelters. The coastline is jagged, but immediately west of Es Caló you'll find some good swimming holes and stretches of blisteringly white sand massaged by what will probably turn out to be the most translucent water you will ever gleefully dive into.

From Es Caló, the road twists up to the island's highest point. Close to the top, beside Restaurante El Mirador, there are spectacular views along the length of the island, whose eastern extremity is an elevated limestone plateau. Most of the coastline is only accessible by boat. A road runs arrow-straight to the island's eastern tip, passing through Es Pilar de la Mola, which comes alive for hippie markets, which are held from 4pm to 9pm each Wednesday and Sunday. At the end of the road are the Far de sa Mola lighthouse, a monument to Jules Verne (who used this setting in one of his novels), a bar and spectacular seascapes.

🛌 Sleeping

Camping is prohibited. Most accommodation caters to package-tour agencies, so is overpriced and/or booked out in midsummer. Rental apartments (a better deal for stays of a week or more) are more common than *hostales* and hotels (of which there are just over 50). Check out www.formentera hotelsguide.com and www.guiaformentera. com.

Astbury Formentera (www.formentera.co .uk) is a UK-based specialist in house and apartment rentals in Formentera.

DON'T MISS

FORMENTERA'S TOP BEACHES

» Platja de Migjorn
» Cala Saona
» Platja de Ses Illetes
» Platja de Llevant

SANT FRANCESC XAVIER

Several *hostales* are scattered about this pleasant town and prices are more realistic than at some of the beach locations.

Searing-white Es Marès (971 32 32 16; www.hotelesmares.com; Carrer Santa María 15; r incl breakfast from €380; ✱🏠⛱), with its decor scheme that includes beach pebbles and driftwood, is dressed up like a miniature version of the island itself. The pain of paying such high prices will be somewhat soothed by the free spa treatments.

CALA SAONA

A white behemoth of a building overlooking the beach, Hotel Cala Saona (971 32 22 43; www.hotelcalasaona.com; s/d incl breakfast €140/180; ☉Jun-Sep; P✱@🏠⛱🍴) offers 116 rooms, a pool, tennis courts and a restaurant. From the best rooms, the view is straight across the beach and out to sea. Its beach bar-restaurant is perfect for a sunset sangria. Prices halve in low season.

ES PUJOLS

Ochre fronted and about 100m inland from the beach, Hostal Voramar (971 32 81 19; www.hostalvoramar.com; Avenida Miramar 25-33; s incl breakfast €124-127, d incl breakfast €160-167; ☉May-Oct; ✱@🏠⛱) has comfortable rooms, most with balcony. For night owls, breakfast is served from 8.30am until noon. Have a workout in the small gym. The same people own the simpler, adjacent Fonda Pinatar (s/d €88/112).

One of the better-value options is the smart Hotel Sa Volta (971 32 81 25; www.savolta.com; Avenida Miramar 94; s €93-103, d €170-190; P✱@🏠⛱🍴), which stands white and proud in the town centre, and has good-sized and well-maintained rooms decorated in a no-fuss style.

SANT FERRAN DE SES ROQUES

A classic for decades, Hostal Pepe (971 32 80 33; Carrer Major 68; s/d incl breakfast €50/60; ☉May–mid-Oct; ✱⛱) sits on the pleasant (and, on summer nights, lively) main street near the village's old sandstone church. Whitewashed with flashes of blue, it has 45 simply furnished, breezy rooms, all with balcony.

PLATJA DE MIGJORN

There's a sprinkling of *hostales* and apartments along Formentera's south beach, but most only deal with tour operators.

At Hostal Ca Marí (971 32 81 80; www.hotelcamari.com; Es Ca Marí; r €103-141, apt €88-124.50; ☉May-Oct; P✱@🏠⛱🍴), rooms and apartments all share gardens, a central bar, a restaurant, a pool and a grocery shop in the little settlement of the same name. The beach, where the *hostal* has its own bar-restaurant, is barely 100m away.

With its stunning beachfront location and minimalist rooms, backpackers are most definitely not welcome at the Gecko Beach Club (971 32 80 24; www.geckobeachclub.com; Es Ca Marí, Platja de Mgjorn; r incl breakfast €270-325; P✱🏠⛱🍴), which falls squarely into the 'oh you're so Ibiza chic' category.

ES CALÓ

In a diminutive fishing hamlet overlooking a small rocky harbour, Hostal Rafalet (971 32 70 16; www.hostal-rafalet.com; s/d €80/110; ✱🏠) is a welcoming *hostal*, where many of the spacious rooms have sea views. Did we say 'sea views'? Sorry, we meant it's so close to the sea that fish might try and cuddle up next to you in bed at night. Downstairs, there's a popular bar and restaurant with a portside terrace where you can gobble up the fish that got in your bed last night.

✗ Eating

Most waterfront eateries offer a standard range of seafood and paella-style options. All those recommended here open from May to October only unless otherwise indicated.

ES PUJOLS

El Caminito (971 32 81 06; www.caminitoformentera.es; Carretera La Savina-Es Pujols; meals €40; ☉dinner Apr-Nov) brings a touch of the *pampa* to the Med. This Argentine grill, one of the best restaurants on the island, serves juicy slabs of meat. It's 1km outside Es Pujols on the road to La Savina.

SANT FERRAN DE SES ROQUES

Pedestrianised Carrer Major has a string of summertime eateries.

Sit on the breezy terrace of Sa Finca (971 32 90 28; Carrer Tarragona; mains €10-15, meals around €30; ☉year-round), in the village centre, and enjoy superlative seafood and tapas. The highlight has to be the paellas, which are all properly cooked and presented and, unlike in most restaurants, if you ask nicely they might even make one for just one person.

PLATJA DE SES ILLETES

In a tastefully renovated mill, Es Molí de Sal (971 18 74 91; www.esmolidesal.es; meals €40-50) boasts a lovely terrace and magnificent sea views. It serves some of Formentera's finest seafood. Try one of the rice dishes or the house speciality, *caldereta de llagosta* (lobster stew).

PLATJA DE MIGJORN

Set amid a greenery-filled dune, Vogamari (☑971 32 90 53; meals €30-35; ☺closed dinner Tue) is a simple island eatery with a broad veranda. It's great for fresh fish, paella or solid meat dishes. Turn off the PM820 at Km 9.5.

Sa Platgeta (☑971 18 76 14; Es Ca Marí, Platja de Migjorn; mains €15, meals €35; ☺Mon-Sat) is, according to some locals, one of the best spots on the island for fresh fish. Planted amid pines just back from a narrow, rock-studded beach, this simple bar-restaurant has a pleasant shady terrace. It's 500m west of Es Ca Marí (follow the signs through the backstreets or take the waterfront boardwalk).

At the eastern extremity of the beach, Restaurante Es Cupiná (☑971 32 72 21; meals around €35) is a big name on the island. In business for nearly 40 years, this breezy restaurant is noted for its freshly cooked fish of the day.

ES CALÓ

S'Eufabi (☑971 32 70 56; www.restauranteseu fabi.com; Carretera La Mola, Km 12.5; mains €10-18, menus €13) dishes up some of the best paella and *fideuá* (a fine noodle variant) on Formentera at a reasonable price. This shady eatery is about 1km east of Es Caló, on the left as you begin the gentle ascent towards Es Pilar de la Mola.

ES PILAR DE LA MOLA

Pequeña Isla (☑971 32 70 68; www.pequena isla.com; Avinguda del Pilar 101; meals €30-35; ☺Tue-Sun), the 'Little Island', has a shady roadside terrace and serves up hearty meat items, fresh grilled fish, paella and other rice dishes, as well as various island specialities, including simmered lamb and fried octopus.

☆ Entertainment

ES PUJOLS

In summer Es Pujols gets lively. Its intense tangle of intertwined bars along or just off Carrer d'Espardell (just back from the waterfront) stay open until 3am or 4am. Customers are 90% Italian – indeed you'd hardly know you were in Spain! Current hot dates include **Bananas & Co** and **Tropicana Cafe**.

Vivi Club (☑691 046904; Avinguda Miramar) is a pleasant music bar with pine trees in the garden. The purple lighting tinges everything, even your cocktails.

SANT FERRAN DE SES ROQUES

An island classic, Fonda Pepe (☑971 32 80 33; Carrer Major 55; ☺May-Oct) is a knockabout bar connected with the *hostal* across the street of the same name. It has been serving *pomadas* (shots of gin and lemon) for decades and attracts a lively crowd of locals and foreigners of all ages and persuasions.

PLATJA DE SES ILLETES

Bigsurlife (☺10.30am-sunset May-Oct) attracts a good-natured and beautiful Italian crowd. The daily event is drinks (huge glass steins of mojito) on the beach for sunset. About 20m before the turn-off for Platja de ses Illetes from the La Savina–Es Pujols road, a parking area is signposted to the left. Another 30m brings you to the beach and bar.

Tiburón (☑659 63 89 45; ☺10am-sunset May-Oct), about 200m further along the strand, is an equally fun beach tavern that tends to attract more locals for fish, salads, sangria and, of course, sunsets.

PLATJA DE MIGJORN

Above the long strand, the scattering of bars range from sophisticated (often Italian-run) chill-out scenes for sipping cocktails to more rough-and-ready affairs.

Blue Bar (☑666758190; www.bluebarfor mentera.com; ☺noon-4am Apr-Oct) is a long-established Formentera favourite that offers good seafood, rice dishes and spadefuls of *buen rollito* (good vibes). At the south's chill-out bar par excellence, everything is blue – seats, sunshades, tables, loos and walls. Why, they even mix a blue Curacao-based cocktail! Take the sandy track at Km 8.

Milan meets the sea at 10.7 (☑971 32 84 85; www.10punto7.com; meals around €30; ☺May-Sep), an Italian-owned bar-restaurant with an international wine list. Sushi is the speciality. The rolling waves below, mellow black-and-white decor and relaxed vibe are perfect for lingering. Take the dirt track at, specifically, Km 10.7.

Xiringuito Bartolo (☺lunch daily, dinner Tue-Sat May-Oct), at the eastern extremity of the beach, must be the world's tiniest beach bar, much loved by islanders. Sitting cheerfully on stilts, it hosts two longish tables. Bartolo serves up drinks and snacks to wander away with if there's nowhere to sit.

🛈 Information

Formentera's main **tourist office** (☎971 32 20 57; www.formentera.es; ⊙10am-8pm Mon-Fri, 10am-3pm Sat & Sun) is beside the ferry landing point in La Savina. There are smaller branches in Es Pujols and opposite the church in Sant Francesc Xavier.

🛈 Getting There & Around

BOAT Regular passenger ferries (one way adult €23.80-26.50, child €14-17; 25 to 35 minutes) run between Ibiza City and La Savina. Return fare is a little under double that of a one-way fare.

Baleària-Trasmapi (www.balearia.com) More than 10 daily. Small car (with passenger) costs €92 one way; a motorcycle cost €32.90; bicycles are free.

Mediterranea-Pitiusa (www.medpitiusa.net) Passengers only; six fast ferries daily.

BUS **Autocares Paya** (☎971 32 31 81; www. autocarespaya.com) runs a regular bus service connecting the main villages, but you're much more flexible on a scooter or bicycle.

CAR & BICYCLE Kiosk after kiosk offering car, scooter and bicycle hire greet you on arrival at La Savina's harbour. Daily rates start at around €8 for a bike, €29 for a motor scooter. A car is superfluous on this tiny island, but they are available for rent, starting at at €35 per day.

TAXI Call ☎971 32 23 42.

Seville & Andalucía

Why Go?

A parched region fertile with culture, a conquered land that went on to conquer, a fiercely traditional place that has accepted rapid modernisation: Andalucía has multiple faces. Here, in the cradle of quintessential Spain, the questions are often as intriguing as the answers. Who first concocted flamenco? How did tapas become a national obsession? Could Cádiz be Europe's oldest settlement? Are those *really* Christopher Columbus' bones inside Seville cathedral? And, where on earth did the audacious builders of the Alhambra get their divine inspiration from? Putting together the missing pieces of the puzzle is what makes travel in Andalucía the glorious adventure that it is, a never-ending mystery trail that will deposit you in places where you can peel off the chequered history in dusty layers: edgy Granada, arty Málaga, vivacious Seville, sleepy Grazalema, rugged Ronda, brassy Marbella – places that lodge in your memory like collected souvenirs, luring you back.

Best Places to Eat

» Vinería San Telmo (p675)
» Arrayanes (p752)
» El Aljibe (p692)
» Casa Curro (p681)

Best Places to Stay

» Hotel Casa 1800 (p673)
» Casa Morisca Hotel (p750)
» Palacio de la Rambla (p768)
» V... (p706)

When to Go
Seville

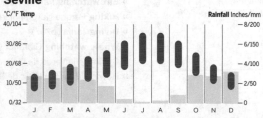

Apr Sombre Semana Santa processions are followed by the exuberance of the spring fairs.

May The weather's still relatively cool; many towns and villages celebrate *romerías* (pilgrimages).

Late Sep The heat diminishes, the crowds go home – but it's still warm enough for the beach.

NATIONAL PARKS

Two of Spain's 14 national parks reside in Andalucía: Doñana in Huelva and Seville provinces, established in 1969, and Sierra Nevada in Granada and Almería provinces, established in 1999.

Fast Facts

» Population: 8.4 million

» Area: 87,268 sq km

» Number of foreign visitors (2011): 7.8 million

» Annual income: €20,000

Planning Your Trip

» Book your accommodation at http://hotels.lonelyplanet.com.

» Andalucía is a region of festivals – research what's on and try to incorporate one or two.

» Check train timetables on www.renfe.es and bus timetables on www.movielia.es.

Resources

» www.andalucia.com

» www.andalucia.org

Spain's Finest Railway

The most spectacular train in Spain? The Ronda–Algeciras line is certainly a contender. Opened in 1892 to allow bored British military personnel bivouacked in Gibraltar access to the (then) hidden wonders of Spain, the line was engineered and financed by a couple of wealthy Brits who furnished the towns at each end with two magnificent Victorian age hotels: the Reina Victoria (Ronda) and the Reina Cristina (Algeciras). Still running on single track, the line traverses some of Andalucía's finest scenery including cork oak forest, Moorish white towns, boulder-strewn mountainscapes and diminutive Thomas-the-Tank-Engine stations. Trains run three times a day in either direction.

FEDERICO GARCÍA LORCA

It is debatable whether you can truly understand modern Anadalucía without at least an inkling of Spain's greatest poet and playwright, Federico García Lorca. Lorca epitomised many of Andalucía's potent hallmarks – passion, ambiguity, exuberance and innovation – and he brought them skilfully to life in a litany of precocious works, including the play *Blood Wedding* and the poem *Romancero Gitano*. Granada produced, inspired and ultimately destroyed Lorca, and it is here that his legacy remains most evident. But, keep your ear to the ground, and you'll feel his influence almost everywhere. Catch a live performance of his work, visit his birth house in Fuente Vaqueros (p755) or just wander the streets and fields of Granada and the Vega and compose your own poetic itinerary.

Best Places for Outdoor Activities

» **Windsurfing/Kitesurfing** Tarifa (p707), Los Caños de Meca (p706)

» **Rock climbing** El Chorro (p725)

» **Birdwatching** Parque Nacional de Doñana (p683)

» **Hiking** Parque Natural Sierra de Grazalema (p703)

» **Diving** Tarifa (p707)

» **Whale-watching** Gibraltar (p711)

» **Cycling** Vía Verde de la Sierra (p705), Cádiz province

» **Horse riding** Sanlúcar de Barrameda (p695)

History

Around 1000 BC or 900 BC, Andalucía's agricultural and mining wealth attracted Phoenician trading colonies to coastal sites such as Cádiz, Huelva and Málaga. In the 8th and 7th centuries BC, Phoenician influence gave rise to the mysterious, legendarily wealthy Tartessos civilisation somewhere in western Andalucía. From the 3rd century BC to the 5th century AD, Andalucía, governed from Córdoba, was one of the most civilised and wealthiest areas of the Roman Empire.

Andalucía was the obvious base for the Muslim invaders who surged onto the Iberian Peninsula from Africa in 711 under Arab general Tariq ibn Ziyad, who landed at Gibraltar with around 10,000 men, mostly Berbers (indigenous North Africans). Until the 11th century Córdoba was the leading city of Islamic Spain, followed by Seville until the 13th century, and finally Granada until the 15th. At its peak in the 10th century, Córdoba was the most dazzling city in Western Europe, famed for its 'three cultures' coexistence of Muslims, Jews and Christians. Islamic civilisation lasted longer in Andalucía than anywhere else on the Iberian Peninsula, and it's from the medieval name for the Muslim areas of the peninsula, Al-Andalus, that the name Andalucía comes.

The Emirate of Granada, the last bastion of Al-Andalus, finally fell to the Reyes Católicos (Catholic Monarchs), Ferdinand and Isabella, in 1492. Columbus' landing in the Americas the same year brought great wealth to Seville and later Cádiz, the Andalucian ports through which Spain's trade with the Americas was conducted. But the Castilian conquerors killed off Andalucía's deeper prosperity by handing out great swaths of territory to their nobles, who set sheep to run on former food-growing lands.

By the late 19th century rural Andalucía was a hotbed of anarchist unrest. During the civil war Andalucía split along class lines and savage atrocities were committed by both sides. Spain's subsequent 'hungry years' were particularly hungry here in the south, and between 1950 and 1970 some 1.5 million Andalucians left to find work in the industrial cities of northern Spain and other European countries.

But tourism, industrial growth and massive European Union (EU) subsidies for agriculture have made a big difference since the 1960s. The left-of-centre Partido Socialista Obrero Español (PSOE; Spanish Socialist Worker Party) has controlled Andalucía's regional government in Seville since 1982. The worst of Andalucian poverty has been eradicated by welfare provision and economic improvement. Education and health care have steadily improved, and the PSOE has given Andalucía Spain's biggest network of environmentally protected areas (though only in the last couple of years has it begun to tackle the rampant overdevelopment of many coastal areas).

Andalucía has been badly affected by the economic meltdown that followed the 2008–09 banking crisis. The region's unemployment rate has hovered above 25% percent, well above the (already poor) national average, and rates among the young (under 24-year-olds) have soared above 50%. Another hard-hit group was Andalucía's army of expats – mostly situated on the Costa del Sol – many of whom were forced to pack up and head home.

Seville

POP 703,000

Some cities have looks. Others have personality. The *sevillanos* (Seville residents) – lucky devils – get both, courtesy of their flamboyant, charismatic, ever-evolving Andalucian metropolis founded, according to mythology, 3000 years ago by the Greek god Hercules. Doused in never-ending sunlight, Sevillee's beauty is relatively easy to uncover; watch pretty girls in polka-dot dresses ride in carriages to the Feria de Abril (April Fair). Its soul is a darker and more complex force. Flamenco was partially born here in the dusty taverns of Triana, and greedy conquistadors once roamed the sinuous streets of El Arenal counting their colonial gold. Tugged by the pull of both forces, it is Seville's capriciousness that leaves the heaviest impression. Come here in April and watch as haunting Semana Santa (Holy Week) metamorphoses into the cacophony of spring fair and you'll wonder whether Bizet's Carmen wasn't more real than imagined.

History

Roman Seville, named Hispalis, was a significant port on the Río Guadalquivir, which is navigable to the Atlantic Ocean 100km away. Muslim Seville, called Ishbiliya, became the most powerful of the *taifas* (small kingdoms) into which Islamic Spain split after the Córdoba caliphate collapsed in 1031. In the 12th century a strict Islamic sect from

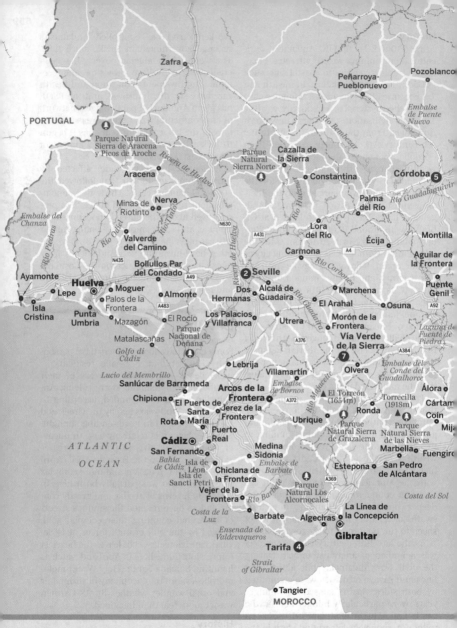

Andalucía Highlights

1 Follow the masses and make a pilgrimage to **Granada's** (p741) Alhambra

2 Choose from some of Andalucía's (and Spain's) best tapas in **Seville** (p659)

3 Stop in one of Spain's finest *paradores* (luxury hotels) in the Renaissance town of **Úbeda** (p767)

4 Get active with wind-surfing, diving, whale-watching or horse-riding in adventure nexus **Tarifa** (p707)

5 Tackle the tangle of Moorish streets in **Córdoba's** (p733) *judería* (Jewish quarter)

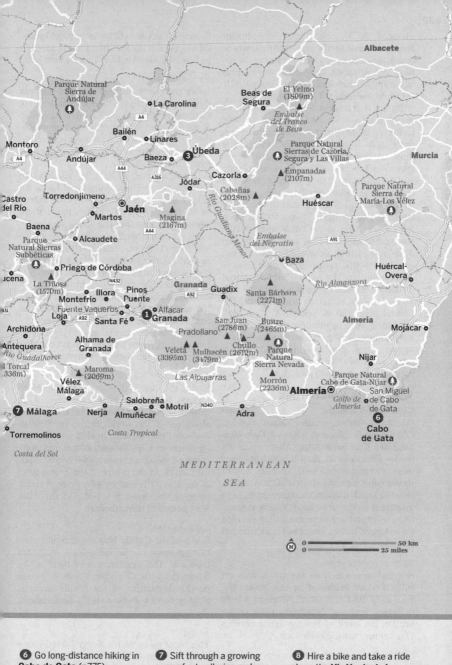

6 Go long-distance hiking in **Cabo de Gata** (p775)

7 Sift through a growing array of art galleries and museums in the city of **Málaga** (p715)

8 Hire a bike and take a ride along the **Vía Verde de la Sierra** (p705)

Morocco, the Almohads, took over Muslim Spain and made Seville capital of their whole realm, building a great mosque where the cathedral now stands. Almohad power eventually crumbled and Seville fell to Fernando III (El Santo, the Saint) of Castilla in 1248.

By the 14th century Seville was the most important Castilian city, and was in sole control of trade with the American colonies from 1503. It rapidly became one of the most cosmopolitan cities on earth. However, over the next 300 years, both plague and the silting up of the river contributed to Seville's long decline. Seville fell very quickly to the Nationalists at the start of the Spanish Civil War in 1936. Things looked up a few decades later in the 1980s when Seville was named capital of the new autonomous Andalucía within democratic Spain, and *sevillano* Felipe González became Spain's prime minister. The Expo 92 international exhibition in 1992 brought to the city millions of visitors, eight new bridges across the Guadalquivir, and the speedy AVE rail link to Madrid. And in the new century, where less is more, Seville is already experimenting with green initiatives, including trams, a metro and bikes that glide quietly alongside antique monuments to past glory.

◎ Sights & Activities

Cathedral & Giralda   CHURCH

(adult/child €8/free; ◎11am-5.30pm Mon-Sat, 2.30-6.30pm Sun Sep-Jun, 9.30am-4.30pm Mon-Sat, 2.30-6.30pm Sun Jul & Aug) After Seville fell to the Christians in 1248 the mosque was used as a church until 1402. Then, in view of its decaying state, the church authorities decided to knock it down and start again. Let's 'construct a church so large, future generations will think we were mad', they decided (or so legend has it). The result is a cathedral 126m long and 83m wide.

Sala del Pabellón

Selected treasures from the cathedral's art collection are exhibited in this room, the first after the ticket office. Much of what's displayed here, as elsewhere in the cathedral, is the work of masters from Seville's 17th-century artistic golden age.

Southern & Northern Chapels

The chapels along the southern and northern sides of the cathedral hold riches of sculpture and painting. Near the western end of the northern side is the Capilla de San Antonio, housing Murillo's 1666 canvas depicting the vision of St Anthony of Padua; thieves cut out the kneeling saint in 1874 but he was later found in New York and put back.

Tomb of Columbus

Inside the Puerta de los Príncipes (Door of the Princes) stands the monumental tomb of Christopher Columbus (Cristóbal Colón in Spanish) – the subject of a continuous riddle – containing what were long believed to be the great explorer's bones, brought here from Cuba in 1898.

Columbus died in 1506 in Valladolid, in northern Spain. His remains lay at La Cartuja monastery in Seville before being moved to Hispaniola in 1536. Even though there were suggestions that the bones kept in Seville's cathedral were possibly those of his son Diego (who was buried with his father in Santo Domingo, Hispaniola), recent DNA tests seemed to finally prove that it really is Christopher Columbus lying in that box. Yet unfortunately, to confuse matters further, the researchers also say that the bones in Santo Domingo could also be real, since Columbus' body was moved several times after his death. It seems that even death couldn't dampen the great explorer's urge to travel.

Capilla Mayor

East of the choir is the Capilla Mayor (Main Chapel). Its Gothic retable is the jewel of the cathedral and reckoned to be the biggest altarpiece in the world. Begun by Flemish sculptor Pieter Dancart in 1482 and finished by others in 1564, this sea of gilt and polychromed wood holds over 1000 carved biblical figures. At the centre of the lowest level is the tiny 13th-century silver-plated cedar image of the Virgen de la Sede (Virgin of the See), patron of the cathedral.

Sacristía de los Cálices

South of the Capilla Mayor are rooms containing some of the cathedral's main art treasures. The westernmost of these is the Sacristy of the Chalices, where Francisco de Goya's painting of the Seville martyrs, *Santas Justa y Rufina* (1817), hangs above the altar.

Sacristía Mayor

This large room with a finely carved stone dome was created between 1528 and 1547: the arch over its portal has carvings of 16th-century foods. Pedro de Campaña's 1547 *Descendimiento* (Descent from the Cross) above the central altar at the southern end, and Francisco de Zurbarán's *Santa Teresa*,

SEVILLE IN...

Two Days

Kick off day one with a visit to the **Alcázar** then wander through the Barrio de Santa Cruz and enjoy lunch at the **Vinería San Telmo**. In the afternoon head over towards the Río Guadalquivir and visit the **Museo de Bella Artes**. Spend the evening on a tapas bar crawl around the Plaza de la Alfalfa.

Devote the morning of day two to Seville **cathedral** before heading up to El Centro to visit the new **Metropol Parasol** and some city-centre shops. In the evening cross over the river to Triana and sample fried fish in Calle del Betis.

Four Days

Chill out on day three in **Parque de Maria Luisa** where you can negotiate its two museums. If you have the energy, hire a Sevici bike and cycle around. Dodge the tapas and treat yourself to a classy dinner at **Restaurante Egaña Oriza**. Return to Santa Cruz in the evening for exotic flamenco happenings at **Casa de la Memoria de Al-Andalus**.

On day four pop into the **Museo del Baile Flamenco** and **El Pabellon de Navegación**. Enjoy a night in the Alameda de Hércules with tapas in **Bar-Restaurante Eslava** and drinks at **Bulebar Café**.

to its right, are two of the cathedral's most precious paintings. The room's centrepiece is the Custodia de Juan de Arfe, a huge 475kg silver monstrance made in the 1580s by Renaissance metalsmith Juan de Arfe.

Cabildo
The beautifully domed chapter house, also called the Sala Capitular, in the southeastern corner, was originally built between 1558 and 1592 as a venue for meetings of the cathedral hierarchy. Hanging high above the archbishop's throne at the southern end is a Murillo masterpiece, *La Inmaculada*.

Giralda
In the northeastern corner of the cathedral you'll find the passage for the climb up to the belfry of the Giralda. The ascent is quite easy, as a series of ramps goes all the way up to the top, built so that the guards could ride up on horseback. The decorative brick tower which stands 104m tall was the minaret of the mosque, constructed between 1184 and 1198 at the height of Almohad power. Its proportions, its delicate brick-pattern decoration, and its colour, which changes with the light, make it perhaps Spain's most perfect Islamic building. The top-most parts of the Giralda – from the bell level up – were added in the 16th century, when Spanish Christians were busy 'improving on' surviving Islamic buildings. At the very top is El Giraldillo, a 16th-century bronze weathervane representing 'faith', which has become a symbol of Seville.

Patio de los Naranjos
Outside the cathedral's northern side, this patio was originally the courtyard of the mosque. It's planted with 66 *naranjos* (orange trees), and a Visigothic fountain sits in the centre. Hanging from the ceiling in the patio's southeastern corner is a replica stuffed crocodile – the original was a gift to Alfonso X from the Sultan of Egypt.

Alcázar CASTLE
(adult/child €7.50/free; ⊙9.30am-7pm Apr-Sep, to 6pm Oct-Mar) If heaven really *does* exist, then let's hope that it looks a little bit like the inside of Seville's Alcázar. Built primarily in the 1300s during the so-called 'dark ages' in Europe, the architecture is anything but dark. Indeed, compared to our modern-day shopping malls and throwaway apartment blocks it could be argued that the Alcázar marked one of history's architectural highpoints. Unesco agreed, making it a World Heritage site in 1987.

Originally founded as a fort for the Cordoban governors of Seville in 913, the Alcázar has been expanded or reconstructed many times in its 11 centuries of existence. In the 11th century, Seville's prosperous Muslim *taifa* (small kingdom) rulers developed the original fort by building a palace called Al-Muwarak (the Blessed) in what's now the western part of the Alcázar. The 12th-century Almohad rulers added another palace east of this, around what's now the Patio del Crucero. Christian Fernando III moved into the

Central Seville

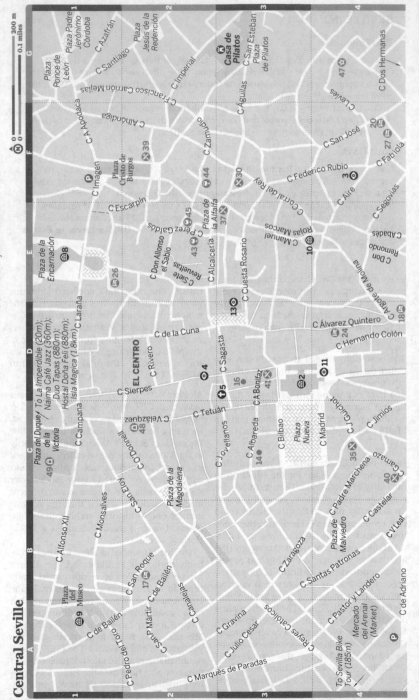

0 0
N 0

200 m
0.1 miles

EL CENTRO

To La Imperdible (20m);
Naima Café Jazz (360m);
Duo Tapas (880m);
Hostal Doña Feli (880m);
Isla Mágica (1.8km)

To Sevilla Bike Tour (185m)

Mercado del Arenal (Market)

Plaza del Museo

Plaza del Duque de la Victoria

Plaza de la Magdalena

Plaza Nueva

Plaza de la Encarnación

Plaza Cristo de Burgos

Plaza de la Alfalfa

Plaza de Pilatos

Casa de Pilatos

Plaza San Esteban

Plaza Ponce de León

Plaza Jesús de la Redención

Plaza Padre Jerónimo Córdoba

C Alfonso XII
C de Bailén
C Pedro del Toro
C de Bailén
C Monsalves
C San Eloy
C O'Donnell
C Velázquez
C Campana
C Sierpes
C de la Cuna
C Rivero
C Sagasta
C Tetuán
C Joyellanos
C Albareda
C Bilbao
C Madrid
C J Guichot
C Padre Marchena
C Gamazo
C Castelar
C V Leal
C de Adriano
C Pastor y Landero
C Reyes Católicos
C Gravina
C Julio César
C Marqués de Paradas
C Santas Patronas
C Zaragoza
C San Roque
C Canalejas
C P Mártir
C Santa
C A Bonifaz
C Albareda
Plaza de Malviedro
C Santas Patronas
C Límios
C Bilbao
C Imagen
C Laraña
C Escarpín
C Pérez Galdós
C Don Alfonso el Sabio
C Siete Revueltas
C Alcaicería
C Cuesta Rosario
C Cuesta Rosario
C Manuel Rojas Marcos
C Corral del Rey
C Zamudio
C Águilas
C Imperial
C Francisco Carrión Mejías
C Alhóndiga
C A Apodaca
C Azafrán
C Santiago
C San José
C Federico Rubio
C Aire
C Segovias
C Abades
C Don Remondo
C Árbote de Molina
C Álvarez Quintero
C Hernando Colón
C San Esteban
C Clevies
C Fabiola
C Dos Hermanas

9
8
26
39
44
30
45
37
43
13
24
18
10
11
2
41
5
4
16
48
14
17
49
47
20
27
3

Alcázar when he captured Seville in 1248, and Christian monarchs later used it as their main residence. Fernando's son Alfonso X replaced much of the Almohad palace with a Gothic one. Between 1364 and 1366 Pedro I created the Alcázar's crown jewel, the sumptuous Mudéjar **Palacio de Don Pedro**.

Patio del León

From the ticket office inside the **Puerta del León** (Lion Gate) you emerge into the **Patio del León** (Lion Patio), which was the garrison yard of the original Al-Muwarak palace. Just off here is the **Sala de la Justicia** (Hall of Justice), with beautiful Mudéjar plasterwork and an *artesonado* (ceiling of interlaced beams with decorative insertions); this room was built in the 1340s by Christian king Alfonso XI, who disported here with one of his mistresses, Leonor de Guzmán, reputedly the most beautiful woman in Spain.

The room leads on to the pretty **Patio del Yeso**, part of the 12th-century Almohad palace reconstructed in the 19th century.

Patio de la Montería

The rooms on the western side of this patio were part of the **Casa de la Contratación** (Contracting House) founded by the Catholic Monarchs in 1503 to control trade with Spain's American colonies. The **Salón del Almirante** (Admiral's Hall) houses 19th- and 20th-century paintings showing historical events and personages associated with Seville; the room off its northern end has an international collection of beautiful, elaborate fans. The **Sala de Audiencias** (Audience Hall) is hung with tapestry representations of the shields of Spanish admirals and Alejo Fernández' 1530s painting *Virgen de los Mareantes* (Virgin of the Sailors), the earliest known painting about the discovery of the Americas.

Palacio de Don Pedro

Posterity owes Pedro I a big thank you for creating this palace (also called the Palacio Mudéjar), the single most stunning architectural feature in Seville.

At the heart of the palace is the wonderful **Patio de las Doncellas** (Patio of the Maidens), surrounded by beautiful arches, plasterwork and tiling. The sunken garden in the centre was uncovered by archaeologists in 2004 from beneath a 16th-century marble covering.

The **Cámara Regia** (King's Quarters), on the northern side of the patio, has stunningly beautiful ceilings and wonderful

Central Seville

plaster- and tile-work. Its rear room was probably the monarch's summer bedroom.

From here you can move west into the little **Patio de las Muñecas** (Patio of the Dolls), the heart of the palace's private quarters, featuring delicate Granada-style decoration; indeed, plasterwork was actually brought here from the Alhambra in the 19th century when the mezzanine and top gallery were added for Queen Isabel II. The **Cuarto del Príncipe** (Prince's Room), to its north, has a superb wooden cupola ceiling trying to re-create a starlit night sky.

The spectacular **Salón de Embajadores** (Hall of Ambassadors), at the western end of the Patio de las Doncellas, was the throne room of Pedro I's palace. The room's fabulous wooden dome of multiple star patterns, symbolising the universe, was added in 1427. The dome's shape gives the room its alternative name, Sala de la Media Naranja (Hall of the Half Orange).

On the western side of the Salón de Embajadores the beautiful Arco de Pavones, named after its peacock motifs, leads into the **Salón del Techo de Felipe II**, with a Renaissance ceiling (1589–91).

Salones de Carlos V

Reached via a staircase at the southeastern corner of the Patio de las Doncellas, these are the much-remodelled rooms of Alfonso X's 13th-century Gothic palace. The rooms are now named after the 16th-century Spanish king Carlos I, using his title as Holy Roman Emperor, Charles V.

Gardens & Exit

From the Salones de Carlos V you can go out into the Alcázar's large and sleepy gardens. Immediately in front of the building is a series of small linked gardens, some with pools and fountains. From one, the **Jardín de las Danzas** (Garden of the Dances), a passage runs beneath the Salones de Carlos V to the **Baños de Doña María de Padilla** (María de Padilla Baths). These are the vaults beneath the Patio del Crucero – originally that patio's lower level – with a grotto that replaced the patio's original pool.

Concerts are sometimes held in the gardens during summer; see www.actidea.com for more information. There is also a fun hedge maze, which will delight children. The gardens to the east, beyond a long wall, are 20th-century creations, but don't hold that against them – they are heavenly indeed.

FREE **Archivo de Indias** MUSEUM
(Calle Santo Tomás; ☺10am-4pm Mon-Sat, to 2pm Sun & holidays) On the western side of Plaza del Triunfo, the Archivo de Indias is the main archive on Spain's American empire, with 80 million pages of documents dating from 1492 through to the end of the empire in the 19th century: a most effective statement of Spain's power and influence during its Golden Age. The building was refurbished between 2003 and 2005.

A short film inside tells its full story, and there are some fascinating original colonial maps and documents.

BARRIO DE SANTA CRUZ

Seville's medieval *judería* (Jewish quarter), east of the cathedral and Alcázar, is today a tangle of atmospheric, winding streets and lovely plant-decked plazas perfumed with orange blossom. Among its most characteristic plazas is Plaza de Santa Cruz, which gives the *barrio* (district) its name. Plaza de Doña Elvira is another romantic perch, especially in the evening.

Hospital de los Venerables Sacerdotes GALLERY
(☑954 56 26 96; Plaza de los Venerables 8; adult/child €4.75/2.40, Sun afternoon free; ☺10am-2pm & 4-8pm) Once a residence for ageing priests, this 17th-century baroque mansion guards what is perhaps Seville's most typical *sevillano* patio – intimate, plant embellished and spirit-reviving. The building's other highlights are its 17th-century church with rich religious murals, and the celebrated painting *Santa Rufina* by Diego Velázquez procured for a hefty €12.5 million by the on-site Centro Velázquez foundation in 2007.

Baños Árabes HAMMAM
(☑955 01 00 25; www.airedesevilla.com; Calle Aire 15; admission from €20; ☺every 2hr 10am-midnight) Jumping on the hamman bandwagon, Seville wins prizes for tranquil atmosphere, historic setting (in the Barrio de Santa Cruz), and Moroccan riad-style decor – living proof that those Moors knew a thing or two about how to relax. For an excellent post-bath pick-me-up, hit the on-site *tetería* (teahouse; p676) for a silver pot of mint tea.

EL CENTRO
The real centre of Seville is the densely packed zone of narrow streets north of the cathedral.

Museo del Baile Flamenco MUSEUM
(www.museoflamenco.com; Calle Manuel Rojas Marcos 3; adult/child €10/6; ☺9.30am-7pm) The brainchild of Sevillana flamenco dancer Cristina Hoyos, this museum, spread over three floors of an 18th-century palace, makes a noble effort to showcase the mysterious art, although at €10 a pop it is more than a little overpriced. Exhibits include sketches, paintings, photos of erstwhile (and contemporary) flamenco greats, plus a collection of dresses and shawls.

Classes, workshops and fantastic concerts are regular occurrences here, and there's the obligatory shop.

Plaza de San Francisco SQUARE
Plaza de San Francisco has been Seville's main public square since the 16th century. The southern end of the **ayuntamiento** (town hall) here is encrusted with lovely Renaissance carving dating from the 1520s and '30s.

Calle Sierpes STREET
Pedestrianised Calle Sierpes, heading north from the Plaza de San Francisco, and the

Seville Cathedral

WHAT TO LOOK FOR

'We're going to construct a church so large, future generations will think we were mad' declared the inspired architects of Seville in 1402 at the beginning of one of the most grandiose building projects in medieval history. Just over a century later their madness was triumphantly confirmed.

To avoid getting lost, orientate yourself by the main highlights. Directly inside the southern (main) entrance is the grand **mausoleum of Christopher Columbus 1** . Turn right here and head into the south-eastern corner to uncover some major art treasures: a Goya in the Sacristía de los Cálices, a Zurbarán in the **Sacristía Mayor 2** , and Murillo's shining Immaculada in the Sala Capitular. Skirt the cathedral's eastern wall taking a look inside the **Capilla Real 3** with its important royal tombs. By now it's impossible to avoid the lure of **Capilla Mayor 4** with its fantastical altarpiece. Hidden over in the northwest corner is the **Capilla de San Antonio 5** with a legendary Murillo. That huge doorway almost in front of you is rarely opened **Puerta de la Asunción 6** . Make for the **Giralda 7** next, stealing admiring looks at the high, vaulted ceiling on the way. After looking down on the cathedral's immense footprint, descend and depart via the **Patio de los Naranjos 8** .

TIPS BOX

» **Queue-dodge** Reserve tickets online at www.servicaixa.com for an extra €1 up to six weeks in advance

» **Pace yourself** Don't visit the Alcazar and Cathedral on the same day. There is far too much to take in

» **Viewpoints** Take time to admire the cathedral from the outside. It's particularly stunning at night from the Plaza Virgen de los Reyes, and from across the river in Triana

Capilla Mayor
Behold! The cathedral's main focal point contains its greatest treasure, a magnificent gold-plated altarpiece depicting various scenes in the life of Christ. It constitutes the life's work of one man, Flemish artist Pieter Dancart.

Patio de los Naranjos
Inhale the perfume of 60 Sevillan orange trees in a cool patio bordered by fortress-like walls – a surviving remnant of the original 12th-century mosque. Exit is gained via the horseshoe-shaped Puerta del Perdón.

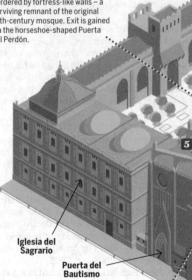

Puerta del Perdón

5

Iglesia del Sagrario

Puerta del Bautismo

Puerta de la Asunción
Located on the western side of the cathedral and also known as the Puerta Mayor, these huge, rarely opened doors are pushed back during Semana Santa to allow solemn processions of Catholic *hermanadades* (brotherhoods) to pass through.

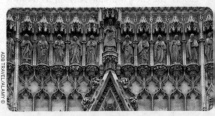

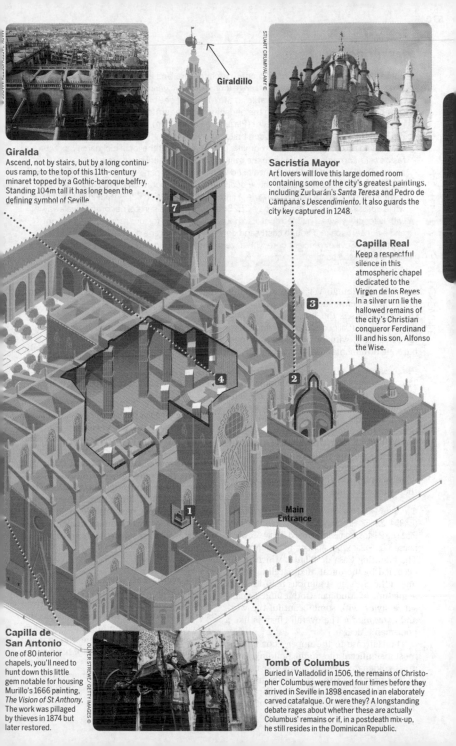

Giralda
Ascend, not by stairs, but by a long continuous ramp, to the top of this 11th-century minaret topped by a Gothic-baroque belfry. Standing 104m tall it has long been the defining symbol of Seville.

Giraldillo

Sacristía Mayor
Art lovers will love this large domed room containing some of the city's greatest paintings, including Zurbarán's *Santa Teresa* and Pedro de Campaña's *Descendimiento*. It also guards the city key captured in 1248.

Capilla Real
Keep a respectful silence in this atmospheric chapel dedicated to the Virgen de los Reyes. In a silver urn lie the hallowed remains of the city's Christian conqueror Ferdinand III and his son, Alfonso the Wise.

Main Entrance

Capilla de San Antonio
One of 80 interior chapels, you'll need to hunt down this little gem notable for housing Murillo's 1666 painting, *The Vision of St Anthony*. The work was pillaged by thieves in 1874 but later restored.

Tomb of Columbus
Buried in Valladolid in 1506, the remains of Christopher Columbus were moved four times before they arrived in Seville in 1898 encased in an elaborately carved catafalque. Or were they? A longstanding debate rages about whether these are actually Columbus' remains or if, in a postdeath mix-up, he still resides in the Dominican Republic.

DON'T MISS

METROPOL PARASOL

Some call him the Ferran Adrià of modern architecture, and it's true, German architect Jurgen Mayer H possesses a strange kind of artistic genius. Who else would have dreamt of constructing a 'flying waffle' in the middle of one of Seville's most traditional shopping squares? Smarting with the audacity of a modern-day Eiffel Tower, the opinion-dividing **Metropol Parasol** (Plaza de la Encarnación), which opened in March 2011, claims to be the largest wooden building in the world. Its undulating honeycombed roof is held up by five giant mushroomlike pillars, earning it the local nickname *Las Setas de la Encarnación*. Six years in the making, the construction covers a former dead zone in Seville's central district once filled with an ugly car park. Roman ruins discovered during the building's conception have been cleverly incorporated into the foundations in the **Museo Antiquarium** (Plaza de la Encarnación; admission €2; ⊙11am-2pm & 3-8pm) while upstairs on level 2 you can pay €1.20 to stroll along a surreal panoramic walkway with killer city views. The Metropol also houses the plaza's former market, a restaurant and a concert space. Though costly and controversial, Mayer's daring creation has slotted into Seville's ancient core with a weird kind of harmony turning (and tilting) the heads of all who pass.

parallel Calle Tetuán/Velázquez are the hub of Seville's fanciest shopping zone. Between the two streets is the 18th-century **Capilla de San José** (Calle Jovellanos; ⊙8am-12.30pm & 6.30-8.30pm), with breathtakingly intense baroque ornamentation.

Plaza Salvador   SQUARE

This plaza, which has a few popular bars, was once the forum of Roman Hispalis. It's dominated by the **Parroquia del Divino Salvador**, a big baroque church built between 1674 and 1712 on the site of Muslim Ishbiliya's main mosque. The interior reveals a fantastic richness of carving and gilding. At sunset, colour from stained-glass windows plays on the carvings to enhance their surreal beauty.

Casa de Pilatos   PALACE, MUSEUM

(☑954 22 52 98; www.fundacionmedinaceli.org; Plaza de Pilatos; admission ground fl only €5, whole house €8; ⊙9am-7pm Apr-Oct, to 6pm Nov-Mar) The haunting Casa de Pilatos, which is still occupied by the ducal Medinaceli family, is one of the city's most glorious mansions. It's a mixture of Mudéjar, Gothic and Renaissance styles, with some beautiful tile work and *artesonado*. The overall effect is like a poor-man's Alcázar.

The staircase to the upper floor has the most magnificent tiles in the building, and a great golden *artesonado* dome above. Visits to the upper floor itself, still partly inhabited by the Medinacelis, are guided. Of interest are the several centuries' worth of Medi-

naceli portraits and a small Goya bullfighting painting.

EL ARENAL

A short walk west from Avenida de la Constitución brings you to the bank of the Río Guadalquivir, lined by a pleasant footpath. The nearby district of El Arenal is home to some of Seville's most interesting sights.

Torre del Oro   MUSEUM

(Paseo de Cristóbal Colón; admission €2; ⊙10am-1.30pm Tue-Sun) This 13th-century Almohad watchtower by the river supposedly had a dome covered in golden tiles, hence its name, 'Tower of Gold'. It was also once used to store the booty siphoned off the colonial coffers by the returning conquistadors from Mexico and Peru. Since then, it has become one of the most recognisable architectural symbols of Seville. Inside is a small maritime museum spead over two floors and a rooftop viewing platform.

Hospital de la Caridad   GALLERY

(Calle Temprado 3; admission €5; ⊙9.30am-1pm & 3.30-7pm Mon-Sat, 9am-12.30pm Sun) The Hospital de la Caridad, a block east of the river, is an art gallery that was once a hospice for the elderly founded by Miguel de Mañara, by legend a notorious libertine who changed his ways after seeing a vision of his own funeral procession.

Inside you'll find some marvellous examples of *sevillano* art of the Siglo de Oro (Golden Age).

Plaza de Toros de la Real Maestranza
DULLRING, MUSEUM

(☎954 22 45 77; www.realmaestranza.es; Paseo de Cristóbal Colón 12; tours adult/child €6.50/2.50; ☺half-hourly 9.30am-8pm, to 3pm bullfight days) In the world of bullfighting, Seville's bullring is the Old Trafford and Camp Nou. In other words, if you're selected to fight here then you've made it. In addition to being regarded as a building of almost religious significance to fans, it's also the oldest ring in Spain (building began in 1758). Slightly robotic guided visits, in English and Spanish, take you into the ring and its museum.

Museo de Bellas Artes
GALLERY

(Fine Arts Museum; Plaza del Museo 9; admission €1.50; ☺9am-8.30pm Tue-Sat, to 2.30pm Sun & holidays; ☎) Housed in the beautiful former Convento de la Merced, Seville's Museo de Bellas Artes does full justice to Seville's leading role in Spain's 17th-century artistic Siglo de Oro. Much of the work here is of the dark, brooding religious type.

The most visually startling room is that of the convent church, which is hung with paintings by masters of *sevillano* baroque, above all Murillo and his rendering of the *Inmaculada Concepción*.

SOUTH OF THE CENTRE
South of Santa Cruz and El Centro, the city opens out into expansive parks and broad streets recently reclaimed by trams, bikes and strollers.

FREE **Antigua Fábrica de Tabacos**
UNIVERSITY

(Calle San Fernando; ☺8am-9.30pm Mon-Fri, to 2pm Sat) Seville's massive former tobacco factory – workplace of Bizet's passionate operatic heroine, Carmen – was built in the 18th century and is the second-largest building in Spain after El Escorial. It's now the university and is wheelchair-accessible.

Hotel Alfonso XIII
LANDMARK

(Calle San Fernando 2) As much a monument as an accommodation option, and certainly more affordable if you come for a cup of coffee as opposed to a room, this striking hotel – conceived as the most luxurious in Europe when it was built in 1928 – was constructed in tandem with the Plaza de España for the 1929 world fair.

The style is classic neo-Mudéjar with glazed tiles and terracotta bricks.

Parque de María Luisa & Plaza de España
PARK

(☺8am-10pm) A large area south of the former tobacco factory was transformed for Seville's 1929 international fair, the Exposición Iberoamericana, when architects adorned it with fantastical buildings, many of them harking back to Seville's past glory or imitating the native styles of Spain's former colonies. In its midst you'll find the large Parque de María Luisa, a living expression of Seville's Moorish and Christian past. Entrance to the park is from the corner of Avenida del Cid and Avenida de Portugal on the southeastern corner of the university (former tobacco factory), about 800m southeast from the cathedral.

Plaza de España, one of the city's favourite relaxation spots, faces the park across Avenida de Isabel la Católica. Around it is the most grandiose of the 1929 buildings, a semicircular brick-and-tile confection featuring Seville tile work at its gaudiest.

On Plaza de América, at the southern end of the park, is Seville's Museo Arqueológico (adult/child €1.50/free; ☺9am-8.30pm Tue-Sat, to 2.30pm Sun & holidays), with plenty to interest. Facing it is the Museo de Artes y Costumbres Populares (☎954 23 25 76; admission €1.50; ☺9am-8.30pm Tue-Sat, to 2.30pm Sun & holidays). Both are wheelchair accessible.

NORTH OF THE CENTRE
Most head north after dark for the nightlife in the Alameda de Hércules, but in the daytime it's worth bringing the kids.

Isla Mágica
AMUSEMENT PARK

(☎902 161 716; www.islamagica.es; adult/child €29/20; ☺high season around 11am-10pm, closed Dec-Mar; ☎) This Disney-goes-Spanish-colonial amusement park provides a great if expensive day out for kids and all lovers of white-knuckle rides. Confirm times before going; hours vary by season. Both buses C1 and C2 run to Isla Mágica.

El Pabellon de la Navegación
MUSEUM

(www.pabellondelanavegacion.es; Camino de los Descubrimientos 2; adult/child €4.90/3.50; ☺to 3pm Sun; ☎) Seville's 'other' futuristic new building may have been overshadowed by its precocious cousin, the Metropol Parasol, but its ultramodern museum and exhibition space, which opened in January 2012, is equally thought-provoking. The architecturally impressive pavilion, which has revived a previous navigation museum that lasted from the 1992 Expo until 1999, resides on the banks

SEVILLE FOR CHILDREN

Many of Seville's adult attractions will appeal to kids on a different level, including the cathedral and the Alcázar, the latter of which has a dedicated booklet for kids, available in most newsagents. The city abounds in open spaces and parks (often with special kids' sections); head for the banks of the Guadalquivir, Parque de María Luisa (⊗8am-10pm Sep-Jun, to midnight Jul & Aug;) and the Jardines de Murillo. Ice-cream and *churros* (long, deep-fried doughnuts) cafes are also ubiquitous. If the tapas get too sophisticated, try a good Italian restaurant. There are many around the Plaza de Alfalfa. Isla Mágica (p671) is specifically targeted at kids, particularly those aged 10 or above. Tours by boat, open-top double-decker bus or horse-drawn carriage also prove popular with kids.

of the Guadalaquivir river on the Isla de la Cartuja. Its permanent collection is split into four parts – navigation, mariners, shipboard life and historical views of Seville – and many exhibits are interactive and kid-friendly.

🎓 Courses

Seville has many dance and flamenco schools; tourist offices and *El Giraldillo* (www.elegirhoy.com) have the details. It is also one of the most popular cities in Spain to study Spanish. The best schools offer both short- and long-term courses at all levels.

Fundación Cristina Heeren de Arte Flamenco FLAMENCO
(☎954 21 70 58; www.flamencoheeren.com; Avenida de Jerez 2) This is by far the best-known school and offers long-term courses in all flamenco arts; it also offers one-month intensive summer courses.

Giralda Center LANGUAGE COURSE
(☎954 22 13 46, 954 21 31 65; www.giraldacenter.com; Calle Mateos Gago 17) Has a friendly atmosphere, plenty of excursions and a reputation for good teaching.

Linc LANGUAGE COURSE
(☎954 50 04 59; www.linc.es; Calle General Polavieja 13) A small, popular school, which is good on cultural activities and excursions.

CLIC LANGUAGE COURSE
(☎954 50 21 31; www.clic.es; Calle Albareda 19) A well-established language centre with a good social scene; courses in business Spanish and Hispanic studies available.

👉 Tours

Horse-drawn carriages wait near the cathedral, Plaza de España and Puerta de Jerez, charging a hefty €50 for up to four people for a one-hour trot around the Barrio de Santa Cruz and Parque de María Luisa areas.

Sevilla Tour BUS TOUR
(☎902 101081; www.sevillatour.com; adult €17, child €7; ⊗7am-8pm) One-hour city tours in open-topped double-decker buses and converted trams with earphone commentary in a choice of languages. The ticket is valid for 48 hours and you can hop on or off along Paseo de Cristóbal Colón (near the Torre del Oro), Avenida de Portugal behind Plaza de España, or the Isla de la Cartuja. Buses typically leave every 30 minutes from 7am to 8pm.

Cruceros Turísticos Torre del Oro BOAT TOUR
(☎954 561692; www.crucerostorredeloro.com; adult/child under 14yr €16/free) One-hour sightseeing river cruises every half-hour from 11am from the river bank by the Torre del Oro. Last departure can range from 6pm in winter to 10pm in summer.

Sevilla Walking Tours WALKING TOUR
(☎902 158226; www.sevillawalkingtours.com; per person €12) Walk around the city like a *sevillano* in the know.

🎉 Festivals & Events

Seville's Semana Santa processions and its Feria de Abril, a week or two later, are worth travelling a long way for, as is the Bienal de Flamenco.

Semana Santa HOLY WEEK
(www.semana-santa.org) Every day from Palm Sunday to Easter Sunday, large, life-sized *pasos* (sculptural representations of events from Christ's Passion) are carried from Seville's churches through the streets to the cathedral, accompanied by processions that may take more than an hour to pass. The processions are organised by over 50 different *hermandades* or *cofradías* (brotherhoods, some of which include women).

The climax of the week is the *madrugada* (early hours) of Good Friday, when some of the most-respected brotherhoods file through the city. The costume worn by the marching penitents consists of a full robe and a conical hat with slits cut for the eyes. The regalia was incongruously copied by America's Ku Klux Klan.

Procession schedules are widely available during Semana Santa, or see the Semana Santa website. Arrive near the cathedral in the early evening for a better view.

Feria de Abril
SPRING FAIR

The April Fair, held in the second half of the month (sometimes edging into May), is the jolly counterpart to the sombre Semana Santa. The biggest and most colourful of all Andalucía's ferias is less invasive (and also less inclusive) than the Easter celebration – it takes place on El Real de la Feria, in the Los Remedios area west of the Guadalquivir.

The ceremonial lighting-up of the fair grounds on the opening Monday night is the starting gun for six nights of *sevillanos'* favourite activities: eating, drinking, dressing up and dancing till dawn.

Bienal de Flamenco
FLAMENCO

(www.bienal-flamenco.org) Most of the big names of the flamenco world participate in this major flamenco festival. Held in the September of even-numbered years.

🛏 Sleeping

There's a good range of places to stay in all three of the most attractive areas – Barrio de Santa Cruz (close to the Alcázar and within walking distance of Prado de San Sebastián bus station), El Arenal (convenient for Plaza de Armas bus station) and El Centro.

Room rates are for each establishment's high season – typically from March to June and again in September and October. During Semana Santa and the Feria de Abril rates are invariably doubled and sell out completely. Book ahead at this time.

Renting a tourist apartment here can be good value: typically costing under €100 a night for four people, or between €30 and €70 for two. Try **Apartamentos Embrujo de Sevilla** (📞627 569919; www.embrujodesevilla.com), which specialises in historic townmansion apartments, or **Sevilla5.com** (📞637 011091, 954 22 62 87; www.sevilla5.com).

BARRIO DE SANTA CRUZ

This old Jewish labyrinth is stuffed with majestic mansions, hidden patios and some very atmospheric accommodation.

🔝 CHOICE Hotel Casa 1800
LUXURY HOTEL €€€

(📞954 56 18 00; www.hotelcasa1800sevilla.com; Calle Rodrigo Caro 6; d €145-198; ✳@🛜) Straight in at number one as Seville's favourite hotel is this newly revived Santa Cruz jewel where the word *'casa'* (house) is taken seriously. This really is your home away from home (albeit a posh one!), with charming staff catering for your every need. Historic highlights include a sweet afternoon tea buffet, plus a quartet of penthouse garden suites with Giralda views.

It's also one of the only places in the city that doesn't hike up its Semana Santa rates to ridiculous levels.

Un Patio en Santa Cruz
HOTEL €€

(📞954 53 94 13; www.patiosantacruz.com; Calle Doncellas 15; s €65-85, d €65-125; ✳🛜📶) Feeling more like an art gallery than a hotel, the Patio has starched-white walls coated in loud works of art, and strange sculptures and preserved plants. The rooms are immensely comfortable, staff are friendly and there's a cool rooftop terrace with mosaic Moroccan tables. It's easily one of the hippest and bestvalue hotels in town.

Hotel Amadeus
HOTEL €€

(📞954 50 14 43; www.hotelamadeussevilla.com; Calle Farnesio 6; s/d €85/95; P✳🛜) Just when you thought you could never find hotels with pianos in the rooms anymore, along came Hotel Amadeus run by an engaging musical family in the old *judería,* where several of the astutely decorated rooms come complete with soundproofed walls and upright pianos, ensuring you don't miss out on your daily practice.

Other perks include in-room classical CDs, wall-mounted violins, and a rooftop terrace with a jacuzzi. Composers and Mozart lovers, look no further.

Hotel Puerta de Sevilla
HOTEL €€

(📞954 98 72 70; www.hotelpuertadesevilla.com; Calle Puerta de la Carne 2; s/d €66/86; P✳🛜) This superfriendly – and superpositioned – hotel is a great mix of chintz and stylish. There's an indoor water feature in the lobby which is lined with superb Seville tile work. The rooms are all flower-pattern textiles, wrought-iron beds and pastel wallpaper.

Hotel Alcántara
HOTEL €€

(📞954 50 05 95; www.hotelalcantara.net; Calle Ximénez de Enciso 28; s/d €68/89; ✳🛜; 🚌1, C3, C4, 21, 23) This small, friendly hotel on a pedestrian street punches above its weight with sparkling modern bathrooms, windows on to the hotel's patio, and pretty floral curtains. It's next door to the Casa de la Memoria Al-Andalus.

Pensión San Pancracio
PENSIÓN €

(☎954 41 31 04; Plaza de las Cruces 9; d €50, s/d without bathroom €25/35) An ideal budget option in Santa Cruz, this old rambling family house has plenty of different room options (all cheap) and a pleasant flower-bedizened patio/lobby. Friendliness makes up for the lack of luxury.

Pensión Córdoba
GUESTHOUSE €€

(☎954 22 74 98; www.pensioncordoba.com; Calle Farnesio 12; s/d €55/75, without bathroom €45/65; ✲) Run by a friendly old couple for the past 30 years, this place is located on a quiet pedestrian street. Rooms are basic but spotless.

Hotel Goya
HOTEL €€

(☎954 21 11 70; www.hotelgoyasevilla.com; Calle Mateos Gago 31; s €39-60, d €65-95; ✲@☎) The gleaming Goya, close to the cathedral, is a popular draw and accepts pets. It's clean, and good value considering its location.

EL ARENAL
A central location and a good mix of accommodation make this river-side neighbourhood worth contemplating as a base.

Hotel Simón
HOTEL €€

(☎954 22 66 60; www.hotelsimonsevilla.com; Calle García de Vinuesa 19; s €60-70, d €95-110; ✲@) A typically grand 18th-century Sevillan house, with an ornate patio and spotless and comfortable rooms, this place gleams way above its two-star rating. Some of the rooms are embellished with rich *azulejos* (tiles).

EL CENTRO
Handily situated for everywhere, El Centro mixes hotel glitter with some real bargains.

EME Catedral Hotel
LUXURY HOTEL €€€

(☎954 56 00 00; www.emecatedralhotel.com; Calle de los Alemanes 27; d €187-348; ✲@☎✉) Take 14 fine old Sevillan houses and knock them into one. Bring in a top designer and Spain's most decorated chef. Carve out a hamman, rooftop pool, four restaurants and slick, striking rooms with red colour accents. Then stick it all nose-to-nose with the largest Gothic cathedral in the world.

The result: EME Catedral Hotel, the city's most talked about new accommodation where ancient Seville has been fused with something a bit more cutting edge. Does it work? Cough up the €200-plus a night and find out.

Oasis Backpackers' Hostel
HOSTEL €

(☎954 29 37 77; www.oasissevilla.com; Plaza de la Encarnación 29; dm/d incl breakfast €15/50; ✲@☎✉) Seville's offbeat, buzzing backpacker central offers 24-hour free internet access. The new location is in Plaza Encarnación, a narrow street behind the Church of the Anunciación. Each dorm bed has a personal safe, and there is a small rooftop pool. There's no curfew; this is Spain!

Hotel San Francisco
HOTEL €€

(☎954 50 15 41; www.sanfranciscoh.com; Calle Álvarez Quintero 38; s/d €55/68; ✲☎) A well-positioned place on a pedestrianised street, the San Francisco is definitely one-star territory, with variable service, dark but clean rooms and wi-fi in the reception only. The hotel is closed in August.

B&B Naranjo
HOSTEL €

(☎954 22 58 40; Calle San Roque 11; s/d €45/65; @☎) Homely pine furniture and restful colours add a touch of warmth at this Centro nook.

NORTH OF THE CENTRE
As this area is a little peripheral to the main sights, you'll need to find a real corker to stay here.

Hotel San Gil
HOTEL €€

(☎954 90 68 11; www.hotelsangil.com; Calle Parras 28; r from €88; ✲☎✉) Shoehorned at the northern end of the Macarena neighbourhood, San Gil's slightly out-of-the-way location is balanced by its proximity to the nightlife of the Alameda de Hercules. A tiled lobby fronts more modern rooms that have large beds and ample space.

Hostal Doña Feli
PENSIÓN €

(☎954 90 10 48; www.hostaldonafeli.com; Calle Jesús del Gran Poder 130; s/d €35/45; ✲) If you're looking for somewhere smart and with real Spanish character close to the nightlife of the Alameda, you can't do much better than this spotless, well-run *hostal* (budget hotel) with rooms piled around a plant-crammed courtyard. Some rooms have baths plus showers.

✖ Eating

In the competition to produce Andalucía's most inventive tapas, Seville wins – hands down. Most tapas bars open at lunchtime as well as in the evening.

For a sit-down meal, restaurants preparing Spanish food open late: ie at 9pm, or nearer 10pm in summer. But with a surfeit of tourists, Seville has plenty of options for earlier dining.

BARRIO DE SANTA CRUZ

Good tapas bars are everywhere in this compact quarter. Wander the narrow streets and allow the atmosphere to draw you in.

TOP CHOICE / **Vinería San Telmo** TAPAS, FUSION €€
(954 41 06 00; www.vineriasantelmo.com; Paseo Catalina de Ribera 4; tapas €3.50, media raciones €10) San Telmo invented the *rascocielo* (skyscraper) tapa, an 'Empire State' of tomatoes, aubergine, goat's cheese and smoked salmon. If this and other creative nougats such as foie gras with quails' eggs and lychees, or exquisitely cooked bricks of tuna, don't make you drool with expectation, then you're probably dead.

Catalina TAPAS €€
(Paseo Catalina de Ribera 4; raciones €10) If your view of tapas is 'glorified bar snacks', your ideas could be blown out of the water here with a creative mix of just about every ingredient known to Iberian cooking. Start with the cheese, aubergine and paprika special. The equally wonderful Vinería San Telmo is next door. Tough choice! Toss a coin.

Bodega Santa Cruz TAPAS €
(Calle Mateos Gago; tapas €2) Forever crowded and with a mountain of paper on the floor, this place is usually standing room only, with tapas and drinks enjoyed alfresco as you dodge the marching army of tourists squeezing through Santa Cruz's narrow streets.

Extraverde TAPAS €
(www.extraverde.es; Plaza de Doña Elvira 8; tapas €2.50-4; 10.30am-11.30pm) Recent to the Santa Cruz scene, Extraverde is a unique bar-shop specialising in Andalucian products such as olive oil, cheese and wine. You can taste free samples standing up, or sit down inside and order full tapas.

Restaurante Egaña Oriza CONTEMPORARY SPANISH €€€
(www.restauranteoriza.com; Calle San Fernando 41; mains €22-32; closed Sat lunch & Sun) Say Basque and you've got a byword for fine-dining these days, so it's not surprising that Basque-run Egaña Oriza is regarded as one of the city's stand-out restaurants. Situated opposite the bus station, this could be your first (and best) culinary treat in Seville.

There's an equally posh tapas spot on the ground floor.

Café Bar Las Teresas TAPAS €
(Calle Santa Teresa 2; tapas €3) The hanging hams look as ancient as the bar itself, a sinuous wrap-around affair with just enough room for two stout waiters to pass carrying precariously balanced tapas plates. The atmosphere is dark but not dingy, the food highly traditional, and the crowd an integrated mix of tourists and Santa Cruz locals.

Cervecería Giralda TAPAS €
(954 22 82 50; Calle Mateos Gago 1; tapas €3.50-5) Exotic tapas variations are merged with traditional dishes in this one-time Muslim bathhouse.

EL ARENAL

Surprisingly lively at night, El Arenal has some good tapas places where most people seem to congregate in the street.

Mesón Cinco Jotas TAPAS €€
(www.mesoncincojotas.com; Calle Castelar 1; tapas €3.80, media raciones €10) In the world of *jamón*-making, if you are awarded 'Cinco Jotas' (Five Js) for your *jamón* (cured ham), it's like getting an Oscar. The owner of this place, Sánchez Romero Carvajal, is the biggest producer of Jabugo ham, and has a great selection on offer.

Enrique Becerra ANDALUCIAN €€€
(954 21 30 49; www.enriquebecerra.com; Calle Gamazo 2; mains €17-25; closed Sat & Sun) Squeeze in with the locals at lunchtime and enjoy some hearty Andalusian dishes. The lamb drenched in honey sauce and stuffed with spinach and pine nuts (€22) is just one of many delectable offerings, but be warned that it charges €2.50 for bread and olives!

EL CENTRO

Plaza de la Alfalfa wears many hats. It is the hub of the tapas scene in the day, a stopping-off point for boisterous families in the early evening, and a fount of late-night bars and clubs after darkness falls. There are a couple of decent Italian restaurants on or around the square if you need a break from the usual Spanish suspects.

Los Coloniales CONTEMPORARY ANDALUCIAN €€
(www.tabernacoloniales.es; cnr Calle Dormitorio & Plaza Cristo de Burgos; tapas €2.50, raciones €10-12) The quiet ones are always the best. It might not look like much from the outside but, take it on trust; Los Coloniales is something very

special. The quality plates line up like models on a catwalk: *chorizo a la Asturiana* (a divine spicy sausage in an onion sauce served on a bed of lightly fried potato, aubergines in honey), and pork tenderloin *al whisky*.

Robles Laredo CONTEMPORARY SPANISH €€
(www.casa-robles.com; Plaza de San Francisco; raciones €9-12) This small Italianite cafe-restaurant is fairly dwarfed by its two huge chandeliers and a vast collection of delicate desserts displayed in glass cases. The tapas are equally refined. Try the foie gras, beef-burgers with truffle sauce, or oysters and whitebait.

Bar Alfalfa TAPAS €
(cnr Calles Alfalfa & Candilejo; tapas €3) It's amazing how many people, hams, wine bottles and other knick-knacks you can stuff into such a small space. No matter: order through the window when the going gets crowded. You won't forget the tomato-tinged magnificence of the Italy-meets-Iberia *salmorejo* (thick gazpacho) bruschetta.

Horno de San Buenaventura CAFE €
(www.hornosanbuenaventura.com; Avenida de la Constitución; pastries from €1; ⊙9am-9pm) There are actually two of these gilded pastry/coffee/snack bars in Seville, one here in Avenida de la Constitución opposite the cathedral and the other (inferior one) in the Plaza de Alfalfa. All kinds of fare are on show, though it's probably best enjoyed for its lazy continental breakfasts (yes, the service can be slow) or a spontaneous late night cake fix.

ALAMEDA DE HÉRCULES
Seville's trendiest nightlife quarter also has some decent eating places overlooking the main pedestrianised park.

Bar-Restaurante Eslava TAPAS, ANDALUCIAN €€
(www.espacioeslava.com; Calle Eslava 3; tapas €4, media raciones €9-13) A legend in its own dinnertime, Eslava shirks the traditional tile-work and bullfighting posters of tapa-bar lore and delivers where it matters; fine food backed up with equally fine service.

There's a 'nouvelle' tinge to the memorable *costillas a la miel* (pork ribs in a honey and rosemary glaze) and vegetable strudel in a cheese sauce, but there's nothing snobby about the atmosphere which is local and pretty fanatical after 9pm. The restaurant overlooks the Plaza de San Lorenzo just off the southwestern corner of the Alameda de Hércules.

Duo Tapas TAPAS, FUSION €€
(Calle Calatrava 10; tapas €3-4.50, media raciones €9-12) Missed by the masses who rarely wander north from the Alameda de Hércules, Duo Tapas is 'new school'. But, what it lacks in *azulejos* and illustrious past patrons, it makes up for in inventive tapas with an Asian twist. Alameda trendies swear by its green chicken with rice and spicy noodles.

TRIANA
The riverside restaurants along riverfront Calle del Betis are at their best around 11pm. Sit outside and enjoy fried seafood with the Torre del Oro reflecting on the river.

Ristorante Cosa Nostra ITALIAN €€
(☑954 27 07 52; Calle del Betis 52; pizzas €8.50-12; ⊙closed Mon; ⑅) Forget the Mafiosi nameplate; this is the best Italian food in Seville and well worth crossing the river for. The pizzas are spun in front of your eyes and the rich creamy risottos ought to have every paella chef in the city looking over their shoulder.

Café de la Prensa SEAFOOD €
(Calle del Betis 8; tapas €3) Tapas were surely invented to be enjoyed next to the river on Triana's ebullient Calle del Betis with the Giralda beckoning in the background. It would be heresy to try anything but the fish here, preferably dipped in chick-pea flour and fried briefly in olive oil.

🍸 Drinking

Bars usually open 6pm to 2am weekdays and 8pm to 3am at the weekend. Drinking and partying really get going around midnight on Friday and Saturday (daily when it's hot). In summer, dozens of open-air late-night bars (*terrazas de verano*) spring up along both banks of the river. Ideal bar-hopping neighbourhoods include the Barrio de Santa Cruz and the web of streets around Plaza de Alfalfa. The Alameda de Hércules is the centre of gay Seville.

⌖TOP CHOICE Baños Árabes Tetería TEAHOUSE
(Calle Aire 15) Seville is no Granada when it comes to exotically infused teahouses, though exceptions should be made for this cushioned comfort zone encased in the pin-dropping tranquillity of the Baños Árabes (p667) in Santa Cruz. With no on-site shisha pipes or yodelling singers, the atmosphere is generated by the edgy art and murmuring intellectuals discussing Almodóvar movies.

El Garlochi
BAR

(Calle Boteros 4) Dedicated entirely to the iconography, smells and sounds of Semana Santa, the ubercamp El Garlochi is a true marvel. A cloud of church incense hits you as you go up the stairs, and the faces of baby Jesus and the Virgin welcome you into the velvet-walled bar, decked out with more Virgins and Jesuses.

La Rebótica
BAR

(Calle Pérez Galdós 11) Two's a crowd in the cramped, sinuous Rebótica, the place to come for cheap shots and 1980s flashbacks accompanied by an appropriately retro soundtrack.

Bulebar Café
BAR, CAFE

(☑954 90 19 54; Alameda de Hércules 83; ⊙4pm-late) This place gets pretty *caliente* (hot) at night, but is pleasantly chilled in the early evening, with friendly staff. Don't write off its spirit-reviving alfresco breakfasts that pitch early-birds with up-all-nighters. The cafe is on the eastern side of the Alameda de Hércules.

Cabo Loco
BAR

(Calle Pérez Galdós 26) Dive bar, hole-in-the-wall, cheap shot heaven, call it what you like. Cabo Loco is heaven for those who don't mind standing room only – alfresco.

☆ Entertainment

Seville is reborn after dark, with live music, experimental theatre and exciting flamenco.

Boss
CLUB

(www.salaboss.es; Calle del Betis 67; admission from €12; ⊙8pm-7am Tue-Sun) Make it past the two gruff bouncers and you'll find Boss a top dance spot, and relatively posh for Triana. The music is highly varied.

La Imperdible
THEATRE

(☑954 38 82 19; www.imperdible.org; Plaza del Duque de la Victoria; adult/child €12/5) This epicentre of experimental arts stages lots of contemporary dance, theatre and flamenco, usually around 9pm. The bar here also hosts varied music events from around 11pm Thursday to Saturday.

Naima Café Jazz
BLUES, JAZZ

(☑954 38 24 85; Calle Trajano 47; ⊙live performances from 11pm) If you're getting tired of flamenco, then you can find respite at this intimate place, which sways to the sound of mellow jazz (live at weekends).

Flamenco

Soleares, flamenco's truest *cante jondo* (deep song; an anguished instrument of expression for a group on the margins of society) was first concocted in Triana; head here to find some of the more authentic clubs. Elsewhere, the city puts on nightly *tablaos* (flamenco shows) at about half a dozen different venues.

TOP CHOICE Casa de la Memoria de Al-Andalus
FLAMENCO

(☑954 56 06 70; www.casadelamemoria.es; Calle Ximénez de Enciso 28; tickets €15; ⊙9pm) This *tablao* in Santa Cruz is without doubt the most intimate and authentic nightly flamenco show outside the Museo del Baile Flamenco, offering a wide variety of *palos* (flamenco styles) in a courtyard of shifting shadows and overhanging plants. Space is limited to 100, so reserve tickets a day or so in advance.

FREE La Carbonería
FLAMENCO

(Calle Levíes 18; admission free; ⊙8pm-4am) During the day there is no indication that this happening place is anything but a large garage. But, come after 8pm and this converted coal yard in the Barrio de Santa Cruz reveals two large bars, and nightly live flamenco (11pm and midnight) for no extra charge.

Casa Anselma
FLAMENCO

(Calle Pagés del Corro 49; ⊙midnight-late Mon-Sat) If you can squeeze in past the foreboding form of Anselma (a celebrated Triana flamenco dancer) at the door you'll quickly realise that anything can happen in here. Casa Anselma (beware: there's no sign, just a doorway embellished with *azulejos*) is the antithesis of a tourist *tablao,* with cheek-to-jowl crowds, thick cigarette smoke, zero amplification and spontaneous outbreaks of dexterous dancing. Pure magic.

Anselma is in Triana on the corner of Calle Alfarería, about 200m from the western side of the Puente de Isabel.

🛍 Shopping

The craft shops in the Barrio de Santa Cruz are inevitably tourist oriented, but many sell attractive ceramic tiles and poster art.

Shoe fetishists beware: Seville has possibly the densest quota of shoe shops on the planet, primarily focused in El Centro around the pedestrianised shopping streets of Calles Sierpes, de la Cuna, Velázquez and

Tetuán. Head to Calle Feria, located a couple of blocks to the north of Plaza de la Encarnación, to look for your handmade flamenco guitar. El Corte Inglés (Plaza del Duque de la Victoria 8; ⊙10am-10pm Mon-Sat) department store occupies four separate buildings a little west, on Plaza de la Magdalena and Plaza del Duque de la Victoria. Further north, Calle Amor de Dios and Calle Doctor Letamendi have more alternative shops. In the traditional tile-making area of Triana, a dozen shops and workshops still offer charming, artistic ceramics around the junction of Calles Alfarería and Antillano Campos.

Casa del Libro BOOKS
(www.casadellibro.com; Calle Velázquez 8) Part of Spain's oldest bookshop chain, this branch is spread over four floors and stocks plenty of multilingual fiction and guidebooks (including this one).

Information

Emergency
Ambulance (⌨061)
Emergency (⌨112)
Policía Local (⌨092)
Policía Nacional (⌨091)

Medical Services
Centro de Salud El Porvenir (⌨954 71 23 23; cnr Avenidas Menéndez y Pelayo & de Cádiz) Public clinic with emergency services.
Hospital Virgen del Rocío (⌨955 01 20 00; Avenida de Manuel Siurot) The main general hospital, 1km south of Parque de María Luisa.

Money
There's no shortage of banks and ATMs in the central area. Santa Justa train station, the airport and both bus stations have ATMs.

Post
Post office (Avenida de la Constitución 32)

Tourist Information
There are regional tourist offices at **Avenida de la Constitución 21** (Avenida de la Constitución 21; ⊙9am-7pm Mon-Fri, 10am-2pm & 3-7pm Sat, 10am-2pm Sun, closed holidays) and **Estación Santa Justa** (⌨954 53 76 26; Estación Santa Justa; ⊙9am-8pm Mon-Fri, 10am-2pm Sat & Sun, closed holidays).
Turismo Sevilla (www.turismosevilla.org; Plaza del Triunfo 1; ⊙10.30am-7pm Mon-Fri) Information on all Sevilla province.

Websites
Discover Sevilla (www.discoversevilla.com) An excellent, comprehensive site.

Explore Seville (www.exploreseville.com) A good, informative site.
Seville Tourism (www.turismo.sevilla.org) The city's official tourism site; its 'Accessible Guide' is especially useful for travellers with a disability.

Getting There & Away

Air
Seville's Aeropuerto San Pablo has a fair range of international and domestic flights. **Iberia** (www.iberia.com) flies direct to Barcelona, Madrid and half a dozen other Spanish cities, as well as to London and Paris. **Spanair** (www.spanair.com) also flies to Madrid and, along with Air Europa (p866) and Vueling (p866), to Barcelona. Vueling also covers Paris, and Amsterdam to Seville.

From the British Isles there are flights with **Easyjet** (www.easyjet.com) from London-Gatwick, and **Ryanair** (www.ryanair.com) from London-Gatwick and London-Stansted. Ryanair also flies to Barcelona, Brussels, Rome and various Italian destinations and, more recently, Marrakech. **Transavia** (www.transavia.com) comes from Paris and **Air Europa** (www.aireuropa.com) handles the Canary Islands. Carrier and schedule information changes frequently, so it's best to check with specific airlines or major online bookers.

Bus
Seville has two bus stations. Buses to/from the north of Sevilla province, Huelva province, Portugal, and most other parts of Spain, including Madrid, use the main **Estación de Autobuses Plaza de Armas** (Avenida del Cristo de la Expiración). This is also the main station for **Eurolines** (www.eurolines.es) and international services to Germany, Belgium, France and beyond. Other buses – primarily those running inside Andalucia (except Huelva) – use the **Estación de Autobuses Prado de San Sebastián** (Plaza San Sebastián). Buses from here run roughly hourly to Cádiz, Córdoba, Granada, Jerez de la Frontera, Málaga and Madrid.

Train
Seville's **Estación Santa Justa** (⌨902 432343; Avenida Kansas City) is 1.5km northeast of the centre. Trains go to/from Madrid (€83.30, 2½ hours, 20 daily), Cádiz (€13.25, 1 hour and 45 minutes, 15 daily), Córdoba (€33.20, 42 minutes, 30 daily), Huelva (€10.05, 1½ hours, three daily), Granada (€24.80, three hours, four daily) and Málaga (€38.70, two hours, 11 daily).

Getting Around

To/From the Airport
The airport is 7km east of the city centre on the A4 Córdoba road. **Los Amarillos** (www.losamarillos.es) runs buses between the airport and Avenida del Cid near the San Sebastián bus station (€2.40, every 15 minutes,

CYCLING SEVILLE

Offsetting decades of driving chaos, the inauguration of Seville's Sevici (☏902 01 10 32; www.sevici.es; ☉7am-9pm) bike-sharing scheme in April 2007 was something of a godsend, even for avowed car-users. Sevici was the second bike-sharing initiative in Spain (there are now nine), opening a couple of weeks after Barcelona's *Bicing* program. Despite subsequent copyists – Paris' Vélib was launched in June 2007 – it remains the fifth largest scheme of its kind in Europe with 2500 bikes. Grab a two-wheeled machine from any one of 250 docking stations and you'll quickly discover that cycling rather suits this flat, balmy metropolis that was seemingly designed with visceral experiences in mind.

Most of Sevici's 250,000 daily users are locals, but visitors can take advantage of the sharing system by purchasing a 7-day pass online for €10 (plus a €150 returnable deposit). Proceed to the nearest docking station, punch in the number from your coded receipt, and hey presto. Seville has 120km of city bike lanes (all painted green and equipped with their own traffic signals) and the first 30 minutes of usage are free. Beyond that, it's €1 for the first hour and €2 an hour thereafter.

Another way of taking advantage of the new cycling infrastructure is to take a bike tour around the city's main sights. Sevilla Bike Tour (www.sevillabiketour.com; adult/child €25/19) runs easy guided three-hour (10km) trips daily starting at 10.30am and 6pm. Meet outside the Torre de Oro. No appointments are required and bikes are provided. Cost is adult/child €25/19.

5.45am-12.45am, less frequent on Sundays). A taxi costs about €22.

Bus

Run by Seville's urban transport authority **Tussam** (www.tussam.es), buses C1, C2, C3 and C4 do useful circular routes linking the main transport terminals and the city centre. The standard ticket is €1.30 but a range of passes is available (from stations and kiosks next to stops) if you're likely to use it a lot.

Car & Motorcycle

Hotels with parking usually charge you €12 to €18 a day for the privilege – no cheaper than some public car parks but at least your vehicle will be close to hand. **Parking Paseo de Colón** (cnr Paseo de Cristóbal Colón & Calle Adriano; per hr up to 10hr €1.20, 10-24hr €13.50) is a relatively inexpensive underground car park.

Metro

First mooted some 30 years ago, Seville's metro system has finally emerged from the darkness and seen the light of day (so to speak). The first line opened in April 2009 and connects Ciudad Expo with Olivar de Quinto (this line isn't that useful for visitors). Three more lines are due for completion by 2017. The standard ticket is €1.35. A one-day travelcard is €4.50.

Tram

Tranvia (www.tussam.es) is the city's sleek tram service, first introduced in 2007. Two parallel lines run in pollution-free bliss between Plaza Nueva, Avenida de la Constitucíon, Puerta de Jerez, San Sebastián and San Bernardo (the latter station was added in 2011). The standard ticket is €1.30 but a range of passes is available if you're likely to use it a lot.

Around Seville

Seville province invites day trips. You'll find Andalucía's best Roman ruins at Itálica. On the rolling agricultural plains east of Seville, fascinating old towns such as Carmona and Osuna bespeak many epochs of history.

CARMONA
POP 27,950 / ELEV 250 M

Perched on a low hill overlooking a wonderful *vega* (valley) that sizzles in the summer heat, dotted with old palaces and impressive monuments, Carmona comes as an unexpected highlight of western Andalucía.

☉ Sights

The tourist office in the Puerta de Sevilla, the impressive fortified main gate of the old town, sells tickets (adults/students and seniors €2/1) for the gate's upper levels.

The Puerta de Córdoba (Calle de Dolores Quintanilla; admission €2; ☉tours min 8 people 11.30am, 12.30pm & 1.30pm Tue, Sat & Sun), in Calle Dolores Quintanilla at the end of the street passing the Iglesia Priorial de Santa María, is an original Roman gate in marvellous repair, framing the fertile Seville countryside that unfolds like a precious, faded rug. South of here is the stark, ruined Alcázar (adult/child €2/1, Mon free; ☉10am-6pm

Mon-Sat, to 3pm Sun & holidays), an Almohad fort that Pedro I turned into a country palace. It was brought down by earthquakes in 1504 and 1755, and part of it is now the site of a luxurious *parador* (state-owned hotel).

Iglesia Prioral de Santa María   CHURCH
(☎954 19 14 82; Plaza Marqués de las Torres; admission €3; ⊙9am-2pm & 5.30-7.30pm Mon-Fri, 9am-2pm Sat) This splendid church was built mainly in the 15th and 16th centuries on the site of the former main mosque. The Patio de los Naranjos by which you enter has a Visigothic calendar carved into one of its pillars. Inside, the plateresque altar is detailed to an almost perverse degree, with 20 panels of biblical scenes framed by gilt-scrolled columns.

FREE **Roman Necropolis**   CEMETERY, RUINS
(☎954 14 08 11; Avenida de Jorge Bonsor; ⊙9am-2pm Tue-Sat 15 Jun–14 Sep, to 5pm Tue-Fri, closed holidays & 1 Jul–31 Aug) Just over 1km southwest of the Puerta de Sevilla is Carmona's impressive Roman Necropolis. You can look down into a dozen family tombs, hewn from the rock.

Museo de la Ciudad   MUSEUM
(City History Museum; ☎954 14 01 28; www.museo ciudad.carmona.org; Calle San Ildefonso 1; adult/child €3/free, Tue free; ⊙11am-7pm Tue-Sun, to 2pm Mon) An interesting background to the town can be explored at the city museum, housed in a centuries-old palace, with pieces dating back to Paleolithic times. The sections on the Tartessos and their Roman successors are highlights: the former includes a unique collection of large earthenware vessels with Middle Eastern decorative motifs, the latter several excellent mosaics.

🛏 **Sleeping & Eating**

Posada San Fernando   BOUTIQUE HOTEL €€
(☎954 14 14 08; www.posadasanfernando.com; Plaza de San Fernando 6; s/d/tr €55/65/100; ❋❄🛜) This excellent-value hotel is located on Carmona's liveliest square. Each room in the 16th-century structure is uniquely appointed, with thoughtfully chosen furniture, fittings and wallpaper, down to the hand-painted tiles in the bathrooms, some with claw-foot tubs.

Parador Alcázar del Rey Don Pedro   HISTORIC HOTEL €€€
(☎954 14 10 10; www.parador.es; Calle Alcázar; r €160-171) Carmona's luxuriously equipped *parador* feels even more luxurious for the ruined Alcázar in its grounds. The beautiful dining room (*menú del día* – daily set menu – €32) overlooks a jaw-dropping (and unexpected) view of the surrounding Vega roasting under the Sevillian sun.

Hostal Comercio   HOSTAL €
(☎954 14 00 18; hostalcomercio@hotmail.com; Calle Torre del Oro 56; s/d €35/50) Inside the Puerta de Sevilla, this old-fashioned inn has 14 spiffy, simple rooms around a plant-filled patio with Mudéjar-style arches. The unpretentious decor is matched by the cordial service, cultivated over generations.

Casa Curro Montoya   TAPAS €
(Calle Santa María de Gracia 13; tapas €2.50; ⊙closed Tue) This friendly, family-run joint opposite the Convento de Santa Clara occupies a narrow hall littered with memorabilia. Long-cultivated family traditions find expression in such items as fresh tuna in a luscious onion sauce, foie-stuffed eggplant and fried *pizcotas* (small sardinelike fishes).

ℹ **Information**
Tourist office (www.turismo.carmona.org; Alcázar de la Puerta de Sevilla; ⊙10am-6pm Mon-Sat, to 3pm Sun & holidays) This helpful tourist office is inside the Puerta de Sevilla.

ℹ **Getting There & Away**
Monday to Friday, Casal runs hourly buses to Seville from the stop on Paseo del Estatuto, but less often on weekends. Two or three buses a day go to Córdoba via Écija from the car park next to the Puerta de Sevilla.

OSUNA
POP 18,000 / ELEV 330M

The legacy of a fabulously wealthy line of dukes who loaned the town its name, Osuna dazzles unsuspecting visitors with its beautifully preserved baroque mansions and impressive Spanish Renaissance monastery filled with art treasures. This startling tableau unfolds like a mirage amid an otherwise empty landscape, as if its cache of architectural and artistic gems were no big thing.

It is 91km southeast of Seville, along the Granada–Seville A92.

◎ **Sights**
The massive buildings on the hill overlooking the centre graphically symbolise the weight of various kinds of authority in old Spain. Behind the town hall, the **Palacio de los Cepeda** (Calle de la Huerta 10) has rows of dramatic columns embellished with the Cepeda family coat of arms. Nearby, the **Cilla del Cabildo Colegial** (Calle San Pedro 16) bears a sculpted representation of Seville's Giralda.

Colegiata de Santa María de la Asunción
MUSEUM

(☑954 81 04 44; Plaza de la Encarnación; admission by guided tour only €3; ☷10am-1.30pm & 4-7pm Tue-Sun May-Sep, 10am-1:30pm & 3.30-6.30pm Oct-Apr) This imposing Renaissance structure overlooks Osuna from the site of the ancient parish church. Its halls contain a wealth of fine art and treasure collected by the House of Osuna, among them a series of paintings by José Ribera, aka 'El Españoleto', and sculpted works by Juan de Mesa.

The guided tour (in Spanish only) also includes the lugubrious underground sepulchre, created in 1548 with its own chapel as the family vault of the Osunas, who are entombed in wall niches.

Monasterio de la Encarnación
MUSEUM

(Plaza de la Encarnación; admission €2.50; ☷10am-1.30pm & 4-7pm Tue-Sun May-Sep, 10am-1.30pm & 3.30-6.30pm Oct-Apr) The former monastery is now Osuna's museum of religious art. Its church is decked with baroque sculpture and art, while the cloister features tiled tableaus depicting various biblical, hunting, bullfighting and monastic scenes that are among the most beautiful of Sevillan tile work. Entry is by guided tour only (in Spanish), led by one of the resident nuns.

🛏 Sleeping & Eating

Hotel Palacio Marqués de la Gomera
HISTORIC HOTEL €€

(☑954 81 22 23; www.hotelpalaciodelmarques.es; Calle San Pedro 20; r/ste €89/139; 🅿❄@🛜) Occupying one of Osuna's finest baroque mansions, this is an exceptionally handsome place to stay, with rooms of princely proportions and quiet luxury. It even boasts its own ornate private chapel off a sumptuous arched courtyard.

TOP CHOICE Casa Curro
TAPAS €

(Plazuela Salitre 5; tapas €2, raciones €8) Here's the tapas bar of your dreams, a marvellous blend of tradition and nouvelle cuisine. Plate after plate issue from the kitchen at the locally popular hall west of the centre: eggplant in shrimp and muscatel sauce, homemade meatballs, Iberian 'secret' in a quince sauce served with wild mushrooms. You'll want to try them all.

❶ Information

Oficina Municipal de Turismo (☑954 81 57 32; www.turismosuna.es; Calle Carrera 82; ☷9.30am-1.30pm & 4-6pm Tue-Sat, 9.30am-

ITÁLICA

Situated in the suburban settlement of Santiponce, 8km northwest of Seville, Itálica (☑955 62 22 66; www.juntadeandalucia.es/cultura/italica; Avenida de Extremadura 2; admission €1.50; ☷8.30am-9pm Tue-Sat, 9am-3pm Sun & holidays Apr-Sep, 9am-6.30pm Tue-Sat, 10am-4pm Sun & holidays Oct-Mar) was the first Roman town in Spain. Founded in 206 BC, it was also the birthplace and home of the 2nd-century-AD Roman emperors Trajan and Hadrian. The partly reconstructed ruins include one of the biggest of all the Roman amphitheatres, broad paved streets, ruins of several houses with beautiful mosaics, and a theatre.

Buses run to Santiponce (€1.30, 40 minutes) from Seville's Plaza de Armas bus station at least twice an hour from 6.35am to 11pm Monday to Friday, and a little less often at weekends. They stop right outside the Itálica entrance.

1.30pm Sun) All the info you will need on the town, including some useful guides.

❶ Getting There & Away

The **bus station** (Avenida de la Constitución) is 500m southeast of Plaza Mayor. Up to 11 daily buses run to Seville's Prado de San Sebastián (1½ hours). The **train station** (Avenida de la Estación) is 1km southwest of the centre, with 10 trains per day to Seville (€10.20, one hour).

HUELVA PROVINCE

To fixed-itinerary travellers, Huelva province is that nodule of land 'on the way to Portugal'. To those willing to drag their heels a little, it's home to the region's best *jamón*, its most evocative fandangos, and Spain's most ebullient *romería* (pilgrimage). Throw in some British-influenced mining heritage, Columbus memorabilia, and possibly Spain's most revered national park, and you've got the makings of an Andalucian break well outside the standard mould.

Huelva

POP 149,000

Blemished by factories and with its historical heritage smashed to pieces in the 1755

SEVILLE & ANDALUCÍA HUELVA

Lisbon earthquake (and not rebuilt), Huelva is never going to win any beauty contests. If you're passing through, there's a clutch of journeyman hotels, and some low-key but poignant Columbus memorabilia to ponder (yes, the great explorer first sailed from here). Alternatively, you can tackle Huelva province's sights on day trips from Seville or from the more salubrious small town of Aracena 100km to the north.

◉ Sights

Huelva's sights don't really merit a plural.

FREE **Museo de Huelva**   MUSEUM
(www.museosdeandalucia.es/cultura/museos/
MHU; Alameda Sundheim 13; ☺2.30-8.30pm Tue, 9am-8.30pm Wed-Sat, 9am-2.30pm Sun) Standing on the Alameda, domain of the early 20th century bourgeoisie, the town museum is stuffed to the gills with art and history. The permanent exhibition concentrates on the province's impressive archaeological pedigree, with interesting items culled from its Roman and mining history. Upstairs, changing exhibits mine the museum's substantial art collection, going back to the 16th century.

🛏 Sleeping & Eating

Hotel Costa de la Luz   HOTEL €
(☏959 25 64 22; www.hotelcostaluzhuelva.com; Calle José María Amo 8 & 10; s/d €31/47; ❄🛜) Located on a quiet pedestrian mall near the main shopping district, this is a perfectly good and central option. Well-maintained, spacious rooms have large bathtubs, nice tiles and super TVs with hundreds of channels. Skip the free breakfast and head around the corner to Café Central. There's a slight discount on Friday and Saturday nights.

Albergue Juvenil de Huelva   HOSTEL €
(☏959 65 00 10; www.inturjoven.com; Avenida Marchena Colombo 14; adult/child incl breakfast €27/16; ❄@🛜🚲; 🚌6) This is a good, modern youth hostel, with 53 rooms around a bright and pleasant courtyard. There are two to six beds per room, all with bathroom. Bike rentals are available. It's 2km north of the bus station: city bus 6 from the bus station stops just around the corner from the hostel, on Calle JS Elcano.

Hotel Familia Condes   BUSINESS HOTEL €€
(☏959 28 24 00; www.hotelfamiliaconde.com; Alameda Sundheim 14; s/d incl breakfast €50/65; 🅿❄@🛜) True, it's housed in a rather soulless block, but this business-class operation

is efficiently run with cordial service, and the fresh-smelling rooms have plenty of space and gleaming orange-toned bathrooms. The convenient location is a short stroll from the cafe-lined Gran Vía.

TOP CHOICE **El Picoteo**   TAPAS €
(Avenida Pablo Rada 5; raciones €9.50) On the north side of Pablo Rada is this casual tapas joint for gourmands in the know. It's usually packed but the kitchen can handle any size crowd. *Bacalao* (codfish) is prepared in many ways (in lobster or Pedro Ximénez wine sauce, for example) and there are plenty of vegetarian items such as eggplant tart stuffed with Gouda cheese.

ℹ Information

Regional tourist office (www.turismohuelva.org; Plaza Alcalde Coto Mora 2; ☺9am-7.30pm Mon-Fri, 9.30am-3pm Sat & Sun)

ℹ Getting There & Away

BUS Most buses from the **bus station** (☏959 25 69 00; Calle Doctor Rubio) are operated by **Damas** (www.damas-sa.es), with service to such destinations as Aracena, Isla Cristina, Moguer, Matalascañas and Faro (Portugal). Socibus runs at least two buses a day to Madrid (€24, 7¼ hours).

TRAIN Three services daily run to Seville (€10, 1½ hours) and once a day to Córdoba and Madrid (€70, four hours) from the **train station** (☏902 432343; www.renfe.com; Avenida de Italia).

Lugares Colombinos

The Lugares Colombinos (Columbus Sites) are the three townships of La Rábida, Palos de la Frontera and Moguer, along the eastern bank of the Tinto estuary east of Huelva. All three played key roles in the discovery of the Americas and can be combined in a single day trip from Huelva, the Doñana area or the nearby coast.

LA RÁBIDA
POP 600

In this pretty and peaceful town, don't miss the 14th-century **Monasterio de La Rábida** (☏959 35 04 11; admission €3; ☺10am-1pm & 4-7pm Tue-Sun), visited several times by Columbus before his great voyage of discovery. On the waterfront below the monastery is the **Muelle de las Carabelas** (Wharf of the Caravels; admission €3.55; ☺10am-2pm & 5-9pm Tue-Fri, 11am-8pm Sat & Sun Jun-Aug, 10am-7pm Tue-Sun Sep-May), where you can board replicas of Columbus' tiny three-ship fleet, crewed by ludicrous mannequins.

PALOS DE LA FRONTERA
POP 8500

In La Rábida's neighbouring town you'll find the **Casa Museo Martín Alonso Pinzón** (959 10 00 41; Calle Colón 24; admission free; ⊙10am-2pm Mon-Fri), once the home of the *Pinta's* captain. Further along Calle Colón is the 15th-century Iglesia de San Jorge, where Columbus and his men took communion before embarking on their great voyage.

If you can't face staying in Huelva itself, try the **Hotel La Pinta** (959 53 05 11; Calle Rábida 79; s/d €41/67) which has a big bar, restaurant (with models of Columbus' ships) and decent-sized clean rooms. Stop to take on supplies yourself at **El Bodegón** (959 53 11 05; Calle Rábida 46; mains €10-23; ⊙closed Tue), a noisy, atmospheric cavern of a restaurant that cooks up fish and meat on wood-fired grills.

MOGUER
POP 16,300

Sleepy Moguer provided many of Columbus' crew. The 14th-century **Monasterio de Santa Clara** (959 37 01 07; www.santa-clara.tk; Plaza de las Monjas; guided tour €3; ⊙10.30am-1pm & 4.30-7pm Tue-Sat, 10.30am-1pm Sun) is where Columbus kept a prayerful vigil the night after returning from his first voyage, in March 1493.

Right across the plaza from the monastery, **Barola** (www.barola.es; Plaza de las Monjas) is a cool, stylish tapas bar in a cavernous reconstructed building with Moorish arches.

There's a helpful **tourist office** (959 37 18 98; Calle Castillo; ⊙10am-2pm & 5-7pm Mon-Sat, 10am-3pm Sun, Mon & holidays) a couple of blocks south of the central Plaza del Cabildo, in Moguer's **castillo**, a dramatic, bare-walled enclosure of Almohad origin, expanded in the 14th century.

❶ Getting There & Away

At least 10 buses a day leave Huelva for La Rábida (15 minutes), with half of them continuing to Palos de la Frontera (20 minutes) and Moguer (30 minutes). The others go on to Mazagón.

Parque Nacional de Doñana

Spain's most celebrated and in many ways most important wildlife refuge, the Doñana National Park, created in 1969, is one of Europe's last remaining great wetlands. Covering 542 sq km in the southeast of Huelva prov-

ince and neighbouring Seville province, this World Heritage site is a vital refuge for such endangered species as the Spanish imperial eagle. It offers a unique combination of ecosystems and a place of haunting beauty that is well worth the effort of getting to. To visit the national park you must take a tour from the Centro de Visitantes El Acebuche on the western side of the park, or from El Rocío at the park's northwestern corner, or from Sanlúcar de Barrameda at its southeastern corner.

Half the park consists of *marismas* (wetlands) of the Guadalquivir delta, the largest area of wetlands in Europe. Almost dry from July to October, in autumn the *marismas* fill with water, attracting hundreds of thousands of wintering waterbirds from the north. As the waters sink in spring, other birds – greater flamingos, spoonbills, storks – arrive, many to nest. The park also has a 28km Atlantic beach, separated from the *marismas* by a band of sand dunes up to 5km wide; and 144 sq km of *coto* (woodland and scrub), which harbours many mammals, including deer, wild boar and semiwild horses.

Interesting areas surrounding the national park are included in the 540-sq-km Parque Natural de Doñana, a separate protected area comprising four distinct zones.

EL ROCÍO
POP 1200

The village of El Rocío overlooks a section of the Doñana *marismas* at the park's northwestern corner. The village's sandy streets bear as many hoofprints as tyre marks, and they are lined with rows of verandahed buildings that are empty most of the time. But this is no ghost town: most of the houses belong to the 90-odd *hermandades* of pilgrim-revellers and their families, who converge on El Rocío every year in the extraordinary Romería del Rocío (see the boxed text, p685). In fact, a party atmosphere pervades the village at most weekends as *hermandades* arrive to carry out lesser ceremonial acts.

◉ Sights & Activities

Deer and horses graze in the shallow water in front of the village, and you might see a flock of flamingos wheeling through the sky in a great pink cloud. The bridge over the river on the A483, 1km south of the village, is another good viewing spot.

Ermita del Rocío   CHURCH
(⊙8am-10.30pm Apr-Sep, 8.30am-8pm Oct-Mar)
In the heart of the village stands the Ermita

del Rocío, built in its present form in 1964. This is the home of the celebrated Nuestra Señora del Rocío (Our Lady of El Rocío), a small wooden image of the Virgin dressed in long, jewelled robes, which normally stands above the main altar. People arrive to see the Virgin every day of the year and especially on weekends, when the brotherhoods of El Rocío often gather here for colourful celebrations.

FREE **Francisco Bernis Birdwatching Centre** BIRDWATCHING
(☑959 44 23 72; ☺9am-2pm & 4-6pm Tue-Sun) About 350m east of the Ermita along the waterfront, this facility backs on the marsh, and flamingos, glossy ibis, spoonbills etc can be observed through the rear windows or from the observation deck. (High-powered binoculars are provided.) The experts here can help you identify species and inform you about which migratory birds are visiting and where to see them.

Sleeping & Eating

Don't bother even trying to find a room at Romería del Rocío time.

Hotel Toruño HOTEL €€
(☑959 44 23 23; www.toruno.es; Plaza Acebuchal 22; s/d incl breakfast €59/80; ☐❄☎) An attractive villa overlooking the *marismas*, Toruño has 30 well-appointed rooms. Some have marsh views, so you can see the spoonbills having their breakfast when you wake. Across the road, the restaurant (mains €12 to €22) dishes up generous portions of well-prepared country and coastal fare.

Hotel La Malvasía HOTEL €€
(☑959 44 38 70; www.lamalvasiahotel.com; Calle Sanlúcar 38; s/d incl breakfast €75/90; ☐❄☎) Overlooking the marshes, this idyllic hotel is located inside a truly magisterial building. Rooms are crushed with character including rustic tiled floors, vintage photos of the town and iron bedsteads in floral designs. Top-level units make great bird-viewing perches.

Pensión Cristina PENSIÓN €
(☑959 44 24 13; Calle El Real 58; s/d €40/60; ☐❄☎) Just east of the Ermita, the Cristina provides reasonably comfortable rooms facing a pleasant patio with lots of plants (though, sadly, no marsh views). There's a popular restaurant (mains €10 to €12) serving paella, venison, seafood and more.

Restaurante El Real ANDALUCIAN €
(Calle Real 7; set lunch €9; ☺8am-7pm Tue-Sun) Opposite the shrine, this may be a tourist-oriented place but one that seems to relish serving outsiders. The food is homemade and there's a pleasant terrace. Be sure to try the *salmorejo* and for dessert the 'heavenly bacon' (flan with pine nuts).

ⓘ Information

Centro de Información Las Rocinas (☺9am-3pm & 4-7pm, to 8pm or 9pm Apr-Aug, to 3pm Sun 15 Jun–14 Sep) Located 1km south on the A483, the centre has national park information and paths to nearby birdwatching hides.
Tourist office (www.turismodedonana.com; Camino de Moguer; ☺9.30am-2pm Tue-Sun) Inside the Museo del Rocío, in the southwestern corner of the village just off the A483.

CENTRO DE VISITANTES EL ACEBUCHE

Twelve kilometres south of El Rocío on the A483, then 1.6km west, you'll find Centro de Visitantes El Acebuche (☑959 43 96 29; ☺8am-9pm May-Sep, to 7pm Oct-Apr; ❄), the national park's main visitor centre. It has an interactive exhibit on the park and paths to birdwatching hides, plus a film show of Iberian lynxes at El Acebuche – the closest visitors can get to them.

National Park Tours

Trips in 20-person all-terrain vehicles from El Acebuche are the only way for ordinary folk to get into the interior of the national park from the western side. Book ahead through Cooperativa Marismas del Rocío (☑959 43 04 32; www.donanavisitas.es; 4hr tour per person €27; ☺8.30am & 3pm Tue-Sun mid-Sep–Apr, 8.30am & 5pm Mon-Sat May–mid-Sep). During spring, summer and holidays, book at least a month ahead, but otherwise a week is usually plenty of notice. Bring binoculars if you can, drinking water in summer and mosquito protection, except in winter. Most guides speak Spanish only. The tour normally starts with a long beach drive, before moving inland. You can be pretty certain of seeing deer and boar, but ornithologists may be disappointed by the limited bird-observation opportunities.

For more specialist trips, try one of the following private operators.

Doñana Reservas BIRDWATCHING
(☑959 44 24 74; www.donanareservas.com; Avenida La Canaliega, El Rocío; 4hr trip 4-12 people per person €35, 10hr trip 3-6 people per person €85) English-speaking guides with expertise in

ROMERÍA DEL ROCÍO

Every Pentecost (Whitsuntide), the seventh weekend after Easter, El Rocío is inundated with up to a million pilgrim-revellers from all corners of Spain in the Romería del Rocío (Pilgrimage to El Rocío). This vast cult festivity revolves around the tiny image of Nuestra Señora del Rocío, which was found here in a tree by a hunter from Almonte back in the 13th century. Carrying it home, the hunter stopped for a rest and the statue miraculously made its own way back to the tree. Before long a chapel was built where the tree had stood (now El Rocío) and pilgrims were making for it.

Today almost 100 *hermandades* (brotherhoods) from around and beyond Andalucía, some comprising several thousand men and women, travel to El Rocío each year on foot, on horseback and in gaily decorated covered wagons pulled by cattle or horses, using cross-country tracks.

Solemn is the last word you'd apply to this quintessentially Andalucian event. The 'pilgrims' dress in bright Andalucian costume and sing, dance, drink and romance their way to El Rocío.

Things reach an ecstatic climax in the early hours of the Monday. Members of the *hermandad* of Almonte, which claims the Virgin for its own, barge into the church and bear her out on a float. Chaotic struggles ensue as others battle with the Almonte lads for the honour of carrying La Blanca Paloma, but somehow good humour survives and the Virgin is carried round to each of the brotherhood buildings, finally returning to the Ermita in the afternoon.

identification of birds, wildflowers, mushrooms and mammals. Tours focus on the marshes and woods in the northern section of the park. Binoculars, telescopes and checklists are provided.

Doñana Nature GUIDED TOUR
(959 44 21 60; www.donana-nature.com; Calle Las Carretas 10; 3½hr trip per person €26) Half-day trips, at 8am and 3.30pm daily, are general interest, although specialised ornithological and photographic trips are also offered. English- and French-speaking guides are available.

Doñana Bird Tours BIRDWATCHING
(959 46 59 47; www.donanabirdtours.com; 9hr trip 1-3 people €150, each extra person €30) Top-class birdwatching tours departing from Villamanrique de la Condesa.

Minas de Riotinto

POP 4100 / ELEV 420M

Tucked away on the southern fringe of the sierra is one of the world's oldest mining districts, so old that even King Solomon of faraway Jerusalem is said to have mined gold here for his famous temple. Though the miners clocked off for the last time in 2001, it's still a fascinating place to explore, with a superb museum and the opportunity to visit the old mines and ride the mine railway.

Minas de Riotinto is the area's hub. The Río Tinto itself rises a few kilometres northeast of town, its name ('Red River') stemming from the deep red-brown hue produced by the reaction of its acidic waters with the abundant iron and copper ores.

Sights & Activities

Museo Minero MUSEUM
(959 59 00 25; www.parquemineroderiotinto.com; Plaza Ernest Lluch; adult/child €4/3; 10.30am-3pm & 4-7pm) This mining museum is a figurative goldmine for devotees of industrial archaeology, taking you through the area's unique history from the megalithic tombs of the 3rd millennium BC to the Roman and British colonial eras and finally the closure of the mines in 2001. The tour includes an elaborate 200m-long recreation of a Roman mine. The museum also features a big display on the railways that served the mines. Pride of place goes to the Vagón del Maharajah, a luxurious carriage built in 1892 for a tour of India by Britain's Queen Victoria, though she never actually rode in it.

Peña de Hierro MINE
(adult/child €8/7; noon-1.30pm & 5.30-7pm) These are old copper and sulphur mines 3km north of Nerva. Here you see the source of Río Tinto, an 65m-deep open-cast mine, and are taken into a 200m-long underground mine gallery. It's essential to book

ahead (online at www.parquemineroderio
tinto.com), and schedules may change.

Ferrocarril Turístico-Minero   TOUR
(☎959 59 00 25; www.parquemineroderiotinto.
com; adult/child €10/9; ☺1pm Mon-Fri & 4.30pm
Sat & Sun Mar–mid-Jun, Oct & Nov, 1.30pm &
5.30pm daily mid-Jul–Sep) A fun way to see the
area (especially with children) is to ride the
old mining train, running 22km (round trip)
through the surreal landscape in restored
early-20th-century carriages.

Trips start at the old railway repair workshops 4km east of Minas de Ríotinto off the
road to Nerva. Commentary is in Spanish.
It's mandatory to book ahead. Tickets may
be purchased either at the museum or the
railway station.

❶ Getting There & Away

From Monday to Friday, **Damas** (www.damas-sa.
es) runs five buses between Minas de Riotinto
and Huelva (€6.30, 1¾ hours), with three on
weekends. There is no public transport to the
Ferrocarril Turístico-Minero.

Aracena & Around
POP 7800 / ELEV 730M

Who knew? The gently folded uplands of
northern Huelva province offer yet another
nuance to rural *andaluz* culture: pastoral,
flower-bedecked hills and sheltered valleys
replete with gnarly oak trees and forag-
ing pigs that produce what many consider
to be the finest cured ham in Spain – the
legendary *jamón iberico*. You can dump
your car here; the region's sleepy, half-
forgotten villages are all linked by good
footpaths that thread out from the regional
nexus of Aracena, a whitewashed market
town that is markedly different in character
to the traditional *pueblos blancos* (white
towns) further east. The 1840-sq-km Parque
Natural Sierra de Aracena y Picos de Aroche
comprises Andalucía's second-largest protected area.

◉ Sights & Activities

The **Cerro del Castillo** is where the old
town originated. Climb to the top of the hill
to view the 13th-century Portuguese-built
castillo and the adjacent **Iglesia Prioral**
(☺9.30am-7pm). A little lower down in Plaza
Alta there's an interesting **Centro de Visitantes** (☎959 12 95 53; Plaza Alta; ☺10am-2pm
& 4-6pm Tue-Sun), which showcases the high-

lights of **Parque Natural Sierra de Aracena
y Picos de Aroche**.

Gruta de las Maravillas   CAVE
(Cave of Marvels; ☎663 93 78 76; Calle Pozo de la
Nieve; tour adult/child €8.50/6; ☺10.30am-1.30pm
& 3-6pm, tours every hr Mon-Fri, every half-hr Sat,
Sun & holidays) Beneath the castle hill is a web
of caves and tunnels carved from the karstic
topography. An extraordinary 1km route
takes you through 12 chambers and past six
underground lakes, all beautifully illuminated and filled with weird and wonderful rock
formations that provided a backdrop for the
film *Journey to the Centre of the Earth*.

Tours are in Spanish but audio guides are
available. You're not allowed to take photos
but a photographer is on hand on the way in
for that obligatory portrait.

Linares de la Sierra   HIKING
Hikes in the Aracena area are legion and the
trails are rarely crowded. If you're on a day
trip from Seville, try the undulating route to
Linares de la Sierra and – time and energy
permitting – continue onto **Alájar** (there's a
return bus from Alájar to Aracena that leaves
at 4pm connecting with the 5pm Aracena–
Seville service). The signposted path is easy
to find on the southwest side of Aracena approximately 500m past the municipal swimming pool. Follow the wide bucolic track as
far as **Linares** (6km), a soporific village renowned for its *llanos* (front-patio mosaics).
From here the path narrows and becomes a
little trickier to navigate, though you'll spot
plenty of snorting pigs and eye-catching wildflowers along the way. Just before the hamlet
of Los Madroñeros, fork right on the 'Caracol'
trail (signposted), which traverses an oak-
sprinkled hillside into Alájar (distance 12km).

You can stay over in Alájar at **La Posada** (☎959 12 57 12; www.laposadadealajar.com;
Calle Médico Emilio González 2; s/d incl breakfast
€45/60), a very cosy inn whose English-
speaking owners are keen walkers. Shop
around in the village for the excellent local
ham. Another walking path heads northwest to the next village, Castaño de Robledo.

🛏 Sleeping & Eating

La Casa Noble   BOUTIQUE HOTEL €€€
(☎959 12 77 78; www.lacasanoble.net; Calle Campito
35; s/d incl breakfast from €165/185; ❋🛜) Describing this as a boutique hotel does it a
disservice. It's a divine palace to luxury, filled
with antiques, over-the-top tile work and
beds as thick and bouncy as something out of

The Princess and the Pea. The dining room has to be seen to be believed! Access is limited to guests 16 years and older.

Molino del Bombo BOUTIQUE HOTEL €
(959 12 84 78; www.molinodelbombo.com; Calle Ancha 4; s/d €36/60; 🕸🅥) Though of recent vintage, this lodging at the top of the town has a rustic style that blends in with Aracena's time-worn architecture. Bright rooms feature frescoes and exposed stone and brick work as design features, and bathrooms are done up as picturesque grottoes. You'll likely want to linger in the salon or courtyard with trickling fountain.

TOP CHOICE **Rincón de Juan** TAPAS €
(627 33 47 66; Calle José Nogales; tapas €1.80, raciones €7-10; 7am-4pm & 6.30pm-midnight Mon Fri, 8am midnight Sat) It's standing room only at this wedge-shaped, stone-walled corner bar, indisputably the finest tapas joint in town. Iberian ham is certainly the star attraction and forms the basis for a variety of *montaditos* (little sandwiches) and *rebanadas* (sliced loaves that feed several people). The homemade sausage, sweet or spicy, is always a good bet.

Café-Bar Manzano TAPAS €€
(959 12 75 13; Calle Campito 9; raciones €9-14; 9am-4:30pm & 8pm-midnight Wed-Mon) This classy terrace cafe on the main plaza is a fine spot to watch Aracena go by and enjoy varied tapas and *raciones* (large tapas servings) that celebrate wild mushrooms and other regional fare. Even out of season, it serves up such tempting toadstools as *tentullos*, *gurumelos* and *tanas*, sauteed or in enticing scrambles.

ℹ️ Information

Municipal tourist office (www.aracena.es; Calle Pozo de la Nieve; 10am-2pm & 4-6pm) Faces the entrance to the Gruta de las Maravillas and sells some maps of the area.

ℹ️ Getting There & Away

The **bus station** (Avenida de Sevilla) is 700m southeast of the Plaza del Marqués de Aracena, on the Seville road. **Damas** (www.damas-sa.es) runs one morning and two afternoon buses from Seville (€6.80, 1¼ hours), continuing on to Cortegana via Alájar or Jabugo. From Huelva, there are two afternoon departures daily (€10, three hours). There is also local service between Aracena and Cortegana via Linares, Alájar and Almonaster La Real.

CÁDIZ PROVINCE

If you had to break off one part of Andalucía to demonstrate to aliens what it looked like, you'd probably choose Cádiz province. Emblematic regional highlights are part of the furniture here: thrillingly sited white towns, craggy mountains, endless olives trees, flamenco in its purist incarnation, the original (and best) fortified sherry, the font of Andalucian horse culture, festivals galore, and – just when you thought you'd half-sussed it out – that idiosyncratic British anomaly, Gibraltar. Stuffed in among all of this condensed culture are two expansive natural parks that cover an unbroken tract of land that runs from Olvera in the north to Algeciras in the south. The same line once marked the blurred frontier between Christian Spain and Moorish Granada, and the ancient border is flecked with huddled 'white towns', many of them given a 'de la Frontera' suffix testifying to their volatile but fascinating history.

Cádiz

POP 125,000

You could write several weighty university theses about Cádiz and still fall a mile short of nailing its essence. Old age accounts for much of the complexity. Cádiz is generally considered to be the oldest continuously inhabited settlement in Europe. Now well into its fourth millennium, the ancient centre is as romantic as it is mysterious, an ocean settlement surrounded almost entirely by water, where Atlantic waves crash against eroded sea walls, municipal beaches stretch for miles, and narrow streets echo with the sounds of cawing gulls and frying fish. Come here for the seafood, the surf, and the cache of intriguing churches and museums that inflict little, if any, damage on your wallet. More importantly, come here for the *gaditanos* (Cádiz residents), an upfront and gregarious populace who have made *alegrías* (upbeat flamenco songs) into an eloquent art form.

History

Cádiz is probably the oldest city in Europe. Historians date its founding to the arrival of Phoenician traders in 800 BC.

In less-distant times, Cádiz began to boom after Columbus' trips to the Americas. He sailed from here on his second and fourth voyages. Cádiz attracted Spain's enemies too: in 1587 England's Sir Francis Drake 'singed the king of Spain's beard' with

Cádiz Province

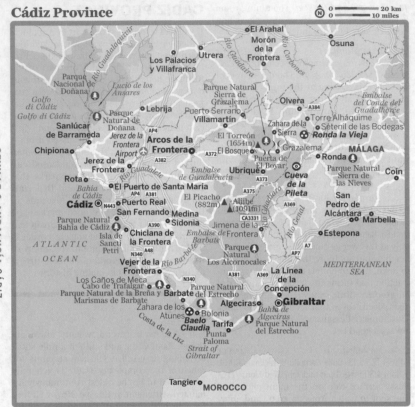

a raid on the harbour, delaying the imminent Spanish Armada. In 1596, Anglo-Dutch attackers burnt almost the entire city.

Cádiz' golden age was the 18th century, when it enjoyed 75% of Spanish trade with the Americas. It grew into the richest and most cosmopolitan city in Spain and gave birth to the country's first progressive, liberal middle class. During the Napoleonic Wars, Cádiz held out under French siege from 1810 to 1812, when a national parliament meeting here adopted Spain's liberal 1812 constitution, proclaiming sovereignty of the people.

The loss of the American colonies in the 19th century plunged Cádiz into a decline from which it is only today recovering, with increased tourism playing a significant role.

The year 2012 was a big one for Cádiz, with the city dolling itself up for the 200th anniversary of La Pepa, Spain's (and the world's) first liberal constitution, signed in 1812.

⊙ Sights & Activities

To understand Cádiz you need to first become acquainted with its barrios. The old city can be split into classic quarters: **Barrio del Pópulo**, home of the cathedral, and nexus of the once prosperous medieval settlement; **Barrio de Santa María**, the old Roma quarter and an important fount of flamenco; **Barrio de la Viña**, a former vineyard that became the city's main fishing quarter; and the **Barrio del Mentidero**, centre of Cádiz' modern nightlife and bar scene.

Plaza San Juan de Dios & Around   SQUARE
Broad Plaza San Juan de Dios is lined with cafes and is dominated by the imposing neoclassical **ayuntamiento** built around 1800. Between here and the cathedral is the Barrio del Pópulo, the kernel of medieval Cádiz and a focus of the city's ongoing sprucing-up program. At the nearby **Roman Theatre** (Campo del Sur; ⊙10am-2.30pm & 5-7pm Wed-Mon) you

can walk along a gallery beneath the tiers of seating. The theatre was discovered by chance in 1980.

Catedral
CHURCH

(Plaza de la Catedral; adult/student €5/3, 7-8pm Tue-Fri & 11am-1pm Sun free; ⊙10am-6.30pm Mon-Sat, 1.30-6.30pm Sun) Cádiz' yellow-domed cathedral is an impressively proportioned baroque-neoclassical construction, but by Spanish standards very sober in its decoration. It fronts a broad, traffic-free plaza where the cathedral's ground-plan is picked out in the paving stones. The decision to build the cathedral was taken in 1716 but the project wasn't finished until 1838, by which time neoclassical elements, such as the dome, towers and main facade, had diluted Vicente Acero's original baroque plan. From a separate entrance on Plaza de la Catedral, climb to the top of the Torre de Poniente (Western Tower; adult/child €4/3; ⊙10am-6pm, to 8pm mid-Jun–mid-Sep) for marvellous vistas.

FREE Museo de las Cortes de Cádiz
MUSEUM

(Calle Santa Inés 9; ⊙9am-6pm Tue-Fri, to 2pm Sat-Sun) More *gratis* Cádiz history, this time in the recently remodelled Museo de las Cortes de Cádiz which is full of memorabilia of the revolutionary 1812 Cádiz parliament. One exhibit jumps out at you: the huge, marvellously detailed model of 18th-century Cádiz, made in mahogany and ivory by Alfonso Ximénez in 1777-79.

The plush new over-hanging viewing gallery decorated with old city maps allows a bird's eye perspective.

Museo de Cádiz
MUSEUM

(Plaza de Mina; admission €1.50; ⊙2.30-8.30pm Tue, 9am-8.30pm Wed-Sat, 9.30am-2.30pm Sun) The Museo de Cádiz, on one of Cádiz' leafiest squares, is the best museum in the province. The ground-floor archaeology section includes two Phoenician marble sarcophagi carved in human likeness, lots of headless Roman statues, plus Emperor Trajan, with head, from the ruins of Baelo Claudia. The fine arts collection, upstairs, features a group of 18 superb canvases of saints, angels and monks by Francisco de Zurbarán.

Also here is the painting that cost Murillo his life, the beautifully composed altarpiece from the chapel of Cádiz' Convento de Capuchinas (the artist died in 1682 after falling from the scaffolding).

Torre Tavira
TOWER

(Calle Marqués del Real Tesoro 10; admission €4; ⊙10am-6pm mid-Sep–mid-Jun, to 8pm mid-Jun–mid-Sep) Northwest of Plaza de Topete, the Torre Tavira has another dramatic panorama of Cádiz and a camera obscura that projects live, moving images of the city onto a screen (sessions start every half-hour).

Coastal Walk
WALKING

This airy 4.5km walk takes at least 1¼ hours. Go north from Plaza de Mina to the city's northern seafront, with views across the Bahía de Cádiz. Head west along the Alameda gardens to the Baluarte de la Candelaria, then turn southwest to the Parque del Genovés, a semitropical garden with waterfalls and quirkily clipped trees. Continue to the Castillo de Santa Catalina (⊉956 22 63 33; admission free; ⊙10.30am-8.30pm, to 7.45pm Nov-Feb), built after the 1596 sacking; inside are an interesting historical exhibit on Cádiz and the sea, and a gallery for exhibitions. Sandy Playa de la Caleta (very crowded in summer) separates Santa Catalina from the 18th-century Castillo de San Sebastián. You can't enter San Sebastián, but do walk along the breezy 750m causeway to its gate. Finally, follow the broad promenade along Campo del Sur to the cathedral.

Playa de la Victoria
BEACH

Normally overshadowed by the rich historical booty, Cádiz' beaches are Copacabana-like in their size and vitality. This lovely, wide strip of fine Atlantic sand stretches about 4km along the peninsula from its beginning at the Puertas de Tierra. At weekends in summer almost the whole city seems to be out here.

Bus 1 (Plaza España–Cortadura) from Plaza de España will get you there, or you can walk along the promenade from Barrio Santa María.

🎭 Festivals & Events

Carnaval
CARNIVAL

No other Spanish city celebrates Carnaval with the verve, dedication and humour of Cádiz, where it turns into a 10-day singing, dancing and drinking fancy-dress party spanning two weekends in February. The fun, abetted by huge quantities of alcohol, is irresistible.

Costumed groups called *murgas* tour the city on foot or on floats, dancing, singing satirical ditties or performing sketches (most of their famed verbal wit will be lost on all

Cádiz

Cádiz

Top Sights

Sights

Sleeping

Eating

Drinking

Entertainment

doors, beautifully tiled floors that adorn bedrooms and bathrooms, and the intricate Moorish arch in the lobby. The hotel has three themes: the first floor is Mudéjar, the second floor is colonial, and the third floor is a mix.

Hotel Patagonia Sur
HOTEL €€

(☏856 17 46 47; www.hotelpatagoniasur.es; Calle Cobos 11; d €80-130; ❄@🖧) The newest establishment in Cádiz' old town, this sleek gem opened in 2009 and offers clean-lined modernity just steps from the 18th century cathedral. Bonuses include its sun-filled attic rooms on the 5th floor with cathedral views and a glass-fronted minimalist cafeteria at street level.

Casa Caracol
HOSTEL €€

(☏956 26 11 66; www.caracolcasa.com; Calle Suárez de Salazar 4; dm/hammock incl breakfast €16/10; @🖧) Casa Caracol is the only backpacker hostel in the old town. Friendly, as only Cádiz can be, it has bunk dorms for four and eight, a communal kitchen, and a roof terrace with hammocks. Green initiatives include recycling, water efficiency measures and plans for solar panels. It's advisable to book through www.hostelworld. com or www.hostelbookers.com as the hostel often fills up.

Hostal Fantoni
HOSTAL €

(☏956 28 27 04; www.hostalfantoni.es; Calle Flamenco 5; s/d €45/65; ❄@) There's a pleasant courtyard disguising more basic (sometimes windowless) rooms, but Fantoni is all about its central location – and you're not going to spend much time in your room in Cádiz anyway.

Hostal Bahía
HOSTAL €€

(☏956 25 90 61; Calle Plocia 5; s/d €60/76) All rooms here are exterior and impeccably looked after, with phone, TV and built-in wardrobes. They're plain and straightforward, but good value.

🍴 Eating

Cádiz' hallowed seafood street is Calle Virgen de la Palma in the Viña quarter. Good un-fancy restaurants are legion here. Try El Faro (www.elfarodecadiz.com; Calle San Félix 15; mains €15-25), decorated with pretty ceramics, or the even grittier Taberna El Albero (cnr Calles San Félix & Virgen de la Palma). In and around Plaza de San Juan de Díos is another good place to dine.

but fluent Spanish speakers). In addition to the 300-or-so officially recognised *murgas,* who are judged by a panel in the Gran Teatro Falla, there are also the *ilegales* – any group that fancies taking to the streets and trying to play or sing.

Some of the liveliest and most drunken scenes are in the working-class Barrio de la Viña, between the Mercado Central and Playa de la Caleta, and along Calle Ancha and around Plaza de Topete, where *ilegales* tend to congregate.

If you plan to be here during Carnaval, book accommodation months in advance.

🛏 Sleeping

Hotel Argantonio
HOTEL €€

(☏956 21 16 40; www.hotelargantonio.com; Calle Argantonio 3; s/d incl breakfast €90/107; ❄@🖧) Welcome to another characterful small-is-beautiful hotel in Cádiz' old quarter. The stand-out features here are the hand-painted

TOP CHOICE El Aljibe TAPAS €€

(www.pablogrosso.com; Calle Plocia 25; tapas €2-3.50, mains €10-15) Refined restaurant upstairs and supercool tapas bar downstairs, El Aljibe on its own is almost reason enough to come to Cádiz. The cuisine developed by *gaditano* chef Pablo Grosso is a delicious combination of the traditional and the adventurous – goat's cheese on nut bread with blueberry sauce, courgette and prawn lasagne...you get the drift?

Atxuri BASQUE, ANDALUCIAN €€

(956 25 36 13; www.atxuri.es; Calle Plocia 7; mains from €12; 1-4.30pm daily & 9-11pm Thu-Sat) One of Cádiz' most decorated and long-standing restaurants, Atxuri fuses Basque and Andalucian influences and the result is a sophisticated range of flavours. *Bacalao* (cod) and high-quality steaks are recurring themes, as you'd expect in a place with Basque roots, but fish and meat tastes are such staples of Andalucian cooking that the boundary between Andalucía and the Basque Country is often deliciously blurred.

Arrocería La Pepa SPANISH €€

(956 26 38 21; Paseo Maritimo 14; paella per person €12-17) To get a decent paella you have to leave the old town behind and head for a few kilometres southeast along Playa de la Victoria – a pleasant, appetite-inducing oceanside walk along a popular jogging route or a quick ride on the No 1 bus. Either method is worth it.

The fish in La Pepa's seafood paella tastes as if it's just jumped the 100m or so from the Atlantic onto your plate.

Freiduría Las Flores SEAFOOD €

(956 22 61 12; Plaza de Topete 4; seafood per 250g €3-8) Cádiz' addiction to fried fish finds wonderful expression here. If it comes from the sea, chances are that it's been fried and served in Las Flores as either a tapa, *ración* (meal-sized serving of tapas) or *media ración* (half a *ración*), or served in an improvised paper cup, fish-and-chips style. You order by weight (250g is the usual order).

If you're finding it hard to choose, order a *surtido* (a mixed fry-up).

La Gorda Te Da De Comer FUSION €

(Calle General Luque 1; tapas €2; 9-11.30pm Mon, 1.30-4pm & 9-11.30pm Tue-Sat) Incredibly tasty food at incredibly low prices amid cool pop-art design. The tastes are fresh and innovative but it's almost always done with a discernibly local twist.

Try the curried chicken strips with Marie-Rose sauce, the deep-fried aubergines with honey or a dozen other mouth-watering concoctions.

Drinking

In the old city, the Plaza de Mina–Plaza San Francisco–Plaza de España area is the main hub of the nocturnal bar scene; things get moving around midnight at most places, but it can be quiet in the first half of the week.

The second hot spot is down Playa de la Victoria, along Paseo Marítimo and nearby in the Hotel Playa Victoria area, about 2.5km from the Puertas de Tierra.

TOP CHOICE Quilla CAFE

(www.quilla.es; Playa de la Caleta; 10am-midnight;) A bookish coffee bar encased in what appears to be the rusty hulk of an old ship overlooking Playa de la Caleta, with pastries, tapas, wine, art expos and free wi-fi – to say nothing of the gratis sunsets.

☆ Entertainment

Head out late, Thursday to Saturday nights, to Punta de San Felipe (known as La Punta) on the northern side of the harbour. Here, a line of disco bars and the big disco **Sala Anfiteátro** (Paseo Pascual Pery; admission €6-8) are packed with an 18-to-25 crowd from around 3am to 6am.

The **Gran Teatro Falla** (956 22 08 34; Plaza de Falla) hosts busy and varied programs of theatre, dance and music.

TOP CHOICE Peña Flamenca La Perla FLAMENCO

(956 25 91 01; www.laperladecadiz.es; Calle Carlos Ollero; admission free) The paint-peeled Peña La Perla set romantically next to the crashing Atlantic surf hosts flamenco nights at 10pm most Fridays, more so in spring and summer. Right beside the ocean just off Calle Concepción Arenal in the Barrio de Santa María, entry is free and the audience is stuffed with aficionados. It's an unforgettable experience.

Barabass BAR, MUSIC

(856 07 90 26; www.barabasscadiz.es; Calle General Muñoz Arenillas 4-6; admission incl 1 drink €10; 10pm-6am) The glamorous Barabass is one of the hippest bars in Cádiz' other nighttime nexus, Playa de la Victoria.

❶ Information

You'll find plenty of banks and ATMs along Calle Nueva and the parallel Avenida Ramón de Carranza. The main post office is in Plaza de Topete next to the central market.

Hospital Puerta del Mar (✆956 00 21 00; Avenida Ana de Viya 21) The main general hospital, 2km southeast of Puertas de Tierra.

Municipal tourist office (Paseo de Canalejas; ⊗8.30am-6pm Mon-Fri, 9am-5pm Sat & Sun)

Regional tourist office (Avenida Ramón de Carranza; ⊗9am-7.30pm Mon-Fri, 10am-2pm Sat, Sun & holidays)

❶ Getting There & Around

Bicycle

Urban Bike (www.urbanbikecadiz.es; Calle Marques de Valderfigo 4; ⊗10am-2pm & 5.30-9pm Mon-Fri, 10am-2pm Sat) Rents bikes for 1/12/24 hours (€3/10/14).

Boat

Catamarans (www.cmtbc.es; Terminal Marítima Metropolitana) leave from the **Terminal Marítima Metropolitana** for El Puerto de Santa María (€2.35) with 18 daily departures Monday to Friday, but just six/five on Saturdays/Sundays.

Bus

Comes (✆956 80 70 59; www.tgcomes.es; Plaza de la Hispanidad) has regular departures from the **bus station** (✆956 80 70 59; Plaza Sevilla) to Arcos de la Frontera (€5.11, one hour), El Puerto de Santa María (€1.56, 45 minutes), Granada (€32.80, 5½ hours), Jerez de la Frontera (€1.72, one hour), Málaga (€24.62, four hours), Ronda (€15, two hours), Seville (€8.68, one hour and 45 minutes), Tarifa (€8.60, 1½ hours) and Vejer de la Frontera (€5.95, one hour and 20 minutes). In addition to some of the above destinations, **Los Amarillos** (www.losamarillos.es) also runs buses to El Bosque, Sanlúcar de Barrameda and Ubrique from the southern end of Avenida Ramón de Carranza. Buses M050 and M051, run by the **Consorcio de Transportes Bahía de Cádiz** (✆956 01 21 00; www.cmtbc.com), travel from Jerez de la Frontera airport to Cádiz' Comes bus station, via Jerez city and El Puerto de Santa María.

Car & Motorcycle

The AP4 motorway from Seville to Puerto Real on the eastern side of the Bahía de Cádiz carries a €5.50 toll. The toll-free A4 is slower.

There's a handily placed **underground car park** (Paseo de Canalejas; per 24hr €9) near the port area.

Train

From the **train station** (✆902 240202), plenty of trains run daily to/from El Puerto de Santa María (€4.10, 30 minutes, 15 daily), Jerez de la Frontera (€5, 40 minutes, 15 daily), Seville (€13.25, one hour and 45 minutes, 15 daily) and Madrid (€72.20, 4½ hours, three daily). The high-speed AVE service from Madrid should operate to Cádiz by 2013.

El Puerto de Santa María

POP 89,000

When you're surrounded by such cultural luminaries as Cádiz, Jerez and Seville, it's easy to get lost in the small print; such is the fate El Puerto de Santa María, a strange oversight considering its stash of well-known icons. Osborne with its famous bull logo (which has become the national symbol of Spain) was founded and retains its HQ here, as do half a dozen other sherry bodegas. El Puerto also claims one of Spain's great bullrings and a weighty bullfighting legacy to go with it. Gastronomy is its other forte. There are more decent tapas bars per head here than almost anywhere else in Spain. Review your itinerary – try to squeeze El Puerto in.

◉ Sights & Activities

The four-spouted **Fuente de las Galeras Reales** (Fountain of the Royal Galleys; Plaza de las Galeras Reales), by the Muelle del Vapor, once supplied water to America-bound ships.

The nearest beach is pine-flanked **Playa de la Puntilla** (🚍26), a half-hour walk from the centre – or take bus 26 (€1) along Avenida Aramburu de Mora. In high summer the beaches furthest out, such as Playa Fuenterrabía, reached by bus 35 from the centre, are least hectic.

Castillo San Marcos   CASTLE
(✆956 85 17 51; Plaza Alfonso X El Sabio; admission Tue free, Thu & Sat €5; ⊗tours 11.30am, 12.30pm & 1.30pm Tue, 10.30am, 11.30am, 12.30pm & 1.30pm Thu & Sat) The castle is open for half-hour guided tours three days a week, with a sampling of Caballero sherry included (the company owns the castle). The highlight is the pre-13th-century mosque (now a church) preserved inside.

Fundación Rafael Alberti   MUSEUM
(✆956 85 07 11; www.rafaelalberti.es; Calle Santo Domingo 25; admission €5, audio guide €1; ⊗11am-2.30pm Tue-Sun) A few blocks inland from Castillo de San Marcos, this place has interesting exhibits on Rafael Alberti (1902–99), one of the great poets of Spain's 'Generation of 27', who grew up here. The exhibits are

well displayed and audio guides in English, German or Spanish (€1) are available.

FREE Plaza de Toros   BULLRING

(Plaza Elías Ahuja; ⊙11am-1.30pm & 6-7.30pm Tue-Sun May-Sep, 11am-1.30pm & 5.30-7pm Tue-Sun Oct-Apr) Four blocks southwest from Plaza de España is El Puerto's grand Plaza de Toros which was built in 1880 and remains one of Andalucía's most beautiful and important bullrings, with room for 15,000 spectators. It's closed on days before and after bullfights. Entry to the bullring is from Calle Valdés.

Sherry Bodegas   WINERY

The best known of El Puerto's seven sherry wineries, Osborne (☎956 86 91 00; www.osborne.es; Calle Los Moros 7; tours in English/Spanish/German €6; ⊙tours 10.30am, 11am, noon & 12.30pm Mon-Fri, 11am & noon Sat) and Terry (☎956 15 15 00; www.bodegasterry.com; Calle Toneleros 1; tour €8, tour & horse show €15; ⊙10.30am & 12.30pm Mon-Fri, noon Sat), offer weekday tours and sometimes add extra tours, including on Saturday, in summer. For Osborne you need to phone ahead; for Terry you don't.

Iglesia Mayor Prioral   CHURCH

(☎956 85 17 16; ⊙8.30am-12.45pm Mon-Fri, 8.30am-noon Sat, 8.30am-1.45pm Sun, 6-8.30pm daily) El Puerto's most splendid church, the 15th- to 18th-century Iglesia Mayor Prioral dominates Plaza de España.

🛏 Sleeping

The tourist office's accommodation list and website helpfully highlight places with wheelchair access.

TOP CHOICE Palacio
San Bartolomé   LUXURY HOTEL €€€

(☎956 85 09 46; www.palaciosanbartolome.com; Calle San Bartolomé 21, El Puerto de Santa María; r €80-175; ❋@🛜🏊) Every now and again along comes a new hotel that blows even the most jaded hotel reviewer out of the water. Fancy a room with its own mini swimming pool, sauna, Jacuzzi, towelling bathrobes and deckchairs? It´s all yours for €175 at the deftly designed San Bart, opened in a former palace in 2010.

If you don't bag the pool room, the others are equally luxurious. Count on four-poster beds, giant showers and a shared on-site gym and spa.

El Baobab Hostel   HOSTEL €

(☎956 54 21 23; www.casabaobab.es; Calle Pagador 37, El Puerto de Santa María; s/d incl breakfast €28/55, dm €22.50; P❋🛜) Just across from the Plaza de Toros in a converted 19th-century building, this small, six-room hostel is the best budget choice in El Puerto, with a homely friendly feel. The interior renovations are tastefully done and the shared bathrooms are spotless.

Hotel Monasterio San Miguel   HOTEL €€€

(☎956 54 04 40; www.hotelesjale.com; Calle Virgen de los Milagros 27; s/d €105/140; P❋@🛜🏊) A gourmet restaurant, a pool in a semitropical garden, and classically elegant rooms await your pleasure at this luxurious converted 18th-century monastery. The on-site restaurant is gourmet and the cafeteria is equally tempting.

🍃 Casa del
Regidor Hotel   BOUTIQUE HOTEL €€

(☎956 87 73 33; www.hotelcasadelregidor.com; Ribera del Río 30; s/d €65/95; ❋@🛜) A converted 18th-century mansion with its original patio. The excellent rooms have all mod cons and solar-heated hot water.

🍴 Eating

El Puerto has one of the best collections of tapas bars of any town of its size in Andalucía. The main streets to look in are the central Calle Luna; Calle Misericordia and Ribera del Marisco to the north; and Avenidas Bajamar and Aramburu de Mora to the south. Seafood is the speciality. For wonderful local cakes, including the speciality *caramelos*, try Cafetería La Merced (Calle Ganada 46).

TOP CHOICE Mesón del Asador   SPANISH, GRILL €€

(www.mesondelasador.com; Calle Misericordia 2; tapas €2.20, mains €12-15) It's a measure of El Puerto's gastronomic nous that, in such a seafood orientated town, there exists a meat restaurant that could compete with any steakhouse in Buenos Aires. The power of the Mesón's delivery is in the smell that hits you as soon as you open the door – chargrilled beef and pork sizzling away on mini-barbecues that are brought to your table.

Try the chorizo, and don't miss the chicken or pork bruschettas.

Aponiente   SEAFOOD, FUSION €€€

(☎956 85 18 70; www.aponiente.com; Puerto Escondido 6; 12-course tasting menu €95; ⊙closed Mon & dinner Sun, closed Jan–mid Mar) Audacious is the word for the bold experimentation of leading Spanish chef Angel León, whose seafood biased *nueva cocina* menu has won a cavalcade of unusual awards, including a Michelin star and a 2011 plug from the *New York Times* citing it as one of 10 restaurants in the world 'worth a plane ride' (not particularly eco, but you get the drift).

The restaurant splits local opinion in traditional El Puerto. Some snort at its prices and pretension, others salivate at the thought of tripe stew, yeast fermented mackerel and creamy rice with micro-seaweeds.

Romerijo
SEAFOOD €

(☑956 54 12 54; Plaza de la Herrería; seafood per 250g from €4.50) A huge, always busy El Puerto institution, Romerijo has two buildings, one boiling the seafood, the other frying it. Choose from the displays and buy by the quarter-kilogram in paper cones to eat at the Formica tables.

Bar Santa María
TAPAS €

(Plaza Galeras Reales; tapas €2-3.50) Chink glasses and compare tapa recipes in this riverfront haven of good taste where fish rules.

🍷 Drinking

Bodega Obregón
BAR

(Calle Zarza 51; ⊙closed Mon) Think sherry's just a drink for grandmas? Come and have your illusions blown out of the water at this spit-and-sawdust-style bar where the sweet stuff is siphoned from woody barrels. Flamenco is supposed to happen Sundays between 12.30pm and 3pm.

ℹ Information

Tourist office (☑956 54 24 13; www.turismo elpuerto.com; Plaza de Alfonso X El Sabio 9; ⊙10am-2pm & 6-8pm May-Sep) The excellent tourist office has new digs right next to the Castillo de San Marcos.

ℹ Getting There & Away

Boat

Catamarans (www.cmtbc.es) leave from in front of the Hotel Santa María bound for Cádiz' Terminal Marítima Metropolitana (€2.35, 30 minutes), with 18 daily departures Monday to Friday and six/five on Saturdays/Sundays.

Bus

Regular bus services connect El Puerto de Santa María's Plaza de Toros to Cádiz (€1.56, 45 minutes), Jerez de la Frontera (€1.60, 20 minutes) and Sanlúcar de Barrameda (€1.67, 15 minutes). Buses to Seville go daily from the train station.

Train

Daily trains go to/from Jerez de la Frontera (€2.20, 10 minutes, 15 daily) and Cádiz (€4.10, 30 minutes, 15 daily) and Seville (€11.10, one hour and 20 minutes, 15 daily).

Sanlúcar de Barrameda
POP 67,000

Sanlúcar is one of those lesser-known Andalucian cities that you'd do well to shoehorn into your itinerary. The reasons? Firstly, there's gastronomy. Sanlúcar cooks up some of the best seafood in the region on a hallowed waterside strip called Bajo de Guía. Secondly, Sanlúcar sits at the northern tip of the esteemed sherry triangle, and the bodegas nestled in the somnolent old town retain a less commercial, earthier quality. Thirdly, situated at the mouth of the Guadalquivir estuary, the city provides a quieter, less trammelled entry point into the ethereal Parque Nacional de Doñana, preferably via boat.

As if that wasn't enough, Sanlúcar harbours a proud nautical history: both Columbus (on his third sojourn) and Portuguese mariner Ferdinand Magellan struck out from here on their voyages of discovery.

With excellent transport links, Sanlúcar makes an easy day trip from Cádiz or Jerez.

◉ Sights

FREE **Palacio de Orleans y Borbon**
PALACE

(cnr Cuesta de Belén & Calle Caballero; ⊙10am-1.30pm Mon-Fri) From Plaza del Cabildo, cross Calle Ancha to Plaza San Roque and head up Calle Bretones, which becomes Calle Cuesta de Belén. Then dogleg up to this beautiful neo-Mudéjar palace in the Old Town that was built as a summer home for the aristocratic Montpensier family in the 19th century and is now Sanlúcar's town hall.

Iglesia de Nuestra Señora de la O
CHURCH

(Plaza de la Paz; ⊙mass 7.30pm Mon-Fri, 9am, noon & 7.30pm Sun) A block to the left from Palacio de Orleans y Borbón, along Calle Caballeros, this medieval church stands out among Sanlúcar's churches for its beautiful Gothic Mudéjar main portal, created in the 1360s, and the richness of its interior decoration, including the Mudéjar *artesonado* ceilings.

Palacio de los Duques de Medina Sidonia
PALACE, MUSEUM

(☑956 36 01 61; www.fcmedinasidonia.com; Plaza Condes de Niebla 1; admission €3; ⊙tours 11am &

noon Mon-Sat, by appointment Sun) Next door to the Iglesia de Nuestra Señora de la O, this was the rambling home of the aristocratic family that once owned more of Spain than anyone else. The house, mostly dating to the 17th century, bursts with antiques, and paintings by Goya, Zurbarán and other famous Spanish artists.

Castillo de Santiago CASTLE
(☑956 08 83 29; www.castillodesantiago.com; Plaza del Castillo de Santiago; ◷guided tours 11am, noon & 1pm Thu-Sun) Located amid buildings of the Barbadillo sherry company, this restored 15th-century castle has great views from its hexagonal Torre del Homenaje (Keep). Entry to the Patio de Armas and its restaurant is free.

☞ Tours

Sherry Bodegas
Sanlúcar produces a distinctive sherrylike wine, known as manzanilla. Several bodegas give tours for which you don't need to book ahead.

Barbadillo Bodega WINERY TOUR
(☑956 38 55 00; www.museobarbadillo.com; Calle Luis de Eguilaz 11; tour €3, museum free; ◷tours noon & 1pm Mon-Sat, in English 11am Tue-Sat, Museo de Manzanilla 10am-3pm Mon-Sat) Near the castle, Barbadillo is the oldest and biggest manzanilla firm. There's also a good manzanilla museum here, which you can visit independently of the tour.

Parque Nacional de Doñana
Boat departures for the Parque Nacional de Doñana leave from Bajo de Guía, 750m northeast from La Calzada. Here, the Centro de Visitantes Fábrica de Hielo (☑956 38 16 35; Bajo de Guía; ◷9am-7pm) provides displays and information on the Parque Nacional de Doñana.

From Bajo de Guía, Viajes Doñana (☑956 36 25 40; viajesdonana@hotmail.com; Calle San Juan 20; ◷8.30am & 4.30pm Tue & Fri May–mid-Sep, 8.30am & 2.30pm Tue & Fri mid-Sep–Apr) and Viajes Correcaminos (☑956 38 20 40; Calle Ramón y Cajal 4) operate 3½-hour guided tours into the national park, at 8.30am and 2.30pm on Tuesday and Friday (the afternoon trips go at 4.30pm from May to mid-September). After the river crossing, the trip is by 20-person 4WD vehicle, visiting much the same spots as the tours from El Acebuche. On the trip, either take mosquito repellent or cover up.

 Festivals & Events

The Sanlúcar summer gets going with the Feria de la Manzanilla, in late May or early June, and blossoms in July and August with jazz, flamenco and classical-music festivals, one-off concerts by top Spanish bands, and Sanlúcar's unique horse races, the Carreras de Caballo (www.carrerassanlucar.es), in which thoroughbred racehorses thunder along the beach during two three-day evening meetings during August.

🛏 Sleeping
Book well ahead at holiday times.

Hotel Posada de Palacio HISTORIC HOTEL €€
(☑956 36 48 40; www.posadadepalacio.com; Calle Caballeros 11, Sanlúcar de Barrameda; s/d from €88/109; P❋@⊛) Plant-filled patios, gracious historical charm and 18th-century luxury add up to one of the best places to stay in this part of Andalucía. There's antique furniture, but it's rarely overdone and never weighs heavily on the surrounds thanks to the high ceilings and abundance of light.

Hotel Barrameda HOTEL €
(☑956 38 58 78; www.hotelbarrameda.com; Calle Ancha 10, Sanlúcar de Barrameda; d incl breakfast €45-65; ❋@⊛) Looking out over the tapas bar action of Plaza Cabildo, this 30-room central hotel has added some stylish modern rooms to its newer wing, with no big price hikes. Throw in a ground floor patio, marble floors, decent art and a roof terrace, and you've nabbed a bargain.

Tartaneros Hotel HOTEL €€
(☑956 38 53 93; www.hoteltartaneros.com; Calle Tartaneros 8; s/d from €85/100; ❋@⊛) This is a century-old industrialist's mansion with assorted fin-de-siècle artefacts and comfortable rooms, located at the inland end of Calzada del Ejército.

✗ Eating
Spain holds few dreamier dining experiences than tucking into ocean-fresh seafood while watching the sun go down over the Guadalquivir at Bajo de Guía, a strip of high-quality but easygoing fish restaurants overlooking the river estuary about 750m northeast of the town centre.

Cafes and bars, many of them serving manzanilla from the barrel, surround Plaza del Cabildo and Plaza San Roque behind it: Casa Balbino (www.casabalbino.com; Plaza del Cabildo 11; tapas €3) is a must for tapas. For some of the best ice cream in Andalucía don't miss **Helados Artesanos** (www. heladostoni.com; Plaza de Cabildo 2), family run since 1896, with videos demonstrating the fine art of ice cream–making rolling behind the counter.

TOP CHOICE **Poma** SEAFOOD €€

(www.restaurantepoma.com; Avenida de Bajo de Guía 6; mains €12-18) You could kick a football on the Guía de Bajo and guarantee it'd land on a decent plate of fish. It just might be Poma, where the *plato variado* comes with about five different varieties of lightly fried species plucked out of the nearby sea and river.

Cafetería Guzmán El Bueno CAFE, DESSERTS €

(Plaza Condes de Niebla 1; dishes €3-8, ☺8.30am-9pm, extended hours Sat & Jul & Aug) Sink into plump cushions surrounded by antique furnishings at the cafe in the Palacio de los Duques de Medina Sidonia. Fare is simple – omelettes, cheese, ham – but the setting is uniquely atmospheric.

Casa Bigote SEAFOOD €€

(www.restaurantecasabigote.com; Avenida Bajo de Guía 10; fish mains €7-14; ☺closed Sun) The most renowned of the Bajo de Guía restaurants is Casa Bigote, which has a classier air than most places and serves only fish and seafood. Its tapas bar across the small lane is always packed.

☆ Entertainment

There are some lively music bars on and around Calzada del Ejército and Plaza del Cabildo, and lots of concerts are held in summer.

ℹ Information

Tourist office (www.turismosanlucar.com; Calzada del Ejército; ☺10am-2pm & 6-8pm Mon-Fri, 10am-12.45pm Sat & 10am-2pm Sun) Multilingual and very helpful staff.

ℹ Getting There & Away

Los Amarillos (☑956 38 50 60; www.losamarillos.es) runs hourly buses to/from El Puerto de Santa María (€1.87, 15 minutes), Cádiz (€4.55, one hour) and Seville (€8.04, 1½ hours) from the bus station on Avenida de la Estación. **Linesur** (☑956 34 10 63) has hourly buses to/from Jerez de la Frontera.

Jerez de la Frontera

POP 211,000

Stand down all other claimants. Jerez, as most savvy Spain-o-philes know, *is* Andalucía. It just doesn't broadcast the fact in the way that Seville and Granada do. As a result, few people plan their trip around a visit here, preferring instead to jump-cut to the glories of the Giralda and the Alhambra. If only they knew. Jerez is the capital of *andaluz* horse culture, stop one on the famed sherry triangle and – cue the protestations from Cádiz and Seville – the cradle of Spanish flamenco. The *bulería*, Jerez' jokey, tongue-in-cheek antidote to Seville's tragic *soleá*, was first concocted in the legendary Roma *barrios* of Santiago and San Miguel. If you really want to unveil the eternal riddle that is Andalucía, start here.

◉ Sights & Activities

Alcázar FORTRESS

(☑956 14 99 55; Alameda Vieja; admission incl/excl camera obscura €5.40/3; ☺10am-7.30pm Mon-Sat, to 2.30pm Sun May–mid-Sep, 10am-5.30pm Mon-Sat, to 2.30pm Sun mid-Sep–Apr) Jerez's muscular yet refined 11th- or 12th-century fortress is one of the best preserved Almohad-era (1140s–1212) relics left in Andalucía. It's noted for its octagonal tower, a classic example of Almohad defensive forts.

You enter the Alcázar via the **Patio de Armas**. On the left is the beautiful *mezquita* (mosque), which was converted to a chapel by Alfonso X in 1264. Beyond the Patio de Armas, the lovely gardens re-create the ambience of Islamic times with their geometrical plant beds and tinkling fountains, while the domed **Baños Árabes** (Arab Baths) with their shafts of light are another highlight. Back on the Patio de Armas, the 18th-century **Palacio Villavicencio**, built over the ruins of the old Islamic palace, contains works of art, but is best known for its bird's-eye view of Jerez from the summit; the palace's tower also contains a **camera obscura**, which provides a picturesque live panorama of Jerez.

TOP CHOICE **Catedral de San Salvador** CATHEDRAL

(Plaza de la Encarnación; admission €5; ☺10.30am-6.30pm Mon-Sat, 12.30-3.30pm Sun) Echoes of Seville colour Jerez' wonderful cathedral, a surprisingly harmonious mix of baroque, neoclassical and gothic styles. Stand-out features are its broad flying buttresses and its

A VERY BRITISH DRINK

It's the names that give it away: Harvey, Sandeman, Terry, Humbert and Osborne. Andalucía's sherry industry might be Spanish in character but it was undisputedly Anglo-Irish in its genesis. You can blame Francis Drake for Britain's sherry obsession. The daring Elizabethan privateer set a precedent in 1587 when he sacked Cádiz and greedily made off with over 3000 barrels of the local *vino*. Before long, the normally undiscerning Brits had developed an incurable taste for Spain's fortified wine – and they wanted more of it. To meet the demand, a whole new industry was inauspiciously born. Early British entrepreneurs included Thomas Osborne Mann, a shopkeeper from Exeter who had resettled in Cádiz; George Sandeman, a Scotsman from Perth; John Harvey from Bristol who concocted the world's first cream sherry, Harvey's Bristol Cream, in the 1860s; and the Garvey and Terry families, both from Southern Ireland. Even Spain's most famous sherry dynasty Gonzalez-Byass – producers of the trademark Tio Pepe brand – was formed from an Anglo-Spanish alliance hatched in 1835 between Andalucian Manuel Maria Gonzalez and his London-based agent (and Englishman) Robert Byass.

intricately decorated stone ceilings. In 2012 the cathedral opened as a musuem showing off its art (including works by Zurbarán and Pacheco), religious garments, and silverware in a series of rooms and chapels behind the main altar.

You can also enjoy an orange tree–lined patio (the church was built on the site of an old mosque) and a 'secret staircase' to nowhere. Named for San Salvador, the building only offically became a cathedral as recently as 1980.

A couple of blocks northeast of the cathedral is Plaza de la Asunción, with the handsome 16th-century Antiguo Cabildo (Old Town Hall) and lovely 15th-century Mudéjar Iglesia de San Dionisio.

Real Escuela Andaluza del Arte Ecuestre
EQUESTRIAN SHOW

(956 31 80 08; www.realescuela.org; Avenida Duque de Abrantes; training sessions adult/child €10/6, exhibición adult/child €19/12; training sessions 11am-1pm Mon, Wed & Fri Sep-Jul, Mon & Wed Aug, noon Tue & Thu Sep-Jul, exhibición noon Tue, Thu & Fri Aug) The famed Royal Andalucian School of Equestrian Art trains horses and riders in equestrian skills, and you can watch them going through their paces in training sessions and visit the Horse Carriage Museum, which includes an 18th-century Binder Hunting Break. The highlight for most is the official exhibición (show) where the handsome white horses show off their tricks to classical music. You can book tickets online for this – advisable for the official shows, which can sell out.

Barrio de Santiago
NEIGHBOURHOOD

Northwest of Plaza de la Asunción, the Barrio de Santiago has a sizeable Roma population. The excellent Museo Arqueológico (956 35 01 33; Plaza del Mercado) here was still undergoing protracted renovations at the time of writing; it is expected to reopen soon. When it does, its impressive collection of local finds includes a 7th-century-BC Greek helmet, found in Río Guadalete, among other highlights. Also in this area is the Centro Andaluz de Flamenco (Andalusian Flamenco Centre; 856 81 41 32; www.centro andaluzdeflamenco.es; Plaza de San Juan 1; 9am-2pm Mon-Fri). Jerez is at the heart of the Seville–Cádiz axis where flamenco originated. This centre is a kind of flamenco museum, library and school, with a different flamenco video screened each day.

Hammam Andalusi
HAMMAM

(Arabic baths; 956 34 90 66; www.hammam andalusi.com; Calle Salvador 6; baths €22, with 15/30-min massage €32/50; 10am-midnight) Jerez is replete with echoes of the city's Islamic past, but there is none more evocative than the Hammam Andalusi. As soon as you enter, you're greeted by the wafting scent of incense and essential oils, and the soothing sound of tinkling water and Arab music. Once inside, you pass, depending on the package you choose, through the three pools (hot, tepid or cold), and you can add a massage and/or a variety of beauty treatments. There's even a chocolate bath (€85). Sessions are limited to 15 people, so be sure to reserve beforehand.

SHERRY BODEGAS

Jerez is home to around 20 bodegas and most are open to visitors, but they're scattered around town and many of them require you to call ahead. The tourist office has up-to-date information.

Bodegas González Byass   WINERY
(Bodegas Tio Pepe; ☎956 35 70 16; www.bodegas tiopepe.com; Calle Manuel María González 12; tour €11, with tapas €16; ☺tours in English & Spanish hourly 11am-6pm Mon-Sat, to 2pm Sun Oct-Apr) Home of the Tio Pepe brand and one of the biggest sherry houses, handily located just west of the Alcázar. Six or seven tours each are given daily in English and Spanish, and a few in German and French. Reservations can be made online.

Bodegas Tradición   WINERY
(☎956 16 86 28; www.bodegastradicion.com; Plaza Cordobeses 3; tours €18; ☺9am-6.30pm Mon-Fri, 10am-2pm Sat Mar-Jun, 8am-3pm Sat Jul & Aug) An interesting bodega, not only for its extra-aged sherries (20 or more years old), but because it houses the Colección Joaquín Rivera, a private Spanish art collection that includes important works by Goya, Velázquez and Zurbarán. Tours (mainly in English and Spanish, with a few in Italian, German and French) of the collection are given three or four times a day.

Bodegas Sandeman   WINERY
(☎956 15 17 11; www.sandeman.com; Calle Pizarro 10; tour in English €7, with tasting €14; ☺tours hourly 11.30am-2.30pm Mon, Wed & Fri, 10.30am & hourly noon-3pm Tue & Thu, 11am, 1pm & 2pm Sat) Has three or four tours each in English, Spanish and German, and one in French.

⚔ Festivals & Events

Jerez has a comprehensive calendar of festive events. These are the biggest highlights:

Motorcycle Grand Prix   MOTORCYCLES
Jerez' **Circuito Permanente de Velocidad** (Racing Circuit; ☎956 15 11 00; www.circuitode jerez.com), on the A382 10km east of town, hosts several motorcycle- and car-racing events each year (usually in March, April or May), including one of the Grand Prix races of the World Motorcycle Championship.

Festival de Jerez   FLAMENCO
(www.festivaldejerez.com) Jerez' biggest celebration of flamenco in late February/early March.

Feria del Caballo   HORSES
(Horse Fair) Jerez' week-long Horse Fair in late April or the first half of May is one of Andalucía's grandest festivals, with music, dance and bullfights as well as all kinds of equestrian competitions and parades.

🛏 Sleeping

Many places almost double their rates for the Motorcycle Grand Prix and Feria del Caballo, and you need to book ahead.

[TOP CHOICE] Hotel Casa Grande   HOTEL €€
(☎956 34 50 70; www.casagrande.com.es; Plaza de las Angustias 3; r €85-105, ste €115-125; [P][✽][@]) This brilliant hotel occupies a carefully restored 1920s mansion. Rooms are spread over three floors and set around a patio, or beside the roof terrace, which has views of Jerez' roof line. All is overseen by the congenial Monika Schroeder, a mine of information about Jerez.

🏠 Hotel Chancillería   HOTEL €€
(☎956 30 10 38; www.hotelchancilleria.com; Calle Chancillería 21; s €55-140, d €80-180; [✽][@][🛜]) Opened in January 2008, this stunning renovation of two 17th-century homes is a discreet temple to good taste. There are many highlights: African art, an original 17th-century wall, a lovely garden, stylish and spacious rooms, a delightful roof terrace and one of Jerez' best restaurants, Sabores.

Nuevo Hotel   HOTEL €
(☎956 33 16 00; www.nuevohotel.com; Calle Caballeros 23; s/d incl breakfast €27/42; [✽][@][🛜][🅿]) One of the most pleasant family-run hotels in Anadalucía, the Nuevo's comfortable rooms are complemented by spectacular *habitación* (room) 208, replete with Islamic-style stuccowork and *azulejos*. You'll wake up thinking you've taken up residence in the Alhambra.

Hotel Bellas Artes   HOTEL €€
(☎956 34 84 30; www.hotelbellasartes.com; Plaza del Arroyo 45; d €69-99; [✽][@][🛜][🅿]) A top-notch palace conversion, the Bellas Artes overlooks the cathedral from its main terrace and suites. An exquisite carved stone corner pillar graces the sand-coloured neoclassical exterior. Strong interior colours contrast with white marble floors. Free-standing bath-tubs further contribute to an old-world ambience, though rooms have all the mod cons.

Hotel Palacio Garvey
HOTEL €€€

(☎956 32 67 00; www.sferahoteles.net; Calle Tornería 24; s/d €224/293; P❄@🛜🏊) The Garvey is a sensational 19th-century neo-classical palace conversion, with part of the ancient city wall visible from the lift and more of it in the gardens. The public areas sport animal prints, large, colourful paintings and Japanese-inspired bowls on low-slung tables, while subtle colours and luxurious leather furniture feature in the 16 individually decorated rooms.

Hostal Fenix
HOSTAL €

(☎956 34 52 91; www.hostalfenix.com; Calle Cazón 7; d incl breakfast from €30; ❄🛜) There's nothing flash about the Fenix, which is part of its charm. Simple rooms are well-maintained by ultrafriendly owners who'll bring you breakfast (included in the price) on a tray to your room. The impressive art adorning the walls is painted by the *dueña* (owner) and her cousin.

Eating

The sherry trade has introduced English and French accents into the local cuisine. Jerez also prizes its cured and grilled meats, and fish. Central Jerez is littered with great tapas bars. The pedestrian streets just north of Plaza del Arenal are a fine place to start.

TOP CHOICE Sabores
CONTEMPORARY ANDALUCIAN €€

(☎956 32 98 35; www.restaurantesabores.es; Chancillera 21; mains from €12) When scrambled eggs go gourmet, you know you're onto something special. In actual fact, the eggs are flambéed with cured ham, but whatever the method, the results are melt-in-your-mouth delicious. You can back it up with dishes such as beef cheek, or creative fish all presented like modern art on your plate.

Not without merit, Sabores is one of Andalucía's best restaurants located in what might be Jerez' best hotel, the Chancillería.

Cruz Blanca
TAPAS €

(www.lacruzblanca.com; Plaza de la Yerva; tapas €1.80-3) The Cruz whips up good seafood, egg, meat and salad offerings and has tables on a quiet little plaza. The marinated fish in a pesto-flecked sauce could steal the crown for Jerez' best meal.

El Gallo Azul
SPANISH €€

(Calle Larga 2; raciones from €11.50) Housed in what has become Jerez' signature building, a circular facade emblazoned with a sherry logo, El Gallo Azul (the blue cockerel) has a restaurant upstairs and tapas at street level. It's also an excellent perch to enjoy an afternoon coffee and a slice of cake as the city springs back to life after the siesta.

Bar Juanito
TAPAS €

(www.bar-juanito.com; Calle Pescadería Vieja 8-10; tapas from €2.20, media raciones €5-7) One of the best tapas bars in Jerez, 60-year-old Bar Juanito, with its outdoor tables and checked tablecloths, is like a slice of village Andalucía in the heart of the city. Its *alcachofas* (artichokes) are a past winner of the National Tapa Competition, but there's so much local cuisine to choose from here and it's all served up with the best local wines.

La Carboná
ANDALUCIAN €€

(☎956 34 74 75; www.lacarbona.com; Calle San Francisco de Paula 2; mains €12.50-16.50; ⊗closed Tue) This popular, cavernous restaurant with an eccentric menu occupies an old bodega with a hanging fireplace that's oh-so-cosy in winter. Specialities include grilled meats and fresh fish, and the quirky quail with foie gras and rose petals.

Mesón El Patio
ANDALUCIAN €€

(Calle San Francisco de Paula 7; mains €8-17; ⊗closed Sun evening & Mon) Combining a touch of refinement with local conviviality, this place occupies a restored sherry warehouse, which means lofty ceilings, warm tones and carved wooden chairs. Above all, the food (a snapshot of Andalucía's obsession with fish and meat dishes) is terrific.

Drinking

A few bars in the narrow streets north of Plaza del Arenal can get lively with an under-30 crowd: try beer bar **Dos Deditos** (Plaza Vargas 1) and wine bar **La Carbonería** (Calle Letrados 7). Northeast of the centre, **La Plaza de Canterbury** (cnr Calles Zaragoza & N de Cañas) has a couple of pubs (one English and one Irish) around a central courtyard that attract a 20s clientele, while music bars northeast on Avenida de Méjico are the late-night headquarters for the 18–25 crowd.

Entertainment

TOP CHOICE El Lagá Tio Parrilla
FLAMENCO

(Plaza del Mercado; show & 2 drinks €25; ⊗10.30pm Mon-Sat) A high quota of Roma (both performers and clientele) ensures that this place wins most plaudits for its regular *tablaos*. Gutsy shows rarely end without

JEREZ' FERTILE FLAMENCO SCENE

Jerez' moniker as the 'cradle of flamenco' is regularly challenged by aficionados in Cádiz and Seville, but the claim has merit. This surprisingly un-touristed city harbours not just one but *two* Roma quarters, Santiago and San Miguel, which, between them, have produced a glut of renowned artists, including Roma singers, Manuel Torre and António Chacón. Like its rival cities to the north and west, Jerez has also concocted its own flamenco *palo*, the intensely popular *bulerías*, a fast rhythmic musical style with the same *compás* (accented beat) as the *soleá*.

Explorations of Jerez' flamenco scene ought to start at the Centro Andaluz de Flamenco (p698), Spain's only bona fide flamenco library where you can pick up information on clubs, performances and singing/dance/guitar lessons. From here you can stroll down Calle Francos and visit legendary flamenco bars such as Damajuana (www.damajuana cafebar.com; Calle Francos 18; ⊙4.30pm-3am Tue-Sun) and El Arriate (Calle Francos 41) where singers and dancers still congregate. To the north, in the Santiago quarter, you'll find dozens of *peñas* (small private clubs) all known for their accessibility and intimacy; entrance is normally free if you buy a drink at the bar. The *peña* scene is particularly fertile during the February flamenco festival, which is arguably Andalucía's finest.

rousing renditions of that old Jerez stalwart – the *bulería*.

Teatro Villamarta THEATRE
(⊉956 35 02 72; www.villamarta.com; Plaza Romero Martínez) Stages a busy program where you can pick up Bizet, Verdi, Mozart and – of course – a dash of flamenco.

Discoteca Oxi CLUB
(www.oxixerez.es; Calle Zaragoza 20; ⊙9pm-6am Wed-Sat) Jerez' ultimate disco has four different rooms and attracts a young crowd who dance till dawn (7am) at weekends. Theme nights are popular.

ⓘ Information

Municipal tourist office (⊉956 33 88 74; www.turismojerez.com; Plaza del Arenal; ⊙9am-3pm & 5-7pm Mon-Fri, 9.30am-2.30pm Sat & Sun)
Provincial tourist office (Airport; ⊙8.15am-2pm & 5-6.30pm Mon-Fri)

ⓘ Getting There & Around

Air

Jerez airport (⊉956 15 00 00; www.aena. es), the only one serving Cádiz province, is 7km northeast of town on the NIV. Over a dozen airlines fly into Jerez from elsewhere in Europe including: Ryanair from Barcelona and London-Stansted (seasonal), Air-Berlin from Mallorca and Düsseldorf (seasonal), and Iberia daily to/from Madrid. Taxis from the airport start at €14. The local airport buses M050 and M051 (€1, 30 minutes) run 12 times daily Monday to Friday and six times daily on weekends. From Jerez this service continues to El Puerto de Santa María and Cádiz.

Bus

The **bus station** (⊉956 33 96 66; Plaza de la Estación) is 1.3km southeast of the centre. Destinations include Seville (€7.50, 1¼ hours, 11 or more daily), Sanlúcar de Barrameda (€1.68, 30 minutes, seven or more daily), El Puerto de Santa María (€1.60, 20 minutes, 15 or more daily), Cádiz (€1.72, one hour, nine or more daily), Arcos de la Frontera (€2.64, 45 minutes, 13 daily) and Ronda (€11.50, three hours, three daily).

Train

Jerez **train station** (⊉956 34 23 19; Plaza de la Estación) is right beside the bus station. Regular trains go to El Puerto de Santa María (€2.20, 10 minutes, 15 daily) and Cádiz (€5, 40 minutes, 15 daily), and 10 or more to Seville (€9.15, 1¼ hours, 15 daily).

Arcos de la Frontera

POP 31,500 / ELEV 185M

Choosing your favourite *pueblo blanco* (white town) is like choosing your favourite Beatles album; they're all so damned good, it's hard to make a definitive decision. Pressured for an answer many people single out Arcos, a larger-than-average white town thrillingly sited on a high, unassailable ridge with sheer precipices plummeting away on both sides. With the Sierra de Grazalema as a distant backdrop, Arcos possesses all the classic white-town calling cards: spectacular location, soporific old town, fancy *parador* and volatile frontier history. The odd tour bus and foreign-owned homestay do little to dampen the drama.

For a brief period during the 11th century, Arcos was an independent Berber-ruled kingdom. In 1255 it was claimed by Christian King Alfonso X for Seville.

◉ Sights

Along the streets east of Plaza del Cabildo, take time to seek out lovely buildings such as the **Iglesia de San Pedro** (Calle Núñez de Prado; admission €1; ⊙10.30am-2pm & 5-7pm Mon-Fri, 11am-2pm Sat), another Gothic baroque confection sporting what is perhaps one of the most magnificent small church interiors in Andalucía (and it's not depressingly dark, either).

Plaza del Cabildo   SQUARE
The old town captures multiple historical eras evoking the ebb and flow of the once-disputed Christian-Moorish frontier. Plaza del Cabildo is the centre of this quarter. Close your eyes to the modern car park and focus instead on the fine surrounding buildings (all old) and a vertiginous **mirador** (lookout) with views over Río Guadalete. The 11th-century **Castillo de los Duques** is firmly closed to the public, but its outer walls frame classic Arcos views. On the plaza's northern side is the Gothic-cum-baroque **Basílica-Parroquia de Santa María** sporting beautiful stone choir stalls and Isabelline ceiling tracery. On the eastern side, the **Parador Casa del Corregidor** hotel is a reconstruction of a 16th-century magistrate's house. If you think you've already seen every possible jaw-dropping vista in Andalucía, drink this one in – preferably over a *café con leche* (half coffee and half warm milk) and accompanying *torta* (piece of cake). Outside is an equally dramatic mirador at the far end of the plaza.

☞ Tours

One-hour guided tours of the old town's monuments and pretty patios start from the tourist office at 11am Monday to Friday.

✵ Festivals & Events

Semana Santa   HOLY WEEK
Holy Week processions through the narrow old streets are dramatic; on Easter Sunday there's a hair-raising running of the bulls.

Fiesta de la Virgen de las Nieves   FLAMENCO
This three-day festival in early August includes a top-class flamenco night in Plaza del Cabildo.

Feria de San Miguel   RELIGIOUS
Arcos celebrates its patron saint with a four-day fair; held around 29 September.

⌬ Sleeping

TOP CHOICE **Parador Casa del Corregidor**   HISTORIC HOTEL €€€
(☑956 70 05 00; www.parador.es; Plaza del Cabildo, Arcos de la Frontera; r from €155; ✳@ⓢ) This rebuilt 16th-century magistrate's residence combines typical parador luxury with another magnificent cliffside setting. Eight of the 24 rooms have balconies with sweeping cliff-top views. Otherwise, most of the rest of the rooms look out onto the pretty Plaza del Cabildo.

Casa Campana   GUESTHOUSE €
(☑956 70 47 87; www.casacampana.com; Calle Nuñez de Prado 4, Arcos de la Frontera; d/apt €50/65; ✳@ⓢ⊕) In the heart of old Arcos, and run by the superfriendly Emma and Jim who are extremely knowledgeable about the local area, Casa Campana has two simple doubles and a massive apartment that's filled with character. The quiet roof terrace is a fine place to relax with good views and a real sense of privacy. Jim has recently added a cafe and ice cream window downstairs.

Hotel El Convento   HOTEL €€
(☑956 70 23 33; www.hotelelconvento.es; Calle Maldonado 2; s/d incl breakfast from €55/70) The nuns who used to live in this beautiful, former 17th-century convent obviously appreciated a good view. Now it's been turned into a slightly chintzy hotel.

Hotel Marques de Torresoto   HOTEL €
(☑956 70 07 17; www.hotelmarquesdetorresoto. com; Calle Marqués de Torresoto 4; s/d €35/50) The deal of the season is waiting in the junglelike inner courtyard of this Arcos gem. Beyond the grand entry the 15 rooms are a little plain with an odd layout, but at this price who's complaining?

Hotel Real de Veas   HOTEL €€
(☑956 71 73 70; www.hotelrealdeveas.com; Calle Corredera 12; s/d incl breakfast €55/70) A superb option inside a lovingly restored building. The dozen or so rooms are arranged around a glass-covered patio and are cool and comfortable. It's one of the few places that has easy car access.

Eating

TOP CHOICE Bar La Cárcel TAPAS €€
(☏956 70 04 10; Calle Deán Espinosa 18; tapas & montaditos €2.50, raciones €8-12; ⊙8am-noon Mon, to late Tue-Sun) A *cárcel* (prison) in name only, this friendly and authentic place offers no-nonsense tapas (bank on fajitas, or aubergine with goat's cheese and honey) with ice-cold *cañas* (glasses of beer) for customers who sit at beer barrels doubling as tables.

Restaurante-Café Babel MOROCCAN, FUSION €€
(Calle Corredera 11; dishes €8-12) Arcos' new Moorish fusion spot has some tasteful decor (the ornate stools were shipped in from Casablanca) and some equally tasty dishes: count on tagines and couscous, or the full Arabic tea treatment with silver pots and sweet pastries.

ℹ Information

The **tourist office** (☏956 70 22 64; Calle Cuesta de Belén 5; ⊙10am-2.30pm & 5.30-8pm Mon-Fri, 10.30am-1.30pm & 5-7pm Sat, 10.30am-1.30pm Sun) is on the old town's main square.

Banks and ATMs are along Calle Debajo del Corral and Calle Corredera.

ℹ Getting There & Away

From the **bus station** (☏956 70 49 77), **Los Amarillos** (www.losamarillos.es) and/or **Comes** (www.tgcomes.es) have daily buses (fewer on weekends) to Cádiz (€5.11, one hour, eight daily), Olvera (€5.81, 1½ hours, three daily), Jerez de la Frontera (€2.64, 45 minutes, 19 daily), Málaga (€16.85, 3½ hours, two daily) and Ronda (€8.75, two hours, two daily).

Parque Natural Sierra de Grazalema & Around

Of all Andalucía's protected areas, Parque Natural Sierra de Grazalema is the most accessible and best set up for lung-stretching sorties into the countryside. Though not as lofty as the Sierra Nevada, the park's rugged pillarlike peaks nonetheless rise abruptly off the plains northeast of Cádiz, revealing precipitous gorges, wild orchids and hefty rainfall (stand aside Galicia and Cantabria, this is the wettest part of Spain, logging an average 2000mm annually). Grazalema is also fine walking country (the best months are May, June, September and October). For the more intrepid there are opportunities for climbing, caving, canyoning, kayaking and paragliding.

The park extends into northwestern Málaga province, where it includes the Cueva de la Pileta. The **Centro de Visitantes** (☏956 72 70 29; Avenida de la Diputación; ⊙10am-2pm & 6-8pm Mon-Sat, 9am-2pm Sun), with limited displays and information, is situated in the village of El Bosque, 20km east of Grazalema village.

GRAZALEMA
POP 2200 / ELEV 825M

A true mountain 'white town', Grazalema looks like it has been dropped from a passing spaceship onto the steep rocky slopes of its eponymous mountain range. Few *pueblos blancos* are as generically perfect as this one, with its spotless whitewashed houses sporting rust-tiled roofs and wrought-iron window bars. Grazalema embraces the great outdoors with hikes fanning out in all directions, but it's also an age-old producer of blankets, honey, meat-filled stews and an adrenalin-filled bull-running festival. There's an artisan textile factory in the town that still employs traditional weaving methods.

🏃 Activities

You're in walking country, so make the most of it. Good hiking info can be procured at the tourist office. Four of the park's best hikes (including the 12.5km El Pinsapar walk through Spain's best-preserved fir woodland) traverse restricted areas and must be booked ahead at the **visitor centre** (☏956 72 70 29; Calle Federico García Lorca 1; ⊙10am-2pm & 5-7pm Mon-Sat, 9am-2pm Sun) in El Bosque. Of the free-access paths, the most dramatic is the 7.2km **Sendero Salto del Cabrero** between Grazalema village and Benaocaz between the Puerto del Boyar that traverses the western flanks of the Sierra del Endrinal. Look out for rare wild orchids along the way.

Horizon ADVENTURE SPORTS
(☏956 13 23 63; www.horizonaventura.com; Calle Corrales Terceros 29, Grazalema) Horizon, a block off Plaza de España, is a highly experienced adventure firm that will take you climbing, bungee jumping, canyoning, caving, paragliding or walking, with English-speaking guides. Prices per person range from around €14 for a half-day walk to around €60 for the 4km underground wetsuit adventure from the Cueva del Hundidero near Montejaque to the Cueva del Gato near Benaoján. Minimum group sizes apply for some activities.

🛏 Sleeping & Eating

🍴 Casa de las Piedras
HOTEL €

(☎956 13 20 14; www.casadelaspiedras.net; Calle de las Piedras 32, Grazalema; s/d/apt €42/48/65; ❋❋☎) Mountain airs and a homely feel go together like Ferdinand and Isabel in the Casa de la Piedras, a 16-room rural hotel with a cozy downstairs lounge and bags of information on park activities. The blankets in the simple but clean rooms are made in Grazalema village.

Restaurante El Torreón
ANDALUCIAN €€

(www.restauranteeltorreongrazalema.com; mains €8-12) This friendly mountain restaurant is where you can take a break from the Cádiz fish monopoly with local chorizo, spinach, soups and the menu speciality, partridge. There's pasta for kids.

❶ Information

The village centre is the pretty Plaza de España, overlooked by the 18th-century Iglesia de la Aurora. Here you'll find the **tourist office** (☎956 13 20 73; ⊙10am-2pm & 4-9pm), with a shop selling local products. Two banks on Plaza de España have ATMs.

ZAHARA DE LA SIERRA
POP 1500 / ELEV 550M

Rugged Zahara, set around a vertiginous crag at the foot of the Sierra de Grazalema, hums with Moorish mystery. For over 150 years in the 14th and 15th centuries, it stood on the old medieval frontier facing off against Christian Olvera, clearly visible in the distance. These days Zahara encapsulates all of the best elements of a classic white town and is popular as a result. Come during the afternoon siesta, however, and you can still hear a pin drop.

The precipitous road over the ultrasteep 1331m Puerto de los Palomas (Doves' Pass) links Zahara with Grazalema (18km) and is a spectacular ride full of white-knuckle switchbacks (try it on a bike!).

Zahara's streets invite investigation, with vistas framed by tall palms and hot-pink bougainvillea. To climb to the 12th-century castle keep, take the path almost opposite the Hotel Arco de la Villa – it's a steady 10- to 15-minute climb. The castle's recapture from the Christians by Abu al-Hasan of Granada, in a night raid in 1481, provoked the Catholic Monarchs to launch the last phase of the Reconquista, which ended with the fall of Granada.

For accommodation choose one of the 17 rooms at Hotel Arco de la Villa (☎956 12 32 30; www.tugasa.com; Paseo Nazarí, Zahara de la Sierra; s/d €36/60; �P❋☎), which is partially built into the rock face. All rooms have jaw-dropping views, but little rural character.

Restaurante Los Naranjos (☎956 12 33 14; Calle San Juan 12; mains €8-12; ⊙9am-11pm) serves hearty hill-country platefuls both indoors and outside under the orange trees and has saved many a hiker's/cyclist's legs.

Zahara village centres on Calle San Juan, where you'll find the natural park's helpful Punto de Información Zahara de la Sierra (☎956 12 31 14; Plaza del Rey 3; ⊙9am-2pm & 4-7pm).

SETENIL DE LAS BODEGAS

While most white towns sought protective status atop lofty crags, the people of Setenil did the opposite and burrowed into the dark caves beneath the steep cliffs of the river Trejo. The strategy clearly worked. It took the Christian armies a 15-day siege to dislodge the Moors from their well-defended positions in 1484. Many of the original cavehouses remain and some have been converted into bars and restaurants. Further afield, you can hike along a 6km path (the Ruta de los Molinos) past ancient mills to the next village of Alcalá del Valle.

The tourist office (Calle Villa; ⊙10am-4pm Tue-Sun) is near the top of the town in the 16th-century Casa Consistorial, which exhibits a rare wooden Mudéjar ceiling. A little higher up is the 12th-century castle (opening hours are sporadic; check at tourist office) captured by the Christians just eight years before the fall of Granada.

Setenil has some great tapas bars; an ideal pit stop while you study its unique urban framework. Start in Restaurante Palermo in Plaza de Andalucía at the top of town and work your way down.

OLVERA

A bandit refuge until the mid-19th century, Olvera has come in from the cold and now supports more family-run farming co-ops than anywhere else in Spain. A white town par excellence, it is also renowned for its olive oil, Renaissance church, and roller-coaster history that started with the Romans.

Built on top of an older church, the neoclassical Iglesia Parroquial Nuestra Señora de la Encarnación (Plaza de la Iglesia; ⊙Mass Sun) was commissioned by the Dukes of Osuna and completed in 1843. Perched

VÍA VERDE DE LA SIERRA

Regularly touted as the finest of Spain's prophetic *vía verdes* (greenways which have transformed old railway lines into traffic-free thoroughfares for bikers, hikers and horse-riders), the Vía Verde de la Sierra between Olvera and Puerto Serrano is one of 17 such schemes in Andalucía. Aside from its wild, rugged scenery, the greenway is notable for four spectacular viaducts, 30 tunnels (with sensor-activated lighting), and three old stations-turned-hotels/restaurants that are spread over a 36km route. Ironically, the train line that the greenway follows was never actually completed. Constructed in the 1920s as part of the abortive Jerez to Almargen railway, the project's private backers went bankrupt during the Great Depression and the line wasn't used. After languishing for decades, it was restored in the early 2000s.

The unique Hotel/Restaurante Estación Verde (☑661 463207; Olvera; s/d/apt €30/50/130) just outside Olvera is the official start of the route. You can hire a multitude of bikes here including tandems, kid's bikes and chariots, from €10 a day. Bike hire is also available at Coripe and Puerto Serrano stations. Other facilities include a kid's playground, exercise machines and the Patrulla Verde, a helpful staff of bike-experts who dole out info and can help with mechanical issues.

A highlight of the Via Verde is the Peñon de Zaframagón, a distinctive crag that acts as a prime breeding ground for Griffon vultures. The Centro de Interpretación y Observatorio Ornitologico (adult/child €2/1; ☉10am-4pm) encased in the former Zaframagón station building 16km west of Olvera allows close up observations activated directly from a high definition camera placed up on the crag.

The Vía Verde de la Sierra is open 365 days a year. Devotee cyclists like to tackle it on hot summer nights under a full moon with head torches.

above it is the 12th-century Nasrid Castillo Árabe (Arab Castle; admission incl Museo Histórico €3; ☉10am-2pm & 6-9pm). Next door in La Cilla (☉10.30am-2pm & 4-6pm Tue-Sun, to 7pm May-Sep), an old grain store of the Dukes of Osuna, you'll find the fascinating Museo 'La Frontera y los Castillos', the Vía Verde de la Sierra Interpretive Centre relating the natural history of the nearby bike path, and the tourist office. All share the same opening times.

For accommodation try the excellent Hotel Sierra y Cal (☑956 13 03 03; www.tugasa. com; s/d €36/60; P✳🐕✳). Bars and restaurants line Avenida Julian Besteiro, including the wonderfully 'local' Bodega La Pitarra (www.bodegalapitarra.com; Julián Besteiro 44; media raciones €8-10).

❶ Getting There & Around

Los Amarillos (☑902 210317; www.losamarillos.es) and Comes (☑902 199208; www.tgcomes.es) run daily buses from Jerez de la Frontera via Arcos de la Frontera to Olvera (€8.22, two hours and 15 minutes, three daily) and Setenil de las Bodegas (€8.88, 2½ hours, three daily). Two of these buses carry on to Málaga (€11.04, two hours and 15 minutes).

Los Amarillos runs twice daily buses either way between Zahara de la Sierra and Ronda (€3,

one hour). Grazalema has buses to/from Ronda (€2.63, 45 minutes, twice daily); El Bosque (€2.35, 30 minutes, one daily), where you can change for Arcos; and Ubrique/Benaocaz (€2.13, 40 minutes, two daily).

Southern Costa de la Luz

Arriving on the Costa de la Luz from the Costa del Sol is like opening the window in a crowded room and gasping in the early-morning sunlight. Bereft of tacky resorts and unplanned development, suddenly you can breathe again. More to the point, you're unequivocally back in Spain; a world of flat-capped farmers and clacking dominoes, grazing cows and Sunday Mass followed by a furtive slug of dry sherry. Don't ask why these wide yellow sandy beaches and spectacularly located white towns are so deserted. Just get out and enjoy them while you still can.

VEJER DE LA FRONTERA
POP 12,800 / ELEV 190M

Vejer – the jaw drops, the eyes blink, the eloquent adjectives dry up. Looming moodily atop a rocky hill above the busy N340, 50km south of Cádiz, this placid yet compact white town is something very special. Yes, there's a cool labyrinth of twisting streets, some serendipitous viewpoints, as well as a ruined castle. But, Vejer possesses something else – soulfulness, an air of mystery, an imperceptible touch of *duende* (spirit).

◉ Sights

Plaza de España has a fantastical Seville-style terracotta and tiled fountain and is surrounded by some amazing eating nooks.

FREE Castle   CASTLE
(Calle del Castillo; ⊙approx 10am-9pm Jun-Sep) Vejer's much-reworked castle has great views from its battlements. Its small museum with erratic opening hours preserves one of the black cloaks that Vejer women wore until just a couple of decades ago (covering everything but the eyes).

Casa del Mayorazgo   HOUSE
(Callejón de La Villa; admission by donation) If the door's open, as it often is, this 15th-century house has a pretty patio and one of just three original towers that kept watch over the city – the views from here, including down onto Plaza de España, are worth the short climb.

🛏 Sleeping & Eating

Here are three more reasons to come to Vejer.

TOP CHOICE V...   BOUTIQUE HOTEL €€€
(☑956 45 17 57; www.hotelv-vejer.com; Calle Rosario 11-13; d €139-199; ❋@) V...(that's V for Vejer not V for five, and, yes, the three dots are part of the name) is one of Andalucía's most exquisite creations, an old world boutique hotel where trendy modern design features (bath-tubs in the middle of the room) mix with antique artifacts (antique doors). The 12 fine rooms all require double takes, and the communal areas include comfy sofas in interesting nooks and a waterfall – wait for it – on a vista-laden roof terrace next to a bubbling Jacuzzi.

Hotel La Casa del Califa   HOTEL €€
(☑956 44 77 30; www.lacasadelcalifa.com; Plaza de España 16; s/d incl breakfast €73/86; ❋@) Rambling over several floors, this gorgeous hotel oozes character. Rooms are peaceful and very comfortable, with Islamic decorative touches. Special 'Emir' service (€43) also bags you fresh flowers, chocolates and champagne. Downstairs there's a superb Middle Eastern restaurant, El Jardín del Califa (mains €8-16; ☑).

La Vera Cruz   CONTEMPORARY ANDALUCIAN €€
(☑956 45 16 83; www.restaurantelaveracruz.es; Calle Shelly 1; mains €12-18; ⊙lunch Tue-Sun, dinner Thu-Sat) Situated in an old convent with slightly limited opening hours, the 'True Cross' specialises in gourmet tapas such as cold anchovy lasagne and glazed ribs with wasabi purée. Local buzz suggests it's the best in town.

☆ Entertainment

Peña Cultural Flamenca
'El Aguilar de Vejer'   FLAMENCO
(Calle Rosario 29; cover charge €3) Part of Vejer's magic is its genuine small-town flamenco scene, best observed in this atmospheric old-town bar/performance space. Singing and guitar lessons are offered Thursday nights.

ⓘ Information

Buses stop beside the **tourist office** (☑956 45 17 36; Avenida Los Remedios 2; ⊙10am-2pm daily, 6-8pm Mon-Sat approx May-Oct), about 500m below the town centre. Also here is a convenient large, free car park.

ⓘ Getting There & Away

Comes (☑902 199208; www.tgcomes.es) buses leave from Avenida Los Remedios. Buses run to Cádiz (one hour) and Barbate (15 minutes) five or six times a day. Buses for Tarifa (45 minutes, 10 daily), Algeciras (1¼ hours, 10 daily), Jerez de la Frontera (1½ hours, two daily), Málaga (2¾ hours, two daily) and Seville (2¼ hours, four daily) stop at La Barca de Vejer, on the N340 at the bottom of the hill. It's a steep 20-minute walk up to town from here or an equally steep €6 in a taxi.

LOS CAÑOS DE MECA
POP 300

The 'chilled' beach village of Los Caños straggles along a series of spectacular open beaches southwest of Vejer. Once a hippie hideaway, Los Caños still has a highly alternative, hedonistic scene, especially in summer with its nudist beaches and a strong gay following. Windsurfing, kitesurfing, surfing, horse riding and hikes in the nearby Parque Natural de la Breña y Marismas de Barbate are all among the activities you can pursue here.

◉ Sights & Activities

At the western end of Los Caños a side road leads out to a lighthouse on an unremarkable spit of land with a famous name – Cabo de Trafalgar – which marks the site of the eponymous battle in 1805. The beach under

JIMENA DE LA FRONTERA

Tucked away in crinkled hills on the cusp of the Parque Natural Los Acornocales, Jimena sits in prime cork oak country with its blanched whiteness and crumbled castle looking out towards Gibraltar and Africa, both magnificently visible from its Nasrid-era citadel. Property-seeking Brits have discovered the town, but it has managed to keep a Spanish village feel. The walking trails here are very special and include treks along the cross-continental E4 (GR7) path which bisects the town, and forays out to Bronze Age cave paintings at Laja Alta. Another rare find is Restaurante El Anón (www.hostalanon. com; Consuelo 34; mains €10-15), a rambling house full of interesting nooks and even more interesting fusion food. It also rents rooms.

The best way arrive in Jimena is on one of Spain's most delightfully scenic railways lines from Ronda (€6.05, one hour, three daily) and Algeciras (€4.10, 40 minutes, three daily). The station is in the village of Los Ángeles (1km from Jimena).

the cliffs here – Playa del Faro – is a popular nudist spot.

Some 5km along the coast northwest of Los Caños, the long beach at El Palmar has Andalucía's best board-surfing waves from about October to May. Several places rent boards and give surfing classes: try Escuela de Surf 9 Pies (☑620 104241; www.9piesescueladesurf.com; board & wetsuit rental per 2/4hr €12/20, classes 2/4hr €27/52), open all year towards the north end of the beach. Trafalgar Surf (☑666 942849; www. trafalgarsurftrip.com; beginners' classes from €35) offers classes in English at the area's best-surfing beach on the day, with free pick-up anywhere along the coast from Los Caños to La Barrosa.

🛏 Sleeping & Eating

For further accommodation options check www.playasdetrafalgar.com or www.placer detrafalgar.com.

Hostal Mini-Golf   HOTEL €€
(☑956 43 70 83; www.hostalminigolf.com; Avenida Trafalgar 251; s €35-60, d €45-70; 🅿🌸🛜🏊) If you can get past the misleading name (there's no golf or even minigolf here), this well-positioned hotel with an onsite restaurant where the road forks to Cabo Trafalgar is probably Caños' best midrange crash pad. Kitesurfing central is just 400m down the road.

El Pirata   SEAFOOD €€
(Avenida Trafalgar 67; mains €9-13; ⊙year-round) Enjoying a superb beachside position, this place seems to sum up Caños' hedonism. Enjoy the excellent seafood at lunchtime and come back in the evening for music and dancing that often drifts out onto the beach.

🍷 Drinking & Entertainment

Good bars include Los Castillejos (⊙Easter-Oct) towards the eastern end of Avenida Trafalgar and super-relaxed Las Dunas (Carretera del Faro de Trafalgar; 🛜) on the road out to Cabo de Trafalgar. Both host live music of various kinds from about midnight and stay open till 2am or 3am.

❶ Getting There & Away

Monday to Friday, there are two Comes buses to/from Cádiz (1¼ hours) to El Palmar (1¼ hours). There's also one morning bus, Monday to Friday, running between Vejer and both places. There may be extra services from Cádiz and even Seville from mid-June to early September.

Tarifa
POP 17,900

Tarifa's tip of Spain location has donned it a different climate and a different personality to the rest of Andalucía. Stiff Atlantic winds draw in surfers, windsurfers and kitesurfers who, in turn, lend this ancient, yet deceptively small settlement a laidback internationalist image that is noticeably (some would say, refreshingly) at odds with the commercialism of the nearby Costa del Sol. While the town acts as the last stop in Spain before Morocco, it also serves as a taste of things to come. Moroccan fusion food is par for the course here, and the walled old town with its narrow whitewashed streets and ceaseless winds could pass for Chefchaouen or Essouria in a film-set.

Tarifa may be as old as Phoenician Cádiz and was definitely a Roman settlement, but it takes its name from Tarif ibn Malik, who led a Muslim raid in AD 710, the year before the main Islamic invasion of the peninsula.

DON'T MISS

BAELO CLAUDIA

In the tiny village of Bolonia hidden on a beautiful bay about 20km up the coast from Tarifa, you'll find the ruins of the most complete Roman town yet uncovered in Spain, Baelo Claudia (956 10 67 97; admission €1.50; ⊗9am-7pm Tue-Sat Mar-May & Oct, to 8pm Tue-Sat Jun-Sep, to 6pm Tue-Sat Nov-Feb, to 2pm Sun year-round). The site – which affords fine views across the water to Africa – includes a theatre where plays are still sometimes staged, a market, forum, temples, and workshops that turned out the products that made Baelo Claudia famous in the Roman world: salted fish and garum, a prized condiment made from fish entrails. There's a good recently opened museum too.

Baelo Claudia's zenith was in the 1st century AD during the reign of Emperor Claudius (AD 41–54).

A hilly 7km side road to Bolonia heads west off of the N340, 15km from Tarifa. A couple of local buses run daily from Tarifa to Bolonia in July and August only.

◉ Sights

Old Town
OLD TOWN

A wander round the old town's narrow streets, which are of mainly Islamic origin, is an appetiser for Morocco. The Mudéjar Puerta de Jerez was built after the Reconquista. Look in at the small but action-packed market (Calle Colón) before wending your way to the mainly 15th-century Iglesia de San Mateo (Calle Sancho IV El Bravo; ⊗9am-1pm & 5.30-8.30pm). South of the church, the Mirador El Estrecho, atop part of the castle walls, has spectacular views across to Africa, located only 14km away.

Castillo de Guzmán
CASTLE

(Calle Guzmán El Bueno; admission €2; ⊗11am-4pm) Originally built in 960 on the orders of Cordoban caliph Abd ar-Rahman III, this fortress is named after Reconquista hero Guzmán El Bueno. In 1294, when threatened with the death of his captured son unless he surrendered the castle to attacking Islamic forces, El Bueno threw down his own dagger for the deed to be done.

Guzmán's descendants later became the Duques de Medina Sidonia, one of Spain's most powerful families. You'll need to buy tickets for the fortress at the tourist office.

Beaches
BEACHES

On the isthmus leading out to Isla de las Palomas, tiny Playa Chica lives up to its name. Spectacular Playa de los Lances is a different matter, stretching northwest for 10km to the huge sand dune at Ensenada de Valdevaqueros.

The low dunes behind Playa de los Lances are a natural park and you can hike across them on a raised boardwalk from the end of Tarifa's concrete promenade.

🏃 Activities

Diving

Diving is generally done from boats around the Isla de las Palomas where shipwrecks, corals, dolphins and octopuses await. Of the handful of dive companies in Tarifa, try Aventura Marina (956 05 46 26; www.aventuramarina.org; Avenida de Andalucía 1), which offers 'Discover Scuba Diving' courses (€75, three hours). One-tank dives with equipment rental and guide cost €50.

Horse Riding

Contemplating Tarifa's wind-lashed coastline (or heading off into the hilly hinterland) on horseback is a terrific way to pass an afternoon or even longer. A one-hour beach ride along Playa de los Lances costs €30, a two-hour beach-and-mountain ride costs €50, while three-/five-hour rides start at €70/80. One recommended place, with excellent English-speaking guides, is Aventura Ecuestre (956 23 66 32; www.aventuraecuestre.com; Hotel Dos Mares, N340 Km79.5), which also has private lessons (one hour €30), pony rides for kids (half-/one hour €15/30) and five-hour rides into the Parque Natural Los Alcornocales. Molino El Mastral (956 10 63 10; www.mastral.com; Carretera Sanctuario de la Luz), 5km northwest of Tarifa, is also excellent.

Whale-Watching

The waters off Tarifa are one of the best places in Europe to see whales and dolphins as they swim between the Atlantic and the Mediterranean between April and October; sightings of some description are almost guaranteed between these months. In addition to striped and bottlenose dolphins, and long-finned pilot whales, orcas (killer whales) and sperm whales, you may also, if you're lucky, see endangered fin whales and the misleadingly named common dolphin. The best months for orcas are July and August, while sperm whales are present in the Strait of Gibraltar from April to July. Of the dozens of whale-watching outfits, not-for-profit **FIRMM** (☑956 62 70 08; www.firmm.org; Calle Pedro Cortés 4; ☺Mar-Oct) is a good bet, not least because its primary purpose is to study the whales, record data and encourage environmentally sensitive tours.

Windsurfing & Kitesurfing

Occupying the spot where the Atlantic meets the Mediterranean, Tarifa's legendary winds have turned the city into one of Europe's premier windsurfing and kitesurfing destinations. The most popular strip is along the coast between Tarifa and Punta Paloma, 10km to the northwest, but you'll see kitesurfers on Tarifa's town beach as well (it's rather a good spectator sport).

Over 30 places offer windsurfing equipment rental and classes (from beginners to experts, young and old). Recommended are **Club Mistral** (www.club-mistral.com) and **Spin Out** (☑956 23 63 52; www.tarifaspinout. com; El Porro Beach, N340 Km75), both of which are signposted off the N340 northwest of town. Kitesurfing rental and classes are available from the same places as for windsurfing, or from **Hot Stick Kite School** (☑647 155516; www.hotsticktarifa.com; Calle Batalla del Salado 41).

Price-wise, for kitesurfing you're looking at €70 for a three hour 'baptism', €135 for a six hour 'initiation', and €180 for a nine hour 'total course'. Equipment rental is €60 per day. You can train in windsurfing, surfing and paddle-boarding (all €50 for two hours).

🛏 Sleeping

High season is typically from the beginning of July to mid-September, and it's essential to phone ahead in August.

IN TOWN

TOP CHOICE **La Casa de la Favorita**   HOTEL, APARTMENT €€
(☑690 180253; www.lacasadelafavorita.com; Plaza de San Hiscio 4, Tarifa; d €60-125; ❄🤶📶📺) A quick internet search will reveal that La Favorita has become a lot of people's favourite recently. It must be something to do with creamy furnishings, the surgical indoor cleanliness, the kitchenettes in every room, the small library, the roof terrace, and the dynamic colorful art.

Posada La Sacristía   BOUTIQUE HOTEL €€
(☑956 68 17 59; www.lasacristia.net; Calle San Donato 8, Tarifa; r incl breakfast €115-135; ❄@🤶) Tarifa's most elegant boutique accommodation is in a beautifully renovated 17th-century town house. Attention to detail is impeccable with 10 stylish rooms, tasteful colour schemes, large comfy beds and rooms on several levels around a central courtyard. Best of all, it has the same prices year-round. Its restaurant is similarly excellent.

Melting Pot   HOSTEL €
(☑956 68 29 06; www.meltingpothostels.com; Calle Turriano Gracil 5; dm/d incl breakfast from €13/35; 🅿🤶🤶) The Melting Pot is a friendly, well-equipped hostel just off the Alameda. The five dorms, for five to eight people, have bunks, and there's one for women only. A good kitchen adjoins the cosy bar-lounge, and all guests get their own keys.

Hostal Africa   HOSTAL €
(☑956 68 02 20; www.hostalafrica.com; Calle María Antonia Toledo 12, Tarifa; s/d €50/65, with shared bathroom €35/50; 🤶) This revamped 19th-century house close to the Puerta de Jerez is one of the best *hostales* along the coast. The owners are hospitable and the rooms sparkle with bright and attractive colours and plenty of space. There's a lovely, expansive roof terrace with an exotic cabana and views of Africa. The *hostal* is open from late December to late January.

🍴 Eating

Tarifa has some excellent breakfast joints and a couple of good Moroccan Arabic–inspired restaurants. The most populous 'eat street' is Paseo de la Alameda, leading northwest from the port.

Bamboo   BREAKFAST €
(Paseo de la Alameda 2; snacks from €4) Was there ever a better place to chill out after some white-knuckle water sports than in Bamboo? Trance music and strong coffee turn kitesurfers into internet-surfers in this trippy zone of dented couches, scattered pouffées and a dude-heavy clientele. The java and savoury panini are produced by the largely Italian staff.

Live music turns up after 10pm at weekends, when luminous green lights make the atmosphere even more trancy.

Mandrágora   MOROCCAN, ARABIC €€
(☑956 68 12 91; Calle Independencia 3; mains €12-18; ☺from 8pm Mon-Sat) Behind Iglesia

de San Mateo, this intimate place serves Andalucian-Arabic food and does so terrifically well. It's hard to know where to start, but the options for mains include lamb with plums and almonds, prawns with *ñora* (Andalucian sweet pepper) sauce, or monkfish in a wild mushroom and sea urchin sauce.

Café Azul Bar   BREAKFAST €
(Calle Batalla del Salado 8; breakfast €3.50-8; ☺9am-3pm, closed Wed winter) This little Italian-owned place packs 'em in every day for Tarifa's best breakfasts. The muesli, fruit salad and yoghurt is large and tasty, or choose one of the excellent crêpes. There's good coffee, juices and shakes, plus *bocadillos* (filled rolls) and cakes.

La Oca da Sergio   ITALIAN €€
(www.la-oca-da-sergio.artesur.eu; Calle General Copons 6; mains €10-16) Italians rule in Tarifa, at least on the food scene. The amiable Sergio, who roams the tables Italian-style armed dexterously with loaded plates and amusing stories, resides over genuine home-country fare. Bank on homemade pasta, wood-oven thin-crust pizzas, cappuccinos and postdinner offers of limoncello.

🍸 Drinking & Entertainment

A large ever-changing contingent of surfing and kiteboarding dudes ensures that Tarifa has a decent bar scene focused primarily on narrow Calle Santísima Trinidad and Calle San Francisco, just east of the Alameda. Don't even bother going out before 11pm. The real dancing starts around 2.30am and ultimate endurance freaks keep bopping until 8am. Many places close on Sunday. Several bars line the southern end of the Alameda. Try **La Ruina** (Calle Santísima Trinidad 2; ☺1-4am), with good electro dance music, or **Bistro Point** (cnr Calles Santísima Trinidad & San Francisco), with a friendly international crowd and good crêpes (€2 to €4).

A handful of more clublike bars stays open longer. There are further bar and club possibilities on Playa de los Lances and outside town.

MOVING ON?

For tips, recommendations and reviews, head to shop.lonelyplanet.com to purchase a downloadable PDF of the Morocco chapter from Lonely Planet's *Mediterranean Europe* guide.

Bar Almedina   BAR, FLAMENCO
(Calle Almedina) Built into the old city walls, this place has a cavernous feel and squeezes a flamenco ensemble into its clamorous confines every Thursday at 10.30pm.

Bear House   BAR
(Calle Sancho IV El Bravo 26; ☺2pm-2am) A sort of wine bar meets surf bar, the slick new Bear House has low cushioned 'chill-out' sofas, a variety of cocktails, football on the big screen, but no bears.

ℹ Information

Centro de Salud (Health Centre; ☎956 02 70 00; Calle Amador de los Ríos) Has emergency service.

Policía Local (☎956 61 41 86; Plaza de Santa María) Local police.

Tourist office (☎956 68 09 93; www.ayto tarifa.com; Paseo de la Alameda; ☺10am-2pm daily, 6-8pm Mon-Fri Jun-Sep) Near the top end of the palm-lined Paseo de la Alameda.

ℹ Getting There & Around

BOAT FRS (☎956 68 18 30; www.frs.es; Avenida Andalucía 16) runs a fast (35-minute) ferry between Tarifa and Tangier in Morocco (one way per adult/child/car/motorcycle €37/20/93/31) up to eight times daily. All passengers need a passport.

BUS Comes (☎956 68 40 38; www.tgcomes. es; Calle Batalla del Salado 13) operates from the small open lot near the petrol station at the north end of Calle Batalla del Salado. It has regular departures to Cádiz, Jerez de la Frontera, La Línea de La Concepción (for Gibraltar), Málaga, Seville and Zahara de los Atunes.

La Línea de la Concepción

POP 63,000

La Línea, 20km east of Algeciras, is the stepping stone to Gibraltar. A left turn as you exit the bus station brings you onto Avenida 20 de Abril, which runs the 300m or so from the main square, Plaza de la Constitución, to the Gibraltar border. The **municipal tourist office** (Avenida Príncipe Felipe; ☺8am-8pm Mon-Fri, 9am-2pm Sat) faces the border.

Buses run about every 30 minutes to/from Algeciras (€2, 30 minutes).

To save queuing at the border, many visitors to Gibraltar park in La Línea, then walk across. The underground **Parking Fo Cona**, just off Avenida 20 de Abril, is the safest place to leave your wheels.

ALGECIRAS – GATEWAY TO MOROCCO

The major port linking Spain with Africa is an ugly industrial town and fishing port notable for producing the greatest flamenco guitarist of the modern era, Paco de Lucía, who was born here in 1947. New arrivals usually make a quick departure by catching a ferry to Morocco, or a bus to Tarifa or Gibraltar.

The bus station is on Calle San Bernardo. Comes (☑956 65 34 56; www.tgcomes.es) has buses for La Línea (30 minutes) every half-hour, Tarifa (30 minutes, 13 daily), Cádiz (2½ hours, 13 daily) and Seville (2½ hours, six daily).

The adjacent train station (☑956 63 10 05) runs services to/from Madrid (€70.90, five hours 20 minutes, two daily) and Granada (€24.80, four hours and 15 minutes, three daily).

The ferry crossing to Tanger with FRS (p710) is cheaper than Tarifa, costing per adult/car one way €23/84. There are also five daily crossings to the Spanish Moroccan enclave of Ceuta (adult/car one way €31/110). To get from the bus station to the port walk approximately 600m east along Calle San Bernardo.

Gibraltar

POP 30,000

Red pillar boxes, fish-and-chip shops, bobbies on the beat, and creaky seaside hotels with 1970s furnishings; Gibraltar – as British writer Laurie Lee once opined – is a piece of Portsmouth sliced off and towed 500 miles south. As with many colonial outposts, 'The Rock', as it's invariably known, tends to overstate its underlying Britishness, a bonus for lovers of pub grub and afternoon tea, but a confusing double-take for modern Brits who thought that their country had moved on since the days of stuffy naval prints and Lord Nelson memorabilia. Stuck strategically at the jaws of Europe and Africa, Gibraltar's Palladian architecture and camera-hogging Barbary apes make an interesting break from the tapas bars and white towns of Cádiz province. Playing an admirable supporting role is its swashbuckling local history; lest we forget, the Rock has been British longer than the United States has been American.

History

In 711 Tariq ibn Ziyad, the Muslim governor of Tangier, landed at Gibraltar to launch the Islamic invasion of the Iberian Peninsula. The name Gibraltar is derived from Jebel Tariq (Tariq's Mountain).

Castilla wrested the Rock from the Muslims in 1462. Then in 1704 an Anglo-Dutch fleet captured Gibraltar during the War of the Spanish Succession. Spain ceded the Rock to Britain in 1713, but didn't abandon military attempts to regain it until the failure of the Great Siege of 1779–83. Britain developed it into an important naval base (bringing in a community of Genoese ship repairers). During the Franco period, Gibraltar was an extremely sore point between Britain and Spain: the border was closed from 1967 to 1985. In 1969 Gibraltarians voted – 12,138 to 44 – in favour of British rather than Spanish sovereignty, and a new constitution gave Gibraltar domestic self-government. In 2002 the UK and Spain held talks about a possible future sharing of sovereignty over Gibraltar, but Gibraltarians expressed *their* feelings in a referendum (not recognised by Britain or Spain), which voted resoundingly against any such idea.

In December 2005 the governments of the UK, Spain and Gibraltar set up a new, trilateral process of dialogue. The parties reached agreement on some issues but tricky topics remain, not least Britain's military installations and 'ownership' of Gibraltar airport. Gibraltarians want self-determination and to retain British citizenship, making joint sovereignty improbable. Few foresee a change in the status quo, but relations are less strained these days. On 18 September 2006 a three-way deal was signed by Spain, Gibraltar and Britain relating to telecommunications on the Rock, Gibraltar airport and other issues, but not sovereignty. Gibraltar airport is currently being expanded, and flights from Spanish cities and other European destinations direct to Gibraltar airport were re-introduced in 2006 (they had been suspended at the time of writing due to lack of demand). In December 2009 a ferry link to mainland Algeciras was reactivated after lying dormant for 40 years.

The mainstays of Gibraltar's economy are tourism, the port and financial services. Investment on the Rock continues apace with a huge luxury waterfront development on

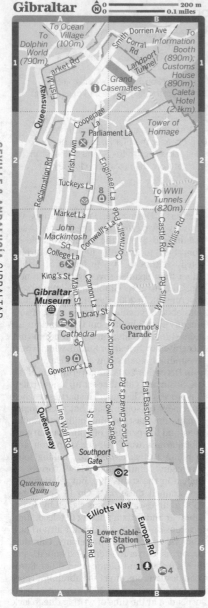

Gibralatar

Gibraltar

◎ **Top Sights**

Gibraltar Museum.................................A4

◎ **Sights**

1 Alameda Botanical Gardens.............B6
2 Trafalgar Cemetery B5

🛏 **Sleeping**

3 Bristol Hotel.......................................A4
4 Rock Hotel B6

🍴 **Eating**

5 Bistro Madeleine................................A4
6 Royal Calpe A3
7 Star Bar...A2

🛍 **Shopping**

8 Bell Books..A2
9 Gibraltar Bookshop A4

◉ Sights & Activities

THE TOWN

Pedestrianised Main St has a typically British appearance (including pubs, imperial statues and familiar British shops), though you'll catch Spanish inflections in the shuttered windows, narrow winding side streets and bilingual locals who have a tendency to start their sentences in English and finish them in Spanish. Most Spanish and Islamic buildings on Gibraltar were destroyed in 18th-century sieges, but the Rock bristles with British fortifications, gates and gun emplacements.

Gibraltar Museum MUSEUM
(Bomb House Lane; adult/child £2/1; ⊙10am-6pm Mon-Fri, to 2pm Sat) Gibraltar's history is swashbuckling to say the least and it quickly unfolds in this fine museum – comprising a labyrinth of rooms large and small – from Neanderthal to medieval to the infamous 18th century siege. Don't miss the well-preserved Muslim bathhouse and an intricately painted 7th-century-BC Egyptian mummy that washed up here in the late 1800s.

Trafalgar Cemetery CEMETERY
(Prince Edward's Road; ⊙8.30am-sunset) Gibraltar's cemetery gives a very poignant history lesson, with its graves of British sailors who died at Gibraltar after the Battle of Trafalgar in 1805.

its western side. Much of the demand for space is being met through extensive land reclamation (reclaimed land currently comprises approximately 10% of the territory's total area).

Alameda Botanical Gardens PARK

(Europa Rd; ☺8am-sunset) These lush gardens make a refreshing break from Gibraltar's inexplicably manic traffic.

Dolphin-Watching

The Bahía de Algeciras has a sizeable year-round population of dolphins and at least three companies run excellent dolphin-watching trips. From about April to September most outfits make two or more daily trips; at other times of the year they make at least one trip daily. Most of the boats go from Watergardens Quay or the adjacent Marina Bay. Trips last from 1½ to 2½ hours. The tourist office has a list of operators, which include **Dolphin World** (☎54481000; Waterport, Ferry Terminal; adult/child £20/10) and **Dolphin Adventure** (☎20050650; www. dolphin.gi; Marina Bay). Advance bookings are essential.

THE ROCK

TOP
CHOICE **Upper Rock Nature**

Reserve NATURE RESERVE

(adult/child incl attractions £10/5, vehicle £2, pedestrian excl attractions £0.50; ☺9am-6.15pm, last entry 5.45pm) Most of the upper parts of the Rock (but not the main lookouts) come within the Upper Rock Nature Reserve; entry tickets include admission to St Michael's Cave, the Apes' Den, the Great Siege Tunnels, the Moorish castle, Military Heritage Centre, the 100-tonne supergun and the 'Gibraltar: A City Under Siege' exhibition. The upper Rock is home to 600 plant species and is the perfect vantage point for observing the migrations of birds between Europe and Africa.

The Rock's most famous inhabitants are the tailless Barbary macaques. Some of the 200 apes hang around the top cable-car station, while others are found at the **Apes' Den** (near the middle cable-car station) and the Great Siege Tunnels. Legend has it that when the apes (which may have been introduced from North Africa in the 18th century) disappear from Gibraltar, so will the British. Summer is the ideal time to see newborn apes, but keep a safe distance to avoid the sharp teeth and short tempers for which they're well known.

About 15 minutes' walk south down St Michael's Rd from the top cable-car station, O'Hara's Rd leads up to the left to **O'Hara's Battery**, an emplacement of big guns on the Rock's summit. A few minutes further down is the extraordinary **St Michael's Cave**, a spectacular natural grotto full of stalagmites and stalactites. In the past, people thought the cave was a possible subterranean link with Africa. Today, apart from attracting tourists in droves, it's used for concerts, plays and even fashion shows. For a more extensive look at the cave system, the **Lower St Michael's Cave Tour** (ticket £8; ☺6pm Wed, 2.30pm Sat) is a three-hour guided adventure into the lower cave area. Wear appropriate footwear. Children must be over 10 years old. Contact the tourist office to arrange a guide.

About 30 minutes' walk north (downhill) from the top cable-car station is Princess Caroline's Battery, housing the **Military Heritage Centre**. From this point one road leads down to the Princess Royal Battery – more gun emplacements – while another leads up to the **Great Siege Tunnels**, a complex defence system hewn out of the Rock by the British during the siege of 1779–83 to provide gun emplacements. The **WWII tunnels** (adult/child £8/free; ☺10am-5pm Mon-Fri), where the Allied invasion of North Africa was planned, can also be visited, but this isn't included on your nature reserve ticket. Even combined, these tunnels constitute only a tiny proportion of more than 70km of tunnels and galleries in the Rock. Note that most of these are off limits to the public.

On Willis's Rd, the way down to the town from Princess Caroline's Battery, you'll find the **'Gibraltar: A City Under Siege'** exhibition, in the first British building on the Rock, and the **Moorish Castle** (Tower of Homage), the remains of Gibraltar's Islamic castle built in 1333.

🛏 Sleeping

Bristol Hotel HOTEL €€

(☎20076800; www.bristolhotel.gi; 10 Cathedral Sq; s/d/tr £63/81/93; [P] [✻] [🛜] [🏊]) Veterans of bucket-and-spade British seaside holidays can wax nostalgic at the stuck-in-the-'70s Bristol with its creaking floorboards, red patterned carpets and Hi-de-Hi reception staff. Arrivals from other climes will enjoy the attractive walled garden, small swimming pool and prime just-off-Main-St location.

Caleta Hotel HOTEL €€€

(☎20076501; www.caletahotel.gi; Sir Herbert Miles Rd; d without/with sea view £110/150) This has a wonderful location overlooking Catalan Bay, on the east side of the Rock, five minutes from town. Its cascading terraces have panoramic sea views, and there's a host of gym and spa facilities. Bedrooms are large and luxurious.

Rock Hotel HOTEL €€€
(☎20073000; www.rockhotelgibraltar.com; 3 Europa Rd; d/ste £160/195; P❋@☎☎) As Gibraltan as the famous wild monkeys, the Rock is more grand dame than chic young newcomer these days, though it's not lacking in facilities. Tick off sea-view rooms, gym, pool, welcome drink, bathrobes and that all-important trouser press you'll never use. Mingle among the conference delegates and retired naval captains and rekindle the empire spirit.

✕ Eating

Goodbye tapas, hello fish and chips. Gibraltar's food is unashamedly British. The staples are pub grub, beer and sandwiches, chippies and stodgy desserts. Grand Casemates Sq has a profusion of cooler, more modern Euro-cafes, though the newest movers and shakers (including some good ethnic places) can be found in Marina Bay's spanking new Ocean Village.

TOP CHOICE Bistro Madeleine CAFE, BISTRO €
(256 Main St; cakes from £3; ⊙9am-11pm; ☎☎) If you've just polished off steak and ale pie in the local pub, come here for your dessert. In this refined, smoke-free bistro Illy coffee is served with big chunks of British-inspired cakes. The toffee and date cake is outstanding.

Royal Calpe PUB €€
(176 Main St; mains £8-12) If halfway through your quintessential Gibraltar pub crawl you get an unstoppable urge for heavily crusted meat pies, fish and chips, and a pint of Caffrey's *without* the cigarette smoke (yes, you can still smoke inside Gibraltar pubs), roll into the Royal Calpe. Its nonsmoking rear conservatory is popular with young mothers, health freaks and the nicotine patch brigade.

Star Bar PUB €€
(12 Parliament Lane; breakfast £3.50-5, mains £5-11; ⊙24hr) Gibraltar's oldest bar, if the house advertising is to be believed, the Star Bar is small, smoky and – judging by the wall art – full of diehard supporters of British football team Tottenham Hotspur. If none of this puts you off, squeeze inside for lamb chops,

Irish fillet, and hake in a Spanish-style green sauce.

Shopping

Gibraltar has lots of British high-street stores, such as Next, Marks & Spencer, Monsoon and Mothercare (all on or just off Main St) and a huge Morrisons supermarket (in Europort at the northern end of the main harbour). Shops are normally open 9am to 7.30pm weekdays, and until 1pm Saturday. There are a couple of good bookshops, including **Bell Books** (☎76707; 11 Bell Lane) and **Gibraltar Bookshop** (☎71894; 300 Main St).

❶ Information

Electricity

Electric current is the same as in Britain: 220V or 240V, with plugs of three flat pins. You'll thus need an adaptor to use your Spanish plug lead, available for £3 to £4 from numerous electronics shops in Main St.

Emergency

Emergency (☎199) For police or ambulance.
Police station (120 Irish Town)

Medical Services

St Bernard's Hospital (☎20079700; Europort) With 24-hour emergency facilities.

Money

The currencies are the Gibraltar pound (£) and pound sterling, which are interchangeable. You can spend euros (except in payphones and post offices), but conversion rates are poor. Change unspent Gibraltar currency before leaving. Banks are generally open from 9am to 3.30pm weekdays; there are several on Main St.

Post

Post office (104 Main St; ⊙9am-4.30pm Mon-Fri & 10am-1pm Sat, 9am-2.15pm Mon-Fri mid-Jun–mid-Sep)

Telephone

To dial Gibraltar from Spain, you now precede the five-digit local number with the code ☎00350; from other countries, dial the international access code, then the Gibraltar country code ☎350 and local number. To phone Spain from Gibraltar, just dial the nine-digit Spanish number.

Tourist Information

Gibraltar has several helpful tourist offices, with information booths at the **airport** (☎73026; ⊙ mornings only Mon-Fri) and **Customs House** (☎20050762; Customs House; ⊙9am-4:30pm Mon-Fri, 10am-1pm Sat).

Tourist office (Grand Casemates Sq; ⊙9am-5.30pm Mon-Fri, 10am-3pm Sat, to 1pm Sun & holidays) Several information desks provide all the information you need about Gibraltar, with plenty of pleasant cafes in the same square where you can read through it all at leisure.

Visas

To enter Gibraltar, you need a passport or EU national identity card. EU, USA, Canadian, Australian, New Zealand and South African passport-holders are among those who do not need visas for Gibraltar. For further information contact Gibraltar's **Immigration Department** (⏃20072500; Joshua Hassan House; ⊙9am-12.45pm Mon-Fri).

⊙ Getting There & Away

Air

Easyjet (www.easyjet.com) flies daily to/from London-Gatwick and three times a week from Liverpool, while **Monarch Airlines** (www.monarch.co.uk) flies daily to/from London-Luton and Manchester. **British Airways** (www.ba.com) flies seven times a week from London-Heathrow. Gibraltar's airport has a brand new terminal right next to the border which opened in November 2011.

Bus

There are no regular buses to Gibraltar, but La Línea de la Concepción bus station is only a five-minute walk from the border.

Car & Motorcycle

Snaking vehicle queues at the 24 hour border and congested traffic in Gibraltar often make it easier to park in La Línea and walk across the border. To take a car into Gibraltar (free) you need an insurance certificate, registration document, nationality plate and driving licence.

Ferry

One **ferry** (www.frs.es) a week sails between Gibraltar and Tangier in Morocco (adult/child one way £46/30, 70 minutes) on Fridays at 7pm. Ferries to/from Tangier are more frequent from Algeciras.

⊙ Getting Around

Bus 5 goes from the border into town (and back) every 15 minutes on weekdays, and every 30 minutes on weekends. The fare is £1. Buses 1, 2, 3 and 4 cover the rest of Gibraltar and are free of charge.

All of Gibraltar can be covered on foot, if you're energetic. You can also ascend to the upper Rock, weather permitting, by the **cable car** (Red Sands Rd; adult/child return £8/4.50, incl entry to Nature Reserve £16/12.50; ⊙every few min 9.30am-8pm Mon-Sat, last cable up 7.15pm, last cable down 7.45pm, to 5pm Oct-Apr). For the Apes' Den, disembark at the middle station.

MÁLAGA PROVINCE

Misty-eyed old men on park benches reminisce about whitewashed fishing villages as blue-eyed invaders from the north pick up the keys to their new Costa del Sol condominiums. Málaga province is where Spain's great tourist experiment went viral, leaving a once-tranquil coastline covered in concrete and a local populace fighting to maintain a semblance of its traditional culture. Odd snippets of the old way of life still exist. The provincial capital, Málaga, is an oasis of old-fashioned Spanishness while, further inland, outside encroachments have been kept to a minimum in eye-catching towns like Antequera and Ronda, and equally spectacular natural features such as the Garganta del Chorro (Chorro Gorge).

Málaga

POP 558,000

The Costa del Sol can seem wholly soulless until you decamp to Málaga, an unmistakably Spanish metropolis curiously ignored by the lion's share of the 11 million tourists who land annually at Pablo Ruíz Picasso International Airport before getting carted off to the golf courses and beaches of 'Torrie' and Fuengirola. Their loss could be your gain. Stubborn and stalwart, Málaga's history is as rich as its parks are green, while its feisty populace challenges *sevillanos* as 24-hour party people. Not known for their timidity in battle, the *malagueños* (residents of Málaga) held out until 1487 against the invading Christian armies and employed equal tenacity when Franco's fascists came knocking in the Spanish Civil War. More recently, Málaga has fought off the less attractive effects of mass tourism and placed a strong bid to become Europe's 2016 Capital of Culture. Work has already started to redevelop its weathered port area.

Málaga endowed the world with another priceless gift – Pablo Picasso, the 20th century's most ground-breaking artist, who was born in a small house in Plaza de Merced in

1881. A couple of excellent museums guard his gigantic legacy.

History

Probably founded by Phoenicians, Málaga has long had a commercial vocation. It flourished in the Islamic era, especially as the chief port of the Emirate of Granada, later reasserting itself as an entrepreneurial centre in the 19th century when a dynamic middle class founded textile factories, sugar and steel mills and shipyards. Málaga dessert wine ('mountain sack') was popular in Victorian England. During the civil war Málaga was initially a Republican stronghold. Hundreds of Nationalist sympathisers were killed before the city fell in February 1937 after being bombed by Italian planes. Vicious reprisals followed.

Málaga has enjoyed a steadily increasing economic spin-off from the mass tourism launched on the nearby Costa del Sol in the 1950s. In recent years, the city has become an important destination in itself.

◉ Sights & Activities

TOP CHOICE Museo Picasso Málaga MUSEUM
(☏902 443377; www.museopicassomalaga.org; Calle San Agustín 8; permanent/temporary collection €6/4.50, combined ticket €8; ◷10am-8pm Tue-Thu & Sun, to 9pm Fri & Sat) The Museo Picasso has an enviable collection of 204 works, 155 donated and 49 loaned to the museum by Christine Ruiz-Picasso (wife of Paul, Picasso's eldest son) and Bernard Ruiz-Picasso (his grandson), and includes some wonderful paintings of the family, including the heartfelt *Paulo con gorro blanco* (Paulo with a white cap), a portrait of Picasso's eldest son painted in the 1920s.

Don't miss the Phoenician, Roman, Islamic and Renaissance archaeological remains in the museum's basement, discovered during construction works.

Málaga Province

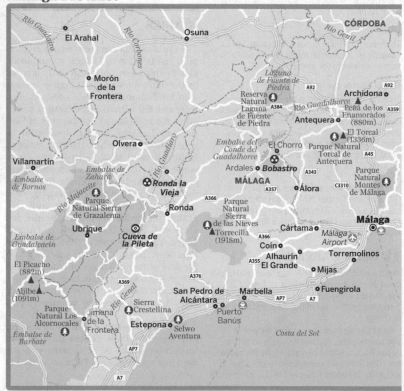

Cathedral CATHEDRAL

(☎952 21 59 17; Calle Molina Lario; cathedral & museum €3.50; ☺10am-6pm Mon-Sat, closed holidays) Málaga's cathedral was started in the 16th century and building continued for some 200 years. From the start, the project was plagued by over-ambition, and the original proposal for a new cathedral had to be shelved. Instead, a series of architects (five in total) set about transforming the original mosque – of this, only the **Patio de los Naranjos** survives, a small courtyard of fragrant orange trees where the ablutions fountain used to be.

Inside, it is easy to see why the epic project took so long. The fabulous domed ceiling soars 40m into the air, while the vast colonnaded nave houses an enormous cedar wood choir. Aisles give access to 15 chapels with gorgeous retables and a stash of 18th-century religious art. Such was the project's cost that by 1782 it was decided that work would stop. One of the two bell towers

was left incomplete, hence the cathedral's well-worn nickname, La Manquita (the one-armed lady). The cathedral entrance is on Calle Císter. The cathedral's **museum** displays a collection of religious items covering a period of 500 years. These include sacred paintings and sculptures, liturgical ornaments, and valuable pieces made of gold, silver and ivory.

Alcazaba CASTLE

(Calle Alcazabilla; admission €2.10, incl Castillo de Gibralfaro €3.40; ☺9.30am-8pm Tue-Sun Apr-Oct) No time to visit Granada's Alhambra? Then Málaga's Alcazaba can provide a taster. The entrance is next to the **Roman amphitheatre**, from where a meandering path climbs amid lush greenery: crimson bougainvillea, lofty palms, fragrant jasmine bushes and rows of orange trees.

Extensively restored, this palace-fortress dates from the 11th-century Moorish period, and the caliphal horseshoe arches, courtyards and bubbling fountains are evocative of this influential period in Málaga's history. Don't miss the small archaeological museum located within the former servants' quarters of the Nazari palace with its exhibits of Moorish ceramics and pottery.

Castillo de Gibralfaro CASTLE

(admission €2.10; ☺9am-9pm Apr-Sep, to 6pm Oct-Mar) One remnant of Málaga's Islamic past is the craggy ramparts of the Castillo de Gibralfaro, spectacularly located high on the hill overlooking the city. Built by Abd ar-Rahman I, the 8th-century Cordoban emir, and later rebuilt in the 14th century when Málaga was the main port for the emirate of Granada, the castle originally acted as a lighthouse and military barracks.

Nothing much is original in the castle's interior, but the airy walkway around the ramparts affords the best views over Málaga. There is also a military museum, which includes a small-scale model of the entire castle complex and the lower residence, the Alcazaba. The model clearly shows the 14th-century curtain wall that connected the two sites and which has been recently restored.

The best way to reach the castle on foot is via the scenic Paseo Don Juan de Temboury, to the south of the Alcazaba. From here a path winds pleasantly (and steeply) through lushly gardened terraces with viewpoints over the city. Alternatively, you can drive

Málaga

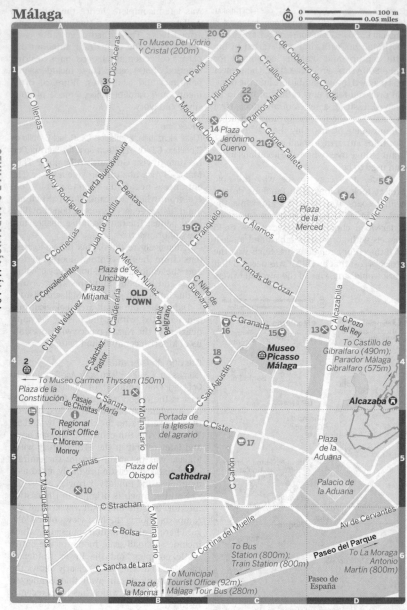

up the Camino de Gibralfaro or take bus 35 from Avenida de Cervantes.

There are plans to build a funicular railway up the hill to the Castillo but no completion date was available at research time.

Museo Carmen Thyssen MUSEUM
(www.carmenthyssenmalaga.org; Calle Compañia 10; adult/child €6/free; ⊙10am-8pm Tue-Sun) One of the city's latest museums opened in 2011 in an aesthetically renovated 16th-century palace in the heart of the city's his-

Málaga

toric centre, the former old Moorish quarter of Málaga. The extensive collection concentrates on 19th-century Spanish and Andalucian art and includes paintings by some of the country's most exceptional painters, including Joaquín Sorolla y Bastida, Ignacio Zuloaga and Francisco de Zurbarán. Temporary exhibitions similarly focus on 19th-century art.

Casa Natal de Picasso   MUSEUM
(Plaza de la Merced 15; admission €1; ⊙9.30am-8pm) For an intimate insight into Picasso's childhood, head to the house where he was born in 1881, which now acts as a study foundation. The house has a replica 19th-century artist's studio and small quarterly exhibitions of Picasso's work. Personal memorabilia of Picasso and his family make up part of the display.

Museo del Vidrio y Cristal   MUSEUM
(Museum of Glass & Crystal; www.museovidrioycristalmalaga.com; Plazuela Santísimo Cristo de la Sangre 2; admission €4; ⊙11am-7pm Tue-Sun) This new glass and crystal museum may not sound the most riveting collection in the world, but it's wonderfully historic, rich and varied. The museum is housed in an 18th-century palatial house, complete with three central patios, in a charmingly dilapidated part of town. Recently restored by aristocratic owner and historian Gonzalo Fernández-Prieto, the private collection concentrates on glass and crystal but also includes antique furniture, priceless carpets, pre-Raphaelite stained glass windows and huge 16th-century ancestral portraits.

Beaches   BEACHES
Sandy city beaches stretch several kilometres in each direction from the port. **Playa de la Malagueta**, handy to the city centre, has some excellent bars and restaurants close by. **Playa de Pedregalejo** and **Playa del Palo**, about 4km east of the centre, are popular and reachable by bus 11 from Paseo del Parque.

⚑ Courses

There are many private language schools in Málaga; try the **Instituto Picasso** (☏952 21 39 32; www.instituto-picasso.com; Plaza de la Merced 20), which runs two-/three-/four-week courses for €285/400/515 starting every fortnight on a Monday. There are four 50-minute lessons a day and the price includes access to cultural activities such as flamenco and cookery courses. Accommodation is also available.

☞ Tours

To pick up the child-friendly, open-topped **Malaga Tour** (☏902 101081; www.malaga-tour. com), head for Avenida Manuel Agustín Heredia or the eastern end of the Paseo del Parque. This hop-on/hop-off tour does a circuit of the city, stopping at all the sights. Tickets are valid for 24 hours. If you're happier on two wheels, you can try Malaga Bike Tours (☑606 978513; www.malagabike tours.eu; Calle Trinidad Grund 1; tours €23). Open tours leave from outside the municipal tourist office in Plaza de la Marina at 9.50am daily. You can book 24 hours ahead. Alternatively, you can travel in old-fashioned style, with a horse-carriage tour of the city that lasts 45 minutes and costs €30. Carriages line up at the Plaza de la Marina end of the Jardines Alcalde Pedro Ruiz Alonzo, along the Paseo del Parque.

✨ Festivals & Events

Semana Santa   HOLY WEEK

Each night from Palm Sunday to Good Friday, six or seven *cofradías* (brotherhoods) bear their holy images for several hours through the city, watched by large crowds.

Feria de Málaga   FAIR

Málaga's nine-day feria (fair), launched by a huge fireworks display on the opening Friday in mid-August, is the most ebullient of Andalucía's summer ferias. Resembling an exuberant Rio-style street party with plenty of flamenco and *fino* (sherry), head for the city centre to be in the thick of it. At night, festivities switch to large fairgrounds and nightly rock and flamenco shows at Cortijo de Torres, 3km southwest of the city centre; special buses run from all over the city.

🛏 Sleeping

El Riad Andaluz   GUESTHOUSE €€

(☑952 21 36 40; www.elriadandaluz.com; Calle Hinestrosa 24; s/d €70/86; ✳@☎) This French-run guesthouse, near the Teatro Cervantes, has eight rooms set around the kind of atmospheric patio that's known as a *riad* in Morocco. The decoration is Moroccan but each room is different, including colourful tiled bathrooms. Breakfast is available.

El Hotel del Pintor   HOTEL €€

(☑952 06 09 81; www.hoteldelpintor.com; Calle Álamos 27; r from €75; ✳@☎) The red, black and white colour scheme of this friendly small hotel echoes the abstract artwork of *malagueño* artist Pepe Bornov, whose paintings are on permanent display throughout the public areas and rooms. Convenient for most of the city's main sights, the rooms in the front can be noisy, especially on a Saturday night.

Parador Málaga Gibralfaro   HISTORIC HOTEL €€€

(☑952 22 19 02; www.parador.es; Castillo de Gibralfaro; r €160-171; P✳☎☏) With an unbeatable location perched on the pine-forested Gibralfaro, Málaga's stone-built Parador is a popular choice, although the rooms are fairly standard. Most have spectacular views from their terraces, however, and you can dine at the excellent terrace restaurant even if you are not a guest at the hotel.

Room Mate Larios   HOTEL €€

(☑952 22 22 00; www.room-matehotels.com; Calle Marqués de Larios 2; s/d € 80/100; ✳@☎) Located on the central Plaza de la Constitución, this hotel is housed in a 19th-century building that has been elegantly restored. Rooms are luxuriously furnished with carpeting throughout and king-sized beds; several rooms have balconies overlooking the sophisticated strut of shops and boutiques along Calle Marqués de Larios. The roof terrace bar is separately owned but easily accessible and boasts stunning views of the cathedral.

Hostal Larios   HOSTAL €

(☑952 22 54 90; www.hostallarios.com; Calle Marqués de Larios 9; s/d €50/60, without bathroom €41/51; ✳) This small hotel may have only one star, but it enjoys a veritable five-star location on Málaga's sophisticated main shopping street. There are just 11 rooms, all washed in dark ochre with original antique double doors, high ceilings, colourful bedcovers and flatscreen TVs. Some rooms have shared bathrooms which, while small, are clean and adequately equipped.

Feel Málaga Hostel   HOSTEL €

(☑952 22 28 32; www.feelmalagahostel.com; Calle Vendeja 25; d €45, without bathroom €35, shared rooms per person from €16 ; @☎) This sparkling new hostel opened in October 2011 and is a welcome addition to Málaga's budget sleeping scene. Located within a suitcase trundle of the city-centre train station, the accommodation is clean and well equipped with a choice of doubles and shared rooms. Bathrooms sport classy mosaic tiles and the top-floor kitchen has all the essentials necessary to whip up a decent meal.

Eating

Málaga's restaurants are well priced and of a good standard due to the largely local clientele. A speciality here is fish fried quickly in olive oil. *Fritura malagueña* consists of fried fish, anchovies and squid. Most of the best eating places are sandwiched in the narrow streets between Calle Marqués de Larios and the cathedral.

 Vino Mio INTERNATIONAL €€
(www.restaurantevino.mio.com; Plaza Jeronimo Cuervo 2; mains €10-15) This Dutch-owned restaurant has a diverse and interesting menu that includes dishes like kangaroo steaks, vegetable stir fries, duck breast with sweet chilli, pasta, and several innovative salads. Tasty international tapas, like hummus and Roquefort croquettes, are also available to tantalise the tastebuds. The atmosphere is contemporary chic with regular art exhibitions and live music, including flamenco.

La Moraga
Antonio Martín CONTEMPORARY ANDALUCIAN €€€
(952 22 41 53; www.lamoraga.com; Plaza Malagueta 4; tapas from €5, mains from €20) This is Michelin-star chef Dani Garcia's second Málaga-based La Moraga (the first is on Calle Fresca in the centre). The concept is based on traditional tapas given the nouvelle treatment – like cherry gazpacho garnished with fresh cheese, anchovies and basil; king prawns wrapped in fried basil leaves; and mini-burgers created from oxtail. The dining spaces have a cool contemporary look and overlook the beach.

Tapeo de Cervantes TAPAS €
(www.eltapeodecervantes.com; Calle Cárcer 8; tapas €4-6; Tue-Sun) This place has caught on big time which, given its squeeze-in space, can mean a wait. Choose from traditional or more innovative tapas and *raciones* with delicious combinations and stylish presentation. Think polenta with oyster mushrooms, chorizo and melted cheese or the more conventional tortilla (potato omelette), spiked with a veg or two.

La Rebaná TAPAS €
(www.larebana.com; Calle Molina Lario 5; tapas €4.20-8.50, raciones €7-11.50) A great, noisy tapas bar near the Picasso museum and the cathedral. Dark wood, tall windows and exposed-brick walls create a modern, minimal, laid-back space. Try the unique foie gras with salted nougat tapa.

Terra Sana HEALTH FOOD €
(www.restaurantesterrasana.com; Calle Alcazabilla; mains €8-10;) One of a small local chain that concentrates on healthy international cuisine. There's a great salad choice, plus wraps, with stuffings like tofu, chicken and *jamón serrano*, plus yoghurt-based sundaes, Indian-style lassies and Mexican quesadillas. There's a children's menu.

Alumbre CONTEMPORARY ANDALUCIAN €€
(www.alumbrebar.com; Calle Strachan 11; mains €11.50-17) Located on a pedestrian street flanked by classy bars and restaurants, Alumbre dishes up arty plates of innovative Andalucian-inspired cooking with its roots in traditional 16th-century dishes. Surprises on the menu include snail croquettes, while more conservative palates may prefer the cuttlefish steak.

🍷 Drinking

On weekend nights, the web of narrow old streets north of Plaza de la Constitución comes alive. Look for bars around Plaza de la Merced, Plaza Mitjana and Plaza de Uncibay.

Bodegas El Pimpi BAR
(www.bodegabarelpimpi.com; Calle Granada 62; 11am-2am) This rambling bar is an institution in this town. The cavernous interior encompasses a warren of rooms with a central courtyard and large open terrace overlooking the recently renovated Roman amphitheatre. Walls are decorated with historic feria posters and photos of celeb-style visitors while the enormous barrels are signed by more well-known folk, including Tony Blair and home boy Antonio Banderas. Tapas and meals also available.

La Tetería TEAHOUSE, CAFE
(Calle San Agustín 9; speciality teas €2.50, breakfasts €2.30-5; 9am-midnight) This place serves heaps of aromatic and classic teas, herbal infusions, coffees and juices, with teas ranging from peppermint to '*antidepresivo*'. You can breakfast on fresh juices and *bocadillos* (filled rolls); there are only crêpes from around 2pm. Sit outside and marvel at the beautiful church opposite or stay inside to enjoy the wafting incense and background music.

Casa Lola BAR
(Calle Granada 46; 11am-4pm & 7pm-midnight) Fronted by traditional blue-and-white tiles, this sophisticated spot specialises in vermouth on tap, served ice cold and costing just a couple of euros. Grab a pew on one of the tall stools perusing the arty decor

and clientele; an ideal spot to kickstart your night out on the town.

El Jardín CAFE, BAR

(☑952 22 04 19; Calle Cañón 1; mains €12.50; ⊙9am-midnight Mon-Thu, 9am-2pm & 5pm-midnight Fri & Sat, 5pm-midnight Sun) A beautiful Viennese-style cafe next to palm-filled gardens behind the cathedral, full of ancient *malagueños* plus the odd inebriated Picasso lookalike. Art-nouveau flourishes and old photographs evoke a pleasant ambience, but not great food. Instead, come for wine or coffee and listen to some young-at-heart septuagenarian pound away on the upright piano.

☆ Entertainment

Málaga's substantial flamenco heritage has its nexus to the northwest of Plaza de la Merced. Venues here include Kelipe (☑692 829885; www.kelipe.net; Calle Pena 11), a flamenco centre which puts on *muy puro* performances Thursday to Saturday at 9.30pm; entry of €15 includes one drink and tapa – reserve ahead. Kelipe also runs intensive weekend courses in guitar and dance. Amargo (Calle R Franquillo 3) offers Friday and Saturday night gigs, while Vino Mio (Calle Alamos) is a small restaurant with an international menu where musicians and dancers fill the wait for the food.

Teatro Cervantes THEATRE

(www.teatrocervantes.com; Calle Ramos Marín; ⊙closed mid-Jul–Aug) The handsome art deco Cervantes has a fine program of music, theatre and dance, including some known names on the concert circuit, like Rufus Wainwright who called Cervantes 'the most beautiful theatre in Europe'.

Onda Pasadena LIVE MUSIC

(Calle Gómez Pallete 5) A congenial combination of older and younger audiences mingle on Tuesdays to listen to jazz, while handclapping is all the rage on Thursdays when flamenco gigs take over.

🛍 Shopping

Central Calle Marqués de Larios and nearby streets have glitzy boutiques and shoe shops in handsomely restored old buildings.

ℹ Information

There are plenty of banks with ATMs on Calle Puerta del Mar and Calle Marqués de Larios, and ATMs in the airport arrivals hall.

In addition to the **municipal tourist office** (Plaza de la Marina; ⊙9am-8pm Mar-Sep, 9am-6pm Oct-Feb), there are also information booths at the main train station, Alcazaba, Plaza de la Merced, main post office and on the eastern beaches.

Hospital Carlos Haya (☑951 03 01 00; Avenida de Carlos Haya) The main hospital, 2km west of the centre.

Policía Local (☑952 12 65 00; Avenida de la Rosaleda 19)

Post pffice (Avenida de Andalucía 1; ⊙8.30am-8.30pm Mon-Fri, 9.30am-2pm Sat)

Regional tourist office (www.andalucia.org; Pasaje de Chinitas 4; ⊙9am-7.30pm Mon-Fri, 10am-7pm Sat, 10am-2pm Sun) There is another branch at the airport; these cover the whole of Málaga and all of Andalucía.

ℹ Getting There & Away

Air

Málaga's **Pablo Picasso Airport** (www.aena.es), the main international gateway to Andalucía, is 9km southwest of the city centre and underwent a considerable expansion in 2010. It is a major hub in southern Spain serving top global carriers, as well as budget airlines.

Boat

Trasmediterránea (☑952 06 12 18, 902 454645; www.trasmediterranea.com; Estación Marítima, Local E1) operates a ferry (7½ hours) daily year-round to/from Melilla, the Spanish enclave in North Africa (passenger/car one way €27/299).

Bus

Málaga's **bus station** (☑952 35 00 61; www.estabus.emtsam.es; Paseo de los Tilos) is just 1km southwest of the city centre. Frequent buses travel along the coasts, and others go to Seville (€30, 2½ hours, six daily), Granada (€10.50, 1½ to two hours, 18 daily), Córdoba (€13.50, 3½ hours, four daily), Antequera (€5, one hour, 13 daily) and Ronda (€9.50, 2½ hours, nine or more daily). Five buses also run daily to Madrid Airport (€36, five hours), and a few go up Spain's Mediterranean coast. There are services to France, Germany, Holland, Portugal and Morocco too.

Car

Numerous local and international agencies (including Avis and Hertz) have desks at the airport.

Train

The Málaga-Renfe train station is near the bus station. Destinations include: Córdoba (€25.90, 2½ hours, 18 daily), Seville (€18.35, 2¾ hours, 11 daily) and Madrid (€87, 2½ hours, 10 daily). Note that for Córdoba and Seville the daily schedule includes faster trains at roughly double the cost.

ℹ Getting Around

To/From the Airport

BUS Bus 75 to the city centre (€1.20, 20 minutes) leaves from outside the arrivals hall every 20 minutes from 7am to midnight. The bus to the airport leaves from the western end of Paseo del Parque, and from outside the bus and train stations, about every half-hour from 6.30am to 11.30pm.

TAXI A taxi from the airport to the city centre costs around €16.

TRAIN Trains run every 20 minutes from 6.50am to 11.54pm to the Málaga-Renfe station and the Málaga-Centro station beside the Río Guadalmedina. Departures from the city to the airport are every 20 minutes from 5.30am to 10.30pm.

Costa del Sol

Splaying from Nerja in the east to Gibraltar in the west, the Costa del Sol juxtaposes cheesy (Torremolinos) with swanky (Marbella) on a coastline that is not renowned for its subtlety. Though the sprawling suburbs and overdeveloped beaches provoke extreme responses from different types of travellers, the Costa – to coin one of its favourite tourist-brochure clichés – really does have 'something for everyone'. If your idea of a good holiday is sandy beaches, pulsating nightclubs, and large, kid-friendly amusement parks, then this famously mild coastline has them all in abundance. If, on the other hand, the very mention of the word 'Torremolinos' sends you into fits of depression, thank your lucky stars that, by sucking up approximately 70% of the region's annual tourists, the Costa del Sol unwittingly keeps the likes of Tarifa, Vejer de la Frontera and Grazalema deliciously tranquil.

A convenient train service links Málaga's Renfe and Aeropuerto stations with Torremolinos (€1.45), Arroyo de la Miel (€1.65) and Fuengirola (€2.25). Buses from Málaga link all the resorts, and services to places such as Ronda, Cádiz, Seville and Granada go from the main resorts.

TORREMOLINOS
POP 48,000

Like an overexposed film star with a fame addiction, Torremolinos' reputation precedes it. Think T-shirt suntans and Union Jack swimming trunks, beer over fish and chips and permanently inebriated 18- to 30-year-olds on elongated stag weekends. Yet, despite being the butt of everything from Monty Python jokes to hysterical tabloid holiday exposés, 'Terrible Torrie' refuses to die. Reinvention is its perennial hallmark. Dogged by a lager-loutish reputation in the 1990s, the resort has successfully embraced its kitsch side and started attracting an older demographic backed up by a strong gay following. Make no mistake: the town of towers *(torres)* and windmills *(molinos)* has life in it yet.

◉ Sights & Activities

Torrie's beaches are wider and longer than some on the *costa* (coast), but are way inferior (and more crowded) than those on the Costa de la Luz. Away from the beach/bar scene, the local attractions are mostly child-oriented.

FREE **Buddhist Stupa** MUSEUM, MONUMENT (Benalmádena Pueblo; ⊙10am-2pm & 3.30-6.30pm Tue-Sat, 10am-7.30pm Sun) The largest Buddhist stupa in Europa is in Benalmádena Pueblo. It rises up, majestically out of place, on the outskirts of the village, surrounded by new housing and with sweeping coastal views. The stupa is open to visitors.

Tivoli World AMUSEMENT PARK (www.tivoli.es; Avenida de Tivoli; admission €7; ⊙6pm-1am) Just five minutes' walk from Benalmádena–Arroyo de la Miel train station, this is the biggest amusement park on the *costa*. The Supertivolino ticket (€12) includes the admission price and gives unlimited access to more than 35 rides.

🍴 Sleeping & Eating

Torremolinos lists 55 hotels in its tourist-office brochures, and in addition to British breakfasts and beer, it has no shortage of good seafood places, many of them lining the Paseo Marítimo in La Carihuela.

Hotel Tropicana HOTEL €€ (☑952 38 66 00; www.hoteltropicana.es; Calle Tropico 6, La Carihuela; s/d €95/120; ℗❄🛜♨♿) A thong's throw from the beach, this pleasant low-rise hotel has attractive homey rooms with warm colour schemes and dazzling white fabrics, a garden of lofty palms and a decent restaurant. It is also perfectly positioned for strolling along the promenade that links Benalmádena Port with Torremolinos.

La Consula
CONTEMPORARY SPANISH €€€

(☑952 436 026; www.laconsula.com; Finca Consula Churriana; set menus €35-50; ⊙lunch Mon-Fri, closed Aug) Located around 6km northwest of Torremolinos in Churriana in a lush setting, La Consula is one of Spain's top culinary schools. The daily menu reflects an innovative twist on traditional Spanish dishes with beautifully crafted plates, not too much froth and drizzle, and faultless delicious flavours. The service is the best you will find anywhere – these students don't want to mess up – and the atmosphere is elegant and formal.

☆ Entertainment

Torrie's nightlife is famous among the hard partying set, international DJs and the gay 'in crowd'. An energetic, fun-loving lot gather at Kaleido (www.kaleido.es; Darsena de Levante, Puerto Marina; ⊙11am-late) near Playa La Carihuela.

❶ Information

Tourist office (www.pmdt.es; Plaza de la Independencia; ⊙9.30am-1.30pm Mon-Fri) There are also offices on **Playa Bajondillo** (Playa Bajondillo; ⊙10am-2pm) and **Playa Carihuela** (Playa Carihuela; ⊙10am-2pm).

FUENGIROLA
POP 71,800

Fuengirola is a genuine Spanish working town, as well as being firmly on the tourist circuit. It attracts mainly Northern European visitors and also has a large foreign resident population, many of who arrived here in the '60s – and stayed (yes, there are a few grey ponytails around). The beach stretches for a mighty 7km, encompassing the former fishing quarter of Los Boliches.

The Hipódromo Costa del Sol (☑952 59 27 00; www.hipodromocostadelsol.es; Urbanización El Chaparral; admission €8; ⊙10pm-2am Sat Jul-Sep), Andalucía's leading horse-racing track with regular racing, is off the N340 at the southwestern end of Fuengirola.

For eating there's Charolais (www.bode gacharolais.com; Calle Larga 14; mains €12-20), a modern tapas bar, a terrace and a rustic-style restaurant emphasising expertly prepared meat dishes. La Picada (Calle de la Pandereta 5; tapas €3, mains €10; ⊙Tue-Sat) piles in the locals with its generously portioned tapas.

The tourist office (☑952 46 74 57; Avenida Jesús Santos Rein 6; ⊙9.30am-2pm & 5-7pm Mon-Fri, 10am-1pm Sat) is about a block from the train station (Avenida Jesús Santos Rein), which runs half-hourly trains to Torremolinos, Málaga airport and Málaga city.

MARBELLA
POP 136,000

Marbella is the Costa del Sol's classiest, and most expensive, resort. This inherent wealth glitters most brightly along the Golden Mile, a tiara of star-studded clubs, restaurants and hotels which stretches from Marbella to Puerto Banús, the flashiest marina on the Costa del Sol, where black-tinted Mercs slide along a quayside of luxury yachts. Marbella has a magnificent natural setting, sheltered by the beautiful Sierra Blanca mountains, as well as an attractive *casco antiguo* (old town).

◉ Sights & Activities

Pretty Plaza de los Naranjos, with its 16th-century town hall, is at the heart of the largely pedestrianised, postcard-perfect old town. Puerto Banús, the Costa del Sol's flashiest marina, is 6km west of Marbella and has a slew of glamorous boutiques and busy restaurants strung along the waterfront.

There are good walks in the Sierra Blanca, starting from the Refugio de Juanar, a 17km drive north of Marbella.

FREE Museo Ralli
MUSEUM

(Urbanización Coral Beach; ⊙10am-2pm Tue-Sat) This superb private art museum exhibits paintings by primarily Latin American and European artists in bright, well-lit galleries. Part of a nonprofit foundation, exhibits include sculptures by Henry Moore and Salvador Dalí, and vibrant contemporary paintings by Argentinian surrealist painter Alicia Carletti and Cuban Wilfredo Lam, plus works by Joan Miró, Chagall and Chirico.

Museo del Grabado Español
MUSEUM

(Calle Hospital Bazán; admission €2.50; ⊙10am-2pm & 5.30-8.30pm) This small art museum in the old town includes works by some of the great masters, including Picasso, Joan Miró and Salvador Dalí, among other, primarily Spanish, painters.

🛏 Sleeping & Eating

TOP CHOICE Claude
BOUTIQUE HOTEL €€€

(☑952 90 08 40; www.hotelclaudemarbella.com; Calle San Francisco 5; s/d €225/250; ❄❂) Situated in the quieter upper part of town, this sumptuous hotel is housed in a 17th-century mansion of some historical significance – it was the former summer home of Napoleon's third wife. The decor successfully marries contemporary flourishes with the original architecture, while claw foot tubs and crystal chandeliers add to the classic historical feel. There are superb views from the rooftop terrace.

Hotel Lima   HOTEL €€
(☑952 77 05 00; www.hotellimamarbella.com; Avenida Antonio Belón; s/d €60/75; ❄☏) Although this hotel does not have a lot of character, it provides a good central base near the beach. The rooms have dark wood furnishings and floral bedspreads, and several have balconies overlooking the leafy street.

Calima   MODERN EUROPEAN €€€
(☑952 76 42 52; www.restaurantecalima.es; Hotel Melia Don Pepé, Calle Jose Melia; mains €22-28; ☉7.30-10pm Tue-Sat & 1.30-3pm Sat) Michelin star chef Dani García cut his culinary teeth at Ronda's famous Tragabuches restaurant and has carried on to acquire considerable fame here, as well as at his chain of smart tapas bars: La Moraga. Dishes are based on contrasts and have tantalising names like 'egg without an egg' and litchis and roses popcorn. The open plan dining space is all steely grey and chrome. Seafood is his forte.

El Estrecho   TAPAS €€
(Calle San Lázaro; tapas €1.50, raciones €5-8) Always crammed, elbow your way to a space in the small back dining room and order from a massive menu that includes tapas like *salmorejo* (Córdoba-style thick gazpacho). This is one of several great tapas bars on this narrow pedestrian street.

🍷 Drinking & Entertainment
The busiest nightlife zone in the Marbella area is at Puerto Banús, where dozens of pubs and varied dance clubs cluster along a couple of narrow lanes behind the marina.

ℹ Information
Tourist office (www.marbella.es; Plaza de los Naranjos 1; ☉9.30am-9pm Mon-Fri) Has plenty of leaflets and a good town map.

ℹ Getting There & Around
Buses to Fuengirola (€3.20, one hour), Puerto Banús (€1.50, 20 minutes) and Estepona (€2.80, one hour) leave about every 30 minutes from Avenida Ricardo Soriano. Other services use the **bus station** (☑952 76 44 00; Avenida Trapiche), 1.2km north of Plaza de los Naranjos.

Bus 7 (€1.10) runs between the bus station and the central **Fuengirola/Estepona bus stop** (Avenida Ricardo Soriano); returning to the bus station, take bus 2 from Avenida Ramón y Cajal.

Marbella's streets are notoriously traffic-clogged. Fortunately there are a number of pay car parks where you can take refuge on arrival.

El Chorro & Bobastro
POP (EL CHORRO): 100

Fifty kilometres northwest of Málaga, Río Guadalhorce and the main railway in and out of Málaga both pass through the awesome Garganta del Chorro, which is 4km long, up to 400m deep and as little as 10m wide. The gorge is a magnet for rock climbers, with hundreds of varied routes of almost every grade of difficulty. Anyone can view the gorge by walking along the railway from the tiny El Chorro village (ask locally for directions). The view provides an adrenalin rush all by itself.

The gorge is particularly famous for the Camino del Rey, a 1m-wide white-knuckle path similar to an Italian *via ferrata* that contours across the sheer rockface on a ledge 100m above the ground. Initially built in 1905 (and traversed by King Alfonso XIII in 1921– hence the name, Path of the King), the path had fallen into severe disrepair by the late 1990s and was closed in 2000 after a couple of tourist deaths. In 2006 €7 million was earmarked by the Andalucian government to restore it. The work is still pending.

Swiss-owned Finca La Campana (☑626 963942; www.fincalacampana.com), popular with adventure lovers, offers half-day climbing courses (€45), caving (€180 for a group of up to four people), kayaking (€20 per person) and mountain-bike rentals (€15 to €18 per day).

Near El Chorro is Bobastro, the hilltop redoubt of 9th-century rebel Omaribn Hafsun, a sort of Islamic Robin Hood, who led a prolonged revolt against Cordoban rule. Ibn Hafsun at one stage controlled territory from Cartagena to the Strait of Gibraltar. From El Chorro village, follow the road up the far (western) side of the valley and after 3km take the signed Bobastro turn-off. Nearly 3km up here, an 'Iglesia Mozárabe' sign indicates a 500m path to the remains of a remarkable little Mozarabic church cut from the rock, the shape so blurred by time that it appears to have been shaped by the wind alone. It's thought that Ibn Hafsun

WORTH A TRIP

ESTEPONA

Estepona was one of the first resorts to attract foreign residents and tourists some 40 years ago and, despite the surrounding development, the centre of the town still has a cosy old-fashioned feel – for good reason; the town's roots date back to the 4th century. A wide promenade overlooks the sandy **Playa de la Rada**; the Puerto Deportivo (port) is the heart and soul of the nightlife, especially at weekends and is also excellent for sea-sports, as well as bars and restaurants. **Buceo Estepona** (☑645 610374; www.buceoestepona.com; Puerto Deportivo; ⊗10am-2.30pm & 4.30-8pm) is a reputable diving outfit. For dining, join the locals for seafood in **La Escollera** (Puerto Pesquero; mains €6-9; ⊗closed Feb). For drinks, try **Puro Beach** (www.purobeach.com; Laguna Village; ⊗noon-late Apr-Oct) in an Asian-inspired beachside complex of bars, restaurants and shops set around lush landscaping.

There are regular buses to Marbella (€2.80, one hour), and Málaga (€7.20, two hours).

converted from Islam to Christianity (thus becoming a Mozarab) before his death in 917 and was buried here. When Córdoba finally conquered Bobastro in 927, the poor chap's remains were taken for grisly posthumous crucifixion outside Córdoba's Mezquita. At the top of the hill, 2.5km further up the road and with unbelievable views, are faint traces of Ibn Hafsun's rectangular *alcázar* (Muslim-era fortress).

Rockfax publishes a comprehensive guidebook on El Chorro and the surrounding crags – listing routes, grades and access information.

❶ Getting There & Away

Once daily trains (except Sunday) run to El Chorro from Málaga (€5.60, 40 minutes), Ronda (€8.80, 70 minutes) and Seville (€18.45, two hours). No buses run to El Chorro. Drivers can get there via Álora (south of El Chorro) or Ardales (west of El Chorro).

Ronda

POP 37,000 / ELEV 744M

Perched on an inland plateau riven by the 100m fissure of El Tajo gorge, Ronda is Málaga province's most spectacular town. It has a superbly dramatic location, and owes its name ('surrounded' by mountains), to the encircling Serranía de Ronda.

Established in the 9th century BC, Ronda is also one of Spain's oldest towns. Its existing old town, La Ciudad (the City), largely dates back to Islamic times, when it was an important cultural centre filled with mosques and palaces. Its wealth as a trading depot made it an attractive prospect for bandits and prof-

iteers and the town has a colourful and romantic past in Spanish folklore.

Ronda was a favourite with the Romantics of the late 19th century, and has attracted an array of international artists and writers, such as David Wilkie, Alexandre Dumas, Rainer Maria Rilke, Ernest Hemingway and Orson Welles.

⊙ Sights & Activities

Plaza de España SQUARE
Directly across the Puente Nuevo is the main square, Plaza de España, made famous by Hemingway in his novel *For Whom the Bell Tolls*. Chapter 10 tells how early in the Civil War the 'fascists' of a small town were rounded up in the *ayuntamiento*, clubbed and made to walk the gauntlet between two lines of townspeople before being thrown off the cliff. The episode is based on events that took place here in Plaza de España. What was the *ayuntamiento* is now Ronda's *parador*.

La Ciudad NEIGHBOURHOOD
Straddling the dramatic gorge and the Río Guadalevín (Deep River) is Ronda's most recognisable sight, the towering **Puente Nuevo**, best viewed from the **Camino de los Molinos**, which runs along the bottom of the gorge. The bridge separates the old and new towns.

The old town is surrounded by massive fortress walls pierced by two ancient gates: the Islamic Puerta de Almocábar which, in the 13th century, was the main gateway to the castle; and the 16th-century Puerta de Carlos V. Inside, the Islamic layout remains intact, and its maze of narrow streets now takes its character from the Renaissance mansions of powerful families whose predecessors accompanied Fernando el Católico in the taking of the city in 1485.

Plaza de Toros
BULLRING

(Calle Virgen de la Paz; admission €5; ⊙10am-8pm) Ronda's Plaza de Toros is a mecca for bullfighting aficionados. In existence for more than 200 years, it is one of the oldest and most revered bullrings in Spain and has also been the site of some of the most important events in bullfighting history.

Built by Martín Aldehuela, the bullring is universally admired for its soft sandstone hues and galleried arches. At 66m in diameter it is also the largest and, therefore, most dangerous bullring, yet it only seats 5000 spectators – a tiny number compared with the huge 50,000-seater bullring in Mexico City. In July the ring is used for a series of fabulous concerts, and opera.

The on-site Museo Taurino is crammed with memorabilia such as blood-spattered costumes worn by Pedro Romero and 1990s star Jesulín de Ubrique. It also includes photos of famous fans such as Orson Welles and Ernest Hemingway, whose novel *Death in the Afternoon* provides in-depth insight into the fear and tension of the bullring.

Behind the Plaza de Toros, spectacular clifftop views open out from Paseo de Blas Infante and the nearby Alameda del Tajo park.

Museo Lara
MUSEUM

(www.museolara.org; Calle de Armiñán 29; adult/child €4/2; ⊙11am-8pm; ⊛) Juan António Lara Jurado has been a collector since the age of 10. Now in his 70s, he still lives above this museum, but his living space is set to shrink as he wants to expand still further. You name it, it is here: priceless, historic collections of clocks, weapons, radios, gramophones, sewing machines, telephones, opera glasses, Spanish fans, scales, cameras and far more.

Walks
WALKING TOUR

The tourist office publishes a series of brochures (€5) highlighting eight easy hikes around Ronda, all of which start in the town itself. Distances range from 2.5km to 9.1km and visit viewpoints, old hermitages and parks. One of the best is the 4.6km **SL-A38**, which starts at Plaza Campillos near the Palacio de Mondragón before tracking down below the gorge (for the classic bridge photo). After winding past some old mills, it loops back uphill into the New Town.

✦ Festivals & Events

During the first two weeks of September, Ronda's Feria de Pedro Romero (an orgy of partying, including the important flamenco Festival de Cante Grande) takes place. It culminates in the Corridas Goyesca (bullfights in honour of legendary bullfighter Pedro Romero).

🛌 Sleeping

Hotel Alavera de los Baños
HOTEL €€

(📞952 87 91 43; www.alaveradelosbanos.com; Hoyo San Miguel; s/d incl breakfast €70/95; ⊛❄) Taking its cue from the Arab baths next door, the Alavera de los Baños has the Hispano-Islamic theme throughout, with Eastern decor and tasty North African–inspired cuisine using predominantly organic foods. Ask for a room on the terrace, as such rooms open out onto a small, lush garden.

Jardín de la Muralla
HISTORIC HOTEL €€

(📞952 87 27 64; www.jardindelamuralla.com; Calle Espíritu Santo 13; s/d incl breakfast €80/91; ⊛@❄) José María has ensured that his historic family home retains plenty of evocative atmosphere with antiques, chandeliers, ancestral portraits and wonderful claw foot bathtubs. The terraced gardens lead to the 15th-century city walls. Pets allowed.

Parador de Ronda
HOTEL €€€

(📞952 87 75 00; www.parador.es; Plaza de España; r €160-171; P⊛@❄❄) Acres of shining marble and deep-cushioned furniture give this modern *parador* a certain appeal. The terrace is a wonderful place to drink in views of the gorge with your coffee or wine, especially at night.

Enfrente Arte
HOTEL €€

(📞952 87 90 88; www.enfrentearte.com; Calle Real 40; r incl breakfast €80-90; ⊛@❄) On an old cobblestoned street, Belgian-owned Enfrente offers a huge range of facilities and funky modern/Eastern decor. It has a bar, pool, sauna, recreation room, flowery patio with black bamboo, film room and fantastic views out to the Sierra de las Nieves. What's more, the room price includes all drinks, to which you help yourself, and a sumptuous buffet breakfast.

Hotel San Gabriel
HOTEL €€

(📞952 19 03 92; www.hotelsangabriel.com; Calle José M Holgado 19; s/d incl breakfast €66/82; ⊛❄) This charming hotel is filled with antiques and photographs that offer insight into Ronda's history – bullfighting, celebrities and all. Ferns hang down the huge mahogany staircase, there is a billiard room, a cosy living room stacked with books and a DVD screening room with 10 velvet-covered seats rescued from Ronda's theatre and autographed photos of several actors, including Bob Hoskins and Isabella Rossellini.

Hotel Montelirio
HOTEL €€€

(☎952 87 38 55; www.hotelmontelirio.com; Calle Tenorio 8; s/d €100/150; ❋≋) Hugging El Tajo gorge, the Montelirio has magical views. The converted *palacio* has been sensitively refurbished, with sumptuous suites. The lounge retains its gorgeous Mudéjar ceiling and opens out onto a terrace complete with plunge pool. The restaurant is similarly excellent.

Hotel Hermanos Macias
HOTEL €

(☎952 87 42 38; www.hermanosmacias.com; Calle Pedro Romero 3; s/d €35/48; P❋) Located above a popular restaurant and bar, the rooms here are excellent value. Rustic-style and simply furnished, several overlook the bustling pedestrian street.

✗ Eating

Traditional Ronda food is hearty mountain fare that's big on stews, trout, game such as rabbit, partridge and quail, and, of course, oxtail. The largest concentration of restaurants is situated in the grid east of Plaza de España, but there are some less-heralded gems just south of the old town in the Barrio San Francisco.

⬡TOP CHOICE Bodega San Francisco
TAPAS €

(www.bodegasanfrancisco.com; Calle Ruedo Alameda; raciones €6-10) With three dining rooms and tables spilling out onto the narrow pedestrian street, this may well be Ronda's top tapas bar. The menu is vast and should suit the fussiest of families, even vegetarians with nine-plus salad choices. Try the *revuelto de patatas* (scrambled eggs with potatoes and peppers). House wine is good.

Bar Restaurant Almocábar
ANDALUCIAN €

(Calle Ruedo Alameda 5; tapas €1.50, mains €10; ⊘1.30-5pm & 8pm-1am Wed-Mon) Almocábar is little touched by the tourist hordes at the top of town. In fact, the tapas are so good that this spot is normally superpacked, and finding a place at the bar can be a challenge. If that's the case, try reserving the restaurant-section *comedor* (dining room).

Restaurante Tragabuches
CONTEMPORARY SPANISH €€€

(☎952 19 02 91; www.tragabuches.com; Calle José Aparicio 1; menus €59-87; ⊘1.30-3.30pm & 8-10.30pm Tue-Sat) Ronda's best and most famous restaurant is a 180-degree turn away from the ubiquitous 'rustic' look and cuisine. Michelin-starred in 1998, Tragabuches is modern and sleek with an innovative menu to match. Choose from three set menus. People flock here from miles away to taste the food, prepared by its creative chef.

Faustino
ANDALUCIAN €

(Calle Santa Cecilía; tapas €1.50, raciones €6-8) This is the real deal, a lively atmospheric tapas bar with plenty of seating space in the open traditional atrium decorated with plants, feria posters and bullfighting and religious pictures. Tapas and *raciones* are generous. Go with the recommendations like *champingnones a la plancha* (grilled mushrooms with lashings of garlic). The only downside is the uncomfortable, if pretty, rustic-style painted chairs. Ouch!

Restaurante Pedro Romero
ANDALUCIAN €€

(☎952 87 11 10; www.rpedroromero.com; Calle Virgen de la Paz 18; menú €16, mains €15-18) Opposite the bullring, this celebrated eatery dedicated to bullfighting turns out classic *rondeño* dishes (dishes from Ronda). This is a good place to try the *rabo de toro* (a tender meat dish made from bull's tail). Vegetarians will doubtless prefer the fried goat's cheese starter served with apple sauce.

🍷 Drinking

New Baco
BAR

(⊘7pm-4am) Get here too early and you may be greeted by footy on the big screen but, later on and definitely at weekends, there are hot DJs and plenty of dancing from midnight.

Tetería Al Zahra
TEAHOUSE

(Calle las Tiendas 17; ⊘4.30pm-midnight) Come here and try a pot of herbal, Moroccan, Pakistani or a host of other teas, all served in pretty Moroccan ceramic teapots and cups and saucers. There are hookahs for smoking, too, and you can settle in for a few hours of sipping, puffing and gossiping.

☆ Entertainment

Círculo de Artistas FLAMENCO
(Plaza del Socorro; admission €23; ☺Mon-Wed May-Sep) Stages flamenco shows in a sumptuous historical building on the square from 10pm, as well as other song and dance performances. Note unconventional timings.

ℹ Information

Banks and ATMs are mainly on Calle Virgen de la Paz and Plaza Carmen Abela.
Muncipal tourist office (www.turismode ronda.es; Paseo de Blas Infante; ☺10am-7.30pm Mon-Fri, 10.15am-2pm & 3.30-6.30pm Sat, Sun & holidays)
Regional tourist office (www.andalucia. org; Plaza de España 1; ☺9am-7.30pm Mon-Fri May-Sep, to 6pm Oct-Apr, 10am-2pm Sat year-round)

ℹ Getting There & Away

Bus

The bus station is at Plaza Concepción García Redondo 2. **Comes** (www.tgcomes.es) has buses to Arcos de la Frontera (€8.75, two hours, two daily), Jerez de la Frontera (€11.50, three hours, three daily) and Cádiz (€15, two hours, three daily). **Los Amarillos** (www.losamarillos. es) goes to Seville via Algodonales, Grazalema, and to Málaga via Ardales.

Train

Ronda's **train station** (☎952 87 16 73; Avenida de Andalucía) is on the line between Bobadilla and Algeciras. Trains run to Algeciras via Gaucín and Jimena de la Frontera. This train ride is incredibly scenic and worth taking just for the views. Other trains depart for Málaga, Córdoba, Madrid and Granada via Antequera. For Seville, ,change at Bobadilla or Antequera.

ℹ Getting Around

Minibuses operate every 30 minutes to Plaza de España from Avenida Martínez Astein, across the road from the train station.

Around Ronda

Ronda is more than a destination in itself. Surrounded by beautiful mountains, it acts as an ideal launching pad for trips into the parks and white towns of Málaga and Cádiz provinces. Hire a car or, even better, a bike, and strike out in earnest. **Cycle Ronda** (☎952

87 78 14; www.cycleronda.com; Calle Serrato 3) can loan you a good pair of wheels for €20 per day.

This area has many traditional houses converted into gorgeous rural accommodation. For information try Ronda's municipal tourist office or www.serraniaronda.org.

CUEVA DE LA PILETA
Palaeolithic paintings of horses, goats, fish and even a seal, dating from 20,000 to 25,000 years ago, are preserved in this large cave (☎952 16 73 43; www.cuevadelapileta. org; Benaoján; adult/child €8/4; ☺hourly tours 10am-1pm & 4-6pm; ♿). 20km southwest of Ronda. You'll be guided by kerosene lamp and one of the knowledgeable Bullón family from the farm in the valley below. A family member found the paintings in 1905. The Cueva de la Pileta is 250m (signposted) off the Benaoján–Cortes de la Frontera road, 4km from Benaoján. Guides speak a little English. If it's busy, you may have to wait, but you can phone ahead to book a particular time.

PARQUE NATURAL SIERRA DE LAS NIEVES
This precious area of rare natural diversity, a Unesco Biosphere Reserve, also has an unusual history of human endeavour. For hundreds of years before refrigeration, the snow sellers of the region would gather at the end of the winter to shovel tonnes of snow into containers and transport it to huge pits, where it was pressed and compacted to form ice, and tightly covered until summer. Mule teams would then transport huge blocks of ice into neighbouring towns, to sell at astronomical prices. Today, this 180-sq-km protected area, southeast of Ronda, offers some excellent walks. Torrecilla (1910m), the highest peak in the western half of Andalucía, is a five- to six-hour (return) walk from Área Recreativa Los Quejigales, which is 10km east by unpaved road from the A376 Ronda–San Pedro de Alcántara road.
Cerro de Hijar (☎952 11 21 11; www.cerro dehijar.com/eng; Carretera del Balneario; d/ste €80/90; ᴘ❀@☎☂), just above the dazzling white village of Tolox and just within the park, sits at 650m above sea level. This tastefully decorated hotel is generous with its room sizes, decoration, sweeping views and the range of activities it cheerfully organises for guests, including mountain biking, guided walks and 4WD excursions.

Antequera

POP 45,000 / ELEV 575M

Antequera is a fascinating town, both architecturally and historically, yet has somehow managed to avoid being on the coach tour circuit – which only serves to add to its charms. The three major influences in the region – Roman, Islamic and Spanish – have left the town with a rich tapestry of architectural gems. The highlight is the opulent Spanish baroque style that gives the town its character and which the civic authorities have worked hard to restore and maintain. There is also an astonishing number of churches here – over 30, many with wonderfully ornate interiors.

◎ Sights

Alcazaba & Around   FORTRESS

The main approach to the Alcazaba (adult/child incl Colegiata de Santa María la Mayor €6/3; ⊙10.30am-2pm & 6-8.30pm Tue-Sun) passes through the Arco de los Gigantes, built in 1585 and incorporating stones with Roman inscriptions. What remains of the Alcazaba affords great views. Just below it is the Colegiata de Santa María la Mayor (Plaza Santa María; adult/child incl Alcazaba €6/3; ⊙10am-2pm & 6-8.30pm), a 16th-century church with a beautiful Renaissance facade.

Museo Municipal   MUSEUM

(Plaza del Coso Viejo; compulsory guided tour €3; ⊙10am-1.30pm & 4.30-6.30pm Tue-Fri, 10am-1.30pm Sat, 11am-1.30pm Sun) Located in the town centre, the pride of the Museo Municipal is the elegant and athletic 1.4m bronze statue of a boy, *Efebo*. Discovered on a local farm in the 1950s, it is possibly the finest example of Roman sculpture found in Spain.

The museum also displays some pieces from a Roman villa in Antequera, where a superb group of mosaics was discovered in 1998. The collection includes a treasure trove of religious items, containing so much silver that you can only visit by guided tour on the half-hour.

Iglesia del Carmen   CHURCH

(Plaza del Carmen; admission €2; ⊙10.30am-1.30pm & 4.30-6pm Tue-Fri, 11am-1.30pm Sat & Sun) Only the most jaded would fail to be impressed by the Iglesia del Carmen and its marvellous 18th-century churrigueresque retable. Magnificently carved in red pine by Antequera's own Antonio Primo, it's spangled with statues of angels by Diego Márquez y Vega, and saints, popes and bishops by José de Medina. While the main altar is unpainted, the rest of the interior is a dazzle of colour and design, painted to resemble traditional tile work.

FREE Dolmen del Romeral   ARCHAEOLOGICAL SITE

(Cerro Romeral; ⊙9am-6pm Tue-Sat, 9.30am-2.30pm Sun) Dolmen de Viera is 1km from the city centre, on the road leading northeast to the A45. In about 2500 BC or 2000 BC the local folk managed to transport dozens of huge rocks from nearby hills to construct these earth-covered tombs for their chieftains.

🛏 Sleeping & Eating

Hotel Coso Viejo   HOTEL €€

(☎952 70 50 45; www.hotelcosoviejo.es; Calle Encarnación 9; s/d incl breakfast €62/78; P❄) This converted 17th-century neoclassical palace is right in the heart of Antequera, opposite Plaza Coso Viejo and the town museum. The comfortable, simply furnished rooms are set around a handsome patio with a fountain and there's an excellent tapas bar and restaurant.

Parador de Antequera   HISTORIC HOTEL €€€

(☎952 84 02 61; www.parador.es; Paseo García del Olmo; s/d €120/145; P❄🛜☼) The Parador is in a quiet area of parkland north of the bullring and near the bus station. It's comfortably furnished and set in pleasant gardens with wonderful views, especially at sunset.

Restaurante La Espuela   CONTEMPORARY ANDALUCIAN €€

(☎952 70 30 31; Calle San Agustín 1; mains €14-18; ⊙1-4pm & 8-11pm Tue-Sun) Located in a pretty restaurant-flanked cul-de-sac off Calle Infante Don Fernando, La Espuela doubles as a cooking school and offers a fine selection of Antequeran specialities, like oxtail with honey and rosemary along with some international fare including pasta dishes. The bow-tied waiters complete the dress-for-dinner feel.

Rincon de Lola   TAPAS €

(www.rincondelola.net; Calle Encarnación 7; tapas €2, raciones €7; ⊙Tue-Sun) A great place to come for inexpensive varied tapas that can give you a taster of local dishes, like *cochinillo* (suckling pig) or the more unusual (for these parts), like sushi.

ℹ Information

Municipal tourist office (☎952 70 25 05; www.antequera.es; Plaza de San Sebastián 7; ☺11am-2pm & 5-8pm Mon-Sat, 11am-2pm Sun)

ℹ Getting There & Away

The **bus station** (Paseo Garcí de Olmo) is found 1km north of the centre. **Alsa** (www.alsa.es) runs buses to Seville (€13, 2½ hours, five daily), Granada (€8, 1½ hours, five daily), Córdoba (€10, two hours and 40 minutes, one daily), Almería (€21, six hours, one daily) and Málaga (€4.30, 1½ hours, two daily). Buses run between Antequera and Fuente de Piedra village (€2, 25 minutes, three daily).

The **train station** (Avenida de la Estación) is 1.5km north of the centre. Six trains a day run to/from Granada (€9.15, 1½ hours, nine daily), and there are four daily to Seville (€31, 1½ hours, 10 daily). Another three run to Málaga or Córdoba, but you'll need to change at Bobadilla.

El Torcal

Sixteen kilometres south of Antequera, nature has sculpted this 1336m mountain into some of the weirdest, most wonderful rock formations you'll see anywhere. Its 12 sq km of gnarled, pillared and deeply fissured limestone began life as seabed about 150 million years ago.

Two marked walking trails, the 1.5km 'Ruta Verde' (Green Route) and the 3km 'Ruta Amarilla' (Yellow Route), start and end near the information centre.

East of Málaga

The coast east of Málaga, sometimes called the Costa del Sol Oriental, is less developed than the coast to the west, although there's an unnerving feeling that the bulldozers are never too far away.

Behind the coast, La Axarquía, a region dotted with white villages (of Islamic origin) linked by snaking mountain roads, climbs to the sierras along the border of Granada province. There's good walking here (best in April and May, and from mid-September to late October). Once impoverished and forgotten, La Axarquía has experienced a surge of tourism and an influx of expat residents in recent years.

NERJA
POP 22,000

Nerja, 56km east of Málaga, is where the Costa del Sol becomes a little easier on the eye, with more precipitous topography and prettier vistas allowing a peek into the Spain that once was. Though locals like to distance themselves from the gaudy resorts further west, Nerja has been similarly inundated by (mainly British) tourists in recent years. Those seeking solitude might want to look elsewhere.

The town's pièce de résistance, right in the centre, is the spectacular **Balcón de Europa**, a palm-shaded walkway that protrudes out into the ocean. The new **Museo de Nerja** (Plaza de España; adult/child €6/3, incl Cueva de Nerja €12.50/6.50; ☺10am-2pm & 4-6.30pm Tue-Sun) traces Nerja's history from cave dwellers to tourist boom and acts as an ideal prelude to a visit to the enormous Cueva de Nerja (p732) 3km north of town.

🛏 Sleeping & Eating

Rooms in the better hotels get booked up well in advance for the summer period.

Hotel Carabeo   HOTEL €€
(☎952 52 54 44; www.hotelcarabeo.com; Calle Carabeo 34; d/ste incl breakfast €85/180; ❋❀@☎≋) Full of stylish antiques, this small, family-run, seafront hotel is set above manicured terraced gardens. There's also a good restaurant and the pool is on a terrace overlooking the sea. The building, an old school house, is on one of the prettiest pedestrian streets in town, festooned with colourful bougainvillea. The hotel is open from April through to October.

TOP CHOICE **Oliva**   MODERN EUROPEAN €€
(☎952 52 14 29; www.restauranteoliva.com; Calle Pintada 7; mains €15-19) Think single orchids, a drum and bass soundtrack and a charcoal grey-and-green colour scheme. In short, this place has class. The menu is reassuringly brief and changes regularly according to what is fresh in season; typical dishes are grilled scallops in a beetroot sauce and sea bass with wasabi, soy and ginger.

Merendero Ayo   SEAFOOD €€
(Playa Burriana; mains €9-13) At this open-air place you can enjoy a plate of paella cooked on the spot in great sizzling pans over an open fire – and even go back for a free second helping. It's run by Ayo, a delightful local character famed for the discovery of the Cueva de Nerja complex, who throws the rice on the *paellera* (paella dish) in a very spectacular fashion, amusing all his guests.

732

ℹ️ Information
Municipal tourist office (☏952 52 15 31; www.nerja.org; Puerta del Mar; ◷10am-2pm & 6-10pm Jul–mid-Sep, 10am-2pm & 5-8pm mid-Sep–Jun) Has plenty of useful leaflets.

ℹ️ Getting There & Away
From the N340 near the top of Calle Pintada, **Alsa** (www.alsa.es) runs regular buses to/from Málaga (€4.15, 1¾ hours, 23 daily), Marbella (€9.50, 1¼ hours, one daily) and Antequera (€8.30, 2¼ hours, two daily). There are also buses to Almería and Granada.

AROUND NERJA
The big tourist attraction is the **Cueva de Nerja** (www.cuevadenerja.es; adult/child €8.50/4.50, incl Museo de Nerja €12.50/6.50; ◷10am-2pm & 4-7.30pm), just off the N340, 3km east of town on the slopes of the Sierra Almijara. The enormous 4km-long cave complex, hollowed out by water around five million years ago and once inhabited by Stone Age hunters, is a theatrical wonderland of extraordinary rock formations, subtle shifting colours and stalactites and stalagmites. Large-scale performances including ballet and flamenco are staged here throughout the summer. About 14 buses run daily from Málaga and Nerja, except Sunday. The whole site is very well organised for large-scale tourism and has a huge restaurant and car park. A full tour of the caves takes about 45 minutes.

Further east the coast becomes more rugged, and with your own wheels you can head out to Playa El Cañuelo and other scenic, if stony, beaches down tracks from the N340, about 8km to 10km from Nerja.

CÓMPETA & AROUND
POP 3500 / ELEV 640M
Comares sits like a snowdrift atop its lofty hill. The adventure really is in getting there. You see it for kilometre after kilometre before a final twist in an endlessly winding road lands you below the hanging garden of its cliff. From a little car park you can climb steep, winding steps to the village. Look for ceramic footprints underfoot and simply follow them through a web of narrow, twisting lanes past the **Iglesia de la Encarnación** and eventually to the ruins of Comares' **castle** and a remarkable summit **cemetery**.

👁 Sights & Activities
A few kilometres down the valley from Cómpeta, Árchez has a beautiful Almohad minaret next to its church. From Árchez a road winds 8km southwest to Arenas, where a steep but driveable track climbs to the ruined Islamic Castillode Bentomiz, which crowns a hilltop. **Los Caballos del Mosquín** (www.horseriding-andalucia.com; Canillas del Albaida; half-day trek €65), just outside Canillas de Albaida, 2km northwest of Cómpeta, offers horse rides in the mountains. An exhilarating long walk is up the dramatically peaked El Lucero (1779m), from whose summit, on a clear day, you can see both Granada and Morocco. This is a demanding full-day return walk from Cómpeta, but it's possible to drive as far up as Puerto Blanquillo pass (1200m) via a slightly hairy mountain track from Canillas de Albaida. From Puerto Blanquillo a path climbs 200m to another pass, the Puerto de Cómpeta. One kilometre down from there, past a quarry, the summit path (1½ hours), marked by a signboard, diverges to the right across a stream bed.

🛏 Sleeping & Eating
You can book houses, apartments and rooms through **Cómpeta Direct** (www.competadirect.com).

The two best restaurants, both serving excellent and varied Spanish/international food, are **El Pilón** (☏952 55 35 12; www.restauranteelpilon.com; Calle Laberinto; mains €11-18.50; ◷7-11pm Mon & Wed-Sat, 1-3.30pm Sun; ✎) and **Alberdini** (www.alberdini.com; Pago La Lomilla 85; mains €9-12; ✎). In summer ask for an upstairs terrace table at either place.

ℹ️ Information
Tourist office (☏952 55 36 85; Avenida de la Constitución; ◷10am-2pm & 3-6pm Tue-Sat) By the bus stop at the foot of the village.

ℹ️ Getting There & Away
Three or four buses run daily from Málaga (€4, 1½ hours) via Torre del Mar.

CÓRDOBA PROVINCE

Ascending over the Sierra Morena from La Mancha, the window into northern Andalucía is Córdoba province, a largely rural area renowned for its olive oil, wine and historic Roman-founded city that, at its zenith, was the capital of Al-Andalus and home to the glittering court of Abd ar-Rahman III.

Córdoba

POP 328,000 / ELEV 110M

Picture a city 500,000 strong embellished with fine architecture and fuelled by a prosperous and diverse economy. Picture universities and libraries filled with erudite artists and wise philosophers. Picture an Islamic caliphate more advanced and civilised than anything else the world had ever known. Picture Córdoba c AD 975.

OK, so this slightly grainy image may be over 1000 years old now, but enough of ancient Córdoba remains to place it in the contemporary top three drawcards of Andalucía. The centrepiece is the gigantic Mezquita, an architectural anomaly and one of the only places in the world where you can worship Mass in a mosque. Surrounding it is an intricate web of winding streets, geranium-sprouting flower boxes and cool intimate patios that are at their most beguiling in late spring.

History

The Roman colony of Corduba, founded in 152 BC, became capital of Baetica province, covering most of today's Andalucía. In 711 Córdoba fell to Muslim invaders and became the Islamic capital on the Iberian Peninsula. It was here in 756 that Abd ar-Rahman I set himself up as emir of Al-Andalus.

Córdoba's heyday came under Abd ar-Rahman III (912–61). The biggest city in Western Europe had dazzling mosques, libraries, observatories and aqueducts, a university and highly skilled artisans in leather, metal, textiles and glazed tiles. And the multicultural court was frequented by Jewish, Arabian and Christian scholars.

Towards the end of the 10th century, Al-Mansour (Almanzor), a fearsome general, took the reins of power and struck terror into Christian Spain with over 50 *razzias* (raids).

Córdoba's intellectual traditions, however, lived on. Twelfth-century Córdoba produced two of the most celebrated of all Al-Andalus scholars: the Muslim Averroës (Ibn Rushd) and the Jewish Maimonides. These polymaths are best remembered for their philosophical efforts to harmonise religious faith with reason.

In 1236 Córdoba was captured by Fernando III of Castilla and became a provincial town of shrinking importance. The decline began to be reversed only with the arrival of industry in the late 19th century. In common with other Andalucian cities in recent years, the culture, artefacts and traditions of Al-Andalus have enjoyed a growing revival of scholarly and popular interest.

Córdoba, along with 14 other Spanish cities (including Málaga), is aspiring to be the 2016 European Capital of Culture. You can check the campaign's status at www.cordoba2016.es.

⊙ Sights & Activities

Opening hours for Córdoba's sights change frequently, so check with the tourist offices for updated times. Most places (except the Mezquita) close on Monday. Closing times are generally an hour or two earlier in winter than in summer.

TOP CHOICE Mezquita
MOSQUE

(Mosque; ☎957 47 05 12; www.mezquitadecordoba.org; Calle Cardenal Herrero; adult/child €8/4, 8.30-10am Mon-Sat free; ⊙10am-7pm Mon-Sat, 8.30-10am & 2-7pm Sun Mar-Oct, 8.30am-6pm Mon-Sat, 8.30-10am & 2-6pm Sun Nov-Feb) Founded in 785, Córdoba's gigantic mosque is a wonderful architectural hybrid with delicate horseshoe arches making this unlike anywhere else in Spain. The main entrance is the Puerta del Perdón, a 14th-century Mudéjar gateway, with the ticket office immediately inside. Also inside the gateway is the aptly named Patio de los Naranjos (Courtyard of the Orange Trees).

Once inside, you can see straight ahead to the mihrab – the prayer niche in the mosque's qibla (the wall indicating the direction of Mecca) that was the focus of prayer. The first 12 transverse aisles inside the entrance, a forest of pillars and arches, comprise the original 8th-century mosque.

In the centre of the building is the Christian cathedral. Just past the cathedral's western end, the approach to the mihrab begins, marked by heavier, more elaborate arches. Immediately in front of the mihrab is the maksura, the royal prayer enclosure (today enclosed by railings) with its intricately interwoven arches and lavishly decorated domes created by Caliph Al-Hakam II in the 960s. The decoration of the mihrab portal incorporates 1600kg of gold mosaic cubes, a gift from the Christian emperoro of Byzantium, Nicephoras II Phocas. The mosaics give this part of the Mezquita the aura of a Byzantium church.

Mezquita

TIMELINE

600 Foundation of the Christian Visigothic church of St Vincent on the site of the present Mezquita.

785 Salvaging Visigoth and Roman ruins, Emir Abd ar-Rahman I converts the Mezquita into a mosque.

822-5 Mosque enlarged in reign of Abd ar-Rahman II.

912-961 A new minaret is ordered by Abd ar-Rahman III.

961-6 Mosque enlarged by Al-Hakam II who also enriches the **mihrab** **1**.

987 Mosque enlarged for the last time by Al-Mansur Ibn Abi Aamir. With the addition of the **Patio de los Naranjos** **2**, the building reaches its current dimensions.

1236 Mosque reconverted into a Christian church after Córdoba is recaptured by Ferdinand III of Castile.

1271 Instead of destroying the mosque, the overawed Christians elect to modify it. Alfonso X orders the construction of the **Capilla de Villaviciosa** **3** and **Capilla Real** **4**.

1300s Original minaret is replaced by the baroque **Torre del Alminar** **5**.

1520s A Renaissance-style cathedral nave is added by Charles V. 'I have destroyed something unique to the world' he laments on seeing the finished work.

2004 Spanish Muslims petition to be able to worship in the Mezquita again. The Vatican doesn't consent.

TIPS BOX

» **Among the oranges** The Patio de los Naranjos can be enjoyed free of charge at any time

» **Early birds** Entry to the rest of the Mezquita is offered free every morning except Sunday between 8.30am and 10am

» **Quiet time** Group visits are prohibited before 10am meaning the building is quieter and more atmospheric in the early morning

Capilla de Villaviciosa
Sift through the building's numerous chapels till you find this gem, an early Christian modification added in 1277 which fused existing Moorish features with Gothic arches and pillars. It served as the Capilla Mayor until the 1520s.

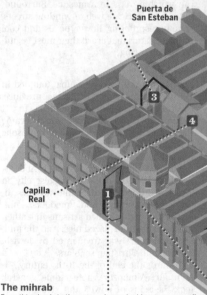

Puerta de San Esteban

3

4

Capilla Real

1

The mihrab
Everything leads to the mosque's greatest treasure – a scallop-shell-shaped prayer niche facing Mecca that was added in the 10th century. Cast your eyes over the gold mosaic cubes crafted by imported Byzantium sculptors.

The cathedral choir
Few ignore the impressive *coro* (choir): a late-Christian addition dating from the 1750s. Once you've admired the skilfully carved mahogany choir stalls depicting scenes from the Bible, look up at the impressive baroque ceiling.

Torre del Alminar
This is the Mezquita's cheapest sight because you don't have to pay to see it. Rising 93m and viewable from much of the city, the baroque-style bell tower was built over the mosque's original minaret.

The Mezquita arches
No, you're not hallucinating. The Mezquita's most defining characteristic is its unique terracotta-and-white striped arches that support 856 pillars salvaged from Roman and Visigoth ruins. Glimpsed through the dull light they're at once spooky and striking.

Puerta del Perdón

Patio de los Naranjos
Abandon architectural preconceptions all ye who enter here. The ablutions area of the former mosque is a shady courtyard embellished with orange trees that acts as the Mezquita's main entry point.

Capilla Mayor
A Christian monument inside an Islamic mosque sounds beautifully ironic, yet here it is: a Gothic church commissioned by Charles V in the 16th century and planted in the middle of the world's third largest mosque.

The maksura
Guiding you towards the mihrab, the maksura is a former royal enclosure where the caliphs and their retinues prayed. Its lavish, elaborate arches were designed to draw the eye of worshippers towards the mihrab and Mecca.

Córdoba

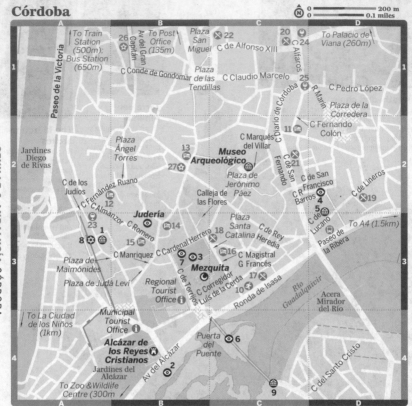

After the Christians captured Córdoba, the Mezquita was used as a church. In the 16th century the centre of the building was torn out to allow construction of a cathedral comprising the **Capilla Mayor**, now adorned with rich 17th-century jasper and marble *retablo,* and the **coro** (choir), with fine 18th-century carved mahogany stalls.

Judería
HISTORIC NEIGHBOURHOOD

Jews were among the most dynamic and prominent citizens of Islamic Córdoba. The medieval *judería,* extending northwest from the Mezquita almost to Avenida del Gran Capitán, is today a maze of narrow streets and whitewashed buildings with flowery window boxes.

The beautiful little 14th-century **Sinagoga** (Calle de los Judíos 20; admission €0.30; 9.30am-2pm & 3.30-5.30pm Tue-Sat, 9.30am-1.30pm Sun & holidays) is one of only three surviving medieval synagogues in Spain and the only one in Andalucía. In the late 1400s it became a hospital for hydrophobics. Translated Hebrew inscriptions eroded in mid-sentence seem like poignant echoes of a silenced society.

In the heart of the *judería*, and once connected by an underground tunnel to the Sinagoga, is the 14th-century **Casa de Sefarad** (www.casadesefarad.es; Calle de los Judíos; admission €4; 10am-6pm Mon-Sat, 11am-2pm Sun). Opened in 2008 on the corner of Calles de los Judíos and Averroes, this small, beautiful museum is devoted to reviving interest in the Sephardic-Judaic-Spanish tradition. There is a refreshing focus on music, domestic traditions and on the women intellectuals (poets, singers and thinkers) of Al-Andalus. A specialist library of Sephardic history is housed here, and there's also a well-stocked shop. A program of live music recitals and storytelling events runs most of the year.

Córdoba

Alcázar de los Reyes Cristianos   CASTLE
(Castle of the Christian Monarchs; Campo Santo de Los Mártires; admission €4, Fri free; ☺10am-2pm & 5.30-7.30pm Tue-Sat, 9.30am-2.30pm Sun & holidays) Built by Alfonso XI in the 14th century on the remains of Roman and Arab predecessors, the castle began life as a palace. It hosted both Fernando and Isabel, who made their first acquaintance with Columbus here in 1486. Its terraced gardens – full of fish ponds, fountains, orange trees, flowers and topiary – are a pleasure to stroll and a joy to behold from the tower.

A hall here displays some remarkable Roman mosaics, dug up from the Plaza de la Corredera in the 1950s. Most notable is a portrait of mythical couple Polyphemus and Galatea, whose story was later retold by Spanish poet Luis de Góngora.

Puente Romano   BRIDGE
The much-restored **Puente Romano** (Roman Bridge) crosses the Guadalquivir just south of the Mezquita. Not far downstream, near the northern bank, is a restored **Islamic water wheel**.

At the southern end of the bridge is the **Torre de la Calahorra** (📞957 29 39 29; adult/child €4.50/3; ☺10am-6pm Oct-Apr, 10am-2pm & 4.30-8.30pm May-Sep), a 14th-century tower with the curious **Roger Garaudy Museum**

of the **Three Cultures** highlighting the intellectual achievements of Islamic Córdoba.

Plaza del Potro   SQUARE
Córdoba's famous Square of the Colt has in its centre a lovely 16th-century stone fountain topped by a rearing *potro* that gives the plaza its name. On its western side is the legendary 1435 inn, **Posada del Potro** (Plaza del Potro 10; admission free; ☺5-9pm Tue-Fri, 10am-2pm Sat), described in *Don Quijote* as a 'den of thieves'.

Palacio de Viana   MUSEUM
(www.palaciodeviana.com; Plaza de Don Gome 2; admission whole house/patios only €6/3; ☺10am-7pm Tue-Fri, 10am-3pm Sat & Sun Sep-Jun, 9am-3pm Tue-Sun Jul & Aug) This stunning Renaissance palace is set around 12 beautiful patios that are a genuine pleasure to visit in the spring. Occupied by the Marqueses de Viana until a few decades ago, the 6500 sq m building is packed with art and antiques. The charge covers a one-hour guided tour of the rooms and access to the patios and garden.

Museo Arqueológico   MUSEUM
(Archaeological Museum; Plaza de Jerónimo Páez 7; admission €1.50; ☺2.30-8.30pm Tue, 9am-8.30pm Wed-Sat, 9am-2.30pm Sun & public holidays) Recently installed in a new wing

while the Renaissance palace that formerly housed the museum is being restored, the exhibit brilliantly covers Córdoba's illustrious history, with an overriding theme of cultural interchange. The building stands upon an archaeological site, the Roman theatre of Colonia Patricia, and the basement level features a walkway through the ruins.

✸ Festivals & Events

Spring and early summer are the chief festival times for Córdoba.

Festival de Los Patios Cordobeses PATIOS (Córdoba Courtyard Festival) A 'best patio' competition with many private courtyards open for public viewing till 10pm nightly (till midnight Friday and Saturday). A concurrent cultural program has flamenco concerts set appropriately in the city's grandest patios, gardens and plazas. The tourist office provides a map of the contestants along with a program of events.

Festival Internacional de la Guitarra MUSIC (International Guitar Festival; www.guitarracordoba.com) A two-week celebration of the guitar, with live performances of classical, flamenco, rock, blues and more; top names play in the city's concert halls and plazas. Held in the first half of July.

🛏 Sleeping

There is plenty of budget accommodation in Córdoba (though finding single rooms for a decent price is not easy). Booking ahead is wise from March to October and essential during the main festivals.

Parador Nacional Arruzafa HISTORIC HOTEL €€€ (☎957 27 59 00; www.parador.es; Avenida de la Arruzafa; r €161; P❄🛜🏊) This *parador* is 3km north of the city centre, fabulously situated

on the site of Abd ar-Rahman I's summer palace. It's a modern affair set amid lush gardens where Europe's first palm trees were planted.

Hospedería Alma Andalusí BOUTIQUE HOTEL €€ (☎957 76 08 88; www.almaandalusi.com; Calle Fernández Ruano 5; s/d €45/100; ❄🛜) The builders of this guesthouse in a quiet section of the *judería* have brilliantly converted an ancient structure into a stylish modern establishment while keeping the rates down. Thoughtfully chosen furnishings, polished wood floors and solid colors make for a comfortable base.

Casa de los Azulejos HOTEL €€ (☎957 47 00 00; www.casadelosazulejos.com; Calle Fernando Colón 5; s/d incl breakfast from €85/107; ❄@🛜) Mexican and Andalucian styles converge in this stylish hotel, where the patio is all banana trees, ferns and potted palms bathed in sunlight. Colonial-style rooms feature tall antique doors, massive beds, walls in lilac and sky blues and floors adorned with the beautiful old *azulejos* that give the place its name.

Hospedería Añil HOSTEL € (☎957 49 15 44; www.sensesandcolours.com; Calle Barroso 4; dm/s/d from €12/30/42; 🛜) This vibrant, superfriendly establishment is aimed at the backpacker set though cuts no corners in the style and comfort department. Primary colours and fanciful murals maintain an upbeat vibe. It's a skip and a jump to either the Mezquita or Plaza de las Tendillas, and there's a terrific flamenco club just across the way.

Hostal Séneca HOSTEL € (☎tel/fax 957 47 32 34; www.cordoba-hostalseneca.com; Calle Conde y Luque 7; dm/s/d incl breakfast from €15/30/50; 🛜) An upgraded version of a longtime backpackers' haunt, the

---

CÓRDOBA FOR CHILDREN

When you and the kids just don't want to look at old stones a moment longer, it's time to head a little way out of town and leave the past behind. Just southwest of Córdoba's city centre and adjoining the **Zoo and Wildlife Centre** (Avenida de Linneo; adult/child €4/2; ⏰10am-7pm Tue-Sun Apr & May, to 8pm Jun-Aug, to 7pm Sep), historic buildings morph into brightly coloured climbing equipment. Welcome to **La Ciudad de los Niños** (☎663 035709; laciudaddelosninos@educasur.es; Avenida Menéndez Pidal; admission free; ⏰10am-2pm & 7-11pm Jun–mid-Sep), Córdoba's City for Kids. A calendar of special events aimed at four- to 12-year-olds runs throughout the summer – check the website for details, or ask at the regional tourist office. Buses 2 and 5 (heading to Hospital Reina Sofia) from the city centre stop here.

Séneca occupies a rambling house with typical Moorish elements. A small cafe-bar supplies breakfast and drinks on a marvellous pebbled patio that's filled with greenery, and there's a kitchen available for guest use. Rooms vary widely – some share a bathroom – so have a look around before checking in.

Hotel Mezquita
HOTEL €€

(☏957 47 55 85; www.hotelmezquita.com; Plaza Santa Catalina 1; s/d €42/74; ❄) One of the best deals in town, the Hotel Mezquita stands right opposite its namesake monument, amid the bric-a-brac of the tourism zone. The 16th-century mansion has large, elegant rooms with marble floors, tall doors and balconies, some affording views of the great mosque.

Hotel Lola
HOTEL €€

(☏957 20 03 05; www.hotellola.es; Calle Romero 3; r incl breakfast €129; ❄ @ 🖤) Individualism and quirky style are the prime ingredients here. Each room, named after an Arab princess, is decorated with large antique beds and covetable items you wish you could take home with you.

✗ Eating

Córdoba has its share of signature food including *salmorejo*, a very thick tomato-based gazpacho (cold vegetable soup), and *rabo de toro* (oxtail). Some restaurants feature recipes from Al-Andalus, such as garlic soup with raisins, honeyed lamb, or meat stuffed with dates and nuts. The local tipple is wine from the nearby regions of Montilla and Moriles, similar to sherry but unfortified.

There are lots of places to eat right by the Mezquita, but beware inflated prices and uninspired food.

TOP CHOICE Taberna San Miguel El Pisto
TAPAS €

(Plaza San Miguel 1; tapas €3, media raciones €5-10; ❂closed Sun & Aug) Brimming with local character, El Pisto is one of Córdoba's best *tabernas* (taverns), both in terms of atmosphere and food. Traditional tapas and *media raciones* are done perfectly, and inexpensive Moriles wine is ready in jugs on the bar. Be sure to try the namesake item, a sort of ratatouille topped with a fried egg.

Bodegas Campos
ANDALUCIAN €€

(☏957 49 75 00; www.bodegascampos.com; Calle de Lineros 32; tapas €5, mains €13-21) One of Córdoba's most atmospheric and famous wine cellar-restaurants, this sprawling hall features dozens of rooms and patios, with oak barrels signed by local and international celebrities stacked up alongside. The bodega produces its own house Montilla, and the restaurant, frequented by swankily dressed *cordobeses* (residents of Córdoba), serves up a delicious array of meals.

La Boca
INTERNATIONAL, FUSION €€

(☏957 47 61 40; www.restaurantelaboca.com; Calle San Fernando 39; mains €11-15; ❂closed Mon dinner & Tue) Trendy for a reason, this cutting-edge eatery whips up exciting global variations on traditional ingredients, then presents them in eye-catching ways: Iberian pork on a bed of Thai noodles? Zuheros cheese garnished with sun-dried tomatoes? Why not? Dine in one of the cosy salons or take a table in the courtyard. Reservations are essential on weekends.

Delorean Bar de Tapas
TAPAS €

(Calle de Alfonso XIII; tapas €0.90; ❂closed Sun) Makes sense that the cheapest tapas in town are amid the alternative club zone – hipsters have to eat too. Cheap but tasty: beyond the burgers, there's eggplant in vinaigrette sauce, *flamenquín* balls, mushroom quesadillas and more. It's a youthful hang-out but it respects one time-honored tradition: free tapas with every beer.

Bar Santos
TAPAS €

(Calle Magistral González Francés 3; tortilla €2.50) The legendary Santos serves the best *tortilla de patata* (potato omelette) in town – and don't the *cordobeses* know it. Thick wedges are deftly removed from giant wheels of the stuff and customarily served with plastic forks on paper plates to take outside and gaze at the Mezquita.

🍽 Amaltea
ORGANIC €€

(☏957 49 19 68; Ronda de Isasa 10; mains €10-16; ❂closed dinner Sun; 🍴) This intimate riverside spot specialises in organic food and wine, with a serious Middle-Eastern influence (Lebanese-style tabbouleh, couscous). There's a good range of vegetarian fare.

🍷 Drinking & Entertainment

Córdoba's liveliest bars are mostly scattered around the newer parts of town and ignite around 11pm to midnight at weekends. Most bars in the medieval centre close around midnight.

SEVILLE & ANDALUCÍA CÓRDOBA

Bodega Guzmán BAR
(Calle de los Judíos 7; ⊙noon to 4pm & 8pm-midnight, closed Thu) Close to the Sinagoga, this atmospheric drinking spot bedecked with bullfighting memorabilia is frequented by both locals and tourists. Montilla wine is dispensed from three giant barrels behind the bar: don't leave without trying some *amargoso* (bitter).

Jazz Café LIVE MUSIC
(Calle Espartería; ⊙8am-late) Not just for jazzbos, this long-standing club is as likely to stage electric blues or belly dancing as its namesake style, attracting a varied crowd until the wee hours. Tuesday nights are reserved for jazz jam sessions.

Café Bar Automático MUSIC BAR
(Calle Alfaros 4; ⊙from 5pm) This is a low-key spot specialising in wacky cocktails and fruit shakes, with alternative rock over a good sound system.

La Pataita de Antonio FLAMENCO
(☏957 49 15 44; www.sensesandcolours.com; Calle Barros 3) 'Antonio' is renowned flamenco dancer Antonio Modéjar, and this is his project: a living space for the art where Young Turks delight aficionados with their dazzling licks. Performances nightly plus matinées Fridays and Saturdays.

Gran Teatro de Córdoba THEATRE
(☏957 48 02 37; www.teatrocordoba.com; Avenida del Gran Capitán 3) This theatre hosts a busy program of concerts, theatre, dance and film, mostly geared to popular Spanish tastes.

Shopping

Córdoba is known for its *cuero repujado* (embossed leather) goods, silver jewellery (particularly filigree) and attractive pottery. You'll find craft shops congregating around the Mezquita.

ℹ Information

Most banks and ATMs are around Plaza de las Tendillas and Avenida del Gran Capitán. The bus and train stations have ATMs.
Hospital Reina Sofía (☏957 21 70 00; Avenida de Menéndez Pidal) Located 1.5km southwest of the Mezquita.
Municipal tourist office (☏902 201774; www.turismodecordoba.org; ⊙9am-2pm & 5-7pm) Opposite the Alcázar de los Reyes Cristianos.
Policía Nacional (☏091; Avenida Doctor Fleming 2) The main police station.

Post office (Calle José Cruz Conde 15)
Regional tourist office (Calle de Torrijos 10; ⊙9am-7.30pm Mon-Fri, 9.30am-3pm Sat, Sun & holidays) Inside the Palacio Episcopal.

ℹ Getting There & Away

Bus

The bus station is behind the train station. Each bus company has its own terminal. **ALSA** (www.alsa.es) runs services to Seville (€10.36, 1¾ hours, six daily), Granada (€12.52, 2½ hours, seven daily), Málaga (€12.75, 2¾ hours, five daily), and Baeza (€10, three hours, one daily). **Secorbus** (☏902 229292; www.socibus.es) operates buses to Madrid (€15.80, 4½ hours, six daily). **Empresa Carrera** (www.autocarescarrera.es) heads south, with several daily buses to Priego de Córdoba, Cabra, Zuheros and Iznájar.

Train

Córdoba's **train station** (☏957 40 02 02; Glorieta de las Tres Culturas) is on the high-speed AVE line between Madrid and Seville. Rail destinations include Seville (€11 to €33, 40 minutes to 1½ hours, 23 or more daily), Madrid (€53 to €68, 1¾ to 6¼ hours, 23 or more daily), Málaga (€22 to €45, 45 minutes to 2½ hours, 16 daily), Barcelona (€138, 4½ hours, four daily). For Granada, change at Bobadilla.

ℹ Getting Around

Bus 3 (€1.20), from the street between the train and bus stations, runs to Plaza de las Tendillas and down Calle de San Fernando, east of the Mezquita. For the return trip, you can pick it up on Ronda de Isasa, just south of the Mezquita.

Taxis from the bus or train station to the Mezquita cost around €7.

For drivers, Córdoba's one-way system is nightmarish, but routes to many hotels and *hostales* are fairly well signposted with a 'P' if they have parking (€12 to €18 per day).

Bicycle Córdoba has installed bicycle lanes throughout town, though they're still little used. Bike rentals are available from **Solobici** (☏957 48 57 66; www.solobici.net; María Cristina 5; per day €15), which also offers regional bike tours.

GRANADA PROVINCE

Who goes to Granada province without first visiting the eponymous city? But once you've paid your respects to Lorca, the Albayzín, and the foppish ghosts of the Alhambra, there's a whole different world waiting on the sidelines. Much of it is rugged and

WORTH A TRIP

MEDINA AZAHARA

Even in the cicada-shrill heat and stillness of a summer afternoon, the Medina Azahara (⟲957 32 91 30; Carretera Palma del Río; admission €1.50; ⊙10am-8.30pm Tue-Sat May–mid-Sep, 10am-6.30pm Tue-Sat mid-Sep–Apr, 10am-2pm Sun year-round) whispers of the power and vision of its founder, Abd ar-Rahman III. The self-proclaimed caliph began the construction of a magnificent new capital 8km west of Córdoba around 936, and took up full residence around 945. Medina Azahara was a resounding declaration of his status, a magnificent trapping of power.

The new capital was amazingly short-lived. Between 1010 and 1013, during the caliphate's collapse, Medina Azahara was wrecked by Berber soldiers. Today, less than a tenth of it has been excavated, and only about a quarter of that is open to visitors.

A new museum on the foundation of one of the excavated buildings blends seamlessly with its surroundings and takes you through the history of the city, with beautifully displayed pieces taken from the site and some amazing interactive displays.

Medina Azahara is signposted on Avenida de Medina Azahara, which leads west out of Córdoba onto the A431.

A taxi costs €37 for the return trip, with one hour to view the site, or you can book a three-hour coach tour for €6.50 to €10 through many Córdoba hotels.

---

mountainous. Granada is home to the mainland's highest mountain peaks (the Sierra Nevada) and its only ski station, while on the range's southern flanks lies the sleeping beauty of the valleys of Las Alpujarras, sprinkled with snaking footpaths and time-stood-still white villages. Granada's coastline, the Costa Tropical, is centred on salt-of-the-earth Almuñécar, an evocative but little-visited Spanish seaside town.

Granada

POP 258,000 / ELEV 685M

Boabdil the Moor wasn't the last departing traveller to shed a farewell tear for Granada, a city of sun-bleached streets and parched earth interspersed with soothing splashes of green, including the woods and gardens that embellish the sultry Alhambra. For those who dig deeper, Granada hides a more elusive allure. This is a place to put down your guidebook and let your intuition lead the way – through mysterious labyrinthine streets and shady Moroccan teterías.

What keeps Granada interesting is its lack of any straightforwardness. Here stands a traditionally conservative city sprinkled with counterculture bohemians, a place where modern graffiti has been sprayed provocatively onto 500-year-old walls. Make no mistake, you'll fall in love here, but you won't always be able to work out why: best idea – don't bother. Instead, immerse yourself in the splendour, and leave the poetic stanzas to the aesthetes. 'Your elegy, Granada, is spoken by the stars which from the heavens perforate your black heart', wrote Federico García Lorca, Granada's most famous man of letters. It's the perfect coda.

History

Granada's history reads like a thriller. Granada began life as an Iberian settlement in the Albayzín district. Muslim forces took over from the Visigoths in 711, with the aid of the Jewish community around the foot of the Alhambra hill in what was called Garnata al Jahud, from which the name Granada derives; *granada* also happens to be Spanish for pomegranate, the fruit on the city's coat of arms.

After the fall of Córdoba (1236) and Seville (1248), Muslims sought refuge in Granada, where Mohammed ibn Yusuf ibn Nasr had set up an independent emirate. Stretching from the Strait of Gibraltar to east of Almería, this 'Nasrid' emirate became the final remnant of Al-Andalus, ruled from the increasingly lavish Alhambra palace for 250 years. Granada became one of the richest cities in medieval Europe.

However, in the 15th century the economy stagnated and violent rivalry developed over the succession. One faction supported the emir, Abu al-Hasan, and his harem favourite Zoraya. The other faction backed Boabdil, Abu al-Hasan's son by his wife Aixa. In 1482 Boabdil rebelled, setting off a confused civil war. The Christian armies invading the emirate took advantage, besieging towns and devastating the countryside, and in 1491 they finally laid siege to Granada. After eight months, Boabdil agreed to surrender the city in return for the Alpujarras and 30,000 gold coins, plus political and religious freedom for his subjects. On 2 January 1492 the conquering Catholic Monarchs, Ferdinand and Isabella, entered Granada ceremonially in Muslim dress. They set up court in the Alhambra for several years.

Jews and Muslims were steadily persecuted, and both groups had been expelled by the 17th century. Granada sank into a deep decline until the Romantics revived interest in its Islamic heritage during the 1830s, when tourism took hold.

When the Nationalists took over Granada at the start of the civil war, an estimated 4000 *granadinos* (residents of Granada) with left or liberal connections were killed, among them Federico García Lorca. Granada has a reputation for political conservatism.

⊙ Sights & Activities

Most major sights are within walking distance of the city centre, though there are buses to save you walking uphill.

TOP CHOICE Alhambra   PALACE

(☏902 441221; www.alhambra-tickets.es; adult/EU senior/EU student/under 8yr €13/9/9/free, Generalife only €6; ⊗8.30am-8pm 16 Mar–31 Oct, to 6pm 1 Nov–14 Mar, night visits 10-11.30pm Tue-Sat Mar-Oct, 8-9.30pm Fri & Sat Nov-Feb) The sheer red walls of the Alhambra rise from woods of cypress and elm. Inside is one of the more splendid sights of Europe, a network of lavishly decorated palaces and irrigated gardens, a World Heritage site and the subject of scores of legends and fantasies.

But at the height of summer, some 6000 visitors tramp through daily, making it difficult to pause to inspect a pretty detail, much less mentally transport yourself to the 14th century. Schedule a visit in quieter months,

Central Granada

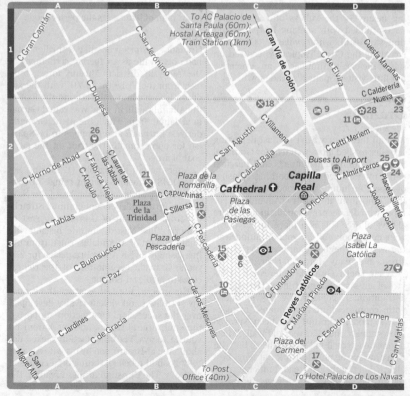

if possible; if not, then book in advance for the very earliest or latest time slot.

The Alhambra takes its name from the Arabic al-qala'a al-hamra (the Red Castle). The first palace on the site was built by Samuel Ha-Nagid, the Jewish grand vizier of one of Granada's 11th-century Zirid sultans. In the 13th and 14th centuries the Nasrid emirs turned the area into a fortress-palace complex, adjoined by a village of which only ruins remain. After the Reconquista (Christian reconquest), the Alhambra's mosque was replaced with a church, and the Convento de San Francisco (now the Parador de Granada) was built. Carlos I (also known as the Habsburg emperor Charles V), grandson of the Catholic Monarchs, had a wing of the palaces destroyed to make space for his huge Renaissance work, the Palacio de Carlos V. During the Napoleonic occupation the Alhambra was used as a barracks and nearly blown up. What you see today has been heavily but respectfully restored.

Palacios Nazaríes

The central palace complex is the pinnacle of the Alhambra's design.

Entrance is through the 14th-century **Mexuar**, perhaps an antechamber for those awaiting audiences with the emir. Two centuries later it was converted into a chapel,

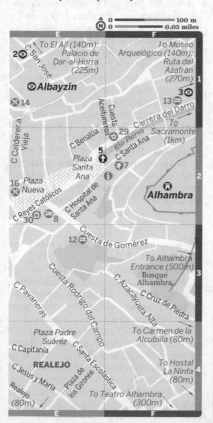

with a prayer room at the far end. Look up here and elsewhere to appreciate the geometrically carved wood ceilings. From the Mexuar you pass into the Patio del Cuarto Dorado. It appears to be a forecourt to the main palace, with the symmetrical doorways to the right, framed with glazed tiles and stucco, setting a cunning trap: the right-hand door leads nowhere but out, but the left passes through a dogleg hall (a common strategy in Islamic domestic architecture to keep interior rooms private) into the Patio de Comares, the centre of a palace built in the mid-14th century as Emir Yusuf I's private residence.

Rooms (which were likely used for lounging and sleeping) look onto the rectangular pool edged in myrtles, and traces of cobalt-blue paint cling to the *muqarnas* (honeycomb vaulting) in the side niches on the north end. Originally, all the walls were lavishly coloured; with paint on the stucco-trimmed walls in the adjacent Sala de la Barca, the effect would have resembled flocked wallpaper. Yusuf I's visitors would have passed through this annex room to meet him in the Salón de Comares, where the marvellous domed marquetry ceiling uses more than 8000 cedar pieces to create its intricate star pattern representing the seven heavens.

Adjacent is the Patio de los Leones (Courtyard of the Lions), built in the second half of the 14th century under Muhammad V, at the political and artistic peak of Granada's emirate. But the centrepiece, a fountain that channelled water through the mouths of 12 marble lions, dates from the 11th century. The courtyard layout, using the proportions of the golden ratio, demonstrates the complexity of Islamic geometric design – the varied columns are placed in such a way that they are symmetrical on numerous axes.

Walking counterclockwise around the patio, you first pass the Sala de Abencerrajes. The Abencerraje family supported the young Boabdil in a palace power struggle between him and his own father, the reigning sultan. Legend has it that the sultan had the traitors killed in this room, and the rusty stains in the fountain are the victims' indelible blood. But the multicoloured tiles on the walls and the great octagonal ceiling are far more eye-catching. In the Sala de los Reyes (Hall of the Kings) at the east end of the patio, the painted leather ceilings depict 10 Nasrid emirs.

On the patio's north side, doors once covered the entrance to the Sala de Dos Hermanas (Hall of Two Sisters). The walls are adorned with local flora – pine cones and acorns – and the band of calligraphy at eye level, just above the tiles, is a poem praising Muhammad V for his victory in Algeciras of 1369, a rare triumph this late in the Islamic game. The dizzying ceiling is a fantastic muqarnas dome with some 5000 tiny cells. The carved wood screens in the upper level enabled women (and perhaps others involved in palace intrigue) to peer down from hallways above without being seen. At the far end, the tile-trimmed Mirador de Lindaraja was a lovely place for palace denizens to look onto the garden below. Traces of paint still cling to the window frames, and a few panels of coloured glass set in the wood ceiling cast a warm glow.

From the Sala de Dos Hermanas a passageway leads past the domed roofs of the baths on the level below and into rooms built for Carlos I in the 1520s and later used by Washington Irving. From here you descend to the pretty Jardín de Lindaraja. In the southwest corner is the bathhouse – you can't enter, but you can peer in at the rooms lit by star-shaped skylights.

You emerge into an area of terraced gardens created in the early 20th century, and the reflecting pool in front of the small Palacio del Partal (Palace of the Portico), the oldest surviving palace in the Alhambra, from the time of Mohammed III (r 1302–09). You can leave the gardens by a gate facing the Palacio de Carlos V or continue along a path to the Generalife.

Alcazaba, Christian Buildings & Museums

The west end of the Alhambra grounds are the remnants of the Alcazaba, chiefly its ramparts and several towers. The Torre de la Vela (Watchtower), with a narrow staircase leading to the top terrace, is where the cross and banners of the Reconquista were raised in January 1492.

By the Palacios Nazaríes, the hulking Palacio de Carlos V clashes spectacularly with its surroundings. In a different setting its merits might be more readily appreciated.

Inside, the Museo de la Alhambra (admission free; ⊙9am-2.30pm Tue-Sat) has a collection of Alhambra artefacts, including the door from the Sala de Dos Hermanas, and the Museo de Bellas Artes (Fine Arts Museum; non-EU/EU citizen €1.50/free; ⊘9am-2pm Mon-Fri) displays paintings and sculptures from Granada's Christian history.

Further along, the 16th-century Iglesia de Santa María de la Alhambra sits on the site of the palace mosque. At the crest of the hill, the Convento de San Francisco, now the Parador de Granada hotel, is where Isabel and Fernando were laid to rest while their tombs in the Capilla Real were being built.

Generalife

From the Arabic *jinan al-'arif* (the overseer's gardens), the Generalife is a soothing arrangement of pathways, patios, pools, fountains, tall trees and, in season, flowers of every imaginable hue. To reach the complex you must pass through the Alhambra walls on the east side, then head back northwest. At the north end is the emir's summer palace, a whitewashed structure on the hillside facing the Alhambra. The courtyards here are particularly graceful; in the second courtyard, the trunk of a 700-year-old cypress tree suggests what delicate shade once graced the patio.

Albayzín   HISTORIC NEIGHBOURHOOD

On the hill facing the Alhambra across the Darro valley, Granada's old Muslim quarter (the Albayzín) is an open-air museum in which you can lose yourself for a whole morning. The cobblestoned streets are lined with gorgeous *cármene*s (large mansions with walled gardens, from the Arabic *karm* for garden). It survived as the Muslim quarter for several decades after the Christian conquest in 1492.

Plaza del Salvador, near the top of the Albayzín, is dominated by the Colegiata del Salvador, a 16th-century church on the site of the Albayzín's main mosque; the mosque's horseshoe-arched patio, cool and peaceful, survives at its western end.

The Arco de las Pesas, off Plaza Larga, is an impressive gateway in the Albayzín's 11th-century defensive wall. If you follow Callejón de San Cecilio from here you'll end up at the Mirador San Nicolás, the Albayzín's premier (and perennially crowded) lookout, with unbeatable views of the Alhambra and Sierra Nevada. Come back here with the world and his wife for sunset, but beware of skilful, well-organised wallet-lifters and bag-snatchers.

Located just east of Mirador San Nicolás, off Cuesta de las Cabras, the Albayzín's first new mosque in 500 years, the Mezquita Mayor de Granada, has been built to serve modern Granada's growing Muslim population.

Another well-placed lookout is the Placeta de San Miguel Bajo, with its lively cafe-restaurants. Close to this square off Callejón del Gallo and down a short lane is the 15th-century Palacio de Dar-al-Horra, a romantically dishevelled mini-Alhambra that was home to the mother of Boabdil, Granada's last Muslim ruler.

Downhill from Placeta de San Miguel Bajo you'll find the lovely Alminar de San José (San José Minaret; Calle San José), a minaret that survives from an 11th-century mosque. Calle San José meets the top of Calle Calderería Nueva, a narrow street famous for its *teterías*, but also a good place to shop for slippers, hookahs, jewellery and North African pottery from an eclectic cache of shops redolent of a Moroccan souk.

Buses 31 and 32 both run circular routes from Plaza Nueva around the Albayzín about every seven to nine minutes from 7.30am to 11pm.

Capilla Real   HISTORIC BUILDING

(Royal Chapel; www.capillareal.granada.com; Calle Oficios; admission €3.50; ⊘10.30am-1.30pm & 4-7.30pm Mon-Sat, 11am-1.30pm & 4-7pm Sun Apr-Oct) The Royal Chapel adjoins Granada's cathedral and is an outstanding Christian building. Catholic Monarchs Isabella and Ferdinand commissioned this elaborate Isabelline-Gothic-style mausoleum. It was not completed until 1521, hence their temporary interment in the Convento de San Francisco.

Isabella and Ferdinand lie in simple lead coffins in the crypt beneath their marble monuments in the chancel, enclosed by a stunning gilded wrought-iron screen created in 1520 by Bartolomé de Jaén. Also here you will find the coffins of Isabella and Ferdinand's unfortunate daughter, Juana the Mad, as well as her husband, Philip of Flanders.

The sacristy contains a small but impressive museum with Ferdinand's sword and Isabella's sceptre, silver crown and personal art collection, which is mainly Flemish but also includes Botticelli's *Prayer in the*

Alhambra

TIMELINE

900 The first reference to *al-qala'at al-hamra* (red castle) atop Granada's Sabika Hill.

1237 Founder of the Nasrid dynasty, Muhammad I, moves his court to Granada. Threatened by belligerent Christian armies he builds a new defensive fort, the **Alcazaba** **1**.

1302-09 Designed as a summer palace-cum-country estate for Granada's foppish rulers, the bucolic **Generalife** **2** is begun by Muhammad III.

1333-54 Yusuf I initiates the construction of the **Palacio Nazaríes** **3**, still considered the highpoint of Islamic culture in Europe.

1350-60 Up goes the **Palacio de Comares** **4**, taking Nasrid lavishness to a whole new level.

1362-91 The second coming of Muhammad V ushers in even greater architectural brilliance exemplified by the construction of the **Patio de los Leones** **5**.

1527 The Christians add the **Palacio de Carlos V** **6**. Inspired Renaissance palace or incongruous crime against Moorish art? You decide.

1829 The languishing, half-forgotten Alhambra is 'rediscovered' by American writer Washington Irving during a protracted sleep-over.

1954 The Generalife gardens are extended southwards to accommodate an outdoor theatre.

MICHAEL TAYLOR / GETTY IMAGES ©

Sala de la Barca
Throw your head back in the anteroom to the Comares Palace where the gilded ceiling is shaped like an up-turned boat. Destroyed by fire in the 1890s, it has been painstakingly restored.

Mexuar

Patio de Machuca

Palacio de Carlos V
It's easy to miss the stylistic merits of this Renaissance palace added in 1527. Check out the ground floor Museo de la Alhambra with artefacts directly related to the palace's history.

6

Palacio Nazaríes

3 Detail

1

2

Puerta de Justica

Alcazaba
Find time to explore the towers of the original citadel, the most important of which – the Torre de la Vela – takes you, via a winding staircase, to the Alhambra's best viewpoint.

DAVID TOMLINSON / GETTY IMAGES ©

Patio de Arrayanes

If only you could linger longer beside the rows of myrtle bushes *(arrayanes)* that border this calming rectangular pool. Shaded porticos with seven harmonious arches invite further contemplation.

Torre de Comares

4

Patio de Arrayanes

Palacio de Comares

The neck-ache continues in the largest room in the Comares Palace renowned for its rich geometric ceiling. A negotiating room for the emirs, the Salón de los Embajadores is a masterpiece of Moorish design.

Baños Reales

Washington Irving Apartments

Jardín de Lindaraja

Sala de Dos Hermanas

Focus on the *dos hermanas* – two marble slabs either side of the fountain – before enjoying the intricate cupola embellished with 5000 tiny moulded stalactites. Poetic calligraphy decorates the walls.

5

Palacio del Partal

Sala de los Abencerrajes

Jardines del Partal

Patio de los Leones

Count the 12 lions sculpted from marble, holding up a gurgling fountain. Then pan back and take in the delicate columns and arches built to signify an Islamic vision of paradise.

Generalife

A coda to most people's visits, the 'architect's garden' is no afterthought. While Nasrid in origin, the horticulture is relatively new: the pools and arcades were added in the early 20th century.

Garden of Olives. Felipe de Vigarni's two fine early-16th-century statues of the Catholic Monarchs at prayer are also here.

Cathedral
CATHEDRAL

(☏958 22 29 59; admission €3.50; ◷10.45am-1.30pm & 4-8pm Mon-Sat, 4-8pm Sun, to 7pm daily Nov-Mar) Granada's cavernous cathedral was commissioned by the Catholic monarchs, but construction began only after Isabella's death, and didn't finish until 1704. The result is a mishmash of styles: baroque outside, by the 17th-century master Alonso Cano, and Renaissance inside, where the Spanish pioneer in this style, Diego de Siloé, directed operations to construct huge piers, white as meringue, a black-and-white tile floor and the gilded and painted chapel. Even more odd, the roof vaults are distinctly Gothic.

Alcaicería & Plaza Bib-Rambla
SQUARE

Just south of the Capilla Real, the Alcaicería was the Muslim silk exchange, but what you see now is a restoration after a 19th-century fire, filled with tourist shops. Just southwest of the Alcaicería is the large and picturesque Plaza Bib-Rambla. Nearby, the handsome, horseshoe-arched 14th-century Corral del Carbon (Calle Mariana Pineda) was once an inn for coal dealers (hence its modern name, meaning Coal Yard). It houses a government-run crafts shop, Artespaña.

Plaza de Santa Ana
SQUARE

Plaza Nueva extends northeast into Plaza de Santa Ana, where the Iglesia de Santa Ana incorporates a mosque's minaret in its bell tower. Along narrow Carrera del Darro is the 11th-century Muslim bathhouse, the Baños Árabes El Bañuelo. Further along is the Museo Arqueológico (Archaeological Museum; ☏958 57 54 08; Carrera del Darro 43; non-EU/EU citizen €1.50/free; ◷2.30-8.30pm Tue, 9am-8.30pm Wed-Sat, 9am-2.30pm Sun), displaying finds from Granada province.

Museo Cuevas del Sacromonte
MUSEUM

(www.sacromontegranada.com; Barranco de los Negros; admission €5; ◷10am-2pm & 5-9pm Tue-Sun) This wide-ranging ethnographic and environmental museum and arts centre in the Roma neighbourhood northeast of the Albayzín is set in large herb gardens and hosts art exhibitions, as well as flamenco and films at 10pm on Wednesday and Friday from June to September.

Monasterio de San Jerónimo
MONASTERY

(Calle Rector López Argüeta 9; admission €3.50; ◷10am-2.30pm & 4-7.30pm) One of the most stunning Catholic buildings in Granada is a little out of the centre. At the 16th-century Monasterio de San Jerónimo, where nuns still sing vespers, every surface of the church has been painted – the stained glass literally pales in comparison.

Gonzalo Fernández de Córdoba, known as El Gran Capitán and the Catholic Monarchs' military man, is entombed here, at the foot of the steps, and figures of him and his wife stand on either side of the enormous gilt retable, which rises eight levels. Almond cookies, baked by the nuns, are for sale at the front desk, to stop your head from spinning.

Monasterio de la Cartuja
MONASTERY

(Paseo de la Cartuja; admission €3.50; ◷10am-1pm & 4-8pm Mon-Sat, 10am-noon Sun) Built between the 16th and 18th centuries by the Carthusian monks themselves, this 16th-century monastery has an imposing sand-coloured stone exterior, but it is the lavish baroque monastery church that people come to see, especially the *sagrario* (sanctuary) behind the main altar, a confection of red, black, white and grey-blue marble, columns with golden capitals, profuse sculpture and a beautiful frescoed cupola.

Huerta de San Vicente
MUSEUM

(☏958 25 84 66; Calle Virgen Blanca; admission only by guided tour in Spanish €3, Wed free; ◷10am-12.30pm & 5-7.30pm Tue-Sun) This house, where Federico García Lorca spent summers and wrote some of his best-known works, is only 1.5km south of the city centre, but still retains the evocative aura of an early-20th-century country villa. Today the modern but handsome Parque Federico García Lorca separates it from whizzing traffic.

To get here, head 700m down Calle de las Recogidas from Puerta Real, turn right along Calle del Arabial, then take the first left into Calle Virgen Blanca.

Hammams de Al Andalus
HAMMAM

(☏902 333334; www.granada.hammamspain.com; Calle Santa Ana 16; bath/bath & massage €22/32) With three pools of different temperatures, plus a steam room and the option of a proper skin-scrubbing massage (*masaje tradicional;* €39), this is your best option in town.

Tours

Cicerone Cultura y Ocio WALKING TOUR
(☑650 541669; www.ciceronegranada.com; tour
€15) Informative walking tours of central
Granada and the Albayzín leave daily from
Plaza Bib-Rambla, at 10.30am, or 11am in
winter.

Alhambra Night Tour CULTURAL TOUR
(☑902 441221; www.alhambra-patronato.es; adult/
child under 12yr €13/free; ⏲10-11.30pm Tue-Sat)
The Palacios Nazaríes are romantically lit in
the evening. You won't get to see as much
as on a day visit, but you won't have to deal
with the same crowds either.

Secret Granada WALKING TOUR
(☑958 20 19 39; www.granadaunderground.
blogspot.com.es; tours €15-30; ⏲9.30am-noon &
4-6.30pm) Explore the tunnels and dungeons
that lie under the city (including the Alhambra). Dug out by the Moors or by Christian
prisoners (no one is certain), they were used
until relatively recently, as many link various
residences and therefore enabled the great
and the good to lead secret lives. Reserve via
the website.

City Sightseeing Tour BUS TOUR
(☑902 101081; www.city-sightseeing.com; adult/
child €18/9; 🚲) Operates Granada's double-
decker city tour bus, with 20 stops at the
main sights. Hop on and off where you like;
the ticket is valid for 24 hours.

✲ Festivals & Events

Feria del Corpus Cristi RELIGIOUS
(Corpus Christi Fair) The big annual fair, which
starts 60 days after Easter Sunday, is a week
of bullfights, dancing and street puppets;
most of the action is at fairgrounds by the
bus station.

**Festival Internacional de
Música y Danza** MUSIC
(www.granadafestival.org) For three weeks in
June and July, first-class classical and modern performance takes over the Alhambra
and other historic sites.

⛏ Sleeping

Granada's strong Moorish bent is reflected
in its hotels, many of which have taken old
medieval mansions and converted them
into Moroccan-style riads. Most of these establishments reside in the Albayzín quarter.
Equally beguiling is Granada's handful of
restored *cármenes*.

As in all Andalucian cities, it's worthwhile
booking ahead during Semana Santa and
Christmas.

ℹ ALHAMBRA ADMISSION

Some areas of the Alhambra can be visited at any time without a ticket, but the highlight
areas can be entered only with a ticket. Up to 6600 tickets are available for each day.
About one third of these are sold at the ticket office on the day, but they sell out early and
you need to start queuing by 7am to be reasonably sure of getting one.

It's highly advisable to book in advance (€1 extra per ticket). You can book up to three
months ahead in two ways:

Alhambra Advance Booking (☑for international calls 0034 934 92 37 50, for national calls
902 888001; www.alhambra-tickets.es; ⏲8am-9pm)

Servicaixa (www.servicaixa.com) Online booking in Spanish and English. You can also buy
tickets in advance from Servicaixa cash machines, but only in the Alhambra grounds.

For internet or phone bookings you need a Visa card, MasterCard or Eurocard. You
receive a reference number, which you must show, along with your passport, national
identity card or credit card, at the Alhambra ticket office when you pick up the ticket on
the day of your visit.

The Palacio Nazaríes is also open for **night visits** (⏲10-11.30pm Tue-Sat Mar-Oct,
8-9.30pm Fri & Sat Nov-Feb). Tickets cost the same as daytime tickets: the ticket office
opens 30 minutes before the palace's opening time, closing 30 minutes after it. You can
book ahead for night visits in the same ways as for day visits.

Buses 30 and 32 (€1.10) both run between Plaza Nueva and the Alhambra ticket office
every five to nine minutes from 7.15am to 11pm, or it's an easy and pleasant walk up the
Cuesta de Gomérez from Plaza Nueva.

GRANADA FOR CHILDREN

With four buildings and eight interactive exhibition areas, Granada's popular **Parque de las Ciencias** (☑958 13 19 00; www.parqueciencias.com; Avenida del Mediterráneo; adult/under 18yr €6/5; ☉10am-7pm Tue-Sat, to 3pm Sun & holidays) should keep the kids happily absorbed for hours. Playing giant chess or threading the Plant Labyrinth are just two activities they can do here. It's about 900m south of the centre, near the Palacio de Congresos conference centre.

If even less intellectual exertion is called for, Parque Federico García Lorca offers refreshing, flat open space for both children and parents. It abounds in broad paved paths and is also a great place to study *granadinos* (Granada residents) at leisure.

Casa Morisca Hotel   HISTORIC HOTEL €€€
(☑958 22 11 00; www.hotelcasamorisca.com; Cuesta de la Victoria 9; d €118-48; ❄@☎) This late-15th-century mansion perfectly captures the spirit of the Albayzín. A heavy wooden door shuts out city noise, and rooms are soothing, with lofty ceilings, fluffy white beds and flat-weave rugs over brick floors. The least expensive ones look only onto the central patio with its fountain – cosily authentic, but potentially claustrophobic for some. The hotel is accessible by taxi.

Carmen de la Alcubilla   HISTORIC HOTEL €€
(☑958 21 55 51; www.alcubilladelcaracol.com; Calle del Aire Alta 12; s/d €100/120; ❄@☎) This exquisitely decorated place is located on the slopes of the Alhambra. Rooms are washed in pale pastel colours contrasting with cool cream and antiques. There are fabulous views and a pretty terraced garden. Ask for the room in the tower for a truly heady experience.

Parador de Granada   HISTORIC HOTEL €€€
(☑958 22 14 40; www.parador.es; Calle Real de la Alhambra; r €315; P❄@☎) It would be remiss not to mention this hotel, the most luxurious of Spain's *paradores*. But it's hard to justify the high price. Yet if you're looking for romance and history (it's in a converted 15th-century convent in the Alhambra grounds) and money is no object...book well ahead.

AC Palacio de Santa Paula   LUXURY HOTEL €€€
(☑902 292293; www.ac-hotels.com; Gran Vía de Colón; r from €170; P❄@❄) As if all the rest wasn't enough, Granada hits five stars with this inspired fusion of neoclassical traditionalism and modern-industrial. The hotel's princely price tag brings you a spa, a snazzy restaurant, lush gardens, a pool, numerous fancy soaps and a red carnation on your bed when you return for an afternoon siesta.

Hotel Zaguán del Darro   HISTORIC HOTEL €€
(☑958 21 57 30; www.hotelzaguan.com; Carrera del Darro 23; s/d €55/70; ❄@) This place offers excellent value for the Albayzín. The 16th-century house has been tastefully restored, with sparing use of antiques. Its 13 rooms are all different; some look out over the Río Darro. There's a good bar-restaurant below, and the main street in front means easy taxi access – but also a bit of evening noise.

Hostal Arteaga   HOSTAL €
(☑958 20 88 41; www.hostalarteaga.com; Calle Arteaga 3; s/d €40/49; ❄@☎) A charming bargain option off the Gran Vía de Colón, just inching into the Albayzín. The rooms are spruced up with lavender walls, striped bedspreads and chequered blue bathroom tiles, for a tidy, modern feel. Stay three nights and you get a free session at the adjacent Baños de Elvira spa.

Hostal Venecia   HOSTAL €
(☑958 22 39 87; www.veneciahostal.es; Cuesta de Gomérez 2; d €42, without bathroom €34; ☎) The house-proud hosts here are as sweet as the flower-and-picture-filled turquoise corridors. The nine rooms overflow with character, and each is different: some have private bathrooms, while others share facilities, and many have small balconies.

Hotel Posada del Toro   BOUTIQUE HOTEL €€
(☑958 22 73 33; www.posadadeltoro.com; Calle de Elvira 25; d/ste €70/108; ❄☎) A lovely small hotel with rooms set around a tranquil central patio. Walls are washed in a delectable combination of pale pistachio, peach and cream, and the rooms are similarly enticing with parquet floors, stucco detailing Alhambra-style, rustic furniture, and small but perfectly equipped bathrooms with double sinks and hydromassage showers. The restaurant offers Spanish dishes such as Galician octopus, as well as pastas and pizza.

Hotel Los Tilos
HOTEL €€

(☎958 26 67 12; www.hotellostilos.com; Plaza Bib-Rambla 4; s/d €55/80; ❀) The spacious rooms, clean and renovated in 2008, overlook Plaza Bib-Rambla, and there are double-glazed windows to shut out the hubbub at night. There's a small but panoramic roof terrace if you don't get your own Alhambra view from your room.

Hotel Palacio de Los Navas
HISTORIC HOTEL €€

(☎958 21 57 60; www.palaciodelosnavas.com; Calle Navas 1; d/ste €86/135; ❀❅) Lovely 16th-century building featuring individually furnished rooms with lots of cool creams and whites, original columns and doors, terracotta tiled floors and desks. The rooms surround a traditional columned patio.

Hotel Fontecruz
HOTEL €€

(☎958 21 78 10; www.fontecruz.com; Gran Vía de Colón 20, d/ste €120/370; ❀@❅) The Fontecruz features large rooms that mix sleek and sumptuous with black-and-white carpeting, dark wood antique-look writing desks and lovely beds. All have at least one shallow balcony. Windows are double-glazed, but rooms overlooking the side street instead of the Gran Vía are noticeably quieter. A rooftop bar yields great views.

Hotel Puerta de las Granadas
HOTEL €€

(☎958 21 62 30; www.hotelpuertadelasgranadas.com; Cuesta de Gomérez 14; r €130; ❀@❅) This small hotel has a prime location just off the Plaza Nueva and halfway up the hill to the Alhambra. The red-and-dark-wood rooms overlook either a back garden (quiet) or the street (a little larger).

Hostal La Ninfa
HOSTAL €

(☎958 22 79 85; www.hostallaninfa.net; Plaza Campo Príncipe; s/d €45/50; ❀❅) The show stopping facade of this hotel, its walls covered with ceramic plaques, sets the scene for the interior which is artistically cluttered and charming. The rooms are brightly painted (think turquoise painted beams) with tiled bedheads and pretty tiled bathrooms. It is a 30-minute uphill trek to the Alhambra from here or you can hop on the bus which stops virtually outside the door.

✖ Eating

Granada is one of the last bastions of that fantastic practice of free tapas with every drink, and some have an international flavour. There are also some good Moroccan and Middle Eastern restaurants, particularly in the Albayzín. There's a revived *granadino* trend for *teterías*, most of which serve light desserts – others offer fuller menus.

NEAR PLAZA NUEVA

Plaza Nueva is rimmed with restaurants, most with alfresco seating. The more obvious places can be a little touristy. For the better nooks hunt around the backstreets or head up Carrera del Darro.

For fresh fruit and veg, head for the large covered Mercado Central San Agustín (Calle San Agustín; ☺closed Sun), a block north of the cathedral.

Ruta del Azafrán
FUSION €€

(www.rutadelazafran.es; Paseo del Padre Manjón 1; mains €13-20) One of the few high-concept restaurants in Granada, this sleek spot with its steely modern interior has an eclectic menu which ranges from Asian-inspired tempuras to broccoli-based pesto, lamb couscous and roasted pork. The terrace outside on the Río Darro is a great place for a snack, but you'll get better service inside.

Parador de Granada
INTERNATIONAL €€€

(☎958 22 14 40; Calle Real de la Alhambra; mains €19-22; ☺8am-11pm) On one side, the Parador de Granada is a hushed, swanky dinner experience, with a Moroccan-Spanish-French menu that also features local goat and venison. On the other, it's a stylish little canteen for sightseers, where even your *bocadillo de jamón* tastes special – and it ought to, considering its €12 price tag. Overall, a bit inflated, but a lovely treat for the location.

Bodegas Castañeda
BAR €

(Calle Almireceros; tapas €2-3, raciones €6-8) An institution among locals and tourists alike, this buzzing bar doles out hearty portions of food (try a hot or cold *tabla,* a platter; a half order, €6, is ample for two) and dispenses drinks from big casks mounted in the walls. The best choice is a lively, herbaceous *vermut* (vermouth) topped with soda. Don't confuse this place with Antigua Bodega Castañeda around the corner, which is not as enticing.

Greens & Berries
INTERNATIONAL €

(Plaza Nueva 1; snacks from €2.50; ❀) Conveniently located for benches in the square, this is a great choice if you want to pick up something healthy, fast and filling. Sandwiches include tasty choices like salmon, avocado and lemon, and goat's cheese and caramelised onion, plus there are soups of the day, fresh fruit smoothies and a wickedly delicious New York cheesecake.

ALBAYZÍN

The labyrinthine Albayzín holds a wealth of eateries all tucked away in the narrow streets. Calle Calderería Nueva is a fascinating muddle of *teterías*, leather shops and Arabic-influenced takeaways.

Arrayanes   MOROCCAN €€

(☎958 22 84 01; www.rest-arrayanes.com; Cuesta Marañas 4; mains €8-15; ⊗from 8pm; ✍) The best Moroccan food in a city that is well known for its Moorish throwbacks? Recline on lavish patterned seating, try the rich, fruity tagine casseroles and make your decision. Note that Restaurante Arrayanes does not serve alcohol.

Samarkanda   LEBANESE €€

(Calle Calderería Vieja 3; mains €8-12; ✍) Despite the rather tired decor, this longstanding Lebanese restaurant is a sound choice, particularly for vegetarian fare. The lentil soup spiked with lemon and cumin is delicious, along with mainstays hummus, *mutabal* (aubergine- and tahini-based dip) and falafel. A finale of *mugle* (cinnamon cream with nuts and orange blossom) should put a smile on your face.

El Ají   MODERN SPANISH €€

(Plaza San Miguel Bajo 9; mains €12-20; ✍) Up in the Albayzín, this chic but cosy neighbourhood restaurant is no bigger than a shoebox but serves from breakfast right through to the evening. Chatty staff at the tiny marble bar can point out some of the highlights of the creative menu (such as prawns with tequila and honey). It's a good place to get out of the sun and rest up, especially if you are hiking up from Plaza Nueva.

Tetería Nazarí   TEAHOUSE

(Calle Calderería Nueva 13) One of the best of Calle Calderería's teahouses complements its aromatic brews with some delicate Arabic pastries.

PLAZA BIB-RAMBLA & AROUND

In the heart of modern Granada, the plaza and its surrounding network of streets cater to a range of tastes and pockets from student to executive. Don't miss the excellent ice cream and *churros*.

Pastelería López-Mezquita   BAKERY

(www.pastelerialopezmezquita.com; Calle Reyes Católicos 39; pastries €2-6; ⊗9am-6.30pm Mon-Sat; ☝) This venerable pastry shop provides great on-the-go snacks – a flaky *empanadilla* filled with bacon and dates, for instance, or a piece of cinnamon-rich *pastela moruna*, a Moorish-style chicken pie. Take a number to order at the counter, or sit down and rest your feet in the back room.

Reca   TAPAS €

(Plaza de la Trinidad; raciones €8; ⊗closed Tue) One of Granada's top tapas places, Reca is always packed with people hungering after its wonderfully presented, modernised versions of classics like couscous and *salmorejo*. It's one of the few bars in the area that serves food through the afternoon, without a break.

Oliver   SEAFOOD €€

(www.restauranteoliver.com; Calle Pescadería 12; mains €12-18; ⊗closed Sun) The seafood bars on this square are a Granada institution, and Oliver is one of the best for food and unflappable service in the middle of the lunch rush. Sleek business types pack in alongside street-sweepers to devour *raciones* of garlicky fried treats at the mobbed bar, which can be ankle deep in crumpled napkins and shrimp shells come 4pm.

Restaurante Chikito   ANDALUCIAN €€

(☎958 22 33 64; www.restaurantechikito.com; Plaza Campillo Bajo 9; mains €17-20; ⊗Thu-Tue) One of the city's most historic restaurants, apparently a favourite of Lorca's (his table is in the corner) and perennially popular with the smart local set. The tapas bar speciality is snails (€5); its walls are plastered with local celeb pics. The adjacent restaurant concentrates on hearty dishes like oxtail stew and pork medallions which it has spent many years getting right. Reservations recommended.

Gran Café Bib-Rambla   CAFE €

(Plaza Bib-Rambla 3; chocolate & churros €4; ☝) Granada's oldest cafe dates back to 1907 when the coffee beans were roasted in the square outside and the milk was brought in daily from surrounding farms. Today, the hot chocolate and *churros* keep locals coming back.

Los Diamantes   SEAFOOD €

(Calle Navas 26; raciones €8-10) This corner bar-restaurant near Plaza del Carmen shows off the Andalucian penchant for frying, particularly seafood. The plates are heaped with an amazing mix of *pescado frito* (fried fish) and succulent prawns. A *caña* (small glass of beer) makes the perfect accompaniment. It attracts a tide of hungry diners, especially around noon.

Café Futbol
CAFE €

(www.cafefutbol.com; Plaza de Mariana Pineda 6; churros €2; 🖶) This three-storey cafe with its butter-coloured walls and gaudy chandeliers dates from 1910 and is generally packed with coiffured señoras, foreign students and families. Elderly white-shirted waiters attend to the morning rush with hot chocolate, fat *churros* and delectable cakes, like the chocolate and custard *tarta san cecilio*. Sit upstairs for views of the square.

🍷 Drinking

The best street for drinking is the rather scruffy Calle de Elvira (try above average **Taberna El Espejo** at No 40), but other chilled bars line Río Darro at the base of the Albayzín, and Campo del Príncipe attracts a sophisticated bunch.

Bodegas Castañeda (p751) and Antigua Castañeda (Calle de Elvira) are the most inviting and atmospheric, with out-of-the-barrel wine and generous tapas to keep things going.

Botánico
BAR

(www.botanicocafe.es; Calle Málaga 3; ⏰1pm-1am) This eco-chic bar and restaurant dishes up healthy Med-inspired cuisine during the day and morphs into a bar and club at dusk with DJs or live music, mainly jazz and blues, after dark. It's named after the peaceful botanical garden across the way which is worth a stroll around if you are here during the day.

Mundra
BAR

(Plaza de la Trinidad; platters €10; ⏰8.30pm-2am Mon-Thu, to 3am Fri-Sat) Overlooking the leafy square, this place has a global-chic feel with its black barrel tables, Buddha statues and chill-out soundracks. There are platters to share for the peckish, including fresh prawns which comes from Motril, and provolone cheese – which doesn't.

☆ Entertainment

The excellent monthly *Guía de Granada* (€1), available from kiosks, lists entertainment venues and places to eat, including tapas bars.

Peña de la Platería
FLAMENCO

(Placeta de Toqueros 7) Buried in the Albayzín warren, Peña La Platería claims to be the oldest flamenco aficionados' club in Spain. It's a private affair, though, and not always open to nonmembers. Performances are usually Thursday and Saturday at 10.30pm – look presentable, and speak a little Spanish at the door, if you can.

Le Chien Andalou
FLAMENCO

(www.lechienandalou.com; Carrera del Darro 7; admission €8; ⏰shows 9pm) This is one of Granada's most atmospheric venues to enjoy some vigorous castanet-clicking flamenco with a varied and professional line-up of musicians and dancers throughout the week. The cavelike surroundings of a renovated *aljibe* (well) create a fittingly moody setting and the whole place has a more genuine feel to it than the Sacramonte coach tour traps. Book through the website.

Boogaclub
DJ

(www.boogaclub.com; Calle Santa Barbara 3; ⏰2pm-6am Mon-Thu, 11pm-7am Fri-Sun) Chill to soulful house, funk, electro and Chicago house then kick up your (high) heels to the international DJs hitting the decks with funk, soul, reggae and tribute sessions (to Amy Winehouse and the like). Karaoke nights, jam sessions and live music. Check the website for the current line-up.

Granada 10
CLUB

(www.granadaten.com; Calle Calderería Nueva 11, admission €10; ⏰from midnight) A glittery converted cinema is now Granada's top club for the glam crowd, who recline on the gold sofas and get hip swivelling to cheesy Spanish pop tunes.

Teatro del Generalife
THEATRE

(Generalife) Created in 1954 by extending the Generalife gardens southward, this outdoor theatre is a Granada rite of passage for summer performances of Lorca plays or live shows by greats such as Paco de Lucía. You can get the performance schedule from the municipal tourist office.

Teatro Alhambra
THEATRE

(☎958 22 04 47; Calle de Molinos 56) Both Teatro Alhambra and the more central Teatro Isabel La Católica (☎958 22 15 14; Acera del Casino) have ongoing programs of theatre and concerts (sometimes flamenco); you may pick up a Lorca play here.

Shopping

Granadino crafts include embossed leather, *taracea* (marquetry), blue-and-white glazed pots, handmade guitars, wrought iron, brass and copper ware, basket weaving and textiles. Look out for these in the Alcaicería and Albayzín, on Cuesta de Gomérez and in the government-run Artespaña in Corral del Carbón.

The Plaza Nueva area is awash with jewellery vendors, selling from rugs laid out on the pavement, and ethnic-clothing shops.

For general shopping try pedestrianised Calle de los Mesones or expensive department store El Corte Inglés.

Tienda Librería de la Alhambra SOUVENIRS
(Calle Reyes Católicos 40) This is a fabulous shop for Alhambra aficionados with a tasteful selection of quality gifts including excellent coffee-table style tomes, children's art books, hand-painted fans, arty stationery and stunning photographic prints which you select from a vast digital library (from €14 for A4 size).

Information

Emergency

Policía Nacional (☎958 80 80 00; Plaza de los Campos) The most central police station.

Medical Services

Hospital Ruiz de Alda (☎958 24 11 00, 958 02 00 09; Avenida de la Constitución 100) Central, with good emergency facilities.

Money

There are plenty of banks and ATMs on Gran Vía de Colón, Plaza Isabel La Católica and Calle Reyes Católicos.

Post

Post office (Puerta Real; ⏲8.30am-8.30pm Mon-Fri, 9.30am-2pm Sat) Often has long queues.

Tourist Information

There are regional tourist offices in **Plaza Nueva** (☎958 22 10 22; Calle Santa Ana 1; ⏲9am-7pm Mon-Sat, 10am-2pm Sun & holidays) and the **Alhambra** (☎902 888001; www.alhambra-tickets.es).

Municipal tourist office (www.granadatur.com; Calle Almona del Campillo 2; ⏲9am-7pm Mon-Fri, to 6pm Sat, 10am-2pm Sun) Sleek, efficient centre opposite the city's Parque Federico García Lorca.

Provincial tourist office (www.turismodegranada.org; Plaza de Mariana Pineda 10; ⏲9am-10pm Mon-Fri, 10am-7pm Sat) Helpful staff with information on the whole Granada region; a short walk east of Puerta Real.

Websites

Turismo de Granada (www.turismodegranada.org) Provincial tourist office.

Where2 (www.where2.es) Excellent, comprehensive English-language website with information on where to eat, sleep, find entertainment or even buy property in Granada.

Getting There & Away

Air

Iberia (☎902 400500; www.iberia.com) flies daily to/from Madrid from **Aeropuerto Federico García Lorca** (www.aena.es), 17km west of the city. There are also flights to Barcelona and the Canary Islands, and seasonally to Paris.

Bus

Granada's bus station is 3km northwest of the city centre. Take city bus 3 to the centre or a taxi for €7. **Alsa** (www.alsa.es) handles buses in the province and across the region, plus a night bus direct to Madrid's Barajas airport (€24.50, six hours). Other destinations include Córdoba (€13.50, 2¾ hours direct, eight daily), Seville (€20.50, three hours direct, 10 daily), Málaga (€10.50, 1½ hours direct, 18 daily) and Las Alpujarras.

Car

Car rental is expensive. **ATA** (☎958 22 40 04; Plaza Cuchilleros 1) has small cars (eg Renault Clio) for approximately €75/48/36 per day for one/two/seven days. You would be better advised to take a taxi to the airport (€18 to €22), where four or five good car-hire operators have offices.

Train

The **train station** (☎958 24 02 02; Avenida de Andaluces) is 1.5km west of the centre, off Avenida de la Constitución. Four trains run daily to/from Seville (€23.85, three hours) and Almería (€16.50, 2¼ hours) via Guadix, and six daily to/from Antequera (€20.50, 1½ hours). Three go to Ronda (€15, three hours) and Algeciras (€25, 4½ hours). For Málaga (€16.50, 2½ hours) or Córdoba (€35.50, 2½ hours) take an Algeciras train and change at Bobadilla. One or two trains go to each of Madrid (€68, four to five hours), Valencia (€52.50, 7½ to eight hours) and Barcelona (€58, 12 hours).

Getting Around

To/From the Airport

The airport is 17km west of the city on the A92. **Autocares J González** (www.autocaresjosegonzalez.com) runs buses between the airport and a stop near the Palacio de Congresos (€3, five daily), with a stop in the city centre on Gran Vía de Colón, where a schedule is posted opposite the cathedral, and at the entrance to the bus station. A taxi costs €18 to €22 depending on traffic conditions and pick-up point.

Bus

Individual tickets are €1.20, or pay €2 for a refillable pass card, then add at least €5, for rides as low as €0.80. Both can be bought with notes or coins from the bus driver. Most lines stop on Gran Vía de Colón; the tourist office dispenses maps and schedules.

Car & Motorcycle

Vehicle access to the Plaza Nueva area is restricted by red lights and little black posts known as *pilonas*, which block certain streets during certain times of the day. If you are going to stay at a hotel near Plaza Nueva, press the button next to your hotel's name beside the *pilonas* to contact reception, which will be able to lower the *pilonas* for you.

Central underground public car parks include **Parking San Agustín** (Calle San Agustín; per hr/day €1.75/20), **Parking Neptuno** (Calle Neptuno) and **Parking Plaza Puerta Real** (Acera del Darro; per hr/day €1.45/17). Free parking is available at the Alhambra car parks.

Taxi

If you're after a taxi, head for Plaza Nueva, where they line up. Most fares within the city cost between €4.50 and €8.50.

Around Granada

Granada is surrounded by a fertile plain called La Vega, planted with poplar groves and crops ranging from melons to tobacco. The Vega was an inspiration to Federico García Lorca, who was born and died here. The Parque Federico García Lorca, between the villages of Víznar and Alfacar (about 2.5km from each), marks the site where Lorca and hundreds, possibly thousands, of others are believed to have been shot and buried by the Nationalists at the start of the civil war.

FUENTE VAQUEROS

The touchingly modest house where Lorca was born in 1898, in this otherwise unremarkable suburb 17km west of Granada, is now the **Casa Museo Federico García Lorca** (☑958 51 64 53; www.museogarcialorca. org; Calle Poeta Federico García Lorca 4; admission €2; ☉guided visits hourly 10am-2pm & 5-7pm Tue-Sat). The place brings his spirit to life, with numerous charming photos, posters and costumes from his plays, and paintings illustrat-

ing his poems. A short video captures him in action with the touring Teatro Barraca.

Ureña (☑958 45 41 54) buses to Fuente Vaqueros (€1.55, 20 minutes) leave from Avenida de Andaluces in front of Granada train station, roughly once an hour from 9am during the week, and at 9am, 11am, 1pm and 5pm on weekends and holidays.

Sierra Nevada

True to their name, Spain's highest mountains rise like icy sentinels behind the city of Granada, culminating in the rugged summit of Mulhacén (3479m), mainland Spain's highest peak. But the snowcapped mountains you see shimmering in the background of all those scenic Alhambra postcards are just the tip of the iceberg. The Sierra Nevada proper stretches 75km west to east from Granada into Almería province. The upper reaches of the range form the 862-sq-km Parque Nacional Sierra Nevada, Spain's biggest national park, with a rare high-altitude environment that is home to about 2100 of Spain's 7000 plant species. Andalucía's largest ibex population (about 5000) is here too. Surrounding the national park at lower altitudes is the 848-sq-km Parque Natural Sierra Nevada. The mountains and Las Alpujarras valleys comprise one of the most spectacular areas in Spain, and the area offers wonderful opportunities for walking, horse riding, climbing, mountain biking and, in winter, good skiing and snowboarding.

ESTACIÓN DE ESQUÍ SIERRA NEVADA

The ski station **Sierra Nevada Ski** (☑902 708090; www.sierranevadaski.com), at Pradollano, 33km from Granada on the A395, often has better snow conditions and weather than northern Spanish ski resorts, so it can get very crowded on weekends and holidays in season. A few of the 85 marked runs start almost at the top of 3395m-high Veleta. There are cross-country routes and a dedicated snowboard area, plus a raft of other activities for nonskiers. In summer you can mountain bike, ride horses and more.

In winter **Tocina** (☑958 46 50 22) operates three daily buses (four on the weekends) to the resort from Granada's bus station (€5/8 one way/return, one hour). Outside the ski season there's just one daily bus (9am from Granada, 5pm from the ski station). A taxi from Granada costs about €50.

Teterías & Hammams

It's 500 years since the Moor uttered his last sigh, but the civilised habits of Al-Andalus' erstwhile rulers live on in many Andalucian cities, in dark, atmospheric *teterías* (tearooms) and elaborate *hammams* (bathhouses). While away lazy evenings in shadowy Moorish leisure facilities embellished with puffed cushions, stuccoed arches and winking lanterns.

Tetería Almedina

1 Liquid refreshment in this Almería establishment (p773) could include anything from an aromatic tea tray of global brews. Try the Moroccan mint or Indian chai accompanied by a plate of delicate Arabic sweets.

Tetería Nazarí

2 A Granada tearoom (p752) popular among students and bohemians, who huddle in the dark corners sharing furtive puffs on the ubiquitous *shishas* (water pipes).

La Tetería

3 Unbeknownst to many, Málaga remained Moorish almost as long as Granada did, meaning that its revitalised *teterías* can claim equal authenticity. You'll find standout brews and cakes at the rather unadventurously named La Tetería (p721), near the Museu Picasso Málaga.

Hammams de Al Andalus

4 Moroccan *hammams* often resemble one-sided wrestling tournaments, but in Andalucía they're a shade more relaxing. Sample the hot baths at Hammams de Al Andalus (p748) before cooling down with a glass of mint tea.

Hammam Andalusi

5 Underrated in almost every department, Jerez harbours plenty of Moorish exoticism, including the Hammam Andalusi (p698) with its unusual 'chocolate bath'.

Right
1. Tea in a *tetería* 2. Hammam Andalusi (p698)

National & Natural Parks

Andalucía's national and natural parks provide visitors with much-needed 'breathing space' between heavy doses of art, culture and history. They also act as important bulwarks against the encroaching development that plagues much of Spain's Mediterranean coast.

Parque Nacional Sierra Nevada

1 Peak-baggers can make for the easily accessible summits of Veleta and Mulhacén (p760), the Spanish mainland's highest peak. The less height-obsessed can ski, cycle, horse-ride, canyon or trek from park access points in Pradollano and Capileira (p759).

Parque Nacional de Doñana

2 A World Heritage–listed rare European wetland, the 542-sq-km Doñana National Park (p683) features copious bird species, large coastal sand dunes and vital water-based ecosystems.

Parque Natural Sierra de Grazalema

3 You can debate all day about Andalucía's finest park, or you can vote with your feet and get up onto the dreamy hiking trails and craggy mountains of this one (p703).

Parque Natural Sierra de Aracena y Picos de Aroche

4 Northern Huelva's *dehesa* ecosystems are the bastion of its finest cured hams, produced in the bucolic oak pastures of one of Andalucía's least-known parks (p686).

Parque Natural de Cabo de Gata-Níjar

5 Remember Spain before mass tourism? No? Then come to Almería's undeveloped littoral (p775) and reacquaint yourself with deserted coastlines and sleepy fishing villages.

Left
1. Sierra Nevada (p755) 2. Cabo de Gata (p775)

Western Sierra Nevada & Alpujarras

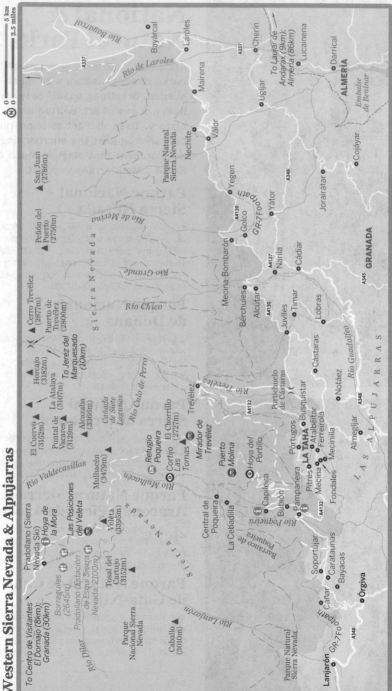

Las Alpujarras

Below the southern flank of the Sierra Nevada lies the 70km-long jumble of valleys known as Las Alpujarras. Arid hillsides split by deep ravines alternate with oasislike white villages set beside rapid streams and surrounded by gardens, orchards and woodlands. An infinity of good walking routes links valley villages and heads up into the Sierra Nevada: the best times to visit are between April and mid-June, and mid-September and early November.

A recent upsurge in tourism, and New Age and foreign (mainly British) settlers has given the area a new dimension.

History

In the 10th and 11th centuries Las Alpujarras, settled by Berbers, was a great silkworm farm for the workshops of Almería. But after Granada fell to Ferdinand and Isabella in 1492, the industry languished and many villages were abandoned.

South from Granada by Gerald Brenan, an Englishman who lived in Las Alpujarras village of Yegen in the 1920s and '30s, gives a fascinating picture of what was then a very isolated, superstitious corner of Spain. Another Englishman, Chris Stewart, settled here more recently, as a sheep farmer near Órgiva. His entertaining best-selling *Driving over Lemons* tells of life as a foreigner in Las Alpujarras in the '90s.

LANJARÓN

Known as 'the gateway to the Alpujarras', Lanjarón's heyday was during the late 19th and early 20th centuries, when it was a fashionable *balneario* (spa). Today, although Lanjarón water is sold all over Spain, the Balneario (958 77 00 137; www.balneariode lanjaron.com; Avenida de la Constitución; 1hr bath €30) is visited largely by elderly Spanish cure-seekers. Yet the town has authentic charms. Traditional family life is lived along its main streets, Avenida de la Alpujarra and Avenida Andalucía. The Museo de Agua (Water Museum; 10am-2pm & 6-9pm Tue-Sun) explores water's link to agriculture, industry and health, along with medicinal qualities of Lanjarón's water. There's an exhibition hall and an audiovisual show.

There are plenty of hotels. Hotel Andalucía (958 77 01 36; www.hotelandalucia. com; Avenida de la Alpujarra 15-17; s/d €42/52;) close to the *balneario* is a good budget option, with clean if bland rooms and an outdoor pool. Eat at seafood restaurant Los Mariscos (Avenida de la Alpujarra 6; mains €8-12), where everything is cooked with fresh ingredients.

The tourist office (Avenida de la Alpujarra), opposite the *balneario*, provides comprehensive information on outdoor activities and accommodation for the entire Alpujarras region.

ÓRGIVA
POP 6500 / ELEV 725M

The western Alpujarras' main town, Órgiva, is a scruffy but bustling place with a big hippie/New Age element. Good places to eat include Baraka (Calle Estación 12; Sat-Thu), located beside the municipal car park in the upper part of town; it has an eclectic menu that includes Moroccan dishes, tofu burgers, shwarmas, delicious brownies and natural juices. Mesón Casa Santiago (Plaza García Moreno; mains €6-12; Mon-Sat) is the best of the bars on the plaza with outside tables and a bricks-and-beams rustic interior.

Stay at Casa Rural Jazmín (958 78 47 95; www.casaruraljazmin.com; Calle Ladera de la Ermita; r €48 65;), a French-run house with four rooms, each decorated in a different style (Asian and Alpujarran rooms are smaller; French and African, larger).

PAMPANEIRA, BUBIÓN & CAPILEIRA
POP 1270 / ELEV 1200–1440M

These small villages clinging to the side of the deep Barranco de Poqueira valley, 14km to 20km northeast of Órgiva, are three of the prettiest, most dramatically sited (and most touristy) in Las Alpujarras. Capileira is the best base for walks.

⊙ Sights & Activities

All three villages have solid 16th-century Mudéjar churches. They also have small weaving workshops, descendants of a textile tradition that goes back to Islamic times, and plentiful craft shops. In Bubión, get a marvellous glimpse of bygone Alpujarras life at the excellent little folk museum Casa Alpujarreña (Calle Real; admission €2; 11am-2pm Sun-Thu, 11am-2pm & 5-7pm Sat & holidays), beside the church.

Eight walking trails, ranging from 4km to 23km (two to eight hours), are marked out in the beautiful Barranco de Poqueira with little colour-coded posts. Their starting points can be hard to find, but they are marked and described on Editorial Alpina's *Sierra Nevada, La Alpujarra* map. Nevadensis (958 76 31 27; www.nevadensis.com),

WORTH A TRIP

TWIN PEAKS

The Sierra Nevada's two highest peaks are Mulhacén (3479m) and Veleta (3395m). Two of three known as Los Tresmiles, because they rise above 3000m, they're on the western end of the range, close to Granada. From the ski station on the mountains' north flank, a road climbs up and over to Capileira, the highest village in the Barranco de Poqueira in the Alpujarras on the south side, but it's closed to motor vehicles on the highest stretch. From late June to the end of October the national park operates two shuttle buses to give walkers access to the upper reaches of the range – or just a scenic guided drive.

One bus runs up from 3km above the ski station, starting at the national park information post at Hoya de la Mora (⊙during bus-service season approx 8.30am-2.30pm & 3.30-7.30pm). The other leaves from the town of Capileira in Las Alpujarras. Tickets are €5 one way or €9 return.

From the end of the bus route on the north side, it's about 4km up Veleta, an ascent of about 370m with 1½ hours' walking (plus stops); or 14km to the top of Mulhacén, with four to five hours' walking. From the Mirador de Trevélez (the end stop on the Capileira side) it's around three hours to the top of Mulhacén (6km, 800m ascent).

If you want to make it an overnight trip, you can bunk down for the night at the Refugio Poqueira (☎958 34 33 49; Mulhacén, Sierra Nevada; per person €15). The refuge is open year-round.

Information

The Centro de Visitantes El Dornajo (☎958 34 06 25; ⊙9.30am-2.30pm & 4.30-7.30pm), about 23km from Granada, on the A395 towards the ski station, has plenty of information on the Sierra Nevada. Knowledgeable, English-speaking staff are happy to help.

at the information office in Pampaneira, offers hikes and treks, 4WD trips, horse riding, mountain biking, climbing and canyoning, all with knowledgeable guides.

🛏 Sleeping & Eating

Book ahead for rooms around Easter and from July to September. Many villages have apartments and houses for rent; ask in tourist offices or check websites such as Turgranada (www.turgranada.es) or Rustic Blue (www.rusticblue.com).

PAMPANEIRA

Opened in 2010, Estrella de las Nieves (☎958 76 39 81; www.estrelladelasnieves.com; Calle Huerto 21; s/d €60/70; [P][🛜][🐖]) just above the town has airy, light and modern rooms with terraces overlooking the rooftops and mountains. Restaurante Casa Diego (Plaza de la Libertad 3; menú €9, mains €6.50-13.50), across from the church, has a pleasant upstairs terrace and serves local trout and ham.

BUBIÓN

Hostal Las Terrazas (☎958 76 30 34; www.terrazasalpujarra.com; Plaza del Sol 7; s/d €22/31,

2-/4-/6-person apt €45/55/72) is located below the main road and near the car park. Traditional Teide Restaurant (☎958 76 30 37; Carretera de Sierra Nevada 2; menús €10) has a good *menú del dia*, while Estación 4 (Calle Estación 4; mains €7-12; ⊙Tue-Sun; [�]) inhabits an old village house.

CAPILEIRA

Hostal Atalaya (☎958 76 30 25; www.hostalatalaya.com; Calle Perchel 3; d without/with view €30/35) is a good budget option, while Finca Los Llanos (☎958 76 30 71; www.hotelfincaloslanos.com; Carretera de Sierra Nevada; s/d €54/76; [🐖]) has tasteful rooms, a pool and a good restaurant. It's also an official Sierra Nevada information point.

Bar El Tilo (Plaza Calvario; raciones €8), Capileira's village tavern, enjoys prime position on a lovely whitewashed square with a terrace. *Raciones* such as *albóndigas* (meatballs in a tomato sauce) are enormous. El Corral del Castaño (Plaza del Calvario 16; menú €10, mains €8.50-14) has an Italian menu and does a local take on gastronomic dishes.

ℹ Information

You'll find ATMs outside the car-park entrance in Pampaneira, and in Capileira at La General (Calle Doctor Castilla).

Punto de Información Parque Nacional de Sierra Nevada (www.nevadensis.com; Plaza de la Libertad; ☉10am 2pm & 4 6pm Tue-Sat, to 3pm Sun & Mon Oct-Mar) Plenty of information about Las Alpujarras and Sierra Nevada; outdoor gear, maps and books for sale. Located in Pampaneira.

Servicio de Interpretación de Altos Cumbres (☎958 76 34 86, 671 564406; picapileira@oapn.mma.es; ☉about 9am-2pm & 4.30-7.30pm) By the main road in Capileira; information mainly about the national park, but also on Las Alpujarras.

PITRES & LA TAHA
POP 800

Pitres (elevation 1245m) is a break from the tourism and souvenirs in the Poqueira Gorge villages, although not quite as pretty. The beautiful valley below it, with five tranquil hamlets (Mecina, Mecinilla, Fondales, Ferreirola and Atalbéitar), all grouped with Pitres in the municipio called La Taha, is particularly fascinating to explore. Its ancient pathways are a walker's delight.

Above Pitres in the tiny hamlet of Capilerilla (and on the E4 footpath) lies Hotel Maravedi (☎958 76 62 92; www.hotelmaravedi.com; s/d/tr €60/80/102), rustic but with all home comforts including satellite TV and private bar-restaurant for clients. In nearby Mecina, welcoming French-run guesthouse L'Atelier (☎958 85 75 01; www.ivu.org/atelier; Calle Alberca 21; s/d incl breakfast €35/50; ☉Mar-Nov; ☑) in an ancient village house also serves gourmet vegetarian/vegan meals (lunch Saturday and Sunday, dinner Wednesday to Monday) and has an art gallery. It also runs vegetarian cooking courses (€50 per day). In peaceful Ferreirola, Sierra y Mar (☎958 76 61 71; www.sierraymar.com; Calle Albaicín; s/d incl breakfast €42/62; ℗☎) has just nine rooms, set around patios and gardens. It is closed in January and February.

TREVÉLEZ
POP 1150 / ELEV 1476M

Trevélez, in a valley almost as impressive as the Poqueira Gorge, claims to be the highest village in Spain (although Valdelinares, Aragón, reaches above 1700m) and produces famous *jamón serrano*.

On a leafy, terraced hillside 1km west of Trevélez, Camping Trevélez (☎958 85 87 35; www.campingtrevelez.net; Carretera Trevélez-Órgiva, Km 1; sites per adult/tent/car/cabin €4.50/5/3.80/19; ☉closed Jan–mid Feb) has ecologically minded owners and a good-value restaurant. Walkers' favourite Hotel La Fragua I (☎958 85 86 26; www.hotellafragua.com; Calle San Antonio 4; s/d €33/45) provides pine-furnished rooms, with a more upmarket annex at La Fragua II (d/tr €55/72). La Fragua is closed early January to early February. Its restaurant, Mesón La Fragua (mains €7.50-12.50), a few doors away, is one of the best in town and worth searching out. In Mesón Joaquín (☎958 85 85 60; Calle Puente; mains €9-14), white-coated *jamón* technicians slice up transparent sheets of the local product, and the trout comes from the wholesaler just behind.

EAST OF TREVÉLEZ

East of Trevélez the landscape becomes barer and more arid, yet there are still oases of greenery around the villages. The central and eastern Alpujarras have their own magic but see far fewer tourists than the western villages.

ℹ Getting There & Away

Alsa (☎958 18 54 80) runs three daily buses from Granada to Órgiva (€5, 1½ hours), Pampaneira (€6, two hours), Bubión (€6.50, 2¼ hours), Capileira (€6.50, 2½ hours) and Pitres (€6.50, 2¾ hours). Two of these continue to Trevélez (€7, 3¼ hours) and Bérchules (€9, 3¾ hours). The return buses start from Bérchules at 5am and 5pm, and from Pitres at 3.30pm. Alsina also runs twice-daily buses from Granada to Cádiar (€8, three hours) and Yegen (€9, 3½ hours).

The Coast

Granada's cliff-lined, 80km-long coast has a hint of Italy's Amalfi about it but is definitively Spanish in flavour. A sprinkling of attractive beach towns is linked by several daily buses to Granada, Málaga and Almería.

ALMUÑÉCAR
POP 27,000

More interesting and certainly more Spanish than anything on the Costa del Sol, Almuñécar is well worth a day's diversion. There's easy access from either Granada or Málaga. The attractive old town, which hugs the coast amid small coves and precipitous cliffs, huddles around the 16th-century Castillo de San Miguel (Santa Adela Explanada; adult/child €2.35/1.60; ☉10.30am-1.30pm & 4-6.30pm Tue-Sat, 10.30am-2pm Sun) and

ARTISAN CRAFTS OF THE ALPUJARRAS

Firecely traditional despite the recent influx of foreign residents, the Alpujarra villages remain bastions of age-old artisan crafts. While this might not look like a typical shopping destination (there's not an insipid shopping mall for miles around), you might just get lucky. Here are some pointers:

Pampaneira

Though it's more famous for its coarsely woven, colourful rugs, the lowest of the Barranco de Poqueira villages is a place for unexpected treats in El Chocolate de la Alpujarra (www.abuelailichocolate.com; Plaza Romanilla 13), where fabulous chocolate is made on-site and includes some wonderful and unusual sweet and savoury flavours ranging from mango to mustard.

Bubión

For a glimpse of the past, visit the French-owned weaving workshop, Nade Taller del Telar (www.tallerdeltelar.com; Calle Trinidad 11; ⊙11am-2.30pm & 5-8.30pm) with its historic enormous looms that come from the Albayzín in Granada. The shawls, sofa throws and blankets, which are made using only natural fabrics, are beautiful and prices start at around €65.

Capileira

Leatherwork is a speciality in the highest Poqueira village. J Brown (Calle Doctor Castilla) (who, despite the name, is Spanish) makes excellent bags, belts and Western-style hats, all from hand. You can watch him at work at the back of the shop.

Pitres

Like the rest of Las Alpujarras region, La Tahá attracts plenty of artists and craftsmen (and women). For exquisite handmade tiles with a definite Moorish influence, check out Alizares Fatima (☑958 76 61 07; Calle Paseo Marítimo 19) on the edge of Pitres, which does beautiful work.

Trevélez

Spain's highest village is famous all over Spain for its cured ham. Jamones González (Calle Nueva) is the place to come if you fancy taking some home. It also sells other local gourmet products.

adjoining Museo Arqueológico (Calle San Joaquín) situated in the basement of an old Roman construction (the schedule and prices are the same as for the Castillo). The breezy seafront is an excellent place to *dar un paseo* (go for a slow evening stroll). Make for the steep pointed headland that divides the two beaches known as the Peñon del Santo.

Just behind Playa de San Cristóbal is a tropical-bird aviary, Parque Ornitológico Loro-Sexi (adult/child €4/2; ⊙11am-2pm & 6-9pm; ⋒).

You can paraglide, windsurf, dive, sail, ride a horse or descend canyons in and around Almuñécar and nearby La Herradura. The tourist office and its website have plenty of information.

🛏 Sleeping & Eating

Hotel Al Najarra
HOTEL €

(☑958 63 08 73; www.hotelnajarra.com; Calle Guadix 12; d/tr €58/81; ✲@⊛✲) This modern hotel isn't bursting with character, but it represents excellent value in Almuñécar, where many properties are a bit tired. The large rooms all open onto terraces or balconies overlooking a back garden and pool.

El Arbol Blanco
ANDALUCIAN €€

(Urbanización Costa Banana; www.elarbolblanco. es; Avenida de la Costa del Sol; mains €8-19; ⊙Thu-Tue; ✲) Run by friendly brothers Jorge and Nacho Rodriguez, the cuisine here includes some creative options, as well as traditional Andalucian dishes, such as their earthy and rich *paletilla de cordero asado* (roast shoulder of lamb).

La Yerbabuena
ANDALUCIAN €€

(Calle Puerta del Mar 4 6; mains €9-18, ☺Wed-Mon) Pass through the front bar to the adjacent dining room with plush cushions, low candles and little pots of *yerba buena* (mint) on every table. The menu of Spanish standards reflects a similar attention to detail, with the best-quality ingredients employed in dishes such as grilled baby lamb and rich asparagus gratin with shrimps.

❶ Information
The main tourist office is 1km southwest, just back from Playa de San Cristóbal, in the rose-pink neo-Moorish Palacete La Najarra with lovely gardens that is a tourist sight in its own right.

❶ Getting There & Away
The **Almuñécar bus station** (☑958 63 01 40; Avenida Juan Carlos I 1) is just south of the N340. At least six buses a day go to Almería (€10, two hours) and Málaga (€6.50, 1¾ hours), eight go to Granada (€7.50, 1½ hours), 11 to

La Herradura (€1, 10 minutes) and 13 to Nerja (€2.50, 30 minutes) and Salobreña (€1.50, 15 minutes). A bus goes to Órgiva (€4, 1¼ hours) at 4.30pm Monday to Saturday.

JAÉN PROVINCE

Jaén province is rarely included in standard Andalucía itineraries, a crying shame for lovers of olive oil, Renaissance architecture, and rugged mountain scenery strafed with rare flora and fauna. The architecture is courtesy of the historic towns of Baeza and Úbeda, and the nature is encased in the expansive Parque Natural de Cazorla (Spain's largest single protected area), while the olive oil is everywhere you look; indeed, it is doubtful if there's a vista in Jaén that doesn't include at least one neat patchwork of olive plantations (the province *alone* accounts for about 10% of the world's olive oil production).

Jaén Province

Jaén

POP 116,000 / ELEV 575M

You don't need to be a genius to deduce what is the pillar of Jaén's economy. With olive plantations pushing right up against the city limits, the health-enhancing 'liquid gold' has long filled the coffers of the local economy and provided rich topping for one of the most dynamic (and least heralded) tapas strips in Andalucía. Surrounding a sentinel-like castle in Jaén's centre is a magnificent Renaissance cathedral worthy of a city twice the size, from which emanate narrow alleys, smoky bars, cavernous *tabernas* and *mucha alegría* (joy). Welcome to Andalucía at its grittiest and understated best.

◉ Sights

Catedral
CATHEDRAL

(Plaza de Santa María; adult/child €5/1.50; ☺10am-6pm Mon-Sat, to noon Sun) The size and opulence of this cathedral, built on the site of an old mosque, dominate and dwarf the entire city. The southwestern facade, set back on Plaza de Santa María, was not completed until the 18th century, and it owes more to the late baroque tradition than to the Renaissance, thanks to its host of statuary by Seville's Pedro Roldán. The overall Renaissance aesthetic is dominant, however, and is particularly evident in the overall size and solidity of the internal and external structures, with huge, rounded arches and clusters of Corinthian columns that lend it great visual strength.

FREE Palacio de Villardompardo
PALACE

(Plaza de Santa Luisa de Marillac; ☺9am-8pm Tue-Fri, 9.30am-2.30pm Sat & Sun) Undergoing renovation at the time of research, (but due to reopen in early 2013) this Renaissance palace houses three excellent attractions: the beautiful 11th-century Baños Árabes (Arab Baths), with a transparent walkway for viewing the excavated baths; the Museo de Artes y Costumbres Populares (Museum of Popular Art & Customs), devoted to the artefacts of the harsh rural lifestyle of pre-industrial Jaén province; and the Museo Internacional de Arte Naïf (International Museum of Naïve Art), with a large international collection of colourful and witty Naive art. You can spend hours lost in the everyday detail so playfully depicted in these works.

Castillo de Santa Catalina
CASTLE

(Cerro de Santa Catalina; admission €3; ☺10am-2pm & 5-9pm Tue-Sun) Watching the city from atop the cliff-girt Cerro de Santa Catalina is the former Islamic fortress Castillo de Santa Catalina, which was undergoing renovation when we visited. However, the *Centro de Interpretacíon* (Interpretation Centre), including audiovisual presentations, should have reopened by the time you read this. Past the castle at the end of the ridge stands a large cross, from where there are magnificent views over the city and the olive groves beyond.

⌷ Sleeping

Parador Castillo de Santa Catalina
HISTORIC HOTEL €€€

(☏953 23 00 00; www.parador.es; Cerro de Santa Catalina; r incl breakfast €142; P✳@☎☲) Next to the castle at the top of the Cerro de Santa Catalina, this hotel has an incomparable setting and theatrically vaulted halls. Rooms are luxuriously dignified with plush furnishings; some have four-poster beds. There is also an excellent restaurant and a bar with terrace seating to maximise the sweeping panoramic views.

Hotel Xauen
HOTEL €

(☏953 24 07 89; www.hotelxauenjaen.com; Plaza del Deán Mazas; s/d incl breakfast €50/60; P✳☎) This hotel has a superb position in the centre of the historic quarter. Communal areas are decorated with large photos of colourful local scenes, while the rooms are a study in beige but good sized. The rooftop bar and solarium have stunning cathedral views.

✗ Eating

The Jaén tapas trail is full of pleasant surprises, especially along tiny Calle del Cerón and Arco del Consuelo.

TOP CHOICE El Gorrión
ANDALUCIAN €

(Calle Arco del Consuelo 7; tapas from €1.50) Lazy jazz plays on the stereo, old newspaper cuttings are glued to the walls, and paintings of bizarre landscapes hang lopsidedly next to oval oak barrels. It feels as though local punters have been propping up the bar for centuries (or at least since 1888, when it opened). The tapas are simple and tradition-

Jaén

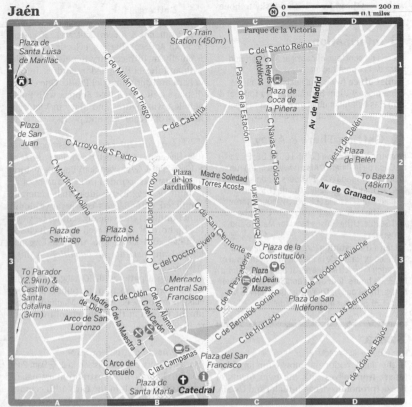

al, and are best enjoyed with the sherry and wine on offer.

Taberna La Manchega ANDALUCIAN €
(www.tabernalamanchegadejaen.com; Calle Bernardo López 12; platos combinados €4-10; ⓧ10am-5pm & 8pm-1am Wed-Mon) This place has been in action since the 1880s and apart from enjoying the great, simple tapas, you can drink wine and watch the local characterful clientele. La Manchega has entrances on both Calle Arco del Consuelo and Calle Bernardo López.

☉ Drinking

Cool drinking spots include **Deán** (Plaza del Deán Mazas; ⓧ11am-late), which has a pulsating late night vibe with its exposed industrial steel piping and pumping music. At **Columbia 50** (Calle del Cerón 6; ⓧ10am-9pm) global coffees and hot chocolates are spiked with everything from Irish whisky to honey and cream.

ℹ Information

There's no shortage of banks or ATMs around Plaza de la Constitución.

Tourist office (www.andalucia.org; Calle de Valparaiso; ☉10am-8pm Mon-Fri, to 1pm Sat & Sun) Has helpful, multilingual staff and plenty of information about the city and province.

ℹ Getting There & Away

From the **bus station** (☎953 25 01 06; Plaza de Coca de la Piñera), **Alsa** (www.alsa.es) runs buses to Granada (€8, 1¼ hours, 12 daily), Baeza (€4, 45 minutes, 11 daily), Úbeda (€5, one hour, 12 daily) and Cazorla (€8.50, 3½ hours, three daily). The Ureña line travels up to Córdoba and Seville. Other buses head for Málaga and Almería.

Jaén's **train station** (☎953 27 02 02; www. renfe.com; Paseo de la Estación) is at the end of a branch line. A train leaves at 8am for Córdoba (€12, 1¾ hours, four daily) and Seville (€29, 2½ hours, three daily). There are also trains to Madrid (€31.50, four hours, three daily).

Baeza

POP 17,000 / ELEV 790M

If the Jaén region is known for anything (apart from olives), it's the twin towns of Baeza (pronounced 'ba-eh-thah') and Úbeda, two shining examples of Renaissance beauty. Smaller Baeza makes a good day trip from Úbeda, some 9km away. It has a richness of architecture that defies the notion that there is little of architectural interest in Andalucía apart from Moorish buildings. Here a handful of wealthy, fractious families, made rich by the wool trade, left a staggering catalogue of perfectly preserved Renaissance churches and civic buildings.

◉ Sights

Opening times of some buildings vary unpredictably.

In the centre of beautiful **Plaza del Pópulo** is the **Fuente de los Leones** (Fountain of the Lions), topped by an ancient statue believed to represent Imilce, a local Iberian princess who was married to Hannibal. On the southern side of the plaza is the plateresque **Casa del Pópulo** dating from about 1540 (and today housing Baeza's helpful tourist office).

FREE **Cathedral**   CATHEDRAL
(Plaza de Santa María; donations welcome; ☉10.30am-1pm & 4-6pm Oct-Mar, 10.30am-1pm & 5-7pm Apr-Sep) Baeza's eclectic cathedral is chiefly in 16th-century Renaissance style, with an interior designed by Andrés de Vandelvira and Jerónimo del Prado. One chapel displays a life-sized Last Supper, with finely detailed wax figures and Mary in Victorian flounces of cream lace and pearls.

FREE **Antigua Universidad** HISTORIC BUILDING
(Old University; Calle del Beato Juan de Ávila; ☉10am-2pm & 4-7pm Wed-Sun) Baeza's historic university was founded in 1538 and became a fount of progressive ideas that generally conflicted with Baeza's conservative dominant families, often causing scuffles between the highbrows and the well-heeled. It closed in 1824, and since 1875 the building has housed an *instituto de bachillerato* (high school).

The main patio, with its elegant Renaissance arches, is open to the public, as is the classroom of poet Antonio Machado, who taught French at the high school from 1912 to 1919.

FREE **Palacio de Jabalquinto**   PALACE
(Plaza de Santa Cruz; admission free; ☉9am-2pm Mon-Fri) Baeza's most extraordinary palace was probably built in the early 16th century for one of the Benavides clan. It has a spectacularly flamboyant facade with pyramidal stone studs typical of Isabelline Gothic style, and a patio with Renaissance marble columns, two-tiered arches and an elegant fountain. A magnificent carved baroque stairway ascends from one side.

Ayuntamiento   HISTORIC BUILDING
(Town Hall; Pasaje del Cardenal Benavides 9) A block north of the Paseo de la Constitución is the *ayuntamiento*, with a marvellous plateresque facade. The four finely carved balcony portals on the upper storey are separated by the coats of arms of the town, Felipe II (in the middle) and the magistrate Juan de Borja, who had the place built. The building was originally a courthouse and, conveniently, a prison.

FREE **Torre de los Aliatares**   TOWER
(Tower of the Aliatares; Plaza de España) The lonely Torre de los Aliatares is one of the few remnants of Muslim Bayyasa (as the town was called by the Muslims), having mi-

raculously survived the destructive Isabel la Católica's 1476 order to demolish the town's fortifications.

🛏 Sleeping & Eating

With such a wealth of building heritage, there are several beautifully restored hotel conversions to choose from in Baeza. Eating-wise, Paseo de la Constitucíon is a good place to start, though there are a few gems hidden in the old town.

TOP CHOICE La Casona del Arco BOUTIQUE HOTEL €€
(☑953 74 72 08; www.lacasonadelarco.com; Calle Sacramento 3, Baeza; r €70; ❋ 🤖 🛜 🐾) A tastefully renovated 16th-century palace in the historic centre with modern comforts, including a spa, and delightful rooms with parquet floors, pale stonework, ochre washed walls and pitched ceilings (or beams). There's a large garden, plus a small pool, and the whole place has a tasteful exclusive feel – at an unexclusive price.

Palacio de los Salcedo HOTEL €
(☑953 74 72 00; www.palaciodelossalcedo.com; Calle San Pablo 8, Baeza; r €60; ❋ 🛜) The only part of this 16th-century palace that is genuine is the facade; the rest is authentic-looking faux, ranging from the intricate carved and painted ceilings to murals, columns and arches. The '80s-style rag rolled paintwork looks dated and some of the gilt furniture is pretty kitsch but, overall, the atmosphere is fittingly historic.

**Mesón Restaurante
La Góndola** ANDALUCIAN €€
(www.asadorlagondola.com; Portales Carbonería 13, Paseo de la Constitución; mains €8-16) A terrific local, atmospheric restaurant, helped along by the glowing, wood-burning grill behind the bar, cheerful service and good food. Try *patatas baezanas*, a vegetarian delight that mixes a huge helping of sautéed potatoes with mushrooms.

**Restaurante Palacio
Sánchez Valenzuela** ANDALUCIAN €€
(Calle San Pablo 24; menú €12, mains €10) Also known as the Nueva Casino, dine in the courtyard of this 16th-century palace, although don't get too excited – the chairs are metal and there is no shade. The setting is still pretty impressive, however, while the food is simple local fare with a well-priced daily menu.

❶ Information

Tourist office (☑953 77 99 82, 953 77 99 83; www.andalucia.org; Plaza del Pópulo; ⏰9am-7.30pm Mon-Fri, 9.30am-3pm Sat, Sun & holidays Apr-Sep) Situated just southwest of Paseo de la Constitución in the 16th-century plateresque Casa del Pópulo, a former courthouse.

❶ Getting There & Away

Alsa (www.alsa.es) runs to Jaén (€4, one hour, 14 daily), Úbeda (€1.05, 15 minutes, 19 daily) and Granada (€11.75, two hours, 10 daily). There are also buses to Cazorla (€4.40, 1¾ hours, three daily), Córdoba (€10.50, 2½ hours, two daily) and Seville (€39.75, 4½ hours, two daily).

The nearest train station is **Linares-Baeza** (☑953 65 02 02; www.renfe.es), 13km northwest of town, where a few trains a day leave for Granada, Córdoba, Seville, Málaga, Cádiz, Almería, Madrid and Barcelona. Buses connect with most trains from Monday to Saturday. A taxi to the train station costs €15.

Úbeda

POP 36,000 / ELEV 760M

Úbeda (*oo*-be-dah) is a slightly different proposition to its little sister, Baeza. Aside from the splendour of its architecture, the town has good tapas bars and restaurants and interesting antique shops, and is home to some of the finest pottery workshops in Spain.

Exposed to the cultural influences of the Italian Renaissance and benefiting from the wealth and privilege of the powerful Molina family, the city turned out what are now considered to be some of the purest examples of Renaissance architecture in Spain. As a result Úbeda (along with neighbouring Baeza) is one of the sole places in Andalucía where you can see stunning buildings and architecture that were *not* built by the Moors.

⊙ Sights

Sacra Capilla del Salvador CHAPEL
(Plaza Vázquez de Molina; adult/child €3/1.50; ⏰10am-2pm & 4-7.30pm Mon-Sat, 11.15am-2pm & 5-8pm Sun) The purity of Renaissance lines is best expressed in this famous chapel, the first of many works executed in Úbeda by celebrated architect Andrés de Vandelvira. A pre-eminent example of the plateresque style, the chapel's main facade is modelled on Diego de Siloé's Puerta del Perdón at Granada's cathedral (p748).

The classic portal is topped by a carving of the transfiguration of Christ, flanked by statues of St Peter and St Paul. The underside of the arch is an orgy of classical sculpture, executed by French sculptor Esteban Jamete, depicting the Greek gods – a Renaissance touch that would have been inconceivable a few decades earlier.

Next door to the *capilla* (chapel) stands the Palacio del Condestable Dávalos. Partly remodelled in the 17th century, the mansion is now Úbeda's luxurious *parador*.

Plaza del 1° de Mayo HISTORIC SITE

This imposing plaza was originally the town's market square and bullring. It was also the grisly site of Inquisition burnings, which local worthies used to watch from the gallery of the Antiguo Ayuntamiento (Old Town Hall) in the southwestern corner.

Leaving no doubt about their political persuasion, locals renamed this square from the former (fascist) Plaza del Generalissimo several years ago.

Sinagoga del Agua HISTORIC SITE

(Calle Roqas 2; admission €4; ☉10am-8.30pm) There is evidence of a considerable Jewish community in Úbeda dating as far back as the 10th century, when it cohabited peacefully with the considerably larger Muslim population. However, it was not until 2006 when this synagogue and former Rabbi's house was discovered by a refreshingly ethical realtor who bought the property to knock down and build apartments – only to discover that every swing of the pickaxe revealed some tantalising archaeological piece of a puzzle.

The result is the city's latest museum, a sensitive recreation of a centuries-old synagogue and Rabbi's house using original masonry whenever possible, some still bearing Jewish symbols, and including capitals, caliphs and arches. A separate women's gallery was discovered in the excavation, as well as a bodega, with the giant urns still in place.

FREE Hospital de Santiago CULTURAL CENTRE

(Calle Obispo Cobos; ☉8am-3pm & 4-10pm Mon-Fri, 11am-3pm & 6-10pm Sat & Sun) Vandelvira's last architectural project is here, the Hospital de Santiago. Completed in 1575, it has often been dubbed the Escorial of Andalucía – a reference to a famous old monastery outside Madrid, which was a precursor to the kind of baroque architecture employed by Vandelvira. It now acts as Úbeda's cultural centre, housing a library, municipal dance school and an exhibition hall. To get

here, turn left along Calle Mesones from the northwest corner of Plaza de Andalucía. The Hospital is a couple of blocks down on your right.

🛏 Sleeping & Eating

Palacio de la Rambla HISTORIC HOTEL €€

(☎953 75 01 96; www.palaciodelarambla.com; Plaza del Marqués de la Rambla 1, Úbeda; d/ste incl breakfast €96/120; ❄🐾) Úbeda's loveliest converted palace has eight gorgeous rooms in the home of the Marquesa de la Rambla. It's not an overstatement to call this one of Andalucía's most stunning places to stay. The ivy-clad patio is wonderfully romantic and entry is restricted to guests only. Each room is clad in precious antiques and has its own salon, so that you feel like you're staying with aristocratic friends rather than in a hotel. Breakfast can be enjoyed in the former bodega or served in your room. This hotel is closed for part of July and August.

Parador Condestable Dávalos HISTORIC HOTEL €€€

(☎953 75 03 45; www.parador.es; Plaza Vázquez de Molina; r €160; ❄🐾🐾) As *paradors* always get the town's best location and building, Úbeda has surrendered its prime spot, looking out over the wonderful Plaza Vázquez de Molina, and has housed the hotel inside an historic monument: the Palacio del Deán Ortega. It has, of course, been comfortably modernised and is appropriately luxurious. It also has the best restaurant in town.

Hotel Postigo HOTEL €

(☎953 75 00 00; www.hotelelpostigo.com; Calle Postigo 5; s/d €40/50; 🐾❄) This appealing small hotel is charmingly situated on a cobbled backstreet with plenty of nearby easy parking. The rooms are spacious and modern with parquet floors and shiny black furnishings. There is a pleasant outside terrace and a large public sitting room with a log fire in the winter.

TOP CHOICE Zeitúm EUROPEAN €€

(www.zeitum.com; Calle San Juán de la Cruz 10; mains €14-20; ☉Tue-Sat, lunch Sun) This restaurant is housed in another heavily historic building, dating from the 14th century, in a former Jewish quarter. Ask the owner to show you the original well and stonework and beams bearing Jewish symbols. It's fascinating stuff and sure makes a change from the cookie-cutter sameness of modern restaurant chains. Olive-oil tastings

DON'T MISS

ANTIQUES & FLAMENCO

The Casa Museo Arte Andalusí (☑953 75 40 14; Calle Narvaez 11; admission €2; ⊘11am-2pm & 5-8pm) is a fascinating private museum and the venue for regular flamenco performances. The first glimpse that this is somewhere special is the original 16th-century heavy carved door. Ring the bell if it is closed.

Owner Paco Castro has lovingly restored this former palace without detracting from its crumbling charm (in other words, it has not metamorphosed into just another 'historical' boutique hotel). Ask him to show you the Star of David etched into one of the original columns in the central patio. Above are balconies and painted Mudéjar-style ceiling and eaves. It is the ideal faded grandeur setting for Paco's fascinating collection of antiques which includes 19th-century ceramics, a 14th-century well, stained glass, ancient millstones, painted tiles, tapestries, intricately carved wooden chests and art work, collected from all over Spain and Morocco.

Downstairs, the former barrel vaulted bodega is lined with photos of Paco and his flamenco chums, including famous maestro Paco de Lucia, who has played here in the past. No promises, of course, but the weekly flamenco show at 9.30pm on Saturday is generally of a high foot-stomping standard (€18, includes a drink). You should book in advance.

are taken seriously here, along with the superb preparation of diverse dishes like steak tartare and a local favourite: partridge salad.

Mesón Restaurante Navarro   ANDALUCIAN €
(Plaza del Ayuntamiento 2; menú €15, raciones €4-12) Always crammed and noisy, the Navarro is a cherished local favourite. Eat your tapas at the bar, or in summer sit out on the sunny plaza. There is also a daily menu with gamey choices like venison and rosemary. Note that the sign just says 'Mesón Restaurante'.

La Taberna   ANDALUCIAN €
(Calle Real 7; mains €6-10; ☷) Children run around screaming, their parents clink glasses and scoff tapas, bar people sweat and work like crazy – a typical Spanish evening scene at this popular tapas bar. Order a drink, get your tapa, and join in. It's good for breakfasts too.

**Taberna
La Imprenta**   CONTEMPORARY ANDALUCIAN €€
(Plaza del Doctor Quesada 1; mains €10-13; ⊘Wed-Mon) This wonderful old print shop, done stylishly and frequented by Úbeda's posh noshers, provides delicious free tapas with your drinks. You can also sit down and eat lobster salad, excellent meat dishes, and saucy little desserts like green apple sorbet with gin on crushed ice.

🛍 Shopping

The typical green glaze on Úbeda's attractive pottery dates back to Islamic times. Several workshops on Cuesta de la Merced and Calle Valencia in the Barrio San Millán, the potters' quarter northeast of the old town, sell their wares on the spot, and the potters are often willing to explain some of the ancient techniques they still use. Alfarería Tito (Plaza del Ayuntamiento 12) has a large selection too. Tito's intricately made blue-and-cream ware is particularly covetable.

ℹ Information

Regional tourist office (☑953 75 08 97; otubeda@andalucia.org; Calle Baja del Marqués 4; ⊘9am-2.45pm & 4-7pm Mon-Fri, 10am-2pm Sat) In the 18th-century Palacio Marqués de Contadero in the old town.

ℹ Getting There & Away

The **bus station** (☑953 75 21 57; Calle San José 6) is located to the northwest in the new part of town. **Alsa** (www.alsa.es) runs to Baeza (€1.05, 15 minutes, 19 daily), Jaén (€5, one hour, 15 daily), Cazorla (€3.85, one hour, five daily), Granada (€11.85, three hours, 10 daily) and Córdoba (€11, 2½ hours, five daily).

Cazorla

POP 8100 / ELEV 885M

Cazorla, 45km east of Úbeda, is a gorgeous foot-of-the-mountains village with a hunting obsession that acts as a gateway to Spain's largest protected park.

◉ Sights

At one end of lovely Plaza de Santa María is the large shell of the Iglesia de Santa María. It was built by Andrés de Vandelvira in the 16th century but was wrecked by Napoleonic troops. A 3.5km round-trip hike starts here to the Ermita San Sebastián via a mirador. Look out for the many species of birds along the route. Alternatively you can take the shorter walk up to the ancient Castillo de la Yedra, which houses the Museo del Alto Guadalquivir (Castillo de la Yedra; admission €1.50; ☉2.30-8pm Tue, 9am-8pm Wed-Sat, 9am-2pm Sun), with art and relics of past local life.

🛏 Sleeping & Eating

Check out some new and wonderful tapas including *rin-ran* (mixed salted cod, potatoes and red peppers), *talarines* (pasta), *gachamiga* (a kind of Spanish polenta) and *carne de monte* (meat – usually venison), as well as Sierra de Cazorla's memorable olive oil – fresh, fruity and slightly bitter.

Hotel Guadalquivir   HOTEL €
(☎953 72 02 68; www.hguadalquivir.com; Calle Nueva 6; s/d €40/50; ❄) Cheap and cheerful, the Guadalquivir has comfortable, blue-hued rooms with pine furniture, TV and heating, though no memorable views. The singles can be a bit cramped, but the hotel is in a central location and equals good value for money.

Bar Las Vegas   TAPAS €
(Plaza de la Corredera 17; raciones €6) The best of Cazorla's bars with barrel tables outside (but little atmosphere within). You can try tasty prawn-and-capsicum *revuelto* (scrambled eggs), as well as the town's top breakfast, *tostadas* (toasted bread) with various toppings, including the classic crushed tomatoes with garlic and olive oil.

Mesón Don Chema   ANDALUCIAN €€
(Calle Escaleras; mains €10-17) Dine under the mounted antlers on game, pork and a variety of meaty mains, plus such sizzling local fare as *huevos cazorleña* (a mixed stew of sliced boiled eggs and chorizo with vegetables).

❶ Information

Oficina de Turismo Municipal (☎953 72 08 75; Paseo del Santo Cristo 19; ☉10am-1pm &

5-7.30pm) The tourist office is located 200m north of Plaza de la Constitución. It has useful information on the Parque Natural de las Sierras de Cazorla, Segura y Las Villas, as well as Cazorla town.

❶ Getting There & Away

Alsa (www.alsa.es) runs buses to Úbeda (€3.85, one hour, five daily), Jaén (€4.40, 1¾ hours, three daily) and Granada (€16, 3¾ hours, three daily). The main stop in Cazorla is Plaza de la Constitución. A few buses run from Cazorla to Coto Ríos in the Parque Natural de las Sierras de Cazorla, Segura y Las Villas, with stops at Arroyo Frío and Torre del Vinagre.

Parque Natural de Cazorla

Filling almost all the eastern side of Jaén province, the Parque Natural de las Sierras de Cazorla, Segura y Las Villas is a stunning region of rugged mountain ranges divided by high plains and deep, forested valleys, and it's one of the best places in Spain for spotting wildlife. At 2143 sq km, it's also the biggest protected area in the country. Walkers stand a good chance of seeing wild boar, red and fallow deer, ibex and mouflon (a large wild sheep). The park also supports 2300 plant species.

The Guadalquivir, Andalucía's longest river, rises in the south of the park and flows north into the Embalse del Tranco de Beas reservoir, then west towards the Atlantic.

Admittedly, you do need wheels to reach some of the most spectacular areas and walks. The best times to visit are between late April and June, and September and October, when the vegetation flourishes and the weather is at its best. In spring, the flowers are magnificent. Peak visitor periods are Semana Santa, July and August.

The park starts just a few hundred metres up the hill east of Cazorla town.

◉ Sights & Activities

The tourist office in the village of Cazorla has maps and descriptions of six park hikes (from 8km to 23km) and seven drives.

RÍO BOROSA WALK

Though it gets busy on weekends and holidays, this walk of about seven hours return (plus stops) is the park's most popular for good reason. It follows the course of Río Borosa upstream to two beautiful mountain lakes: an ascent of 500m in the course of 12km from Torre del Vinagre. Using the bus to Torre del Vinagre, you can do it as a day trip from Cazorla (but confirm bus schedules before setting off). You can top up your water bottle at good, drinkable springs along the walk; the last is at the Central Eléctrica hydroelectric station.

A road signed 'Central Eléctrica', opposite Torre del Vinagre, soon crosses the Guadalquivir and, within 1km, reaches the marked start of the walk, on your right beside Río Borosa. The first section is an unpaved road, crisscrossing the tumbling river on bridges. After 4km, where the road starts climbing to the left, take a path forking right. This takes you through a beautiful 1.5km section, where the valley narrows to a gorge, Cerrada de Elías, and the path takes you to a wooden walkway to save you from swimming. Rejoining the main track, continue for 3km to the Central Eléctrica hydroelectric station. Just past this, a sign points you on up towards the Laguna de Valdeazores. This path will lead you, via some dramatic mountain scenery and two tunnels supplying water to the power station (there's room to stay dry as you go through), to reservoir Laguna de Aguas Negras, then the natural Laguna de Valdeazores.

HORNOS & EL YELMO

The small village of Hornos sits atop a high rocky outcrop with a romantic ruined castle and panoramic views over the northern end of the Embalse del Tranco. The southern approach is awe-inspiring. About 10km northeast of Hornos is the Puerto de Horno de Peguera pass and junction. One kilometre north from here, a dirt road turns left to the top of El Yelmo (1809m), one of the most distinctive mountains in the north of the park. It's 5km to the top, an ascent of 360m – driveable, but better as a walk, with superb views and griffon vultures wheeling around the skies (plus paragliders and hanggliders on weekends). At a fork after 1.75km, go right.

SEGURA DE LA SIERRA

The most spectacular village inside the park, Segura sits 20km north of Hornos, perched on an 1100m hill crowned by a castle. When taken in 1214 by the Knights of Santiago, Segura was one of the very first Christian conquests in Andalucía.

As you reach the upper part of the village, there's a tourist office (Calle Cortijos Nuevos; ⏱10.30am-2pm & 6.30-8.30pm) beside the Puerta Nueva arch. Segura's two main monuments are normally left open all day, every day, but check before proceeding.

The Baño Moro (Calle Baños Moro 1; ⏱10.30am-2pm Wed-Sun), built about 1150, has three elegant rooms (for cold, tepid and hot baths) with horseshoe arches and barrel vaults studded with skylights. The castle, at the top of the village, has Islamic (or maybe even earlier) origins. From its three-storey keep there are great views across to El Yelmo and far to the west.

🧭 Tours

A number of operators offer trips to the park's less accessible areas, plus other activities. Hotels and camping grounds in the park can often arrange for them to pick you up.

Tierraventura ADVENTURE TOURS
(📞953 71 00 73, 953 72 20 11; www.aventuracazorla.com; Calle Ximénez de Rada 17) Multiadventure activities including canoeing, hiking, canyon descents and rock climbing.

🛏 Sleeping & Eating

There's plenty of accommodation in the park, much of it dotted along the A319 north of Empalme del Valle. At peak times it's worth booking ahead. Most restaurants in the park are part of hotels or *hostales*.

Camping is not allowed outside the organised camping grounds.

Hotel Noguera de la Sierpe HOTEL €€
(📞953 71 30 21, www.hotelnoguveradelasierpe.com; Carretera del Tranco Km 44.5, Parque Natural de las Sierras de Cazorla, Segura y Las Villas; s/d €60/90, 4-person chalet €120; P🐾🏊) A paradise for hunting aficionados, run by an equally fanatical proprietor who has decorated the place with stuffed animals and photos of his exploits. The hotel is housed in a converted *cortijo* (farmhouse) and overlooks a picturesque lake. You can arrange riding sessions at the hotel's stables.

Los Abedules APARTMENT €
(📞953 12 43 08; www.losabedules-cazorla.com; Los Peralejos, Apt 44, Parque Natural de las Sierras de Cazorla, Segura y Las Villas; 2-/4-person apt €50/70; P🏊) Surrounded by olive groves, this is an ideal spot for walkers with fully furnished, comfortable apartments and a salt-water pool for cooling down after a long day's hike. It's run by an English couple; Diane is a qualified therapist in a number of alternative therapies, including reflexology and Reiki. Pets welcome.

SEVILLE & ANDALUCÍA PARQUE NATURAL DE CAZORLA

❶ Information

The main information centre is the **Centro de Interpretación Torre del Vinagre** (☺10am-2pm & 4-7pm), 16km north of Empalme del Valle on the A319. Kids will enjoy the interactive AV exhibits about the park's flora and fauna. The Museo de Caza (Hunting Museum) with stuffed park wildlife, is in an adjoining building; a more cheerful botanic garden is just along the road.

Editorial Alpina's 1:40,000 *Sierra de Cazorla*, which covers the south of the park and is available in English, and *Sierra de Segura*, which covers the north, are the best maps, showing selected walks that are described in accompanying booklets. You may be able to get the maps locally, but don't count on it.

❶ Getting There & Away

Carcesa (☎953 72 11 42) runs two buses daily (except Sunday) from Cazorla's Plaza de la Constitución to Empalme del Valle, Arroyo Frío, Torre del Vinagre and Coto Ríos. Pick up the latest timetable from the tourist office. No buses link the northern part of the park with the centre or south, and there are no buses to Segura de la Sierra or Hornos. **Alsa** (www.alsa.es) runs a bus from Jaén, Baeza or Úbeda to La Puerta de Segura (€12, three hours, three daily).

ALMERÍA PROVINCE

Way out east, the gritty working port of Almería and its arid hinterland lie half-forgotten on Andalucía's most unblemished stretch of coastline. Defiantly Spanish with a strong Moorish history, the Costa del Sol–style tourist juggernaut has yet to arrive in this neck of the woods, although Clint Eastwood dropped by in the 1960s to make his trilogy of spaghetti westerns amid scenery more reminiscent of the Wild West than southern Spain. Lying in the rain shadow of the Sierra Nevada, Almería is the Iberian Peninsula's sunniest and driest region, and the site of Europe's only desert. Modern greenhouse farming techniques have recently turned its parched landscapes into a horticultural powerhouse and a huge centre for immigrant labour.

Almería

POP 190,000

Don't underestimate sun-baked Almería, a tough waterside city with an illustrious history and a handful of important historical monuments to prove it. While the queues form outside Granada's Alhambra, mere trickles of savvy travellers head for Almería's equally hefty Alcazaba fortress, which lords it over a city that once served as chief sea outlet for the 10th-century Córdoba caliphate. Today Almería is an increasingly prosperous port with a thriving agribusiness sector and a strong flamenco tradition enshrined in its distinctive *tarantos*.

◉ Sights & Activities

Alcazaba
FORTRESS

(Calle Almanzor; adult/EU citizen €1.50/free; ☺9am-8.30pm Tue-Sun Apr-Oct, to 6.30pm Tue-Sun Nov-Mar) A looming fortification with great curtainlike walls rising from the cliffs, the Alcazaba was built in the 10th century by Abd ar-Rahman III, the greatest caliphate of Al-Andalus, and was the most powerful Moorish fortress in Spain. It lacks the intricate decoration of the Alhambra, but it is nonetheless a compelling monument.

The interior is divided into three distinct sections. The lowest area, the Primer Recinto, was the civic centre, with houses, baths and other necessities – now replaced by lush gardens and water channels. From the battlements you can see the Muralla de Jayrán, a fortified wall built in the 11th century.

In the Segundo Recinto you'll find the ruins of the Muslim rulers' palace, built by Almotacín (r 1051–91), under whom medieval Almería reached its peak. Within the compound is a chapel, the Ermita de San Juan, once a mosque. The highest part, the Tercer Recinto, is a fortress added by the Catholic Monarchs. Its keep is used as a gallery for painting, photography (and similar) exhibitions (9am to 8.30pm Tuesday to Sunday).

Almería Cathedral
CATHEDRAL

(Plaza de la Catedral; admission €3; ☺10am-2pm & 4-5pm Mon-Fri, 10am-2pm Sat) Almería's weighty cathedral is at the heart of the old part of the city below the Alcazaba. Begun in 1524, its fortresslike appearance, with six towers, reflects the prevalence of pirate raids from North Africa during this era.

The interior has a Gothic ribbed ceiling and is trimmed with jasper and local marble. The chapel behind the main altar contains the tomb of Bishop Diego Villalán, the cathedral's founder, whose broken-nosed image is the work of Juan de Orea, who also created the Sacristía Mayor with its fine carved stonework.

Centro Andaluz de Fotografía
GALLERY

(Andalucian Photographic Centre; 950 26 96 80; Calle Pintor Diaz Molina, 9; 11am-2pm & 5.30-9.30pm) Whether you are a keen photographer or an overheated sightseer, you will enjoy the edgy and memorable images here.

Museo Arqueológico
MUSEUM

(Carretera de Ronda 91; non-EU/EU citizen €1.50/free; 2.30-8.30pm Tue, 9am-8.30pm Wed-Sat, 9am-2.30pm Sun) Almería's modern Museo Arqueológico presents finds from Los Millares and other ancient settlements in the region, as well as Roman and Islamic traces. Even if pot shards and bone fragments normally make you yawn, don't skip this – it's a rare example of multimedia technology deployed to excellent effect, touched with a uniquely Spanish flair for the macabre.

FREE Aljibes de Jayrán
HISTORIC SITE

(950 27 30 39; Calle Tenor Iribarne; 10am-2pm Mon-Fri) North of Plaza de las Flores, the Aljibes de Jayrán were built in the early 11th century to supply the city's water. They're well preserved, and are the venue for regular exhibitions, and for the Peña El Taranto (p774), the city's top club of flamenco *aficionados*. There are occasional concerts open to the public.

Beaches
BEACHES

A long, grey-sand beach fronts the palm-lined Paseo Marítimo. It is east of the city's centre.

Hammam Aíre de Almería
HAMMAM

(www.airedealmeria.com; Plaza de la Constitución 5; entry incl 15min massage €35; 10am-10pm) Opened in 2011, this new hammam occupies a wonderful setting on the Plaza de la Constitución, a 17th-century arcaded square that was once the city's main Arab souq. Facilities exude a feeling of tranquillity with a marble and warm brick interior, and three baths: the frigidarium (16°C), the tepidarium (36°C) and the caldarium (40°C), as well as a range of aromatherapy massages. The hammam also incorporates a hotel and a bar.

Sleeping

Hotel Catedral
HOTEL €€

(950 27 81 78; www.hotelcatedral.net; Plaza de la Catedral 8; r €70; @) Cosied up to the cathedral and built with the same warm honey-coloured stone, the building dates from 1850 and has been sensitively restored. Rooms are large, with luxury touches and the sun terrace has heady cathedral views.

Hotel Nuevo Torreluz
HOTEL €

(950 23 43 99; www.torreluz.es; Plaza de las Flores 10; r €54; P) Opened in 2012 this reformed four-star enjoys a superb position on this small square in the heart of the historic centre. Rooms are on the small size but well equipped and comfortable with warm colour schemes. A statue of John Lennon in the centre of the plaza is apparently in recognition of the several months he lived in Almería back in the '60s.

Plaza Vieja Alejandro
HOTEL €€

(950 28 20 96; www.plazaviejahl.com; Plaza de la Constitución 5; r €80-110; P) Part of the stunning Hammam Aíre de Almería, the rooms here are spacious and modern with high ceilings, lots of glass and shiny wood, soft natural colours and vast photo-friezes of local sights like the Cabo de Gato.

Eating

Most of the best tapas bars lie in the triangle between Plaza Pablo Cazard, Puerta de Putchería and the cathedral.

TOP CHOICE Tetería Almedina
TEAHOUSE €

(www.restauranteteteriaalmedina.com; Calle Paz 2, off Calle de la Almedina; teas €3, mains €7-12; 11am-11pm Tue-Sun;) This lovely little cafe in the old city serves a fascinating range of teas, delectable sweets and good couscous. It's run by a group dedicated to restoring and revitalising the old city, and functions as a sort of casual Islamic cultural centre. There's usually live music on Sundays, in addition to art shows and similar.

Casa Puga
TAPAS €

(www.barcasapuga.es; Calle Jovellanos 7; drink & tapa €2.20) Shelves of ancient wine bottles are the backdrop for a tiny cooking station that churns out small saucers of stews, griddled goodies such as mushrooms, and savoury *hueva de maruca* (smoked fish roe).

Plaza de Cañas
TAPAS €

(www.plazadecanas.com; Calle Martín 20; drink & tapa €2.20) Presents traditional combos such as *remojón* (salt cod, orange and potatoes) with style.

Casa Joaquín
SEAFOOD €€

(950 264 359; Calle Real 111; mains €14-21; closed Sat dinner, Sun & Sep) Reserve one of the few tables for lunch if you're really

serious about your seafood. If you don't mind standing, you can jostle at the bar for platters of baby clams swimming in garlic, delicately fried pieces of monkfish liver and other briny treats. There is no menu.

Aljaima MOROCCAN €€
(www.restauranteajaima.es; Calle Jovellanos 12; tapas €2.10, tagines €14-18) The interior here resembles a *riad* in the medina with traditional tiling – even on the ceiling – richly patterned fabrics, and Moroccan-themed artwork and photographs. The food is deeply traditional. Go for one of the tagines, like chicken and lemon.

Drinking & Entertainment

Habana Cristal CAFE
(Calle Altamira 6; cocktails €3.80; ⊙7am-10pm) One of Almería's most emblematic and well-known cafes with a vast choice of coffees, including the winter-warming Habana Negra with Swiss chocolate, Tia Maria and Cointreau. There's a large outside terrace.

C Bar BAR
(www.hotelcatedral.net; Plaza de la Catedral 8; ⊙noon-midnight) Part of the Hotel Catedral, this slick bar has a young fashionable vibe with its giant blackboards, minimalist furniture and innovative tapas like raspberry, gin and basil sorbet.

Peña El Taranto FLAMENCO
(www.eltaranto.net) Hidden in the renovated Aljibes Árabes (Arab Water Cisterns), this is Almería's top flamenco club. Live performances (€20), open to the public, often happen at weekends. Local hero Tomatito still sometimes plays here.

Information

There are numerous banks on Paseo de Almería.
Main post office (behind Plaza Ecuador)
Municipal tourist office (Ayuntamiento, Plaza de la Constitución 1; ⊙10am-1pm & 5.30-7.30pm Mon-Fri, 10am-noon Sat)
Policía local (local police; ☑950 62 12 06; Calle Santos Zárate 11)
Regional tourist office (Parque de Nicolás Salmerón; ⊙9am-7pm Mon-Fri, 10am-2pm Sat & Sun) Provides more free leaflets and brochures.

ⓘ Getting There & Away
Air

Almería **airport** (☑950 21 37 00; www.aena. es), 10km east of the city centre, receives flights from several European countries. **Easyjet** (www. easyjet.com) flies from London-Gatwick, **Ryanair** (www.ryanair.com) from Stansted, East Midlands (UK) and Madrid, **Thomas Cook Airlines** (www. thomascook airlines.co.uk) from Manchester and London-Gatwick (seasonally), and **Monarch Airlines** (www.monarch.co.uk) from Birmingham. **Air-Berlin** (www.airberlin.com) flies from Mallorca and **Transavia** (www.transavia.com) from Amsterdam. **Iberia** (www.iberia.com) flies direct to/from Barcelona, Madrid and Seville.

Boat

For Morocco, **Acciona Trasmediterránea** (www. trasmediterranea.es), **Ferrimaroc** (☑950 27 48 00; www.ferrimaroc.com) and **Comarit** (☑950 23 61 55; www.comarit.es) sail from the passenger port to Melilla and/or Nador (eight hours). Prices start at €55 for a one-way adult fare.

Bus

Destinations served from the clean, efficient **bus station** (☑950 26 20 98) include Granada (€13, 2¼ hours, eight daily), Málaga (€17, 3¼ hours, eight daily), Murcia (€18, 2½ hours, seven daily), Madrid (€44, 10 hours, three daily) and Valencia (€37, 8½ hours, five daily).

Train

Direct trains run to/from Granada (€16.50, 2¼ hours, four daily), Seville (€40, 5½ hours, four daily) and Madrid (€45.50, 6¼ hours, one daily).

ⓘ Getting Around
City bus 20 (€1, 30 minutes) runs to the centre, near Avenida de Federico García Lorca, on weekdays approximately every 50 minutes from 7.33am to 10.33pm, and on Saturday and Sunday every 1½ hours between 7.25am and 10.25pm. A taxi costs about €22.

Around Almería

Beyond Benahadux, north of Almería, the landscape becomes a series of canyons and rocky wastes that look straight out of the Arizona badlands, and in the 1960s and '70s filmmakers shot around 150 westerns here.

The movie industry has left behind three Wild West town sets that are open as tourist attractions. **Mini Hollywood** (www.oasyspar quetematico.com; adult/child €20/10; ⊙10am-9pm, Sat & Sun only Oct-Apr), the best known and best preserved of these, is 25km from Almería on the N340 Tabernas road. Parts of more than 100 movies, including *A Fistful of Dollars* and *The Good, the Bad and the Ugly*, were filmed here. At 5pm (and 8pm from mid-June to mid-September) a hammed-up bank hold-up and shootout is staged (dialogue in Spanish, of course). Rather bizarrely, the ticket includes entry to the adjoining **Reserva Zoológica**. You will need your own vehicle to visit from Almería.

Cabo de Gata

If you can find anyone old enough to remember the Costa del Sol before the bulldozers arrived they'd probably say it looked a bit like Cabo de Gata. Some of Spain's most beautiful and least crowded beaches are strung between the grand cliffs and capes east of Almería city, where dark volcanic hills tumble into a sparkling turquoise sea. Though Cabo de Gata is not undiscovered, it still has a wild, elemental feel and its scattered fishing villages (remember them?) remain low-key. You can walk along, or not far from, the coast right round from Retamar in the northwest to Agua Amarga in the northeast (61km), but beware – the sun can be intense and there's often little shade.

It's worth calling ahead for accommodation over Easter and in July and August.

Parque Natural de Cabo de Gata-Níjar covers Cabo de Gata's 60km coast plus a slice of hinterland. The park's main information centre is the **Centro de Inter-**pretación Las Amoladeras (☑950 16 04 35; ⊙10am-2pm & 5.30-9pm mid-Jul-mid-Sep, to 3pm Tue-Sun mid-Sep-mid-Jul), about 2.5km west of Ruescas.

SAN MIGUEL DE CABO DE GATA

Fronted by a long straight beach, this scruffy village isn't the best introduction to the park. It's composed largely of holiday houses and apartments (deserted out of season), and resembles a detached suburb of Almería. Press on to the Faro, or start hiking in San José and use this as your end point.

South of the village stretch the **Salinas de Cabo de Gata**, which are salt-extraction lagoons. In spring many migrating greater flamingos and other birds call in here: by late August there can be 1000 flamingos. An 11km trail circumnavigates the *salinas*, equipped with strategically placed viewing hides. You should see a good variety of birds from here any time except in winter, when the *salinas* are drained, but you really need binoculars to appreciate the scene.

San José is a better place to stay unless you want to camp at the extremely well-run **Camping Cabo de Gata** (☑950 16 04 43; sites per adult, caravan, car & power supply €17.28, bungalow €71-112), 1km from the beach; it has all the necessary amenities, including a restaurant. It's 2.5km north of the village by dirt roads.

Cabo de Gata

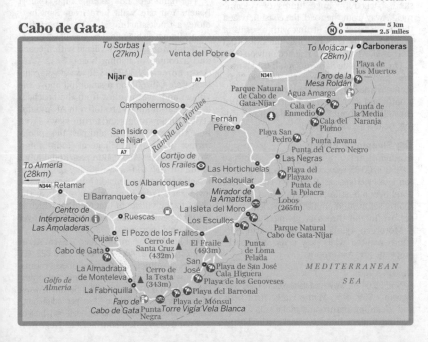

FARO DE CABO DE GATA & AROUND

Beyond the Salinas de Cabo de Gata, a narrow road winds 4km round the cliffs to the Faro de Cabo de Gata, the lighthouse at the promontory's tip. A turn-off by Café Bar El Faro, just before the lighthouse, leads to the Torre Vigía Vela Blanca, an 18th-century watchtower atop 200m cliffs, with awesome views. Here the road ends but a walking and cycling track continues down to Playa de Mónsul (one hour on foot).

SAN JOSÉ
POP 550

San José, spreading round a bay on the eastern side of Cabo de Gata, is a mildly chic resort in summer, but it remains a small, pleasant, low-rise place and is a base for both watery and land-bound activities. Out of season you may have the place almost to yourself.

The road from the north becomes San José's main street, Avenida de San José, with the beach and harbour a couple of blocks down to the left.

Some of the best beaches on Cabo de Gata lie along a dirt road southwest from San José. Playa de los Genoveses, a broad strip of sand about 1km long with shallow waters, is 4.5km away. Playa de Mónsul, 2.5km further from town, is a shorter length of grey sand, backed by huge lumps of volcanic rock. Away from the road, the coast between these two beaches is strung with a series of isolated, sandy, cove beaches, the Calas del Barronal, which can be reached only on foot.

On Avenida de San José you'll find a natural park information office (950 38 02 99; Avenida de San José 27; 10am-2pm & 5-8pm), a bank and an ATM. The information office can tell you about bicycle rental, horse riding, boat trips and diving.

Sleeping & Eating

Atalaya Hotel   HOTEL €€
(950 38 00 85; www.atalayahotel.net; Avenida de San José; r incl breakfast €75;) This central hotel over a bustling restaurant and bar has rooms set around small terraces. The owners are in the throes of giving the rooms a Moroccan-style update with warm burgundy-painted walls, low beds and sparkling slate grey bathrooms.

Hostal Aloha   HOSTAL €
(950 38 04 61; www.hostalaloha.com; Calle Cala Higuera; r €55;) White walls, firm beds and gleaming bathrooms make this an appealing budget hotel to start with. Throw

in the enormous pool on the back terrace, and it's one of the best deals in San José. It's a few blocks back from the beach; to reach it, turn left off the main street at the tourist office.

MC San José   HOTEL €€€
(950 61 11 11; www.hotelesmcsanjose.com; Carretera El Faro; d incl breakfast €139;) The MC is the best of both hotel worlds: chic boutique design, with just 32 rooms and plenty of stylish details, but with the kind of hospitality that only comes from a local family. It's open all year round and there is a reasonable Chinese restaurant on the ground floor.

Acá Charles   INTERNATIONAL €€
(Avenida de San José 51; mains €14-19) Opened in 2012, this place has all the locals enthusing about the sophisticated menu where seafood doesn't necessarily take central stage. Dishes include truffles, crispy Serrano ham and fresh green asparagus with polenta.

SAN JOSÉ TO LAS NEGRAS

The rugged coast northeast of San José allows only two small settlements, the odd fort and a few beaches before the village of Las Negras, 17km away as the crow flies. The road spends most of its time ducking inland.

The hamlet of Los Escullos has a short beach. You can walk here from San José, along a track starting at Cala Higuera bay. One kilometre beyond Los Escullos, La Isleta del Moro is a tiny village with a beach and a couple of fishing boats. Casa Café de la Loma (950 38 98 31; www.degata.com/laloma; s/d €40/60), on a small hill above the village and five minutes from the beach, is a 200-year-old house restored in Al-Andalus style with airy rooms and terrific views. From here the road heads inland past the spooky former gold-mining village of Rodalquilar, worth a detour. About 1km past Rodalquilar is the turn-off to Playa del Playazo, a good beach between two headlands, 2km along a level track. From here you can walk near the coast to the village of Las Negras, which is set on a pebbly beach and largely given over to seasonal tourism.

On Las Negras' main street, Hostal Arrecife (950 38 81 40; Calle Bahía 6; s/d €28/40) has cool, quiet, well-maintained rooms, some with sea views from their balconies. Camping La Caleta (950 52 52 37; www.vayacamping.net/la caleta; sites per adult/tent/car €5.60/6.70/5.60; year-round;) lies in a separate cove 1km south of Las Negras. It can be fiercely hot in summer, but there is a good pool. Other accommodation in Las Negras is mostly holiday apartments and houses to let. **Restaurante La Palma** (mains €12-24), overlooking the beach, plays good music and serves a huge array of fish dishes.

LAS NEGRAS TO AGUA AMARGA

There's no road along this secluded, cliff-lined stretch of coast, but walkers can take an up-and-down path of about 11km, giving access to several beaches. **Playa San Pedro**, one hour from Las Negras, is the site of a ruined hamlet (with castle), inhabited erratically by hippies and naturists. It's 1½ hours on from there to Cala del Plomo beach, with another tiny village, then 1½ hours further to Agua Amarga.

Drivers must head inland from Las Negras through Hortichuelas. A mostly unsealed road heads northeast, cross-country from the bus shelter in Fernán Pérez. Keep to the main track at all turnings, and after 10km you'll reach a sealed road running down from the N341 to Agua Amarga, a chic and expensive but still low-key former fishing village on a straight sandy beach.

Breezy beachfront **Hostal Restaurante La Palmera** (☑950 13 82 08; www.hostalrestau rantelapalmera.com; Calle Aguada; d low/high season €60/90) has 10 bright rooms all with sea views, and its restaurant (mains €11 to €19) is Agua Amarga's most popular lunch spot.

Chic, slick **MiKasa Suites & Spa** (☑950 13 80 73; www.mikasasuites.com; Carretera Carboneras; r incl breakfast €55-85; ✴❋☎) is an elegant, comfortable, romantic hideaway for the long-weekend crowd. There's a poolside restaurant, **Restaurante La Villa** (☑950 13 80 73; mains €10-18; ⊘closed Nov-Mar), and more expensive food (by the sound of it) in the on-site spa – ever heard of caviar facials or algae wraps?

Top spot for food on the beach is **Costamarga** (Playa de Aguamarga; mains €11-16; ✴) which does fish, of course, but it also has a considerable menu section devoted to seasonal vegetables, such as artichoke hearts with ham.

❶ Getting There & Away

Alsa (☑902 422242; www.alsa.es) connects Almería to El Cabo de Gata (€3, one hour, six daily) and Las Negras (€5, 1¼ hours, one daily Monday to Saturday). **Autocares Bernardo** (www.autocaresbernardo.com) runs buses from Almería to San José (€2.65, 1¼ hours, four Monday to Saturday, two Sunday). It also runs

one bus to La Isleta del Moro (€2.65, 1¼ hours) on Monday and Saturday. **Autocares Frahermar** (www.frahermar.com) in Almería runs to/from Agua Amarga (€5.50, 1¼ hours) once on Monday, Wednesday, Friday, Saturday and Sunday; service increases to daily in July and August. There is no bus service connecting towns within the park.

Mojácar

Tucked away in an isolated corner of one of Spain's most traditional regions lies Mojácar, a town that was almost abandoned in the mid-20th century until a foresighted local mayor started luring artists and others with giveaway property offers. Although the tourists have arrived, Mojácar has retained its essence.

There are actually two towns here: old Mojácar Pueblo, a jumble of white, cube-shaped houses on a hilltop 2km inland, and Mojácar Playa, a modern beach resort.

◉ Sights & Activities

Exploring Mojácar Pueblo is mainly a matter of wandering the mazelike streets, with their bougainvillea-swathed balconies, stopping off at craft shops, galleries and boutiques. **El Mirador del Castillo** (⊘11am-11pm or later), at the topmost point, provides magnificent views. The fortress-style **Iglesia de Santa María** (Calle Iglesia) dates from 1560 and may have once been a mosque.

The most touching spot is the **Fuente Mora** (Moorish Fountain) in the lower part of the old town. Though remodelled in modern times, it maintains the medieval Islamic tradition of making art out of flowing water.

South of Mojácar Playa, the beaches are quieter, and once you get to the fringes of town, there are a number of more secluded areas. Several beyond the **Torre de Macenas**, an 18th-century fortification right on the sand, are naturist beaches. There is a pleasant wide promenade that stretches for around 3km north from the Hotel Best Indalo.

🛏 Sleeping & Eating

El Mirador del Castillo   HOSTAL €€
(☑950 47 30 22; www.elcastillomojacar.com; El Mirador del Castillo; d €80, without bathroom €60; ✴❋☎) Up at the top of Mojácar's hill, this laid-back *hostal* is part of a larger art centre and retreat, with a cafe-bar as well. The atmosphere is resolutely bohemian, but even

with some peeling paint, it manages to stay just the right side of characterful, with richly coloured walls and art books on the bedside tables.

La Taberna
TAPAS €

(Plaza del Caño 1, Mojácar Pueblo; tapas & platos combinados from €4) Good tapas and tasty vegetarian bites get everyone cramming into this thriving little restaurant inside a warren of intimate rooms, full of chatter and belly-full diners. Located next to an evocative 11th-century Moorish arch, to get here, head downhill and pass through the old city gate – just on the right, you'll see the tiny tapas *plancha* (griddle) in action.

ⓘ Information

Tourist office (☏950 61 50 25; www.mojacar. es; Calle Glorieta 1; ⊙10am-2pm & 5-7.30pm Mon-Fri, 10.30am-1.30pm Sat) Very helpful tourist office; just off Mojácar Pueblo's Plaza Nueva.

ⓘ Getting There & Around

There is a bus stop at the foot of Mojácar Pueblo and another at the Parque Comercial in Mojácar Playa. **Enatcar/Alsa** (www.alsa.es) runs buses to/from Almería (€7, 1¼ hours, four on weekdays, two on weekends), Granada (€19, four hours, two daily) and Madrid (€38, eight hours, two daily). Buses to Alicante, Valencia and Barcelona go from Vera, 16km north, which is served by several daily buses from Mojácar (€1.50, 50 minutes, nine daily).

Extremadura

Includes »

Best Places to Eat

» Atrio (p784)

» Restaurante Torre de Sande (p784)

» La Finca (p792)

» Casa Benito (p801)

» Casa Juan (p791)

Best Places to Stay

» Hotel Casa Don Fernando (p782)

» Túnel del Hada (p794)

» Hospedería del Real Monasterio (p790)

» Posada dos Orillas (p787)

» El Jardín del Convento (p795)

Why Go?

Visiting Extremadura is like traversing old Spain, from the country's finest Roman ruins to beautiful medieval cities and villages. Mérida, Cáceres and Trujillo rank among the country's best-preserved historical settlements, while *extremeño* villages have a timeless charm, from the remote hills of the north to beguiling Zafra on the cusp of Andalucía in the south.

This is a region of big skies and vast swathes of sparsely populated land with isolated farmhouses. Wooded sierras rise along the region's northern, eastern and southern fringes, while the raptor-rich Parque Nacional de Monfragüe is arguably Extremadura's most dramatic corner.

Relatively few foreign travellers make it this far. Spaniards, however, know it as a place to sample some of inland Spain's finest food, especially roasted meats and the pungent and creamy Torta del Casar cheese.

When to Go
Cáceres

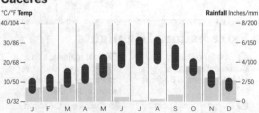

Apr The Valle del Jerte becomes a spectacular white sea of cherry blossom.

Jul–Aug Mérida's 2000-year-old Roman theatre hosts the Festival de Teatro Clásico.

Sep The summer heat has lost its sting and there are few tourists; this is a prime time to visit.

CENTRAL EXTREMADURA

If you have time to visit just one region, make it this one; the heart of Extremadura is home to some of Spain's prettiest towns: Cáceres, Trujillo and Guadalupe.

Cáceres

POP 95,030

The Ciudad Monumental (old town) of Cáceres is truly extraordinary. Narrow cobbled streets twist and climb among ancient stone walls lined with palaces and man-

Extremadura Highlights

❶ Stroll the Ciudad Monumental's evocative cobbled streets in **Cáceres** (p780)

❷ Clamber over Spain's finest Roman ruins in **Mérida** (p798)

❸ Travel to **Trujillo** (p785), medieval home town of some of Latin America's most infamous conquistadors

❹ Spot majestic birds of prey as they wheel over the **Parque Nacional de Monfragüe** (p797)

❺ Check out the mighty impressive Roman bridge over the Tajo in peaceful **Alcántara** (p785)

❻ Admire the fabulous art collection in the extraordinary monastery of **Guadalupe** (p789)

❼ Explore the half-timbered villages of **La Vera** (p791) and marvel at the cherry blossom of adjacent **Valle del Jerte** (p794)

❽ Pace the quiet lanes of the restored historic museum village of **Granadilla** (p796)

sions, while the skyline is decorated with turrets, spires, gargoyles and enormous storks' nests. Protected by defensive walls, it has survived almost intact from its 16th-century heyday. At dusk or after dark, when the crowds have gone, you'll feel like you've stepped back into the Middle Ages. Stretching at its feet, the lively and arcaded Plaza Mayor is one of Spain's finest public squares.

◉ Sights

Ciudad Monumental's name captures it all. The churches, palaces and towers are hugely impressive although few people actually live here and there are just a handful of bars and restaurants.

Plaza de Santa María & Around SQUARE, HISTORIC BUILDING
Enter the Ciudad Monumental from Plaza Mayor through the 18th-century **Arco de la Estrella**, built wide for the passage of carriages. The **Concatedral de Santa María** (Plaza de Santa María; admission €1; ⊙9.30am-2pm & 5.30-8.30pm Mon-Sat, 9.30-11.50am & 5.30-7.15pm Sun May-Sep), a 15th-century Gothic cathedral, creates an impressive opening scene. At its southwestern corner is a modern statue of San Pedro de Alcántara, a 16th-century *extremeño* ascetic (his toes worn shiny by the hands and lips of the faithful). Inside, there's a magnificent carved 16th-century cedar altarpiece, noble tombs and chapels, and a small ecclesiastical museum featuring monstrances and priestly vestments. Climb the **bell tower** for views.

Also on the plaza are the **Palacio Episcopal** (Bishop's Palace), the **Palacio de Mayoralgo** and the **Palacio de Ovando**, all in 16th-century Renaissance style. Just off the plaza's northeastern corner is the **Palacio Carvajal** (Calle Amargura 1; admission free; ⊙9am-9pm Mon-Fri, 10am-2pm & 5-8pm Sat, 10am-2pm Sun). Within this late-15th-century mansion, there's a modern display on the province's attractions and the provincial tourist board, which can help out with information on the region.

Just to the west of the plaza lies the domed **Palacio Toledo-Moctezuma**, once home of a daughter of the Aztec emperor Moctezuma, brought to Cáceres as a conquistador's bride; the palace now houses the municipal archives. Heading back through Arco de la Estrella, you can climb the 12th-century **Torre de Bujaco** (Plaza Mayor; adult/child €2/free; ⊙10am-2pm & 5.30-8.30pm Mon-Sat, 10am-2pm Sun Apr-Sep, 10am-2pm & 4.30-7.30pm Mon-Sat, 10am-2pm Sun Oct-Mar), home to an interpretative display. From the top there's a good stork's-eye view of the Plaza Mayor.

Plaza de San Jorge SQUARE
Southeast of Plaza de Santa María, past the Renaissance-style **Palacio de la Diputación**, is Plaza de San Jorge, above which rises the **Iglesia de San Francisco Javier** (Iglesia de la Preciosa Sangre; Plaza de San Jorge; adult/child €1/free; ⊙10am-2pm & 5.30-8.30pm Mon-Sat), an 18th-century Jesuit church; the views from the towers would be wonderful, were it not for the chicken wire. Around the corner, the **Centro Divulgación Semana Santa** (Cuesta de la Compañía; admission free; ⊙10am-2pm & 5.30-8.30pm) has exhibits on Easter celebrations in Cáceres atop 18th-century cisterns. Due east of the plaza is the **Arco del Cristo**, a Roman gate.

Plaza de San Mateo & Around SQUARE
From Plaza de San Jorge, Cuesta de la Compañía climbs to Plaza de San Mateo and the **Iglesia de San Mateo**, traditionally the church of the land-owning nobility and built on the site of the town's mosque. The soaring wooden altarpiece is an impressive sight at the end of the single nave with its high Gothic vaulting.

Just to the east is the **Torre de las Cigüeñas** (Tower of the Storks). This was the only Cáceres tower to retain its battlements when the rest were lopped off in the late 15th century. It houses occasional art exhibitions.

Below the square is the excellent **Museo de Cáceres** (Plaza de las Veletas 1; non-EU/EU citizens €1.20/free; ⊙9am-2.30pm & 5-8.15pm Tue-Sat, 10.15am-2.30pm Sun) in a 16th-century mansion built over a 12th-century *aljibe* (cistern), a surviving element of Cáceres' Islamic castle. It has an impressive archaeological section and an excellent fine-arts display (open mornings only), with works by Picasso, Miró, Tàpies and other renowned artists.

Other nearby buildings include the **Palacio de los Golfines de Arriba** (Calle de los Olmos 2), where Franco was declared head of state in 1936, and the **Casa Mudéjar** (Cuesta de Aldana 14), which still reflects its Islamic influence in its brickwork and 1st-floor window arches.

🏃 Activities

El Aljibe de Cáceres HAMMAM
(☏927 22 32 56; www.hammamcaceres.com; Calle de Peña 5; ⊙10am-2pm & 4-10pm Sun-Thu, to midnight Fri & Sat) This beautifully indulgent

Cáceres

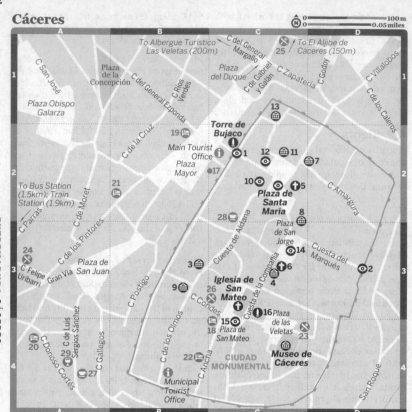

EXTREMADURA CÁCERES

re-creation of an Arab-style bath experience combines soothing architecture and a range of treatments. The basic thermal bath with aromatherapy starts from €15; throw in a massage and you'll pay €22.

Tours

Asociación de Guías Turísticas WALKING TOUR
(Tourist Guides Association; ☎927 21 72 37; Plaza Mayor 2) These guides lead 1½- to two-hour tours (€5) in Spanish around the Ciudad Monumental at least twice daily from May to September, with only morning tours on Sunday. Tours start from its office on Plaza Mayor, and tours in English can be arranged with advance notice.

Festivals & Events

Womad WORLD MUSIC
(World of Music, Arts and Dance; www.womadcaceres.com) For three fiesta-fuelled days in mid-May, Cáceres stages a long-running edition of Womad, with international bands playing in the old city's squares.

Fiesta de San Jorge LOCAL FIESTA
From 21 to 23 April the town celebrates the Fiesta de San Jorge in honour of its patron saint.

Sleeping

TOP CHOICE Hotel Casa Don Fernando BOUTIQUE HOTEL €€
(☎927 21 42 79; www.casadonfernando.com; Plaza Mayor 30; d €60-140; ❄☞) The classiest mid-range choice in Cáceres, this boutique hotel sits on Plaza Mayor directly opposite the Arco de la Estrella. Spread over four floors, the designer rooms and bathrooms are tastefully chic; superior rooms (€30 more than the standards) have the best plaza views and come with free minibar. Attic-style top-floor rooms are good for families.

Cáceres

EXTREMADURA CÁCERES

Atrio
BOUTIQUE HOTEL €€€

(☏927 24 29 28; www.restauranteatrio.com; Plaza de San Mateo 1; r €240-325; P❊🛜🏊) Impeccable modern styling and some serious pieces of contemporary art characterise this excellent fusion of five-star boutique hotel and one of Spain's most garlanded restaurants. The location in the heart of the old town is impressive, and neither the sleek rooms nor the solicitous personal service will disappoint.

Parador de Cáceres
HOTEL €€€

(☏927 21 17 59; www.parador.es; Calle Ancha 6; s/d €139/173; P❊@🛜) A substantial makeover has given this 14th-century Gothic palace in the old town a swish modern look to its interiors, with bedrooms and bathrooms exhibiting a distinctively nonmedieval level of style and comfort. If you're driving here, pay close attention to the directions they give you when booking.

Hotel Don Carlos
HOTEL €€

(☏927 22 55 27; www.hoteldoncarloscaceres. com; Calle Donoso Cortés 15; s/d €48/68; P❊🛜) Rooms are tastefully decorated with bare brick and stone at this welcoming small hotel, sensitively created from a long-abandoned early-19th-century house. There are two artists among the owner's family, hence plenty of original artwork. Parking costs €9.

Hotel Iberia
HOTEL €

(☏927 24 76 34; www.iberiahotel.com; Calle de los Pintores 2; s/d €46/60; ❊) Located in an 18th-century former palace just off Plaza Mayor, this friendly and family-run 36-room hotel has public areas that look like old-world museum pieces, decorated with antique furnishings. The rooms are great for this price, with parquet floors and art on the walls. It's a good, traditional choice in a top location.

Albergue Turístico Las Veletas
HOSTEL €

(☏927 21 12 10; lasveletas@hotmail.com; Calle del General Margallo 36; dm €18-20; ❊🛜) This modern hostel, with its homey rear garden with flowers, offers agreeable accommodation in rooms with three to six beds. Reserve in advance, since it works primarily with groups. Meals are available for €8. Discount for pilgrims.

Eating

From the restaurants and cafes flanking the Plaza Mayor, you can watch the swallows and storks swoop and glide among the turrets of the old city. Stick to a drink and simple tapas, however, as the food here tends to be overpriced and indifferent. There's a better-quality tapas scene around nearby Plaza de San Juan.

Atrio
MODERN SPANISH €€€

(☎927 24 29 28; www.restauranteatrio.com; Plaza de San Mateo 1; menus €99-119) With a stunning new location in the heart of old Cáceres, the city's fine-dining highlight seems to be going from strength to strength. Service that manages to be both formal and friendly backs up the wonderful culinary creations. The focus is on local produce of the highest quality; there's a degustation menu chosen by the chef or you can pick from a selection of daily specials to make up your own menu.

Restaurante Torre de Sande
FUSION €€€

(☎927 21 11 47; www.torredesande.com; Calle Condes 3; meals €35-45; ☉lunch & dinner Tue-Sat, lunch Sun) Dine in the pretty courtyard on dishes like *salmorejo de cerezas del Jerte con queso de cabra* (cherry-based cold soup with goat's cheese) at this elegant gourmet restaurant in the heart of the Ciudad Monumental. More modestly, stop for a drink and a tapa at the interconnecting *tapería* (tapas bar), which has appealing streetside tables.

Madruelo
MODERN SPANISH €€

(☎927 24 36 76; www.madruelo.com; Calle Camberos 2; mains €14-20) This intimate and soberly decorated restaurant is where *cacereños* in the know will go for high-class modern Spanish cuisine at a fair price. Excellent grilled meats are complemented by rices, a range of foie gras dishes and the odd dish from elsewhere in the Mediterranean like moussaka.

La Tahona
TAPAS, SPANISH €€

(www.latahonarestaurante.com; Calle Felipe Uribarri 4; mains €12-19; ☉lunch & dinner Mon-Sat, lunch Sun) Part gallery part eatery, this buzzy side-street choice has an upmarket but almost exuberant feel. Succulent meats cooked in a wood oven are the speciality here, but there's a wide choice which can be munched on in the downstairs tapas bar or in the quieter atmosphere upstairs. Service is friendly and helpful.

El Racó de Sanguino
SPANISH €€

(☎927 22 76 82; www.racodesanguino.es; Plaza de las Veletas 4; tapas €2.50, mains €14-20; ☉lunch & dinner Tue-Sat, lunch Sun) Tables and wicker chairs spread beneath the sloping, timber ceiling within, while romantics can head for the candlelit tables outside. Carlos Sanguino has created a traditional *extremeño* menu with the focus on locally produced ingredients of quality.

Drinking

Just beyond the walls on the southern side of the Ciudad Monumental, around Calles Pizarro and Luis Sergios Sánchez, is a zone of popular nocturnal hang-outs, staying open until around 3am. The new part of the city also offers plenty of action, including several clubs, in an area known as La Madrila on and around Calle Doctor Fleming.

El Corral de las Cigüeñas
CAFE

(www.elcorralcc.com; Cuesta de Aldana 6; ☉8am-1pm Mon & Tue, 8am-1pm & 6pm-3am Wed-Fri, 10am-3am Sat, 5pm-1am Sun) The secluded courtyard with its lofty palm trees and ivy-covered walls just inside the Ciudad Monumental is the perfect spot for a quiet drink in relaxing surroundings and also does worthwhile breakfasts (€2.20 to €3.40). It has snacks at other times and sometimes live music in the evenings.

La Traviata
BAR

(Calle de Luis Sergios Sánchez 8) Has floral wallpaper, original tiles, arches and a terrace.

Babel Café-Bar
CAFE, BAR

(Calle de Luis Sergios Sánchez 7) Does coffees, cocktails, art exhibitions and film screenings depending on the day and the hour.

Shopping

Plenty of places around town sell *extremeño* cheeses (especially the strong, creamy Torta del Casar), cured meats and other foods.

Information

Main tourist office (www.turismoextremadura.com; Plaza Mayor 3; ☉8.30am-2.30pm & 4-6pm or 5-7pm Mon-Fri, 10am-2pm Sat & Sun) At the entrance to the Ciudad Monumental. Opens later in the afternoon in summer.

Municipal tourist office (☎927 24 71 72; http://turismo.ayto-caceres.es; Calle de los Olmos 11; ☉10am-2pm & 4.30-7.30pm)

Getting There & Away

The **bus station** (☎927 23 25 50; www.estacionautobuses.es; Calle Túnez 1) has services to Madrid (€24 to €33, 3¾ hours, seven daily), Trujillo (€4.37, 40 minutes, eight daily), Plasencia (€4.30, 50 minutes, up to five daily) and Mérida (€5.60, one hour, two to five daily).

Up to five trains per day run to/from Madrid (€27, four hours), Plasencia (€5, 1¼ hours) and Mérida (€6.05, one hour).

ℹ Getting Around

Bus L1 from outside the train station – close to the bus station – heads to central Plaza Obispo Galarza.

Valencia de Alcántara

POP 6130

This pretty town is 7km from the Portuguese frontier and its well-preserved old centre is a curious labyrinth of whitewashed houses and mansions. One side of the Old Town is watched over by the ruins of a medieval castle and the 17th-century Iglesia de Rocamador.

The surrounding countryside is known for its cork industry as well as for around 50 ancient dolmens (stone circles of prehistoric monoliths).

Two buses run Monday to Friday from Cáceres (€5.20, 1½ hours).

Alcántara

POP 1630

Alcántara is Arabic for 'the Bridge', and sure enough, below this remote Extremaduran town, a magnificent Roman bridge (204m long, 61m high and much reinforced over the centuries) spans the Río Tajo below a huge dam retaining the Embalse de Alcántara. An inscription above a small Roman temple honours the original architect. From the bridge, a beautiful 20km circuit follows the river then loops up into the hills via a village and a prehistoric menhir. Spot rare birds of prey and black storks along the way.

The town retains old walls, a ruined castle, several imposing mansions and the enormous Renaissance Convento de San Benito (www.fundacionsanbenito.com; Calle Trajano; admission by free hourly guided visit; ⊙10.30am-1.30pm & 5-7pm Wed-Sat, 10.30am-1.30pm Sun). This was built in the 16th century to house the Orden de Alcántara, an order of Reconquista knights, part-monks part-soldiers, who ruled much of western Extremadura as a kind of private fiefdom. The highlights of the down-at-heel monastery include the Gothic cloister and the perfectly proportioned three-tier loggia.

Located just outside town, the Hospedería Conventual de Alcántara (☏927 39 06 38; www.hospederiasdeextremadura.es; Carretera del Poblado Iberdrola; r €70-120; P ❋ @ ⚲ ☀) is a very comfortable and stylish modern hotel that enjoys a marvellous setting in an old monastery.

Four buses run Monday to Friday to/from Cáceres (€5.30, 1½ hours).

Trujillo

POP 9690

Wander into the Plaza Mayor and you could be forgiven for thinking that you have stumbled onto the filmset of a historical blockbuster. The square is surrounded by baroque and Renaissance stone buildings topped with a skyline of towers, turrets, cupolas, crenellations and nesting storks. Beyond, the illusion continues with a labyrinth of mansions, leafy courtyards, fruit gardens, churches and convents. Trujillo truly is one of the most captivating small towns in Spain.

Hometown of many prominent conquistadors, Trujillo came into its own only after the colonisation of the Americas. Then, Francisco Pizarro and his cronies enriched their birthplace with a grand plaza and series of impressive Renaissance palaces that make the town what it is today.

◉ Sights

Plaza Mayor   SQUARE

Trujillo's main square is one of Spain's most spectacular plazas, with a large equestrian statue of the conquistador Francisco Pizarro, by American Charles Rumsey, looking down on it. Apparently, Rumsey originally sculpted it as a statue of Hernán Cortés to present to Mexico, but Mexico, which takes a dim view of Cortés, declined it, so it was given to Trujillo as Pizarro instead.

ℹ TICKETS, TOURS & TIMES

The Trujillo tourist office sells **combined tickets** (€4.70 or €5.30), which include a comprehensive guidebook (some English text at the back) and cover entry to four or five monuments, including the castle, interpretation centre and Iglesia de Santiago. It's €7.95 if you want to join one of the two-hour **guided tours** (in Spanish); they leave from the tourist office daily at 11am and 5pm and include eight monuments.

In summer, sights stay open longer in the afternoons (from 5pm to 8.30pm).

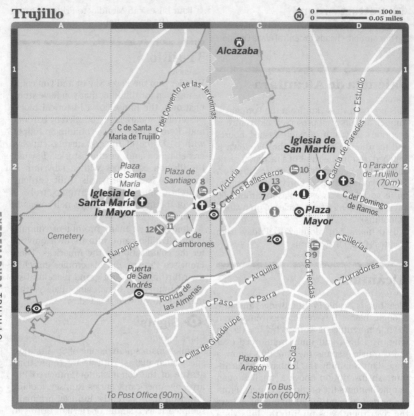

Trujillo

On the south side of the plaza, carved images of Pizarro and his lover Inés Yupanqui (sister of the Inca emperor Atahualpa) decorate the corner of the 16th-century **Palacio de la Conquista**. To the right is their daughter Francisca Pizarro Yupanqui with her husband (and uncle), Hernando Pizarro. The mansion was built in the 1560s for Hernando and Francisca after Hernando – the only Pizarro brother not to die a bloody death in Peru – emerged from 20 years in jail for murder.

Iglesia de San Martín CHURCH
(adult/child €1.40/free; ⊙10am-2pm & 4-7pm) Overlooking the Plaza Mayor is the 16th-century Iglesia de San Martín, with delicate Gothic ceiling tracing in its single nave, stunning stained-glass windows and a grand 18th-century organ (climb up to the choir loft for the best view).

Palacio de los Duques de San Carlos CONVENT, MANSION
(admission €1.40; ⊙9.30am-1pm & 4.30-6.30pm Mon-Sat, 10am-12.30pm Sun) On a corner of the Plaza Mayor rears the solid presence of the 16th-century Palacio de los Duques de San Carlos, nowadays a convent for the Jerónimo order, but open for visits and for selling its homemade biscuits. Its treasures are the sober classical patio and a grand granite staircase crowned with a painting of the family crest: a two-headed eagle. The distinctive brick chimneys were built in Mudéjar style.

Iglesia de Santa María la Mayor CHURCH
(adult/child €1.40/free; ⊙10am-2pm & 4-7pm) This 13th-century church has a mainly Gothic nave and a Romanesque tower that you can ascend for fabulous views. It also has tombs of leading Trujillo families from the Middle Ages, including that of Diego García de Paredes (1466–1530), a warrior of legendary strength who, according to Cervantes, could stop a mill wheel with one finger. The church's magnificent altarpiece includes 25 brilliantly coloured 15th-century paintings in the Flemish style, depicting scenes from the lives of Mary and Christ.

Alcazaba CASTLE
(adult/child €1.40/free; ⊙10.30am-2pm & 4.30-7pm) At the top of the hill, Trujillo's castle of 10th-century Islamic origin (evident by the horseshoe arch just inside the main entrance), later strengthened by the Christians, is impressive although bare. Patrol the battlements for magnificent sweeping views. One tower contains the hermitage of Our Lady of the Victory, Trujillo's patron. Stick a 50-cent coin in a slot to see her spin around in her alcove.

Torre del Alfiler TOWER, INTERPRETATION CENTRE
(Calle de los Ballesteros; admission €1.40; ⊙10am-2pm & 4.30-7.30pm) Once part of the defensive walls guarding the fortress, this tower later became a fortified aristocratic dwelling. It holds an interpretative display about Trujillo and Extremadura history, and offers fine views over the Plaza Mayor.

Iglesia de Santiago CHURCH
(adult/child €1.40/free; ⊙10.30am-2pm & 4.30-7.30pm) Coming up from the Plaza Mayor, you pass through the **Puerta de Santiago**. To its right is the Iglesia de Santiago, the oldest church in Trujillo, founded in the 13th century by the Knights of Santiago (look for their scallop-shell emblem). It's studded with coats of arms and has a fine 14th-century altarpiece and the locally revered sculpture of Cristo de las Aguas. Check out the recreated sacristan's room, and the permanent Nativity scene in the choir.

City Walls WALLS
The 900m of walls circling the upper town date from Muslim times. The western end is marked by the **Puerta del Triunfo** (Gate of Triumph), through which it is said conquering Christian troops marched in 1232, when they wrested the city from the Muslims.

⚔️ Festivals & Events

Fiestas de Trujillo LOCAL FIESTA
The town's annual Fiestas de Trujillo, with music, theatre and plenty of partying, are spread over a few days around the first Saturday in September.

🛏️ Sleeping

⧉ Posada dos Orillas HISTORIC HOTEL €€
(☑927 65 90 79; www.dosorillas.com; Calle de Cambrones 6; d Sun-Thu €70-90, Fri & Sat €80-107; ❄🛰) This tastefully renovated 16th-century mansion is in a great location in the walled town. Rooms replicate Spanish colonial taste and are named for the countries in which towns called Trujillo are found. Personal service from the owners is excellent here, and there are sharp off-season prices that make it the best deal in town.

El Mirador de las Monjas HOTEL €€
(☑927 65 92 23; www.elmiradordelasmonjas.com; Plaza de Santiago 2; s/d incl breakfast Mon-Thu €50/60, Fri-Sun €60/70; ❄) High in the old town, this six-room *hostería* attached to a quality restaurant has spotless, light, modern rooms decorated in minimalist style. The upstairs ones with sloping ceilings and pleasant vistas are slightly better than the ones below, but all are great value and feature excellent bathrooms.

EXTREMADURA & THE AMERICAS

Extremeños jumped at the opportunities opened up by Columbus' discovery of the Americas in 1492.

In 1501 Fray Nicolás de Ovando from Cáceres was named governor of all the Indies. He moved the Hispaniola town of Santo Domingo to a new location and made it his capital. With him went 2500 followers, many of them from Extremadura, including Francisco Pizarro, illegitimate son of a minor noble family from Trujillo. In 1504 Hernán Cortés, from a similar family in Medellín, arrived in Santo Domingo.

Both young men prospered. Cortés took part in the conquest of Cuba in 1511 and settled there. Pizarro, in 1513, accompanied Vasco Núñez de Balboa (from Jerez de los Caballeros) to Darién (Panama), where they 'discovered' the Pacific Ocean. In 1519 Cortés led a small expedition to what's now Mexico, rumoured to be full of gold and silver. By 1524, with combined fortitude, cunning, luck and ruthlessness, Cortés and his band had subdued the Aztec empire.

Pizarro returned to Spain and, before returning to the New World, visited Trujillo, where he received a hero's welcome and collected his four half-brothers, as well as other relatives and friends. Their expedition set off from present-day Panama in 1531, with just 180 men and 37 horses, and managed to capture the Inca emperor Atahualpa, despite the 30,000-strong Inca army. Pizarro demanded an enormous ransom, which was paid, but Trujillo's finest went ahead and executed Atahualpa anyway. The Inca empire, with its capital in Cuzco and extending from present-day Colombia to Chile, soon fell to a backdrop of casual brutality, broken alliances, cynical realpolitik and civil war between Pizarro and his longtime ally, Diego de Almagro. Pizarro was eventually assassinated by the executed Almagro's son and is buried in the cathedral of Lima, Peru.

About 600 people of Trujillo made their way to the Americas in the 16th century, so it's no surprise that there are several other Trujillo towns in Central and South America. Conquistadors and colonists from all over Spain also took with them the cult of the Virgen de Guadalupe in eastern Extremadura; it remains widespread throughout Latin America.

NH Palacio de Santa Marta   HOTEL €€
(☑927 65 91 90; www.nh-hoteles.es; Calle Ballesteros 6; s/d from €75/90; P✹@🖦🅰) Just above the Plaza Mayor, this hotel occupies a 16th-century palace and combines somewhat anodyne modern chambers with beautiful original features. There's a summer-only pool with views across the rooftops; if you want the prime vistas over the square, upgrade to a deluxe room.

Parador de Trujillo   HISTORIC HOTEL €€€
(☑927 32 13 50; www.parador.es; Calle Santa Beatriz de Silva 1; s/d €135/168; P✹@🅰🅰) No surprise that this *parador* is also a former 16th-century convent; there's an agreeable overdose in this town. Rooms are large with terracotta-tiled floors and understated historical touches. Go for the historical ambience, not the upbeat atmosphere. It's in the winding back streets of the Old Town, east of the Plaza Mayor.

Hostal Nuria   HOSTAL €
(☑927 32 09 07; www.hostal-nuria.com; Plaza Mayor; s/d €30/45, apt €60-90; ✹🅰) Rooms here are modern and comfortable; there are no frills, but the location on Plaza Mayor is hard to beat. You'll spend most of your time looking out the window onto the plaza if you're in rooms 204 or 205. There's a busy downstairs bar-restaurant.

🍴 Eating

Mesón Alberca   TRADITIONAL SPANISH €€
(Calle de Cambrones 8; mains €11-17; ☺Thu-Sun) A pretty ivy-clad terrace or dark-timber tables laid with gingham tablecloths create a choice of warm atmospheres for sampling classic *extremeño* cooking. The specialities here are oven roasts and local cheeses. The regional set menu is excellent value at €24.50.

Restaurante La Troya   TRADITIONAL SPANISH €
(Plaza Mayor 10; menus €15) Famed for its copious servings of no-frills *comida casera* (home-style cooking), Troya enjoys a prime location on the main town square. On entering, you'll be directed to one of several dining areas, to be presented with plates of tortilla and chorizo, followed by a three-course

menú. It's all about quantity, and queues stretch out the door on weekends.

ℹ Information

Tourist office (📞927 32 26 77; www.turis motrujillo.com; Plaza Mayor; ⏰10am-2pm & 4.30-7.30pm)

ℹ Getting There & Away

The **bus station** (📞927 32 12 02; Avenida de Miajadas) is 750m south of Plaza Mayor. There are services to/from Madrid (€17.63 to €29.85, three to 4¼ hours, five daily), Cáceres (€3.34, 40 minutes, eight daily) and Mérida (€8.25, 1½ hours, three daily), among other destinations.

Guadalupe

POP 2060

Centred on its palatial monastery, a treasure-trove of art, architecture and history, this sparkling white village is like a bright jewel set in the green crown of the surrounding ranges and ridges of the Sierra de Villuercas. There are thick woods of chestnut, oak and cork meshed with olive groves and vineyards, offering plenty of good walking options.

👁 Sights

While the monastery is the obvious highlight, take some time to wander the picturesque streets off the Plaza Mayor.

TOP CHOICE Real Monasterio de Santa María de Guadalupe
MONASTERY, CHURCH

(📞927 36 70 00; www.monasterioguadalupe.com; Plaza Santa María de Guadalupe; church admission free, monastery by guided tour adult/child €4/1.50; ⏰church 8.30am-9pm, monastery 9.30am-1pm & 3.30-6.30pm) Guadalupe's renowned **monastery** is located, according to legend, on the spot where a shepherd found an effigy of the Virgin, hidden years earlier by Christians fleeing the Muslims. The church received royal patronage from Alfonso XI and became an Hieronymite monastery in the late 14th century. The figure of the Virgin, a black Madonna made from cedar wood, was so revered in the 16th century that she was made patron of all Spain's New World territories. Columbus was particularly devoted to her and, after his fragile fleet survived a terrible tempest on his first voyage, made a pilgrimage of thanks here shortly after returning. The Virgen de Guadalupe, patron of Extremadura, remains a key figure for many

South American and Filipino Catholics. Now cared for by Franciscan monks, this is still one of Spain's most important pilgrimage sites.

Hurried guided tours of the monastery (in Spanish only, one hour) leave on the half hour. At the complex's centre is a lovely late-14th-century Mudéjar cloister decorated with paintings telling the history of the Virgin and miracles she wrought. There are three **museums** spaced around it. The first, in the former refectory, has richly embroidered vestments and altarcloths from various historical periods. The second has a fine collection of illuminated choral songbooks from the 15th century onwards, while the gallery includes three paintings by El Greco (St Andrew, the Assumption, and St Peter), a sombre late Goya (*Confession in Prison*), a fine *Ecce Homo* by Pedro de Mena, a handful of monks by Francisco de Zurbarán and a beautiful little ivory crucifixion attributed to Michelangelo.

In the majestic **sacristía** (sacristy) hangs a series of superb canvases (1638–47) by Zurbarán. There are some exalted works here, none better than the *Temptation of St Jerome,* the stern ascetic saint seemingly at odds with the elaborate baroque decoration of this chamber. Other paintings portray scenes of past monastery life, symbolising the various monastic virtues. The **Relicario-Tesoro** holds spooky relics of martyr saints and a rather vulgar display of treasure, including a 200,000-pearl cape for the Virgin. The **camarín**, a chamber behind the altarpiece, has an image of the Virgin that is revolved for the faithful to kiss a fragment of her mantle; you can elect to do this when your tour ends.

Inside the **church**, the black Virgin's image occupies the place of honour lit up within the soaring *retablo* (altarpiece), separated from the main body of the nave by a fine plateresque *reja* (grille). The fantastic walnut choir is an 18th-century work with an immense lectern, while the fabulous baroque organs are visited on the tour.

🏃 Activities

The tourist office has several maps describing easy-to-medium circular routes of three to five hours.

Ruta de Isabel la Católica
HIKING

One splendid walking option is to take any Miajadas- or Cáceres-bound bus to the village of **Cañamero**, southwest of Guadalupe, and hike back along a well-signed 15km trail that retraces the steps of pilgrims coming to Guadalupe from the south – including Reyes Católicos (the Catholic Monarchs), Isabel and Fernando, after the fall of Moorish Granada.

Sleeping

TOP CHOICE Hospedería del Real Monasterio
HISTORIC HOTEL €€

(927 36 70 00; www.monasterioguadalupe.com; Plaza Juan Carlos I; s/d €49/71; P ✳ 🛜) Centred on the Real Monasterio's beautiful Gothic cloister, this old-fashioned hotel gives you the chance to live it up in a national monument without paying *parador*-style prices. There's a sumptuous patio just off the lobby and a palpable historical ambience. High-ceilinged rooms are all different: darkish, venerable but comfortable and astonishingly reasonably priced.

Parador de Guadalupe
HISTORIC HOTEL €€€

(927 36 70 75; www.parador.es; Calle Marqués de la Romana 12; s/d €119/148; P ✳ 🛜 ⛶) This place occupies a converted 15th-century hospital and 16th-century religious school opposite the Guadalupe monastery. Spacious rooms are tastefully decorated and the cobbled courtyard is delightful, with its lemon and orange trees surrounded by a cloister-like colonnade with arches.

Cerezo II
HOSTAL €

(927 15 41 77; www.hostalcerezo2meson.com; Plaza Mayor 23; s/d €35/48; ✳) On the main square, Cerezo II has attractive modern rooms, decorated in earthy colours with classy thick quilts.

Eating

Cheap restaurants around the Plaza Mayor offer no-frills Extremadura cooking at low prices. The Parador de Guadalupe has a quality restaurant.

Hospedería del Real Monasterio
SPANISH €€

(927 36 70 00; www.monasterioguadalupe.com; Plaza Juan Carlos I; mains €10-22) Dine grandly under the arches of the magnificent Gothic cloister or in the dining halls, rich with 17th-century timber furnishings and antique ceramics. There's a competent range of both meat and fish dishes, and most of the desserts are rustled up in the kitchen. Set meals are €20 if you are staying.

Information

Tourist office (927 15 41 28; www.turismo extremadura.com; Plaza Mayor; ⏰10am-5pm Wed-Fri, to 2pm Sat & Sun) On the square below the monastery.

Getting There & Away

Buses stop on Avenida Conde de Barcelona near the town hall, a two-minute walk from Plaza Mayor. **Mirat** (927 23 48 63; www.mirat.net) runs two services Monday to Friday (and one on Sunday) to/from Cáceres (€10.80, 2¼ hours) via Trujillo. **Samar** (902 25 70 25; www.samar. es) has one to three daily buses to/from Madrid (€16.83, four hours). Timetables are displayed in the tourist-office window.

NORTHERN EXTREMADURA

The western reaches of the Cordillera Central mountain range arch right around pretty Plasencia from the Sierra de Gredos in the east to the Sierra de Gata in the west. In the region's northeast you'll find three lovely valleys: La Vera, Valle del Jerte and Valle del Ambroz. Watered by mountain streams and dotted with ancient villages, the valleys offer fine walking routes and accommodation.

Plasencia

POP 41,450

This pleasant, bustling town is the natural hub of northern Extremadura. Rising above a bend of the Río Jerte, it retains long sections of its defensive walls. It has an earthy and attractive old quarter of narrow streets, Romanesque churches and stately stone palaces, many emblazoned with noble coats of arms.

Sights

Catedral
CATHEDRAL

(Plaza de la Catedral; Catedral Nueva admission free, Catedral Vieja €1.50; ⏰9am-1pm & 5-7pm Mon-Sat, 9am-1pm Sun) Plasencia's cathedral is actually two-in-one. The 16th-century Catedral Nueva is a Gothic-Renaissance blend with a handsome plateresque facade, soaring *retablo* (altarpiece) and intricately carved choir stalls. Within the Romanesque Catedral Vieja are classic 13th-century cloisters surrounding a trickling fountain and lemon trees. Also on view is the soaring octagonal Capilla de San Pablo with a dramatic 1569 Caravaggio painting of John the Baptist.

Plaza Mayor SQUARE
In Plasencia life flows through the lively, arcaded Plaza Mayor, meeting place of 10 streets and scene of a Tuesday farmers' market since the 12th century. The jaunty fellow striking the hour atop the Gothic **town hall** is El Abuelo Mayorga, unofficial symbol of the town.

FREE **Centro de Interpretación**
Torre Lucía WALLS, INTERPRETATION CENTRE
(Calle Torre Lucía; ☉10am-2pm & 5-7pm Tue-Sat) The best-preserved defensive tower of the old city wall, located at the top of the old town, tells the history of medieval Plasencia through video, models and artefacts, and provides access to a walkable chunk of the wall.

⨳ Sleeping

Parador de Plasencia HISTORIC HOTEL €€€
(☎927 42 58 70; www.parador.es; Plaza San Vicente Ferrer; s/d €142/177; P❄☎) This *parador* is a classic – still oozing the atmosphere and austerity of its 15th-century convent roots, with massive stone columns, soaring ceilings and a traditional Renaissance cloister. The rooms are far from monastic, being luxuriously furnished with rugs and rich fabrics.

Palacio Carvajal Girón HOTEL €€
(☎927 42 63 26; www.palaciocarvajalgiron.com; Plaza Ansano 1; r €100-130; P❄☎❄) A mightily impressive conversion job on a formerly ruined palace in the heart of the old town has resulted in this chic Plasencia address. Rooms have modern fittings with crisp white linen juxtaposed with original features of the building – a most successful combination. There's both an indoor and outdoor pool, and very attractive public areas.

Hotel Rincón Extremeño HOTEL €
(☎927 41 11 50; www.hotelrincon.com; Calle Vidrieras 6; s/d €35/45; ❄☎) This friendly and unpretentious hotel on a narrow street just off Plaza Mayor has a great location and clean, if unmemorable, rooms above a popular local restaurant. This is the heart of Plasencia's eating zone, with many good choices within a few minutes' walk.

✕ Eating

At lunchtime and sunset, the bars and terraces surrounding Plaza Mayor fill up with eager punters downing the local red, *pitarra*, and munching complimentary *pinchos*

(tapas). Narrow Calle Vidrieras running off it has lots of bars and restaurants also worth investigating.

TOP CHOICE **Casa Juan** SPANISH €€
(☎927 42 40 42; www.restaurantecasajuan.com; Calle Arenillas 5; mains €13-15; ☉Fri-Wed) Tucked down a quiet lane, French-owned Casa Juan does well-prepared *extremeño* meat dishes, such as shoulder of lamb and suckling pig. Try the homemade melt-in-the-mouth foie gras or the expertly hung local *retinto* beef. Fairly priced wines from all around Spain seal the deal.

ⓘ Information

Municipal tourist office (☎927 42 38 43; www.plasencia.es; Calle Santa Clara 4; ☉9am-2pm & 4-/pm Mon-Fri, 10am-2pm & 4-7pm Sat & Sun)
Regional tourist office (☎927 01 78 40; www.turismoextremadura.com; Calle Torre Lucía; ☉9am-2pm & 4-6pm Mon-Fri, 10am-2pm Sat & Sun) Open mornings only in high summer.

ⓘ Getting There & Away

The **bus station** (☎927 41 45 50; Calle de Tornavacas 2) is east of Plaza Mayor. The train station is off the Cáceres road, about 1km southwest of town.

Up to five buses daily run to/from Cáceres (€4.30, 50 minutes), Madrid (€17.22, 3½ hours) and Salamanca (€8.91, two hours). Others serve smaller destinations around northern Extremadura.

Trains depart three to four times daily from Plasencia to Madrid (€22.05, three hours), Cáceres (€5, one hour) and Mérida (€11.35, 2½ hours).

La Vera

Surrounded by mountains often still capped with snow as late as May, the fertile La Vera region produces raspberries, asparagus and, above all, *pimentón* (paprika), sold in charming old-fashioned tins and with a distinctive smoky flavour. Typical, too, are half-timbered houses leaning at odd angles, their overhanging upper storeys supported by timber or stone pillars.

⊙ Sights & Activities

Monasterio de Yuste MONASTERY
(www.patrimonionacional.es; Cuacos de Yuste; adult/child €9/4; ☉10am-8pm Apr-Sep, 10am-6pm Oct-Mar) In a lovely setting 2km above the

village of Cuacos de Yuste, this monastery is where Carlos I of Spain (also known as Carlos V of Austria) came in 1557 to prepare for death after abdicating his emperorship over much of Western and Central Europe. If you have an interest in Spanish history, it's fascinating to see the royal apartments, including the bedroom where he died in September 1558. A doorway allowed this religious monarch to see, from his deathbed, the Hieronymite monks giving mass in the single-naved church alongside. Carlos was buried behind the high altar, but his son Felipe (Philip) II later had him moved to El Escorial. Two cloisters and a collection of religious art (as well as copies of Titians that Carlos brought with him) are other features. There are good information panels in English, and a detailed audioguide (€6). It may be a working monastery once again by the time you visit, as a community of Polish monks was due to move here. Free for EU citizens the last three hours on Wednesdays and Thursdays.

Walking
HIKING

There are many marked trails winding between various villages in La Vera. One of them is the 10km section of the **Ruta del Emperador**, which leads from Jarandilla to the Yuste monastery.

🛌 Sleeping & Eating

Most villages have well-signposted camping grounds and *casas rurales* with rooms to let. Local dishes include *cabrito a la caldereta* (stewed kid) and *migas* (breadcrumbs fried with garlic, peppers and pork).

TOP CHOICE Haldón Country
RURAL HOTEL €€

(☎927 57 10 04; www.hotelhaldoncountry.com; Finca El Haldón, Robledillo de la Vera; s/d incl breakfast €84/135; P❋☎☲) This exquisite rural hotel, just off the main road between Jarandilla and Villanueva, is a haven of peace and relaxation. Set in extensive grounds, it has airy, light modern rooms decorated with original art and balanced by the heavier elegance of the library and billiard room. The atrium holds a heated pool, there's a small spa, and the welcome from the hosts is genuine. Substantially cheaper midweek.

Parador de Jarandilla
HISTORIC HOTEL €€€

(☎927 56 01 17; www.parador.es; Avenida de García Prieto 1, Jarandilla de la Vera; s/d €135/168; P❋☎☲) Be king of the castle for the night at this 15th-century castle-turned-hotel.

Carlos I stayed here for a few months while waiting for his monastery digs to be completed. Within the stout walls and turrets are period-furnished rooms, plus a classic courtyard where you can dine royally from the restaurant menu.

La Casa de Pasarón
CASA RURAL €€

(☎927 46 94 07; www.pasaron.com; Calle de la Magdalena 18, Pasarón de la Vera; s/d €60/85; P❋☎) Follow the signs to this handsome family house, where the ground floor dates from 1890. Rooms are bathed in light with terracotta tiles and lashings of white linen and paintwork. Pretty attic rooms with sloping ceilings cost a little more. The restaurant is excellent, but only opens if there are enough people.

La Vera de Yuste
CASA RURAL €

(☎927 17 22 89; www.laveradeyuste.com; Calle Teodoro Perianes 17, Cuacos de Yuste; s/d €40/60; ❋) This real gem is set in two typical 18th-century village houses near the Plaza Mayor. The beamed rooms have chunky rustic furniture and the garden is a delight, surrounded by rose bushes with a small courtyard and vegetable patch. Dinner available.

Casa Rural Parada Real
CASA RURAL €

(☎927 17 96 05; www.paradareal.com; Calle Chorrillo 28, Garganta La Olla; s/d €40/50; ❋☎) Painted a fetching dark pink, this attractive *casa rural* is in a lovely location for strolling, at the top of the main street, and has wrought-iron balconies and bright no-fuss rooms. There's a fine downstairs restaurant (mains €10 to €16).

Camping Jaranda
CAMPGROUND €

(☎927 56 04 54; www.campingjaranda.es; sites per adult/tent/car €4.45/4.60/4.60; ⊙mid-Mar–mid-Sep; P☲) Located beside a gurgling brook, 1.25km west of Jarandilla, Camping Jaranda provides sketch maps for local walks. There's a terraced cafe, plenty of shade and bungalows and cabins (€66 to €109). You can rent tents here.

TOP CHOICE La Finca
SPANISH €€

(☎927 66 51 50; www.villaxarahiz.com; Ctra 203, Km 32.8, Jaraíz de la Vera; mains €15-24; ⊙Tue-Sun; ☎) Offering spectacular sierra views from the terrace and the upmarket dining room, this hotel restaurant just below Jaraíz is one of La Vera's best bets for smart regional food, featuring local peppers and other quality Extremadura produce. There's also a bar with an amazing array of gin-and-tonic choices.

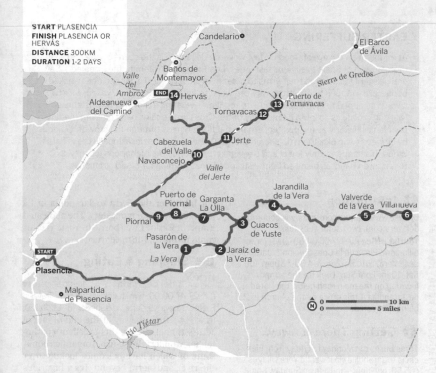

Driving Tour
La Vera & Valle del Jerte

❯ These adjacent rural areas are famous for *pimentón* (paprika) and cherries respectively; both have lovely traditional architecture dignifying the string of villages perched on their hillsides. There are plenty of good accommodation options if you'd like to break the journey overnight; see opposite.

Head out from Plasencia into La Vera, stopping in prettily situated **1 Pasarón** with its fine 16th-century palace of the Condes de Osorno. Next is **2 Jaraíz**, the *pimentón* HQ.

Tracking northeast, **3 Cuacos de Yuste** is rich in typical half-timbered houses and lovely plazas. Beyond, **4 Jarandilla**, famous as a tobacco town, is one of the most appealing stops. The castle-like church, built by the Templars, has an ancient font from the Holy Land.

Next, explore **5 Valverde** – home of the Easter ritual of Los Empalaos – whose lovely Plaza de España is lined with timber balconies, and **6 Villanueva**. Double back to **7 Garganta La Olla**, a steeply pitched village with overhanging balconies and centuries-old inscriptions above the doors.

It's uphill from here on the spectacular drive over the **8 Puerto de Piornal** pass, heading down the other side into the Valle del Jerte. **9 Piornal's** high altitude makes it a good base for sierra walking and enables perfect curing of its famous ham.

Turn right onto the valley's main road. **10 Cabezuela del Valle** has fine houses with wooden balconies on and around its Plaza de Extremadura. The valley's main town and cherry centre is **11 Jerte**, with atmospheric tunnel-like streets and a pretty plaza. There's good hiking around here.

Head on up the valley to the huddled old quarter of **12 Tornavacas**, trailhead for the Ruta del Emperador that crosses back to La Vera.

Beyond Tornavacas, climb steeply for 6km to the **13 Puerto de Tornavacas** pass to the Sierra de Gredos in Ávila province. Otherwise, head back down the valley to Plasencia, or take the steep winding side-road between Jerte and Cabezuela over a dramatic pass to **14 Hervás** in the Valle del Ambroz.

EASTER SUFFERING

At midnight on the eve of Good Friday, Valverde de la Vera is the scene of one of the more bizarre of Spain's religious festivities, **Los Empalaos** (literally 'the Impaled'). Several penitent locals strap their arms to a beam (from a plough) while their near-naked bodies are wrapped tight with cords from waist to fingertips. Barefoot, veiled, with two swords strapped to their backs and – to top it all – wearing a crown of thorns, these 'walking crucifixes' follow a painful Way of the Cross. Iron chains hanging from the timber clank sinisterly as the penitents make painful progress through the crowds. Guided by *cirineos* (who pick them up should they fall), the *empalaos* occasionally cross paths. When this happens, they kneel and rise again to continue their laborious journey. Doctors stay on hand, as being so tightly strapped does nothing for blood circulation.

❶ Information

Browse www.aturive.com and www.comarca delavera.com, two useful websites.

Tourist office (☏927 56 04 60; www.jaran dilla.com; Plaza de la Constitución 1, Jarandilla de la Vera; ☺10am-2pm & 4.30-7.30pm Tue-Sat, 10am-2pm Sun) Look for the temporary location on the main road below the Parador de Jarandilla if this office by the church is still being renovated.

❶ Getting There & Away

Three buses run Monday to Friday from Plasencia to Jarandilla via lower La Vera villages (€5.50, one hour), and one on Sunday. Some continue further up the valley.

Valle del Jerte

This valley, separated from La Vera by the Sierra de Tormantos, grows half of Spain's cherries and is a sea of white blossom in early spring. Visit in May and every second house is busy boxing the ripe fruit.

◉ Sights & Activities

A route from La Vera through the valley is a great option for a driving tour (see p793).

Walking Routes   HIKING

There are excellent walks for all levels in the Valle del Jerte, some along the pretty gorge, Garganta de los Infiernos. The main trailhead is at the Centro de Interpretación de la Naturaleza (☏927 01 49 36; ☺9am-2pm & 4-6pm) 2.5km from central Jerte; it has a nature exhibition and route information, including the easy stroll to the natural pools of Los Pilones (two hours return from Jerte itself). From Los Pilones, you can head on to Cabezuela (four hours). Further up the valley, Tornavacas is the launchpad for the seven- to nine-hour, 28km Ruta del Empera-

dor hike over the sierra to Jarandilla in La Vera via the Yuste monastery. The abdicated Emperor Carlos I was borne to Yuste via this route in the mid-16th century.

⬛ Sleeping & Eating

Túnel del Hada   BOUTIQUE HOTEL €€
TOP CHOICE
(☏927 47 00 00; www.tuneldelhada.com; Travesía Fuente Nueva 2, Jerte; d/superior d €128/160; P❄⬛⬛) Tucked away at the end of one of Jerte's tunnel streets, this excellent spa hotel has wonderfully stylish, romantic rooms, some of which have balconies looking over the river and sierra beyond. It's a luxurious but friendly place, with an upmarket restaurant and supercomfortable beds. You can nearly always get a better deal than the official rates we list here.

El Cerezal de los Sotos   CASA RURAL €€
(☏927 47 04 29; www.elcerezaldelossotos.net; Calle de las Vegas, Jerte; d incl breakfast €86; P❄⬛⬛) The valley is known for *casas rurales* like this one. It is a quiet, homey stone house dating from 1890, with beams, an open fireplace and spacious attractive rooms set amid cherry orchards and sweeping lawns above the river. Follow the signs over the bridge from Jerte. Dinner available (€19).

Antigua Posada   CASA RURAL €
(☏927 17 70 19; www.antiguaposada.com; Calle Real de Abajo 32, Tornavacas; s/d incl breakfast €40/58; ⬛) Occupying a lovely old 18th-century dwelling in the heart of Tornavacas, this exceptionally welcoming house offers great value for well-kept rooms, a home-from-home feel and great sightseeing and walking advice on the surrounding area.

Camping Río Jerte   CAMPGROUND €
(☏927 17 30 06; www.campingriojerte.com; sites per adult/tent/car €5.10/5.10/5.10, 4-6 person

bungalows €88-110; P⊛) Located 1.5km southwest of Navaconcejo, facilities include a volleyball court. To cool off, choose from the adjacent natural riverside pool or a standard artificial one.

Valle del Jerte SPANISH €€

(☑927 47 04 48; www.donbellota.com; Gargantilla 16, Jerte; mains €13-19; ⊗lunch & dinner Tue-Sat, lunch Sun) This warmly decorated restaurant near the main plaza serves local specialities such as trout and *cabrito* (kid). Service is on the fussy side, but the excellent wine selection and delicious desserts make up for it.

ℹ Information

Jerte tourist office (☑927 47 04 53; www. turismovalledeljerte.com; Avenida Ramón y Cajal, Jerte; ⊗10am-2pm & 5-8pm Mon, Tue & Thu-Sat, 10.30am 1.30pm Sun) Located on the main road.

ℹ Getting There & Away

One to four buses daily from Plasencia serve Jerte and other valley towns, some going on to Madrid.

Valle del Ambroz

This broader valley west of the Valle del Jerte is split by the Vía de la Plata and the A66 motorway.

HERVÁS
POP 1200

Hervás is a lively and handsome town with a picturesque old quarter. It makes a great base for exploring the area.

◉ Sights

Hervás has Extremadura's best surviving barrio judío (Jewish quarter); it thrived until the tragic 1492 expulsion of the Jews, when most families fled to Portugal. Seek out Calles Rabilero and Cuestecilla, then, for a fine view, climb up to the Iglesia de Santa María, on the site of a ruined Templar castle.

Museo Pérez Comendador-Leroux GALLERY

(☑927 48 16 55; Calle Asensio Neila; admission €1.20; ⊗4-8pm Tue, 11am-2pm & 4-8pm Wed-Fri, 10.30am-2pm Sat & Sun) Within an impressive 18th-century mansion, the Museo Pérez Comendador-Leroux houses works by Hervás-born 20th-century sculptor Enrique Pérez Comendador and his wife, the French painter Magdalena Leroux. Entry is free on Sundays.

Museo de la Moto Clásica MUSEUM

(www.museomotoclasica.com; Carretera de la Garganta; adult/child €10/free; ⊗10.30am-1.30pm & 4-7pm Mon-Fri, 10.30am-7.30pm Sat & Sun) Set in distinctive conical-roofed buildings 200m north of the river, this museum offers great views, a fabulous collection of more than 300 classic motorcycles, as well as cars and horse-drawn carriages.

⊨ Sleeping & Eating

There are several excellent places to eat scattered through the Old Town.

TOP CHOICE **El Jardín del Convento** HOTEL €€

(☑927 48 11 61; www.eljardindelconvento.com; Plaza del Convento 22; r €65-100, cottage €110; ⊛⊚) On the edge of the Jewish quarter, with a fabulous garden, all roses, vegetables and tranquil seating space that makes for very rural relaxation, this is a wonderful place to stay. The rooms are all different and full of character, with wooden floors, exposed stone walls and period furniture. There's also a small

EXTREMADURA VALLE DEL AMBROZ

VÍA DE LA PLATA

The name of this ancient highway (aka Ruta de la Plata) probably derives not from the word for 'silver', but the Arabic *bilath*, meaning tiled or paved. But it was the Romans in the 1st century who laid this artery that originally linked Mérida with Astorga and was later extended to the Asturian coast. Along its length moved goods, troops, travellers and traders. Later, it served as a pilgrim route for the faithful walking from Andalucía to Santiago de Compostela. Neglected and virtually abandoned until a few decades ago, it's now justifiably promoted. From Seville, it's a 1000km walk or cycle to Santiago or a similar distance to Gijón. Entering Extremadura south of Zafra, the well-marked route passes through Mérida, Cáceres and Plasencia, then heads for Salamanca in Castilla y León. Parts of the original road remain, supplemented by newer sections. It's closely paralleled by the A66 motorway. Take a look at www.rutadelaplata.com or pick up the guide (€3) from tourist offices on the route.

bungalow, a fabulous breakfast room and up-stairs terrace, and excellent hospitality.

Albergue de la Vía de la Plata   HOSTEL €

(☎927 47 34 70; www.alberguesviaplata.es; Paseo de la Estación; dm incl breakfast €20; P@⊕) Owner Carlos runs this delightful hostel with warmth and enthusiasm. The setting is an evocative converted train station over-looking the disused tracks. Rooms and the communal areas are brightly furnished and there's a bar and kitchen.

La Tapería del Convento   TAPAS €

(www.lataperiadelconvento.es; Calle Convento 45; raciones €5-10; ⊙Thu-Tue) This small bar is a great destination for no-frills, but extremely tasty, dishes at low prices and in huge quantities. You get a decent free tapa with your glass of wine too. Local cheeses feature heavily and are also available for sale.

❶ Information

Tourist office (☎927 47 36 18; www.valleam broz.com; Calle Braulio Navas 6; ⊙10am-2pm & 4.30-7.30pm Tue-Fri, 10am-2pm Sat & Sun)

❶ Getting There & Away

One to four buses a day run between Cáceres, Plasencia and Salamanca via the Valle del Ambroz, calling by Hervás (€2.61 from Plasencia).

GRANADILLA

About 25km west of Hervás, the ghost village of Granadilla (admission free; ⊙10am-1pm & 4-8pm Tue-Sun Apr-Oct, to 6pm Nov-Mar) is a beguiling reminder of how Extremadura's villages must have looked before the rush to modernisation. Founded by the Moors in the 10th century but abandoned in the 1960s when the nearby dam was built, the village's traditional architecture has been painstakingly restored as part of a government educational project.

You enter the village through the narrow Puerta de Villa, overlooked by the sturdy castle. From here, the cobblestone Calle Mayor climbs up to the delightfully rustic Plaza Mayor. Some buildings function as craft workshops or exhibition centres in summer; make sure also to walk your way along the top of the Almohad walls, with evocative views of village, lake and pinewoods.

Coria

POP 13,050

This pretty, small market town lies south of the Sierra de Gata and is a good gateway to it. Massive and largely intact protective walls, marked by four gates, enclose the historic quarter of town. The Romans called the place Caurium; after a period of decay, its splendour was revived under the Moors, when it was briefly the capital of a small Islamic state.

◉ Sights & Activities

FREE **Catedral**   CATHEDRAL

(Plaza de la Catedral; museum admission €2; ⊙10.30am-2pm & 4.30-7pm Mon-Sat, 9.30am-2pm Sun) The primarily Gothic cathedral has intricate plateresque decoration around its north portal. It occupies a well-used sacred site: there was a Visigothic cathedral here, then the main mosque, then a Romanesque cathedral before this one was built. The interior highlight is a high sober gold altarpiece; around the cloister is a small ecclesiastical museum. On the plain below is a fine stone bridge, abandoned in the 17th century by Río Alagón, which now takes a more southerly course.

FREE **Museo de la Cárcel Real**   MUSEUM

(Calle de las Monjas 2; ⊙10.30am-2pm & 5.30-8.30pm) Once the town prison, this building houses Coria's tiny two-storey archaeological museum. Step inside the dark, poky celda del castigo (punishment cell), then see how the cushy 1st-floor cells differed from the plebs' prison below.

Convento de la Madre de Dios   CONVENT

(Calle de las Monjas; admission €1.50; ⊙10am-12.15pm & 4-6.15pm) The Convento de la Madre de Dios is a thriving 15th-century convent with an elegant cloister. The sisters sell a variety of delicious homemade sweets and pastries.

🛏 Sleeping & Eating

Palacio Coria   HOTEL €€

(☎927 50 64 49; www.hotelpalaciocoria.es; Plaza de la Catedral; s/d incl breakfast €70/86; P❄🛜) In a 17th-century former bishop's palace next to the cathedral, this sumptuous accommodation successfully couples modern comfort and convenience with heady palatial surrounds. There are excellent weekend deals.

El Bobo de Coria   SPANISH €€

(Calle de las Monjas 6; mains €10-14; ⊙Tue-Sun) Particularly strong on local mushrooms in season, 'the Idiot of Coria' (named after a

Velázquez painting), with its eclectically rustic decor, is also rich in traditional Extremadura dishes.

ℹ️ Information

Tourist office (☏927 50 13 51; http://turismo .coria.org; Avenida de Extremadura 39; ⊙9.30am-2pm & 5-7pm Mon-Fri, 10am-2pm Sat & Sun)

ℹ️ Getting There & Away

The **bus station** (☏927 50 01 10; Calle de Chile) is in the new part of town. Buses run to/from Plasencia (€5.60, 50 minutes, four Monday to Friday, one Sunday) and Cáceres (€7.50, 3½ hours, three to four Monday to Friday and one Sunday).

Parque Nacional de Monfragüe

Spain's 14th and newest national park is a hilly paradise for birdwatchers. Straddling the Tajo valley, it's home to spectacular colonies of raptors and more than 75% of Spain's protected species. Among some 175 feathered varieties are around 300 pairs of black vultures (the largest concentration of Europe's biggest bird of prey) and populations of two other rare large birds: the Spanish imperial eagle and the black stork. The best time to visit is between March and October, since many bird species winter in Africa.

Signed walking trails, both loops and point-to-point hikes, criss-cross the park. The best base is the pretty hamlet of Villareal de San Carlos, from where most trails leave. The EX208 road also traverses the park and you can drive to several of the hides and lookout points. The hilltop Castillo de Monfragüe, a ruined 9th-century Islamic fort, has sweeping views; the castle can also be reached via an attractive 1½-hour walk from Villareal. Arguably the best spot is the Mirador del Salto del Gitano, a lookout point along the main road. From

EXTREMADURA PARQUE NACIONAL DE MONFRAGÜE

> **WORTH A TRIP**
>
> ## SIERRA DE GATA & LAS HURDES
>
> The adjoining Sierra de Gata and Las Hurdes hillscapes form one of Spain's most remote corners, with country villages making traditional products, and a good smattering of *casas rurales* for a relaxing rural getaway.
>
> From Coria, gateway to the Sierra de Gata, head northwest on EX109 to Hoyos, which has some impressive mansions. The solid sandstone mass of its 16th-century Iglesia de Nuestra Señora del Buen Varón is surrounded on three sides by wide plazas and balconies bright with cascading flowers.
>
> Northwest of here is the sierra's most delightful village, San Martín de Trevejo, with traditional houses overlooking cobblestoned lanes. In Valverde del Fresno a great small hotel, A Velha Fábrica (☏927 51 19 33; www.avelhafabrica.com; Calle Carrasco 24, Valverde del Fresno; s/d incl breakfast €60/90; ℗❄️🛜🐕), is set in a former textile mill. In these villages people speak their own isolated dialect, a unique mix of Spanish and Portuguese.
>
> Heading northeast from Hoyos, you arrive in Las Hurdes region, which has taken nearly a century to shake off its image of poverty, disease, and chilling tales of witchcraft and even cannibalism. In 1922 the miserable existence of the *hurdanos* prompted Alfonso XIII to declare during a horseback tour, 'I can bear to see no more'. The austere, rocky terrain yields only small terraces of cultivable land along the riverbanks. In the hilly terrain, donkeys and mules remain more practical than tractors while clusters of beehives produce high-quality honey.
>
> The village of Caminomorisco has a tourist office (☏927 43 53 29; www.todohur des.com; Avenida de Las Hurdes, Caminomorisco; ⊙10am-2pm & 4.30-7.30pm Wed-Sun). From here, head further north, deviating off EX204 to explore remote villages such as Casares and Ladrillar, with traditional stone, slate-roofed houses huddled in clusters. Set aside a day to walk the PR40, a near-circular 28km route from Casares that follows ancient shepherd trails. From nearby Nuñomoral, in the Río Hurdano valley which forms the heart of the region, a picturesque side valley leads to El Gasco, from where there's a particularly good one-hour return walk to El Chorro de la Meancera, a 70m waterfall.
>
> Buses are scarce in the Sierra de Gata and Las Hurdes area. There are weekday buses from Plasencia to major villages in the region, and some services from Coria.

here, there are stunning views across the river gorge to the Peña Falcón crag, where you may spot raptors.

Research is still being carried out as to whether the highly endangered Iberian lynx (previously thought to be present in only two small populations in Andalucía) is present in the park.

☞ Tours

The Centro de Visitantes in Villareal de San Carlos runs free guided walks at weekends; prior reservations by telephone are required.

Many of the hotels and *casas rurales* that surround the park also offer guided tours, either on foot or by 4WD. Other private organisations offering a range of tours include the following:

Birding in Extremadura   BIRDWATCHING
(☎927 31 93 49; www.birdingextremadura.com) Run by British ornithologist Martin Kelsey.

Iberian Nature   BIRDWATCHING
(☎676 784221; www.extremadurabirds.net) Bird-watching experts who also offer guided hikes.

Monfragüe Natural   BIRDWATCHING
(☎638 520891; www.monfraguenatural.com) A variety of excursions, including wildlife-watching, horse riding and kayaking.

**Rutas Dehesas
de Monfragüe**   HIKING, BIRDWATCHING
(☎605 732252; www.rutasdehesasdemonfrague.com) Guided walks and drives in the park and vicinity.

🛌 Sleeping

Casa Rural Monfragüe   CASA RURAL €
(☎927 19 90 02; www.monfraguerural.com; Calle de Villareal 15, Villareal de San Carlos; s/d incl breakfast €39/55; ❄🛜) This light-filled *casa rural* has large, brightly painted rooms in a lovely stone building directly opposite the park's information centre. There's an attractive bar-restaurant downstairs serving solid Extremadura fare, and the owners have another *casa rural* a few doors down. They rent bikes and binoculars and can arrange tours.

Hospedería Parque de Monfragüe   HOTEL €€
(☎927 45 52 78; www.hospederiasdeextremadura.es; Km 39; d incl breakfast €108; P❄@🛜🏊🐕) This tranquil four-star hotel on the northern edge of Torrejón el Rubio looks out across the plains to the national park, with pretty views all around. Spacious slate-walled rooms come with squeaky floors and a TV with internet. Duplexes are good for families, and there's a decent restaurant (mains €17 to €24). Prices can halve off-season.

Camping Monfragüe   CAMPGROUND €
(☎927 45 92 33; www.campingmonfrague.com; sites per adult/tent/car €4.20/4.20/3.80, 2-/4-person bungalows €50/90; P🐕) Precisely 14km north of Villareal on the EX208 is this shady camping ground, with a restaurant, shop and pool, plus homey bungalows complete with front porches. It rents out bikes and does inexpensive four-hour 4WD guided tours of the park (€30).

ℹ Information

Centro de Visitantes (☎927 19 91 34; www.monfrague.com; Villareal de San Carlos; ⊙9.30am-7.30pm, from 9am Sat & Sun) Staff also run interpretation centres at various points around the park, including two in the village of Villareal just down the street from here. You can reserve free guided visits to cave paintings near the Castillo de Monfragüe here.

ℹ Getting There & Away

Public transport through the park is restricted to one bus each way Monday to Friday between Plasencia and Torrejón el Rubio; it stops in Villareal de San Carlos. The nearest train station is at Monfragüe, 18km north of Villareal de San Carlos.

SOUTHERN EXTREMADURA

The landscape in this region is a beguiling combination of flat plains, which, further south, subtly change to a gentle, more pastoral, landscape. The main attraction is the Roman city of Mérida, but don't miss the lovely towns of Olivenza and Zafra.

Mérida

POP 57,800

Mérida, capital of Extremadura, was once also capital of the Roman province of Lusitania and is remarkable for having the most impressive and extensive Roman ruins in all of Spain. The ruins lie sprinkled around the town, often appearing in the most unlikely corners, and one can only wonder what still lies buried beneath the modern city.

⊙ Sights

ROMAN REMAINS

Teatro Romano RUIN

(Calle Álvarez de Buruaga; ⊙9.30am-7.30pm Jun-Sep, 9.30am-1.45pm & 4-6.15pm Oct-May) The stunning Roman theatre, built around 15 BC to seat 6000 spectators, has a dramatic and well-preserved two-tier stage building of Corinthian columns; the stage's facade (*scaenae frons*) was inaugurated in AD 105. The theatre hosts performances during the Festival del Teatro Clásico in summer. The adjoining Anfiteatro, opened in 8 BC for gladiatorial contests, held 14,000. Outside the main gate, the Casa del Anfiteatro, the remains of a 3rd-century mansion, has some reasonable floor mosaics.

Los Columbarios RUIN

(Calle del Ensanche, ⊙9.30am-1.45pm & 5-7.15pm Jun-Sep, 9.30am-1.45pm & 4-6.15pm Oct-May) This Roman funeral site is well documented in Spanish and illustrated. A footpath connects it with the Casa del Mitreo (Calle Oviedo; adult/child €4/free; ⊙9.30am-1.45pm & 5-7.15pm Jun-Sep, 9.30am-1.45pm & 4-6.15pm Oct-May), a 2nd-century Roman house with several intricate mosaics (especially the partial but beautiful remains of the *mosaico cosmológico,* with its allegories and bright colours) and a well-preserved fresco.

Puente Romano BRIDGE

Don't miss the extraordinarily powerful spectacle of the Puente Romano over the Río Guadiana. At 792m in length with 60 granite arches, it is one of the longest bridges built by the Romans. The altogether more modern Puente Lusitania, a sleek suspension bridge designed by Santiago Calatrava, mirrors it to the northwest.

Arco de Trajano RUIN

(Calle de Trajano) The imposing 15m-high archway isn't known to have anything to do with Trajan, but it was situated on one of Mérida's main Roman streets and may have served as an entrance to a sacred area.

Templo de Diana RUIN

(Calle de Sagasta) Inaccurately named, for it's now known to have been dedicated to the Imperial cult, this temple stood in the municipal forum, where the city government was based. Parts were incorporated into a 16th-century mansion built within it. The restored forum's Pórtico del Foro (Calle de Sagasta) is just along the road.

COMBINED TICKET

Admission to most of Mérida's Roman sites is via a combined ticket, which costs €12 for adults, €6 for students and pensioners, and is free for children under 12. It includes entry to the Teatro Romano and Anfiteatro, Casa del Anfiteatro, Los Columbarios, Casa del Mitreo, Alcazaba, Circo Romano, Basílica de Santa Eulalia and the Zona Arqueológica de Morería. Also included is a comprehensive guide (available in English) to the monuments. The ticket has no time limit and can be bought from any of the sights.

Circo Romano RUIN

(Avenida Juan Carlos; ⊙9.50am-1.45pm & 5-7.15pm) The remains of the 1st-century Circo Romano, which could accommodate 30,000 spectators, represent the only surviving hippodrome of its kind in Spain. Inside you can see brief footage in Spanish about Diocles, a champion *auriga* (chariot racer) who served his apprenticeship in Mérida before going on to the big league in Rome.

Acueducto de los Milagros RUIN

(Calle Marquesa de Pinares) The Acueducto de los Milagros, highly favoured by nesting storks, once supplied the Roman city with water from the dam at Lago Proserpina, about 5km out of town. There's another aqueduct, San Lázaro, near the Circo Romano.

OTHER SIGHTS

Museo Nacional de Arte Romano MUSEUM

(http://museoarteromano.mcu.es; Calle de José Ramón Mélida; adult/child €3/free, EU seniors & students free; ⊙9.30am-3.30pm & 5.30-8.30pm Tue-Sun Jul-Sep, shorter hours rest of year) On no account should you miss this fabulous museum, which has a superb collection of statues, mosaics, frescoes, coins and other Roman artefacts, all beautifully displayed. There's heaps of information but you never feel it's an overload. Designed by the architect Rafael Moneo, the soaring brick structure makes a remarkable home for the collection.

Alcazaba FORTRESS

(Calle Graciano; ⊙9.30am-1.45pm & 5-7.15pm Jun-Sep, 9.30am-1.45pm & 4-6.15pm Oct-May) This large Islamic fort was built in the 9th century on a site already occupied by the Romans and Visigoths. Down below, its pretty

Mérida

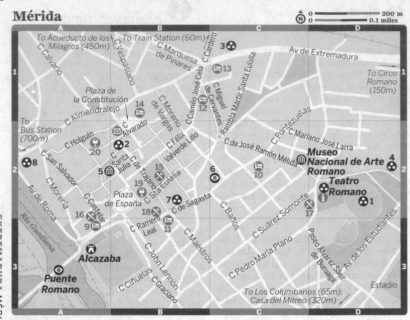

Mérida

goldfish-populated *aljibe* (cistern) reuses Visigothic marble and stone slabs, while the ramparts look out over the Río Guadiana. When Mérida was conquered by the Christians in 1230, the knightly order of Santiago restored the fort, which had fallen into disrepair. The 15th-century monastery in its northeast corner now serves as regional goverment offices. Admission is part of the combined Roman sights ticket.

FREE **Museo de Arte Visigodo** MUSEUM
(Calle de Santa Julia; ☉10am-2pm & 4-6pm Tue-Sat, 10am-2pm Sun) Many of the Visigothic objects unearthed in Mérida are exhibited in this archaeological museum, just off Plaza de España. It's a fascinating insight into a little-

known period of Spanish history. Opening hours are extended from July to September.

Basílica de Santa Eulalia RUIN, CHURCH
(Avenida de Extremadura; ⊙9.50am-1.45pm & 5-7.15pm) Built in the 5th century in honour of Mérida's patron saint, the basilica was reconstructed in the 13th century. Beside it, a museum and excavated areas enable you to identify Roman houses, a 4th-century Christian cemetery and the original 5th-century church. Admission is part of the combined Roman sights ticket.

Zona Arqueológica de Morería RUIN
(Avenida de Roma; ⊙9.50am-1.45pm & 5-7.15pm) This excavated Moorish quarter contains the remains of a cemetery, walls and houses dating from Roman to post-Islamic times.

🌟 Festivals & Events

Festival del Teatro Clásico THEATRE
(www.festivaldemerida.es; admission €12-39; ⊙around 11pm most nights Jul & Aug) This prestigious summer festival, held at the Roman theatre and amphitheatre, features Greek and more recent drama classics, plus music and dance.

Feria de Septiembre LOCAL FIESTA
(www.merida.es) Mérida lets its hair down a little later than most of Extremadura at its September Fair (1 to 15 September).

🛏 Sleeping

TOP CHOICE Aparthotel Capitolina APARTMENT €€
(☎924 31 86 54; www.apartamentoscapitolina.com; Calle Castelar 1; s/d/q incl breakfast €72/96/160; ❋🤶🛜) Just down from Plaza de España, these appealing and spacious apartments sit above a quality restaurant and are very well kept. Each has two double bedrooms, and extra beds can be added for kids as needed. All have a proper kitchen, with breakfast food included. There's a lovely upstairs terrace offering river views, and benevolent management.

TOP CHOICE La Flor de al-Andalus HOSTAL €
(☎924 31 33 56; www.laflordeal-andalus.es; Avenida de Extremadura 6; s/d €33/45; ❋🛜) If only all hostales were this good. Describing itself as a 'boutique hostal', La Flor de al-Andalus has rooms beautifully decorated in Andalucian style, friendly service and a good location within walking distance of all the main sites. This is hotel standard at a great price.

Try to avoid the rooms on the ground floor by the reception. Breakfast available for €3.

Hotel Adealba HOTEL €€
(☎924 38 83 08; www.hoteladealba.com; Calle Romero Leal 18; d incl breakfast from €96.30; ℗❋🛜) This chic but cordial hotel occupies a 19th-century town house close to the Templo de Diana and does so with a classy, contemporary look. The designer rooms have big windows (some with balcony), a minimalist feel, and there's a compact onsite spa complex. It's cheaper midweek. Valet parking available.

Parador Vía de la Plata HISTORIC HOTEL €€€
(☎924 31 38 00; www.parador.es; Plaza de la Constitución 3; s/d €128/161; ℗❋🛜🏊) You're sleeping on the site of a Roman temple in a building that started life as a convent; the lounge was a former chapel, then served as both hospital and prison. In the gardens, the assembled hunks of Roman, Visigothic and Mudéjar artefacts give a brief canter through Mérida's architectural history. Rear-room balconies look onto a quiet garden with fountains.

Hotel Cervantes HOTEL €€
(☎924 31 49 61; www.hotelcervantes.com; Calle Camilo José Cela 8; s/d €45/65; ℗❋🛜) Excellent value for this fairly standard Spanish hotel makes it a good Mérida deal. The location is central, and the service is friendly. The bar-restaurant serves a bacon-and-egg breakfast.

Hostal Alfarero HOSTAL €
(☎924 30 31 83; www.hostalalfarero.com; Calle de Sagasta 40; d €50; ❋🛜) Just down the hill from the Roman museum, this welcoming budget option is built around a little patio. The upstairs rooms have much more natural light than the darkish downstairs ones. There are also cheaper rooms available that share a bathroom (doubles €35).

🍴 Eating

There are numerous restaurants aimed at tourists around the Roman theatre, offering lunchtime set menus for €9 or so.

TOP CHOICE Casa Benito SPANISH €€
(Calle San Francisco 3; tapas €3.30, mains €14-22) Squeeze onto a tiny stool in the wood-panelled dining room, prop up the bar or relax on the sunny terrace for tapas at this bullfighting enthusiasts' hang-out, its walls plastered with photos, posters and memorabilia

EMERITA AUGUSTA

The Roman city of Emerita Augusta, centred on the site of modern Mérida, was founded by Augustus in 25 BC as a colony for veterans of Rome's campaigns in Cantabria; the Roman name translates roughly as 'bachelors' or 'discharged soldiers' from the army of Augustus. The location also served the strategic purpose of protecting a nearby pass and the bridge over the Río Guadiana. The city prospered and became the capital of the Roman province of Lusitania (which included modern-day Portugal) and one of the empire's most important cultural and political centres, with a population of 40,000 in its heyday. After the fall of the Western Roman Empire, the city became the Visigothic capital of Hispania in the 6th century and its monuments remained largely intact. The city later passed into Muslim hands in the 8th century and has been Christian since 1230. During Napoleon's 19th-century invasion of Spain, many of Mérida's monuments were destroyed.

from the ring. The tapas are original and supertasty; the upstairs restaurant specialises in roasts and is also a fine choice.

Tábula Calda   SPANISH €€
(www.tabulacalda.com; Calle Romero Leal 11; meals €20-25; ⊘lunch & dinner Mon-Sat, lunch Sun) This inviting space, with tilework and abundant greenery, serves up well-priced meals (including set menus from €12 to €24.50) that cover most Spanish staples. It effortlessly combines traditional home cooking, thoughtful presentation and subtle innovations.

El Yantar   TAPAS €
(www.jamoneselyantar.com; Paseo Álvarez Sáez de Buruaga 12; raciones €7-20) A step up in class from the touristy restaurants clustered around the Roman theatre entrance, this is a place to try high-quality Extremadura hams, patés and cheeses, accompanied by underrated Ribera del Guadiana wines. There's a pleasant terrace, competent service, and a shop to buy anything you liked the taste of.

Casa Nano   SPANISH €€
(www.casanano.com; Calle Castelar 3; mains €10-17; ⊘Mon-Sat) Tucked behind Plaza de España, the *simpático* staff here serve up hearty traditional dishes such as *cordero a la ciruela* (lamb with plums) and tasty *patatas al rebujón* (fried potatoes with garlic and ham). We also recommend the three-course *menú extremeño* (€23.50). Eat in the secluded dining room or head outside for a table on the quiet pedestrian street.

🍸 Drinking

The best place to enjoy an early evening drink is at one of the kiosk-bars on Plaza de España. You'll find a more diverse selection of bars in and around Plaza de la Constitución.

La Moett   BAR
(www.lamoett.com; Plaza de España 2; ⊘4pm-late) Under the arches of the Ayuntamiento on the Plaza de España's northeastern side, La Moett is a classy option for a coffee or after-dinner *copa,* with tables on the square.

La Tahona Nueva   BAR, LIVE MUSIC
(Calle Alvarado 5; ⊘5pm-late) There's a classy courtyard draped with bougainvillea at La Tahona, plus a cavernous bar area with a stage for regular live gigs ranging from flamenco to blues and jazz.

Jazz Bar   BAR, LIVE MUSIC
(Calle Alvarado 10; ⊘4pm-2am Tue-Sat; 🛜) This jazz stalwart has a sophisticated scene with regular exhibitions and live jazz once or twice a week at 10pm.

ℹ️ Information

Tourist office (✆924 33 07 22; www.turismo merida.org; Calle Álvarez Sáenz de Buruaga; ⊘9am-8pm) Next to the Teatro Romano.

ℹ️ Getting There & Around

From the **bus station** (✆924 37 14 04; Avenida de la Libertad), across the river via the Puente Lusitania, destinations include Badajoz (€4.67, one hour, five to nine daily), Seville (€13.37, 2½ hours, five daily), Cáceres (€5.60, 50 minutes, two to four daily), Trujillo (€8.25, 1¼ hours, three daily) and Madrid (€26.40 to €41, four to 4½ hours, eight daily).

There are trains to Madrid (€33 to €35, 4½ to 6½ hours, five daily), Cáceres (from €4.50, one hour, six daily) and Seville (€16.85, four hours, one daily) via Zafra (€4.50, 50 minutes, three daily).

Badajoz

POP 151,570

Just 4km from Portugal, the sprawling industrial city of Badajoz is not Extremadura's prettiest or most interesting one, but its historic centre is worth a visit if you're passing by. Founded by the Muslims in the 9th century, Badajoz has been battled over by invading armies for centuries – the Portuguese, French, Spanish and British all wreaked their fury upon the city. During the Spanish Civil War, the Nationalists carried out atrocious massacres when they took Badajoz in 1936.

◎ Sights & Activities

Alcazaba   FORTRESS
The walled Alcazaba lords it on the hilltop above the centre. Climb the ramparts that enclose the 8-hectare site that was once a thriving community, with a medina, baths, mosques and houses. Guarding all is the **Torre Espantaperros** (Scare-Dogs Tower), symbol of Badajoz, constructed by the Moors and topped by a 16th-century Mudéjar bell tower. At its feet is the unusual **Plaza Alta**, dating back to 1681, with its highly decorative burgundy, grey and white facades. Within the fort area, a restored Renaissance palace houses the **Museo Arqueológico Provincial** (admission free; ◎10am-3pm Tue-Sun), with artefacts from prehistoric times through to Tartessian, Roman, Islamic and medieval Christian periods.

FREE **Museo Extremeño e Iberoamericano de Arte Contemporáneo**   GALLERY
(Meiac; www.meiac.es; Calle Museo 2; ◎10am-1.30pm & 5-8pm Tue-Sat, 10am-1.30pm Sun) Badajoz' pride and joy, this commanding modern building dedicated to Spanish, Portuguese and Latin American contemporary art houses a wide-ranging collection of avant-garde painting and sculpture.

FREE **Museo de Bellas Artes**   GALLERY
(Calle del Duque de San Germán 3; ◎10am-2pm & 4-6pm Tue-Sat, 10am-2pm Sun) This excellent gallery has Zurbarán, Morales, Picasso and Dalí on show, plus striking works by the 19th-century Badajoz-born artist Felipe Checa.

Baraka Al Hammam   HAMMAM
(☏924 25 08 26; www.baraka-al-hammam.com; Plaza de la Soledad 14; ◎sessions 10am, noon, 6pm & 8pm daily, plus 10pm Fri & Sat) This beautiful recreation of the Arab-style bath experience has beguiling architecture and a range of treatments – the basic session costs €20.

★ Festivals & Events

Feria de San Juan   LOCAL FIESTA
Badajoz' big bash is the Feria de San Juan, celebrated for a full week around 24 June.

Carnaval   CARNIVAL
(www.carnavalbadajoz.es) Running a close second to the Feria de San Juan are the town's Carnaval celebrations in the build-up to Lent, among the most elaborate in Spain.

🛏 Sleeping

Hotel San Marcos   HOTEL €
(☏924 22 95 18; www.hotelsanmarcos.es; Calle Meléndez Valdéz; r €54; P🅿🛰) Top value is to be had at this superfriendly city-centre hotel with good facilities. Rooms are a good size, equipped with fridge and safe, and most have a balcony of some sort and plenty of light. Bathrooms are sleek and modern, many with hydromassage showers.

Hostal Niza I   HOSTAL €
(☏924 22 31 73; www.hostal-niza.com; Calle del Arco Agüero 34; s/d €27/43; 🅿🛰) Look beyond the bland chip marble floors and anaemic colour scheme, as the rooms here are clean and comfortable. Hostal Niza II across the road is basically an overspill with virtually identical decor.

🍴 Eating

The streets running westwards from the Plaza de España are rich in tapas and restaurant options, especially Calle Muñoz Torrero.

El Claustro   TAPAS €€
(☏924 20 17 21; Plaza de Cervantes 13A; tapas €3.50-4, mains €12-18; ◎noon-midnight Mon-Sat) The fashionable stone-clad interior, hung with edgy artwork, is fronted by a buzzy tapas bar serving generous, innovative snacks. The chandelier-lit dining room dishes up larger portions in more formal surrounds.

Cocina Portuguesa   PORTUGUESE €
(www.cocinaportuguesa.com; Calle Muñoz Torrero 7; mains €8-12) As you're so close to the frontier, why not try some cross-border cuisine? This home-style family restaurant near the cathedral has a fine range of *bacalao* (cod) dishes and other Portuguese favourites such as *caldo verde* (green vegetable soup).

MOVING ON?

For tips, recommendations and reviews, head to shop.lonelyplanet.com to purchase a downloadable PDF of the Alentejo chapter from Lonely Planet's *Portugal* guide.

La Casona Alta   TAPAS, SPANISH €€
(www.tabernalacasona.com; Plaza Alta; tapas €1.80-3, mains €9-14; ⊙lunch & dinner Mon-Sat, lunch Sun) With chairs on Badajoz' prettiest square and a bustling bar area with barrel tables, you can choose from a healthy menu of *raciones* or more substantial dishes in the downstairs Moorish-influenced restaurant.

 Drinking

Late-night bars are scattered around the streets near the cathedral.

Espantaperros Café   JAZZ
(Calle Hernán Cortés 14; ⊙7pm-3am Mon-Thu & 4pm-4am Fri-Sun) Among the liveliest options near the cathedral, it has live jazz nightly.

 Information

Tourist office (☑924 22 49 81; www.turismo extremadura.com; Pasaje de San Juan; ⊙10am-2pm & 5-7.30pm Mon-Fri, 10am-2pm Sat & Sun) Just off Plaza de España.

 Getting There & Around

Buses run to/from Mérida (€4.67, one hour, five to nine daily), Madrid (from €30.65, 4½ to 5½ hours, nine daily), Lisbon (€25 to €32, three hours, three daily) and Seville (€15.35, three hours, six daily) via Zafra (€6.07, 1¼ hours).

Around Badajoz

ALBURQUERQUE
POP 5620

Looming large above this small town, 38km north of Badajoz, is the intact **Castillo de la Luna**. The centrepiece of a complex frontier defence system of forts, the castle was built on the site of its Islamic predecessor in the 13th century and subsequently expanded. From the top, views take in the Portuguese frontier. It was closed at time of research as a drawn-out project to build a hotel within it dragged on; check with the Badajoz tourist office if it's opened yet.

Alburquerque is served by two to five buses Monday to Saturday from Badajoz.

OLIVENZA
POP 12,010

Pretty Olivenza, 24km south of Badajoz, clings to its Portuguese heritage – it has only been Spanish since 1801. The cobbled centre is distinctive for its whitewashed houses, typical turreted defensive walls and penchant for blue-and-white ceramic tile work.

Smack-bang in its centre is the 14th-century **castle**, dominated by the **Torre del Homenaje**, 36m high, from which there are fine views. The castle houses an **ethnographic museum** (www.elmuseodeolivenza. com; admission €1; ⊙11am-2pm & 5-8pm Tue-Fri, 10am-2pm & 5-8pm Sat, 10am-2pm Sun), with a collection of toy cars on the 1st floor. The most impressive section of the original **defensive walls** is around the 18th-century **Puerta del Calvario**, on the western side of town. There's a small tourist office on the same square.

Hotel Palacio de Arteaga (☑924 49 11 29; www.palacioarteaga.com; Calle Moreno Nieto 5; s/d €70/84; P❋🛜) is a historic conversion in the heart of town and features spacious modern rooms around a pretty patio. Friendly **Casa Maila** (www.casamaila.com; Calle Colón 3; mains €11-19) is great for delicious free tapas or more elaborate restaurant mains.

Buses to Badajoz (€1.60, 30 minutes) run almost hourly during the week.

Zafra
POP 16,580

Gleaming white Zafra resembles an Andalucian *pueblo blanco* and it's a serene, attractive stop between Seville and Mérida. Originally a Muslim settlement, Zafra's narrow streets are lined with baroque churches, old-fashioned shops and traditional houses decorated by brilliant red splashes of geraniums.

◉ **Sights**

Zafra's 15th-century **castle**, a blend of Gothic, Mudéjar and Renaissance architecture, is now a *parador* and dominates the town. **Plaza Grande** and the adjoining **Plaza Chica**, arcaded and bordered by bars, are the places to see Zafra life.

FREE **Convento de Santa Clara**   CONVENT
(www.museozafra.es; Calle Sevilla 30; ⊙11am-2pm & 5-6.30pm Tue-Sun) Just off the main shopping street, this imposing 15th-century Mudéjar convent was originally designed

as a holy resting place for the remains of the powerful local Feria dynasty. It's still a working convent with cloistered nuns; the museum has a gilded chapel and there are interesting insights (in Spanish) into the lives of these sisters, who also sell pastries.

FREE **Iglesia de la Candelaria** CHURCH
(Calle Tetuán; ⊗10.30am-1pm & 6.30-8.30pm Mon, Tue & Thu-Sat, 11am-1pm Sun) This 16th-century church is worth a look for its fine altarpieces.

🛌 Sleeping

Accommodation prices rise sharply for the feria in late September or early October.

Hotel Plaza Grande HOTEL €
(☑924 56 31 63; www.hotelplazagrande.com; Calle Pasteleros 2; s/d incl breakfast €28/40; ❋☏) The genial owner has created a gem of a hotel here, right on Plaza Grande and quite a bargain. Go for room 108, with its corner balconies overlooking the plaza (room 208 is the same but with windows instead of balconies). Decor is terracotta accentuated by cream paintwork and muted earth colours. The downstairs restaurant and bar are reliably good.

Parador Hernán Cortés HOTEL €€€
(☑924 55 45 40; www.parador.es; Plaza Corazón de María 7; s/d €129/161; ⓟ❋☏☎) They say a man's home is his castle: here it's the reverse. The large rooms are richly decorated with burgundy-coloured fabrics and antiques. The marble-pillared courtyard is truly magnificent, while the secluded pool is surrounded by ivy and turrets. The restaurant is excellent.

Hotel Huerta Honda HOTEL €€
(☑924 55 41 00; www.hotelhuertahonda.com; Calle López Asme 1; s/d/superior d €64/80/104; ⓟ❋☏☎) There are two grades of rooms here: standards are contemporary, stylish and supremely comfortable, with lots of browns and beiges; while 'Gran Clase' are sumptuous, with four-poster beds, timber ceilings and antiques. Whichever you choose, this place is outstanding. The bougainvillea-draped courtyard has views of the castle next door.

🍴 Eating

La Rebotica SPANISH €€
(☑924 55 42 89; www.lareboticadezafra.com; Calle Boticas 12; mains €15-21; ⊗lunch & dinner Tue-Sat, lunch Sun) This restaurant in the heart of the old town offers a traditional meaty menu, including *rabo de toro* (ox tail) and five different pork fillet dishes, subtly prepared by Dutch chef Rudy Koster.

Josefina SPANISH €€
(☑924 55 17 01; Calle López Asme 1; mains €16-22; ⊗lunch & dinner Tue-Sat, lunch Sun) On the edge of the old town, this mother-and-son team serve up succulent traditional food with a modern twist. The eating area is rather staid, but the service is warm and the dishes full of flavour.

Gastro-Bar Baraka TAPAS €
(Plaza Grande 20; raciones €7-13; ⊗7pm-midnight Mon-Wed, 7pm-3am Thu, 1pm-3am Fri-Sun) Gastro-Bar Baraka adds a touch of sophistication to Plaza Grande's charm. The food here ranges from creative *tostas* (open sandwiches on toasted bread; €3 to €4) to more substantial *raciones*. Enjoy these dishes on a balmy summer's evening with a glass of red in the lamplit square – bliss. Downstairs, there's a groovy bar (open Thursday to Sunday) inhabiting the 15th-century cisterns.

ℹ️ Information

Municipal tourist office (☑924 55 10 36; www.rutadelaplata.com; Plaza de España 8A; ⊗10am-1.30pm & 6-7.30pm Mon-Sat) The tourist office is on Plaza de España, the main square.

ℹ️ Getting There & Away

Zafra is on the main bus routes linking Seville (€9.32, 1¾ hours) to the south with Mérida (from €4.30, 65 minutes) and Badajoz (€6.07, 1¼ hours). Trains also pass through.

Around Zafra

Roads through the rolling Sierra Morena into Andalucía head southwest through Fregenal de la Sierra into northern Huelva province, and southeast into the Parque Natural Sierra Norte in Seville province.

In **Fregenal de la Sierra**, highlights include the 13th-century **castle** (Plaza Constitución; admission free; ⊗10.15am-2.45pm & 5.15-7.15pm Wed-Sun) – enter through the adjacent tourist office – which houses a bullring among other buildings, and nearby Santa María church. On Tuesday and Friday mornings there is a lively market in the main square.

Walled and hilly **Jerez de los Caballeros**, 42km west of Zafra, was a cradle of conquistadors. It has a 13th-century castle that was built by the Templars. They refused to lay down arms when the order was suppressed and came to a sticky end. You can wander around at will, but it's basically just the impressive walls that are preserved. There are several handsome churches, three with towers emulating the Giralda in Seville.

Quiet **Burguillos del Cerro**, southwest of Zafra, is overlooked by a 15th-century castle atop a grassy hill.

One weekday bus runs between Zafra and Fregenal de la Sierra (€2.63, one hour), and one Monday to Saturday to Jerez de los Caballeros (€2.84, one hour) via Burguillos.

Understand Spain

›

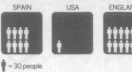
Spain Today

Economic Crisis

It can be hard to remember, but Spain was, not so long ago, the envy of Europe. Its economy was booming and the whole country seemed brimful of optimism. Then things fell apart. In 2008, unemployment stood at around 6%. Four years later, one out of every four Spaniards (over 5.5 million people) can't find work. Old-timers you speak to can't remember a time this bad, with businesses closing their doors forever, including many that weathered civil war and dictatorship down through the decades. A left-of-centre government that waited painfully long to recognise that a crisis was looming was replaced in November 2011 with a right-of-centre one promoting a deep austerity drive that threatens the generous welfare state on which Spaniards have come to depend – strangling the life out of the economy, say some, or taking much-needed remedial action to correct years of spending beyond our means, counter others. Whoever is correct, there is worrying talk of Spain becoming the next Greece. Where did it all go wrong? Spain's economy was heavily reliant on construction and tourism, two industries that are exceptionally susceptible to economic downturns. Its property market also spiralled out of control for far too long: prices rose exponentially, prompting banks to hand out money to those who simply couldn't afford to pay it back. What began in 2008 shows no signs of abating, and it's almost impossible these days to have a conversation in Spain without reference to *la crisis*.

» Population: 47.04 million (2012)

» GDP: 1.537 trillion

» GDP per capita (2011): US$30,600

» Annual inflation (2011): 3.1%

» Unemployment (2012): 24.4%

» Internet domain: es

Spain's Young

If Spain's economic numbers make for depressing reading, those relating to the country's younger generation can seem catastrophic. Almost one out of every two young Spaniards is out of work, and there is talk of an entire generation being lost to the economic downturn. The disparity be-

Top Books

Ghosts of Spain (Giles Tremlett) An account of modern Spain and the hangover from its past.
Everything but the Squeal (John Barlow) A fun guide to northern Spain's food culture.
A Handbook for Travellers (Richard Ford) This 1845 classic is witty and informative.
A Pilgrim in Spain (Christopher Howse) Amusing reflections from a veteran Spain-watcher.
The New Spaniards (John Hooper) Highly readable journey through three decades (until 2006) of democratic Spain.

Top Films

¡Bienvenido, Mr Marshall! (1952)
Jamón, jamón (1992)
Flamenco (1995)
Todo sobre mi madre (1999)
Mar adentro (2004)
Volver (2006)
Alatriste (2006)

belief systems
(% of population)

94 — Roman Catholic

6 — Other (mostly Islam)

if Spain were 100 people

74 would speak Castilian Spanish
17 would speak Catalan
7 would speak Galician
2 would speak Basque

tween salaries – the *mileuristas* (earning up to €1000 a month) became a *cause célèbre* in the media – and still-high house prices means that Spaniards are taking ever longer to move out of home. And for the first time in decades, younger people are leaving the country in search of opportunity in greater numbers than there are immigrants wanting to come to Spain.

Reclaiming the Streets

And yet, many of Spain's young and restless have refused to play the role of victims. On 15 May 2011, the *indignados* (the indignant ones) took over the iconic Plaza de la Puerta del Sol in the centre of Madrid in a peaceful sit-in protest. Their popularity maintained by social media networks, they stayed for months, the forerunner to numerous such movements around the world, including Occupy Wall Street and its offshoots. The protests, which drew Spaniards from all walks of life, were driven by a dissatisfaction with mainstream politics, and a desire to overturn some of the more unfair aspects of Spanish economic life; among these is the requirement that homeowners with homes repossessed by banks must continue to pay their mortgage (ie the bank gets the house *and* the money). While it was business as usual during the 2011 elections, which swept the conservative Popular Party to power, the *indignados'* public meetings and prominent media presence continue, prompting many to hope that a new kind of politics may have been born. With the economy in freefall and Spain's government forced to seek a massive bailout for its banking industry from the EU, protesters returned to the streets of Madrid and other Spanish cities in growing numbers in 2012. By the middle of the year, deep budget cuts prompted large and almost daily protests, including a march on the capital by miners from Asturias. Heavy government crackdowns on protesters only served to heighten the sense of crisis.

» Area: 505,370 sq km
» Highest point on mainland: Mulhacén (3479m)
» Number of national parks: 14
» Length of coastline: 4964km
» Longest border: 1214km (Portugal)
» Shortest border: 1.2km (Gibraltar)

Top Flamenco

Una leyenda flamenca (El Camarón de la Isla) Great music by the all-time flamenco master.
Canciones hondas (Ketama) Rocky flamenco fusion.
Lágrimas negras (Diego El Cigala) Flamenco with Cuban rhythms.

Flamenco (Enrique Morente) Modern flamenco's late creative talent joined by guitar greats.
Paco de Lucía antología (Paco de Lucía) The life's work of the great flamenco guitarist.
Pokito a poko (Chambao) Flamenco chill.

Top Conversations

The economy From boom to spectacular bust in a few short years.
A lost generation Spain's youngsters can't take a trick.
People on the streets Can people power turn it all around?

History

Early Spaniards painted prehistoric art at the Cueva de Altamira between 15,000 and 10,000 BC. After 1000 BC, Phoenician and Greek traders from the eastern Mediterranean established settlements on Spain's southern and eastern coasts. They were supplanted by the Carthaginians, who in turn were replaced by the Romans. Rome ruled Iberia from 200 BC to AD 400, bringing stability and prosperity. After the Roman Empire disintegrated, the Visigoths, a Germanic tribe, took control of the peninsula until Muslim forces invaded from North Africa in AD 711 and rapidly overran the peninsula. The Muslims (Moors) would become the dominant power for four centuries, and a potent one for four centuries after that. Islamic culture and power centred first on Córdoba (756–1031), then Seville (c 1040–1248) and lastly Granada (1248–1492). Islamic Spain developed medieval Europe's most cultured society.

From small beginnings in Asturias, on Spain's northern coastal strip, Christian kingdoms such as León, Castilla (Castile), Aragón and Portugal gradually regained territory in the eight-centuries-long Reconquista. The last Muslim kingdom, Granada, fell in 1492 to the Reyes Católicos (Catholic Monarchs) Isabel (Isabella) of Castilla and Fernando (Ferdinand) of Aragón, whose marriage had united the two most powerful Christian states. The same year, Genoese sailor Christopher Columbus (Cristóbal Colón to Spaniards) found several Caribbean islands on a voyage financed by the Spanish crown, leading to the Spanish conquest of large parts of the Americas and a flood of silver from the new empire. The 16th century saw Spain at the peak of its power under kings Carlos I and Felipe II, who ruled large swaths of Europe.

Silver shipments shrank drastically in the 17th century, initiating three centuries of decline in which Spain lost all of its foreign possessions and sank into stagnation and widespread poverty. Internal wars and a widening wealth gap between rich and poor fomented social unrest and political radicalisation in the late 19th and early 20th centuries. Spain

Spain History Books

» *The Story of Spain* by Mark Williams

» *Spain: A History* by Raymond Carr

» *A History of Spain* by Simon Barton

» *A Concise History of Spain* (Cambridge Concise Histories) by WD & CR Phillips

TIMELINE	c 1.2 million BC	c 22,000 BC	c 15,000–10,000 BC
	Europe's earliest-known humans leave their fossilised remains in the Sima del Elefante at Atapuerca, near the northern city of Burgos.	Neanderthal humans die out on the Iberian Peninsula – perhaps due to climatic changes during the last Ice Age, or perhaps because they were displaced by Homo sapiens arriving from Africa.	Palaeolithic (Old Stone Age) hunters of the Magdalenian culture paint beautiful, sophisticated animal images in caves at Altamira and other sites along Spain's northern coastal strip.

became irretrievably polarised between left and right during the Second Republic (1931–36). This led to the Spanish Civil War (1936–39), in which the right-wing Nationalists, led by General Francisco Franco, defeated the left-wing Republicans. Franco then ruled as a dictator until his death in 1975, after which King Juan Carlos I engineered a return to democracy. Three decades of steady economic progress followed, but Spain has since fallen on hard times and faces a troubled economic future.

The Original Spaniards

Spain can make a convincing claim to be the cradle of European humanity – in 2007, Europe's oldest human remains (a mere 1.2 million years old) were discovered at Atapuerca (p191), near the northern city of Burgos. More recently, the much-visited Cueva de Nerja (p732) in Andalucía was one of many haunts of the earliest Homo sapiens on the Iberian Peninsula, the Cro-Magnons, who probably arrived from Africa around 35,000 years ago. In northern Spain, wonderful (and Unesco World Heritage–listed) cave paintings from the Palaeolithic (Old Stone Age), especially at Altamira (p475), are the country's most superb legacy of prehistoric humanity. After the end of the last Ice Age in about 8000 BC, further new peoples arrived, again probably from North Africa, while the Neolithic (New Stone Age) reached Spain from Mesopotamia and Egypt around 6000 BC. Contacts with northern Europe are evident with the appearance of megalithic tombs (dolmens), dating back to between 3000 BC and 2000 BC; the best dolmens are at Antequera in Andalucía.

Early Traders & Invaders

Spain's rich natural resources and settled societies eventually attracted the interest of more sophisticated societies around the Mediterranean. The first arrivals came chiefly to trade; later, emerging Mediterranean imperialist states sought to exert military control.

The Phoenicians, Greeks & Celts

By about 1000 BC the Phoenicians, a Semitic people from present-day Lebanon, began arriving on Spanish shores to exchange perfumes, jewellery, oil, ivory, wine and textiles for Spanish silver and bronze, and establish coastal trading colonies at places like Almuñécar (which they called Ex or Sex), Cádiz (Gadir) and Huelva (Onuba). In the 7th century BC Greek traders reached Spain, too, establishing settlements mainly along the Mediterranean coast – the biggest was Emporion (Empúries) at L'Escala in Catalonia.

As well as iron, the Phoenicians and Greeks brought with them several things now considered quintessentially Spanish – the olive tree, the grapevine and the donkey – along with other useful skills and items such as writing, coins, the potter's wheel and poultry.

Top Prehistoric Sites

» Cueva de Altamira, near Santillana del Mar

» Atapuerca, near Burgos

» Cueva de Tito Bustillo, Ribadesella

» Dolmens, Antequera

» Cueva de la Pileta, near Ronda

» Siega Verde, near Ciudad Rodrigo

Dating back to at least the 9th century BC, Cádiz was founded by Phoenician traders and is the oldest continually inhabited city in the whole of the Iberian Peninsula, and possibly even Europe.

218 BC

Roman legions arrive in Spain during the Second Punic War, initiating the 600-year Roman occupation of the peninsula; it takes two centuries to subdue all local resistance.

1st to 3rd centuries AD

Pax Romana (Roman Peace), a period of stability and prosperity. The Iberian Peninsula is divided into three provinces: Baetica (capital: Córdoba); Lusitania (Mérida) and Tarraconensis (Tarragona).

MICHAL BOUDIN / ALAMY ©

» Cueva de Altamira (p475)

Around the same time as the Phoenicians brought iron technology to the south, the Celts (originally from Central Europe) brought it – and beer-making – to the north. Celts and Iberians who merged on the *meseta* (the high tableland of central Spain) are known as Celtiberians. Celts in northwestern Spain typically lived in sizeable hill-fort towns called *castros*, some of which can still be seen.

From about the 6th century BC the Phoenicians and Greeks were pushed out of the western Mediterranean by Carthage, a former Phoenician colony in modern Tunisia that established a flourishing settlement on Ibiza. After losing out to Rome in the First Punic War (264–241 BC), which was fought for control of Sicily, Carthage conquered southern Spain. The Second Punic War (218–201 BC) saw Carthaginian general Hannibal march his elephants on from here and over the Alps to threaten Rome, but also saw Rome bring legions to fight Carthage in Spain. Rome's victory at Ilipa, near Seville, in 206 BC, gave it control of the Iberian Peninsula. The first Roman town in Spain, Itálica, was founded near the battlefield soon afterwards.

The Romans

The Romans held sway on the Iberian Peninsula for 600 years. It took them 200 years to subdue the fiercest of local tribes, but by AD 50 most of Hispania (as the Romans called the peninsula) had adopted the Roman way of life. The Basques, though defeated, were never Romanised like the rest.

Rome's legacy was huge, giving Hispania a road system, aqueducts, temples, theatres, amphitheatres and bathhouses, along with the religion that still predominates today – Christianity – and a Jewish population who were to play a big part in Spanish life for over 1000 years. The main languages still spoken on the Iberian Peninsula – Castilian Spanish, Catalan, Galician and Portuguese – are all versions of the colloquial Latin spoken by Roman legionaries and colonists, filtered through 2000 years of linguistic mutation. It was also the Romans who first began to cut (for timber, fuel and weapons) the extensive forests that in their time covered half the *meseta*. In return, Hispania gave Rome gold, silver, grain, wine, fish, soldiers, emperors (Trajan, Hadrian, Theodosius) and the literature of Seneca, Martial, Quintilian and Lucan.

The Visigoths

The Pax Romana (Roman Peace; the long, prosperous period of stability under the Romans) in Spain began to crumble in the 3rd and 4th centuries AD when Germanic tribes began to sweep across the Pyrenees. The Visigoths, another Germanic people, sacked Rome itself in 410, but later became Roman allies. When the Germanic Franks pushed the Visigoths

Spanish History Index (vlib.iue.it/ hist-spain) provides countless internet leads for those who want to dig deeper, with everything from geographical studies to society, culture and politics.

Top Roman Remains

» Mérida
» Segovia
» Itálica
» Tarragona
» Baelo Claudia, Bolonia
» Lugo
» Villa Romana La Olmeda

AD 53	4th to 7th centuries AD	711	718
Future Roman Emperor Trajan is born in Itálica to a wealthy senator. His imperial rule will begin in 98 and see the Roman Empire reach its greatest extent.	Germanic tribes enter the Iberian Peninsula, ending the Pax Romana. The Visigoths establish control and bring 200 years of relative stability in which Hispano-Roman culture survives.	Muslims invade Iberia from North Africa, overrunning it within a few years, becoming the dominant force on the peninsula for nearly four centuries, and then a potent one for four centuries more.	Christian nobleman Pelayo establishes the Kingdom of Asturias in northern Spain. With his victory over a Muslim force at the Battle of Covadonga around 722, the Reconquista begins.

out of Gaul in the 6th century, they settled in the Iberian Peninsula, making Toledo their capital.

The roughly 200,000 Visigoths maintained a precarious hold over the millions of more-sophisticated Hispano-Romans, and culturally, the Visigoths tended to ape Roman ways. They left little mark on the Spanish landscape, although the Visigothic church (p176) at Baños de Cerrato, near Palencia, which dates from 661, is reckoned to be the oldest surviving church in the country. The Visigoths' principal lasting impact on Spanish history lies in the fact that Visigothic nobility headed the small Christian kingdoms that survived the Muslim conquest of 711 and began the eight-century Reconquista, which eventually reasserted Christianity in the Iberian Peninsula. Common names of Visigotic origin, such as Fernando, Roderigo, Fernández and Rodríguez, are still reminders of the Visigoths' role in the Spanish story.

Moorish Spain

Following the death of the Prophet Mohammed in 632, Arabs had carried Islam through the Middle East and North Africa. With the disintegration of the Visigothic kingdom through famine, disease and strife among the aristocracy, the Iberian Peninsula was ripe for invasion.

If you believe the myth, the Muslims were ushered into Spain by the sexual adventures of the last Visigoth king, Roderic, who reputedly seduced Florinda, the daughter of the governor of Ceuta on the Moroccan coast. The governor, Julian, sought revenge by approaching the Muslims with a plan to invade Spain, and in 711 Tariq ibn Ziyad, the Muslim governor of Tangier, landed at Gibraltar with around 10,000 men, mostly Berbers (indigenous North Africans). Roderic's army was decimated, probably near Río Guadalete or Río Barbate in western Andalucía, and he is thought to have drowned while fleeing the scene. Visigothic survivors fled north and within a few years the Muslims had conquered the whole Iberian Peninsula, except for small areas behind the mountains of the Cordillera Cantábrica in the north. Their advance into Europe was only checked by the Franks at the Battle of Poitiers in 732.

The name given to Muslim-controlled territory on the peninsula was Al-Andalus. Its frontiers shifted constantly as the Christians strove to regain territory in the stuttering 800-year Reconquista. Up to the mid-11th century the frontier between Muslim and Christian territory lay across the north of the peninsula, roughly from southern Catalonia to northern Portugal, with a protrusion up to the central Pyrenees.

Islamic cities such as Córdoba, Seville and Granada boasted beautiful palaces, mosques and gardens, universities, public baths and bustling *zocos* (markets). Al-Andalus' rulers allowed freedom of worship to Jews and Christians (known as *mozárabes*, Mozarabs) under their rule. Jews

Best Moorish Monuments

» Alhambra, Granada

» Mezquita, Córdoba

» Albayzín, Granada

» Alcázar, Seville

» Giralda, Seville

» Aljafería, Zaragoza

» Alcazaba, Málaga

Richard Fletcher's *Moorish Spain* is an excellent short history of Al-Andalus (the Muslim-ruled areas of the peninsula) and assumes little or no prior knowledge of the subject. For a modern take on Spain's Moorish history, track down Jason Webster's *Andalus: Unlocking the Secrets of Moorish Spain*.

756	929	1031	1035
Abd ar-Rahman I establishes himself in Córdoba as the emir of Al-Andalus (the Islamic areas of the peninsula) and launches nearly three centuries of Cordoban supremacy.	Abd ar-Rahman III inaugurates the Córdoba Caliphate, under which Al-Andalus reaches its zenith and Córdoba, with up to half a million people, becomes Europe's biggest and most cultured city.	The Córdoba Caliphate disintegrates into dozens of *taifas* (small kingdoms) after a devastating civil war. The most powerful *taifas* include Seville, Granada, Toledo and Zaragoza.	Castilla, a county of the northern Christian kingdom of León (successor to the kingdom of Asturias), becomes an independent kingdom and goes on to become the leading force of the Reconquista.

mostly flourished, but Christians had to pay a special tax, so most either converted to Islam (to be known as *muladíes* or *muwallad*) or left for the Christian north.

The Córdoba Emirate & Caliphate

Almohad rule saw a cultural revival in Seville, and the great Cordoban philosopher Averroës (1126–98) exerted a major influence on medieval Christian thought with his commentaries on Aristotle, trying to reconcile science with religion.

Initially Al-Andalus was part of the Caliphate of Damascus, which ruled the Islamic world. In 750 the Umayyads were overthrown by a rival clan, the Abbasids, who shifted the caliphate to Baghdad. One aristocratic Umayyad survivor made his way to Spain and established himself in Córdoba in 756 as the independent emir of Al-Andalus, Abd ar-Rahman I. It was he who began construction of Córdoba's Mezquita, one of the world's greatest Islamic buildings. In 929 ruler Abd ar-Rahman III gave himself the title caliph, launching the Caliphate of Córdoba (929–1031), during which Al-Andalus reached its peak of power and lustre. Córdoba in this period was the biggest and most dazzling city in Western Europe. Astronomy, medicine, mathematics and botany flourished and one of the great Muslim libraries was established in the city.

Later in the 10th century the fearsome Cordoban general Al-Mansour (or Almanzor) terrorised the Christian north with 50-odd forays in 20 years. He destroyed the cathedral at Santiago de Compostela in northwestern Spain in 997 and forced Christian slaves to carry its doors and bells to Córdoba, where they were incorporated into the great mosque.

THE MOORISH LEGACY

Muslim rule not only set Spain's destiny quite apart from that of the rest of Europe, but left an indelible imprint on the country. This is despite the fact that Islam itself was effectively eradicated from the 16th century until the late 20th century, when it returned with new immigrants from North Africa. Great architectural monuments such as the Alhambra in Granada and the Mezquita in Córdoba are the stars of the Moorish legacy, but thousands of other buildings large and small are Moorish in origin (including the many churches that began life as mosques). The tangled, narrow street plans of many a Spanish town and village, especially in the south, date back to Moorish times, and the Muslims also developed the Hispano-Roman agricultural base by improving irrigation and introducing new fruits and crops, many of which are still widely grown today. The Spanish language contains many common words of Arabic origin, including the names of some of those new crops – *naranja* (orange), *azúcar* (sugar) and *arroz* (rice). Flamenco, though brought to its modern form by Roma people in post-Moorish times, has clear Moorish roots. It was also through Al-Andalus that much of the learning of ancient Greece and Rome (picked up by the Arabs in the eastern Mediterranean) was transmitted to Christian Europe, where it would exert a profound influence on the Renaissance.

1091	1160–73	1195
North African Muslim Almoravids invade the peninsula, unifying Al-Andalus, ruling it from Marrakesh and halting Christian expansion. Almoravid rule crumbles in the 1140s: Al-Andalus splits into *taifas*.	The Almohads, another strict Muslim sect from North Africa, conquer Al-Andalus. They make Seville their capital and revive arts and learning.	The Almohads inflict a devastating defeat on Alfonso VIII of Castilla at the Battle Of Alarcos, near Ciudad Real – the last major Christian reverse of the Reconquista.

OLIVER STREWE / GETTY IMAGES ©

» Alcázar, Seville (p663)

But after Al-Mansour's death the caliphate collapsed in a devastating civil war, ending Umayyad rule, and in 1031 it finally broke up into dozens of *taifas* (small kingdoms).

The Almoravids & Almohads

Political unity was restored to Al-Andalus by the invasion of a strict Muslim sect of Saharan nomads, the Almoravids, in 1091. The Almoravids had conquered North Africa and were initially invited to the Iberian Peninsula to support Seville, one of the strongest *taifas,* against the growing Christian threat from the north. Sixty years later a second Berber sect, the Almohads, invaded the peninsula after overthrowing the Almoravids in Morocco. Both sects roundly defeated the Christian armies they encountered in Spain.

But while the Almohad's successors, the Nasrids, retreated to Granada and contributed to the splendours of the Alhambra, the Christian armies of the Reconquista were finally closing in.

The Reconquista

The Christian Reconquest of the Iberian Peninsula began in about 722 at Covadonga, Asturias, and ended with the fall of Granada in 1492. It was a stuttering affair, conducted by Christian kingdoms that were as often at war with each other as with the Muslims. But the Muslims were gradually pushed back as the Christian kingdoms of Asturias, León, Navarra, Castilla and Aragón in the north, and Portugal in the southwest, developed. The Christians eventually succeeded in turning the whole Iberian Peninsula into a redoubt of Roman Catholicism, which it has remained ever since.

An essential ingredient in the Reconquista was the cult of Santiago (St James), one of the 12 apostles. In 813 the saint's supposed tomb was discovered in Galicia. The city of Santiago de Compostela grew around the site, to become the third-most popular medieval Christian pilgrimage goal after Rome and Jerusalem. Christian generals experienced visions of Santiago before forays against the Muslims, and Santiago became the inspiration and special protector of soldiers in the Reconquista, earning the sobriquet *Matamoros* (Moor-slayer). Today he is the patron saint of Spain.

Castilla Rises

Covadonga lies in the Picos de Europa mountains, where some Visigothic nobles took refuge after the Muslim conquest. Christian versions of the battle there tell of a small band of fighters under their leader, Pelayo, defeating an enormous force of Muslims; Muslim accounts make it a rather less important skirmish. Whatever the facts of Covadonga, by 757 Christians controlled nearly a quarter of the Iberian Peninsula.

**Recon-
quista
Castles on
the Web**

» Castles of Spain (www.castillosnet.org, in Spanish)

» Castles of Spain (www.castlesof spain.co.uk)

» Castles in Spain (http://spain forvisitors.com/archive/features/castlesinspain.htm)

1212	1218	1248	1469
Combined armies of the northern Christian kingdoms defeat the Almohads at Las Navas de Tolosa in Andalucía. The momentum of the Christian–Muslim struggle swings decisively in favour of the Christians.	The University of Salamanca is founded by Alfonso IX, King of León, making it the oldest – and still the most prestigious – university in the country.	Having captured Córdoba 12 years earlier, Castilla's Fernando III takes Seville after a two-year siege, making the Nasrid Emirate of Granada the last surviving Muslim state on the peninsula.	Isabel, the 18-year-old heir to Castilla, marries Fernando, heir to Aragón and one year her junior, uniting Spain's two most powerful Christian states.

The Asturian kingdom eventually moved its capital south to León and became the Kingdom of León, which spearheaded the Reconquista until the Christians were set on the defensive by Al-Mansour in the 10th century. Castilla, initially a small principality within León, developed into the dominant Reconquista force as hardy adventurers set up towns in the no-man's-land of the Duero basin. The capture of Toledo in 1085, by Alfonso VI of Castilla, led the Seville Muslims to call in the Almoravids from North Africa.

In 1212 the combined armies of the Christian kingdoms routed a large Almohad force at Las Navas de Tolosa in Andalucía. This was the beginning of the end for Al-Andalus: León took the key towns of Extremadura in 1229 and 1230; Aragón took Valencia in the 1230s; Castilla's Fernando III El Santo (Ferdinand the Saint) took Córdoba in 1236 and Seville in 1248; and Portugal expelled the Muslims in 1249. The sole surviving Muslim state on the peninsula was now the Emirate of Granada.

Granada Falls

Castilla and Aragón laboured under ineffectual monarchs from the late 14th century until the advent of Isabel and Fernando, the Catholic Monarchs, a century later.

In 1476 Emir Abu al-Hasan of Granada refused to pay any more tribute to Castilla, spurring Isabel and Fernando to launch the Reconquista's final crusade, against Granada, with an army largely funded by Jewish loans and the Catholic Church. The Christians took full advantage of a civil war within the Granada emirate, and on 2 January 1492 Isabel and Fernando entered the city of Granada at the beginning of what turned out to be the most momentous year in Spanish history.

The surrender terms were fairly generous to Boabdil, the last emir, who got the Alpujarras valleys south of Granada and 30,000 gold coins. The remaining Muslims were promised respect for their religion, culture and property, but this didn't last long.

Jews & Muslims Expelled

The Catholic Monarchs' Christian zeal led to the founding of the Spanish Inquisition to root out those believed to be threatening the Catholic Church. The Inquisition focused first on *conversos* (Jews converted to Christianity), accusing many of continuing to practise Judaism in secret. Then, in April 1492, under the influence of Grand Inquisitor Tomás de Torquemada, Isabel and Fernando ordered the expulsion of all Jews who refused Christian baptism. Up to 100,000 converted, but some 200,000 – the first Sephardic Jews – left Spain for other Mediterranean destinations. The bankrupt monarchy seized all unsold Jewish property. A talented middle class was gone.

Aragón was one of the most powerful kingdoms in medieval Spain, a crown created in 1137 when Ramón Berenguer IV of Catalonia married Petronilla, heiress of Aragón, to create a formidable new Christian power block in the northeast, with Barcelona as its power centre.

Gile Tremlett's *Catherine of Aragón: The Spanish Queen of Henry VIII* brings to life all the scheming and intrigue of royal Europe in the 16th century through the story of Isabel and Fernando's daughter.

1478	January 1492	April 1492	October 1492
Isabel and Fernando, the Reyes Católicos (Catholic Monarchs), stir up religious bigotry and establish the Spanish Inquisition that will see thousands killed between now and its abolition in 1834.	Isabel and Fernando capture Granada, completing the Reconquista. Boabdil, the last Muslim ruler, is scorned by his mother for weeping 'like a woman for what you could not defend like a man'.	Isabel and Fernando expel Jews who refuse Christian baptism. Some 200,000 leave, establishing Jewish communities around the Mediterranean; Spain's economy suffers from the loss of their knowledge.	Christopher Columbus, funded by Isabel and Fernando, lands in the Bahamas, opening up the Americas to Spanish colonisation. The bulk of Spanish maritime trade shifts from Mediterranean to Atlantic ports.

Cardinal Cisneros, Isabel's confessor and overseer of the Inquisition, tried to eradicate Muslim culture too. In the former Granada emirate he carried out forced mass baptisms, burnt Islamic books and banned the Arabic language. After a revolt in Andalucía in 1500, Muslims were ordered to convert to Christianity or leave. Most (around 300,000) underwent baptism and stayed, becoming known as *moriscos* (converted Muslims), but their conversion was barely skindeep and they never assimilated. The *moriscos* were finally expelled between 1609 and 1614.

Spain & the Americas
Conquering a New World

In April 1492 the Catholic Monarchs granted Genoese sailor Christopher Columbus (Cristobal Colón in Spanish) funds for his long-desired voyage across the Atlantic in search of a new trade route to the Orient.

Columbus sailed from the Andalucian port of Palos de la Frontera on 3 August 1492, with three small ships and 120 men. After a near mutiny

Medieval Jewish Sites

» *Judería* (Jewish quarter), Toledo

» The Call, Girona

» Ribadavia, Galicia

» *Judería,* Córdoba

» Horvác, Extremadura

HISTORY

THE CATHOLIC MONARCHS

Few individuals in any time or place have had such an impact on their country's history as Spain's Reyes Católicos, Isabel of Castilla and Fernando of Aragón. Indeed, Spain owes its very existence to their marriage in 1469 (which effectively united the Iberian Peninsula's two biggest Christian kingdoms) and to their conquest of Granada (1492) and annexation of Navarra (1512).

Isabel, by all accounts, was pious, honest, virtuous and very determined, while Fernando was an astute political operator – a formidable team. Isabel resisted her family's efforts to marry her off to half a dozen other European royals before her semi-clandestine wedding to Fernando at Valladolid – the first time the pair had set eyes on each other. They were second cousins; she was 18 and he 17. Isabel succeeded to the Castilian throne in 1474, and Fernando to Aragón's in 1479. By the time Isabel died in 1504, the pair had achieved the following:

» set up the Spanish Inquisition (1478);

» completed the Reconquista by conquering Granada (1492);

» expelled all Jews (1492) and Muslims (1500) who refused to convert to Christianity;

» helped to fund Columbus' voyage to the Americas (1492), opening the door to a vast overseas empire for Spain;

» crushed the power of Castilla's rebellious nobility.

Today Isabel and Fernando lie side by side in the beautiful Gothic church they commissioned as their own mausoleum, Granada's Capilla Real (p745).

1494	1512	1521	1533
The Treaty of Tordesillas (near Valladolid) divides recently discovered lands west of Europe between Spain and Portugal, giving the Spanish the right to claim vast territories in the Americas.	Fernando, ruling as regent after Isabel's death in 1504, annexes Navarra, bringing all of Spain under one rule for the first time since Roman days.	Hernán Cortés, from Medellín, Extremadura, conquers the Aztec empire in present-day Mexico and Guatemala with a small band of conquistadors, in the name of the Spanish crown.	Francisco Pizarro, from Trujillo, Extremadura, conquers the Inca empire in South America with a small band of conquistadors, in the name of the Spanish crown.

as the crew despaired of sighting land, they finally arrived on the island of Guanahaní, in the Bahamas, and went on to find Cuba and Hispaniola. Columbus returned to a hero's reception from the Catholic Monarchs in Barcelona, eight months after his departure. Columbus made three more voyages, founding the city of Santo Domingo on Hispaniola, finding Jamaica, Trinidad and other Caribbean islands, and reaching the mouth of the Orinoco and the coast of Central America. But he died impoverished in Valladolid in 1506, still believing he had reached Asia.

Brilliant but ruthless conquistadors such as Hernán Cortés and Francisco Pizarro followed Columbus' trail, seizing vast tracts of the American mainland for Spain. By 1600 Spain controlled Florida, all the biggest Caribbean islands, nearly all of present-day Mexico and Central America, and a large strip of South America. The new colonies sent huge cargoes of silver, gold and other riches back to Spain, where the crown was entitled to one-fifth of the bullion (the *quintoreal;* royal fifth). Seville enjoyed a monopoly on this trade and grew into one of Europe's richest cities.

Entangled in the Old World

Isabel and Fernando embroiled Spain in European affairs by marrying their five children into the royal families of Portugal, the Holy Roman Empire and England. After Isabel's death in 1504 and Fernando's in 1516, their thrones passed to their grandson Carlos I (Charles I), who arrived in Spain from Flanders in 1517, aged 17. In 1519 Carlos also succeeded to the Habsburg lands in Austria and was elected Holy Roman Emperor (as Charles V) – meaning he now ruled all of Spain, the Low Countries, Austria, several Italian states, parts of France and Germany, and the expanding Spanish colonies in the Americas.

Carlos spent only 16 years of his 40-year reign in Spain and at first the Spanish did not care for a king who spoke no Spanish and who appropriated their wealth. Castilian cities revolted in 1520–21 (the Guerra de las Comunidades; War of the Communities), but were crushed. Eventually the Spanish came round to him, at least for his strong stance against the new threat of Protestantism, and his learning of Spanish.

European conflicts soaked up the bulk of the monarchy's new American wealth, and a war-weary Carlos abdicated shortly before his death in 1556, retiring to the Monasterio de Yuste (p791) in Extremadura and dividing his many territories between his son Felipe II (Philip II; r 1556–98) and his brother Fernando. Felipe got the lion's share, including Spain, the Low Countries and the American possessions, and presided over the zenith of Spanish power, though his reign is a study in contradictions. He enlarged the American empire and claimed Portugal on its king's death in 1580, but lost Holland after a long drawn-out rebellion. His navy defeated the Ottoman Turks at Lepanto in 1571, but the Spanish Armada of

Atmosphere of the Middle Ages

» Sos del Rey Católico, Aragón

» Albarracín, Aragón

» Santiago de Compostela

» Morella, Valencia

» La Taha, Las Alpujarras

» Santo Domingo de la Calzada, La Rioja

» Ávila

» Albayzín, Granada

1556–98	1561	c 1600–1660	1609–14
Reign of Felipe II, the zenith of Spanish power. The American territories expand into the modern United States, and enormous wealth arriving from the colonies is used for grandiose architectural projects.	The king makes the minor country town of Madrid capital of his empire. Despite many new noble residences, the overwhelming impression is one of squalor.	Spain enjoys a cultural golden age with the literature of Cervantes and the paintings of Velázquez, Zurbarán and El Greco scaling new heights of artistic excellence as the empire declines.	The *moriscos* (converted Muslims) are expelled from Spain in a final purge of non-Christians that undermines an already faltering economy.

1588 was routed by England. He was a fanatical Catholic who spurred the Inquisition to new persecutions, yet readily allied Spain with Protestant England against Catholic France. He received greater flows of silver than ever from the Americas, but went bankrupt. Felipe too died in a monastery – the immense one at San Lorenzo de El Escorial, which he himself had had built and which stands as a sombre monument to his reign.

Riches to Rags

Spain's impotent response to its American windfall came home to roost over the 17th, 18th and 19th centuries. Under a series of comically inept rulers, it lost nearly all its foreign possessions, sank into deep economic malaise and internal wars, and wound up as a stagnant backwater untouched by the currents of industry, democracy, national unification and colonial expansion that swept Western Europe.

Hapless Habsburgs

Seventeenth-century Spain was immortalised on canvas by great artists such as Velázquez, El Greco, Zurbarán and Murillo, and in words by the likes of Miguel de Cervantes (author of *El ingenioso hidalgo Don Quijote de la Mancha*) and the prolific playwright Lope de Vega. But while the arts enjoyed a golden age, a trio of weak, backward-looking Habsburg monarchs, a highly conservative Church and an idle nobility allowed the economy to stagnate, leading to food shortages. Spain lost Portugal and faced revolts in Catalonia, Sicily and Naples. Silver shipments from the Americas shrank disastrously. And the sickly Carlos II (Charles II; r 1665–1700), known as El Hechizado (the Bewitched), failed to produce children, a situation that led to the War of the Spanish Succession.

Enlightened Bourbons

Carlos II bequeathed his throne to his young relative Felipe V (Philip V; r 1700–46), who also happened to be second in line to the French throne. Meanwhile the Austrian emperor Leopold wanted to see his own son Charles (a nephew of Carlos II) on the Spanish throne. During the resulting War of the Spanish Succession (1702–13), Spain lost its last possessions in the Low Countries to Austria, and Gibraltar and Menorca to Britain. Felipe V renounced his right to the French throne but held on to Spain. He was the first of the Bourbon dynasty, still in place today.

This was Europe's Age of Enlightenment, but Spain's powerful Church and Inquisition were at odds with the rationalism that trickled in from France. Two-thirds of the land was in the hands of the nobility and Church, and underutilised, and large numbers of males, from nobles to vagrants, were unwilling to work. Carlos III (Charles III; r 1759–88)

Echoes of America

» Trujillo, Extremadura

» Lugares Colombinos, near Huelva

» Casa-Museo de Colón, Valladolid

» Columbus' Tomb, Seville Cathedral

» Tordesillas, near Valladolid

» Palacio de Sobrellano, Comillas

» Museo de América, Madrid

1701	1702–13	1805
Felipe V, first of the Bourbon dynasty, takes the throne after the Habsburg line dies out with Carlos II. Felipe being second in line to the French throne causes concern across Europe.	Rival European powers support Charles of Austria against Felipe V in the War of the Spanish Succession: Felipe survives as king but Spain loses Gibraltar and the Low Countries.	A combined Spanish–French fleet is defeated by British ships under Nelson at the Battle of Trafalgar. Spanish sea power is effectively destroyed, and discontent against the king's pro-French policies grows.

DENNIS K JOHNSON / GETTY IMAGES ©

» Trafalgar Cemetery (p712)

expelled the backward-looking Jesuits, transformed the capital Madrid, built new roads to the provinces and tried to improve agriculture, but food shortages still fuelled unrests.

Echoes of the Napoleonic Wars

» Cabo de Trafalgar, Los Caños de Meca

» Trafalgar Cemetery, Gibraltar

» Museo de las Cortes de Cádiz, Cádiz

» Xardín de San Carlos, A Coruña

The Peninsular War

Carlos IV (Charles IV; r 1788–1808) was dominated by his Italian wife, Maria Luisa of Parma, who saw to it that her favourite, the handsome royal guard Manuel Godoy, became chief minister. When France's Louis XVI, cousin to Carlos IV, was guillotined in 1793 in the aftermath of the French Revolution of 1789, Spain declared war on France – only for Godoy to make peace with the French Republic two years later. In 1805 a combined Spanish–French navy was beaten by the British fleet, under Admiral Nelson, off the Cabo de Trafalgar, putting an end to Spanish sea power.

In 1807 Napoleon Bonaparte and Godoy agreed to divide Britain's ally Portugal between them. French forces poured into Spain, supposedly on the way to Portugal, but by 1808 this had become a French occupation of Spain, and Carlos IV was forced to abdicate in favour of Napoleon's brother Joseph Bonaparte (José I). In Madrid crowds revolted, as immortalised by Goya, and across the country Spaniards took up arms guerrilla-style, reinforced by British and Portuguese forces led by the Duke of Wellington. A national Cortes (Parliament) meeting at Cádiz in 1812 drew up a new liberal constitution, incorporating many of the principles of the American and French prototypes. The French were finally driven out after their defeat at Vitoria in 1813.

Bourbon Baubles

» Palacio Real, Madrid

» Palacio Real, Aranjuez

» La Granja de San Ildefonso, near Segovia

My Throne – No, Mine

An increasingly backward and insular Spain in the 19th century frittered away its energies on internal conflicts between liberals (who wanted vaguely democratic reforms) and conservatives (the Church, the nobility and others who preferred the earlier status quo), and sank to depths of poverty and exploitation that spawned growing social unrest.

Meanwhile Spain's American colonies took advantage of its problems and seized their independence. Fernando's dithering over his successor resulted in the First Carlist War (1833–39). During the war violent anticlericalism emerged, religious orders were closed and, in the Disentailment of 1836, church property and lands were seized and auctioned off by the government. The army emerged victorious from the fighting.

Throughout the mid-19th century the Spanish throne was constantly under threat, which led to another Carlist War (1872–76), fought between three factions, each supporting different claimants to the throne. In 1873 the liberal-dominated Cortes proclaimed the country a federal republic.

1808–13	1814	1809–24	1833–39
French forces occupy Spain; Carlos IV abdicates in favour of Napoleon's brother, José I. The ensuing Peninsular War sees British forces helping the Spanish defeat the French.	Fernando VII becomes king and revokes the 1812 Cádiz Constitution (an attempt by Spanish liberals to introduce constitutional reforms) just weeks after agreeing to uphold its principles.	Most of Spain's American colonies win independence as Spain is beset by problems at home. By 1824 only Cuba, Puerto Rico, Guam and the Philippines are under Spanish rule.	The First Carlist War, triggered by disputes over the succession between backers of Fernando VII's infant daughter, Isabel, and his brother, Carlos. Isabel will eventually become queen.

But this First Republic had lost control of the regions and the army put Isabel II's son Alfonso on the throne as Alfonso XII (r 1874–85), in a coalition with the Church and landowners.

The Great Divide

By the late 19th century industry had finally arrived in Barcelona, Madrid and some Basque cities, attracting migrants from the countryside and bringing both prosperity and squalid slums to the cities. But in rural areas the old problems of underproduction, oligarchic land ownership and mass poverty persisted, while society and politics became increasingly polarised between left and right.

Revolutionaries & Separatists

The anarchist ideas of the Russian Mikhail Bakunin reached Spain in the 1860s and rapidly gained support in cities as well as in the countryside. In the 1890s and the 1900s anarchists bombed Barcelona's Liceu opera house, assassinated two prime ministers and killed 24 people with a bomb at King Alfonso XIII's wedding to Victoria Eugenic of Battenberg in May 1906. Socialism grew more slowly than anarchism because of its less dramatic strategy of steady change through parliamentary processes.

Parallel with the rise of the left was the growth of Basque and Catalan separatism. In Catalonia this was led by big business interests. In the Basque country, nationalism emerged in the 1890s in response to a flood of Castilian workers into Basque industries: some Basques considered these migrants a threat to their identity. In 1909 a contingent of Spanish troops was wiped out by Berbers in Spanish Morocco. The government's decision to call up Catalan reservists sparked the so-called Semana Trágica (Tragic Week) in Barcelona, which began with a general strike and turned into a frenzy of violence. The government responded by executing many workers.

Spain stayed neutral during WWI and enjoyed an economic boom, but anarchist and socialist numbers grew, inspired by the Russian Revolution, and political violence and mayhem continued, especially in lawless Barcelona.

First Dictatorship

Alfonso XIII (r 1902–30) had a habit of meddling in politics (his reign saw 33 different governments), and when 10,000 Spanish soldiers were killed by Berbers at Anual in Morocco in 1921, the finger of blame pointed directly at the king. However, in 1923 General Miguel Primo de Rivera, an eccentric Andalucian aristocrat, led an army rising in support of Alfonso and established his own mild dictatorship.

HISTORY

During the First Republic some Spanish cities declared themselves independent states, and some, such as Seville and nearby Utrera, even declared war on each other.

FIRST REPUBLIC

1872–76	1898	1923–30	1931
The Second Carlist War, between three different monarchist factions, brings Isabel II's son, Alfonso XII, to the throne after the brief, chaotic First Republic of 1873.	Spain loses Cuba, Puerto Rico, Guam and the Philippines, its last remaining colonies, after being defeated in the Spanish–American War by the US, which declared war in support of Cuban independence.	General Miguel Primo de Rivera launches an army rising in support of King Alfonso XIII and then establishes himself as dictator. He retires and dies in 1930.	Alfonso XIII goes into exile after Republicans score sweeping gains in local elections. Spain's Second Republic is launched, left-wing parties win a national election, and a new constitution enfranchises women.

Primo was a centralist who censored the press and upset intellectuals. Anarchists went underground. Primo founded industries, improved roads, made the trains run on time and built dams and power plants. But in 1930, facing increasing opposition and an economic downturn following the Wall Street Crash of October 1929, he resigned.

Spain Before the Civil War

» *As I Walked Out One Midsummer Morning* (Laurie Lee)

» *South from Granada* (Gerald Brenan)

» *The Spanish Labyrinth* (Gerald Brenan)

» *Modern Spain, 1875–1980* (Raymond Carr)

Second Republic

National elections in 1931 brought in a government composed of socialists, republicans and centrists. A new constitution gave women the vote, granted autonomy-minded Catalonia its own parliament, legalised divorce, stripped Catholicism of its status as official religion, and banned priests from teaching. But anarchist disruption, an economic slump and disunity on the left all contributed to right-wing parties winning the next election, in 1933. One new force on the right was the fascist Falange, led by José Antonio Primo de Rivera, son of the 1920s dictator.

By 1934 violence was spiralling out of control. Catalonia declared itself independent (within a putative federal Spanish republic), and workers' committees took over the northern mining region of Asturias. A violent campaign against the Asturian workers by the Spanish Legion (set up to fight Moroccan tribes in the 1920s), led by generals Francisco Franco and José Millán Astray, split the country firmly into left and right.

In the February 1936 elections the right-wing National Front was narrowly defeated by the left-wing Popular Front, with communists at the fore. Violence continued from both sides. On 17 July 1936 the Spanish army garrison in Melilla, North Africa, rose up against the Popular Front government, followed the next day by garrisons on the mainland. The leaders of the plot were five generals, among them Francisco Franco. The civil war had begun.

The Civil War

The civil war split communities, families and friends, killed an estimated 350,000 Spaniards (some writers say 500,000), and caused untold damage and misery. Both sides committed atrocious massacres and reprisals. The rebels, who called themselves Nationalists because they believed they were fighting for Spain, shot or hanged tens of thousands of supporters of the republic. Republicans did likewise to Nationalist sympathisers, including some 7000 priests, monks and nuns.

At the start of the war many of the military and the Guardia Civil police force went over to the Nationalists, whose campaign quickly took on overtones of a crusade against the enemies of God. In Republican areas, anarchists, communists or socialists ended up running many towns and cities, and social revolution followed.

1933–35	1936	1936–39	1938
Right-wing parties win a new election; political violence spirals and a ruthless army operation against workers in Asturias irrevocably polarises Spain into left- and right-wing camps.	The left-wing National Front wins a national election. Right-wing 'Nationalist' rebels led by General Francisco Franco rise up against it, starting the Spanish Civil War.	The Spanish Civil War: the Nationalist rebels, under Franco, supported by Nazi Germany and Fascist Italy, defeat the USSR-supported Republicans. About 350,000 people die in fighting and atrocities.	The Nationalists defeat the Republicans' last major offensive, in the Ebro Valley, with 20,000 killed. The Soviet Union ends its support for the Republican side.

Nationalist Advance

Most cities with military garrisons fell immediately into Nationalist hands – this meant almost everywhere north of Madrid except Catalonia and the north coast, as well as parts of Andalucía. Franco's force of legionnaires and Moroccan mercenaries was airlifted to Seville by German warplanes in August. Essential to the success of the revolt, they moved northward through Extremadura towards Madrid, wiping out fierce resistance in some cities. At Salamanca in October, Franco pulled all the Nationalists into line behind him.

Madrid, reinforced by the first battalions of the International Brigades (armed foreign idealists and adventurers organised by the communists), repulsed Franco's first assault in November and then endured, under communist inspiration, over two years' siege. The International Brigades never numbered more than 20,000 and couldn't turn the tide against the better-armed and -organised Nationalist forces.

Nazi Germany and Fascist Italy supported the Nationalists with planes, weapons and men (75,000 from Italy, 17,000 from Germany), turning the war into a testing ground for WWII. The Republicans had some Soviet planes, tanks, artillery and advisers, but other countries refused to become involved (although some 25,000 French fought on the Republican side).

Republican Quarrels

With Madrid besieged, the Republican government moved to Valencia in late 1936 to continue trying to preside over the quarrelsome factions on its side, which encompassed anarchists, communists, moderate democrats and regional separatists.

In April 1937 German planes bombed the Basque town of Guernica (Gernika), causing terrible casualties; this became the subject of Picasso's famous pacifist painting which now hangs in Madrid's Centro de Arte Reina Sofía (p79). All the north coast fell to the Nationalists that year, while Republican counter-attacks near Madrid and in Aragón failed. Meanwhile divisions among the Republicans erupted into fierce street fighting in Barcelona, with the Soviet-influenced communists completely crushing the anarchists and Trotskyites who had run the city for almost a year. The Republican government moved to Barcelona in autumn 1937.

Nationalist Victory

In early 1938 Franco repulsed a Republican offensive at Teruel in Aragón, then swept eastward with 100,000 troops, 1000 planes and 150 tanks, isolating Barcelona from Valencia. In July the Republicans launched a last offensive in the Ebro Valley. This bloody encounter, won by the Nationalists, cost 20,000 lives. The USSR withdrew from the war in September

Civil War Reads

» *For Whom the Bell Tolls* (Ernest Hemingway)

» *Homage to Catalonia* (George Orwell)

» *Blood of Spain* (Ronald Fraser)

» *The Spanish Civil War* (Hugh Thomas)

» *The Battle for Spain* (Antony Beevor)

1939

The Nationalists take Barcelona in January. The Republican government flees to France, Republican forces evaporate and the Nationalists enter Madrid on 28 March. Franco declares the war over on 1 April.

1939–50

Franco establishes a right-wing dictatorship. Spain stays out of WWII but is later excluded from NATO and the UN and suffers a damaging international trade boycott.

» Puerta de Alcalá, Madrid (p90)

1938, and in January 1939 the Nationalists took Barcelona unopposed. The Republican government and hundreds of thousands of supporters fled to France. The Republicans still held Valencia and Madrid, and had 500,000 people under arms, but in the end their army simply evaporated. The Nationalists entered Madrid on 28 March 1939 and Franco declared the war over on 1 April.

Franco's Dictatorship

Instead of postwar reconciliation, more bloodletting ensued: an estimated 100,000 people were killed or died in prison after the war. The hundreds of thousands imprisoned included many intellectuals and teachers; others fled abroad, depriving Spain of a generation of scientists, artists, writers, educators and more. For 36 years Franco maintained absolute power. Regional autonomy aspirations were simply not tolerated. The army provided many government ministers and enjoyed a most generous budget. Catholic supremacy was also fully restored.

WWII & the Years of Hunger

Despite Franco's overtures to Hitler, Spain remained on the sidelines of WWII. In 1944 Spanish leftists launched a failed attack on Franco's Spain from France; small leftist guerrilla units continued a hopeless struggle in parts of the north, Extremadura and Andalucía until the 1950s.

After WWII Franco's Spain was excluded from the UN and NATO, and suffered a UN-sponsored trade boycott that helped turn the late 1940s into Spain's *años de hambre* (years of hunger). With the onset of the Cold War, however, the US wanted bases in Spain, and Franco agreed to the establishment of four, in return for large sums of aid. In 1955 Spain was admitted to the UN.

Economic Miracle

In 1959 a new breed of technocrats in government, linked to the Catholic group Opus Dei, engineered a Stabilisation Plan, which brought an economic upswing. Spanish industry boomed, modern machinery, technology and marketing were introduced, transport was modernised and new dams provided irrigation and hydropower.

The recovery was funded in part by US aid, and remittances from more than a million Spaniards who had gone to work abroad, but above all by tourism, which was developed initially along Andalucía's Costa del Sol and Catalonia's Costa Brava. By 1965 the number of tourists arriving in Spain was 14 million a year.

A huge population shift from rural regions to the cities and tourist resorts took place. Many Andalucians went to Barcelona.

Films Set in Franco's Spain

» *Pan's Labyrinth* (2006)

» *The Spirit of the Beehive* (1973)

» *¡Bienvenido, Mr Marshall!* (Welcome, Mr Marshall!; 1952)

» *Las 13 rosas* (The 13 Roses; 2007)

1955–65	1959	1975	1976
Spain is admitted to the UN after agreeing to host US bases. The economy is boosted by US aid and mass tourism on the Costa Brava and Costa del Sol.	Euskadi Ta Askatasuna (ETA; Basque Homeland and Freedom) is founded, aiming to gain Basque independence. The terrorist group will go on to murder over 800 people, including Franco's prime minister in 1973.	Franco dies and is succeeded by King Juan Carlos I. The monarch had been schooled by Franco to continue his policies but soon demonstrates his desire for change.	The king appoints Adolfo Suárez as prime minister. Suárez engineers a return to democracy. Left-wing parties are legalised, despite military opposition, and the country holds free elections in 1977.

The Final Decade

By the 1960s, after two-and-a-half decades of Franco's rule, the jails were still full of political prisoners and large garrisons were maintained outside every major city. Over the next decade, labour unrest grew and discontent began to rumble in the universities. The Basque terrorist group Euskadi Ta Askatasuna (ETA; Basque Homeland and Freedom) gave cause for the declaration of six states of emergency between 1962 and 1975.

In what seemed like a safe bet, Franco chose as his successor Prince Juan Carlos, the Spanish-educated grandson of Alfonso XIII. In 1969 Juan Carlos swore loyalty to Franco and the Movimiento Nacional. Cautious reforms by Franco's last prime minister, Carlos Arias Navarro, provoked violent opposition from right-wing extremists. Spain seemed to be sinking into chaos when Franco died on 20 November 1975.

New Democracy

Juan Carlos I, aged 37, took the throne two days after Franco died. The new king's links with the dictator inspired little confidence in a Spain now clamouring for democracy, but Juan Carlos had kept his cards close to his chest and takes much of the credit for the successful transition to democracy that followed. In July 1976 he appointed Adolfo Suárez, a 43-year-old former Franco apparatchik with film-star looks, as prime minister. To general surprise, Suárez got the Cortes to approve a new, two-chamber parliamentary system, and in 1977 political parties, trade unions and strikes were all legalised. The Movimiento Nacional was abolished.

Suárez's centrist party, the *Unión de Centro Democrático* (UCD; Central Democratic Union), won nearly half the seats in the new Cortes in 1977. A new constitution in 1978 made Spain a parliamentary monarchy with no official religion. In response to the fever for local autonomy, by 1983 the country was divided into 17 'autonomous communities' with their own regional governments controlling a range of policy areas. Personal and social life enjoyed a rapid liberation after Franco. Contraceptives, homosexuality and divorce were legalised, and the Madrid party and arts scene known as the *movida madrileña* formed the epicentre of a newly unleashed hedonism that still reverberates through Spanish life.

The Suárez government granted a general amnesty for deeds committed in the civil war and under the Franco dictatorship. There were no truth commissions or trials for the perpetrators of atrocities. For the next three decades Spain cast barely a backward glance.

Through the 1980s and '90s, under their new constitution and multiparty political spectrum, Spaniards became steadily richer, better educated and more liberated than ever before. But not everything in the orchard was orange blossom: ETA terrorism cost hundreds of lives, economic progress was sometimes stained by corruption, and the tussles

FRANCO

Paul Preston's *Franco* is the big biography of one of history's little dictators – and it has very little to say in the man's favour. Conspiracy theorists will love Peter Day's *Franco's Friends: How British Intelligence Helped Bring Franco to Power in Spain*.

1978	1981	1982–96	1986
A new constitution, overwhelmingly approved by referendum, establishes Spain as a parliamentary democracy with no official religion and the monarch as official head of state.	On 23 February a group of armed Guardia Civil led by Antonio Tejero attempt a coup by occupying the parliament building. The king denounces them on national TV; the coup collapses.	The centre-left Partido Socialista Obrero Español (PSOE; Spanish Socialist Workers' Party) is led by Felipe González. Despite an economic boom the government is associated with scandals and corruption.	Spain joins the European Community (now the EU). Along with its membership of NATO since 1982, this is a turning point in the country's post-Franco international reacceptance.

over regional autonomy between Madrid and the Basque Country and Catalonia seemed to have no end. But Spain's changes of government were orderly, electoral affairs, the economic graphs moved in a general upward direction and the improvement in ordinary people's lives was steady.

The PSOE & the PP

The main left-of-centre party, the Partido Socialista Obrero Español (PSOE; Spanish Socialist Workers' Party), led by a charismatic young lawyer from Seville, Felipe González, came second in the 1977 election and then won power with a big majority in 1982. González was to be prime minister for 14 years. The PSOE's young and educated leadership came from the generation that had opened the cracks in the Franco regime in the late 1960s and early 1970s. Unemployment rose from 16% to 22% by 1986. But that same year Spain joined the European Community (now the EU), bringing on a five-year economic boom. The middle class grew ever bigger, the PSOE established a national health system and improved public education, and Spain's women streamed into higher education and jobs.

In 1992 – the 500th anniversary of the fall of Granada and Columbus' first voyage to the Americas – Spain celebrated its arrival in the modern world by staging the Barcelona Olympics and the Expo 92 world fair in Seville. But the economy was in a slump and the PSOE was mired in scandals. By 1996 unemployment was running at 23%, the highest in Western Europe. It came as no surprise when the PSOE lost the 1996 general election.

The party that won the 1996 election was the centre-right Partido Popular (PP; People's Party), led by José María Aznar, a former tax inspector from Castilla y León. The PP had been founded by a former Franco minister, Manuel Fraga, something its opponents never let it forget. Aznar promised to make politics dull, and he did, but he presided over eight years of solid economic progress, winning the 2000 election as well. The PP cut public investment, sold off state enterprises and liberalised sectors such as telecommunications, and during the Aznar years Spain's economy grew a lot faster than the EU average, while unemployment fell dramatically.

Spain Reinvented

On 11 March 2004, just three days before the national elections, Madrid was rocked by 10 bombs on four rush-hour commuter trains heading into the capital's Atocha station. When the dust cleared, 191 people had died and 1755 were wounded, many of them seriously. It was the biggest such terror attack in the nation's history. Madrid was in shock and, for

> Paul Preston's searing *The Spanish Holocaust: Inquisition and Extermination in Twentieth-Century Spain* lays bare the brutality of Spain's civil war (neither side comes out well) and the oppression by victorious Franco forces after the war.

CIVIL WAR

1992
Barcelona holds the Olympic Games, putting Spain in the international spotlight and highlighting the country's progress since 1975. Madrid is European Capital of Culture and Seville hosts a world expo.

1996
Disaffection with PSOE sleaze gives the centre-right Partido Popular (PP), led by José María Aznar, a general election victory, at the start of a decade of sustained economic growth.

OLIVER STREWE / GETTY IMAGES ©

» Seville Cathedral (p662)

24 hours at least, this most clamorous of cities fell silent. Then, some 36 hours after the attacks, more than three million *madrileños* streamed onto the streets to protest against the bombings, with a further eight million marching in solidarity in cities across Spain.

The PP government insisted that the ETA was responsible. But as evidence mounted that the attack might have come from a radical Islamic group in reprisal for the government's unswerving support for the deeply unpopular invasion of Iraq, angry Spaniards turned against the government. In a stunning reversal of pre-poll predictions, the PP was defeated by the PSOE, whose leader, José Luis Rodríguez Zapatero, led the Socialists back to power after eight years in the wilderness.

In addition to withdrawing Spanish troops from Iraq, the new government gave Spain a makeover by introducing a raft of liberalising social reforms. Gay marriage was legalised, Spain's arcane divorce laws were overhauled, almost a million illegal immigrants were granted residence, and a law seeking to apportion blame for the crimes of the Civil War and Franco dictatorship entered the statute books. Although Spain's powerful Catholic Church cried foul over many of the reforms, the changes played well with most Spaniards even as the Catholic Church bussed in demonstrators en masse to protest.

The PSOE government won another four years at elections in 2008, albeit with a reduced majority that forced it to rely on smaller regional parties in order to govern. But the early signs of economic crisis quickly contributed to the sense of a government almost immediately under siege. Prime Minister Zapatero's delay in acknowledging the crisis sealed the government's fate, and it was defeated by the PP of Prime Minister Mariano Rajoy in a landslide on 20 November 2011. With the highest unemployment in Europe and an economy in freefall, the new government faced a daunting task.

Modern Spain Reading

» *Ghosts of Spain* (Giles Tremlett)

» *The New Spaniards* (John Hooper)

» *Juan Carlos: Steering Spain from Dictatorship to Democracy* (Paul Preston)

» *Roads to Santiago: Detours & Riddles in the Land and History of Spain* (Cees Nooteboom)

---

11 March 2004	14 March 2004	October 2008	November 2011
A terrorist bombing on 10 Madrid commuter trains kills 191 people. The following day, an estimated 11 million people take to the streets across Spain.	The PSOE led by José Luis Rodríguez Zapatero sweeps to power and ushers in eight years of Socialist rule, characterised by sweeping changes to social legislation.	Spain's unemployment rate soars from less than 6% to 12.3% in a single month. Spain's finance minister admits that Spain has entered 'its deepest recession in half a century'.	The conservative Popular Party, led by Mariano Rajoy (who had been defeated in 2004 and 2008), sweeps to power in national elections, ending eight years of Socialist Party rule.

Architecture

As you look up at the arches of the great Roman aqueduct in Segovia, you can almost see centurions marching beneath it. With the gentle bubbling of its cool fountains, the Alhambra conjures up Spain's Islamic era as if from a dream. On a grey winter's day, along the echoing corridors of the Monasterio de Santo Domingo de Silos' Romanesque cloisters, the Middle Ages seem to return in all their mystical fervour. Towering, at times half-ruined, castles dot the countryside from Catalonia to Castilla. To gaze up, eyes turned to God, at the great Gothic cathedrals of Burgos, Palma de Mallorca and Toledo, you can feel the awe they must have inspired when first raised. And who isn't carried away by the whimsy of Gaudí's Modernista fantasies dotting the streets of Barcelona?

Spain's architecture presents one of the broadest and richest testimonies in Europe to thousands of years of building ingenuity. The journey starts with the simple stone housing of the Celtiberian tribes, but Spain's long Islamic history is where the real story begins. The fusion of Middle Eastern and European aesthetics is unique in Europe: the Moorish heyday produced extravagant masterpieces, while after the Reconquista architects reacted strongly against Islamic styles with austere Romanesque structures. Meanwhile, others slyly integrated them, as in the case of Mozarabic and Mudéjar designs. The love of ornament carried on well into the Renaissance, when Spanish designers developed the ornate plateresque style, which in turn paved the way for the staggering confections of the baroque period. In the late 19th century, Modernista geniuses in Barcelona pushed walls and ceilings into all-new shapes, a process continued by Spain's ground-breaking contemporary architects.

Ancient Spain

The tribes that first inhabited the Iberian Peninsula were collectively known as Celtiberians. In the northwest part of the country (and in Portugal), the so-called Castro culture of the Bronze Age (9th century BC) is named for the *castro* (walled hamlet made up of circular stone houses, clustered together like cupcakes in a bakery box). *Castro* culture and architecture survived until at least the 2nd century AD. Among the better preserved *castro* ruins are those at A Guarda (p541), on Galicia's southern coast, and near Coaña (p493) in Asturias.

Later, the Greeks and Carthaginians remained primarily on the coast and left little behind. The Romans, however, made more of an impact – architectural and otherwise – across the peninsula after the 2nd century BC. The 1st-century emperor Trajan, who expanded the empire to its furthest limits, was born at Itálica, near modern-day Seville. In Extremadura, Augusta Emerita (now Mérida) was one of the most influential cities in the western Roman Empire, and continued to hold sway until it was conquered by the Arabs in 713 AD. It has the longest Roman bridge still standing, working reservoirs and a vast amphitheatre.

In the 1920s, a replica of Seville's Giralda jutted above the old Moorish-looking Madison Square Garden in New York City; it was later torn down. Another replica fares better, standing tall above Kansas City, Missouri – a sister city to Seville.

GIRALDA

The Visigothic Period

The Visigoth reign lasted fewer than three centuries between the last vestiges of the Roman Empire and the rise of the Islamic one, beginning in 711 AD. Accordingly, the architectural legacy is small: very little survived. During the Islamic era many Visigothic churches were neglected, and during the Catholic Reconquista many more were destroyed to make way for grander structures.

But what remains shows a remarkably attractive style – humbler than the Romans', but solidly built with smooth dressed stones and decorated with reliefs of abstract plant forms and crosses that are reminiscent of Byzantine styles. Another characteristic of this period is the arch with slightly indented sides, creating a faint horseshoe shape. It would later become associated purely with Moorish architecture, as Syrian architects had also developed the arch.

Reputedly the oldest Visigothic church in Spain, the Basílica de San Juan (p176) in Baños de Cerrato, in the province of Palencia, was constructed in 661 and consecrated by King Recceswinth. It has a horseshoe-shaped entrance door and friezes of intertwined circles. Ermita de Santa María de Lara (p191), at Quintanilla de las Viñas in Burgos province, is probably the last church built under the Visigoths, as archaeologists have dated it to around 700. Only about a third of it survives, but in the outline of the building one can see numerous smaller rooms, another feature of Visigothic structures.

The Introduction of Islam

About 70 years after the first Islamic incursion into Spain, Córdoba was well established as the new capital of the western end of the empire. In 784 Syrian architects set to work on the grand Mezquita (p733), conjuring their homeland with details that echo the Umayyad Mosque in Damascus, such as delicate horseshoe arches and exquisite decorative tiles with floral motifs. But even from the beginning, this Islamic architecture in Spain was a synthesis: the building's most distinctive feature – more than 500 columns that crowd the interior of the mosque – were repurposed from Roman and Visigothic ruins.

In the centuries that followed, Moorish architecture incorporated trends from all over the Islamic empire. The technique of intricately carved stucco detailing was developed in 9th-century Iraq, while *muqarnas* (honeycomb vaulting) arrived via Egypt in the 10th century. Square minarets, such as the Giralda (p662) in Seville (now a church tower), came with the Almohad invasion from Morocco in the 12th century.

The better remnants of the Islamic era are in Andalucía, although the Aljafería (p373) in Zaragoza is a beautiful exception. Perhaps the most magnificent creation is the core of Granada's Alhambra (p742), the Palacios Nazaríes (Nasrid Palaces). From the 13th to the 15th century, architects reached new heights of

SPANISH ARCHITECTURE

210 BC–AD 409 Roman

Bridges, waterworks, walls, whole cities – the Romans build to last, and to inspire later traditions.

409–711 Visigothic

Invaders from the north build sturdy stone churches with simple decoration and horseshoe arches.

711–1492 Moorish

Horseshoe arches, square minarets, intricate geometric design – this synthesis of styles from across the Islamic empire includes Mozarabic (Islamic-look buildings in Christian territory).

1100–1700 Mudéjar

Post-Reconquista work by Muslims, carrying on the Moorish tradition of decoration and adapting it to more common materials.

1100–1300 Romanesque

Essentially the anti-Moorish, with spare decoration and proportions based on Byzantine churches. Look for heavy, perfectly semicircular arches.

1200–1600 Gothic

Churches nearly take flight: flying buttresses enable ceilings to soar, and arches become pointy to match.

1400–1600 Plateresque

The pinnacle of Spain's Renaissance, a dazzling ornate style of relief carving on facades.

elegance, creating a study in balance between inside and outside, light and shade, spareness and intricate decoration. Eschewing innovation, the Alhambra refined well-tried forms, as if in an attempt to freeze time and halt the collapse of Moorish power, which, at the time, was steadily eroding across the peninsula.

Hybrid Styles: Mozarabic & Mudéjar

The real creativity in architecture came as a byproduct of the *convivencia*, when Muslim, Christian and Jewish cultures cross-pollinated. By the 10th century, Moorish rule had produced a class of people called Mozarabs – practicing Christians who lived in Islamic territory and spoke Arabic. When Mozarab artisans moved or travelled north into Christian Spain, they took elements of classic Islamic construction with them. As a result, the Monasterio de San Miguel de Escalada (p183), east of León, imitates the Mezquita, with horseshoe arches atop leafy Corinthian capitals reused from Roman buildings. Many arches are boxed in by an *alfiz* (a rectangular decorative frame typically filled with geometric or abstract vegetal decoration), around the upper portion of the arch. This became a signature detail in Mozarabic architecture.

The 11th-century Ermita de San Baudelio (p198), beyond Berlanga de Duero in Soria province, resembles Visigoth churches in its constricted layout. But it was covered in lavish frescoes of Middle Eastern camels and elephants, as well as hunting scenes that resemble those in old Syrian Umayyad palaces. (Most of the frescoes have since been removed to museums.) Because these Mozarabic buildings crossed religious boundaries, they could be called the first truly Spanish architectural style to emerge after the rise of Islam.

Later, as the Reconquista started to gain ground, another border-crossing class emerged: Mudéjars (the Muslims who stayed on in now-Catholic Spain). Mudéjar artisans, largely disenfranchised, offered cheap labour and great talent. The Mudéjar style, in evidence from the 12th century on, is notable first for the use of relatively inexpensive materials – gone were the days of lavish government commissions, and the Roman stones had all been used up. Instead, brick, tile and plaster were worked with incredible skill to conjure opulence, with some of the best extant examples in Aragon and Castilla. Teruel in particular is dotted with intricate brick towers, trimmed in glazed tiles.

Only one unruly part of northern Spain, in what is now Asturias, was never conquered by the Muslims. During the 9th century a unique building style emerged, exaggerating Visigothic styles. The Palacio de Santa María del Naranco, for instance, has dramatically elongated proportions, delicate relief carvings and tall, thin arches.

MUQARNAS MATH

Unique to Islamic architecture, honeycomb vaulting (*muqarnas* in Arabic) is essentially stacks of tiny corbels (vaults that stick up and out, and are designed to hold weight), cut into various shapes and assembled in horizontal tiers. The Sala de Dos Hermanas in Granada's Alhambra is composed of more than 5000 tiny cells.

Massed together on a ceiling, these tiny vaults resemble wasps' nests or stalactites, but there is nothing organic about their construction – they are the product of a rigorous geometrical process. For a culture that valued science and maths and was obsessed with geometrical intricacy, *muqarnas* is the natural next step from two dimensions to three – so natural, in fact, that it appears to have developed simultaneously in both North Africa and Iran.

A full *muqarnas* dome is essentially a negative sculpture – the world's most elaborate jelly mould. Scholars have spent countless hours analysing various examples of *muqarnas* and rendering them in two-dimensional plans to reveal the near-endless variations in tesselation, rotational symmetry and component shapes. The most common general type, especially in Spain, is the square lattice, so named because it is usually built into a dome set on a square base. Squinches in the corners of the square create an octagon, and from there, smaller shapes are added in tiers to smooth the transition from square base to round dome.

Another telltale Mudéjar feature is extravagantly decorated timber ceilings done in a style called *artesonado*. They can be barrel vaults, but the most typical style is a flat wood ceiling made of interlocking beams that are inset with multicoloured wood panels in geometric patterns. In the Alhambra, the ceilings installed by later Catholic occupants may not be quite as intricate as earlier Islamic work in the same complex, but the style is remarkably consistent, even as it incorporates the new rulers' coats of arms.

From Romanesque to Gothic

While the tide was turning against the Muslims, the Romanesque style was sweeping medieval Europe, taking root in Spain in part because it was the aesthetic opposite of Islamic fashions – architect and art historian Josep Puig i Cadafalch posited that each Romanesque detail was a systematic riposte to an Islamic one. These buildings were spare, angular and heavy, inspired by the proportions of classical structures. Many of these Romanesque churches, monasteries, bridges and pilgrims' hospices were not-so-subtle statements about the success of the Reconquista.

Romanesque structures had perfectly semicircular arches – none of the stylised horseshoe look that had come before. In churches, this was expressed in a semicylindrical apse (or, in many cases, triple apse), a shape previously found in Byzantine churches. The round arch also graced doorways, windows, cloisters and naves. Entrances supported stacks of concentric arches – all the more eye-catching because they were often the only really decorative detail. Some great, lesser-known examples include the Iglesia de San Martín (p176) in Frómista, and Sant Climent de Taüll (p343), one of many fine examples in the Catalan Pyrenees. Later, during the 12th century, the Spanish began to modify these semicircles, edging towards the Gothic style, as they added pointed arches and ribbed vaults. The Monasterio de la Oliva (p452) in Navarra was among the first to show such features, and cathedrals in Ávila (p137), Sigüenza (p231), Tarragona (p363) and Tudela all display at least some transitional elements.

Meanwhile, in northern Europe, everyone was marvelling at the towering cathedrals made possible by the newfangled flying buttresses. The idea caught on in Spain by the 13th century, when the cathedrals at Burgos (p186), León (p178) and Toledo (p205) were built. Their models were basically French, but the Spaniards soon introduced other elements. Some changes were subtle, such as placing choir stalls in the centre of the nave, but one was unmissable: the towering, decorative *retablo* (altarpiece) that graced the new churches. Spanish Gothic architects also devised the star vault, a method of distributing weight with ribbed vaults projecting out from a central point.

Many great buildings were begun at the height of Romanesque fashion but not completed until long after the Gothic style had gained the upper hand. The cathedral in Burgos, for instance, was begun in 1221 as a relatively sober construction, but its 15th-century spires are a product of German-inspired late-Gothic imagination. Mudéjar influences also still made themselves felt, particularly in the use of brick rather than stone. Toledo boasts many gloriously original buildings with a Gothic-Mudéjar flair, as does part of Aragón, where the fanciful brick structures have been declared a Unesco World Heritage site.

1650–1750 Churrigueresque

Spain's special twist on baroque – literally, as spiral columns were all the rage, along with gold-leaf everything.

1888–1911 Modernisme

The Spanish version of art nouveau took a brilliant turn in Barcelona, and the city hasn't been the same since.

1975–present Contemporary Architecture

Spain's architecture has headed off in previously unimaginable directions since the death of Franco.

Roman Relics

» Aqueduct, Segovia

» Roman theatre, Mérida

» City walls, Lugo, Galicia

» Museu d'Història de Tarragona, Catalonia

» Itálica, Seville

» Baelo Claudia, Andalucía

» Villa Romana La Olmeda, Castilla y León

Decorative Details

The history of architecture in Spain seems to be an ongoing struggle between austere simplicity and mind-boggling decoration. Perhaps it's too soon to declare a winner, but all things baroque, intricate and elaborate appear to have the edge.

Alhambra, Granada

1 The pinnacle of Islamic architecture in Spain, Alhambra (p742) piles on the ornament in the form of plaster so finely carved it resembles lace, and swirling calligraphy that creates an overall effect. Richly coloured ceramic tiles are quintessential Andalucía.

Aljafería, Zaragoza

2 Wood ceilings with a complex inlay in geometric patterns were perfected under Islamic rule and carried into the Reconquista by Mudéjar artisans. Lie down in the middle of the room (p373) to gawk properly – it's worth it.

Park Güell, Barcelona

3 Catalonia's capital bursts with Antoni Gaudí's visions, especially the eye-popping tiles in Park Güell (p268). Structure and surface merge perfectly: the mosaics seem to grow organically from the odd bulging forms to which they're applied.

Monasterio de La Cartuja, Granada

4 The Carthusian monks went for baroque in a big way – the monastery (p748) is extreme. The sacristy, where the priests would dress, is trimmed in mirrors, marquetry cabinets and dizzying black-and-white tiles.

Universidad Civil, Salamanca

5 Plateresque craftsmen carved Salamanca's rich sandstone (p144) within an inch of its life; the facade crawls with crests, lions, griffins, skulls, the pope and a tiny frog, said to bring luck to whoever can spot it.

Clockwise from top left
1. Alhambra, Granada (p742) 2. Aljafería, Zaragoza (p373) 3. Park Güell, Barcelona (p268)

Gothicism displayed odd local variants. The Catalan approach was more sober, bereft of pinnacles. Architects developed incredibly broad, unsupported vaults without the use of flying buttresses. In contrast, the Isabelline Gothic look, inspired by the Catholic queen, is a decorative mash-up, reflecting her fondness of Islamic exotica and heraldic imagery. It's on display in Toledo's San Juan de los Reyes (p208), where Gothic arches meet intricately carved and painted wood ceilings, and the Capilla Real (p745) in Granada, where she and King Ferdinand are buried – their initials form a decorative band around the outside, perhaps inspired by the calligraphy in the Alhambra.

It wasn't only religious buildings that flourished during this period. Most of the innumerable castles scattered across the country went up in Gothic times. Many never saw action and were not intended to – an extraordinary example is the sumptuous castle at Coca (p164), in Segovia. In Barcelona, some marvellous civil Gothic architecture can be admired, including the Saló del Tinell in the one-time royal palace in the Barri Gòtic and the Reials Drassanes, the once-mighty shipyards now home to the Museu Marítim (p251).

The Gothic fascination lasted into the 16th century, when there was a revival of pure Gothic, perhaps best exemplified in the new cathedral (p146) in Salamanca, although the Segovia cathedral (p158) was about the last, and possibly most pure, Gothic structure raised in Spain.

> The Camino de Santiago is also an architecture pilgrimage route, for such Romanesque beauties as the Monasterio de Santo Domingo de Silos, the smaller cloister in the Monasterio de las Huelgas in Burgos, the restored Iglesia de San Martín in Frómista and the cathedral itself in Santiago de Compostela.

Renaissance & Plateresque

The effects of the pan-European Renaissance began to show in Spain at the end of the 15th century. The intellectual boom did not yield a single unified style, but inspired the uniquely Spanish vision of plateresque, which drew partly on Italian styles but was also an outgrowth of the Isabelline Gothic look. It is so named because facade decoration was so ornate that it looked as though it had been wrought by *plateros* (silversmiths). To visit Salamanca, where the Spanish Renaissance first took root, is to receive a concentrated dose of the most splendid work in the genre. The university (p144) facade is a virtuoso piece, featuring busts, medallions and a complex floral design that covers the wall like an unfurled carpet. Not far behind in intensity comes the facade of the Convento de San Esteban (p146), where the main facade arch is studded with a thousand flowerlike forms, glowing in the warm local sandstone.

A more purist Renaissance style, reflecting classical proportions and styles already established in Italy and France, prevailed in Andalucía. Symbolically and physically, the aesthetic finds its maximum expression in the Palacio de Carlos V (p745) that the emperor erected smack in the middle of the Moorish pleasure palaces in Granada's Alhambra. It's the only example of the Renaissance circle-in-a-square ground plan in Spain.

The Renaissance wild card was Juan de Herrera, whose work bears almost no resemblance to anything else of the period because it is so austere. His masterpiece is the palace-monastery complex of San Lorenzo de El Escorial (p130), a study in cubes (he had written a book on this very subject). He discarded typical classical decorative orders, leaving vast granite surfaces bare. The look was imitated in numerous monasteries for more than a century.

> Ildefonso Falcones' best-selling historical novel *La catedral del mar* (The Cathedral of the Sea) tells the juicy tale of the construction of the Santa María del Mar cathedral in Barcelona in the 13th century.

Baroque & Churrigueresque

In the late 17th century, Spanish architects took to the heady frills and spills of baroque in a big way. Aside from the late-18th-century Cádiz cathedral (p689), there are very few from-scratch baroque buildings in Spain. But no matter: the exuberant decoration is so eye-catching that it easily overtakes the more sober earlier buildings to which it's attached. The leading exponents of this often overblown style were the Churriguera brothers, three sons of a respected sculptor who specialised in *retablos,* the enormous carved-wood altar backdrops. One of the sons, José Benito, was court architect for Carlos II from 1690 to 1702; in his obituary he was dubbed 'the Michelangelo of Spain'.

The hallmark of churrigueresque is the so-called Solomonic column, a delightful twisting pillar that, especially when covered in gold leaf or vines, seems to wiggle its way to the heavens. José Benito later pioneered the more severe estipite column, shaped like an inverted cone.

Later practitioners took the Churrigueras' innovations and ran with them. The Carthusian monks of Granada, for instance, built the Monasterio de Nuestra Señora de la Asunción (p748; more commonly called La Cartuja) by hand. The *sancta sanctorum* around the tabernacle is mind-boggling, crammed with saints, gilt skulls and intricate marble inlay. Likewise, Narciso Tomés' gold-leaf-trimmed altarpiece in the Catedral de Toledo is a later baroque masterwork.

Modernisme & Art Deco

At the end of the 19th century, Catalonia was the powerhouse of Spain, and Barcelona's prosperity unleashed one of the most imaginative periods in Spanish architecture. The architects at work here, who drew on prevailing art nouveau trends as well as earlier Spanish styles, came to be called the Modernistas. Chief among them, Antoni Gaudí sprinkled Barcelona with jewels of his singular imagination. They range from his immense, unfinished Sagrada Família (p257) to the simply weird Casa Batlló (p265) and the only slightly more sober La Pedrera (p265). Though Gaudí is most associated with a certain, well, gaudiness, his structural approach owed more to the austere era of Catalan Gothic, which inspired his own inventive work with parabolic arches.

Two other Catalan architects, Lluís Domènech i Montaner and Josep Puig i Cadafalch, don't have the immediate name recognition, but their works are Barcelona landmarks. Domènech i Montaner's Palau de la Música Catalana (p252), for instance, matches Gaudí in exuberance and use of decorative tile. Puig i Cadafalch, who studied under Domènech i Montaner, built town houses such as Casa Amatller (p265).

While Barcelona went all wavy, Madrid embraced the rigid glamour of art deco. This global style arrived in Spain just as Madrid's Gran Vía (p76) was laid out in the 1920s – the boulevard was the perfect blank slate for architectural creation. One of the more overwhelming caprices from that era is the Palacio de Comunicaciones on Plaza de la Cibeles (p89).

The playful nature of Modernisme and art deco came to a quick end shortly after Franco took over in 1936, stifling architectural creativity for decades.

Contemporary Innovation

Post-Franco, Spain has made up for lost time. Ambitious urban redevelopment programs revamped cityscapes such as Barcelona, where the 1992 Olympics inspired a harbour makeover. More recently in Madrid, the Cuatro Torres business area sprouted skyscrapers by Spanish and international star architects.

Local heroes include Santiago Calatrava, who built his reputation with swooping, bone-white bridges. In 1996 he designed the futuristic Ciudad de las Artes y las Ciencias (p557; City of Arts and Sciences) complex in Valencia. In 2000 he also built the Sondika Airport, in Bilbao, which has been nicknamed La Paloma (the Dove), for the winglike arc of its aluminium skin.

Catalan Enric Miralles had a short career, dying of a brain tumour in 2000 at the age of 45, but his Mercat de Santa Caterina (p253) in Barcelona shows brilliant colour and inventive use of arches. His Gas Natural

ARCHITECTURE

Baroque Baubles

» Monasterio de Nuestra Señora de la Asunción, Granada

» Plaza Mayor, Salamanca

» Cathedral facade, Santiago de Compostela

» Cathedral, Murcia

» Real Academia de Bellas Artes de San Fernando, Madrid

Robert Hughes' *Barcelona* is a thorough, erudite history of the city, with an emphasis on architecture. The Gaudí chapters provide special insight into the designer's surprisingly conservative outlook.

building, also in Barcelona, is a poetic skyscraper that juts both vertically and horizontally. Both were completed after his death by his widow, Italian architect Benedetta Tagliabue.

In 1996 Rafael Moneo won the Pritzker Prize, the greatest international honour for living architects, largely for his long-term contributions to Madrid's cityscape, such as the revamping of the Atocha railway station (p82). His renovation of the Palacio Villahermosa into the Thyssen-Bornemisza Museum (p87) in Madrid blends in subtly with the urban fabric. The Kursaal Palace in San Sebastían, finished in 1999, is eye-catching – still staunchly functional, but shining, like two giant stones swept up from the sea.

Moneo may so far be the only Pritzker winner from Spain, but the country has become something of a Pritzker playground. It's perhaps this openness – even hunger – for outside creativity that marks the country's built environment today. Norman Foster designed the metro system in Bilbao, completed in 1995; the transparent, wormlike staircase shelters have come to be called *fosteritos*. But it was Frank Gehry's 1998 Museo Guggenheim (p409) in the same city that really sparked the quirky-building fever. Now the list of contemporary landmarks includes Herzog & de Meuron's deep-blue Edifici Fòrum on Barcelona's waterfront; Jean Nouvel's spangly, gherkin-shaped Torre Agbar (p267), also in Barcelona; Richard Rogers' dreamy, wavy Terminal 4 at Madrid's Barajas airport; Oscar Niemeyer's flying-saucerish Centro Cultural Internacional Avilés (p490) in Asturias; and Zaha Hadid's whalelike bridge-cum-pavilion for the Zaragoza Expo.

Although construction has slowed almost to a halt in Spain since the economic crash of 2008, watch out for Norman Foster's facelift of the Camp Nou Stadium in Barcelona, where coloured glass will create a modern cathedral, and Zaha Hadid's Spiral Tower, also in Barcelona, which resembles a precarious stack of rectangular dinner plates.

Outside Spain, Rafael Moneo is best known for the 2002 Cathedral of Our Lady of Angels, in downtown Los Angeles, California.

MONEO

Spain's Master Painters

The Golden Century – Velázquez & Friends

The star of the 17th-century art scene, which became known as an artistic Golden Age, was the genius court painter, Diego Rodríguez de Silva Velázquez (1599–1660). Born in Seville, Velázquez later moved to Madrid as court painter and composed scenes (landscapes, royal portraits, religious subjects, snapshots of everyday life) that owe their vitality not only to his photographic eye for light, contrast and the details of royal finery, but also to a compulsive interest in the humanity of his subjects so that they seem to breathe on the canvas. With Velázquez any trace of the idealised stiffness that characterised the previous century's spiritless mannerism fell by the wayside. His masterpieces include *Las meninas* (Maids of Honour) and *La rendición de Breda* (Surrender of Breda), both in the Museo del Prado (p82).

Another shining light of the period was Francisco de Zurbarán (1598–1664), who is best remembered for the startling clarity and light in his portraits of monks.

Goya & the 19th Century

There was nothing in the provincial upbringing of Francisco José de Goya y Lucientes (1746–1828), who was born in the village of Fuendetodos in Aragón, to suggest that he would become one of the towering figures of European art. Goya began his career as a cartoonist in the Real Fábrica de Tapices (Royal Tapestry Workshop) in Madrid. Illness in 1792 left him deaf; many critics speculate that his condition was largely responsible for his wild, often merciless style that would become increasingly unshackled from convention. By 1799 Goya was appointed Carlos IV's court painter.

Several distinct series and individual paintings mark his progress. In the last years of the 18th century he painted enigmatic masterpieces, such as *La maja vestida* (The Young Lady Dressed) and *La maja desnuda* (The Young Lady Undressed), identical portraits but for the lack of clothes in the latter. The Inquisition was not amused by the artworks, which it covered up. Nowadays all is bared in Madrid's Museo del Prado.

The arrival of the French and the war in 1808 had a profound impact on Goya. Unforgiving portrayals of the brutality of war are *El dos de mayo* (The Second of May) and, more dramatically, *El tres de mayo* (The Third of May). The latter depicts the execution of Madrid rebels by French troops.

Goya spent the last years of his life in voluntary exile in France, where he continued to paint until his death.

Velázquez so much wanted to be made a Knight of Santiago that in *Las meninas* he cheekily portrayed himself with the cross of Santiago on his vest, long before his wish was finally fulfilled.

VELÁZQUEZ

In addition to Madrid, Zaragoza's Museo Camón Aznar (p374) has an outstanding collection of Goya etchings.

Picasso, Dalí & the Others – the Shock of the New

In the early years of the 20th century, the genius of mischievous *malagueño* (Málaga native) Pablo Ruiz Picasso (1881–1973) came like a thunderclap. A child when he moved with his family to Barcelona, Picasso was formed in an atmosphere laden with the avant-garde freedom of Modernisme.

Picasso must have been one of the most restless artists of all time. His work underwent repeated revolutions as he passed from one creative phase to another. From his gloomy Blue Period, through the brighter Pink Period and on to cubism – in which he was accompanied by Madrid's Juan Gris (1887–1927) – Picasso was nothing if not surprising. Picasso consistently cranked out paintings, sculptures, ceramics and etchings until the day he died. A good selection of his early work can be viewed in Barcelona's Museu Picasso (p249), while the Museo Picasso Málaga (p716) has more than 200 Picasso works. The remaining works are scattered around different galleries, notably Madrid's Centro de Arte Reina Sofía (p79).

Separated from Picasso by barely a generation, two other artists reinforced the Catalan contingent in the vanguard of 20th-century art: Dalí and Miró. Although he started off dabbling in cubism, Salvador Dalí (1904–89) became more readily identified with the surrealists. This complex character's 'hand-painted dream photographs', as he called them, are virtuoso executions brimming with fine detail and nightmare images dragged up from a feverish and Freud-fed imagination. Preoccupied with Picasso's fame, Dalí built himself a reputation as an outrageous showman and shameless self-promoter. The single best display of his work can be seen at the Teatre-Museu Dalí (p326) in Figueres.

Slower to find his feet, Barcelona-born Joan Miró (1893–1983) developed a joyous and almost childlike style that earned him the epithet 'the most surrealist of us all' from French writer André Breton. His later period is his best known, characterised by the simple use of bright colours and forms in combinations of symbols that represented women, birds (the link between earth and the heavens) and stars (the unattainable heavenly world, source of imagination). The Fundació Joan Miró (p273) in Barcelona and the Fundació Pilar i Joan Miró (p614) in Palma de Mallorca are the pick of the places to see his work.

Spain's Best Contemporary Artists

The death of Franco acted as a catalyst for the Spanish art movement. New talent sprang up, and galleries enthusiastically took on anything revolutionary, contrary or cheeky. The 1970s and 1980s were a time of al-

GOYA

Reach into the tortured mind of one of Spain's greatest artists with the help of Robert Hughes' riveting work *Goya*.

GOYA'S BLACK PAINTINGS

Goya saved his most confronting paintings for the end. After he retired to the Quinta del Sordo (Deaf Man's House) in Madrid, he created his nightmarish *Pinturas negras* (Black Paintings), which now hang in the Museo del Prado in Madrid. The *Saturno devorando a su hijo* (Saturn Devouring His Son) captures the essence of Goya's genius, and *La romería de San Isidro* (A Pilgrimage to San Isidro) and *El akelarre* (*El gran cabrón*; The Great He-Goat) are profoundly unsettling. The former evokes a writhing mass of tortured humanity, while the latter two are dominated by the compelling individual faces of the condemned souls of Goya's creation.

PICASSO'S GUERNICA

It was market day in the small Basque town of Guernica on the morning of 26 April 1937. At the same time that market-goers poured into the town from outlying villages, a squadron of aeroplanes was making its way to Guernica. Over the next few hours Hitler's Condor Legion, in agreement with Franco, dropped hundreds of bombs on the town and killed between a couple of hundred to well over 1000 civilians.

Shortly afterwards, Picasso, who was based in Paris at the time, was commissioned by the Republican government of Madrid to produce the paintings for the Spanish contribution to the Paris Exposition Universelle. As news of the bombings filtered out of Spain, Picasso committed his anger to canvas: it was a poignant memorial to the first use of airborne military hardware to devastating effect. You can see the *Guernica* in Madrid's Centro de Arte Reina Sofía.

most childish self-indulgence. Things have since calmed down but there's still much activity.

Basques Eduardo Chillida (1924–2002) and Jorge Oteiza (1908–2003) were two of Spain's leading modern sculptors, active throughout their lives almost to the end of their days.

Seville's Luis Gordillo (b 1934) started his artistic career with surrealism, from where he branched out into pop art and photography. His later work in particular features the serialisation of different versions of the same image.

Antonio López (b 1936) is considered the father of the so-called Madrid hyperrealism. One of his grandest works is the incredibly detailed *Madrid desde Torres Blancas* (Madrid from Torres Blancas).

Mallorcan Miquel Barceló (b 1957) is one of the country's big success stories. His work is heavily expressionist, although it touches on classic themes, from self-portraiture to architectural images.

Barcelona's Susana Solano (b 1946) is a painter and, above all, sculptor, considered to be one of the most important at work in Spain today.

Jaume Plensa (b 1955) is possibly Spain's best contemporary sculptor and has displayed his work around the world.

Check out www.
arteespana.com,
an interesting
website that covers broad swaths
of Spanish art
history, and
where you can
buy art books or
even models of
monuments.

The Spanish Table

Spanish cooking has taken the world by storm in recent years, and deservedly (if belatedly) so. While that has a whole lot to do with gastronomic innovation by Spanish chefs, wonderful flavours and astonishing regional variety, it's also because eating in Spain is a way of living, one of the most important things in life. Whole philosophies surround this cuisine of which locals are fiercely proud, and so many moments of a Spaniard's life are either devoted to food or impossible to imagine without it.

In order to understand the enduring appeal of Spanish cooking, it's necessary to take a journey into the heart of Spanish cuisine and, in the process, unlock the secrets to the essential elements of one of the world gastronomy's most pleasurable tales.

The Laws of Spanish Cooking

The laws of traditional Spanish cooking are deceptively simple: take the freshest and finest ingredients and interfere with them as little as possible. While the rest of the world was developing sophisticated sauces, Spanish chefs were experimenting with subtlety, creating a combination of tastes in which the flavour of the food itself was paramount. Nowhere is this more evident than in the humble art of tapas – bite-sized morsels whose premise is so simple as to have the hallmarks of genius – where carefully selected meats, seafood or vegetables are given centre stage and allowed to speak for themselves. Such are the foundations on which Spanish cooking is built.

If simplicity is the cornerstone of Spanish cooking, it's the innovation and nouvelle cuisine emerging from Spanish kitchens that has truly taken the world by storm. Celebrity chefs have developed their own culinary laboratories, experimenting with all that's new while never straying far from the principles that underpin traditional Spanish cuisine.

Tapas

Many would argue that tapas are Spain's greatest culinary gift to the world. While devotees of paella and *jamón* (cured ham) can make a convincing counterclaim, what clinches it for us is the fact that the potential variety for tapas is endless.

Anything can be a tapa, from a handful of olives or a slice of *jamón* on bread to a *tortilla de patatas* (Spanish potato omelette) served in liquefied form. That's because tapas are the canvas upon which Spanish chefs paint the story of a nation's obsession with food, the means by which they show their fidelity to traditional Spanish tastes even as they gently nudge their compatriots in never-before-imagined directions. By making the most of very little, tapas serve as a link to the impoverished Spain of centuries past. By re-imagining even the most sacred Spanish staples,

The Food of Spain & Portugal – A Regional Celebration, by Elisabeth Luard (2005), demystifies the food and wine of the various Spanish regions with recipes and the context from which they arise.

tapas are the culinary trademark of a confident country rushing head-long into the future. And the national pastime of *ir de tapear* (going out to eat tapas) is so deeply ingrained in Spanish culture that tapas are as much a social event as they are a much-loved culinary form.

The undoubted king of tapas destinations is the Basque Country in general (where tapas are called *pintxos*), and San Sebastián in particular. Although good tapas can be found anywhere, other places with especially fine tapas include Madrid, Zaragoza and most cities in Andalucía.

The Origin of Tapas

There are many stories concerning the origins of tapas.

One of the most common explanations derives from the fact that medieval Spain was a land of isolated settlements and people on the move – traders, pilgrims, emigrants and journeymen – who had to cross the lonely high plateau of Spain en route elsewhere. All along the route, travellers holed up in inns where the keepers, concerned about drunken men on horseback setting out from their village, developed a tradition of putting a *tapa* (lid) of food atop a glass of wine or beer. The purpose was partly to keep the bugs out, but primarily to encourage people not to drink on an empty stomach.

Another story holds that in the 13th century, doctors of King Alfonso X advised him to accompany his small sips of wine between meals with small morsels of food. So enamoured was the monarch with the idea that he passed a law requiring all bars in Castile to follow suit.

In Andalucía in particular, it is also claimed that the name 'tapa' attained widespread usage in the early 20th century when King Alfonso XIII stopped at a beachside bar in Cádiz province. When a strong gust of wind blew sand in the king's direction, a quick-witted waiter rushed to place a slice of *jamón* atop the king's glass of sherry. The king so much enjoyed the idea (and the *jamón*) that, wind or no wind, he ordered another and the idea stuck.

Jamón

There is no more iconic presence on the Spanish table than cured ham from the high plateau, known as *jamón*. Every *tasca* (tapas bar) has it. The *jamón* from Extremadura or Salamanca is considered to be the finest, although the Teruel region of Aragón makes a convincing claim for membership to such an elite group. *Chorizo, salchichón* and *lomo* (different types of cured pork sausages) are also made from acorn-fed pigs.

Jamón: A Primer

Spanish *jamón* is, unlike Italian prosciutto, a bold, deep red and well marbled with buttery fat. At its best, it smells like meat, the forest and the field. Like wines and olive oil, Spanish *jamón* is subject to a strict series of classifications. *Jamón serrano* refers to *jamón* made from white-coated pigs introduced to Spain in the 1950s. Once salted and

THE SPANISH TABLE

JAMÓN

The recipe for cured meats such as *jamón* (ham) is attributed to a noble Roman, Cato the Elder, who changed the course of Spanish culinary history with his tome *De Re Rustica*.

BOOKS ABOUT SPANISH FOOD

Apart from being really good reads, the following books capture the essence and spirit of Spanish food and what it means in Spanish culture:

» *A Late Dinner: Discovering the Food of Spain* (Paul Richardson) Rich in anecdotes and insight.

» *Everything but the Squeal: A Year of Pigging Out in Northern Spain* (John Barlow) Fun, food-inspired travels through the Basque Country and Galicia.

» *World Food: Spain* (Lonely Planet) Out of print but worth tracking down.

semidried by the cold, dry winds of the Spanish sierra, most now go through a similar process of curing and drying in a climate-controlled shed for around a year. *Jamón serrano* accounts for approximately 90% of cured ham in Spain.

Jamón ibérico – more expensive and generally regarded as the elite of Spanish hams – comes from a black-coated pig indigenous to the Iberian Peninsula and a descendant of the wild boar. Gastronomically, its star appeal is its ability to infiltrate fat into the muscle tissue, thus producing an especially well-marbled meat. If the pig gains at least 50% of its body weight during the acorn-eating season, it can be classified as *jamón ibérico de bellota,* the most sought-after designation for *jamón.*

For an authoritative and comprehensive periodical on Spanish gastronomy, check www.foods fromspain.com, which overflows with recipes and ideas for culinary explorations of Spain.

Paella

We'll let you into a secret: a *really* good paella can be surprisingly hard to come by in Spanish restaurants. Why? For a start, saffron is extremely expensive, prompting many restaurants to cut corners by using yellow dye number 2. Secondly, many restaurant owners play on the fact that every second foreign visitor to Spain will order a paella while in the country, but few will have any idea about what a good paella should taste like. Spaniards are much more discerning when it comes to their national dish, so check out the clientele before sitting down and ordering.

The base of a good paella always includes short-grain rice, garlic, parsley, olive oil and saffron. The best rice is the *bomba* variety, which opens out accordion fashion when cooked, allowing for maximum absorption while remaining firm. Paella should be cooked in a large shallow pan to enable maximum contact with the bottom of the pan where most of the flavour resides. And for the final touch of authenticity, the grains on the bottom (and only on the bottom) of the paella should have a crunchy, savoury crust known as the *socarrat.* Beyond that, the main paella staples are *paella valenciana* (from Valencia, where paella has its roots and remains true to its origins), which is cooked with chicken, beans and sometimes rabbit, and the more widespread *paella de mariscos* (seafood paella), which should be bursting with shellfish.

Olive Oil

Olive oil is the foundation on which so much Spanish cooking is built.

Wines from Spain (www.winesfrom spain.com) is the best website covering Spanish wine, with detailed but accessible sections on history, grape varieties and all the Spanish wine-producing regions.

Spain is the world's largest olive-oil producer. There are more than 100 million olive trees in Andalucía; a remarkable 20% of the world's olive oil originates in Jaén province, which produces more olive oil than Greece; and Jaén's more-than-4500 sq km of olive trees constitute the world's largest man-made forest. Southern Spain's olive groves were originally planted by the Romans, but the production of *az-zait* (juice of the olive) – from which the generic Spanish word for olive oil, *aceite,* is derived – was further developed by the Muslims.

The best olive oils are those classified as 'virgin' (which must meet 40 criteria for quality and purity) and 'extra virgin' (the highest-quality olive oil, with acidity levels no higher than 1%).

The most common type of olive used for making olive oil is the full-flavoured and (sometimes) vaguely spicy Picual, which dominates the olive groves of Jaén province and accounts for 50% of all Spanish olive production. It takes its name from its pointed *pico* (tip) and is considered ideal for olive oil due to its high proportion of vegetable fat, natural antioxidants and polyphenol; the latter ensures that the oil keeps well and maintains its essential qualities at a high cooking temperature.

Another important type of olive is the Hojiblanco. Its oil, which keeps for less time and should be stored in a cool dark place, is said to have a taste and aroma reminiscent of fruits, grass and nuts.

SPAIN'S BEST WINE MUSEUMS

The following museums are where you really should start your journey into the world of Spanish wine. Most are interactive (allowing you to familiarise yourself with the various grape aromas), many host tastings, and all put the wineries you're about to visit into their proper historical context.

» **Museo del Vino** (p460), Haro – La Rioja
» **Dinastía Vivanco** (Museo de la Cultura del Vino; p461), Briones – La Rioja
» **Villa Lucia** (p460), Laguardia – La Rioja
» **Quaderna Via**, Estella – Navarra
» **Museo de la Viña y el Vino de Navarra** (p452), Olite – Navarra
» **Museo Provincial del Vino** (p195), Peñafiel – Ribera del Duero, Castilla y León
» **Espacio de Vino** (p396), Barbastro – Somontano, Aragón
» **Museo del Vino** (p378), Cariñena – Aragón's largest wine-growing area

Wine

Spain's internationally acclaimed wine industry boasts the largest area (1.2 million hectares) of wine cultivation in the world, and accounts for more than 30% of land under vine in the EU; France and Italy can only muster around 25% each.

All of Spain's autonomous communities, with the exceptions of Asturias and Cantabria, are home to recognised wine-growing areas. With so many areas to choose from, and with most Spanish wines labelled primarily according to region or classificatory status rather than grape variety, a little background knowledge can go a long way.

Spanish wine is subject to a complicated system of wine classification with a range of designations marked on the bottle. These range from the straightforward *vino de mesa* (table wine) to *vino de la tierra*, which is a wine from an officially recognised wine-making area. If an area meets certain strict standards for a given period and covers all aspects of planting, cultivating and ageing, it receives Denominación de Origen (DO; Denomination of Origin) status. There are currently more than 60 DO-recognised wine-producing areas in Spain.

An outstanding wine region gets the much-coveted Denominación de Origen Calificada (DOC), a controversial classification that some in the industry argue should apply only to specific wines, rather than every wine from within a particular region. At present, the only DOC wines come from La Rioja in northern Spain and the small Priorat area in Catalonia.

Other important indications of quality depend on the length of time a wine has been aged, especially if in oak barrels. The best wines are often, therefore, marked with the designation '*crianza*' (aged for one year in oak barrels), '*reserva*' (two years ageing, at least one of which is in oak barrels) and '*gran reserva*' (two years in oak and three in the bottle).

More than half of Spain's wine production comes from Castilla-La Mancha, with Catalonia, Extremadura and Valencia making up the top four. Better-known wine-producing regions such as La Rioja and Castilla y León trail in fifth and sixth place respectively.

Flamenco

Flamenco's passion is clear to anyone who has heard its melancholic strains in the background of a crowded Spanish bar or during an uplifting live performance. And yet, flamenco can seem like an impenetrable world of knowledgeable but taciturn initiates. Most people's entry point into the genre comes in a single uplifting moment when flamenco's raw passion suddenly transports you to another place, where joy and sorrow can threaten to overwhelm you. The performer's gift for sparking this kind of response is known as *duende* (spirit), and if you experience it once, you'll quickly become one of flamenco's lifelong devotees.

Seville's Museo del Baile Flamenco trawls through flamencos past and present and, with its frequent flamenco classes, gives you the chance to perfect your sevillana.

SEVILLANA

The Birth of Flamenco

Flamenco's origins have been lost to time. Some have suggested that it derives from Byzantine chants used in Visigothic churches. But most musical historians agree that it probably dates back to a fusion of songs brought to Spain by the *gitanos* (Roma people) with music and verses from North Africa crossing into medieval Muslim Andalucía. Flamenco as we now know it first took recognisable form in the 18th and early 19th centuries among *gitanos* in the lower Guadalquivir valley in western Andalucía. The Seville, Jerez de la Frontera and Cádiz axis is still considered flamenco's heartland and it's here, purists believe, that you'll encounter the most authentic flamenco experience.

Flamenco – the Essential Elements

A flamenco singer is known as a *cantaor* (male) or *cantaora* (female); a dancer is a *bailaor* or *bailaora*. Most of the songs and dances are performed to a blood-rush of guitar from the *tocaor* or *tocaora* (male or female flamenco guitarist). Percussion is provided by tapping feet, clapping hands and sometimes castanets.

Flamenco *coplas* (songs) come in many different types, from the anguished *soleá* or the intensely despairing *siguiriya* to the livelier *alegría* or the upbeat *bulería*. The first flamenco was *cante jondo* (deep song), an anguished instrument of expression for a group on the margins of society. *Jondura* (depth) is still the essence of pure flamenco.

The traditional flamenco costume – shawl, fan and long, frilly *bata de cola* (tail gown) for women, and flat Cordoban hats and tight black trousers for men – dates from Andalucian fashions in the late 19th century.

Flamenco Legends

The great singers of the 19th and early 20th centuries were Silverio Franconetti and La Niña de los Peines, from Seville, and Antonio Chacón and Manuel Torre, from Jerez de la Frontera. Torre's singing, legend has it, could drive people to rip their shirts open and upturn tables. The dynamic dancing and wild lifestyle of Carmen Amaya (1913–63), from Barcelona, made her the *gitana* dance legend of all time. Her long-time partner Sabicas was the father of the modern solo flamenco guitar, inventing a host of now-indispensable techniques.

After a trough in the mid-20th century, when it seemed that the *tablaos* (touristy flamenco shows emphasising the sexy and the jolly) were in danger of taking over, *flamenco puro* got a new lease of life in the 1970s through singers such as Terremoto, La Paquera, Enrique Morente, Chano Lobato and, above all, El Camarón de la Isla (whose real name was José Monge Cruz) from San Fernando near Cádiz.

Some say that Madrid-born Diego El Cigala (b 1968) is El Camarón's successor. This powerful singer's biggest-hitting albums are *Lágrimas negras* (Black Tears; 2003), and *Dos lágrimas* (Two Tears; 2008), which mix flamenco with Cuban influences.

Paco de Lucía, born in Algeciras in 1947, is the doyen of flamenco guitarists. So gifted is he that by the time he was 14 his teachers admitted that they had nothing left to teach him. De Lucía has transformed the flamenco guitar into an instrument of solo expression with new techniques, scales, melodies and harmonics that have gone far beyond traditional limits.

Many of the most talented flamenco stars have spent time in prison, and each year Spain's penitentiary system holds *El Concurso de Cante Flamenco del Sistema Penitenciario* (The Prison Flamenco Competition).

Flamenco Today

Rarely can flamenco have been as popular as it is today, and never so innovative.

Universally acclaimed is José Mercé, from Jerez. Estrella Morente from Granada (Enrique's daughter and internationally best known for being the 'voice' behind the 2006 film *Volver*), Miguel Poveda (from Barcelona) and La Tana from Seville are young singers steadily carving out niches in the first rank of performers.

Dance, always the readiest of flamenco arts to cross boundaries, has reached its most adventurous horizons in the person of Joaquin Cortés, born in Córdoba in 1969. Cortés fuses flamenco with contemporary dance, ballet and jazz in spectacular shows with music at rock-concert amplification.

Among guitarists, listen out for Manolo Sanlúcar from Cádiz; Tomatito from Almería; and Vicente Amigo from Córdoba and Moraíto Chico from Jerez, who both accompany today's top singers.

Flamenco Fusion

What started with the experimentation of Paco de Lucía has seen musicians mixing flamenco with jazz, rock, blues, rap and other genres.

The seminal recording was a 1977 flamenco-folk-rock album *Veneno* (Poison) by the group of the same name, centred on Kiko Veneno and

THE SHRIMP FROM THE ISLAND

Possibly the most important flamenco singer of all time, José Monge Cruz (aka Camarón de la Isla; Shrimp of the Island) did more to popularise flamenco over the last 30 years than anyone else. Born to *gitano* (Roma people) parents, Camarón started his career at a young age by singing in local bars. Eventually he met that other great of flamenco, guitarist Paco de Lucía, with whom he recorded nine much-praised albums between 1969 and 1977. Later in his career Camarón worked with one of Paco's students, Tomatito.

Camarón was an intense introvert and hated publicity, but so extraordinary was his talent that publicity was to hound him everywhere he went and, so many say, it was eventually to lead him to an early grave in the best live-fast, die-young rock-star fashion. He was idolised for his voice by flamenco fans across the world, and it was his fellow *gitanos* who really elevated him almost to the status of a god.

He died of lung cancer in 1992 at the age of just 42. It's estimated that more than 100,000 people attended his funeral. The Shrimp's best recordings include *La leyenda del tiempo*, *Soy gitano* and *Una leyenda flamenca*.

FLAMENCO RESOURCES

» **Flama** (www.guiaflama.com) Good for upcoming concerts and background info.

» **Duende: A Journey into the Heart of Flamenco** (Jason Webster) The author's gripping journey through the underbelly of flamenco.

» **Camarón** (2005) A terrific biopic of El Camarón de la Isla, directed by Jaime Chávarri.

» **Bodas de sangre** (1981) and **Flamenco** (1995) These two Carlos Saura films are flamenco classics; the former is a film version of Federico García Lorca's dramatic play of the same name.

» **Centro Andaluz de Flamenco** (www.centroandaluzdeflamenco.es) The website of the Andalucian Centre for Flamenco.

Raimundo Amador, both from Seville. Kiko remains an icon of flamenco fusion, mixing rock, blues, African and flamenco rhythms with witty lyrics focusing on snatches of everyday life. Amador later formed the group Pata Negra, and produced four fine flamenco-jazz-blues albums before going solo.

The group Ketama, originally from Granada, has successfully mixed flamenco with African, Cuban, Brazilian and other rhythms for two decades. Cádiz' Niña Pastori arrived in the late 1990s with an edgy, urgent voice singing jazz- and Latin-influenced flamenco.

Eleven-strong Barcelona-based band Ojos de Brujo mixes flamenco with reggae, Asian and even club dance rhythms.

Málaga's Chambao successfully combines flamenco with electronic beats on its albums such as *Flamenco Chill* (2002) and *Pokito a poko* (Little by Little; 2005). Its latest is 2009's *En el fin del mundo*.

Concha Buika, a Mallorcan of Equatorial Guinean origin, possesses a beautiful, sensual voice. Her albums *Buika* (2005) and *Mi niña Lola* (2006) are a captivating melange of African rhythms, soul, jazz, hip hop, flamenco and more.

Probably nobody upsets the purists quite as much as Mala Rodríguez does with her socially aware combination of flamenco and rap. *Malamarismo* (2007) is a classic of her unique genre and her latest *Dirty Bailarina* (2010) looks set to repeat her earlier successes.

Flamenco World (www.flamenco-world.com) is an online shop that stocks absolutely everything and anything flamenco-based. Its website also contains numerous interviews and news features.

Seeing Flamenco

Flamenco is easiest to catch in Seville, Jerez de la Frontera, Granada and Madrid. The best places for live performances are *peñas* (clubs where flamenco fans band together). The atmosphere in such places is authentic and at times very intimate, proof that flamenco feeds off an audience that knows its flamenco. Most Andalucian towns have dozens of *peñas,* and most tourist offices have lists of those open to visitors. The other, easier, option is to attend a performance at a *tablao,* which hosts regular shows put on for largely undiscriminating tourist audiences – the quality can be top-notch, even if the gritty atmosphere of the *peñas* is lacking.

The following are some of the best flamenco festivals:

» **Festival Flamenco** (p102), Madrid (February)

» **Festival de Jerez** (p699), Jerez de la Frontera (February to March)

» **Suma Flamenca** (p102), Madrid (June)

» **Festival Internacional de la Guitarra** (p738), Córdoba (June to July)

» **Festival Internacional del Cante de las Minas**, La Unión, Murcia (August)

» **Bienal de Flamenco** (p673), Seville (September)

Bullfighting

An epic drama of blood and sand or a cruel blood 'sport' that has no place in modern Spain? This most enduring and controversial of Spanish traditions is all this and more, at once compelling theatre and an ancient ritual that sees 40,000 bulls killed in around 17,000 fights every year in Spain. Perhaps it was best summed up by Ernest Hemingway – a bullfighting aficionado – who described it as a 'wonderful nightmare'.

Bullfighting took off in the mid-18th century. King Carlos III stopped it late in the century, but his successors dropped the ban. By the mid-19th century, breeders were creating the first reliable breeds of *toro bravo* (fighting bull), and a bullfighting school had been launched in Seville.

The Basics

The matador (more often called the *torero* in Spanish) is the star of the team. Adorned in his glittering *traje de luces* (suit of lights), it is his fancy footwork, skill and bravery before the bull that has the crowd in raptures or in rage, depending on his (or very occasionally her) performance. A complex series of events takes place in each clash, which can last from about 20 to 30 minutes (there are usually six fights in a programme). *Peones* (the matador's 'footmen' whose job it is to test the strength of the bull) dart about with grand capes in front of the bull; horseback *picadores* (horsemen) drive lances into the bull's withers; and *banderilleros* (flagmen) charge headlong at the bull in an attempt to stab its neck. Finally, the matador kills the bull, unless the bull has managed to put him out of action, as sometimes happens.

If you do plan to attend a bullfight, it's important to understand what you're about to experience. The bull's back and neck are repeatedly pierced by the lances, resulting in quite a lot of blood. The bull gradually becomes weakened through blood loss before the *torero* delivers the final sword thrust. If done properly, the bull dies instantly from this final thrust, albeit after bleeding for some time from its other wounds. If the coup de grace is not delivered well, the animal dies a slow death. When this happens, the scene can be extremely disturbing.

When & Where

The bullfighting season begins in the first week of February with the fiestas of Valdemorillo and Ajalvir, near Madrid, to mark the feast day of San Blas. Elsewhere – especially in the two Castillas and Andalucía – *corridas* (bullfights) and *encierros* (running of the bulls through town), as in Pamplona (see the boxed text, p444), are part of town festivals. By October, you'd be hard-pressed to find a *corrida* anywhere in the country.

Bullfighting Legends

The most extraordinary matador of the moment is Madrid's José Tomás. After a stellar career, he retired in 2002, only to make a spectacular

ANIMAL RIGHTS

The Asociación para la Defensa de los Derechos del Animal (ADDA; www .addaong.org) is a Spanish animal-rights and antibullfighting organisation. Other antibull-fighting organisations are the World Society for the Protection of Animals (WSPA; www.wspa.org.uk) and People for the Ethical Treatment of Animals (PETA; www.peta. org).

GREAT ANGLO-AMERICAN BULLFIGHTERS

Ernest Hemingway loved watching the bullfight, but some of his countrymen preferred action to observation. Sidney Franklin was the first English-speaking *torero* (bullfighter) to take the alternative, in 1945 in Madrid's Las Ventas, one of the largest rings in the bullfighting world. He was followed by Californian John Fulton (a painter and poet) in 1967. Best of all was Arizona-born Robert Ryan. Now retired, he is a man of many facets – writer, poet, painter, sculptor and photographer. Englishman Henry Higgins, known in Spain as Enrique Cañadas, something of an adventurer and pilot, was also keen to take to the ring, while his countryman, Mancunian Frank Evans ('El Inglés'), retired in 2005.

return a few years later. At the fiestas of San Isidro in Madrid on 5 June 2008, he cut four bulls' ears (the cutting off of an ear of the dead bull is a mark of admiration) for his performance – something that hadn't been seen for decades. Says the austere Tomás: 'Living without bullfighting isn't living'. Two weeks later, in another epic afternoon, bulls gored him severely in the thighs three times. After recovering from his injuries he returned to the ring and continued to dazzle audiences, but in April 2010, during a fight in Mexico, he was severely injured after being gored in the groin. At the time of writing, his career hangs in the balance.

Other great fighters include El Cordobés, El Juli, Manuel Jesú (El Cid) and Miguel Ángel Perera.

The Bullfighting Debate

The popular image of Spain would have us all believe that every Spaniard is a die-hard bullfighting fan, but this couldn't be further from the truth. While bullfighting remains strong in some parts of the country, notably Andalucía, in other areas such as Galicia, Cantabria and other northern regions it's never really been a part of local culture. A recent poll found that just 17% of Spaniards under 25 had any interest in bullfighting, compared with 41% of those aged over 64. Similar polls suggest that three-quarters of Spaniards have no interest in the sport.

Today there's a large, growing antibullfighting movement in Spain. The Socialist government banned children under 14 from attending bullfights in 2006 and forbade state-run TV from broadcasting live coverage of bullfights (some private broadcasters continued to televise). This latter decision was later overturned by the newly elected Popular Party government, and live broadcasts of bullfighting (at 6pm) resumed on the state-run channel in September 2012. The bullfighting world was given a further blow when the Catalan government's ban on bullfighting officially became law on 1 January 2012 (see the boxed text, p367). On the flip side, though, bullfighting does still have some fans in high places. In 2008 around €600 million of public money, including some from European funds, was given to the bullfight breeding industry, and King Juan Carlos is on record as saying: 'The day the EU bans bullfighting is the day Spain leaves the EU'.

That this is a debate at all in Spain owes a little to bullfighting's waning popularity and arguably more to the country's growing integration with the rest of Europe since the late 1970s. The fall in bullfighting's popularity has fostered some antibullfighting organisations, such as Madrid-based Equanimal (www.equanimal.org). But the greatest impetus has come from groups beyond Spanish shores, such as the League Against Cruel Sports (www.leagueagainstcruelsports.org). For information on creative protests against bullfighting, see www.runningofthenudes.com.

Survival Guide

Directory A-Z

Accommodation

Spain's accommodation is generally of a high standard, from small, family-run *hostales* to the old-world opulence of *paradores*.

Officially, places to stay are classified into *hoteles* (hotels; one to five stars), *hostales* (one to three stars) and *pensiones* (basically small private hostales, often family businesses in rambling apartments; one or two stars). These are the categories used by the annual *Guía Oficial de Hoteles*, sold in bookshops, which lists almost every such establishment in Spain (except for one-star *pensiones*) with approximate prices.

Checkout time in most establishments is generally noon.

Reservations

Although there's usually no need to book ahead for a room in the low or shoulder seasons, booking ahead is generally a good idea, if for no other reason than to avoid a wearisome search for a room. Most places will ask for a credit-card number or will hold the room for you until 6pm unless you let them know that you'll be arriving later.

Seasons

Prices throughout this guidebook are high-season maximums. You may be pleasantly surprised if you travel at other times. What constitutes low or high season depends on where and when. Most of the year is high season in Barcelona or Madrid, especially during trade fairs that you're unlikely to be aware of. August can be dead in the cities, but high season along the coast. Winter is high season in the ski resorts of the Pyrenees and low season in the Balearic Islands (indeed, the islands seem to shut down between November and Easter). Finding a place to stay without booking ahead in July and August in the Balearics and elsewhere along the Mediterranean Coast can be difficult.

Weekends are high season for boutique hotels and *casas rurales* (rural homes), but low season for business hotels (which often offer generous specials then) in Madrid and Barcelona. Always check out hotel websites for discounts.

Prices

At the lower end of the budget category there are dorm beds (from €17 per person) in youth hostels or private rooms with shared bathrooms in the corridor. If you're willing to pay a few euros more, there are many budget places, usually *hostales*, with good, comfortable rooms and private bathrooms. In relatively untouristed or rural areas, the prices of some boutique or other hotels can sometimes drop into the budget category, especially during low season.

Spain's midrange hotels are generally excellent; you should always have your own private bathroom, and breakfast is sometimes included in the room price. Boutique hotels, including many that occupy artistically converted historical buildings, largely fall into this category and are almost always excellent choices.

And a final word about terminology. A *habitación doble* (double room) is frequently just that: a room with two beds (which you can often shove together). If you want to be sure of a double bed *(cama matrimonial),* ask for it!

Accommodation Types

APARTMENTS, VILLAS & CASAS RURALES

Throughout Spain you can rent self-catering apartments and houses from one night

---

BOOK YOUR STAY ONLINE

For more accommodation reviews by Lonely Planet authors, check out http://hotels.lonelyplanet.com. You'll find independent reviews, as well as recommendations on the best places to stay. Best of all, you can book online.

upwards. Villas and houses are widely available on the main holiday coasts and in popular country areas.

A simple one-bedroom apartment in a coastal resort for two or three people might cost as little as €30 per night, although more often you'll be looking at nearly twice that much, and prices jump even further in high season. More luxurious options with a swimming pool might come in at anything between €200 and €400 for four people.

Rural tourism has become immensely popular, with accommodation available in many new and often charming *casas rurales*. These are usually comfortably renovated village houses or farmhouses with a handful of rooms. They often go by other names, such as *cases de pagès* in Catalonia, *casas de aldea* in Asturias, *posadas* and *casonas* in Cantabria and so on. Some just provide rooms, while others offer meals or self-catering accommodation. Lower-end prices typically hover around €30/50 for a single/double per night, but classy boutique establishments can easily charge €100 or more for a double. Many are rented out by the week.

Agencies include the following:

Apartments-Spain (www. apartments-spain.com)
Associació Agroturisme Balear (www.rusticbooking. com)
Atlas Rural (www.atlasrural. com)
Casas Cantabricas (www. casas.co.uk)
Cases Rurals de Catalunya (www.casesrurals.com)
Escapada Rural (www. escapadarural.com)
Fincas 4 You (www.fincas 4you.com)
Guías Casas Rurales (www. guiascasasrurales.com)
Holiday Serviced Apartments (www.holidayapart ments.co.uk)
Owners Direct (www.owners direct.co.uk)

ACCOMMODATION PRICE RANGES

Throughout this guidebook, the order of accommodation listings is by author preference, and each place to stay is accompanied by one of the following symbols (the price relates to a double room with private bathroom):

» € less than €65
» €€ from €65 to €140
» €€€ more than €140

The price ranges for Madrid and Barcelona are inevitably higher:

» € less than €75
» €€ from €75 to €200
» €€€ more than €200

Ruralka (www.ruralka.com)
Rustic Rent (www.rusticrent. com)
Rusticae (www.rusticae.es)
Secret Destinations (www. secretdestinations.com)
Secret Places (www.secret places.com)
Top Rural (www.toprural.com)
Traum Ferienwohnungen (www.traum-ferienwohnungen. de)
Villas 4 You (www.villas4you. co.uk)
Vintage (http://vintagetravel. co.uk)

CAMPING & CARAVAN PARKS

Spain has around 1000 officially graded *campings* (camping grounds). Some of these are well located in woodland or near beaches or rivers, but others are on the outskirts of towns or along highways. Few of them are near city centres, and camping isn't particularly convenient if you're relying on public transport. Tourist offices can always direct you to the nearest camping ground. Camping grounds are officially rated as first class (1ªC), second class (2ªC) or third class (3ªC). There are also some that are not officially graded, usually equivalent to third class. Facilities generally range from reasonable to very good, although any camping ground can be crowded and noisy at busy times (especially July and August). Even a third-class camping ground is likely to have hot showers, electrical hook-ups and a cafe. The best ones have heated swimming pools, supermarkets, restaurants, laundry service, children's playgrounds and tennis courts. Camping grounds usually charge per person, per tent and per vehicle – typically €5 to €9 for each. Children usually pay a bit less than adults. Many camping grounds close from around October to Easter. You sometimes come across a *zona de acampada* or *área de acampada*, a country camping ground with minimal facilities (maybe just tap water or a couple of barbecues), little or no supervision and little or no charge. If it's in an environmentally protected area, you may need to obtain permission from the local environmental authority to camp there. With certain exceptions – such as many beaches and environmentally protected areas and a few municipalities that ban it – it is legal to camp outside camping grounds (but not within 1km of official ones!) Signs usually indicate where wild camping is not allowed. If in doubt, you can always check with tourist offices.

PRACTICALITIES

» **Currency** Euro

» **Electric current** 220V, 50Hz

» **Smoking** Banned in all enclosed public spaces.

» **Weights & measures** Metric

» **Major newspapers** Centre-left *El País* (www.elpais.com); centre-right *El Mundo* (www.elmundo.es); and right-wing *ABC* (www.abc.es). The widely available *International Herald Tribune* includes an eight-page supplement of articles from *El País* translated into English (www.elpais.com/misc/herald/herald.pdf).

» **Radio** Radio Nacional de España (RNE)'s Radio 1, with general interest and current affairs programs; Radio 5, with sport and entertainment; and Radio 3 (Radio d'Espop). Stations covering current affairs include the left-leaning Cadena Ser, or the right-wing COPE. The most popular commercial pop and rock stations are 40 Principales, Kiss FM, Cadena 100 and Onda Cero.

» **TV** Spain's state-run Televisión Española (TVE1 and La 2) or the independent commercial stations (Antena 3, Tele 5, Cuatro and La Sexta). Regional governments run local stations, such as Madrid's Telemadrid, Catalonia's TV-3 and Canal 33 (both in Catalan), Galicia's TVG, the Basque Country's ETB-1 and ETB-2, Valencia's Canal 9 and Andalucía's Canal Sur. Cable and satellite TV is becoming widespread.

You'll need permission to camp on private land.

Useful websites:

Guía Camping (www.guiacampingfecc.com) Online version of the annual *Guía Camping* (€13.60), which is available in bookshops around the country.

Campinguía (www.campinguia.com) Comments (mostly in Spanish) and links.

Campings Online (www.campingsonline.com/espana) Booking service.

CAMAS, FONDAS & HOSPEDAJES

At the budget end of the market, places listing accommodation use various names to describe themselves. In broad terms, the cheapest are usually places just advertising *camas* (beds), *fondas* (traditionally a basic eatery and inn combined, though one of these functions is now often missing) and *casas de huéspedes* or *hospedajes* (guesthouses). Most such places will be bare and basic. Bathrooms are likely to be shared, although if you're lucky you may get an in-room *lavabo* (washbasin). In winter don't hesitate to ask for extra blankets.

PENSIONES

A *pensión* is usually a small step up from the previous types in standard and price. Some cheap establishments forget to provide soap, toilet paper or towels. Don't hesitate to ask for these items.

HOSTALES

Hostales are in much the same category, although a small step up again from *pensiones*. In both cases the better ones can be bright and spotless, with rooms boasting full en-suite bathroom – *baño privado*, most often with a *ducha* (shower) rather than bathtub – and usually a TV, air-conditioning and/or heating.

HOTELS

The remainder of establishments call themselves *hoteles* and run the gamut of quality, from straightforward roadside places, bland but clean, through to charming boutique gems and on to superluxurious hotels. Even in the cheapest hotels, rooms are likely to have an attached bathroom and there will probably be a restaurant.

Among the more tempting hotels for those with a little fiscal room to manoeuvre

are the 90 or so **Paradores** (☑ in Spain 902 547979; www.parador.es), a state-funded chain of hotels in often stunning locations, among them towering castles and former medieval convents. Similarly, you can find beautiful hotels in restored country homes and old city mansions, and these are not always particularly expensive. A raft of cutting-edge, hip design hotels with cool staff and a New York feel can be found in the big cities and major resort areas. At the top end you may pay more for a room with a view – especially sea views or with a *balcón* (balcony) – and will often have the option of a suite.

Many places have rooms for three, four or more people where the per-person cost is lower than in a single or double, which is good news for families.

Many of the agencies listed under Apartments, Villas & Casas Rurales also have a full portfolio of hotels.

MONASTERIES

An offbeat possibility is staying in a monastery. In spite of the expropriations of the 19th century and a sometimes rough run in the 20th, numerous monastic orders have survived across the country. Some offer rooms to outsiders – often fairly austere monks' or nuns' cells.

Monastery accommodation is generally a single-sex arrangement, and the idea in quite a few is to seek refuge from the outside world and indulge in quiet contemplation and meditation. On occasion, where the religious order continues ancient tradition by working on farmland, orchards and/or vineyards, you may have the opportunity to work too.

Useful resources include the following:

Guía de Monasterios (www.guiasmonasterios.com)

Alojamientos Monásticos de España A guidebook to Spain's monasteries by Javier de Sagastizabal and José Antonio Egaña, although it's in need of an update.

REFUGIOS

Mountain shelters (refugios) for walkers and climbers are liberally scattered around most of the popular mountain areas (mainly the Pyrenees), except in Andalucía, which has only a handful. They're mostly run by mountaineering and walking organisations. Accommodation, usually bunks squeezed into a dorm, is often on a first-come, first-served basis, although for some refugios you can book ahead. In busy seasons (July and August in most areas) they can fill up quickly, and you should try to book in advance or arrive by mid-afternoon to be sure of a place. Prices per person range from nothing to €15 or more a night. Many refugios have a bar and offer meals (dinner typically costs around €8 to €12), as well as a cooking area (but no cooking equipment). Blankets are usually provided, but you'll have to bring any other bedding yourself. Bring a torch too.

The Aragonese Pyrenees are particularly well served

with refugios; check out the following:

Albergues & Refugios de Aragón (www.alberguesyrefugiosdearagon.com) To make reservations in refugios and albergues (refuges).

Federación Aragonesa de Montañismo (FAM; ☎976 22 79 71; www.fam.es; 4th fl, Calle Albareda 7) The FAM in Zaragoza can provide information, and a card will get you substantial discounts on refugio stays.

YOUTH HOSTELS

Spain's 250 or so youth hostels – albergues juveniles, not be confused with hostales (budget hotels) – are often the cheapest places for lone travellers, but two people can usually get a better double room elsewhere for a similar price.

The hostel experience in Spain varies widely. Some hostels are only moderate value, lacking in privacy, often heavily booked by school groups, and with night-time curfews and no cooking facilities (although if there's nowhere to cook there's usually a cafeteria). Others, however, are conveniently located, open 24 hours and composed mainly of small dorms, often with a private bathroom. An increasing number have rooms adapted for people with disabilities. Some even occupy fine historic buildings.

Most Spanish youth hostels are members of the **Red Española de Albergues Juveniles** (REAJ, Spanish Youth Hostel Network; www.reaj.com), the Spanish representative of Hostelling International.

Most of the REAJ member hostels are also members of the youth hostel association of their region (Andalucía, Catalonia, Valencia etc). Each region usually sets its own price structure and has a central booking service where you can make reservations for most of its hostels. You can also book directly with hostels themselves.

Central booking services include:

Andalucía (☎902 510 000; www.inturjoven.com)
Catalonia (☎93 483 83 41; www.xanascat.cat)
Valencia (☎902 225 552; www.gvajove.es)

Prices at youth hostels often depend on the season, and vary from about €15 to €21 for those under 26 (the lower rate is usually applied to people with ISIC cards too) and between €18 and €28 for those 26 and over. In some hostels the price includes breakfast. A few hostels require you to rent sheets (around €2 to €5 for your stay) if you don't have your own or a sleeping bag.

Most hostels require you to have a HI card or a membership card from your home country's youth hostel association. You can obtain a HI card in Spain at most hostels.

A growing number of hostel-style places not connected with HI or REAJ often have individual rooms as well the more typical dormitory options. Prices can vary greatly as, not being affiliated to any organisation, they are not subject to any pricing system. A good resource for seeking out hostels, affiliated or otherwise, is **Hostel World** (www.hostelworld.com).

Finally, you will sometimes find independent albergues offering basic dormitory accommodation for around €10 to €18, usually in villages in areas that attract plenty of Spanish walkers and climbers. These are not specifically youth hostels – although the clientele tends to be under 35. They're a kind of halfway house between a youth hostel and a refugio. Some will rent you sheets for a couple of euros, if you need them.

Business Hours

Standard opening hours are for high season only and tend to decrease outside that time.

Banks 8.30am-2pm Mon-Fri; some also open 4-7pm Thu and 9am-1pm Sat

Central post offices 8.30am-9.30pm Mon-Fri, 8.30am-2pm Sat

Nightclubs midnight or 1am to 5am or 6am

Restaurants lunch 1-4pm, dinner 8.30pm-midnight or later

Shops 10am-2pm & 4.30-7.30pm or 5-8pm; big supermarkets and department stores generally open 10am-10pm Mon-Sat

Customs Regulations

Duty-free allowances for travellers entering Spain from outside the EU include 2L of wine (or 1L of wine and 1L of spirits), and 200 cigarettes or 50 cigars or 250g of tobacco.

There are no duty-free allowances for travel between EU countries but equally no restrictions on the import of duty-paid items into Spain from other EU countries for personal use. You *can* buy VAT-free articles at airport shops when travelling between EU countries.

Discount Cards

At museums, never hesitate to ask if there are discounts for students, young people, children, families or seniors.

Senior Cards Reduced prices for people over 60, 63 or 65 (depending on the place) at various museums and attractions (sometimes restricted to EU citizens) and sometimes on transport.

Student Cards Discounts (usually half the normal fee) for students. You will need some kind of identification (eg an International Student Identity Card; www.isic.org) to prove student status. Not accepted everywhere.

Youth Card Travel, sights and youth hostel discounts with the European Youth Card (www.euro26.org), known as Carnet Joven in Spain. The International Youth Travel Card (IYTC; www.istc.org) offers similar benefits.

Electricity

Electrical plugs in Spain can also be round, but will always have two round pins. The bottom image is for Gibraltar.

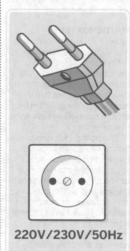

220V/230V/50Hz

240V/50HZ

Embassies & Consulates

The embassies are located in Madrid. Some countries also maintain consulates in major cities, particularly in Barcelona.

Australia (91 353 66 00; www.spain.embassy.gov.au; Paseo de la Castellana 259D, 24th fl, Madrid)

Canada Barcelona (932 70 36 14; Carrer d'Elisenda de Pinós 10); Madrid (91 382 84 00; www.espana.gc.ca; Paseo de la Castellana 259D, Torre Espacio, Madrid); Málaga (95 222 33 46; Plaza de la Malagueta 2)

France Barcelona (93 270 30 00; www.consulfrance-barce lone.org; Ronda de l'Universitat 22B); Madrid (91 423 89 00; www.ambafrance-es.org; Calle de Salustiano Olózaga 9) Has further consulates in Bilbao and Seville.

Germany Barcelona (93 292 10 00; www.barcelona. diplo.de; Passeig de Gràcia 111); Madrid (91 557 90 00; www.spanien.diplo.de; Calle de Fortuny 8)

Ireland Barcelona (93 491 50 21; Gran Via de Carles III 94); Madrid (91 436 40 93; www.embassyofireland.es; Paseo de la Castellana 46)

Japan (91 590 76 00; www. es.emb-japan.go.jp; Calle de Serrano 109, Madrid; M Gregorio Marañon)

Morocco Barcelona (932 89 25 30; Calle Bejar 91); Madrid (91 563 10 90; www.emba jada-marruecos.es; Calle de Serrano 179; M Santo Domingo) Has further consulates-general in Algeciras, Almería, Bilbao, Seville, Tarragona and Valencia.

Netherlands Barcelona (934 19 95 80; Avinguda Diagonal 611); Madrid (91 353 75 00; espana.nlembajada. org; Torre Espacio, Paseo de la Castellana 259D; Avenida del Comandante Franco 32) Has further consulates in Palma de Mallorca, Seville and Torremolinos.

FOOD PRICE RANGES

Throughout this book, the order of restaurant listings follows the author's preference, and the following price ranges refer to a standard main dish:

» € less than €10
» €€ from €10 to €20
» €€€ more than €20

New Zealand (☎91 523 02 26; www.nzembassy.com/spain; 3rd fl, Calle de Pinar 7, Madrid)
UK Barcelona (☎93 366 62 00; Avinguda Diagonal 477; Hospital Clinic); Madrid (☎91 714 62 00; http://ukinspain.fco. gov.uk; Paseo de la Castellana 259D, Torre Espacio, Madrid); Palma de Mallorca (☎902 109 356; Carrer del Convent dels Caputxins 4, Edifici B) Has further consulates in Alicante, Bilbao, Ibiza and Málaga.
USA Barcelona (☎93 280 22 27; barcelona.usconsulate.gov; Passeig de la Reina Elisenda de Montcada 23-25; ⓂFGC Reina Elisenda); Madrid (☎91 587 22 00; http://spanish.madrid. usembassy.gov/; Calle de Serrano 75, Madrid) Has consular agencies in A Coruña, Fuengirola, Palma de Mallorca, Sevilla and Valencia.

Food

For an in-depth guide to Spanish cuisine as well as practical information for travellers, turn to our planning feature Eat and Drink Like a Local (p36) and the essay The Spanish Table (p840).

Gay & Lesbian Travellers

Homosexuality is legal in Spain and the age of consent is 13, as it is for heterosexuals. In 2005 the Socialist president, José Luis Rodríguez Zapatero, gave the country's conservative Catholic foundations a shake with the legalisation of same-sex marriages in Spain.

Lesbians and gay men generally keep a fairly low profile, but are quite open in the cities. Madrid, Barcelona, Sitges, Torremolinos and Ibiza have particularly lively scenes. Sitges is a major destination on the international gay party circuit; gays take a leading role in the wild Carnaval (www.sitges.com/carnaval) there in February/March. As well, there are gay parades, marches and events in several cities on and around the last Saturday in June, when Madrid's **gay and lesbian pride march** (www.orgullogay.org) takes place.

Useful Resources

In addition to the following resources, Barcelona's tourist board publishes *Barcelona – The Official Gay and Lesbian Tourist Guide* biannually, while Madrid's tourist office has a useful 'Gay & Lesbian Madrid' section on the front page of its website (www.esmadrid.com).

Chueca (www.chueca.com) Forums, news and reviews.
GayBarcelona (www.gaybarcelona.com) News and views and an extensive listings section covering bars, saunas, shops and more in Barcelona and Sitges.
Gay Iberia (Guía Gay de España; www.gayiberia.com) Gay guides to Barcelona, Madrid, Sitges and 26 other Spanish cities.
Gay Madrid 4 U (www.gaymadrid4u.com) A good overview of gay bars and nightclubs.
Guía Gay de España (http://guia.universogay.com) Countrywide listings.
LesboNet (www.lesbonet.org) A lesbian site with contacts, forums and listings.
Night Tours.com (www.nighttours.com) A reasonably good guide to gay nightlife and other attractions in Madrid, Barcelona and seven other Spanish locations.
Orgullo Gay (www.orgullogay. org) Website for Madrid's gay and lesbian pride march and links to gay organisations across the country.
Shangay (www.shangay.com) For news, upcoming events, reviews and contacts. It also publishes *Shanguide*, a Madrid-centric biweekly magazine jammed with listings (including saunas and hardcore clubs) and contact ads. Its companion publication *Shangay Express* is better for articles with a handful of listings and ads. They're available in gay bookshops and gay or gay-friendly bars.

Organisations

Casal Lambda (☎93 319 55 50; www.lambdaweb.org; Carrer de Verdaguer i Callís 10; ⓂUquinaona) A gay and lesbian social, cultural and information centre in Barcelona's La Ribera.
Colectivo de Gais y Lesbianas de Madrid (Cogam; ☎91 522 45 17, 5-9pm Mon-Fri 91 525 00 70; www.cogam.es; Calle de la Puebla 9; ⓂCallao or Gran Vía) Has an information office and social centre, and runs an information line (☎91 523 00 70).
Coordinadora Gai-Lesbiana Barcelona (☎93 298 00 29; www.cogailes.org; Carrer de Violant d'Hongria 156; ⓂPlaça del Centre) Barcelona's main coordinating body for gay and lesbian groups. It also runs an information line, the **Línia Rosa** (☎900 601601).
Federación Estatal de Lesbianas, Gays, Transexuales & Bisexuales (☎902 280669; www.felgt.org; 1st fl, Calle de las Infantas 40) A national advocacy group, based in Madrid, that played a leading role in lobbying for the legalisation of gay marriages.
Fundación Triángulo (☎91 593 05 40; www.fundacion triangulo.es; 1st fl, Calle de Melendez Valdés 52; ⓂIglesia)

Another source of information on gay issues in Madrid.

Health

Spain has an excellent health-care system.

Availability & Cost of Health Care

If you need an ambulance, call ☎061. For emergency treatment, go straight to the *urgencias* (casualty) section of the nearest hospital.

Farmacias offer valuable advice and sell over-the-counter medication. In Spain, a system of *farmacias de guardia* (duty pharmacies) operates so that each district has one open all the time. When a pharmacy is closed, it posts the name of the nearest open one on the door.

Medical costs are lower in Spain than many other European countries, but can still mount quickly if you are uninsured. Costs if you attend casualty range from nothing (in some regions) to around €80.

Altitude Sickness

If you're hiking at altitude, altitude sickness may be a risk. Lack of oxygen at high altitudes (over 2500m) affects most people to some extent. Symptoms of Acute Mountain Sickness (AMS) usually develop during the first 24 hours at altitude but may be delayed by up to three weeks. Mild symptoms include headache, lethargy, dizziness, difficulty sleeping and loss of appetite. AMS may become more severe without warning and can be fatal. Severe symptoms include breathlessness, a dry, irritative cough (which may progress to the production of pink, frothy sputum), severe headache, lack of coordination and balance, confusion, irrational behaviour, vomiting, drowsiness and unconsciousness.

Treat mild symptoms by resting at the same altitude until recovery, usually for

a day or two. Paracetamol or aspirin can be taken for headaches. If symptoms persist or become worse immediate descent is necessary; even 500m can help. Drug treatments should never be used to avoid descent or to enable further ascent.

Hypothermia

The weather in Spain's mountains can be extremely changeable at any time of year. Proper preparation will reduce the risks of getting hypothermia: always carry waterproof garments and warm layers, and inform others of your route.

Hypothermia starts with shivering, loss of judgment and clumsiness. Unless rewarming occurs, the sufferer deteriorates into apathy, confusion and coma. Prevent further heat loss by seeking shelter, warm dry clothing, hot sweet drinks and shared body warmth.

Bites & Stings

Nasty insects to be wary of are the hairy reddish-brown caterpillars of the pine processionary moth (touching the caterpillars' hairs sets off a severely irritating allergic skin reaction), and some Spanish centipedes have a very nasty but nonfatal sting.

Jellyfish, which have stinging tentacles, are an increasing problem at beaches along the Mediterranean coastline.

The only venomous snake that is even relatively common in Spain is Lataste's viper. It has a triangular-shaped head, grows up to 75cm long, and is grey with a zigzag pattern. It lives in dry, rocky areas, away from humans. Its bite can be fatal and needs to be treated with a serum, which state clinics in major towns keep in stock.

Water

Tap water is generally safe to drink in Spain. If you are in any doubt, ask *¿Es potable el agua (de grifo)?* (Is the (tap) water drinkable?). Do not drink water from rivers

or lakes as it may contain bacteria or viruses that can cause diarrhoea or vomiting.

Insurance

A travel-insurance policy to cover theft, loss, medical problems and cancellation or delays to your travel arrangements is a good idea. Paying for your ticket with a credit card can often provide limited travel-accident insurance and you may be able to reclaim the payment if the operator doesn't deliver. Worldwide travel insurance is available at lonelyplanet.com/travel_services. You can buy, extend and claim online anytime – even if you're on the road.

Internet Access

Wi-fi is increasingly available at most hotels and in some cafes, restaurants and airports; generally (but not always) it's free. Connection speed often varies from room to room in hotels, so always ask when you check in.

Good internet cafes that last the distance are increasingly hard to find; ask at the local tourist office. Prices per hour range from €1.50 to €3.

Language Courses

Among the more popular places to learn Spanish are Barcelona, Granada, Madrid, Salamanca and Seville. In these places and elsewhere, Spanish universities offer good-value language courses.

The **Escuela Oficial de Idiomas** (EOI; www.eeooiinet.com) is a nationwide language institution where you can learn Spanish and other local languages. Classes can be large and busy but are generally fairly cheap. There are branches in many major cities. On the website's opening page, hit 'Centros' under 'Comunidad' and then 'Centros en la Red' to get to a list of schools.

Private language schools as well as universities cater for a wide range of levels, course lengths, times of year, intensity and special requirements. Many courses have a cultural component as well as language. University courses often last a semester, although some are as short as two weeks or as long as a year. Private colleges can be more flexible. One with a good reputation is **Don Quijote** (www.donquijote.com), with branches in Barcelona, Granada, Madrid, Salamanca and Valencia.

It's also worth finding out whether your course will lead to any formal certificate of competence. The Diploma de Español como Lengua Extranjera (DELE) is recognised by Spain's Ministry of Education and Science.

Legal Matters

If you're arrested you will be allotted the free services of an *abogado de oficio* (duty solicitor), who may speak only Spanish. You're also entitled to make a phone call. If you use this to contact your embassy or consulate, the staff will probably be able to do no more than refer you to a lawyer who speaks your language. If you end up in court, the authorities are obliged to provide a translator.

In theory, you are supposed to have your national ID card or passport with you at all times. If asked for it by the police, you are supposed to be able to produce it on the spot. In practice it is rarely an issue and many people choose to leave passports in hotel safes.

The Policía Local or Policía Municipal operates at a local level and deals with such issues as traffic infringements and minor crime. The Policía Nacional (☑091) is the state police force, dealing with major crime and operating primarily in the cities. The military-linked Guardia Civil

(created in the 19th century to deal with banditry) is largely responsible for highway patrols, borders, security, major crime and terrorism. Several regions have their own police forces, such as the Mossos d'Esquadra in Catalonia and the Ertaintxa in the Basque Country.

Cannabis is legal but only for personal use and in very small quantities. Public consumption of any illicit drug is illegal. Travellers entering Spain from Morocco should be prepared for drug searches, especially if you have a vehicle.

Maps
Small-Scale Maps

Some of the best maps for travellers are by Michelin, which produces the 1:1,000,000 *Spain Portugal* map and six 1:400,000 regional maps covering the whole country. These are all pretty accurate and are updated regularly, even down to the state of minor country roads. Also good are the GeoCenter maps published by Germany's RV Verlag.

Probably the best physical map of Spain is *Península Ibérica, Baleares y Canarias* published by the **Centro Nacional de Información Geográfica** (CNIG; ☑955 56 93 20; edificio Sevilla 2, 8th fl, módulo 7, Avenida San Francisco Javier 9, Madrid), the publishing arm of the **Instituto Geográfico Nacional** (IGN; www.ign.es; Calle General de Ibáñez de Ibero 3, Madrid). Ask for it in good bookshops.

Walking Maps

Useful for hiking and exploring some areas (particularly in the Pyrenees) are Editorial Alpina's *Guía Cartográfica* and *Guía Excursionista y Turística* series. The series combines information booklets in Spanish (and sometimes Catalan) with detailed maps at scales ranging from 1:25,000 to 1:50,000. They are an indispensable hikers'

tool but have their inaccuracies. The Institut Cartogràfic de Catalunya puts out some decent maps for hiking in the Catalan Pyrenees that are often better than their Editorial Alpina counterparts. Remember that for hiking only, maps scaled at 1:25,000 are very useful. The CNIG also covers most of the country in 1:25,000 sheets.

You can often pick up Editorial Alpina publications and CNIG maps at bookshops near trekking areas, and at specialist bookshops such as these:

Altaïr (☑93 342 71 71; www.altair.es; Gran Via de les Corts Catalanes 616, Barcelona)

Altaïr (☑91 543 53 00; www.altair.es; Calle de Gaztambide 31; ◷10am-2pm & 4.30-8.30pm Mon-Fri, 10.30am-2.30pm Sat; ⓂArgüelles, Madrid)

La Tienda Verde (☑91 535 38 10; www.tiendaverde.es; Calle Maudes 23, Madrid)

De Viaje (☑91 577 98 99; www.deviaje.com; Calle de Serrano 41; ◷10am-8.30pm Mon-Fri, 10.30am-2.30pm & 5-8pm Sat; ⓂSerrano, Madrid)

Librería Desnivel (☑902 248848; www.libreriadesnivel.com; Plaza de Matute 6, Madrid)

Quera (☑93 318 07 43; www.llibreriaquera.com; Carrer de Petritxol 2, Barcelona)

Money

The most convenient way to bring your money is in the form of a debit or credit card, with some extra cash for use in case of an emergency.

ATMs

Many credit and debit cards can be used for withdrawing money from *cajeros automáticos* (automatic teller machines) that display the relevant symbols such as Visa, MasterCard, Cirrus etc. Remember that there is usually a charge (around 1.5% to 2%) on ATM cash withdrawals abroad.

Cash

Most banks and building societies will exchange major foreign currencies and offer the best rates. Ask about commissions and take your passport.

Credit & Debit Cards

Can be used to pay for most purchases. You'll often be asked to show your passport or some other form of identification. Among the most widely accepted are Visa, MasterCard, American Express (Amex), Cirrus, Maestro, Plus, Diners Club and JCB. If your card is lost, stolen or swallowed by an ATM, you can call the following telephone numbers toll free to have an immediate stop put on its use: **Amex** (☑1800 528 2122, 91 572 03 03), **Diners Club** (☑902 401 112), **MasterCard** (☑900 971231) and **Visa** (☑900 991124).

Moneychangers

You can exchange both cash and travellers cheques at exchange offices – which are usually indicated by the word cambio (exchange). Generally they offer longer opening hours and quicker service than banks, but worse exchange rates and higher commissions.

Taxes & Refunds

In Spain, value-added tax (VAT) is known as IVA (ee-ba; impuesto sobre el valor añadido). Visitors are entitled to a refund of the 18% IVA on purchases costing more than €90.16 from any shop, if they are taking them out of the EU within three months. Ask the shop for a cash back (or similar) refund form showing the price and IVA paid for each item, and identifying the vendor and purchaser. Then present the refund form to the customs booth for IVA refunds at the airport, port or border from which you leave the EU.

Tipping

Menu prices include a service charge. Most people leave some small change if they're satisfied: 5% is normally fine and 10% extremely generous. Porters will generally be happy with €1. Taxi drivers don't have to be tipped but a little rounding up won't go amiss.

Travellers Cheques

Can be changed (you'll often be charged a commission) at most banks and building societies. Visa, Amex and Travelex are widely accepted brands with (usually) efficient replacement policies. Get most of your cheques in fairly large denominations (the equivalent of €100 or more) to save on any per-cheque commission charges. It's vital to keep your initial receipt, and a record of your cheque numbers and the ones you have used, separate from the cheques themselves.

Post

The Spanish postal system, **Correos** (☑902 197 197; www.correos.es), is generally reliable, if a little slow at times.

Postal Rates & Services

Sellos (stamps) are sold at most estancos (tobacconists' shops with 'Tabacos' in yellow letters on a maroon background), as well as at post offices.

A postcard or letter weighing up to 20g costs €0.70 from Spain to other European countries, and €0.85 to the rest of the world. For a full list of prices for certificado (certified) and urgente (express post), go to www.correos.es (in Spanish) and click on 'Calculador de Tarifas'.

Sending Mail

Delivery times are erratic but ordinary mail to other Western European countries can take up to a week (although often as little as three days); to North America up to 10 days; and to Australia or New Zealand (NZ) between 10 days and three weeks.

Public Holidays

The two main periods when Spaniards go on holiday are Semana Santa (the week leading up to Easter Sunday) and August. At these times accommodation in resorts can be scarce and transport heavily booked, but other places are often half-empty.

There are at least 14 official holidays a year – some observed nationwide, some locally. When a holiday falls close to a weekend, Spaniards like to make a puente (bridge), meaning they take the intervening day off too. Occasionally when some holidays fall close, they make an acueducto (aqueduct)! Here are the national holidays:

Año Nuevo (New Year's Day) 1 January

Viernes Santo (Good Friday) March/April

Fiesta del Trabajo (Labour Day) 1 May

La Asunción (Feast of the Assumption) 15 August

Fiesta Nacional de España (National Day) 12 October

La Inmaculada Concepción (Feast of the Immaculate Conception) 8 December

Navidad (Christmas) 25 December

Regional governments set five holidays and local councils two more. Here are the common dates:

Epifanía (Epiphany) or **Día de los Reyes Magos** (Three Kings' Day) 6 January

Jueves Santo (Good Thursday) March/April – not observed in Catalonia and Valencia

Corpus Christi June – the Thursday after the eighth Sunday after Easter Sunday

Día de Santiago Apóstol (Feast of St James the Apostle) 25 July

Día de Todos los Santos
(All Saints Day) 1 November
Día de la Constitución
(Constitution Day)
6 December

Safe Travel

Most visitors to Spain never feel remotely threatened, but a sufficient number have unpleasant experiences to warrant an alert. The main thing to be wary of is petty theft (which may of course not seem so petty if your passport, cash, travellers cheques, credit card and camera go missing). What follows is intended as a strong warning rather than alarmism. In other words, be careful but don't be paranoid.

Scams

There must be 50 ways to lose your wallet. As a rule, talented petty thieves work in groups and capitalise on distraction. Tricks usually involve a team of two or more (sometimes one of them an attractive woman to distract male victims). While one attracts your attention, the other empties your pockets. More imaginative strikes include someone dropping a milk mixture on to the victim from a balcony. Immediately a concerned citizen comes

up to help you brush off what you assume to be pigeon poo, and thus suitably occupied you don't notice the contents of your pockets slipping away.

Beware: not all thieves look like thieves. Watch out for an old classic: the ladies offering flowers for good luck. We don't know how they do it, but if you get too involved in a friendly chat with these people, your pockets almost always wind up empty.

On some highways, especially the AP7 from the French border to Barcelona, bands of delinquents occasionally operate. Beware of men trying to distract you in rest areas, and don't stop along the highway if people driving alongside indicate you have a problem with the car. While one inspects the rear of the car with you, his pals will empty your vehicle. Another gag has them puncturing tyres of cars stopped in rest areas, then following and 'helping' the victim when they stop to change the wheel. Hire cars and those with foreign plates are especially targeted. When you do call in at highway rest stops, try to park close to the buildings and leave nothing of value in view. If you do stop to change a tyre and find yourself getting unsolicited

aid, make sure doors are all locked and don't allow yourself to be distracted.

Even parking your car can be fraught. In some towns fairly dodgy self-appointed parking attendants operate in central areas where you may want to park. They will direct you frantically to a spot. If possible, ignore them and find your own. If unavoidable, you may well want to pay them some token not to scratch or otherwise damage your vehicle after you've walked away. You definitely don't want to leave anything visible in the car (or open the boot (trunk) if you intend to leave luggage or anything else in it) under these circumstances.

Theft

Theft is mostly a risk in tourist resorts, big cities and when you first arrive in a new city and may be off your guard. You are at your most vulnerable when dragging around luggage to or from your hotel. Barcelona, Madrid and Seville have the worst reputations for theft and, on very rare occasions, muggings.

Anything left lying on the beach can disappear in a flash when your back is turned. At night avoid dingy, empty city alleys and backstreets, or anywhere that just doesn't feel 100% safe.

Report thefts to the national police. You are unlikely to recover your goods but you need to make this formal *denuncia* for insurance purposes. To avoid endless queues at the *comisaría* (police station), you can make the report by phone (☏902 102112) in various languages or on the web at www.policia.es (click on Denuncias). The following day you go to the station of your choice to pick up and sign the report, without queuing.

Telephone

The reasonably widespread blue payphones are easy to use for international and domestic calls. They accept

---

GOVERNMENT TRAVEL ADVICE

The following government websites offer travel advisories and information for travellers:

Australian Department of Foreign Affairs & Trade (www.smartraveller.gov.au)

Canadian Department of Foreign Affairs & International Trade (www.voyage.gc.ca)

French Ministere des Affaires Etrangeres Europeennes (www.diplomatie.gouv.fr/fr/conseils-aux-voyageurs_909)

New Zealand Ministry of Foreign Affairs & Trade (www.safetravel.govt.nz)

UK Foreign & Commonwealth Office (www.fco.gov.uk)

US Department of State (www.travel.state.gov)

coins, *tarjetas telefónicas* (phonecards) issued by the national phone company Telefónica and, in some cases, various credit cards. Calling from your computer using an internet-based service such as Skype is generally the cheapest option.

Collect Calls

Una llamada a cobro revertido (an international collect call) is simple. Dial ☑99 00 followed by the code for the country you're calling:

Australia ☑900 99 00 61
Canada ☑900 99 00 15
France ☑900 99 00 33
Germany ☑900 99 00 49
Ireland ☑900 99 03 53
Israel ☑900 99 09 72
New Zealand ☑900 99 00 64
UK for BT ☑900 99 00 44
USA for AT&T ☑900 99 00 11, for Sprint and various others ☑900 99 00 13

Mobile Phones

Spain uses GSM 900/1800, which is compatible with the rest of Europe and Australia but not with the North American GSM 1900 or the system used in Japan. From those countries, you will need to travel with a tri-band or quadric-band phone.

You can buy SIM cards and prepaid time in Spain for your mobile (cell) phone (provided you own a GSM, dual- or tri-band cellular phone). This only works if your national phone hasn't been code-blocked; check before leaving home. Only consider a full contract if you plan to live in Spain for a while.

All the Spanish mobile phone companies (Telefónica's MoviStar, Orange and Vodafone) offer *prepagado* (prepaid) accounts for mobiles. The SIM card costs from €50, which includes some prepaid phone time. Phone outlets are scattered across the country. You can then top up in their shops or by buying cards in outlets,

such as *estancos* (tobacconists) and newsstands.

On 1 July 2010 the EU's new Roaming Regulation came into force. It reduced roaming charges and set in place measures designed to prevent travellers from running up massive bills. Check with your mobile provider for more information.

Phone Codes

Mobile (cell) phone numbers start with 6. Numbers starting with 900 are national toll-free numbers, while those starting 901 to 905 come with varying costs. A common one is 902, which is a national standard rate number, but which can only be dialled from within Spain. In a similar category are numbers starting with 800, 803, 806 and 807.

International access code ☑00
Spain country code ☑34
Local area codes None (these are incorporated into listed numbers)

Phonecards

Cut-rate prepaid phonecards can be good value for international calls. They can be bought from *estancos*, small grocery stores, *locutorios* (private call centres) and newsstands in the main cities and tourist resorts. If possible, compare the rates. Many private operators offer better deals than those offered by Telefónica. *Locutorios* specialising in cut-rate overseas calls have popped up all over the place in bigger cities.

Useful Phone Numbers

Emergencies ☑112
English-speaking Spanish international operator ☑1008 (for calls within Europe) or ☑1005 (rest of the world)
International directory inquiries ☑11825 (a call to this number costs €2)
National directory inquiries ☑11818

Operator for calls within Spain ☑1009 (including for domestic reverse-charge (collect) calls)

Time

Time zone Same as most of Western Europe (GMT/UTC plus one hour during winter and GMT/UTC plus two hours during the daylight-saving period).

Daylight saving From the last Sunday in March to the last Sunday in October.

UK, Ireland, Portugal & Canary Islands One hour behind mainland Spain.

Morocco Morocco is on GMT/UTC year-round. From the last Sunday in March to the last Sunday in October, subtract two hours from Spanish time to get Moroccan time; the rest of the year, subtract one hour.

USA Spanish time is USA Eastern Time plus six hours and USA Pacific Time plus nine hours.

Australia During the Australian winter (Spanish summer), subtract eight hours from Australian Eastern Standard Time to get Spanish time; during the Australian summer, subtract 10 hours.

12- and 24-hour clock Although the 24-hour clock is used in most official situations, you'll find people generally use the 12-hour clock in everyday conversation.

Tourist Information

All cities and many smaller towns have an *oficina de turismo* or *oficina de información turística*. In the country's provincial capitals you will sometimes find more than one tourist office – one specialising in information on the city alone, the other carrying mostly provincial or regional information. National and natural parks also often have their own visitor centres offering useful information.

Turespaña (www.spain.info) is the country's national tourism body, and it operates branches around the world. Check the website for office locations.

Travellers with Disabilities

Spain is not overly accommodating for travellers with disabilities but some things are slowly changing. For example, disabled access to some museums, official buildings and hotels represents a change in local thinking. In major cities more is slowly being done to facilitate disabled access to public transport and taxis; in some cities, wheelchair-adapted taxis are called 'Eurotaxis'. Newly constructed hotels in most areas of Spain are required to have wheelchair-adapted rooms. With older places, you need to be a little wary of hotels who advertise themselves as being disabled-friendly, as this can mean as little as wide doors to rooms and bathrooms, or other token efforts.

Organisations

Accessible Madrid (www.esmadrid.com) Madrid's tourist office website has some useful information (type 'Accessible' into their search box). You can download the free, generally outstanding 152-page *Madrid Accessible Tourism Guide;* it covers everything from sights, restaurants and transport to itineraries through the city. The site also allows you to download a list of wheelchair-accessible hotels, and a PDF called 'Lugares Accesibles', a list of wheelchair-friendly restaurants, shopping centres and museums.

Accessible Travel & Leisure (☑01452-729739; www.accessibletravel.co.uk) Claims to be the biggest UK travel agent dealing with travel for people with a disability, and encourages independent travel.

Barcelona Turisme (☑93 428 52 27; www.barcelona-access.com) Website devoted to making Barcelona accessible for visitors with a disability.

ONCE (Organización Nacional de Ciegos Españoles; ☑91 577 37 56, 91 532 50 00; www.once.es; Calle de Prim 3, Madrid; ⓂChueca or Colón) The Spanish association for the blind. You may be able to get hold of guides in Braille to a handful of cities, including Madrid and Barcelona, although they're not published every year.

Society for Accessible Travel & Hospitality (☑212-447 7284; www.sath.org; 347 5th Ave, Ste 610, New York, USA) Although largely concentrated on the USA, this organisation can provide general information.

Visas

Spain is one of 26 member countries of the Schengen Convention, under which 22 EU countries (all but Bulgaria, Cyprus, Ireland, Romania and the UK) plus Iceland, Norway, Liechtenstein and Switzerland have abolished checks at common borders.

The visa situation for entering Spain is as follows:

Citizens or residents of EU & Schengen countries No visa required.

Citizens or residents of Australia, Canada, Israel, Japan, New Zealand and the USA No visa required for tourist visits of up to 90 days.

Other countries Check with a Spanish embassy or consulate.

To work or study in Spain A special visa may be required – contact a Spanish embassy or consulate before travel.

Extensions & Residence

Schengen visas cannot be extended. You can apply for no more than two visas in any 12-month period and they are not renewable once in Spain. Nationals of EU countries, Iceland, Norway, Liechtenstein and Switzerland can enter and leave Spain at will and don't need to apply for a *tarjeta de residencia* (residence card), although they are supposed to apply for residence papers.

People of other nationalities who want to stay in Spain longer than 90 days have to get a residence card, and for them it can be a drawn-out process, starting with an appropriate visa issued by a Spanish consulate in their country of residence. Start the process well in advance.

Volunteering

Volunteering possibilities in Spain include the following:

Earthwatch Institute (www.earthwatch.org) Occasionally Spanish conservation projects appear on its program.

Go Abroad (www.goabroad.com) At last count it had links to 56 different volunteering opportunities in Spain.

Sunseed Desert Technology (www.sunseed.org.uk) This UK-run project, developing sustainable ways to live in semi-arid environments, is based in the hamlet of Los Molinos del Río Agua in Almería.

Transitions Abroad (www.transitionsabroad.com) A good website to start your research.

Women Travellers

Travelling in Spain as a woman is as easy as travelling anywhere in the Western world. That said, you should be choosy about your accommodation. Bottom-end fleapits with all-male staff can be insalubrious locations to bed down for the night. Lone women should also take care in city streets at night – stick with the crowds. Hitching for solo women travellers, while feasible, is risky.

Spanish men under about 40, who've grown up in the liberated post-Franco era, conform far less to old-fashioned sexual stereotypes, although you might notice that sexual stereotyping becomes a little more pronounced as you move from north to south in Spain, and from city to country.

Work

Nationals of EU countries, Switzerland, Liechtenstein, Norway and Iceland may freely work in Spain. If you are offered a contract, your employer will normally steer you through any bureaucracy.

Virtually everyone else is supposed to obtain a work permit from a Spanish consulate in their country of residence and, if they plan to stay more than 90 days, a residence visa. These procedures are well-nigh impossible unless you have a job contract lined up before you begin them.

You could look for casual work in fruit picking, harvests or construction, but this is generally done with imported labour from Morocco and Eastern Europe, with pay and conditions that can often best be described as dire.

Translating and interpreting could be an option if you are fluent in Spanish and have a language in demand.

You can start a job search on the web at sites such as **Think Spain** (www.thinkspain. com).

Language Teaching

This type of work is an obvious option for which language-teaching qualifications are a big help. Language schools abound and are listed under 'Academias de Idiomas' in the *Yellow Pages*. Getting a job is harder if you're not an EU citizen, and the more reputable places will require prospective teachers to have TEFL qualifications. Giving private lessons is another avenue, but is unlikely to bring you a living wage straight away.

Sources of information on possible teaching work – in a school or as a private tutor – include foreign cultural centres such as the British Council and Alliance Française, foreign-language bookshops, universities and language schools. Many have noticeboards where you may find work opportunities

or can advertise your own services.

At **Pueblo Inglés** (www. puebloingles.com), native English-speakers (not necessarily qualified teachers) can get work conversing with Spaniards in English at summer camps and other locations.

Tourist Resorts

Summer work on the Mediterranean coasts is a possibility, especially if you arrive early in the season and are prepared to stay a while. Check any local press in foreign languages, such as the Costa del Sol's *Sur In English,* which lists ads for waiters, nannies, chefs, babysitters, cleaners and the like.

Yacht Crewing

It is possible to stumble upon work as crew on yachts and cruisers. The best ports to look include (in descending order) Palma de Mallorca, Gibraltar and Puerto Banús.

In summer the voyages tend to be restricted to the Mediterranean but, from about November to January, many boats head for the Caribbean. Such work is usually unpaid and about the only way to find it is to ask around on the docks.

Transport

GETTING THERE & AWAY

Spain is one of Europe's top holiday destinations and is well linked to other European countries by air, rail and road. Regular car ferries and hydrofoils run to and from Morocco, and there are ferry links to the UK, Italy, the Canary Islands and Algeria.

Flights, cars and tours can be booked online at lonelyplanet.com.

Entering Spain

Immigration and customs checks (which usually only take place if you're arriving from outside the EU) normally involve a minimum of fuss, although there are exceptions.

Your vehicle could be searched on arrival from Andorra. Spanish customs look out for contraband duty-free products destined for illegal resale in Spain. The same generally goes on arrival from Morocco or the Spanish North African enclaves of Ceuta and Melilla. In this case the search is for controlled substances. Expect long delays at these borders, especially in summer.

The tiny principality of Andorra is not in the European Union (EU), so border controls remain in place.

Passport

Citizens of the 27 EU member states and Switzerland can travel to Spain with their national identity card alone. If such countries do not issue ID cards – as in the UK – travellers must carry a full valid passport. All other nationalities must have a full valid passport.

By law you are supposed to carry your passport or ID card with you in Spain at all times.

Air

There are direct flights to Spain from most European countries, as well as North America, South America, Africa, the Middle East and Asia. Those coming from Australasia will usually have to make at least one change of flight.

High season in Spain generally means Christmas, New Year, Easter and roughly June to September. This varies depending on the specific destination. You may find reasonably priced flights to Madrid available in August because it is stinking hot and everyone else has fled to the mountains or the sea. As a general rule, November to March is when airfares to Spain are likely to be at their lowest, and the intervening months can be considered shoulder periods.

Airports & Airlines

All of Spain's airports share the user-friendly website and flight information telephone number of **Aena** (☏902 404704; www.aena.es), the national airports authority. To find more information on

---

CLIMATE CHANGE & TRAVEL

Every form of transport that relies on carbon-based fuel generates CO_2, the main cause of human-induced climate change. Modern travel is dependent on aeroplanes, which might use less fuel per kilometre per person than most cars but travel much greater distances. The altitude at which aircraft emit gases (including CO_2) and particles also contributes to their climate change impact. Many websites offer 'carbon calculators' that allow people to estimate the carbon emissions generated by their journey and, for those who wish to do so, to offset the impact of the greenhouse gases emitted with contributions to portfolios of climate-friendly initiatives throughout the world. Lonely Planet offsets the carbon footprint of all staff and author travel.

each airport, choose English and click on the drop-down menu of airports. Each airport's page has details on practical information (including parking and public transport) and a full list of (and links to) airlines using that airport. They also have current flight information.

Madrid's Aeropuerto de Barajas is Spain's busiest (and Europe's fourth- or fifth-busiest, depending on the year) airport. Other major airports include Barcelona's Aeroport del Prat and the airports of Palma de Mallorca, Málaga, Alicante, Girona, Valencia, Ibiza, Seville and Bilbao. There are also airports at A Coruña, Almería, Asturias, Jerez de la Frontera, Murcia, Reus and Seville.

Land

Spain shares land borders with France, Portugal and Andorra.

Apart from shorter cross-border services, **Eurolines** (www.eurolines.com) are the main operators of international bus services to Spain from most of Western Europe and Morocco.

In addition to the rail services connecting Spain with France and Portugal, there are direct trains between Zurich and Barcelona (via Bern, Geneva, Perpignan and Girona), and between Milan and Barcelona (via Turin, Perpignan and Girona). For these and other services, visit the website of **Renfe** (www.renfe.com), the Spanish national railway company.

Andorra

Regular buses connect Andorra with Barcelona (including winter ski buses and direct services to the airport) and other destinations in Spain (including Madrid) and France. Regular buses run between Andorra and Barcelona's Estació d'Autobusos de Sants (€27.50, three hours).

France
BUS

Eurolines (www.eurolines.fr) heads to Spain from Paris and more than 20 other French cities and towns. It connects with Madrid (17¾ hours), Barcelona (14¾ hours) and many other destinations. There is at least one departure per day for main destinations.

CAR & MOTORCYCLE

The main road crossing into Spain from France is the highway that links up with Spain's AP7 tollway, which runs down to Barcelona and follows the Spanish coast south (with a branch, the AP2, going to Madrid via Zaragoza). A series of links cuts across the Pyrenees from France and Andorra into Spain, as does a coastal route that runs from Biarritz in France into the Spanish Basque Country.

TRAIN

The principal rail crossings into Spain pierce the Franco-Spanish frontier along the Mediterranean coast and via the Basque Country. Another minor rail route runs inland across the Pyrenees from Latour-de-Carol to Barcelona.

In addition to the options listed below, two or three TGV (high-speed) trains leave from Paris-Montparnasse for Irún, where you change to a normal train for the Basque Country and on towards Madrid. Up to three TGVs also put you on track to Barcelona (leaving from Paris Gare de Lyon), with a change of train at Montpellier or Narbonne. For more information on French rail services, check out the **SNCF** (www.voyages-sncf.com) website.

There are plans for a high-speed rail link between Madrid and Paris. In the meantime, these are the major cross-border services:

Paris-Austerlitz to Madrid-Chamartín (chair/sleeper class €157.20/172.60, 15 hours, one daily) *Trenhotel Francisco de Goya* runs via Les Aubrais, Blois, Poitiers, Vitoria, Burgos and Valladolid.

Paris-Austerlitz to Barcelona–Estacio de Franca (chair/sleeper class €173.60/203.40, 12 hours, one daily) *Trenhotel Joan Miró* runs via Les Aubrais, Limoges, Figueres and Girona.

Montpellier to Lorca (€105, 13 hours, daily) Talgo service along the Mediterranean coast via Girona, Barcelona, Tarragona and Valencia.

Portugal
BUS

Avanza (902 020999; www.avanzabus.com) runs two daily buses between Lisbon and Madrid (€37.50, 7½ to nine hours, two daily).

Other bus services run north via Porto to Tui,

BUS PASSES

Travellers planning broader European tours that include Spain could find one of the following passes useful.

Busabout (in the UK 084 5026 7514; www.busabout.com; 7-11 Bressenden Place, London) is a UK-based hop-on/hop-off bus service aimed at younger travellers. Its network includes more than 30 cities in nine countries, and the main passes are of interest only to those travelling a lot beyond Spain (where there are five stops).

Eurolines (www.eurolines.com) offers a high-season pass valid for 15 days (adult/under 26 years €350/295) or 30 days (€460/380). This pass allows unlimited travel between 51 European cities, but the only Spanish cities included are Barcelona, Madrid and Alicante.

RAIL PASSES

InterRail Passes

InterRail (www.interrailnet.com) passes are available to people who have lived in Europe for six months or more. They can be bought at most major stations and student travel outlets, as well as online.

Children's InterRail passes (half the cost of the adult fare) are for children aged four to 11; youth passes for people aged 12 to 25; and adult passes for those 26 and over. Children aged three and under travel for free.

InterRail has a **Global Pass** encompassing 30 countries that comes in four versions, ranging from five days' travel in 10 days to a full month's travel. Check out the website for a full list of prices.

The InterRail **one-country pass** for Spain can be used for three, four, six or eight days in one month. For the eight-day pass you pay €476/311/205 for adult 1st class/adult 2nd class/youth 2nd class.

Eurail Passes

Eurail (www.eurail.com) passes are for those who've lived in Europe for less than six months and are supposed to be bought outside Europe. They're available from leading travel agencies and online.

For most of the following passes, children aged between four and 11 pay half-price for the 1st-class passes, while those aged under 26 can get a cheaper 2nd-class pass. Again, the website has a full list of prices, including special family rates and other discounts.

Eurail Global Passes are good for travel in 23 European countries; forget it if you intend to travel mainly in Spain. Passes are valid for 15 or 21 consecutive days, or for 10 or 15 days within one month. There are also one-, two- or three-month passes.

The **Eurail Select Pass** provides between five and 15 days of unlimited travel within a two-month period in three to five bordering countries.

Eurail also offers a one-country **Spain Pass** and several **two-country regional passes** (Spain-France, Spain-Italy and Spain-Portugal). You can choose from three to 10 days' train travel in a two-month period for any of these passes. The 10-day Spain Pass costs €434/348 for 1st/2nd class.

As with all Eurail passes, be sure you will be covering a lot of ground to make these worthwhile. Check some sample prices in euros for the places you intend to travel on the **Renfe** (www.renfe.com) website, to compare.

Santiago de Compostela and A Coruña in Galicia, while local buses cross the border from towns such as Huelva in Andalucía, Badajoz in Extremadura and Ourense in Galicia.

CAR & MOTORCYCLE

The A5 freeway linking Madrid with Badajoz crosses the Portuguese frontier and continues on to Lisbon, and there are many other road connections up and down the length of the Spain–Portugal border.

TRAIN

From Portugal, the main line runs from Lisbon across Extremadura to Madrid.

Lisbon to Madrid (chair/sleeper class €63.20/91.40, 9¼ hours, one daily)

Lisbon to Irún (chair/sleeper class €73.80/103.50, 14½ hours, one daily)

Sea

Ferries run to mainland Spain regularly from the Canary Islands, Italy, North Africa (Algeria, Morocco and the Spanish enclaves of Ceuta and Melilla) and the UK. Most services are run by the Spanish national ferry company, **Acciona Trasmediterránea** (☎902 454645; www.tras mediterranea.es). You can take vehicles on most routes.

A useful website for comparing routes and finding links to the relevant ferry companies is www.ferrylines.com.

Algeria

Acciona Trasmediterránea runs year-round ferries between Almería and Ghazaouet, with further departures for Oran from May to September.

France

A new service operated by **LD Lines** (www.ldlines.com) now sails between Gijón and Saint-Nazaire (14 hours, three times weekly).

Italy

Most Italian routes are operated by **Grimaldi Lines** (www.grimaldi-lines.com).

Genoa to Barcelona (19 hours, three weekly)

Civitavecchia (near Rome) to Barcelona (20½ hours, six weekly)

Livorno (Tuscany) to Barcelona (19½ hours, three weekly)

Porto Torres (Sardinia) to Barcelona (12 hours, daily April to December)

Morocco

Tangier to Algeciras (1½ hours, up to eight daily) Buses from several Moroccan cities converge on Tangier to make the ferry crossing to Algeciras, then fan out to the main Spanish centres.

Tangier to Barcelona (24 to 35 hours, weekly)

Tangier to Tarifa (35 minutes, up to eight daily)

Nador to Almería (five to eight hours, up to three daily)

UK

From mid-March to mid-November or October, **Brittany Ferries** (☑0871 244 0744; www.brittany-ferries. co.uk) runs the following services:

Plymouth to Santander (20 hours, weekly)

Portsmouth to Santander (24 hours, weekly)

Portsmouth to Bilbao (24 hours, twice weekly)

GETTING AROUND

Spain's network of train and bus services is one of the best in Europe and there aren't many places that can't be reached using one or the other. The tentacles of Spain's high-speed train network are expanding rapidly with every passing year, while domestic air services are plentiful over longer distances and on routes that are more complicated by land.

Air

Spain has an extensive network of internal flights. These are operated by Spanish airlines and a handful of low-cost international airlines, which include the following:

Air Berlin (www.airberlin. com) Madrid to Valencia, Palma de Mallorca, Ibiza, Seville, Jerez de la Frontera, Alicante, Bilbao and Santiago de Compostela.

Air Europa (www.aireuropa. com) Madrid to Ibiza, Palma de Mallorca, Vigo and Santiago de Compostela.

EasyJet (www.easyjet.com) Madrid to Ibiza, Menorca, Asturias (Gijón) and Santiago de Compostela.

Iberia (www.iberia.es) Spain's national airline and its subsidiary, Iberia Regional-Air Nostrum, have an extensive domestic network.

Ryanair (www.ryanair.com) Numerous domestic Spanish routes.

Volotea (www.volotea.com) New budget airline that flies domestically and internationally.

Vueling (www.vueling.com) Spanish low-cost company with loads of domestic flights within Spain, especially from Barcelona.

Bicycle

Years of highway improvement programs across the country have made cycling a much easier prospect than it once was, although there are few designated bike lanes. Cycling on *autopistas* (tollways) is forbidden. Driver attitudes are not always that enlightened, so beware, and cycling in most major cities is not for the faint-hearted.

If you get tired of pedalling, it is often possible to take your bike on the train. All regional trains have space for bikes (usually marked by a bicycle logo on the carriage), where you can simply load the bike. Bikes are also permitted on most *cercanías* (local-area trains around big cities such as Madrid and Barcelona). On long-distance trains there are more restrictions. As a rule you have to be travelling overnight in a sleeper or couchette to have the (dismantled) bike accepted as normal luggage. Otherwise, it can only be sent separately as a parcel. It's often possible to take your bike on a bus – usually you'll just be asked to remove the front wheel.

Hire

Bicycle rental is not as widespread as in some European countries, although it's becoming more so, especially in the case of *bici todo terreno* (mountain bikes), and in Andalucía, Barcelona and popular coastal towns. Costs vary considerably, but expect to pay around €10 per hour, €15 to €20 per day, or €50 to €60 per week.

Zaragoza and Seville are among those cities to have introduced public bicycle systems with dozens of automated pick-up/drop-off points around the city. These schemes involve paying a small subscription fee which then allows you to pick up a bicycle at one location and drop it off at another.

Boat

Ferries and hydrofoils link the mainland (La Península) with the Balearic Islands and Spain's North African enclaves of Ceuta and Melilla.

The main national ferry company is **Acciona Trasmediterránea** (☑902 45 46 45; www.trasmediterranea. es). It runs a combination of slower car ferries and modern, high-speed, passenger-only fast ferries and hydrofoils. On overnight services between the mainland and the Balearic Islands you can opt for seating or sleeping accommodation in a cabin.

Bus

There are few places in Spain where buses don't go. Numerous companies provide bus links, from local routes between villages to fast inter-city connections. It is often cheaper to travel by bus than by train, particularly on long-haul runs, but also less comfortable.

Local services can get you just about anywhere, but most buses connecting villages and provincial towns are not geared to tourist needs. Frequent weekday services drop off to a trickle, if they operate at all, on Saturday and Sunday. Often just one bus runs daily between smaller places during the week, and none operate on Sundays. It's usually unnecessary to make reservations; just arrive early enough to get a seat.

On many regular runs (say, from Madrid to Toledo) the ticket you buy is for the next bus due to leave and *cannot* be used on a later bus. Advance purchase in such cases is generally not possible. For longer trips (such as Madrid to Seville or to the coast), and certainly in peak holiday season, you can (and should) buy your ticket in advance. On some routes you have the choice between express and stopping-all-stations services.

In most larger towns and cities, buses leave from a single *estación de autobuses* (bus station). In smaller places, buses tend to operate from a set street or plaza, often unmarked. Locals will know where to go and where to buy tickets.

Bus travel within Spain is not overly costly. The trip from Madrid to Barcelona starts from around €29 one way. From Barcelona to Seville, which is one of the longest trips (15 to 16 hours), you pay up to €89 one way.

People under 26 should inquire about discounts on long-distance trips.

Among the hundreds of bus companies operating in Spain, the following have the largest range of services:

ALSA (☑902 422242; www.alsa.es) The biggest player, this company has routes all over the country in association with various other companies.

Avanza (☑902 020999; www.avanzabus.com) Operates buses from Madrid to Extremadura, western Castilla y León and Valencia via eastern Castilla-La Mancha (eg Cuenca), often in association with other companies.

Socibus & Secorbus (☑902 229292; www.socibus.es) These two companies jointly operate services between Madrid and western Andalucía, including Cádiz, Córdoba, Huelva and Seville.

Car & Motorcycle

Every vehicle should display a nationality plate of its country of registration and you must always carry proof of ownership of a private vehicle. Third-party motor insurance is required throughout Europe. A warning triangle and a reflective jacket (to be used in case of breakdown) are compulsory.

Automobile Associations

The **Real Automóvil Club de España** (RACE; ☑902 404545; www.race.es; Calle de Eloy Gonzalo 32, Madrid) is the national automobile club. They may well come to assist you in case of breakdown, but in any event you should obtain an emergency telephone number for Spain from your own insurer or car rental company.

Driving Licence

All EU member states' driving licences are fully recognised throughout Europe. Those with a non-EU licence are supposed to obtain a 12-month International Driving Permit (IDP) to accompany their national licence, which your national automobile association can issue, although in practice car rental companies and police rarely ask for one. People who have held residency in Spain for one year or more should apply for a Spanish driving licence.

Fuel & Spare Parts

Gasolina (petrol) in Spain is pricey, but generally slightly cheaper than in its major EU neighbours (including France, Germany, Italy and the UK).

Petrol is about 10% cheaper in Gibraltar than in Spain and 15% cheaper in Andorra.

You can pay with major credit cards at most service stations.

Hire

To rent a car in Spain you have to have a licence, be

BEATING PARKING FINES

If you've parked in a street parking spot and return to find that a parking inspector has left you a parking ticket, don't despair. If you arrive back within a reasonable time after the ticket was issued (what constitutes a reasonable time varies from place to place, but it is rarely more than a couple of hours), don't go looking for the inspector, but instead head for the nearest parking machine. Most machines in most cities allow you to pay a small penalty (usually around €5) to cancel the fine (keep both pieces of paper just in case). If you're unable to work out what to do, ask a local for help.

TRANSPORT CAR & MOTORCYCLE

ROAD DISTANCES (KM)

	Alicante	Badajoz	Barcelona	Bilbao	Córdoba	Granada	A Coruña	León	Madrid	Málaga	Oviedo	Pamplona	San Sebastián	Seville	Toledo	Valencia	Valladolid
Badajoz	696																
Barcelona	515	1022															
Bilbao	817	649	620														
Córdoba	525	272	908	795													
Granada	353	438	868	829	166												
A Coruña	1031	772	1118	644	995	1043											
León	755	496	784	359	733	761	334										
Madrid	422	401	621	395	400	434	609	333									
Málaga	482	436	997	939	187	129	1153	877	544								
Oviedo	873	614	902	304	851	885	340	118	451	995							
Pamplona	673	755	437	159	807	841	738	404	407	951	463						
San Sebastián	766	768	529	119	869	903	763	433	469	13	423	92					
Seville	609	217	1046	933	138	256	947	671	538	219	789	945	1007				
Toledo	411	368	692	466	320	397	675	392	71	507	510	478	540	458			
Valencia	166	716	349	633	545	519	961	685	352	648	803	501	594	697	372		
Valladolid	615	414	663	280	578	627	455	134	193	737	252	325	354	589	258	545	
Zaragoza	498	726	296	324	725	759	833	488	325	869	604	175	268	863	396	326	367

aged 21 or over and, for the major companies at least, have a credit or debit card. Smaller firms in areas where car hire is particularly common (such as the Balearic Islands) can sometimes live without this last requirement. Although those with a non-EU licence should also have an IDP, you will find that national licences from countries such as Australia, Canada, New Zealand and the USA are usually accepted without question.

Auto Europe (www.auto-europe.com) US-based clearing house for deals with major car rental agencies.

Autos Abroad (www.autosabroad.com) UK-based company offering deals from major car rental agencies.

Avis (☏902 180854; www.avis.es)

Europcar (☏902 105030; www.europcar.es)

Hertz (☏91 749 77 78; www.hertz.es)

Ideamerge (www.ideamerge.com) Renault's car-leasing plan, motor-home rental and much more.

National/Atesa (☏902 100101; www.atesa.es)

Pepecar (☏807 414243; www.pepecar.com) Local low-cost company, but beware of 'extras' that aren't quoted in initial prices.

Insurance

Third-party motor insurance is a minimum requirement in Spain and throughout Europe. Ask your insurer for a European Accident Statement form, which can simplify matters in the event of an accident. A European breakdown-assistance policy such as the AA Five Star Service or RAC Eurocover Motoring Assistance is a good investment.

Car-hire companies also provide this minimum insurance, but be careful to understand what your liabilities

and excess are, and what waivers you are entitled to in case of accident or damage to the hire vehicle.

Road Rules

Blood-alcohol limit: 0.05%. Breath tests are common, and if found to be over the limit you can be judged, condemned, fined and deprived of your licence within 24 hours. Fines range up to around €600 for serious offences. Nonresident foreigners may be required to pay up on the spot (at 30% off the full fine). Pleading linguistic ignorance will not help – the police officer will produce a list of infringements and fines in as many languages as you like. If you don't pay, or don't have a Spanish resident to act as guarantor for you, your vehicle could be impounded.

Legal driving age for cars 18 years.

Legal driving age for motorcycles & scooters 16

(80cc and over) or 14 (50cc and under) years. A licence is required.

Motorcyclists Must use headlights at all times and wear a helmet if riding a bike of 125cc or more.

Overtaking Spanish truck drivers often have the courtesy to turn on their right indicator to show that the way ahead of them is clear for overtaking (and the left one if it is not and you are attempting this manoeuvre).

Roundabouts (traffic circles) Vehicles already in the circle have the right of way.

Side of the road Drive on the right.

Speed limits In built-up areas, 50km/h (and in some cases, such as inner-city Barcelona, 30km/h), which increases to 100km/h on major roads and up to 120km/h on *autovías* and *autopistas* (toll-free and tolled dual-lane highways, respectively). Cars towing caravans are restricted to a maximum speed of 80km/h.

Hitching

Hitching is never entirely safe in any country in the world, and we don't recommend it. Travellers who decide to hitch should understand that they are taking a small but potentially dangerous risk. People who do choose to hitch will be safer if they travel in pairs and let someone know where they are planning to go.

Hitching is illegal on *autopistas* and *autovías*, and difficult on other major highways. Choose a spot where cars can safely stop before highway slipways, or use minor roads. The going can be slow on the latter, as the traffic is often light.

Local Transport

Most of the major cities have excellent local transport. Madrid and Barcelona have extensive bus and metro systems, and other major cities also benefit from generally efficient public transport. By European standards, prices are relatively cheap.

Bus

Cities and provincial capitals all have reasonable bus networks. You can buy single tickets (usually between €1 and €1.50) on the buses or at tobacconists, but in cities such as Madrid and Barcelona you are better off buying combined 10-trip tickets that allow the use of a combination of bus and metro, and which work out cheaper per ride. These can be purchased in any metro station and from some tobacconists and newspaper kiosks.

Regular buses run from about 6am to shortly before midnight and even as late as 2am. In the big cities a night bus service generally kicks in on a limited number of lines in the wee hours. In Madrid they are known as *búhos* (owls) and in Barcelona more prosaically as *nitbusos* (night buses).

Metro

Madrid has the country's most extensive metro network. Barcelona follows in second place with a reasonable system. Valencia, Bilbao, Seville and Palma de Mallorca also have limited but nonetheless useful metro systems. Tickets must be bought in metro stations (from counters or vending machines), or sometimes from *estancos* (tobacconists) or newspaper kiosks. Single tickets cost the same as for buses (around €1.50). The best value for visitors wanting to move around the major cities over a few days are the 10-trip tickets, known in Madrid as Metrobús (€12) and in Barcelona as T-10 (€9.25). Monthly and seasonal passes are also available.

Taxi

You can find taxi ranks at train and bus stations, or you can telephone for radio taxis.

A MEMORABLE NORTHERN TRAIN JOURNEY

The romantically inclined could opt for an opulent and slow-moving, old-time rail adventure in the colourful north of Spain.

Catch the **Transcantábrico** (www.transcantabrico. feve.es) for a journey on a picturesque narrow-gauge rail route, from Santiago de Compostela (by bus as far as O Ferrol) via Oviedo, Santander and Bilbao along the coast, and then a long inland stretch to finish in León. The eight-day trip costs up to €3900 per person (you can shave €150 off the price by booking more than six months in advance), and can also be done in reverse. There are just six or seven departures a year, which works out almost monthly from May to September. The package includes various visits along the way, including the Museo Guggenheim in Bilbao, the Museo de Altamira, Santillana del Mar, and the Covadonga lakes in the Picos de Europa. The food is as pleasurable for the palate as the sights are for the eyes, with some meals being eaten on board but most in various locations.

The trains don't travel at night, making sleeping aboard easy and providing the opportunity to stay out at night.

In larger cities taxi ranks are also scattered about the centre, and taxis will stop if you hail them in the street – look for the green light and/or the *libre* sign on the passenger side of the windscreen. The bigger cities are well populated with taxis, although you might have to wait a bit longer on a Friday or Saturday night. No more than four people are allowed in a taxi.

Daytime flagfall (generally to 10pm) is, for example, €2.15 in Madrid, and up to €3.10 after 10pm and on weekends and holidays. You then pay €1 to €1.20 per kilometre depending on the time of day. There are airport and luggage surcharges. A cross-town ride in a major city will cost about €7 to €10 – absurdly cheap by European standards – while

a taxi between the city centre and airport in either Madrid or Barcelona will cost €25 or €35 with luggage.

Tram

Trams were stripped out of Spanish cities decades ago, but they're making a timid comeback in some. Barcelona has a couple of new suburban tram services in addition to its tourist Tramvia Blau run to Tibidabo. Valencia has some useful trams to the beach, while various limited lines also run in Seville, Bilbao, Murcia and, most recently, Zaragoza.

Train

Renfe (☎902 243402; www.renfe.com) is the excellent national train system that runs

most of the services in Spain. A handful of small private railway lines also operate.

You'll find *consignas* (left-luggage facilities) at all main train stations. They are usually open from about 6am to midnight and charge from €3 to €5 per day per piece of luggage.

Spain has several types of trains, and *largo recorrido* or *Grandes Líneas* (long-distance trains) in particular have a variety of names.

Alaris, Altaria, Alvia, Arco and Avant Long-distance intermediate-speed services.

Cercanías For short hops and services to outlying suburbs and satellite towns in Madrid, Barcelona and 11 other cities.

Euromed Similar to the Tren de Alta Velocidad Española

Train Routes

CHEAPER TRAIN TICKETS

Train travel can be expensive in Spain, but there are a couple of tricks worth knowing.

For a start, **Renfe** (www.renfe.com) offers up significant discounts on a limited number of tickets on just about every major route, but you have to be quick to get one. The discounted tickets go on sale exactly two months before the date of travel, and most are quickly snapped up not long after midnight (Spanish time) – if you wait until morning, you'll almost certainly miss out, especially on more popular routes. If you can organise yourself that far in advance, play around with the dates on the Renfe website to make sure you have the right date (it will say *'No se han encontrado trenes'* if you've gone too far into the future), then lie in wait.

An easier way to save a little money is to remember that return tickets cost considerably less than two one-way tickets. If there's a chance you'll be returning on the same route sometime over the coming months (usually three months is the limit), keep your original ticket and then present it when buying the return.

cost as much as €139 (it could work out significantly cheaper if you book well in advance).

Children aged between four and 12 years are entitled to a 40% discount; those aged under four travel for free (except on high-speed trains, for which they pay the same as those aged four to 12). Buying a return ticket often gives you a 10% to 20% discount on the return trip. Students and people up to 25 years of age with a Euro<26 Card (Carnet Joven in Spain) are entitled to 20% to 25% off most ticket prices.

On overnight trips within Spain on *trenhoteles* it's worth paying extra for a *litera* (couchette; a sleeping berth in a six- or four-bed compartment) or, if available, single or double cabins in *preferente* or *gran clase* class. The cost depends on the class of accommodation, type of train and length of journey. The lines covered are Madrid–La Coruña, Barcelona–Córdoba–Seville, Barcelona–Madrid (and on to Lisbon) and Barcelona–Málaga, as well as international services to France.

(AVE) trains, they connect Barcelona with Valencia and Alicante.

Regionales Trains operating within one region, usually stopping all stations.

Talgo and Intercity Slower long-distance trains.

Tren de Alta Velocidad Española (AVE) High-speed trains that link Madrid with Albacete, Barcelona, Burgos, Córdoba, Cuenca, Huesca, Lerida, Málaga, Seville, Valencia, Valladolid and Zaragoza. There are also Barcelona–Seville and Barcelona–Málaga services. In coming years Madrid–Cádiz and Madrid–Bilbao should also come on line.

Trenhotel Overnight trains with sleeper berths.

Classes & Costs

All long-distance trains have 2nd and 1st classes, known as *turista* and *preferente*, respectively. The latter is 20% to 40% more expensive.

Fares vary enormously depending on the service (faster trains cost considerably more) and, in the case of some high-speed services such as the AVE, on the time and day of travel. Tickets for AVE trains are by far the most expensive. A one-way trip in 2nd class from Madrid to Barcelona (on which route only AVE trains run) could

Reservations

Reservations are recommended for long-distance trips, and you can make them in train stations, Renfe offices and travel agencies, as well as online. In a growing number of stations you can pick up prebooked tickets from machines scattered about the station concourse.

Language

WANT MORE?

For in-depth language information and handy phrases, check out Lonely Planet's *Spanish Phrasebook*. You'll find it at **shop .lonelyplanet.com**, or you can buy Lonely Planet's iPhone phrasebooks at the Apple App Store.

Spanish *(español)* – or Castilian *(castellano)*, as it is also called – is spoken throughout Spain, but there are also three co-official, regional languages: Catalan *(català)*, spoken in Catalonia, the Balearic Islands and Valencia; Galician *(galego)*, spoken in Galicia; and Basque *(euskara)*, which is spoken in the Basque Country and Navarra.

The pronunciation of most Spanish sounds is very similar to that of their English counterparts. If you read our coloured pronunciation guides as if they were English, you'll be understood. Note that kh is a throaty sound (like the 'ch' in the Scottish *loch*), r is strongly rolled, ly is pronounced as the 'lli' in 'million' and ny as the 'ni' in 'onion'. You may also notice that the 'lisped' th sound is pronounced as s in Andalucia. In our pronunciation guides, the stressed syllables are in italics.

Where necessary in this chapter, masculine and feminine forms are marked with 'm/f', while polite and informal options are indicated by the abbreviations 'pol' and 'inf'.

BASICS

Hello.	Hola.	o·la
Goodbye.	Adiós.	a·dyos
Yes./No.	Sí./No.	see/no
Excuse me.	Perdón.	per·don
Sorry.	Lo siento.	lo syen·to
Please.	Por favor.	por fa·vor
Thank you.	Gracias.	gra·thyas
You're welcome.	De nada.	de na·da
How are you?	¿Qué tal?	ke tal
Fine, thanks.	Bien, gracias.	byen gra·thyas

What's your name?

¿Cómo se llama Usted?	ko·mo se lya·ma oo·ste (pol)
¿Cómo te llamas?	ko·mo te lya·mas (inf)

My name is ...

Me llamo ...	me lya·mo ...

Do you speak English?

¿Habla inglés?	a·bla een·gles (pol)
¿Hablas inglés?	a·blas een·gles (inf)

I don't understand.

No entiendo.	no en·tyen·do

ACCOMMODATION

hotel	hotel	o·tel
guesthouse	pensión	pen·syon
youth hostel	albergue juvenil	al·ber·ge khoo·ve·neel
I'd like a ... room.	Quisiera una habitación ...	kee·sye·ra oo·na a·bee·ta·thyon ...
single	individual	een·dee·vee·dwal
double	doble	do·ble
air-con	aire acondicionado	ai·re a·kon·dee·thyo·na·do
bathroom	baño	ba·nyo
window	ventana	ven·ta·na

How much is it per night/person?

¿Cuánto cuesta por noche/persona?	kwan·to kwes·ta por no·che/per·so·na

Does it include breakfast?

¿Incluye el desayuno?	een·kloo·ye el de·sa·yoo·no

DIRECTIONS

Where's ...?
¿Dónde está ...?   don·de es·ta ...

What's the address?
¿Cuál es la dirección?   kwal es la dee·rek·thyon

Can you please write it down?
¿Puede escribirlo,   pwe·de es·kree·beer·lo
por favor?   por fa·vor

Can you show me (on the map)?
¿Me lo puede indicar   me lo pwe·de een·dee·kar
(en el mapa)?   (en el ma·pa)

at the corner	*en la esquina*	en la es·kce·na
at the traffic lights	*en el semáforo*	en el se·ma·fo·ro
behind ...	*detrás de ...*	de·tras de ...
in front of ...	*enfrente de ...*	en·fren·te de ...
left	*izquierda*	eeth·kyer·da
next to ...	*al lado de ...*	al la·do de ...
opposite ...	*frente a ...*	fren·te a ...
right	*derecha*	de·re·cha
straight ahead	*todo recto*	to·do rek·to

EATING & DRINKING

What would you recommend?
¿Qué recomienda?   ke re·ko·myen·da

What's in that dish?
¿Que lleva ese plato?   ke lye·va e·se pla·to

I don't eat ...
No como ...   no ko·mo ...

Cheers!
¡Salud!   sa·loo

That was delicious!
¡Estaba buenísimo!   es·ta·ba bwe·nee·see·mo

Please bring us the bill.
Por favor, nos trae   por fa·vor nos tra·e
la cuenta.   la kwen·ta

I'd like to book a table for ...	*Quisiera reservar una mesa para ...*	kee·sye·ra re·ser·var oo·na me·sa pa·ra ...
(eight) o'clock	*las (ocho)*	las (o·cho)
(two) people	*(dos) personas*	(dos) per·so·nas

Key Words

bottle	*botella*	bo·te·lya
breakfast	*desayuno*	de·sa·yoo·no
(too) cold	*(muy) frío*	(mooy) free·o
dinner	*cena*	the·na
food	*comida*	ko·mee·da
fork	*tenedor*	te·ne·dor

Numbers

1	*uno*	oo·no
2	*dos*	dos
3	*tres*	tres
4	*cuatro*	kwa·tro
5	*cinco*	theen·ko
6	*seis*	seys
7	*siete*	sye·te
8	*ocho*	o·cho
9	*nueve*	nwe·ve
10	*diez*	dyeth
20	*veinte*	veyn·te
30	*treinta*	treyn·ta
40	*cuarenta*	kwa·ren·ta
50	*cincuenta*	theen·kwen·ta
60	*sesenta*	se·sen·ta
70	*setenta*	se·ten·ta
80	*ochenta*	o·chen·ta
90	*noventa*	no·ven·ta
100	*cien*	thyen
1000	*mil*	meel

glass	*vaso*	va·so
highchair	*trona*	tro·na
hot (warm)	*caliente*	ka·lyen·te
knife	*cuchillo*	koo·chee·lyo
lunch	*comida*	ko·mee·da
market	*mercado*	mer·ka·do
(children's) menu	*menú (infantil)*	me·noo (een·fan·teel)
plate	*plato*	pla·to
restaurant	*restaurante*	res·tow·ran·te
spoon	*cuchara*	koo·cha·ra
vegetarian food	*comida vegetariana*	ko·mee·da ve·khe·ta·rya·na

Meat & Fish

beef	*carne de vaca*	kar·ne de va·ka
chicken	*pollo*	po·lyo
duck	*pato*	pa·to
lamb	*cordero*	kor·de·ro
lobster	*langosta*	lan·gos·ta
pork	*cerdo*	ther·do
prawns	*camarones*	ka·ma·ro·nes
tuna	*atún*	a·toon
turkey	*pavo*	pa·vo
veal	*ternera*	ter·ne·ra

Fruit & Vegetables

apple	*manzana*	man·tha·na
apricot	*albaricoque*	al·ba·ree·ko·ke
banana	*plátano*	pla·ta·no
beans	*judías*	khoo·dee·as
cabbage	*col*	kol
capsicum	*pimiento*	pee·myen·to
carrot	*zanahoria*	tha·na·o·rya
cherry	*cereza*	the·re·tha
corn	*maíz*	ma·eeth
cucumber	*pepino*	pe·pee·no
fruit	*fruta*	froo·ta
grape	*uvas*	oo·vas
lemon	*limón*	lee·mon
lettuce	*lechuga*	le·choo·ga
mushroom	*champiñón*	cham·pee·nyon
nuts	*nueces*	nwe·thes
onion	*cebolla*	the·bo·lya
orange	*naranja*	na·ran·kha
peach	*melocotón*	me·lo·ko·ton
peas	*guisantes*	gee·san·tes
pineapple	*piña*	pee·nya
plum	*ciruela*	theer·we·la
potato	*patata*	pa·ta·ta
spinach	*espinacas*	es·pee·na·kas
strawberry	*fresa*	fre·sa
tomato	*tomate*	to·ma·te
vegetable	*verdura*	ver·doo·ra
watermelon	*sandía*	san·dee·a

Other

bread	*pan*	pan
cheese	*queso*	ke·so
egg	*huevo*	we·vo
honey	*miel*	myel
jam	*mermelada*	mer·me·la·da

Signs

Abierto	Open
Cerrado	Closed
Entrada	Entrance
Hombres	Men
Mujeres	Women
Prohibido	Prohibited
Salida	Exit
Servicios/Aseos	Toilets

Question Words

How?	*¿Cómo?*	ko·mo
What?	*¿Qué?*	ke
When?	*¿Cuándo?*	kwan·do
Where?	*¿Dónde?*	don·de
Who?	*¿Quién?*	kyen
Why?	*¿Por qué?*	por ke

rice	*arroz*	a·roth
salt	*sal*	sal
sugar	*azúcar*	a·thoo·kar

Drinks

beer	*cerveza*	ther·ve·tha
coffee	*café*	ka·fe
(orange) juice	*zumo (de naranja)*	thoo·mo (de na·ran·kha)
milk	*leche*	le·che
red wine	*vino tinto*	vee·no teen·to
tea	*té*	te
(mineral) water	*agua (mineral)*	a·gwa (mee·ne·ral)
white wine	*vino blanco*	vee·no blan·ko

EMERGENCIES

Help!	*¡Socorro!*	so·ko·ro
Go away!	*¡Vete!*	ve·te

Call ...!	*¡Llame a ...!*	lya·me a ...
a doctor	*un médico*	oon me·dee·ko
the police	*la policía*	la po·lee·thee·a

I'm lost.
Estoy perdido/a. es·toy per·dee·do/a (m/f)

I'm ill.
Estoy enfermo/a. es·toy en·fer·mo/a (m/f)

It hurts here.
Me duele aquí. me dwe·le a·kee

I'm allergic to (antibiotics).
Soy alérgico/a a soy a·ler·khee·ko/a a
(los antibióticos). (los an·tee·byo·tee·kos) (m/f)

Where are the toilets?
¿Dónde están los don·de es·tan los
servicios? ser·vee·thyos

SHOPPING & SERVICES

I'd like to buy ...
Quisiera comprar ... kee·sye·ra kom·prar ...

I'm just looking.
Sólo estoy mirando. so·lo es·toy mee·ran·do

GALICIAN

Galician is the official language of the Autonomous Community of Galicia and is also widely understood in the neighbouring regions of Asturias and Castilla y Léon. It's very similar to Portuguese. Galicians are likely to revert to Spanish when addressing a stranger, especially a foreigner, but making a small effort to communicate in Galician will always be welcomed.

Hello.	Ola.	I don't understand.	Non entendo.
Good day.	Bon dia.	Could you speak in Castilian, please?	Pode falar en español, por favor?
Goodbye.	Adeus./Até logo.		
Many thanks.	Moitas grácias.	What's this called in Galician?	Como se chama iso en galego?
Do you speak English?	Fala inglés?		

Can I look at it?
¿Puedo verlo? — pwe·do ver·lo

I don't like it.
No me gusta. — no me goos·ta

How much is it?
¿Cuánto cuesta? — kwan·to kwes·ta

That's too expensive.
Es muy caro. — es mooy ka·ro

Can you lower the price?
¿Podría bajar un poco el precio? — po·dree·a ba·khar oon po·ko el pre·thyo

There's a mistake in the bill.
Hay un error en la cuenta. — ai oon e·ror en la kwen·ta

ATM	cajero automático	ka·khe·ro ow·to·ma·tee·ko
internet cafe	cibercafé	thee·ber·ka·fe
post office	correos	ko·re·os
tourist office	oficina de turismo	o·fee·thee·na de too·rees·mo

TIME & DATES

What time is it?	¿Qué hora es?	ke o·ra es
It's (10) o'clock.	Son (las diez).	son (las dyeth)
Half past (one).	Es (la una) y media.	es (la oo·na) ee me·dya
At what time?	¿A qué hora?	a ke o·ra
At ...	A la(s) ...	a la(s) ...
morning	mañana	ma·nya·na
afternoon	tarde	tar·de
evening	noche	no·che
yesterday	ayer	a·yer
today	hoy	oy
tomorrow	mañana	ma·nya·na

Monday	lunes	loo·nes
Tuesday	martes	mar·tes
Wednesday	miércoles	myer·ko·les
Thursday	jueves	khwe·bes
Friday	viernes	vyer·nes
Saturday	sábado	sa·ba·do
Sunday	domingo	do·meen·go

TRANSPORT

Public Transport

boat	barco	bar·ko
bus	autobús	ow·to·boos
plane	avión	a·vyon
train	tren	tren
first	primer	pree·mer
last	último	ool·tee·mo
next	próximo	prok·see·mo
a ... ticket	un billete de ...	oon bee·lye·te de ...
1st-class	primera clase	pree·me·ra kla·se
2nd-class	segunda clase	se·goon·da kla·se
one-way	ida	ee·da
return	ida y vuelta	ee·da ee vwel·ta
aisle seat	asiento de pasillo	a·syen·to de pa·see·lyo
station	estación	es·ta·thyon
ticket office	laquilla	ta·kee·lya
timetable	horario	o·ra·ryo
window seat	asiento junto a la ventana	a·syen·to khoon·to a la ven·ta·na

I want to go to ...
Quisiera ir a ...   kee·sye·ra eer a ...

At what time does it arrive/leave?
¿A qué hora llega/sale?   a ke o·ra lye·ga/sa·le

Does it stop at (Madrid)?
¿Para en (Madrid)?   pa·ra en (ma·dree)

Which stop is this?
¿Cuál es esta parada?   kwal es es·ta pa·ra·da

Please tell me when we get to (Seville).
¿Puede avisarme   pwe·de a·vee·sar·me
cuando lleguemos   kwan·do lye·ge·mos
a (Sevilla)?   a (se·vee·lya)

I want to get off here.
Quiero bajarme aquí.   kye·ro ba·khar·me a·kee

Driving & Cycling

I'd like to   Quisiera   kee·sye·ra
hire a ...   alquilar ...   al·kee·lar ...
  4WD   un todo-   oon to·do-
    terreno   te·re·no
  bicycle   una   oo·na
    bicicleta   bee·thee·kle·ta
  car   un coche   oon ko·che
  motorcycle   una moto   oo·na mo·to

---

child seat   asiento de   a·syen·to de
    seguridad   se·goo·ree·da
    para niños   pa·ra nee·nyos
helmet   casco   kas·ko
mechanic   mecánico   me·ka·nee·ko
petrol   gasolina   ga·so·lee·na
service station   gasolinera   ga·so·lee·ne·ra

How much is it per day/hour?
¿Cuánto cuesta por   kwan·to kwes·ta por
día/hora?   dee·a/o·ra

Is this the road to (Barcelona)?
¿Se va a (Barcelona)   se va a (bar·the·lo·na)
por esta carretera?   por es·ta ka·re·te·ra

(How long) Can I park here?
¿(Por cuánto tiempo)   (por kwan·to tyem·po)
Puedo aparcar aquí?   pwe·do a·par·kar a·kee

The car has broken down (at Valencia).
El coche se ha averiado   el ko·che se a a·ve·rya·do
(en Valencia).   (en va·len·thya)

I have a flat tyre.
Tengo un pinchazo.   ten·go oon peen·cha·tho

I've run out of petrol.
Me he quedado sin   me e ke·da·do seen
gasolina.   ga·so·lee·na

BASQUE

Basque is spoken at the western end of the Pyrenees and along the Bay of Biscay – from Bayonne in France to Bilbao in Spain, and inland, almost to Pamplona. No one quite knows its origin, but the most likely theory is that Basque is the lone survivor of a language family that once extended across Europe, and was wiped out by the languages of the Celts, Germanic tribes and Romans.

Hello.   Kaixo.   **Please.**   Mesedez.
Goodbye.   Agur.   **Thank you.**   Eskerrik asko.
How are you?   Zer moduz?   **You're welcome.**   Ez horregatik.
Fine, thank you.   Ongi, eskerrik asko.   **Do you speak English?**   Ingelesez ba al dakizu?
Excuse me.   Barkatu.   **I don't understand.**   Ez dut ulertzen.

Basque Signs

In many towns in the Basque region street names and signs are changing from Spanish to Basque. Not everyone uses these new names though, and many maps remain in Spanish, which can make navigating a little tricky for travellers. In this book we've provided the most commonly used version or have included both Spanish and Basque. Here are some Basque words commonly used in signs, followed by their Spanish counterpart and English translation:

aireportua   aeropuerto (airport)
erdialdea   centro (city centre)
jatetxea   restaurante (restaurant)
kalea   calle (street)
kale nagusia   calle mayor (main street)
komunak   servicios (toilets)

kontuz   atención (caution/beware)
nekazal turismoak   casas rurales (village/farmstead accommodation)
ongi etorri   bienvenido (welcome)
turismo bulegoa   oficina de turismo (tourist office)

CATALAN

The recognition of Catalan as an official language in Spain is the end result of a regional government campaign that began when the province gained autonomy at the end of the 1970s. Until the Battle of Muret in 1213, Catalan territory extended across southern France, taking in Roussillon and reaching into the Provence. Catalan was spoken, or at least understood, throughout these territories and in what is now Catalonia and Andorra. In the couple of hundred years that followed, the Catalans spread their language south into Valencia, west into Aragón and east to the Balearic Islands. It also reached Sicily and Naples, and the Sardinian town of Alghero is still a partly Catalan-speaking outpost today. Catalan is spoken by up to 10 million people in Spain.

In Barcelona you'll hear as much Spanish as Catalan. Your chances of coming across English speakers are also good. Elsewhere in the province, don't be surprised if you get replies in Catalan to your questions in Spanish. However, you'll find that most Catalans will happily speak to you in Spanish, especially once they realise you're a foreigner. This said, the following Catalan phrases might win you a few smiles and perhaps help you make some new friends.

Hello.	Hola.	Monday	dilluns
Goodbye.	Adéu.	Tuesday	dimarts
Yes.	Sí.	Wednesday	dimecres
No.	No.	Thursday	dijous
Please.	Sisplau./Si us plau.	Friday	divendres
Thank you (very much).	(Moltes) gràcies.	Saturday	dissabte
You're welcome.	De res.	Sunday	diumenge
Excuse me.	Perdoni.		
May I?/Do you mind?	Puc?/Em permet?	1	un/una (m/f)
I'm sorry.	Ho sento./Perdoni.	2	dos/dues (m/f)
		3	tres
What's your name?	Com et dius? (inf)	4	quatre
	Com es diu? (pol)	5	cinc
My name is ...	Em dic ...	6	sis
Where are you from?	D'on ets?	7	set
Do you speak English?	Parla anglès?	8	vuit
I understand.	Ho entenc.	9	nou
I don't understand.	No ho entenc.	10	deu
Could you speak in	Pot parlar castellà	11	onze
Castilian, please?	sisplau?	12	dotze
How do you say ... in	Com es diu ... en	13	tretze
Catalan?	català?	14	catorze
		15	quinze
I'm looking for ...	Estic buscant ...	16	setze
How do I get to ...?	Com puc arribar a ...?	17	disset
Turn left.	Giri a mà esquerra.	18	divuit
Turn right.	Giri a mà dreta.	19	dinou
near	a prop de	20	vint
far	a lluny de	100	cent

GLOSSARY

Unless otherwise indicated, the following terms are from Castilian Spanish. The masculine and feminine forms are indicated with the abbreviations 'm/f'.

ajuntament – Catalan for *ayuntamiento*

alameda – tree-lined avenue

albergue – refuge

albergue juvenil – youth hostel

alcázar – Muslim-era fortress

aljibe – cistern

artesonado – wooden Mudéjar ceiling with interlaced beams leaving a pattern of spaces for decoration

autopista – tollway

autovía – toll-free highway

AVE – Tren de Alta Velocidad Española; high-speed train

ayuntamiento – city or town hall

bailaor/bailaora – male/female flamenco dancer

baile – dance in a flamenco context

balneario – spa

barrio – district/quarter (of a town or city)

biblioteca – library

bici todo terreno (BTT) – mountain bike

bodega – cellar (especially wine cellar); also a winery or a traditional wine bar likely to serve wine from the barrel

búhos – night-bus routes

cabrito – kid

cala – cove

calle – street

callejón – lane

cama – bed

cambio – change; also currency exchange

caña – small glass of beer

cantaor/cantaora – male/female flamenco singer

capilla – chapel

capilla mayor – chapel containing the high altar of a church

carmen – walled villa with gardens, in Granada

Carnaval – traditional festive period that precedes the start of Lent; carnival

carretera – highway

carta – menu

casa de huéspedes – guesthouse; see also *hospedaje*

casa de pagès – *casa rural* in Catalonia

casa rural – village, country house or farmstead with rooms to let

casco – literally 'helmet'; often used to refer to the old part of a city; more correctly, *casco antiguo/histórico/viejo*

castellano/a (m/f) – Castilian; used in preference to *español* to describe the national language

castellers – Catalan human-castle builders

castillo – castle

castro – Celtic fortified village

català – Catalan language; a native of Catalonia

catedral – cathedral

cercanías – local train network

cervecería – beer bar

churrigueresco – ornate style of baroque architecture named after the brothers Alberto and José Churriguera

ciudad – city

claustro – cloister

CNIG – Centro Nacional de Información Geográfica; producers of good-quality maps

cofradía – see *hermandad*

colegiata – collegiate church

coll – Catalan for *collado*

collado – mountain pass

comarca – district; grouping of *municipios*

comedor – dining room

comunidad – fixed charge for maintenance of rental accommodation (sometimes included in rent); community

conquistador – conqueror

copa – drink; literally 'glass'

cordillera – mountain range

coro – choir; part of a church, usually the middle

correos – post office

Cortes – national parliament

costa – coast

cruceiro – standing crucifix found at many crossroads in Galicia

cuesta – lane, usually on a hill

custodia – monstrance

dolmen – prehistoric megalithic tomb

embalse – reservoir

encierro – running of the bulls Pamplona-style; also happens in many other places around Spain

entrada – entrance

ermita – hermitage or chapel

església – Catalan for *iglesia*

estació – Catalan for *estación*

estación – station

estación de autobuses – bus station

estación de esquí – ski station or resort

estación marítima – ferry terminal

estany – Catalan for *lago*

Euskadi Ta Askatasuna (ETA) – the name stands for Basque Homeland & Freedom

extremeño/a (m/f) – Extremaduran; a native of Extremadura

fallas – huge sculptures of papier mâché (or nowadays more often polystyrene) on wood used in Las Fallas festival of Valencia

farmacia – pharmacy

faro – lighthouse

feria – fair; can refer to trade fairs as well as to city, town or village fairs that are basically several days of merrymaking; can also mean a bullfight or festival stretching over days or weeks

ferrocarril – railway

festa – Catalan for *fiesta*

FEVE – Ferrocarriles de Vía Estrecha; a private train company in northern Spain

fiesta – festival, public holiday or party

fútbol – football (soccer)

gaditano/a (m/f) – person from Cádiz

gaita – Galician version of the bagpipes

gallego/a (m/f) – Galician; a native of Galicia

gitanos – the Roma people

glorieta – big roundabout (traffic circle)

Gran Vía – main thoroughfare

GRs – *(senderos de) Gran Recorrido;* long-distance hiking paths

guardia civil – military police

hermandad – brotherhood (including men and women), in particular one that takes part in religious processions

hórreo – Galician or Asturian grain store

hospedaje – guesthouse

hostal – cheap hotel

huerta – market garden; orchard

iglesia – church

infanta/infante – princess/prince

IVA – *impuesto sobre el valor añadido,* or value-added tax

jamón – cured ham

jardín – garden

judería – Jewish *barrio* in medieval Spain

lago – lake

librería – bookshop

lidia – the art of bullfighting

locutorio – private telephone centre

madrileño/a (m/f) – person from Madrid

malagueño/a (m/f) – person from Málaga

manchego/a (m/f) – La Manchan; a person from La Mancha

marcha – action, life, 'the scene'

marismas – wetlands

marisquería – seafood eatery

medina – narrow, maze-like old section of an Arab or north African town

mercado – market

mercat – Catalan for *mercado*

meseta – plateau; the high tableland of central Spain

mihrab – prayer niche in a mosque indicating the direction of Mecca

mirador – lookout point

Modernista – an exponent of Modernisme, the architectural and artistic style influenced by art nouveau and sometimes known as Catalan Modernism, whose leading practitioner was Antoni Gaudí

monasterio – monastery

morería – former Islamic quarter in a town

movida – similar to *marcha;* a *zona de movida* is an area of a town where lively bars and discos are clustered

mozárabe – Mozarab (Christian living under Muslim rule in early medieval Spain)

Mozarabic – style of architecture developed by Mozarabs, adopting elements of

classic Islamic construction to Christian architecture

Mudéjar – Muslims who remained behind in territory reconquered by Christians; also refers to a decorative style of architecture using elements of Islamic building style applied to buildings constructed in Christian Spain

muelle – wharf or pier

municipio – municipality, Spain's basic local administrative unit

muralla – city wall

murgas – costumed groups

museo – museum

museu – Catalan for *museo*

nitbus – Catalan for 'night bus'

oficina de turismo – tourist office; also *oficina de información turística*

parador – luxurious state-owned hotels, many of them in historic buildings

parque nacional – national park; strictly controlled protected area

parque natural – natural park; a protected environmental area

paseo – promenade or boulevard; to stroll

paso – mountain pass

pasos – figures carried in Semana Santa parades

pelota vasca – Basque form of handball, also known simply as *pelota,* or *jai-alai* in Basque

peña – a club, usually of flamenco aficionados or Real Madrid or Barcelona football fans; sometimes a dining club

pensión – small private hotel

pinchos – tapas

pintxos – Basque tapas

piscina – swimming pool

plaça – Catalan for *plaza*

plateresque – early phase of Renaissance architecture

noted for its intricately decorated facades

platja – Catalan for *playa*

playa – beach

plaza – square

plaza de toros – bullring

port – Catalan for *puerto*

PP – Partido Popular (People's Party)

PRs – *(senderos de) Pequeño Recorrido;* short-distance hiking paths

PSOE – Partido Socialista Obrero Español (Spanish Socialist Workers Party)

pueblo – village

puente – bridge; also means the extra day or two off that many people take when a holiday falls close to a weekend

puerta – gate or door

puerto – port or mountain pass

punta – point or promontory

rambla – avenue or riverbed

rastro – flea market; car-boot sale

REAJ – Red Española de Albergues Juveniles, which is the Spanish HI youth hostel network

real – royal

Reconquista – the Christian reconquest of the Iberian Peninsula from the Muslims (8th to 15th centuries)

refugi – Catalan for *refugio*

refugio – mountain shelter, hut or refuge

Renfe – Red Nacional de los Ferrocarriles Españoles; the national rail network

retablo – altarpiece

Reyes Católicos – Catholic monarchs; Isabel and Fernando

ría – estuary

río – river

riu – Catalan for *río*

rodalies – Catalan for *cercanías*

romería – festive pilgrimage or procession

ronda – ring road

sacristía – sacristy; the part of a church in which vestments, sacred objects and other valuables are kept

sagrario – sanctuary

sala capitular – chapter house

salinas – salt-extraction lagoons

santuario – shrine or sanctuary

Semana Santa – Holy Week, the week leading up to Easter Sunday

Sephardic Jews – Jews of Spanish origin

seu – cathedral (Catalan)

sidra – cider

sidrería – cider house

sierra – mountain range

tablao – tourist-oriented flamenco performances

taifa – small Muslim kingdom in medieval Spain

tasca – tapas bar

techumbre – roof

teleférico – cable car; also called *funicular aéreo*

terraza – terrace; pavement cafe

terrazas de verano – open-air late-night bars

tetería – teahouse, usually in Middle Eastern style, with low seats around low tables

torero – bullfighter

torre – tower

trascoro – screen behind the *coro*

turismo – means both tourism and saloon car; *el turismo* can also mean 'tourist office'

urgencia – emergency

vall – Catalan for *valle*

valle – valley

villa – small town

VO – abbreviation of *versión original;* a foreign-language film subtitled in Spanish

zarzuela – Spanish mix of theatre, music and dance

behind the scenes

SEND US YOUR FEEDBACK

We love to hear from travellers – your comments keep us on our toes and help make our books better. Our well-travelled team reads every word on what you loved or loathed about this book. Although we cannot reply individually to postal submissions, we always guarantee that your feedback goes straight to the appropriate authors, in time for the next edition. Each person who sends us information is thanked in the next edition – the most useful submissions are rewarded with a selection of digital PDF chapters.

Visit **lonelyplanet.com/contact** to submit your updates and suggestions or to ask for help. Our award-winning website also features inspirational travel stories, news and discussions.

Note: We may edit, reproduce and incorporate your comments in Lonely Planet products such as guidebooks, websites and digital products, so let us know if you don't want your comments reproduced or your name acknowledged. For a copy of our privacy policy visit lonelyplanet.com/privacy.

OUR READERS

Many thanks to the travellers who used the last edition and wrote to us with helpful hints, useful advice and interesting anecdotes:

Miguel Abella, Jorge Alegre, Miguel Angel, Miguel Angel Dieguez, Cagri Araci, Merce Arguelles, CJ Armstrong Jr, Anisa Atlasi, Abigail Bakker, Valerie Ballester, Vaskor Basak, Mike Bechley, Konstantin Bettenhausen, Enrique Bonggo, Andrea Brandle, Deana Briggs, Ursina Burkhard, Melanie Cardew, Cristina Castellvi Sarbakhshe, Michael Cooke, Annabel Cowley, Claire De Brabandere, Chad Dehmler, Nicole Dicke, Belén Echeandia, Robin Eyre, Mario Falzon, Rob Ferguson, Natalia Fernández, Regina Fouquin, Michael Gogolen, Edwina Golombek, Tana Gomis, Paz Gonzalez, S González, Bob Gunning, Helen Haines, Theresa Hansen, Stefan Hornke, Richard Hume, Jennifer Jader, Max Jordan, Jose Jurado Pacheco, Giselle La Rock, Beate Lang, Tim Laslavic, May Lee, Micaela Levine, Shihe Ma, Nacho Martin, Marthissa März, Monica Massari, Travis Massey, Jim Mill, Cristina Montes, Jamie Murrie, Rika Nauck, Hedi Nore, Paul Ormrod, Carrie Osgood, David Owens, Sheila Padden, Barry Parks, José Manuel Perulero, Shirley Qin, Daryl Reilly, Alina Riskute, Michael Ritzert, Andy Roberts, Michal Rudziecki, Jesse Sammons, Jose A Sanchez, Hans Schmidt, Fernando Schonfeldt Lecuona, James Scott, Gill Smith, Martyn Swan, Wenjie Tang, Paloma Tejedor, Sharon Toner, Barry Tunnah, Karen Valom, Eric Van Adelsberg, Margaret Vile, Miriam Waite, Mark Webster, Neville Wells, Ken Westmoreland, David White, Amy Williamson, Yishay Yateh, Adriane Yeo

AUTHOR THANKS
Anthony Ham

During a decade of living in Madrid, I have been welcomed and assisted by many people whose lives and stories have become a treasured part of the fabric of my own. A huge thank you to my wonderful team of coauthors, and to the wise Dora Whitaker at Lonely Planet. It was my great fortune a week after arriving in Madrid to meet my wife and soulmate, Marina, who has made this city a true place of the heart. And to my daughters, Carlota and Valentina: truly you are Madrid's greatest gifts of all.

Stuart Butler

First and foremost, I must once again thank my wife Heather for all her love and support, and my young son, Jake, for putting up with daddy being away so much – and to them both for their help in such devotion to researching the *pintxos* of San Sebastián and Bilbao. Thank you also to my coauthor Miles Roddis for stepping in at short notice – twice! *Gracias* to all the tourist office staff, hotel and restaurant owners, and everyone else who helped out with my chapters.

Anna Kaminski

I'm very grateful for all the great advice from friends, locals and tourism staff. In particular, I'd like to thank my long-suffering flatmates – Pete and Andrea, Dawn for uncomplainingly traipsing around Costa Brava with me, Tony in Taüll, Matthew Tree for providing perspective, David and Eva for the warm hospitality, Fernando in Sitges, José and María in Cadaqués, and to Salvador Ortiz-Carboneres for teaching me. A big thank you to Anthony Ham for the support and advice, to Dora Whitaker for entrusting me with this task, and the rest of the Lonely Planet team.

Miles Roddis

Thanks, as always and ever, to Ingrid, who keeps me on the right track in both my life and my writing. Nudges, winks and a smirk or two towards Poppy and Lily for their insights into Valencia after dark.

Brendan Sainsbury

Many thanks to all the untold bus drivers, tourist info volunteers, sherry pourers, flamenco singers and innocent bystanders who helped me during my research, particularly to Dora Whitaker for offering me the gig, Anthony Ham for his coordinating skills, and Josephine Quintero, John Noble and Daniel Schechter for their backup. Special thanks to my wife Liz and six-year-old son Kieran for their company in countless bars, buses, flamenco clubs and hotel rooms.

Regis St Louis

I'm grateful for all the great advice from locals, expats and tourism staff. In particular, I'd like to thank Eric Mills, Sol Polo, Maria Asunción Guardia, Margherita Bergamo Meneghini, Meritxell Checa Esteban and friends, Carine Ferry, Laura of Runnerbean, and Diego in Barri Gotic. Thanks also to editors Dora Whitaker and Angela Tinson, and Vesna Maric for tips on the road. Finally, big hugs to my wife and daughters for their continued support.

Andy Symington

I owe gratitude to many people in tourist offices, on streets, in cabs. Particular thanks to the SPP team and Anthony Ham, to José Eliseo Vázquez González and Carmen Rodríguez Aláez for logistical, moral and culinary support, to Alejandra Abulafia, Javier de Celis Sánchez, Lourdes Villa Diez, Mario Urbano Martín, Zoraida Vaquero Menéndez and Darío Castro Pérez for regional expertise, to Richard Prowse for transport, and to my family for encouragement. And, most importantly, *mil gracias* to Elena Vázquez Rodríguez, travel companion, soulmate and so much more.

ACKNOWLEDGMENTS

Climate map data adapted from Peel MC, Finlayson BL & McMahon TA (2007) 'Updated World Map of the Köppen-Geiger Climate Classification', *Hydrology and Earth System Sciences*, 11, 163344.
Barcelona Metro Map © TMB Metro 2010
Madrid Metro Map © Diseño Raro S.L. 2010
Illustrations pp84, 258, 276, 668, 734, 746 by Javier Zarracina.
Cover photograph: Segovia Cathedral, Christian Kober/AWL.

THIS BOOK

This guidebook was commissioned in Lonely Planet's London office. It was researched and written by a dedicated team of authors. Anthony Ham coordinated the group, which comprised Stuart Butler, Anna Kaminski, John Noble, Miles Roddis, Brendan Sainsbury, Regis St Louis and Andy Symington. Anthony, Stuart, John, Miles and Brendan all contributed to previous editions, as did Damien Simonis, Josephine Quintero, Zora O'Neill, Sarah Andrews, Arpi Armenakian Shively, Susan Forsyth, Fiona Adams, Mark Armstrong, Fionn Davenport, Tim Nollen, Andrea Schulte-Peevers, Corinne Simcock, Daniel Schechter, Des Hannigan, Richard Sterling, Elizabeth Swan and Dr Caroline Evans.

Commissioning Editor
Dora Whitaker

Coordinating Editor
Branislava Vladisavljevic

Coordinating Cartographer Peter Shields

Coordinating Layout Designer Mazzy Prinsep

Managing Editors Annelies Mertens, Angela Tinson

Managing Cartographers Shahara Ahmed, Mark Griffiths, Diana Von Holdt

Managing Layout Designers Jane Hart

Assisting Editors Susie Ashworth, Andrew Bain, Andrea Dobbin, Lorna Goodyer, Carly Hall, Elizabeth Jones, Anne Mason, Joanne Newell, Kristin Odijk, Charlotte Orr, Charles Rawlings-Way, Tracy Whitmey

Assisting Cartographers Jeff Cameron, Csanad Csutoros, Xavier Di Toro, Rachel Imeson, Joelene Kowalski, Gabriel Lindquist, Samantha Tyson

Assisting Layout Designers Clara Monitto, Jacqui Saunders

Cover Research Naomi Parker

Internal Image Research Claire Gibson

Illustrator Javier Zarracina

Thanks to Imogen Bannister, Basque Tour, Elin Berglund, Nigel Chin, Daniel Corbett, Laura Crawford, David Elexgaray, Ryan Evans, Jennifer Fernández, Larissa Frost, Chris Girdler, Itziar Herran, Jouve India, Gabrielle Innes, Andi Jones, Oihana Lazpita, Chris Lee Ack, Kate McDonell, Wayne Murphy, Mardi O'Connor, Trent Paton, Susan Paterson, Martine Power, LUR Publicaciones, Kirsten Rawlings, Raphael Richards, Jonathan Ricketson, Averil Robertson, Dianne Schallmeiner, Amanda Sierp, Helena Smith, Iñigo Uriarte, Gerard Walker

index

how to use this book

These symbols will help you find the listings you want:

- 👁 Sights
- 🐬 Beaches
- 🏃 Activities
- 🎓 Courses
- 👆 Tours
- 🎉 Festivals & Events
- 🛏 Sleeping
- 🍴 Eating
- 🍷 Drinking
- ☆ Entertainment
- 🛍 Shopping
- ℹ Information/Transport

Look out for these icons:

- **TOP CHOICE** Our author's recommendation
- **FREE** No payment required
- 🍃 A green or sustainable option

Our authors have nominated these places as demonstrating a strong commitment to sustainability – for example by supporting local communities and producers, operating in an environmentally friendly way, or supporting conservation projects.

These symbols give you the vital information for each listing:

- ☏ Telephone Numbers
- ⊘ Opening Hours
- P Parking
- ⊘ Nonsmoking
- ❄ Air-Conditioning
- @ Internet Access
- 📶 Wi-Fi Access
- 🏊 Swimming Pool
- 🥗 Vegetarian Selection
- 📖 English-Language Menu
- 👪 Family-Friendly
- 🐾 Pet-Friendly
- 🚍 Bus
- ⛴ Ferry
- Ⓜ Metro
- Ⓢ Subway
- 🚊 Tram
- 🚉 Train

Reviews are organised by author preference.

Map Legend

Sights
- 🐬 Beach
- ⚑ Buddhist
- 🏰 Castle
- ✝ Christian
- ☸ Hindu
- ☪ Islamic
- ✡ Jewish
- ❶ Monument
- 🏛 Museum/Gallery
- ✪ Ruin
- ✪ Winery/Vineyard
- 🦁 Zoo
- ◉ Other Sight

Activities, Courses & Tours
- 🤿 Diving/Snorkelling
- 🛶 Canoeing/Kayaking
- ⛷ Skiing
- 🏄 Surfing
- 🏊 Swimming/Pool
- 🚶 Walking
- 🏄 Windsurfing
- ✪ Other Activity/Course/Tour

Sleeping
- 🛏 Sleeping
- ⛺ Camping

Eating
- ✕ Eating

Drinking
- ☕ Drinking
- ☕ Cafe

Entertainment
- ✪ Entertainment

Shopping
- 🛍 Shopping

Information
- ✉ Post Office
- ℹ Tourist Information

Transport
- ✈ Airport
- ⊗ Border Crossing
- 🚌 Bus
- ⬥●⬥ Cable Car/Funicular
- ◌ Cycling
- ⛴ Ferry
- ⬥Ⓜ⬥ Monorail
- P Parking
- Ⓢ S-Bahn
- ⊖ Taxi
- ⊕ Train/Railway
- ⊖ Tram
- ⊖ Tube Station
- Ⓤ U-Bahn
- Ⓜ Underground Train Station
- • Other Transport

Routes
- Tollway
- Freeway
- Primary
- Secondary
- Tertiary
- Lane
- Unsealed Road
- Plaza/Mall
- Steps
-)═(Tunnel
- Pedestrian Overpass
- Walking Tour
- Walking Tour Detour
- Path

Boundaries
- ––– International
- ––– State/Province
- –– Disputed
- –– Regional/Suburb
- Marine Park
- Cliff
- Wall

Population
- ★ Capital (National)
- ◉ Capital (State/Province)
- ● City/Large Town
- ● Town/Village

Geographic
- ⌂ Hut/Shelter
- ⛯ Lighthouse
- ◉ Lookout
- ▲ Mountain/Volcano
- ◉ Oasis
- ❶ Park
-)(Pass
- ⌖ Picnic Area
- ◉ Waterfall

Hydrography
- River/Creek
- Intermittent River
- Swamp/Mangrove
- Reef
- Canal
- Water
- Dry/Salt/Intermittent Lake
- Glacier

Areas
- Beach/Desert
- Cemetery (Christian)
- Cemetery (Other)
- Park/Forest
- Sportsground
- Sight (Building)
- Top Sight (Building)

Miles Roddis

Valencia & Murcia; Mallorca, Menorca & Ibiza Miles and his wife, Ingrid, have lived for over 20 years in a shoebox-sized apartment in the Barrio del Carmen, Valencia's oldest and most vital quarter. He's the author or coauthor of more than 50 Lonely Planet guidebooks, including *Valencia & the Costa Blanca*, *Valencia Encounter*, *Walking in Spain*, *Canary Islands* and seven editions of the book you're holding. He loves Fallas about twice a decade, and gets the hell out of town in intervening years.

Brendan Sainsbury

Andalucía An expat Brit, now living near Vancouver, Canada, Brendan once worked in Andalucía as a guide leading cultural and hiking trips in the hills of Grazalema. He fell unashamedly for the region's romantic charms when he met his future wife in a small white village near Ronda in 2003. He's been back numerous times since, and has developed a special passion for flamenco guitar and the city of Granada. Brendan also writes for Lonely Planet on Cuba, Italy and Mexico.

Regis St Louis

Barcelona Regis first fell in love with Catalunya on a grand journey across Iberia in the late 1990s. Subsequent trips cemented his relationship with Barcelona, one of his favourite cities on the planet. Memorable outings from his most recent trip include morning runs in Barceloneta, evening concerts in the Ciutat Vella and feasting on perhaps the last *calçots* of the season. Regis is also the author of *Barcelona*, and he has contributed to dozens of other Lonely Planet titles. He lives in Brooklyn, New York.

Read more about Regis at:
lonelyplanet.com/members/regisstlouis

Andy Symington

Castilla-La Mancha; Extremadura Andy hails from Australia but has been living in Spain for over a decade, where, to shatter a couple of stereotypes of the country, he can frequently be found huddled in sub-zero temperatures watching the tragically poor local football team. He has authored and coauthored many Lonely Planet guidebooks and other publications on Spain and elsewhere; in his spare time he walks in the mountains, embarks on epic tapas trails, and co-bosses a rock bar.

OUR STORY

A beat-up old car, a few dollars in the pocket and a sense of adventure. In 1972 that's all Tony and Maureen Wheeler needed for the trip of a lifetime – across Europe and Asia overland to Australia. It took several months, and at the end – broke but inspired – they sat at their kitchen table writing and stapling together their first travel guide, *Across Asia on the Cheap*. Within a week they'd sold 1500 copies. Lonely Planet was born.

Today, Lonely Planet has offices in Melbourne, London and Oakland, with more than 600 staff and writers. We share Tony's belief that 'a great guidebook should do three things: inform, educate and amuse'.

OUR WRITERS

Anthony Ham

Coordinating Author; Madrid; Castilla y León; Aragón In 2001 Anthony fell in love with Madrid on his first visit to the city. Less than a year later, he arrived on a one-way ticket, with not a word of Spanish and not knowing a single person. Having recently passed the 10-year mark in Madrid, he still adores his adopted city as much as the first day he arrived. When he's not writing for Lonely Planet, Anthony writes about and photographs Spain, Africa and the Middle East for newspapers and magazines around the world.

Stuart Butler

Basque Country, Navarra & La Rioja; Valencia & Murcia; Mallorca, Menorca & Ibiza Stuart's first childhood encounters with Spain, in Parque Nacional de Doñana and on family holidays along the north coast, left lasting impressions. When he was older he spent every summer on the Basque beaches, until one day he found himself unable to tear himself away – he has been there ever since. His travels for Lonely Planet, and various surf magazines, have taken him beyond Spain to the shores of the Arctic, the deserts of Asia and the forests of Africa. His website is stuart butlerjournalist.com.

Read more about Stuart at:
lonelyplanet.com/members/stuartbutler

Anna Kaminski

Catalonia Anna's love affair with Spain began in 2001 during a summer Spanish course in Santander and continued, unabated, in spite of a nasty bout of salmonella. Over the last decade she has found herself returning every year, both for research and pleasure – be it to hike in the Pyrenees, kitesurf in Tarifa, or go tapas bar–hopping in San Sebastián, Granada and Madrid. Memorable moments from her most recent trip include almost running out of petrol on a lonely mountain road and visiting the former home of the late, great Dalí. Anna currently calls Barcelona home.

John Noble

Cantabria & Asturias; Santiago de Compostela & Galicia John, originally from England's Ribble Valley, has lived in an Andalucian mountain village since 1995. In that time he has travelled lengthily all over Spain and helped write every edition of Lonely Planet's *Spain* and *Andalucía* guides. He loves returning to faraway parts of the country like Galicia and the north coast, with their completely different landscapes, climate, people and culture, and being reminded just how diverse Spain is.

Read more about John at:
lonelyplanet.com/members/ewoodrover

OVER
PAGE | MORE
WRITERS

Published by Lonely Planet Publications Pty Ltd
ABN 36 005 607 983
9th edition – Mar 2013
ISBN 978 1 74220 051 4
© Lonely Planet 2013 Photographs © as indicated 2013
10 9 8 7 6 5 4 3 2
Printed in China